GREAT JEWISH QUOTATIONS

GREAT JEWISH
JEWISH
Quotations

Selected and annotated by
ALFRED J. KOLATCH

jD | **Jonathan David Publishers, Inc.**
Middle Village, New York 11379

Great Jewish Quotations

No part of this book may be reproduced in any form
without the prior written consent of the publisher.
Address all inquiries to:

Jonathan David Publishers, Inc.
68-22 Eliot Avenue
Middle Village, New York 11379

2 4 6 8 10 9 7 5 3 1

Library of Congress Cataloging-in-Publication Data
Great Jewish quotations / [compiled] by Alfred J. Kolatch.
   p. cm.
   ISBN 0-8246-0369-9
   1. Judaism—Quotations, maxims, etc.   2. Jews—Quotations.
   I. Kolatch, Alfred J., 1916–   .
   BM43.G69   1994
   296—dc20   93-38747
                                                        CIP

Book design by Marcy Stamper

Printed in the United States of America

Contents

Acknowledgments

Deep appreciation is hereby expressed to the many individuals whose various contributions have helped advance this book.

Among those who deserve special thanks are:

- My son David for his persistence in settling for nothing less than editorial excellence.

- My wife, Thelma, for her valuable suggestions after reading the manuscript.

- Allison G. Mastropieri for typing the entire text and keeping track of each write and rewrite.

- Diane L. Purr for helping with the Biographical Notations.

- Kathy Ann Gluszak for her computer wisdom.

- Fiorella deLima for her efficient handling of the work-in-progress.

- Judy Press for preparing a superb index.

- Marcy Stamper for design and layout of the text.

- Dorothy Wachtenheim for the jacket design.

- The entire staff of Jonathan David Publishers for their willingness to pitch in whenever needed.

Introduction

WHAT MAKES A QUOTATION GREAT? A quotation may be characterized as great if it has become memorable as a result of its originality, its literary power, its special insight into a current or universal event, its humor, or its inspirational value. A quotation may also be considered great even if it lacks these positive qualities but lives on in the public memory by virtue of its having been written or spoken by a person of renown.

WHAT MAKES A QUOTATION JEWISH? For the purposes of this book, a quotation is considered Jewish if it was spoken or written by a member of the Jewish faith or if it touches on a Jewish theme regardless of the person's religion or heritage.

While the entries in *Great Jewish Quotations* extend from biblical times to the present, special attention has been devoted to those statements made by Jews or about Jews and Judaism relatively recently, specifically within the last few decades of the twentieth century.

In this volume the reader may expect to find:

▫ an assortment of quotations from the Bible and Talmud that are relevant to modern living;

▫ expressions of understanding and appreciation for the Jewish contribution to civilization by literary notables such as Erich Segal, Herman Wouk, Leon Uris, Saul Bellow, Alfred Kazin, A. B. Yehoshua, and Cynthia Ozick;

▫ analyses of the important legal issues of the day by jurists and attorneys such as Louis Brandeis, Benjamin Cardozo, Felix Frankfurter, Ruth Bader Ginsburg, Stephen G. Breyer, and Alan Dershowitz;

▫ speculation on the nature of God and the values of religion by clerics and scholars such as Baruch Spinoza, Mordecai M. Kaplan, Walter Kaufmann, Martin Buber, Solomon Schechter, and Abraham Joshua Heschel;

▫ reflections and perspectives on the Holocaust by prominent figures such as Steven Spielberg, Henry Siegman, Emil Fackenheim, Billy Graham, and Martin Niemöller;

▫ statements by women in the forefront of the struggle for equal rights such as Henrietta Szold, Bella Abzug, Betty Friedan, and Ida Nudel;

▫ a diversity of views on how to solve the Arab-Israeli conflict by politicians such as Yitzhak Rabin, Yasser Arafat, Shimon Peres, Ezer Weizman, and Abba Eban;

▫ quotations relating to the importance of the Zionist ideal and the Land of Israel by advocates such as Theodor Herzl, Ezra Stiles, Henrietta Szold, Abraham Isaac Kook, Oscar S. Straus, Allen Ginsberg, Golda Meir, Marie Syrkin, and Edward I. Koch;

- opinions and attitudes of artists and sports figures such as Leonard Bernstein, Marlon Brando, Frank Sinatra, Red Buttons, Milton Berle, Jerome Kern, Barbra Streisand, Howard Cosell, Sandy Koufax, Hank Greenberg, Marc Chagall, and Ben Shahn;

- expressions of affection and concern for the Jewish citizens of America by U.S. presidents such as George Washington, John Adams, Abraham Lincoln, Grover Cleveland, Woodrow Wilson, Warren G. Harding, Calvin Coolidge, Franklin D. Roosevelt, Harry S Truman, John F. Kennedy, and Bill Clinton;

- encouraging and complimentary statements by non-Jewish religious leaders such as Pope John XXIII, Pope John Paul II, John (Cardinal) O'Connor, and Jerry Falwell;

- disparaging statements and calumnies by religious figures such as Martin Luther, Jimmy Swaggart, Gerald K. Smith, Jesse Jackson, and Louis Farrakhan;

- anti-Semitic prejudices promoted by prominent personalities such as Henry Ford and Charles Lindbergh;

- open expressions of philo-Semites such as Mark Twain, Émile Zola, and Robert Louis Stevenson.

In preparing *Great Jewish Quotations,* in the interests of accuracy I have wherever possible tried to trace to their original sources the quotations selected for inclusion. Even so, as John Bartlett points out in the Preface to the first edition of his *Familiar Quotations,* published in 1855, the process may be "imperfect in some respects." Nonetheless, difficult as it is to achieve absolute accuracy, since many of the quotations were written or spoken as far back as biblical times, great care has been taken to note the correct source for each entry. Where secondary sources have been used, they are noted as well.

Great Jewish Quotations is arranged alphabetically by the individual being quoted. Each entry is explicitly annotated, indicating the source and date of the quotation and, where useful, the context in which it was spoken or written. It is hoped that this feature, together with the detailed index, will make this work a practical source for writers, public speakers, speechwriters, and students of all stripes searching for an apt illustration to drive home a specific point or expand upon a theme.

As it highlights the basic thinking and attitudes of prominent scholars, statesmen, writers, philosophers, entertainers, and others who have represented the cutting edge of society in their day, this volume can also serve to help one recall events of importance that have long been forgotten. Furthermore, by placing all quotations under the name of the author, rather than dispersing them according to subject matter, historians, biographers, writers, and students in general will quickly be able to discern the evolution in thinking of some of the individuals quoted. This is evident, for example, as one studies the changing attitudes of Chaim Weizmann, Theodor Herzl, Henry Kissinger, Jesse Jackson, or Henry Ford.

The reader will note that each quotation is introduced by a concise heading which, in most cases, will serve to offer a sense of what the quotation aims at conveying.

Appended to the body of the work is a section entitled Biographical Notations, followed by a detailed index designed to help the reader locate material with ease.

THE QUOTATIONS

Abba ben Acha

GOLDEN CALF AND TABERNACLE

It is hard to fathom this people's character: they give for the Golden Calf, and they give for the Holy Tabernacle.

Quoted in the talmudic tractate Shekalim (Mishna 1:11).

□

Abba ben Chanina

REDUCING SUFFERING

He who visits the sick reduces his suffering by one-sixtieth.

Quoted in the talmudic tractate Nedarim (39b).

□

Abba ben Zavda

BURDEN AND PRIVILEGE

Even though [the Jewish people] have sinned, they are still [called] Israel.... Thus people say: a myrtle, though it stands among reeds, is still called a myrtle.

Implying that Israel is a name of honor as long as its people are faithful to God. Quoted in the talmudic tractate Sanhedrin (44a).

□

Abba ben Zavina

BE TRUE TO YOURSELF

If you are a Jew, be a Jew; if a heathen, be a heathen!

From the Jerusalem Talmud, Sheviit (4:2).

□

Abbahu

PERSECUTED AND PERSECUTOR

A man should always strive to be of the persecuted and not of the persecutors, for among birds none are more persecuted than doves and pigeons, yet only these were de-clared by Scripture to be fit [as sacrifices] for the altar.

Quoted in the talmudic tractate Bava Kamma (93a).

HIGH PRAISE FOR PENITENTS

In the place where penitents stand even the wholly righteous cannot stand.

Quoted in the talmudic tractate Berachot (34b).

SCENE AT SINAI

When God gave the Torah [to Israel] no bird twittered, no fowl flew, no ox lowed...the sea did not roar, the creatures did not speak; the whole world was wrapped in breathless silence. Then the voice went forth: I am the Lord Thy God.

Quoting his teacher Rabbi Yochanan in Midrash Exodus Rabba (29:9).

□

Mahmoud Abbas

TURNING A NEW PAGE

We have come to this point because we believe that peaceful coexistence and cooperation are the only means for reaching understanding and for realizing the hopes of the Palestinians and the Israelis. The agreement we will sign reflects the decision we made in the Palestine Liberation Organization to turn a new page in our relationship with Israel.

Statement made at the signing of the peace accord between Israel and the Palestine Liberation Organization in a ceremony at the White House on Monday, September 13, 1993.

A PALESTINIAN STATE

The Israelis can say whatever they want. We want a Palestinian state, and after it is established it will have a confederative relationship with Jordan. That is our preference; that is our goal. And we will achieve it in time.

A statement to the London-based newspaper Al-Khiat.

□

Abbaye

WHO IS POOR?
We have a tradition that says: "He who lacks knowledge is poor."

Quoted in the talmudic tractate Nedarim (41a).

LEARN WHILE YOUNG
The lessons of youth are not easily forgotten.

Quoted in the talmudic tractate Shabbat (21b).

MARK OF INSINCERITY
Speak not one thing with the mouth and another with the heart.

Quoted in the talmudic tractate Bava Metzia (49a).

HOW NEWS TRAVELS
Your friend has a friend and your friend's friend has a friend.

Quoted in the talmudic tractate Ketubot (109b).

PEASANTS AND KINGS
When a peasant becomes king, he does not take the basket off his shoulder.

Quoted in the talmudic tractate Megilla (7b).

□

Lyman Abbott

THE MORAL LAW
The fundamental principle of the Hebraic commonwealth was that there are great moral laws...not dependent upon the will of monarch, oligarchy, aristocracy, or public assembly.

From his Life & Literature of Ancient Hebrews *(1901).*

THE EDUCATED MAN
I hope the time will come when the laws and literature of the ancient Hebrews will be studied in all of our schools as now are studied the laws and literature of the ancient Greeks and Romans, and when it will be universally recognized that no man ignorant of the laws and literature of the ancient Hebrews is a well-educated man.

From The 250th Anniversary of Jews in the U.S. *(1905).*

□

Abdel-Latif

MOSLEM VIEW OF MAIMONIDES
Moses, the son of Maimun, visited me, and I found him to be a man of very high merit, but governed by an ambition to take the first place, and to make himself acceptable to men in power. Besides medical works, he has written a philosophical book [*The Guide of the Perplexed*] for the Jews, which I have read; I consider it a bad book, which is calculated to undermine the principles of religion through the very means which are apparently designed to strengthen them.

Reporting on his meeting with Maimonides, held in 1192 at the request of Saladin, the sultan of Egypt and Syria. Quoted in Heinrich Graetz's History of the Jews *(1894).*

□

Rajai Abdo

BIDING HIS TIME
I want Palestinian self-rule.... If this is my aim, I must accept the concept of peace and coexistence with the Jewish state of Israel, at least for the time being.

Quoted in The Jerusalem Post, *December 10, 1993.*

□

Abdullah

NEGOTIATING WITH ARABS
During the last thirty years, you have grown and strengthened yourselves. Your achievements are many. We cannot disregard you and we must compromise with you. There is no quarrel between you and Arabs. The quarrel is between the Arabs and the British, who brought you to Palestine; and between you and the British, who have not kept their promises to you.

At a secret meeting with Golda Meir on November 17, 1947, twelve days before the United Nations voted on the partition of Palestine. The king said that he was prepared to go along with partition if the Jews would agree to the establishment of a Hebrew Republic within Transjordan, with himself as sovereign.

□

Irving Abella

SENSITIVE ANTENNAE
We Jews, who have grown up in the shadow of the Holocaust, have extra sensitive antennae, and mine are now waving frantically. There is a palpable rise of nativism and xenophobia and anti-Semitism throughout the world, and Canada is no exception....

From an address delivered at the World Conference on Anti-Semitism and Prejudice in a Changing World, held in Brussels, Belgium, July 1992.

JEWISH PARANOIA

I heard from him [Nahum Goldmann], that classic paranoid Jewish story of those two Jews walking down a street on a wonderful afternoon, the sun was shining, it was the first day of summer, and they were having a wonderful time, when suddenly a flock of birds flew by, and did what birds do. And one Jew looks at the other, shrugs his shoulders and says, "For the *goyim* they sing."

Ibid.

UNCHALLENGED LIES

The Nazis taught us one thing, that lies that go unchallenged become mistaken for truths, they become policies and ultimately they become murder. Of all the organs in the human body, as Rabbi [Abraham] Heschel once warned us, the tongue is by far the most dangerous. We know that there is no panacea for hate. But we can try to quarantine it.

Ibid.

□

(Patriarch) Abraham

FINDING A WIFE

Put your hand under my thigh and I will make you swear by the Lord, the God of heaven and the God of earth, that you will not take a wife for my son from the daughters of the Canaanites among whom I dwell, but will go to the land of my birth to get a wife for my son Isaac.

Exacting a promise from his senior servant, whom he sends on a mission to find a wife for Isaac (Genesis 24:3–4).

□

Israel Abrahams

NEW TESTAMENT AND THE JEWISH GENIUS

From one point of view the New Testament is, after the Hebrew Bible, the most momentous and greatest product of the Jewish genius, and from another point of view several of its constituent parts were alien to that genius.

Quoted by Joseph Leftwich in the Foreword to his Jewish Omnibus *(1933).*

WE ARE ALL ZIONISTS

All over the world Jews are resolved that our common Judaism shall not be crushed out by short-sighted fanatics for local patriotism; and, in so far as Zionism strengthens this sense of the solidarity of our common Judaism, we are all Zionists.

From a 1905 statement quoted by J. H. Hertz in A Book of Jewish Thoughts *(1917).*

THE SOIL OF GENIUS

The Jewish genius is not of the kind that plants its seed and leaves it for the silent centuries to assimilate it and mature its fruits. It needs living hearts for its soil, and the whole world is only wide enough to provide them.

From his Jewish Life in the Middle Ages *(1896).*

□

Morris Abram

AFTER FIFTY YEARS

I don't give a damn what else they put in there. The thing they did not want to put in was anti-Semitism—that has taken 50 years.

Commenting on the fact that the United Nations Commission on Human Rights, in a March 1994 resolution, is required to look into incidents of anti-Semitism in addition to discrimination against Arabs and Moslems.

WORDS COUNT

Some say trials in international courts of law amount to nothing but words. I say words have meaning and consequence in this world. As incitements to action they can change the course of human history. Consider the words of the Declaration of Independence, or, conversely, those of the Ayatollah Khomeini.

From testimony given on April 21, 1993, before Senator Dennis DeConcini's Committee on the UN Commission on Security and Cooperation (also known as the Helsinki Commission). Abram was then chairman of the "UN Watch" project of the World Jewish Congress.

IN UNION THERE IS STRENGTH

Man is, by nature, a follower, particularly of the fashionable. I felt lonely in the South, fighting anti-Semitism and racism.... In union there is strength. Our diverse communities around the world require the support of an international network which allows them to speak, backs them up and connects them to other communities.

From an address to the World Conference on Anti-Semitism and Prejudice in a Changing World, held in Brussels, Belgium, July 1992. Abram was then serving in Geneva as U.S. Permanent Representative to the United Nations.

JEWS WHO MADE A DIFFERENCE

In 1943, when Supreme Court Justice Felix Frankfurter heard news of the extermination of Jews from an agent of the Polish underground, he said he did not "have the strength to believe it." But another Jew in President Roosevelt's administration, Treasury Secretary Henry Morgenthau, Jr., went out and investigated the response of the State Department to Nazi anti-Semitism. He delivered his damning report to the President in early 1944. It was only after this action that President Roosevelt initiated his much delayed response to the Holocaust.

Ibid.

NEEDS OF ALL MINORITIES

Jesse Jackson, despite his bows to the rainbow coalition, is now essentially a separatist, supported by a chief proponent of separatism, Louis Farrakhan, who calls whites "devils" and utters physical threats against a black journalist for abiding by the professional standards of his peers. No matter how many blacks are persuaded to register [to vote] by Mr. Jackson's charismatic leadership, political goals cannot be gained in a climate in which black needs are separated from the needs of others and assigned to a black politician.

From an article written by Abram when serving as vice chairman of the United States Commission on Civil Rights. Quoted in The New York Times Magazine, *June 10, 1984.*

THE ISRAELI-ARAB DISPUTE

I am now convinced that nothing Israel does will cause the Arab world as a whole, or the world as represented in the UN, to accept the fact of Israel. If the objection is not to the settlements, it's going to be to Jerusalem. If not Jerusalem it's going to be the Golan Heights.... If it isn't Golan, the drumbeat will concentrate on the "racist" nature of the state.

From a letter written to The New York Times *in August 1980, after returning from a visit to Israel.*

REAGAN'S FAUX PAS

Bitburg was the mistake of a friend, not the sin of an enemy.

Commenting on President Ronald Reagan's visit to the military cemetery in Bitburg, Germany, where Nazi officers were buried. From The New York Times, *May 10, 1985.*

¤

S. Z. Abramov
TRADE RATHER THAN AID

In the first two decades American help to Israel was characterized by "aid." This was inevitable. But circumstances have changed. Traditional "aid" is no longer the only response needed. In the future, the relationship of American Jewry to Israel must be governed by the principle of "Trade rather than aid."

From a December 1967 article in The Jewish Spectator. *This is in keeping with the thinking of Yigal Allon (q.v.).*

¤

Robert Abrams
STRESSING WHAT UNITES

Those who hate us in this world see us as one. Let us learn something from our enemies. Let us in fact be and remain a unified single people. We must be able to conduct an appropriate dialogue on the critical issues that confront our community in a spirit of solidarity which stresses what unites us as Jews, not what divides us.

From a speech delivered in March 1994 at the installation of Rabbi Louis Frishman as president of the New York Board of Rabbis.

¤

Ismail Ibrahim Abuhayy
I LIFT MY HEAD AGAIN

For forty years I have no identity. I am pushed from here to there. I am shunned by the world.... But when I hear this news, I lift my head. Today I am a citizen from Gaza.

From an interview with a Los Angeles reporter on September 13, 1993, after the signing of the peace accord between Israel and the PLO.

¤

Bella Abzug
THE LONELY CONGRESSWOMAN

When I was elected to the House in 1970.... I was lonely and an oddity, a woman, a Jew, a New York lawyer, a feminist, a Nixon opponent from way back, a peace activist who passionately opposed American involvement in Indochina and just as strongly favored aid to democratic Israel.

> *Noting after her election in 1970 that she was one of only twelve women in Congress and the only Jew.*

WITH JUSTICE FOR ALL

Judaism has had a very profound effect on me. Jews believe you can't have justice for yourself unless other people have justice as well. That has motivated much of what I've done.

> *Commenting on the adoption by the United Nations of its "Zionism equals racism" resolution.*

ORDERING A LIFE

You try to adjust the family situation to the realities of your life. You don't put one ahead of the other. There is a balance, and you strive to keep that balance. The family grows with it. And the kids also know that the mother is a woman, wife, and lawyer. A total person. It makes them better people.

> *Explaining how she combined her public and private lives. Quoted in Elinor and Robert Slater's* Great Jewish Women *(1994).*

¤

Dean Acheson

AJC'S POLICY

Joe, I'm going to save you a lot of time. I've been studying this thing all morning, and I'm ready to say to you that the partition of Palestine and the creation of a Jewish state is American policy not only because of your Jewish interests but for a number of other reasons, collateral, which I couldn't and can't go into, and if you will get the American Jewish Committee, which is a great non-Zionist organization, to back us up it will be a great help both to Palestine and to America.

> *From a 1947 letter to Joseph Proskauer of the American Jewish Committee after a meeting with Nahum Goldmann. The Committee was now able to go on record for Jewish statehood.*

¤

André Aciman

GOSSIP, NOT RESEARCH

Gossip is what people do best in the Middle East. It was my main source in the book—never research, just gossip. And if as a kid you have a penchant for gossip, then you will have epics to write about later in life.

> *Commenting on the source of information for his* Out of Egypt *(1994), an account of four generations of Sephardic life in Alexandria, Egypt.*

ECHOES OF THE PAST

I wanted to come back tomorrow night, and the night after and the one after that as well, sensing that what made leaving so fiercely painful was the knowledge that there would never be another night like this, that I would never eat soggy cakes along the coast road in the evening, not this year or any other year, nor feel the baffling, sudden beauty of that moment when, if only for an instant, I had caught myself longing for a city I never knew I loved.

> *Ibid. Looking back after thirty years at his last night in his native Alexandria, the city from which he was expelled in the 1960s.*

MEMORY AND JEWISHNESS

Memory is not something that's fortuitous for Jews. Judaism is founded on the idea of re-membering, and re-remembering, and remembering that you should not forget. That's what marks us Jewish, I think.

> *From an interview in the* Forward, *February 3, 1995.*

¤

Gary Ackerman

HAS JUSTICE BEEN SERVED?

The issue no longer is whether justice was done in sentencing, but that justice is not served when Pollard is presently serving more time than any person convicted of spying for a friendly foreign government—unless the U.S. declared war on Israel without telling us.

> *From a November 1993 address delivered at a protest in Washington, DC, demanding that Jonathan Pollard be released from prison.*

¤

(Lord) Acton

ADMIRATION FOR DISRAELI

He [Benjamin Disraeli] was quite remarkable enough to fill a volume of Éloge. Someone wrote to me yesterday that no Jew for 1,800 years has played so great a part in the world.

That would be no Jew since St. Paul; and it is very startling.

In a letter to Mrs. Drew dated April 24, 1881.

❏

Herbert Baxter Adams

JEWS NOT JEWELS

Not jewels but Jews were the real financial basis of the first expedition of Columbus.

From his Columbus and His Discovery of America *(1892).*

PROPHECY AND HISTORY

Hebrew prophecy was history and Hebrew history was prophecy.

From an 1892 article in Johns Hopkins University's Studies in Historical and Political Science.

❏

Joey Adams

THE YELLOW HEART

I was the only guy in the army awarded the yellow heart.

Quoted in Henry D. Spalding's Encyclopedia of Jewish Humor *(1969).*

❏

John Adams

TO MORDECAI M. NOAH

I wish your nation [of Jews] may be admitted to all privileges of citizens in every country of the world. This country has done much. I wish it may do more; and annul every narrow idea in religion, government, and commerce. Let the wits joke; the philosophers sneer! What then? It has pleased the Providence of the 'first cause,' the universal cause, that Abraham should give religion, not only to Hebrews, but to Christians and Mahometans, the greatest part of the modern civilized world.

In response to a communication from Mordecai M. Noah, containing the address that he had delivered at the consecration of New York's Mill Street Synagogue on May 28, 1818.

MANIFESTATION OF ESTEEM

Dear Sir:

How is it possible this old fellow [Voltaire] should represent the Hebrews in such a contemptible light? They are the most glorious nation that ever inhabited this earth. The Romans and their empire were but a bauble in comparison to the Jews. They have given religion in three quarters of the globe and have influenced the affairs of mankind more, and happily than any other nation, ancient or modern.

Yours to the last,
John Adams

A letter dated December 31, 1808, from the retired second president of the United States to his cultured friend, Judge Francis Adrian Van der Kemp (1783–1825) in which he attacks Voltaire's derogatory attitude toward the Bible and the Jewish people. Discovered in 1947 in the archives of the Historical Society of Pennsylvania by the society's librarian, Rabbi Isidore S. Meyer.

VOLTAIRE'S SLANDERS

If I were an atheist, and believed in blind eternal fate, I should still believe that fate had ordained the Jews to be the most essential instrument for civilizing nations. If I were an atheist of the other sect, who believe or pretend to believe, that all is ordained by chance, I should believe that chance had ordered the Jews to preserve and propagate to all mankind that doctrine of a supreme, intelligent, wise, almighty Sovereign of the Universe, which I believe to be the great essential principle of all morality and consequently of all civilization.

From a letter to F. A. Van Der Kemp dated July 13, 1815.

❏

Adda ben Ahaba

SLEEPING WITH ANGER

Anger never went to bed with me.

From the talmudic tractate Taanit (20b).

❏

Joseph Addison

POSITIVE SIDE OF THE DIASPORA

They [the Jews] are so disseminated through all the trading parts of the world that they are become the instruments by which the most distant nations converse with one another, and by which mankind are knit together in a general correspondence. They are like the pegs and nails in a great building, which, though they are but little valued in themselves, are absolutely necessary to keep the whole frame together.

From The Spectator, *September 27, 1712.*

HEBREW'S GRACE AND BEAUTY

Hebrew idioms run into the English tongue with a particular grace and beauty.... They give a force and energy to our expressions, warm and animate our language, and convey our thoughts in more ardent and intense phrases than any that are to be met with in our own tongue.

Ibid.

¤

Alfred Adler

FIGHTING FOR PRINCIPLES

It is easier to fight for one's principles than to live up to them.

Quoted in Lionel Blue's Jewish Guide to the Here and Hereafter (1988).

¤

Cyrus Adler

A LINK IN A CHAIN

I will continue to hold my banner aloft. I find myself born into a people and a religion. The preservation of my people must be for a purpose, for God does nothing without a purpose. His reasons are unfathomable to me, but on my own reason I place little dependence; test it where I will, it fails me. The simple, the ultimate in every direction is sealed to me.... The courses of the planets are no harder to explain than the growth of a blade of grass. Therefore am I willing to remain a link in the great chain.

From his I Have Considered the Days (1941).

WOOING DOCTOR SCHECHTER

I believe that eight cities claim the honor of being the birthplace of Homer. I cannot recall how many people claim the honor of having been instrumental in bringing Doctor Schechter to the United States.

Reminiscing about the coming of Solomon Schechter to America to become president of the Jewish Theological Seminary.

CALL FOR AN ORGANIZED JEWISH COMMUNITY

The affairs of the Jews in the United States as a religious and social body are of such importance that there should be in existence a representative body which may act for all of them with authority.

Expressing the need for a unified Jewish voice in America to protest the persecution of Jews in Russia, which was climaxed by

the Kishinev pogrom in 1903. The American Jewish Committee was formed as a result. From an article in *American Hebrew, 1906.*

RESPONSE TO THE FEARFUL

If three and a half million Jews in America cannot maintain Judaism without a constant stream of immigrants, then they are unworthy of Judaism.

*Commenting on the ominous predictions that American Jewry will not be able to survive the new restrictive immigration law passed by Congress in 1921. From an article in *American Hebrew, September 26, 1924.*

ARYAN MYTH

Now I want to say, with great calmness, and fully understanding the meaning of the words, that this theory [that the German nation is composed of Aryans] is an absolute lie. There is no Aryan race. As far as we know there never has been one. There is not a single biologist, or ethnologist, or anthropologist in the world who believes in the Aryan race.

From his 1939 presidential address to the American Jewish Committee. Quoted in the American Jewish Yearbook, 1939–40.

¤

Felix Adler

ON THE TREK TO THE GOAL

On the way to the highest goal I must take my fellow-beings with me.

From his Life and Destiny (1903).

INQUIRING OF THE DEAD

In the Hebrew religion the spiritual part of man was conceived not as ghostly, but under the attribute of holy. It is a significant fact that stories of ghosts or apparitions are almost absent from the Old Testament; and necromancy, which attempts to come into communication with the dead, that is, to deal with ghosts, was especially abhorrent.

Quoted in J.H. Hertz's Pentateuch and Haftorahs (1961).

¤

Morris Adler

I BELIEVE BECAUSE...

I believe because Judaism opens wide the door that leads me into the heart of all mankind....

I believe because being frail, I reach for

strength; being sorrowful I need comfort; being erratic I wish to be guided; being proud I wish to be elevated to humility; and being a searcher I seek the assurance that my quest is not doomed to futility.

I believe since having entered the world as a Jew by birth, I wish to leave it as a Jew by worth.

From Jewish Information *magazine, Vol. 6, No. 1 (1966).*

LIFE OF A RABBI

His is essentially a life of pathos.... For he is isolated at the very center of the community he "leads" and serves as the spokesman of a group tradition at a time when the group has become all but traditionless.

From his May I Have a Word with You? *(1967).*

CHOOSING LIFE

To man is given the freedom to chart his path in life, and his is the responsibility for the choice he makes. If man were bereft of such freedom of choice, righteousness and wrong, good and evil would have no essential meaning, and morality would be an empty phrase.

Ibid.

IF I WERE A CHRISTIAN

I happen to be a Jew.... By virtue of my training, my conditioning, my environment, my social inheritance, the fact of my Jewishness penetrates every fiber, determines my feelings and reactions, and has contributed largely to the creation of the man that I am....

If I were a Christian, I would similarly recognize the accident of my Christian birth and would therefore not give to that fact such an exalted importance as to make those seem inferior who are not as "fortunate" as I in the matter of accident of birth.

Ibid.

CREATION: A PROCESS

Creation is not a completed event, permitting God to withdraw into a cosmic vastness outside of it. Creation is a dynamic, ongoing process.

Ibid.

A VOICE IN THE DESERT

Out of the desert, with all of its danger, came the Torah, which is our proudest possession and gives to our group-life as Jews its most authentic character and to all humanity the most valid promise of continuing creative contributions to the total fund of human understanding. That voice spoke in the desert.

From his Voice Still Speaks *(1968).*

RIGHTEOUS MAN WITH A FLAW

Nowhere did Noah show a feeling of sadness and pathos that an entire generation was to be lost, and the world destroyed....

Noah was a righteous man; Noah deserves to be in the circle of the great. But there was a fatal flaw in Noah, and so he did not become the father of a new religion, a new faith, and a new community. He lacked compassion and, because he lacked compassion, he forfeited that far greater place in history that might have been accorded him.

Ibid.

□

Rachel Adler

WOMEN AND KADDISH

The experience which made me a feminist was my grandmother's death. I loved her greatly and wanted her to have a *Kaddish*. Since she had no male relative, I asked if I might assume this responsibility. I was told that I could not say *Kaddish* because I was a woman, but that for $350 I could hire a man to say *Kaddish* for her.

From Lilith *magazine, Winter 1976-77.*

□

Samuel Adler

NEW ROBES FOR NEW TIMES

Religion must change her dress according to the times and the climate...according to the dictates of advanced science, enlightened insight, more cultured taste, broadening conditions of life—in short, according to the needs of the world today.

From an 1860 sermon preached at Congregation Anshe Chesed in New York City.

□

S. Y. Agnon

A PRAYERFUL SIGH

One sigh uttered in prayer is of more avail than all the choirs and singers.

Quoted in Israel Argosy *magazine, 1952.*

□

Jacob B. Agus

THE MEANING OF REVELATION

The word of God in the heart of man is not an auditory hallucination, but a power, a deposit of energy, a momentary upsurge toward a higher level of being.

From an essay in Condition of Jewish Belief *(1966), compiled by the editors of* Commentary *magazine.*

REVELATION: ONGOING PROCESS

The human spirit, in its alternation from worship to free creativity and back again, is the self-revelation of the universal spirit. This process cannot be complete, or exclusive, or unique. It is an ongoing movement in the culture of a people as in the life of an individual. The entire panoply of religion and the diverse fields of culture are "the commentary," as Hillel put it.

Ibid.

JUDGING RELIGIOUS PRACTICES

In religion, no law or practice may be judged in isolation from the general context of the life of faith.

Ibid.

IMAGES OF THE MESSIAH

So paradoxical is the Messianic idea that it glows as the brightest of stars on the horizon, when seen in perspective from the distance, and it turns into dust and ashes, like a glowing ember, if it is brought too close and grasped too tightly. As in the case of the God-idea itself, we must beware to resist the popular temptation to fashion earthly images of the Messiah, who is the symbol of the Goal of life.

From Jewish Frontier *magazine, July 1952.*

□

Ahad Ha-am

LEARNING, LEARNING, LEARNING

Learning, learning, learning—that is the secret of Jewish survival.

From a September 18, 1910 letter to Judah Magnes.

ON HEBREW WRITERS

The less their ability, the more their concert.

From a February 10, 1897 letter to A. Ravnitski, referring to Hebrew writers of the time.

PALESTINE: A SPIRITUAL CENTER

In Palestine we can and should found for ourselves a spiritual center of our nationality.

From his 1892 article "Dr. Pinsker & His Pamphlet."

UNIQUENESS OF THE SABBATH

More than Israel has guarded the Sabbath, the Sabbath has guarded Israel.

From his Al Parashat Derachim (At the Crossroads) *(1895–1913).*

PREREQUISITE FOR STATEHOOD

Palestine will become our spiritual center only when the Jews are a majority of the population and own most of the land.

From a July 27, 1903 letter. Quoted in Leon Simon's Ahad Ha-am: Essays, Letters, Memoirs *(1946).*

SOURCE OF STRENGTH

The heart of the Jewish people has always been in the Bet Ha-Midrash; there was the source from which they drew the strength and the inspiration that enabled them to overcome all difficulties and withstand all persecutions. If we want to go on living, we must restore the center to the Bet Ha-Midrash, and make that once more the living source of Judaism.

Ibid. From an October 26, 1915 letter to B. Benas and I. Raffalowich.

FOUNDATIONS OF THE FUTURE

We Jews have been taught by our history to appreciate the real value of laying foundations for future developments. Our share, as a people, in the building up of the general culture of Humanity has been nothing else than the laying of its foundations long before the superstructures were built by others.

Ibid. From an August 12, 1918 letter to Chaim Weizmann.

IMPORTANCE OF NATIONAL SPIRIT

What is national existence if not the existence of a national spirit? What is a nation's importance if not the importance of the spiritual treasures it has added to human culture?

Quoted in Ha-Shiloah *magazine, Volume 6, 1902.*

HOME OF HEALING

The national center will not be a "secure home of refuge" for our people, but it will be a home of healing for its spirit.

From his Summa Summarum *(1912).*

ARISTOCRATS OF HISTORY

Our very existence in dispersion is possible only because we feel ourselves to be "the aristocrats of history."

From an April 17, 1910 letter to A. V. Ravnitzki.

SOURCE OF SALVATION

Israel's salvation will be realized by prophets, not by diplomats.

From his 1897 essay entitled "The First Zionist Congress."

INADVISABILITY OF SEEKING STATEHOOD

After two thousand years of untold...suffering, the Jewish people cannot possibly be content with attaining at last to the position of a small and insignificant nation, with a State tossed about like a ball between its powerful neighbors.

From a speech at the First Zionist Congress (1897) in which he favored a national spiritual center—rather than a political entity—in Palestine.

TREATMENT OF ARABS

Yet what do our brethren do in Palestine? Just the very opposite! Serfs they were in the lands of the Diaspora and suddenly they find themselves in freedom, and this change has awakened in them an inclination to despotism. They treat the Arabs with hostility and cruelty, deprive them of their rights, offend them without cause, and even boast of these deeds.

From a statement made in 1891, after noting that the new Zionist settlers were not relating to the Arabs respectfully. He observed: "We think that the Arabs are all savages who live like animals and do not understand what is happening around them. This is, however, a great error." Ahad Ha-am's statement created a storm of indignation.

LOATHING BOYCOTTS

I am in general absolutely opposed to all forms of boycott. Even in childhood I detested the Jerusalem *herem* [religious boycott proclaimed by Orthodox rabbis], and this feeling has remained in my heart to this day, even if the boycott emanates from the Hebrew Teachers' Union. Call it *herem* or call it boycott, I loathe it. If I were in Palestine, I would fight this loathsome practice with all my might. I do not care if they call me a reactionary, or even traitor; what was ugly in my eyes thirty years ago remains ugly now.

In a May 19, 1914 statement protesting the boycott proclaimed by the Hebrew teachers

of Palestine against the Jewish Institute of Technology in Haifa because it allowed an "alien" language (other than Hebrew) to be the language of instruction.

ACHING HEART

As to the war against the Jews in Palestine, I am a spectator from afar with an aching heart, particularly because of the want of insight and understanding shown on our side to an extreme degree. As a matter of fact, it was evident twenty years ago that the day would come when the Arabs would stand up against us.

From a July 9, 1911 letter to a friend in Jaffa in which he reiterates his complaint that Zionists were unwilling to understand the Arabs living in Palestine.

MISSION OF THE PROPHET

The past and the future are the Prophet's whole life, each completing the other. In the present he sees nothing but a wilderness, a life far removed from his ideal; and therefore he looks before and after. He lives in the future world of his vision and seeks strength in the past out of which that vision-world is quarried.

From his essay "Moses," included in Selected Essays of Ahad Ha-am, *translated by L. Simon (1912).*

UNDOING THE SLAVE MENTALITY

Pharaoh is gone, but his work remains; the master has ceased to be master, but the slaves have not ceased to be slaves. A people trained for generations in the house of bondage cannot cast off in an instant the effects of that training and become truly free, even when the chains have been struck off.

Ibid.

JUDAISM AND REASON

His task was to so shape the content and form of Judaism that it could become a bulwark on which the nation could depend for its continued survival. There is, however, this great difference between Maimonides and his predecessors: whereas for the latter the bulwark was a Judaism placed above reason, for Maimonides it was a Judaism identified with reason.

From a 1904 essay entitled "The Supremacy of Reason," written in commemoration of the seven-hundredth anniversary of the death of Moses Maimonides.

SPIRITUAL FREEDOM

I have no need to exalt my people to Heaven, to trumpet its superiority above all other nations, in order to find a justification for its existence. I at least know why I remain a Jew—or, rather, I can find no meaning in such a question, any more than if I were asked why I remain my father's son.

From his essay entitled "Slavery in Freedom."

WHERE JUDAISM DIFFERS

We cannot conceive Christianity without Jesus, or even Islam without Mohammed.... For Judaism, God is the only ideal of absolute perfection, and He only must be kept always before the eye of man's inner consciousness....

From his essay entitled "Jewish and Christian Ethics."

MOSES AND JESUS

Moses died in his sin, like any other man. He was simply God's messenger, charged with the giving of His Law; his image is not an essential part of the very fabric of the religion. Thus the Jewish teachers of a later period found nothing to shock them in the words of one [Rabbi Jose] who said in all simplicity: "Ezra was worthy to be the bearer of the Law to Israel, had not Moses come before him" (Sanhedrin 21b). Could it enter a Christian mind, let us say, to conceive the idea that Paul was worthy to be the bearer of the "message," had not Jesus come before him?

Ibid.

COMING OF THE MESSIAH

His importance lies not in himself, but in his being the messenger of God for the bringing of redemption to Israel and the world. Jewish teachers pay much more attention to "the days of the Messiah" than to the Messiah himself. One of them even disbelieved altogether in a personal Messiah, and looked forward to a redemption effected by God Himself without an intermediary; and he was not therefore regarded as a heretic.

Ibid.

THE BLOOD LIBEL SYNDROME

This [blood libel] accusation is the solitary case in which the general acceptance of an idea about ourselves does not make us doubt whether all the world can be wrong, and we right, because it is based on an absolute lie. Every Jew who has been brought up among Jews knows as an indisputable fact that throughout the length and breadth of Jewry there is not a single individual who drinks human blood for religious purposes.... "But," you ask, "is it possible that everybody can be wrong and the Jews right?" Yes, it is possible: the blood accusation proves it possible.

Quoted in Joseph Telushkin's Jewish Wisdom *(1994).*

Ahikar

FROM FRYING PAN INTO FIRE

Young swallows fell out of their nest. A cat caught them and said, "If it were not for me, great evil would have befallen you." Said they, "Is this why you put us in your mouth?"

From the Book of Tobit in the Apocrypha.

Akavya ben Mehalalel

HOW TO AVOID SINNING

Remember three things, and you will avoid sin: whence you came, whither you go, and to whom you must account.

Quoted in the talmudic tractate Ethics of the Fathers (3:1).

Akiba ben Joseph

GOD, THE MERCIFUL ONE

Whatever the All Merciful does is all for the good.

Quoted in the talmudic tractate Berachot (60b).

ON VISITING THE SICK

He who does not visit the sick is comparable to one who has shed blood.

Quoted in the talmudic tractate Nedarim (40a).

A MOST NOTEWORTHY BOOK

The most noteworthy day in history is the one on which the Song of Songs was composed. All the other Hagiographa books are holy, but this one is the Holy of Holies.

Quoted in the Mishna Yada'yim (3:5).

ON CAPITAL PUNISHMENT

The condemning judge must fast on the day of execution.

From the Midrash Sifra on Leviticus (19:26).

MUTUAL BENEFIT

More than the calf wishes to suckle [its mother], does the cow wish to be suckled.

> Quoted in the talmudic tractate Pesachim (112a).

A SPECIAL LOVE

Beloved is man, for he was created in the image of God.

> From the talmudic tractate Ethics of the Fathers (3:18).

KEEP CHANTING

Chant it every day! Chant it every day!

> Suggesting that this is the best way to remember your studies. Quoted in the talmudic tractate Sanhedrin (99b).

FREE-WILL PARADOX

Everything is foreseen, but man is given freedom of will.

> Quoted in the talmudic tractate Ethics of the Fathers (3:19).

PROOF OF GOD'S PRESENCE

As a house implies a builder, a dress a weaver, a door a carpenter, so the world proclaims God, its Creator.

> From the Midrash Temura (3).

CHERISH YOUR INDEPENDENCE

Treat your Sabbath as a weekday, rather than be dependent on men [to provide you with supplies for observing the holy day].

> Ibid.

REMARRIAGE ADVICE

Do not marry a divorced woman during her husband's lifetime. For a master said: When a divorced man marries a divorced woman, there are four minds in bed.

> Ibid.

Abu Alaa

A BIRTHDAY PRESENT

This agreement is your birthday present.

> Statement made to Israeli Foreign Minister Shimon Peres by the senior PLO negotiator after the secret peace accord with Israel was signed in Oslo, Norway, on August 20, 1993, Peres' seventieth birthday.

Joseph Albo

THE ETERNAL TORAH

The Torah will never change, for truth is unchangeable.

> From his Sefer Ha-Ikkarim (1428).

CRUELTY TO ANIMALS

In the killing of animals there is cruelty; it accustoms one to the bad habit of shedding innocent blood.

> Ibid.

GOD'S OMNIPOTENCE

We cannot imagine that even God can make a part equal to the whole; or a diagonal of a square equal to one of its sides; or two contradictory propositions true at the same time.

> Ibid. Addressing the philosophical question often asked: Can God make an object that is so heavy that He Himself cannot lift it?

William Foxwell Albright

DISEASED CONSCIENCE

In view of the incredible viciousness of his attacks on Judaism and the Jews, which continued at least until 1943, Gerhard Kittel must bear the guilt of having contributed more, perhaps than any other Christian theologian, to the mass murder of millions of Jews by the Nazis; an apologia pro vita sua written by him about the beginning of 1946 [presumably Kittel's defense statement...] painted an utterly amazing picture of a diseased conscience.

> In condemnation of the prominent Protestant-German theologian who supported the Nazi policy of defaming Judaism.

ARCHAEOLOGY AND THE BIBLE

The uniqueness of the Bible, both as a masterpiece of literature and as a religious document, has not been lessened, and nothing tending to disturb the religious faith of Jew or Christian has been discovered [by archaeologists].

> This view, expressed in 1932, was widely accepted by scholars.

◻

(Rabbi) Alexandri

GRIEVING WIDOWER

The world is darkened for him whose wife has died in his lifetime.

> *To which Jose ben Chanina and Abbahu added: "His steps grow shorter" and "his wit is diminished." Quoted in the talmudic tractate Sanhedrin (22a).*

◻

Muhammed Ali

THOSE JEWISH BRAINS

There's my Jewish brains [pointing to his accountant and financial advisor]. Get those Jewish brains around you—the best in the world.

> *At a 1971 news conference.*

◻

Fred Allen

JACK BENNY'S MONEY

I don't want to say that Jack Benny is cheap, but he's got short arms and carries his money low in his pockets.

> *Quoted in Irving A. Fein's* Jack Benny.

◻

George E. Allen

GLADSTONE VS. DISRAELI

Gladstone: Mr. Disraeli, you will probably die by the hangman's noose or a vile disease.
Disraeli: Sir, that depends upon whether I embrace your principles or your mistress.

> *Quoted in his* Presidents I Have Known.

◻

Steve Allen

JEWS AS INFERIOR

Perhaps my own personal early background, a thoroughly anti-Semitic culture, enables me to perceive more clearly than most certain realities of Jewish–Gentile relations in the United States. Anti-Semites, whether of the truly vicious or almost casual type, perceive Jews as inferior.... On the contrary, they are superior.

> *From his introduction to Tim Boxer's* Jewish Celebrity Hall of Fame *(1987).*

IMPRESSIVE RECORD OF SUCCESSES

Comprising, as they do, a remarkably small percentage of the population of our nation they [the Jews] have distinguished themselves to a strikingly disproportionate degree.... Although Jews number only about three percent of our population, they have been awarded 27 percent of the Nobel prizes won by American scientists.

> *Ibid.*

◻

Woody Allen

AGNOSTICISM

If only God would give me some clear sign! Like making a large deposit in my name in a Swiss bank.

> *From an article in* The New Yorker, *November 5, 1973.*

CHOOSING BETWEEN TWO EVILS

More than any other time in history, mankind faces a crossroads. One path leads to despair and utter hopelessness. The other, to total extinction. Let us pray we have the wisdom to choose correctly.

> *From a 1980 speech to a graduating class.*

THE ODD COUPLE

The lion and the calf shall lie down together but the calf won't get much sleep.

> *Quoted in* The New Republic, *August 31, 1974.*

GOD, AN UNDERACHIEVER

If it turns out that there is a God, I don't think that he's evil. But the worst that you can say about him is that basically he's an underachiever.

> *From the 1975 film* Love and Death.

AFRAID TO DIE?

It's not that I'm afraid to die. I just don't want to be there when it happens.

> *Ibid.*

HILARIOUS GROUCHO

Groucho Marx was the best comedian this country ever produced.... [He] combined a totally original physical conception that was hilarious with a matchless verbal delivery.

> *Quoted in Darryl Lyman's* Jewish Comedy Catalog *(1989).*

DRAMA VS. COMEDY

Drama is like a plate of meat and potatoes. Comedy is rather like a dessert; a bit like meringue.

> *Quoted in Graham McCann's* Woody Allen *(1990).*

WOODY THE FILMMAKER

I draw my ideas from everything I've done and everything that interests me.... You can have 600 jokes in your film and if two gags are Jewish, the picture will be perceived as Jewish comedy. This is a false perception, I think.

> *When asked if he thought of himself as a Jewish filmmaker. Quoted in Elinor and Robert Slater's* Great Jewish Men *(1996).*

◻

Yigal Allon

ISRAEL'S ECONOMY

If every American Jew were to purchase just one Israeli shirt or dress a year, its economy would be out of the doldrums.

> *From an address delivered in the 1960s when he was serving as Israeli's minister of labor.*

◻

Abu-Yussuff Almansur

THE JEW-BADGE

If I knew that the converted Jews had adopted the Mahometan [Mohammedan] belief with an upright heart, then I would allow them to intermarry with the Mussulmans [Moslems]. If, on the other hand, I were convinced that they are still skeptics, I would put them to the sword, enslave their children, and confiscate their goods. But I am doubtful about this point; therefore they shall appear distinguished by a hateful uniform.

> *Upon requiring that converted Jews wear distinctive garb. The practice was imitated by Pope Innocent III with the introduction of the yellow "Jew-Badge" in November 1215. Quoted in Heinrich Graetz's* History of the Jews *(1894).*

◻

Menachem Alon

ISRAELI LAW AND HALACHA

In Israel, there always has been—I believe this will only continue to escalate—conflict between Halacha [Jewish religious law] and Israeli jurisprudence.... We are a unique country in that sense, in which nationality and religion are one and the same.... This is why I believe the Supreme Court must have in its midst someone of high caliber who is acquainted with the law and Halacha.

> *Upon completing, on November 24, 1993, sixteen years on Israel's Supreme Court and retiring at the mandatory age of seventy. From an interview with Netty C. Gross in* The Jerusalem Post, *February 4, 1994.*

GOMEL AND GIMLA'UT

A judge who has reached the age of retirement has to say the prayer of thanks to God, [known as] *Gomel*, that he came out of the process sound in both body and soul.

> *Ibid. In a play on the Hebrew term* gimla'ut, *meaning "retirement."*

IGNORANT JUDGES

The problem of Jewish law in the Supreme Court today is principally one of ignorance on the part of the justices. The tragedy is that justices simply don't know because they didn't study it [Jewish law]. I've been teaching at the Hebrew University's law school for forty years and, when I mention to my students *Shulchan Aruch, Even Ha-ezer* [the codified part of Jewish law which pertains to family law], they ask me which publishing house I am referring to....

I yearn for the days of the *apikorsim* [heretics]. Why? Because an *apikores* has made an intellectual decision, meaning he knows something to begin with. Here, there's no one to argue with.

> *Ibid.*

THOSE WERE THE DAYS

Those were the best years of my life. We sat and studied days, nights. It was total immersion. It was a place where you studied for the sake of knowledge. No diplomas were given.

> *Recalling the eight years of rigorous study in the Jerusalem Hebron Yeshiva, beginning in 1936 when he was thirteen years old.*

ON EUTHANASIA

A lethal injection, which might be allowed in Holland, would be considered murder by both American jurisprudence and Halacha [Jewish law].

> *Explaining his April 1993 ruling in denying the request for detaching the life-support system from a severely ill two-year-old Tay-Sachs patient.*

◻

Shulamit Aloni

NEGOTIATING WITH THE PLO

The State of Israel should proclaim that it is ready to negotiate and discuss peace with every party, not excepting the PLO, on condition that the PLO recognizes the right of the State of Israel to a sovereign existence as the state of the Jewish people....

If the PLO were to refuse, however, it would be evident that it is they who close the door to negotiations; they who are the aggressive and violent party that does not wish to reach a peace agreement; they whose objective it is to destroy the existing sovereign State of Israel, a member state of the UN, together with its inhabitants and achievements.

From a symposium that appeared in Moment *magazine, March 1976.*

A HUMAN LIBBER

I'm not a "women's libber." I am a "human libber." I put human rights above women's rights. I hate classifications and labeling.

A comment to a caller on her twice-weekly Israeli radio program, After Office Hours.

◻

Gil Carl Alroy

ERODING ISRAEL'S POSITION

As soon as the PLO utters some vague words of acceptance of UN resolutions—which is not improbable—Washington will rush to interpret such gobble as final "recognition" of the Jewish state, which must fully face the consequences. A similar condition may come about with Washington continuing to erode Israel's position, bit by bit, until Israel awakens one day to find herself in bed with Arafat, without having had any say in the matter.

From a symposium that appeared in Moment *magazine, March 1976.*

SHIFT IN AMERICAN POLICY

The real problem for Israel is not with the PLO, but with Washington. The root question is whether there really is a place in the radical shift of American policy under Kissinger for a strong and confident Jewish state. To me, it seems that Kissinger, having made his confrontation in the fateful days of October 1973 and afterward with Israel, rather than with the

Arabs, has made possible an era in which the Jewish people is in jeopardy.

Ibid.

◻

Robert Alter

CRITIQUE OF HUGH NISSENSON

Nissenson is...the only genuinely religious writer in the whole American Jewish group. His fiction represents an attempt to follow the twisting, sometimes treacherous ways between God and man; his stories reach out for Jewish experiences in Eastern Europe, in Israel and in America, in an effort to discover what Jews do with their faith in a God who so often seems conspicuous by his absence.

A critique of Nissenson's early writings, which include A Pile of Stones *(1965),* Notes from the Frontier *(1968),* In the Reign of Peace *(1972), and* My Own Ground *(1976).*

LANGUAGE OF THE BIBLE

Language in the biblical stories is never conceived as a transparent envelope of the narrated events, or as an aesthetic embellishment of them, but as an integral and dynamic component—an insistent dimension—of what is being narrated. With language God creates the world; through language He reveals His design in history to men. There is a supreme confidence in an ultimate coherence of meaning through language which informs the biblical vision.

From an article in Commentary *magazine, which he expanded upon in his* Art of Biblical Narration *(1981).*

◻

Nathan Alterman

CREATION OF A NATION

And when I saw the African Jew bending over the furnace,
To draw out the ingot of red-hot steel,
And passing it with his tongs to the immigrant from the Balkans,
I saw a people standing firm on its foundations.

Quoted in Shimon Peres' From These Men: Seven Founders of the State of Israel *(1979).*

Murray Altman

EPISCOPALIAN JEW

I always knew that the first Jew who ran for President would be an Episcopalian.

> *Alluding to Senator Barry Goldwater, Republican candidate for the U.S. presidency in 1964. Although Goldwater's father was Jewish, his mother was Episcopalian.*

WASPY RABBI

It is even better to have a Wasp name when you're applying for a job as rabbi in some congregations.

> *Ibid.*

Jean Amery

TO DIE LIKE DOGS

Let the hungry be fed and the poor be welcome and the Jews shall die like dogs.

> *Publicizing a sign sighted beneath a crèche in Austria on Christmas 1938, emphasizing the degradation of the Nazi regime. Amery was an Auschwitz survivor.*

Yehuda Amichai

MAN AT THE CENTER

Once I sat on the stairs at the gate of David's Tower and put two heavy baskets next to me. A group of tourists stood there around their guide and I served as their orientation point. "You see that man with the baskets? A bit to the right of his head, there's an arch from the Roman period. A bit to the right of his head." But he moves, he moves!! I said to myself: redemption will come only when they are told: You see over there the arch from the Roman period? Never mind: but next to it, a bit to the left and lower, sits a man who bought fruit and vegetables for his home.

> *From his* Yehuda Amichai: A Life of Poetry 1948–1994 *(1994).*

CANDLES THAT REMEMBER

There are candles that remember for twenty-four hours,
As the label says. And there are candles that remember for eight hours.
And there are eternal candles that promise the memory of a man to his sons.

> *Ibid.*

Yigal Amir

ON GOD'S ORDERS

I acted alone on God's orders, and I have no regrets.

> *After being arrested for assassinating Prime Minister Yitzhak Rabin in Tel Aviv on November 4, 1995.*

Yehuda Amital

THE GAMBLE

I think there is a good chance that this [September 13, 1993 peace accord between Israel and the Palestinians] will prevent war.... I fear that with the rise of Hamas there would be a danger of Iran's involvement in the conflict, and then the distance to war is not great.... One thing is clear, anyone who thinks it is possible to continue the status quo without an explosion is living in a fool's paradise. The status quo would bring an explosion; it would bring Hamas and fundamentalism.

> *From an interview in* The Jerusalem Post, *November 13, 1993.*

(Prophet) Amos

CHOSEN FOR WHAT?

You alone have I singled out of all the families of the earth. That is why I will visit upon you all your sins.

> *From the Book of Amos (3:2).*

Morey Amsterdam

CAPONE AND ME

Maybe they thought I had a machine gun in my cello case, but the racket guys loved me. Al Capone called me "Kid." He'd pick me up and drive me out to his home in Cicero. He'd cook spaghetti for me, and I'd play Italian songs for him.

> *Recalling his relationship with Al Capone as a teenager in the late 1920s. Quoted in Darryl Lyman's* Jewish Comedy Catalog *(1989).*

Jawad al-Anani

BANNING OF SCHINDLER'S LIST

People are going to ask me: Is this the time to sympathize with what happened almost fifty years ago, when the massacre in Hebron took place four weeks ago?

Explaining plans to ban the movie Schindler's List *in Jordan. The February 1994 Hebron massacre left thirty-nine Moslems dead while at prayer in a mosque.*

Marc D. Angel

NOW I AM AN ORPHAN

Being a rabbi, I officiated at the funeral [of my mother]. During the eulogy, I found myself saying, "Now I am an orphan. My brothers and sister are orphans." Even as I said those words, I felt that they were surprising. The word orphan usually connotes helplessness. But I, my brothers and sister were married, had families of our own. We were not helpless. We were adults in the middle of our own lives. Nevertheless, I felt orphaned. And years later, I still feel so. The death of a parent changes one's life in practical and abstract ways. I don't think that one ever stops missing a deceased parent.

From his essay entitled "On the Death of a Parent," which appears in The Hadassah Magazine Jewish Parenting Book *(1989), edited by Roselyn Bell.*

Charles Angoff

THE MYSTERY OF WOMEN

The mystery of women is largely the product of the romantic imagination of men.

From an article in American Mercury, *September 1950.*

Mordecai Anielewicz

A LIFE FULFILLED

I cannot describe the conditions in which the Jews of the ghetto are now living. Only a few exceptional individuals will be able to survive such suffering.... It is impossible to light a candle, for lack of air. Greetings to you who are outside. Perhaps a miracle will occur and we shall see each other again one of these days. It is extremely doubtful. The last wish of my life has been fulfilled. Jewish self-defense has become a fact. Jewish resistance and revenge have become actualities.

I am happy to have been one of the first Jewish fighters in the ghetto.

Where will rescue come from?

From his last letter, dated April 23, 1943. On May 8th he died with his colleagues in the command bunker at 18 Mila Street. He was twenty-four years old.

Anonymous

DISCOVERING ONE'S IDENTITY

I thought of myself as a Russian, not as a Jew. Then after the war, I found that it did not make any difference what I thought about myself—I was a Jew on the books. I was a Jew to the director of the institute where I worked. Very well. I became a Jew to myself.

From a description by a Russian Jew. Quoted in an article by Harrison Salisbury in The New York Times *after a 1955 visit to Russia.*

TODAY I SHALL BE GLAD

From tomorrow on, I shall be sad,
From tomorrow on.
Today I shall be glad!
What is the use of sadness?—tell me that!
Why should I grieve tomorrow—today?
Tomorrow may be so good, sunny.
Tomorrow the sun may shine for us again.
We will no longer be sad.
From tomorrow on I shall be sad,
From tomorrow on!
Not today! No! Today I will be glad.
And every day—no matter how bitter it be,
I shall say:
From tomorrow on I shall be sad,
Not today.

A poem entitled "Motele," left behind by a young child who perished in the Warsaw Ghetto uprising.

WHO WAS JOB?

Job never was and never existed.

Quoted in the talmudic tractate Bava Batra (15a). The Midrash Genesis Rabba (57:4) ascribes the quote to Rabbi Simeon ben Lakish.

TRIUMPH OF LOVE

Here I can't even get a date, and that guy's in solitary and gets engaged!

In reaction to the announcement that Jonathan Pollard, a convicted Israeli spy, became engaged while serving time in an American prison. Quoted by Jonathan Mark in The Jewish Week, *December 3–9, 1993.*

GILDING THE LILY

The letters of the Torah Scroll must not be gilded.

Quoted in the talmudic tractate Sefer Torah (1:7).

MAN'S THREE NAMES

Every man has three names: one his father and mother gave him, one others call him, and one he acquired himself.

Quoted in Ecclesiastes Rabba (7:1).

HAIRCUT RITUAL

The king has his hair trimmed every day; the High Priest, every eve of the Sabbath; and the common priest, once in thirty days.

Quoted in the talmudic tractate Sanhedrin (22b).

LOQUACIOUS LADIES

Ten measures of talk were bequeathed to the world. Nine were taken by women and the one was left for the entire world.

Quoted in the talmudic tractate Kiddushin (49b).

LESSON IN HUMILITY

Fortunate is the generation whose ruler [is humble enough that he] brings a sacrifice for a sin he has committed unwittingly.

Quoted in the name of the Rabbis in the talmudic tractate Hora'yot (10b).

PLAGIARISM DISCOURAGED

Everyone who quotes a statement in the name of him who said it brings deliverance to the world.

Quoted in the talmudic tractate Ethics of the Fathers (6:6).

A FATHER'S OBLIGATION

A father is obligated, concerning a son, to circumcise him, to redeem him [if he is a first-born of his mother], to teach him Torah, to see that he marries, and to teach him a craft.

Quoted in the name of the Rabbis in the talmudic tractate Kiddushin (29a).

ON BEING PLIABLE

A person should always be as pliable as a reed and as unyielding as a cedar.

Quoted in the name of the Rabbis in the talmudic tractate Taanit (20a).

RECIPROCATING RESPECT

Fortunate is the generation in which great men pay attention to persons of lesser stature, and all the more so when the less educated heed the advice of the more learned.

Quoted in the talmudic tractate Rosh Hashana (25b).

WHEN GOD IS SILENT

I believe in the sun even when it is not shining. I believe in love even when not feeling it. I believe in God even when He is silent.

An inscription on the wall of a cellar in Cologne, Germany, where Jews hid from the Nazis.

BEING EVER GRATEFUL

If a Jew breaks a leg, he says, "Praised be God that I did not break both legs." If he breaks both legs, he says, "Praised be God that I did not break my neck."

Yiddish folksaying.

DISBELIEVING THE INEVITABLE

Every man knows that he must die, but no one believes it.

Yiddish folksaying.

FRIENDLY ENEMIES

A mother-in-law and daughter-in-law do not ride in the same cart.

Yiddish folksaying.

SHOFAR-BLOWING TECHNIQUE

An ox has a long tongue, and yet can't blow the shofar.

Yiddish folksaying.

UNDERSTATING THE OBVIOUS

For borsht you don't need any teeth.

Yiddish folksaying.

LETTING OFF STEAM

If God lived on earth, people would break his windows.

Yiddish folksaying.

WITHHOLDING GOOD WISHES

To a doctor you mustn't wish a good year.

Yiddish folksaying.

FULL HEART

When the heart is full, the eyes overflow.

Yiddish folksaying.

THE COMPANY ONE KEEPS

Whoever goes to sleep with dogs gets up with fleas.

Yiddish folksaying.

Taking It Out on God

Because he is angry at the cantor he [a congregant] doesn't say "Amen."

Yiddish folksaying.

Psychic Litvaks

A Litvak [Lithuanian] is so clever he repents even before he sins.

Yiddish folksaying.

Charitable Jews

Jews are very charitable: when you say "good morning," they reply "good year."

Yiddish folksaying.

Money for Emergencies

Somehow, there is always money for *matzos* and shrouds.

Yiddish folksaying.

Self-reliance

You can't chew with somebody else's teeth.

Yiddish folksaying.

Ignorance Is Bliss

The luck of the ignoramus is that he doesn't know that he doesn't know.

Yiddish folksaying.

Overexposure

Houseguests and fish spoil on the third day.

Yiddish folksaying.

Spitting in the Well

Don't spit in the well. You may have to drink from it later.

Yiddish folksaying.

Painless Troubles

A boil is no trouble—under the other fellow's armpit.

Yiddish folksaying.

You Can't Take It With You

Shrouds have no pockets.

Yiddish folksaying.

How to Become Wealthy

If we didn't have to eat, we'd all be rich.

Yiddish folksaying.

Peace and War

An insincere peace is better than a sincere war.

Yiddish folksaying.

When Praise Is in Order

All brides are beautiful; all the dead are pious.

Yiddish folksaying.

Shifting Blame

When the girl doesn't know how to dance, she says the musicians don't know how to play.

Yiddish folksaying.

Two Ears, One Mouth

God gave man two ears and one mouth so he might hear much and say little.

Yiddish folksaying.

Personal Quirks

Every person has his own *meshugaas* [craziness].

Yiddish folksaying.

Growing into a Fool

Whoever is a child at twenty stays a fool till one hundred.

Yiddish folksaying.

It Takes Ten to Pray

Nine rabbis can't make a *minyan* [quorum for prayer], but ten cobblers can.

Yiddish folksaying.

The Physically Impossible

You can't dance at two weddings at the same time, nor can you sit on two horses with one buttocks.

Yiddish folksaying.

Always Accept

If they offer it to you, take it. If they take it from you, yell!

Yiddish folksaying.

Test of Devotion

One father supports ten children, but ten children do not support one father.

Yiddish folksaying.

Potatoes: The Poor Man's Menu

Zuntig—bulbes,
Montig—bulbes,
Dinstig un mitvoch—bulbes,
Donershtig un freitig—bulbes.
Ober Shabes in a novineh, a bulbe kigele!
Un zuntig vaiter, bulbes.

Translation
Spuds on Sunday,

Spuds on Monday,
Tuesday and Wednesday—spuds!
Thursday and Friday—spuds!
But the treat on the Sabbath is a pudding
of potatoes!
And on Sunday, once again, it is—spuds!

Yiddish folksong.

CONCENTRATION CAMP PRAYER

O Lord, remember not only the men and women of goodwill but also those of ill will. But do not remember the suffering they have inflicted upon us; remember the fruits we brought thanks to this suffering, our comradeship, our loyalty, our humility, the courage, the generosity, the greatness of heart which has grown out of this; and when they come to judgment, let all the fruits that we have borne be their forgiveness.

Found on a piece of wrapping paper in Ravensbrück concentration camp.

WHY ANIMALS DON'T SPEAK

The Holy One, blessed be He, has consideration for the dignity of mankind and, knowing their needs, He shut the mouth of beasts [making them dumb]. For had they been able to speak, it would have been impossible to put them to the service of man or to stand one's ground against them. For here was this ass, the most stupid of all beasts, and there was [Balaam] the wisest of all wise men, yet as soon as she opened her mouth he could not stand his ground against her!

From the Midrash Numbers Rabba (20:14), explaining why after the heathen prophet's encounter with his ass (Numbers 22), it was established that it is best for man that animals should be unable to speak.

WE ARE ALL EQUAL

A king of flesh and blood stamps his image on a coin, hence all coins look and are alike; but the King of Kings has stamped every man with the seal of the first man, yet no man is like any other.

Quoted in the talmudic tractate Sanhedrin (Mishna 4:5).

GIVING WITHOUT LOSING

It often happens that when one is eager to perform a *mitzva* [a commandment, such as giving charity], the Evil Impulse says to him: "Why do you want to reduce your wealth? Instead of giving to others, give it to your children." But man's Good Impulse says to him: "Give to a worthy cause. Just as the light [brightness] of a lamp is not diminished even if

a million candles are lighted from it, so will he who fulfills any commandment [by acts of charity] not suffer a diminution of his possessions."

Quoted in the Midrash Exodus Rabba (26:3) in a comment on the verse "The lifebreath of man is the lamp of the Lord" (Proverbs 20:27).

SOUNDS, SIGHTS, SMELLS

Three things restore a man's good spirits: [beautiful] sounds, sights, and smells.

Quoted in the talmudic tractate Berachot (57b).

ENHANCING SELF-ESTEEM

Three things enhance a man's self-esteem: a beautiful home, a beautiful wife, and beautiful clothes.

Ibid.

CURIOUS QUAKER WOMAN

Art thou a Jew, one of God's Chosen People?...May I examine thee?...Hmpf! Thou art no different from us.

Observation of a Quaker woman after examining the first Jew she ever met. Quoted in Max Dimont's Jews in America *(1978).*

ON DOCTOR'S FEES

A doctor who charges nothing is worth nothing.

Quoted in the talmudic tractate Bava Kamma (85a).

UNITY OF MANKIND

If any man saves a single human being, Scriptures considers it as if he had saved the whole world. And man was created singly [Adam alone, and not all mankind at one time] so that no one shall ever say, "My father was greater than your father [making us all equal]."

Quoted in the talmudic tractate Sanhedrin (Mishna 4:5). Later sources changed the words "human being" to "Israelite" (Jew).

RIGHTEOUS GENTILE

*Chasiday u-mot ha-olam
Der unvergessliche Lebenretter [sic] 1200
verfolgter Juden.*

Epitaph on the tombstone of Oskar Schindler (1908–1924), who is buried in the Latin cemetery of Mount Zion, Israel. The first line in Hebrew reads "Righteous Gentiles." The second line in German reads: "The unforgettable savior of 1,200 persecuted Jews."

WITH GOD'S HELP

Oy, if God would only help me until He helps me!

> *Quoted in Henry D. Spalding's* Encyclopedia of Jewish Humor *(1969).*

RAISING AN ORPHAN

Anyone who rears an orphan, boy or girl, in his own home is considered by Scripture to be his biological parent.

> *Quoted in the talmudic tractate Megilla (13a).*

NONLEVEL PLAYING FIELD

You cannot compare one who has bread in his basket with one who has no bread in his basket.

> *Quoted as a saying of the Rabbis in the talmudic tractate Yoma (18b).*

A JEW IS A JEW IS A JEW

A Jew and a hunchback are walking down the street. They pass a synagogue. The Jew says to the hunchback, "I used to be a Jew." And the hunchback counters, "I used to be a hunchback."

> *A popular anecdote.*

FROM MOSES TO MOSES

From Moses, the prophet, till Moses [Maimonides] there has not appeared his equal.

> *A folksaying popular with adherents of the twelfth-century Spanish scholar.*

MARTYRED MURDERER

A million Arabs aren't worth the fingernail of one Jew.

> *Statement by a rabbi eulogizing Dr. Baruch Goldstein, who murdered over forty Palestinians while they were praying in a mosque in Hebron on Friday morning February 25, 1994.*

ACKNOWLEDGING THANKFULNESS

It is forbidden for a man to enjoy anything of this world without [first reciting] a blessing, and if anyone does he commits a sacrilege.

> *Quoted in the name of the Rabbis in the talmudic tractate Berachot (35a).*

GREAT CELEBRATION

He who has not seen the rejoicing that took place at the ceremony of water-drawing has never seen a celebration in his life.

> *Called* Simchat Bet Ha-sho'eva *in Hebrew, this ceremony took place in Temple times at the conclusion of the first day of Sukkot. Water was poured on the altar to induce a rainy season. Quoted in the talmudic tractate Sukka (51b).*

BAD CHARACTER TRAIT

Whoever eats in the street is like a dog; and some [Rabbis] say that he is unfit to testify.

> *Quoted in the talmudic tractate Kiddushin (40b).*

FOR THE SAKE OF PEACE

We support the poor of the heathen along with the poor of Israel, and visit the sick of the heathen along with the sick of Israel, and bury the poor of the heathen along with the dead of Israel [if there is no one else to bury them]—all for the sake of peace.

> *Quoted in the name of the Rabbis in the talmudic tractate Gittin (61a).*

WORST KIND OF THEFT

Stealing from a Gentile is worse than stealing from a Jew because it involves the profanation of God's name.

> *Quoted in the Tosefta Bava Kamma (10:15).*

WHO IS SICK?

When a poor man eats chicken, one of them is sick.

> *A popular folksaying.*

WHEN THE TREES TREMBLED

When iron was created, the trees began to tremble. Said iron to them: Why do you tremble? Let none of your wood enter me [to form a handle] and not one of you will be injured.

> *A folksaying first mentioned in Genesis Rabba (5:10).*

JEWISH RACISM

All Swedes, get out of the water.... Take those Swedes out of the water. They probably don't realize that it's time to light the candles.

> *Abusive language used by lifeguards at a pool in a park near Tel Aviv on July 1, 1994. Ethiopian Jews are known as "Swedes."*

MAN'S TWO POCKETS

Everyone must have two pockets, so that he can reach into the one or the other, according to his needs. In his right pocket are to be the words: "For my sake was the world created," and in his left: "I am but dust and ashes."

> *A chassidic teaching. Quoted in Martin Buber's* Ten Rungs *(1947).*

WORLD WAR II ANTI-SEMITISM

First man killed—Mike Murphy
First man to sink a Jap warship—Colin Kelly

First man to down five Jap planes—Eddie
O'Hara
First man to get four new tires—Abie Cohen

> *Quoted in* Bluejacket, *December 31, 1942,
> a base newspaper of the U.S. Naval Train-
> ing School in Memphis, Tennessee.*

PORK DITTY

I had a piece of pork, I put it on a fork
And gave it to the curly-headed Jew
Pork, Pork, Pork, Jew, Jew, Jew.

> *An anti-Jewish jingle reportedly sung by
> schoolchildren throughout America. From an
> essay by Jonathan D. Sarna entitled "The
> Pork on the Fork: A Nineteenth-Century
> Anti-Jewish Ditty," which appeared in* Jew-
> ish Social Studies, *Vol. 45, No. 2 (1982).*

UPS AND DOWNS

Yom assal, yom bassal. One day honey, the
next day onions.

> *A Judeo-Arabic expression, especially
> popular in Iraq.*

◻

Solomon (Rappoport) Anski

COVERED WITH SILVER

There is glass in the window and in the
mirror, but in the mirror the glass is covered
with a little silver; now, lo and behold, no
sooner is a little silver added than you cease
to see others and see only yourself.

> *From his play* The Dybbuk *(1918).*

SIN MUST BE PURIFIED

As the goldsmith refines gold in his powerful flame, as the farmer winnows the grain
from the chaff, so must sin be refined of its
uncleanness, until only its holiness remains.

> *Ibid.*

◻

Mary Antin

THE PAST IS MINE

It is not I that belong to the past, but the
past that belongs to me.

> *From her* Promised Land *(1912).*

THE JEWISH PREFERENCE

There is never a Jewish community without
its scholars, but where Jews may not be both
intellectuals and Jews, they prefer to remain
Jews.

> *Ibid.*

SCARS OF INTEGRATION

All the processes of uprooting, transporta-
tion, replanting, acclimatization, and development took place in my own soul. I felt the
pang, the fear, the wonder, and the joy of it. I
can never forget, for I bear the scars. But I
want to forget—sometimes I long to forget. I
think I have thoroughly assimilated my past—
I have done its bidding—I want now to be of
today. It is painful to be consciously of two
worlds, the Wandering Jew in me seeks forgetfulness. I am not afraid to live on and on, if
only I do not have to remember too much. A
long past vividly remembered is like a heavy
garment that clings to your limbs when you
would run.

> *Ibid. Recounting how she tried desperately
> to discard her dearly held Jewish heritage so
> she might become a fully integrated Ameri-
> can and put her Russian past behind her.*

◻

Austin J. App

DENYING THE HOLOCAUST

Not finding the Nazis guilty of real war
crimes at all commensurate with the monstrous ones of the victors, they resorted to the
only alternative open to hypocrites and liars,
namely to fabricate a mass atrocity. This they
did with the legend of the six million Jews
"gassed."...This is a fabrication and swindle.

> *From his book* A Straight Look at the Third
> Reich *(1974), in which he denies the Holo-
> caust and accuses the Jews of directing Al-
> lied policy.*

◻

Aharon Appelfeld

UNAPPROACHABLE EXPERIENCES

I have confronted the Holocaust head on
when this is possible, but certain experiences
in life are unapproachable. They cannot be explored in a meaningful way. They can shock
and they can stun, but they cannot be compre-
hended.

> *From an article that first appeared in* The
> Jewish Advocate *of Boston.*

THE UNFATHOMABLE

The deaths of millions remain too astonishing a phenomenon to explore in a literary situation. A writer should deal with individuals.

> *Ibid.*

HOLOCAUST AS METAPHOR

The Holocaust is a central event in many people's lives, but it has also become a metaphor for our century. There cannot be an end to speaking and writing about it.

A comment that appeared in The New York Times, *November 15, 1986.*

LIFE AFTER AUSCHWITZ

Today I can't imagine myself as a Jew without being religious.... I can't imagine any form of Jewish life without prayer and the synagogue. I came to that because after looking inside myself, I felt there is meaning to life, even after Auschwitz, and so there is the obligation to continue. If there is meaning, then there is God. Faith gives us a chance. It is up to us what to do with it.

From an article in the Baltimore Jewish Times. *Quoted in Anne Roiphe's* Season for Healing *(1988).*

ENLARGEMENT OF VISION

To be a decent citizen after the experience of Auschwitz is doubtless a considerable personal achievement and a social contribution, but it cannot be interpreted as a spiritual victory.

From his Beyond Despair: Three Lectures and a Conversation with Philip Roth *(1994).*

SUPPRESSING THE HOLOCAUST

For many years the members of my generation were concerned with the concealment and repression or, to use a harsher word, the suppression of memory.

Ibid.

WHAT REMEMBERING MEANS

To remember, you have to do something concrete. Study the Bible seriously. Study Talmud. Learn Yiddish and Hebrew. Then you're speaking the language the victims spoke. Then you will be in the circle where your parents or ancestors lived. Otherwise what does remembering mean?

From an interview in The Reporter of Women's American ORT, *Winter 1994–95.*

MY HOME

Jewishness is my home. I mean the people, their lives, their learning. My home is Jewish history, Jewish character, Jewish fate.

Ibid.

TO BE A WRITER

You are a writer or not a writer. I don't accept the term "Holocaust writer." I write about Jews and non-Jews, about Western Jews and Western civilization.

Ibid.

LANGUAGE OF THE ABSURD

To my surprise he [Franz Kafka] spoke to me not only in my mother tongue, but also in another language which I knew intimately, the language of the absurd. I had come from the camps and the forests, from a world that embodied the absurd, and nothing in that world was foreign to me. What was surprising was this: How could a man who had never been there know so much, in precise detail, about that world?

My real world was far beyond the power of the imagination.

From his Beyond Despair: Three Lectures and a Conversation with Philip Roth.

❑

Miriam Arad

PREDICTING THE FUTURE

As Mr. [Yitzhak] Rabin once observed, there's no predicting Middle East affairs. No one foresaw Sadat's trip to Jerusalem, the Iran-Iraq war, the split in the PLO and the *brogez* [anger] between Arafat and Assad.... Not only did no one foresee any of it, they foresaw a whole lot of other things that never happened.

From her Randomalia *(1988).*

❑

Yitzak Arad

SILENCE OF THE CHURCH

All of us know about the silence of the Church at that time [of the Holocaust]. If the Church had raised its voice, many more Jews would have survived. It would have caused more Christians to help Jews, and Jewish survival often depended on the local population.

A statement made after conducting Cardinal John O'Connor of New York through Yad Vashem in Jerusalem.

❑

Suha Tawil Arafat

MRS. ARAFAT SPEAKS

He [Yasser Arafat] simply cannot walk away from it now—it's gone too far. And, if we stop this process now, there will be massacre after massacre, just like Bosnia. But, if we go ahead, then we will get the economic prize [foreign investment for Gaza and the West Bank] and the political prize will follow that. We're a tiny country, and we have no choice. We must coexist with the Israelis, and we can learn a lot from them: about agriculture, economic development, women's rights. I grew up in a house where Israelis were coming and going all the time. So, you see, for me making peace with them is not at all strange.

From an interview with Mary Anne Weaver in which Yasser Arafat's wife speaks out against the rumors that her husband might abandon the peace process initiated with Israel on September 13, 1993. Quoted in The New Yorker, *May 16, 1994.*

No Hiding from Death

His life is under constant threat, but he's prepared me for the day, if it comes. He often says that you have to be a believer, that nobody takes more than is written in his destiny, and that when death comes it will come whether you are hiding in a castle, in a villa, or walking down the street.

Ibid. Responding to whether she fears Arafat will be assassinated.

Mrs. Arafat, the Feminist

I have told my husband that if he denies women equality, I will be in the vanguard of women on the streets, protesting outside his office in the new Palestinian state. I also feel very strongly that polygamy must be banned. My husband says that it is justified in the Koran, but he is simply wrong. I have told him again and again that I will not tolerate legitimate mistresses in Palestine, and for me that is what polygamy is. But I am not confronting him on religious grounds. I am challenging him on social and economic grounds.

Ibid.

Helping Our Husbands

Time will give us the answers that yes, Arafat was right.... He is a man of peace and the only one who can deliver it.... I would like to tell Madame Rabin, let's sit together and help our husbands to make peace together.

In an interview in Tunis with CNN on Monday, September 13, 1993, the day on which Israel and the PLO signed a peace accord at the White House.

✡

Yasser Arafat

Self-rule vs. Statehood

The Palestinian state is within our grasp. Soon the Palestinian flag will fly on the walks, the minarets, and the cathedrals of Jerusalem.

Upon the announcement that Israel and the Palestinians were reaching a peace agreement. Reported in The New York Times, *September 3, 1993.*

Letter to Rabin

The signing of the Declaration of Principles marks a new era in the history of the Middle East. In firm conviction thereof, I would like to confirm the following PLO commitments:

The PLO recognizes the right of the State of Israel to exist in peace and security.

The PLO accepts United Nations Security Council Resolutions 242 and 338.

The PLO commits itself to the Middle East peace process and to a peaceful resolution of the conflict between the two sides and declares that all outstanding issues relating to permanent status will be resolved through negotiations.

The PLO considers that the signing of the Declaration of Principles constitutes a historic event, inaugurating a new epoch of peaceful coexistence, free from violence and all other acts which endanger peace and stability. Accordingly, the PLO renounces the use of terrorism and other acts of violence and will assume responsibility over all PLO elements and personnel in order to assure their compliance, prevent violence and discipline violators.

In view of the promise of a new era and the signing of the Declaration of Principles and based on Palestinian acceptance of Security Council Resolutions 242 and 338, the PLO affirms that those articles of the Palestinian Covenant which deny Israel's right to exist, the provisions of the Covenant which are inconsistent with the commitments of this letter are now inoperative and no longer valid. Consequently, the PLO undertakes to submit to the Palestinian National Council for formal approval and necessary changes in regard to the Palestinian Covenant.

The text of a September 9, 1993 letter to Yitzhak Rabin in which the Palestine Liberation Organization renounces terrorism and recognizes Israel's right to exist.

Battle of Our Lives

The battle for peace is the most difficult battle of our lives. It deserves our utmost efforts because the land of peace yearns for a just and comprehensive peace.

> *At the White House signing of the Israeli-Palestinian peace accord on September 13, 1993.*

OUR NATIONAL AUTHORITY

I know it [declaring a Palestinian state] is a problem for Israelis, so we'll declare our "national authority," which is really a state.

> *From an interview with* U.S. News and World Report *following the signing of the September 13, 1993 peace accord.*

CONFEDERATION, NOT STATEHOOD

We have taken a decision not to go in the direction of an independent state, but toward confederation with Jordan.

> *Foreign Minister Peres quoting Arafat after a conversation in Switzerland early in 1994.*

I AM HIS EXCELLENCY

I am not Mr. Chairman. I am His Excellency, the President of Palestine.

> *When responding to Swedish Prime Minister Carl Bildt's greeting at a meeting in Stockholm in December 1993.*

THE HAND THAT MILLIONS KISSED

Millions of Moslems kiss my hand, and you [the Israelis] treat me like a hostage. I'd have no problem stepping outside and declaring within one minute that it's all called off, that it's all a mistake—and nothing would happen to me.

> *Toward the end of a summit meeting between Arafat and Yitzhak Rabin in Cairo on December 12, 1993, when the September 13, 1933 peace accord seemed to be falling apart because Rabin would not agree to Arafat's demands.*

HEBRON MASSACRE

I know. I am an expert. No one can kill 65 and injure 256 alone. No one. There is no Rambo.

> *Suggesting a conspiracy behind the Hebron massacre of February 25, 1994, in which Palestinians engaged in prayer were gunned down by Dr. Baruch Goldstein. Quoted in* The Jerusalem Report, *March 24, 1994.*

ULTIMATE GOAL

From here in Gaza, we will go to the Ibrahim mosque [the Machpela Cave in Hebron], we will go to Nablus, Jenin, Tulkarm, Kalkiya, Bethlehem, Ramallah and then, after Hebron, Jerusalem, Jerusalem, Jerusalem to pray there

together....

We have vowed to our martyrs that we will pray for them in Jerusalem, which is the first site, the site of the prophet Mohammed and the birthplace of Jesus....

The promise is alive, it is alive and the pledge is alive. We have lots of work to do to build our Palestinian National Authority and then our free independent Palestinian state.

> *From a speech delivered in Gaza on July 1, 1994.*

INVITORS AND INVITEES

They [the Israelis] haven't the right to offer him invitations. It is my duty and my responsibility to offer the invitations to all my brothers and to all my friends to visit the holy city. This is the jurisdiction of the Palestinians and I appreciate very much that King Hussein will come to visit the holy city together with me. This is an invitation from me to His Majesty.

> *At a news conference in July 1994 after Israel invited King Hussein to visit Jerusalem, claiming that doing so was his prerogative.*

THE COMING JIHAD

I tell those who are making operations here and there, they should remember we are making a reconciliation agreement. We should respect it because the Prophet Mohammed respected his reconciliation with the atheists.... This is the stage of the great jihad to construct our homeland of Palestine and Jerusalem its capital.

> *Referring to recent Hamas attacks. From an October 1994 speech to students at Gaza's Al-Azhar University. Quoted in* The Jerusalem Post, *November 5, 1994.*

ON JERUSALEM

We are now in the midst of negotiations, but if the Israelis think that we do not have alternatives—by Allah [I swear that] they are mistaken. The Palestinian people is ready to sacrifice the last boy and the last girl in order for the Palestinian flag to fly over the walls of Jerusalem, its mosques and its churches.

> *From an August 6, 1995 speech delivered at Al-Azhar University. Quoted in an article by Ze'ev B. Begin in* The Jerusalem Report, *November 16, 1995.*

MY FAMILY

You are my family now.

> *Upon visiting and kissing Leah Rabin, widow of slain Israeli leader Yitzhak Rabin, and Rabin's grandchildren during the week of shiva. Quoted in* Newsday, *November 28, 1995.*

Isaac Arama

JEWS AND GENTILES

Every truly righteous Gentile is equal to a son of Israel.

> *Quoted in his fifteenth-century philosophical commentary on the Torah,* Akedat Yitzchak, *chapter 60. This view is also found in Joseph Caro's* Code of Jewish Law *(Yoreh Deah 367:1).*

Abdel Rahman Aref

FATAL PROGNOSTICATION

We shall, God willing, meet in Tel Aviv and Haifa.

> *Iraq's president in an address to his air force officers in June 1967, just before the Six-Day War.*

MINCING NO WORDS

Our goal is clear: to wipe Israel off the map.

> *In a statement prior to the 1967 Six-Day War.*

Hannah Arendt

THE ANONYMITY OF DEATH

The concentration camps, by making death itself anonymous [that is, making it impossible to find out whether a prisoner is dead or alive], robbed death of its meaning as the end of a fulfilled life. In a sense they took away the individual's own death, proving that thenceforth nothing belonged to him and he belonged to no one. His death merely set a seal on the fact that he had never existed.

> *From her* Origins of Totalitarianism *(1951).*

FULL EXTENT OF IMMORTALITY

Aristotle explicitly assures us that man, insofar as he is a natural being and belongs to the species of mankind, possesses immortality; through the recurrent cycle of life, nature assures the same kind of being-forever to things that are born and die as to things that are and do not change.

> *From her* Between Past and Future *(1961).*

THE BANALITY OF EVIL

It was as though in those last minutes he [Eichmann] was summing up the lessons that this long course in human wickedness had taught us—the lesson of the fearsome, word-and-thought-defying banality of evil.

> *From her* Eichmann in Jerusalem: A Report on the Banality of Evil *(1963).*

EICHMANN'S DEFENDER

Adolf Eichmann went to the gallows with great dignity.

> *Ibid. In her book, Arendt debunks the idea that Eichmann and the Germans were solely responsible for what happened to the Jews—a view for which she was highly criticized.*

PUNISHMENT AS A DETERRENT

No punishment has ever possessed enough power of deterrence to prevent the commission of crimes. On the contrary, whatever the punishment, once a specific crime has appeared for the first time, its reappearance is more likely than its initial emergence could have been.

> *Ibid.*

THE SEARCH FOR LIGHT

Even in the darkest of times we have the right to expect some illumination, and that such illumination may come less from theories and concepts than from the uncertain, flickering, and often weak light that some men and women, in their lives and work, will kindle under almost all circumstances and shed over the time-span that was given them on earth.

> *From her* Men in Dark Times *(1968).*

THE CONVERSION OF REVOLUTIONARIES

It is well known that the most radical revolutionary will become a conservative on the day after the revolution.

> *From an article in* The New Yorker, *September 12, 1970.*

THINKING VS. ACTING

Under conditions of tyranny it is far easier to act than to think.

> *Quoted in W.H. Auden's* A Certain World *(1970).*

SOURCE OF TRUTH

Human truth never resides in the exception, not even in the exception of the persecuted but only in what is, or should be, the rule. It was out of this insight that Kafka's Zionist tendencies sprang. He affiliated himself with the movement that wanted to liquidate the exceptional position of the Jews, to make them into a "people like all other peoples." He, possibly the last of the great European writers, could certainly not have desired to become a nationalist.

From her Secret Tradition: Eight Essays *(1976).*

☼

Moshe Arens

EVERY JEW A SURVIVOR

Every Jew living today and every Jew born in the future is really a survivor of the Holocaust. They would not be alive, or born, if Hitler had had his way. We have a special obligation to assure the defeat of Hitler, to assure the existence of the Jewish people, and to assure that the message of the Jewish people will continue to come out of Zion. That can only be achieved here in Israel.

Quoted in Merrill Simon's Moshe Arens: Statesman and Scientist Speaks Out *(1988).*

CAMP DAVID NEGOTIATIONS

The facts are in—books have been written by participants in the Camp David talks about the negotiations held before and after. The historical record is clear that the Carter administration applied very severe, undue pressure on Israel to make concessions that really were contrary to Israel's best interests.

Ibid.

WHO IS A JEW?

From a proactive perspective, a Jew is a person who perceives himself (or herself) as being Jewish and accountable to demonstrate that Jewishness in a self-defined way. It may mean being strictly observant, being affiliated with a synagogue, being a member of a Jewish organization, and/or donating money or time to some Jewish cause. However demonstrated, it is an indication of commitment to being a Jew.

Ibid.

BATTLE OF CULTURE

This is not a conflict between Jews and Arabs, this is a conflict between two cultures. This is a conflict between two value systems. Until the Arab world adopts Western value systems, Israel has to keep its guard up and defend itself.

From an address to a group of Likud supporters on February 5, 1995.

THE GOLAN PROBLEM

We shouldn't give it [the Golan Heights] back, and anybody who thinks that if there are American troops on the Heights, it's OK for Israel to turn the Heights over to Syrian control, simply doesn't understand the problem.

Ibid.

UNCONSCIONABLE BEHAVIOR

I'm not in touch with Baker [today]. He was here in Israel but he didn't contact me. I'm not surprised. I think Baker realized that he behaved in an unconscionable manner toward me and I haven't forgotten it. And he knows that.

Claiming that U.S. Secretary of State James Baker tried to undermine the Shamir government, using aid as a lever to pressure Israel. From an interview in The Jerusalem Post, *February 11, 1995.*

NO SMILES FROM ASSAD

The fear I have is reading the paper in the morning that a deal has been done. If we lose the Golan, and I hope we don't, then Israel is going to be in danger. The only reason we haven't given back the Golan is that [Syrian leader] Assad is not ready to smile at Israel.

Ibid.

COMPUTER WRITING

I didn't realize how easy it is to write on a computer. I could write ten books.

Ibid. After writing his first book, Broken Covenant *(1995).*

☼

Judah Arieh

REVELATION IS NEVER-ENDING

His [God's] revelation is continuous. New aspects of the Torah unfold constantly. The more we study it, the more it expands.

From his Sefat Emet *(1926).*

☼

Chaim Arlosoroff

CONFLICTING VIEWS

To the revolutionaries, the Jew is the capitalist, against whom pogroms are instigated; to the capitalist, on the other hand, he is the revolutionary who should not be allowed to see the light of day.

Quoted in Shlomo Avineri's Arlosoroff *(1989).*

TRUE NATIONALISM

Our nationalism is the nationalism of the hungry and the starved. We are all property-less, we are all naked; all of us, as a nation, are a proletarian people.

We do not stoop to conquer, as do those European nations who are proud of their sword; we do not have the power to conquer. We need all the power we can muster in order to survive, to keep our identity, our culture, our being and our future.

Ibid.

ARAB NATIONALISM

An Arab movement does exist. It would be pernicious for us to belittle it, or to rely on bayonets, be they Jewish or English, to sup-press it. You can rely on bayonets only for a limited period of time, but not for decades.

Ibid.

POLITICS OF COMPROMISE

We have only one way—the way of peace, and only one policy—the policy of mutual un-derstanding. It is especially important to say these things now, in a moment of rage and anger.... Because of existing conditions, Jews and Arabs are pushed into one path, and therefore they are in need of the politics of compromise.

Ibid.

POLITICS OF PEACE

The Arabs, too, will have to understand that they have no other way except the poli-tics of peace, that the determination of the Hebrew nation to build its national home in Eretz Israel is irrevocable. They should know that the more this land is soaked with Jewish blood, the more obstinate will be our will to strike roots in it.

Ibid.

◻

Richard Armey

FREUDIAN SLIP?

I don't have to listen to Barney Fag—Bar-ney Frank—haranguing in my ear because I made a few bucks off a book I worked on.

A January 1995 comment about Represen-tative Barney Frank of Massachusetts, an avowed homosexual.

◻

Matthew Arnold

BEAUTY AND HOLINESS

The Hebrews believed in the beauty of ho-liness; the Greeks believed in the holiness of beauty.

By attribution.

THE NATURE OF CONSCIENCE

The governing idea of Hellenism is spon-taneity of consciousness, that of Hebraism, strictness of conscience.

From his Culture and Anarchy *(1869).*

INCOMPARABLE ISAIAH

The Hebrew language and genius are seen in the Book of Isaiah at their perfection—this has naturally had its effect on the English translators of the Bible, whose Version no-where perhaps rises to such beauty as in this "Book."

Quoted in Joseph H. Hertz's Pentateuch and Haftorahs *(1961).*

◻

Reuben Arnold

THE LEO FRANK CASE

The most horrible persecution of a Jew since the death of Christ.

Commenting on the indictment and trial of his client, who was convicted of murdering a thirteen-year-old employee, Mary Phagan, in April 1913. Quoted in The Atlanta Con-stitution, *October 26, 1913.*

◻

Beatrice Arthur

ANIMAL RIGHTS

I think fur coats should have a label on them saying how they became fur coats. Peo-ple don't know the indignity, the horror, that animals go through.

Quoted in Darryl Lyman's Jewish Comedy Catalog *(1989).*

◻

Max Arzt

LOVING GOD SINCERELY

We need to advance from affiliation to af-firmation, from external compliance to inner conviction. Solomon Schechter, the great

Anglo-American theologian, called our attention to the truism that one cannot love God with his father's heart.

From his Justice and Mercy *(1963).*

TESTING CONSTANCY OF CHARACTER

Constancy of character is tested whenever a crisis occurs and a decision is called for. We readily sustain our principles when no sacrifice is entailed. But too often we rationalize their abandonment when the situation calls for heroic disregard of immediate personal comfort or interest.

Ibid.

¤

Sholem Asch

ORIGIN OF CHRISTIAN VALUES

All the values which unfolded in Christianity—love, pity, patience, insight, restraint, the essentials of our civilization—are Jewish values.

From his What I Believe *(1941).*

WHEN THE WORLD HELD ITS BREATH

It lasted an eternity, it lasted an instant. It was an incident in human history not to be measured with the limited apprehension of man, but belonging to the province of the Eternal and the infinite of Divinity. And therefore it is impossible to speak of the duration of the exalted episode. Only when the voice of God ceased from speaking did the world fall back into its framework of time and space; and only then did Israel experience the fullness of fear. It was a peculiar dread of the ungraspable. They did not know where they were, whether on the earth or still hovering in space with God, held by an invisible power to the flying mountain.

From his Moses *(1951), translated by Maurice Samuel.*

MESSIANISM: JEWISH SPIRITUAL TERRITORY

The Messianic ideal gave birth to the world-destiny of Christianity. We have no part and no partnership with the Church. Our roads divided very early. This is not the place to make accusations....

But we have a deep part and a close relationship with that glorious figure—one of the brightest stars in Israel's sky—Jesus of Nazareth, and with all that has to do with him. With all that he stands for, with his whole Jewish environment. It is spiritual Jewish territory, which belongs to the Jewish writer. He

blooms in the garden of the Jewish spirit—and who will tell me that the fruit of this tree is forbidden to me?

From an essay entitled "My Faith," included in Great Yiddish Writers of the Twentieth Century *(1969), translated by Joseph Leftwich.*

UNIVERSAL ARTIST

I am not a Yiddish artist, I am a universal artist.

Defining himself. Quoted in Charles A. Madison's Yiddish Literature *(1971).*

¤

Isaac Asimov

THE DYNAMICS OF CHANGE

It is change, continuing change, inevitable change, that is the dominant factor in society today. No sensible decision can be made any longer without taking into account not only the world as it is, but the world as it will be.

From an article published in The Encyclopedia of Science Fiction, *edited by Robert Holdstock (1978).*

¤

Edward Asner

ACTIVIST FOR HUMAN RIGHTS

Though I find some Jews these days certainly lacking in Jewish soul, I credit a lot of it to my Jewish soul and Jewish awareness. Jews never knew when the blow would fall on them. So if we find some people drifting from that path, from that thought of progressivism, that thought of constant concern for human rights, then maybe they're feeling awfully comfortable and safe in America to be able to forget about the past so easily.

Responding to the question, "Why are you so obsessed with progressive ideals?" From Tim Boxer's Jewish Celebrity Hall of Fame *(1987).*

IT'S GOOD TO HAVE A DREAM

Growing up, we identified comfortably with Israel and the creation of a homeland, always talking about a homeland. Most of the time we thought it was a dream. It was part of the ritual. It's good to have a dream.

Ibid.

NO ATHEISTS IN FOXHOLES

There are times when I want to say I absolutely believe in Him, and there are times I would say I am not sure what belief is. There are no atheists in the foxholes. I rarely, if ever, have been in touch with Him or He with me.

Ibid.

A Jew Must Be Better

A Jew to me is special, supposedly inspired to rise above the levels perhaps established for others. If we sink to the same levels, then to me there is no importance to being a Jew or any drive to maintain the identification.

Ibid.

¤

Hafez al-Assad

Yes and No

It's now up to the Israelis: Sometimes we hear yes, sometimes no. More no. Maybe they are not good at saying yes.

Commenting on the Middle East Peace Conference in 1992.

Triple Talk

I said we decided not to obstruct the agreement. I did not say we will obstruct those who oppose it. It is not our specialty, responsibility or right to repress those who oppose this agreement or those who oppose anything else.... We decided not to obstruct the agreement. We said it is up to the Palestinian people and their organizations.

In an October 1, 1993 interview with Charlayne Hunter-Gault of PBS in which the Syrian president speaks out on the September 13, 1993 peace accord between Israel and the PLO.

In Honor We Shall Make Peace

Syria seeks a just and comprehensive peace with Israel as a strategic choice that secures Arab rights, ends the Israeli occupation and enables our peoples in the region to live in peace, security and dignity. In honor we fought, in honor we negotiate, and in honor we shall make peace. We want an honorable peace for our people and for the hundreds of thousands who paid their lives in defense of their countries and their rights.

Excerpt from a news conference with U.S. President Bill Clinton and the President of Syria, held in Geneva, Switzerland, January 16, 1994.

¤

W. H. Auden

Squandered Solicitude

I know that all the verse I wrote, all the positions I took in the thirties, didn't save a single Jew from Auschwitz.

Quoted in What Did They Think of the Jews? *(1991), edited by Allan Gould.*

Incipient Anti-Semitism

Anti-Semitism is, unfortunately, not only a feeling which all Gentiles at times feel, but also, and this is what matters, a feeling of which the majority of them are not ashamed.

Quoted in Joseph Telushkin's Jewish Wisdom *(1994).*

¤

Ephraim Auerbach

The Collective and Individual Sabbath

The Sabbath has never ceased to be with us a source of creative activity, of artistic and ethical inspiration. From ancient days to our own time the Sabbath is a living figure, with which both the collective imagination of the folk and the individual vision of the artist are busily engaged the whole time. The ordinary Jew in the street and the ordinary Jewess created their own Sabbath in the image of their own feeling, pulsating with their own fervent faith.

From his essay, "The Song of Sabbath." Reprinted in Joseph Leftwich's anthology The Way We Think *(1969).*

¤

Shlomo Avineri

Israel's Conflict with the PLO

Israel should not enter into talks with the PLO. The PLO, as presently constituted, is aimed explicitly and unequivocally at the destruction of the State of Israel. This aim is rooted in a number of deeply held ideological conceptions, the primary among them expressed in Article 20 of the PLO Charter. This Article states that the Jews are not a nation and hence have no claim for national sovereignty or national self-determination....

Unlike many fellow academics, both in Israel and abroad, I do not envisage any magic formula for the resolution of the conflict, precisely because it is not a conflict about boundaries or territories, or even the fate of the

Palestinians, but because it is a conflict about the legitimacy of Israel's existence.

> *From a symposium that appeared in* Moment *magazine, March 1976.*

◻

(Rabbi) Avira

THE PRUDENT MAN

A man should always eat and drink less than his means allow, clothe himself in accordance with his means, and honor his wife and children more than his means allow, for they are dependent upon him and he is dependent upon "Him who spake and the world came into being."

> *Quoted in the talmudic tractate Chulin (84b).*

◻

Bernard Avishai

BRAINPOWER MORE VALUABLE THAN OIL

Israel is on the verge of a new prosperity, grounded in a new political economy—both of which will engender a new basis for peace. When Palestinians finally begin building their national life, they will discover that they could do worse than live between Tel Aviv and Amman. All sides will discover that the new global economy needs imaginative political arrangements, not outdated notions of self-determination that have long confounded peacemakers....

This turnaround reflects a vast change in global competition. Brainpower is now more valuable than oil, and Israel has some of the biggest proven reserves of it.

> *Following the famous Rabin-Arafat handshake on September 13, 1993. From an Op-Ed essay in* The New York Times, *September 29, 1993.*

◻

Colette Avital

KNOWING FACTS REDUCES FEAR

Violence is not part and parcel of Jewish tradition. Religious leaders have a moral obligation to lead their communities better in the sense of toleration. I strongly appeal to the Orthodox community—which is not uniformly against the government of Israel or the peace plan—and to those who incite, to reconsider [their actions].... If people knew the facts better, they would have less reason for concern.

> *From a wide-ranging interview with the editors of* The Jewish Week *to mark Avital's first anniversary as Israel's consul general in New York. Reported in* The Jewish Week, *December 31, 1993–January 6, 1994.*

A PEOPLE WITH A MEMORY

We are a people with a memory and a past and there can't be a future unless we know our history.

> *A comment made at an April 1994 ceremony, initiated by the Ronald S. Lauder Foundation and dedicated to the preservation of the Auschwitz-Birkenau concentration camps.*

INCITEMENT TO MURDER

[Rabbi Abraham Hecht's remarks] didn't cause anger on a personal level, but it was something that caused concern on a public level because it was an incitement to murder.

> *Referring to a statement made on Israeli television by the president of the Rabbinical Alliance of America. Hecht said that according to Torah law, Prime Minister Yitzhak Rabin could be killed as a traitor to the Jewish people because of the land givebacks called for in the Israeli–Palestinian peace agreements.*

Israel Baal Shem Tov

TORAH INTERPRETATION

The Torah is eternal, but its explanation is to be made by the spiritual leaders of Judaism...in accordance with the age.

Quoted in Solomon Schechter's Studies in Judaism *(1896).*

"UNITY" OF GOD

People should get to know what the unity of God really means. To attain a part of this indivisible unity is to attain the whole. The Torah and all its ordinances are from God. If I therefore fulfill but one commandment in and through the love of God, it is as though I have fulfilled them all.

Ibid.

SYNAGOGUE EVERYWHERE

A man needs no fixed places to say his prayers, no synagogues; among the trees of the forest, everywhere one can pray.

Quoted in S. A. Horodetzky's Leaders of Hasidism *(1928).*

SPARK OF HOLINESS

Everything created by God contains a spark of holiness.

Quoted by Solomon Anski in his play The Dybbuk *(1918).*

THE FEAT OF CREATION

Unless we believe that God renews the work of Creation every day, our prayers and our observance of the commandments becomes routine and jaded. As it is written in the Book of Psalms (71:9): "Cast me not off in the time of old age"—that is to say, do not let my world grow old.

Quoted in Nahum Glatzer's In Time and Eternity *(1946).*

LOVE AND COMPASSION

I cannot enter there. The house is full to the brim of teaching and prayer.... During the day the people speak here words without true devotion, without love and compassion, words that have no wings. They remain between the walls, they squat on the floor, they grow layer by layer like decaying leaves until the decay has packed the house to overflowing and there is no longer room for me in there.

Explaining why he once stood at the threshold of a synagogue but refused to enter. Quoted in Martin Buber's Legend of the Baal Shem *(1955).*

UNIQUENESS OF EXISTENCE

God never does the same thing twice. That which exists is unique, and it happens but once.

Ibid.

UNIQUENESS OF MAN

Every man should know that since Creation no other man ever was like him. Had there been another, there would be no need for him to be. Each is called on to perfect his unique qualities. And it is his failure to heed this call which delays the Messiah.

From Die Chassidischen Bücher *(1927).*

DRAWING CLOSE TO GOD

When a father starts to teach his child to walk, he stands in front of him and holds out his hands on either side of the child so that he cannot fall, and the boy goes toward his father. But the moment the child is close, his father withdraws a little and holds his hands farther apart. As the father does this again and again, the child learns to walk.

Responding to a question about God's seeming remoteness, put to him by a disciple. Quoted in William B. Silverman's Rabbinic Wisdom and Jewish Values *(1971).*

SOURCE OF BEAUTY

If the image of a beautiful woman, or any lovely thing, comes suddenly to mind, let one say to himself: The source of such beauty must be the divine force which envelops the universe. So why be attracted only to a part? Better be drawn to the All.

By attribution.

SPIRIT COUNTS

The important thing is not how many separate commandments we obey, but the spirit in which we obey them.

Ibid.

LEAVING ROOM FOR GOD

There is no room for God in a person who is full of himself.

Ibid.

¤

Isaac Babel

ODESSA AND ITS FAMOUS VIOLINISTS

All the folk in our circle—brokers, shopkeepers, clerks in banks and steamship offices—used to have their children taught music.... And in fact, in the course of ten years or so our town supplied the concert platforms of the world with infant prodigies. From Odessa came Elman, Zimbalist, Gabrilowitsch. Odessa witnessed the first steps of Jascha Heifetz.

From his "Awakening," a story about his childhood in Odessa (after 1905) in which his father, Emmanuel, hopes that Isaac, his favorite son, would become a famous musician.

EVEN GOD MAKES MISTAKES

If you need my life you may have it, but all make mistakes, God included. A terrible mistake has been made, Aunt Pesya. But wasn't it a mistake on the part of God to settle Jews in Russia, for them to be tormented worse than in Hell? How would it hurt if the Jews lived in Switzerland, where they would be surrounded by first-class lakes, mountain air, and nothing but Frenchies? All make mistakes, God not excepted.

Words spoken by Benya Krik, the gangster boss of Jewish Odessa, in Babel's story, "How It Was Done in Odessa."

¤

Lauren Bacall

OOZING CHARACTER

Bogie was a very complicated, fascinating man...character just oozed out of his pores.

Explaining what attracted her to Humphrey Bogart, whom she married on May 21, 1945, when she was twenty-one years old. Quoted in Elinor and Robert Slater's Great Jewish Women *(1994).*

SUMMING UP

He drank, he was an actor, and he was *goyim*.... No one has ever written a romance better than we lived it.

Ibid.

ENOUGH IS ENOUGH

Is it ever going to stop? Bogart's been dead for years. And being a widow is not exactly a profession, you know. It's time I was allowed a life of my own, to be judged and thought of as a person, as me.

Ibid. Objecting to constantly being called "Bogie's Baby" by his fans.

ON BEING DIFFICULT

I have a reputation for being difficult and I suppose in a way I'm like Barbra [Streisand] in that I'm a perfectionist. If that's difficult, then I'm difficult.

Ibid. Responding to critics after the completion of Mr. North, *her twentieth film.*

PROUD OF MY ROOTS

[I am] just a nice Jewish girl from New York. Going back through my life now, the Jewish family feeling stands proud and strong, and at least I can say I am glad I sprang from that. I would not trade those roots—that identity.

From her memoirs, Lauren Bacall by Herself *(1979).*

¤

Roger Bacon

PREREQUISITE TO UNDERSTANDING THE BIBLE

It is impossible that the quality of one language should be preserved in another.

Referring to Bacon's contention that a knowledge of Hebrew is a prerequisite to an understanding of the Bible. Quoted in A.B. Burke's Opus Majus of Roger Bacon *(1928).*

¤

Leo Baeck

HOW TO SEEK GOD

To avoid wrong and to seek good means to know God.

From his Essence of Judaism *(1936).*

PURPOSE OF PRAYER

The purpose of prayer is to leave us alone with God.

Ibid.

JUDAISM AND SOCIAL ACTION

In Judaism social action is religiosity, and religiosity implies social action.

Ibid.

ADDING MEANING TO LIFE

Through faith man experiences the meaning of the world; through action he is to give it meaning.

Ibid.

INDEPENDENCE OF THE SOUL

The thought underlying the Messianic conception is that the soul must not allow itself to be subjugated to anyone but God.

Ibid.

BOUNDS OF THE STATE

Religion may be the concern of a people, but it must never become a concern of the state.

Ibid.

MAN'S CREED

Man's creed is that he believes in God, and therefore in mankind....

Ibid.

ETHICAL MONOTHEISM

Only in Israel did an ethical monotheism exist, and wherever else it is found later on, it has been derived directly or indirectly from Israel.

Ibid.

WHERE THE REAL LIFE IS

The life of man means more than the narrowness of existence in this world. With all its deficiencies and limitations, its pain and suffering, it is, as the old Rabbinic metaphor says, but a place of "preparation," an "ante-chamber"; it is only the "life of the hour." The true life is the "eternal life."

Ibid.

GOD IS ONE

He is the One, and therefore man must decide for Him, in contrast to and over and against all else, and must serve Him only and no power of nature or fate....

Ibid.

LOVE THY NEIGHBOR

Service of God consists in what we do to our neighbor.

Ibid.

BOWING ONLY TO GOD

We stand before our God.... We bow to Him, and we stand erect before man.

From a prayer he distributed to synagogues throughout Germany in 1938 to be read on Yom Kippur.

JEWISH PIETY

Piety, especially Jewish piety, respects the little—the little man, the little matter, the little task, the little duty. Through the little, religion meets the greatness that lies behind.

By attribution.

ON TRANSLATING TEXTS

All translation is commentary.

From his Pharisees *(1947).*

A CREATIVE MINORITY

We Jews are, as it were, the sons of the revolution, the daughters of the revolution. We should be aware of it. We can always be what Dr. Toynbee calls a "creative minority."

From his Judaism *(1949).*

ABOVE ALL THAT COMES AND GOES

In the language of the Bible the word *berit* became a characteristically religious word, one of these words in which the idea of great interrelatedness, the great unity of all, of mystery and ordered certainty seeks to express itself. The God-given order was to find expression in this term.... The Old Aramaic translation of the Bible translated *berit* as *ka'yama* [that which is established], indicating that which is above all change, above all that comes and goes.

From his People of Israel *(1965).*

□

Gemaliel Bailey

JEWS AS SLAVE-DEALERS

The Davises [of Petersburg, Virginia]...are the great slave-traders. They are Jews [who] came to that place many years ago as poor peddlers....These men are always in the market, giving the highest price for slaves. During the summer and fall they buy them up at low prices, trim, shave, wash them, fatten them so that they may look sleek, and sell them to great profit.

Quoted by Harriet Beecher Stowe in her little-known commentary on Uncle Tom's Cabin. *From a letter she received from Dr. Bailey.*

◻

James A. Baker

CALLING THE WHITE HOUSE

Everybody over there [in Israel] should know that the telephone number [of the White House] is 1-202-456-1414. When you're serious about peace, call us.

Criticizing Israel's conditions for peace talks before the U.S. Congress in June 1990.

MIDEAST FRUSTRATION

Nothing has made my job of trying to find Arab and Palestinian partners for Israel more difficult than by being greeted by a new settlement [in the West Bank] every time I arrive in the Middle East.

In testimony before Congress in May 1991.

ARAFAT'S LAST CHANCE

Today, the Palestinian people enjoy a unique opportunity: a chance for the first time in over 40 years to enjoy peace, to build a society, to raise their children without bitterness or fear.

If you miscalculate, if you fail to show the courage necessary to build a true peace, they may lose it all. And, as lucky as you are, Mr. Chairman, there will be no second chance.

An open letter to Yasser Arafat published in Moment *magazine, December 1993.*

COURAGEOUS ACTION

Prime Minister Rabin and Foreign Minister Peres did not negotiate out of charity. Their actions were based...on an accurate calculation of Israel's short- and long-term interests.

Like you, the Israeli leadership showed great personal and political courage. Like you, they will pay a price if the dynamic for peace falters. But there the symmetry ends. If the peace agreement fails, the Labor government may lose an election. The Palestinians will lose a future.

Ibid.

◻

Eliyahu Bakshi-Doron

ENOUGH WARS

The situation in Israel is terrible and we pray that God should give peace....When I speak of peace, they [the PLO] want war. There is not a single Jew who does not want peace. We have had enough wars. Jews want to serve God. We are never out to conquer.

From a speech delivered in New York during his visit to the United States in April–May 1994.

◻

James Baldwin

BLACKS FACING JEWS

The Negro facing a Jew, hates, at bottom, not his Jewishness but the color of his skin.... But just as a society must have a scapegoat, so hatred must have a symbol. Georgia has the Negro, and Harlem has the Jew.

From his Notes of a Native Son *(1957).*

◻

Arthur James Balfour

CHRISTENDOM'S DISGRACE

The treatment of the [Jewish] race has been a disgrace to Christendom, a disgrace which tarnishes the fair fame of Christianity even at this moment, and which in the Middle Ages gave rise to horrors which whoever makes himself acquainted with even in the most superficial manner, reads of with shuddering and feelings of terror lest any trace of blood guiltiness then incurred should have fallen on the descendants of those who committed the deeds.

From a speech during a debate in the British Parliament on May 2, 1905.

TOWARD A JEWISH STATE

Dear Lord Rothschild,

I have much pleasure in conveying to you, on behalf of His Majesty's government, the following Declaration of Sympathy with Jewish Zionist aspirations which has been submitted to, and approved by, the Cabinet:

"His Majesty's Government view with favour the establishment in Palestine of a national home for the Jewish people, and will use their best endeavours to facilitate the achievement of this object, it being clearly understood that nothing shall be done which may prejudice the civil and religious rights of existing non-Jewish communities in Palestine, or the rights and political status enjoyed by Jews in any other country."

I should be grateful if you would bring this declaration to the knowledge of the Zionist Federation.

Yours sincerely,
Arthur James Balfour

A declaration issued on November 2, 1917 by the British Foreign Office, through a letter to a member of the House of Lords, declaring England's favoring the establishment of a Jewish homeland in Palestine.

□

Lucille Ball

IT'S WEDGWOOD!

You shmuck! It's Wedgwood!

A note left under the plate of her dinner guest, Jack Carter, who she was sure would lift the plate to check the trademark.

□

Bernard J. Bamberger

GOD AS A LIVING POWER

I hold to the faith—which does not seem to me unreasonable—that there is a cosmic root out of which man's values grow. I believe that man's strivings, above all his ethical strivings, are not irrelevant to the universe. I believe man has some kinship with ultimate reality. Or, in more traditional language—though no language is adequate—I believe in God as a living power.

From an essay in Condition of Jewish Belief *(1966), compiled by the editors of* Commentary *magazine.*

WHO IS A JEW?

I shall not be willing to read out of Jewish life any persons who want to be a part of it.

Ibid.

□

William Bankhead

THE MAILED FIST

When democracy yields to dictatorship, the Jew is the first to feel the mailed fist of arbitrary power....Wherever democracy reigns supreme, the Jew is accorded equal treatment.

From an address to B'nai Brith, May 9, 1938.

□

Ehud Barak

ISRAEL ON THE GOLAN

From a professional military perspective I would say that we have to be on at least part of it in order to defend Israel. But the government will decide, and then we [the military] will specify what security arrangements are best given that decision.

From an interview with David Makovsky during a tour of the Golan Heights and southern Lebanon. Reported in U.S. News and World Report, *December 26, 1994.*

THE BEST HOPE

On the one hand, the Palestinians are weak. On the other hand, they are perceived by [Israeli] citizens to be the source of terror and day-to-day frictions; and they legitimize pan-Arabic hostility toward Israel. So long as we reduce terror without damaging any of Israel's vital interest by smoothing relations with them, then it will be more difficult to motivate hostile acts against us from Benghazi [Libya] or Tehran.

Ibid.

□

Molly Lyons Bar-David

DEATHBED BLESSING

"Jane! Jane! My child!—Jane, what is this radiance that glows around you?"

"It is the Jewishness in me, Mother."

"If that is so, then God bless you, my saintly child."

The mother and daughter clung in love, and wept together in the joy of consolation.

The next day, the aged mother passed away in peace.

Writing about the conversion of her Catholic friend Devorah Wigoder, who was being urged by her brother, a priest, to renounce her desire to convert to Judaism so as to ease the anguish of their dying mother. From an article in Jewish Affairs, March 1967, *published in South Africa.*

□

David Bar-Ilan

A VIEW OF THE PLO

A Palestinian state for me is like asking Saddam Hussein to be your neighbor. With the PLO and Saddam Hussein, it's the same type of thinking, the same kind of political philosophy and same kind of enmity toward Israel.

What we are doing now is shaking hands with Saddam Hussein, and asking him to live across the street from us in Jerusalem and across the suburbs in Tel Aviv. They will be on the high ground, overlooking Israel. And a sovereign state cannot be demilitarized, any more than Hitler's Germany was demilitarized.

Reacting to the peace accord signed between Israel and the PLO on September 13, 1993.

◻

Bar Kappara

EVIL SPEECH

If a person hears an unworthy remark, he should plug his finger into his ear.

Quoted in the talmudic tractate Ketubot (5a).

◻

Salo W. Baron

THE JEWISH PEOPLE

To Judaism the existence of the Jewish people is essential and indispensable, not only for its realization in life, but for its very idea; not only for its actuality, but for its potentiality. The Jewish religion without the "chosen people" is unthinkable. Neither could it, like the other religions, be transplanted from the Jewish to another people. No matter how many adherents it might gain in the outside world, the physical extinction of the Jewish people would sound the death knell of Judaism.

From his Social & Religious History of the Jews (1952).

GERMS THAT THREATEN

A communicable disease can be combated not only by fighting the germs but also by strengthening the resistance of the body under attack. Jews can do very little about fighting anti-Semitism...but they certainly can go on strengthening the morale of their own people.

From The American Zionist.

◻

Roseanne Barr

ROSEANNE AS RALPH

Above anyone on earth, I adore Jackie Gleason. That's what I want my series to be— *The Honeymooners,* only I'm Ralph.

Quoted in Darryl Lyman's Jewish Comedy Catalog (1989).

BRAINWASHED WOMEN

Men have actually brainwashed women into thinking that in order to be successful you have to be exactly like the men. And what I'm trying to say more than anything is no, you don't. I mean they're going to evolve us out of the human race if we let them. As soon as they figure out cloning, forget it. They won't need us for anything.

Ibid.

I NEVER APOLOGIZE

I never apologize for what I say. And that's what sets me apart from a lot of other women comics.

Ibid.

◻

Karl Barth

DAY OF REST

A being is free only when it can determine and limit its activity. God's creative activity has its limit in the rest from His works determined by Himself, i.e., the rest of the seventh day. His freedom revealed in this rest is a first criterion of the true deity of the Creator in the biblical saga.

Commenting on the day of rest established in the second chapter of the Book of Genesis. From his Church Dogmatics (1958).

◻

Bernard M. Baruch

HOOVER'S BRAIN

Facts to Hoover's brain are as water to a sponge; they are absorbed into every tiny interstice.

Quoted in D. Hinshaw's Herbert Hoover: American Quaker.

HUMAN RELATIONS

Even when we discover basic truths about human affairs, it is another thing to overcome human failings—the greed, hatred, sloth, or whatever it is that keeps us from acting on those truths. In a laboratory, men follow truth wherever it may lead. In human relations, men have a supreme talent for ignoring truth, and denying facts they do not like. That is why the ancient messenger who brought bad tidings was put to death.

We would all do well to echo Thomas Huxley's prayer: "God give me strength to face a fact even though it slay me."

From his Baruch: The Public Years (1960).

HUMAN NATURE IN WASHINGTON

I have had the opportunity to know many of the men who have dominated the history of this [twentieth] century. Most of them were unusually well endowed with character and ability, but I have learned that human nature in Washington is very little different from human nature in Wall Street—or Main Street—that, indeed, there is very little difference between the "great" man and the "common" man. I have learned the truth of the observation that the more one approaches great men the more one finds that they are men.

> *Ibid.*

WHY BARUCH ADMIRED WILSON

Remembering my own college days, when the fact of being a Jew had been enough to bar me from fraternities, I admired [Woodrow] Wilson's blunt attack of the [eating] clubs [at Princeton]. Moreover, his two years as Governor of New Jersey had marked him as an imaginative and effective leader; and the New Freedom he talked about touched in me an awakening, though still ill-defined, political philosophy.

> *Ibid. Explaining why he would vote for Woodrow Wilson, a Democrat, rather than for Theodore Roosevelt, for whom he had voted in 1904.*

THE DIRTY PRESIDENTIAL CAMPAIGN

There is one issue in this [1928] campaign and that is religion. Whoever put it there, no matter how it got there, it is there and the filth and dirt is enough to make one boil!

> *Ibid. In a letter to William Gibbs McAdoo, commenting on Al Smith's defeat for the presidency in 1928.*

HITLER AND PEACE

I never had the slightest illusion about Hitler. At a time when most people were inclined to dismiss his boasts and threats as the hollow ranting of an excitable demagogue, I was one of that small minority in the democracies, of whom Churchill was the most prominent, who took Hitler seriously. By 1935 I was saying in public speeches: "Hitler and peace! The very terms are antithetical. He is today the greatest menace to world safety."

> *Ibid.*

PLIGHT OF HITLER'S VICTIMS

When Hitler instituted his "final solution" of the "Jewish question"—the gas chambers and ovens of the concentration camps—some of my relatives were among his victims. I was profoundly conscious of the need for a place of refuge, not only for Jews but for others of all faiths and nationalities whom Hitler had marked for destruction. Regrettably, refugees had few places to go; the democracies found many excuses for not opening their doors.

> *Ibid. Commenting on a trip to Europe in the summer of 1938.*

THE COLD WAR

Let us not be deceived. We are today in the midst of a cold war.

> *From a September 16, 1947 speech delivered before the South Carolina state legislature.*

ON ADVISING THE JEWS

I do best in the high grass.

> *In response to a question posed by Harry Golden as to why Baruch doesn't advise Jews, since he had advised so many U.S. presidents. From Golden's autobiography,* The Right Time *(1969).*

OLD AGE

To me old age is always fifteen years older than I am.

> *Commenting on the occasion of his eighty-fifth birthday. Reported in* Newsweek *magazine, August 29, 1955.*

GOVERNMENT OF THE PEOPLE

We must remember that the people do not belong to the government but that governments belong to the peoples.

> *From an address to the United Nations Atomic Energy Commission, June 14, 1946.*

NOTHING IS INCURABLE

There are no such things as incurables; there are only things for which man has not found a cure.

> *From an address to the President's Committee on Employment of the Physically Handicapped, April 30, 1954.*

SELL WHEN RISING

Repeatedly in my market operations I have sold a stock while it was rising—and that has been one reason why I held onto my fortune.

> *Quoted in* The New York Times *obituary, June 21, 1965.*

GETTING ALL THE FACTS

If you get all the facts, your judgment can be right. If you don't get all the facts, it can't be right.

> *Quoted in* The St. Louis Post-Dispatch, *June 21, 1965.*

PRAISE AND BE PRAISED

Be quick to praise. People like to praise those who praise them.

> *Ibid.*

THOSE WHO ASK WHY

I'm not smart. I try to observe. Millions

saw the apple fall but Newton was the one who asked "why."

> Quoted in the New York Post, June 24, 1965.

PREPARE A PONTOON

We can't always cross a bridge until we come to it; but I always like to lay down a pontoon ahead of time.

> Quoted in A. K. Adams's Home Book of Humorous Quotations.

FOR WHOM TO VOTE

Vote for the man who promises the least; he'll be the least disappointing.

> Quoted in Meyer Berger's New York.

A MOST CHERISHED LESSON

To mind my own business.

> When asked the most important lesson he had learned in his lifetime. Quoted in The St. Louis Post-Dispatch, June 21, 1965.

BALANCING OUR NEEDS

The limit on what our economy can stand is what we are willing to discipline and organize ourselves to do. It may not be possible to have the defenses we need and everything else we crave. But we have the resources for as large an effort as may be necessary, provided we are willing to curb the fancied wants which conflict with that effort.

> From his autobiography, From My Own Story.

IMPORTANCE OF CHARACTER

During my eighty-seven years I have witnessed a whole succession of technological revolutions. But none of them has done away with the need for character in the individual or the ability to think.

> Ibid.

TERROR OF WEAPONRY

The terror created by weapons has never stopped men from employing them.

> From a speech to the United Nations Atomic Energy Commission, June 14, 1946.

THE ATOM BOMB

Science has taught us how to put the atom to work. But to make it work for good instead of for evil lies in the domain dealing with the principles of human duty. We are now facing a problem more of ethics than physics.

> Ibid.

THE QUICK AND THE DEAD

We are here to make a choice between the quick and the dead.

> Ibid.

◻

Simon Baruch

EARNING AND SPENDING

No, my son, I'm not impressed. What I want to know is—how will you spend the money you have earned?

> Comment by Bernard Baruch's father after Bernard told him, in 1900, that he had become a millionaire. Quoted in Elinor and Robert Slater's Great Jewish Men (1996).

◻

Baruch of Medzebozh

HIDE AND SEEK

Picture two children playing hide-and-seek. One hides but the other does not look for him. God is hiding and man is not seeking. Imagine His distress.

> Explaining the idea of a hidden God. Quoted in Elie Wiesel's Souls on Fire (1972).

◻

Lia Bass

WOMAN RABBI IN BRAZIL

Once I was accepted [as a student at the seminary], it suddenly hit me—how big this was and how long the process. I realized I was doing something radically different from what any woman in my country had done before.

> Prior to her ordination as a rabbi in 1994 by the Jewish Theological Seminary of America. From a profile in Masoret magazine, Spring 1993.

◻

Yehuda Bauer

ANTI-SEMITISM: AN ACQUIRED CODE

Anti-Semitism is a code in Western civilization. It's not a genetic code. Nobody is born with anti-Semitic genes. It's an acquired code, you see, transmitted by culture, transmitted by tradition. It is part of the positive achievements of Western civilization, my friends....

But precisely because it is not a genetic code, there is a possibility of fighting it, because it is a culturally transmitted code.

> From an address to the World Conference on Anti-Semitism and Prejudice in a Changing World, held in Brussels, Belgium, July 1992.

True Meaning of Holocaust

Just as I said that anti-Semitism is a code in Western civilization, the Holocaust is becoming a cultural code in our civilization. When you want to say something extreme about society you call it a Holocaust; you misuse the term. You cheapen it; you trivialize it, but you use it!...When you turn it into a cultural discrimination, you deny that Holocaust is murder!

Ibid.

◻

Philip Baum

Pollard's Opponents

Pollard's advocates are terrible people.... They've charged me and others, that we're traitors to the Jewish people. I think it's a discredit to them.... So what! Their position must be judged on its merits.

Protesting the condemnation of Jews who oppose the pardoning of Jonathan Pollard for spying against the United States. Quoted in The Jewish Week, *December 10–16, 1993.*

Where Are We Going?

The basis for Jewish association in the past has been anti-Semitism, religion, nostalgia, history, Yiddishkeit and nationalism. None of them seem to work anymore....We are on our own now. We can't draw on other things to provide us with a sense of gratification and a sense of worth. All of the old structures we had were for the old crises. Where are we going now?

After becoming executive director of the American Jewish Congress in April 1994, succeeding Henry Siegman.

◻

Vicki Baum

A Loved Woman

A woman who is loved always has success.

From her Grand Hotel *(1931).*

The Art of Staying Married

Marriage always demands the greatest understanding of the art of insincerity possible between two human beings.

From her And Life Goes On *(1931).*

To Be a Jew

To be a Jew is a destiny.

Ibid.

◻

José Bautista

All the Way

I go all the way with it. Shabbat, Chanukah, all the way.

Rachel Cohen, the mother of the dark-skinned, right-handed pitcher for the San Francisco Giants (in 1995), left the Soviet Union in the 1930s and settled in the Dominican Republic. José married a Jewish woman in 1983. Aside from Eric Helfand and Doug Johns of Oakland and Shawn Green of Toronto, in 1995 he was the only Jew in the Major Leagues.

◻

Augustin Cardinal Bea

Vatican II on Anti-Semitism

[It must be acknowledged] honestly and clearly what God has accomplished in the Jewish people and through them, the whole human race.

After being appointed by Pope John XXIII as president of the Secretariat for Promoting Christian Unity. Quoted in his Church and the Jewish People *(1966).*

◻

Jedaiah ben Abraham Bedersi

Last in Time, First in Rank

Go my heart to the left or right, but believe—believe all that our great master and teacher, Moses the son of Maimon, believed. He was the last of the Geonim in time, but first in rank, and there is none among the Sages of Israel since the days of the Talmud who could compare to him.

With this praise of Moses Maimonides, Bedersi concludes his prose-poem Bechinat Olam *("Evaluation of the World").*

Facing the Inevitable

How can my flesh be delighted, when I am informed that I shall live long, since there is no escape from the destruction of death?

Ibid.

Max Beerbohm

ZANGWILL THE BORE

He [Israel Zangwill] is an old bore. Even the grave yawns for him.

From his Herbert Beerbohm Tree *(1920).*

Richard Beer-Hofman

ACCEPTING GOD'S WILL

Lord, whate'er Thy will imposes on me
I'll bear like a crown, not like a yoke.

From his Jacob's Dream *(1919).*

THE STAGE OF FATE

We are judged by different laws than other peoples; whether we like it or not, what we Jews do takes place on a stage our fate has built. The good and the bad habits of other peoples are taken for granted and accepted. But the whole world is allowed to loll in the audience, gaping at the Jews.

Quoted in Harry Zohn's Jewish Role in Austrian Literature *(1986).*

HAVING BEEN A JEW

When I no longer am, and when those who read German then wish to number me among their own, I will have been a German poet. But I will have one advantage: that I can look back on a long line of forebears who, in all their afflictions, never abandoned their God.

Ibid.

SPLIT PERSONALITY

By substance I am definitely a Jew, functionally definitely an Austrian.

Ibid.

Menachem Begin

MUTILATION OF THE LAND

The Homeland has not been liberated, but utilized Eretz Israel will be restored to the people of Israel. All of it and forever.

Reacting to the UN partition plan which the General Assembly passed on November 29, 1947.

REMEMBERING THE HOLOCAUST

If I forget the extermination of the Jews, may my right hand wither, may my tongue stick to my palate if I cease to think of you, if I do not keep the extermination of the Jews in memory even at my happiest hour.

From an oath he asked his followers to take when, in 1952, he opposed Israel's negotiation of a reparation agreement with Germany. Based on a verse from Psalm 137 beginning: "If I forget thee, O Jerusalem, let my right hand wither..." Quoted in Tom Segev's Seventh Million *(1993).*

AMERICAN JEWS AND ISRAEL

I venture to say that I have served the Jewish people for more than 50 years. My old eyes have seen much: two world wars, seven other wars, jail and concentration camp; five years underground—deprivation, starvation and more.

Given this experience—which you will admit is not small—I permit myself to express astonishment why a man like you has to organize American Jews in order to publish a statement which lends—not, God forbid, intentionally—comfort to those who gleefully declare: Look, the Jews of America are turning their backs on Israel.

In response to a letter from Professor Leonard Fein of Brandeis University in which the prime minister is critical of a statement first published in Israel in May 1980 and signed by 250 distinguished Israelis, and now signed by 56 active members and leaders of American Jewry. Both letters were reported in The Jerusalem Post International Edition, *July 22–August 2, 1980.*

CARING FOR OUR CHILDREN

Jews have the right to criticize the government of Israel in which I serve as prime minister—at any given moment, any second, any hour, day and night. But I, too, have the right to ask of them to understand one thing at least: On matters that relate to the national security of the little nation in Eretz Israel, please refrain from proffering advice, at least in public, within earshot of our enemies who conspire to do us evil. Remember, please, the simple fact that we care for our children and grandchildren—and they, these little children, live *here.*

Ibid.

ISRAEL BELONGS TO ALL JEWS

Ever since I learned Zionism from Ze'ev Binyamin Herzl and Ze'ev Jabotinsky, I believe with all my heart that Eretz Israel belongs to the whole Jewish people and not only to those Jews who live in it. Hence, I have no objection to Jews who live in the Diaspora criticizing the policy of the Israel government of the day; by its very democratic nature, it is transient.

Ibid.

AUTONOMY FOR PALESTINIAN ARABS

Yes, indeed there is the problem of the Palestinian Arabs. Never did we seek to do them wrong. The absolute historic truth is that they inflicted on themselves all the wrongs done to them. By their own hand and that of their leaders they suffered. You should know that as long as we fought the British for the liberation of Eretz Israel from colonial rule there was total peace between Jew and Arab in the country, and then, on the morrow of November 29, 1947, they, the Palestinian Arabs, attacked us to literally annihilate us. The truth is that my colleagues and I wish, to the extent possible, to redress that wrong, which the Arabs brought upon themselves when they strove to deprive us not only of the land of our forefathers but also of our lives. Hence, the idea of the autonomy for the Arab inhabitants of Judea, Samaria and the Gaza District, which is totally our idea.

Ibid.

SHALOM, SALAAM, FOREVER

No more wars; no more bloodshed. Peace unto you. Shalom, salaam, forever.

On signing the Egyptian–Israeli peace treaty in Washington, DC, March 26, 1979.

CHOOSING LIFE

Better a condemnation and no reactor, than a reactor and no condemnation.

Reacting to the 1981 decision of Israel to bomb the nuclear reactor in Iraq.

PUNISHMENT AND THREATS

A week ago the Knesset adopted the Golan law, and again you declare that you are "punishing" Israel. What kind of talk is that, "punishing" Israel? Are we a vassal state? A banana republic? Are we fourteen-year-old boys, that if they don't behave they have their knuckles smacked? I will tell you of whom this government is composed. It is composed of men who fought, risked their lives and suffered. You cannot and will not frighten us with punishments and threats.... The people of Israel have lived for 3,700 years without a memorandum

of understanding with America and will continue to live without it for another 3,700 years.

From a letter addressed to President Ronald Reagan and Secretary of State George Shultz in December 1981, after Israel annexed the Golan Heights and the U.S. threatened to withhold financial aid. Quoted in Eric Silver's Begin: The Haunted Prophet *(1984).*

ADVANCE NOTICE

My generation, dear Ron, swore on the Altar of God that whoever proclaims the intent of destroying the Jewish state or the Jewish people, or both, seals his fate.

From a letter to U.S. President Ronald Reagan. Quoted in the London Observer, *January 2, 1983.*

◘

Yosef Begun

BELIEF IN GOD AND PLURALISM

I can't say I am a strong Orthodox Jew now, but I continue to respect Jewish tradition and religion. It seems to me that a Jew cannot deny the existence of God. Maybe a Jew can be non-observant, but if a person decides that he wants to be a Jew, he cannot exist without the idea of God.... The Torah has seventy faces and every one of them is God.

From an interview with Walter Ruby, one of the most prominent refuseniks. Begun was released from Christopol Prison in 1987. While there, he became a very observant Jew. From an article in The Jewish World, *October 15–21, 1993.*

AT HOME WITH ALL JEWS

I myself feel comfortable davening in Reform, Conservative or Orthodox synagogues. The only Jews I don't respect are those extremists who say, "Only my way is the right way."

Ibid.

A RETURN TO LIFE

Freedom is more complicated than prison. When I got to Israel, I was overwhelmed by the beauty of the country and its people, but also dismayed by such negative realities as hostility among Jews and the fierce political conflicts. I was saddened at first, but came to understand that life is life, and I had to get used to all sides of life. When a person is freed from a long stay in prison, he has to learn how to live all over again.

Ibid.

PRISONER OF ZION

I was willing to be arrested for Zion in Russia. I am certainly willing to be arrested for Zion in Israel.

Commenting on having been arrested for campaigning that new settlements continue to be established on the West Bank. Reported in The Jerusalem Post, *February 12, 1994.*

◻

S. N. Behrman

AN UNBELIEVABLE CHARACTER

A character who, if he did not exist, could not be imagined.

From Oscar Levant's introduction to A Smattering of Ignorance.

◻

Yossi Beilin

AN OCCUPIER IS AN OCCUPIER

An occupier is an occupier is an occupier. There is no such thing as a benevolent occupation.

From a statement made at a news conference in January 1984.

JEWISH AMERICAN ESTABLISHMENTS

There is no doubt that most US Jews are moderate, liberal and pragmatic, and would like to see a compromise solution between us and the Arabs. On the other hand, the Jewish American establishments are much more extreme—again, not all of them, but the large majority.

Responding to criticism of his attack, in the summer of 1993, on American Jewish organizations for being "right wing" and for questioning their loyalty to the Rabin government.

THE OSLO CHANNEL

Rabin gave the green light for several people who thought the same way as I did, to try, in parallel, to get a dialogue going with the PLO. If he and Peres had been opposed when I informed them about the Oslo channel, it would have been the easiest thing in the world for them to put a stop to it.

In defense of charges that he, as deputy foreign minister to Shimon Peres, surreptitiously led Peres and Prime Minister Rabin by the nose in arranging the Oslo meetings which led to the eventual signing of a PLO–Israel peace accord on September 13, 1993. From an article by Leslie Susser in The Jerusalem Report, *December 30, 1993.*

A PRIME MINISTER'S JOB

A prime minister of Israel is prime minister 24 hours a day. Literally. He does not have a moment to himself. It's a very heavy sacrifice, which would leave no time for social thinking or writing, and I'm not sure I'm ready to make it.

Ibid. Denying he has aspiration to become prime minister of Israel.

ISRAEL: A RICH COUNTRY

If our economic situation is better than in many of your countries, how can we go on asking for your charity? You want me to be the beggar and say we need money for the poor people. Israel is a rich country, I'm sorry to tell you.

Comment made in January 1994 to a gathering of the Women's International Zionist Organization.

THE GOLAN MISTAKE

I would not have set up settlements on the Golan Heights. That was a mistake from the beginning. But now they are there and I believe if there will be territorial compromise on the Golan, those settlements that will come under Syrian sovereignty will remain under Syrian sovereignty.

Ibid.

NO ISRAELI STARVES

No one is starving in Israel. No one in Israel starves for bread because society has taken care of that.

Ibid.

CALL FOR POLITICAL CLARITY

My main expectation is that...Assad will be much clearer about a peace accord with Israel. And if he does indeed say the words we expect—such as diplomatic relations, open borders, economic relations, and so on—he will find Israel definitely prepared to go towards peace with Syria.

Statement made following the summit meeting between U.S. President Bill Clinton and Syrian President Haffez el-Assad on January 16, 1994, in Geneva, Switzerland.

THE POPE SPEAKS

It is one thing if we condemn an anti-Semitic incident in, say, Argentina. But it is quite another if the Pope does.

Comment made after he and his team concluded an eighteen-month-long negotiation with the Vatican to establish diplomatic relations. The Fundamental Agreement between the Holy See and the State of Israel was signed in December 1993.

VATICAN-ISRAEL RELATIONS

Behind the agreement are thousands of years of history full of hatred, fear and ignorance...but before us are many years of light.

Ibid.

SCUDS BURSTING IN AIR

When I started writing this book, I could not have foreseen in my wildest dreams that part of it would be written between one alarm siren and the next, while scud missiles travelling some 400 miles in six or seven minutes fell on homes in Tel Aviv and the surrounding area.

From the Preface from his Israel: A Concise Political History *(1992).*

◻

Moshe Bejski

HOLOCAUST ICONOCLAST

During the war, as long as he [Oskar Schindler] could produce kitchenware and sell it on the black market, he could make a lot of money. But he was unable to work normally after the war. A group of survivors in Israel raised some money for him when he was hard up. If we sent $3,000-$4,000, he spent it in two or three weeks, then phoned to say he didn't have a penny.... If Schindler had been a normal man, he would not have done what he did. Everything he did put him in danger. I once asked him why he did it. He answered: "I knew the people who worked for me. When you know people, you have to behave towards them like human beings."

From an article by Eric Silver in The Jerusalem Report, *December 30, 1993, in which the retired judge of the Israeli Supreme Court, who had been a draftsman in Schindler's enamelware factory and helped forge documents, speaks of the Schindler who saved 1,200 lives.*

◻

Harry Belafonte

YOU'RE FINE, HESH

My Jewish friend asked me, "Where do you want to go?" "To the best hospital," I told her, "the Israeli Field Army Hospital, which served in Rwanda without taking sides." After examining me, the Israeli doctor said, "Hesh, you're fine," and we then spent Friday night with the Israelis.

From an address at the 25th Anniversary Gala Awards Dinner of the American Associates for Ben-Gurion University of the Negev, held at New York's Plaza Hotel, September 18, 1995. Hesh is a common Yiddish name for Harry. Belafonte had picked up a parasite during a visit to Rwanda.

◻

Samuel Belkin

PHILOSOPHY OF INTEGRATION

Our philosophy is one of integration and we firmly deny that our integration in the American community in any way implies the abrogation of even one iota of our sacred tradition.

From his Essays in Traditional Jewish Thought *(1969).*

MEMORY AND FORGETFULNESS

God has endowed man with two great gifts: memory and forgetfulness, differentiating him from the irrational animals in nature. If man had no memory, civilization could not continue; if man lacked forgetfulness, he could not endure the pain of life's grim experiences.

From the Introduction to Understanding Bereavement and Grief *(1977), edited by Norman Linzer.*

◻

August Bell

ANTI-SEMITISM AND SOCIALISM

Anti-Semitism is the Socialism of fools.

From his Antisemitismus and Social-demokratie *(1893).*

◻

Hilaire Belloc

TAMPERING WITH GOD

It's their [the Jews'] own bloody fault; they should have left God alone.

Quoted in Joseph Telushkin's Jewish Wisdom *(1994).*

◻

Saul Bellow

A FACT OF JEWISH LIFE

What you do know is that there is one fact of Jewish life unchanged by the creation of a Jewish state: you cannot take your right to live for granted.

In his To Jerusalem and Back: A Personal Account *(1976), which reveals his heartfelt reaction to contemporary Israeli society.*

I WANT, I WANT, I WANT

There was a disturbance in my heart, a voice that spoke there and said, I want, I want, I want! It happened every afternoon, and when I tried to suppress it it got even stronger.... It never said a thing except I want, I want, I want!

From his Henderson the Rain King *(1959).*

ON BEING HUMAN

I am simply a human being, more or less.

From his Herzog *(1964).*

THE RIGHT WAY TO WRITE

I have a trunk full of manuscripts. The main reason for rewriting is not to achieve a smooth surface, but to discover the inner truth of your characters.

After admitting that he rewrote his famous 1964 novel Herzog *fifteen to twenty-five times.*

THE DOUBLE CURSE

As though to be Jewish weren't trouble enough, the poor woman was German, too.

From his Mr. Sammler's Planet *(1970).*

MODERN SODOM AND GOMORRAH

New York makes one think of the collapse of civilization, about Sodom and Gomorrah, the end of the world. The end wouldn't come as a surprise here. Many people already bank on it.

Ibid.

BODY AND SOUL

The body, she says, is subject to the forces of gravity. But the soul is ruled by levity, pure.

From the title story in his Him with His Foot in His Mouth & Other Stories *(1984).*

SOURCE OF BOREDOM

Boredom is the shriek of unused capacities.

From his Adventures of Augie March *(1953).*

CITIES AND CIVILIZATIONS

There haven't been civilizations without cities. But what about cities without civilizations?

Ibid.

ACCEPT THE MIXTURE

We make what we can of our condition with the means available. We must accept the mixture as we find it—the impurity of it, the tragedy of it, the hope of it.

From his introduction to Great Jewish Short Stories *(1963), which discusses the plight of the Jewish writer in America.*

ON BEING VIGILANT

The only real distinction at this dangerous moment in human history and cosmic development has nothing to do with medals and ribbons. Not to fall asleep is distinguished. Everything else is mere popcorn.

From his Humboldt's Gift *(1975).*

THE PLACE OF ART

I feel that art has something to do with the achievement of stillness in the midst of chaos. A stillness which characterizes prayer, too, and the eye of the storm. I think that art has something to do with an arrest of attention in the midst of distractions.

Quoted in George Plimpton's Writers at Work *(1967).*

❑

Richard Belzer

MOTHER'S KITCHEN

There is a definite connection between being funny and being Jewish. The toughest room I ever played was my mother's kitchen.

From a June 1986 speech at the Jewish Museum in New York City.

A COSTLY LESSON

You learn to cherish certain people more and stop wasting time.

Statement made following his 1984 bout with cancer.

❑

Yossi Ben-Aharon

WHO WANTS PEACE MORE?

You don't want peace any more than I want peace, and I don't claim to want it more than you. That kind of question has no justification and no basis. Yitzhak Shamir doesn't want peace any less than Shimon Peres wants peace. They just have completely different ideas of how to go about getting it.

In response to a question posed on Israel television as to whether Shamir had really been interested in peace or just wanted to stay at the negotiating table to satisfy the United States.

❑

Elijah Benamozegh

MANKIND AND ISRAEL

Mankind cannot rise to the essential principles on which society must rest unless it meets with Israel. And Israel cannot fathom the deeps of its own national and religious tradition unless it meets with mankind.

Quoted by Aimé Pallière in The Unknown Sanctuary *(1979).*

¤

Ben Azzai

A Time and a Place

Every man has his hour and every thing has its place.

From the talmudic tractate Ethics of the Fathers (4:3).

¤

Ben Bag Bag

Safeguarding Privacy

Do not enter your neighbor's premises without permission, even to retrieve something that belongs to you.

Quoted in the talmudic tractate Bava Kamma (27b).

¤

Michael Ben-Chorin

When Walls Speak

With graffiti, the walls speak, not the author.

Claiming credit for some of the anti-Rabin slogans appearing in the Golan Heights after the September 1993 Israeli–PLO peace accords signed in Washington, DC.

A War for Our Homes

Yitzhak Rabin and all the leftists who are with him are reading things all wrong. They think: Begin gave back the Sinai, Rabin will do it with Golan. In the Sinai it was colonialism; you never saw a Jew on tractors. This is a war for our homes.

Protesting the 1993 Israeli-PLO peace accord. Quoted in Stuart Schoffman's article in The New Republic, *January 3, 1994.*

¤

Stephen Vincent Bénet

Union Superpatriots

Judah P. Benjamin, the dapper Jew,
Sela-sleek, black-eyed, lawyer and epicure,
Able, well-hated, face alive with life,
Looked around the council-chamber with the slight

Perpetual smile he held before himself
Continually like a silk-ribbed fan.
Behind the fan, his quick, shrewd, fluid mind
Weighed Gentiles in an old balance.
The mind behind the silk-ribbed fan
Was a dark prince, clothed in an Eastern stuff,
Whose brown hands cupped about a crystal egg
That filmed with coloured cloud.
The egg stared searching.

From his poem "John Brown's Body." Judah P. Benjamin, of Virginia, elected to the U.S. Senate in 1852, served as secretary of war and secretary of state in Jefferson Davis's Cabinet and became a prime target for denunciation by Union superpatriots.

¤

Meron Benevisti

West Bank Settlements

Many of the Jewish residential areas in the West Bank no longer fit the classification "settlement."...Now, whole towns of apartment houses and villas are being built.... As bedroom communities with only a little of their own light industry and virtually no serious farming, they have the potential of becoming Israel's new suburbs.

They have also begun to attract a non-ideological breed of middle class Israelis who are moving to the West Bank.... A recent study has found that the land made available by the Begin Government for Israeli settlement is much more extensive than previously known, covering 55 to 65 percent of the entire West Bank.

Quoted by Rabbi Balfour Brickner in an article in the Jewish Spectator, *Winter 1983.*

Five Minutes to Midnight

It is not that it is beyond the point of no return. It is five minutes to midnight.

Ibid.

¤

Ely Ben-Gal

Historians: A Chosen People

Perhaps now we can accept in a certain way that we were chosen: not God's chosen people, but the exact opposite, the people selected to be backed against the wall. So perhaps it is because of what we need—for ourselves, and using you as intermediary—to have a ceremony and a medal. We need it to be able to say to our children that they must not lose faith in humanity, that in our worst moments of abjection, we were not alone.

Speaking to fellow historians in 1990 at the Diaspora Museum in Tel Aviv.

ٱ

David Ben-Gurion

ISRAEL'S IMMUTABILITY

No Jew has the right to yield the rights of the Jewish people in Israel. No Jew has the authority to do so. No Jewish body has the authority to do so. Not even the entire Jewish people alive today has the authority to yield any part of Israel. It is the right of the Jewish people over generations, a right which under no condition can be canceled. Even if Jews in a specific period proclaim they are relinquishing this right, they have neither the power nor the authority to deny this right to future generations. No concession of this type is binding or obligates the Jewish people.

From a 1937 speech before the Zionist Congress in Basle, Switzerland.

FIGHTING THE WHITE PAPER

We shall fight Hitler as though there were no White Paper, and we shall fight against the White Paper as though there were no Hitler.

From a September 1939 declaration in response to England's issuance of the White Paper on May 17, 1939, restricting Jewish immigration to Palestine.

BLESSED BE THE GUN

Blessed be the gun that fired on the *Atalena.*

Spoken in June 1948 when a vessel bearing the name Atalena *brought arms and ammunition to Israel, supplies that were to be divided between the Irgun underground army and the official Haganah army under the provisional government of Ben-Gurion. Ben-Gurion had a change of heart and broke the agreement. The ship headed out to sea, was fired upon by the Haganah, and blown up with all the ammunition still on board.*

SOURCE OF THE ZIONIST VISION

I believe that the Zionist vision does not emanate from persecution...but that it is deeply impressed in the Jewish people's desire for national existence; in its historical willpower to maintain its independence on the soil of the homeland in which it sprouted and in which its national genius was molded.

From a World Zionist Organization release, extracted from his writings.

RUSSIAN JEWRY

I believe a day will come when Russian Jewry will once again contribute of its strength to the Jewish people and to Eretz Israel.

Ibid.

TRAILBLAZING ISRAEL

I believe in our moral and intellectual advantages, in our ability to be a unique people capable of blazing the path and serving as an example for the redemption of the human race.

Ibid.

PEACE PROSPECTS

I believe in the possibilities of peace and in the prospects of peace in the world at large and in the Middle East in particular—despite everything.

Ibid.

MURDERERS AS HEIRS

Let not the murderers of our nation also be its heirs.

Comment during the debate in 1952 supporting the view that Israel should accept reparations from the Germans.

PLACING ALLEGIANCE

The Jews of the United States, as a community and as individuals, have only one political attachment and that is to the United States of America. They owe no political allegiance to Israel....The government and the people of Israel fully respect the right and integrity of the Jewish communities in other countries to develop their own mode of life and their indigenous social, economic and cultural institutions in accordance with their own needs and aspirations.

Backing down from his previous position after an August 1950 meeting in Jerusalem with Jacob Blaustein, president of the American Jewish Committee.

NOT YET A NATION

It is an exiled people still in the desert longing for the flesh-pots of Egypt. It cannot be considered a nation until the Negev and Galilee are settled, until millions of Jews immigrate to Israel and until moral standards necessary to the ethical practice of politics and the high values of Zionism are sustained.

In a 1969 statement, near the end of his life.

A DESPICABLE BOOK

One of the most despicable books about Jews ever to be written by anyone of Jewish origin.

> Commenting on Boris Pasternak's Doctor Zhivago, *which earned him the Nobel Prize in 1958.*

SEARCHING FOR EICHMANN

Adolf Eichmann—that's the man who must be brought to justice if he is still alive.

> Words uttered in 1945, shortly after World War II, even before Israel became a state. The search ended in a suburb of Argentina in May 1960, fifteen years later.

TO HELL WITH ANTI-SEMITES

If the anti-Semites want to hate, let them hate, and let them go to hell.

> From a letter in which he condemned those who expressed fear over repercussions that might follow the capture and trial of Adolf Eichmann in 1961.

THE GREATEST MIRACLE

The Jewish people, returned to its own land, has been the greatest miracle of world history.

> After the United Nations invited Israel to be a member.

AN ELECTRIFYING MOMENT

A short time ago, one of the greatest of Nazi war criminals, Adolf Eichmann, who was responsible together with the Nazi leaders for what they called the "final solution of the Jewish question"—that is, the extermination of six million Jews of Europe—was found. [He] is already under arrest in Israel, and will shortly be put on trial under the Nazis and Nazi Collaborators Law.

> In a statement read on May 23, 1960 before a packed meeting of the Israeli Knesset, which was stunned by the spectacular announcement.

WHO IS A JEW?

A Jew is a Jew and finished. Every human being who comes to me and tells me "I'm a Jew," and I have no reason to think he's saying it for some criminal purpose, I'll accept him as a Jew.

> Commenting in the 1960s on the case of Commander Shalit, a Jewish atheist and his Scottish non-Jewish wife, also an atheist. The couple wanted their children to be registered as Jews.

THE DOVISH BEN-GURION

We have no need of the [Golan] Heights because we won't remain there.

> A notation in his diary after the 1967 Six-Day War. Quoted in Dan Kurzman's Ben-Gurion: Prophet of Fire *(1983).*

TROTSKY AND LENIN

Trotsky was no statesman. What sort of policy is "No peace and no war"? It is a Jewish contrivance. If it is to be peace, then one must pay the price—which is sometimes very heavy—for it. If it is to be war—then one must take the terrible risk involved. Lenin understood this. And although it may be that from an intellectual standpoint Trotsky was superior to Lenin, politically speaking Lenin understood the Russian people and this was the reason that he became their true leader.

> Quoted in Shimon Peres' From These Men: Seven Founders of the State of Israel *(1979).*

NEVER SATISFIED

What is satisfaction? What is the good of it? If a man becomes satisfied, what is he to do then? A man who is satisfied no longer yearns, no longer dreams, no longer creates, no longer makes demands. No. I have never known a single moment of satisfaction.

> Ibid. In response to a question posed by a twelve-year-old school girl: "Mr. Ben-Gurion, at what time in your life did you feel the greatest satisfaction?"

A TIME TO DANCE

Now they are dancing, but tomorrow we shall find ourselves at war.

> Ibid. Comment made when the United Nations voted in favor of the establishment of the State of Israel. Ben-Gurion stayed in his room while the entire country was celebrating.

A NAME THAT WILL LIVE ON

His name will live forever in the annals of the Jewish people. We feel confident that American Jewry will be proud of this great and gallant man who has given his life for the liberation of Israel.

> From a cable sent to Mickey Marcus's wife, Emma, after he was mistakenly killed by a Jewish sentry on June 10, 1948. Quoted in Max Eichhorn's Joys of Jewish Folklore *(1981).*

LIKE A MOURNER AT A FEAST

I feel no gaiety in me, only deep anxiety. I am like a mourner at a feast.

Confided to a friend on May 14, 1948, after having read to the newly elected parliament the proclamation that the Jewish state in Palestine is to be called Israel.

ISRAEL SPEAKS ONLY FOR ISRAELIS

The State of Israel represents and speaks only on behalf of its own citizens, and in no way presumes to represent or speak in the name of the Jews who are citizens of any other country.

From an address delivered in Jerusalem, August 23, 1950.

CREATIVE ABILITY

Not the absorption capacity of the land, but the creative ability of a people, is the true yardstick with which we can measure the immigration potentialities of the land.

From a speech to the Palestine Labor Party (1931).

MIRACLES AND REALISM

In Israel, in order to be a realist you must believe in miracles.

From an October 5, 1956 interview on CBS television.

THE MEANS TO AN END

The State is not in itself an aim: it is a means to an end, the end of Zionism.

From an August 13, 1948 speech.

INGREDIENTS FOR NATIONAL INDEPENDENCE

Without moral and intellectual independence, there is no anchor for national independence.

Ibid.

PEOPLE AND COUNTRY

This country made us a people: our people made this country.

Remarks at the Anglo-American Commission of Inquiry, March 19, 1946.

ON ARAB FRIENDSHIP

There will be not only peace between us and the Arabs...but close friendship and cooperation.

Ibid.

NUCLEUS OF A NATION

We have gathered up human particles... and combined them into the fruitful and creative nucleus of a nation revived...; in the desolate spaces of a ruined and abandoned Homeland, we have...built villages and towns, planted gardens and established factories; ...we have breathed new life into our muted and abandoned ancient language.... Such a marvel is unique in the history of human culture.

From his farewell address to the Knesset, December 7, 1953.

PAST AND PRESENT

Our past is not only behind us, it is in our very being.

From the Israel Government Year Book *(5712).*

THE MAKING OF A JEW

The real miracle of Palestine is the Jew who masters the labor of orchard and garden, field and vineyard, quarry and harbor, water and power, factory and craft, highway and byway. That sort of Jew the Diaspora never made.

Quoted in M. Nurock's Rebirth and Destiny *(1954).*

A UNIVERSE DIVIDED

The outlook of the ghetto divided the universe into two: this world for the gentiles—the hereafter for the Jews.

Ibid.

NOT BY MIGHT

The State of Israel will prove itself not by material wealth, not by military might or technical achievement, but by its moral character and human values.

From a statement made in March 1949.

DEAR RACHEL

There is hope, dear Rachel, that peace is approaching, not quickly, but slowly, slowly...and, it appears to me that by the end of this century, the prophecy of Isaiah will be fulfilled.

From a 1970 letter written three years before he died, to his life-long secret love, Rachel Beit-Halachmi. Reported by Dan Kurzman in The New York Times, *September 19, 1993.*

CRIME OF WEAKNESS

We Jews have been accused of many crimes. Yet our one indictable crime in history has been the crime of weakness. Be assured that we shall never be guilty of that crime again.

A declaration of national commitment issued in 1952.

A PEACEFUL COOPERATIVE

The best way of teaching is by example, and our goal here [in Israel] is to build a cooperative commonwealth of free men.

From an article in The New York Times Magazine, *September, 24, 1961.*

HERZL AND WEIZMANN

Two great men rose in the cause of Zionism—Herzl and Weizmann. It is difficult to find, in the history of any one nation, two men who had so powerful an influence over the lives of their fellows, yet who were so very different, not only in their capabilities, but in the relationship they bore to their people.

Herzl came from the outer world. He was a typical assimilated Jew with no knowledge of his people's culture nor any acquaintance with the Jewish masses.... Weizmann was the exact opposite in a number of essential respects: for one thing, he was first and foremost a *Jewish* Jew. He was born in a small hamlet within the Pale of Jewish Settlement in Russia; he was bred in the lap of Judaism, amongst the masses of Israel.

From an essay evaluating the life and career of Chaim Weizmann. Quoted in Meyer Weisgal's Chaim Weizmann: A Biography by Several Hands *(1963).*

GREATEST JEWISH AMBASSADOR

Weizmann was the greatest Jewish emissary to the Gentile world. He was an ambassador to the Gentiles, the most gifted and fascinating envoy the Jewish people ever produced.... Weizmann fascinated the Gentiles with his *Jewish* grandeur, his Jewish profundity, his genius for depicting for them the deepest and most intimate emotions of the people of Israel.

Ibid.

TO CHAIM, WITH LOVE

Our line should be the Mandate—or a State. For as long as Britain rules Palestine she must carry out the Mandate as the League of Nations intended.... If Britain is unable or unwilling to carry out the Mandate, she should agree to the establishment of a Jewish State, even if not in the whole of Palestine, but at once.... Whatever your views are on all this you remain for me the elect of Jewish history, representing beyond compare the suffering and the glory of the Jews. And wherever you go you will be attended by the love, and faithful esteem of me and of my colleagues.

From an October 28, 1946 letter to Chaim Weizmann, who was in London recuperat-

ing from a second eye operation. Quoted in Abba Eban's profile of Weizmann, "Tragedy and Triumph." Quoted in Chaim Weizmann: A Biography by Several Hands *(1963).*

CONGRATULATIONS ARE IN ORDER

On the establishment of the Jewish State we send our greetings to you, who have done more than any other living man towards its creation. Your stand and help have strengthened all of us. We look forward to the day when we shall see you at the head of the state established in peace.

The message sent to Chaim Weizmann on the day after the United States recognized Israel as an independent state.

A MAN FOR THE AGES

[He will be] taking his place in the eternal history of the Jewish people alongside the great figures of the past—the Patriarchs and Kings, the Judges, Prophets and spiritual leaders who have woven the fabric of our national life for four thousand years.

From a statement issued upon the death of Chaim Weizmann, at the age of 77, on November 9, 1952.

◻

Ben Hey-Hey

EARNING THE REWARD

In keeping with the effort is the reward [in Aramaic *lefum tzaara agra*].

Quoted in the talmudic tractate Ethics of the Fathers (5:26).

◻

Hadassa Ben-Itto

PROTOCOLS OF THE ELDERS OF ZION

If you ask me what to my mind is one of the most dangerous phenomena in promoting anti-Semitism through the ages, I would say that mostly it is libels against the Jewish people. And if we go back, it is libels, like the blood libels, like the poisoning of the wells, like the *Protocols of the Elders of Zion....*

I won't go into the whole story of the Protocols. I will just say this. To my mind, if there is one single document which is the most dangerous in the context of anti-Semitism, the most dangerous to the Jewish people, it is the *Protocols of the Elders of Zion.* Not because it perpetuates the old myth of a Jewish plan and conspiracy to dominate the world, but because this document is a political document. It's not an old tale of black-clad people, conniving in an old Prague cemetery where Satan is also present and so on and so forth, and everybody knows it's fiction. This purports to be a political document composed during the first Zionist Congress in Basel, in 1897, and quoting chapter and verse what happened there with the names of the people who wrote it.

From an address to the World Conference on Anti-Semitism and Prejudice in a Changing World, held in Brussels, Belgium, July 1992.

◻

Isaac Benjacob

UP ONE DAY, DOWN ANOTHER

O earth: Today I am on you, tomorrow you will be on me.

From his Pirchay Tzafon *(1841)*

◻

Judah Philip Benjamin

A DISTINGUISHED PAST

It is true that I am a Jew, and when my ancestors were receiving their Ten Commandments from the immediate hand of Deity, amidst the thunderings and lightnings of Mt. Sinai, the ancestors of the distinguished gentleman who is opposed to me were herding swine in the forest of Scandinavia.

His reply to a fellow U.S. senator who referred to him as "that Jew from Louisiana."

◻

Yosef Ben-Moshe

THE BIG MAC'S MENACE

When a Jew, a pure soul, eats an impure animal, it destroys his soul, and he becomes a jungle man, an evil animal....This causes people to leave the homeland and mixed marriages. It's worse than Hitler. McDonald's is contaminating all of Israel and all of the Jewish people.

After McDonald's opened its nonkosher restaurant in Jerusalem in 1995. He added that this will "lead to bank robberies, murders, decadence, and corruption."

◻

Jack Benny

IF IT HURTS IT ISN'T FUNNY

The public today demands more of its humor than a laugh at any price. It resents too much insulting, too much cynicism. In short, the public likes good comedy, but it likes good taste even better.... Nobody gets hurt on our program. Its all in the spirit of fun. We try to follow one simple rule: if it hurts, it isn't funny.

From a 1940s comment decrying all forms of violence in programming. Quoted in Darryl Lyman's Jewish Comedy Catalog *(1989).*

CHERISHING SELF-RESPECT

I wouldn't want people to think I'm desecrating this holiday by working on it. I wasn't thinking of the Jews. I wouldn't like the Gentiles to think I didn't respect my religion.

To an assistant on the eve of Yom Kippur, when he was preparing for his Sunday program schedules to begin in Los Angeles at 4:00 p.m. Benny suddenly realized that on the East Coast it would be after sundown when the program aired. Quoted in Elinor and Robert Slater's Great Jewish Men *(1996).*

HURTFUL GAGS

There are enough basic concepts in life to poke fun at. Funny things happen to us all the time....If a gag is hurtful, I don't need it.

Ibid.

THE INDIAN RABBI

I was born in Waukegan a long, long long time ago. As a matter of fact, our rabbi was an Indian...he used a tomahawk...I was eight days old...what did I know?

Quoted in Irving A. Fein's Jack Benny.

◻

Miriam Ben-Porat

TO TELL THE TRUTH

I craft my findings and conclusions in the reports in the driest of terms so that they speak for themselves. They do not contain even one single superfluous or irritating word. My objective is to state the truth without giving personal offense, yet without concealing facts. In the eyes of the state comptroller, all people must be equal.... Even the prophet Moses said he had to give a complete accounting to the people for all their contributions to construct the Sanctuary. When asked if he was not satisfied that God trusted him, Moses replied that while God can read his heart and mind, human beings cannot, and so they must be shown.

From a portrait by Asher Wallfish and Evelyn Gordon in The Jerusalem Post, *July 10, 1993. Countering the criticism to which she was subject. She also quoted the old Russian proverb: "If you tell the truth, all you get is a beating."*

□

Ben Sira

ON CAPRICE

Do not seek to be a ruler if you have not the strength to subdue caprice.

This proverb was a permanent fixture on David Ben-Gurion's desk.

WE ALL GROW OLD

Dishonor not the old; we shall all be numbered among them.

From the apocryphal book Wisdom of Ben Sira (8:6).

AGE AND EXPERIENCE

Much experience is the crown of the aged.

Ibid (25:6).

WEALTH AND HEALTH

There is no wealth like health.

Ibid (30:16).

NO PERMISSION TO SIN

Say not: "God has led me astray," for He does not desire sin. No one is bidden to be godless, and to no one did He give permission to sin.

Ibid (15:12).

TOMORROW'S TROUBLES

Do not worry about tomorrow's troubles, for you cannot know what the day may bring. Tomorrow may come and you will be no more, so you worry about a world which is not yours.

Ibid. Quoted in the talmudic tractate Yevamot (63b).

□

Norman Bentwich

HISTORICAL OVERSIGHT

It is a melancholy reflection upon the history of the Jews that they have failed to pay due honor to their two greatest philosophers. Spinoza was rejected by his contemporaries from the congregation of Israel; Philo-Judaeus was neglected by the generations that followed him.

From the Preface to his biography, Philo-Judaeus of Alexandria (1940).

□

Yoram Ben-Ze'ev

AN OBLIGING PRESIDENT

When he wears his presidential suit, *noblesse oblige*. The position demands of him that he keep a certain distance and we don't call him Chaim or, as Aura does, Vivian. But he is easygoing and informal with people on a personal level. I've never had to take my feet off the table when he comes into this office. And you can certainly tell him a dirty joke. He has a terrific sense of humor.

Commenting on Israeli president Chaim Herzog, who served from 1984 to 1993.

□

Ben Zoma

WHO IS RICH?

Who is rich? He who is satisfied with his fate.

Quoted in the talmudic tractate Avot (4:1).

HOW BLESSED AM I

Let us consider how much effort Adam had to exert before he could eat a piece of bread. He had to plow a field and sow the seed and harvest the grain, then bind and thresh and winnow and select the grains. After that he ground the wheat, sifted the flour, kneaded the dough and baked it, and only then could he eat bread. But I rise in the morning and find it all prepared and ready for my use.

Quoted in the talmudic tractate Berachot (58a).

□

Nicholai A. Berdyayev

BEARERS OF THE CROSS

Perhaps the saddest thing to admit is that those who rejected the Cross have to carry it, while those who welcomed it so often engaged in crucifying others.

From his Christianity and Anti-Semitism.

MUTUAL UNDERSTANDING

Jews and Christians are rapidly changing their attitudes towards one another. They are now entering a totally new phase of mutual understanding. In our contemporary world, which seems to be growing more and more ir-religious, the strength of the Jews lies in the resistance which they offer, together with Christians, against the new paganism.

From an article in Religion, February 1939.

◘

Gertrude Berg

GETTING OLD

So the legs are a little short, the knees maybe knock a little, but who listens?

From her Molly and Me *(1961).*

THE REAL AND THE UNREAL

I think that we all live in worlds that are part real, part unreal, sometimes wishing that the real might be touched with just a little of the unreal.... My profession has been making believe. Almost every day I move from my real apartment to a stage apartment. I write words for characters who never were but aren't too different from people I've really known. I have enjoyed this double identity so much that I've never really asked myself "Why?"

Quoted in Darryl Lyman's Jewish Comedy Catalog *(1989).*

CATALOG OF FAULTS

Certainly I have faults, but why should I torture myself? I know that I'm addicted to soda water, that I try every new diet I hear about, that department stores are my downfall, and that I'm very weak when it comes to noodle soup (with lots of noodles). I also like to eavesdrop on other people's conversations, and I have a total recall for everybody else's mistakes. Aside from that I'm normal—normal enough not to want to write a confession.

Ibid.

◘

Elmer Berger

AMERICAN COUNCIL FOR JUDAISM

We exist to fight Zionism, because we believe it is inimical to the best interests of American Jews. We believe we should be Jews by religion and by heritage, but that we are not Jews by nationality, a concept which Zionism fosters.

Zionism claims that all Jews, regardless of where they live, automatically have a double nationality—that of their host country and of Israel—and thus they must accept a double loyalty. We believe Americans of Jewish faith have no national rights or obligations except as equal, responsible citizens of the United States.

Stating the purpose and platform of the anti-Zionist American Council for Judaism, which he helped found in 1943 together with former members of the American Jewish Committee. Reported in The New York Times, *July 16, 1967.*

◘

Samuel Hugo Bergman

CONTRIBUTION OF HASIDISM

There is always the danger in Judaism that Jewish law will become arid, lifeless and cold. There always remains a fear that the live current which created *halakha* (law) will no longer be creative. The danger lurks in the not too distant future that religious life will be completely eradicated unless a new life is injected into it. These perils jeopardize not only all religious life but especially Judaism, which is founded on the practical and ritual applications of theological principles. Here, I believe, lies the greatness of Hasidism. It transforms the deed *(mitzvah)* into a vibrant and living act, and fills the law with life and meaning.

Quoted by Shlomo Shamir in the journal Panim El Panim, *Sivan 1961.*

CAPITAL PUNISHMENT

I believe with perfect faith that clemency for this man will halt the chain of hatred and bring the world a bit of salvation. Equally certain am I that a death sentence...will help the devil with a great victory in the world.

Joining a chorus opposing the death penalty for Adolf Eichmann. To which Attorney General Gideon Hausner, the prosecutor, responded, "We owe it to the Holocaust survivors to impose the punishment."

◘

Martin Bergmann

REMEMBERING AND FORGETTING

To be traumatized and in mourning inevitably affects a group's ability to assess current threats and deal with them effectively and realistically. Therefore we have to steer a careful line between not forgetting and excessive remembering. Too much stress on remembrance is an oppressive way to live. It is often overlooked that the process of mourning should ultimately lead to some measure of resolution and resignation without despair.

Urging that the Jewish people would do well abandoning its preoccupation with a tragic past. Quoted in Anne Roiphe's Season for Healing *(1988).*

◘

Henri Bergson

SALVATION THROUGH LITERATURE

Anyone who is thoroughly familiar with the

language and literature of a people cannot be wholly its enemy.

> From his Two Sources of Morality & Religion *(1935).*

GOD AS LOVE

God is love, and the object of love: herein lies the whole contribution of mysticism.

> *Ibid.*

THE FLUCTUATING MIND

There is no state of mind, however simple, which does not change every minute.

> *Quoted in Elinor and Robert Slater's* Great Jewish Men *(1996).*

CAUSE AND EFFECT

Action is what matters. We are present where we act....What is found in the effect was already in the cause.

> *Ibid.*

□

Eliezer Berkovits

ELIXIR OF LIFE

The enjoyment of the Sabbath is neither spiritual nor material; it is wholly human. Body and spirit celebrate the Sabbath in communion. The Jew who keeps the Sabbath may say that the material enjoyments of the day enhance his spiritual elation and that his spiritual elation renders the material enjoyments more gratifying. In the unifying act of the *mitzvah* the Sabbath acts as "a spice" to the palate and as an exhilarating joy for the spirit of man.

> From his God, Man and History *(1959).*

SABBATH MEALS

One celebrates the day not only by meditation and prayer, but also by wearing Sabbath clothes and by partaking of the Sabbath meals. The Sabbath meal itself is a *mitzvah;* it is a divine service. And if properly performed, it is a service of a far higher quality than that of prayer and meditation alone; it is the service of the whole man.

> *Ibid.*

SUFFERING SERVANT OF GOD

God's chosen people is the suffering servant of God. The majestic fifty-third chapter of Isaiah is the description of Israel's martyrology through the centuries [and] the way Christianity treated Israel through the ages only made

Isaiah's description fit Israel all the more tragically and truly.

> From his Faith After the Holocaust *(1973), in which he disputes the Christian claim that the suffering servant in Isaiah refers to Jesus.*

BEYOND HISTORY

God is responsible for having created a world in which man is free to make history. There must be a dimension beyond history in which all suffering finds its redemption through God. This is essential to the faith of a Jew. The Jew does not doubt God's presence, though he is unable to set limits to the duration and intensity of His absence.

> *Ibid.*

WHO WERE THE NAZIS?

In order to pacify the Christian conscience it is said that the Nazis were not Christians. But they were all the children of Christians.

> *Ibid.*

MAN AND HISTORY

Man can only exist because God renounces the use of power on him. This...means that God cannot be present in history through manifest material power. Such presence would destroy history. History is the area of human responsibility and its product.

> *Ibid.*

MAKING ROOM FOR HISTORY

God is mighty for He shackles His omnipotence and becomes *powerless* so that history may be possible.

> *Ibid.*

TORAH AND THE HUMAN CONDITION

The humanization of the Word of God requires that in applying the Torah to the human condition, one takes into consideration human nature and all its needs, human character and its problems, the human condition in its forever-fluctuating dimension, the Jew and the Jewish people in their unique historical reality.

> From his Not in Heaven: The Nature and Function of Halakha *(1984).*

ALL JEWS ARE BROTHERS

How far are you [Conservative and Reform Jews] willing to go for the sake of the more comprehensive *mitzvah* of Jewish unity?...In the Orthodox camp there are certain psychological impediments that have to be overcome. It is time that Orthodox rabbis face without dogmatism the issue of their relationship to rabbis of the non-Orthodox denominations. Judged in the light of the real situation, it is just not true that the latter, because of their Conservative or Reform interpretation of Judaism, are incapable of *yirat shama'yim*.

Ibid.

FUNDAMENTALISM AND JUDAISM

Only non-Jews have been fundamentalists. Never Jews who took their place within Judaism. For them every word of the Torah and, of course, every commandment, has its source in God; but the *meaning* of the revealed word or commandment is given in the oral tradition....The oral tradition is the Jews' protection against fundamentalism.

From an essay in Condition of Jewish Belief *(1966), compiled by the editors of* Commentary *magazine.*

THE TRUE RELIGION

Judaism is the one true religion—for the Jew. As for the rest of mankind, Judaism teaches that the righteous of all nations have a share in the world to come.

Ibid.

JUDEO-CHRISTIAN FANTASY

Judaism is Judaism because it rejects Christianity, and Christianity is Christianity because it rejects Judaism. What is usually referred to as the Judeo-Christian tradition exists only in Christian and secularist fantasy. As far as Jews are concerned, Judaism is fully sufficient. There is nothing in Christianity for them.

Quoted in Egal Feldman's Dual Destinies: The Jewish Encounter with Protestant America *(1990).*

STRANGLED CREATIVITY

It is very likely that in the Holocaust 80% or more of the creative vitality of the Jewish people was strangled.

From an interview with The Jerusalem Post's *Ernie Meyer, shortly before Professor Berkovits' death in 1992.*

□

William Berkowitz

INNER STRENGTH

In the face of all the difficulties from without, the Jew was strong from within. He maintained an inner pride and inner dignity that no tyrant could destroy. The Jew of the past knew the value and strength of Judaism. He was aware of its ethical teachings and familiar with its message. He was convinced of his own

people's eternal role that needed to be carried forward in each generation. Thus he was inwardly secure, even though he was constantly threatened from without.

From the Introduction to his Ten Vital Jewish Issues *(1964).*

SHVER TZU ZEIN A YID

Sholem Aleichem, whose gifted pen and unusual humor helped brighten a darkened Jewish horizon at the turn of the century, left us a rich legacy of wise and introspective sayings from which many have drawn and quoted. Across the years, one of his classic expressions was: *Shver tzu zein a Yid*, "It's difficult to be a Jew." To be sure, this was no exaggeration. Indeed, in this pithy saying Sholem Aleichem summarized decades, if not centuries, of Jewish existence and survival.

Ibid.

□

Adolf A. Berle

NO SILLY IDLE DREAM

Looked upon by many as a silly or idle dream for years, there is now something resembling a probability that there will arise in Palestine a Jewish state under the protectorate of the great powers, or some of them, which will have a significance to the world far beyond, probably, what even its most ardent advocates dream.

From his World Significance of a Jewish State *(1918).*

□

Milton Berle

GREAT COMEDIAN

Henny Youngman is one of the great comedians of our generation. This is not only my opinion, it's Henny's as well.

From the Foreword to Henny Youngman's How Do You Like Me So Far? *(1963).*

THE PRESSURE TO STAR

I have a lot of regrets about things I did and said, for the way I pushed and shoved and bullied during those hysterical years. My only defense, which is no defense, is the pressure. [If a youth becomes a star too early, it will be] a miracle if that kid doesn't grow up to be a man who believes he's Casanova, Einstein, and Jesus Christ all rolled into one.

Quoted in Darryl Lyman's Jewish Comedy Catalog *(1989).*

DEFINING A COMMITTEE

Committees are places where people keep minutes and waste hours.

Quoted in Morris Mandel's Affronts, Insults, and Indignities *(1975).*

◻

Irving Berlin

GOD BLESS AMERICA

God bless America,
Land that I love;
Stand beside her and guide her
Through the night with a light from above.

A song written in 1917 and first sung by Kate Smith on Armistice Day, 1938.

ON BEING A SUCCESS

The toughest thing about success is that you've got to keep on being a success.

From an interview with Ward Morehouse in Theatre Arts *magazine, February 1958.*

PLAYING IN NEW HAVEN

I write a song to please the public—and if the public doesn't like it in New Haven, I change it!

Commenting on what made his music so timely and popular. Quoted in Elinor and Robert Slater's Great Jewish Men *(1996).*

◻

Isaiah Berlin

TYPES OF INTELLECTUALS

There exists a great chasm between those, on one side, who relate everything to a single central vision....and, on the other side, those who pursue many ends, often unrelated and even contradictory....The first kind of intellectual and artistic personality belongs to the hedgehogs, the second to the foxes.

From his Hedgehog and Fox *(1953).*

LIBERTY IS LIBERTY

Liberty is liberty, not equality or fairness or justice or human happiness or a quiet conscience.

From his Two Concepts of Liberty *(1958).*

HEIGHT OF HUMILITY

All my life I have been greatly overestimated.... I am all for it. Long may it last.

Quoted in Avishai Margalit's essay in The New Republic, *February 20, 1995.*

WHAT JEWS HAVE IN COMMON

What do you think is common to all Jews? I mean, to the Jew from San'a, from Marrakech, from Riga, from Glasgow? A sense of social unease. Nowhere do almost all Jews feel entirely at home.

Ibid. Answering his own question.

YES AND NO

I am a devoted Anglophile, not an Englishman.

Ibid. Responding to whether he feels at home in England.

◻

Saul Berman

WOMEN IN JEWISH LAW

The first step [in solving the dissatisfaction of women over the lack of equality with men] is to call a moratorium on apologetics. It is one thing to recognize the problems and to attempt to understand the theological, halakhic, economic, and cultural factors which produced them. It is a completely different matter, both dishonest and dysfunctional, to attempt through homiletics and scholasticism to transform problems into solutions and to reinterpret discrimination to be beneficial.

From his essay "The Status of Women in Halakhic Judaism," which appeared in The Jewish Woman *(1976), edited by Elizabeth Kolkun.*

◻

Chaim Bermant

BECOMING A JEW AGAIN

When it became clear that in spite of his wealth and prominence he [Robert Maxwell] would never become an establishment figure, he reverted to his origins and became a Jew again.... His reconversion was not an overnight phenomenon and the process must have been helped by the adverse publicity he provoked, not a little of which had distinct anti-Semitic undertones....Once he became a Jew again, it was inevitable that he should become a super-Jew, not in the religious sense, but the nationalist one.

From an article in the London Jewish Chronicle. *Quoted in Elisabeth Maxwell's* Mind of My Own: My Life With Robert Maxwell *(1994).*

Sarah Bernhardt

A PROUD JEW

I, too, am the daughter of the great Jewish people!

Quoted in Elinor and Robert Slater's Great Jewish Women *(1994).*

Isaac W. Bernheim

DENUNCIATION OF ZIONISM

Zionism, political and otherwise, of the imported or domestic brand, was not...a thing to our liking, nor can it ever receive our support. Here [Germany] is our Palestine, and we know no other.

From a 1921 address delivered to the council of the Union of American Hebrew Congregations by an opponent of political Zionism.

David S. Bernstein

BLACK ANTI-SEMITISM

Now that the white radicals (again disproportionately Jewish) who never left the universities are tenured professors and administrators, it is only natural that they would continue their affinity for radical black politic. However, they didn't envision—although they should have—that their indigenous American Leftist movement would take the same turn to virulent anti-Semitism that every other international Marxist movement has.

From an address presented at the World Conference on Anti-Semitism and Prejudice in a Changing World, held in Brussels, Belgium, July 1992.

Leonard Bernstein

BERNSTEIN WILL DO

I'll do as Bernstein or not at all.

When it was suggested, in 1943, that he change his name after he was appointed assistant to Artur Rodzinski, conductor of the New York Philharmonic.

KEEP REHEARSING

All the world is a stage, with audiences searching for the perfect play. We may not reach perfection—this is not a utopian world—but all of us can strive toward that perfection.

To do that: keep rehearsing.

From an address to a Philadelphia gathering at which he was being honored.

TECHNIQUE AND COMMUNICATION

Technique is communication: the two words are synonymous in conductors.

Quoted in the London Times, *June 27, 1989.*

Louis J. Bernstein

WHAT IS RIGHT

For us, the only guidelines must be what is right, and not what the right says.

When criticized by the ultra-Orthodox for his addressing a convention of Conservative rabbis.

Claude Berri

LOYAL JEWISH ATHEIST

I am more French than the French.... If you are a Jew, you must know where you come from. If your family is Jewish, you are a Jew, no question. But my culture is French and I am an atheist. My religion is art.

From a profile in The Jerusalem Report, *January 27, 1994. Berri's father was a Polish Jew; his mother was of Rumanian-Jewish extraction.*

James D. Besser

NIXON AND THE JEWS

Nixon's career, in a way, was a kind of mirror reflecting a changing Jewish political universe. Like most of this country's political leaders, Nixon went from an indifference about Israel to a kind of support—sometimes grudging, almost always pragmatic—and an understanding that in many ways, Israel's interests are parallel to those of the United States.

An evaluation of the life of the thirty-seventh president of the United States after his death in April 1994. From The Jewish Week, *April 29–May 5, 1994.*

Karl Best

LAST SNIPERS OF LIBERALISM

The Jewish question is the dynamite with which we shall blow up the redoubts where the last snipers of liberalism have dug themselves in nations who abandon their Jews and thereby give us their previous judaized form of life, based on false ideals of freedom.

A statement by the German SS leader on July 27, 1942.

□

Bruno Bettelheim

INABILITY TO ACT IN SELF-DEFENSE

The vast majority of my fellow prisoners were not Jews but German gentiles. Beholden to ghetto thinking; only what happened to the Jews counted; they were not interested in what happened to the gentiles. But lacking interest they could not learn from it. Those Jews who were interested and learned from it were able to save themselves.... It was not a shunning of violence that explains Jewish suffering under the Nazis, but rather an inability to act in self-defense...*as a Jew.*

From a 1962 speech delivered at the Eighth Annual Rosenwald Lecture of the American Council for Judaism.

ACCEPTING RESPONSIBILITY

Blaming others or outside conditions for one's own misbehavior may be the child's privilege; if an adult denies responsibility for his own actions, it is another step towards personality disintegration.

Reflecting upon the actions of fellow inmates in Nazi concentration camps. From his In-formed Heart (1971).

□

David Biale

THE HOLOCAUST IN A HUMAN CONTEXT

The Holocaust needs to be divorced from what it tells us about Jewish history and connected instead to the other special dilemmas of contemporary politics. Remembering the Holocaust cannot prevent a recurrence.

Quoted in Anne Roiphe's Season for Healing (1988).

□

Chaim Nachman Bialik

I LOVE TEL AVIV

I love Tel Aviv...because all of it, from the foundation to the coping, was established by our own hands...because we need not feel oblig-

ated to anyone for its good points or apologetic for its bad points. Is not this the whole aim of our redemption....to be owners of our body and soul, masters of our spirit and creation?

Quoted in M. Obadiah's Mi-pee Bialik (5691).

THE TASTE OF WINE

To know the taste of wine, it is not necessary to drink the whole barrel.

Ibid.

SMALL BUT IMPORTANT

In creative work, never consider quantity. Obadiah consists of one chapter, yet it found its place in the Book of Books.

Ibid.

A NEED FOR POETRY

As long as the soul animates man, and longs for light and thirsts for beauty, man needs the fountain of poetry.

Ibid.

INTUITION AND CREATION

Intuition precedes all creation.

Ibid.

FIGHTING GOD

Why do they *pray* to Me? Tell them to *thunder* against Me. Let them raise their fists against Me and claim recompense for their shame!

From his classic poem "In the City of Slaughter" (1904), prompted by the Kishinev pogrom.

YEARNING TO BELONG

The misery at home, the bitter orphanhood, weighed heavily on me. I was invited by relatives to a wedding party. The light and music filled my heart, which thirsted so badly to feel joy again. Like a madman I danced barefoot to the music. I forgot myself, but my heart longed to join a circle, to cleave to something, to belong.

Quoted in David Aberbach's Bialik (1988).

CHERISHING OUR LEGENDS

Legends are the beautiful little stones lapped by the sea for centuries and generations until they are cast up on the shore, polished and smooth. Legends pass from generation to generation. Everything superfluous falls away. What remains is the best, the beautiful, and most worthy of keeping and remembering.

> *Describing the meaning of legends to Hebrew writer M. J. Berdichewsky.*

SAY THIS AT MY FUNERAL

After I am dead
Say this at my funeral:
There was a man who exists no more.
That man died before his time,
And his life's song was broken off halfway.
He had one more poem,
And that poem has been lost
For ever.

> *Part of his 1904 poem "Acharay Moti [After My Death]."*

SELF-PROPELLED YIDDISH

Hebrew one has to speak, while Yiddish speaks on its own [*Yiddish ret zich alayn*].

> *Although Bialik was the poet laureate of Hebrew letters, he preferred to speak in Yiddish.*

¤

Louis Binstock

CLOCK OF LIFE

Our clock of life, wound up in the womb, begins to run down at the very moment of birth. Every day we die a little.

> *From his* Power of Faith *(1952).*

¤

Trudi Birger

KEEPING A PROMISE

I fulfilled my ideal. In the concentration camp, after a wonderfully rich childhood, I vowed that if I were to survive, I would devote myself to helping needy children.

> *From a 1993 interview in Jerusalem. The author of* A Daughter's Gift of Love *has concentrated her efforts on education and health care. In 1980, in Jerusalem, she established a free dental clinic that treats Moslem and Jewish children as well as Ethiopian and Russian immigrants.*

¤

Stephen Birmingham

MEDIA INFLUENCE

The most important question to be asked is whether the fact of Jews in the media affects the media's treatment of the news and, as Agnew claims, foreign policy. Most media experts and observers feel that it does not at all....

It is safe to say that, although the Jewish media dismiss the Agnew charges as absurd and unfounded, they are nonetheless sensitive—very sensitive to them. The trouble is that many people will take him (Agnew) seriously, much as an earlier generation took another demagogue, Henry Ford, seriously when he publicized the spurious *Protocols of the Learned Elders of Zion* in his Dearborn newspaper. There was dark talk then of an "international conspiracy" of Jews to control the world's money. Now there will be more conspiracy talk.

> *From a 1976 article in* More *magazine in which Birmingham refutes claims the former vice-president makes in his book* The Canfield Decision *that "a Jewish cabal" exists in the media, that it influences U.S. policy towards the support of Israel, and plots favorable coverage for the Jewish state.*

¤

Nathan Birnbaum

JUDAISM AND THE WORLD-TO-COME

The pious of the Gentiles will inherit the world to come. The Jew is not the Almighty's only child, for whom alone the world to come is open. He is a child whom God has chosen for priority in religion, giving him the Holy Torah. Judaism is not the appointed guardian of the world-to-come. It is therefore not a recruiting religion among the peoples.

> *From an essay by an early collaborator of Theodor Herzl, the man who coined the word "Zionism."*

¤

Milton Birnbaum

SINS AND VIRTUES

You might consider following up this excellent series [on the deadly sins] with another called "The Seven Virtues: Faith, Hope, Charity, Prudence, Justice, Fortitude and Temperance." I wonder if you'd be able to find writers who could speak with experiential authority on these virtues. Offhand, only two people come to mind: Mother Teresa and Elie Wiesel.

> *From a letter to the editor of* The New York Times Book Review, *August 22, 1993.*

Otto von Bismarck

DER ALTE JUDE

Der alte Jude, das ist der Mann [the old Jew, he is the man].

> *Pointing to Disraeli, as he responds, at the Congress of Berlin, as to who was "the center of gravity at the Congress." Quoted in Henry Kissinger's* Diplomacy *(1994).*

RIGHTS OF JEWS

I shall never agree to have the constitutionally accorded rights of the Jews curtailed in any wise.

> *His reply to a question of Moritz Behrend in 1880, as to whether he was in agreement with anti-Semitism.*

(Rabbi) Bisna

NO ONE IS TROUBLE-FREE

There is no person in the world who is not plagued by troubles.

> *Quoted in the Midrash Yalkut Shimoni on Ekev (450).*

Joey Bishop

GIVING SOMETHING BACK

No matter how great the comedian, if he didn't do something for humanity, I disliked him to a certain level.

> *Quoted in Darryl Lyman's* Jewish Comedy Catalog *(1989).*

A JEWISH ORCHESTRA

I'd like to work one club—just one club—where they have a Jewish orchestra and Spanish people dancing.

> *Ibid.*

Harry A. Blackmun

CHANUKAH AND CHRISTMAS

Chanukah, like Christmas, is a cultural event as well as a religious holiday. Indeed, the Chanukah story always has had a political or national as well as a religious dimension: it tells of national heroism in addition to divine intervention. Just as some Americans celebrate Christmas without regard to its religious significance, some nonreligious American Jews celebrate Chanukah as an expression of ethnic identity, and as a cultural or national event, rather than as a specifically religious event.

> *From his ruling in the case of* County of Allegheny v. ACLU *(1989).*

LEVEL PLAYING FIELD

If the city [of Pittsburgh] celebrates both Christmas and Chanukah as secular holidays, then its conduct is beyond the reach of the Establishment Clause. Because government may celebrate Christmas as a secular holiday, it follows that government may also acknowledge Chanukah as a secular holiday.

> *Ibid.*

CHANUKAH GELT

The tradition of giving Chanukah *gelt* [money] has taken on greater importance because of the temporal proximity of Chanukah to Christmas. Indeed, some have suggested that the proximity of Christmas accounts for the social prominence of Chanukah in this country. Whatever the reason, Chanukah is observed by American Jews to an extent greater than its religious importance would indicate: in the hierarchy of Jewish holidays, Chanukah ranks fairly low in religious significance. The socially heightened status of Chanukah reflects its cultural or secular dimension.

> *Ibid.*

James G. Blaine

FAUST REVISITED

The Mephistopheles of the Southern Confederacy.

> *A description of Judah P. Benjamin, the brilliant lawyer, in S. I. Nieman's* Judah Benjamin.

William Blake

TRUE CHRISTIANS

If humility is Christianity, you, Jews, are the true Christians!

> *From his* Selections from Jerusalem *(1804–1820).*

Michael Blankfort

PEACE OF SPIRIT

In the communion of Judaism, the identification with my people, my active affection for the Land of Israel, my faltering efforts to live by the precepts of the Prophets, I have found a peace of the spirit.... It is a way of life and understanding by which, as a human being, an American, a Jew and a writer, I can view with more meaning the world around me and the world within.

From his Education of a Jew.

AN ORTHODOX ILLITERATE

During that time [that he was attending *cheder*—that is, Hebrew school] I learned how to read the Hebrew prayer book and Torah Hebrew, chanted without the vowel signs, and with a speed and accuracy which were miracles of learning by rote. I understood, however, no more than one one-thousandth of what I read.... To be blunt, I was an Orthodox illiterate.

After the publication of his second "Jewish" book, The Strong Hand. *His first was* The Juggler. *Both created controversy in Jewish circles.*

□

Jacob Blaustein

LIFE IN AMERICA

To American Jews, America is home. There, exist their thriving roots; there, is the country which they have helped to build; and there, they share its fruits and its destiny. They believe in the future of a democratic society in the United States under which all citizens can live on terms of equality.

After a confrontation in August 1950 with David Ben-Gurion, who had been insisting on massive American immigration to the State of Israel.

□

J. David Bleich

SAFETY AND SURVIVAL

When you are riding in a horse and wagon and pass the door of a church, if the driver does not cross himself, get off immediately.

A Yiddish folksaying he recalls hearing from his great-grandmother when he was a child. Quoted in David Dalin's American Jews and the Separatist Faith *(1993).*

□

Wolf Blitzer

CHILDREN EXCITEMENT

We are little children. We get excited when we meet big stars.

Commenting on the Washington press corps' fawning reaction upon meeting Barbra Streisand backstage after a Maryland concert.

□

Ernst Bloch

THE STRUGGLE GOES ON

For the Jews are not yet weary. They will not fail. They are like heart cells and do not allow themselves to slacken.

Quoted in Silvia Markun's Ernst Bloch *(1985).*

□

Harold Bloom

AN AMERICAN JEWISH CULTURE

Our writers and speculators just have not been original enough until now, and probably will not be for some time to come.

Articulating why he believes we do not have, as yet, an American Jewish culture. From his essay "Masks of the Normative," which appeared in Orot: A Jewish Journal at Yale, *Volume 1, Number 1, Autumn 1985.*

THE DOMAIN OF FOOLS

I realized early on that the academy and the literary world alike—and I don't think there really is a distinction between the two— are always dominated by fools, knaves, charlatans and bureaucrats. And that being the case, any human being, male or female, of whatever status, who has a voice of her or his own, is not going to be liked.

From an interview in Criticism in Society, *edited by I. Salusinski (1987).*

□

Michael Bloomberg

CALLING GOD

I'm not terribly religious, but I am terribly sensitive to the fact that it's my heritage. I don't spend time *davening* [praying]. If I don't call God, he won't call me.

Describing his relationship to Judaism. From an interview in The Jerusalem Report, *March 9, 1995.*

UJA AND THE "RELIGIOUS"

I won't give too much money to the UJA, because of the hold the religious have on Israel. I have one wish: Shoot all the clerics.

Ibid.

SUPER SALESBOY

I was in some senses an achiever. I was an Eagle Scout, and sold more Christmas wreaths than anyone.

Ibid.

□

Léon Blum

PROMOTING JUSTICE

All my life I have hoped to see an alleviation of the suffering of the world's disinherited. Should I then now, when the opportunity comes to me to assure those of France a larger measure of justice, abandon them? I accept the challenge which comes to me as a Jew and as a citizen of France.

After a delegation of Jews in 1836 urged him to decline the premiership in a Leftist coalition for fear of anti-Semitic repercussions.

DEFINING A FREE MAN

The free man is he who does not fear to go to the end of his thoughts.

From a comment to Jules Renard. Quoted in John Gunther's Inside Europe.

□

William E. Bohn

SOCIALISM RECONSIDERED

I cannot think of Abe Cahan without recalling one great scene, some months after Roosevelt had started on his New Deal. The Socialists, believing in a set of inherited stereotypes, thought that nothing good could come out of a "capitalist" party. Before a great gathering of Socialists at Madison Square Garden, Abe Cahan, just returned from Europe, bluntly told all of the assembled theorists that they ought to give up their slogans and support Roosevelt in his concrete proposals. I can picture him standing there, the little man on the wide platform, saying plainly, in simple words, what he had to say. No one thinking back to that time can realize what a shock he sent through that crowd.

From his article entitled "Abraham Cahan: A Great American," which appeared in The New Leader, *September 17, 1951.*

□

Ben Zion Bokser

FENCES AND ROADS

The tragedy is that many people build fences around their lives, instead of open roads.

From his sermon in Best Jewish Sermons of 5713 *(1953), edited by Saul I. Teplitz.*

OPEN ROAD

The open road of spiritual life extends also to the past and the future.

Ibid.

EFFECTIVE CRITICISM

There are three prerequisites for effective criticism, according to the Talmud, and they apply to anyone who seeks to correct his neighbor, which is the ultimate goal of all preachment. The person to be corrected must be willing to accept criticism, the critic must know how to criticize, and he must himself be virtuous enough to merit the role of being a critic.

From the Introduction to Alfred J. Kolatch's Sermons for the Sixties *(1965).*

HEART AND MIND

Men can know with the heart and not only with the mind.

Ibid.

□

Sonny Bono

FRANKLY SPEAKING

Barney, I want to keep watching you, if you don't mind, because you're the best I've ever seen. I haven't figured out what the hell you do, but it's good.

At a 1995 Washington National Press Club dinner at which sharp-tongued Barney Frank, congressman from Massachusetts, was present.

□

Hyman (Harry) Bookbinder

FREEDOM TO LOBBY

It was presumably proper for industry to express its views; it was perfectly understandable that Saudi Arabia itself would spend lavish sums on the highest-priced lobbyists and lawyers; it was okay for 21 other Arab embassies to express their views; it was only natural that Mobil and other oil companies would expand their "public service" advertising programs to promote the AWACS sales...then just as surely Americans concerned with the very security of their co-religionists in Israel...are no less entitled to freedom of advocacy.

> *From a statement made in 1981 after the Reagan administration won the battle to sell AWACS (Airborne Warning and Control System) to Saudi Arabia and criticized Jews for opposing the sale.*

Now We All Know

I tell students that their generation will not ever have the same excuse some in my generation invoke, that they "did not know." We all know now, and we must act.

> *Upon his return from visiting Auschwitz and other death camps in 1980.*

Path to Self-fulfillment

Government's principal purpose must be to implement the great promise of America the securing of life, liberty, and the pursuit of happiness. Above all, this has meant for me the lifting of discriminatory barriers to self-fulfillment—race, religion, national origin.

> *Quoted in* Who's Who in America *(1992–1993).*

¤

Daniel J. Boorstin

Extravagant Expectations

We expect too much of the world. Our expectations are extravagant in the precise dictionary sense of the word—"going beyond the limits of reason or moderation." They are excessive.

> *From his* Image *(1961).*

Disappointed People

Never have people been more the masters of their environment. Yet never has a people felt more deceived and disappointed. For never has a people expected so much more than the world could offer.

> *Ibid.*

God as Image

What preoccupies us, then, is not God as a fact of nature, but as a fabrication useful for a God-fearing society. God himself becomes not a power but an image.

> *Ibid.*

Land of Dreams

America has been a land of dreams, a land

where the aspirations of people from countries cluttered with rich, cumbersome, aristocratic, ideological pasts can reach for what once seemed unattainable.

> *Ibid.*

¤

Victor Borge

Weight of a Smile

A smile is the shortest distance between people.

> *Explaining how he arrives at intimacy with his audience. Quoted in Darryl Lyman's* Jewish Comedy Catalog *(1989).*

Keeping in Control

With an orchestra you have to play up to standard, but I'm never tense in solo performance, because there I can always talk my way out of a mistake.

> *Ibid.*

Thanks and Thanks Again

I want to thank my parents for making this possible—and I want to thank my children for making this necessary.

> *Ibid. A classic quip with which he ends his concerts.*

My Greatest Fault

Being the recipient of physical and mental facilities assigned to me before my birth, I am convinced that, as custodian, my efforts toward accomplishments consist mainly of a reasonable amount of discipline and devotion to elementary decency. Perhaps part of my good fortune may be credited to my faults, of which the greatest is modesty.

> *Ibid.*

¤

Ludwig Börne

German and a Jew

Yes, because I was born a slave, I love freedom more than you. Yes, because I was raised in bondage, I understand freedom better than you. Yes, because I was born without a fatherland, I wish for a fatherland more passionately than you, and because my birthplace was no larger than Judengasse (Jews' Lane), and foreign parts began beyond the locked gates, the city is no longer enough as a fatherland for me, nor is a region or a province; only the truly vast fatherland is enough, as far as its language reaches.

> *Quoted in* Börne's Work *(1986), edited by Helmut Bock and Walter Dietze.*

□

Ber Borochov

NATIONAL SUICIDE

Death and suicide are the most radical reliefs from disease. Similarly, assimilation is the most radical solution to the Jewish problem. If there were no Jews, there would be no suffering from the Jewish tragedy. Nevertheless, no medical expert would advise a patient to take poison for a cure.... Only to us Jews have self-appointed "physicians" had the audacity, the shamelessness, to preach national suicide.

> *From his* Nationalism and the Class Struggle *(1937).*

□

Eugene Borowitz

PATCHWORK THEOLOGY

Cohen's God, Baeck's mystery, Kaplan's peoplehood, Buber's Covenant and Heschel's Prophetic Sympathy, will not mesh together. The premises on which they are founded substantially contradict one another.

> *In his* Choices in Modern Jewish Thought, *arguing against the idea that a patchwork theology can be created by selecting the most appealing elements from prominent thinkers.*

JEWISH CONTRIBUTION TO CIVILIZATION

What Judaism can contribute to the world is not, then, an idea or a concept....

What Judaism can uniquely give the world is Jews, men, and equally important, communities that live by their social, messianic hopes and try to effectuate them in day-to-day reality.... No other human institution has yet shown the capability that Judaism has of transforming a statistically large number of individuals into socially motivated persons and groups.

> *From an essay in* Condition of Jewish Belief *(1966), compiled by the editors of* Commentary *magazine.*

LAMENTABLE JEWISH LEADERSHIP

What other religious groups in America... can boast of men who are zealously committed to interfaith activities, but who have no faith of their own, who worship in no church with any degree of regularity, and who observe no commandments but those that their organizational participation requires or common American decency requires?

> *From his* New Jewish Theology in the Making *(1968).*

□

Leon Botstein

THE JEWISH INFLUENCE

Being Jewish is the most important social and cultural part of my life. It defined my relationship to my world more decisively than anything else.

> *Quoted in the* Forward, *October 20, 1995.*

REVERSE DISCRIMINATION

I don't think reverse discrimination is serious. I don't think there are a lot of Jews out there who are sitting unemployed because some black got the job. That's just a scare tactic.

> *Ibid.*

THE MANY FACES OF JUDAISM

In the modern age, there are many varieties of adhering metaphorically and also practically to a sense of faith without a fundamentalist definition.

> *Ibid. Expressing discontent with the monolithic nature of Orthodox Judaism.*

□

Phyllis Bottome

TO BE A JEW

To be a Jew...is to be strong with a strength that has outlived persecutions. It is to be wise against ignorance, honest against piracy, harmless against evil, industrious against idleness, kind against cruelty!

> *From her* Mortal Storm.

□

Barbara Boxer

WISDOM IN YOUTH

When I look at you, I see the exuberance of youth, the exaggeration of youth and the loveliness of youth, along with some of the problems of youth.... Just because you're young doesn't mean your opinion doesn't mean something.

> *In support of Joshua Steiner at the hearings before the Senate Banking Committee on August 2, 1994, the purpose of which was to investigate Treasury Department contacts with the White House in the Whitewater matter. Twenty-eight-year-old Steiner, chief of staff to Treasury Secretary Lloyd Bentsen, had kept a diary which was proving embarrassing to his superiors.*

□

Milton Bracker

THE CREMATORIUM

It is certain that the crematorium, the hooks, the gas orifices, the dissection slab, and the urns were not used for mere decoration.

> *Reporting in* The New York Times, *December 5, 1944, after a visit to an abandoned Nazi concentration camp.*

□

Louis D. Brandeis

HAZARDS OF A FREE SOCIETY

[He held] that it is hazardous to discourage thought, hope, or imagination; that fear breeds repression; that repression breeds hate; that hate menaces stable government; that the path of safety lies in the opportunity to discuss freely supposed grievances and proposed remedies; and that the fitting remedy for evil councils is good ones.

> *From his decision in the 1927 Supreme Court case of* Whitney v. California.

PURPOSE OF THE STATE

Those who won our independence believed that the final end of the State was to make men free to develop their faculties; and that in its government the deliberative forces should prevail over the arbitrary. They valued liberty both as an end and as a means. They believed liberty to be the secret of happiness and courage to be the secret of liberty.

> *Ibid.*

THE RIGHT TO ORGANIZE

America cannot develop citizens unless the workingmen possess industrial liberty; and industrial liberty is impossible if the right to organize be denied.

> *From an article in* Collier's Weekly, *September 14, 1912.*

INALIENABLE RIGHT TO PRIVACY

[The framers of our constitution] conferred, as against the government, the right to be left alone—the most comprehensive of rights and the right most valued by civilized men. To protect that right, every unjustifiable intrusion by the government upon the privacy of the individual, whatever the means employed, must be deemed a violation of the Fourth Amendment. And the use, as evidence in a criminal proceeding, of facts ascertained by such intrusion must be deemed a violation of the Fifth.

> *From his decision in the 1928 Supreme Court case of* Olmstead v. United States.

MULTIPLE LOYALTIES

Multiple loyalties are objectionable only if they are inconsistent. A man is a better citizen of the United States for being also a loyal citizen of his state, and of his city; for being loyal to his family, and to his profession or trade; for being loyal to his college or his lodge.

> *From his* Jewish Problem *(1915).*

AMERICANISM AND ZIONISM

Loyalty to America demands that each American Jew become a Zionist.

> *Ibid.*

JEWISH GIFTS TO THE WORLD

The Jews gave to the world its three greatest religions, reverence for law, and the highest conceptions of morality.

> *Ibid.*

LIFE'S MISUNDERSTANDINGS

Nine-tenths of the serious controversies which arise in life result from misunderstanding.

> *From an address to a Boston typothetae, April 22, 1904.*

A PLACE FOR THE JEWISH SPIRIT

Shall we, with our inheritance, do less than the Irish, the Serbians, or the Bulgars? And must we not, like them, have a land where the Jewish life may be naturally led, the Jewish language spoken, and the Jewish spirit prevail?

> *From his* Call to the Educated Jew *(1916).*

A NATION IS BORN

The Jewish Renaissance has come—the nation is reborn, and the Jewish State in its beginning is already here.

> *From an April 1915 address.*

AMERICAN AND JEWISH IDEALS

The twentieth-century ideals of America

have been the ideals of the Jew for more than twenty centuries.

Quoted in The Menorah Journal, *January 1915.*

A RETURN TO SPIRITUALITY

The educated descendants of a people which in its infancy cast aside the Golden Calf and put its faith in the invisible God cannot worthily in its maturity worship worldly distinction and things material.

Ibid.

JEWISH BROTHERHOOD

Persecution made the Jew's law of brotherhood self-enforcing. It taught them the seriousness of life; it broadened their sympathies; it deepened their passion for righteousness; it trained them in patient endurance, in persistence, in self-control, and in self-sacrifice.

Ibid.

DEFINITION OF GRAFT

Getting an advantage at the expense of somebody else—that really is what graft is.

Reported in Boston American, *July 22, 1905.*

OVERRATED AND UNDERRATED

The ability of big men is overrated, and that of small men underrated. Give a man opportunity and responsibility, and he will grow.

From a statement in A. Lief's Brandeis Guide to the Modern World *(1941).*

A RESPECT FOR LAW

To secure respect for law, we must make the law respectable.

From an October 15, 1912 speech.

FUNCTION OF THE PRESS

The function of the press is very high. It is almost holy. It ought to serve as a forum for the people, through which the people may know freely what is going on. To misstate or suppress the news is a breach of trust.

From an article in Collier's Weekly, *March 23, 1912.*

THE PATH OF PROGRESS

America has believed that in differentiation, not in uniformity, lies the path of progress.

From a Boston address, April 6, 1915.

REACHING FOR PERFECTION

The new nationalism adopted by America proclaims that each race or people, like each individual, has the right and duty to develop, and that only through such differentiated development will high civilization be attained.

From "True Americanism," a July 4, 1915 address.

THE STRUGGLE FOR LIBERTY

Let us recognize that we Jews are a distinct nationality of which every Jew, whatever his country, station, or shade of belief, is necessarily a member. Let us insist that the struggle for liberty shall not cease until equality of opportunity is accorded to nationalities as to individuals.

From an April 25, 1915 address.

LIFE IS TOO SHORT

I have only one life, and it is short enough. Why waste it on things I don't want most?

Quoted in Current Literature, *March 1911.*

NOTHING IS IMPOSSIBLE

Most of the things worth doing in the world had been declared impossible before they were done.

Statement made during arbitration proceedings affecting the New York cloak industry, October 13, 1913.

PRESERVING THE JEWISH SPIRIT

The Jewish spirit, so long preserved, the character developed by so many centuries of sacrifice, should be preserved and developed further, so that in America as elsewhere the sons of the race may in the future live lives and do deeds worthy of their ancestors.

From his Brandeis on Zionism *(1942).*

THE JEWISH NAME

It is not wealth, it is not station, it is not social standing and ambition, which makes us worthy of the Jewish name, of the Jewish heritage. To be worthy of them, we must live up to and with them. We must regard ourselves as custodians. Every young man here must feel that he is the trustee of what is best in Jewish history.

Ibid.

CULTURAL PLURALISM

Every American Jew who aides in advancing the Jewish settlement in Palestine, though he feels that neither he nor his descendants will ever live there, will be a better man and a better American for doing so.

Quoted in Elinor and Robert Slater's Great Jewish Men *(1996).*

DEFINING A "GOOD BARGAIN"

The old idea of a good bargain was a transaction in which one man got the better of another. The new idea of a good contract is a transaction which is good for both parties to it.

From a 1912 address at Brown University.

EMPATHY FOR CORELIGIONISTS

When men and women of Jewish blood suffer—because of that fact—and even if they suffer from quite different causes—our sympathy and our help goes out to them instinctively in whatever country they may live.

A comment inspired by the unjust conviction of Leo M. Frank, falsely accused of murdering Mary Phagan, a thirteen-year-old employee, in April 1913. Quoted in Jacob de Haas's Louis D. Brandeis *(1929).*

HOMEWARD BOUND

You have brought me back to my people.

After listening to an address by European Zionist leader Nahum Sokolow in 1913.

BEING LED BY REASON

If we would guide by the light of reason, we must let our minds be bold.

From a closing statement in the case of New State Ice Co. *v.* Liebman.

¤

Marlon Brando

ACADEMY AWARDS

The [Oscar] ceremony has its roots in Hollywood's obsession with self-promotion; people in the business have a passion for paying tribute to one another. I suspect it stems from the fact that so many of them are Jewish. It is a part of their faith to recognize and reward good works and be honored for them.

From his autobiography, Brando: Songs My Mother Taught Me *(1994).*

NEW YORK OF THE 1940S

The extraordinary European Jews [who immigrated to New York] were enriching the city's intellectual life with an intensity that has probably never been equaled anywhere during a comparable period of time. I was raised largely by these Jews. I lived in a world of Jews. They were my teachers; they were my employers; they were my friends. They introduced me to a world of books and ideas that I didn't know existed.

Reminiscing about New York. Reported in the New York Post, *October 3, 1994.*

ACTOR'S GURU

Virtually all acting in motion pictures stems from her, and she had an extraordinary effect on the culture of her time. I don't think audiences realize how much we are in debt to her, to other Jews and to the Russian theater for most performances we see now.

Commenting on the contribution of Stella Adler (who died in 1994) to the theater and her influence upon actors.

¤

Algirdas Brazauskas

REPENTANT LITHUANIA

From this podium, where many heads of state have stood—in the very heart of your history and of your state—I, the president of Lithuania, bow my head to the memory of the more than 200,000 Jews of Lithuania who were killed. I ask you for your forgiveness for those Lithuanians who ruthlessly murdered, shot, deported and robbed Jews.

The memory of the hundreds of thousands of Jews who lived in Lithuania and of their suffering does not allow many among my decent countrymen to remain at peace with themselves.

From an emotional March 1995 address before the Knesset, in Jerusalem.

¤

Eric Breindel

ANTI-SEMITISM AND ANTI-ZIONISM

What I think you have in the mainstream media is a pronounced anti-Israel bias. And there are times when the anti-Israel bias crosses the line into what we would want to call genuine anti-Semitism, or if you will, anti-Zionism. Anti-Zionism is a cloak for anti-Semitism.

From an address delivered at the World Conference on Anti-Semitism and Prejudice in a Changing World, held in Brussels, Belgium, July 1992.

CROWN HEIGHTS POGROM

The Crown Heights episode [in August 1991] was a pogrom not vastly dissimilar to the many that took place in Eastern Europe during the last years of the nineteenth century and the first decades of the twentieth century....

The entire episode, which virtually no black public figure condemned, and which was actually incited in the black print and radio media, made it abundantly plain that Jews concerned with anti-Semitism in American life could no longer dismiss as marginal the particular phenomenon of black anti-Semitism.

Ibid. Referring to an auto accident in which a car driven by a chassidic Jew flew out of control and ran down a black child. A rumor spread that the private Jewish ambulance crew ignored the fatally injured child, which led to three nights of anti-Semitic rioting.

Discomfort with Totalitarianism

Their experience made me profoundly suspicious of totalitarian societies and movements. The degree to which the left seemed to sympathize either with the Soviet Union or with budding revolutionary regimes in the Third World... made me decidedly uncomfortable.

After noting the harrowing experiences of his parents during the Holocaust. Quoted in The Jewish Week, *November 25–December 1, 1994.*

The Holocaust and Israel

After the Holocaust, anybody who is any way conscious of the historical implications of that event began to see Israel as central to continued Jewish life.

Ibid.

What's Best for America

I'm never really engaged with political issues as a Jew per se. I don't pretend it's as a Jew I feel the way I do. My issues turn primarily on how I feel is the best way for society to arrange itself and what's best for America and American life.

Ibid.

□

David Brenner

Tiny Star of David

I wear a tiny Magen David [Star of David] on a thin gold chain around my neck. I wear it in memory of one of the more than one million Jewish children murdered by the Nazis in World War II.

When asked if he knew any of the children, he responded, "I knew every one of them." Quoted in Darryl Lyman's Jewish Comedy Catalog *(1989).*

Living a Footrace

I have always felt like I am in a footrace with Death. I know that one day he is going to win, but until then I am going to give him one helluva good race.

Ibid.

□

Jimmy Breslin

Battling Bella

Some came early, others came late. Bella has been there forever.

Commenting on Bella Abzug's involvement in the peace movement. From his Daily News *column, October 1970.*

□

Isaac Breuer

Zionism Is Not the Answer

The attempt of Zionism to lead Israel, nation and land, into the "normalcy" of the other nations, has no future. It is only God's kingly will, God's revealed Torah, that can shelter Israel, the people and the land, in Jerusalem's two-fold peace.

Quoted in Leo Jung's Judaism in a Changing World *(1939).*

□

Stephen G. Breyer

The Establishment Clause

I think it's fairly well established in case law that the Establishment Clause means at bottom that the Government of the United States is not to favor one religion over another, nor religion over nonreligion, so that people's area of personal belief is their area. They can practice it themselves, and they should, and it's terribly important. And they certainly can pass it on to their children, and that's terribly important. That persons who are agnostic, persons who are Jewish, persons who are Catholic, persons who are Presbyterian, all religions, and nonreligion too, is on an equal footing as far as the Government is concerned. That's the basic principle.

In response to a question posed by Colorado's Senator Hank Brown at the July 13, 1994 Senate Judiciary Committee hearing on Breyer's nomination to the Supreme Court.

Importance of Consensus

Consensus is important because law is not theoretical; law is a set of opinions and rules that lawyers have to understand, judges have to understand them, lower court judges have to understand them, and eventually the labor union, the business, small business, everyone else in the country has to understand how they are supposed to act or not act according to law.

> *Ibid. Breyer's reply to a question posed by Senator Howell Heflin.*

SCRUTINIZING OUR SUPREME JUDGES

It's appropriate in an era when people can find out about you so quickly through the media that millions of people would like to have a look at you, and the Senate is the instrument of that look....This institution is right because people should have a look at me in a society where the ultimate source of authority is the court.

> *Finding no fault with the difficult Senate confirmation process to which nominees for the Supreme Court are put. From a speech at a forum sponsored by the New York lawyers chapter of American ORT.*

A FIDUCIARY NOTION

The rabbi made an interesting point, that the Jewish notion of *tzedakah* related not so much to the notion of charity, but...to justice and law. The notion of looking out for another person is part of a fiduciary notion, the obligation of human beings to use our talents for the benefit of others.

> *Commenting on a sermon he had heard in London during a 1994 High Holiday service.*

WALL OF SEPARATION

I think of Jefferson. I think of a wall.

> *Referring to Thomas Jefferson's view that the Constitution stands for a wall of separation between Church and State.*

FUNCTION OF THE LAW

[What the law] is supposed to do, seen as a whole, is allow people to live together in a society where they have many different views...so that they can work productively together.

> *From a statement on the occasion of his nomination by President Bill Clinton in 1994. Quoted in Elinor and Robert Slater's Great Jewish Men (1996).*

PRACTICAL JUDAISM

I think of what Hillel said: "If I am not for myself, who will be for me, but if I am only for myself, what am I? And if not now, when?" I've always thought of the practical nature of Jewish religious beliefs and the way they're involved in making this world a better place, requiring people to have a sense of justice and to think about other people.

> *Ibid. When asked how Judaism had affected his public career.*

COMPLETE ACCEPTANCE

Here I am absolutely Jewish. I am appointed to the Supreme Court, and there's already another Jewish member [Ruth Bader Ginsburg], and there's no issue for or against. My parents and grandparents would never have believed it. It's the kind of ideal that many people have aspired to in terms of the place of a Jew in public life. It's neither a qualification nor a disqualification.

> *Ibid.*

NO BARGAINING

[In the Supreme Court] there's no bargaining. People here don't build consensus through bargaining. Insofar as there is agreement, it tends to be the result of listening to each other's point of view.

> *Ibid.*

¤

Fanny Brice

AS YOU ARE

Let the world know you as you are, not as you think you should be, because sooner or later, if you are posing, you will forget the pose, and then where are you?

> *Quoted in Norman Katkov's Fabulous Fanny (1952).*

THE AUDIENCE SPEAKS

Your audience gives you everything you need. They tell you. There is no director who can direct you like an audience.

> *Ibid.*

JEWISH IDENTIFICATION

I never did a Jewish routine that would offend my race, because I depended on my race for the laughs. In anything Jewish I ever did, I wasn't standing apart making fun. I was the race, and what happened to me onstage is what could happen to my people. They identified with me, which made it all right to get a laugh, because they were laughing at me as much as at themselves.

> *After being criticized for singing comedy routines that were thought to be offensive. Quoted in Elinor and Robert Slater's Great Jewish Women (1994).*

WOMAN'S PLACE IS THE HOME

I always hoped I'd have a boy and a girl, and I had them. I always hoped the boy would have talent, and not the girl, and it worked out that way. Because, as I realize it, I didn't want my daughter to have a career. Because if a woman has a career, she misses an awful lot.

Ibid.

REPRESSED EMOTIONS

Being a funny person does an awful lot of things to you. You feel that you must never get serious with people. They don't expect it, and they won't take it from you. You are not entitled to be serious. You are a clown. And maybe that is what made me dislike emotion. Once I cried in the movies, and I covered my face and bent my head. I admired the Chinese all my life because they would never show any feeling.

Quoted in Darryl Lyman's Jewish Comedy Catalog *(1989).*

□

Balfour Brickner

ON FAMILY RIGHTS

My religious tradition is one that has revered and sanctified human life for nearly four thousand years.... It is precisely because of this regard for that sanctity that we see as most desirable the right of any couple to be free to produce only that number of children whom they felt they could feed and clothe and educate properly....

From testimony before Senator Birch Bayh's Subcommittee on Constitutional Amendments, March 7, 1974, supporting a woman's right to control her own body.

□

John Bright

A SENSE OF PEOPLEHOOD

Above all, there was in Israel's heritage a feeling of tribal solidarity between people and God that must have contributed more than we can guess to that intensely strong sense of peoplehood so characteristic of her for all time to come.

From his History of Israel *(1981).*

SELF-ADMIRATION

He is a self-made man, and worships his creator.

Quoted in A. K. Adams's Home Book of Humorous Quotations.

□

Herb Brin

DAYS OF AWE

A blade of grass upon a timeless land
I stand alone
Tossed by winds of eternity.
A falling leaf upon a shifting sand
I seek my God
Alone, in the Days of Awe.

From his Wild Flowers *(1965).*

MARCH OF TIME

I wear the childhood smile of joy
To see a baby with a toy
And when he cries my soul is torn
The child at birth one day will mourn
The loss of youth, the loss of dream:
The child must learn to scream.

Ibid.

SIGH WITH ME

To Andalusia have I come
Back to Andalusia
Have I come
To this Jerusalem of Spain
Slain in flame.
Walk my troubled stones
These shadowed pathways to my roots
And sigh with me.
And sigh with me.

From his My Spanish Years and Other Poems *(1985).*

THE GREATEST HUMAN CRIME

If there were a thousand Holocaust memorials in the world—in Berlin or even in Warsaw alone—they would hardly bring justice to the greatest human crime in history. They would not be enough to raise mirrors to a world of indecency that tolerated the tragedy.

From an article in Heritage Southwest Jewish Press, *January 14, 1994.*

□

Ruth F. Brin

GOD OF MEN AND MOUNTAINS

God of men and mountains,
Master of people and planets,
Creator of the universe:
I am afraid.
I am afraid of the angels
Thou hast sent to wrestle with me:
The angel of success
Who carries a two-edged sword,
The angels of darkness

Whose names I do not know,
Then angel of death
For whom I have no answer.
I am afraid of the touch
Of Thy great hand on my feeble heart.
Yet must I turn to Thee and praise Thee,
Awful and great though Thou art,
For there is none else.

From her Time to Search *(1959).*

TO SIGNIFY FAITH

He who cannot sing must speak
He who cannot speak must gesture
He who cannot gesture must bow his head,
But all must worship.

Ibid.

KADDISH FOR MOTHER

I stand to recite the proper prayer
"Extolled and magnified is the Lord,"
But you mock me on the empty air,
Though you cannot hear nor speak a word
You cannot knit, your hands are still,
Yet I know your strength, your mind, your will.
Why did you go when warmth was in the air
Before you saw your trillium once again?
The grief for my father is old and rare
But now for you I grieve as I began,
Torn from you, weeping, with sobbing breath,
In the bitter green season of your death.

Ibid.

◘

Arthur Brisbane

ROLE MODEL

Benny Leonard has done more to conquer anti-Semitism than a thousand textbooks have done.

Commenting on the well-liked lightweight boxing champion who led a clean and honorable life. Leonard retired from the ring in 1924, undefeated.

◘

Max Brod

DESTINY REPEATED

Our destiny repeats itself because we create it.

From his Master *(1951).*

FAULTS AND VIRTUES

A curious people these Jews, with glaring faults and shining virtues.

Ibid.

JEWISH SENSITIVITY

My experience of Judaism was "pleasant." I was not ashamed of my origin; it would never have occurred to me that there might be anything disgraceful in it. Nor was I particularly proud of my people. The atmosphere that surrounded me was one of absolute normalcy. For a long while things Jewish did not concern me at all, but I had not forgotten them. The sensitivity that seizes many a Western Jew if even the slightest allusion is made to his association with his people—this oversensitivity, which is a particularly distasteful sign of weakness and insecurity, was totally alien to me.

From his Valiant Living *(1960).*

KAFKA'S ALIENATION

[*The Castle* depicts] the special feeling of a Jew who would like to put down roots in alien surroundings, who strives with all the strength of his soul to draw closer to the strangers around him, to become completely like them—and who cannot achieve this union.

Ibid. Expressing the loneliness and isolation felt by his friend Franz Kafka.

◘

Joseph A. Brodsky

THE YEVREI

I wasn't ashamed of being a Jew, nor was I scared of admitting it.... Everyone in my class [in Russia] knew I was a Jew—a *Yevrei.*

From his book Less Than One *(1981).*

HAPPY COMBINATION

I'm the happiest combination you can think of. I'm a Russian poet, an English essayist, and a citizen of the United States.

Upon receiving the Nobel Prize for literature in 1987.

◘

Edgar Bronfman

MEETING HALFWAY

Perhaps we cannot rebuild our ties with the black community. But, my friends, we can try. One conference like this does not end racism, xenophobia, or anti-Semitism. One speech does not make the Reverend Jesse Jackson a Zionist.

But his condemnation of anti-Semitism, and his clear support of the State of Israel here in

Brussels, have demonstrated his willingness to go more than half way. So must we!!

From an address delivered at the World Conference on Anti-Semitism and Prejudice in a Changing World, held in Brussels, Belgium, July 1992.

THE UN AND ANTI-SEMITISM

Neither the UN nor its Commission on Human Rights has yet to condemn in any resolution anti-Semitic incitement to hatred or specific acts of anti-Semitism, whether in isolation or in conjunction with the more general phenomena of racism, intolerance and xenophobia.

In a 1993 meeting with United Nations Secretary General Boutros Boutros-Ghali.

SORROW, PRIDE, AWE

We stand here in sorrow. We stand here with pride. We stand here in awe.

From a statement made on April 19, 1993 in Warsaw, Poland, at the commemoration of the fiftieth anniversary of the Warsaw Ghetto uprising against the Nazis.

UNIVERSAL JEWISH EDUCATION

[It is] the duty of my generation and my children's generation to see to it that Jewish schools are available and affordable...[and] that every Jewish child who wants a Jewish education can get one, regardless of ability to pay.

From a speech to 3,000 delegates at the Council of Jewish Federation's General Assembly, held in Denver, Colorado, in November 1994, in which he said that the Jewish community should see to it that 50,000 to 100,000 Jewish teens go to Israel each summer.

NON-JEWISH JEWS

Anti-Semitism is not the [main] problem in America anymore. The problem is the non-Jewishness of the Jews.

Advocating that more money be spent to fight assimilation rather than anti-Semitism. From an interview in the Forward, *November 1994.*

NEW PRIORITIES SOUGHT

Anti-Semitism is a terrible thing, and the ADL does a good job monitoring and combating it. My only point is that with their huge overheads, organizations might serve the Jewish people better by merging, so that more resources can be directed toward Jewish education. I fear that if we don't reprioritize, in

a few generations there won't be any Judaism left due to assimilation.

Commenting on the February 1995 report of the Anti-Defamation League that anti-Semitic incidents were increasing, and on the duplication of efforts to deal with them.

Jacob Bronowski

ALWAYS SECOND BEST

The world is made of people who never quite get into the first team and who just miss the prizes at the flower show.

From his Face of Violence *(1954).*

THE WISH TO HURT

The wish to hurt, the momentary intoxication with pain, is the loophole through which the pervert climbs into the minds of ordinary men.

Ibid.

ON MANAGING THE WORLD

We have to understand that the world can only be grasped by action, not by contemplation. The hand is more important than the eye....The hand is the cutting edge of the mind.

From his Ascent of Man *(1973).*

Mel Brooks

A COMIC TO BREAST-BEATERS

Look at Jewish history. Unrelieved lamenting would be intolerable. So, for every 10 Jews beating their breasts, God designated one to be crazy and amuse the breast-beaters. By the time I was five I knew I was that one.

Quoted by Stuart Schoffman in The Jerusalem Report, *December 30, 1993.*

THE WHEEL TURNS

We mock the thing we are to be. Yes, yes, we make fun of the old; then we become them.

Quoted in Darryl Lyman's Jewish Comedy Catalog *(1989).*

THE TWO-THOUSAND-YEAR-OLD MAN

When I became him, I could hear five thousand years of Jews pouring through me.

Ibid. Explaining that his famous "two-thousand-year-old man" comic character is a pastiche of everyone around him.

GREAT EXPERIENCES

There are only a handful of things that have genuinely touched me in my life: When I first heard Bix Beiderbecke play his cornet; when I first walked by a painting by Soutine; when I first read Tolstoy; when I first saw my wife, Anne Bancroft, on the stage in *Miracle Worker;* and when Sid Caesar alternately made me laugh and cry while doing his version of *Pagliacci* on our TV show. It was the thrill of the discovery of a true genius.

Ibid.

FEELING OF ALIENATION

I may be angry at God or at the world, and I'm sure that a lot of my comedy is based on anger and hostility.... It comes from a feeling that, as a Jew and as a person, [I] don't fit into the mainstream of American society.

Ibid.

¤

Chaim Brovender

A BAD INVESTMENT

When the Intifada started, our present prime minister said it would be over in a few weeks. It hasn't ended. They've done it. They've done it well. Do we have an option to become a country of murderers, to spend all our time killing and being killed? Is that the future of the Jewish people in Israel? Is that what we waited for for 2,000 years?

Quoted in The Jerusalem Post, *February 12, 1994.*

¤

Cecil Brown

NOT SO ODD OF GOD

But not so odd
As those who choose
A Jewish God,
But spurn the Jews.

In response to William Norman Eiver's verse, "How odd of God to choose the Jews."

¤

Robert McAfee Brown

ROOTS OF CHRISTIANITY

Christians cannot understand who they are apart from Judaism. Not only do both Catholicism and Protestantism have their historical roots in Judaism, but their theological and liturgical roots as well, and they therefore stand in a different relationship to Judaism than to other world religions. Judaism is not just another world religion....It is that religion par excellence which helps to define for them who they are, with which both must come to terms, and apart from which neither can understand itself or the other.

From his Ecumenical Revolution *(1967).*

¤

Robert Browning

THE BEST IS YET TO BE

Grow old along with me!
The best is yet to be,
The last of life, for which the first was made.

From his poem "Rabbi Ben Ezra" (1864).

ISRAEL'S UNSHAKEN FAITH

By the torture prolonged from age to age,
By the infamy, Israel's heritage,
By the Ghetto's plague, by the garb's disgrace,
By the badge of shame, by the felon's place,
By the branding tool, by the bloody whip,
And the summons to Christian fellowship.

Quoted in J.H. Hertz's Pentateuch and Haftorahs *(1961).*

¤

Lenny Bruce

THE REAL JEW

Now a Jew, in the dictionary, is one who is descended from the ancient tribes of Judea, or one who is regarded as descended from that tribe. That's what it says in the dictionary; but you and I know what a Jew is—*One Who Killed Our Lord....* And although there should be a statute of limitations for that crime, it seems that those who neither have the actions nor the gait of Christians, pagan or not, will bust us out, unrelenting dues, for another deuce.

From one of his classic comedy routines. Quoted in The Essential Lenny Bruce, *edited by John Cohen (1967).*

THE TRUE ART FORM

The only honest art form is laughter, comedy. You can't fake it...you can't.

Ibid.

ON TRUTH

What is truth today may be a damn lie next week.

Ibid.

JEWISH AND "GOYISH"

If you live in New York or any other big city, you are Jewish. It doesn't matter even if you're Catholic; if you live in New York, you're Jewish. If you live in Butte, Montana, you're going to be *goyish* even if you're Jewish....

Jewish means pumpernickel bread, black cherry soda and macaroons. *Goyish* means Koolaid, Drake's cakes, and lime jello. Trailer parks are so *goyish* that Jews won't go near them.

Ibid.

◘

Martin Buber

GOD AFTER AUSCHWITZ

Can one still speak to God after Auschwitz? Can one still, as an individual and as a people, enter at all into a dialogue relationship with Him? Dare we recommend to the survivors of Auschwitz, the Jobs of the gas chambers, "Call to Him, for He is kind, for His mercy endures forever"?

From his essay "Dialogue Between Heaven and Earth" in Will Herberg's Four Existentialist Theologians *(1958).*

EXPERIENCING CREATION

Creation—happens to us, burns into us, changes us, we tremble and faint, we submit. Creation—we participate in it, we encounter the creator, offer ourselves to him, helpers and companions.

From his I and Thou *(1970).*

BETWEEN I AND THOU

The spirit is not in the I, but between I and Thou. It is not like the blood that courses in you, but like the air in which you breathe. Man lives in the spirit if he is capable of responding to his Thou. He is capable of it if he enters into the relationship with his whole nature. It is solely his capacity for relationships that enables man to live in the spirit.

Ibid.

CHILDREN OF GOD

After the heavenly sacred fact of being a child of God, nothing is as great in human existences as the earthly sacred fact of being a brother of men.

From a 1952 address to the Brotherhood Movement of the Jewish Theological Seminary of America.

UNIQUENESS OF THE INDIVIDUAL

Every person born into this world represents something new, something that never existed before, something original and unique... there has never been anyone like him in the world, for if there had been someone like him, there would have been no need for him to be in the world.

From his Hasidism and Modern Man *(1972).*

GOD AS A PERSON

The description of God as a Person is indispensable for everyone who like myself means by "God" not a principle, and like myself means by "God" not an idea, but who rather means by "God," as I do, Him who—whatever else He may be—enters into a direct relation with us men in creative, revealing, and redeeming acts, and thus makes it possible for us to enter into a direct relationship with Him.

From his Way of Response *(1971).*

PLEA FOR COEXISTENCE

Let us beware of considering and behaving toward anyone who is foreign and as yet insufficiently known to us as if he were inferior! Let us beware of doing ourselves what has been done to us! I must confess that I am horrified at how little we know the Arabs...both they and we love this country and seek its future welfare; as we love the country and together seek its welfare, it is possible for us to work together for it.

Speaking out against Revisionist Zionism, a movement founded by Jabotinsky, on the eve of the sixteenth Zionist Congress in August 1929.

KING DAVID HOTEL BOMBING

The way of violence does not lead to liberation or healing but only to renewed decline and enslavement.... These events will bring what they will in their wake. We must repent and change our ways, whatever will happen now, lest an even greater catastrophe befall us. It is our obligation to elevate the sacred law [of life] to ensure that it not be undermined, that the people as a people protect it from all subverters.

Condemnation of the Irgun in July 1946 when, under the leadership of Menachem Begin, it blew up the central government offices in the King David Hotel, in Jerusalem, killing eighty people.

THE IMAGE OF GOD

Whether or not we know it, what we really mean when we say that a god is dead is that the images of God vanish and that therefore an image, which up to now was regarded and worshipped as God, can no longer be so regarded and so worshipped.

From his Israel and the World *(1963).*

IMAGES AND APPEARANCES

There is Peter as he wishes to appear to Paul, and Paul as he wishes to appear to Peter. Then there is Peter as he really appears to Paul, that is, Paul's image of Peter which in general does not in the least coincide with what Peter wishes Paul to see; and similarly there is the reverse situation. Further, there is Peter as he appears to himself, and Paul as he appears to himself. Lastly, there are the bodily Peter and the bodily Paul. Two living beings and six ghostly appearances which mingle in many ways in the conversation between the two. Where is there room for any genuine interhuman life?

From his Knowledge of Man *(1965).*

LOVING GOD MEANS LOVING PEOPLE

If anyone tells you that he loves God and does not love his fellow man, you will know that he is lying.

From his Ten Rungs: Hasidic Sayings *(1947).*

MAN MUST JUDGE HIMSELF

If a man does not judge himself, all things will judge him, and all things will become messengers of God.

Ibid.

THE MYSTERIOUS SPIRITUAL SUBSTANCE

The Baal Shem teaches that no encounter with a being or a thing in the course of our life lacks a hidden significance. The people we live with or meet with, the animals that help us with our farmwork, the soil we till, the materials we shape, the tools we use, they all contain a mysterious spiritual substance which depends on us for helping it towards its pure form, its perfection.

Ibid.

ESSENCE OF ZIONISM

Zion is greater than a piece of land in the Near East. Zion is greater than a Jewish commonwealth in this land. Zion is memory, admonition, promise. Zion is...the foundation stone of the messianic upbuilding of humanity. It is the unending task of the Jewish people.

From his Zion and Youth *(1918).*

MYSTERY OF THE MISSING NUMBER

They asked Rabbi Levi Yitzhak: "Why is the first page number missing in all the tractates of the Babylonian talmud? Why does each begin with the second [the number bet]." He replied: "However much a man may learn, he should always remember that he has not even gotten to the first page.

From his Tales of the Hasidim *(1947).*

A BLESSING ON YOUR HEAD

Be healthy and strong as a *goy!*

Ibid. A blessing conferred by eighteenth-century chassidic rabbi Meshullam Zusya whenever he met a Jewish boy.

RECONCILING ARAB-ISRAELI DIFFERENCES

We considered, and still consider, it our duty to understand, to honor the claim which is opposed to ours, and to endeavor to reconcile both claims. We could not and cannot renounce the Jewish claim: something even higher than the life of our people is bound up with this land, namely, its work, its divine mission. But we have been and still are convinced that it must be possible to find some compromise between this claim and the other, for we love this land and we believe in its future; since such love and such faith are surely present on the other side as well, a union in the common service of the land must be within the range of possibility. Where there is faith and love, a solution may be found even to what appears to be a tragic opposition.

Quoted in Anne Roiphe's Season for Healing *(1988).*

GOAL OF RELIGIOUS MOVEMENTS

Genuine religious movements do not seek to offer man the solution to the mystery of the world, they seek to equip him to live through the power of that mystery; they do not seek to teach him about the nature of God but to show him the path where he can encounter God.

From his speech at the reopening of the Frankfort Jewish Lehrhaus in 1936.

CLEMENCY FOR EICHMANN

Our belief is that concluding Eichmann's trial with his execution will diminish the image of the Holocaust and falsify the historical and moral significance of this trial.

From a letter to Israeli President Yitzhak Ben Zvi cosigned by nineteen other prominent individuals.

THE FUTURE OF JUDAISM

For Judaism has not only a past, despite all it has already created, it has, above all, not a past but a future. Judaism has, in truth, not yet done its work, and the great forces active in this most tragic and incomprehensible of people have not yet written their very own word into the history of the world.

> *Quoted in Elinor and Robert Slater's* Great Jewish Men *(1996).*

◻

Patrick J. Buchanan

CATHOLICISM AND INTELLECTUALS

Anti-Catholicism is the anti-Semitism of the intellectual.

> *Quoted in the* London Observer, *December 5, 1991.*

THE WEST BANK

Listen, my friend, I've just come back from Mississippi and over there when you talk about the West Bank they think you mean Arkansas.

> *A comment made during his 1992 campaign for the U.S. presidency. Quoted in London's* Spectator, *March 13, 1992.*

BUCHANAN UNMASKED

Michael, I think you're the best argument I've seen for the Spanish Inquisition.

> *Snide remark of CNN's "far right" moderator to his Jewish colleague, senior editor of* The New Republic, *Michael Kinsley, in a 1994 Good Friday debate on the subject "Faith in America."*

BUCHANAN VS. ROSENTHAL

There are only two groups that are beating the drums for war in the Middle East: the Israeli defense ministry and its amen corner in the United States.

> *In an appearance on* The McLaughlin Group *television discussion show. A.M. Rosenthal branded Buchanan "an anti-Semite" in his September 19, 1990 op-ed column in* The New York Times.

◻

Art Buchwald

ON DOING THE RIGHT THING

United States foreign policy is going through its most difficult phase. Not only are we having trouble convincing our Western al-lies and our Latin American friends that we are doing the right thing, but we're having a heck of a time persuading our own university students and professors.

> *From his May 20, 1965 syndicated column when criticism of U.S. policy in Vietnam and the Dominican civil strife was rife.*

ON ARAFAT'S BEARD GROWTH

There seems to be a lot of leaders in the Middle East who don't shave every day. By the same token they refuse to grow beards. They prefer a four- to six-day growth, but no more. My source believes they're all using the same razor blade.

> *From his collection of humorous pieces,* Laid Back in Washington *(1981).*

THE POPE'S WARDROBE

All John Paul's raiments are made by hand. I have it on the highest authority that he spends more money on one cape than Menachem Begin spends on his entire wardrobe.

When it comes to headgear, there isn't a statesman in the world who can hold a candle to one of the Pope's skullcaps.

> *Ibid.*

PRAYERS OF JEWS

Well, as you know, the stations are fighting for ratings and the kookier you are, the more chance you have of making the news. For example, if you made a statement that God doesn't hear the prayers of Jews, we could get you on all three networks.

> *Ibid. Referring to the 1980 statement of Reverend Baily Smith: "God Almighty does not hear the prayer of a Jew."*

GOD AND AMERICAN POLITICS

Some fundamentalist sects, known as the Moral Majority, are spending wads of money to defeat anybody whose voting record doesn't go along with their interpretation of the Bible.... I always thought the nice thing about God was that he stayed out of American politics.

> *Ibid.*

JOINING THE ESTABLISHMENT

If you attack the establishment long enough and hard enough, they will make you a member of it.

> *Quoted in the* International Herald Tribune, *May 24, 1989.*

Pearl Buck

CREATIVE JEWISH BLOOD

Often when I found in China an artist of unusual talent, or a mind more vivid than others among my students, the chances were good that he had Jewish blood in him. It is a creative strain.

From her My Several Worlds *(1954).*

¤

Roy Bullock

GETTING THE DIRT

I am by no stretch of the imagination a spy. I'm a researcher.

Answering accusations in December 1993 that he picked through garbage, posed as an Arab-American activist, and tapped phones as an operative of the Jewish Anti-Defamation League.

¤

Simcha Bunam of Przysucha

CONSTANT RENEWAL

The Lord created the world in a state of beginning. The universe is always in an incomplete state, in the form of its beginning. It is not like a vessel at which the master works to finish it; it requires continuous labor and renewal by creative forces. Should these cease for only a second, the universe would return to primeval chaos.

Quoted in Louis Newman's Hasidic Anthology *(1944).*

¤

Avraham Burg

HEBREW-SPEAKING GOYIM

The Jewish people have to look in the mirror and say not who is a Jew but what is a Jew. A Hebrew-speaking soldier is not necessarily a Jew. There is a risk that my children might become Hebrew-speaking *goyim*.

During an April 1995 Dialogue with the President [of Israel] on Jewish Identity. Bemoaning that Israeli youth often "do not know the difference between Kaddish *and* Kiddush."

CATASTROPHIC ZIONISM

Catastrophic Zionism, with Jews fleeing for their lives, is over.

Ibid.

LIMITED EXPOSURE

Six weeks of "Israel Experience" is not enough against 18 years of *shiksas*.

Commenting in 1995 on his plans as new head of the Jewish Agency to expand Jewish education in the Diaspora to more than a brief visit to Israel.

TRIPLE JEOPARDY

It is not permissible that a Jew is robbed of his life, murdered, and then robbed after his death.

Claiming, in 1996, that the extent of unclaimed Swiss bank funds belonging to Holocaust victims has not yet been revealed.

¤

Joseph Burg

THE CLASSIC MINORITY

All over the world, we Jews are a minority. Only in Israel are we a majority. As a nation that for two thousand years was a classic minority of the world, Jews have a moral obligation and a political obligation to show how to behave in a country where they are the majority.

From an address to the World Conference on Anti-Semitism and Prejudice in a Changing World, held in Brussels, Belgium, July 1992.

¤

Walter Burkhardt

THE SUFFERING SERVANTS

[Jews are] a people that has survived every persecution and borne ceaseless witness to the suffering servant of Yahweh. God is here, and He speaks to and through the Jew, His suffering servant.

Quoted in Anne Roiphe's Season for Healing *(1988).*

¤

George Burns

NO MEMORABILIA, NO SCRAPBOOKS

I'm not interested in anything that happened yesterday. I'm interested in what I'm going to do today and what I'm going to do tomorrow. I've got no memorabilia, no scrapbooks. I don't keep anything. All I got is what you see.

Responding to why his office was so Spartan, with few framed pictures or momentos.

GETTING PAID TO PRAY!

What upset me was when my grandmother died and you had to have a *minyan* to pray. I don't know if I should tell you this story, but I will. You had to have ten people for a *minyan*. We could only get seven. The other three we had to pay. We had to pay them fifty cents each to pray or they wouldn't do it. That stuck with me all my life. I couldn't imagine anybody getting paid for praying.

From a 1987 interview.

SWEET SMELL IN ADVERSITY

Dear Gracie, here's eleven roses. The twelfth one is you.

> *In his less affluent days when he did not have enough money to send his wife twelve roses as he would have wished. Quoted in True Story magazine.*

MAKING JOLSON HAPPY

It was easy enough to make Jolson happy at home. You just had to cheer him for breakfast, applaud wildly for lunch, and give him a standing ovation for dinner.

> *Quoted in M. Freedland's Jolson.*

OH, GEORGE!

Sometimes I get carried away with the part I played in *Oh, God!* Yesterday, when I was on an elevator, a woman got on and said, "Nice day." I said, "Thank you."

> *From one of his comedy routines. Quoted in Darryl Lyman's Jewish Comedy Catalog (1989).*

TURNING AGE INTO HUMOR

Thanks for the standing ovation. I'm at the point now where I get a standing ovation just for standing.... They're talking about making a movie of my life. I hope they do it quick—I'd like to see it.

> *Ibid. From his comedy routines as he approached his one hundredth birthday in 1996.*

□

George Bush

SELF-CONTRADICTION

This body cannot claim to seek peace and at the same time challenge Israel's right to exist.

> *In a September 1991 speech to the United Nations General Assembly, urging the repeal of the 1975 UN resolution equating Zionism with racism. In December the Assembly revoked the resolution by a vote of 111 to 25, with 13 abstentions.*

□

Samuel Henry Butcher

PROPHETS DO NOT DESPAIR

In the absence of Hope and of an ideal of progress, we strike upon one great difference between the classical Greeks and the Hebrews .... In the darkest hour of adversity the Prophets did not despair of Israel.

> *From his Some Aspects of the Greek Genius (1893).*

□

Red Buttons

NOSTALGIA: I LOVE IT

I have all the cantorial tapes. I ride in my Bentley in Beverly and play the music. I stop for a light and people in the other cars look at me while I blast the cantorial sound on my stereo. It's nostalgia, I love it.

> *Referring to tapes of the great cantor Yossele Rosenblatt, which he loves to listen to. As a youngster, Buttons sang in the choir that accompanied the cantor. Quoted in Tim Boxer's Jewish Celebrity Hall of Fame (1987).*

NO ETHNIC JOKES

I don't do any of the Polish jokes. I don't believe in degrading any people. I think it's very dangerous. I don't like it, never did it. It was never my kind of comedy. When you're making fun of people, you're making of them something less than what they are.

> *Ibid.*

REAL ESTATENIKS

I was in Tokyo at a small fundraising breakfast to buy the rest of Los Angeles.

> *From his 1995 one-man show entitled Buttons on Broadway.*

ONE FOR ALL

I was in Osaka at a small reunion of kamikaze pilots whose motto is, "Live and let live."

> *Ibid.*

□

(Lord) George Gordon Byron

WANDERING TRIBES

Tribes of the wandering foot and weary
   breast,
How shall ye flee away and be at rest?
The wild dove hath her nest, the fox his cave,
Mankind their country—Israel, but the grave.

> *Lamenting Israel's lack of a land of its own. From his "Hebrew Melodies" (1815).*

S. Parkes Cadman

FREEDOM FOR ALL

The denial of freedom to the Jew denies it to the Gentile. Any impairment of justice for Israel impairs universal justice and ultimately corrupts and enslaves the nation guilty of the offense.

> *Quoted in Joseph L. Baron's* Stars and Sand *(1943).*

¤

Julius Caesar

OUR FRIENDS, THE JEWS

We are sorrowed to hear that decrees have been issued against our friends, which make it impossible for them to live according to their ancestral customs.

> *Quoted in Sam Waggenaar's* Pope's Jews *(1974).*

¤

Sid Caesar

I BELIEVE IN SOMETHING

I believe in something. I don't know if there is a God. I believe there is an energy, a force. Everything is energy and nothing disappears. The conservation law is at work.

> *Quoted in Tim Boxer's* Jewish Celebrity Hall of Fame *(1987).*

¤

Abraham Cahan

THE IMMIGRANT'S HIGHEST PRIORITY

A tenement house kitchen turned...into a classroom, with the head of the family and his boarder bent over an English school reader... is a common spectacle....

The poor laborer...will pinch himself to keep his child at college, rather than send him to a factory....

> *The future editor of the* Forward *newspaper, himself an immigrant, expresses appreciation for the immigrant's concentration on educating himself and his children. From an article in* The Atlantic Monthly, *July 1898.*

ENDORSEMENT OF ZIONISM

There was a time when battles and disputes about [Zionism] used to flare forth between parties and groups. I am convinced that this is now a thing of the past.... In millions and millions of Jewish hearts a warm feeling has developed, a glorious hope that, in Palestine, a Jewish home is growing.

> *After a visit to Palestine in 1924, and after the outbreak of Arab violence in 1929, Cahan no longer withheld his endorsement of Zionism.*

TAILOR-MADE GIRLS

Foreigners ourselves, and mostly unable to write English, we had Americanized the system of providing clothes for the American woman of moderate or humble means.... Indeed, the Russian Jew had made the average American girl a tailor-made girl.

> *From his* Rise of David Levinsky *(1917).*

¤

Sammy Cahn

LOVE AND MARRIAGE

Love and marriage
Love and marriage
　go together like a horse and carriage.
Dad was told by mother
　you can't have one without the other.

> *Lyrics to a popular 1955 song with music by James Van Heusen.*

JEWS ARE DESTINED TO BE IMMORTAL

I believe the Jew was destined to be immortal because of persecution and the constant desire to eliminate him. I really believe in my heart that if the Jews were left alone, they could very well lose that immortality.

> *Quoted in Tim Boxer's* Jewish Celebrity Hall of Fame *(1987).*

◻

Cain

EVADING RESPONSIBILITY

Am I my brother's keeper?

His reply to God's question: "Where is your brother, Abel?" (Genesis 4:19).

FOR THE SIN OF FRATRICIDE

My punishment is greater than I can bear.

When he was condemned to wander the earth after killing his brother, Abel.

◻

Edward N. Calisch

SHAKESPEARE'S JEWISH VILLAINS

The great wrong that Shakespeare did the Jewish people was...that by emphasizing at every evil point Shylock's race and religion, he made him as a type of his people.... Shakespeare painted many other villains...yet never did he associate their religious creed with them.

From his Jew in English Literature *(1909).*

◻

Raphael Cantoni

INTERVENTION OF PIUS XII

The Church and the papacy have saved Jews as much and in as far as they could save Christians.... Six million of my co-religionists have been murdered by the Nazis, but there could have been many more victims, had it not been for the efficacious intervention of Pius XII.

Quoted in Pinchas Lapide's Last Three Popes and the Jews *(1967).*

◻

Eddie Cantor

MAKING A SUCCESS

It takes twenty years to make an overnight success.

Quoted in The New York Times Magazine, *October 20, 1963.*

EXPERIENCING JOLSON

There was something electric about him [Al Jolson] that sent a thrill up your spine. He sang and talked; but he was more than just a singer or an actor—he was an experience.

From his Take My Life.

◻

Nina Beth Cardin

PASSIONATE LIVING

Live Judaism passionately. Whether your preference is for the prophetic legacy of social and political action; the talmudic model of untangling the knots of logic and laying them out end to end; the philosophical, mystical, liturgical, ritual or national; learn it, do it, live it passionately.

From Hadassah Magazine, *June–July 1993.*

◻

Benjamin Cardozo

DEATH PENALTY

The death penalty will seem to the next generation as it seems to many even now, an anachronism too discordant to be suffered, mocking with grim reproach all our clamorous professions of the sanctity of life.

From his Law and Literature *(1931).*

HEROIC HOURS

The heroic hours of life do not announce their presence by drum and trumpet.

Ibid.

MATRIX OF ALL FREEDOMS

Freedom of expression is the matrix, the indispensable condition of nearly every other form of freedom.

From a brief in the 1937 Palko v. Connecticut *case.*

WOOING JUSTICE

Justice is not to be taken by storm. She is to be wooed by slow advances.

From his Growth of the Law *(1924).*

LOGIC AND THE SOCIAL SCIENCES

Not logic alone, but logic supplemented by the social sciences becomes the instrument of advance.

Ibid.

A PRINCIPLE OF GROWTH

There is danger in perpetual quiescence as well as in perpetual motion...a compromise must be found in a principle of growth.

Ibid.

SPIRIT OF RELIGION

The submergence of self in the pursuit of an ideal, the readiness to spend oneself without measure, prodigally, almost ecstatically for something intuitively apprehended as great and noble, spend oneself one knows not why some of us like to believe that this is what religion means....

At the commencement exercises of a rabbinical school. Quoted in an article by Edgar J. Nathan, Jr., in American Jewish Yearbook, *1939–40.*

PRECIOUS SPIRITUAL VALUES

In persecution and contumely they [the Jews] knew that there were values of the spirit greater than any others, values for whose fruits they would have to wait perhaps a hundred years, perhaps a thousand, values whose fruits might elude them altogether, yet values to be chosen unfalteringly uncomplainingly with cheer and even joy.

Ibid.

□

Shlomo Carlebach

GREATEST THING IN THE WORLD

Kinderlach, teireh kinderlach, gedenksha, precious children, remember: The greatest thing in the world is to do someone a favor.

One of the messages he enjoyed imparting to his followers.

LOOKING FOR JERUSALEM

Almost a thousand hippies came with me. We were collecting kids on the street like a parade. They weren't just looking for drugs and music, they were looking for Jerusalem.

After announcing at the Berkeley Folk Festival in 1966: "Holy brothers and sisters, my dear chevra *[compatriots], I'm going to* shul *tonight and you're all invited."*

SERVING GOD IN JOY

What we need is synagogues filled with love, not appeals for money. We have to stop underestimating our young people who are burning with longing for something holy and heavenly in their lives. We need to make much more space for our holy sisters. The male rabbis drove our young people out of the synagogue, maybe our holy sisters will bring them back. The problem is not never again; the problem is never before. Let there be a new light. A new *Yiddishkeit*. And I promise you all our children will dance with us by the Holy Wall in Jerusalem. Please let it be.

From Hadassah Magazine, *June–July 1993.*

ATTRACTING THE YOUTH

The [Lubavitcher] *rebbe* told me to go out into the world. He called me in one day, when he became the *rebbe* in 1951 and said, "God gave you so much talent to talk to people, you have to go out and talk to young people today."

From his last interview, on October 20, 1994, describing what launched his career as a peripatetic singer looking for lost souls all over the world.

□

(King) Juan Carlos

STRUGGLING FOR SURVIVAL

The search for an identity and respect for the traditions that characterize the Jewish people have been forged in the setting of countless adverse and difficult circumstances: unjust and unnecessary expulsions, persecution and intolerance, culminating, more recently, in the tragedy of the Holocaust. From all this adversity, the Jewish people were able to draw teachings with a view to consolidating their faith and their traditions, in an exemplary struggle for their survival.

Today's Spain is proud of its close kinship with the [Jewish] community, which has contributed in a very special way to the prosperity of this great country.

From a 1987 address delivered to the Sephardic Community of Los Angeles at a special ceremony held at Temple Tifereth Israel.

□

Abraham Isaac Carmel

NO REDUCED PRICES

Judaism does not and cannot offer any season tickets to Heaven at reduced prices. Every pilgrim travels under his own steam, so to speak. The Jew believes that he, as all men, has sufficient willpower, assisted by prayer, to resist any evil inclination. He does not require an extravagant sacramental system, born of human ingenuity rather than Divine revelation, to snatch him from the fires of God's anger.

From his autobiography, So Strange My Path *(1964), written after this Roman Catholic priest converted to Judaism in 1963.*

Joseph Caro

A THIEF IS A THIEF

A thief is a thief, whether he steals much or little, from Jew or Gentile.

From his Code of Jewish Law (Shulchan Aruch), *Choshen Mishpat 369.*

WHO IS A GOY?

Let it be known that wherever [in this *Code of Jewish Law*] the words *akum, goy* and *nachri* are used, the reference is to those who did not recognize the True God, who did not believe in His revelation, and were far from morality; but the people on whose land we live and whose government protects us believe in God and in revelation and in ethics.

An introductory statement in the Vilna edition of his Code of Jewish Law.

Jimmy Carter

ON ISRAELI SECURITY

For thirty years we have stood at the side of the proud and independent nation of Israel. I can say without reservation...the United States will never support any agreement or any action that places Israel's security in jeopardy.

At a 1978 White House ceremony in observance of the thirtieth anniversary of the State of Israel.

ISRAEL'S RIGHT TO EXIST

The United States government and I personally oppose an independent Palestinian state—and unless and until they recognize Israel's right to exist and accept Resolution 242 as a basis for peace, we will neither recognize nor negotiate with the PLO.

From a September 1980 statement.

ON PALESTINIANS

We do favor a homeland or an entity wherein the Palestinians can live in peace.... My own preference is that they not be an independent nation but be tied in some way with the surrounding countries, making a choice, for instance, between Israel and Jordan.

In a December 1977 statement during the Camp David Summit meetings.

THE SUPREME COMPLIMENT

If you're interested in moving to America, I'd be more than happy to appoint you to the Supreme Court.

To Aharon Barak, legal advisor to the Israeli team at the 1978 Camp David negotiations with Egypt. Carter was impressed by Barak's even temperament and by the key parts of the peace accord drafted by him. A few months later Barak was appointed to the Israeli Supreme Court and in 1995 became its Chief Justice.

THE DIVERSE PALESTINIANS

The PLO is comprised of highly diverse Palestinians; it's a mistake to characterize all Palestinians or all those who support the PLO as terrorists. That's a way to denigrate or condemn an entire race of people. And I think that's a serious mistake.

There's no doubt that the PLO has been involved in and has often publicly supported terrorist acts which I deplore profoundly, and which, I think, work contrary to their own interests and the interests of the Palestinians.

From an interview with a Moment *magazine editor, March 1984.*

BEGIN ON THE WEST BANK

I don't believe that Prime Minister Begin or his successor has any intention of relinquishing any portion of the West Bank or Gaza. And this is a crux of the problem.

Ibid.

ON HYMAN RICKOVER

With the exception of my father, no other person has had such a profound impact on my life [as Admiral Hyman Rickover].

At a January 1980 ceremony in which Hyman Rickover, "Father of the Nuclear Navy," was awarded the Medal of Freedom.

THE HOLOCAUST

The most unspeakable crime in the whole of human history.

Commenting on the Holocaust and the importance of the United States Holocaust Memorial Museum, in Washington, DC.

Stephen L. Carter

NO ONE IS BEYOND CRITICISM

The ghastly experience of the Holocaust no more immunizes Israel from moral correction than the ghastly oppressions of slavery and Jim

Crow immunize those of us who are black. Thus, it is no more anti-Semitic to criticize Israel for, say, its policies toward West Bank Arabs than it is racist to criticize such black Americans as Louis Farrakhan for making anti-Semitic remarks.

From his Culture of Disbelief: How American Law and Politics Trivialize Religious Devotion *(1993).*

CLASSROOM PRAYER

As a child in Washington, DC, I attended a public school at which, each morning, one of the children would read a psalm aloud. But only the Christian children participated. There were, as I recall, perhaps three Jewish children out of a class of twenty-five or thirty. As the rest of us listened to the psalms, they would read books.... How, I often wondered, do they feel at this moment? I didn't know then, I don't know now.

Ibid.

A HIERARCHY OF SUFFERING

We enact a terrible threat to the unity of humanity when we construct a hierarchy of suffering, by arguing that one oppression is worse than another. This argument is what has led to the tragic and absurd spectacle of blacks and Jews occasionally sniping at one another over which was a greater evil, slavery or the Holocaust.

Ibid.

BEQUEATHING A RELIGIOUS TRADITION

It was wonderful to see the way religion permeated their lives. Since then I've always wanted a religious tradition to hand down to my kids.

From a 1993 interview in People *magazine in which the black Yale law professor described the period in his youth when he lived with a Jewish family in Upstate New York.*

PROTECTING RELIGIOUS PEOPLE

The idea behind the separation of church and state is that government was dangerous, not religion.... [The Founding Fathers were concerned about] protecting religious people from government, not the other way around.

Ibid.

¤

David Cassuto

A VISION OF JERUSALEM

Jerusalem is, first and foremost, the city of its residents. But it is also—and prominently —the capital of the State of Israel, as well as the focal city of the entire Jewish people. It also has prime importance to the three monotheistic religions, and Israel has amply proven its readiness to protect their interests. So my vision of Jerusalem is as a city under exclusive Israeli rule that preserves the rights of all who regard it as holy.

From a July 1994 discussion on the future of the Holy City.

¤

Umberto Cassuto

THE TORAH: A PEOPLE'S BOOK

The Torah was not intended specifically for intellectuals but for the entire people, which is not concerned with philosophic or theological speculation. It uses ordinary language plainly and without sophistication and pays no heed to inferences that later readers who are accustomed to ways of thinking wholly alien to the Bible may draw from its works.

From his From Adam to Noah *(1961).*

¤

Emanuel Celler

JOHNNY-COME-LATELY ZIONISTS

The Nazi terrors had brought many Johnny-come-latelies into the Zionist fold. I suppose I could be counted among those. The reasons were of compelling force. No country would take the Jews.... There were Jews already in Palestine who since before the turn of the century were draining the marshes, reviving the tired, wasted soil, building for the day of statehood.

Noting how American Jews became involved in pro-Zionist activity after World War II.

A LOSING BATTLE

When I finally rose to talk, I knew it was in vain. I used every device at my command. I pleaded and I reassured and realized finally they simply didn't want any more "wops, dagoes, Hebrews, hunkies, bulls."

Fighting a losing battle to convince Congress to pass an emergency immigration bill that would have allowed more Polish Jews to enter the U.S. Instead, a bill restricting immigration was passed in 1921 and was signed by President Warren G. Harding. From his autobiography, You Never Leave Brooklyn *(1953).*

¤

Ze'ev Chafetz

ASTROLOGERS AND PROPHECY

I recently heard a story about the editor of the British tabloid *The Sun*, who was forced, for reasons of economy, to fire a number of staff members. To most of them he broke the bad news in a conventional message of regret, but to the paper's astrologer he sent a letter which began: "Dear Sir: As you will no doubt have foreseen...."

From an article in The Jerusalem Report, *December 16, 1993.*

MASQUERADES TO BE AVOIDED

This year's list of celebrity no-nos includes Tonya Harding, Lorena and John Wayne Bobbitt, Rabbi Shlomo Goren, Mike Tyson, Saddam Hussein, Woody Allen, Admiral Bobby Ray Inman, Michael Lerner, Michael Jackson, Evans and Novak, Dr. Ruth Westheimer, Dr. George Habash, the Baba Barukh, the Menendez brothers, LaToya Jackson, Rabbi Ovadia Yosef (you'll never find the right clothes anyway), Vladimir Zhirinovsky, Heidi Fleiss, Rabbi Eliezer Schach and Snoopy Doggy Dog. And Barry Manilow.

Listing famous persons one should not be identified with when selecting a costume for the 1994 Purim party. From his article in The Jerusalem Report, *February 24, 1994.*

THE SHIMON PERES LOOK

Just don an elegant dark suit, slick back your hair, slip on a pair of rose-colored glasses and you, too, can look like the foreign minister of Israel.... The Peres ensemble also comes with a life-sized, inflatable Yasser Arafat love doll.

Ibid.

DIFFERENT PEOPLES

We simply are two different peoples. Two generations ago most of the Israeli Jews and most of the American Jews were European Jews or children of European Jews. They had a lot in common—Yiddish, Jewish food.... Two generations have passed. The Israeli Jews are more Israeli. American Jews are more American.

A comment made at a June 1994 conference on Israeli–Diaspora relations convened by President Ezer Weizman.

THE LAW OF RETURN

[The Law of Return made sense] at a time when most Jews were not intermarried, when large communities were still at risk, when Israel was desperate for warm bodies and nobody really wanted to come here anyway.

From an article in The Jerusalem Post, *August 11, 1994, in which he claims that too many social misfits, lunatics, and unemployables have made Israel a "dumping ground."*

¤

Marc Chagall

MEMORIES

Paris! My second Vitebsk!

Upon his first visit to Paris in 1910, when he settled in Montmarte and lived on a meager budget.

VITEBSK UNVISITED

I would have been afraid not to recognize my town, and in any event I have carried [it] forever in my heart.

Upon visiting Russia in June 1973 after a fifty-year absence. He was reunited with his sisters but refused to visit Vitebsk, his home town.

TO BE AN ARTIST

The artist must penetrate into the world, feel the fate of human beings, of peoples, with real love. There is no art for art's sake. One must be interested. One must be interested in the entire real of life.

Quoted in The Jewish Spectator, *September 1951.*

TESTING A PICTURE

When I am finishing a picture I hold some God-made object up to it—a rock, a flower, the branch of a tree or my hand—as a kind of final test. If the painting stands up beside a thing man cannot make, the painting is authentic. If there's a clash between the two, it is bad art.

Quoted in the Saturday Evening Post, *December 1962.*

BEYOND POVERTY

What poverty surrounded my youth, what trials my father had with us nine children. And yet he was always full of love and in his way a poet. Through him I first sensed the existence of poetry on this earth. After that I felt it in the nights, when I looked into the dark sky. Then I learnt that there was also another world. This brought tears to my eyes, so deeply did it move me.

From his autobiography, Marc Chagall *(1966).*

◻

Chama ben Chanina

FEET AND FATE

Man's feet are his fate; they lead him to where he is wanted.

Quoted in the Jerusalem Talmud, tractate Kila'yim (9:4).

IMITATING GOD

As He [God] clothes the naked, visits the sick, comforts mourners, and buries the dead so you do likewise.

Quoted in the talmudic tractate Sota (14a).

KEEN MINDS

As "iron sharpens iron" [Proverbs 27:17], so do two scholars sharpen one another's mind in law.

Quoted in the talmudic tractate Taanit (7a).

◻

Walter M. Chandler

THE BITTER LOAD OF HATRED

In every century of history, with their hands tied behind them and their hearts burdened to the breaking point with a bitter load of hatred and persecution, Jews have yet managed...to plant in the garden of life, in the soil of the soul, the most beautiful and fragrant flowers that bloom and blossom there.

From an address to the U.S. Congress on October 10, 1913 about the Jews of Rumania.

◻

(Rabbi) Chanina

GUARDIAN OF THE PEOPLE

Pray for the welfare of the government. Were it not that people stand in awe [fear] of it, men would swallow each other alive.

Quoted in the talmudic tractate Ethics of the Fathers (3:2).

◻

Chanina ben Dosa

GOD'S LOVE

He in whom his fellowman takes delight, God takes delight as well.

From the talmudic tractate Ethics of the Fathers (3:10).

◻

Chanina ben Pappa

HOLY ROBBERS

To enjoy this world without [first reciting] a benediction is tantamount to robbing the Holy One.

Quoted in the talmudic tractate Berachot (35b).

◻

Charles Chaplin

THE GREAT DICTATOR

I did this picture for the Jews of the world.

After the release of his movie The Great Dictator *in 1940, which makes a direct connection between Nazism and anti-Semitism. Patricia Erens, in her* Jew in American Cinema *(1984), commented: "[The film] was worth at least three [military] divisions."*

◻

Sherm Chavoor

HERO OF THE 1972 MUNICH OLYMPICS

After the [1968] Olympic trials the swimmers went to train at Colorado Springs. Mark [Spitz] ran into a lot of anti-Semitism from his teammates.... Some of the older guys really gave it to him. They tried to run him right off the team. It was "Jew-boy" this and "Jew-boy" that. It wasn't a kidding type of thing, either. I heard it with my own ears.

He didn't know how to handle it. He tried to get ready for a race and he'd get so wound up he'd come up with all sorts of imaginary sicknesses: sore throat, headache, like that. He was psyched.

Mark Spitz's swimming coach, noting that anti-Semitism definitely affected Spitz's swimming.

◻

Chayim of Zans

PRAYING TO PRAY

Before praying, I pray that during my prayers I will be praying.

By attribution.

Gennady Chazanov

HITLERIAN-TYPE COMPLIMENT

No fascist has paid such a compliment to a comedian since Adolf Hitler attacked Charles Chaplin.

Upon being called a potential spy by Vladimir Zhirinovsky because he held dual Israeli and Russian citizenship. Quoted in The Jerusalem Report, *January 13, 1994.*

(Rabbi) Chelbo

AN ANNOYING ITCH

Proselytes are as troublesome to Israel as a sore on the skin.

Quoted in the talmudic tractate Yevamot (109b) and also in the tractate Nidda (13b).

RELUCTANT DEPARTURE

When a man leaves the synagogue, he should not take long steps.

So as not to give the impression that he is eager to depart from the House of God. The scholar Abaye added: "But when one goes to the synagogue, it is a pious deed to run." Quoted in the talmudic tractate Berachot (6b).

BLESSINGS THROUGH A WIFE

One must always observe the honor due his wife, because blessings come to man's home only on account of his wife.

Quoted in the talmudic tractate Bava Metzia (59a).

Eliyohu Cherikover

RADICAL JEWISH WOMEN

The Jewish woman devoted herself to the revolutionary movement with special fervor....The [Russian] revolution changed the entire character of the radical Jewish woman, much faster, and probably much more deeply, than it did that of the Jewish man.

Quoted in Naomi Shepherd's Price Below Rubies: Jewish Women as Rebels and Radicals *(1993).*

Maxine Chernoff

MAGIC OF THE JEWS

In Steve Stern's universe, where survival is the magic the Jews have practiced for cen-turies, history can never die, and anything that can be imagined can be—and is—believed.

From a review of Steve Stern's Three Novellas *in* The New York Times Book Review, *January 2, 1994.*

Abraham Chill

A SOUL-STIRRING EXPERIENCE

The proper performance of a *mitzvah* [com-mandment] is a soul-stirring experience which raises the Jew to unprecedented spiritual heights in his urge to seek out and communi-cate with God.

From his Mitzvot: The Commandments and Their Rationale *(1994).*

Jacques Chirac

ACKNOWLEDGING GUILT BELATEDLY

France, the homeland of the Enlightenment and of the rights of man, a land of welcome and asylum, on that day omitted the irrepara-ble. Breaking its word, it handed those who were under its protection over to their execu-tioners. We owe them [the victims] an ever-lasting debt.

At a ceremony in Paris, July 16, 1995, marking the anniversary of the first mass arrests of Jews in Paris. His predecessor, François Mitterrand, always argued that the Vichy government was responsible: "I will not apologize in the name of France," he always said.

FRENCH CULPABILITY

These dark hours forever sully our history and are an insult to our past and our traditions. Yet, the criminal folly of the occupiers was sec-onded by the French, by the French state.

Ibid.

(Rabbi) Chisda

ON EATING VEGETABLES

I never ate vegetables. When I was poor I did not eat them because they stimulate an appetite, and I had nothing with which to sat-isfy it. When I became rich I did not eat them because I preferred to eat meat and fish.

Quoted in the talmudic tractate Shabbat (140b).

FIRST CHILD A GIRL

If one's first child is a girl, this is a good sign for future children.

> *Quoted in the talmudic tractate Bava Batra (141a).*

ON BEING A TYRANT

A man should never terrorize his household.

> *Quoted in the talmudic tractate Gittin (6b).*

UNSTABLE HOME

Infidelity in a home is like a worm in a poppy plant.... Anger in a home is like a worm in a sesame plant.

> *Quoted in the talmudic tractate Sota (3b).*

ON ABROGATING BIBLICAL LAW

A rabbinic court may lay down a condition which abrogates a biblical law.

> *From the talmudic tractate Yevamot (89b).*

�‍◌

Chiya bar Abba

THE RIGHTEOUS AND THE WICKED

The righteous are called living in death; the wicked are called dead even when alive.

> *Quoted in the talmudic tractate Berachot (18a).*

KEEPING SECRETS

When wine goes in, secrets come out.

> *Noting that the Hebrew words* ya'yin *(wine) and* sod *(secret) have the same numerical value, each adding up to seventy. Quoted in the talmudic tractate Sanhedrin (38a).*

STRIKING A BLOW AT GOD

The hatred of heathen nations toward the Jews—to what can this be compared? To a person who hated the king and wished to harm him, but could not. So what did he do? He approached a statue of the king and was about to demolish it, but was suddenly overcome by fear, realizing if he were caught he would be executed for treason. So, instead, he took an iron stake and began to strike the base to undermine its foundation, feeling confident that in time the statue would collapse. In like manner do heathens plan to provoke God, but finding that they cannot accomplish this, they attack and persecute the Jews instead.

> *Quoted in Midrash Exodus Rabba (51:5).*

◌

Noam Chomsky

WHEN SCIENCE IS AT A LOSS

As soon as questions of will or decision or reason or choice of action arise, human science is at a loss.

> *From a March 30, 1978 television interview.*

◌

(King) Christian X

THE YELLOW STAR

If the Germans want to put the yellow Jewish star in Denmark, I and my whole family will wear it as a sign of the highest distinction.

> *To the leaders of Danish Lutheran Church on October 11, 1943.*

NO JEWISH PROBLEM

But you see, there isn't any Jewish problem here. We do not consider ourselves inferior to them.

> *In response to the Nazi order that anti-Jewish legislation be introduced in Denmark.*

◌

Warren Christopher

SETTLING DISPUTES

Negotiations do work; peace is possible. We have not yet seen the end of contention in the Middle East, but we are changing the manner of contention. We are coming closer to the day when disputes that were once inflamed by the argument of force will now be settled by the force of argument.

> *Upon signing the PLO–Israeli peace accord, on May 4, 1994, in Cairo, Egypt.*

◌

Joseph Churba

"OCCUPIED" TERRITORY

It is one thing to argue that the establishment of new Jewish settlements on the West Bank does not promote the cause of peace, and quite another to encumber the issue by declaring such settlements illegal.

On the legal side, Israel's capture and control of western Palestine, historically known as Judea and Samaria, does not represent occupation of foreign territory. Indeed, the foreign occupation was the illegal and unrecognized annexation of the West Bank by Jordan, whose internationally recognized frontier ended at the Jordan River.

From a letter to the editor of The New York Times, August 25, 1977.

◻

Winston Churchill

A MOST HORRIBLE CRIME

[The "Final Solution" is] probably the greatest and most horrible crime ever committed in the whole history of the world.

July 1944 communication to British Foreign Secretary Anthony Eden.

A JEWISH HOMELAND

It is manifestly right that the scattered Jews should have a national centre and a national home to be re-united, and where else but in Palestine, with which for three thousand years they have been intimately and profoundly associated? We think it will be good for the world, good for the Jews, good for the British Empire, but also good for the Arabs who dwell in Palestine...they shall share in the benefits and progress of Zionism.

From a statement made in 1921. Quoted in Benjamin Netanyahu's A Place Among the Nations (1993).

AN ASTOUNDING RACE

And it may well be that this same astounding [Jewish] race may at the present time be in the actual process of producing another system of morals and philosophy, as malevolent as Christianity was benevolent, which, if not arrested, would shatter irretrievably all that Christianity has rendered possible. It would almost seem as if the gospel of Christ and the gospel of Antichrist were destined to originate among the same people; and that this mystic and mysterious race had been chosen for the supreme manifestations both of the divine and the diabolical.

From his article "Zionism Versus Bolshevism: A Struggle for the Soul of the Jewish People," which appeared in The Illustrated Sunday Herald, February 8, 1920.

WEIZMANN EULOGY

Those of us who have been Zionists since the days before the Balfour Declaration know what a heavy loss Israel has sustained in the death of Chaim Weizmann, who was famed and respected throughout the free world, and whose son was killed fighting for us. Weizmann led his people back to the Promised Land, where we have seen them invincibly installed in a sovereign state.

While addressing the Lord Mayor's Banquet in London, he learned of the death of Weizmann. Churchill departed from his prepared text to eulogize an old friend.

VINDICATION WILL COME

None has suffered more cruelly than the Jew the unspeakable evils wrought on the bodies and spirits of men by Hitler and his vile regime. The Jew bore the brunt of the Nazis' first onslaught upon the citadels of freedom and human dignity. He has borne and continues to bear a burden that might have seemed to be beyond endurance. He has not allowed it to break his spirit; he has never lost the will to resist. Assuredly in the day of victory the Jew's sufferings and his part in the struggle will not be forgotten. Once again, at the appointed time, he will see vindicated those principles of righteousness which it was the glory of his fathers to proclaim to the world.

Statement on the one-hundredth anniversary issue of London's Jewish Chronicle, November 14, 1941.

◻

Tansu Çiller

YAD VASHEM EXPERIENCE

I am shocked by my visit to Yad Vashem. Human suffering of this magnitude defies meaning; the tragedy experienced by the Jewish nation is the most terrible crime ever committed against humanity. The ability of the Jewish nation to overcome the horror is worthy of admiration. I pray for all the victims.

During an official visit to Israel in November 1994.

LOVE CONNECTION

I consider you my connection of love. You have a role to play in the history of the peace process. You are our [Turkish] ambassadors. I am proud of you, and I thank you.

At a warm reception she received at Bat-Yam where, in November 1994, more than two thousand Turkish immigrants from all over Israel came to greet her.

◻

Willy Claes

ANTI-SEMITISM: BELGIAN VIEW

Anti-Semitism, a specific form of racism, like other forms of intolerance, must be considered a social disease rooted in, and feeding on, a variety of ills like prejudice, chauvinism, xenophobia and many more. One could add the specific dimension, derived from the Diaspora of the Jews, placing them as minorities amidst the people of the world. An old Zionist saying puts it this way: "No need to explain anti-Semitism, it is too permanent and too irrational...."

From an address delivered at the World Conference on Anti-Semitism and Prejudice in a Changing World, held in Brussels, Belgium, July 1992.

◻

Grover Cleveland

A Debt Repaid

It is time for the unreserved acknowledgment that the toleration and equal opportunity accorded the Jews of the United States have been abundantly repaid to us.

I know that human prejudice—especially that growing out of race or religion—is cruelly inveterate and lasting. But wherever in the world prejudice against the Jews still exists, there can be no place for it among the people of the United States, unless they are heedless of good faith, recreant to the underlying principles of their free government, and insensible to every pledge involved in our boasted equality of citizenship.

From a 1905 address at the celebration of the 250th anniversary of the settlement of Jews in the United States.

◻

Bill Clinton

Head without Heart

The Holocaust reminds us forever that knowledge divorced from values can only serve to deepen the human nightmare, that a head without a heart is not humanity.

From a speech delivered on April 22, 1993 at the dedication of the United States Holocaust Memorial Museum in Washington, DC.

Sadness and Hope

I believe that this museum will touch the life of everyone who sees it, that no one who sees it will emerge without being changed.

This is a place of deep sadness, but it will also become a sanctuary of bright hope. Here on the town square of our national life...we dedicate the United States Holocaust Memorial Museum,

and so bind one of the darkest lessons in history to the hopeful soul of America.

Ibid.

Web of Hatred

Today we bear witness to an extraordinary act in one of history's defining dramas—a drama that began in a time of our ancestors when the word went forth from a sliver of land between the River Jordan and the Mediterranean Sea. That hallowed piece of earth, that land of light and revelation, is the home to the memories and dreams of Jews, Muslims and Christians throughout the world....

For too long the young of the Middle East have been caught in a web of hatred not of their own making. For too long they have been taught from the chronicles of war; now we can give them the chance to know the season of peace. For them we must realize the prophecy of Isaiah, that the cry of violence shall no more be heard in your land, nor wrack nor ruin within your borders. The children of Abraham, the descendants of Isaac and Ishmael, have embarked together on a bold journey. Together today with all our hearts and all our souls, we bid them *Shalom, Salaam*. Peace.

From a speech on the South Lawn of the White House on Monday, September 13, 1993, before the peace accord between Israel and the Palestine Liberation Organization was signed by Shimon Peres and Mahmoud Abbas in the presence of Yitzhak Rabin and Yasser Arafat.

Making Peace with the Enemy

Ever since Harry Truman first recognized Israel, every American president...has worked for peace between Israel and her neighbors. Now the efforts of all who have labored before us bring us to this moment—a moment when we dare to pledge what for so long seemed difficult even to imagine: that the security of the Israeli people will be reconciled with the hopes of the Palestinian people, and there will be more security and more hope for all.

Today the leadership of Israel and the Palestine Liberation Organization will sign a declaration of principles on interim Palestinian self-government. It charts a course toward reconciliation between two peoples who have both known the bitterness of exile. Now both pledge to put old sorrows and antagonisms behind them and to work for a shared future shaped by the values of the Torah, the Koran and the Bible. Let us salute also today the Government of Norway, for its remarkable role in nurturing this agreement.

Ibid.

WALLS OF ANGER AND SUSPICION

We have been granted the great privilege of witnessing this victory for peace. Just as the Jewish people this week celebrate the dawn of a new year, let us all go from this place to celebrate the dawn of a new era, not only for the Middle East but for the entire world.

The sound we heard today, once again as in ancient Jericho, was of trumpets toppling walls, the walls of anger and suspicion between Israeli and Palestinian, between Arab and Jew. This time, praise God, the trumpets herald not the destruction of that city but its new beginning.

Ibid.

ON VOTING PREFERENCES

Too many of us are still unwilling to vote for people who are different than we are.

During the 1993 campaign for mayor of New York City, when the president of the United States appeared to advocate the reelection of David Dinkins, the incumbent black mayor.

A "STATICLESS" PROPOSAL

If I'm going to propose, we might as well have a good line.

In a telephone call explaining to Judge Ruth Bader Ginsburg that owing to the bad phone connection, he'd have to call her back to offer her the Supreme Court job.

TAKING RISKS FOR PEACE

When I first met Prime Minister Rabin last year, almost a year ago this week, he said that he would be willing to take risks for peace, and certainly, he has been. Sometimes the opposition that he faces at home reminds me of the opposition I face from time to time. But clearly, he has been willing to take risks for peace. I told him if he should be willing to take those risks, then it was my responsibility as the President of the United States to minimize those risks. And I have tried to do that.

In an April 1994 address to the World Jewish Congress Governing Board, in Washington, DC.

IRONCLAD COMMITMENT

Our commitment to maintaining and enhancing the security of Israel is ironclad.

Ibid.

CURRENCY OF HOPE

The awful power of ancient arguments and the raw wounds of recent wars have left gener-

ations of Israelis, Jordanians, and Palestinians unable to imagine, much less build, a life of peace and security. Today King Hussein and Prime Minister Rabin give their people a new currency of hope and the chance to prosper in a region of peace.

From remarks made in Washington, DC, on July 25, 1994, just before King Hussein of Jordan and Prime Minister Yitzhak Rabin of Israel signed a declaration ending the state of war that had existed between Jordan and Israel for forty-six years.

TWENTY-FIRST-CENTURY SPOKESWOMAN

Her words and her judgments will help to shape our nation today and well into the twenty-first century.

At the August 10, 1994 White House ceremony at which Ruth Bader Ginsburg was sworn in as the 107th Supreme Court justice.

HEALING WOUNDS

I say to the people of Israel and Jordan, now you must make this peace real. To turn no-man's land into everyman's home; to take down the barbed wire; to remove the deadly mines; to help the wounds of war to heal; open your borders, open your hearts. Peace is more than an agreement on paper, it is a feeling, it is activity, it is devotion.

An excerpt from remarks delivered on October 26, 1994 at the signing of the Israeli-Jordanian peace accord at the Arava Crossing, Israel.

HEARTS OF LOVE

Here, you people will drink water from the same well and savor together the fruit of the vine. As you seize this moment, be assured that you will redeem every life sacrificed along the long road that brought us to this day. You will take the hatred out of hearts and you will pass along to your children a peace for the generations.

Ibid.

FAREWELL, FRIEND

Shalom, chaver [Goodbye, friend].

Upon learning of the assassination of Israeli Prime Minister Yitzhak Rabin on Saturday, November 4, 1995, following a peace rally in Tel Aviv.

AN UNUSUAL ARRAY

Today, my fellow citizens of the world, I ask all of you to take a good hard look at this picture. Look at the leaders from all over the Middle East and around the world who have journeyed here today for Yitzhak Rabin and for peace. Though we no longer hear his deep and booming voice, it is he who has brought us together again here, in word and deed, for peace.

From his November 6, 1995 eulogy for Yitzhak Rabin, noting the array of leaders from all parts of the world assembled to pay tribute to the assassinated prime minister of Israel.

Hillary Rodham Clinton

THE WHITE HOUSE MENORAH

This country is made up of all faiths, and the menorah is a wonderful addition to the collection.

After being presented with a Chanukah menorah in December 1993. The candelabrum graces the lobby of the White House West Wing, near the Oval Office, as part of a new permanent crafts collection consisting of sixty-five pieces. Donated by artist Zachary J. Oxman, of Hillsboro, Virginia, in 1993.

LEARNING TALMUD

I am interested in learning Talmud.

After the signing of the peace treaty between Israel and Jordan on October 16, 1994, Rabbi Menachem Genack, kashrut director of the Orthodox Union, told her that "the concept that each child is a gift [from God] is found in the Talmud."

Arthur A. Cohen

COMMONALITY OF SUFFERING

The Jew need not learn to hear the Christian speak of the Christ nor must the Christian learn to hear the Jew speak of the dominion of Torah in the time of the Messiah; but both must come to hear in each other the sounds of truth.... It is the commonalty of human suffering that is the commonalty of Christian and Jew; and there must come, as a miracle of Grace, a means of expressing that shared experience.

From his Myth of the Judeo-Christian Tradition *(1971).*

SUPERNATURAL VOCATION OF THE JEW

The rediscovery of the supernatural vocation of the Jew is the turning point of modern Jewish history, for the Jewish people is not a fact of history but an article of faith.

From his Natural and Supernatural Jew *(1963).*

Eliot A. Cohen

CONSEQUENCES OF THE 1993 MIDDLE EAST PEACE ACCORD

For the PLO's leaders, formal recognition of Israel's legitimacy meant a far greater concession—and far greater personal risks—than did Yitzhak Rabin's meeting with Arafat on the White House lawn [on September 13, 1993]. The Palestinian leadership, which Abba Eban once said never missed an opportunity to miss an opportunity, accepted a compromise that will abate the war that has raged between Arab and Jew for the better part of a century.

From an article in The New Republic, *December 6, 1993.*

Gerson D. Cohen

ASPECTS OF ASSIMILATION

A frank appraisal of the periods of great Jewish creativity will indicate that not only did a certain amount of assimilation and acculturation not impede Jewish continuity and creativity but that in a profound sense this assimilation or acculturation was even a stimulus to original thinking and expression and, consequently, a source of renewed vitality.

From a 1966 commencement address delivered at a Hebrew teachers' college.

FAMILY AND COMMUNITY

The Jewish family never sustained the Jew. That is a myth that is being perpetuated by people who are dissatisfied with the synagogue and find themselves failures. The family, as a unit in a strongly organized community, had very little to do except to generate, feed, and clothe kids. The community educated them. Where? In the street, in the marketplace, in the synagogue, in the house of study, in the assembly hall. The family today is being asked to do things which it can't possibly do. It is called upon to replace community, to provide leisure, love, respect, satisfaction, fulfillment. But that's impossible, because we can't do these things in isolation. We can do them only as a community.

From a 1979 address delivered to the Jewish Educators Assembly convention.

Haim Cohen

THE "WHO IS A JEW?" QUESTION

Should a man who regards Israel as his homeland, and who is passionately imbued with the desire to live here, but who is a Christian by religion, be denied entrance [as a Jew] through the portals of the country for that reason only? I, for my part, am willing to accept only the first part of the government's definition of a Jew: a person who in good faith declares himself to be Jewish.

One of the justices of the Israeli Supreme Court renders the minority opinion in the case of Father Daniel, born Oswald Refeisen of Jewish parents in Poland. He tried unsuccessfully to enter Israel in 1958 under the Law of Return.

Henry Cohen

WHY BE JEWS?

I recall Abraham Cronbach, *olav ha-shalom,* once saying cryptically: "We are Jews because we want to be Jews."

My wanting has to do with a stubborn refusal to deny that which I feel to be very much a part of me.

My wanting has to do with the ease I feel with people who will not let the world forget the Holocaust and will not turn their backs on Israel.

My wanting has to do with the radical freedom I prize when my mind searches for the meaning of God and man. I cherish the thought that almost wherever my mind roams I can find within the Jewish community someone to join me in my dissent.

My wanting has to do with feeling at home with a tradition that has usually given high marks to man and, even in the midst of despair, held out hope for mankind.

From his Why Judaism: A Search for Meaning in Jewish Identity *(1973).*

Hermann Cohen

HISTORY VS. LOGIC

An anti-Semite may prove "logically" that Jesus never existed and may yet continue to prove "historically" that the Jews had crucified him.

Quoted in Hayyim Greenberg's Inner Eye *(1953).*

PATRON SAINT OF THE JEWISH PEOPLE

The Sabbath became the most effective patron saint of the Jewish people....The ghetto Jew discarded all the toil and trouble of his daily life when the Sabbath lamp was lit. All insult and outrage was shaken off. The love of God, which returned to him the Sabbath each seventh day, restored to him also his honor and human dignity even in his lowly hut.

From his Die Religion der Vernunft aus den Quellen des Judentums *(1919).*

DEFINING CHRISTIANITY

What you call Christianity, I call Prophetic Judaism.

In a remark to F. A. Lange.

WITCHCRAFT VS. MONOTHEISM

Not to realize the vital necessity of these laws concerning witchcraft and the vital duty of its extirpation, is to fall a victim to the superstition that witchcraft was mere harmless make-believe that did not call for any drastic punishment. At the bottom of this skeptical attitude towards the laws of witchcraft is indifference towards the unique value of monotheism.... It is a question of "to be or not to be" for the ethical life.

Quoted in J. H. Hertz's Pentateuch and Haftorahs *(1961).*

ESSENCE OF REVELATION

This is the most general sense of revelation: that God comes into relation with man.

From his Religion of Reason Out of the Sources of Judaism *(1972).*

TO BE CONTENT

The Jew, in spite of all his most base daily occupations, has, as a rule, at the same time been a scholar. As scholar, he could become a wise man, and as a wise man the basic mood of the Jew could become contentment with this earthly lot.

Ibid.

WHAT JEWISH HOLIDAYS HAVE WROUGHT

Considering the suffering that pervades the whole historical life of the Jew, it is surely a wonder that he could continually maintain such equanimity, such genuine humor, without which he would never have been able to lift himself again and again from the deepest humiliation to proud heights. The Jewish holidays have brought about this wonder for him.

Ibid.

THE BLESSING OF THE SABBATH

The Sabbath effectively eliminates the differences that exist because of the work people do. The artisan, too, becomes his own master. Having one's weekly rest on a specific day puts the worker and his master on equal footing.... All indignities were shaken off. God's love, which gave him the Sabbath every seventh day, also gave him back his honor and human dignity in his low-ceilinged hut.

Ibid.

PROTECTING THE STRANGER

The stranger was to be protected, although he was not a member of one's family, clan, religion, community, or people; simply because he was a human being. In the stranger, therefore, man discovered the idea of humanity.

Quoted in Richard Schwartz's Judaism and Global Survival *(1987).*

□

Jack J. Cohen

HOLDING OUT HOPE

There is no doubt that a Holocaust could now be in the making. Holocaust is on the minds of people here [in Israel]. I have no reason to assume that Arab terrorists have any other purpose in mind. They have stated it. The sense of the Holocaust has never left the people in this country. There are isolated moments of calmness when people would like to forget, but these are few and far between. I hold the hope that maybe some of the Arab leaders are prepared to be satisfied at some point. They might say: "Let the Jews in Israel live. We've got them to the point where they're no threat to us."

February 1974 remarks quoted in The Christian Century *magazine, December 11, 1974.*

LAND AND THE JEWS

You have to see present-day Israel through biblical eyes. Read the Bible as Jewish history, people settling into a land. The land was always a problem—a dream, a reality, a horror, something that people sang about. The Judaism of the Jewish people is a culture rooted in time and space. It's as material as you can make it.

Ibid.

ON DEVELOPING PATIENCE

There are prejudices, there are inequalities here [in Israel], as there are everywhere in the world.... I'm very self-critical, and I'm critical with my own people, and my problem frequently as a Jew is to catch myself, and be as sympathetic with my fellow Jews as I am with the Arabs. But, I'm learning to be as critical of the Arabs as I am of the Jews, and maybe I'm becoming normal here.

From a 1977 interview. Reported in Frank Epp's The Israelis: Portrait of a People in Conflict *(1980).*

THE EARTH IS THE LORD'S

I think that the earth is the Lord's and the fullness thereof, and we are all here on more or less long-term or short-term leases. We do not have an absolute right to any soil.... The sentiments that are attached to this land are factors that have to be taken into account, but they in themselves are not, and should not be decisive. What seems to me to be decisive is the opportunity for people to develop their own authenticity, without doing too much harm to someone else.

Ibid.

□

Jonathan Cohen of Lünel

PRAISE FOR MAIMONIDES

Since the death of the last of the Rabbis of the Talmud, there has not been such a man in Israel.

Paying homage to Maimonides for his great erudition.

□

Morris Raphael Cohen

A PHILOSOPHER'S BUSINESS

The business of a philosopher is well done if he succeeds in raising genuine doubts.

From his Dreamer's Journey *(1949).*

BEAUTY AND KNOWLEDGE

It is the appreciation of beauty and truth, the striving for knowledge, which makes life worth living.

Ibid.

BREATHING ROOM

A richer American culture can come only if the Jews, like other elements, are given a chance to develop under favorable conditions their peculiar genius.

Ibid.

SCHOOLING COMES FIRST

The people of Neshwies...wore rags on their feet and ate white bread only on the Sabbath, but no child went without schooling.

Ibid.

SYMBOL OF CONTINUITY

Men cling to sanctified phrases not only because of the insights they contain but even more because, through ritual and repetition, they have become redolent with the wine of human experience.... The ritual may be diluted by English and by modernisms, but the Hebraic God is still a potent symbol of the continuous life of which we individuals are waves.

Ibid.

SELF-CONTROL AND SELF-WORTH

Self-control is not worth a farthing unless we build up a great self worth controlling.

From an article in The New Republic, *August 31, 1918.*

MANIFESTATION OF GOD

The glory of God is not visible except to those who are profoundly moved by compassion for their fellow-men.

Ibid.

IN DEFENSE OF CEREBRAL LABOR

I don't believe in this superstitious prejudice that only the man who works with his hands is socially useful.

From his Reflections of a Wandering Jew *(1950).*

PALLBEARERS OF THE PAST

We will live not as pallbearers of a dead past, but as the creators of a more glorious future.

From an article in the International Journal of Ethics *(1915).*

□

Pamela Cohen

JEWISH ROOTS EXPOSED

[Vladimir Volfovich] Zhirinovsky is a classic example of a person of Jewish origin who made his political career as an enemy of the Jewish people. He represents a grave danger to the Jewish community of Russia and to the world. Stories about Zhirinovsky's Jewish background should not be used to divert the world's attention from this threat.

Quoted in an article by Joseph Polakoff that appeared in Heritage Southwest Jewish Press, *December 24, 1993, in which she points out that Zhirinovsky was born on April 26, 1946 to a Russian woman married to a Jewish lawyer who died when Vladimir was a baby.*

□

Rina Cohen

THE RIGHT OF RETURN

You can't tell a ninety-year-old [Russian] Jew he can't come to Israel because he's sick. We have the Law of Return. Every Jew has the right to come here, no matter how sick he is, no matter if he has one foot in the grave. Even if it comes out of my taxes.

Quoted in The Jerusalem Post, *July 9, 1994.*

□

Seymour Cohen

HOW TO BECOME HUMAN

God wants us to become human.... When we realize our potential, when we make the most of ourselves, when we live up to our resources, when we strive for a better world, when we complete ourselves, when we realize our limitations and also our strength, then we become human.

From his sermon in Best Jewish Sermons of 5713 (1953), *edited by Saul I. Teplitz.*

□

Steven M. Cohen

SPEAKING TO A NEW GENERATION

He's trying to establish his own personality, and he's speaking to younger, more secular, more intellectual Israelis who see the current Diaspora-Israel relationship as insulting. They are upset with what they perceive to be rich American Jews who come to Israel, throw their weight around and make Israelis speak English.

Commenting on the outspoken views of Yossi Beilin, Israel's deputy foreign minister, referred to by Yitzhak Rabin as "Peres' Poodle." Quoted in The Jewish Week, *February 11–17, 1994.*

Dan Cohn-Sherbak

THE CHARACTER OF JEWISH MYSTICISM

In their study of Jewish mysticism, students make a number of interesting points. They note that Jewish mysticism is in numerous respects different from mysticism in other religious traditions: it is reserved for the few; it is scholarly in character; it is essentially speculative in nature. In other religions—such as Buddhism and Hinduism—mysticism is largely contemplative and open to all.

From an article in The Jewish Spectator, *Fall 1985.*

Steve Cokely

JEWS, BLACKS, AND AIDS

The AIDS epidemic is a result of doctors, especially Jewish ones, who inject AIDS into blacks.

From a 1988 speech to the Nation of Islam.

Samuel Taylor Coleridge

THE STATESMAN'S BEST MANUAL

I persist in avowing my conviction that the inspired poets, historians and sententiaries of the Jews are the clearest teachers of political economy; in short, that their writings are the statesman's best manual.

From his Lay Sermon *(1816).*

Christopher Columbus

ON THE EXPULSION OF THE JEWS

So after having expelled the Jews from your dominions [in 1492], Your Highnesses, in the same month of January, ordered me to proceed with sufficient armament to the said region of India.

From a letter to the king and queen of Spain that opens his Journal of the First Voyage.

Eric Conrad

YEARNING FOR THE INDEFINABLE

By teaching others, she [Montague] taught herself. By praying with others, she was helped to formulate her own thoughts and to put into words the yearning for the Indefinable that was smoldering within her.

From his Lily H. Montague: Prophet of a Living Judaism.

Calvin Coolidge

THE FAITH OF LIBERTY

The Jewish faith is predominantly the faith of liberty. From the beginnings of the conflict between the colonies and the mother country, they were overwhelmingly on the side of the rising revolution....

It is easy to understand why a people with the historic background of the Jews should thus overwhelmingly and unhesitatingly have allied themselves with the cause of freedom. From earliest colonial times, America has been a new land of promise to this long-persecuted race.

From an address delivered at the laying of the cornerstone of the Jewish Community Center in Washington in 1925. Quoted in Foundations of the Republic *(1926).*

CHARITY, LIBERTY, PROGRESS

Every inheritance of the Jewish people, every teaching of their secular history and religious experience, draws them powerfully to the side of charity, liberty and progress.

Ibid.

Aaron Copland

MUSIC IS JEWISH

I think of music as Jewish, because it's dramatic, it's intense, it has a certain passionate lyricism to it. I can't imagine it written by a *goy*.

Quoted in Elinor and Robert Slater's Great Jewish Men *(1996).*

Carl H. Cornill

UNIQUENESS OF KING DAVID

The king who did more for the worldly greatness and earthly power of Israel than anyone else was a genuine Israelite in that he appreciated also Israel's religious destiny; he was no soldier-king, no conqueror of common stamp, no ruler like any one of a hundred others, but he is the truest incorporation of the distinctive character of Israel—a unique personality in the history of the world.

Quoted in J.H. Hertz's Pentateuch and Haftorahs *(1961).*

PROPHET OF MANKIND

The whole history of humanity has produced nothing which can be compared in the remotest degree to the prophecy of Israel. Through prophecy Israel became the prophet of mankind. Let this never be overlooked nor forgotten: the costliest and noblest treasure that man possesses he owes to Israel and to Israelitic prophecy.

From his Prophets of Israel *(1894).*

❑

Howard Cosell

MASSACRE IN MUNICH

I was never brought up in a religious home or observed any religious ritual. I'd go to the synagogue with my father on Yom Kippur, but it was never anything formal. It took an experience like Munich to awaken me.

I left those Games knowing who I was, what I was all about. I knew that forever more, no matter what happened in my life, I was Jewish, and very proud of it.

From a 1990 interview in which he recalled witnessing the brutal assassination of eleven Israeli athletes at the 1972 Olympics in Munich, Germany.

❑

Irwin Cotler

CANADIAN MULTICULTURALISM

The organizing motif in Canada has always been multi-culturalism as distinct from the idea of the melting pot. Canadian society had always had a kind of tribal character defined of course by the two founding communities, the Anglophone and the Francophone, and for us the consequence has been that Jews do not feel apologetic or defensive about giving expression to what might be called Jewish tribalism. We are just another part of the Canadian mosaic.

From a December 1980 interview with the editor of Moment *magazine.*

INTERLOCKING AGENDAS

Canadian policy in very diverse areas has a Jewish dimension—and so, too, what Canadian Jews say and do about things like the Middle East or Soviet Jewry has consequences for Canada at large. If, for example, we are dealing with a matter relating to Israel, we must bear in mind that we are not making the case for Israel or for Israelis; we're making the case in Canada, and for a Canadian foreign policy. Our advocacy must be "Canadianized," lest it fall on deaf ears. Put differently: We seek support for Israel's cause not on the grounds that it is a Jewish cause but on the grounds that it is a just cause.

Ibid.

❑

Norman Cousins

THE HUMAN SPECIES

The major problem on earth is not the bomb. The bomb is actually the product of the problem. The main problem is that the human imagination has not yet expanded to the point where it comprehends its own essential unity. People are not yet aware of themselves as a single interdependent species requiring the proper performance of certain vital services if the human race is to be sustained.

From an article in Saturday Review, *July 21, 1962.*

WHERE EDUCATION HAS FAILED

The great failure of education—not just in the United States but throughout most of the world—is that it has made man group conscious rather than species-conscious. It has celebrated man's institutions but not himself. It has attached value to the things man does but not to what man is. Man's power is heralded but the preciousness of life is unsung.

...There are national anthems but no anthems for humanity.

Ibid. April 9, 1966.

❑

Rachel Cowan

JEWISH COMMUNAL NEEDS

We need to make our community more joyful, educated, creative and welcoming. Let's make our synagogues spiritually deeper, our commitment to social justice more active. Let's bring new ideas into our Jewish world: women's perspectives on ritual, theology and leadership; outreach to Jews who are struggling with illness, grief and loneliness; awareness that our environment is God's creation and needs our action to protect it; authentic Jewish traditions of meditation to deepen our spiritual life. And let's see in the phenomenon of intermarriage an opportunity to bring new Jews into our community.

From Hadassah Magazine, *June–July 1993.*

Samuel Sullivan Cox

JERUSALEM AND THE JEW

In the full blaze of history, one cannot help but feel that this [Jerusalem] is especially the city of the Jews. Christians may fight for and hold its holy places; Moslems may guard from all other eyes the tombs of David and Solomon; the site of the temple on Mount Moriah may be decorated by the mosques of Omar and Aksa; but if ever there was a material object on earth closely allied with a people, it is this city of Jerusalem with the Jews.

From an 1882 editorial in his Orient Sun Beams. *Quoted in an essay by Moshe Davis in* With Eyes Toward Zion *(1977).*

Gordon A. Craig

WAGNER'S ANTI-SEMITISM

[Richard Wagner] combined a hidden admiration for the Jews' success in surviving centuries of oppression with strong doubts about the ability of his own people to retain its individuality in conditions of free competition. He expressed his anxieties in attacks upon the Jews as enemies of German culture.

From his Germans *(1982), in which he sums up the source of Wagner's anti-Semitism.*

Abraham Cronbach

EISENHOWER AND THE ROSENBERGS

On June 16, 1953, the forty-seventh anniversary of my ordination, I conversed with President Dwight D. Eisenhower in the Presidential office of the White House Annex. I had been invited to join three Christian clergymen in beseeching the President for clemency toward Julius and Ethel Rosenberg, sentenced to be executed on June 18.... I remarked, "Mr. President, all of us are dedicated to the interests of America. All of us are solicitous that America shall suffer no harm. Would not America be adequately safeguarded if, instead of death, the penalty of the Rosenbergs would be imprisonment, no matter how long?... Life is full of problems that baffle our intelligence. All of us need the guidance of God. Mr. President, may you have the guidance of God!"

Quoted in Critical Studies in American Jewish History *(1971).*

CRIME AND PUNISHMENT

To those who maintain that the punishment was just, I should like to say a few words. It is an ancient Jewish maxim that if, after a law has been violated, the violator has been punished, the violation is to be regarded as canceled. The defendant ceases to be a defendant. Matters become as if the violation had never occurred. That Jewish maxim is so noble and so worthy that it ought to be adopted by people everywhere. According to that maxim, Julius and Ethel Rosenberg are now innocent—innocent even if judged from the harshest point of view.

Ibid. Remarks made at the funeral of Julius and Ethel Rosenberg, on June 21, 1953, after Rabbi Cronbach's plea for clemency was turned down by President Eisenhower on June 16th.

Walter Cronkite

PRAISE FOR GOLDA MEIR

She [Golda Meir] lived a life under pressure that we, in this country, would find impossible to understand. She is the strongest woman to head a government in our time and for a very long time past.

From a television broadcast after Golda Meir's death in 1978.

Richard H. S. Crossman

A CHRISTIAN DISEASE

Racialism is a universal [disease], anti-Semitism an exclusively Christian disease.

From an article in The New Statesman, *November 19, 1960.*

Billy Crystal

BAR MITZVA SPEECH

I delivered my Bar Mitzva speech with an Oklahoma [southern] accent.

So enamored was he of his baseball idol, Oklahoma-born Mickey Mantle, that he tried to imitate him in every way. Quoted by Bob Costas during his eulogy of Mantle on August 15, 1995, in Dallas, Texas.

◻

John Cardinal Csernoch

ANTI-SEMITISM IN HUNGARY

I know no difference between men. A close friendship binds me to the Chief Rabbi of Budapest, a very worthy and wise man, for whom I avow the greatest esteem. There are honest and dishonest persons: this is the only difference that I recognize among men.

It is not true that the Catholic Church favors the anti-Semitic agitation.... I am watchful that the Hungarian clergy not only do not participate in it, but rather reprove it in the most decisive manner under all circumstances.

From a January 2, 1925 declaration.

◻

Michael J. Curley

VICTORY OVER A MAD MAN

Long after Hitler is dead and forgotten the Jews will still be living in Germany. At least I know the Catholic Church will be living in Germany. Hitler cannot destroy her, and Goebbels cannot propagandize her out of existence.

Germany has gone mad, but not all the people of Germany are mad. There are Germans who continue to love and serve God; they are not all of the Nazi spirit of a Hitler and a Goebbels. They will continue to withstand persecution and hate and injustice; they will continue to be true to God; they will obey God rather than a mad man.

From an address delivered before the Holy Comforter Church, in Washington, DC, November 13, 1938.

◻

Adam Czerniakow

DEPTHS OF DESPAIR

I am powerless, my heart trembles in sorrow and compassion. I can no longer bear all this.

From a secret diary he kept of the destruction of Warsaw Jewry. In July 1942, he committed suicide.

D

Dalai Lama

A Model Community

We Tibetans wonder if we can follow your example.

Expressing admiration for the Jewish community's tenacity in retaining its identity. Statement made in April 1993 after attending the opening of the U.S. Holocaust Memorial Museum in Washington, DC.

¤

Thomas Daly

A Model for Our Times

What makes Wiesel a model for our times is that he emerged from the scalding horror of the European nightmare concerned not only about his own people but about all of humanity.

Comment made while presenting the Award for Religious and Racial Understanding to Elie Wiesel at Queens College, New York, in April 1994.

¤

Alfonse D'Amato

Dictator Assad

I say to Hafiz al-Assad: You're not a president. You're a criminal. You're a killer. You're a dictator. And we want our people released now.

At a rally outside Syria's UN mission, demanding the free emigration of Syrian Jews. Quoted in The Jerusalem Report, *December 30, 1993.*

¤

Uri Dan

Operation Entebbe

It was not until the commandos had already landed at Entebbe, that [Prime Minister] Rabin instructed Eran [Director General of the Prime Minister's office] to phone Israeli Ambassador Simcha Dinitz, via a special line to Washington, and to instruct him to advise the White House that a special operation was under way. Dinitz was taken completely by surprise. He gasped, and asked for details. But he was told that he would not know any more for another hour or so.

Dinitz notified his close friend, Henry Kissinger, who responded with manifest satisfaction, "I expected that Israel would act."

It was only after the famous 90 minutes when the last Israeli Hercules had left the airport [with the rescued hostages] that Dinitz got the phone call from Rabin that told him what had happened. He passed the news along to both the White House and to Kissinger. This time, Kissinger was somewhat more composed. He told Dinitz, "You know, all day Saturday we were getting bits and pieces of information at the State Department. But when I was consulted, I told my people to brush them aside."

From an article in Moment *magazine, December 1976.*

¤

John C. Danforth

Christians and the Holocaust

It is not possible to recognize the magnitude of the Holocaust without admitting the complicity of Christians.... The [U.S. Holocaust Memorial] Museum will guarantee that, for generations to come, Americans will never forget the horrors of the past.

From a sermon delivered at a special ecumenical service held at Washington's National Cathedral on April 18, 1993. Senator Danforth is also an Episcopal priest.

¤

Gabriele D'Annunzio

The Stuff of Dreams

The Jews are a people of artists, of intrinsic dreamers. That's what makes them achieve the impossible, and that is why they have survived.

Quoted in Hunterberg's Tragedy of the Ages.

Dante

JEPHTHAH'S VOW

Be strong
To keep your vow; yet be not perverse—
As Jephthah once, blindly to execute a rash
resolve.
Better a man should say, I have done
wrong
Than keeping an ill vow, he should do
worse.

From his Divine Comedy, *Paradiso.*

◻

Abraham Danzig

THE WORST SIN

A sin against man is far more reprehensible
than a sin against God.

Quoted in The Jewish Encyclopedia,
Volume IV (1905).

◻

Mahmoud Darwish

TIME TO DEPART

The time has come for you to go.
Live where you like, but not among us.
Die where you please, but not among us.
Get out of our soil, our sea, our wheat, our
salt, our wounds.
[Get] out of the memory of our memories....

*Written in 1988 by the poet laureate of the
Palestinian national movement, expressing
his people's attitude toward the Jewish
settlers living in their midst.*

◻

(King) David

LAMENT OVER A SON

My son, Absalom! O my son, my son, Absalom! If only I had died instead of you, O Absalom, my son. My son!

*Lamenting the death of his son, whose hair
got tangled in the branches of a tree while
he rode his mule; he was left hanging.
II Samuel 19:1.*

ELI, ELI, LAMA AZAVTANI?

My God [Eli], my God, why hast Thou forsaken me?

*From Psalm 22, verse 2. Christians often
change the word* azavtani *to* zevachtani
*("sacrificed me") and connect it to the
Crucifixion.*

STRONGER THAN A SPEAR

You have come against me with a sword
and a spear and a javelin, but I come against
you in the name of the Lord of Hosts.

*In his confrontation with the Philistine Go-
liath. From I Samuel 17:45.*

A NOBLE ELEGY

How have the mighty fallen! Tell it not in
Gath, nor in the streets of Ashkelon, lest the
daughters of the Philistines rejoice, lest the
daughters of the enemy exult.

*In mourning the tragic death of King Saul
and his three sons as described in I Samuel
31:8 and I Samuel 1:17ff.*

GRIEVING FOR JONATHAN

O Jonathan, I am distressed for you, my
brother Jonathan. Your love to me was more
wonderful than the love of women.

How have the mighty fallen, and the
weapons of war perished!

From II Samuel 2:26–27.

THE LORD AS SHEPHERD

The Lord is my Shepherd, I shall not want.

From the Book of Psalms 23:1.

BEAUTIFUL LIVES

Saul and Jonathan,
Loved and beautiful in their lives,
And in their deaths they were undivided—
They were swifter than eagles,
Stronger than lions.

O daughters of Israel,
Weep for Saul,
Who clothed you in scarlet with fineries,
Who added a gold ornament to your clothing.

How have the heroes fallen
In the midst of war!
Jonathan,
On your high places slain!

It is hard for me,
My brother Jonathan;
You were very beautiful to me.
Your love was more wondrous to me
Than the love of women.

*Lament for Jonathan. From II Samuel
1:23–27.*

◻

Israel Davidson

MAIDSERVANT OF HEBREW

A generation or two ago Yiddish was regarded as a jargon by the people who read it,
and the very men who wrote it had the feeling

that they were sacrificing their literary talents on the altar of utilitarianism. Those fond of figurative language called Yiddish the "maidservant" of Hebrew. Today, this maidservant has become her own mistress.

Quoted in the Foreword to Joseph Leftwich's Jewish Omnibus *(1933).*

It Is Later Than You Think

There is an American proverb which I think is not only false but pernicious in its implication. America prides itself on having coined the saying, "Time is money." This is a false statement and leads to serious error. The only case in which time and money are alike is that there are some people who do not know what to do with their money, and still others who are so unfortunate as not to know what to do with time either. But, otherwise, time is infinitely more precious than money, and there is nothing common between them. You cannot accumulate time; you cannot regain time lost; you cannot borrow time; you can never tell how much time you have left in the Bank of Life. Time is life.

From a commencement address at the Jewish Theological Seminary of America. Quoted in a profile of Davidson by Louis Finkelstein in the American Jewish Yearbook *(5700/1939–40). Inside the cover of a watch carried by Professor Davidson were the words, "It is later than you think."*

A Good Five-cent Cigar

I learned long ago to appreciate a five-cent cigar as much as a fifteen-cent one. We professors can afford to choose our friends but we cannot afford to choose our cigars.

From a letter to his fellow (Protestant) chaplain at Sing Sing and Dannemore prisons, the Reverend Francis H. Pierce.

Books without Readers

I continue to write books which people continue not to read, but the proofreader and I are having a good time.

Ibid.

◻

Jo Davidson

Destruction of an Old Myth

Here in Israel they are killing the myth that there is a physical type of Jew. The thing that's so startling here is that Jews from India are so Indian and Jews from Persia so Persian.

Quoted by D.A. Schmidt in The New York Times, *December 19, 1951.*

◻

Sammy Davis, Jr.

Sharing Grief

I share your grief and your sorrow. When I saw the destruction that the fire did to your synagogue, my Jewish heart wept as all of us are now weeping. I tell you from the bottom of my heart that they can burn our synagogues, they can set fire to our Torah, they can torch our holy books—but they can never destroy our spirit.

We must respond to this challenge as one people united in their determination that our spirit is still strong and vibrant.

A comment made after attending a service held in the basement of the arson-struck Young Israel Synagogue in Hartford, Connecticut, in August 1983. The sanctuary was destroyed by the fire.

Why I Became a Jew

[I converted to Judaism] because I wanted to be part of that strong and steadfast tradition that withstood and overcame thousands of years of bigotry and persecution. I assure you that this persecution, too, shall pass. We will rebuild this synagogue, and we shall glory in the light that it will radiate for all our Jewish brethren and for all people everywhere.

Ibid.

Who's Face?

With this *punim* [face] who else could I be?

Responding to a woman who asked, "Are you really Sammy Davis?"

◻

Lucy Dawidowicz

Power Game

Hitler did not blame the Jews in order to gain power; he gained power, in large measure, to persecute the Jews. Hatred of Jews constituted his essence, rather than being a political strategy. Nothing proves this better than this final statement to the German people urging them, "above all," to go on fighting the Jews.

From her War Against the Jews *(1975).*

The Holocaust in Perspective

It is important to know about the Holocaust, to talk about it. That's what I've tried to do. On the other hand, you have to put it in the perspective of all of Jewish existence.

> *The editor of* The Holocaust Reader *(1976) objects to what she calls "the Holocaust industry" and those who would "vulgarize" it by an outpouring of books and films on the subject.*

WOMEN RABBIS

To my mind, the assumption by a woman of rabbinic or priestly function in the synagogue undermines the very essence of Jewish tradition.

> *From her* Jewish Presence: Essays in Identity and History *(1977).*

WHERE THE BLAME BELONGS

The enormity [of the Holocaust] is not in our suffering but in their evil. It is their history, *goyische* [Gentile] history, that stands outside of what has been normative human experience—even for evil doing. If the old moral positions are no longer valid after the Holocaust, it is not our problem. It's their problem. If only they would realize it.

> *Ibid.*

IMMIGRATION RESTRICTIONS

It is a paradox of Jewish history that the anti-Semitism propagated in the United States after the First World War wrought more damage to the European Jews than to the American Jews. The restriction of immigration in accordance with the national-origins quota prevented hundreds of thousands of Jews from entering America in years to come when the difference was a difference between life and death.

> *From her* On Equal Terms: Jews in America, 1881–1981.

ANOTHER HISTORY

In the early 1850s, a mutual friend introduced [Leopold] Zunz to Heinrich Graetz, saying that Graetz was planning to publish a history of the Jews. "Another history of the Jews!" Zunz exclaimed. "Another history," Graetz retorted, "but this time a *Jewish* history!"

> *From her* What Is the Use of Jewish History? *(1993).*

HOLOCAUST ACTIVITY

There's no business like *Shoah* [Holocaust] business.

> *By attribution.*

□

Clarence Day

LANGUAGE OF GOD

Aside from a few odd words in Hebrew, I took it completely for granted that God had never spoken anything but the most dignified English.

> *From "Father Interferes with the Twenty-third Psalm" in his* Life with Father *(1957).*

□

Moshe Dayan

PUNISHMENT ENOUGH

The only revenge I would take on the captured Egyptian soldiers would be to make them eat the same food our boys eat.

> *After the defeat of Egypt in the June 1967 Six-Day War.*

A TWO-WAY STREET

The Arabs may have all the oil, but we have all the credit cards.

> *Calming the apprehension that Jews might suffer as a result of the Arab boycott following the 1967 Six-Day War victory.*

ISRAEL OF THE HEART

The people of Israel were exiled from their land, but their land was never exiled from their hearts. In whatever country they dwelt throughout the nineteen Diaspora centuries, they yearned for their homeland, Israel.

> *From his* Living with the Bible *(1978).*

FOR LOVE OF HOMELAND

To one who was born in Israel, love of homeland was not an abstraction. The Rose of Sharon and Mount Carmel were very real to me, as were the sweet-scented blossom and the hills whose paths I climbed.

> *Ibid.*

ISRAEL: DREAM AND REALITY

My parents who came from another country sought to make the Israel of their imagination, drawn from descriptions in the Bible, their physical homeland. In somewhat the reverse way, I sought to give my real and tangible homeland the added dimension of historical depth, to bring to life the strata of the past which now lay beneath the desolate ruins and archaeological mounds—the Israel of our patriarchs, our judges, our kings, our prophets.

> *Ibid.*

FOUNDING FATHERS

The people closest to me were the founders of our nation, the patriarchs Abraham, Isaac and Jacob. They wandered over the length and breadth of the land with a staff in their hand, a knotted stick fashioned from the branch of an oak, the strongest and stoutest of trees.... They left the homes of their parents, parted from their brethren, and embarked on their lonesome path. They carried a weighty burden—a new faith, a new nation, a new land.

Ibid.

□

Yael Dayan

PEACE ON PROBATION

The Declaration of Principles, the "breakthrough" of mutual recognition, the PLO flags flying in Jericho, the historic handshake—all are being measured now through rifle sights or with dagger blades.

The bulldozed road has become a pitted dirt-track. The horizon has dwindled down to the next junction, and no one can see the mountaintop any longer. The word "peace" has been put on probation, depending on the number of attacks and weekly violations of order.

From an article in The Jerusalem Post, *December 18, 1993.*

□

Massimo d'Azeglio

REPAIRING THE DAMAGE

Let us extend our hands to our Jewish brothers and repair the damage caused by the outrageous insults they had to endure from those who do not merit the name Christian.

Commenting on the horrible living conditions in the ghetto of Rome and the fate of its Jews in 1848, three centuries after the ghetto was established. Quoted in Sam Waagenaar's Pope's Jews *(1974).*

□

Moshe Dechter

THE BACKS OF OTHER JEWS

The majority of those [Soviet Jews] who have left or who are still to leave have, in a sense, gotten a free ride: they are riding out on the backs of those in Israel who generated the movement for Soviet Jewish rights, including the right to leave. They are riding out on the

backs of that handful of noble Russian Zionists who risked their freedom and their lives for those rights... They have a great moral obligation to Israel, which they can assuredly be called upon to discharge. They can legitimately be called upon to give back something to the state that made it possible for them to leave as Jews.

From an article in The Jewish Week, *December 3–9, 1993.*

□

Charles de Gaulle

VITIATION OF VICHY

Be assured that since we have repudiated everything that has falsely been done in the name of France after June 23rd [1940], the cruel decrees directed against French Jews can and will have no validity in Free France. These measures are not less a blow against the honor of France than they are an injustice against her Jewish citizens.

From a message to the American Jewish Congress, dated November 11, 1940, in light of the betrayal of French independence by the Vichy government.

□

Jacob de Haas

ISRAEL'S WANDER-LAND

The territory is unique in that it has only one page in all human history—it was Israel's wander-land for forty years.

From his Theodor Herzl *(1927).*

□

Maurice de Hirsch

HUMANITY IS MY HEIR

My son I have lost, but not my heir; humanity is my heir.

A reply to a message that he had lost his son (1887).

□

Louis de Jong

HOPING AGAINST HOPE

It may be true that over a hundred thousand Jews were deported, but it is equally true that the Dutch underground tried to save 25,000 Jews. I would like to add that many Jews, my own parents among them, refused the help that was offered them because they believed that deportation gave them a better chance to survive than going into hiding.

From a 1990 Harvard lecture. Quoted in Eva Fogelman's Conscience & Courage *(1994).*

◻

Jerry della Femina

FOOD MAVENS

Always have a restaurant where 40 to 50 percent of your clientele is Jewish. They make the best customers. That's why I'm looking at Greenwich—it's so near Westchester.

Upon opening a new restaurant in Greenwich, Connecticut. "My goal is to ring New York City with restaurants," he added.

◻

Joseph del Medigo

BOOKS LIKE SOULS

It seems to me that books are subject to the same process as souls: they migrate from one body to another. Not by chance are "son" and "book" designated in Latin by the same term, liber. And so it is in the case of scholarly books that are translated from one language into another, in a different style, in other words, and in changed order. The language becomes different but the content is the same.

Quoted in Nahum Glatzer's In Time and Eternity *(1946).*

◻

Cecil B. DeMille

VAUDEVILLE AT ITS HEIGHT

There was a Lasky touch, a Lasky finish and polish about his productions that made them unique.... If the bill included a Lasky musical, you left the vaudeville theater well satisfied and with a lilt. Lasky was a showman's showman.

From his Autobiography, *commenting on the quality of Jesse L. Lasky's productions.*

◻

Alan M. Dershowitz

MORE CHUTZPAH

American Jews need more chutzpah. Notwithstanding the stereotype, we are not pushy or assertive enough for our own good and for the good of our more vulnerable brothers and sisters in other parts of the world.

From his Chutzpah *(1991).*

THE "SHANDA" FACTOR

The byword of past generations of Jewish Americans has been *shanda*—fear of embarrassment in front of our hosts. The byword of the next generation should be *chutzpah*—assertive insistence on first-class status among our peers.

Ibid.

AMERICA IS DIFFERENT

We are not a "Christian nation" or even a "Judeo-Christian nation." Nor are we an Anglo-Saxon people or a white people. A majority does not a national character make, as evidenced by the obvious fact that we are not a woman's nation, just because a majority of our citizens are female. We are truly a diverse nation of immigrants, where all are equal under law.

Ibid.

STEREOTYPING THE JEWS

Reverend [Jesse] Jackson, some people think you are an anti-Semite. I now understand that such a characterization misses the point. You are simply ignorant about the Jewish community. You just don't know what we are about. You don't understand our complexity. And therefore you tend to stereotype, in much the same way that many whites—including Jews—who don't know the black community tend to stereotype your people.

Ibid. After Jackson's comment that many Jews have a commitment to both progressive causes and the cause of Israel.

A HUMAN RIGHTS DOCUMENT

Something is wrong. Zionism is still a dirty word. When I walk around Harvard with my button that says I am a proud Zionist, people look at me as if I'm making an admission, as if it were the '50s and I'm wearing a button that says I am a communist.

We have not taught our young people how to explain the Law of Return, one of the great human rights documents of the 20th century. They think it's an exclusionary, apartheid-type of legislation when in fact it is the ultimate affirmative action to the world's failure to open its doors to the Jews.

From an April 1993 speech at an American Zionist organization luncheon.

HISTORICAL OBLIGATION

Though I was brought up as an Orthodox Jew, my interest in the survival of the Jewish community did not crystallize until the days leading up to the Six-Day War. The fear of another Holocaust directed against a vulnerable Jewish community made me think hard about the inaction of American Jews during World War II and the silence of American Jewry toward oppressed Jews in Russia and elsewhere.... As a safe and secure American Jew, I knew then that I had a moral and historical obligation to use whatever power I possessed to help avoid the historic cycle of oppression directed against vulnerable Jews.

Quoted in Hadassah Magazine, *March 1994.*

THE ORTHODOX DERSHOWITZ

My Orthodoxy, my observance totally filled my Jewish quota. I didn't have to think of anything else.

Discussing his early youth. From an interview with Elinor and Robert Slater. Quoted in their Great Jewish Men *(1996).*

THE DOUBTING DERSHOWITZ

I was never that theological. I was always something of a skeptic and a doubter. I was a terrible Yeshiva student because I was always raising questions. I had to reconcile evolution with the story of Creation. So I was a bad religious student but I was observant. My father's attitude was: It doesn't matter if you have doubts, come to synagogue.

Ibid.

SO I BECAME A LAWYER

I never thought I had talents in anything else. I was told by my Yeshiva teachers that I wasn't too bright, but I had a good mouth so I should either be a lawyer or a Conservative rabbi. It was one of the most insulting things you could tell a young Orthodox Jewish boy. I didn't want to be a rabbi, so I became a lawyer.

Ibid.

IDENTIFYING WITH SOVIET JEWRY

I identified with the Soviet Jewry movement even more than I did with Israel because I felt that I could have been a Soviet Jew.

Ibid.

A PLEA FOR CLEMENCY

He pleaded guilty. He fully cooperated. He helped the government in its damage assessment. He spied for a country which was an ally of the United States.... These are not defenses, but those certainly argue against the maximum possible punishment, which is what he got.

Arguing for a reduced sentence for Jonathan Pollard, who had been convicted of spying for Israel against the United States.

FUHRMAN AND HITLER

The Jewish outrage at a black man [Johnnie Cochran] making reference to Hitler seemed a bit overdone, especially since many Jews seem to make far more outrageous Hitler comparisons with far less criticism. Ben-Gurion compared Begin to Hitler. Several Israeli and American rabbis have compared Rabin to Hitler. The former director of the ADL called Farrakhan a "Black Hitler."

Countering the many letters criticizing O. J. Simpson's defense lawyer, Johnnie Cochran, for comparing Los Angeles rogue-cop Mark Fuhrman to Hitler in the trial summation in September 1995. From his article in The Jerusalem Report, *November 16, 1995.*

❏

Giscard d'Estaing

THE ELEVATION OF WOMEN

Madame Simone Veil has symbolized the rise of women to the highest positions of responsibility in French society. By her simplicity, her dignity, her competence, she has illustrated the indispensable contribution of women in the public life.

When Veil was elevated to preside over the European Parliament in June 1979.

❏

Gotthard Deutsch

TEETERING ON THE BRINK

You of the snobocratic Jewish ministry will drive me in my old age into the ranks of Zionism, for no mattering how confused and chimerical their ideas may be, there is at least self-respect in their camp.

From a letter to his friend, Rabbi Joseph Stolz, January 11, 1917.

SOCIAL CONSCIOUSNESS

I am not only a Jew, but an official Jew. Nevertheless, a strike on a railroad or in a coal mine touches me more deeply than the possibility of being rejected by a fashionable summer resort hotel or even a country club, should

I ever have had the ambition of knocking at their doors.

From a May 24, 1920 communication to Leon Kellner in which the former president of Hebrew Union College, an outspoken pro-German protagonist during World War I, explains the kind of person he is.

○

Israel Deutsch

MESSIANIC BELIEF

It is the comforting and uplifting faith in Messiah which has sustained the Jews through the fateful times of oppression.

From an address delivered on July 2, 1839.

○

Isaac Deutscher

THE MESSAGE OF JUDAISM

The world has compelled the Jew to embrace the nation-state and to make of it his pride and hope just at a time when there is little or no hope left in it. You cannot blame the Jews for this; you must blame the world. But Jews should at least be aware of the paradox and realize that their intense enthusiasm for "national sovereignty" is historically belated....

I hope, therefore, that, together with other nations, the Jews will ultimately become aware—or regain the awareness—of the inadequacy of the nation-state and that they will find their way back to the moral and political heritage that the genius of the Jews who have gone beyond Jewry has left us—the message of universal human emancipation.

In his essay "The Non-Jewish Jew," based on a lecture to the World Jewish Congress during Jewish Book Week in February 1958.

○

Eliezer Diamond

RUTH: THE HEROINE

If ever I loved a woman I neither saw nor met, it is Ruth, the heroine of the biblical book that bears her name. My love affair with Ruth is a longstanding one and, as in many affairs of the heart, affection preceded comprehension. For the longest time, I could not understand what drew me to her.

From the Spring 1993 issue of Masoret *magazine.*

○

Charles Dickens

ALL JEWS ARE ALIKE

Men find the bad among us easily enough. They take the worst of us as samples of the best; they take the lowest of us as presentations of the highest; and they say, "All Jews are alike."

Spoken by Riah in his Our Mutual Friend *(1865).*

○

Morris Dickstein

ILLUSORY MR. HOWE

He was not in and of the Jewish world, but in a sense an emissary from it to a larger cosmopolitan world.

Opening comments at a day-long April 1994 conference at the City University of New York paying tribute to Irving Howe, who died in May 1993.

○

(Rabbi) Dimi

YOUTH AND OLD AGE

Youth is a crown of roses; old age a crown of [heavy to bear] willow-rods.

Quoted in the talmudic tractate Shabbat (152a).

○

Max Dimont

SMOTHERING JEWISH HISTORY

For all too long, Jews and Christians have distorted Jewish history with so many pious frauds and smothered it with so much pious mythology that at times it has been difficult for scholar or layman to perceive its real grandeur.

In the Preface to his Indestructible Jews *(1971).*

AMERICAN JUDAISM

To those who view purist Orthodoxy as the only authentic Judaism, American Judaism is nothing but a wasteland.

From the Introduction to his Jews in America *(1978).*

ESSENCE OF SURVIVAL

The Jews have survived friendly bedrooms, persecutions, expulsions, concentration camps. But there was always a commitment to Judaism, which permitted Jewish history to march unimpeded into the next challenge.

Ibid.

JEWISH SOCIALISM

Jewish socialism laid the foundation for an important segment of both the American labor movement and much of the social legislation of President Franklin Delano Roosevelt's New Deal. Whereas the communists viewed socialism as scientific materialism, the Jewish socialists thought of it as ethical humanism. They were impelled toward their social goals by moral indignation rather than by rational hate.

Ibid. Referring to the four decades from 1880 to 1920.

¤

Thomas Dine

UNFORGIVABLE INDISCRETION

I don't think mainstream Jews feel very comfortable with the ultra-Orthodox. It is a class thing, I suppose. Their image is "smelly." That's what I'd say now that you've got me thinking about it. Hasids and New York diamond dealers.

United Jewish Appeal people have told me several times that they don't want to fly El Al because of "those people."... But I fly El Al to Israel because it is direct. Yes, TWA flies direct, too. But it is low class, like the Orthodox. Yes, that's still the image. Still the poor immigrant image. That's the perception of a lot of people I mix with.

In a 1989 interview with Israeli journalist David Landau. Reported in Landau's Piety and Power: The World of Jewish Fundamentalism *(1993). Because of this statement, Dine was forced to resign his position as head of AIPAC (American Israel Public Affairs Committee), the Washington-based Israel lobby, a position he had filled successfully.*

¤

Simcha Dinitz

THEORETICAL VS. PRACTICAL ANTI-SEMITISM

Rutskoi was very sympathetic to Israel.... He spoke with me very strongly about the anti-Semitic forces existing in Russia. He said he was very concerned that unless they dealt with anti-Semitism with a strong hand it might move from theoretical to real violence. We're basically a country with a totalitarian tradition, and in such a country, the line between theoretical and practical anti-Semitism is a very thin one.

Reporting on a 1992 meeting with the then vice-president under Boris Yeltsin. Dinitz was negotiating to permit the Jewish Agency to operate freely in Russia.

NO MORE JEWISH "REFUGEES"

Israel cannot erase anti-Semitism. But it did erase the term "refugee" from the Jewish dictionary. With the establishment of Israel, no more are boats roaming the seas with people looking for a home. Every Jew has a home now when he decides to live in it. There never will again be Jewish refugees.

In an address delivered at the World Conference on Anti-Semitism and Prejudice in a Changing World, held in Brussels, Belgium, July 1992.

LAME EXCUSE

I shop at Syms.

The spendthrifty former Jewish Agency chief executive trying to prove that he is a very modest spender and shops at low-price stores.

¤

Benjamin Disraeli

A JEW WITH PRIDE

Yes, I am a Jew, and when the ancestors of the right honourable gentleman were brutal savages in an unknown island, mine were priests in the Temple of Solomon.

In reply to a taunt by Daniel O'Connell, who accused Disraeli of being a descendant of "miscreant" Jews.

FOR LOVE OF FAMILY

A man, however fallen, who loves his home, is not wholly lost.

Quoted in J. H. Hertz's Book of Jewish Thoughts *(1917).*

THE BLANK PAGE

Your Majesty, you know that in most editions of the Holy Bible there is the Old Testament and then there is the New Testament, and in between the two there is an empty, blank page. I am that blank page.

His response to Queen Victoria, who was puzzled about her prime minister. Disraeli had been converted into the Anglican faith at age thirteen yet never cut his ties to the Jewish people.

FIRST LOVE

The magic of first love is the ignorance that it can ever end.

From his Henrietta Temple *(1837).*

ISRAEL SURVIVES

Empires and dynasties flourish and pass away; the proud metropolis becomes a solitude, the conquering kingdom even a desert: but Israel still remains.

From his Alroy *(1833).*

I WILL RETURN

Though I sit down now, the time will come when you will hear me.

From his Maiden Speech in Parliament, ecember 7, 1837.

SLIPPERY CLIMB

Yes, I have climbed to the top of the greasy pole.

Ibid. Reminiscing upon his election as prime minister.

INSTITUTIONS FROM A NATION

Individuals may form communities, but it is institutions alone that can create a nation.

From an 1866 speech in Manchester, England.

POLITICAL LARCENY

His life has been a great appropriation clause. He is a burglar of the other's intellect.... There is no statesman who has committed political petty larceny on so great a scale.

Commenting on the character of Prime Minister Sir Robert Peel. From a speech to the House of Commons on May 15, 1847.

ON MRS. DISRAELI

She is an excellent creature, but she never can remember which came first, the Greeks or the Romans.

About his wife, Mary Ann. By attribution.

EVOLUTION REJECTED

The question is this: Is man an ape or an angel? My lord, I am on the side of the angels. I repudiate with indignation and abhorrence of these new-fangled theories.

From a November 25, 1864 speech before the Diocesan Conference in Oxford.

NO ROOM FOR FAILURE

We belong to a race that can do everything but fail.

Quoted in J. de Haas's Theodore Herzl *(1927).*

THE GRUMBLER

His temper naturally morose, has become licentiously peevish. Crossed in his Cabinet, he insults the House of Lords, and plagues the most eminent of his colleagues with the crabbed malice of a maundering witch.

Criticizing the Earl of Aberdeen in an 1853 letter to the press.

UNCOUPLED MARRIAGES

I have always thought that every woman should marry, and no man.

From his Lothair *(1870).*

FATAL BOOKS

Books are fatal: they are the curse of the human race. Nine-tenths of existing books are nonsense, and the clever books are the refutation of that nonsense. The greatest misfortune that ever befell man was the invention of printing.

Ibid.

CIVILITIES OF MAN

Increased means and increased leisure are the two civilizers of man.

From a speech in Manchester, England, April 3, 1872.

PRIDE OF AUTHORSHIP

An author who speaks about his own books is almost as bad as a mother who talks about her own children.

At a banquet in his honor given by Glasgow University, November 19, 1873.

JERUSALEM AND THE WORLD

Jerusalem at midday in midsummer is a city of stone in a land of iron with a sky of brass.... The view of Jerusalem is the history of the world; it is more, it is the history of earth and heaven.

From his Tancred *(1847).*

A CALL FOR PATIENCE

Everything comes if a man will only wait.

Ibid.

WHAT IS CHRISTIANITY?

Christianity is Judaism for the multitude.

Quoted in Nahum Sokolow's History of Zionism *(1919).*

IN DEFENSE OF JEWS

It is as a Christian that I will not take upon me the awful responsibility of excluding from the legislature those who are from the religion in the bosom of which my Lord and Saviour was born.

> *Speaking in the House of Commons in defense of Lionel de Rothschild, who won several elections to the Parliament but was not permitted to serve for some time because he was a Jew. Quoted in Stanley Weintraub's* Disraeli: A Biography *(1993).*

INSECT WORSHIP

If a traveler were informed that such a man was leader of the House of Commons, he may begin to comprehend how the Egyptians worshipped an insect.

> *In evaluating Lord John Russell. Quoted in Morris Mandel's* Affronts, Insults, and Indignities *(1975).*

THREE KINDS OF LIES

There are three kinds of lies: lies, damned lies, and statistics.

> *Ibid.*

THE RULE OF LIFE

Religion should be the rule of life, not a casual incident.

> *From his* Internal Marriage *(1834).*

LEARNING FROM EXPERIENCE

Experience is the child of thought, and thought is the child of Action. We cannot learn men from books.

> *From his* Vivian Grey *(1826).*

MOTHER OF ENJOYMENT

Variety is the mother of Enjoyment.

> *Ibid.*

MAN AND CIRCUMSTANCES

Man is not a creature of circumstances. Circumstances are the creatures of man.

> *Ibid.*

LITTLE MINDS

Little things affect little minds.

> *From his* Sybil *(1845).*

LIVING A CIRCLE

We, all of us, live too much in a circle.

> *Ibid.*

TRUTH IN ACTION

Justice is truth in action.

> *From a February 11, 1851 speech.*

THE WORLD IS A WHEEL

The world is a wheel, and it will all come round right.

> *From his* Endymion.

STAGES OF MAN

Youth is a blunder; manhood a struggle; old age a regret.

> *From his* Coningsby *(1844).*

THE MANLY MAN

Life is too short to be little. Man is never so manly as when he feels deeply, acts boldly, and expresses himself with frankness and with fervour.

> *Ibid.*

ㅁ

Roland B. Dixon

SEMITIC NOSES

The proportion of so-called "Semitic" noses is very much greater among the non-Jewish population.

> *From his* Racial History of Man *(1923).*

ㅁ

Robert Dole

ON LOBBYISTS

You can't say one word [of criticism about Israel] without the whole apparatus...coming down on top of you.... I don't believe any one group—whether it's the Israeli lobby or any other lobby—should in effect run our foreign policy.... In my view, if you're friends, and I think I am a friend, you ought to be able to discuss things out in the open without being pounced on by the Israeli lobby.

> *Commenting on such organizations as AIPAC (American Israel Public Affairs Committee), the pro-Israel lobby. From a January 20, 1990 appearance on the* Evans and Novak *television program in which the senator proposed a five percent cut in aid to Israel.*

A DAY TO REMEMBER

I've been around here for a while and I can't remember a day like today.

> *After listening to the speeches of King Hussein of Jordan and Yitzhak Rabin of Israel on July 26, 1994, celebrating the end of a state of war between the two nations.*

RELOCATING THE AMERICAN EMBASSY

What are we waiting for? The time has come to move beyond letters, expressions of support and sense-of-Congress resolutions.

At the AIPAC's annual policy conference on May 8, 1995, urging that the American Embassy be moved from Tel Aviv to Jerusalem.

¤

Nelson Doubleday

ANTI-SEMITISM IN BASEBALL

Well, I guess the Jew boys have gotten to you.

When he learned in September 1992 that the Jewish owners of the Chicago White Sox and Milwaukee Brewers, Jerry Reinsdorf and Bud Selig, were urging that Fay Vincent be ousted as commissioner of baseball. Quoted in John Helyar's Lords of the Realm: The Real History of Baseball *(1994).*

¤

Kirk Douglas

LOOK TO THE WOMAN

If you want to know about a man, you can find out an awful lot by looking at who he married.

Quoted in London's Daily Mail, *September 9, 1988.*

THE END OF THE MATTER

All this talk about equality. The only thing people really have in common is that they are all going to die.

Quoted in Roberts Shelton's No Direction Home *(1986).*

TO BE A JEW

It took me a long time to learn that you didn't have to be a rabbi to be a Jew.

From a 1994 speech at the Los Angeles Synagogue for the Performing Arts.

THE NAZI LOOK

Of course, I was always proud to be a Jew, even though it would have been easier for me not to be. I remember when I auditioned as a young actor in a Yiddish theater in New York. They looked at me and said: "If we have a part for a Nazi, we'll call you."

Ibid.

YOM KIPPUR IS SPECIAL

Throughout my life, when I was moving farther and farther from Judaism, I always clung to a single thread—Yom Kippur. On that one day I fasted. I might be shooting it out with Burt Lancaster or John Wayne, or battling Laurence Olivier and his Romans [in *Spartacus*], but I always fasted.

Ibid.

NEVER TOO LATE

I hope it's not too late.

If God is a patient God, maybe he'll give me enough time to learn the things I need to know to understand what it is that makes us Jews the conscience of the world.

Ibid.

¤

Dov Ber of Mezeritch

THE OPEN ROAD

To live the life of a good man is to follow the call of the open road [*Derech nikra tzadik*].

Quoted by Rabbi Ben Zion Bokser in Best Jewish Sermons of 5713 *(1953), edited by Saul I. Teplitz.*

THE STAGE OF NOTHINGNESS

For an object to undergo a change, it must first go through a stage of being nothing. This state is nothing more than a primal state that came before Creation; a state of chaos that no man can imagine. It is much like a planted seed: before it can sprout, it must rot away to nothing and lose its very seed-hood. Now the name for this rung is *chochma*, for *chochma* is the stage in thought where nothing is as yet tangible.

By attribution.

¤

Lorenzo Dow

OUT-JEWING JEWS

Jews cannot flourish among Yankees, who are said to out-Jew them in trading.

From his Dealings of God, Man and the Devil *(1833).*

¤

Olin Downes

VIOLIN PRODIGY

It seems ridiculous to say that he [Yehudi Menuhin] showed a mature conception of Beethoven's concerto, but that is the fact.... A boy of eleven proved conclusively his right to be ranked, irrespective of his years, with outstanding interpreters of this music.

Commenting after a 1928 solo appearance of the child prodigy at Carnegie Hall.

◻

Fran Drescher

A JEWISH TV CHARACTER

I'm the only Jew on TV who isn't afraid to say I'm Jewish or talk about being Jewish. I'm the one who teaches these people [the show's non-Jewish family] how to have a real Christmas. I'm the one that shows them that family and togetherness are what's important. This was a show about a Jew who is having a Christmas every Jew dreams of. To deny that growing up, it seemed like Christmas was a more fun holiday—if anybody wasn't honest about that, they're bullshitting themselves.

Defending the role she plays in The Nanny, *a CBS situation comedy that she conceived, coproduces, and writes with her husband, Peter Marc Jacobson. Quoted by Sheli Teitelbaum in* The Jerusalem Report, *April 21, 1994.*

◻

Samuel R. Driver

LESSON OF THE PLAGUES

The story of the plagues is drawn with unfading colours, and its typical and didactic significance cannot be overrated. It depicts the impotence of man's strongest determination when it essays to contend with God, and the fruitlessness of all human efforts to frustrate His purposes.

Quoted in J.H. Hertz's Pentateuch and Haftorahs *(1961).*

◻

Don Drysdale

O, TO BE JEWISH

I bet right now you wish I was Jewish too.

Comment made to Los Angeles Dodgers manager Walt Alston after the pitcher had given up six runs in the third inning of the first game of the 1965 World Series. It fell on Yom Kippur and Sandy Koufax refused to pitch that day.

◻

Simon M. Dubnow

MILITARY VS. SPIRITUAL DISCIPLINE

The spiritual discipline of the [religious] school came to mean for the Jew what military discipline is for other nations.

From his Jewish History *(1903).*

INNER AND OUTER BEAUTY

The Hellenes paid homage first and foremost to external beauty and physical strength; the Judeans to inner beauty and spiritual heroism.

Ibid.

LOVE OF LEARNING

In those gloomy, tumbledown Jewish houses, intellectual endeavor was at white heat. The torch of faith blazed clear in them.... In the abject, dishonored son of the Ghetto was hidden an intellectual giant.

Ibid.

TAPPING THE JEWISH SOUL

The first part of Jewish history, the biblical part, is a source from which, for many centuries, millions of human beings have derived instruction, solace, and inspiration.... But a time will come—perhaps it is not very far off—when the second half of Jewish history, that people's life after the biblical period, will be accorded the same treatment. The thousand years' martyrdom of the Jewish People, its unbroken pilgrimage, its tragic fate, its teachers of religion, its martyrs, philosophers, champions—this whole epic will, in days to come, sink deep into the memory of men. It will speak to the heart and conscience of men, and secure respect for the silvery hair of the Jewish People.

Quoted in J. H. Hertz's Pentateuch and Haftorahs *(1961).*

SAD SEDER NIGHT

We celebrated the Seder with the Winawars. We ate our *matza* in tears and silence. We read the Haggadah and tried to chant its songs, but the mood was lacking. The question *Ma nishtana....* "Why is this night different..." went unanswered. There is no answer. We are just slaves, given to shame and slaughter.

Noted in his diary in 1915, after the outbreak of war in 1914 between Germany and Russia, which brought untold suffering to the Jewish people. Quoted in Chaim Raphael's Feast of History *(1972).*

LEAGUE OF NATIONS OBITUARY

Now that the League of Nations is dead, the Jewish people has no one to whom to appeal. Its only support are the progressive forces of humanity.

In a November 1938 letter to his student Dr. Tcherikover, residing in Paris.

AT ONE WITH HUMANITY

What is to be done? If there is war, we should recruit volunteers in the anti-Hitlerist armies. We shall exist or we shall perish together with humanity.

From a letter dated May 4, 1939.

JEWS, WRITE IT DOWN

Jews, don't forget! Write it down! Write everything down. Tell everything that is happening.

His last words before being executed by the Nazis in Riga, Latvia, in December 1941. He was eighty-one years old.

¤

Marcel Dubois

THE OPEN WOUND

It was like a Barnum and Bailey circus.... When we meet, Jews and Christians, even in the most beautiful communion, there is still an open wound that separates us.

Comment made in February 1994 at the International Jewish–Christian Conference held in Jerusalem. Quoted in The Jerusalem Report, *April 21, 1994.*

¤

Abraham G. Duker

DIVERSITY IN AMERICA

Every Jew carries his own *Shulchan Aruch* [*Code of Jewish Law*].

Commenting in 1949 on the diversity of religious observance in America. Quoted in the Proceedings of the American Jewish Historical Society, *Vol. 39, September 1949–June 1950.*

THE FOURTH GENERATION

While there has been a marked return to Jewish affiliation and identification among the "third generation"—the grandchildren of the immigrants—the position of the fourth generation remains a puzzle, particularly in view of its limited Jewish education and narrow Jewish contacts within a particular synagogue, class or association.

Indeed, it is possible to note both positive and negative trends, signs of hope and despair, in a community estimated to be five to six million strong and in various stages of acculturation to American life and of readjustment to Jewishness.

From "Some Trends Affecting American Jewish Life." Quoted in Jacob Fried's Jews in the Modern World, *Volume II (1962).*

¤

John Foster Dulles

ON ZIONISM

We were in the present jam [in the Middle East] because the past Administration has always dealt with the area from a political standpoint and had tried to meet the wishes of the Zionists in this country, and that had created a basic antagonism with the Arabs.

From a Department of State memorandum, October 21, 1955.

¤

Profiat Duran

A DESIRE FOR LEARNING

The House of Learning should be beautiful and pleasing in structure. This increases the desire for learning, and strengthens the memory because the viewing of pleasing forms and beautiful reliefs and drawings rejoices the heart and strengthens the mind.

An exhortation that artistic expression be encouraged.

¤

Andrea Dworkin

THE FACE OF REALISM

Being a Jew, one learns to believe in the reality of cruelty and one learns to recognize indifference to human suffering as a fact.

From her Letters from a War Zone *(1978).*

¤

Bob Dylan

WHEN TO CALL A MAN A MAN

How many roads must a man walk down
Before you can call him a man?

From the 1962 song "Blowin' in the Wind."

RECALLING THE PAST

"Equality," I spoke the word
As if a wedding vow.
Ah, but I was so much older then,
I'm younger than that now.

From the 1964 song "My Back Pages."

LET'S JUST BE FRIENDS

I don't want to fake you out,
Take or shake or forsake you out,
I ain't lookin' for you to feel like me,
See like me or be like me.
All I really want to do
Is, baby, be friends with you.

From his Writings and Drawings *(1973).*

Abba Eban

HOLOCAUST LEGACY

The legacy of the Holocaust is still acutely relevant to an understanding of Israel's consciousness today. It explains the obsessive concern with physical security; the innate suspicion of Gentile intentions; the firm conviction that Israel's small sovereignty is a minimal justice in comparison to the vast inheritance of Arab freedom in eighteen states.

> *From his Introduction to* Hannah Senesh: Her Life & Diary *(1971).*

ON BEING JEWISH

If six million people are killed only because they are Jews, then being Jewish must obviously be something very important indeed. For its own health and sanity, mankind must come to terms with the Jewish condition.

> *Ibid.*

ETERNAL OPTIMISTS

Never was this people stronger than [in] its moment of weakness, never more hopeful than in its hour of despair.

> *From a 1952 address.*

MISSED OPPORTUNITY

Our Arab neighbors never lost a chance of missing an opportunity.

> *Commenting on the Arab League meeting in Khartum on September 1, 1967, when the Arabs rejected the Israeli proposal for peace and declared: "No peace, no bargaining, no recognition, and no negotiation with Israel."*

ON CHAIM WEIZMANN

Here was a lecturer in Manchester, not very high ranking in the Zionist hierarchy, who decided that if some of his friends would help him with train fare to London three times a week, he would get the British government, then the most powerful in the world, to adopt the Zionist program and he would then go on and get the rest of the family of nations to adopt the Zionist program. I call that a typical Zionist attitude—90 percent fantasy and 10

percent reality. But three years later, these things happened.

> *Reflecting upon the power of one individual—in this case Chaim Weizmann—to alter history. From an interview with Sue Fishkoff in* The Jerusalem Post, *November 7, 1992.*

CONSENT FOR COEXISTENCE

The security of a nation-state depends not exclusively on its territorial configuration, but also and mainly, upon its inner cohesion, the rhythm of solidarity between its citizens, the capacity to share common memories and devotions. In the historic 1947 U.N. debate, when an Arab delegate urged that "Arabs and Zionists should be *forced* to accept the 'axiom' of a single state," the Canadian delegate quietly remarked: "Mutual consent is necessary for living together. Without consent there must be separation." Ironically, it was the Zionist camp which then applauded that remark.

> *From an essay in* Tikkun *magazine, Vol.1, No. 2.*

PALESTINIAN AND ISRAELI INTERESTS

If Israel were able safely to disengage from the tasks of ruling the densely populated Arab areas of the West Bank and Gaza, it would not only be making a concession to Palestinian rights; it would also be serving Israel's values and interests.

> *Ibid.*

ACCEPTANCE OF CRITICISM

There are some who ask whether Diaspora Jews should express themselves about Israel's predicaments at all. I can only say this: If we say to Diaspora Jews that we want your money and we want your political support but we don't want to hear your opinion; if we say that Jewish support must have a financial and political but not an intellectual dimension, then the Jewish Diaspora will probably accept that limitation but will subside into silence, leaving the Israeli cause diminished.

> *From* Moment *magazine, December 1980.*

ATTAINING WISDOM

History teaches us that men and nations behave wisely once they have exhausted all other alternatives.

From a speech delivered in London, December 16, 1970.

PRODDING ANCIENT ROOTS

There is no other modern nation whose motives of existence and action require such frequent reference to distant days. This is true of Israel in the Diaspora, as it is of Israel in the community of nations.... I recall Kierkegaard's words: "Life must be lived forward, but can only be understood backward."

From the Foreword to his My People: The Story of the Jews *(1968).*

NEED FOR CONSENSUS

Since Palestinian statehood is neither improbable nor necessarily catastrophic, an opposition party that cherishes truth and national solidarity should be seeking consensus with the government on how to ensure that such a state is as innocuous and even as creative as it can be. There is, after all, no way back to Gaza.

From an article in Heritage Southwest Jewish Press, *June 17, 1994.*

AMERICAN JEWS VIEW ISRAEL

American Jews have always been a few months or years behind [developments in the Middle East]. They still think of Israel as a quivering and whimpering victim liable to go out of existence....

From an address at a conference on Israel–Diaspora relations convened in June 1994 by Israeli President Ezer Weizman.

ENEMIES OF ISRAEL

For American Jews, an enemy of Israel is someone who agrees with Israel [only] 95 percent of the time.

Ibid.

¤

A. Roy Eckhardt

WHY SIX MILLION JEWS PERISHED

The few voices that were raised [during the Holocaust] merely helped to make the general stillness louder. When at the beginning of the crisis Protestant and Catholic organizations were asked by the American Jewish community to call upon our government to stand by Israel, there was no institutional response. The U.S. Conference of Catholic Bishops gave no word and the National Council of Churches was content to urge "compassion and concern for all the people of the Middle East."...The fact is that church groups either ignored the entire problem or announced a policy of neutralism.

From his Elder and Younger Brothers: The Encounter of Christians and Jews *(1968).*

INVENTORS OF ANTI-SEMITISM

Opposition to Jews is the one constant of Christian history.

From his Your People, My People: The Meeting of Jews and Christians *(1974).*

AUSCHWITZ AND THE CHURCH

Could there be a more damning judgment upon the Church of our century than this one—that not until after the day of Auschwitz did Christians see fit to fabricate a correction of the record?

Ibid.

ANTI-SEMITISM IN CHRISTIAN SCRIPTURE

To shut my eyes to the anti-Semitic proclivities of the Christian Scripture is indefensible.

From a 1971 statement.

¤

Anthony Eden

EXCUSES, EXCUSES

Hitler might well take us up on such an offer and there simply are not enough ships in the world to handle them.

According to Harry Hopkins this was the March 1943 response of the British foreign secretary when Jewish leaders pleaded that sixty to seventy thousand Bulgarian Jews be moved to Turkey.

¤

Henry Morris Edmonds

NOT A WORD OF APPRECIATION

We have taken your Bible over and made it ours, and said never a word of appreciation of the genius for God which produced it...We have called peace a Christian attitude, forgetting that it was a Jew who first used those words, which now belong to humanity, about beating swords into plowshares and spears into pruning hooks.

Quoted in the Federal Council Bulletin, *June 1931.*

◻

Jonathan Edwards

JEWS AND THEIR LAW

[The Jews] had a very superstitious and extravagant notion of their law...as if it were the prime, grand, and indeed the only rule of God's proceeding with mankind.

From a sermon in his Original Sin *(1970).*

MISTAKEN NOTION

One reason why the Jews looked upon themselves as better than the Gentiles, and called themselves holy and the Gentiles sinners, was that they had the law of Moses.

Ibid.

◻

David Max Eichhorn

SINCERE CONVERTS

The question that may be asked is, "How much of the conversion was dependent upon a real belief in the principles of Judaism and how much upon convenience?" We have an example in Norma Shearer, who converted to Judaism when she married the late Irving Thalberg. She became the president of the sisterhood of Rabbi Magnin's synagogue in Los Angeles. Then her next husband was a Catholic, and she converted to Roman Catholicism and married him. So we certainly cannot claim Norma Shearer as a very sincere convert.

Quoted in William Berkowitz's Ten Vital Jewish Issues *(1964).*

◻

Adolf Eichmann

VOICE OF INNOCENCE

There are other men who can look upon such actions. I cannot. At night I cannot sleep. I dream. I cannot do it.

Statement made in July 1941 after being ordered by Gestapo Chief Heinrich Muller to observe the mass murders being conducted in some concentration camps.

THE GREAT CAPTURE OF ADOLF EICHMANN

Ich bin Adolf Eichmann.

The immediate response to the first question put to Eichmann after he was taken captive by an Israeli team who had been stalking him in Buenos Aires, Argentina, in the spring of 1960.

EARLY ATONEMENT

If it would give greater significance to the act of atonement, I am ready to hang myself in public.

Upon his capture in May 1960. Quoted in Moshe Pearlman's Capture and Trial of Adolf Eichmann *(1963).*

NO REGRETS

To sum it up, I regret nothing.

While awaiting trial in Israel in 1960.

HARA-KIRI EICHMANN-STYLE

I shall gladly jump into the pit, knowing that in the same pit there are five million enemies of the state.

Reported to have so commented during his last visit to Theresienstadt in April 1945.

VOLUNTARY CONFESSION

I, the undersigned, Adolf Eichmann, state herewith of my own free will: Since my true identity has now been revealed, I realize that there is no point in my continuing to try to evade justice. I declare myself willing to proceed to Israel and to stand trial there before a competent court.

It is understood that I will receive legal counsel and I shall try to give expression, without any embroidery, to the facts relating to my last years of service in Germany, so that a true picture of the events may be transmitted to future generations. I am submitting this declaration of my own free will; I have not been promised anything and I have not been threatened. I want at last to achieve inner peace.

As I am unable to remember all the details and may also mix things up, I request that I be helped by the placing at my disposal of documents and testimonies to assist me in my endeavor to establish the truth.

Handwritten by Eichmann in Buenos Aires, Argentina, immediately after his capture. The note was written in German.

TRUCKS FOR JEWS

One million Jews for ten thousand trucks. One hundred Jews for each truck, a low price. But the trucks must be new, with all accessories, and they must be winterized. Throw in a few tons of coffee, tea, chocolate, and soap.

A proposal made to Yoel Brand, a Hungarian Jew. The deal never went through.

LAST WORDS

After a short while, gentlemen, we shall all meet again. So is the fate of all men. I have lived believing in God and I die believing in

God. Long live Germany. Long live Argentina. Long live Austria. These are the countries with which I have been most closely associated, and I shall not forget them. I greet my wife, my family and my friends. I had to obey the rules of war and my flag.

Uttered near midnight on May 31, 1962, just before the noose was placed over his head. Then, two flaps of the trap door opened and Eichmann dropped to his death.

□

Ricardo Eichmann

EICHMANN'S SON CONFESSES

I hate the Nazis and I'm glad my father is not with us now.... When I think about the suffering he caused, then I would say, yes, his punishment was justified.

From a 1995 interview with a German newspaper.

□

David Einhorn

CANCER OF THE UNION

Does the Negro have less ability to think, to feel, to will? Does he have less of a desire to happiness? Was he born not to be entitled to all these? Does the Negro have an iron neck that does not feel a burdensome yoke? Does he have a stiffer heart that does not bleed when...his beloved child is torn away from him?

From one of his many sermons on the problem of slavery, which he called "the cancer of the Union."

SLAVERY MUST BE ABOLISHED

The end never justifies the means. Slavery is immoral and must be abolished.... There are even immigrant Jews who are so blinded as to be enthusiastic for secession and slavery.

Ibid.

REBELLION AGAINST GOD!

Is it anything else but a deed of Amalek, rebellion against God, to enslave human beings created in His image?... Can *that* Book mean to raise the whip and forge chains, which proclaims, with flaming words, in the name of God: "Break the bonds of oppression, let the oppressed go free and tear every yoke!"

A rejoinder to Rabbi Morris J. Raphall's sermon in which he preached that the Bible does not consider slaveholding to be a sin. Einhorn's attack was published in his Sinai, *February–March 1861, a monthly German-language journal first issued in 1856.*

EVALUATING PEOPLE

Once we start to evaluate people by the country of birth, next will come an evaluation by religion; and in this case surely, the Jews, the so-called crucifiers of the crucified, will be in great danger.

Ibid.

COMMON DESTINIES

America of the future will not rest on slave chains or belittling its adopted citizens. It will also give up its disinterestedness in the fate of other peoples of the world.

Comparing the destiny of Jews and America. Both are to fight for justice the world over.

□

Albert Einstein

ON HIS THEORY

By an application of the theory of relativity to the taste of readers, today in Germany I am called a German man of science, and in England I am represented as a Swiss Jew. If I come to be regarded as a *bête noire*, the descriptions will be reversed, and I shall become a Swiss Jew for the Germans and a German man of science for the English!

From an article in the London Times, *November 28, 1919.*

WHAT SHOULD BE

Knowledge of what *is* does not open the door directly to what *should be*. One can have the clearest and most complete knowledge of what *is* and yet not be able to deduct from that what should be the *goal* of our human aspirations.

From his Out of My Later Years *(1936).*

HIGH DESTINY

It is only to the individual that a soul is given. And the high destiny of the individual is to serve rather than to rule.

Ibid.

YEARS OF MATURITY

I live in that solitude which is painful in youth, but delicious in the years of maturity.

Ibid.

EDUCATION'S ESSENCE

Education is that which remains when one has forgotten everything he learned in school.

Ibid.

THE GOOSESTEPPER

If someone can enjoy marching to music in rank and file, I can feel only contempt for him; he has received his large brain by mistake, a spinal cord would have been enough.

Ibid.

KNOWLEDGE RENEWED

Knowledge of truth alone does not suffice; on the contrary this knowledge must continually be renewed by ceaseless effort, if it is not to be lost. It resembles a statue of marble which stands in the desert and is continuously threatened with burial by the shifting sand. The hands of service must ever be at work, in order that the marble continue lastingly to shine in the sun.

Ibid.

LIP SERVICE

The road to perdition has ever been accompanied by lip service to an ideal.

Ibid.

GOD IS SUBTLE

God is subtle, but He is not malicious.

In a remark after first visiting Princeton University in April 1921.

GOD IS SLICK

God is slick, but He ain't mean.

Restating in 1946 his original statement of 1921: "God is subtle, but He is not malicious."

EVERYONE LOVES A WINNER

If my theory of relativity is proved successful, Germany will claim me as a German and France will claim me as a citizen of the world. Should my theory prove untrue, France will say I am a German and Germany will say I am a Jew.

From a December 1929 address delivered at the Sorbonne, in Paris.

MORALITY IS NOT DIVINE

The scientist is possessed by the sense of universal causation. The future, to him, is every whit as necessary and determined as the past. There is nothing divine about morality; it is a purely human affair. His religious feeling takes the form of a rapturous amazement at the harmony of natural law, which reveals an intelligence of such superiority that, compared with it, all the systematic thinking and acting of human beings is an utterly insignificant reflection.

From his World As I See It *(1934).*

REGAINING SELF-RESPECT

We Jews should once more become conscious of our existence as a nationality and regain the self-respect that is necessary to a healthy existence.

Ibid.

TRUE VALUE

The true value of a human being is determined primarily by the measure and sense in which he has attained to liberation from the self.

Ibid.

NOBLE TEACHERS

Academic chairs are many, but wise and noble teachers are few.

Ibid.

HOME OF THE JEWISH SPIRIT

Palestine is not primarily a place of refuge for the Jews of Eastern Europe, but the embodiment of the reawakening corporate spirit of the whole Jewish nation.

Ibid.

STATE AND MAN

The state is made for man, not man for the state.

Ibid.

DISQUALIFIED FOR LIFE

The man who regards life and that of his fellow creatures as meaningless is not merely unfortunate but almost disqualified for life.

Ibid.

FEATURES OF JEWISH TRADITION

The pursuit of knowledge for its own sake, an almost fanatical love of justice, and the desire for personal independence—these are the features of Jewish tradition which make me thank my stars that I belong to it.

Ibid.

ANTIDOTE TO ANTI-SEMITISM

Before we can effectively combat anti-Semitism, we must first of all educate ourselves out of it, and out of the slave-mentality which it betokens. Only when we respect ourselves can we win the respect of others; or rather, the respect of others will then come of itself.

Ibid.

NEGATION OF SUPERSTITION

Judaism is not a creed; the Jewish God is

simply a negation of superstition, an imaginary result of its elimination.

Ibid.

IRRECONCILABLE OPPONENTS

Those who rage today against the ideals of reason and of individual freedom, and seek to impose an insensate state of slavery by means of brutal force, rightly see in the Jews irreconcilable opponents.

Ibid.

ON GOD'S EXISTENCE

Now I know there is a God in heaven.

After listening to child prodigy Yehudi Menuhin's violin performance in Berlin in 1928.

EXPERIENCING THE MYSTERIOUS

The most beautiful thing we can experience is the mysterious. It is the source of all true art and science.

From his What I Believe *(1930).*

CONCERN FOR MAN

Concern for man himself and his fate must always form the chief interest of all technical endeavors, concern for the great unsolved problems of the organization of labor and the distribution of goods—in order that the creations of our mind shall be a blessing and not a curse to mankind. Never forget this in the midst of your diagrams and equations.

From an address delivered at the California Institute of Technology in 1931.

INEVITABILITY OF WAR

As long as there are sovereign nations possessing great power, war is inevitable.

Commenting on the atomic bomb. From an article in The Atlantic Monthly, *November 1945.*

THE ATOMIC BOMB

I do not believe that civilization will be wiped out in a war fought with the atomic bomb. Perhaps two-thirds of the people of the earth might be killed, but enough men capable of thinking, and enough books, would be left to start again, and civilization could be restored.

Ibid.

MENACE OF ATOMIC ENERGY

Since I do not foresee that atomic energy is to be a great boon for a long time, I have to say that for the present it is a menace. Perhaps it is well that it should be. It may intimidate

the human race into bringing order into its international affairs, which, without the pressure of fear, it would not do.

Ibid.

GOD DOES NOT GAMBLE

I shall never believe that God plays dice with the world.

Quoted in Philipp Frank's Einstein, His Life and Times *(1947).*

GOD PLAYING DICE

You believe in a dice-playing God, and I in the perfect rule of law within a world of objective reality.

From a letter to physicist Max Born. Quoted in Born's Natural Philosophy of Cause and Chance *(1949).*

ON SPINOZA

I believe in Spinoza's God who reveals Himself in the orderly harmony of what exists, but not in a God who concerns Himself with the fates and actions of human beings.

When asked if he believes in God.

THE CATHOLIC CHURCH AND HITLER

Only the Catholic Church protested against the Hitlerian onslaught on liberty. Up till then I had not been interested in the Church, but today I felt a great admiration for the Church, which alone has had the courage to struggle for spiritual truth and moral liberty.

From a 1940 comment. Quoted in Pinchas Lapide's Last Three Popes and the Jews *(1967).*

ON JEWISH LEARNING

I believe that the establishment of Jewish institutions for scientific studies, especially those of a non-religious nature, has become a necessity dictated by self-respect. We cannot be content merely to be tolerated in non-Jewish institutions as students, teachers and research workers, but must strive to achieve a situation also in this domain in which we shall be not only recipients but also donors.

From a letter to Dr. Bernard Revel, president of Yeshiva College, dated June 16, 1934, in response to an invitation to attend that year's commencement exercises and accept an honorary Doctor of Humane Letters. Professor Einstein declined the invitation.

TASK OF PHYSICISTS

The supreme task of the physicist is to arrive at those universal elementary laws from which the cosmos can be built up by pure deduction. There is no logical path to these laws;

only intuition, resting on sympathetic under-standing of experience, can reach them.

From a 1918 address.

MEASLES OF MANKIND

Nationalism is an infantile disease. It is the measles of the human race.

In a 1921 comment to George Sylvester Viereck. Quoted in Albert Einstein: The Human Side, *by Helen Dukas and Banesh Hoffman (1979).*

HEBREW UNIVERSITY

Unfortunately, the universities of Europe today are for the most part nurseries of chau-vinism and of a blind intolerance of all things foreign to the particular nation or race of all things bearing the stamp of a different individ-uality.... On this occasion of the birth of our [Hebrew] University I should like to express the hope that our University will always be free from this evil, that teachers and students will always preserve the consciousness that they serve their people best when they main-tain its union with humanity and with the highest human values.

From his About Zionism *(1930).*

JEWISH INDIVIDUALITY

The Jewish problem cannot be solved by the assimilation of the individual Jew to his environment. Jewish individuality is too strong to be effaced by such assimilation and too conscious to be ready for such self efface-ment.... The establishment of a National Home for the Jewish people in Palestine would raise the status and dignity of those who would remain in their native countries and would thereby materially assist in improving the relations between Jew and non-Jew.

Ibid.

HONESTY AND CHARACTER

The German Jew who works for the Jewish people and for the Jewish home in Palestine no more ceases to be a German than the Jew who becomes baptized and changes his name ceases to be a Jew.... The antithesis is not be-tween Jew and German, but between honesty and lack of character. He who remains true to his origin, race and tradition will also remain loyal to the state of which he is a subject. He who is faithless to the one will also be faithless to the other.

Ibid.

THEORY OF RELATIVITY SIMPLIFIED

Madam, I was once walking in the country on a hot day with a blind friend and said I could do with a drink of milk.

"Milk?" said my friend. "Drink I know; but what is milk?"

"A white liquid," I replied.

"Liquid I know," said the blind man, "but what is white?"

"Oh, the color of a swan's feathers."

"Feathers I know. What is a swan?"

"Swan? A bird with a crooked neck."

"Neck I know—but what is this crooked?"

Thereupon I lost patience. I seized his arm and straightened it. "That's straight," I said. Then I bent it at the elbow. "And that's crooked."

"Ah," cried the blind man, "Now I know what you mean by milk!"

When asked by a woman to tell her about relativity in a few simple words. Attributed in Long Week End, *by Robert Graves and Alan Hodge (1963).*

TO BE YOUNG AGAIN

If I would be a young man again and had to decide how to make my living, I would not try to become a scientist or scholar or teacher. I would rather choose to be a plumber or a peddler in the hope to find that modest degree of independence still available under present circumstances.

Quoted in The Reporter, *November 18, 1954.*

SCIENCE AND RELIGION

Science without religion is lame, religion without science is blind.

From an article in Science, Philosophy, and Religion: A Symposium *(1941).*

DRIFTING TOWARDS CATASTROPHE

The unleashed power of the atom has changed everything save our modes of think-ing and we thus drift toward unparalleled catastrophe.

From a telegram sent to prominent Ameri-cans on May 24, 1946.

AN ABSOLUTE PACIFIST

I am an absolute pacifist...It is an instinc-tive feeling. It is a feeling that possesses me, because the murder of men is disgusting.

From an interview with Paul Hutchinson. Reported in The Christian Century, *August 28, 1929.*

Thinking Ahead

I never think of the future. It comes soon enough.

From a December 1930 interview.

On Imagination

Imagination is more important than knowledge.

From his On Science.

Explaining Relativity

When a man sits with a pretty girl for an hour, it seems like a minute. But let him sit on a hot stove for a minute, and it's longer than any hour. That's relativity.

By attribution.

Harmonious Life

I feel that you are justified in looking into the future with true assurance, because you have a mode of living in which we find the joy of life and the joy of work harmoniously combined. Added to this is the spirit of ambition which pervades your very being, and it seems to make the day's work like a happy child at play.

From a 1931 New Year's greeting.

Achieving Peace

Peace cannot be kept by force. It can only be achieved by understanding.

From his Notes on Pacifism.

Standing Before God

Before God we are all equally wise—equally foolish.

From his Cosmic Religion.

Living Selflessly

Only a life lived for others is a life worth living.

From an article in Youth, *June 1932.*

Monument to Loyalty

This monument shall serve as a reminder for us who have survived to remain loyal to our people and to the moral principles cherished by our fathers. Only through such loyalty may we hope to survive this age of moral decay.

At the monument to the martyred Jews of the Warsaw Ghetto, April 19, 1948.

Personal Prisons

Everyone sits in the prison of his own ideas.

By attribution.

The Jewish Preference

Looking at the Jews as such, I can't say I enjoy it much. Looking at the rest I'd say I'll be Jewish any day.

Quoted in Albert Einstein as Philosopher and Scientist *(1955), edited by Paul Arthur Schilpp.*

No Alternative

Producing an atom bomb, I was certainly aware of the terrible menace to mankind should the enterprise succeed. But the likelihood that the Germans were working on the same problem with good prospects of success forced me to undertake this step. I had no other choice, although I have always been a convinced pacifist.

From his My View of Life *(1953), edited by Carl Seelig.*

¤

Judah David Einstein

Jewish Password

Shema Yisrael was on the lips of those who suffered and were tortured for the sake of the Law.... It is the password by which one Jew recognizes another in every part of the world.

From his article "Shema," included in The Jewish Encyclopedia *(1905).*

¤

Maurice N. Eisendrath

The Believing Jew

The believing Jew has a faith to live by, a heritage to be proud of, a task and a challenge to be discharged. The non-believing Jew, since he jettisons his religion for the merely ethical (if even that), will deny himself those sources of religious experience and those elements of the Jewish faith which seek to answer the basic religious questions of man: What is the meaning and significance of my existence? Whence do I come and whither am I bound? Why is this "yoke of the Torah" placed upon me?

From an essay in Condition of Jewish Belief *(1966), compiled by the editors of* Commentary *magazine.*

¤

Dwight D. Eisenhower

On Clemency for the Rosenbergs

According to Federal law, there is no such thing as "imprisonment no matter how long."

State laws provide for long terms of incarceration. With Federal law it is otherwise. According to Federal law, the Rosenbergs would be eligible for parole in fifteen years. Besides, there are times when nothing but death is a deterrent. After our invasion of Europe, the inhabitants of a certain area complained bitterly about the misconduct of some American soldiers. The people had to arm themselves with pitchforks and other makeshift weapons to prevent pillage and rape. All of that stopped after I had two of the malefactors publicly hanged. On one occasion some law-defying soldiers were offered the alternative of imprisonment or of service in the front lines. Every one of them chose imprisonment. There are times when death is the only effective penalty.

In response to a plea by Rabbi Abraham Cronbach, on June 16, 1953, that the President grant clemency to Julius and Ethel Rosenberg, who had been sentenced to be executed for stealing U.S. atomic bomb secrets for the Soviet Union. Quoted in Critical Studies in American Jewish History *(1971).*

FORESTALLING THE DENIERS

In one room, where there were piled up twenty or thirty naked men, killed by starvation, [General] George Patton would not even enter. He said that he would get sick if he did so. I made the visit deliberately, in order to be in a position to give firsthand evidence of these things, if ever in the future there develops a tendency to charge these allegations merely to "propaganda."

After visiting the Nazi concentration camp at Ohrdruf, Germany. Quoted in Harry James Cargas's Shadows of Auschwitz.

□

Ira Eisenstein

THE PURSUIT OF PEACE

Here are hundreds of men and women like myself. They are praying for peace. They all have the same idea that I have. They hate war. So do I. They are my brothers. Hundreds of us, with one heart and one mind, are pledging allegiance to this ideal. We will win out in the end. We must win out. We will change the world and make the world give up the madness of war. God is with us.

From his What We Mean By Religion *(1938).*

FAITH, HOPE, AND PATIENCE

Jews have a four-thousand-year history to draw upon. Those who know that history, make it part of their consciousness, and identify themselves with it should have (and I believe, on the whole, do have) a sensitivity to social evils which others might not have. They know what homelessness means, what exile, religious persecution, and political disability mean. They know what it means to suffer anxiety and frustration. They understand faith and hope and patience.

From an essay in Condition of Jewish Belief *(1966), compiled by the editors of* Commentary *magazine.*

□

Rafael Eitan

JEWISH ROOTS

I'm speaking as a secular Jew. Whoever abandons these sites abandons his roots.

From a 1995 speech condemning the abandoning of Joseph's tomb and other religious sites in Judea and Samaria.

□

William Norman Eiver

HOW ODD OF GOD

How odd
of God
to choose
the Jews.

From his Week-End Book *(1924).*

□

Stuart E. Eizenstat

AMERICAN MIDDLE EAST POLICY

The American desire to enhance its influence in the Arab world was evident in the Eisenhower–Dulles years, when Moslem countries were organized into a defense alignment against Soviet penetration; in the Rogers Plan to pre-determine Israel's boundaries; in the successful American effort to block Israel's complete victory over the Egyptian Third Army during the 1973 Yom Kippur War and on into our own day. It seems incredible today to recognize that no Israeli prime minister was an official guest of a president of the United States until Lyndon Johnson invited Levi Eshkol to the White House, nearly two decades after the establishment of the State.

From Moment *magazine, March 1984.*

¤

Daniel J. Elazar

Watershed of Jewish History

June 1967 marked a watershed in contemporary Jewish affairs. The Six-Day War united the members of the generation that witnessed the founding of the state with those of a new generation, one that grew up accepting the existence of Israel as a matter of fact, only to encounter suddenly the harsh possibility of its destruction, making both generations deeply aware of the shared fate of all Jews, and the way that fate is now bound up with the political entity that is the State of Israel.

On the impact of the 1967 Six-Day War. From an article in American Jewish Yearbook *(1969).*

Open to Seduction

We do not have a government that seems to be able to say 'no' despite its intentions. It is rather like Ado Annie, the girl in the musical "Oklahoma!" who could not say no. No matter how much she thought that she should and she wanted to when she started, fundamental urges led her to give in to seduction every time. Not surprisingly, the potential seducers figured that out early on and took full advantage of it. So have ours.

Assessing the peace process that was set in motion by Yitzhak Rabin and Shimon Peres upon the signing of the peace accord with the Palestine Liberation Organization on September 13, 1993. Quoted by Emanuel Rackman in his Jewish Week *column, December 3–9, 1993.*

¤

Akiva Eldar

Holy Jerusalem

For Jews, Jerusalem is motherhood and apple pie.

Commenting on the proposed transfer of the American embassy from Tel Aviv to Jerusalem. From a May 12, 1995 op-ed essay in The New York Times.

¤

(Rabbi) Eleazar

A Pearl Is a Pearl Is a Pearl

When a righteous man dies, he dies only for his own generation. It is like a man who loses a pearl. Wherever it may be, the pearl continues to be a pearl. It is lost only to its owner.

Commenting on the immortality of the soul. Quoted in the talmudic tractate Megilla (15a) in the name of Rabbi Chanina.

Fasting vs. Charity

Fasting is more efficacious than [giving] charity.... One is performed with a man's money, the other with his body.

Quoted in the talmudic tractate Berachot (32b).

Disciples of the Wise

The disciples of the wise increase peace in the world.

Ibid.

Prayers and Tears

Ever since the Temple was destroyed the gates of prayer have been closed...but though the gates of prayer are closed, the gates of tears are not closed.

Quoted in the talmudic tractates Berachot (32b) and Bava Metzia (59a).

Reason for Exile

The Holy One, blessed be He, did not exile Israel among the nations save for one reason: so that they might encourage proselytes to join their ranks.

Quoted in the talmudic tractate Eruvin (87b).

Giving Anonymously

A man who gives charity in secret is greater than Moses our teacher.

Quoted in talmudic tractate Bava Batra (9b).

Encouraging Good-doers

He who stimulates others to do good is greater than the doer.

Ibid (9a).

A World of Kindness

He who executes charity and justice is regarded as though he had filled the entire world with kindness.

Quoted in talmudic tractate Sukka (49b).

◻

Eleazar ben Arach

HAVE A READY ANSWER

Be eager to study the Torah and be prepared with an answer for the unbeliever.

Quoted in talmudic tractate Ethics of the Fathers (2:14).

◻

Eleazar ben Azariah

TRUE REPENTANCE

For transgressions of man against God, the Day of Atonement atones; but for transgressions against a fellow-man the Day of Atonement does not atone, unless and until he has conciliated his fellow-man and redressed the wrong he had done him.

Quoted in the talmudic tractate Yoma (Mishna 8:9).

BLIND OBEDIENCE

Say not, "I do not want forbidden food, forbidden clothes, or forbidden sexual relations." Rather say, "I do indeed want these but will not have them, because my Father in Heaven forbade them."

From the Midrash Sifra on Leviticus (20:36).

THE SUSTAINING FACTOR

If there is no bread, there can be no Torah, and if there is no Torah, there can be no bread.

Quoted in the talmudic tractate Ethics of the Fathers (3:17).

◻

Eleazar ben Pedat

FIRST WIFE

If a man divorces his first wife, even the altar [Temple] sheds tears.

Quoted in the talmudic tractate Gittin (90b).

THE MESSIAH'S COMING

Messiah will come in a generation fit for extinction.

Quoted in Midrash Pesikta Rabbati.

◻

Eleazar ben Shammua

PILLAR OF RIGHTEOUSNESS

The world rests on a single pillar: righteousness.

Quoted in the talmudic tractate Chagiga (12b).

◻

Eleazar ben Yair

CRY FROM MASADA

We prefer death to slavery.

Quoted in Flavius Josephus's Jewish War (first century C.E.)

◻

Eleazar Ha-Kappar

ISRAEL'S REDEMPTION

Israel was redeemed because they had not changed their names, abandoned their language, borne tales, or practiced immorality.

Quoted in the Midrash Mechilta on Exodus (12:6).

◻

Eleazar of Modin

NO ULTERIOR MOTIVES

If one wishes to adopt Judaism, in the name of God and for the sake of Heaven, welcome and befriend him, do not repel him.

From the Midrash Mechilta to Exodus (18:6).

◻

Yaffa Eliach

HOLOCAUST MEMOIRS

Holocaust memoirs are like apple pie and motherhood. People are sometimes reluctant to pass judgment on them.

Commenting on the spate of survivors' memoirs being published. Quoted in Publishers Weekly *magazine, May 8, 1995.*

◻

Mordechai Eliahu

UNDER GOD'S UMBRELLA

God-fearing Jews should not carry an umbrella on the Sabbath even if it was opened on Friday.

A declaration issued in 1992.

◻

Arie Lova Eliav

AN OUTSPOKEN DOVE

Israel should make a general declaration of intent, that for full peace it is ready to give up the occupied territories [from the Six-Day

War] with some adjustments agreed upon and negotiated between the parties. I have said the same for nine years, and the lack of such a declaration has already brought, and will still bring, havoc upon us.

Proposing that a Palestinian state is necessary for peace. From a symposium in Moment magazine, March 1976.

UNDERESTIMATING THE PALESTINIANS

Israel must under no circumstances underestimate the Palestinian Arab armed organizations.... These armed Palestinian Arabs know that they are courting death, and that out of every ten setting out only one or two will return alive to their bases, while the rest will either be killed in battle or captured and sent to prison for long terms. Anyone who says that people going into battle under such circumstances are "yellow Arbooshes" or "rabble" doesn't know what he is talking about.

From his Land of the Heart *(1973).*

□

(Rabbi) Eliezer

DEEP WELL OF KNOWLEDGE

If all seas were ink and all reeds pens, and heaven and earth scrolls, and all mankind scribes, that would not suffice to write the Torah that I have learned, even though I have garnered from it no more than a man could take by dipping the tip of his painting brush into the sea.

Quoted in the Midrash Song of Songs Rabba (1:3). A similar quotation is ascribed to Rabbi Joshua.

THE POWER OF LAW

Let the Law pierce the mountain.

Expressing the importance of letting the Law take its course and not force parties to submit to arbitration once a decision has been rendered. Quoted in the talmudic tractate Sanhedrin (6b) and Yevamot (92a).

□

Eliezer ben Yaakov

STOLEN GOODS

A benediction over stolen things is blasphemy.

Quoted in the talmudic tractate Bava Kamma (94a).

□

(Prophet) Elijah

THE WICKED KING AND QUEEN

The dogs shall devour Jezebel in the field of Jezreel. All of Ahab's progeny who die in the town shall be devoured by dogs, and all who die in the open field shall be devoured by the birds of the sky.

Proclaiming the punishment that God will exact upon King Ahab and Queen Jezebel for killing Naboth and taking his vineyard after he refused to sell it (I Kings 21:23–24).

A DOUBLE CRIME

Would you murder and also take possession?

Castigating King Ahab for murdering Naboth and then confiscating his property (I Kings 21:19).

□

Elijah ben Solomon
(Gaon of Vilna)
REPUDIATION OF HASIDIM

It is the duty of every believing Jew to repudiate and remove them.... They have sinful hearts and are like a plague on the body of Israel.

Commented in 1796 after the hasidim had spread a rumor that the Gaon regrets having attacked and repudiated their views.

□

Charles William Eliot
THE HIGHEST VALUES

The highest conception of God, man, and nature are all Jewish.

From a November 1905 address.

□

George Eliot
CHRISTIAN VIEW OF JEWS

The usual attitude of Christians towards Jews is—I hardly know whether to say more impious or more stupid, when viewed in the light of their professed principles.... They hardly know Christ was a Jew. And I find men, educated, supposing that Christ spoke Greek. To my feeling, this deadness to the history which has prepared half our world for us, this inability to find interest in any form of life that is not clad in the same coat-tails and flounces as our own, lies very close to the worst kind of irreligion.

From her letter to Harriet Beecher Stowe (1876). Quoted in J. W. Cross's Life as Related in Her Letters and Journals *(1884).*

LOW-GRADE JUDAISM

My Gentile nature kicks most resolutely against any assumption of superiority in the Jews, and is almost ready to echo Voltaire's vituperation. I bow to the supremacy of Hebrew poetry, but much of their early mythology, and almost all their history, is utterly revolting.... Everything specifically Jewish is of low grade.

From George Eliot's Life *(1885), edited by J. W. Cross. Quoted in Joseph L. Baron's* Stars and Sand *(1943).*

MARRIAGES ARE MADE IN HEAVEN

"The Omnipresent," said a Rabbi, "is occupied in making marriages." The levity of the saying lies in the ear of him who hears it; for by marriages the speaker meant all the wondrous combinations of the universe, whose issue makes for good and evil.

Quoted in Israel Abrahams's Book of Delight *(1912).*

DENYING THE PAST

When it is rational to say, "I know not my father or my mother, let my children be aliens to me, that no prayer of mine may touch them," then it will be rational for the Jew to say, "I will seek to know no difference between me and the Gentile, I will not cherish the prophetic consciousness of our nationality—let the Hebrew cease to be, and let all his memorials be antiquarian trifles, dead as the wallpaintings of a conjectured race."

From her Daniel Deronda *(1876).*

ARISTOCRATIC TRAGIC HEROES

The Jews are among the aristocracy of every land. If a literature is called rich in the possession of a few classic tragedies, what shall we say of a national tragedy lasting for fifteen hundred years, in which poets and the actors were also the heroes.

Ibid.

□

Elisha ben Avuya

CLEAN SLATE

He who studies as a child—to what may he be compared? To ink written on a new sheet of paper. But he who studies in his old age—to

what may he be compared? To ink applied to aging paper.

Quoted in the talmudic tractate Ethics of the Fathers (4:25).

THE HIGHEST PRIORITY

Saving a life supersedes the Sabbath.

Quoted in the Midrash Mechilta on Exodus (31:13).

□

Havelock Ellis

NO JEWISH PROBLEM

For me indeed there has never been any Jewish question. The background from which I come had no Jewish element, save indeed the Bible, which for me is Jewish throughout and has an importance I would never belittle.

Even in later life when I have gained many friends who are Jews, and experienced in large measure those qualities of generosity and receptivity which often mark the Jew, I have been conscious of no Jewish problem. Myself English in the narrowest sense, the Jew is not more alien to me than the Cornishman or the Irishman, or even many so-called Englishmen, often less so....

From his essay "The Jewish Question," which appeared in Questions of Our Day *(1936).*

□

Marc Ellis

PALESTINIANS AND THE HOLOCAUST

Jews cannot be healed of the trauma of the Holocaust unless Palestinians are healed of their trauma of displacement.

From a March 1995 lecture at the United States Holocaust Museum in Washington, DC.

□

Amos Elon

SABRA HUMOR

Sabra [native Israeli] humor hardly excels in the kind of biting, yet humane, self-irony that is the hallmark of traditional Jewish humor. It is cooler, a bit distant, or abstract in the shaggy-dog style. In his humor, the *sabra* is critical not of himself, but of the high-sounding pathos of the older generation.

Quoted in Lewis Glinert's Joys of Hebrew *(1992).*

ロ

Menachem Elon

WHO ISN'T A JEW?

The Jewish people, over 2,000 years of Jewish and world history, determined that [followers of Jesus] shall no longer be considered members of the Jewish people, that they removed themselves from the people and shall not come within it.

Expressing the unanimous 1987 ruling of the Israeli Supreme Court in the case of three Messianic Jewish families (followers of Jesus) who sought to obtain Israeli citizenship from the Ministry of the Interior, claiming their rights as Jews under the Law of Return.

ロ

Motti Elon

SLOGANEERING JUDAISM

We are not "Now" people. I don't want Peace Now and I don't want Moshiah Now. Of course I support both concepts—peace and the coming of the Messiah—but I object to the easy sloganeering. I want a deep, abiding faith in the eternal nature of Israel and the Jewish people.

Quoted in The Jerusalem Post, *November 26, 1994.*

WELCOME TO THE POPE

I would welcome the pope. Absolutely. He's a vital personality and a man of deep faith. This sort of visit could only be beneficial. But I would not extend an invitation in the spirit of forgetting. And I would be totally disinterested in pursuing a discussion, for example, regarding what they [the Vatican] consider a pet theme—turning Jerusalem into an international city.

We are here in Israel and there is nothing to apologize for, nor any reason not to speak openly about the past. The question is, Will I forget who I am and why I am here or will I hold on to the concept of the 'eternal Israel' and integrate it into the new reality? Who should the burden be on of accepting the new reality, us or the pope?

Ibid. Concerning the debate in 1994 about inviting John Paul II to Jerusalem.

WHERE IS OUR PLACE?

I think it's rather disgraceful when [our leaders] lack the strength of character to state things clearly and at the right moment. I still don't understand, for example, why Jews are not allowed on the Temple Mount, why there is a total capitulation on that subject. And of course I ask this question while stating that I only support the rabbinate's position on this subject. Nevertheless it prompts the question: where is our just place in this world, after all?

Ibid.

A LIGHT UNTO THE NATIONS

While I understand the desire not to be a nation which dwells alone, I wonder sometimes where is our pride, where is the commitment to our being the light unto the nations? It is an idea that Ben-Gurion himself espoused.

Ibid.

ロ

Jacob Emden

SENSE OF TOUCH

The wise men of other nations claim that there is disgrace in the sense of touch, but this is not the view of our Torah. To us the sexual act is worthy, good, beneficial even to the soul. No other human activity compares with it. When performed with pure and clean intention, it is certainly holy.

Quoted in Neil Shister's article "Sex: Professional and Lay People," which appeared in Moment *magazine, December 1976.*

RIGHTEOUS CHRISTIAN PRINCIPLES

The Christians...have many admirable traits and righteous principles.... Happy are they and happy are we when they treat us according to their faith!

From the Preface to his Seder Olam *(1757). Quoted in Leo Jung's* Judaism in a Changing World *(1939).*

THE NAZARENE

The Nazarene wrought a double kindness on the world; he supported the Torah of Moses with full strength,...and sought to perfect Gentiles with ethical qualities.

Ibid.

THE LAND CONNECTION

Everyone in Israel [that is, every Jew] must in his heart steadfastly resolve to go to Eretz Israel and to remain there. But if he cannot go himself, he should, if his circumstances permit—whether he be a craftsman or a merchant—support some person in that country, and so do his part in restoring the Holy Land, which has been laid waste, by maintaining one of its rightful inhabitants.... The mistake our parents made was that of ignoring this precious land, and thereby they caused much suffering in the generations that came after them.

From the Introduction to his prayerbook. Quoted in Nahum Glatzer's In Time and Eternity *(1946).*

◻

Ralph Waldo Emerson

MELTING POT

In this continent—asylum of all nations...all the European tribes...will construct a new race, a new religion, a new state.

Entry in his Journal *(1845). Quoted in Abraham Karp's* Haven and Home *(1985).*

RACE AND THE JEW

Race is a controlling influence in the Jew, who, for two millenniums, under every climate, has preserved the same character and employments.

From his English Traits: Race *(1856).*

SUFFERANCE IS THE BADGE

The sufferance, which is the badge of the Jew, has made him, in these days, the ruler of the rulers of the earth.

From his Conduct of Life: Fate *(1860).*

THE CHARM OF STUDY

You cannot bring me too good a word, too dazzling a hope, too penetrating an insight from the Jews. I hail everyone with delight, as showing the riches of my brother, my fellow soul, who could thus think and thus greatly feel. Zealots eagerly fasten their eyes on the differences between their creed and yours, but the charm of study is in finding the agreements, the identities, in all the religions of men.

From a May 28, 1869 speech.

QUALITIES OF GREATNESS

The Hebrew nation compensated for the insignificance of its members and territory by its religious genius, its tenacious belief; its poems and histories cling to the soil of this globe like the primitive rocks.

From his address "The Man of Letters" (1863), in Lectures and Biographical Sketches *(1884).*

PROMISING POET

The poems have important merits, and I observe that my poet gains in skill as the poems multiply, and she may at last confidently say, I have mastered the obstructions, I have learned the rules.

From an undated letter to Emma Lazarus.

◻

Eliot Engel

ISRAEL AND THE VATICAN

By establishing relations with Israel, the Vatican would recognize the common heritage shared by Christians and Jews, as well as send a meaningful message of acceptance and tolerance to the entire world community.

Statement made in 1993 prior to the Vatican's recognition of the State of Israel in 1994.

◻

Friedrich Engels

MARX'S GOAL

Marx was above all a revolutionary, and his great aim in life was...the emancipation of the modern proletariat.

From his March 17, 1883 remarks eulogizing Karl Marx. Quoted in F. Mehring's Karl Marx.

◻

Moshe Chaim Ephraim

DANCING A CAPPELLA

I heard this from my grandfather: Once a fiddler played so sweetly that all who heard him began to dance, and whoever came near enough to hear joined in the dance. Then a deaf man who knew nothing of music happened along, and to him all he saw seemed the action of madmen—senseless and in bad taste.

Recalling what his grandfather, the Baal Shem Tov, had said.

◻

Ephron the Hittite

A BURIAL SITE FOR SARAH

My lord, do hear me! A piece of land worth 400 shekels of silver—what is that between you and me? Go and bury your dead.

Spoken to Abraham when his wife Sarah died and he wished to buy a burial site for her in Hebron, land owned by the Hittites (Genesis 23:15).

Benjamin Epstein

ANTI-SEMITISM IN AMERICA

Our capacity for social development is unlimited. Barring some major world catastrophe, American anti-Semitism will continue to decrease. You can tell it in the attitudes of our cultural, religious and political leaders. You can tell it in the great growth of community organization in the United States, the process of people banding together on behalf of many democratic causes. You can tell it in the development of modern education in the United States, which, with human-relations education as its base, is capable of producing a generation of Americans emotionally rich and fulfilled, incapable of joining a hate movement or even tolerating one.

But the phenomenon of anti-Semitism is deep-rooted; it will not die in our time. And before it does it will claim many more victims.

From his essay "Anti-Semitism Today: An Epilogue," included in Jews in the Modern World *(1962), edited by Jacob Fried.*

Yechiel Michal Epstein

RISING FOR BENEDICTIONS

Gentiles join their hands in prayer, signifying that their hands are bound. We express the same idea by putting our feet together when we rise for the Benedictions. This symbolizes greater humility; for with the hands bound, one can still run for pleasure, but not with the feet bound.

From his Kitzur Shnay Luchot Ha-berit *(1683).*

Desiderius Erasmus

MAKING OF A CHRISTIAN

If hating Jews makes one a true Christian, then we all are outstanding Christians.

Quoted in Joseph Telushkin's Jewish Wisdom *(1994).*

John Erskine

EVERYONE HAS RELIGION

Nearly every one has religion, at least in the sense that he knows what church he is staying away from.

By attribution.

Esau

SELLING A BIRTHRIGHT

Behold, I am about to die. What profit shall the birthright bring me?

Speaking to Jacob when pleading for some of the pottage Jacob had prepared. Quoted in the Book of Genesis (25:31).

Levi Eshkol

I DO NOT DANCE

Mein teire ambassador: Ich tanz nisht.
My dear ambassador: I do not dance.

President Eshkol's response (in Yiddish) to Abraham Harman, Israel's ambassador to the United States, who had suggested, during a 1964 visit to the White House, that Eshkol invite the First Lady to dance with him after Lyndon Johnson had invited Eshkol's wife, Miriam, to dance.

Rabaud Saint Étienne

A CALL FOR FREEDOM

I demand liberty for the nation of the Jews, always condemned, homeless, wandering over the face of the whole globe, and doomed to humiliation. Banish forever the aristocracy of thought, the feudal system of opinion, which desires to rule others and impose compulsion upon them.

From a speech before the French National Assembly after the revolution, at the end of the eighteenth century. Quoted in Heinrich Graetz's History of the Jews *(1894).*

(Pope) Eugenius IV

SOCIALIZING WITH JEWS

We decree and order that from now on, and for all time, Christians shall not eat or drink with Jews, nor admit them to feasts, nor cohabit with them, nor bathe with them. Christians shall not allow Jews to hold civil honors over Christians, or to exercise public offices in the state.

A decree issued in 1442.

Eli N. Evans

FEELING FOR THE SOUTH

I am not certain what it means to be both a Jew and a Southerner, to have inherited the Jewish longing for a homeland while being raised with the southerner's sense of home. The conflict is deep in me—the Jew's involvement in history, his deep roots in the drama of man's struggle to understand deity and creation. But I respond to the Southerner's commitment to place, his loyalty to the land, to his own tortured history, the strange bond beyond color that Southern blacks and whites discover when they know one another.

Commenting on Pickett's failed charge toward the Northern lines at Gettysburg in July 1863. Quoted in his Provincials: A Personal History of the Jews in the South *(1973).*

Eve

BLAMING THE SERPENT

The serpent duped me, and I ate.

In response to God's asking Eve why she ate from the forbidden fruit in the Garden of Eden and also gave some to Adam (Genesis 3:13).

Myrlie Evers-Williams

BLACKS AND JEWS

There are significant pressures in both communities to divide us. Extremist rhetoric makes dialogue difficult. We in the African-American community do not sanction extremist, hate-filled rhetoric.... Jewish Americans have played prominent roles in our history. There is appreciation in our community for the solidarity and support from Jewish Americans over the years.

A 1995 statement before the World Jewish Congress Commission on Intergroup Relations by the newly elected head of the NAACP.

Yair Evron

THE NATIONAL IDENTITY OF PALESTINIANS

Mrs. [Golda] Meir's position denying the existence of a Palestinian nation was neither based on fact nor conducive to a constructive de-escalation of the Arab-Israeli conflict. There is no question that there is a Palestinian national entity. At the same time it is important to remember that Palestinians living in the West Bank, the Gaza Strip, and in what is now Jordan, have several levels of national identifications and adherences. They certainly feel Palestinian. They also have a basic feeling of belonging to the "Arab nation." And many of them identify at least partly with Jordan as well.

Co-chairman of the Strategic Studies Division of the Davis Institute of International Relations at Hebrew University. From a symposium in Moment *magazine, March 1976.*

Jonathan Eybeshitz

ALL FOR ONE, BUT NOT ONE FOR ALL

Let a Jew sustain material loss, let him find himself the victim of political persecution, and all his fellow-Jews will rush to his rescue...Yes, ...we do love one another. But that love is purely physical. Of spiritual love, that is, love for the soul of our neighbor, there is but little in our midst. One may fritter away one's life in unseemly practices, and none will venture to remonstrate with him.

From his Ya-arot Davash *(1779). Quoted in Israel Bettan's* Studies in Jewish Preaching *(1939).*

Walter Eytan

THE INTIFADA

The Arabs threw away their chances [for peaceful coexistence] in 1947 and have been keeping them buried ever since. *Intifada,* a term familiar to all since 1987, means a "shaking off." The Arab states and the Palestinian Arabs have done their utmost to shake off the Jews, not only since the independence of Israel but at least since the Balfour Declaration of 1917 and the League of Nations Mandate of 1922–48.

Quoted in Hadassah Magazine, *March 1991.*

RESPONDING TO STONE-THROWING

For every incident of stone-throwing by Arab youths, 10 settlements should be built. When we have settled the land, all the Arabs will be able to do about it will be to scurry around like drugged roaches in a bottle.

Suggesting a response to the Intifada *of the 1980s.*

Rose Eytinge

HUMOROUS MR. LINCOLN

When I was presented to the President, he took my hand, and holding it while he looked down upon me from his great height said, "So this is the little lady that all us folks in Washington like so much!" Then with a portentous shake of his head but with a twinkle in his eye, he continued, "Don't you ever come around here asking me to do some of those impossible things you women always ask for, for I would have to do it and then I would get into trouble."

Recalling when she was invited to the White House by Abraham Lincoln. Recorded in her memoirs.

(Prophet) Ezekiel

DRIED BONES

Our bones are dried up and our hope is lost.

From the Book of Ezekiel (37:11).

Emil L. Fackenheim

THE "614TH COMMANDMENT"

Jews are forbidden to hand Hitler posthumous victories. They are commanded to survive as Jews, lest the Jewish People perish.... They are commanded to remember the victims of Auschwitz, lest their memory perish. They are forbidden to despair of man and his world, and to escape into either cynicism or otherworldliness, lest they cooperate in delivering the world over to the forces of Auschwitz. Finally, they are forbidden to despair of the God of Israel, lest Judaism perish.... A Jew may not respond to Hitler's attempt to destroy Judaism by himself cooperating in its destruction.

From his Jewish Return into History *(1978).*

PROOF OF GOD'S EXISTENCE

The universe we find ourselves in is an infinitely more complex and more wonderful construction than a clock. Is it likely, as the atheists maintain, that, while the clock was made for a purpose and according to a craftsman's design, the universe is only an accidental collection of atoms? Only an insane person would say this about the clock.... Just as the clock is evidence for the clockmaker, the universe is evidence for a universemaker—for God.

From his Paths to Jewish Belief *(1968).*

EVIDENCE OF THE "INFINITE MIND"

Wherever we find life, it is charged with purpose. We can see this in even the very lowest forms of life. For example, when an amoeba is hungry, it reaches out for food, forms itself into new shapes, and surrounds what it wants to eat. It acts with a purpose—to satisfy its hunger. This is the wonder that we cannot understand.

Ibid.

THE DIVINE MEETS MAN

In revelation, the Divine meets the human: It does not remain in inaccessible transcendence. While meeting the finite human, It yet remains in divine infinity: the finite is not idolatrously deified. And It enters into the human situation: It does not force the human into a mystic surrender of its finitude. The Divine commands, and commands humans in their humanity.

From an essay in Condition of Jewish Belief *(1966), compiled by the editors of* Commentary *magazine.*

THE MESSIANIC WORLD

Whereas Christian ethical life is lived in the context of a grace which has already redeemed the world, Jewish ethical life is premessianic, and finds grace primordially in the commandments, a grace which makes possible a human share in the preparation of the messianic kingdom.

Ibid.

MODEL OF EVERY JEW

I revere Abraham who lived the human paradox to the extreme and yet had faith that it was not fatal.... Abraham waits for us, as the potential father of every Jew aspiring to be a good Jew; for he teaches us to live courageously the ethical under the moral law, in an existence which requires divine love superseding the ethical if it is to be healed of its tragic tensions. Hence we can confess with Kierkegaard: "No one is so great as Abraham! Who is capable of understanding him?"

Commenting on the Akeda *(the "binding" of Isaac). From his* Quest for Past and Future: Essays in Jewish Theology *(1968).*

PARTNERS WITH GOD

Judaism believes in the co-workership of God and man, in the covenant between God and Israel, and in God's availability in prayer; and the...relationship implied in these beliefs can be thought of only in quasi-personal terms.

Ibid.

SANCTIFICATION OF LIFE

In the Warsaw ghetto Rabbi Isaac Nissenbaum, a famous and respected Orthodox rabbi, made the statement—much quoted by Jews of all persuasions in their desperate efforts to defend, preserve, and hallow Jewish life against an enemy sworn to destroy it all—that this was a time not for *kiddush ha-Shem* [martyrdom] but rather for *kiddush ha-chayim* [the sanctification of life]. It is a time for *kiddush ha-chayim* still. The Jewish people have passed through the Nazi antiworld of death; thereafter, by any standard, religious or secular, Jewish life ranks higher than Jewish death, even if it is for the sake of the Divine name.

From his What Is Judaism? *(1987).*

THE NEW CYRUS

Harry Truman was the new Cyrus. He knew that if we, the Jewish people, came back to Jerusalem a second time, it would be a boon to both Christianity and Islam. There will be true peace in Jerusalem when both Islam and Christianity come to worship there, not in spite of being there but because of it.

Quoted in The Jerusalem Post, *April 29, 1995.*

FACING TERRORISM

I have been careful to be in the middle of the political debate, but let this country survive, even if it means that we must be oppressors. Is there an alternative? We are under siege. What we certainly don't need is to be taught by these S.O.B.s the morality of the Jewish people. I am sure there have been grievous excesses, and this must be criticized and ended, but it's a big step from there to attacking the occupation [of the West Bank] as such, and anyone doing so must show that there is a non-self-destructive alternative.

Ibid. Making the point that the Israeli army must dirty its hands (as Sartre pointed out in his play Dirty Hands*) for the sake of a greater cause, and so that Israel is not victimized by terrorists who are praised as "martyrs."*

◻

Clifton Fadiman

NEGATIVE WRITING

My notion is that Miss [Gertrude] Stein has set herself to solve, and has succeeded in solving, the most difficult problem in prose composition—to write something that will not arrest the attention in any way, manner, shape, or form.

Quoted in B. L. Reid's Art by Subtraction.

BORING WRITING

Miss Stein was a past master in making nothing happen very slowly.

From The Selected Writings of Clifton Fadiman: *"Puzzlements."*

◻

Lewis Fagen

THE MIND OF SCHINDLER

I don't know what his [Schindler's] motives were, even though I knew him very well. I asked him and I never got a clear answer, and the film doesn't make it clear, either. But I don't give a damn. What's important is that he saved our lives.

Commenting on Steven Spielberg's Academy Award–winning movie Schindler's List, *in which Fagen, now of Boca Raton, Florida, was portrayed as Ludwik Feigenbaum of Cracow. Quoted in David Margolick's article in* The New York Times, *February 13, 1994.*

◻

Jerry Falwell

CONDEMNATION OF ANTI-SEMITISM

The Jews are the apple of God's eye...Anyone who hates Jews is stupid.

From his Sunday morning sermon, March 11, 1984.

ANTI-SEMITISM AND SATAN

Anti-Semitism was produced by Satan himself as an antithesis to the God of heaven who selected and ordained the Jewish people as His own chosen family.

From his Strength for the Journey: An Autobiography *(1987).*

VOLUNTARY PRAYER

I favor the return of voluntary prayers to the public schools. I oppose mandated or officially written prayers.

From Merrill Simon's Jerry Falwell and the Jews *(1984).*

ON FIGHTING ANTI-SEMITISM

I personally feel a heavy responsibility to educate the American people on the importance of supporting the State of Israel and Jewish people everywhere. I am training thousands of pastors to do the same...how they can do their part in the future to stamp out anti-Semitism.

Ibid.

CALLING OF THE CHURCH

World evangelization is an irrevocable calling to the Church. There is nothing anti-Semitic about this evangelistic calling. To share Christ is part of our faith.

Ibid.

ON JEWISH CONVERSION

In my mind, a Jew converting to Christianity does not abandon, in the slightest sense of the word, his wonderful Old Testament heritage. In reality, a Christian Jew is simply a son of Abraham who, having studied the evidence, has concluded that Jesus Christ is indeed the Messiah so often promised in the Old Testament.

Ibid.

HOMOSEXUALITY CONDEMNED

When the Lord created the world, He created Adam and Eve, not Adam and Steve.

From a sermon.

¤

Moishe Farjoun

THE MOST POWERFUL NOISE

Sure, those Habad people do a lot, but they make too much noise about it. Take their loudspeaker trucks every Friday afternoon, driving through town blaring their announcements about candlelighting time. I agree with what Reb Oosher Zaltz says: "What are they making all that noise for? Remaining silent is so powerful that it outshouts the most powerful outcry."

Comment of a Sephardic guide in Safed on the recent influx of Bratzlav and Habad groups. From an article by Moshe Kohn in The Jerusalem Post, *August 8, 1975.*

¤

Louis Farrakhan

LIBELOUS TALK

[The Jews are] bloodsuckers whom Jesus condemned in the plainest of language.

From an October 1985 address delivered before 25,000 followers at New York's Madison Square Garden.

THE MAN WON'T CRAWL

You're telling me that I've got to build a track record, meaning like Jesse [Jackson]? Jesse hasn't breached the gap between himself and the Jews. He's constantly apologizing and trying to do nice things, and running all over

the world to make it right with them. And it's not right yet. Farrakhan don't intend to do this. Never! I'm a man, brother. God has made me a man, and I don't see nothing on this earth of power that I should crawl to. Nothing!...

Do you mean to tell me that the Jews have never done any evil to black people? And if I point it out, does that mean I hate Jews? Is there no pain on our side? Were [the Jews] involved in the slave trade? Yes they were. And the Jews must be brought to account for this.

From a January 1994 Amsterdam News *interview with editor-in-chief and publisher Wilbert Tatum.*

I'M NOT AN ANTI-SEMITE

I'm neither a racist nor an anti-Semite. But if I point out your evil tracks in the sands of time, don't blame me.

Responding to charges of bigotry in a December 1993 speech to supporters at a rally in New York City.

THE FARRAKHAN/JACKSON ALLIANCE

I came into the light of the media as a helper of Reverend Jesse Jackson in his bid to become the nominee [for U.S. president] of the Democratic party in 1984.... Unfortunately, that was a very, very negative coming, primarily because in my judgment many Jews feared Reverend Jackson's growing prominence because of his even-handed policy toward Israel and her Arab neighbors and some of these Jewish organizations, having connections in the media, used the words that I spoke during the Jackson campaign out of context. And so I was lambasted by the press, but have weathered all the storms and by the grace of God have come out on top.

From an interview with Barbara Kleban Mills, correspondent for People *magazine, September 17, 1990.*

GUTTER RELIGION

Judaism is a gutter religion.

From a June 1984 radio broadcast.

BLOODSUCKERS

You suck the blood of the black community, and you feel we have no right now to say something about it.

From a February 1990 speech at Michigan State University.

INTERNATIONAL INTRIGUE

We know that Jews are the most organized, rich and powerful people, not only in America but in the world.... They are plotting against us even as we speak.

From a January 28, 1994 speech in Harlem.

SPEAKING THE TRUTH

I cannot say to Jewish people if I speak the truth that I'm sorry for speaking the truth. That's what prophets are sent to do. And Israel had many prophets, and the prophets had to speak the truth to the sins of the Children of Israel.

From a conversation with correspondent Scott Minerbrook. Reported in U.S. News & World Report *prior to the Million Man March on Washington, DC, which took place on Monday, October 16, 1995.*

SINS OF JEWS

Why if I point out sins of Jews am I considered anti-Semitic, and I'm not considered anti-black when I call black people and all of us on the carpet for our shortcomings? It's wrong to call me anti-Semitic.

Ibid.

A MESSAGE TO JEWS

If you could sit with Arafat, where there's rivers of blood between, why can't you sit down with us, and there's no blood.

Calling for an improvement in black–Jewish relations in a speech delivered at the Million Man March on Washington in October 1995.

❑

(King) Faud

HUMAN BEING OR JEW?

I treat you as a human being, not as a Jew.

Henry Kissinger explaining to Golda Meir how the king of Saudi Arabia welcomed him. To which Golda responded: "You know, Mr. Secretary, some of your best friends are human beings."

❑

Mordecai Ze'ev Feierberg

LIGHT A CANDLE!

Blow out the light of the *Galut* [Diaspora]— a new candle must be lit!

From his Le-an? *(1898). Quoted in S. Halkin's* Modern Hebrew Literature *(1950).*

❑

Jules Feiffer

ENRICHED VOCABULARY

I used to think I was poor. Then they told me I wasn't poor, I was needy. Then they told me it was self-defeating to think of myself as needy, I was deprived. Then they told me deprived was a bad image, I was underprivileged. Then they told me underprivileged was overused, I was disadvantaged. I still don't have a dime. But I sure have a great vocabulary.

Quoted in William Safire's Political Dictionary *(1968).*

❑

Leonard Fein

WELCOME TO AMERICA

America was ready to open its heart only to those who viewed themselves as "wretched refuse"—inferior cultures which they will discard.

From an address to the opening session of the YIVO Annual Conference, June 6, 1971. Quoted in Aviva Cantor's Jewish Women/ Jewish Men *(1994).*

JEWS AND LIBERAL CHRISTIANS

Jews have not fared well, recently, at the hands of liberal Christians. The general sense within the Jewish community, encouraged in a major way by the call of the National Council of Churches for the recognition of the PLO [Palestine Liberation Organization] is that our erstwhile allies on the moderate left have abandoned us, that they are insensitive not only to Israel's plight but also to the dangers of anti-Semitism. Among the Evangels, however, there is much support for Israel and its safety, support which holds that the Second Coming depends on the ingathering of the Jews in the Holy Land—followed, to be sure, by their conversion to Christianity.

From Moment *magazine, December 1980.*

UNDESERVED AWARD

I am unaware of any service whatsoever that [Jerry] Falwell has performed for the State of Israel—save for not attacking it...and it is demeaning to suggest that he has.

Ibid. After being awarded, under the aegis of the Jabotinsky Foundation, a medal for distinguished service to the State of Israel.

INVOKING LOVE FOR ZION

Each who loves Zion affirms as he is able, as he is given to understand the meaning of affirmation.... Zion wants not only the love of its people, but their wisdom, too. For there is a name to Zion's dream; its name is peace, the time of the wolf and the lamb.

> Urging that each person "celebrate" Israel's thirty-sixth birthday as he comprehends its significance. From Moment magazine, May 1984.

Keeping the Wound Alive

To be a Jew in America is to carry with you the consciousness of limitless savagery. It is to carry that consciousness with you not as an abstraction, but as a reality; not, God help us all, only as a memory, but also as a possibility.

> From his Where Are We? The Inner Life of America's Jews (1988), in which he encourages Jews to bring into the open the hurt caused by the Holocaust.

Jews as Community

The core method of Judaism is community. Ours is not a personal testament, but a collective and public commitment.... What defines the Jews as Jews is community; not values, not ideology.

> Ibid.

Israel-Diaspora Tension

You can't say aliya is the ideal and the diaspora is [simply] valid. There's a tension there. You're the stars, we're the ushers, the financial backers and the enthusiastic audience to your productions. We can't accept this role. We have our own less auspicious but equally important theatrical production. Our diaspora palate has been richer than yours, our product more useful.

> From a speech at a conference of Israel-Diaspora relations convened in June 1994 by President Ezer Weizman. Quoted in The Jewish Week, July 1–7, 1994.

Support for Israel

Let Israel's enemies take no comfort. There is debate and division among the Jews, and these will continue, for the matters at issue are momentous. But they take place within a context; to ignore the context is to misinterpret the debate. The support of the Jewish people for a free and independent Jewish state of Israel is profound and enduring. Our quarrels with each other—more settlements or less or none, a Greater Israel solution or a Jordanian solution or an independent Palestine solution—reflect the anguished search of a beleaguered people for a corner of safety and quiet in a world where Jews have been, for the most part, dispensable.

> Upon his return from a lengthy trip to Israel. From an Op-Ed article in The New York Times, July 19, 1980.

□

Henry L. Feingold

Crisis of Faith

A secular Jew believes one can be Jewish without being Judaic.... Faith had become a separate component of American Jewish identity, and for a growing number it played little role in their lives.

> Evaluating Jewish life in the 1920s. From his Time for Searching: Entering the Mainstream, 1920–1945 (1992).

□

Dianne Feinstein

Solace in Catholicism

I was the first Jew at Sacred Heart, and it turned out to be a pretty good recipe. In Judaism you believe in a code of morality and ethics to live as the one God would have you live. In Catholicism, it is more a day-to-day code, and I eventually found a lot of solace in the Catholic Church.

> Quoted in Elinor and Robert Slater's Great Jewish Women (1994).

A Confirmed Jew

I have always considered myself Jewish.

> Ibid. Noting that her three husbands were all Jewish.

□

Moshe Feinstein

Women and Mitzvot

Their [women's] motivation is fundamentally a complaint against God and His Torah. Their intention is not a truthful desire to serve Him and their actions do not constitute a mitzvah [commandment]. Their disrespect for our Torah and our sages amounts to nothing less than blasphemy.

> Commenting on women who put on talitot (prayershawls) and tefilin (phylacteries) when they pray. Quoted in Moment magazine, April 1994.

(Emir) Feisal

ACCORD BETWEEN ARABS AND JEWS

The two main branches of the Semitic family, Arabs and Jews, understand one another, and I hope that as a result of the interchange of ideas at the Peace Conference, which will be guided by the ideals of self-determination and nationality, each nation will make definite progress towards the realization of its aspiration. Arabs are not jealous of Zionist Jews, and intend to give them fair play; and the Zionist Jews have assured the Nationalist Arabs of their intention to see that they, too, have fair play in their respective areas.

> *From a statement by the newly coronated king of Syria after a meeting with Jewish leaders in London, England. Published in* The Times, *December 12, 1918. Earlier, Chaim Weizmann had met with Feisal at Aqaba to work out the understanding.*

PRO-ZION ARABS

We Arabs, especially the educated among us, look with the deepest sympathy on the Zionist movement. Our deputation here in Paris is fully acquainted with the proposals submitted yesterday by the Zionist Organization to the Peace Conference, and we regard them as moderate and proper. We will do our best, in so far as we are concerned, to help them through: we will wish the Jews a most hearty welcome home.

> *After signing a Treaty of Friendship with Zionist leaders in London on January 3, 1919. From a letter to Felix Frankfurter dated March 3, 1919.*

Avraham Feld

HANGING OUT WITH KORESH

I hung out with him day and night; slept in his apartment, ate with him, and got drunk with him.... [Koresh] felt that his message was going against a wall of rabbinic Judaism and that the darkness of the Talmud prevented his light from penetrating.

He said he was Jewish [through his maternal grandmother], but if you questioned him enough, he said it [his distress] was because of his belief in Jesus. When he was drunk, he said he was the Messiah.

> *Reporting on his contacts with David Koresh, who had lived and studied in Jerusalem before establishing his Branch Davidian cult headquarters in Waco, Texas. From a report by Haim Shapiro in the July 17, 1993 issue of* The Jerusalem Post.

Edward Feld

PULVERIZED OPTIMISM

[After the Holocaust] all optimistic liberalism evaporates. Any simple trust in the basic and inevitable goodness is forfeited, any faith in the long-range victory of a general and progressive meliorism is dispelled. We now know the depths of humanity's capacity for evil. We are different because of the Holocaust, terribly different.

> *From his* Spirit of Renewal *(1991).*

David Feldman

SEXUAL RESTRAINT AND DISCIPLINE

Judaism imposes certain restraints and discipline in this area of life that are intended to safeguard both persons and sex itself from abuse. In its proper setting sex is a *mitzva* [commandment].... The sex act itself is described in classic Jewish sources as both good and holy. The Jewish sex ethic, then, affirms sexual pleasure in the disciplined structure of family life and holds the restraints of civilization to be the means of holiness.

> *From his* Birth Control in Jewish Law *(1968).*

Tovah Feldshuh

HAPPY WITH HER NAME

I am very happy to be who I am. Having kept this name [Tovah] has harnessed me for Jewish affairs and I am grateful for that. All the Jewish charities mean a great deal to me. They are in the business of making lives work.

> *Quoted in Tim Boxer's* Jewish Celebrity Hall of Fame *(1987).*

Edna Ferber

TO HITLER, WITH CONTEMPT

To Adolf Hitler, who made me a better Jew and a more understanding and tolerant human being, as he has millions of other Jews, this book is dedicated in loathing and contempt.

> *The dedication in her autobiography,* Peculiar Treasure *(1939).*

SONS AND MOTHERS

Men often marry their mothers.

From her Saratoga Trunk *(1941).*

CLOSED MINDS

A closed mind is a dying mind.

From a 1947 radio broadcast.

BIG ISN'T BETTER

Big doesn't necessarily mean better. Sunflowers aren't better than violets.

From her Giant *(1952).*

¤

Ferdinand and Isabella

EXPULSION FROM SPAIN

And as it is found and appears, that the said Jews, wherever they live and congregate, daily increase in continuing their wicked and injurious purposes; to afford them no further opportunity for insulting our holy Catholic faith, and those whom until now God has been pleased to preserve, as well as those who had fallen, but have amended and are brought back to our holy mother church, which, according to the weakness of our human nature and diabolical suggestion that continually wages war with us, may easily occur, unless the principal cause of it be removed, which is to banish the said Jews from our kingdoms....

Therefore we command this our edict to be issued, whereby we command all Jews and Jewesses, of whatever age they may be, that live, reside, and dwell in our said kingdoms and dominions, as well natives as those who are not, who in any manner or for any cause may have come to dwell therein, that by the end of the month of July next, of the present year, 1492, they depart from all our said kingdoms and dominions...under pain that if they do not perform and execute the same, and are found to reside in our said kingdoms and dominions, or should in any manner live therein, they incur the penalty of death, and confiscation of all their property to our treasury.

From the edict for the expulsion of the Jews, March 30, 1492.

¤

Max Ferguson

JUDAISM IS JOY

I spent the first 30 years of my life giving my mother a hard time about being too Jewish and the last few years giving her a hard time about not being Jewish enough.... Judaism is joy. Bottom line is joy—top line, middle line, bottom line. Even the Kaddish is a reaffirmation of life.

After the renowned artist discovered his roots in the late 1980s. Quoted in Joan Schwartz Michel's article in Hadassah Magazine, *March 1994.*

TAPPING JEWISH ROOTS

I guess there's always been something in me, my Yiddish *neshoma*, waiting to be tapped. In many ways I was running full speed from it. At a certain point I just turned around and faced it.

Ibid.

¤

Lion Feuchtwanger

POWER OF THE BOOK

They [the Jews] had no state holding them together, no country, no soil, no king, no form of life in common. If, in spite of this, they were one, more one than all the other peoples of the world, it was the Book that sweated them into unity.

From his Power *(1925).*

SUFFERING STRENGTHENS

It is only the strong who are strengthened by suffering; the weak are made weaker.

From a 1940 article in the Paris Gazette.

JEWISH HEARTBEAT

My brain thinks like a cosmopolitan, my heart beats like a Jew.

Quoted in One Hundred Small Works *(1956), a collection compiled by Wolfgang Berndt.*

DEFINING JUDAISM

Judaism is a shared mentality, a shared intellectual attitude. It is the agreement of all who belong to this group, the "consensus omnium" on all crucial problems. It is the concord and agreement of a three-thousand-year-old tradition on what is good and bad, fortune and misfortune, desirable or hateful, agreement on the fundamental views concerning God and man.

Ibid.

○

Johann Fichte

SOLVING THE JEWISH PROBLEM

Grant them civil rights? I see no other way of doing this except to cut off all their heads on one night and substitute other heads without a single Jewish thought in them.

Quoted in Joseph Telushkin's Jewish Wisdom *(1994).*

○

Ben Field

TWO GREAT BREASTS

I look around and see how fortunate is the American writer of Jewish birth. He sits on two knees, he is suckled by two great breasts. Walt Whitman is his own, and so is Sholem Aleichem.

Quoted in Caravan: A Jewish Quarterly Omnibus *(1962).*

○

Totie Fields

PAIN AND AFFLICTION

I see life a little differently now. I have a different set of values than I did before. I don't waste time on nonsense when I can see beauty in flowers, in trees and in the faces of people around me.

Laughing saves me, too. If I took the amputation seriously, everyone around me would be sad. It's not too bad to lose a leg. I had two of them. But I only have one sense of humor to lose.

My father was blind. I learned from him that you only feel sad for people in pain. He wasn't in pain. Neither am I. I feel terrific every morning when I get up.

In April 1976 the comedienne underwent surgery for the removal of her left leg. With the aid of an artificial limb, within one year, she was up and about, resuming her career. Questioned about her successful recovery and high spirits, this was her response.

○

Irving Fineman

RAPE OF DINAH

Much as I abhorred what they [Simeon and Levi] were doing, I could hardly make war on my sons. But when I looked upon the foul thing they had done after all my teaching, I thought how like it was to the behavior of a child who, left unwatched, will break the careful training of its mother and befoul itself.

Referring to the story in Genesis (34) about the rape of Dinah and the distress of Jacob over the outrageous revenge taken upon Hamor and his son Shechem and all the townspeople for the dastardly act. From his novel Jacob.

○

Fyvush Finkel

IT'S A MIRACLE

I can tell you one thing: For Ray Walston [who plays the part of Judge Bone in the television series *Picket Fences*] it's nothing new to be successful. For me, it's a miracle.

After winning the 1994 Emmy for Best Supporting Actor in his role as an attorney who will stop at nothing to defend his client.

○

Louis Finkelman

WE ARE ALL ALIKE

No matter how different cultures are, most people, simple people, are everywhere the same. They love their children. They are willing to take great risks to find a better place for their children. They want things to be better for their children.

Quoting his mother's advice on welcoming strangers. From Moment *magazine, December 1980.*

○

Louis Finkelstein

THE PRICE OF SUCCESS

Nations have been wrecked because they lacked an overriding moral goal to which individuals could commit themselves. History shows us that when we become success-dominated, we lose sight of our real reasons for living.

From "The Businessman's Moral Failure," an article that appeared in Fortune *magazine, September 1958.*

RISKING THE WORLD

Certain ancient rules apply with equal force to Jew and Christian, atheist and agnostic, to all men in all situations. These immutable laws are expressed in various ways. The Pentateuch reveals the Decalogue and the Golden Rule of Leviticus 19:18: "Thou shalt love thy neighbor as thyself."...

Yet these and other binding commandments are often violated in the American business community. A man fears he may be risking his business if he obeys them, forgetting, however, that if he violates them he risks the world.

Ibid.

MEASURING SUPERIORITY

Rabbi Israel Salanter found two boys quarreling over which was the taller. One forced the other to stand in a ditch to settle the argument. Seeing this, Rabbi Israel sadly commented, "Isn't this characteristic of the world where to prove his superiority man must prove others inferior? After all, the same purpose could have been achieved by standing on a chair!"

Ibid.

TIME IS LIFE

On the inside cover of Professor Israel Davidson's watch was the inscription, "It is later than you think." Once, addressing the students of the Jewish Theological Seminary at a Commencement, he said, "There is an American proverb which I think is not only false but pernicious in its implication. America prides itself on having coined the saying, "Time is money." This is a false statement and leads to serious error. The only case in which time and money are alike is that there are some people who do not know what to do with their time and some who do not know what to do with their money, and still others who are so unfortunate as not to know what to do with either. But, otherwise, time is infinitely more precious than money, and there is nothing common between them. You cannot accumulate time; you cannot regain time lost; you cannot borrow time; you can never tell how much time you have left in the Bank of Life. Time *is* life.

From his evaluation of the life of Israel Davidson (1870–1939) in the American Jewish Yearbook, *Vol. 41 (1939–40).*

MORAL DECISIVENESS

The art and science of life are even more exacting in their demands than any others. The penetration of moral decisiveness into every aspect of life, and indeed the very conception of life as a science and an art, involves sacrifice of the immediate and tangible for the future and the intangible.

From his Pharisees *(1940).*

EXEGESIS AND CUSTOMS

Customs create exegesis, not exegesis customs.

Ibid.

UNITY WITHOUT UNIFORMITY

Out of man's present spiritual chaos may emerge an ordered, pluralistic universe of thought. It will be a universe in which the principle of federalism is applied to the realm of the spirit, as it has been in the realm of political life. Unity will be achieved with no sacrifice of liberty; cooperation without imposing uniformity.

Ibid.

JEWISH CEREMONIES

The fundamental concept of the Jewish ceremonial system is that God continually reveals Himself in nature, in history, and in man's daily life. Each ceremony seeks to emphasize some aspect of this Divine revelation, and thus becomes a means for communion between man and God.

From the essay "Jewish Religion: Its Beliefs and Practices," in his book The Jews: Their History, Culture and Religion *(1949).*

FAILED PROPHET

The conversion of American Jews to other faiths is proceeding at such an alarming rate that, within the next generation or two, Judaism may cease to have any significance in American life.... The stream of conversion of Jews to other faiths has become a river, particularly in the case of boys who have been overseas, all very sensitive.

From a statement made at the outset of a fundraising campaign for the Jewish Theological Seminary of America. Reported in the Brooklyn Jewish Examiner, *March 8, 1946.*

AMERICA THE SAVIOR

America saved not only our lives but our souls.

From an address delivered in 1976 at the U.S. bicentennial celebration in Newport, Rhode Island.

¤

David "Dudu" Fisher

IN LOVE WITH JEAN VALJEAN

I cried throughout the whole show. It was like a butterfly seeing another life from the cocoon. At the end of the show I was sitting in my seat alone, my eyes swollen, when I suddenly felt a tap on my shoulder. A man said, "Excuse me, sir, the show is over." And I said, "No, sir, the show is not over. The show is just beginning." I saw [it] again and again and I said to my manager I wanted to audition for the part.

> *After seeing* Les Misérables *in London for the first time.*

LIFE WITHOUT HUGO

In the yeshiva they thought we could get on in life without Victor Hugo. It happened I could not.

> *Ibid.*

ON BEING A JEW FIRST

I'm a religious man. There are borders I won't cross. I'm a Jew first, an Israeli second and an artist third.

> *Commenting on his refusal to perform in the theater on the Sabbath or Jewish holidays.*

LIKE PRAYING BEFORE THE ARK

In the show [*Les Misérables*] I'm singing from the heart. It's exactly the same when I'm standing in front of the Ark.

> *Commenting on the emotion with which he portrays the role of Jean Valjean in* Les Misérables.

▢

Eddie Fisher

ELIZABETH TAYLOR'S CONVERSION

She sincerely believed in what she had done. Then she forgot all about it. We didn't go to synagogue. We celebrated Yom Kippur only once.

> *Commenting on Elizabeth Taylor's conversion to Judaism by Reform rabbi Max Nussbaum before she married Fisher.*

A JEW FIRST AND ALWAYS

I think it is too late for me. For what I have been through and what I have found, it is too late for me to find a nice Jewish girl in show business. The woman I have now is not Jewish, but she is a very spiritual woman, very religious in her thinking. As a matter of fact, she has changed a lot of my thinking. Not as far as being a Jew. I am a Jew, first and always. Proud that I am a Jew. That is my *shtoltz* [pride].

> *Quoted in Tim Boxer's* Jewish Celebrity Hall of Fame *(1987).*

I BELIEVE

I have a deep concern for Israel. I am a Zionist. I believe in America; I believe in Israel.

> *Ibid. When asked how he expresses his Jewishness.*

A SPECIAL ATTRACTION TO NON-JEWISH WOMEN

I couldn't help being attracted to beautiful women, almost always women who were not Jewish, because they were forbidden. And I was excited when they responded to me, whatever their motives. Going out with a pretty *shiksa*, going to bed with her, was like spending a lot of money—a way of proving I was no longer a poor Jew from the slums of Philadelphia. I was somebody.

> *From his autobiography,* Eddie: My Life, My Loves.

▢

Eugene Fisher

SHOAH MEANS HOLOCAUST

When I started working in this field, I could not presume a Catholic audience would understand what I meant when I spoke about the Holocaust. Today I don't need to explain Holocaust to use it, and can use the Hebrew term *Shoah*, and will tell them that it means Holocaust.

> *After noting Pope John Paul's usage of the term* Shoah *before a group of rabbis who met with him on Saturday night, October 7, 1995, during a visit to the New York Metropolitan area.*

▢

Max M. Fisher

MESSAGE ISRAEL BRINGS

Out of this land [Israel] once came a great message to the world: justice, freedom and human dignity. And we Jews, we choose to believe that out of this land will yet come another such message. To be given a chance to make our contribution to that goal, to be able to do our part by re-establishing our people, to build for the peace that will surely come, to have a small share in creating that Israel.... All this is a privilege beyond price.

> *From a 1971 address to the newly reconstituted Jewish Agency. Quoted in Abraham Karp's* Haven and Home *(1985).*

▢

Edward H. Flannery

THE GREAT HATRED

It was Judaism that brought the concept of a God-given universal moral law into the world. [Consequently] the Jew carries the burden of God in history, and for this has never been forgiven.

> *Quoted in* The New York Times, *November 30, 1974.*

□

Edmond Fleg

THOUGHT AND REALITY

I have long since renounced the puerile atheism, and even the agnosticism, of my first philosophical ambitions. Spencer and Kant are now alike powerless to influence me. I no longer believe that spirit can come from matter, evolution or no evolution, if matter has not received spirit. I no longer believe that reality is unknowable; to feel it unknowable is already in some fashion, to know it; and if we are able, when thinking it, to impose on it the forms of our thought, then there must be, between our thought and reality, some relation of harmony.

> *Quoted in the South African magazine* Jewish Affairs, *August 1965.*

WHY I AM A JEW

I am a Jew because wherever there is suffering, the Jew weeps.
I am a Jew because whenever there is despair, the Jew hopes.
I am a Jew because the message of our faith is the oldest and the newest.

> *From his essay "Why I Am a Jew" (1929).*

REGRETS OF LATER YEARS

I regretted my years at college.... I should have studied Hebrew, learned to know my race, its origins, its beliefs, its role in history, its place among the human groups of today; to attach myself through it to something that should be I, and something more than I, to continue through it something that others had begun and that others after me would carry on.

> *Ibid.*

A MOST HUMAN PEOPLE

The Jew has suffered so much hurt, he has endured so many injustices, experienced so completely the misery of life, that pity for the poor and the humiliated has become second nature to him. And in his agonized wanderings, he has seen at close range so many men of all races, and of all countries, different everywhere and everywhere alike, that he has understood, he has felt in the flesh of his flesh, that Man is one as God is One. Thus was formed a people which may have the same vices and the same virtues as other peoples, but which is without doubt the most *human* of all peoples.

> *Ibid.*

□

Abraham Flexner

FOOTSTOOL OF EDUCATION

Without ideals, without effort, without scholarship, without philosophical continuity, there is no such thing as education.

> *From his* Universities *(1930).*

BORROWING FOR EDUCATION

Nations have recently been led to borrow billions for war; no nation has ever borrowed largely for education. Probably no nation is rich enough to pay for both war and civilization. We must make our choice; we cannot have both.

> *Ibid.*

A CALL FOR HARD WORK

The prevailing philosophy of education tends to discredit hard work.

> *Ibid.*

□

David Flusser

THE COMING OF THE MESSIAH

When he comes, we will simply ask him: "Tell me, sir, is this your first visit?"

> *In an address to a group of clerics in which he told them that Jews as well as Christians were awaiting the Messiah.*

□

Ferdinand Foch

VALIANT JEWS OF FRANCE

I greet you as representatives of the Jewish people. I thank you for what the Jewish people did in the War. They displayed great valor on the field of battle, taking the offensive as men throughout the struggle. You have reason to be proud of your race.

> *Statement made to a delegation of American rabbis in 1921.*

□

Jerome D. Folkman

MIXED MARRIAGES AND INTERMARRIAGES

In popular speech, we use "intermarriage" and "mixed marriage" almost synonymously.

We really should not do it. We should be more accurate in our language. When we refer to intermarriage we mean a marriage contracted between two people who were not originally of the same faith [and which] one of them converts to the religion of the other so as to give the family one faith. By mixed marriages, we mean a family in which there is no such conversion and in which each one tries to maintain his own religious identification.

> *Quoted in William Berkowitz's* Ten Vital
> Jewish Issues *(1964).*

◻

Gerald R. Ford

ON SOVIET JEWRY

These people are very good people. I will help you. If these people were to come here, they would never go on welfare.

> *Responding to a personal plea from Mayor
> Edward I. Koch of New York to permit
> Soviet Jews to come to the United States
> without regard to quota restrictions.*

◻

Henry Ford

FEAR OF THE JEWS

International financiers are behind all war. They are what is called the international Jew— German Jews, French Jews, English Jews, American Jews. I believe that in all those countries except our own the Jewish financier is supreme.... Here the Jew is a threat.

> *In a 1920 interview with J. J. O'Neill of the
> New York World. Quoted in Howard M.
> Sachar's* History of the Jews in America
> *(1992).*

MAKING AMENDS

I deem it to be my duty as an honorable man to make amends for the wrong done to the Jews as fellow-men and brothers, by asking their forgiveness for the harm that I have unintentionally committed...and by giving them the unqualified assurance that henceforth they may look to me for friendship and goodwill.

> *Expressing regret in 1926 for his previously
> expressed anti-Semitic views. From a letter
> to Louis Marshall, prominent Jewish leader.*

A FORD APOLOGY

I confess that I am deeply mortified that this journal [*The Dearborn Independent*] which is intended to be constructive and not destructive, has been made the medium for resurrecting exploded fictions, for giving currency to the so-called Protocols of the Wise Men of Zion, which have been demonstrated, as I learn, to be gross forgeries, and for contending that the Jews have been engaged in a conspiracy to control the capital and the industries of the world, besides laying at their door many offenses against decency, public order and good morals.

> *From a letter to Louis Marshall, dated
> June 30, 1927, Dearborn, Michigan. Quoted
> in the* American Jewish Yearbook *(1927).*

PRAISE FOR THE JEWISH PEOPLE

I am fully aware of the virtues of the Jewish people as a whole, of what they and their ancestors have done for civilization and for mankind and toward the development of commerce and industry, of their sobriety and diligence, their benevolence and their unselfish interest in the public welfare.

> *Ibid.*

◻

Henry Ford II

DEFIANCE OF THE ARAB BOYCOTT

We feel we have the right to compete in any market in the world willing to accept us as an industrial citizen.

> *A November 1966 statement defying the
> Arab League's blacklisting of the Ford Motor
> Co. because it licensed an Israeli company
> to assemble Ford trucks and tractors.*

◻

Harry Emerson Fosdick

PROGNOSIS FOR RELIGIOUS TOLERANCE

It is particularly fitting that a Christian should help introduce this volume to its American readers. Here is a story, told without malice by a Jew, which, nonetheless, lays on the Christian conscience a burden of guilt and responsibility.... Only as Jews and Christians recognize together the folly of their prejudices, the suicidal nature of their mutual antagonisms, the common guilt of their estrangement, and the great gain in their cooperation, can any desirable future be foreseen.

> *From his Foreword to Cecil Roth's* Jewish
> Contribution to Civilization *(1940).*

A PERSON FIRST

One says of a man that he is black or brown, a Jew, a Roman Catholic, a Japanese, a

German, an employer, an employee. I answer that first of all he is a person, of whom it is my business to think, and with whom it is my business to deal, as an individual.

> *From his* Victorious Living.

ARABS UNDER JEWISH RULE

I would regard it as an injustice to the Arabs to put them under Jewish rule without their consent.

> *A comment made after the creation of the Jewish State in 1948. From his* Living of These Days: An Autobiography *(1956).*

DUAL LOYALTIES

We resent the Zionist endeavor to make the State of Israel the center of patriotism for American Jews. The Jewish people here are American like all the rest of us, and Judaism is not a nationalistic cult, but is one of the great universal faiths.

> *Ibid. A statement issued in 1960. Quoted in Egal Feldman's* Dual Destinies: The Jewish Encounter with Protestant America *(1990).*

DIRE PROPHESY

[Zionism] must forego grasping ambition for political dominance and turn its back on chauvinistic nationalism. It must cease its absurd pretense that into this poor land as a place of refuge millions of persecuted Jews from southeastern Europe can be poured.... But if the partisans of political Zionism, as now seems probable, are allowed to force the issue, I am willing to risk my reputation on prophecy: Zionism will end in tragedy.

> *From his* Pilgrimage to Palestine *(1928).*

¤

Marvin Fox

LIFE WITHOUT TORAH

I believe, because I cannot afford not to believe. I believe as a Jew, in the divinity of Torah, because without God's Torah I have lost the ground for making my own life intelligible and purposeful.

> *From an essay in* Condition of Jewish Belief *(1966), compiled by the editors of* Commentary *magazine.*

¤

Abraham H. Foxman

RECOGNIZING ANTI-SEMITISM

A few years ago, a justice of the Supreme Court of the United States declared that while he could not define obscenity, he knew it when he saw it. That is the way we Jews feel about anti-Semitism. We definitely know it when we read it, see it, or hear it, and we certainly feel it when it breeds violence against us.

> *In an address to the World Conference on Anti-Semitism and Prejudice in a Changing World, held in Brussels, Belgium, July 1992.*

JESSE JACKSON'S RECORD

I will, with your permission at this point, say a few words about the Reverend Jesse Jackson and his appearance this morning. I welcome, as we all do, the Reverend Jesse Jackson's effort at reconciliation with the Jewish community. I welcome, as you do, anything that Jackson says which unqualifiably confronts and rejects anti-Semitism and those who give it voice....

But having stated that fervent hope, I must also note that Jackson's record on anti-Semitism and other issues of deep concern to the Jewish community is not a blank slate....

For Reverend Jackson's opposition to anti-Semitism to be meaningful, his speech will have to be delivered in Crown Heights and the ghettos of Bedford Styvesant, and to the black student unions around the country. Reverend Jackson's words of opposition to anti-Semitism will have to be buttressed by credible action, which will build a constructive relationship to the benefit of both our communities.

> *Ibid.*

TOLERANCE FOR INTOLERANCE

There's a greater tolerance for intolerance today. In this society there is a new permissiveness that almost sanctions hate.

> *Speaking out in 1993 after the ADL was attacked for "creating" anti-Semitism.*

SYNAGOGUE OF SATAN

I don't expect her to be a great judge of lyrics, but how many people were involved in the production of that record?

> *Ibid. Referring to Madonna's recording of "Immaculate Conception," where she sings the lyric "Jews worshipping at the Synagogue of Satan."*

QUIVERING ANTENNAS

When our antennas quiver, we don't have the luxury to conduct a deep study. We should speak out, and if we err, I would rather err on the side of speaking out. Erring the other way could cost us dearly.

> *Ibid.*

ISRAEL'S RIGHT TO GOVERN ITSELF

Jews all of a sudden have individual rights but not group rights. Everybody has the right to self determination, but not the Jews. That belief made possible the 1975 United Nations resolution equating Zionism with racism. Israel is also the only country in the world that does not have the right to designate its own capital.

Ibid.

NEED FOR A SCAPEGOAT

If the Nation of Islam wants to better the plight of African-Americans, how does this message of hate, of attacking and defaming other people, help? How does it alleviate violence and injustice? Why this need to scapegoat Jews, who have historically shared with the African-American community the pain and anguish of prejudice?

Commenting on an anti-Semitic February 19, 1994 speech, delivered in Baltimore, Maryland, by Nation of Islam spokesman Khalid Abdul Muhammed.

NEW TOLERANCE FOR ANTI-SEMITISM

Fifty years after the Holocaust, there is a new tolerance for anti-Semitism. All of us, in Israel and in the US, have to recognize these two contradictory trends, and work harder than ever to see that those who preach anti-Semitism are excluded from the world community.

From his column in The Jerusalem Post, *June 25, 1994.*

SEPARATING CHURCH AND STATE

I have no objection to Jews or Christians being elected to public office, but if they are elected they cannot in any way be influenced by their religious beliefs.... Legislators should vote against murder because that's what the majority of people want, not because legislators believe God says that murder is wrong.

From a telephone conversation that Pat Robertson reported he had with Foxman after the appearance of David Cantor's Religious Right: The Assault on Tolerance and Pluralism in America, *in which Robertson claims that he was attacked without provocation.*

CRITIQUING THE RELIGIOUS RIGHT

The problem with issuing a critique of the religious right movement is that much of what this movement says it wants is right: most of us value strong families, better schools, a government that upholds the commitment to religious liberty.

[But] the religious right's simple insistence on organized prayer and Christianized curricula flaunts constitutional and democratic considerations.

Ibid. From the Foreword.

PRAYER IN PUBLIC SCHOOLS

Those who seek to intrude organized prayer into America's public schools do not seek to intrude a minority's prayer. An organized school prayer in this country would inevitably be either a Christian prayer or some unsatisfactory secularized variation. Furthermore, school prayer likely would be merely the first salvo in a campaign to "Christianize" America.

From his column in the January 1995 issue of On the Frontline, *the monthly publication of the Anti-Defamation League.*

A SPIRITUAL PROTEST

I can no longer pray in a synagogue with a spiritual leader who spouts such hate-filled rhetoric and who harbors such intolerance toward others.

From a 1995 letter in which he announced his resignation from an Orthodox synagogue of which he was a member for more than twenty years. He was protesting the vitriolic attacks of the rabbi against Israeli Prime Minister Yitzhak Rabin's government for its efforts to make peace with the Palestinians.

PIED PIPER

He could be a pied piper of reconciliation and atonement.... Instead, he continues to be the pied piper of bigotry, racism, and anti-Semitism.

Questioning the sincerity of Louis Farrakhan's call for a reconciliation between blacks and Jews at the Million Man March on Washington, DC, in October 1995.

◊

Anatole France

DEPTHS OF DESPAIR

There is not in all the universe a creature more unhappy than I. People think me happy. I have never been happy for one day, not for a single hour.

Revealing his feelings after being adored for his brilliance by his many loyal friends and admirers.

◊

Anne Frank

DEAR DIARY

I hope I shall be able to confide in you completely, as I have never before been able to do in anyone before, and I hope that you will be a great support and comfort to me.

At age thirteen, addressing the diary she kept while in hiding from the Nazis, who occupied Holland in 1942. From Anne Frank: Diary of a Young Girl *(1952).*

SUNSHINE AND JOY

I looked out of the open window, over a large area of Amsterdam, over all the roofs and on to the horizon, which was such a pale blue that it was hard to see the dividing line. As long as this exists, I thought, and I may live to see it, this sunshine, these cloudless skies, while this lasts I cannot be unhappy.

A February 23, 1944 diary entry.

HAPPINESS IS CONTAGIOUS

Whoever is happy will make others happy too. He who has courage and faith will never perish in misery!

A March 7, 1944 diary entry.

HOPING AGAINST HOPE

We have been pointedly reminded that we are in hiding, that we are Jews in chains.... We Jews mustn't show our feelings, must be brave and strong, must accept all inconveniences and not grumble.... Sometime this terrible war will be over. Surely the time will come when we are people again, and not just Jews.

An April 11, 1944 diary entry.

MUTUAL RESPONSIBILITY

Is discord going to show itself while we are still fighting, is the Jew once again worth less than another? Oh, it is sad, very sad, that once more, for the umpteenth time, the old truth is confirmed: what *one* Christian does is his own responsibility, what *one* Jew does is thrown back at all Jews.

A May 22, 1944 diary entry.

COMING OF AGE

One of the many questions that have often bothered me is why women have been, and still are, thought to be so inferior to men. It's easy to say unfair, but that's not enough for me; I'd really like to know the reason for this great injustice.

A June 13, 1944 diary entry.

IN SPITE OF EVERYTHING

In spite of everything, I still believe that people are really good at heart.

A July 15, 1944 diary entry.

WE ARE RESPONSIBLE

[Daddy] said: "All children must look after their own upbringing." Parents can only give good advice or put them on the right paths, but the final forming of a person's character lies in their own hands.

Ibid.

SOLACE FROM NATURE

The best remedy for those who are afraid, lonely, or unhappy is to go outside, somewhere where they can be quite alone with the heavens, nature, and God. Because only then does one feel that all is as it should be and that God wishes to see people happy, amidst the simple beauty of nature. As long as this exists, and it certainly always will, I know that then there will always be comfort for every sorrow.... And I firmly believe that nature brings solace in all troubles.

Ibid.

FOREVER AN OPTIMIST

I hear the ever approaching thunder, which will destroy us, too. I can feel the sufferings of millions and yet, if I look up into the heavens, I think that it will all come [out] right, that this cruelty too will end, and that peace and tranquility will return again.

One of the last entries in her diary before being captured by the German police in August 1944.

□

Barney Frank

SHARP RETORT

Nobody has ever called my mother Mrs. Fag.

After the House of Representative majority leader, Dick Armey of Texas, called him (in 1995) "Barney Fag," which Armey later claimed was a slip of the tongue. Frank is an avowed homosexual.

I YIELD

I yield the floor to Abraham Lincoln.

After Henry Hyde, the Republican congressman from Illinois, and an historian, made reference to historical figures.

ON SCHOOL PRAYER

[Anti-Semitism] made me distrust anyone who wants to come along and impose a kind of uniform orthodoxy on America. I say to my friends, who like the idea of school prayer in principle, that they should understand it ain't going to be *Shma Yisrael*.

> *From an interview in* The Jerusalem Report, *April 6, 1995.*

JEWS IN POLITICS

We have two Jewish women in the Senate from California [Dianne Feinstein and Barbara Boxer]. You can now get elected as a Jew from almost anywhere. In my own lifetime, I have seen anti-Semitism in politics diminish substantially.

> *Ibid.*

LIFE IN THE MINORITY

It's never been easy for me to think of myself as part of a natural majority. I cannot think of any basic characteristic where I'm in the majority. I'm gay. I'm Jewish. I'm male. I'm even left-handed.

> *Quoted in* The New Republic, *March 6, 1995.*

SPEAKING OF THE SPEAKER

He [Newt Gingrich] has one of the most consistently anti-gay records in the Congress. When three members of the House in 1994 said they would never hire a gay person under any circumstances, and some of us criticized them, he defended them. When Dee Mosbacher, the lesbian daughter of Robert Mosbacher, got her father to meet with National Gay and Lesbian Task Force people in 1992, nine Republican members of the House wrote him a letter and denounced him. One of those members was Gingrich.

> *Ibid. Gingrich became Speaker of the House in 1994.*

◘

Hans Frank

WISHFUL THINKING

I ask nothing of the Jews, except that they should disappear.... We must destroy the Jews wherever we meet them and whenever opportunity presents offers.

> *A December 16, 1941 pronouncement in Poland.*

ETERNAL GUILT

A thousand years will pass and the guilt of Germany will not be erased.

> *From a statement made in 1946 at the Nuremberg Trials.*

◘

Ellen Frankel

JUDAISM AND THINGS ENGLISH

Going to synagogue in England is like seeing *My Fair Lady* in Yiddish: it's familiar but completely incongruous. At the *bimah* [platform] stands Henry Higgins in top hat and *tallis:* in the women's gallery high above the sanctuary, kibbitzing and chattering sits a bevy of matronly Eliza Doolittles, wearing plumed, furred and flowered hats to rival the Queen's. The rabbi sits stiffly by the ark, trussed up with rabbinic robe and medieval English lawyer's collar. At the close of the Orthodox service all congregants reverently intone an English prayer for Queen Elizabeth, Prince Charles and the Queen Mother.

> *From* Moment *magazine, May 1980.*

◘

Zechariah Frankel

ATTAINING RESPECTABILITY

A people without a center or a government of its own can never attain to honor among the nations of the world. We must therefore demonstrate that the desire for rebirth still lives within us.

> *Quoted in Louis Ginzberg's* Students, Scholars, and Saints *(1928).*

POSITIVE-HISTORICAL JUDAISM

Positive-Historical Judaism...[is] my Judaism.

> *From a speech in Frankfurt, Germany, July 18, 1845.*

JEWISH COMMUNAL LINK

Hebrew is the historical chain which links all the dispersed parts of our people into one national body. If we drive it out of Jewish communal life in Germany...we destroy our national unity, and become strangers to all other Jews.

> *From a letter to Abraham Geiger in 1845.*

◘

Felix Frankfurter

REMEMBER THE NAME

Some day you will be proud to have known the owner of that name.

> *After one of his college professors made an anti-Semitic remark about his name.*

ON SALUTING THE FLAG

One who belongs to the most vilified and persecuted minority in history is not likely to be insensible [sic] to the freedom guaranteed by our Constitution.... But as judges we are neither Jew nor Gentile, neither Catholic nor agnostic.... As a member of this Court I am not justified in writing my private notions of policy into the Constitution, no matter how deeply I may cherish them.

> In siding with the state against a dissenting minority (Jehovah's Witnesses) in the question of saluting the flag. The case was West Virginia State Board of Education v. Barnette (1943).

TO LEAVE AS A JEW

I came into the world a Jew, and although I did not live my life entirely as a Jew, I think it is fitting that I should leave as a Jew. I don't want to be one of these pretenders and turn my back on a great and noble heritage.

> From a conversation with playwright and producer Garson Kanin, who had interviewed the Supreme Court justice. Reported in a 1964 article in The Atlantic Monthly.

PROCEDURAL SAFEGUARDS

The history of liberty has largely been the history of the observance of procedural safeguards.

> From his 1943 brief in the case of McNabb v. United States.

ON BEING TOLERANT

If err we must, let us err on the side of tolerance.

> Quoted in The New York Times Magazine, November 23, 1952.

THE GOOD SOCIETY

When there are repressions, or inhibitions, or fears, or timidities, or prudences, you can't have a good society.

> Quoted in The New York Times, February 23, 1965.

GOVERNMENT AN ART

Government is neither business, nor technology, nor applied science. It is the art of making men live together in peace and with reasonable happiness.

> From an article in The New Republic, October 31, 1928.

THE HEAVENLY SUPREME COURT

He loathed being President and being Chief Justice was all happiness for him. He fought against being President and yielded to the acceptance of that heritage because of the insistence of Mrs. Taft—very ambitious in that direction. It had always been the ambition of his life to be on the Supreme Court. Taft once said that the Supreme Court was his notion of what heaven must be like.

> Describing the life of William Howard Taft, the twenty-seventh president of the United States. From his Reminiscences (1947).

APPEASEMENT OF A DICTATOR

I wonder if Joe Kennedy [father of President John F. Kennedy and U.S. ambassador to Great Britain in 1938] understands the implication of public talk by an American ambassador. Such public approval of dictatorships, in part even, plays into their hands.

> In a letter to President Franklin Roosevelt condemning the ambassador for using his post to urge the appeasement of Hitler, claiming that only economics counted—trade, finance, deals—not how the Nazis chose to rule. Quoted by A. M. Rosenthal in his New York Times column, January 4, 1994.

HISTORIAN, PHILOSOPHER, JUDGE

A judge should be compounded of the faculties that are demanded of the historian and the philosopher and the prophet. The last demand upon him—to make some forecast of the consequences of his action—is perhaps the heaviest. To pierce the curtain of the future, to give shape and visage to mysteries still in the womb of time, is the gift of imagination.

> From Of Laws & Life & Other Things That Matter: Papers & Addresses of Felix Frankfurter 1956–1963, edited by Philip B. Kurland (1969).

MARRIAGE NOT A CRIME

The reason I don't perform marriages is because marriages aren't considered federal offenses.

> Quoted in Morris Mandel's Affronts, Insults, and Indignities (1975).

¤

Victor E. Frankl

THE PRECIOUS GIFT OF FREE CHOICE

We who lived in concentration camps can remember the men who walked through the huts comforting others, giving away their last piece of bread. They may have been few in number, but they offer sufficient proof that everything can be taken from a man but one thing: the last of the human freedoms—to choose one's attitude in any given set of circumstances, to choose one's own way.

From his Man's Search for Meaning *(1985).*

¤

Benjamin Franklin

HEROIC ANCIENT PEOPLE

The Jews were acquainted with several Arts and Sciences long e'er the Romans became a People, or the Greeks were known among the Nations. Indeed, if the Greeks had been acquainted with the songs of Moses...or the Romans had ever known the odes of David... they would never have spoke of the Jews with so much Contempt.... I believe I might fairly challenge all the Antiquity of the Heathens, to present us with an Ode of more beautiful sentiments, and greater Elegancy than the Lamentations over Saul and Jonathan.

From an article in The Pennsylvania Gazette.

¤

Earl Emil Franzos

EPITOME OF HATRED

Each country has the kind of Jews it deserves.

From an article in the Neue Freie Presse, *March 31, 1875.*

¤

Frederick of Baden

DR. HERZL, NOBLE MAN

Doctor, you know, of course, the Zionist movement and its leader, Dr. Herzl. Yes, Dr. Herzl is a noble man, who placed himself at the head of the organization without any self-seeking and out of the purest motives. The Governments have as yet, unfortunately, no true understanding of the cause, but that will come in time. Thank God, we do not need such havens of refuge for our German Jews; but we do need them for your coreligionists in the East and North.

From an audience he granted to Jewish leader Dr. A. Berliner on July 25, 1899.

¤

George M. Fredrickson

JEWISH SUCCESS STORY

The success of Jews, despite virulent anti-Semitism, was due in large part to the advantage of being not merely on the right side of the American color line but also of being unusually skilled and well educated for an immigrant group.

From a review of Ronald Tokakis's Different Mirror: History of Multicultural America, *in* The New York Times Book Review, *August 22, 1993.*

¤

Max Freedman

THE ESSENCE OF FRANKFURTER

Small, quick, articulate, jaunty, Frankfurter was inexhaustible in his energy, and his curiosity, giving off sparks like an overcharged electric battery. He loved people, loved conversation, loved influence, loved life. Beyond his sparkling personal qualities, he had an erudite and incisive legal intelligence, a resourceful approach to questions of public policy, and a passion for raising the standards of public service.

From his Roosevelt and Frankfurter: Their Correspondence, 1928–1945.

¤

Solomon B. Freehof

JUDAISM AND PROSELYTISM

Would that Christianity had the same respect for Judaism as Jewish law has for Christianity! The Christian missionary mandate leads them to hope that Judaism will disappear into Christianity. We have no such hope and therefore no such mandate. The list of 613 commandments contains no commandment to proselytize.

From an essay in Condition of Jewish Belief *(1966), compiled by the editors of* Commentary *magazine.*

THE POWER OF PRAYER

A man should praise God even for misfortunes as much as he praises Him for happiness [say the Rabbis in the Talmud]. Whether this lofty courage is attainable by the average Jew or not, he learns to feel and to express, or perhaps to express and thus to feel, a constant sense of gratitude to the Master of the Universe. Prayer in Israel teaches man to overcome bitterness and self-pity; to think not of what the world owes him, but what he owes the world and God. It is not primarily piteous pleading but is essentially grateful communion with the Infinite.

From his Small Sanctuary *(1942).*

THE BIBLE AND THE PRAYERBOOK

The Bible is the meaning of Judaism; the prayerbook its method. The Bible is doctrine; the prayerbook is spiritual training.

Ibid.

GOD AND PRAYER

Prayer is the search for harmony between man and God, the quest for communion between the finite and the infinite.

Ibid.

◻

Eliyah Frej

SLIP OF MIND

The court said I stole merchandise. I said I bought it, I just couldn't remember from whom.

After having served a nine-year prison sentence in Israel. Quoted in The Jerusalem Report, *February 24, 1994.*

◻

Abbé Frémont

DUTY OF A CHRISTIAN

I do not evade the responsibilities which duty imposes on me, and I tell you as a Christian, as a priest, before the holy altars which hear me, that when I peruse the history of the past, one of the saddest pages before my eyes is that which relates the hateful persecutions heaped upon the sorrowful remnants of Israel over such a long period of time.... Gentlemen, these things must be denounced energetically, denounced in order that Catholics may not bear the responsibility for the same.

Quoted in Joseph L. Baron's Stars and Sand *(1943).*

◻

Sigmund Freud

SEX BEHAVIOR

Homosexuality is assuredly no advantage, but is nothing to be ashamed of, no vice, no degradation. It cannot be classified as an illness.

From a 1935 letter to a mother concerned about her son's homosexuality. Expressing a viewpoint adopted by a unanimous vote of the Board of the American Psychiatric Association in 1973.

NATURAL HOMOSEXUALITY

Natural homosexuality is something pathological; it is an arrested development.

Quoted in Dr. Joseph Wortis's Fragments of an Analysis with Freud *(1954).*

MY IDENTITY

My parents were Jews, and I remained a Jew myself.

From his Autobiographical Study *(1935).*

THE ADVANTAGE OF BEING JEWISH

Only to my Jewish nature did I owe the two qualities which have become indispensable to me on my hard road. Because I was a Jew I found myself free from many prejudices which limit others in the use of their intellects.

From a May 6, 1926 speech to the B'nai B'rith in Vienna, Austria. From B'nai B'rith magazine, June 1936.

JEWISH CHARACTERISTICS

In some respects, indeed, the Jews are our superiors. They do not need so much alcohol as we do in order to make life tolerable; crimes of brutality, murder, robbery and sexual violence are great rarities among them; they have always set a high value on intellectual achievement and interest; their family life is more intimate; they take better care of the poor; charity is a sacred duty to them, since we have allowed them to cooperate in our cultural tasks, they have acquired merit by valuable contributions in all the spheres of science, art and technology, and they have richly repaid our tolerance. So let us cease at last to hand them out favours when they have claim to justice.

From his article "A Comment on Anti-Semitism" in Volume 23 of the Complete Works. *Quoted in Raphael Patai's* Jewish Mind *(1977). Freud pretended that the statement is a quotation from an anonymous Christian writer.*

RELIGION AS ILLUSION

Religion is an illusion and it derives its strength from its readiness to fit in with our instinctual wishful impulses.

From Lecture 35 in his New Introductory Lectures on Psycho-Analysis *(1933).*

THE ROYAL ROAD

The interpretation of dreams is the royal road to a knowledge of the unconscious activities of the mind.

From his Interpretation of Dreams *(1900).*

SECRET TREASURE

[The Jewish people] has met misfortune and ill-treatment with an unexampled capacity for resistance, it has developed special character-traits and incidentally has earned the hearty dislike of every other people....

We know the reason for this behaviour and what their secret treasure is. They really regard themselves as God's chosen people, they believe that they stand especially close to Him and this makes them proud and confident.

From his last book, Moses and Monotheism *(1939).*

JUDAISM: THE FATHER RELIGION

Judaism had been a religion of the father; Christianity became a religion of the son. The old God the Father fell back behind Christ; Christ, the Son, took his place, just as every son had hoped to do in primeval times.

Ibid.

THE $64,000 QUESTION

Why the people of Israel adhered to their God all the more devotedly the worse they were treated by Him, that is a question we must leave open.

Ibid.

YEARNING FOR FATHER

It is the longing for the father that lives in each of us from his childhood days.

Ibid.

A LIVING TRADITION

It is honor enough for the Jewish people that it has kept alive such a tradition and produced men who lent it their voice, even if the stimulus had first come from the outside, from a great stranger.

Ibid.

HATRED FOR JUDAISM

We must not forget that all the people who now excel in the practice of anti-Semitism became Christians only in relatively recent times, sometimes forced to it by bloody compulsion. One might say they all are "badly christened"; under the thin veneer of Christianity they have remained what their ancestors were, barbarically polytheistic. They have not yet overcome their grudge against the new religion which was forced on them.... The hatred for Judaism is at bottom hatred for Christianity.

Ibid.

HUMAN PRIVILEGE

Neurosis seems to be a human privilege.

Ibid.

LET YOUR SON GROW UP AS A JEW

If you do not let your son grow up as a Jew, you deprive him of those sources of energy which cannot be replaced by anything else. He will have to struggle as a Jew and you ought to develop in him all the energy he will need for the struggle. Do not deprive him of that advantage.

Statement made to Max Graf. Quoted in Psychoanalytical Quarterly, *1942.*

SPIRITUAL VALUES

We Jews have always known how to respect spiritual values.

From a November 30, 1938 letter to Jacob Meitlis.

POWER OF IDEAS

We [Jews] preserved our unity through ideas, and because of them we have survived to this day.

Ibid.

RELIGION AS NEUROSIS

Religion is comparable to a childhood neurosis.

From his Future of an Illusion *(1949).*

SELF-EFFACEMENT

This determination of self-criticism may make clear why it is that a number of the most excellent jokes...should have sprung into existence from the soil of Jewish national life.... I do not know whether one often finds a people that makes so merry unreservedly over its own shortcomings.

From his Wit and Its Relation to the Unconscious *(1917).*

THE ABSENCE OF JEWISH CONCERNS

My father spoke the sacred language, as well as German. He let me grow up in complete ignorance of everything that concerns Judaism.

Quoted in Masoret *magazine, Fall 1993.*

ON JUNG

Jung is *meshuga.*

In a comment to his friend and disciple Sandor Ferenczi. Quoted in The Correspondence of Sigmund Freud and Sandor Ferenczi *(1994).*

WHEN THE FATES TAKE OVER

There is no medicine against death, and against error no rule has been found.

The inscription by Freud under a pen and ink portrait drawn of him by artist Robert Kastor in 1925.

NO SCAPEGOATS

Since I am profoundly irreligious...there is no one I can accuse.

Upon the death in 1920 of his beloved daughter, Sophie. From a letter he wrote to Sandor Ferenczi.

WHAT BOUND ME TO JUDAISM

What bound me to Judaism was, I must confess, not belief and not national pride.... Other considerations...made the attractiveness of Judaism and Jews irresistible.... Because I was a Jew I found myself free from many prejudices which limited others in the use of their intellect, and being a Jew, I was prepared to enter opposition and to renounce agreement with the "compact majority."

From a letter he wrote in 1926 to his fellow lodge brothers who celebrated his seventieth birthday, which he was unable to attend because of illness.

THE BEST FIVE YEARS

My goodness, woman, don't stand there talking to me—hurry home! You have already wasted the five best years!

His response to a mother whose child was five years old and had not yet begun his education.

ON JESUS

Jesus could have been an ordinary deluded creature.

In a letter to Oskar Pfister.

IMAGINING OUR OWN DEATH

It is indeed impossible to imagine our own death, and whenever we attempt to do so we can perceive that we are in fact still present as spectators.... At bottom no one believes in his own death.

From an essay, "Thoughts for the Times on War and Death," written in 1915, six months after the start of World War I.

SHREWD MATCHMAKER

The matchmaker asks: "What do you require of your bride?" The answer: "She must be beautiful, rich, and educated."

"All right," says the matchmaker. "But I make that three matches."

From The Standard Edition of the Complete Psychological Works *(1905).*

□

Betty Naomi Friedan

BECOMING COMPLETE

It is easier to live through someone else than to become complete yourself.

From her Feminine Mystique *(1963).*

THE INNER VOICE

The time is at hand when the voices of the feminine mystique can no longer drown out the inner voice that is driving women on to become complete.

Ibid.

THE FEMININE MYSTIQUE

The feminine mystique says that the highest value and the only commitment for women is the fulfillment of their own femininity. It says that the great mistake of Western culture, throughout most of its history, has been the undervaluation of this femininity. It says this femininity is so mysterious and intuitive and close to the creation and origin of life that man-made science may never be able to understand it.... The mistake, says the mystique, the root of women's troubles in the past, is that women envied men, women tried to be like men, instead of accepting their own nature, which can find fulfillment only in sexual passivity, male domination and nurturing maternal love.

Ibid.

WOMEN AND THEIR POTENTIAL

The problem that has no name—which is simply the fact that American women are kept from growing to their full human capacities—is taking a far greater toll on the physical and mental health of our country than any known disease.

Ibid.

A JEW AND A PIG'S VALVE

I had heart surgery and they put in a pig's valve as a substitute for my own. But my Jewish heart rejected it. So they had to do a second operation to replace the pig's valve with a human one.

Quoted in a profile in Hadassah Magazine, *November 1993.*

FEMINISM AND DIVERSITY

I hate all this political correctness stuff. I don't think there's one definition of pure feminism. We've got to allow for diversity.

Ibid.

JUDAISM AND FEMINISM

Down through the generations in history my ancestors prayed, "I thank Thee, Lord, I was not created a woman," and from this day forward I trust that women all over the world will be able to say, "I thank Thee, Lord, I *was* created a woman."

From a speech delivered on August 26, 1970 at a rally of Women's Strike for Equality, attended by fifty thousand people in New York City.

WOMEN'S EQUALITY AND ANTI-SEMITISM

[The battle for women's equality] was really a passion against injustice which originated from my feelings of the injustice of anti-Semitism.

Quoted in Howard M. Sachar's History of the Jews in America *(1992).*

IN BUT NOT IN

When you're a Jewish girl who grew up on the right side of the tracks in the Midwest, you're marginal. You're in, but you're not, and you grew up an observer.

Quoted in Elinor and Robert Slater's Great Jewish Women *(1994).*

THE JEWISH FAMILY

Feminism is not a threat to the Jewish family. Family is basic to the survival of Jews. The liberation of women to full personhood will only help in the strengthening and evolution of the family.

Ibid.

JOINING A MINYAN

It moves me very much, in that small hotel room, to watch young Naamah Kelman, an American-born Israeli, daughter of 13 generations of rabbis, in her white prayer shawl, leading us in the ancient rituals only men have been allowed to perform. And tears came to my eyes as I join the young women in prayer: "Blessed are You, O God, who has made me free. Blessed are You, O God, who has made me in Your image."

Referring to the fact that she had been invited to help form a minyan (quorum of ten) for morning prayers. From her article in The New York Times Magazine, October 28, 1984.

FEMININE BREAKTHROUGH

I had never considered myself religious. I am a daughter of the secular city. For me, as for other Jewish feminists, religion perpetuated the patriarchal tradition that denied women access to Judaism's most sacred rituals and enshrined them within the strict confines of their biological role. But when women like me broke through to our authentic personhood as women, we also found the strength to dig deep into ourselves on other levels.

From her article in The New York Times Magazine, October 18, 1984.

¤

Maurice Friedberg

A 1973 PROGNOSTICATION

A significant number of the country's [USSR's] Jews are eager to emigrate, and some succeed. Nevertheless, there can be little doubt that the majority will remain in the country of their birth, whether by reasoned choice, by inertia, or because they will not receive official permission to leave.

From a 1973 essay entitled "Soviet Jews, Nationalism and Dissent," which was featured in Present Tense *magazine.*

¤

Harry Friedenwald

IN DEFENSE OF NEGRO RIGHTS

We Jews have had such a long experience in segregation, and we found it so intolerable, that I would never actively promote such a movement. I consider any such restrictions based upon color, race or religion as the manifestations of such injustice that I could not take a hand in it. This country cannot endure permanently a caste system with a caste of untouchables.

Writing to his son Jonas on October 22, 1929, countering the bigoted appeal "to protect our neighborhood from Negro invasion."

WEALTHY NON-ZIONISTS

The wealthy...have for the most part been indifferent to the appeal of Zionism. The power of the magnet is not felt by gold!

Quoted in Zionism *(1916), by P. Goodman and A. D. Lewis.*

¤

Israel Friedlaender

EVERYTHING HAS ITS PLACE

Every form of existence in nature, be it an object, a man, or a nation, has its own distinct place in the Universe, which can truly be filled only by itself—and by no other.

From his Past and Present: Selected Essays *(1919).*

FOR THE LOVE OF ISRAEL

The love of *Eretz Yisroel* [Israel] was the torch that illumined the thorny path of our people. It was the anchor that kept our ship from drifting out into the boundless ocean.

Ibid.

EXPOSING JUDAISM'S TRUE COLORS

If Judaism is to be preserved amidst the new conditions, if, lacking as it does, all outward support, it is still to withstand the pressure of the surrounding influences, it must again break the narrow frame of a creed and resume its original function as a culture, as the expression of the Jewish spirit and the whole life of the Jews.

Ibid.

THE SUN OF THE BIBLE

The Sun of the Bible radiates warmth and strength, and has called into being a system of morality, which has become the corner-stone of human civilization.

Ibid.

ABOLISHING GOD'S LAWS

What human being can claim a right to abolish laws given by the Almighty?

From his Jewish Religion *(1922).*

NO NEED TO BE PERFECT

A race which, in the face of uninterrupted and unparalleled persecution...has managed to preserve its mental and moral vigor, and has remained a powerful factor in the life of civilized humanity, can well afford to own to its share of human frailty.

From his Jews of Russia and Poland *(1915).*

◻

Michael Friedlander

EDEN AS SYMBOL

As the life of Adam and Eve in the Garden of Eden was free from care and trouble, and such a life was the ideal of human hopes and wishes, the Garden of Eden became the symbol of man's happiness in its perfection, such as will fall to the good and the righteous.

In his Jewish Religion *(1891).*

THE MESSIANIC NATURE

Those who believe in a superhuman nature of Messiah are guilty of idolatry.

Ibid.

LEGAL BUT UNETHICAL

There are transactions which are legal and do not involve any breach of law, which are yet base and disgraceful. Such are all transactions in which a person takes advantage of the ignorance or embarrassment of his neighbour for the purpose of increasing his own property.

Quoted in J. H. Hertz's Pentateuch and Haftorahs *(1961).*

◻

Lee M. Friedman

JEWS IN THE CLOTHING INDUSTRY

The history of the Jew in nineteenth-century America is marked by his development of the clothing industry. Starting in the 1830's with factories that produced crude, cheaply-made clothing, he developed the industry so well that, by the end of the century, dresses for women and suits for men, of good quality and cut, were being produced in such quantities that their price was within reach of most people.

From his Pilgrims in a Strange Land.

◻

Milton Friedman

FRANKLY, I'M A JEW

I do not go around making a great fuss about the fact that I am a Jew, but when the issue comes up I am very frank that I am Jewish.

From an interview with Elinor and Robert Slater. Quoted in their Great Jewish Men *(1996).*

◻

Theodore Friedman

CROSSING THE ABYSS

We are tightrope walkers treading a rope stretching across the abyss.... We cannot move lightly across the rope unless we look ahead towards the goals that beckon us and forget the abyss below.

From his sermon in Best Jewish Sermons of 5713 *(1953), edited by Saul I. Teplitz.*

Thomas L. Friedman

FOCUS ON ISRAEL

Quite simply, the West has a fascination and preoccupation with the story of Israel, a curiosity about it, an attraction and even an aversion to it that is out of all proportion to the nation's size. And equally, Israel has an uncanny ability to inject itself into the news like no other country of four million people.

From an article in The New York Times, *February 1, 1987.*

Pavel Friedman

I NEVER SAW ANOTHER BUTTERFLY

For seven weeks I've lived in here,
Penned up inside this ghetto.
But I have found what I love here.
The dandelions call to me
And the white chestnut branches in the
 court.
Only I never saw another butterfly....
Butterflies don't live in here,
in the ghetto.

From a poem dated June 4, 1942. Born in Prague on January, 7, 1921, Pavel was deported to Terezin on April 26, 1942. He died in Auschwitz on September 29, 1944.

David Frishman

FULL OF PRAYER

Brethren, give me a God, for I am full of prayer!

From his poem Ha-yadata. *Quoted in Meyer Waxman's* History of Jewish Literature *(1930).*

Erich Fromm

VOICE OF MAN'S CONSCIENCE

Man is the only creature endowed with conscience. His conscience is the voice which calls him back to himself, it permits him to know what he ought to do in order to become himself, it helps him to remain aware of the aims of his life and to the norms necessary for the attainment of these aims.

From his Man for Himself: An Inquiry into the Psychology of Ethics *(1947).*

A FUNDAMENTAL PRINCIPLE

Do not do to others what you would not have them do to you is one of the most fundamental principles of ethics. But it is equally justifiable to state: *Whatever you do to others, you also do to yourself.*

Ibid.

THE PRICE OF SELFISHNESS

Selfish persons are incapable of loving others, but they are not capable of loving themselves either.

Ibid.

ALL PART OF ONE

In essence, all human beings are identical. We are all part of One; we are One. This being so, it should not make any difference whom we love. Love should be essentially an act of will, of decision to commit my life completely to that of one other person.

From his Art of Loving *(1956).*

MAN AS AN EMPTY SHELL

Man must strive to recognize the truth and can be fully human only to the extent to which he succeeds in his task. He must be independent and free, an end in himself and not the means for any other person's purposes. He must relate himself to his fellow man lovingly. If he has no love, he is an empty shell even if his were all power, wealth, and intelligence. Man must know the difference between good and evil, he must learn to listen to the voice of his conscience and to be able to follow it.

From his Psychoanalysis and Religion *(1950).*

THE PLACE OF THE STATE

The state must perish if man becomes tied to it in such a way that the welfare of the state, its power and its glory become the criteria of good and evil.

Ibid.

ABSURDITY OF THEOLOGY

The logical consequence of Jewish monotheism is the absurdity of theology. If God has no name, there is nothing to talk about. However, any talk about God—hence all theology—implies using God's name in vain, in fact, it brings one close to idolatry.

From his You Shall Be As Gods *(1967).*

CAUSE OF DESTRUCTIVENESS

Destructiveness is the outcome of outlived lives.

From his Escape from Freedom *(1941).*

FROM FREEDOM TO ANXIETY

Freedom, although it has brought [modern man] independence and rationality, has made him isolated and, thereby, anxious and powerless.

Ibid.

THE MOST IMPORTANT CREATION

Man's nature, his passion and anxieties, are a cultural product; as a matter of fact, man himself is the most important creation and achievement of the continuous human effort, the record of what we call history.

Ibid.

MODERN SOCIETY

The structure of modern society affects man in two ways simultaneously: he becomes more independent, self-reliant, and critical, and he becomes more isolated, alone, and afraid.

Ibid.

WHO IS DEAD?

In the nineteenth century the problem was that God was dead; in the twentieth century the problem is that man is dead.

From his Sane Society *(1955).*

GOOD AND EVIL

Good is all that serves life; evil is all that serves death. Good is reverence for life, all that enhances life, growth, unfolding. Evil is all that stifles life, narrows it down, cuts it into pieces. Joy is virtuous and sadness is sinful.

From his Heart of Man: It's Genius for Good and Evil *(1964).*

Moshe Gafni

THE REFORM MOVEMENT

Letting a Reform rabbi sit on the Tel Aviv religious council is the equivalent of letting a terrorist into the General Staff headquarters. The Reform are terrorists, not rabbis.

During a March 1995 Knesset debate on conversions in which he blasted both the Reform and Conservative movements.

❏

Joseph Galiber

TEACHING THE HOLOCAUST

We were slaves. We were protected as chattel. The Jews were not even a commodity. No one protected them.

In commentary as a co-sponsor of an April 1994 piece of legislation introduced in the New York State legislature to teach about the Holocaust in public schools.

❏

Paul Gallico

MAKING A HIT

Andy is forced to parade his religion and commercialize it whether he wants to or not.... Every time Andy comes to bat he feels he must make a hit, not only for John McGraw, his teammates and the City of New York, but for the Jewish race as well, which is a large order.... It looks to me as though these days the baseball magnates are enslaving not only the bodies of their hired help but their souls as well.

Writing in the New York Daily News *at the time of Andy Cohen's opening day heroics in 1928. He condemned Giants manager McGraw's exploitation of Cohen's Jewishness. Quoted in Peter Levine's* Ellis Island to Ebbets Field *(1992).*

❏

John Galsworthy

I DON'T LIKE 'EBREWS

I don't like 'ebrews. They work harder; they're more sober; they're honest; and they're everywhere.

Spoken by a character in his play Loyalties *(1922).*

PROUD TO BE A JEW

You can call me a damned Jew. My race was old when you were all savages. I am proud to be a Jew.

Ibid.

❏

Mohandas K. Gandhi

ADVICE TO JEWS

If ever there could be justifiable war in the name of humanity, a war against Germany—to prevent the wanton persecution of a whole race—would be completely justified.

If I were a Jew and were born in Germany and earned my livelihood there, I would claim Germany as my home, even as the tallest gentile may, and challenge him to shoot me or cast me into a dungeon. I would refuse to be expelled or to submit to discriminating treatment.

From an article in his weekly Bombay newspaper, December 6, 1938.

❏

Hy Gardner

"I DO" TO ADIEU

If the divorce rate keeps increasing, part of the marriage vow will have to be changed from "I do" to *"adieu."*

Quoted in Morris Mandel's Affronts, Insults, and Indignities *(1975).*

○

Moses Gaster

JEWISH HEROES

The Jewish heroes were not men of battle, but men of faith.

From his Maaseh Book *(1934).*

○

Theodor H. Gaster

GOD AND HIS PARTNERS

Judaism has a central, unique and tremendous idea that is utterly original—the idea that God and man are partners in the world and that, for the realization of His plan and the complete articulation of this glory upon earth, God needs a committed, dedicated group of men and women.

From a speech delivered at the American Council for Judaism conference, April 30, 1954.

THE SOURCE OF POWER

The story of the hero retrieved in infancy from a river may perhaps reflect the primitive notion that charismatic men draw their special qualities from water, the primordial, uncontaminated element, which is the primal source of power and wisdom.

From his Myth, Legend, and Custom in the Old Testament *(1969).*

○

Peter Gay

UNIQUE STORIES

When refugees meet and exchange stories about their escape from Hitler and their lives abroad, each has a unique story to tell, yet each story is like all the others: a life bravely made over but also a dream lost forever.

From his Jews of Germany: A Historical Portrait *(1978).*

○

Abraham Geiger

REACHING FOR GOD

Longing after the Highest and Noblest, attachment to the Whole, soaring up to the Infinite, despite our finiteness and limitedness—this is religion.

From his Judaism and Its History *(1866).*

IGNORANCE CANONIZED

Canonization of ignorance has never been the rule in Israel.

Ibid.

ORIGINAL SIN

Judaism has not allowed the doctrine of original sin to be grafted onto it.

From his History of Judaism *(1865).*

UNADULTERATED JUSTICE

Sympathy and compassion are great virtues, but even these feelings must be silenced in the presence of justice.

Quoted in J. H. Hertz's Pentateuch and Haftorahs *(1961).*

○

Marc Gellman

KILLING OF A FETUS

I had never apologized for being pro-civil rights on the basis of the Bible; why should I apologize for being pro-life on the basis of the Talmud.... I am still uncertain about how my view on abortion ought to be translated, if at all, into public policy, but I know that the killing of a fetus is not a morally neutral act.

From an essay in David Dalin's American Jews and the Separatist Faith *(1993).*

○

Eugene Genovese

HOW JEWS REACT

Attack the Italians and they'll go after you with a baseball bat. Attack the Jews and they'll call a conference at the 92nd Street Y.

Comment at a May 1994 conference discussing the Jewish reaction to black anti-Semitism.

○

Henry George

THE MOSAIC CODE

It is not the protection of property, but the protection of humanity, that is the aim of the Mosaic Code. Its sanctions are not directed to securing the strong in heaping up wealth so much as to preventing the weak from being crowded to the wall.

From his "Moses: A Lecture" (1878), included in The Writings of Henry George *(1898).*

MOSAIC LAW AND HUMAN FREEDOM

The Hebrew commonwealth was based upon the individual—a commonwealth whose ideal it was that every man should sit under his own vine and fig-tree, with none to vex him or make him afraid; a commonwealth in which none should be condemned to ceaseless toil; in which for even the beast of burden there should be rest.

Quoted in J. H. Hertz's Pentateuch and Haftorahs *(1961).*

ISRAEL THE PHOENIX

Israel—a people who have been overthrown, crushed, scattered; who have been ground, as it were, to very dust, and flung to the four winds of heaven; yet who, though thrones have fallen, and empires have perished, and creeds have changed, and living tongues have become dead, still exist with a vitality seemingly unimpaired.

Ibid.

ON THE WRITING OF SONGS

You should not write songs for *your* people, but for *the* people.

From an undated letter to Emma Lazarus.

□

Richard Gephardt

TWO HISTORIC SPEECHES

I daresay that the two speeches we heard today were the most moving, dramatic and historic speeches that any of us have ever heard.

After listening to King Hussein of Jordan and Yitzhak Rabin of Israel speak before a joint session of Congress on July 26, 1994, celebrating the end of a state of war between the two nations.

□

(The) Gerer Rebbe

SATAN'S GOAL

Now behold Satan has come and confused the world. There are threats from the leaders of the Zionists that a powerful danger is lurking behind our walls and that the power of the enemies of Israel is prevailing—Heaven forbid. It is therefore all the more incumbent upon us to protect ourselves from confusing the masses of the people. Everyone who has a brain in his head will realize that the Zionists, through their nonsensical writings, will only increase hostility; if they continue in their brazenness

to spread the libel that we are in revolt against the peoples and that we are a danger to the lands in which we reside, then their evil prophecy will be fulfilled—Heaven forbid.

From a 1901 statement castigating the Zionist influence. Quoted in Zionism Reconsidered *(1970), edited by Michael Selzer.*

□

Gersonides

GOD'S FOREKNOWLEDGE

God foreknows...the only possibilities open to a man is his freedom, not the particular decisions he will make.

From his Sefer Milchamot Adonai *("Book of the Wars of the Lord"), which was severely attacked by traditionalists.*

□

Elliot Gertel

WHAT JESSE JACKSON HAS NOT SAID

As dismayed as we are by things Jackson has said and done, we are also dismayed by what he has not said and not done. How do you explain reports that in 1985 Jackson did not respond when Mayor Teddy Kollek of Jerusalem called upon him to intercede for Ethiopian Jews stranded in the Sudan? Or why, as columnist Eugene Kennedy pointed out in *The New York Times* (Tuesday, July 26, 1988), did Jackson not speak out when Chicago mayoral aide Steve Cokely accused the Jews of an international conspiracy to control the world and attributed the AIDS epidemic to "doctors, especially Jewish ones, who inject AIDS into blacks?" What did Jackson think when Farrakhan invited Cokely to join his staff after Cokely had made vicious remarks about Jackson himself? What kind of friend is Farrakhan after all?

From an article in The Jewish Spectator, *Fall 1988.*

□

Bon Claude Gerville

JEWISH BENEFICENCE

No citizen has proved himself more zealous for liberty than the Jew...none has displayed more sense of order and justice, none shown more benevolence towards the poor or more readiness in voluntarily contributing towards the expenses of the district.

From the French statesman's speech at Paris City Hall, January 29, 1790. Quoted in Heinrich Graetz's History of the Jews *(1891–98).*

Estelle Getty

FEELING SAFE

It was still very exciting. The people are still gung ho for their country. It's very nice to go there. What a feeling to see the policemen are Jews. It's a total Jewish environment. There's a sense of safety you feel, everybody being your own people. You stand there and watch a garbage truck go by, a police car, a cement mixer. It was a wonderful experience.

After a visit to Israel, where she observed how Americanized Israel had become with its discos and bars. Quoted in Tim Boxer's Jewish Celebrity Hall of Fame *(1987).*

André Gide

SUPERNATIONALIST

If saving an innocent Dreyfus involves any injury to the French state, everything should be done to make Dreyfus guilty, so that France may remain unstained.

From a letter to a friend in 1898 concerning the trial of Alfred Dreyfus.

Miep Gies

JUST DOING MY DUTY

I am not a hero. I stand at the end of the long, long line of good Dutch people who did what I did or more—much more—during those dark and terrible times years ago, but always like yesterday in the hearts of those of us who bear witness.... I have never wanted special attention. I was only willing to do what was asked of me and what seemed necessary at the time.

Known in Anne Frank's diary as Miep van Santen. Quoted in Eva Fogelman's Conscience & Courage *(1994).*

Neil Gilman

DEALING WITH LIFE

No more than anyone else do I know beyond question what will happen to me after I die. What I do know, however, is that what I believe about those events will decisively affect how I deal with my one and only life here on earth. And that, ultimately, is what religion is all about.

From an essay in Masoret *magazine, Fall 1993.*

Newt Gingrich

ISRAEL AND THE U.S. EMBASSY

Israel is the only sovereign state where outsiders dictate where they may or may not have their capital—and that's wrong.

Upon sponsoring a 1995 bill in the U.S. House of Representatives that would move the U.S. embassy from Tel Aviv to Jerusalem by 1999.

ARABS: GROW UP

Israel's Arab neighbors ought to grow up. Israel is a sovereign nation and has earned the right to choose its own capital.

Urging the relocation of the American embassy from Tel Aviv to Jerusalem. At the annual policy conference of the American Israel Public Affairs Committee (AIPAC), May 8, 1995, in Washington, DC.

Allen Ginsberg

THE END OF THE STORY

This is the end
the redemption from Wilderness
way for the Wonderer
House sought for All
black handkerchief washed clean by weeping.

From his Kaddish *(1959).*

FALSE GODS

The Jews always complained, kvetching about false gods, and erected the biggest false God, Jehovah, in the middle of western civilization.

From his poem "World Karma," which appeared in White Shroud *(1986).*

THE BEAT GENERATION

I saw the best minds of my generation destroyed by madness, starving, hysterical, naked, dragging themselves through the Negro streets at dawn looking for a fix.

From his book of poetry entitled Howl *(1986).*

Martin D. Ginsburg

SUPPORTIVE RELATIONSHIPS

I have been supportive of my wife since the beginning of time, and she has been supportive of me. It's not sacrifice, it's family.

Following the nomination of his wife, Ruth Bader Ginsburg, to the U.S. Supreme Court in June 1993.

¤

Ruth Bader Ginsburg

ABORTION AND PRIVACY

The emphasis must be not on the right to abortion, but on the right to privacy and reproductive control.

Quoted in Ms. *magazine, April 1974.*

DEPLORING DISCRIMINATION

I think rank discrimination against anyone is against the tradition of the United States and is to be deplored.

In discussing her views about bias based on sexual orientation, at her confirmation hearing before the Senate Judiciary Committee on July 29, 1993.

A TRIBUTE TO MOTHER

I pray that I may be all that she [my mother] would have been had she lived to an age when women could aspire and achieve and daughters are cherished as much as sons.

From her emotional 1993 statement after she was selected by President Bill Clinton to occupy the U.S. Supreme Court seat vacated by Byron R. White. Tears streamed down the President's face as he listened to her words.

¤

Louis Ginzberg

HALAKHIC ESSENCE

It is only in the *Halakha* that we find the mind and character of the Jewish people exactly and adequately expressed.

From his Students, Scholars and Saints *(1928).*

THE SYSTEMLESS SYSTEM

The most significant feature of the rabbinical system of theology is its lack of system.

Ibid.

LAW AS AN END IN ITSELF

The dietary laws are not incumbent upon us because they conduce to moderation, nor the family laws because they further chastity. The law as a whole is not the means to an end, but the end in itself; the Law is active religiousness, and in active religion lies what is specifically Jewish.

Ibid.

JEWISH NATIONALISM

Is not Jewish nationalism an empty phrase if we do not connect with it Jewish religion and Jewish ethics, Jewish culture and the Jewish mode of life which gave it its individuality?

Ibid.

WATER ON A ROCK

Drops of water continually falling upon a rock will finally wear it away though the first drips seem to produce no effect at all. It is the same with self-discipline; its effects cannot fail to penetrate our hearts if we practice it continually.

Ibid.

AN ORIGINAL CREATION

The school is the most original institution created by post-biblical Judaism.

Ibid.

SCRIBES AND PROPHETS

The Scribes succeeded where the Prophets had failed. Through them the teachings proclaimed in the schools of the Prophets became the common property of the whole people.

Ibid.

THE HOLY LANGUAGE

The recollection that it was the Hebrew language in which the Revelation was given, in which the Prophets expressed their high ideals, in which generations of our fathers breathed forth their suffering and joys, makes this language a holy one for us.

Ibid.

¤

Natalia Levi Ginzburg

A GENERATION APART

And we are a people without tears. The things that moved our parents do not move us at all.

From her Little Virtues *(1962).*

¤

Rudolph Giuliani

ISRAEL AND AMERICA

Israel has been the strongest and truest friend America can possibly have. We have a shared commitment to democracy, to what we believe government should be, and a shared memory of lives lost together.

From a speech to an Amit Women's benefit held at the Hilton Hotel in New York City in November 1994.

SING "DAYENU"

Not only will I use it, I will sing it.

> *Responding to Rabbi Arthur Schneier, who advised the New York mayor attending his 1995 seder that he can use the refrain "dayenu" when skirmishing with the press or City Council.*

Washington Gladden

ANTI-JEWISH PREJUDICE

I have no doubt that prejudice against the Jews has been raised, unwittingly, by the teachings of Church and Sunday School. Christian teachers of all grades ought to explain more carefully than they sometimes do, that the Jews, with all their prejudice, were the very best people in the world when our Lord came to earth, possessing the purest morality, honoring the family as it was honored by no other nation. We ought to keep it before our children that Jesus himself was a Jew; that all the apostles were Jews, that Christianity was planted in Asia and Europe by Jews.

> *Quoted in Joseph L. Baron's Stars and Sand (1943).*

Joseph B. Glaser

ON MISTREATMENT OF INDIANS

The American Indian has received the most outrageous treatment of any people in history at the hands of the United States and, perhaps, at the hands of anyone at any time, anywhere in the world. A Jew has to take a deep breath before making such a statement, but I believe it is true.

> *From Reform Judaism magazine, Spring 1984.*

Jacob Glatstein

COME BACK, DEAR GOD

We've both turned universal.
Come back, dear God, to a land
no bigger than a speck.
Dwindle down to only ours.
I'll go around with homely sayings
suitable for chewing over in small places.
We'll both be provincial.
God and His poet
Maybe it will go sweeter for us.

> *Translated from the Yiddish by Cynthia Ozick.*

Glückel of Hameln

MESSAGE FOR POSTERITY

Always remember, children, that the core of the Torah is, "Thou shalt love thy neighbor as thyself." Remember this, even though in our days we rarely find it so; and so few there are who love their fellowmen with all their heart. On the contrary, if man can contrive to ruin his neighbor, nothing pleases him more.

> *From her Memoirs of Glückel of Hameln, written as a testament to her children in 1690, in the city of Hamburg, after she was widowed at age forty-four.*

TRUST ONLY IN YOURSELVES

Hereafter trust only in yourselves, for now there is no man and no friend on whom you may rely, and even if you had many friends; if you needed their aid, you could not rely on them. When one has no need thereof, everyone wishes to befriend him, but when he stands in want of friends, they are not, as the story goes, to be found.

> *Ibid. Advice to her children after the death of her husband in 1689.*

LEFT TO FLOUNDER

But who is now my comforter? To whom shall I pour out my soul? Where shall I turn? All my life my beloved companion listened to my troubles, and they were many; he comforted me so that somehow they would soon vanish. But now...I am left to flounder in my woe.

> *Ibid. Upon the loss of her husband.*

Joseph Paul Goebbels

THE BARBARIC NAZI PLAN

Beginning with Lublin, the Jews in the General Government are now being evacuated eastward. The procedure is a pretty barbaric one and not to be detailed here more precisely. Not much will remain of the Jews. On the whole it can be said that about 60 percent of them will have to be liquidated whereas only about 40 percent can be used for forced labor.

The former Gauleiter of Vienna, who is to carry out this measure, is doing it with considerable discreetness and according to a procedure that does not attract too much attention. A judgment is being visited upon the Jews that, while barbaric, is fully deserved by them.

The prophecy which the Führer made about them for having brought on a new world war is beginning to come true in a most terrible manner. One must not be sentimental in these matters. If we did not fight the Jews, they would destroy us. It's a life-and-death struggle between the Aryan race and the Jewish bacillus.

From a March 1942 entry in his diary.

TROUBLESOME JEWS

The [Jewish] question is causing us a lot of trouble. Everywhere, even among our allies, the Jews have friends to help them...I believe both the British and Americans are happy that we are exterminating the Jewish riff-raff.

Ibid.

THE HEIGHT OF HATE

A Jew is for me an object of physical disgust. I vomit when I see one.... It is a fact...I treasure an ordinary prostitute above a married Jewess.

Quoted in John Gunther's Inside Europe.

GOEBBEL'S PARABLE

Certainly the Jew is a human being. But then the flea is a living thing too; only not a pleasant one. Since the flea is not a pleasant thing, we are not obliged to keep it and let it prosper...our duty is rather to exterminate it. Likewise with the Jews.

A 1929 statement.

□

Hermann Goering

SETTLING ACCOUNTS

Should the Reich become involved in an international conflict in the foreseeable future, we in Germany will have to think about settling our accounts with the Jews.

At a high-level Nazi meeting in November 1938.

FROM GOERING TO HEYDRICH TO EICHMANN

As supplement to the task that was entrusted to you in the decree dated 24 January 1939, namely to solve the Jewish question by emigration and evacuation in the most favourable way possible, given present conditions, I herewith commission you to carry out all necessary preparations with regard to the organizational, substantive and financial viewpoints, for a total solution of the Jewish question in the German sphere of influence in Europe.

From a July 31, 1941 letter he sent to Reinhard Heydrich, Chief of Security Police, who was delegated to coordinate the "Jewish problem." Heydrich, in turn, gave orders to Adolf Eichmann, who had administrative responsibility for the Holocaust as a whole.

□

Johann Wolfgang von Goethe

A FACT THAT'S NOT A FACT

Christ cannot possibly have been a Jew. I don't have to prove that scientifically. It is a fact.

Quoted by John Gunther in The Nation, *February 6, 1935.*

A LOVE-HATE SCENARIO

I was opposed to the new law regarding Jews, which permitted intermarriage between members of both faiths.... I do not hate the Jews. The aversion which I felt against them in my early youth was more timidity before the mysterious, the ungraceful. The scorn which used to stir within me was more a reflection of the Christian men and women around me. Only later, when I became acquainted with many talented and refined men of this race, respect was added to the admiration which I entertained for this people that created the Bible, and for the poet who sang the Song of Songs.

It is despicable to pillory a nation which possesses such remarkable talents in art and science.

Quoted in Joseph Baron's Stars and Sand *(1943).*

□

Sherwood Goffin

THIS LAND IS OUR LAND

This land is your land,
This land is my land,
From the Negev Desert
To the Heights of Golan.
From the port of Haifa
To Maale Adumim,
This land was made for you and me.

A new set of lyrics to Woody Guthrie's folk classic, "This Land Is Your Land." Written and performed in 1994 by the cantor of New York's Lincoln Square Synagogue.

ۃ

Herbert Gold

To Be a Jew

I was thought to be a Jew because I was so named by others. I learned by being one that Jew is more than epithet. The content of tenuous community, risk, and history makes me feel immortal even though I'm not. No matter what happens to me, I am continuous with a past which was worthy of better than me; a present when others died to be Jews; a future constructed equally of fate and intention.... I am a part of history, not merely a kid on a streetcorner or a man making out okay.

> *From his* My Lost Two Thousand Years *(1972).*

A Unique Fate

I'm not sure what my destiny as a Jew means—or what the destiny of the Jews means—except that it is a unique fate, a peculiar devotion to world and spirit wrapped together.

> *Ibid.*

ۃ

Michael Gold

Revolutionary on a Soapbox

O workers' Revolution, you brought hope to me, a lonely, suicidal boy. You are the true Messiah. You will destroy the East Side when you come, and build there a garden for the human spirit.

O Revolution that forced me to think, to struggle and to live.

O great Beginning!

> *From his* Jews without Money *(1930).*

ۃ

Arthur J. Goldberg

When Religion Misses the Mark

Religion, it seems to me, functions in an ivory tower in a quiet and respectable vacuum—when it ceases to inform and inspire, when it misses its social opportunity, when it fails to have impact on people and state. As you well know, the prophets were in the thick of it; their voices rose above the people, and they were eagerly heeded. And what was their

message if not chiefly an ethical interpretation of the law?

> *From a 1966 address at the Jewish Theological Seminary of America.*

On Being Our Brother's Keeper

No law can require us to be our brother's keeper, as individual citizens or as a nation. But ethically, we do care. I believe that this deeper, ethical concern is ingrained in most Americans. It is latent within us, as part of our national character.

> *Ibid.*

Open-mouthed Diplomats

Modern diplomats approach every problem with an open mouth.

> *Quoted in Morris Mandel's* Affronts, Insults and Indignities *(1975).*

No Illusions about Peace

I have no illusions that peace can be achieved rapidly, but I have every confidence that it is going to be possible to inch toward it, inch by agonizing inch.

> *At his inauguration as U.S. ambassador to the United Nations on July 26, 1965.*

ۃ

Hank Goldberg

Who's the Meshuggener?

I just thought you should know that these guys are *meshuggeh* and I don't know what they are up to.

> *Attacking the defense attorneys in the 1995 O. J. Simpson murder trial for their theory about the blood evidence. Defense attorney Barry Sheck responded by incorrectly correcting Goldberg's Yiddish, saying: "I don't want to correct you, but it's* meshuggener."

ۃ

J. J. Goldberg

New Front Burner Pot

The peace accord [signed between Israel and the PLO in Washington, DC, on September 13, 1993] puts on the front burner the question of whether Israel or the Diaspora will be the center of identity for the next generation of American Jews.

> *Examining the issues and emotions evoked by the signing. From* The Jerusalem Report, *December 2, 1993.*

¤

Michael Goldberg

LYNCHPIN OF THE WORLD

Jews should survive because they are the lynchpin in [God's] redemption of the world.

From his Why Should Jews Survive?
(1995).

¤

Reuben Goldberg

ON CHANGING THE WORLD

I can't change the world; I'll leave that to the young men—the men who can get angry every day the way I used to. When you come down to it, the world has to change itself. I suppose human nature is better now than it was eighty years ago, but it's got a long way to go, and I can't wait for it.

From an interview with R.W. Apple, Jr., of
The New York Times, *April 24, 1964.*

¤

Whoopi Goldberg

JEWISH AMERICAN PRINCESS EXPOSED

Send chauffeur to your favorite butcher shop.... Have your cook [prepare seasoning].... Watch your nails [when closing the bag, and]... Hand bag to the cook. Go dress for dinner... [By the time dinner is ready] you must be exhausted.

One of many recipes contributed by residents of Litchfield County, Connecticut, to Cooking in Litchfield Hills, *a 1993 book whose sale benefits the Elliott Pratt Education Center, an environmental organization. When criticized for being anti-Semitic, Goldberg's publicist, Brad Caralli, responded: "Whoopi is Jewish...she is certainly not anti-Semitic."*

¤

Harry Golden

ROAD TO SUCCESS

I write, edit, and publish *The Carolina Israelite.* Nineteen years ago I started with 600 subscribers, now I have almost 45,000. Recently people have begun to ask me to what I attribute the success of my little personal journal. The answer is a simple one: I waited.

From the Introduction to his For 2¢ Plain
(1959).

CARUSO AND ROOSEVELT

Two of the most beloved Christians in the history of the American-Jewish community were Enrico Caruso and Theodore Roosevelt. I doubt whether anyone else, before or since, has ever enjoyed the same degree of reverence and devotion.

Ibid.

PEOPLE OF THE BOOK

Our people are known as People of the Book. It is the Book [Bible] and other books which have sustained us, and books laid the foundation of this entire better world in which we live.

Ibid.

CREATING AN INVENTORY

I once sat down to read the *Universal Jewish Encyclopedia.* I know how silly it sounds for a man to claim that he has read an encyclopedia, but that is exactly what I did.... I knew this would be a good investment. What I did was create an inventory, and one which is not even taxable.

Ibid.

A WORRISOME HERO

Lindbergh frightened me because he was a legitimate American hero, he was respectable in a way Fritz Kuhn was not, and he was rich.... Lindbergh didn't make my hands shake with palsy, but he made my brow crease with worry. What he did was to disguise the moral issue of barbarism versus civilization in a realistic appraisal—that somebody was going to win the war, and we had to get along with that somebody, who was probably going to be Hitler.

From his autobiography, The Right Time
(1969).

BUILDING SECURITY

You are never safer than when you are fighting for somebody else—when you fight for others, you build a wall of security around yourself.

Ibid. From an address to a Jewish organization.

ONLY IN AMERICA

It [*Only in America*] was a success because it was a "Jewish" book with a difference. A large majority of Jewish writers fall into two camps. There are the apologists who argue in their books that the Jews are the same as everyone else—they play basketball—and there are the historians who blow a few details out of all perspective to prove the Jews are patriots.

Ibid.

◻

Leib Goldhirsch

WHY GO TO SHUL

A Jew is a Jew like a Frenchman is a Frenchman. No race of people can survive long without a ritual and some degree of discipline. These people are my people—the people I live with, the people with whom I came to America. My beloved friend Dudya Silverberg goes to *shul* to talk to God, and I go to *shul* to talk to Dudya.

Questioning his father about why he attended synagogue regularly. From Harry Golden's autobiography, The Right Time *(1969).*

◻

Louis Golding

ACHIEVING HEROIC DIGNITY

The ungainly figure of the Wandering Jew...acquires a heroic dignity when one realizes that he could have thrown off his rags, and clad himself in scarlet, and enjoyed peace and quiet and affluence, by pronouncing one single word—a word which he did not pronounce.

From his Jewish Problem *(1938).*

◻

William Golding

CHILDHOOD SICKNESS

Childhood is a disease—a sickness that you can grow out of.

Quoted in London's Guardian, *June 22, 1990.*

◻

Abraham Goldman

WHAT A GIRL NEEDS TO KNOW

Girls do not have to learn much. All a Jewish girl needs to know is how to prepare gefilte fish, cut noodles fine, and give the man plenty of children.

To his studious daughter Emma, after she objected to the husband he had selected for her at age fifteen.

◻

Ari Goldman

JEWISH FATHERING

One of my fondest boyhood memories is getting up early on Saturday mornings to walk to *shul* with my dad. It was a special time. My father would take my hand in his and begin to sing a *Shabbos* song. His baritone voice would echo through the empty streets, and I would join in with my youthful soprano.

More than school, more than the synagogue, more than any teacher, it was on those walks that I learned to be a Jew. I think it was also then that my father planted the seeds that enable me to be a nurturing Jewish father for my own boy.

From his essay entitled "Jewish Fathering," which appears in The Hadassah Magazine Jewish Parenting Book *(1989), edited by Roselyn Bell.*

◻

Emma Goldman

ESPOUSING UNPOPULAR CAUSES

The history of progress is written in the blood of men and women who have dared to espouse an unpopular cause, as, for instance, the black man's right to his body, or woman's right to her soul.

From her "What I Believe," which appeared in New York World, *1908.*

BLESSED ARE THE POOR

Heaven must be an awfully dull place if the poor in spirit live there.

From an essay in Mother Earth, *April 1913.*

THE STATE IDEA

The Russian Revolution has demonstrated beyond doubt that the State idea, State Socialism, in all its manifestations...is entirely and hopelessly bankrupt.

From her My Further Disillusionment *(1924).*

THE GOAL OF ANARCHISM

Anarchism, then, really, stands for the liberation of the human mind from the dominion of religion; the liberation of the human body from the dominion of property; liberation from the shackles and restraints of government.

From her Anarchism and Other Essays *(1910).*

◻

Fred Goldman

A FATHER'S ANGUISH

This is *not* the Fuhrman trial. This is a trial about the man who murdered my son.

> *After the defense team at the 1995 O. J. Simpson murder trial began focusing attention on the rogue detective Mark Fuhrman rather than on his slain son, Ronald, and Nicole Brown Simpson.*

◻

Solomon Goldman

THE ROOTS OF JUDAISM

Judaism is rooted forever in the soil, blood, life-experience and memory of a particular folk—the Jewish people.

> *From his* Crisis and Decision *(1938).*

◻

Nahum Goldman

SURVIVAL IN THE DIASPORA

It may sound paradoxical, but it may be true, nevertheless, that Zionism will hereafter be judged by its efforts for Jewish survival outside Israel more than by its efforts on behalf of Israel.

> *From an address in December 1953 to the First American Zionist Assembly meeting in New York City.*

DEGENERATION OF A LEADER

As the State of Israel was established without any serious attempt to reach a settlement with the Arabs, the outcome was inevitable... [with the result that this country has turned into] a banalization of Jewish destiny, a desecration of the tragic and heroic nature of our people's history...a greater disaster than Auschwitz.

> *From an article in the German weekly* Die Welt, *bastion of the German intellectual left. Reported in* The Jerusalem Post, *July 27–August 2, 1980.*

◻

Herbert Goldstein

HOW PRAYER IS ANSWERED

Prayer serves not only as a petition to God, but as an influence upon ourselves. Our Sages, centuries ago, voiced the thought echoed by the great poet George Meredith, who declared, "He who rises from his worship a better man,

his prayer is answered." Prayer has the double charm of bringing God down to man, and lifting man upward to God.

> *From his* Letter on Prayer.

◻

Israel Goldstein

I'LL DO IT GOD'S WAY

We have our own preferences, our own commitments, perhaps our own prejudices as Conservative Jews. But we should be tolerant, perhaps more than a certain Episcopalian clergyman who was having an argument with a Unitarian clergyman. Finally, the Episcopalian, with a great show of expansive tolerance, said to his Unitarian colleague, "Well, my friend, you do it your way. I'll do it God's way."

> *In a dialogue with Rabbi William Berkowitz at the Institute of Adult Jewish Studies in New York. Quoted in Berkowitz's* Ten Vital Jewish Issues *(1964).*

SAFEGUARD OF JEWISH SURVIVAL

When Mr. Ben-Gurion speaks of Zionism as a scaffolding, and says that now that the building is here, the State is here, and it is time to remove the scaffolding, he does an injustice to all that Zionism has meant from the beginning and means today. Zionism has its own independent values and purposes. Even after Israel no longer needs United Jewish Appeal dollars from the United States or elsewhere, Zionism will still be necessary as one of the great safeguards of Jewish survival in the world. For Zionism is based upon the fundamental concept of the oneness of the Jewish people.

> *Ibid.*

JUDAISM AND THE CATHOLIC CHURCH

While it is true that the Catholic Church offers some kind of analogy [to the make-up of the Jewish people], it is not quite the same thing because we Jews are more than a church. You cannot really find any analogies.

> *Ibid.*

ACTIVE PROSELYTIZING

While I believe in the universal values of Judaism, I do not believe in aggressive, active proselytzing. Different, however, is the individual case of conversion at the request of a person who wants to accept our faith. Even then, we must convert people only in the old Jewish tradition—pushing them away with the one hand and drawing them nearer with the other, pointing out the difficulties, the problems, and then when that person still insists upon becoming a Jew, by all means welcoming him.

Ibid.

◘

Jonah Goldstein

THREE WORLDS

Jews have three worlds: *die velt* ["this world"], *yene velt* ["the other world"], and Roosevelt.

Expressing the confidence that American Jews placed in Franklin D. Roosevelt after he was elected to the U. S. presidency in 1932 and introduced the New Deal.

◘

Barry Goldwater

MY HERITAGE

I am proud of my heritage. My grandparents and my father were Jews. My mother was a Christian, an Episcopalian. I have a high regard for the American Jewish community.

In response to a question posed in 1964 when he was the Republican candidate for the U.S. presidency.

◘

Samuel Goldwyn

STAR PRODUCTION

God makes stars. I just produce them.

Quoted in London's Daily Express, *May 16, 1939.*

FAMOUS GOLDWYNISM

For years I have been known for saying, "Include me out."

From a speech to students at Balliol College, Oxford, England, on March 1, 1945.

JEW PLAYING JEW

You can't have a Jew play a Jew. It won't work.

Commenting on his casting of Frank Sinatra in the move version of Guys and Dolls *after it had been played on Broadway by Sam Levene.*

ON VISITING A DOCTOR

Anyone who goes to a doctor ought to have his head examined.

By attribution.

AUTOBIOGRAPHIES

I don't think anybody should write his autobiography until after he's dead.

Quoted in Arthur Marx's Goldwyn: The Man Behind the Myth *(1976).*

◘

Goliath

DAVID FACING THE GIANT

Am I a dog that you come after me with sticks? Come to me, and I will give your flesh to the fowls of the air and to the beasts of the field.

From the First Book of Samuel (17:43–44), where Goliath addresses David, who comes to battle the Philistine giant with only a stick, a slingshot, and five smooth stones picked out of a brook.

◘

Abraham Golomb

ETERNAL JEWS

There is no "eternal Jewish people," and there never was one. The idea "eternal Jews" means only a section, large or small, a branch of the Jewish people in each generation, which in that generation creates the Jewish people. And it too is constantly shedding dry branches and leaves.

From his essay "What Is Jewish Tradition?" Reprinted in Joseph Leftwich's anthology, The Way We Think *(1969).*

JUDAISM'S VIBRANCY

The first and most important principle of Jewish tradition is a negative one. "No graven images" keeps Jewishness from getting tied up with any fixed bodily idea. Everything in Judaism must remain fluid—streaming, changeable, on the running board of history; everything in Jewishness must be with and go with its people in exile; God Himself must.

Ibid.

◘

David Golovensky

DANGER OF COMPROMISE

The Torah is not static. It develops, but it develops according to the pattern and the formula of the *halakha*.... The Will of God cannot be compromised. We believe that compromise does not strengthen but weakens. One compromise inevitably introduces another and leads to a third.

You remember the story of the man who willed his home to a charity with the provisos that he live in it during the rest of his life, that he would pay for the minor repairs, and that the major repairs be handled by the beneficiary.

After a few years a friend of his asked how the arrangement has worked out. The donor said, "Wonderful. I didn't have to pay for a single repair, because when the minor repairs came along, I waited until they became major." So too with compromise; you may start with a minor compromise, but the minor leads to a major. We believe that the more complex life becomes, and it is becoming more and more complex all the time, the more do we need the disciplines of religion.

In a 1960 dialogue with Rabbi William Berkowitz at the Institute of Adult Jewish Studies in New York. Reported in Berkowitz's Ten Vital Jewish Issues *(1964).*

□

Ellen Goodman

BEHAVIOR AND FEELINGS

The truth is that we can overhaul our surroundings, renovate our environment, talk a new game, join a new club, far more easily than we can change the way we respond emotionally. It is easier to change behavior than feelings about that behavior.

From her Turning Points *(1979).*

LIVING WITH CERTAINTY

When you live alone, you can be sure that the person who squeezed the toothpaste tube in the middle wasn't committing a hostile act.

From her Close to Home *(1979).*

□

Hirsh Goodman

JERUSALEM: SYMBOL OF HARMONY

Of all the many problems facing us along the road to peace, Jerusalem is perhaps, ironically, one of the easiest to resolve. That the city can remain the united capital of Israel and, at the same time, serve as the functional capital of Palestinian self-rule, are not mutually exclusive.... All that's needed is for sloganism to be forsaken and logic and goodwill allowed to prevail.

From his column in The Jerusalem Report, *November 4, 1993.*

NEW CHANCE FOR PEACE

I listen carefully as defense experts pontificate on the question of whether Israel can afford to give up the Golan or not. Like Israeli right-wing politicians, they are speaking yesterday's language. The cardinal strategic question is not whether or not Israel can afford to give up the Golan, but whether Israel can afford to give up what seems to be a real chance of peace with Syria.

Reflecting on the significance of the January 16, 1994 press conference following the Geneva meeting of Presidents Clinton and Assad in which Assad declared: "In honor we fought; in honor we negotiate; and in honor we shall make peace." From his column in The Jerusalem Report, *January 20, 1994.*

FAILED EXPERIMENT

If one were asked today to assess the success or failure of the settlement movement, the conclusion would be unavoidable: It has been an abysmal failure.... An estimated 30 percent of Israelis living in the territories moved for economic reasons, not ideological ones. Twenty-five percent of all settlers polled recently, openly admit that if awarded adequate compensation, they would pack up and leave tomorrow.

Expressing how futile the settlement effort has been. From his column in The Jerusalem Report, *January 27, 1994.*

LIVING FIVE LIFETIMES

To have lived in Israel for thirty years is to have lived five lifetimes. The pace of events is stunning. Things that should be etched in memory become fleeting moments in the rush of history. The intensity is omnipresent and, often, oppressive. Each morning the news brings yet another cause for concern, another threat, another reason why life here can never seem to be normal.

Ibid.

□

Paul Goodman

AFFIRMATIVE ACTION

The Jewish outcry against quotas, which barred them from the academic world, from job opportunities, and from housing, had no echo in the society. There was no "Affirmative Action" to meet *their* grievances. Should anyone wonder, therefore, that the mere mention of quotas...is disturbing to the Jewish community?... Should they make peace with a process which has bitter echoes in their history?

From Jewish Frontier *magazine, October 1972.*

¤

Mikhail Gorbachev

INFORMATION PLEASE

If there is any country in which Jews enjoy the political and other rights they do in our country, I would like to hear about it.

At an October 1985 press conference.

¤

Nadine Gordimer

ANTI-APARTHEID ADVOCATE

I don't think that my Jewishness is an influence, and I get rather annoyed when people say that my opposition to racism comes from being Jewish. It's a terrible deflection if you have self-interest in acting against racism. It distressed me that in my own country [South Africa] there have been such paradoxes among Jews.

Responding to those who believe that her Jewish heritage influenced her political activity and her criticism of apartheid.

ISRAEL'S DISGRACE

I think for all Jews it was a sorrow, really, and a shame. I can't accept all the explanations about "what other friends does Israel have?" For Israel to have friends like [former president P. W. Botha] is a disgrace.

Explaining that she hesitated to visit Israel because of Israel's cooperation with South Africa in defense weapons.

¤

Jacob Gordin

WHY JEWS ARE DESPISED

Brothers, Jews, think it over why are you despised, why does no one have pity on you? Why are different elements in the Russian society so united in hating you? Is this only a religious hatred? [And he answers:] It is our love for money, our arrogance, our usury, innkeeping and the middlemen occupations and all the other dishonest deeds that enrage the Russian population against us.

From an appeal that appeared in Russian newspapers in 1881.

¤

Robert Gordis

SPOKESMEN FOR JEWISH LAW

Only those who recognize the authority of Jewish law should have a voice in determining its character.

Upon being elected vice-president of the Rabbinical Assembly of America in June 1942.

KADDISH JUDAISM

[The synagogue has been] emptied of one function after the other. [It has been] forced to be little more than a mortuary chapel for *Kaddish* and *Yizkor.*

Quoted in the Proceedings of the Rabbinical Assembly of America, *Vol. 10, 1946.*

MAINSTREAM CONSERVATIVE JUDAISM

We accept as fundamental to vital Jewish religion the principle of *Torah min Ha-shamayim,* "The Torah as a revelation of God."... This conception need not mean that the process of revelation consisted of the dictation of the Torah by God, and its passive acceptance by men.

From his Judaism for the Modern Age *(1955).*

ONGOING REVELATION

The idea of a progressive and growing revelation is not merely compatible with faith in its divine origin, but is the only view that reckons with the nature of the human participant in the process.

Ibid.

POSTULATES OF CONSERVATIVE JUDAISM

The maintenance of the twin principles of authority and development in Jewish law... together with the emphasis upon the worldwide peoplehood of Israel—these are the basic postulates of Conservative Judaism.

From an article in the 1951 Central Conference of American Rabbis Year Book.

WHERE DENOMINATIONS DIFFER

Reform declared that Judaism has changed throughout time and that Jewish law is no longer binding. Orthodoxy denies both propositions, insisting upon the binding character of Jewish law and negating the view that Judaism has evolved. Conservative Judaism agrees with Orthodoxy in maintaining the authority of Jewish Law and with Reform that Judaism has grown and evolved through time.

From his Judaism in a Christian World *(1966).*

EXPLOITATION OF THE ENVIRONMENT

To claim that [the verse in Genesis 1:28, "Fill the earth and master it"] provides justification for the exploitation of the environment, leading to the poisoning of the atmosphere, the pollution of our water, and the spoilation of natural resources is...a complete distortion of the truth. On the contrary, the Hebrew Bible and the Jewish interpreters *prohibit* such exploitation.

...All animal life and all growing and life-giving things have rights in the cosmos that man must consider, even as he strives to ensure his own survival. The war against the spoilation of nature and the pollution of the environment is therefore the command of the hour and the call of the ages.

> *From* Congress Bi-Weekly *magazine, April 1971.*

o

Aaron David Gordon

ZIONISM IN THE DIASPORA

It is the task of Zionism in the Diaspora to transform the Jews domiciled there into workers and producers. There, too, the chief thing is creation, not wealth.

> *Quoted in S. Spiegel's* Hebrew Reborn *(1930).*

o

Judah Leib Gordon

A JEW FOR ALL PLACES

Be a man when in the world and a Jew at home!

> *From his 1863 poem* Hakitza Ami *("Awake My People").*

A SOBER PEASANTRY

Israel is ready to show to the nations a phenomenon the like of which has never been seen: a peasantry not given to drink, laborers not given to brawls.

> *From a letter to J. Syrkin, July 14, 1892. Quoted in* Igrot.

o

Albert Gore, Jr.

IMPOSSIBLE QUESTIONS

We are reduced to silence filled with the infinite pool of feeling that has created all the words for humility, heartbreak, helplessness and hope in all the languages of the world.

> *At the April 1993 dedication of the United States Holocaust Memorial Museum in Washington DC.*

THE BIG STRETCH

This might be a stretch, but my injury reminds me of this week's Torah portion.

> *From a speech made at the 63rd annual meeting of the General Assembly of the Council of Jewish Federations, held in Denver, Colorado, in November 1994. He was walking with a cane as a result of an injury to his Achilles' heel. The crowd roared with delight even before the Vice-President mentioned Jacob and his injury described in the Torah portion* Va-yeshlach.

ON THE TORAH PORTION

It's good to know that so many of you are familiar with the Torah portion.

> *Ibid. Continuing his comment in reaction to the audience's roar of laughter.*

CONCERN FOR THE ENVIRONMENT

I believe that the purpose of life is to glorify God, and one cannot accomplish that goal while heaping contempt on God's creation.... Teach your communities about the religious basis of concern for this planet. Teach in Hebrew school, preach from the *bima*, join forces with congregations of other faiths. Don't hesitate to lobby Washington when we are wrong or when we can do right.

> *Speaking at the Jewish Theological Seminary of America's 102nd commencement exercises in May 1995.*

o

Shlomo Goren

RELIGIOUS VS. SECULAR LAW

It is clear that, according to *Halacha*, a soldier who receives an order that runs contrary to Torah law should uphold the *Halacha*, and not the secular order. And since settling the Land is a commandment, and uprooting the settlements is breaking the commandment, the soldier should not carry out an order to uproot settlements.

> *From an interview in* Hatzofeh *magazine, December 1993.*

ON UPROOTING SETTLEMENTS

This [Rabin] government does not lean on the majority of Jewish support, but rather on Arab votes. According to Halacha, it does not have the authority of a majority, and therefore government directives to uproot the Jewish settlements do not have the authority of the majority of the people.

A December 1993 comment on the Rabin government's agreement to return to the PLO territory on which Jewish settlements exist.

IN DEFIANCE OF THE LAW

I don't give a hoot about the government's threats. As far as I am concerned, they can put me on trial or send me to jail.

Comments made at a December 1993 Israeli Cabinet meeting after the police threatened to investigate him for calling on soldiers to disobey orders to uproot West Bank settlements.

FEUDING RABBIS

I call upon the rabbis in the world and the Jews of Great Britain, who hold the city of Jerusalem and the land of Israel sacred, to spew this dangerous man [Immanuel Jakobovits] from our midst.

Vehemently attacking the Chief Rabbi of Britain for his 1980 statement that Israel can arrive at an accommodation with the Arabs.

□

Maxim Gorky

ZIONISM AS UTOPIA

I am told Zionism is a Utopia. I do not know; perhaps. But inasmuch as I see in this Utopia an unconquerable thirst for freedom, one for which the people will suffer, it is for me a reality. With all my heart I pray that the Jewish people, like the rest of humanity, may be given spiritual strength to labor for its dream and to establish it in flesh and blood.

Quoted in The Macabbean, *April 1902.*

□

Chaim Grade

EULOGIZING YIDDISH WRITERS

I weep for you with all the letters of the alphabet.

In a letter to Yiddish writer David Bergelson after he and twenty-three other Russian–Jewish intellectuals were imprisoned in Moscow's Lubianka Prison on August 12, 1952 and were murdered on orders from Stalin.

□

Heinrich Graetz

MAKING ROOM FOR JEWISH HISTORY

It is the heartfelt aspiration of the author that this historical work in its English garb may attain its object of putting an end to the hostile bearing against the Jewish race, so that it may no longer be begrudged the peculiar sphere whereto it has been predestined through the events and sorrows of thousands of years, and it may be permitted to fulfill its appointed mission without molestation.

From the Preface to the 1891 English translation of his monumental History of the Jews, *which appeared in the German between 1853 and 1876.*

THINKING AND SUFFERING

Thinking became just as characteristic a feature of the Jews as suffering.

Ibid.

FIXATED ON HOPE

In its journey through the wilderness of life...the Jewish people has carried along the Ark of the Covenant, which breathed into its heart ideal aspirations, and even illumined the badge of disgrace affixed to its garment with a shining glory.... Such a people, which disdains its present and has the eye fixed steadily on its future, which lives as it were on hope, is on that very account eternal, like hope.

Ibid.

THE JEWISH SPIRIT

The Babylonian Amoraim [talmudic scholars] created the dialectic, close-reasoning, Jewish spirit, which in the darkest days preserved the dispersed nation from stagnation and stupidity. It was...the eternal spring which kept the mind ever bright and active.

Ibid.

□

Billy Graham

A MOVING MOMENT

That was one of the few times when I stood before an audience and I wept because it's so moving to me. I think *Schindler's List* has helped remind people [about the Holocaust]—and it could happen again. I think to keep it alive is wonderful, and television is the main medium to do that.

Recalling having laid a wreath at Auschwitz as the press looked on. Quoted in The Jewish Week, *January 10, 1995.*

ᗡ

Alexander Granach

A CONVERSATION WITH GOD

Mama has blessed the candles, always interspersing prayer with personal conversation; she has always spoken to God like a grown daughter to her father, reminding him of his responsibilities and duties. It is the same every week.

> *From his* There Goes a Man: A Novel About Life *(1945)*.

ᗡ

Ulysses S. Grant

GRANT'S ORDER #11

The Jews, as a class, violating every regulation of trade established by the Treasury Department and also departmental orders, are hereby expelled from the Department [of the Tennessee] within twenty-four hours.

> *From Order #11, issued on December 17, 1862. As soon as President Abraham Lincoln was apprised of the matter, he canceled the decree.*

UNPRECEDENTED DIPLOMATIC ENTERPRISE
Executive Mansion
December 8, 1870

The bearer of this letter, Mr. Benjamin Peixotto...has accepted the important, though unremunerative position of U.S. Consul to Roumania....

Mr. Peixotto has undertaken the duties of his present office...as a missionary work for the benefit of the people he represents—a work in which all citizens will wish him the greatest success.

> *The letter carried by Benjamin F. Peixotto, when he was appointed by U.S. President Ulysses S. Grant to help alleviate the plight of Jews in Rumania.*

ᗡ

Rebecca Gratz

EARLY PLEA FOR TOLERANCE

The whole spirit of religion is to make men merciful, humble and just.... Unless the strong arm of power is raised to sustain the provisions of the Constitution of the United States, securing to every citizen the privilege of worshipping God according to his own conscience, America

will no longer be the happy asylum of the oppressed and the secure dwelling place of religion.

> *From a letter to her brother Ben in 1844 after Catholic churches were burned in Philadelphia in protest by the Protestant majority of the large influx of newcomers from Ireland.*

ᗡ

Solomon Grayzel

EUROPE'S FAILURE

Jewish life in Europe was not a failure. Europe had failed.

> *From his* History of the Jews *(1952)*.

THE HUMAN SPIRIT

The Jews have always lived in the very centre of world events so that their experiences in any period have reflected the state of the human spirit.

> *From the Foreword to his* History of the Contemporary Jews *(1960)*.

ᗡ

Andrew M. Greeley

FAMILY FIGHT

By us Irish, we should be so lucky to have an Irving Howe...I serve due warning to other *goyim* [non-Jews] who sit back and watch the debate that Irving Howe will stir up with *World of Our Fathers*: it's a family fight and, while they may nitpick, most American Jews will quite justifiably be proud of Howe's accomplishment.

> *In a review of Irving Howe's* World of Our Fathers *(1976) in* Moment *magazine, March 1976.*

ᗡ

Arthur Green

SEARCHING FOR INNOVATIVE SPIRITUALITY

I would also like to see there be a silent [Friday evening] *Kabbalat Shabbat* service in our cities, where the beginning of the holy day is marked with candle lighting, a period of wordless chanting, a long time of silent awareness of the change of light in that mysterious hour (there should be a natural light-source or view of the outdoors, and no artificial lighting except Shabbat candles), and ended with a shared kiddush.

From his lecture "Judaism for the Post-Modern World," delivered on December 12, 1994 at Hebrew Union College—Jewish Institute of Religion, in Cincinnati, Ohio.

□

Hannah Green

NO GUARANTEES

I never promised you a rose garden. I never promised you perfect justice.

From her I Never Promised You a Rose Garden *(1964).*

□

Mrs. J. R. Green

CHARISMATIC SOLOMON SCHECHTER

That wild man of stupendous genius.

Commenting on the wild-haired Lecturer on Rabbinics at Cambridge University, England.

□

Blu Greenberg

FEMINISM AND JEWISH SURVIVAL

Since we are Jews, we need not buy the whole package of feminism.... Feminism, for all its worth in upgrading the status of Jewish women, does not bode well in its entirety for Jewish survival. Some of its directions may be wrong—or even destructive—when judged from a Jewish perspective.

From her essay "Judaism and Feminism," which appears in The Jewish Woman, *edited by Elizabeth Koltun (1976).*

THE LAST WITNESSES

The life of every [Holocaust] survivor is a miraculous gift and a precious resource to the Jewish community. They have suffered for all of us, and we must be ready to hear the whole story each witness has locked up inside—whomever will listen.

From her essay "Talking to Kids About the Holocaust," which appears in The Hadassah Magazine Jewish Parenting Book, *edited by Roselyn Bell (1989).*

WHERE TO INVEST

One area in which we should invest greater sums is popular Jewish culture. Novels, television, theater, the arts—creations that can stir

the emotions and spirit of the neutral or indifferent. We must create some new and easy markers through which marginal Jews can identify themselves and find access to Judaism; the traditional markers seem not to be working for this group.

From Hadassah Magazine, *June–July 1993.*

NEW MEANS OF COMMUNICATION

In early marriage, when passion and romance dominate, *niddah* [menstrual period] allows and encourages a man and woman to develop other techniques of communication. Not every peak emotion may be expressed through sex; nor can every newly married spat be settled in bed. One also learns quickly that sex cannot be used as a reward or punishment. If sex is being regulated by a force "out there," it becomes less a matter of one or the other controlling or manipulating.

Ibid. From her article "Intergrating Mikveh and Modernity," which appeared in Sh'ma *magazine, January 1980.*

ORTHODOX WOMEN RABBIS

Orthodox women should be ordained because it would constitute a recognition of their new intellectual accomplishments and spiritual attainments; because it would encourage greater Torah study; because it offers wider female models of religious life.

From her article "Is Now the Time for Orthodox Women Rabbis?" which appeared in Moment *magazine, December 1993.*

ORTHODOX LEADERSHIP

The Orthodox community encourages a brain drain. Jewish women with fine minds are being wooed by secular society to make their contribution there, while the door to Jewish scholarship remains, in great part, closed.

From her On Women and Judaism: A View from Tradition *(1981).*

□

Hank Greenberg

A SPECIAL RESPONSIBILITY

After all, I was representing a couple of million Jews among a hundred million gentiles and I was always in the spotlight.... I felt a responsibility. I was there every day and if I had a bad day, every son of a bitch was calling me names so that I had to make good.... As time went by I came to feel that if I, as a Jew, hit a home run, I was hitting one against Hitler.

> *Commenting on the 1938 season when he hit fifty-eight home runs and was approaching Babe Ruth's 1927 record of sixty home runs in one season.*

BASEBALL HERO

There was added pressure being Jewish. How the hell could you get up to home plate every day and have some son of a bitch call you a Jew bastard and a kike and a sheenie and get on your ass without feeling the pressure. If the ballplayers weren't doing it, the fans were. I used to get frustrated as hell. Sometimes I wanted to go in the stands and beat the shit out of them.

> *Ibid.*

◻

Hayim Greenberg

THE CHATHAM SQUARE CEMETERY

One of the earliest documents about the Jews in America fills me with dismay. It is the petition that the Jews of New Amsterdam, which became New York, presented to Stuyvesant to let them purchase a plot of land for a cemetery. I believe that Jewish life in America began with that small burial ground in Chatham Square in New York, in 1656. Not a synagogue, or a Beth Hamedrash, a yeshiva, or a club, but a graveyard. Death, not life.

> *From his essay "A Glance into the Future." Reprinted in Joseph Leftwich's* The Way We Think *(1969).*

THE CHOOSING PEOPLE

Perhaps the Jewish doctrine of the chosen people may be interpreted in this way: Jews are not a chosen people, but a choosing people. According to the Haggada God went around to nation after nation with the Torah, speaking to each in its own language, offering the Torah to each of them, but without success, till the Jews said that they would accept the Torah and keep it. The Jews chose the One God, and the Jews chose the one and only true Torah. How can we apply the usual standards to a people with such an aristocratic choosiness?

> *Ibid.*

SECURITY, EQUALITY, AND DIGNITY

Security and equality cannot bring man happiness...but they can bring him something no less important—dignity—a sense of social value and individual worth.

> *From his essay "To a Communist Friend," included in his book* The Inner Eye *(1953).*

ENDS AND MEANS

Ends and means in politics are analogous to form and content in art. Form in art is not merely technique; means in politics are not merely instruments. The content must be felt in the form. The means must contain the basic elements of the end. When this minimal harmony between ends and means is lacking, we get the stake at which the Holy Inquisition burns unbelievers to save their souls.

> *Ibid.*

A VARIETY OF EXILES

Galut. Wherever Jews live as a minority where they are not politically or socially independent, where they rely on the good graces of the non Jewish majority and are subject to the everyday pressures of its civilization and mode of life, such a place is Galut [Exile].... If, in a general sense, Exile may be conceived of symbolically as night, then there are some Exiles of pitch black night, and some where the night is moonlit.

> *From his essay "Jewish Culture and Education in the Diaspora." Included in* The Hayim Greenberg: Anthology, *edited by Marie Syrkin (1968).*

HEADS HELD HIGH

Let others be ashamed of what they did to us in exile. We have every reason to consider our exile past with heads proudly lifted.

> *Ibid.*

LACKADAISICAL JEWRY

May God not punish me for my words, [but] the fact that in recent months Jews have not produced a substantial number of mentally deranged persons is hardly a symptom of health.

> *From "Bankrupt," a February 1943 article about American Jewry. Quoted in* Hayim Greenberg: Anthology, *edited by Marie Syrkin (1968).*

◻

Irving Greenberg

HEIGHT OF INDIGNITY

Now that [the victims of the Holocaust] have been cruelly tortured and killed, boiled into soap, their hair made into pillows and their bones into fertilizer, their unknown graves and the very fact of their death denied to them, the theologian would inflect [sic] on them the only indignity left: that is, insistence that it was done because of their sins.

> *From an essay in* Auschwitz: Beginning of a New Era? Essays on the Holocaust *(1977), edited by Eva Fleischner.*

QUESTION OF CHOICE

I, too, believe that choice should play a greater role in our religion, but having thought about it for 10 years, I think the movement toward pure choice is excessive. Life is more subtle than that. There remains an element of election, which birth represents; an element of the given, which the body represents.

The Jewish response is that we are not pure birth or tribe, but we are not pure choice either. Biology does speak. This does greater justice to the embodied situation.

> *Presenting the Orthodox view in the debate over whether one is to be considered a Jew only if his mother is a Jew, or if he is to be considered a Jew even if only his father is a Jew. Orthodox and other traditional Jews, unlike Reform Jews, refuse to accept "patrilineal" Jews as Jewish. Quoted in an essay by Peter Steinfels in* The New York Times, *August 7, 1993.*

CBMS AND DSMS

The breakthrough to peace demands not CBMs [confidence-building measures] but DSMs [defense-shattering moves]. True, the other side may exploit the move rather than reciprocate. But, by risking all, one may move the other's heart.

Israel and the PLO have started the peace process. A number of CBMs have been taken. But we still lack a defense-shattering move. Unlike Sadat, Arafat has not risked all. What will it take? An unequivocal denunciation of the violence? A statement of regret for past murderous excesses? A showdown with the radicals?

> *Calling for gestures that will give meaning to the reluctant handshake of September 13, 1993. From an essay in* The Jerusalem Report, *December 30, 1993.*

◘

Sidney Greenberg

MOUNTAINS OF MOMENTS

Just as there are mountains in space, there are mountains in time. Just as there are high places, so are there high moments.... We can and do make mountains out of moments.

> *From his sermon in* Best Jewish Sermons of 5713 *(1953), edited by Saul I. Teplitz.*

COLLECTIVE WISDOM

From the heights afforded by the collective wisdom and experience of Israel's poets and prophets, psalmists and sages, and distilled through our prayerbook, we obtain a proper perspective upon life, upon our destiny in it, and our relationship to one another.

> *Ibid.*

◘

Uri Zev Greenberg

PAST AND FUTURE MEET

Whatever will be in the future already was in the past.

> *Quoted in* Israel Argosy *magazine, Autumn 1952.*

◘

Gary Greenebaum

RELATIONSHIPS TO EFFECT CHANGE

We live in an urban environment where it is not enough to make friends with some powerful white people. We must build coalitions based on real relationships that will protect our rights and promote our interests. It's not enough to smile at each other and then go our ways. And it's not about jumping up and down and yelling that this or that person committed an anti-Semitic act. We must have relationships with enough people so that we can find a way to meet and effect change.

> *Commenting in his capacity as president of the Los Angeles Police Commission. Quoted in* Hadassah Magazine, *April 1994.*

◘

(Pope) Gregory VII

CONTROLLING THE JEWS

As we feel impelled to congratulate you on the progress of your fame, so at the same time must we deprecate the harm you do. We admonish your Highness that you must cease to suffer the Jews to rule over the Christians and exercise authority over them. For to allow the Christians to be subordinate to the Jews, and to subject them to their judgment, is the same as oppressing God's Church and exalting

Satan's synagogue. To wish to please Christ's enemies means to treat Christ himself with contumely.

From a 1080 letter addressed to Castilian King Alonso VI, who employed Jewish advisors and used them on diplomatic missions. Quoted in Heinrich Graetz's History of the Jews *(1894).*

CRUSADERS CONDEMNED

[They] plot impious designs against the Jews and pay no heed to the fact that the proof for the Christian faith comes, as it were, from their archives and that, as the prophets testified, although they should be as the sands of the sea, yet in the end of days a remnant of them shall be saved, because the Lord will not forever spurn His people.... They do not sufficiently consider that...those to whom God wants to be merciful are not to be compelled to the grace of baptism unless they want it voluntarily.

From a letter he sent to archbishops and bishops.

α

William Lindsay Gresham

A WHOLE NEW FORM OF MAGIC

He [Harry Houdini] hurled at the universe a challenge to bind, fetter, or confine him so that he, in turn, could break free. He triumphed over manacles and prison cells, the wet-sheet packs of insane asylums, webs of fish net, iron boxes bolted shut—anything and everything human ingenuity could provide in an attempt to hold him prisoner.

From his Houdini *(1975).*

α

Joel Grey

WHERE PEOPLE REALLY PRAY

My father didn't like the baloney of the big stentorian rabbis who stand up there and pontificate about life. They were more English than the English people. He preferred to go to the more humble *shul* [synagogue] where men really come with their *talis* [prayershawl], a storefront on Beverly Boulevard where, when they blew the *shofar,* it went right through you. They really *davened* [prayed]. He felt much more connected to that, and so did I.

Quoted in Tim Boxer's Jewish Celebrity Hall of Fame *(1987).*

PLAYING A JEW

I've never played a Jew before. I've played Nazis and Irishmen, and WASPs—but never a Jew. It feels good.

Commenting on the part he played in Grand Tour, *the 1979 musical adaptation of a play by S. N. Behrman. His role was that of a Polish Jew escaping from the Nazis.*

α

Alex Grobman

TRIVIALIZING THE HOLOCAUST

It seems to me that she is equating what happened in the Holocaust with other acts of violence, and that is wrong. The Holocaust was unique. It was a Jewish event, primarily. The death of the Six Million was not a by-product of the war. These murders were intended to destroy the Jewish people. These murders were ends in themselves.

What happened to Jews in the Holocaust should become a paradigm for evil because it is unprecedented.

Complaining that artist Judy Chicago has been trivializing the Holocaust by proclaiming its universality. From an article by Ari L. Noonan in Heritage Southwest Jewish Press, *September 23, 1994.*

α

Earl A. Grollman

BEING TRUTHFUL WITH CHILDREN

We should not tell the youngsters what they will later need to unlearn. Fairy tales and half-truths have to be avoided, as well as the delusion that someday the loved one will return. Imaginative fancy only gets in the child's way at a time when he is having trouble enough distinguishing the real from the make believe.

Insisting that children be taught the reality of death. From his Explaining Death to Children *(1969).*

α

Andrei Gromyko

ON THE JEWISH PLIGHT

As is well known, the aspirations of an important part of the Jewish people are bound up with the question of Palestine, and with the future structure of that country. It is not surprising, therefore, that both in the General Assembly and in the meetings of the Political Committee of the Assembly a great deal of attention was given to this aspect of the matter. This interest is comprehensible and completely justified. The Jewish people suffered extreme misery and deprivation during the last war. It can be said, without exaggeration, that the sufferings and miseries of the Jewish people are beyond description.

From a speech delivered to the UN General Assembly on May 14, 1947.

ON THE PARTITION OF PALESTINE

The representatives of the Arab states claim that the partition of Palestine would be an historic injustice. But this view of the case is unacceptable, if only because, after all, the Jewish people has been closely linked with Palestine for a considerable period in history.

Ibid.

□

Peter Grose

FAILED LEADERSHIP

The options open to the United States government were pitifully few. But even the possibilities scarcely came up for discussion.... Roosevelt's guilt, the guilt of American Jewish leadership and the dozens [of] others in positions of responsibility, was that most of the time they failed to try.

Condemning the Jewish and non-Jewish leadership for not doing enough to save Jewish lives during the Holocaust. From his Israel in the Mind of America (1983).

THE AMERICAN–ISRAEL BOND

The Americans see something of themselves in Israel. Even as they go their own way, in pursuit of their own national interest, Americans and Israelis are bonded together like no two other sovereign people.... Israel restored and adopted the vision and the values of the American dream. Each, the United States and Israel, grafted the heritage of the other onto itself.

Ibid.

□

David Grossman

SUDDENLY...A HUMAN TOUCH

After so many years of being fed hatred and suspicion against Palestinians, and the Palestinians being fed hatred and suspicion against us, suddenly there will be a human touch between two peoples.

Of course, who knows if it will work? But

we know what doesn't work. The present situation doesn't work. We all feel that we live in the worst alternative possible.

Reacting to the September 13, 1993 peace accord signed between Israel and the Palestine Liberation Organization in Washington, DC.

□

Richard Grossman

GRADATIONS OF INJUSTICE

Today we had [Chaim] Weizmann, who looks like a weary and more humane version of Lenin, very tired, very ill.... He spoke for two hours with a magnificent mixture of passion and scientific detachment.... He is the first witness who has frankly and openly admitted that the issue is not between right and wrong, but between the greater and the lesser injustice.

Commenting on the activity of the Anglo-American Commission. From an entry in his diary dated March 8, 1946.

□

Philip Guedalla

ARGUMENT FOR ZIONISM

In the last resort, if the highest argument for Zionism is to be found in the prophet Isaiah, the case for it on the narrowest grounds is—[the] Kishineff [pogrom].

From his Supers and Supermen (1920).

□

Edgar A. Guest

SPEAKING OF HANK GREENBERG

Came Yom Kippur—holy fast day world wide over to the Jew—
And Hank Greenberg to his teaching and the old tradition true
Spent this day among his people and he didn't come to play.
Said Murphy to Mulrooney, "We shall lose the game today!
We shall miss him on the infield and shall miss him at the bat,
But he's true to his religion—and I honor him for that!"

From his poem "Speaking of Greenberg," written after the 1934 baseball season when Hank Greenberg refused to play on September 19th because it was Yom Kippur. His team, the Detroit Tigers, was in a close pennant race that year.

⌐

Betya Gur

FREE TO BE OBJECTIVE

I'm a loner and I'll stay a loner. But I think in my line of work—reviewing books—it's best that I steer clear of the literary scene. That way you don't get influenced by the personalities. And it gives me a freer hand reviewing their books. Besides, meeting writers isn't as exciting as reading their books. I never try to meet anyone I write about, even when I worship their work, as with Zach. And I use the word advisedly.

> *From an interview in* The Jerusalem Post, *January 1, 1984.*

⌐

Sidney S. Guthman

REMEMBRANCES OF MARTIN LUTHER KING

I marched with Dr. King in Alabama. And I was in his presence but twice more. Once was at the remarkable rally in Washington when, sitting beneath the rostrum on a grassy hill, I heard that unforgettable "I Have a Dream" speech.

The second time was at a convention of the Rabbinical Assembly on March 25, 1968. He was introduced by my late teacher, his friend and comrade in the struggle for civil rights, Rabbi Abraham Joshua Heschel. We greeted him by singing "We Shall Overcome" in Hebrew, and he was visibly moved. He told us that he had heard that song in many languages, but never in Hebrew!

He spoke of his revulsion for anti-Semitism and his agony over the Holocaust. He lauded Israel as "an oasis of brotherhood and democracy."

> *From one of his sermons.*

⌐

Jakob Guttman

WHEN WILL THE MESSIAH COME?

Judaism does not hold that the Messiah redeems mankind from sin, but declares that when mankind shall have set itself free from the sway of sin through *its own powers of amendment,* and shall have matured to true moral perfection, *then,* for it, the *Messiah will have come.*

> *Quoted in S. Bernfeld's* Foundation of Jewish Ethics *(1929).*

H

(Prophet) Habakkuk

People of Faith

A righteous person lives by his faith.

From the Book of Habbakuk (2:4).

¤

Emile Habibi

Hope for Palestinians

I feel as if the most sublime goals of my life are coming true. I have lived through the tragedy of my people in 1947.... This agreement gives me great hope that we have reached the end of the road of the tragedy of the Palestinian Arab people. So I am very happy and feel great satisfaction.

Reacting to the peace accord signed between Israel and the PLO on September 13, 1993.

¤

Gershon Hacohen

Warriors and Women

Men have always been warriors just as women have been whores.

Speaking to a twelfth-grade Jerusalem class. Quoted in The Jerusalem Report, *February 23, 1995.*

¤

Solomon Ha-Cohen

Law Not Needed

What? Pass a law against counterfeit money? You must be a scoundrel indeed if you need such a law to keep you honest!

From his Responsa *(1594).*

¤

Hai Gaon

Business with Relatives

Transact no business with your kith and kin.

From his Musar Haskel *(c. 1000). Quoted in Benzion Halper's* Post-Biblical Hebrew Literature *(1921).*

All Is for the Best

Delight in what comes from God, and say, "This, too, is for the best."

Ibid.

Life a Disease

Life is a terrible disease, cured only by death.

Ibid.

¤

Devorah Halberstam

A New Survivor

I was born in 1956, eleven years after the [Second World] war ended. But now I am a survivor of the Holocaust. A heart consumed with hatred took the life of my beloved son, Ari, shattering the lives of our entire family forever.

From a plea in April 1994 to Suffolk County legislators to urge the state to pass antibias laws. Her sixteen-year-old son was killed on the Brooklyn Bridge while traveling in a van with other students who had been to the hospital to pray for the ailing Lubavitcher rebbe, *Menachem Schneerson.*

¤

Moshe Halbertal

The Naked and the Dead

When I was first taken to Yad Va-shem [the holocaust memorial in Jerusalem] as a child, I saw a picture of a group of Jewish women standing naked before Nazi guns and awaiting execution. This photograph made me reluctant to visit Yad Va-shem again, because in my parents' house there is a single picture of my grandmother who perished in the Holocaust, and I feared that I might see my grandmother among the naked women. I knew that she would not have wished to be seen in such a manner, and I did not wish to sin against her memory. The picture in Yad Va-shem was not only a document, it was also an obscenity, and I refused to be fascinated by it.

> *From his review of* The Seventh Million: The Israelis and the Holocaust *(1993) in* The New Republic, *October 18, 1993.*

¤

H. R. Haldeman

NIXON ON THE MEDIA

February 1, 1972: There was considerable discussion [in the Nixon White House] of the terrible problem arising from total Jewish domination of the media, and agreement was that this was something that would have to be dealt with. [Reverend Billy] Graham...says that there are satanic Jews, and that that's where our problem arises.

> *From his* Haldeman Diaries *(1994). Graham denies that he ever made such a statement.*

PREPARING FOR CHINA

February 9, 1972: Made the [wise]crack, in reviewing the press list, of whether there were any non-Jews going in the press corps to China.

> *Ibid.*

¤

Eliezer Halevi

HOW TO TREAT A WIFE

Husbands must honor their wives more than themselves, and treat them with tender consideration.

> *From his* Tzava'a *(c.1350). Quoted in Israel Abrahams's* Hebrew Ethical Wills *(1926).*

¤

Yehuda Halevi

THE MEANING OF GODLINESS

The servant of God does not withdraw himself from secular contact lest he be a burden to the world and the world to him; he does not hate life, which is one of God's bounties granted to him.... On the contrary, he loves this world and a long life, because they afford him opportunities of deserving the world to come: The more good he does, the greater is his claim on the world to come.

> *From his* Kuzari *(c. 1135).*

A NOBLE CREATURE

This is the true greatness, which descended direct from Adam. He was the noblest creature on earth. Therefore you rank above all the other inhabitants of the earth.

> *Ibid.*

THE SABBATH QUEEN

The Sabbath is the choicest fruit and flower of the week, the Queen whose coming changes the humblest home into a palace.

> *Ibid.*

JEWS IN THE DIASPORA

The Jewish people in the Diaspora is a body without a head or heart.... Indeed, it is not even a body, but scattered bones.

> *Ibid.*

APPROACHING GOD

Man can approach God only by doing His commands.

> *Ibid.*

GENTLEMEN JEW

Be a gentleman in the street and a Jew at home; a brother to your [gentile] fellow and a [loyal] servant to your king.

> *From* The Selected Poems of Jehuda Halevi *(1924), translated from the Hebrew by Nina Salaman.*

CLINGING TO GOD

When far from Thee, I die
while yet in life;
But if I cling to Thee, I live,
though I should die.

> *Ibid.*

FRUITLESS WISDOM

Let not the wisdom of the Greeks beguile
thee,
Which hath no fruit but only flowers.

> *Ibid.*

WHERE THE HEART IS

My heart is in the East,
And I am in the ends of the West.
How then can I taste what I eat,
And how can food to me be sweet?

> *Ibid. A lament over his being unable to settle in his beloved Jerusalem.*

GOD REVEALED

Remove lust from the midst of thee;
Thou wilt find thy God within thy bosom
Moving gently.

> *Ibid.*

SEARCHING FOR GOD

Lord, where shall I find You?
High and hidden is Your place.
And where shall I not find You?
The world is full of Your glory.
I have sought Your nearness,
With all my heart I called You,
And going out to meet You
I found You coming to meet me.

Ibid.

LONGING FOR JERUSALEM

Oh, city of the world, most chastely fair,
In the far west, behold, I sigh for thee....
Oh, had I eagles' wings I'd fly to thee,
And with my falling tears make moist thine
earth....
Oh, that I might embrace thy dust, the sod
Were sweet as honey to my fond desire.

Ibid.

IN SEARCH OF PEACE

Zion! Wilt thou not ask if peace be with thy
captive?

*According to a legend, when Yehuda Halevi
approached Jerusalem on a visit in 1141, an
Arab horseman trampled him to death as he
was reciting these words.*

READY ACCEPTANCE

He who accepts the Torah without scrutiny
and arguments is better off than he who inves-
tigates and analyzes.

*Quoted in Samuel Caplan and Harold
Ribalow's* Great Jewish Books *(1983).*

□

David Weiss Halivni

BURDEN OF THE BLESSED

A person cannot live with the feeling that
they have achieved the highest. The Nobel
Prize did not become an end, rather a new beginning. He [Wiesel] realizes that the Nobel
Prize was given to him as "Mr. Jew," and therefore he owes it to the Jewish people. In a sense
it entails a greater responsibility. It has imposed a burden on him; the possibility of ex-
tending help, because of his connections, is
much bigger. There is nothing more frightening
for a sensitive person than having power.

*Commenting upon the effect the receipt of
the Nobel Prize has had on Elie Wiesel.
Quoted in Yosef I. Abramowitz's article in*
Moment *magazine, February 1994.*

□

Hillel Halkin

FEAR OF RESPONSIBILITY

What living in Israel means above all is
taking upon oneself *as a Jew* full responsibility
for the human condition in the 20th century—
whether this condition involves the existential
terrors of secularism, the bloody clashes of national sovereignties, or the dehumanizing aspects of a technology-based modern society. In
this respect Israel has become the psychiatrist's couch for the Jewish people. To lie down
on that couch, to live in this land, can be a
painful and disillusioning experience in which
long-operative defense mechanisms are broken down and long-held fantasies must be sur-
rendered. It is no wonder that many diaspora
Jews are reluctant to take such a step.

From an article in The Jewish Spectator,
Winter 1978.

□

Granville Stanley Hall

BE PROUD OF YOUR TRADITION

Do not conceal, but magnify and be proud
of your race, your names and your religion....
Train your children in Hebrew, and tell in your
homes the magnificent traditions of your race.

*From a speech at the cornerstone laying of
Congregation Shaaray Torah, in Worcester,
Massachusetts, April 29, 1906.*

□

Monty Hall

SAY YES FIRST

I say yes first. Everybody else I know says
no first. Then you have to grab him and twist
his arm. I find it a lot easier that if you are free,
do it. Do it! Be a *mensch*, do it, help somebody.

Quoted in Tim Boxer's Jewish Celebrity Hall
of Fame *(1987).*

THE HALL PHILOSOPHY

I don't charge $20,000 like Henry Kissinger,
because I am Monty Hall and Monty Hall
charges nothing. He wants the money to stay
with the charity.

Ibid.

Ben Halpern

OPENING AN ARAB–ISRAELI DIALOGUE

As for the Arabs, we feel a measure of our guilt towards them. We all know and understand out of what necessity we came to it...how much justice validates that which we did.... Yet we must aspire to proper neighborly relations built upon the feeling of mutual guilt between ourselves and the Arab peoples. Let us, then, first of all do what is incumbent upon us to do.

From a 1967 essay in an Israeli publication. Quoted in Murray Polner's American Jewish Biographies *(1982).*

Shaul Hameed

"INFLUENTIAL JEWS" SYNDROME

If what goes on [with the Muslims] in Bosnia happened to six million Jews, they would have brought down the world...because they control the media [the instruments of power].

In an address at a 1993 pan-Asian Islamic conference held in Colombo, Sri Lanka.

Yoram Hamizrachi

PEACE IS IMPOSSIBLE

I am not happy with the situation, but I don't agree with the Israeli politicians talking about peace. There is no chance for any kind of peace between us and the Arabs. Believe me, I am not a hawk and I am not against peace, but I am also not a dove—just saying okay, peace, peace.... I know it is very nice in our time to talk about peace but I don't talk about peace because I don't believe it.

From a 1977 interview reported in Frank Epp's Israelis: Portrait of a People in Conflict *(1980).*

WHY TRUST ARABS?

I am a member of a nation whose first lesson was not to trust anybody. Why should I trust the Arabs? I don't trust, and I don't give a damn about what they think about me. My father was always pro-Arab. He likes to eat with them, he likes to sit with them, he likes to drink with them, he talks their language. But he will never forget that he has also fought against them four times. So to drink and to talk with someone is one side of the story, but on the other hand, you have to fight him one day.

Ibid.

Julius Hammerslough

APPRECIATION FOR LINCOLN

It is, above all, fitting in this land where the Hebrews have won so proud a name and are so greatly respected and honored that they should thus show their love and veneration for the fallen chief of the nation, whose wisdom, honesty and purity of purpose were so highly appreciated by foreign nations and who was so beloved at home.

In an appeal for funds, dated May 30, 1865, to be used for the erection of the Abraham Lincoln monument in Springfield, Illinois.

Hamnuna

THE IMPORTANCE OF EDUCATION

Jerusalem was destroyed only because people neglected to send their children to school.

Quoted in the talmudic tractate Shabbat (119b).

Learned Hand

A SELF-MADE NAME

A self-made man may prefer a self-made name.

Referring to Samuel Goldfish's request to change his name to Samuel Goldwyn. Quoted in Bosley Crowther's Lion's Share *(1957).*

Hannah

A WOMAN'S PRAYER

O Lord of Hosts: If Thou wilt take notice of my troubles and remember me; if Thou wilt not forget me and grant me a son, I will give him to the Lord for all the days of his life.

Quoted in II Samuel (1:11).

Isaac H. Harby

REFORM JUDAISM AND THE REFORMATION

The pen of Luther was a great intellectual lever which shook the papal supremacy to its foundation. Why may not the virtuous example of a few Israelites then shake off the bigotry of the ages from their countrymen? Our principles are rapidly pervading the whole mass of Hebrews throughout the United States.

Comparing his efforts early in the nineteenth century to introduce Reform Judaism to America to the Reformation of Martin Luther. Quoted in Max Dimont's Jews in America *(1978).*

□

Warren G. Harding
HEBRAIC MORTAR
Hebraic mortar cemented the foundations of American democracy.

At the cornerstone-laying ceremony of the Washington (DC) Jewish Center.

ON THE TREATMENT OF JEWS
We fail lamentably where we do not preach effectively tolerance as well as justice and security and respect for the rights of others as much as liberty. And while I hold these views as to all peoples, irrespective of race or creed or condition, I am especially earnest in my protests against the frequent reversions to barbarity in the treatment of the Jewish citizens of many lands, a people who have commanded always my admiration by their genius, industry, endurance, patience and persistence, the virtue and devotion of their domestic lives, their broad charity and philanthropy and their obedience to the laws under which they live.

Quoted in Samuel Walker McCall's Patriotism of the American Jew *(1924).*

□

Yehoshafat Harkabi
PASSING THE BURDEN OF PROOF
Israel should declare readiness to recognize the legitimate interests or rights of the Palestinians and negotiate with the PLO, provided the Palestinians recognize simultaneously the legitimacy of Israel. Such a step, too, would pass the burden of proof to the Arabs or Palestinians. One cannot be sanguine at all that the Palestinians are ready to make such a change in their national doctrines. Their adherence to the unamended National Covenant from July 1968 testifies to this.

From a symposium in Moment *magazine, March 1976.*

□

Cyril Harris
THE ROOTS OF COMPASSION
He was proud to acknowledge the Jewish roots of his compassion.

From his 1995 eulogy delivered at the funeral of Joe Slovo, Nelson Mandela's associate and advisor.

□

Maria Harris
SOURCE OF NOURISHMENT
I am...indebted to the rich, poetic, everfruitful Jewish tradition itself, not only the past but present. I am nourished continually by its insights, and as a "stranger in its land" to use a Jubilee phrase, I acknowledge my indebtedness to the people of that land.

From the Acknowledgments in her Jubilee Time: Celebrating Women, Spirit, and the Advent of Age *(1995).*

SIGNIFICANCE OF RITUAL
Rituals help particular groups of people to interpret themselves at important times in their lives.

Ibid.

□

Leon Harrison
HELD TO A HIGHER STANDARD
The Jew must be gold to pass for silver; he is deemed guilty until he is proved innocent; he alone is not judged by his best, but by his worst. He is attacked not only by the ignorant through lack of knowledge, but by the scholar through lack of sympathy.

From his Religion of a Modern Liberal *(1931).*

□

Alan Hart
KISSINGER'S MACHINATIONS
When Golda had finished her long and detailed account of the Yom Kippur War, I suggested to her that the only conclusion to be drawn was that Henry Kissinger in effect made use of [Anwar] Sadat [of Egypt] to set up the Israelis for a limited war, to teach them a lesson, in order for him to begin a peace initiative on his own terms.... Without a pause for re-

flection, Golda replied: "That is what I believe. That is what we believe. But we cannot ever say so...what I mean is that we cannot even say so to ourselves."

> *Reporting in his* Arafat: A Political Biography *(1984) on a four-hour interview with Golda Meir a few weeks before her death from cancer in November 1979.*

BLOCKING GOLDA'S IMPORTUNING

Golda also told me how she was constantly on the telephone to Nixon "begging" him to begin the airlift of fighter planes and tanks to replace those Israel had lost in the opening hours of the [Yom Kippur] war. At the end of her graphic account of these telephone talks, I asked her whether she suspected that Kissinger was blocking her requests. She replied, "I'm sure that is exactly what was happening. And that's one of the reasons why I insisted on going to Washington myself."

> *Ibid.*

ם

Jeffrey Hart

WHY ISRAEL IS SPECIAL

I can understand why Israel in fact has become sacred. The history of the twentieth century is, to put it mildly, unique. The Holocaust is a sort of hole in the cosmos, a guarantor of the existence of evil. It is an equivalent for Jews of the Crucifixion. Israel then became the equivalent of the Redemption. This is true even for relatively secular Jews. Judaism has never successfully separated God and Tribe. The people itself is the God carrier. I think that from a full experience of the twentieth century I am willing to accept the sacredness of Israel as a religious fact.

> *Comment made after the assassination of Israeli Prime Minister Yitzhak Rabin on November 4, 1995. Quoted in a statement by William F. Buckley, Jr., founder of the* National Review.

ם

Bret Harte

NO JEW AT THIS HOTEL

You'll allow Miss McFlimsey her diamonds
    to wear,
You'll permit the Van Dams at the waiters
    to swear,

You'll allow Miss Decollete to flirt on the
    stair,
But, as to an Israelite, pray have a care.

> *Attacking Judge Henry Hilton, administrator of the exclusive Grand Union Hotel in Saratoga, New York, for his refusal to allow banker Joseph Seligman, the most prominent Jew in the U.S., to register. The desk clerk greeted him with the following prepared statement: "Mr. Seligman, I am required to inform you that Judge Hilton has given instructions that no Israelites shall be permitted in the future to stop at this hotel." The hotel had been suffering from a decline in business and one of the reasons given was that "ostentatious" and "vulgar" Jews were driving away Gentiles.*

ם

David Hartman

BEING JUDGED OBJECTIVELY

The Zionist quest for normalcy should free the Jewish people of any myth about the unique moral and spiritual powers of the Jewish soul. In taking upon ourselves responsibility for a total society, we must allow ourselves to be judged by the same standards as we have judged others.

> *In his* Living Covenant *(1985).*

LOOKING CLOSELY AT OURSELVES

Our newly gained sense of belonging and power enables us to look critically and honestly both at ourselves and at the *halakhic* [Jewish legal] tradition without the apologetic stance so characteristic of a community that saw itself as a persecuted and vulnerable minority. A community that feels dignified and secure in its identity and place in the world can allow itself the mature activity of honest critical self-appraisal.

> *Ibid.*

ISRAELIS AND PALESTINIANS TOGETHER?

The soul of our nation is being put to the test. Our testimony to the moral integrity of Jewish history will be determined by the way we deal with the issue of the Palestinians. Of course, we must be certain that our survival in our own country is not threatened. Our security needs and our sense of being at home should never be undermined. We can be totally uncompromising in our demands for security and at the same time cognizant of the Palestinians' quest for political, economic, and cultural dignity. While we must cherish the sacredness of our own human life, our urgent need for security does not require that we deny the political and cultural renaissance of the Palestinian people. Both can live and flourish together. Most Israelis believe that there can be more than one dignified people in this land.

> *From the Introduction to his* Conflicting Visions: Spiritual Possibilities of Modern Israel *(1990).*

THE NONOBSERVANT MAJORITY IN ISRAEL

In building a nation-state, nonobservant Jews in Israel have found a rich and satisfying Jewish life. It is distasteful and vulgar to approach them from a paternalistic, authoritarian perspective. Traditional *halakhic* Jews cannot enter into a serious dialogue with the majority of Israelis if we infantilize and trivialize the Jewish society they have created.

> *Ibid.*

JUDAISM'S OBLIGATION

When I came here, I didn't have the language. Although I knew Hebrew, I didn't speak Hebrew, and I didn't think in Hebrew. I thought in English. Language is a real problem, especially for a philosopher. If I were a surgeon or a plumber it would have been easier.

I came here because I knew my Judaism had to be historical. I came here not because I was persecuted, and not because I was a failure, but because my Judaism was on trial. If Judaism means anything in the modern world, it's going to have to transform a society. If it can't, then it's dead.

> *Upon moving to Israel from Montreal after the Six Day War. From a 1977 interview, reported in Frank Epp's* Israelis: Portrait of a People in Conflict *(1980).*

SINGING ONE'S OWN SONG

In Israel, Judaism has an opportunity to sing a total song—not an unfinished symphony, but a total symphony. No one's stopping us. We have an autonomous culture.

> *Ibid.*

THE JEWISH ANCHOR

God who is worshipped through the *mitzvot* [commandments] anchors the Jew within the historical and makes him or her understand that God's home lies within the temporal. The revealed commandments constitute a total way of life that must be implemented within the framework of human history.

> *Quoted in Lewis Glinert's* Joys of Hebrew *(1992).*

STARTING POINT FOR CONTINUITY

Are we going to face honestly the fact that we have lost our identity as a people of Torah?... The issue of our time is, how do we retrieve the power of Sinai?... We all face that issue. [It is for Jews now to admit to each other their longing for that lost faith] to feel the pain of that reality and tell it to another Jew— not as a solution, but so that we can meet to talk about it.

> *From an address at a June 1994 conference convened by Israel's President Ezer Weizmann on Israel-Diaspora relations.*

¤

Khalad Hassan

KISSINGER THE LIAR

Alan, I've told you many times before, and no doubt I'll have to tell you many times in the future, this man Kissinger is a big liar.

> *Comment to Alan Hart describing the political maneuverings during the Yom Kippur War period. Reported in Hart's* Arafat: A Political Biography *(1984).*

SHARON'S SECRET VOW

I just heard a terrible story and it happens to be true. I know I've checked it. It concerns our famous General [Ariel] Sharon. Do you know what that lunatic has just done.... He's sworn a secret oath. He's taken a vow that if this or any future government of Israel attempts to withdraw from the West Bank, he'll set up headquarters there and fight to the death to prevent a withdrawal.... He's mad enough to nuke the whole Arab world provided he can find a way to protect this little country from the fall-out!

> *Ibid.*

¤

(Crown Prince) Hassan of Jordan

THE PRINCE AND HIS HORSE

People have accused me for years of trying to put the economic cart before the political horse. I don't really think that it is a fair accusation. Today, I may be one of the few people in the region who has a horse at all.

> *Defending himself against charges that he has not projected the importance of Israel sufficiently in his vision of the new Benelux-type arrangement for the turbulent Middle East. Quoted in* The Jerusalem Report, *December 16, 1993.*

Judith Hauptman

EGALITARIAN JUDAISM

What troubles Jewish women today is that the movement for equalization ended before real equalization was reached.... We hope that we will soon see a reinstitution of the process so admirably evolved and applied by the earlier rabbis, an improvement in the lot of women, and a vindication of the essential Jewish tradition.

From the article "Women's Liberation in the Talmudic Period," which appeared in Conservative Judaism *magazine, Summer 1972.*

Rita E. Hauser

A TOTALLY INDEPENDENT FEMINIST

[Men try] to discourage women by arguing that a woman has to be tough, bitchy and hardshelled. I want to show that this is not so. A woman can be natural, feminine, pretty—and tough when she must be, too.

From a 1978 interview in The New York Times.

Gideon Hausner

SOME SHINING LIGHTS

In the darkness that engulfed Europe there were some shining lights. The Jewish people have a long memory; it will never forget its benefactors as it will not forget its foes. Their names [will] be engraved in our memory forever, as we still [bear] in thankful memory the name of Cyrus of Persia, who enabled the exiles to return to the promised land.

Paying tribute to non-Jews who risked their lives to save Jews. Quoted in Eva Fogelman's Conscience & Courage *(1994).*

A DEBT TO SURVIVORS

We owe it to the Holocaust survivors to impose the punishment.

Countering the view of some prominent Israelis who advocated that Eichmann's death sentence be commuted.

Goldie Hawn

ADVICE FROM A FATHER

My daddy said that if you think you're too big for your britches just go stand in the ocean and feel how small you really are. I always remember that.

A lesson recalled after making a $30,000,000 seven-picture deal with Disney Pictures in the spring of 1991.

John Hay

AN UNCOMPROMISING VOICE

The political disabilities of the Jews in Rumania, their exclusion from the public service and the learned professions, the limitations of their civil rights and the imposition upon them of exceptional taxes, involving as they do wrongs repugnant to the moral sense of liberal modern peoples, are not so directly in point for my present purpose as the public acts which attack the inherent right of man as a breadwinner in the ways of agriculture and trade. The Jews are prohibited from owning land, or even from cultivating it as common laborers. They are debarred from residing in the rural districts. Many branches of petty trade and manual production are closed to them in the overcrowded cities, where they are forced to dwell and engage, against fearful odds, in the desperate struggle for existence. This government cannot be a tacit party to such an international wrong. It is constrained to protest treatment to which the Jews of Rumania are subjected, not alone because it has unimpeachable ground to remonstrate against the resultant injury to itself, but in the name of humanity.

In 1902, at President Theodore Roosevelt's direction, the secretary of state sent this stiff note to Rumania.

Malcolm Hay

CHURCH FATHERS AND THE JEWS

The Church, conscious that Christianity is founded on Judaism, recognized their right to live and to practice their religion without interference.... This right, however, was conditioned by the stipulation, which the Fathers of the early Church had often emphasized, that they were to live in a state of misery and degradation. The sons of the bondwoman must be kept in subjection to the sons of the freewoman.

From his Foot of Pride *(1950).*

Early Popes and the Jews

The Popes of the Middle Ages often intervened, not always effectively, to defend Jews against personal violence, but seldom wrote a line to condemn the ill-will which made such violence inevitable.

Ibid.

¤

William Randolph Hearst, Jr.

A Most Memorable Leader

[Ben-Gurion] had an inner strength and dedication that flowed from his mind and body to all those with whom he came in contact. [His dynamism was such that he] communicated greatness and strength of will in ordinary human contact. His personality transformed a simple moment into an unforgettable experience.

From his Hearsts: Father and Son *(1993), in which he says that his father spoke of the "legendary" Ben-Gurion as one of the three most memorable leaders he met during his long journalistic career.*

¤

Abraham Hecht

I Apologize

For my part, I wish to repudiate any words and actions of anger.... We must not use hurtful words, but rather come together as fellow Jews in love—with trust and respect.

In an October 23, 1995 letter of apology to Israeli Prime Minister Yitzhak Rabin issued after Hecht's October 18th missive on behalf of his right-wing Orthodox Rabbinical Alliance of America, which encouraged Israeli soldiers to disobey all orders issued to remove Jews from their West Bank settlements and for encouraging the assassination of Rabin.

The Rabbi and the Pope

The truth is, I would feel more at home with the Pope than with a Reform rabbi.

After being selected as one of twenty-five rabbis chosen to meet with Pope John Paul II on October 7, 1995, during his visit to New York.

A Message for the Pope

I'm not interested in taking pictures with the Pope. My community doesn't even know who he is.

Ibid. Insisting that his only purpose in joining the group meeting with the Pope was to ask him to require Catholics to obey the seven Noahide laws.

¤

Ben Hecht

Militancy of the Irgun

Every time you [the Irgun] blow up a British arsenal, or wreck a British jail, or send a British railroad train sky high, or rob a British bank, or let go with your guns and bombs at the British betrayers or invaders of your homeland, the Jews of America make a little holiday in their hearts.

From an ad placed in The New York Times *in 1946 encouraging the Irgun violence in Palestine. The Zionist leadership disavowed the activity of the Irgun.*

Yeast of Civilization

The Jews are the yeast in the bread of civilization which causes it to grow.

From his autobiography, A Child of the Century *(1954).*

Entertainers of America

What a troupe they were in their heyday! What a wild yap of wit and sweet burst of song came surging out of the Jewish slums of the twenties! The Marx Brothers, Al Jolson, George Jessel, Fanny Brice, Eddie Cantor, Jack Benny, Jack Pearl, Bennie Fields, Lou Holtz, Ed Wynn, Joe Laurie, the Howard Brothers, Julius Tannen, Phil Baker, Phil Silvers, Milton Berle, Belle Baker, Harry Richman, Ben Bernie, the Ritz Brothers, Smith and Dale, Ben Welch, Harry Green, Ray Samuels, Jackie Osterman, George Burns—these are some of them.... In their presence Jewishness was not Jewishness. It was a fascinating Americanism.

Ibid.

¤

Eli Hecht

Swindler's List

I am sick and tired of this generation identifying Judaism with suffering. Why is it imperative for our children and young people to visit Holocaust museums? Why do they need to hear lectures about skinheads and neo-nazis and growing anti Semitism...?

Commenting on Steven Spielberg's film Schindler's List, *which Hecht called "Swindler's List." From a letter sent to* The Los Angeles Times. *Quoted in* Heritage Southwest Jewish Press, *January 21, 1994.*

Jascha Heifetz

THE JOB OF TEACHERS

The greatest job of teachers is to cultivate talent until it ripens for the public to reap its bounty.

Commenting on the art of teaching music. From an article in Newsweek *magazine, February 11, 1963.*

Samuel Heilman

STRUGGLING OVER IDENTITY

In our own times we continue to struggle with the question of where to draw the line of identity.... Should we emphasize inclusion or exclusiveness, ritual or ethics, feeling or praxis, the community or the individual? Is our model the European or the North African diaspora; biblical or modern Israel; Vilna, Casablanca, New York or Jerusalem?

From an article in Moment *magazine, February 1994.*

BORN-AGAIN JEWS

As an involved Jew, I am frankly far more concerned about those Jews who don't care at all than those who do care and argue about defining who and what a Jew is. Those who have ceased to care where to draw the line are the real Jewish victims of modernity. Their Jewish identity has died.

Ibid.

Eugene Heimler

WHAT I LEARNED IN BUCHENWALD

It was in Buchenwald that I learnt from Jews, Christians, Moslems and pagans, from Englishmen, Serbs, Rumanians, Albanians, Poles and Italians that I was only one more suffering insignificant man.... That I am not in any way superior, that I am not different from others, that I am but a link in the great chain, was among the greatest discoveries of my life. From then on I resolved to support those who fell, even as I had been supported.... It may be that I would have learnt this without the lesson of Buchenwald. But I would have learnt it much later—perhaps too late.

From his Night of Mist *(1959).*

Heinrich Heine

HEROES OF THE BIBLE

I see now [upon studying the Bible] that the Greeks were only handsome striplings, while the Jews were always men—powerful, indomitable men—who fought and suffered on every battlefield of human thought. How small Sinai appears when Moses stands upon it!

From his Confessions *(1854).*

THE REAL MOSES

Formerly, I felt no special affection for Moses, probably because the Hellenic spirit was paramount in me, and I could not pardon the legislator of the Jews his hatred against the plastic arts. I did not see that, notwithstanding his hostility to art, Moses was a great artist, and possessed the true artistic spirit. But this spirit was directed by him, as by his Egyptian compatriots, to colossal and indestructible undertakings.... However, he built human pyramids, carved human obelisks; he took a poor shepherd family and created a nation from it, a great, eternal holy people, a people of God, destined to outlive the centuries, and to serve as a pattern to all other nations, even as a prototype to the whole of mankind: he created Israel.

Ibid.

PORK-EATING JUDAISM

The religion of the Scotch Protestants is simply pork-eating Judaism.

Ibid.

CONVOLUTED LOGIC

How strange! The very people who had given the world a God, and whose whole life was inspired by devotion to God, were stigmatized as deicides!

Ibid.

NOBLE HOUSE OF ISRAEL

The writer of these pages might well be proud that his ancestors belong to the noble house of Israel, that he is a descendant of those martyrs who gave the world a God and an ethic, who struggled and suffered on all the battlefields of ideas.

Ibid.

HEINE'S BAPTISM

An entrance ticket to European society.

Explaining his submission to baptism in 1825.

JERUSALEM IN DESOLATION

She for whom the Rabbi languished was a woebegone poor darling; Desolation's very image, And her name: Jerusalem.

A lament over the destruction of the Holy City.

BIRTHING OF A BOOK

A book, like a child, needs time to be born. Books written quickly—within a few weeks—make me suspicious of the author. A respectable woman does not bring a child into the world before the ninth month.

From his Thoughts and Fancies *(1869).*

COMRADES IN MISERY

My ancestors did not belong to the hunters so much as to the hunted, and the idea of attacking the descendants of those who were our comrades in misery goes against my grain.

From his Nordeney *(1826).*

A CHASTE RACE

The Jews are a chaste, temperate, I might say an abstract race, and in purity of morals they are most nearly allied to the Germanic races.

From his Shakespeare's Maidens: Jessica *(1838).*

FROM EXILE TO HOMELAND

He who does not know exile will not understand how luridly it colors our sorrows, how it pours the darkness of night and poison into all our thoughts.... Only he who has lived in exile knows what love of fatherland is—patriotism with all its sweet terrors and its nostalgic trials.

From his Ludwig Börne *(1840). Quoted in F. Eiven's* Poetry and Prose of Heinrich Heine *(1948).*

FROM THE VULGAR TO THE PURE

Jews are of the stuff of which gods are made; today trampled under foot, tomorrow worshipped on the knees. While some of them crawl in the filthy mire of commerce, others rise to the loftiest peaks of humanity.... You will find among them every possible caricature of vulgarity, and also the ideas of purest humanity.

Ibid.

TWIST OF FATE

Other seasons, other songbirds,
Other songbirds, other songs.
They perchance could give me pleasure
Had I only other ears!

From his "Atta Troll" (1841).

ABHORRENCE OF HUNTING

I cannot comprehend, when I see such a noble animal [deer] how educated and refined people can take pleasure in its chase or death.

From his Harzreise *(1824).*

RELIGION AND PHILOSOPHY

The moment a religion seeks support from philosophy, its ruin is inevitable.... Religion, like every other form of absolutism, should be above justification.

From his Germany from Luther to Kant. *(1834).*

FREEDOM'S ACCENT

Since the Exodus freedom has spoken with a Hebrew accent.

Ibid.

DEISM: OUTDATED

Pantheism is the public secret in Germany. In fact, we have outgrown deism. We are free and do not want a thundering tyrant; we are grown up and require no fatherly care. Nor are we the bungled work of a great mechanic. Deism is a religion for slaves, for children, for Genevese, for watchmakers.

Ibid.

COLORS OF MY HOUSE

Noble sir! Would you be my knight, then you...must sew yellow wheels upon your mantle, or bind a blue-striped scarf about your breast. For these are my colors, the colors of my house, named Israel, the unhappy house mocked at on the highways and byways by the children of fortune.

From his Rabbi von Bacharach *(1840). Quoted in G. Karpeles's* Jewish Literature *(1895).*

SEDER SOUNDS

Jews who long have drifted from the faith of their fathers...are stirred in their inmost parts when the old, familiar Passover sounds chance to fall upon their ears.

Ibid.

PRICE OF CARELESSNESS

He who reaches for a rose with a careless hand must not complain if he is stuck by thorns.

Ibid.

I LIKE YOUR COOKING

I could not be one of you. I like your cooking much better than I like your religion. No. I could not be one of you; and I suspect that even at the best of times, under the rule of your King David, in the best of your times, I would have run away from you and gone to the temples of Assyria and Babylon, which were full of love and the joy of life.

Ibid. The lead character speaking to the rabbi, emphasizing his distaste for orthodoxy.

STAYING ON THE RIGHT SIDE

As Christians act, so do Jews [*Wie es sich Christeld so Judelt es sich*].

An expression that has become a folksaying.

MEDICINE CHEST

The Bible: that great medicine chest of humanity.

Quoted in F. Ewen's Poetry and Prose of Heinrich Heine *(1948).*

THE GREAT EQUALIZER

Powder makes men equal. A citizen's musket fires as well as a nobleman's.

From his English Fragments *(1831).*

TURNING WITH THE WIND

The weathercock on a church spire, though made of iron, would soon be broken by the storm-wind if it did not understand the noble art of turning to every wind.

Ibid.

EVERY MAN A WORLD

Every single man is a world which is born and which dies with him; beneath every gravestone lies a world's history.

From his Munich to Genoa *(1828).*

SOMETIMES BETTER, SOMETIMES WORSE

The Jews when good are better, and when bad are worse, than the Christians.

From his Gedanken und Einfälle *(1869).*

WHAT A JEW CANNOT BELIEVE

No Jew can ever believe in the divinity of another Jew.

Ibid.

PRINCESS SABBATH

Of a prince by fate thus treated is my song.
His name is Israel,
And a witch's spell has changed him
To the likeness of a dog....
But on every Friday evening
On a sudden, in the twilight,
The enchantment weakens, ceases,
And the dog once more is human.

From his "Princess Sabbath" (1851).

THE WORLD A HOSPITAL

Life is a disease, the whole world a hospital, and Death is our physician.

From his "City of Lucca" (1829).

ASK ME WHAT I AM

Ask me not what I have, my
    loved one,
Ask me rather what I am.

From his Early Poems.

SOLDIER FOR FREEDOM

I really do not know whether I deserve that a laurel wreath be laid on my coffin.... But ye may lay a sword on my coffin, for I was a brave soldier in the war of freedom for mankind.

From his Journey from Munich to Genoa *(1828).*

GREEK AND JEWISH VALUES

The contrasts are boldly paired,
Love of pleasure in the Greek, and thought
    of God in the Judean,
Oh! this conflict will never end,
The true must always contend with the
    beautiful.

Expressing his continuing struggle to harmonize the pure morality of Judaism and the symmetrical beauty of Hellenism. Quoted in Heinrich Graetz's History of the Jews *(1894).*

SURGING SENSE OF PRIDE

Now I perceive that the Greeks were only handsome youths, but the Jews have always been men, powerful, stubborn men, not only in days of yore, but even at present, in spite of eighteen centuries of persecution and misery. I have since learned to know them better, and to value them more highly, and if pride of descent were not always a foolish contradiction, I might feel proud of the fact that my progenitors were members of the noble house of Israel, that I am a descendant of those martyrs who have given a God and morality to the world, and who have fought and suffered on all the battle-fields of thought.

Ibid. Expressing pride in belonging to an ancient aristocracy toward the end of a life in which he struggled with a love-hate relationship to Judaism.

PRAISE FOR THE POTATO

Why do you sing about the rose? It is the aristocrat of flowers. Why don't you sing the praise of the democratic potato, which is food for the people?

Quoted in Lionel Blue's Jewish Guide to the Here and Hereafter *(1988).*

SECURING SYMPATHY

I bequeath all my property to my wife on the condition that she remarry immediately. Then, there will be at least one man to regret my death.

> Quoted in Morris Mandel's Affronts, Insults, and Indignities (1975).

HORSES AND ASSES

The aristocracy is composed chiefly of asses—asses who talk about horses.

> Ibid.

ISRAELITE AND JEW

When people talk about a wealthy man of my creed, they call him an Israelite; but if he is poor they call him a Jew.

> From his manuscript papers.

ON THE BURNING OF BOOKS

Where books are burned, human beings will be burned too.

> Quoted in The Times Literary Supplement, London, March 17, 1961.

EQUAL OF ROTHSCHILD

And may God withdraw his favors if it is not true, Herr Doktor. I sat next to Salomon Rothschild and he treated me as an equal, as if I were "famillionaire."

> From his autobiographical Reisebilder (1826–1831).

□

Joseph Heller

THAT'S SOME CATCH

"There was only one catch and that was Catch-22, which specified that a concern for one's own safety in the face of dangers that were real and immediate was the process of a rational mind. Orr was crazy and could be grounded. All he had to do was ask; and as soon as he did, he would no longer be crazy and would have to fly more missions.... If he flew them he was crazy and didn't have to; but if he didn't want to he was sane and had to...."

"That's some catch, that Catch-22," he [Yossarian] observed.

"It's the best there is," Doc Daneeka agreed.

> From his Catch-22 (1961).

SELF-MADE MAN

He was a self-made man who owed his lack of success to nobody.

> Ibid.

PRIZES AND PARADES

Like Olympic medals and tennis trophies, all they signified was that the owner had done something of no benefit to anyone more capably than everyone else.

> Ibid.

□

Lillian Hellman

CREATIVITY

God forgives those who invent what they need.

> From her Little Foxes (1939).

THE COSTLY FIGHT

It doesn't pay well to fight for what we believe in.

> From her Watch on the Rhine (1941).

TAKING THE FIFTH

I am not willing, now or in the future, to bring bad trouble to people who, in my past association with them, were completely innocent of any talk or any action that was disloyal or subversive. I do not like subversion or disloyalty in any form and if I had ever seen any I would have considered it my duty to have reported it to the proper authorities. But to hurt innocent people whom I knew many years ago in order to save myself is, to me, inhuman and indecent and dishonorable. I cannot and will not cut my conscience to fit this year's fashions.

> From her May 1952 testimony before the House Committee on Un-American Activities, which investigated suspected Communist sympathizers. For this statement she was blacklisted throughout the 1950s.

THE GIFT OF BEING BORN A JEW

I myself make very anti-Semitic remarks, but I get very upset if anybody else does. I wasn't brought up as a Jew. I know almost nothing about being one —I'm sorry to say—though not sorry enough to go to the trouble of learning.... [I] decided a long time ago that I was very glad I was born a Jew. Whether brought up as one or not, somewhere in the background there was the gift of being born a Jew.

> From a 1981 interview. Quoted in Elinor and Robert Slater's Great Jewish Women (1994).

Ernest Hemingway

THE MANLY STEIN

Gertrude Stein and me are just like brothers.

Quoted by John Malcolm Brinnin.

❑

Brian Henderson

JEWISH GUILT

The root cause of the crisis in the legal aid system is Jewish mothers.... Jewish mothers are infamous for advising their offspring to become doctors or dentists or lawyers, or marry a doctor or dentist or lawyer. And the result is we have too many of all three in this province.

A 1995 comment on Ontario, Canada radio that prompted violent criticism.

❑

Burton Hendricks

WAVE OF ANTI-SEMITISM

The one prejudice which would seem to have no decent cause for existence in the free air of America is one that is based on race and religion. Yet the most conservative American universities are openly setting up bars against the unlimited admittance of Jewish students; the most desirable clubs are becoming more rigid in their inhospitable attitude toward Jewish members; a weekly newspaper, financed by one of the richest men in America, has filled its pages for three years with a virulent campaign against this element in our population; secret organizations have been established for the purpose of "fighting" the so-called "Jewish predominance in American life"; Congress has passed and the President has signed an immigration law—it is just as well to be frank about the matter—to restrict the entrance of Jews from Eastern Europe.

From his Jews in America *(1923).*

❑

Louis Henkin

A TRUSTED FRIEND

He [Felix Frankfurter] began to talk to me about this [arrangements for a Jewish funeral] several years ago when he was still in good health. Particularly he spoke of it last year. Frankfurter was very much occupied with the manner in which he would take leave from the world. He did not want a public funeral. Only friends were to attend. But he wanted a ceremony which would make known to the world that he died as a Jew.... I suggested that I say the *Kaddish* and Frankfurter said "fine."

Revealing to Garson Kanin the instructions that Felix Frankfurter had left with him about arrangements for his funeral. Henkin, a practicing Orthodox Jew, was a colleague and close personal friend of the Supreme Court justice. Reported in The Jewish Press, *March 19, 1965.*

❑

Michael Henry

TEFILLIN AND CRICKET

You may be very good Jews and none the worse for it in any walk of life. Your right arm will fling a cricket ball none the less deftly because your left arm had worn the *tefillin* [phylacteries] an hour before you went to the playground.

Recalling his school days in London and the many English sports in which he was engaged. From his Sabbath Readings *(1876).*

❑

Nat Hentoff

DEPTHS OF DESPAIR

If I were to hear one morning through bullhorns that all Jews are to report to Grand Central Station, I would not be entirely surprised.

From an article in The Village Voice. *Quoted in Aviva Cantor's* Jewish Women/Jewish Men *(1994).*

❑

Will Herberg

DELUSIVE SELF-SUFFICIENCY

"Turning [*teshuvah*]" is the fusion of repentance and grace. It points at one and the same time to man's action in abandoning his delusive self-sufficiency so as to turn to God, and to God's action in giving man the power to break the vicious circle of sin and turn to the divine source of his being....

Because it is the delusion of self-sufficiency that must be overcome before the healing work of God becomes available to us, we obviously cannot hope to achieve our salvation through our own works, however meritorious.

From his Judaism and Modern Man *(1951).*

IDEALISM GONE SOUR

Cynicism is, after all, simply idealism gone sour.

Ibid.

THE HIGHER LAW

Hebraic religion cannot and will not admit that society is the whole of life or that any social institution whatever is above judgment and criticism in terms of the "higher law" revealed in the divine imperative. It says *no* to society or the state or the church when any of these dares to exalt itself and call for the worship of total allegiance.

Ibid.

MORALITY WITHOUT GOD

Morality ungrounded in God is indeed a house built upon sand, unable to stand up against the vagaries of impulse and the brutal pressures of power and self-interest.

Ibid.

JEWS TO AMERICAN EYES

Today, if the American Jew is to regard himself as a Jew, and if he is to be so regarded by his non-Jewish neighbors and friends, some religious association, however vague, is necessary. The only way in which the Jew can integrate himself into American society is in terms of a religious community.

From his Religious Trends in American Jewry *(1955).*

ULTIMATE QUESTIONS

We live in an age when ultimate questions have, quite unaccountably, become immediate questions.

Ibid.

BATTLE OF FAITH

Faith is a never-ending battle against self-absolutization and idolatry; it is a battle which has to be fought every moment of life because it is a battle in which the victory can never be final. But although never final, victory is always possible....

Ibid.

HANDLING EVIL

The real moral peril consists not so much in choosing what in our best judgment seems to be the lesser evil; such choice is entailed by the very process of living. The real moral peril consists in trying to make a virtue out of necessity, in converting the lesser evil we choose, merely because we choose it, into a positive good.

Ibid.

PREOCCUPATION WITH RITUAL

Mr. Wouk devotes very little space to the *inwardness* of Jewish faith...he is mostly preoccupied with the externals of observance and behavior.... These externals are important but they are not that faith itself.

Ibid. In his evaluation of Herman Wouk's This Is My God.

SELF-IDOLIZATION

Ultimately all idolatry is worship of the self projected and objectified: all idolization is self-idolization.

Ibid.

AMERICANIZATION OF THE JEW

Trade unionism helped very materially to obtain acceptance for the immigrant Jewish worker in the United States, for it was trade unionism, along with the public school, that constituted for the mass of immigrant Jews their first real initiation into American institutional life. As a trade unionist, the immigrant Jew began to speak a "language" that Americans could understand.

From his article "The Jewish Labor Movement in the United States," included in the American Jewish Yearbook *(1952).*

¤

Johann Gottfried Herder

THE BEAUTY OF HEBREW

It is worth studying the Hebrew language for ten years in order to read [the highly poetic] Psalm 104 in the original.

Quoted in J. H. Hertz's Daily Prayer Book *(1948).*

¤

Robert Travers Herford

JUDAISM'S GENTLE TOUCH

The tone of the great Jewish writers in reference to Christianity was as different from that of their opponents as light from darkness. Criticism and dissent were of course to be found in Jewish writings, but not the execration which filled so many Christian pages.

From a 1919 article in Menorah Journal. *Quoted in Bevan and Singer's* Legacy of Israel *(1927).*

CONTINUOUS REVELATION

The Pharisees survived because they had developed a type of Judaism which was not dependent on the Temple and its ritual, but had its roots in the synagogue and the school.... The Pharisees were able to do this because they were the only exponents of Judaism who discovered in it the principle of continuous revelation.

Ibid.

JEWISH CONTRIBUTION TO HUMANITY

Can it be doubted that it has been and is a substantial benefit to the human race that there should be, amongst its members, and especially its Christian members, this nonconformist nation, to represent liberty of thought, freedom of conscience, independence of judgment, the right of the human mind to settle for itself its relation with God?

Ibid.

THE OPTIMIST

If Israel is the stubborn nonconformist among the nations, he is also the unconquerable optimist.

Ibid.

NEEDING NOTHING

The Jews...never have needed anything that Paul or any other Christian missionary had to offer them.

From his Judaism in the New Testament Period *(1928).*

SPIRITUALITY OF THE FLESH

Jewish thought never identified "the flesh" with the evil impulse, nor regarded flesh and spirit as hostile to one another.

Ibid.

GOD SPEAKING TO MAN

It was for the prophet to find God, for the Psalmist to praise Him; in prophecy God speaks to man, in psalmody man sings to God. The prophet makes religion, the Psalmist experiences and acclaims it.

Ibid.

CREATION OF THE SYNAGOGUE

The Temple was the altar, the Synagogue was the hearth, and the sacred fire burned on each of them. With the fall of the Temple, the fire was quenched on the altar, stamped out under the heel of the conqueror; but it still glowed on the hearth.... In all their long history, the Jewish people have done scarcely anything more wonderful than to create the Synagogue. No human institution has a longer continuous history, and none has done more for the uplifting of the human race.

Quoted in J. H. Hertz's Pentateuch and Haftorahs *(1961).*

◻

Agnes G. Herman

GAY CONDUCT

Behavior that is different from our own makes us uncomfortable. Two men holding hands in synagogue and embracing each other to say "Good *Shabbos*" is distasteful to many Jews. Two women dancing together at a bar mitzva party is acceptable, as is men dancing together at a traditional wedding. But should the dancers be acknowledged gays, outrage would be the response. It is clear that not all Jews can evidence their life-style in the synagogue.

In her essay "Parenting a Homosexual Child," which appears in The Hadassah Magazine Jewish Parenting Book *(1989), edited by Roselyn Bell.*

◻

Jerry Herman

JEWS AND MUSICAL COMEDIES

You know how amazing it is that, except for a handful like Cole Porter, almost everybody in musical comedy on Broadway have been Jews... I think it has something to do with growing up in a Jewish home where there is melodic singable music. They all came from that atmosphere. I grew up in a home where there was always Yiddish and Hebrew songs.... Cole Porter said when he wanted to be super melodic he'd put a Jewish melody in his song. An example is "I Love Paris."

Quoted in Tim Boxer's Jewish Celebrity Hall of Fame *(1987).*

◻

Ruhama Hermon

DIPLOMATIC TALK

I must say that the Likud did a very good job in the last 15 years in telling American Jews the importance of the Golan Heights and Judea and Samaria.... And I think it will be a little hard now to convince them, after all these years, why we can give up some territory.

But I will try to say to people that I, too, in the past, wanted—and still do want—the Golan Heights to be in Israel. I want to be protected by these Heights always, and I want to live in a bigger Israel. If you ask me directly: I want it.

But I know that this is impossible. If I want to achieve peace, I know I have to give some things up. And I tell them that living in Israel, and sending my son to the army, that can change a person. Sometimes you feel that a piece of land is less important than his life.

From a portrait by Allison Kaplan Sommer in The Jerusalem Post, *July 31, 1993.*

❏

John Hersey

A GLORIOUS HERITAGE

The Jewish faith is ancient. Through centuries and generations it has come down to you. You are the product of its traditions of humility, of the Torah, of family bonds, of hard work, of love of music and art...traditions, above all, of being persecuted.... The heritage is in your heart, it's a glorious heritage and you should be proud of it.

From his The Wall *(1950).*

❏

Seymour Hersh

KISSINGER HALF-TRUTHS

[Kissinger] lied about his role in the [Watergate] wiretapping and his knowledge of the Plumbers was widely assumed in the Washington press corps, and even inside the Watergate Special Prosecution Force, but Kissinger was permitted to slide by with his half-truths and misstatements.

From an essay entitled "Kissinger and Nixon in the White House," which appeared in Atlantic Monthly *magazine, May 1982.*

❏

Harry Hershfield

SPEAKING OF NEW YORK

It is a city where everyone mutinies but no one deserts.

Quoted in The New York Times, *December 5, 1965.*

BETWEEN DAY AND NIGHT

The difference between a wife and a mistress is the difference between day and night.

Quoted in Morris Mandel's Affronts, Insults, and Indignities *(1975).*

❏

Joseph H. Hertz

FACING DEATH

To rail at life, to rebel against destiny, is of little avail. We cannot lay down terms to life. Life must be accepted on its own terms.

Explaining the significance of the keria *(rending the garment) ceremony. From his* Pentateuch and Haftorahs *(1961).*

THE MEANING OF THE SHEMA

That opening sentence of the Shema rightly occupies the central place in Jewish religious thought; for every other Jewish belief turns upon it; all goes back to it; all flows from it.

Ibid. Referring to "Hear, O Israel, the Lord is our God, the Lord is One" (Deuteronomy 6:4).

MOSES IN THE HAGGADA

Only once, indirectly in a quotation, does the name of Moses occur at all in the whole Seder.

Ibid. Underscoring that God, not a human leader, saved Israel.

GARDEN OF EDEN

Is the narrative literal or figurative, and is the Serpent an animal, a demon or merely the symbolic representation of Sin? Various have been the answers to these questions; and none of them are of cardinal importance to the Faith of a Jew. There is nothing in Judaism against the belief that the Bible attempts to convey deep truths of life and conduct by means of allegory. The Rabbis often taught by parable; and such method of instruction is, as is well known, the immemorial way among Oriental people.

Ibid.

THE TRINITY AND MONOTHEISM

Trinitarianism has at times been indistinguishable from tritheism; i.e., the belief in three separate gods.... Judaism recognizes no intermediary between God and man; and declares that prayer is to be directed to God alone, and to no other being in the heavens above or on earth beneath.

Ibid.

❏

Arthur Hertzberg

EDUCATE, EDUCATE, EDUCATE

For the last century we have bet our survival on the idea that together we should fight our enemies. This has failed. We can hope to succeed only if we teach the young, and ourselves, the texts and rhetoric of the tradition.

The future, if there is to be one, is in learning "and thou shalt teach these words diligently unto your children." All else is vanity.

From Hadassah Magazine, *June–July 1993.*

CHOSEN PEOPLE

The essence of Judaism is the affirmation that the Jews are the chosen people; all else is commentary.

From an essay in Condition of Jewish Belief *(1966), compiled by the editors of* Commentary *magazine.*

A DIVINELY APPOINTED RELIGION

Classical Judaism believes that the many faiths of man all play a role in the divine scheme. What Judaism does contend is that its divinely appointed role is uniquely its own, and that that appointment is both its task and its destiny.

Ibid.

PROOF OF GOD'S CHOICE

The Catholics have great difficulty admitting the Jewish nature of the Holocaust because of the basic tenets of their theology. At the center of the unknowable mystery, the mystical heart of Catholicism, is the belief that God sacrificed one third of the Holy Trinity. The concept of suffering as both a quality of God's and a sign of redemption is at the core of Catholic belief. When the Jews lost one third of their living body to the cross of Auschwitz, it reawakened the question that maybe they really are God's chosen people.

Quoted in Anne Roiphe's Season for Healing *(1988).*

PALESTINIAN RIGHTS

Palestinans, too, are human beings, and we have a moral obligation to defend their rights when violated; if you cannot think that way, you simply aren't a Jew. Period.

From a 1988 essay in Present Tense *magazine.*

THE COMING OF THE MESSIAH

The Lubavitcher rebbe knows that the Messiah is coming; and I wonder what is going to happen to his Hasidim [followers] when the rebbe, as is inevitable, goes on to his eternal reward and the Messiah has not come. As I keep insisting, if the Messiah were coming in our century, that tarrying no-good should have come to Auschwitz; and if he didn't come to Auschwitz, I don't think he is coming to the West Bank.

Ibid.

DEFENDING A WEAKENED HERITAGE

A generation which began in the 1930s believing in its own capacity to succeed is less confident now, more aware of problems than hopeful of their solutions.... The prevailing mood today is not thus going forward boldly to new adventure. It is rather one of defending a heritage which we weakened in the boldness of the ardor of many of my contemporaries for grand solutions.

From the Introduction to his Being Jewish in America *(1979), a book of essays.*

WAITING FOR MASS ALIYA

The tragic truth is that the very element in Jewish life which created Zionism and for whom it was intended, those who really need a Jewish country in which to live out their contemporary selves without fear of evaporating, have chosen to do everything for Israel except go there.... We cannot wait for Israel to be more pleasant and less full of problems.

From an article entitled "Mass Aliya for the Moderates," which appeared in Jewish Chronicle, *August 29, 1980.*

I DO NOT DUCK

Knowing from the very beginning that I was going to plow my own furrow, I was not going to give anyone the handle which said, "He ducked." I don't duck, I do not duck.

Explaining why he volunteered to serve as a military chaplain during the Korean War.

PUTTING IT ON THE LINE

We are rabbis who have nothing going for us except our own passion, our own conviction, our own lives and what we are willing to put them on the line for.

From an address to a rabbinical convention in 1975.

AFFIRMATION AND BELIEF

The momentum of Jewish experience in America is essentially spent. Ethnicity will no doubt last for several more generations, but it is well on the way to becoming a memory. But a community cannot survive on what it remembers; it will persist only because of what it affirms and believes.

From his Jews in America *(1989).*

CREATION'S BLUEPRINT

God left something of the primal chaos and charged mankind with the task of making order and bringing justice to finish Creation itself. The blueprint for that task was prepared before Creation. It was a book, the Torah, which God rolled out before Him, and made the world according to its prescriptions. Later, He gave this book to Moses and his people at Mount Sinai.

From the Foreword to Joseph Gikatilla's Gates of Light *(1994).*

DEGRADING DREYFUS

At the Ecole Militaire that day [January 5, 1895, when Captain Alfred Dreyfus was court-martialed and convicted of treason] the Jewish people learned an upsetting lesson. Even in a liberal republic, in France, their freedom was not secure. They could not always depend on the goodwill of others. In the next century Jews would have to continue to fight for a more inclusive society and to acquire some power in their own hands.

From an article entitled "Dreyfus: 100 Years After," which appeared in Hadassah Magazine, *January 1995.*

TOUCHY-FEELY JUDAISM

The problem with this [Jewish renewal approach] is that it is all for immediate experience; it is touchy-feely Judaism. It's lovely to learn how to tie *tzitzit* together, but where are the texts as to why we should wear it, or the committment to put it on?

Dismissing the approach to Judaism of the chavura *movement of the 1970s and 1980s, arguing that these "renewalists" place the study of mysticism before Talmud and do not address the need for day schools. Quoted in* The Jewish Week, *August 12–18, 1994.*

◻

J. O. Hertzler

OBLITERATING A CULTURAL IRRITANT

The Jew must be completely assimilated. Any old allegiance to his "chosen people" idea will have to disappear; he must consciously remove characteristics of behavior which are recognizably Jewish; he must deliberately mold himself and his life on Gentile patterns.... He will have to be completely absorbed ethnically, that means he will have to marry with non-Jews, generation after generation, until he has no grandparents who were considered as Jews and no children who by chance might have any distinguishing "Jewish" characteristics.

From an essay in Jews in a Gentile World: The Problem of Anti-Semitism *(1942), edited by Graeber and Britt.*

◻

Theodor Herzl

THE TRUMPED-UP DREYFUS CASE

What made me into a Zionist was the [1894] Dreyfus Case.... At that time I was living in Paris as a newspaper correspondent and attended the proceedings of the military court until they were declared secret. I can still see the defendant coming into the hall in his dark artillery uniform trimmed with braid. I still hear him give his credentials: "Alfred Dreyfus, Captain of Artillery," in his affected nasal voice. And also the howls of the mob in the street in front of the Ecole Militaire, where he was degraded, still ring unforgettably in my ears: "Death! Death to the Jews!" Death to Jews all because this one was a traitor?

Quoted in Abba Eban's My People: The Story of the Jews *(1968).*

RECEIVING AN ALIYA

In deference to religious considerations, I went to the synagogue on Saturday. The head of the congregation called me up to the Torah. I had the brother-in-law of my Paris friend Beer, Mr. Markus of Meran, drill the *broche* [blessing] into me. I was more excited than all the [Zionist] Congress days. The few Hebrew words of the *broche* caused me more anxiety than my welcoming and closing address and the whole direction of the proceedings.

From the September 9, 1897 entry in his diary. He had not used the Hebrew language since his Bar Mitzva in Budapest, Hungary, twenty-four years earlier.

HERZL'S ENEMIES

The Jews who are comfortable are, all of them, my enemies. Thus I have the right to be the greatest anti-Semite of all.

From an entry in his diary. At that time it was as unpopular to be a Zionist as it is today unpopular not to be a Zionist.

THE SABBATH

Zionism was the Sabbath of my life.

From an entry in his diary, January 24, 1902.

FOUNDING THE STATE

Were I to sum up the Basel Congress in a word—which I shall guard against pronouncing publicly—it would be this: At Basel I founded the Jewish State.

If I said this out loud today, I would be answered by universal laughter. Perhaps in five years, and certainly in fifty, everyone will know it. The foundation of a State lies in the will of the people for a State, yes, even in the will of one sufficiently powerful individual. Territory is only the material basis; the State, even when it possesses territory, is always something abstract. The Church State exists even without it; otherwise the Pope would not be sovereign.

> *From an entry in his diary, September 3, 1897, in which he notes what transpired at the First Zionist Congress, convened in Basel, Switzerland, from August 29 to August 31. At the Congress delegates from sixteen countries adopted the Basel Program advocating large-scale migration to Palestine.*

APPRECIATING THE HUMAN BODY

What a marvelous machine it is, the human body. A chemical laboratory, a powerhouse. Every movement, voluntary or involuntary, full of secrets and marvels!

> *From an entry in his diary, January 24, 1902.*

THE GREAT MOMENT

The great moment has found a small people.

> *From an entry in his diary, May 1, 1900.*

LEAVE US IN PEACE

We are a people, *one* people. We have everywhere tried honestly to integrate with the national communities surrounding us and to retain only our faith. We are not permitted to do so.... In vain do we exert ourselves to increase the glory of our fatherlands by achievements in art and in science and their wealth by our contributions to commerce.... We are denounced as strangers.... If only they would leave us in peace.... But I do not think they will.

> *From Der Judenstaat ("The Jewish State"), the first extracts of which were published in London's Jewish Chronicle on January 17, 1896. Herzl did not care if the tract of land Jews would settle would be in Argentina or Palestine.*

CRUSHED BY ANTI-SEMITISM

I am in favour of conversion. For me the matter is closed but it bothers me greatly for my son Hans. I ask myself if I have the right to sour and blacken his life as mine has been soured and blackened.... Therefore one must baptize Jewish boys before they must account for themselves, before they are able to act against it and before conversion can be construed as weakness on their part. They must disappear into the crowd.

> *While he considered baptizing his son, he said, "I myself would never convert." Quoted in Amos Elon's Herzl (1976).*

GREATNESS BY EXAMPLE

The world will be freer by our liberty, richer by our wealth, greater by our greatness.

> *From his Jewish State (1896).*

SALVATION OF THE JEW

The Jews have but one way of saving themselves—a return to their own people and an emigration to their own land.

> *Ibid.*

THE ESSENTIAL STATE

The Jewish state is essential to the world; therefore it will be created.

> *Ibid.*

DECLINE IN JEWISH SELF-RESPECT

The Jews too faithfully say "Amen" to the anti-Semitic slogan that we earn our living off the "feeder" nations and that if it were not for them we should be forced to starve to death. This is another indication of the decline of our self-respect under the onslaught of false accusations.

> *Ibid.*

WEAKENED BY SUFFERING

No people has had so many misconceptions published about it as have the Jews, and we are so depressed, so weakened by our history of suffering, that we ourselves repeat the lies of our calumniators, actually believing them as completely as they do.

> *Ibid.*

HERZL'S JEWISH FLAG

I would suggest a white flag with seven gold stars: the white field symbolizing our pure life; the stars, the seven golden hours of our working day.

> *Ibid.*

ZIONISM'S AIM

Zionism aims to create for the Jewish people a publicly recognized and legally secured home in Palestine.

> *From his Basel Program (1897).*

LET STRANGERS BE COUNTED AS BROTHERS

It would be immoral if we would exclude anyone, whatever his origin, his descent, or his religion, from participating in our achievements. For we stand on the shoulders of other civilized peoples.... What we own we owe to the preparatory work of other peoples. Therefore, we have to repay our debt. There is only one way to do it, the highest tolerance. Our motto must therefore be, now and ever: Man, you are my brother.

> *From his novel* Altneuland *(1902), the last book he wrote to serve as a testament to the movement he founded and the future state he envisioned.*

HERZL'S DREAM

If you will it, it is no dream.

> *Ibid.*

BRANCHES OF MISERY

Judaism is a mass shelter for misery, with branches all over the world.

> *Ibid.*

SELF-HELP

If a people cannot help itself, it cannot be helped at all.

> *From an address before the First Zionist Congress, August 29, 1897.*

THE FOUNDATION STONE

We are here to lay the foundation stone of the house which is to shelter the Jewish nation.

> *Ibid. His opening words to the First Zionist Congress.*

SOLVING THE JEWISH PROBLEM

On the day the plough is again in the strengthened hands of the Jewish farmer, the Jewish question will be solved.

> *Ibid. August 31, 1897.*

ENGLAND FOREVER

England the great! England the free! England, with her eyes scanning the seven seas, will understand us.

> *From an address before the Fourth Zionist Congress, 1900.*

THE FORGOTTEN HESS

Everything that we have tried is already in his book. Since Spinoza, Jewry has brought forth no greater spirit than this forgotten Moses Hess.

> *From a 1901 diary entry.*

WHERE LEADERSHIP BELONGS

I am not better nor more clever than any of you. But I remain undaunted and that is why the leadership belongs to me.

> *In a conversation with friends. Quoted in Walter Laqueur's* History of Zionism *(1972).*

□

Aura Herzog

FIVE IN ONE

I feel as if I'm married to five men in one.

> *Commenting on the distinction of her husband, Chaim Herzog, as a lawyer, diplomat, soldier, businessman, and writer.*

□

Chaim H. Herzog

PEACE ON THE HORIZON

Viewed historically, the Yom Kippur War constituted a watershed in the Israel–Arab conflict, and led to the first peace agreement Israel signed with any Arab state—the biggest and most important in the Middle East....

The war proved, as Sadat understood, that Israel could be reached only by way of peace, not through war; since the 1979 treaty was signed, not a single Israeli or Egyptian soldier has fallen on the peaceful border between Israel and Egypt.

> *From his article in* The Jerusalem Post, *September 18, 1993.*

RESPECT BUT SUSPECT

I do not want to reject the arrangement per se; it is perfectly possible that we are looking at a breakthrough for which we've been waiting for so many years of struggle. If there is even the smallest chance of bringing to an end the constant, tragic funeral marches to our cemeteries we should grab it.

But at the same time too much haste may make this arrangement very dangerous.

Our approach must be [in accordance with the rabbinic injunction] "honor him, but suspect him." First, the PLO must prove that it can rule the area and stop the intifada.

> *Ibid. Reacting to the peace accord reached between Israel and the Palestine Liberation Organization.*

THE MAN WAS NOTICED

He scaled the heights of human endeavor. Kings and princes waited on him. Many admired him. Many disliked him. But none was indifferent to him.... Few are the persons who stride across the stage of human experience and leave their mark. Robert Maxwell was one of them.

> *From his eulogy delivered at the 1991 Jerusalem funeral of friend Robert Maxwell, with whom he served in the British army during World War II. Quoted in Elisabeth Maxwell's* Mind of My Own: My Life with Robert Maxwell *(1994).*

Isaac Halevi Herzog

FROM FATHER TO SON

My son, strive to know yourself, to know and understand your Judaism, your wonderful, unique history, the inseparable connection of your people with the patriarchs and the prophets....

My son, the future of your great, martyred people lies in your hands! Resolve now firmly to hold fast to Israel's inalienable divine heritage, to work for the spiritual and material welfare of your historic people, and for the land divinely promised to Abraham, Isaac, and Jacob. May you become a source of blessing to yourself, to those dear to you, and to the entire house of Israel. Amen!

From a Bar Mitzva message to his son.

LOSS OF A GREAT MAN

The death of Pope Pius XII is the loss of a great man to the world at large. Catholics are not alone in lamenting his passing.

Quoted in Pinchas Lapide's Last Three Popes and the Jews *(1967).*

Abraham Joshua Heschel

HOLINESS IN TIME

On the Sabbath we try to become attuned to *holiness in time*. It is a day when we are called upon to share in what is eternal in time, to turn from the results of creation to the mystery of creation; from the world of creation to the creation of the world.

From his Sabbath: Its Meaning for Modern Man *(1975).*

ISLAND OF STILLNESS

In the tempestuous ocean of time and toil there are islands of stillness where man may enter a harbor and reclaim his dignity. The island is the seventh day, the Sabbath, a day of detachment from things, instruments and practical affairs as well as of attachment to the spirit.

Ibid.

JUDAISM AND TIME

Judaism is a religion of time aiming at the sanctification of time.

Ibid.

CONNECTING WITH THE SACRED

Judaism teaches us to be attached to holiness in time, to be attached to sacred events, to learn how to consecrate sanctuaries that emerge from the magnificent stream of a year.

Ibid.

RITUAL AND TIME

Jewish ritual may be characterized as the art of significant forms in time, as architecture of time. Most of its observances—the Sabbath, the New Moon, the festivals, the Sabbatical and the Jubilee year—depend on a certain hour of the day or season of the year.

Ibid.

SABBATH ARMISTICE

The Sabbath is a day for being with ourselves, a day of armistice in the economic struggle with our fellowman and the forces of nature.

Ibid.

GREATER THAN RELIGION

We must insist upon loyalty to the unique and holy treasures of our own tradition and at the same time [acknowledge] that in this aeon of religious diversity may be the providence of God.... [The ecumenical spirit was] born of the insight that God is greater than religion, that faith is deeper than dogma...and that religion involves the total situation of man, his attitudes and deeds, and must therefore never be kept in isolation.

From his Insecurity of Freedom *(1966).*

DEATH AS ARRIVAL

Death may be the beginning of exaltation, an ultimate celebration, a reunion of the divine image with the divine source of being. Dust returns to dust while the image, the divine stake in man, is returned to the bundle of life. Death is not sensed as a defeat but as a summation, an arrival, a conclusion.

From an article in Conservative Judaism *magazine, Fall 1973.*

OLD AGE

May I suggest that man's potential for change and growth is much greater than we are willing to admit, and that old age be regarded not as the age of stagnation but as the *age of opportunities for inner growth.*

The years of old age...are indeed formative years, rich in possibilities to unlearn the follies of a lifetime, to see through inbred self-deceptions, to deepen understanding and compassion, to widen the horizon of honesty, to refine the sense of fairness.

From his essay "To Grow in Wisdom," which appeared in Judaism *magazine, Spring 1977.*

SENSE OF THE INEFFABLE

Religion begins with the sense of the ineffable, with the awareness of a reality that discredits our wisdom, that shatters our concepts. It is, therefore, the ineffable with which we must begin, since otherwise there is no problem; and its perception to which we must return since otherwise no solution will be relevant.

In his Man Is Not Alone *(1951).*

A SUPREME BEING

God is of no importance unless He is of supreme importance.

Ibid.

WHAT GOD MEANS TO US

It is tragically true that we are often wrong about God, believing in that which is not God, in a counterfeit ideal, in a dream, in a cosmic force, in our own father, in our own selves. We must never cease to question our own faith and ask what God means to us.

Ibid.

MEANING OF REVELATION

Revelation means that the thick silence which fills the endless distance between God and the human mind was pierced, and man was told that God is concerned with the affairs of man; that not only does man need God, God is also in need of man.

Ibid.

WHEN FAITH IS REAL

Faith is real only when it is not one-sided but reciprocal. Man can rely on God if God can rely on man.

Ibid.

RECOGNIZED BY OUR ACTIONS

Reflection alone will not procure self-understanding. The human situation is disclosed in the thick of living. By whatever we do, by every act we carry out, we either advance or obstruct the drama of redemption; we either reduce or enhance the power of evil.

Quoted in Tikkun *magazine, Volume 1, No. 1.*

IMPATIENCE OF THE PROPHETS

A student of philosophy who turns from the discourses of the great metaphysicians to the orations of the prophets may feel as if he were going from the realm of the sublime to an area of trivialities. Instead of dealing with the timeless issues of being and becoming, of matter and form, of definitions and demonstrations, he is thrown into orations about widows and orphans, about the corruption of judges and affairs of the market place. Instead of showing us a way through the elegant mansions of the mind, the Prophets take us to the slums. Their breathless impatience with injustice may strike us as hysteria.... But if such deep sensitivity to evil is to be called hysterical, what name should be given to the abysmal indifference to evil which the prophet bewails?

Quoted in Tikkun *magazine, Volume 1, No. 2.*

COMPREHENDING THE SUPERNATURAL

We must, of course, give up hope of ever attaining a valid concept of the supernatural in an objective sense, yet since for practical reasons it is useful to cherish the idea of God, let us retain that idea and claim that while our knowledge of God is not objectively true, it is still symbolically true [as Kant taught].

In his essay "Toward an Understanding of Halacha," included in Seymour Siegel's Conservative Judaism and Jewish Law (1977).

CEREMONIES AND MITZVOT

Let us be frank. Too often a ceremony is the homage which disbelief pays to faith. Do we want such homage?

Judaism does not stand on ceremonies.... Jewish piety is an answer to God, expressed in the language of *mitzvot* rather than in the language of *ceremonies*. The *mitzvah* rather than the ceremony is our fundamental category. What is the difference between the two categories?

Ceremonies whether in the form of things or in the form of actions are required by custom and convention; *mitzvot* are required by Torah. Ceremonies are relevant to man; *mitzvot* are relevant to God. Ceremonies are folkways; *mitzvot* are ways to God.

Ibid.

RELIGION AND SYMBOLS

It has become a [not acceptable] truism that religion is largely an affair of symbols.

Ibid.

RELIGION TO ME

To me, religion included the insights of the Torah, which is a vision of man from the point of view of God.

Ibid.

TO BE GOOD

Man cannot be good unless he strives to be holy.

Ibid.

GOD'S WILL

The meaning of life is to do His will.

Ibid.

GOD'S NAME

The ineffable Name, we have forgotten how to pronounce it. We have almost forgotten how to spell it. We may totally forget how to recognize it.

Ibid.

SPIRITUAL SENSITIVITY

Sensitivity to spiritual meaning is not easily won; it is the fruit of hard, constant devotion, of insistence upon remaining true to a vision.

Ibid.

KEEPING THE LEVEL HIGH

Let us beware lest we reduce Bible to literature, Jewish observance to good manners, the Talmud to Emily Post.

Ibid.

GOD IN HIDING

God is hiding in the world. Our task is to let the divine emerge from our deeds.

From his God in Search of Man *(1976).*

SPECULATION DOES NOT LEAD TO FAITH

Understanding God is not attained by calling into session all arguments for and against Him, in order to debate whether He is a reality or a figment of the mind. God cannot be sensed as a second thought, as an explanation of the origin of the universe. He is either the first and the last, or just another concept.

Ibid.

TREE LEAVES

Israel is the tree, we are the leaves. It is the clinging to the stem that keeps us alive.

Ibid.

A MAMMOTH TOOL BOX

Human beings have indeed become primarily tool-making animals, and the world is now a gigantic tool box for the satisfaction of their needs.... Nature as a tool box is a world that does not point beyond itself. It is when nature is sensed as mystery and grandeur that it calls upon us to look beyond it. The awareness of grandeur and the sublime is all but gone from the modern mind.

Ibid.

GOD'S WITNESSES

What is unique about Jewish existence?

The fact that ours is not a free association with the Bible. We are her offspring, her outcome. Her spirit is our destiny. What is our destiny? To be a community in whom the Bible lives on.... "Ye are my witnesses, says the Lord, and I am God" (Isaiah 43:12).

From his Israel: An Echo of Eternity *(1967).*

MONSTROSITY OF INEQUALITY

That equality is a good thing, a fine goal, may be readily accepted. What is lacking is a sense of the monstrosity of inequality.... A person cannot be religious and indifferent to other human beings' plight and suffering.

From an address delivered at the 1963 United Synagogue Biennial Convention.

THE SIN OF FORGETTING

The gravest sin for a Jew is to forget—or not to know—what he represents.

From his Earth Is the Lord's *(1950).*

DAWN AND DUSK

We are God's stake in human history. We are the dawn and the dusk, the challenge and the test.

Ibid.

SONG OF GOD

The divine sings in noble deeds.

Ibid.

BEHIND ALL GOOD DEEDS

The meaning of man's life lies in his perfecting the universe. He has to distinguish, father and redeem the sparks of holiness scattered throughout the darkness of the world.

Ibid.

TOUCHSTONE OF CIVILIZATION

We are Jews as we are men. The alternative to our Jewish existence is spiritual suicide, disappearance, not conversion into something else. Judaism has allies, partners, but no substitute. It is not a handmaiden of civilization but its touchstone.

Ibid.

IRRELIGION AS POISON

Mankind does not have the choice of religion and neutrality. Irreligion is not opiate but poison. Our energies are too abundant for living indifferently. We are in need of an endless purpose to absorb our immense power if our souls are not to run amok.

Ibid.

REAL PRAYER

The focus of prayer is not the self. A man may spend hours meditating about himself, or be stirred by the deepest sympathy for his fellow man, and no prayer will come to pass. Prayer comes to pass in a complete turning of the heart toward God, toward His goodness and power.

From his Man's Quest for God *(1954).*

THE BRIDGE TO HOLINESS

A wide stream of human callousness separates us from the realm of holiness. Neither an individual man nor a single generation can by its own power erect a bridge that would reach that realm. For ages our fathers have labored in building a sacred bridge. We who have not crossed the stream must beware lest we burn the bridge.

Ibid.

DEFINING FAITH

Faith is an act of man who, transcending himself, responds to Him who transcends the world.

From his Between God and Man *(1959).*

SUICIDE VS. MARTYRDOM

According to Albert Camus, "There is only one really serious philosophical problem; and that is suicide."

May I differ and suggest that there is only one really serious problem; and that is martyrdom. Is there anything worth dying for?

From his Who Is Man? *(1965).*

IS GOD DEAD OR ALIVE?

The problem of religious thinking is not only whether God is dead or alive, but also whether we are dead or alive to His realness. A search for God involves a search of our own measure, a test of our own spiritual potential.

Ibid.

ARE WE ALONE?

Are we alone in the wilderness of time, alone in the dreadfully marvelous universe, of which we are a part and where we feel like strangers? Is there a Presence to live by?

Ibid.

TO BE IN GOD'S PRESENCE

How embarrassing for man to be the greatest miracle on earth and not to understand it! How embarrassing for man to live in the shadow of greatness and to ignore it, to be a contemporary of God and not to sense it!

Ibid.

GOD'S DREAM

God's dream is...to have mankind as a *partner* in the drama of continuous creation.

Ibid.

CHISEL AND MARBLE

For man, to *be* is to *play* a part in a cosmic drama.... Am I not both the chisel and the marble?

Ibid.

HALACHA AND AGADA

Halacha is the string, *Agada* is the bow. When the string is tight, the bow will evoke a melody.

From his Passion for Truth *(1986).*

PEOPLE I MOST ADMIRE

When I was young, I admired clever people. Now that I am old, I admire kind people.

Quoted in Joseph Telushkin's Jewish Wisdom *(1994).*

¤

Moses Hess

A JEW IS A JEW IS A JEW

The converted Jew remains a Jew no matter how much he objects to it.

From his Rome and Jerusalem *(1862).*

FORWARD MARCH

March forward, Jews of all lands! The ancient fatherland of yours is calling you.... March forward, ye noble hearts! The day on which the Jewish tribes return to their fatherland will be epoch-making in the history of humanity.

Ibid.

POTENTIAL SAVIORS

Every Jew has within him the potentiality of a Messiah, and every Jewess that of a Mater Dolorosa.

Ibid.

ON THE REBIRTH OF ISRAEL

Every Jew, even the convert to Christianity, shares in the responsibilities of the rebirth of Israel.

Ibid.

ACHIEVING INNER EMANCIPATION

The Germans so long and so thoroughly demonstrated to us that our nationality is an obstacle to our "inner" emancipation that we ultimately believed it ourselves and did every-thing we could to prove ourselves worthy of the blond Germanic lineage by denying our origins.

> *Ibid.*

STRANGERS ALWAYS

We shall always remain strangers among [European] nations; they may emancipate us out of a feeling of humanity and justice, but will never ever respect us until we accept *ubi bene ibi patria* as our maxim and dogma, and put our great individual national memories in second place.

> *Ibid.*

Alan Hevesi

A JEWISH AWAKENING

When I got into politics, I was suddenly confronted with the hugely influential and im-portant New York Jewish community with a Jewish agenda. I was a part of it, but I didn't know I was a part of it.

> *Following his election as comptroller of the City of New York in November 1993. From an interview in* The Jewish Week, *December 3–9, 1993.*

Ferenc Hevesi

THE YELLOW STAR

The yellow star will [one day] be removed from us, but a mark of humiliation will always show on the breasts of those who forced us to wear this star and those who by their indiffer-ence allowed this to happen.

> *Consoling his people when in 1944 the new regime ordered Jews to wear the Star of David and confiscated their property.*

Reinhard Heydrich

JUDENREIN EASTERN EUROPE

It may be safely assumed that in the future there will be no more Jews in the annexed Eastern Territories.

> *From an August 1941 letter to Heinrich Himmler.*

(Rabbi) Hezekiah

SUPERFLUOUS OBSERVANCE

He who is exempt from the obligation of performing a precept [*mitzva*] and performs it nevertheless is called ignorant.

> *Quoted in the Jerusalem Talmud, Berachot (2:9) and Shabbat (1:1).*

Marvin Hier

NO GOING BACK

No Israeli government, Likud or Labor, will ever be able to change what happened in the White House ceremony. No Israeli govern-ment will be able to pretend not to speak to the PLO. When Washington stages an event of this magnitude, in front of the Supreme Court, the world's leading diplomats, former presi-dents, former secretaries of state, members of Congress, you can't go back.

> *Commentary on the significance of the peace accord between Israel and the Palestine Lib-eration Organization, signed at the White House on September 13, 1993.*

CHARISMA PERSONIFIED

Louis Farrakhan is a charismatic person. Whatever we may think of him, he's a great or-ator. He can affect people.

> *Commenting in 1995 on the danger of the Reverend Farrakhan and his aides traveling around Europe to speak at universities and suggesting that the world's problems are the fault of the Jews.*

Dov Hikind

SELECTIVE JUSTICE

Unfortunately, the liberal establishment is very selective, and because they did not agree with the philosophy of Rabbi Meir Kahane, they considered him expendable. Where was the sense of justice for a Jew, a sense of justice that he was assassinated and nothing hap-pened? Are they willing to say by their silence that taking this life was OK?

> *Comment made after El Sayyid Nosair was acquitted of slaying Kahane. From a news report.*

RACISM AND COLOR

I tell my kids, "You don't like something di-rected against the Jewish people, so don't you be guilty of it. There is no reason for hate or racism or anti-Semitism.... I'm not a friend of David Dinkins [mayor of New York City] but the reason has nothing to do with the color of his skin. But most of those who are [for him] are for him *because* of the color of his skin. That's also racism.

> *Ibid.*

□

Raoul Hilberg

DENYING REALITY

The Jews...did not always have to be deceived. They were capable of deceiving themselves.

> *From his* Destruction of European Jewry *(1967), in which he concludes that Jews deliberately avoided resistance because they refused to believe they were doomed.*

□

Ben Hill

ANTI-SEMITISM IN THE BLACK MEDIA

You're talking about a warmonger nation that's in bed with South Africa. That's got the blood of black men on their hands. That's cutting diamonds and dealing in weighing gold that's coming out of the mines of South Africa. And you want to paint some lovey-dovey picture about tending sheep and the Holocaust. Hey, send them back to Germany. Don't be giving me that lovey-dovey story.

> *Statement made on WGST, the major black radio station in Atlanta, Georgia, in response to a caller. From an ADL report on anti-Semitism in the black community. Recalled by Eric Breindel in his address to the World Conference on Anti-Semitism in a Changing World, held in Brussels, Belgium, July 1992.*

□

Hillel the Elder

PUTTING ONESELF FIRST

If I am not for myself, who will be for me? But if I care only for myself, what am I? And if not now, when?

> *Quoted in the talmudic tractate Ethics of the Fathers (1:14).*

LOVE PEACE AND PURSUE IT

Be of the disciples of Aaron, one who loves peace and pursues it, who loves all men and brings them near to the Torah.

> *Ibid (1:12).*

RESERVE JUDGMENT

Judge not your neighbor until you have stood in his shoes.

> *Ibid (2:4).*

DON'T PROCRASTINATE

Do not say, "I will study when I have leisure." Perhaps you will never have leisure.

> *Ibid.*

CHARACTERISTICS TO BE SHUNNED

An empty-headed person does not fear sin, an ignorant one cannot be pious, one who is too bashful [to ask questions] cannot become learned, an irritable man cannot teach, and he that is engrossed in business cannot become a Sage.

> *Ibid (2:5).*

BE A MENSCH

Where there are no men, strive to be a man.

> *Ibid.*

THE PLACE I LOVE

It is to the place that I love that my feet lead me.

> *Quoted in the talmudic tractate Sukka (53a).*

THE CENTER OF THE UNIVERSE

If I am here, everyone is here, but if I am not here, who is here?

> *Ibid. A declaration made during the water-drawing ceremony on Sukkot.*

RECIPROCAL VISITATIONS

God says: "If you will come to my house, I will come to yours."

> *Ibid.*

ESSENCE OF THE TORAH

What is hateful unto you, do not do to your neighbor. That is the whole Torah and the rest of it is commentary. Now go forth and learn it.

> *Responding to a heathen who wanted to be taught the whole Torah while standing on one foot. Quoted in the talmudic tractate Shabbat (31a).*

ISRAEL: SONS OF PROPHETS

If they [the Jews] are not prophets, they are the sons of prophets.

> *Ibid (66b).*

ACQUIRING ANXIETY

The more possessions, the more aggravation.

> *Quoted in the talmudic tractates Ethics of the Fathers (2:8).*

STUDYING IN DEPTH

He that has repeated his lesson one hundred times is not to be compared to one who has reviewed it one hundred and one times.

In response to a comment by Ben Hey-Hey. Quoted in the talmudic tractates Chagiga (9b) and Sanhedrin (99a).

¤

Hillel's Disciples

IS LIFE WORTH LIVING?

It would have been better if man had not been created; but inasmuch as he has been created, let him examine his actions.

Quoted in the talmudic tractate Eruvin (13b).

¤

Morris Hillquit

UNADULTERATED SOCIALIST

If elected to Congress, I will not consider myself the special representative of the...special interests of this district, but the representative of the Socialist Party and the interests of the working class of the country.

Though a Jew, Hillquit did not identify with specific Jewish interests. He was defeated in the 1908 New York congressional race. Quoted in The New York Call, *September 12, 1908.*

A RIGHT TO BE BAD

This is the old trick of the ruling classes. It is the same old trick Booker T. Washington worked on the Negroes.... "Don't assert yourselves or else you will incur the hatred of the ruling classes.... Be gentle slaves and you will be all right." And I say to you as a citizen to citizens, as a Jew to Jews, you don't have to be good; you have the right to be as bad as the rest of the world.

Appealing to immigrant Jewish voters in his race for mayor of New York City in 1917. He told them that if he were elected by Jewish votes, the American tradition of tolerance would be imperiled. Quoted in The New York Times, *November 4, 1917.*

¤

Gertrude Himmelfarb

ABSOLUTE LIBERALITY

Liberals learned at a fearful cost the lesson that absolute power corrupts absolutely. They have yet to learn that absolute liberality corrupts absolutely.

From her On Liberty and Liberalism *(1974).*

RESCUING THE ADJECTIVE "VICTORIAN"

Values, as we now understand that word, do not have to be virtues; they can be beliefs, opinions, attitudes, feelings, habits, conventions, preferences, prejudices, even idiosyncrasies—whatever any individual, group, or society happens to value, at any time, for any reason.

From her De-moralization of Society: From Victorian Virtues to Modern Values *(1995).*

¤

Milton Himmelfarb

YOUNG INTELLECTUALS

Most of the symposiasts have a smattering of Jewish culture—a peculiar position for intellectuals to be in.

Commenting on the caliber of the participants in Commentary *magazine's April 1961 symposium entitled "Jewishness and the Younger Intellectuals," in which thirty-one intellectuals took part.*

A PROVIDENTIAL ORDER

In the last third of the twentieth century we may be beginning to believe again that the history of the Jews points to some kind of providential order, which—for reasons having to do not with our merits, but at most with the merits of the Fathers—has a special place for it.

From an article entitled "The 1967 War," which appeared in Commentary *magazine, October 1967.*

JEWS AND POLITICS

What was old about the 1980 election is that Jews as a group are still unassimilated politically.... And they still worry about Israel. What was new was very new: fewer than one-half voted for the Democrats [because of] the desire for a strong resolute America and a secure Israel.

From an article entitled "Are Jews Becoming Republican?" which appeared in Commentary *magazine, August 1981.*

¤

Heinrich Himmler

GERMAN PRIDE

Among ourselves it should be mentioned quite frankly and yet we will never speak of it publicly. I mean the evacuation of the Jews, the extermination of the Jewish race.... Most of you must know what it means when a hundred corpses are lying side by side or five hundred or a thousand. To have stuck it out and at the same time—apart from exceptions caused by human weakness—to have remained decent men, that is what has made us hard. This is a page of glory in our history, which has never been written and is never to be written.

In an October 1943 address to SS generals in Poznan.

"SACRED" ORDERS

The Occupied Eastern Territories are to become free of Jews. The execution of this grave order has been placed on my shoulders by the Führer.

From a July 1942 letter to a senior SS official.

THE FINAL SOLUTION

We have the moral right, we have the duty with regard to our people, to kill this race that wants to kill us.

Ibid.

◻

Paul von Hindenburg

NO ROOM FOR PREJUDICE

The Jewish people have given to humanity some of its greatest men. Germany is proud to have among its citizens a scholar of the caliber of Professor Einstein....

No, there is no room for intolerance and prejudice, if permanent world peace is to be established. That is why I granted you this interview, despite my aversion to talking for the press, in order to make it clear once and for all that democratic Germany will not tolerate any prejudice towards any race or creed.

In an interview with Miriam Sterner that appeared in American Jewish World, *June 29, 1928.*

◻

Emil G. Hirsch

ON ATHEISM AND AGNOSTICISM

The belief in God is merely the outcome of the belief in man. God is the apex of the pyramid, not the base. Man is the cornerstone; and from the true conception of man have the Jewish thinkers risen to the noblest conception of the Deity. Those are shallow who talk of their

agnosticism and parade their atheism. No one is an agnostic and no one is an atheist, except he have neither pity for the weak nor charity for the erring; except he have no mercy for those who need its soothing balm.

From a sermon he preached in 1893.

A FUNDAMENTAL QUESTION

The question fundamental for man to ask is not "What is God?" but "What is He for us as men?" What is God for man is indeed the basic inquiry of Judaism, and to it Judaism gives a clear and definite answer: God for man stands in the consciousness of man's dignity.

From his article "The Sociological Center of Religion," which appeared in The Reform Advocate, *Volume 11 (1896).*

THE IDEA OF SIN

Sin is not an offense against God, but against our humanity. It is not a state which came to us and which we cannot throw off; it is an act of our own. Sin is anti-social conduct, due to the want of resistance on our part to the influences of the animal world behind us, selfishness, or to the legacy of a phase of civilization over which and beyond which we should have passed on.

Ibid.

REINTERPRETING PRAYER

True worship is not a petition to God; it is a sermon to our own selves. The words which are its raiments are addressed to us. They speak of God and the divine in man, and thus make man find in himself the God that so often is forgotten when the battle rages and the batteries roar.

Ibid. Volume 14 (1897).

BEAUTY OF HOLINESS

The Greeks stressed the holiness of beauty; the Jews emphasized the beauty of holiness.

From a sermon quoted in Louis Ginzberg's Students, Scholars and Saints *(1928).*

◻

Richard G. Hirsch

NATURE OF THE HOLOCAUST

The Holocaust was more than a physical destruction of the Jews. It was an attempt to obliterate the Jewish people from the world. It had roots for 2,000 years in anti-Semitism, nourished and cultivated by various political, social and economic factors. I don't think the same situation obtains in the Middle East today. I would not place [Anwar] Sadat or [Yasser] Arafat in the same category with Hitler. I don't think there's an effort by the Arabs to wipe the Jewish people off the face of the earth.

From an article in The Christian Century *magazine, December 11, 1974.*

JEWISH SURVIVAL PROSPECTS

Jews can't simply be led to the slaughter, for they have the means to defend themselves. The Jewish people will not permit themselves to be destroyed. I think God will not be God without the Jewish people. This doesn't mean that either God or the Jewish people is linked for all time inextricably to the State of Israel. But as I now look at the plight of Jews around the world, the survival of the Jewish people is at this moment inextricable from the survival of the Jewish State.

Ibid.

✡

Samson Raphael Hirsch

A JEW'S CATECHISM

The Jew's catechism is his calendar.

Explaining how the commandments (mitzvot) *are tied to special Hebrew dates. Quoted by Arthur Spier in the Foreword to his* Comprehensive Hebrew Calendar *(1981).*

DUTIES BUT NO DOGMAS

Judaism enjoins 613 duties [*mitzvot*], but knows no dogmas.

From his Nineteen Letters of Ben Uziel *(1899). Translated by Bernard Drachman.*

BE A BLESSING

First become a blessing to yourself that you may be a blessing to others.

Ibid.

BODY AND SPIRIT

Respect your own body as the receptacle, messenger, and instrument of the spirit.

Ibid.

NUMBERS DO NOT COUNT

Truth does not concern itself with the number of its adherents.

Ibid.

MEDITATION IS NOT ENOUGH

A life of seclusion, devoted only to meditation and prayer, is not Judaism.

Ibid.

TO BE RESPECTED

Be a Jew; be it really and truly...then will you be respected, not in spite of it but because of it.

Ibid.

A CHERISHED IDEAL

Israel's most cherished ideal is the universal brotherhood of mankind.

Ibid.

THE TRUE HASID

The true *hasid* is he who devotes himself in love entirely to the service of the Higher Power, who...does not withdraw from the world, but lives in it, with it, and for it.

Ibid.

JUDAISM DEFINES MAN

Whoever in his time, with his equipment of powers and means, in his condition, fulfills the will of God toward the creatures that enter into his circle, who injures none and assists every one according to his power, to reach the goal marked out for it by God—he is a man!

Ibid.

GUILT AND PUNISHMENT

Judaism teaches that the greater the man the stricter the standard by which he is judged, and, if he fails to measure up, the greater will be his guilt and punishment.

Commenting on Numbers 20:12. From his translation and commentary on the Pentateuch.

THE ONE GOD IS MY GOD

The foundation of Jewish life is not merely that there is only one God, but the conviction that this One, only, and true God is *my* God, my sole Ruler and Guide in all that I do.

From his comment on Exodus 20:2: "I am the Lord your God who brought you out of the land of Egypt."

GOD'S WORD AND HUMAN JUDGMENT

Do we mean what we say when, in the circle of fellow-worshippers, we point to the written word of the Torah and declare that God gave us these teachings, that these are his teachings, the teachings of truth and that he thereby implanted in us everlasting life? Is all this a mere mouthing of high sounding phrases? If not, then we must keep those commandments, fulfill them in their original and unabbreviated form. We must observe them under all circumstances and at all times. This word of God must be accepted by us as an eternal standard, transcending all human judgment.

From an essay in Jeschurun *(1854–55).*

◻

Samuel Hirsch

THE WORK OF JUDAISM

The perfectibility of mankind on this earth is the characteristic work of Judaism.

Quoted in D. Philipson's Reform Movement in Judaism *(1907).*

◻

Adolf Hitler

ANTI-SEMITIC FURY

I shall have gallows erected, in Munich for example in the Marienplatz, as many as traffic permits. Then the Jews will be hanged, one after another, and they will stay hanging until they stink.... As soon as one is untied, the next will take his place, and that will go on until the last Jew in Munich is obliterated. Exactly the same thing will happen in the other cities until Germany is cleansed of its last Jew.

From a private talk with Major Josef Hell in 1922. Quoted in Paul Johnson's History of the Jews *(1987).*

FALSE PROPHET

Today I want to be a prophet once more: If international finance Jewry inside and outside of Europe should succeed once more in plunging nations into another world war, the consequence will not be the Bolshevization of the earth and thereby the victory of Jewry, but the annihilation of the Jewish race in Europe.

From a January 30, 1939 speech explicitly stating the Nazi intention to destroy the Jews. Quoted in Raoul Hilberg's Destruction of the European Jews *(1967).*

MISGUIDED PREDICTION

They [the Jews] are our old enemy as it is, they have experienced at our hands an upsetting of their ideas, and they rightfully hate us as much as we hate them.... The war will not end as the Jews imagine it will, namely with the uprooting of the Aryans, but the result of this war will be the complete annihilation of the Jews.

From a January 1942 Berlin speech marking the ninth anniversary of Nazi rule over Germany.

DECEITFUL THEORY

[Democracy], the deceitful theory that the Jew would insinuate—namely, that theory that all men are created equal.

From his Mein Kampf *(1925–26).*

WAR FOR DOMINATION

It is true we Germans are barbarians; that is an honored title to us. I free humanity from the shackles of the soul; from the degrading suffering caused by the false vision called conscience and ethics. The Jews have inflicted two wounds on mankind: circumcision on its body and conscience on its soul. They are Jewish inventions. The war for the domination of the world is waged only between these two camps alone, the Germans and the Jews. Everything else is but deception.

Ibid.

ON GERMAN JEWRY

In America you exclude any would-be immigrants you do not care to admit. You regulate their number. Not content with that, you prescribe their physical condition. Not content with that, you insist on the conformity of their political opinions. We demand the same right in Germany. We have no concern with the Jews of other lands, but we are very much concerned about the anti-German elements within our country. We demand the right to deal with these elements as we see fit. Jews have been the intellectual proponents of subversive anti-German movements, and as such they must be dealt with.

From an article by H.R. Kaltenborn in The New Republic, *February 14, 1933.*

DOING THE LORD'S WORK

I believe today that I am acting in the sense of the Almighty Creator. By warding off the Jews I am fighting for the Lord's work.

From a 1936 speech before the Reichstag.

EARLY HITLER DOCTRINE I

Rational anti-Semitism, however, must lead to a systematic legal opposition and elimination [*Beseitigung*] of the special privileges that Jews hold, in contrast to the other aliens living among us (aliens' legislation). Its final objective must unswervingly be the removal [*Entfernung*] of the Jews altogether.

From an early 1920s document in Hitler's own hand. Quoted in Lucy Dawidowicz's War Against the Jews 1933–45 *(1975).*

EARLY HITLER DOCTRINE II

Removal of the Jews from our nation, not

because we would begrudge them their existence—we congratulate the rest of the whole world on their company [great merriment], but because the existence of our own nation is a thousand times more important to us than that of an alien race.

Ibid.

PROPHET OF DOOM

I have often been a prophet in my life and was generally laughed at. During my struggle for power, the Jews primarily received with laughter my prophecies that I would someday assume the leadership of the state.... I suppose that the once resounding laughter of Jewry in Germany is now choking in their throats.

From a January 30, 1939 speech before the Reichstag.

◻

Remi Hoeckman

CHURCH/SYNAGOGUE RELATIONS

We want to deal with the Jewish people out of our religious base and dialogue—not on a confrontational level but out of love. We have a great deal of historic guilt, but the last thirty years have proven that major pronouncements by our Church and Church leaders have turned things around.... If we are to be closer, we must now reach people's minds and hearts or nothing will change. We cannot address only issues of society and human rights, like anti-Semitism. Until now we lacked the theological dimension. It is important that we develop a relationship based on each other's faith.

From an address to members of the Center for Christian-Jewish Understanding. Quoted in its Summer 1994 Newsletter.

◻

Malcolm Hoenlein

LESSONS TO BE TAUGHT

The Holocaust is central to the Jewish experience. The lessons have to be communicated and taught in order to enable future generations to...avoid the mistakes made at that time. On the other hand, we have to give young Jews positive experiences...not just *tsuris* ["troubles"]. We have to share with them the excitement.... The [emancipation of the]

Soviet, Syrian and Ethiopian Jews are miracles in our time.

Comment made following the 1993 opening of the United States Holocaust Museum in Washington, DC. Reported in Hadassah Magazine, *April 1994.*

◻

Eric Hoffer

WHEN A VICTOR MUST SUE FOR PEACE

Yes, Jews are a peculiar people. Things permitted to other nations are forbidden to the Jews. Other nations drive out thousands, even millions of people and there is no refugee problem. Russia did it. Poland and Czechoslovakia did it. Turkey drove out a million Greeks and Algeria a million Frenchmen. Indonesia threw out Heaven knows how many Chinese—and no one says a word about refugees. In the case of Israel, the displaced Arabs have become eternal refugees, and everyone insists that Israel must take back every single Arab.

Other nations when victorious on the battlefield dictate peace terms. But when Israel is victorious it must sue for peace.

I have a premonition that will not leave me: As it goes with Israel, so will it go with all of us. Should Israel perish, the holocaust will be upon us. Israel must live!

In response to Arnold Toynbee, who after the Six-Day War of 1967 called the displacement of the Arabs an atrocity greater than any committed by the Nazis.

◻

Abbie Hoffman

ADVICE FROM A YIPPIE LEADER

We have to be in touch with them. We have to keep the bridges open to the Palestinians. We have to keep talking away, explaining and using the right language so it's not so easily said that you're anti-Semitic. We have to point out that the other policy isn't working.

Criticizing Menachem Begin's policies of the 1980s, which he describes as being "based on hysteria and disgrace."

POLITICS VS. TACTICS

I hate your politics, but I love your tactics.

A comment made to Rabbi Meir Kahane after the latter splashed a full-page ad in The New York Times *in 1969 showing a Jewish goon squad armed with lead pipes and baseball bats ready to take on black militants. The text read: "Is this any way for a nice Jewish boy to behave?"*

□

Atago Hokuzan

JAPANESE ANTI-SEMITISM

The degree to which countries retain a democratic character is precisely the degree to which they are subject to the Jewish dictatorship.... The extent to which the so-called fascist countries are totalitarian and espose ethnic nationalism is precisely the extent to which they have thrown off the Jewish yoke.

Quoted in Goodman and Miyazawa's Jews in the Japanese Mind: The History and Uses of a Cultural Stereotype *(1994).*

□

Samuel Holdheim

THE MISSION IDEA

It is the destiny of Judaism to pour the light of its thoughts, the fire of its sentiments, the fervor of its feelings, upon all the souls and hearts on earth. It is the Messianic task of Israel to make the pure law of morality of Judaism the common possession and blessing of all the peoples on earth.

Quoted in W. Gunther Plaut's Rise of Reform Judaism *(1963).*

□

Ernest F. Hollings

SNIDE CHARACTERIZATION

The Senator from B'nai Brith.

Characterizing Senator Howard Metzenbaum during a 1981 Senate debate concerning voluntary prayer in public schools. Senator Arlen Spector of Pennsylvania reprimanded Hollings. Hollings apologized, saying, "I said it only in fun."

□

Abiel Holmes

CIVILITY TOWARD JEWS

While admitted into most countries for the purpose of trade and commerce, instead of being treated with that humanity and tenderness which Christianity should inspire, they are often persecuted and condemned as unworthy of notice or regard. Such treatment tends to prejudice them against our holy religion, and to establish them in their infidelity [to resist conversion].

From the 1978 biography of his famous father-in-law, the Reverend Ezra Stiles. Quoted in Joseph L. Blau and Salo W. Baron's Jews of the United States 1790–1840.

□

John Haynes Holmes

CRITICAL EVALUATION

Even the moderate Zionists show a disquieting tendency to take for granted Jewish ascendancy. They do not think at all in terms of violence or oppression. Yet they were silent when England and her allies tore to tatters the nationalistic aspiration of the Moslem world. They have refused the request of the Palestinian Arabs, presented in not immoderate terms, for co-operation in securing some form of popular government, and thus have conspired, as an obstructive minority backed by alien power, to deny to the majority their public rights.

A statement made after a 1929 visit to Palestine.

IF CHRISTIANS WERE CHRISTIANS

If Christians were Christians, there would be no anti-Semitism. Jesus was a Jew. There is nothing that the ordinary Christian so dislikes to remember as this awkward historical fact. But it happens, nonetheless, to be true.

From his Sensible Man's View of Religion *(1933).*

THE DEBT OWED JUDAISM

Such is the debt which Christianity owes to Judaism! Not Jesus merely, nor the Bible, the Church and the Sunday, but the whole substance of Christian teaching.

Ibid.

WHY CHRISTIANS HATE JEWS

We find here an explanation at least, and a very important one, of why Christians dislike and persecute Jews. They hate them and would get rid of them because they are heavily indebted to them. This is a very simple law of psychology.

From a sermon delivered at the Community Church, New York City, January 17, 1943.

◻

Oliver Wendell Holmes

ODE TO CIVILIZED HUMANITY

In the midst of all triumphs of Christianity, it is well that the stately synagogue should lift its walls by the side of the aspiring cathedral, a perpetual reminder that there are many mansions in the Father's earthly house as well as in the heavenly one; that civilized humanity, longer in time and broader in space than any historical form of belief, is mightier than any one institution or organization it includes.

From an article in American Hebrew *magazine, April 4, 1890.*

MODESTY AND CIVILITY

The Jews are with us as a perpetual lesson to teach us modesty and civility.

Ibid.

◻

Barry Holtz

ONE-WAY DOORS

Today I saw an old woman try to enter a
  supermarket
The wrong way.
She hadn't mastered the electric doors.
What a world for her, I thought, where
  doors
Never get touched by hands and only open
  one way.

From his "Yahrzeit Poem," which appeared in Response *magazine, Summer 1974.*

◻

Benjamin Hooks

PLEA FOR CLEMENCY

Dear President Clinton:

I have recently reviewed the facts in the case of Jonathan Pollard and have concluded that the term of his sentence is unduly harsh and unjust. I am therefore respectfully urging you to grant Mr. Pollard executive clemency.

As a lawyer and a minister, as well as a former judge and CEO of the NAACP, I have rarely encountered a case in which government arbitrariness was so clear-cut and inexcusable....

As inexcusable as Mr. Pollard's acts were, he was [sic] never been accused of treason or harming our nation. His crime was limited to aiding a close ally and this should have mitigated against such a harsh punishment.

In a July 1993 appeal to grant Pollard executive clemency limited to the seven years already served.

INCOMPETENT PEOPLE

I don't know how we could have any more incompetent people anywhere in this nation, unless they openly wore Ku Klux Klan robes.

Condemning Ronald Reagan's choice of Morris B. Abram and his two co-nominees to the United States Commission on Civil Rights.

◻

Earnest A. Hooton

A JEWISH POSSESSION

Superior intelligence is preeminently the possession of the Jewish people.... It has enabled them to produce genius with such a frequency that it becomes monotonous and irksome to less gifted peoples.

From Anthropological Appraisal *magazine, May 15, 1938.*

◻

Herbert Hoover

NAZI BLOW TO CIVILIZATION

These individuals are taking Germany back four hundred and fifty years in civilization to Torquemada's expulsion of the Jews from Spain. They are bringing to Germany not alone the condemnation of the public opinion of the world. These men are building their own condemnation by mankind for centuries to come....

It is still my belief that the German people, if they could express themselves, would not approve these acts against the Jews. But as they cannot so express themselves, it is the duty of men everywhere to express indignation not alone at the suffering these men are imposing upon an innocent people but at the blow they are striking at civilization itself.

From a radio address released by the Federal Council of the Churches of Christ in America, November 14, 1938.

JEWS HELPING JEWS

There is no brighter chapter in the whole history of philanthropy than that which could be written of the work of the American Jews in the last nine years.

From a 1923 statement. Quoted in Joseph C. Heyman's article "Twenty-Five Years of American Aid to Jews Overseas," which appeared in American Jewish Yearbook, *1939–40.*

ON A JEWISH STATE

I have watched with genuine admiration the steady and unmistakable progress made in the rehabilitation of Palestine which, desolate for centuries, is now renewing its youth and vitality through the enthusiasm, hard work and self-sacrifice of the Jewish pioneers who toil there in spite of peace and social justice.

Expressing support for a Jewish State in Palestine at a Zionist Organization of America dinner.

◻

Levi Isaac Horowitz
PRIDE IN JEWISH IDENTITY

We are faced with a generation of young people who lack knowledge and understanding of what living a Jewish life means, and we must declare ourselves partners in their guilt. Today's youth have not rejected Judaism after studying and understanding it; they have ignored it because of misconceptions, a lack of interest, and their own struggle for identity and meaning in life. The young person who says, "I am proud to be a Jew," should indeed be proud. It is our responsibility to give him that spirit and pride in being a Jew.

From "Understanding Ourselves Through Others," an article that appeared in The Jewish Observer, *May–June 1980.*

◻

(Prophet) Hosea
SOWING THE WIND

They that sow the wind shall reap the whirlwind.

From the Book of Hosea (8:7).

MORE IMPORTANT THAN RITUAL

For I desire righteousness [*chesed*], not
    sacrifice,
And knowledge of God more than burnt
    offerings.

Ibid (6:6).

◻

Edward M. House
THE SILENT JEW

The objection to [Walter] Lipmann is that he is a Jew, but unlike other Jews he is a silent one.

Assuring President Woodrow Wilson in 1918 that the criticism of his selection of Walter Lipmann to help draft the Fourteen Points is unfounded.

◻

Oliver Otis Howard
EXEMPLARY JEWISH SOLDIERS

It is impossible for me to do justice to those who served with me under my command who are known to be of Hebrew extraction. I would hardly be justified without their permission to give their names.... I can assure you, my dear sir, that, intrinsically, there are no more patriotic men to be found in the country than those who claim to be of Hebrew descent, and who served with me in parallel commands or more directly under my instructions.

From a January 2, 1892 letter addressed to Simon Wolf. Quoted in Wolf's American Jew as Patriot Soldier and Citizen *(1895).*

◻

Irving Howe
IN PRAISE OF OBSCURE MEN

We need not overvalue the immigrant Jewish experience in order to feel a lasting gratitude for having been part of it. A sense of natural piety toward one's origins can live side by side with a spirit of critical detachment....

The story of the immigrant Jews is all but done. Like all stories of human striving, it ought to be complete, with its beginning and its end, at rest in fulfillment and at ease with failure. A story is the essential unit of our life, offering the magical imperatives of "so it began" and "so it came to an end." A story encompasses us, justifies our stay, prepares our leaving. Here, in these pages, is the story of the Jews, bedraggled and inspired, who came from eastern Europe. Let us now praise obscure men.

Hinting at the probable fate and future of American Jews in the final two paragraphs of his World of Our Fathers *(1976).*

MULTIPLE POINTS OF VIEW

Commentary [magazine] is widely regarded as representing *the* point of view of American Jews. But the Jewish community rarely has, or should have, only one point of view. Yet in the absence of significant opposition, the increasingly strident conservatism of *Commentary* comes to be seen as representative of the political and cultural outlook of the American Jews. And that seems to me highly unfortunate.

In an interview with William Novak in Moment *magazine, March 1976.*

FEEL FREE TO SCREAM

Whatever strong disagreements I've had with Norman Podhoretz, I do share with him a very strong sentiment against what might be called Jewish repressiveness, or Jewish gentility. If you want to scream and yell, you should feel free to scream and yell. Even if the gentiles don't like it.

Ibid.

SIGN OF STRENGTH

You know, the only way to avoid divisions of opinion is to destroy democracy. And I believe that's too high a price for Israel or anywhere else. I don't believe divisions of opinion are signs of weakness. I believe this is a sign of the great strength of Israel.

From a statement at a peace conference held in Washington, DC, on June 23, 1980.

MASTER FUNDRAISER

He [Abraham Sachar] turned to Jews of East European origin who had grown wealthy during the war years, men mostly lacking in education yet worshipful of the idea of it. Sachar milked this layer of the newly rich Jewish bourgeoisie with a skill that it would have taken a heart of gold not to admire.

Recounting how the president of Brandeis University succeeded in raising funds. From his Margin of Hope: An Intellectual Autobiography *(1982).*

BEING JEWISH

I think being Jewish means, among other things, that you don't feel quite at home in the world.

From a 1992 interview. Quoted in The Jewish Week, *April 22–28, 1994.*

¤

Langston Hughes

BLAMING JEWS

When hard luck overtakes you
Nothin' for you to do...
Gather up yo' fine clothes
An sell 'em to de Jew.
Jew takes yo' fine clothes,
Gives you a dollar an' a half...
Go to de bootleg's,
Git some gin to make you laugh.

From his classic 1937 poem "Hard Luck," in which the Jewish-owned pawnshops are linked to the sad plight of the blacks.

¤

Cordell Hull

TRAGEDY REMEMBERED

Of all the inhuman and tyrannical acts of Hitler and his Nazi lieutenants, their systematic persecution of the Jewish people—men, women and children—is the most debased. The fate of these unhappy people must be ever before us in the efforts we are making today for the final victory; at the moment of triumph, under the terms of the Atlantic Charter, the United Nations will be prepared not only to redeem their hopes of a future world based upon freedom, equality and justice but to create a world in which such a tragedy will not again occur.

From a statement to a rabbinical delegation on November 2, 1942.

¤

Hubert H. Humphrey

FROM HUBERT TO HARRY

Dear Harry:

What's this I hear about you closing down [your newspaper] *The Carolina Israelite?* This whole world of ours will never be the same if you do that, but I can well understand that there comes a time when a fellow wants to take it a little easier; in fact, I am beginning to feel that way myself. These are the most difficult and trying of days.

From a February 1968 letter to Harry Golden.

¤

(Rabbi) Huna

SOCIAL ROBBERY

He who does not return a greeting is called a robber.

From the talmudic tractate Berachot (6b).

REPEAT OFFENDERS

As soon as a person has committed a sinful act and has repeated it, it has become unto him permissible.

Quoted in the talmudic tractate Moed Katan (27b).

UNCONTROLLABLE BREACH

Strife is compared to an opening made by a rush of water that widens as the water presses through it.

Quoted in the talmudic tractate Sanhedrin (7a).

◻

Huna ben Yehoshua

ON WALKING BAREHEADED

May I be rewarded for never walking four cubits [six feet] without a headcovering.

Quoted in the talmudic tractate Shabbat (118b). A similar quotation is ascribed to Nachman ben Isaac's mother (Shabbat 156b).

◻

Sol Hurok

GREASING THE SKIDS

There are two ways of writing a bad review.

Commenting how, by sending birthday and Christmas gifts to reviewers, he was able to influence them to be a bit more generous. Quoted in Harlow Robinson's Last Impresario *(1994).*

◻

Fanny Hurst

RICH PEOPLE

Some people think they are worth a lot of money just because they have it.

A 1952 comment.

◻

(King) Hussein

SECRET MEETINGS

I've met all the Israeli prime ministers except for Menachem Begin, including the present prime minister [Yitzhak Rabin] and his predecessor, Yitzhak Shamir.

Revealing, at a meeting with U.S. Jewish leaders, past secret contacts with Israeli officials. Quoted in The Jerusalem Report, *February 24, 1994.*

WAR IS OVER

Mr. Speaker, the state of war between Israel and Jordan is over.... I have come before you today to demonstrate that we are ready to open a new era in our relations with Israel.

From an address on July 26, 1994 before a joint session of the U.S. Congress.

A BEAUTIFUL DAY

Out of all the days of my life, I do not believe there is one such as this.

After U.S. President Bill Clinton escorted the king into the White House Rose Garden to join Yitzhak Rabin at a welcoming ceremony on July 25, 1994, when both leaders signed a declaration ending the state of war between Israel and Jordan.

NO MORE DEATH

We will always cherish the memory and honor all those who have fallen over the years from amongst all of our peoples. I believe they are with us on this occasion and at this time, as we come together to insure—God willing—that there will be no more death, no more misery, no more suspicion, no more fear, no more uncertainty of what each day might bring, as has been the case in the past.

An excerpt from remarks made on October 26, 1994, at the signing of the Israel–Jordanian peace accord at the Arava Crossing, Israel.

PEACE WITH DIGNITY

This is peace with dignity. This is peace with commitment. This is our gift to our peoples and the generations to come. It will herald the change in the quality of life of people. It will not be simply a piece of paper ratified by those responsible, blessed by the world. It will be real....

Ibid.

BROTHER AND FRIEND

He had courage, he had vision, and he had a commitment to peace. As long as I live, I'll be proud to have known him, to have worked with him, as a brother and as a friend and as a man, and the relationship of friendship that we had is something unique, and I'm proud of that.

From his eulogy of slain Israeli Prime Minister Yitzhak Rabin, on November 6, 1995.

◻

Faisal al-Husseini

A SMALL STEP

I would hope that it would be a bigger first step, but it is the beginning.

Comment of the senior PLO leader in the West Bank upon the signing of the Israeli–PLO peace accord in Cairo, Egypt, on May 4, 1994.

¤

Thomas H. Huxley

THAT STRANGE WORD "PHARISEE"

Of all the strange ironies of history, perhaps the strangest is that the word "Pharisee" is current as a term of reproach among the theological descendants of the sect of Nazarenes who, without the martyr spirit of those primitive Puritans, would never have come into existence. They, like their historical successors, our own Puritans, have shared the general fate of the poor wise men who save cities.

Quoted in Louis Finkelstein's Pharisees *(1940).*

¤

(Père) Hyacinthe

JEWISH SIDE OF JESUS

It is an historic fact that he [Jesus] instituted no rite, no sacrament, no Church. Born a Jew, he wished to live and to die a Jew, and from the swaddling clothes of circumcision to the embalmed shroud of sepulchre, followed only the rites of his religion.

Quoted in Aimé Pallière's Unknown Sanctuary *(1979).*

¤

Paula Hyman

FAMILY AND COMMUNITY

It can be argued that...the nature of the Jewish community served to preserve the traditional Jewish family rather than that the Jewish family preserved Judaism.... The theory that women are culture bearers is one which many women are inclined to accept without challenge, despite its inaccuracy, because it is flattering. It connotes power and a recognition of the value of the mothering role.

From a 1975 address before the American Jewish Congress.

Joseph ibn Caspi

THE BELIEVING JEW'S GUIDE

How can I know God and that He is one, unless I know what knowing means and what constitutes unity? No one really knows the true meaning of loving God and fearing Him, unless he is acquainted with natural science and metaphysics, for we love not God as a man loves his wife and children, nor do we fear Him as we would a mighty man. I do not say that all men can reach this intellectual height, but I maintain that it is the degree of highest excellence, though those who stand below it may still be good. Strive, thou, my son, to attain this degree; yet be not hasty in commencing metaphysical studies, and constantly read moral books.

From his book Sefer Ha-musar. *Quoted in Israel Abrahams's* Jewish Life in the Middle Ages *(1958).*

◻

Abraham ibn Chasdai

LIVE POSITIVELY

Rejoice in what you have; sigh not for what you lost.

From his Ben Ha-melech Ve-ha-nazir *(c.1230).*

◻

Abraham ibn Ezra

GOD IS EVERYWHERE

I see Thee in the starry field,
I see Thee in the harvest's yield,
In every breath, in every sound,
An echo of Thy name is found.
The blade of grass, the simple flower,
Bear witness to Thy matchless power.
Elixirs of Life
A pretty maiden, a cup of wine, a beautiful garden, the song of a bird, and the murmur of a brook are the cure of the lover, the joy of the lonely, the wealth of the poor, and the medicine of the sick.

Quoted in Meyer Waxman's History of Jewish Literature *(1930).*

THE JEWS OFFER PSALMS

The Arabs sing of love and passion,
The Romans of war and vengeance,
The Greeks of science and speculation,
The Hindus of proverbs and riddles,
The Jews offer psalms to the Lord of hosts.

Quoted in Yochanan Alemano's Shaar Ha-cheshek *(1790).*

THE BIG SIN

A little sin is a big sin when committed by a big man.

In his commentary on Genesis (32:9).

MAN'S PURPOSE IN LIFE

Man eats to live, he does not live to eat.... He was created to serve God and to cleave to Him, not to accumulate wealth and erect buildings which he must leave behind.

From his Yesod Mora *(1158).*

RASHI: A SHINING STAR

A star shone forth in France. A mighty commentary he wrote on Torah. Therefore he is called *Parshandat* ["Interpreter of the Law"].

In admiration of Rashi, the great eleventh-century commentator.

◻

Moses ibn Ezra

A MOST DELIGHTFUL COMPANION

A book is the most delightful companion.... An inanimate thing, yet it talks.... It stimulates your latent talents. There is in the world no friend more faithful and attentive, no teacher more proficient.... It will join you in solitude, accompany you in exile, serve as a candle in the dark, and entertain you in your loneliness. It will do you good, and ask no favor in return. It gives, and does not take.

From his twelfth-century Shirat Yisrael.

SINCERE THOUGHTS

Words which emerge from the heart enter the heart.

Ibid.

SELF-CONFIDENCE UNLIMITED

In spite of those who hate and envy me
At all times high will rise my eminence.
They aimed their arrows at my heart
But the hands of God deflected them.

Quoted in Raphael Patai's Jewish Mind
(1977).

WISDOM OF THE ANCIENTS

I will make the wisdom of the ancients my
      portion...
When I dive into the sea of their knowledge,
I bring forth pearls to adorn my neck...
They are light to my eyes, they
are music to my ears,
They are honey to my palate,
they are savor to my nostril.

From The Selected Poems of Moses ibn
Ezra, *edited and translated H. Brody and S.
DeSolis Cohen (1934).*

DREAMS AND DEATH

Man's years are dreams; death alone can
tell their meaning.

Ibid.

SABBATH AND CREATION

To remember the Sabbath is to remember
that God created the world.

*From his comment on the fourth command-
ment (Exodus 20:8).*

¤

Solomon ibn Gabirol

A NOBLE PEDIGREE

What is the most impressive pedigree? Lovingkindness.

From his Mivchar Ha-peninim *("Pearls of
Wisdom"), c. 1050.*

AN ENDLESS SEARCH

Man is wise only while in search of wisdom; when he imagines he has attained it, he
is a fool.

Ibid.

BURNING THE MIDNIGHT OIL

A sage who was asked, "Why are you wiser
than your friends," said, "Because I spent
more on oil than they on wine."

Ibid.

NUMBERING OUR DAYS

When told that a certain man had acquired
great wealth, a sage asked, "Has he also acquired the days in which to spend it?"

Ibid.

SEEK THE TRUTH

Be not ashamed to learn truth from any
source.

Ibid.

PLANNING FOR ETERNITY

Plan for this world as if you were to live forever; plan for the hereafter as if you were to
die tomorrow.

Ibid.

LEARNING THAT ENDURES

Learning in old age is like writing on sand;
learning in youth is like engraving on stone.

Ibid.

ON RETRACTING WORDS

I can retract what I did not say, but I cannot retract what I have already spoken.

Ibid.

FACING REALITY

If we believe that no misfortune will befall
us, it is as though we desired not to exist at all.
Because misfortunes are a necessary condition
of the passing of worldly things.

Quoted in Lionel Blue's Jewish Guide to the
Here and Hereafter *(1988).*

MAN IS UNLIKE GOD

Thou art One, and Thou art exalted above
abasement and falling—not like a man, who
falls when he is alone.

From his Keter Malchut *("Kingly Crown").*

SIXTEEN GOING ON EIGHTY

I am the mastersinger and song is my
slave.... Though I am but sixteen, I have the
wisdom of a man of eighty.... I am filled with
wrath when I behold fools parading as wise
men.... They deem their song superior to mine,
whereas they do not even understand it.

Quoted in Chaim Potok's Wanderings
(1978).

A LIQUID OFFERING

I pray, prone before my King,
I bend to him my face and knee,
My heart His sacrifice shall be,
My tear His liquid offering...

Ibid.

ON TO BETTER LANDS

Woe to thee, land of my foes,
In thee I have no portion,
Whether joy or sorrow be thy lot.

Encouraging his soul in its resolve to forget Spain and its inhospitable climate. Quoted in Heinrich Graetz's History of the Jews *(1894).*

SEARCHING FOR WISDOM

How shall I forsake wisdom?
I have made a covenant with her.
She is my mother, I her dearest child;
She hath clasped her jewel about my neck.
Shall I cast aside the glorious ornament?
While life is mine, my spirit shall aspire
Unto her heavenly heights.
I will not rest until I find her source.

Ibid. Singing the praises of his beloved philosophy.

◻

Bachya ibn Pakuda

MAN'S REAL DUTY

He who does no more than his duty is not doing his duty.

From his Chovot Ha-levavot *("Duties of the Heart"), 1040.*

THE REAL ENEMY

Every man's enemy is within himself.

Ibid.

THINKING POSITIVELY

Scholars passed by a dead dog. "How awful its smell!" they said. Their master responded: "How white its teeth!"

Ibid.

TESTING YOUR SINCERITY

There is an old saying: If you wish to find out whether your motive is pure, test yourself in two ways: whether you expect recompense from God or anyone else, and whether you would perform the act in the same way if you were alone, unbeknown to others.

Ibid.

TRUE HUMILITY

He who is humble before God will not only do good to all men, but he will speak kindly to them and about them;...will never relate anything shameful about them; and will forgive them for any shameful things they may say about him.

Ibid.

BEARING TROUBLES

The humble [person]...bears troubles with greater fortitude than do the proud.

Ibid.

PEN OF THE HEART

The tongue is the pen of the heart and the messenger of the distant soul.

Ibid.

PLACING PRAISE AND BLAME

If you want to praise, praise God; if you want to blame, blame yourself.

Quoted in Solomon Schechter's Seminary Addresses *(1959).*

◻

Alsaid ibn Sina

HIGH PRAISE FOR MOSHE BEN MAIMON

Galen's art heals only the body,
But Abu Amram's the body and soul.
With his wisdom he could heal the sickness of ignorance.

Singing the praises of the man Arabs called Abu Amram Musa ibn Maimon (Moses Maimonides), who had won great fame in the Arab world as a physician and a scholar.

◻

Judah ibn Tibbon

BOOKS AS COMPANIONS

My son! Make your books your companions, let your bookcases and shelves be your pleasure grounds and gardens. Bask in their paradise, gather their fruit, pluck their roses, take their spices and their myrrh.

From a testament addressed to his son, Samuel. Quoted in Israel Abrahams's Hebrew Ethical Wills *(1926).*

ADVICE TO A WRITER

My son! If you write, read it through a second time, for no man can avoid slips. Let not any consideration of hurry prevent you from revising a short epistle. Be punctilious as to grammatical accuracy, in conjugation and genders, for the constant use of the vernacular sometimes leads to error in this regard. A man's mistakes in writing bring him into disrepute; they are remembered against him all his days.

Ibid.

Solomon ibn Verga
I SHALL REMAIN A JEW

A shipload of Jewish refugees from Spain, swept by the plague, was compelled to land on a desolate coast. Among them was a man, his wife and two children. As they struggled on through the waste, the wife died. The man carried his two sick children, but at last he fainted from fatigue and hunger. When he awoke, he found his two children dead by his side. He rose to his feet and said in his grief: "Lord of the universe, much hast Thou done to make me forsake my faith. But know for a certainty that nothing which Thou hast brought, or may still bring, over me will make me change. Despite everything, I am a Jew and I shall remain a Jew!"

From his Shevet Yehuda *(1550). Quoted in Solomon Schechter's* Seminary Addresses *(1915).*

Henrik Ibsen
LEARNING HOW TO WAIT

For fortune such as I have enjoyed I have to thank America. My amply furnished library I owe to Germany's later schools. From France, again, I get my waistcoats, my manners, and my spice of wit; from England an industrious hand, and keen sense for my own advantage. The Jew taught me how to wait.

From his play Peer Gynt *(1867).*

(Rabbi) Iddi
DEFINING A RIGHTEOUS PERSON

He who is good to Heaven [God] and good to man, he is a righteous man who is good. He who is good to Heaven but not good to man, he is a righteous man who is not good.

Quoted in the talmudic tractate Kiddushin (40a).

(Rabbi) Ila'i
MANIFESTATION OF CHARACTER

A person manifests his character in three ways: by his cup [how he handles liquor], his purse [how he conducts business], and his anger [how he controls himself].

Quoted in the talmudic tractate Eruvin (65b). Some rabbis add a fourth quality: "By his laughter."

Leon Ilutovich
IN MEMORY OF POLISH JEWRY

Our goal is to plant three million trees in memory of the three million Polish Jews who perished in the Holocaust. For a thousand years and until World War II, over three million Jews in Poland constituted the largest Jewish center in Europe. The Polish Jewry Memorial Forest in the hills of Jerusalem will stand out as a lasting tribute and a living memorial to the Jewish community in Poland which is no more.

From a speech at the initiation of the forest project in 1993.

Naftali Herz Imber
THE GREAT HOPE

As long as in our heart of hearts
There throbs a Jewish soul,
And in the Orient, in Zion,
We envision our goal,
Our cherished hope is not yet lost,
The ancient hope not dampened—
To regain our fatherland,
Where David once encamped.

From his 1876 poem "Hatikva."

Samuel Jacob Imber
A WOMAN'S SOUL

Would you know a woman? Her soul has seven seals.

Quoted in Joseph Leftwich's Golden Peacock *(1939).*

William Ralph Inge
INFLUENCES ON JEWISH THOUGHT

It was either under Persian influence or by a parallel development of thought that Judaism came to believe in a future life, a resurrection, a last judgment, heaven and hell, a cosmic duel between right [sic] and darkness, and a divine Saviour. A cynic might even say that we owe more to Zarathustra than to Moses.

From a 1950 sermon delivered at Modern Church Union, Cambridge, England.

PROTESTANTS AND JEWS

At the Reformation the composite elements flew apart.... The Catholic became two-thirds a pagan; the Protestant, at least in England, two-thirds a Jew.

Ibid.

□

(Pope) Innocent III

DESTINED TO WANDER

The Jews, like the fratricide Cain, are doomed to wander about the earth as fugitives and vagabonds, and their faces must be covered with shame. They are under no circumstances to be protected by Christian princes, but, on the contrary, to be condemned to serfdom. It is, therefore, discreditable for Christian princes to receive Jews into their towns and villages, and to employ them as usurers in order to extort money from Christians. They (the princes) arrest Christians who are indebted to Jews, and allow the Jews to take Christian castles and villages in pledge; and the worst of the matter is that the Church in this manner loses its tithes.

It is scandalous that Christians should have their cattle slaughtered, and their grapes pressed by Jews, who are thus enabled to take their portion, prepared according to their religious precepts, and hand over the leavings to the Christians.

A still greater sin is it that this wine prepared by Jews should be used in the Church for the sacrament of the Lord's Supper.

Whilst the Christians are excommunicated for favoring the Jews, and their land is laid under the ban, the Jews are all the time laughing in their sleeves at the fact that, on their account, the harps of the Church are hung on willows, and that the priests are deprived of their revenues.

> *From a 1208 pastoral letter in which the Pope denounced princes and kings who were favorably disposed toward the Jews. Quoted in Heinrich Graetz's* History of the Jews *(1894).*

□

(Pope) Innocent IV

PAPAL DEFENSE OF JEWS

What a shame it is that they should be more miserable under Christian princes than their ancestors were under Pharaoh.

> *From his* Letter in Defense of the Jews *(1247).*

A CALL FOR KINDNESS

If the Christian religion were to give careful heed and rightly analyze by use of reason how

inhuman it is and how discordant with piety for it to afflict...the remnant of the Jews,...it would, at least, extend the solace of human kindness to those whom it holds, as it were, in tribute.

> *Ibid. Referring to an unproved accusation that Jews had nailed a girl to the Cross, and the draconian measures taken against them.*

□

Eugene Ionesco

KARL MARX AND MESSIANISM

Despite his atheism, Marx cannot be understood without the Bible. His myth of a perfect society, surmounting history, beyond history, is in fact the biblical myth of Paradise on Earth.... What is Marxism if not Messianism?

> *Remarks made at the 1973 Jerusalem Book Fair.*

□

(Patriarch) Isaac

SACRIFICE OF ISAAC

Here is the fire and the wood, but where is the sheep for the burnt offering?

> *Addressing his father, Abraham, who was taken to Mount Moriah to be purified. From the Book of Genesis (22:7).*

DECEPTION OF ISAAC

The voice is the voice of Jacob, but the hands are the hands of Esau.

> *Commenting when his son Jacob appears before him to be blessed and is dressed in his brother Esau's clothing (Genesis 27:22).*

□

(Rabbi) Isaac

HARD WORK PAYS OFF

If a man says to you, "I have worked hard and not succeeded," do not believe him.

If he says, "I have not worked hard and have nevertheless succeeded," do not believe him.

If he says, "I have worked hard and succeeded," believe him.

> *Quoted in the talmudic tractate Megilla (6b).*

MORE PRECIOUS THAN CHARITY

He who gives a coin to a poor man obtains

six blessings, but he who addresses him with words of comfort obtains eleven blessings.

A statement based on a verse in the Book of Isaiah (58:7). Quoted in the talmudic tractate Bava Batra (9b).

ESTATE PLANNING

A man should always divide his assets into three parts: one third [should be invested] in real estate; a second in merchandise; and a third in readily transportable articles.

Quoted in the talmudic tractate Bava Metzia (42a).

BLACK AND WHITE

The milk of black goats and the milk of white goats is one and the same.

Commenting on the equality of all men. Quoted in Midrash Genesis Rabba (87:5).

¤

Isaac ben Nappacha

IT ALL STEMS FROM SINAI

Everything the Prophets were to prophesy, and everything Sages of future generations were destined to teach, they received it all from Sinai.

Quoted in Midrash Exodus Rabba (28:6).

A PRECIOUS GIFT

A handful of flour brought by a poor man voluntarily [as a sacrifice] is more precious than two handfuls of incense brought by the High Priest.

Quoted in Midrash Ecclesiastes Rabba (4:6).

¤

Moses Isaac

PASSPORT TO THE WORLD-TO-COME

A tailor who does not appropriate some of his customer's cloth, a cobbler who patches with good leather, a storekeeper who gives the correct weight and a full measure, will have a greater portion in the world-to-come than many a rabbi.

Quoted in J. Mark's Gedolim Fun Unzer Dor (1927).

¤

Walter Isaacson

KISSINGER FROM FURTH

Though [Henry] Kissinger, the refugee from Furth [Germany], did not need to be taught

about the Holocaust, some in Israel believed that Kissinger the [U.S.] Secretary of State might.

In his biography entitled Kissinger (1993).

KISSINGER AND THE HOLOCAUST

For Kissinger, the Holocaust destroyed the connection between God's will and the progress of history—a tenet that is at the heart of the Jewish faith.... After witnessing the Nazi horror, Kissinger would abandon the practice of Judaism.

Ibid.

¤

(Prophet) Isaiah

REASONABLE ROAD

Come now, and let us reason together, saith the Lord: though your sins be as scarlet, they shall be as white as snow; though they be red like crimson, they shall be as wool.

Urging his listeners to adopt a more compassionate way of life. From the Book of Isaiah (1:18).

VISION OF UNIVERSAL PEACE

They shall beat their swords into plowshares, and their spears into pruning hooks. Nation shall not lift up sword against nation, neither shall they learn war anymore.

Ibid (2:4). The same quotation appears in the Book of Micha. Inscribed on the Isaiah Wall, across the street from the United Nations.

IDYLLIC PEACE

The wolf shall lie down with the lamb, the leopard shall couch with the kid.... And a little child shall lead them.

Ibid (11:6).

SABBATH DELIGHT

And you shall call the Sabbath a delight.

Ibid (58:13).

¤

Ishmael ben Elisha

THE ESSENCE OF LIVING

It is a wheel [*galgal*] that revolves in the world.

A similar expression was used by Benjamin Disraeli, implying that what goes around comes around.

ON ABORTION

It is a capital crime to destroy an embryo in the womb.

Quoted in the talmudic tractate Sanhedrin (57b).

◻

Edward L. Israel

THE OUTSPOKEN RABBI

You may sincerely feel that because of my official position [as a rabbi], I have no right to interest myself in public controversies where I feel that a moral issue is at stake. If this is your point of view, I am sorry that I cannot follow you in it. As I interpret religion, it is the application of the individual conscience to the problems of life.... For one to keep silent merely because he may be expressing an adverse opinion is a type of moral cowardice to which I cannot submit.

From a statement in his Temple's (Har Zion) bulletin, Baltimore, Maryland, May 16, 1929.

◻

Richard J. Israel

PRIORITIZING JEWISH LIFE

I would give priority to personal change over institutional change.... There are foods we should and should not eat. We must organize our lives so they are in touch with the Jewish calendar, Shabbat and holidays. We must actively attach ourselves to Jewish community

here and in Israel. We must have *tzedaka* [charity] lines in our personal budgets. We must engage in continuing Jewish learning. Without individual change, structural change won't help. With it structural change becomes possible.

From Hadassah Magazine, June–July 1993.

◻

Isaac Israeli

DOCTOR'S FEES

The more you demand for your service, the greater will it appear in the eyes of the people. Your art will be looked down upon by people you treat for nothing.

In his Doctor's Guide (tenth century).

CARING FOR THE POOR

Make it your special concern to visit and treat poor and needy patients, for in no other way can you find more meritorious service.

Ibid.

◻

Moses Isserles

TIME TO CHANGE

If anything arises that the former teachers knew not or were not called upon to decide, then surely a change is as necessary as any alteration mentioned in the Talmud.

Quoted in D. Philipson's Reform Movement in Judaism (1907).

Vladimir Jabotinsky

HOPE MUCH

I hope always, I desire much, I expect little.

Quoted in Jewish Affairs *magazine, July 1950.*

USING JEWISH BLOOD

Jewish blood is the best for oiling the wheels of progress.

Quoted in his War and the Jew *(1942).*

ANTI-SEMITISM WORKSHOP

Germany—and in this respect Austria was one with her long before the *Anschluss*—has ever been the paramount workshop of modern anti-Semitism.

Ibid.

SAVE YOURSELVES

For three years, I have been imploring you, Jews of Poland, the crown of world Jewry, appealing to you, warning you unceasingly that the catastrophe is near. My hair has turned white and I have grown old over these years, for my heart is bleeding that you do not see the volcano which will soon begin to spew forth its fires of destruction.... Listen to my words at this, the twelfth hour. For God's sake: let everyone save himself, so long as there is time to do so, for time is running short.

From a speech in Warsaw on August 10, 1938, one year before the Nazis invaded Poland. Quoted in Benjamin Netanyahu's Place Among the Nations: Israel and the World *(1993).*

□

Henry "Scoop" Jackson

FREEDOM OF MOVEMENT

Everyone has the right to leave any country, including his own, and to return to his country.

In a March 1973 amendment to a trade bill opposed by U.S. President Richard Nixon linking the right of Soviet citizens to emigrate. Jackson's amendment was based on the rights affirmed in the Universal Declaration of Human Rights.

THREAT TO KUWAIT

I would remind the chairman of the [U.S. Senate] Foreign Relations Committee that it is not Israel—as he suggests—that threatens Kuwait—but Iraq which was, as late as last week, engaged in military activity that may have as its objective the eventual control of that oil rich sheikdom. It is not Israel that threatens Saudi Arabia—but Yemen to the south, Soviet-supported Iraq and Syria to the north, and Egypt to the west. It is not Israel that is in Oman, but rather the stability of Oman is threatened by a smoldering insurgency backed by the Communist Chinese.

I believe that a strong Israel, like a strong Iran, is vital to America's interests in the Middle East and the Persian Gulf.

Comment recorded in the Congressional Record, *Monday, May 21, 1973.*

ARAB-ISRAELI SOLUTION

I, for one, believe that we must leave to the parties themselves the task of finding a solution to the Arab–Israeli dispute; and the crucial first step toward that objective is for the Arab States to agree to direct negotiations with Israel.

Ibid.

ENERGY AND THE MIDDLE EAST

It is time for the Administration to speak some plain truths to the American people: our energy crisis does not result from the Arab-Israeli dispute and it did not arise out of the Yom Kippur war. Without the dispute, without the war, indeed, even without the existence of the State of Israel, we would have faced an energy crisis this year and for several years to come. Saying this will not solve the shortages we face, but it will help the American people to understand that the oil weapon is a pea shooter and not a howitzer.

Ibid. From an address before the Senate, Wednesday, December 19, 1973.

¤

Jesse Jackson

POISONOUS WEED

Zionism is a kind of poisonous weed that is choking Judaism.... We have the real obligation to separate Zionism from Judaism.

Quoted in Sol Stern's article entitled "Jews, Blacks, and Jesse Jackson," which appeared in Reform Judaism *magazine, Spring 1984.*

WE DO NOT STAND ALONE

This struggle against prejudice is our struggle. If we do not fight it together, we shall lose terribly, at a great cost, as we have lost so many times in the past. If we try to stand alone, we may survive for a year, or a decade, or even a generation, but our children shall pay the price with their tears.

And yet we do not stand alone. We stand on the shoulders of the great men and women who have come before us. We have a great legacy to turn to and to learn from. Surely heaven is smiling today with Dr. Martin Luther King and Rabbi Abraham Heschel, two men with whom I studied and worked, for surely they bless this meeting as another step in their lifelong work of bridge-building and making us whole.

In an address to the World Conference on Anti-Semitism and Prejudice in a Changing World, held in Brussels, Belgium, July 1992.

PRO-ISRAEL CREDENTIALS

I support Israel's right to exist with security, with internationally recognized boundaries. I am equally convinced that Israeli security and Palestinian justice are two sides of the same coin.

Before the B'nai B'rith district convention in Washington, DC, July 1993.

IN DEFENSE OF ARAFAT

Arafat is educated, urbane, reasonable. I think his commitment to justice is an absolute one.

From an article in Penthouse *magazine, February 1981.*

ARAFAT THE HERO

One who does not think Arafat is a true hero does not read the situation correctly.

From a September 27, 1979 interview in the Israeli newspaper Maariv *during Jackson's trip to the Middle East. At that time he embraced Yasser Arafat and fired up a Palestinian crowd as they carried him on their shoulders, shouting, "Jackson! Arafat!"*

GENESIS OF THE CONFLICT

The conflict [with the Jews] began when we [blacks] started our quest for power.

From a statement in The New York Times, *August 19, 1979.*

SHARE THE WEALTH

When it came to the division of power, we did not get from the Jews the slice of the cake we deserved.... The Jews do not share with us control of wealth, broadcasting stations and other centers of power.

From an interview on the television program 60 Minutes, *September 16, 1979.*

GUILT TRIP

I am sick and tired of hearing about the Holocaust and having the United States put in the position of a guilt trip.

Quoted in Newsweek *magazine, October 8, 1979.*

LEGACY OF HESCHEL AND KING

We must thrust off all of the excess baggage of fear, prejudice and intolerance and strengthen our historic alliance.... These two [Rabbi Abraham Heschel and Rev. Martin Luther King] who tore down walls, building bridges; their devotion to social justice, freedom, unity, coalition and peace—their legacy beckons to us to take our struggle to the next stage and face this day's challenge.

From a speech on December 5, 1994 before a crowd of 1,000 at Manhattan's Park Avenue Synagogue.

I WAS ALWAYS THERE

I walked with Rabbi Heschel, I was there in Skokie when the neo-Nazis wanted to march, I was there in Bitburg, I confronted Gorbachev on Soviet Jewry, I asked Assad to free the Syrian Jews.

From an interview with The Jewish Week, *December 9–15, 1994.*

¤

Michael Jackson

JEW ME/SUE ME

Jew me,
Sue me,
Everybody do me.
Kick me,

Kike me,
Don't you black or white me.

Lyrics of the song "They Don't Care About Us," which was included in his album History, *released in June 1995. Jackson insisted that the lyrics are not anti-Semitic. However, after much criticism, he modified the lyrics and re-recorded the song.*

VOICE OF THE ACCUSED

I am the voice of the accused and the attacked. I am the voice of everyone. I am the skinhead. I am the Jew, I am the black man, I am the white man. I am not the one who was attacking.

Ibid. Explaining that the lyrics of "They Don't Care About Us" were intended to call attention to social problems.

MY BEST FRIENDS

My accountants and lawyers are Jewish, my three best friends are Jewish...Steven Spielberg, Jeffrey Katzenberg and David Geffen... and Michael Milken.

From an interview with ABC-TV personality Diane Sawyer, defending the original lyrics of "They Don't Care About Us."

◘

(Patriarch) Jacob

THE HAIRY BROTHER

My brother is a hairy man and I am smooth-skinned.

Explaining to his mother, Rebecca, why it would be difficult to fool Isaac. From the Book of Genesis *(27:11).*

◘

Benno Jacob

ONLY ONE HUMAN SPECIES

Of beasts it [Genesis 1:25] says that they were created "of every kind." Not so of man; there is only one human species.

Commenting on the uniqueness of man. From his Das Erste Buch der Torah; Genesis *(1934).*

◘

Joe Jacobs

SORE LOSER

We wuz robbed!

After the title bout between Max Schmeling and Jack Sharkey on June 21, 1932. Jacobs managed Schmeling.

SAFE HAVEN

I should of stood in bed.

After leaving his sickbed to attend the 1935 World Series in Detroit, Michigan, and betting on the loser.

◘

Joseph Jacobs

A BLAZING COMET

It is impossible to convey any adequate idea of the genial radiance and *élan* of Schechter's personality at this period. At the height of his physical and mental vigor, appreciated for the first time his true value, surrounded by an ever-increasing circle of admiring friends, he burst upon us as a blazing comet in the intellectual sky.

The period referred to is 1882, when, as a young man, Claude G. Montefiore met Solomon Schechter in Berlin and persuaded him to come to England to act as his tutor.

THE BIBLE AND THE JEWS

If it be true, as it obviously is, that the Bible is a creation of the Jews, it is also true, though not so obvious, that the Jews are a creation of the Bible.

From his Jewish Contributions to Civilization *(1919).*

LOOKING BACK

Man is made by history. It is history that causes the men of historic nations to be more civilized than the savage. The Jew recognizes that he is made what he is by the history of his fathers, and he feels he is losing his better self so far as he loses his hold on his past history.

Ibid.

◘

Louis Jacobs

REJECTION OF POLYTHEISM

Judaism stands or falls on the rejection of polytheism as it is compatible with dualism or trinitarianism.... The believing Jew still recites the *Shema* ["Hear, O Israel" prayer] as plying the pure monotheistic doctrine on which Judaism as a religion is based.

From his Jewish Theology *(1975).*

WHAT THE WORLD OWES ISRAEL

It becomes obvious that we are not discussing a dogma incapable of verification, but the recognition of sober historical fact. The world owes Israel the idea of the One God of righteousness and holiness.... Clearly, God used Israel for this great purpose.

Ibid.

□

Edward Jacobson

TRUMAN AND WEIZMANN

Harry, all your life you have had a hero. You are probably the best read man in America on the life of Andrew Jackson.... Well, Harry, I too have a hero, a man I never met but who is, I think, the greatest Jew who ever lived.... I am talking about Chaim Weizmann. He is an old man and a sick man, and he has come all the way to America to see you. Now you refuse to see him because you were insulted by some of our American Jewish leaders.... It doesn't sound like you, Harry.

> *Imploring President Harry Truman, his old friend and one-time Kansas City business partner, in March 1948, to allow his hero, Chaim Weizmann, to have a presidential audience so that he might make the Zionist case personally. (Truman had been speaking about his hero, Andrew Jackson.) Truman finally acquiesced, saying, "All right, you bald-headed son of a bitch, I'll see him."*

□

Immanuel Jakobovits

STATUS SYNDROME

The American Jew wants to achieve something that is in a way unattainable—that he will be granted equal rights not only as an individual, but that as a group the Jews must also enjoy equality.... But constituting less than three percent of the total society, it is not likely that he will ever achieve actual equal status with the remaining ninety-seven percent. And therefore there is a greater degree of self-consciousness about being Jewish in the United States than I find to exist in Britain.

> *In an interview with Ellen Frankel that appeared in* Moment *magazine, May 1980.*

WHY ROCK THE BOAT

British Jews don't like innovation and experimentation. They prefer to take the tried paths of past experience rather than the uncertainties of unknown ways.... And that is one of my problems, because whenever I make a new suggestion, the first reaction is, we've managed for three hundred years, why rock the boat?

Ibid.

ON JEWISH SURVIVAL

The question is not whether we will survive, but who and how many will survive. And this will depend on the degree to which we can try and recapture the masses of our young people to the thrills of Jewish learning and Jewish living.

Ibid.

ON WELCOMING PROSELYTES

If Jews are born as Jews and they ignore Jewish law, reject Jewish law, may not even remember that they are Jews, we still recognize them as Jews. We say, *"Yisroel af al pi shechata Yisroel hu."* A Jew, even though he may be baptized, we still look upon him as a Jew. He is our child. He is born into our people. You cannot escape from Judaism. If, however, we are to adopt a Jew, if we are to invite one who is not born Jewish to assume these responsibilities and make him into one of ourselves, we can ask to be assured that he will be an asset to us. If he will be a liability, if he will become a law-breaker, why should we impose the burden on him?

> *In a 1960 dialogue with Rabbi William Berkowitz at the Institute of Adult Jewish Studies in New York. Reported in Berkowitz's* Ten Vital Jewish Issues *(1964).*

MISPLACED JEWISH ENERGY

Would it not be a catastrophic perversion of the Jewish spirit if brooding over the Holocaust were to become a substantial element in the Jewish purpose, and if the anxiety to prevent another Holocaust were to be relied upon as an essential incentive for Jewish activity?

> *Expressing his need to shift emphasis from "survival of Jews to survival of Judaism." Quoted in Anne Roiphe's* Season for Healing *(1988).*

HITLER'S ALLIES

Silence, indifference and inaction were Hitler's principle allies.

> *Quoted in London's* Independent, *December 5, 1989.*

ARAB ACCOMMODATION

I am one of all-too-few Orthodox rabbis who have consistently advocated an accommodation with our Arab neighbors for political, moral, religious—and indeed security—reasons.

In this post-colonial age, it is unacceptable for Jews to rule over two million Arabs. It is also painfully demoralizing for Israeli society and for the army in particular.

Moreover, it compromises the Jewish character of the state—not to mention the supreme Jewish ideal of peace. At the same time, the situation breeds despair leading to terrorism. And it makes future wars, with ever-escalating casualties, inescapable.

From an article in The Jerusalem Post, *May 28, 1994.*

RELIGION AND CHARACTER-BUILDING

Schools which do not provide religious training are career factories, turning out morally indifferent robots; they fail in their principal task to produce upright, idealistic and consecrated citizens of sturdy moral fibre.

Ibid.

NATURE'S GRANDEUR

Jews today are the most urbanized people on earth, and as a result many of us have become divorced from nature and insensitive to its thrills and quiet inspiration. Most Jews somehow seem to prefer the loud clanging of a dance orchestra to the mystic eloquence of a rushing mountain stream or the sweet, soothing music of a humming bird.

From a 1965 High Holiday sermon to his New York congregation. Quoted in Chaim Bermant's biography Lord Jakobovits *(1990).*

NO BENDING, NO COMPROMISING

I am resolved to preserve the Orthodox traditions of my office and the predominantly traditional character of our community...I have not become Anglo Jewry's First Minister in order to preside over the liquidation of British Judaism.

Ibid. Remarks made at his brief installation ceremony, in 1965, as Chief Rabbi of the British Commonwealth.

WHAT WE OWE SOCIETY

The accent today is on demands not obligations. Everyone thinks of what society owes to him, not what he owes to society.

Ibid. From an address to the directors of Albert Hall a few months after his induction in 1965 as Chief Rabbi of the British Commonwealth. The theme is strikingly familiar to that of U.S. President John F. Kennedy in his 1961 inaugural speech.

PEANUTS FOR MONKEYS

If you pay peanuts, you get monkeys.

Commenting on the reason it was difficult to recruit suitable candidates for the rabbinate. Quoted in Chaim Bermant's biography Lord Jakobovits *(1990).*

◻

(Rabbi) Jannai

THE SUPERIOR EGG

An egg is superior [in food value] to the same quantity of any other food.

Quoting his teacher Rabbi Judah the Prince. From the talmudic tractate Berachot (44b).

◻

Jacob Javits

CHANGING IDENTITY

I am frequently asked whether anti-Semitism played a role in my initial cold welcome to the Senate. It is possible.... But...I never attributed anything that happened to me to anti-Semitism.... A personal snub or problem can be dealt with, but if you succumb to the paranoia that your opponent is fighting you because of your religion or ethnic background, then you might as well give up entirely, because there is no way to change your identity.

From his autobiography, in which he advised aspiring politicians.

◻

Thomas Jefferson

LEARNING ABOUT JEWISH HISTORY

Sir:—I thank you for the discourse on the consecration of the Synagogue in your city, with which you have been pleased to favor me. I have read it with pleasure and instruction, having learnt from it some valuable facts in Jewish history which I did not know before. Your sect by its sufferings has furnished a remarkable proof of the universal spirit of religious intolerance inherent in every sect, disclaimed by all while feeble, and practiced by all when in power. Our laws have applied the only antidote to this vice, protecting our religious, as they do our civil rights, by putting all on an equal footing. But more remains to be done, for although we are free by the law, we are not so in practice; public opinion erects itself into an Inquisition, and exercises its office with as much fanaticism as fans the flames of an *Auto-de-fe.*

In response to a communication from Mordecai M. Noah containing the address Noah had delivered at the consecration of New York City's Mill Street Synagogue on May 28, 1818.

EARLY JEWISH REFORM EFFORTS

I am little acquainted with the liturgy of the Jews or their mode of worship but the reformation proposed and explained appears entirely reasonable. Nothing is wiser than that all our institutions should keep pace with the advance of time and be improved of human mind.

In response to a letter from Isaac Harby (died 1828), a founder of the Reformed Society of Israelites, who had sent Jefferson a copy of their resolution stating that they would no longer be bound by blind observance. Quoted in Max Dimont's Jews in America *(1978).*

ADDING INSULT TO INJURY

[I have] ever felt regret at seeing a sect, the parent and basis of all those of Christendom, singled out by all of them for a persecution and oppression which proved they have profited nothing from the benevolent doctrines of him whom they profess to make the model of their principle and practice.

I have thought it a cruel addition to the wrongs which that injured sect [the Jews] have suffered, that their youth should be excluded from the instructions in science afforded to all others in our public seminaries, by imposing upon them a course of Theological Reading which their consciences do not permit them to pursue; and in the University lately established there, we have set the example of ceasing to violate the rights of conscience by any injunction on the different sects respecting their religion.

From a letter to Joseph Marx. Quoted in Saul K. Padover's Democracy by Thomas Jefferson *(1939).*

¤

Adolph Jellinek

VERY SPIRITUAL PEOPLE

Where is there another people on earth, among whom studies which aimed only at truth and the development of the spiritual life were cultivated with such pure, devoted and selfless love as in Israel?

Quoted in J. H. Hertz's Book of Jewish Thoughts *(1917).*

¤

(Prophet) Jeremiah

EPITOME OF MEEKNESS

Like a lamb led to slaughter.

From the Book of Jeremiah (11:19).

NO BALM IN GILEAD

Is there no balm in Gilead? Is there no physician there?

Ibid (8:22).

PRAY FOR PEACE

Seek the peace of the city whither I have caused you to be carried away captive, and pray unto the Lord for it; for in the peace thereof shall you have peace.

Ibid (29:7).

CHILDREN PAYING THE PRICE

The fathers have eaten sour grapes, and the children's teeth are set on edge.

A popular ancient quotation from the Book of Jeremiah (31:29). Also quoted in the Book of Ezekiel (18:2).

CRY OF PEACE

They offer healing offhand for the wounds of My people, saying, "All is well, all is well," when nothing is well.

Ibid (6:14, 8:11). Speaking in the name of God.

WHEREIN MAN MAY GLORY

Thus said the Lord:
Let not the wise man glory in his wisdom;
Let not the strong man glory in his strength;
Let not the rich man glory in his riches.
But only in this should one glory:
In his earnest devotion to Me.
For I the Lord act with kindness, justice and equity in the world;
For in these I delight.

Ibid (9:22). It is on this note that Maimonides concludes his Guide of the Perplexed *(III:54).*

¤

George A. Jessel

A FINE MAN

I know Governor Thomas E. Dewey and Mr. Dewey is a fine man. Yes, Dewey is a fine man. So is my Uncle Morris. My Uncle Morris shouldn't be president; neither should Dewey.

Quoted in Morris Mandel's Affronts, Insults, and Indignities *(1975).*

GREATEST ENTERTAINER

He was a no-good son of a bitch. But he was the greatest entertainer I've ever seen.

An evaluation of Al Jolson twenty years after Jessel had eulogized him magnificently at Jolson's funeral in October 1950. Quoted in Michael Freedland's Jolson *(1972).*

Erica Jesselson

WHAT YOU CAN TAKE WITH YOU

What you create and leave behind is your good name. You created it with your own hands and heart. The rest you can't take with you. His credo was that the *mitzvah* was only fulfilled when it was done anonymously.... With all of his diverse interests, his heart was in this edifice.

> *Commenting after a room in the UJA–Federation building on East 59th Street in New York City was dedicated to her millionaire philanthropist husband, Ludwig Jesselson, April 25, 1994.*

Ahmed Jibril

ARAFAT IS DOOMED

Undoubtedly, when Arafat took this [September 13, 1993 peace accord] step, he knew he had the considerable support of the US administration. He also had Israeli support. We also know that Arafat is going to Gaza and Jericho knowing that he has billions of dollars. Yet all of this will not deter the general popular indignation.

We feel that neither the Shin Bet nor the Mossad will be able to protect Arafat. The CIA wasn't able to protect Sadat.

> *Comment made following the signing of the peace accord with Israel on September 13, 1993. From an interview with journalist Steve Rodan. Reported in* The Jerusalem Post, *November 27, 1993.*

WHO WILL KILL ARAFAT?

I am not saying that I personally will kill Arafat. I am saying that the people will not be lenient with a man who has given away 90 percent of their land. When Arafat is killed, the accord [the Israel–PLO declaration of principles] will fade away.

> *Ibid.*

ARAFAT IS A JEW

[Arafat is a] Jew who works for the Israeli secret service and infiltrated the PLO. I have proof that Arafat belongs to a Moroccan-Jewish family, from the Kaddoua family.

> *Ibid.*

Ali Jiddah

I WANT REAL PEACE

This agreement is killing me emotionally. I felt sad and very bitter. I went back to the period when I was arrested, to my experiences in prison, the suffering with my brothers. I went back to the convoys of martyrs and their mothers.

I've spent the best days of my life in prison, and I'm one of the people who really needs peace, for my child, who I don't want to experience what I went through. But we are not heading toward a stable peace....

I want peace, but real peace between equals. This is artificial, and it won't last long.

> *A reaction to the September 13, 1993 peace accord between Israel and the PLO. Jiddah spent seventeen years in Israeli prisons for planting a bomb that wounded seven Israelis in Jerusalem in 1968.*

Job

SACRED COVENANT

I made a covenant with my eyes; how then could I [lustfully] look upon a maiden?

> *From the Book of Job (31:1).*

TEMPUS FUGIT

My days are swifter than a weaver's shuttle.

> *Ibid (7:6).*

CURSE MY BIRTH

Cursed be the day I was born, and the night on which it was announced: "A male-child is being born."

> *Ibid (3:3).*

FAITH DESPITE ADVERSITY

Naked came I out of my mother's womb,
And naked shall I return there;
The Lord gave, and the Lord has taken away;
Blessed be the name of the Lord.

> *Ibid (1: 21), after being advised that his children were dead and all his property was in ruins.*

WISDOM OF THE AGED

With the ancient is wisdom and in length of days understanding.

> *Ibid (12:12).*

SUPREME FAITH

Though He slay me, yet, will I trust in Him.

Ibid (13:15).

MAN IS BORN TO TROUBLE

Man, born of woman, is of few days and full of trouble.

Ibid (4:1).

◻

Richard M. Joel

JUDAISM ON CAMPUS

We need to ensure that our young people include Jewishness as a defining feature in their lives. College is a time of great personal growth when students make decisions about their future. The community must support campus organizations that connect young Jews to their Jewishness. The community must also encourage these organizations to reach beyond their traditional constituencies to nurture connections with the many who are not being touched.

Quoted in Hadassah Magazine, *June–July 1993.*

◻

John I of Castille

ESTABLISHMENT OF A GHETTO

In the first place from now on all Jews and Jewesses, Moors and Moorish women of My kingdoms and dominions shall be and live apart from the Christian men and women in a section or part of the city or village or any place where they have resided. It shall be surrounded by a wall and have but one gate through which one could enter it. All Jews and Jewesses, Moors and Moorish women shall live in the said enclosure thus assigned to them and in no other place or house outside it. They shall begin to move thereto within eight days after these places are assigned to them. And if some Jews or Jewesses, Moors or Moorish women should stay outside the said enclosure, he or she shall by that very fact lose all his or her possessions. The body of such a Jew or Jewess, Moor or Moorish woman shall likewise be at My mercy to impose upon him or her any corporal punishment according to my discretion.

An edict issued in 1412. Quoted in Benjamin Netanyahu's Scattered Among the Nations *(1993).*

◻

(Pope) John XXIII

THE SECOND CRUCIFIXION

We realize now that many, many centuries of blindness have dimmed our eyes, so that we no longer see the beauty of Thy Chosen People and no longer recognize in their faces the features of our first-born brother. We realize that our brows are branded with the mark of Cain. Centuries long has Abel lain in blood and tears, because we have forgotten Thy love. Forgive us the curse which we unjustly laid on the name of the Jews. Forgive us, that with our curse, we crucified Thee a second time.

A prayer composed shortly before his death in 1963, hoping to make amends with the Jewish people.

◻

(Pope) John Paul II

ON THE HOLOCAUST

[The Holocaust was] the great tragedy of our times. We must do all in our power never to let it happen again.

A statement made to a visiting rabbi. Quoted in The Jerusalem Report, *April 21, 1994.*

CALL FOR ETERNAL VIGILANCE

It is not enough that we remember; for in our own day, regrettably, there are many new manifestations of the anti-Semitism, xenophobia and racial hatred which were the seeds of those unspeakable crimes. History cannot permit all that to happen again.... With the help of Almighty God, we can work together to prevent the repetition of such heinous evil.

At an April 1994 meeting with survivors of the Holocaust, during a Vatican concert hosted by the Pope, in which he paid tribute to the Six Million Jewish martyrs.

BIG BROTHER TO CHRISTIANS

The attitude of the Church toward the people of God's Old Testament—the Jews—can only be that they are our elder brothers in the faith. I have been convinced of that from my youngest years in my native town of Wadowice.

From an interview in 1994 with Tad Szule, a former New York Times *reporter writing the Pope's biography.*

CONDEMNATION OF ANTI-SEMITISM

A consideration of centuries-long cultural conditioning could not prevent us from recognizing that the acts of discrimination, unjustified limitation of religious freedom, oppression, also on the level of civil freedom, in regard to the Jews were, from an objective point of view, gravely deplorable manifestations. Yes, once again, through myself, the Church, in the words of the well-known declaration *Nostra Aetate,* "deplores the hatred, persecutions, and displays of anti-Semitism directed against the Jews at any time and by anyone." I repeat, "By anyone."

I would like once more to express a word of abhorrence for the genocide decreed against the Jewish people during the last war, which led to the holocaust of millions of innocent victims.

> *From a speech delivered on April 13, 1986 in Rome's Central Synagogue, overlooking the Tiber River. Translated from the Italian by the Vatican.*

BOND WITH JUDAISM

The Jewish religion is not "extrinsic" to us, but in a certain way is "intrinsic" to our own religion. With Judaism, therefore, we have a relationship which we do not have with any other religion. You are our dearly beloved brothers, and in a certain way, it could be said that you are our elder brothers.

> *Ibid. The Pope refers to paragraph four of the* Nostra Aetate *during his 1986 speech to the Jewish community of Rome.*

BLAME NOT THE JEWS

No ancestral or collective blame can be imputed to the Jews as a people for "what happened in Christ's passion." Not indiscriminately to the Jews of that time nor to those who came afterward nor to those of today. So any alleged theological justification for discriminatory measures or, worse still, for acts of persecution is unfounded. The Lord will judge each one "according to his own works," Jews and Christians alike.

> *Ibid.*

MEMORIES OF YOUTH

I remember very clearly the Wadowice Synagogue, which was near our High School. I have in front of my eyes the numerous worshippers who during their holidays pass on their way to pray. If you are able to be there in Wadowice in the month of May [1989], tell all who are gathered there that together with them I venerate the memory of their so cruelly killed co-religionists and compatriots and also the place of worship which the invaders destroyed.

> *From a letter to his childhood friend Jerzy Kluger, to be read if he wished at the dedication of the rebuilt synagogue.*

RESOLUTION OF A DISPUTE

By the will of the Church you are to move now to a different site in Oswieçim [Auschwitz].

> *In an April 1993 letter to fourteen Roman Catholic Carmelite nuns who were told to move to another convent within the diocese in the Auschwitz area or return to where they came from nine years earlier.*

I DON'T TOLERATE YOU

I don't *tolerate* you. I'm not going to tolerate you, because according to my religion I'm called to love you. Because if you are my brother I can't tolerate you. How can one *tolerate* one's brother? One must *love* one's brother.

> *During a 1991 visit to Poland, speaking to members of all faiths.*

THE RIGHT OF ISRAEL

It must be understood that Jews, who for 2,000 years were dispersed among the nations of the world, decided to return to the land of their ancestors. This is their right.

> *In a 1994 interview in* Parade *magazine.*

JERUSALEM AND THE JEWISH PEOPLE

Jews ardently love Jerusalem and in every age venerate her memory, abundant as she is in many remains and monuments from the time of David, who chose her as the capital, and of Solomon, who built the Temple there. Therefore, they turn their minds to her daily, one may say, and point to her as the sign of their nation.... For the Jewish people who live in the State of Israel and who preserve in the land such precious testimonies to their history and their faith, we must ask for the desired security and the due tranquillity that is the prerogative of every nation and condition of life and of progress for every society.

> *From a papal letter issued in 1984.*

PRAYING TO ONE GOD

I can vividly remember the Jews who gathered every Saturday at the synagogue behind our school. Both religious groups, Catholics and Jews, were united, I presume, by the awareness that they pray to the same God.

> *From his* Crossing the Threshold of Hope *(1994).*

CHRISTIANITY'S ELDER BROTHER

The Second Vatican Council's Declaration *Nostra Aetate* is the result of the Catholic Church's reflections on this relationship. The Council contributed greatly to the development of the awareness that the children of Israel are our "elder brothers."

Ibid.

CHERISHING SIGNIFICANT RELATIONSHIPS

On my pastoral journeys around the world I always try to meet representatives of the Jewish community. But a truly exceptional experience for me was certainly my visit to the synagogue of Rome. The history of the Jews in Rome is a unique chapter in the history of the Jewish people.

Ibid.

MESSAGE OF AUSCHWITZ

Auschwitz, perhaps the most meaningful symbol of the Holocaust of the Jewish people, shows to what lengths a system constructed on principles of racial hatred and greed for power can go. To this day, Auschwitz does not cease to admonish, reminding us that anti-Semitism is a great sin against humanity, that all racial hatred inevitably leads to the trampling of human dignity.

Ibid.

ELECTED PEOPLE

This extraordinary people continues to bear signs of its divine election. I said this to an Israeli politician once and he readily agreed, but was quick to add: "If only it could cost less!" Israel has truly paid a high price for its "election."

Ibid.

ALL GOD'S CHILDREN

Why? Aren't we all God's children?

His response, as a youth, to his friend Jerzy Kluger, who came to visit him in church after a woman expressed surprise at seeing a Jewish boy there. From Gian Franco Svidercoschi's Letter to a Jewish Friend *(1994).*

COHABITING WITH THE JEWS

A man lives events on the basis of his own experiences. I belong to that generation for whom cohabitation with the Jews, the Israelites, was a fact of everyday life.

From a statement made in June 1991, in Warsaw, to the representatives of the Polish Jewish community.

□

Lyndon B. Johnson

LOST AND FOUND

You have lost a good friend, but you have found a better one in me.

Remarks to a Jewish delegation that called upon the President after John Kennedy's assassination on November 22, 1963.

THE SIX-DAY WAR PROGNOSTICATION

My generals are always right about other people's wars and often wrong about ours.

Spoken to Abba Eban in the White House Oval Office a few months after the June 1967 Six-Day War. The president reminded Eban of the earlier evaluation of the Pentagon, which was that if war broke out, Israel would be victorious in less than seven days.

□

Paul Johnson

PURPOSE AND DESTINY

No people has ever insisted more firmly than the Jews that history has a purpose and humanity a destiny.

From his History of the Jews *(1987).*

JUDENREIN

The world without Jews would have been a radically different place.

Ibid.

JEWS ARE STILL IN HEBRON

When the historian visits Hebron today, he asks himself: Where are all those peoples which once held the place? Where are the Canaanites? Where are the Edomites? Where are the ancient Hellenes and the Romans, the Byzantines, the Franks, the Mameluks and the Ottomans? They have vanished into time, irrevocably. But the Jews are still in Hebron.

Ibid.

HISTORY OF THE JEWS

When I was working on my *History of Christianity*, I became aware for the first time in my life of the magnitude of the debt Christianity owes to Judaism. It was not, as I had been taught to suppose, that the New Testament replaced the Old; rather, that Christianity gave a fresh interpretation to an ancient form of monotheism, gradually evolving into a different religion but carrying with it much of the moral and dogmatic theology, the liturgy, the institutions and the fundamental concepts of its forebear.

Ibid. From the Prologue.

DOCTORING THE TRUTH

The need to avert the face from the Jewish facts led her [Lillian Hellman] to doctor truth with fiction. As late as 1955 she was associated with a dramatization of *The Diary of Anne Frank* that virtually eliminated the Jewish element in the tragedy.

> *Criticizing Hellman's sanitizing of Anne's character by an attempt to universalize her.*

¤

Richard Mentor Johnson

THE FOURTH COMMANDMENT

We are aware that a variety of sentiment exists among the good citizens of this nation on the subject of the Sabbath day; and our government is designed for the protection of one as much as for another. The Jews, who in this country are as free as Christians, and entitled to the same protection from the laws, derived their obligation to keep the Sabbath day from the Fourth Commandment of their decalogue and, in conformity with that injunction, pay religious homage to the seventh day of the week, which we call Saturday. One denomination of Christians among us, justly celebrated for their piety, and certainly as good citizens as any other class, agree with the Jews in the moral obligation of the Sabbath and observe the same day.

> *From "The Sunday Mail Report," presented to the United States Senate on January 19, 1829. Reprinted in* Selected Addresses and Papers of Simon Wolf *(1926).*

¤

Al Jolson

MISTER HARDING

> Harding, You're the Man for us.
> We think the country's ready
> For another man like Teddy.
> We need another Lincoln
>   To do the country's thinkin'
>   Mist-er Hard-ding
>   You're the man for us.

A campaign song he wrote and sang in 1919, electioneering for Warren G. Harding, the Republican candidate for the presidency facing James M. Cox.

¤

(Rabbi) Jonathan

VALUE OF A GOOD DEED

Whoever performs one good deed [*mitzva*] in this world [can expect that it will] precede him on his journey to the world-to-come...and whoever commits one transgression in this world, it will cling to him until the Day of Judgment.

> *The aphorism is ascribed to Rabbi Jonathan by Rabbi Samuel ben Nachmani in the talmudic tractate Sota (3b).*

¤

Jonathan ben Joseph

ON IGNORANCE

Who is ignorant? He who does not educate his children.

> *Quoted in the talmudic tractate Sota (22a).*

¤

Leroi Jones

ON BEING A GOOD JEWISH-AMERICAN

Mainstream American literature is characterized by the Jewish intelligence right now. They have evolved so that the thrust of their energy is stable enough to define itself reflectively. Their work reflects the struggle and the thrust of a group breaking into the mainstream America. Theirs is still a psychological struggle, how to be a good Jewish American or, now that I am a Jew and in the mainstream, what does that mean.

As for black literature, it must function to bring us to an awareness that we are who we are—that is a weak, powerless, enslaved people—or it must give us the energy or the spirit to do something about our situation.

> *From his* Raise Race Rays Raze *(1971).*

¤

Erica Jong

BEWARE OF THE MAN

Beware of the man who wants to protect you; he will protect you from everything but himself.... Beware of the man who denounces his mother; he is a son of a bitch.

> *From her essay "Seventeen Warnings in Search of a Feminist Poem."*

THE BOOK I HAD TO WRITE

I never *dreamed* it would find a wide audience. It seemed to me the book I *had* to write whether it was ever published or not.... For the first time I was writing as if my life depended on it, and to some extent it did.

> *Remarked during a lecture at Hofstra College after her* Fear of Flying *was published (1973).*

THE TRAIL OF TALENT

Everyone has talent. What is rare is the courage to follow the talent to the dark place where it leads.

Quoted in William Packard's Craft of Poetry *(1974).*

SEEKING ADVICE

Advice is what we ask for when we really know the answer but wish we didn't.

From her How to Save Your Own Life *(1977).*

THE RHYTHM OF DIVORCE

There is rhythm to the enduring of a marriage just like the rhythm of a courtship—only backward. You try to start again but get into blaming over and over. Finally, you are both worn out, exhausted, hopeless.

Ibid.

(Rabbi) Jose

A TIME FOR ANGER

Do not try to placate a person when he is in the heat of anger.

Quoted in the talmudic tractate Berachot (7a) in the name of Rabbi Yochanan.

BORN AGAIN

One who has become a convert to Judaism is like a child newly born.

Expressing the point that all of his previous sins (as an idolater) are forgiven. Quoted in the talmudic tractate Yevamot (22a).

Czarny Josef

I AM AUTHENTIC

Had I known that such a thing would happen, I wouldn't have taken upon myself and stood up in court in Jerusalem. It's very painful. You have no idea how painful. I never imagined.

I am not an expert on all these things. Only I, I Czarny Josef. Am I not authentic? Am I not authentic? Am I not authentic? I am authentic.

Response to his testimony, given at the Jerusalem trial of John Demjanjuk, that the man on trial was Ivan the Terrible, the sadistic guard at the Nazis' Treblinka death camp. Josef exploded when on July 29, 1993 the Israeli Supreme Court overturned the conviction and death sentence of Demjanjuk because new evidence that had been obtained from Soviet archives cast doubt on whether this Ivan (Russian for John) was actually Ivan the Terrible.

(Rabbi) Joseph

ASSIGNING BLAME

It is not the mouse that is the thief; the hole [from which it emerges] is the thief.

Quoted in the talmudic tractate Gittin (45a). To which his colleague Rabbi Abbaye responded: "If there were no mouse, what could the hole accomplish?"

Jacob Joseph

KEEPING VOTERS HONEST

The laws of the country must be obeyed even as are religious laws. Hence it is our duty to admonish all our brethren who are not legally entitled to vote, to keep away from the voting places.

A proclamation issued on November 16, 1888.

TURNING THE OTHER CHEEK

Those who oppose my regulations [governing *shechita*] that animals are to be treated with humane consideration, it is a question of business with them, a question of gaining a livelihood.... Believe me, I have not the least sense of resentment in my heart for all the evil they speak and publish against me.

Expressing understanding and a forgiveness towards those in rebellion, in 1888, against his newly issued rules governing ritual slaughtering.

Morris Joseph

ESSENCE OF PASSOVER

Passover has a message for the conscience and the heart of all mankind. For what does it commemorate? It commemorates the deliverance of a people from degrading slavery, from most foul and cruel tyranny. And so, it is Israel's—nay, God's protest against unrighteousness, whether individual or national. Wrong, it declares, may triumph for a time, but even though it be perpetrated by the strong on the weak, it will meet with its inevitable retribution at last.

In his Judaism as Creed and Life *(1903).*

SOUL AS A STATE OF BEING

Heaven is not a place, for the liberated soul knows neither place nor time. It is a state of being. Its joys are not the sordid joys of the senses, for the senses perish with the body. They are the joys of the spirit. The bliss of being near God...that is heaven.

Ibid.

A Man's Worth

The divine test of a man's worth is not his theology but his life.

Ibid.

When God Is No God

God has not made the world and left it to its fate. Exalted above the heavens, He yet takes a deep and loving interest in human joys and sorrows. It is impossible to think otherwise. The Supreme Being is bound by his own nature to care for His handiwork. An unsympathizing God is no God.

Ibid.

The Jews' Affirmation

It is in no arrogant temper that we claim to be the chosen people. We thereby affirm, not that we are better than others, but that we ought to be better.

Ibid.

Passover Message

Passover affirms the great truth that liberty is the inalienable right of every human being.

Ibid.

The Seal of a Jew

Judaism is something more than a badge, something more than a birthmark; it is a life. To be born a Jew does not declare any of us to be of the elect; it only designates us for enrollment among the elect. God signs the covenant, but we have to seal it—to seal it by a life of service.

Ibid.

Mankind's Creed

While Judaism in its entirety is for the Jew, its creed and its ethics are for mankind.

Ibid.

Self-control and Self-sacrifice

It ought to be the pride of the modern Jew and every child should be taught to feel it—that his religion demands from him a self-abnegation from which other religionists are absolved; that the price to be paid for the privilege of belonging to the hierarchy of Israel is continuous and conscious self-sacrifice.

Quoted in J. H. Hertz's Pentateuch and Haftorahs *(1961).*

The Price of Intermarriage

Every Jew who contemplates marriage outside the pale must regard himself as paving the way to a disruption which would be the final, as it would be the culminating disaster in the history of his people.

Ibid.

Peace: A Jewish Ideal

There are worse things, it is true, than war; but the worst of them is the belief that war is indispensable. Such a belief is fatal to the ultimate establishment of universal peace. The Jew who is true to himself will labour with especial energy in the cause of peace. The war-loving Jew is a contradiction in terms. Only the peace-loving Jew is a true follower of his Prophets.

Ibid.

ם

Flavius Josephus

Pride in Jewish Law

We possess a code excellently designed to promote piety, friendly relations...and humanity toward the world, besides justice, hardihood and contempt of death.

From his Against Apion *(first century C.E.).*

Essential Task

Above all we [the Jews] pride ourselves on the education of our children, and regard as the most essential task in life the observance of our laws.

Ibid.

Outstretched Hand

To all who desire to come and live under the same laws with us, our lawgiver gives a gracious welcome.

Ibid.

The Reward That Counts

The reward of such as live exactly according to the laws is not silver or gold, not a garland of olive branches or of smallage, nor any such public sign of commendation; but every good man is content with the witness that his own conscience bears him.

Ibid.

Respectful of Tradition

Never may I live to become so abject a captive as to abjure my race or forget the traditions of my forefathers!

From his Jewish War *(first century C.E.).*

SIMPLE MAN

Moses bore himself as a simple commoner, who desired in nothing to appear different from the crowd, save only in being seen to have their interests at heart.

From his Antiquities *(first century C.E.).*

JEWISH LAW

Though we be deprived of our wealth, of our cities, or of other advantages we have, our laws [Torah] continue immortal.

Quoted in the Preface to Louis Ginzberg's Legends of the Jews *(1909).*

ON MINGLING SPECIES

Nature does not rejoice in the union of things that are not in their nature alike.

Commenting on the biblical law relating to shaatnez (the mixing of species). Quoted in J. H. Hertz's Pentateuch and Haftorahs *(1961).*

□

Joshua

THE DAY THE SUN STOOD STILL

Stand still, O sun, at Gibeon,
O moon in the valley of Aijalon.

Asking for the Lord to prolong the day so that the Israelites might defeat the Amorites in battle (Joshua 10:12).

□

Joshua ben Chananya

A SEASONING CALLED SABBATH

We have a certain seasoning, called Sabbath, which lends an unusual flavor to our dishes; but it works only for him who observes the Sabbath.

From the talmudic tractate Shabbat (119a).

RIGHTEOUS GENTILES

Righteous Gentiles have a share in the world-to-come.

Quoted in the Tosefta, Sanhedrin (13:2).

□

Joshua ben Karcha

MAN'S GLORY

The glory of a face is its beard.

Quoted in the talmudic tractate Shabbat (152a).

PEACE THROUGH ARBITRATION

Settlement by arbitration is a meritorious act.... Surely, where there is strict justice there is no peace, and where there is peace there is no strict justice. But what is the kind of justice with which peace abides? We must answer: arbitration.

Implying that the strict application of the law does not always set both parties to peace. Quoted in the talmudic tractate Sanhedrin (6b).

THE LOWLY THORNBUSH

No place is devoid of God's presence, not even a thornbush.

Quoted in Midrash Exodus Rabba (2:5). In answer to the question, "Why did God choose a thornbush from which to speak to Moses?"

□

Joshua ben Levi

ETERNAL ISRAEL

As an olive tree does not lose its foliage in summer or winter, so Israel will never be lost, here or hereafter.

Quoted in the talmudic tractate Menachot (53b).

THE VALUE OF PEACE

Great is peace. Peace is to the world as leaven is to dough.

Quoted in the minor talmudic tractate Derech Eretz Zuta, final chapter.

RELIVING THE REVELATION

If any man teaches his son Torah, it is as if he had received it from Mount Sinai. For it is said, when you make the words of Torah known to your children and children's children, it is like the day that you stood before the Lord your God in Horeb.

Quoted in the talmudic tractate Berachot (21b).

A HEAVENLY VOICE SPEAKS

A heavenly voice proclaims daily from Mt. Horeb: Woe to men who scorn the Torah!

Quoted in the talmudic tractate Ethics of the Fathers (6:2).

INCONSISTENCIES OF HALACHA

The *halacha* [religious law] would not be a true mirror of Jewish life if it were free from all logical inconsistencies.

Ibid.

◘

(Rabbi) Josiah

ADVICE TO JUDGES

If the judgment you are about to pronounce is as clear to you as the morning light, deliver it; if not, be silent.

Quoted in the talmudic tractate Sanhedrin (7b).

◘

(Dr.) Jossy

DEATH OF A HERO

Officer Yoni, leader of the rescue and the only fatality, was brought to us literally in death throes. There was nothing we could do for him apart from covering his body in a quiet corner in order to preserve his dignity and prevent further suffering among the hostages who were with us.

Reporting on the death of Lieutenant Colonel Jonathan Netanyahu, who led the July 4, 1976 Entebbe raid in Uganda. From an interview in the spring of 1977 reported in Frank Epp's Israelis: Portrait of a People in Conflict *(1980).*

A TEMPORARY HIGH

At the time of a historic mission like this [the Entebbe raid], your morale goes up; but it doesn't stay up for a long time; it goes back to some sort of base line. I would liken it perhaps to the difference between the qualities of steel and iron. If you try to magnetize steel, it's very difficult, but once it's magnetized it holds. Iron, on the other hand, is very easy to magnetize, but it loses its magnetization quickly. We can compare the people of Israel to the bar which becomes quickly electrified, and very soon afterwards drops back to normal. Maybe we've had too many immunizations. Maybe.

Ibid.

◘

James Joyce

IRELAND'S INFAMOUS ACCOMPLISHMENT

Ireland has the honor of being the only country which never persecuted the Jews.... Because she never let them in.

From his Ulysses *(1914).*

◘

Judah

A BROTHER'S PLEA

Please let your servant remain as a slave to my lord instead of the boy, and let the boy go back with his brothers.

Pleading with his brother Joseph to release Benjamin, who had been arrested for "stealing" Joseph's goblet. Quoted in the Book of Genesis (44:33).

◘

Judah bar Ila'i

THE POWER OF CHARITABLE ACTS

Rock is strong
But iron shatters it.
Fire melts iron;
Water extinguishes fire;
Clouds carry away water,
And wind drives away clouds;
Man can withstand the wind,
But fear conquers man;
Wine dispels fear,
But sleep overcomes wine.
And death rules over sleep.
But more powerful than all ten
Are sweet acts of charity and lovingkindness.

After having witnessed the martyrdom of his beloved teacher Rabbi Akiba, who was put to death by the Romans.

LITERAL TRANSLATIONS

If one translates a verse literally, he is a liar; and if he embellishes upon it, he is a blasphemer and a libeler.

Quoted in the talmudic tractate Kiddushin (49a).

SAND AND STARS

These people have been compared to sand and stars: when they fall, they fall as low as the sand, and when they rise as high as the sky.

Quoted in the talmudic tractate Megilla (16a).

◘

Judah ben Tema

BE EAGER TO DO GOD'S WILL

Be bold as a leopard, swift as an eagle, fleet as a deer, and strong as a lion to do the will of your Father in Heaven.

Quoted in the talmudic tractate Ethics of the Fathers (5:22).

▢

Judah the Prince

MAN UNDER SURVEILLANCE

Be aware of three things and you will not fall into sin. Know what is above you: a seeing eye and a hearing ear, and [never forget] all your deeds are recorded in a book.

Quoted in the talmudic tractate Ethics of the Fathers (2:2).

PREPARING FOR LIFE

If one does not teach his son an occupation, it is as if he teaches him thievery.

Quoted in the talmudic tractate Kiddushin (30b).

SELF-DISCIPLINE

Although I am lenient with others, I am strict with myself.

Quoted in the talmudic tractate Berachot (22a).

A BLESSING FOR SPRING

If one goes out in the days of Nissan [springtime] and sees the trees sprouting, he should say: "Blessed is He who has allowed nothing to be lacking in His world, and has created so many good creations such as trees, which bring enjoyment to mankind."

Quoted in the talmudic tractate Berachot (43b).

KING OF ISRAEL

David, king of Israel, is alive and full of vigor.

The phrase used to signal the beginning of the New Month. From the talmudic tractate Rosh Hashana (25a).

REWARD FOR SABBATH OBSERVANCE

He who keeps one Sabbath properly is accounted as if he had observed all the Sabbaths from Creation to the Resurrection.

Quoted in the Midrash Mechilta on Exodus (31:13).

LEARNING FROM PUPILS

I learned much from my teachers, more from my colleagues, and most from my pupils.

Quoted in the talmudic tractate Taanit (7a).

THE POWER OF CHARITY

Great is charity for it brings Redemption closer.

Quoted in the talmudic tractate Bava Batra (10a).

▢

Leo Jung

THE END OF THE MATTER

One day, sooner or later, you and I will be called away and what will matter, beyond tears and shock, is that we have somebody worthy, able and willing to take our place.

From his sermon in Best Jewish Sermons of 5713 (1953), edited by Saul I. Teplitz.

LIFE IS PURPOSEFUL

We Jews believe that there is nothing accidental in the cosmos, nor in the history of mankind. There should be nothing accidental or careless in our conduct.

Ibid.

Farouk Kaddoumi

THE ULTIMATE AIM

There is no way that we will relinquish one grain of the Palestinian land. We will not rest until the occupiers are thrown out.

Comment made after the PLO took control of Gaza and Jericho in 1994.

□

Pauline Kael

JEWS HAVE NO DIGNITY

For [Woody Allen] Jewishness means his own kind of schlumpiness, awkwardness, hesitancy.... In Woody Allen's films Jews have no dignity. That's just about how he defines them and why he's humiliated by them.

Commenting on Woody Allen as the quintessential self-hating Jew. From an article in The New Yorker, *October 27, 1980.*

□

Franz Kafka

GREAT TRANSFORMATION

As Gregor Samsa awoke one morning from uneasy dreams, he found himself transformed in his bed into a gigantic insect.

From his Metamorphosis *(1915).*

PRIVATE ENTRANCE

No one else could ever be admitted here, since this gate was made only for you. I am now going to shut it.

From his Parables and Paradoxes *(1946).*

SOURCE OF SIN

We are sinful not merely because we have eaten of the Tree of Knowledge, but also because we have not yet eaten of the Tree of Life.

Ibid.

THE MESSIAH'S ARRIVAL

The Messiah will come only when he is no longer necessary; he will come only on the day after his arrival; he will come, not on the last day, but on the very last.

Ibid.

THE WORLD AT YOUR FEET

You do not have to leave the room
Remain standing at your table and listen.
Do not even listen, simply wait.
Do not even wait.
Be quite still and solitary.
The world will freely offer itself to you.
To be unmasked.
It has no choice
It will roll in ecstasy at your feet.

Ibid.

WARDING OFF DESPAIR

Anyone who cannot cope with life while he is alive needs one hand to ward off a little of his despair over his fate...but with his other hand he can jot down what he sees among the ruins, for he sees different and more things than the others; after all, he is dead in his own lifetime and the real survivor.

Ibid.

HESITATION BEFORE BIRTH

If there is a transmigration of souls, then I am not yet on the bottom rung. My life is a hesitation before birth.

From the Diaries of Franz Kafka, *January 24, 1922 entry.*

TORMENTED

Not one calm second is granted to the Western Jew. Everything has to be earned, not only the present and the future but also the past—something after all which perhaps every human being has inherited—this too must be earned; it is perhaps the hardest work.

Ibid.

NEED FOR A PERMANENT FAITH

Man cannot live without a permanent faith in something indestructible in himself.

Quoted in Masoret *magazine, Fall 1993.*

NOT NOT-JEWISH

[She is] a common and yet astounding phenomenon. Not Jewish and yet not not-Jewish, not German and yet not not-German, crazy about the movies, about operettas and comedies, covers her face with powder and veils, possesses an inexhaustible and nonstop store of the brashest Yiddish expressions, in general very ignorant, more cheerful than sad—that is about what she is like.

Describing Julie Wohryzek, the new young lady who has entered his life in 1919, in a letter to his friend Max Brod. From his Letters to Friends, Family, and Editors *(1977).*

CONCERNS OF WOMEN

It is strange how little sharpsightedness women possess; they only notice whether they please, then whether they arouse pity, and finally, whether you look for compassion from them. That is all; come to think of it, it may even be enough, generally speaking.

Ibid. Reacting negatively to Brod who, in a communication, wrote about "real girls."

THE EFFECT OF MARRIAGE

There were separate obstacles, as there always are, but then life consists in facing such obstacles.... This manifests itself in the fact that from the moment I make up my mind to marry I can no longer sleep, my head burns day and night, life can no longer be called life, I stagger about in despair.

Explaining to his father why he did not marry. From Letter to His Father *(1953).*

WHAT IS LOVE

Love is everything that enhances, widens, and enriches our life.

From his Letters to Felice *(1967).*

INNER TURMOIL

A torrent of anxiety descends upon me continually. What I want one minute I don't want the next. When I have reached the top of the stairs, I still don't know the state I will be in when I enter the apartment.... My memory is very bad, but even the best of memories could not help me to write down accurately even a short paragraph which I have thought out in advance and tried to memorize.

Ibid.

MAN OF LETTERS

I consist of literature and am unable to think of anything else.

Describing his life and career before dying of cancer on June 3, 1924.

ABSENCE OF COMMONALITY

What do I have in common with the Jews? I hardly have anything in common with myself and ought to go and stand quietly in a corner grateful that I can breathe.

In a letter to Max Brod. Quoted in Franz Kafka: Letters From 1902 to 1924, *edited by Max Brod.*

LOSS OF FOOTING

To get away from Judaism is what most of those who began to write in German wanted, usually with the vague approval of their fathers (this vagueness was an infuriating thing); that is what they wanted, but with their little back legs they were glued to the Judaism of their fathers, and their little front legs could find no new footing. Their despair over this was their inspiration.

Ibid.

BOOKS WORTH READING

I believe that the only books worth reading are the ones that bite and sting. If the book we are reading does not wake us up with a blow to the head, what are we reading it for?

Ibid.

THE VEGETARIAN

Now I can look at you in peace; I don't eat you anymore.

While viewing fish at an aquarium. Quoted in Richard Schwartz's Judaism and Vegetarianism *(1988).*

¤

Israel Meir Kagan

DARKNESS BEFORE DAWN

Despair not. It is darkest before dawn.... Before light was created, all was darkness "upon the face of the deep."

From his Chafetz Chaim *(1873). Quoted in M. M. Yoshor's* Saint and Sage *(1937).*

SECRET OF LONGEVITY

All my life I taught the message of the Psalmist, and I tried to practice what I preached. I was careful with the use of my tongue, and I urged others to do likewise. This was a prescription for a long life. I feared that if I were to die young I would prove the Psalmist wrong. I would have not proved that one can prolong one's life by the use of proper speech. Now that I have been blessed to reach age 80, I need fear no longer.

Responding to disciples who questioned why he wanted them to make a party for him on his eightieth birthday.

LIFE IS NEVER BAD

Never say that life is bad or life is hopeless, my son. When one is ill and the doctor prescribes a medicine, the medicine may be bitter, but it is not bad. It is meant to cure the sick. Life may sometimes be very bitter, but it is never bad.

The response to a man who complained that his life was terribly bad and completely useless.

ᴑ

Meir Kahane

ON EXPELLING ARABS

I have a program in which I call for the transfer of Arabs out of Israel. Give me the power and I'll take care of them by transferring them out of Israel—which is another way of saying expulsion!...In 1945 the Poles and the Czechs transferred—expelled, threw out—12 million ethnic Germans from Silesia, the Sudetenland, Danzig and so on. It was ratified at Potsdam; it's part of international law today. Truman, Attlee, Stalin—nobody said anything about that. I have no intention of losing my country to Arab bullets or Arab babies.

In an interview with Walter Reich in Moment magazine, January–February 1985.

SECULAR ZIONISM AND THE JEWISH STATE

Secular, political Zionism came into being to create a Jewish state. A Jewish state means, at the least, a state with a majority of Jews.... You can have a democratic state or you can have a Jewish state or you can have an Arab state, but you can't have a democratic Jewish state.

Ibid.

IDEALISTS AT WORK

I once asked Begin how he felt when he learned that thirty or forty Jews were killed in the bombing of the King David Hotel [during the British Palestine Mandate years]. Begin told me he felt horrible. That's exactly how I felt after the Hurok bombing.

When asked how he felt about his Jewish Defense League's 1972 bombing of the office of impresario Sol Hurok, who had been a major promoter of Soviet musical talent. A young Jewish secretary was killed in the blast.

ᴑ

Madeline Kahn

LOVE AND THE FUNNY WOMAN

Men don't feel comfortable being romantic with a funny woman.

Explaining why her love-life suffered. Quoted in Darryl Lyman's Jewish Comedy Catalog (1989).

ᴑ

Bernard Kalb

BREAKING THE FAST

It's just absolutely the most marvelous party in town.

Commenting on the gathering at Helene and William (Bill) Safire's house in the Washington suburb of Chevy Chase on Wednesday night October 4, 1995, after the Yom Kippur fast. These gatherings, which started twenty-three years ago, brought together Supreme Court Justice Stephen G. Breyer, Clinton advisor Richard Morris, and scores of other political celebrities.

ᴑ

Carmela Efros Kalmanson

UNITING BODY AND SOUL

I can only speak for myself, but my tie to the Jewish state is such that when it is threatened physically, I feel threatened emotionally. The only way I know to unite body and soul, to make myself feel whole, is to go to Israel.

In reaction to Iraq's launching of SCUD missiles into Israel during the 1991 Gulf War. Quoted in Hadassah Magazine, March 1991.

ᴑ

Kalonymos ben Kalonymos

BURDEN UPON BURDEN

Cursed be he who told my father the news...a son is born to you. Woe to him whose children are males. What a grievous yoke awaits them. Whole armies of prohibitions and commandments lie in wait for them—all the 613 commandments, positive and negative. Who can fulfill all these? No man, no matter how diligent he may be, can withstand whole regiments. It is impossible to save oneself. One remains a sinner and lawbreaker.

From his fourteenth-century social satire Even Bochan ("Testing Stone"). Quoted in Max Dimont's Jews in America (1978).

□

Kalonymos ben Yehuda

DEATH RATHER THAN BAPTISM

Yea, they slay us and they smite,
Vex our souls with sore affright;
All the closer cleave we, Lord,
To thine everlasting word.
Not a line of all their Mass
Shall our lips in homage pass;
Though they curse, and bind, and kill,
The living God is with us still.
We still are Thine, though limbs are torn;
Better death than life forsworn.
From dying lips the accents swell,
"Thy God is One, O Israel";
And bridegroom answers unto bride,
"The Lord is God, and none beside,"
And, knit with bonds of holiest faith,
They pass to endless life through death.

> *Composed after the Crusader massacre
> of the Jews of Xanten, near the Rhine, on
> June 27, 1096. Quoted in J. H. Hertz's*
> Pentateuch and Haftorahs *(1961).*

□

Immanuel Kant

NATION OF SWINDLERS

The Jews cannot claim any true genius, any truly great man. All their talents and skills revolve around stratagems and low cunning.... They are a nation of swindlers.

> *Quoted in Alan Dershowitz's* Chutzpah *(1991).*

□

Aryeh Kaplan

GIVING THOUGHT TO YOUR THOUGHTS

It is strange that most people have never given a thought to their thoughts. Thoughts are so much part of our being that we take them for granted. One of the first steps in meditation is learning how not to take our thoughts for granted.

> *From his* Jewish Meditation: A Practical
> Guide *(1985).*

DISCOVERING GOD

As you continue to explore what is most meaningful to you, you may come to a point where you feel that you are reaching a new threshold. You may find yourself pondering not only the meaning of your own life, but the very meaning of existence in general.

At this point, you will have discovered God.

> *Ibid.*

GOD IS "IN THERE"

We often think of God as being "out there," far away from the world. But it is important to realize that God is also "in there"—in the deepest recesses of the soul.

> *Ibid.*

THE SPIRITUAL SIDE OF FOOD

The most important discipline of Judaism involves the *blessing*. When a blessing is recited before eating, then the act itself becomes a spiritual undertaking. Through the blessing, the act of eating becomes a contemplative exercise. Just as one can contemplate a flower or a melody, one can contemplate the act of eating.

> *Ibid.*

□

Chaim Kaplan

APPEAL TO THE LEADER

Can the world sit silent? Will evil always be triumphant? O Leader of the world, where are You? But He who sits in heaven laughs.

> *Reacting to a law in mid-1940 demanding
> complete confinement to the ghetto area.*

WARSAW GHETTO PASSOVER I

The synagogues are closed, but in every courtyard there is a [Passover] holiday service, and cantors sing the prayers and hymns in their sweet voices. In every home the signs of the holiday are manifest.... The people run around carrying packages of *matzah* as if the sword of sabotage were not hovering over their heads.

> *Describing the resourcefulness of Jews in the
> ghetto who were celebrating the first Passover
> on April 24, 1940. From his secret diary
> (which he kept in Hebrew) that was published
> in 1966 under the name* Scroll of Agony.

WARSAW GHETTO PASSOVER II

We are faced with a Passover of hunger and poverty, without even "the bread of affliction." For eating and drinking there is neither *matzah* or wine. For prayer there are no synagogues or houses of study.

> *Ibid. Describing the 1941 Passover in the
> Warsaw Ghetto.*

HISTORICAL MISSION

Some of my friends and acquaintances who know the secret of my diary urge me, in their despair, to stop writing.... I feel that continuing this diary to the very end of my physical and spiritual strength is a historical mission which must not be abandoned.

> *Ibid.*

¤
Deborah B. Kaplan
PASSING THE TORCH

I worry at least as much as the next Jewish mother, but I look at my children and grand-children with a sense of faith, and an unsaid prayer, that the Jewish people will endure.... My concern is not just Jewish survival, but the kind of Jewish world we will pass on to the next generations.

In her June–July 1993 President's Column in Hadassah Magazine.

¤
Louis Kaplan
THE NEW FACE OF FUNDAMENTALISM

I am deeply troubled by the resurgence of fundamentalism in Judaism and Christianity. These may and will be modulated in time, but secularism and liberalism have lost even more of their attractiveness, as they have failed to deliver on their promises.

From The Jewish Spectator, Winter 1978.

THE LEVERAGE OF FATE AND FAITH

Our historic experience is long enough to *disabuse* us of the illusion of continuous, uninterrupted progress. It also should immunize us against the views of *defeatism*. Naive optimism and/or despair are not what Jewish history and especially our present situation *demand of us*. We must be realists whose faith in man and in God the Creator of all will enable us to cope with the evil in the world and with our own frailties. The world needs the leverage our *fate* and *faith can provide*.

Ibid. Spring 1978.

¤
Mordecai M. Kaplan
WAITING FOR THE TRUTH

We cannot afford to wait with our health until we know the final truth about our bodies and minds. Neither can we afford to wait with our ethical and spiritual health until we know the ultimate truth about the world and God.

From his Not So Random Thoughts (1966).

NOT A VETO

The ancient authorities are entitled to a vote—but not to a veto.

Ibid.

RELIGIOUS MATURITY

It is a sign of childishness to accept the great religious myths as literal truths, a sign of adolescence to regard them as delusion, and a sign of maturity to appreciate their spiritual implications.

Ibid.

TAKING THE BIBLE SERIOUSLY

The foremost problem in Jewish religion is how to get Jews to take the Bible seriously without taking it literally.

Ibid.

RELIGION IN ACTION

People whose religion begins and ends with worship and ritual practices are like soldiers forever maneuvering but never getting into action.

Ibid.

KEEPING THE HOLY HOLY

Those to whom every inherited folly is holy are mainly to blame for there being so many to whom everything holy is folly.

Ibid.

AIM OF THE TORAH

The difference between our Torah and other ancient and modern law codes is that the chief aim of those law codes is to establish law and order in society, whereas the chief aim of the Torah is to enable man to become fully human.

Ibid.

SEEKERS OF GOD

We shall not come to experience the reality of God unless we go in search of Him. To be seekers of God, we have to depend more upon our own thinking and less upon tradition. Instead of acquiescing passively in the traditional belief that there is a God, and deducing from that belief conclusions which are to be applied to human experience and conduct, we must accustom ourselves to find God in the complexities of our experience and behavior.... Only by way of participation in human affairs and strivings are we to seek God.

From his Meaning of God in Modern Jewish Religion (1962).

THE POWER BEHIND SALVATION

When we believe in God, we believe that reality—the world of inner and outer being, the world of society and nature—is so constructed as to enable man to achieve salvation.

Ibid.

GOD AS A PROCESS

Modern scientific and philosophic thought regards all reality not as something static but as energy in action. When we say that God is Process, we select, out of the infinity of processes in the universe, that complex of forces and relationships which makes for the highest fulfillment of man as a human being, and identify it by the term *God*. In exactly the same way, we select, among all the forces and relationships that enter into the life of the individual, those which make for his highest fulfillment and identify them by the term person. *God* and *person* are thus correlative terms, the meaning of each being relative to and dependent on that of the other, like *parent* and *child, teacher* and *pupil, citizen* and *state. God is the Process by which the Universe produces persons, and persons are the Processes by which God is manifest in the individual.*

> From his Questions Jews Ask *(1956).*

IMPLICATION OF JEWISH PEOPLEHOOD

The political implication of Jewish peoplehood is the concern of Jews everywhere with the freedom, stability, and security of the State of Israel.

> *Ibid.*

GOD AS A MAGNETIC FORCE

A magnetic needle, hung on a thread or placed on a pivot, assumes of its own accord a position in which one end of the needle points north and the other south. So long as it is free to move about, all attempts to deflect it will not get it to remain away from its normal direction. Likewise, man normally veers in the direction of that which makes for the fulfillment of his destiny as a human being. That fact indicates the functioning of a cosmic Power which influences his behavior. What magnetism is to the magnetic needle, Godhood or God is to man.

> *Quoted in* Contemporary Jewish Thought, *edited by Simon Noveck.*

PURPOSE AND MEANING OF JEWISH EXISTENCE

The purpose of Jewish existence is to be a people in the image of God. The meaning of Jewish existence is to foster in ourselves as Jews, and to awaken in the rest of the world a sense of moral responsibility in action.

> *From his* Purpose and Meaning of Jewish Existence *(1964).*

ON THE FEAR OF BEING JEWS

Our emancipation will not be complete until we are free of the fear of being Jews.

> *From his* Future of the American Jew *(1948).*

THE "CHOSEN PEOPLE" CONCEPT

We...advocate the elimination from our own liturgy of all references to the doctrine of Israel as the Chosen People.

> *Ibid.*

RELIGION'S ESSENCE

The essence of religion is the human quest for salvation.

> *Ibid.*

KNOWING ONESELF

An individual is a person when and because he knows himself as such; a group is a people when and because it knows itself as such.

> *Ibid.*

RENDEZVOUS WITH DESTINY

If you have a rendezvous with destiny, be sure to come on time.

> *From* The Reconstructionist, *April 7, 1950.*

DEMANDS OF JEWISH IDENTITY

Jewish identity demands of the individual Jew that he so come to know the Jewish people, its entire history, its civilization, and its destiny as to experience the reality of its God. This God, YHWH, is that aspect of the Jewish people which renders it more than the sum of its individual, past, present, and future [parts], and gives meaning to all its virtues, sins, successes, and failures.

> *From his* If Not Now, When?, *co-authored with Arthur Cohen (1973).*

WHY REMAIN JEWS?

What the Jewish people should mean to the individual Jew may be illustrated by the famous answer given by George Malory, one of the greatest mountain climbers, when asked why he wanted to climb Everest. He simply replied, "Because it is there." Likewise when we are asked, "Why remain Jews?" the only reason we should feel called upon to give is: "Because Jewish people is here and we are part of it."

> *From his* New Zionism *(1955).*

JUDAISM AND THE STATUS QUO

Jewish religion absolutely refuses to make peace with the *status quo* which it considers as godless because, despite the outward form of law and respectability, it is based upon the rule of might and not of right.

From his Judaism as a Civilization *(1934).*

ESSENCE OF A CIVILIZATION

A civilization is not a deliberate creation. It is as spontaneous a growth as any living organism. Once it exists it can be guided and directed, but its existence must be determined by the imperative of a national tradition and the will to live as a nation. Civilization arises not out of planned cooperation but out of centuries of inevitable living, working, and striving together.

Ibid.

JUDAISM AS A PRIVILEGE

Before the beginning of the nineteenth century, all Jews regarded Judaism as a privilege. Since then, most Jews have come to regard it as a burden.

Ibid.

¤

Attar Abu Karas

UNEMPLOYED TERRORIST

Ever since the deal [between Israel and the PLO] was signed in Washington [on September 13, 1993] and Arafat renounced terrorism, I've been unemployed.

A lament by the leader of Fatah's Intifada Committee in Gaza.

¤

Menachem M. Kasher

THE BROTHERHOOD OF MAN

Ben Azzai laid down a fundamental teaching of Judaism. For in the verse quoted [Genesis 5:1], the scholar saw the basic declaration of human brotherhood: By tracing back the whole of the human race to one single ancestor, created by one God, the Bible taught that all men have *one* Creator—the heavenly Father—and *one* ancestor—the human father.

From his Encyclopedia of Biblical Interpretation *(1953).*

¤

Abraham I. Katsch

HEBRAIC IDEALISM AND THE REVOLUTIONARY WAR

It becomes clear that Moses' warning and Samuel's admonition against monarchy actu-

ated the policy of our United States, at the crossroads of colonial life during the third quarter of the eighteenth century. Hebraic idealism spurred our fathers to challenge monarchy and persuaded them to offer their blood in the Revolutionary War.

Ibid. From an essay in his Bar Mitzvah *(1955).*

REAL MEANING OF EQUALITY

To Khrushchev or any other Russian leader anti-Semitism means pogroms akin to physical extermination as done by the Nazis. Well, this is not going on in Russia today and therefore the Russian leaders are really disturbed when they are accused of Anti-semitism. They are not aware that you can have spiritual genocide as well as physical. Also, take the term "equality," to us "equality" means the right to be different and not be penalized for the difference. With them it is the reverse. Equality means the right *not* to be different, and if you are different then you are penalized for this difference.

In a 1960 dialogue with Rabbi William Berkowitz at the Institute of Adult Jewish Studies in New York. Quoted in Berkowitz's Ten Vital Jewish Issues *(1964).*

¤

Shmuel Katz

THE CHARACTER OF HAMAS

It is surely time that Washington, and indeed the West in general, awaken to the real dimensions and character of Hamas. Its methods are revolutionary and violent; it seeks to dominate the Arab world and become the leader of all Moslems. It sees itself as the flaming sword of Islam, designed to exact vengeance not only on Israel but on the West at large. It will not be long before the reach of its arms include Europe.

Commenting on the banishment from Israel of four hundred Hamas terrorists in 1992.

¤

Berl Katznelson

FOR LOVE OF HOMELAND

Our love of homeland springs from the timeless verses of the Book of Books, from the very sound of the biblical names. We loved an abstract homeland, and we planted this love in our soul and carried it with us wherever we went throughout the generations.

> Urging the rejection of the 1937 British proposal to partition the Land of Israel. Quoted in Moshe Dayan's Living with the Bible (1978).

EVALUATION OF BEN-GURION

Nobody knows Ben-Gurion's shortcomings better than I do. The man is obstinate, he has theatrical tendencies and entrenched opinions and he's like me in that he quarrels with everybody, but he's the greatest Jew that we have, straightforward, strong-minded, and a democrat to his fingertips.

> Quoted in Shimon Peres' From These Men: Seven Founders of the State of Israel (1979).

DAY OF MOURNING

Israel has always kept its day of mourning, the day of the loss of its freedom. And on this day [the ninth of Ab], in every generation, the Jew sees *himself* as the man whose world is in ruins.

> Ibid.

NO NEED TO REINVENT THE WHEEL

A generation that renews and creates things from scratch must under no circumstances reject the legacy of past generations. What is needed is to restore the ancient tradition of life and use it to strengthen this progressive generation.

> Ibid.

SIGNIFICANCE OF JEWISH HOLIDAYS

The Jewish year is thickly sown with days of far deeper significance than anything to be found in the calendars of other peoples.

> Ibid.

THE OLD HAGGADAH

I don't care for modern versions of the Haggadah. It may be that new expressions are to some extent appropriate to our times, but they detract from the primeval historical force. Words are not born in the dictionary. The dictionary confirms them. It is the past that gives them content and meaning.

> Ibid.

◘

David Kaufmann

A PASSIONATE LONGING

All the weaning of the centuries, all the enlightenment of modern times, have been un-

able to banish a longing for that land from their hearts.

> From his George Eliot and Judaism (1877).

◘

Walter Kaufmann

POWERS OF GOD

Faith in immortality, like belief in God, leaves unanswered the ancient question: Is God unable to prevent suffering, and thus not omnipotent? Or is He able and not willing it and thus not merciful? And is He just?

> After turning to Lutheranism he returned to Judaism, favoring a humanistic approach. From his Faith of a Heretic (1961).

◘

Yechezkel Kaufmann

IRRITANTS THAT BREED ENMITY

Wherever there is contact between [different] religious, ethnic, and economic groups there necessarily develop irritations and quarrels that breed enmity. As a result of the dispersion [of the Jews] the areas of contact between Israel and other peoples increased immeasurably.

> From his Hebrew classic Gola Ve-nechar (1954).

JEWISH UNIQUENESS

The great rule of history is that every people, when it lives under conditions of exile, is absorbed among its neighbours. How, then, is it possible to explain the fact that the Jewish people clung to the forms of its national existence and maintained its unique national character in spite of the natural effect of social conditions?

It was no external factor, nor even the so-called biological urge to survive, but *the special power that was latent in Israel's religious culture that was responsible for its unique place among the nations.* The true basis for its uniqueness was its religion, for the sake of which it preserved its separateness from the nations.

> Ibid. Quoted by David Ben-Gurion in his essay "Vision and Redemption," reprinted in Jews in the Modern World (1962), edited by Jacob Fried.

LIFE TO THE DEAD

The remembering of a man's name after his death brings renewed life to his soul in the world beyond. The name is a conduit which connects the two worlds, the worlds of the living and the dead. When the dead who are buried among their people and families, and their names are remembered by them, it is as though they continue to participate in life upon earth.

From his Religion of Israel (Toldot Ha-emuna Ha-Yisraelit), *1937. Quoted by Haim Gevaryahu, who lost his son Reuven in the Yom Kippur War, in his article entitled "A Name and Remembrance to the Soldiers Who Fell in the Yom Kippur War," which appeared in* Dor Le-dor *magazine, Fall 1974.*

BATTLE WITH IDOLATRY

No patriarch is charged with a prophetic mission; the first apostolic prophet is Moses. Nowhere in Genesis is there reference to a battle with idolatry. The divine covenants with the patriarchs promise personal protection and future material blessings. But they never involve a fight with idolatry, nor do the patriarchs ever appear as reproaching their contemporaries for idolatry. Indeed, there is no religious contrast between the patriarchs and their surroundings.

Ibid.

◻

Alfred Kazin

ALIENATION

I still thought of myself then as standing outside America. I read as if books would fill my every gap, remedy my every flaw, let me in at last into the great world that was anything just out of Brownsville.

Expressing his struggle to enter the greater society and escape his Brownsville (Jewish) upbringing. From his A Walker in the City *(1951).*

LIBRARY LOVE

I liked reading and working out my ideas in the midst of that endless crowd walking in and out of 315 looking for *something.*... There was something about the vibrating empty rooms early in the morning—light falling through the great tall windows, the sun burning the smooth tops of the golden tables as if they had been freshly painted—that made me restless with the need to grab up every book, press into every single mind right there on the open shelves. My book was building itself.

Recalling the time in his youth spent in the famous Reading Room (No. 315) at the 42nd Street New York Public Library. From his memoirs, New York Jew *(1978).*

SOUR RESPONSES

A dupe of intellectual pride so overweening that he is incapable of making distinctions between totalitarian and democratic societies, between oppressors and victims.

Commenting on Noam Chomsky's defense of those professors who deny the Holocaust. From his article in Dimensions, Vol. 4, No. 1 *(1988).*

JEWISH CONTRIBUTION TO AMERICA

I don't think that there has been anywhere in the history of the Jewish people anything quite like the influence that Jewish intellectuals have exerted on American culture.

Quoted in Abraham Karp's Haven and Home *(1985).*

REWARDS OF WRITING

To write is in some way to cut the seemingly automatic pattern of violence, destructiveness, and death wish. To write is to put the seeming insignificance of human existence into a different perspective. It is the need, the wish, and, please God, the ability to reorder our physical faith.

From Telling Lives: The Biographer's Art *(1981), edited by Marc Pachter.*

A FASCINATING CRITIC

[Edmund] Wilson is not like other critics; some critics are boring even when they are original; he fascinates even when he is wrong.

Quoted in Max J. Herzberg's Reader's Encyclopedia of American Literature *(1962).*

◻

Wolfe Kelman

ATTRACTION OF CONSERVATISM

I can't tell you of five Conservative rabbis who have joined the other two movements. That tells you something. After all, we're not giving away lollipops to new members.

In praise of the growth and vitality of the Rabbinical Assembly.

◻

Kemal Ataturk

THE JEWS OF TURKEY

We have in our midst faithful elements who have linked their destiny with that of the dominant element the Turkish people. Above all, the Jews, having proved their loyalty to this nation and fatherland, have led hitherto a comfortable existence and will continue in the future to live prosperously and happily.

From a February 2, 1923 statement.

◻

Jack Kemp

HARDLINE ON SYRIA

I have never trusted Hafez al-Assad. I have always been skeptical of Assad. Israel and the U.S. should be very careful and skeptical about putting their trust in Assad.... [The Syrians] should be required to get out of Lebanon before Israel has to back out of the Golan. It is a matter of good faith. They need to prove that they are part of the civilized world, and that they stopped promoting terror. They should disarm the Hezbollah.

From an interview with the Forward, *January 13, 1995, at the twentieth-anniversary commemoration in Jerusalem of the Jackson-Vanik Amendment, which linked American granting most-favored-nations status to the Soviet Union with freedom of Jewish emigration.*

THE GREATEST MITZVAH

We have to realize that many men and women around the world are still not free. The highest *mitzvah* [good deed] is to save the captive, to provide refuge, to provide hope, to provide opportunity.

From an October 1995 address to a group of supporters of the Hebrew Immigrants Aid Society (HIAS).

◻

Thomas J. Keneally

SCHINDLER'S JEWS

One of the commonest sentiments of Schindler Jews is still "I don't know why he did it." It can be said to begin with that Oskar was a gambler, was a sentimentalist who loved the transparency, the simplicity of doing good; that Oskar was by temperament an anarchist who loved to ridicule the system; and that beneath the hearty sensuality lay a capacity to be outraged by human savagery, to react to it and not to be overwhelmed. But none of this, jotted down, added up, explains the doggedness with which, in the autumn of 1944, he prepared a final haven for [the Jews who worked in his Kraków factory].

Acknowledging his inability to explain Oskar Schindler's metamorphosis "from hustling opportunist to self-disregarding savior." Quoted in a review by Stanley Kaufmann in The New Republic, *January 24, 1994.*

◻

John F. Kennedy

ISRAEL AND AMERICA

Friendship for Israel is not a partisan matter; it is a national commitment.

In an August 1960 address to the national convention of the Zionist Organization of America.

YOUTHFUL LEADERSHIP

The Jewish people, ever since David slew Goliath, have never considered youth as a barrier to leadership.

From an address to the Zionist Organization of America during his 1960 campaign for the presidency.

TO GOLDA

I think that it is quite clear that in case of any invasion, the U.S. would come to the support of Israel.

In December 1962, after a meeting in Palm Beach, Florida, with Israeli Foreign Minister Golda Meir.

TO NEW YORK'S JEWS

You know, I was elected by the Jews of New York, and I would like to do something for the Jewish people.

In a comment to David Ben-Gurion, who was visiting New York after Kennedy's razor-thin presidential victory over Richard Nixon in 1960. Quoted in Howard M. Sachar's History of the Jews in America *(1992).*

◻

Robert F. Kennedy

RACE FOR THE SENATE

There's still a deep scar for what the Church did to the Jews—it goes back to the Middle Ages. My brother was up against the same thing, but Jack's advantage in New York was that his opponent was Nixon and the Jews could not take Nixon. My opponent, on the other hand, is a man greatly admired and, from what I have seen, greatly beloved by the Jewish people. Furthermore, the Jews, since the days of the Cossacks, look with suspicion on the investigator, and that's all I've ever really been so far, an investigator and a cop.

Explaining to Harry Golden why Jews were annoyed with Golden's support of Kennedy, who was opposing Kenneth Keating in the 1964 race for New York's Senate seat. Keating was considered the Jews' best friend in Washington.

◻

Joseph Kerler

DEAR MOTHER RUSSIA

Dear land where I was cradled,
Farewell!
I leave you now,
Not like a beaten dog
Who, at a whistle or a pat,
Is pathetically ready to bound back
And wag his tail...
I go with heavy heart,
With leaden steps,
With each step
I tear away
Pieces of earth
Soaked with my blood.
I wrench my eye away
I wrench my heart away
And wish you:
Let all be well with you!

*An appeal dated November 18, 1969, sent
to the Russian folksinger Nechama Lifshitz,
who managed to leave the USSR early in
1969. Kerler was repeatedly refused an exit
visa. Quoted in the South African magazine
Jewish Affairs, January 1971.*

◻

Jerome Kern

AMERICAN MUSIC MAN

Irving Berlin has no place in American
music. He *is* American music.

*Quoted in Elinor and Robert Slater's Great
Jewish Men (1996).*

◻

Morris N. Kertzer

BENEFIT OF THE PROTESTANT REFORMATION

We Jews worry about the separation of
Church and State more than any other group.
I think we associate the established Church
with Catholicism rather than Protestantism.
You know we Jews achieved emancipation because of the Protestant Reformation. We are
here the beneficiaries of the Protestant Reformation. We became first-class citizens in the
world only because of what the Protestants
did. If there had been no Protestants, if this
were a Catholic world, you and I would still be
second-class citizens.

*In a 1960 dialogue with Rabbi William
Berkowitz at the Institute of Adult Jewish
Studies in New York. Quoted in Berkowitz's
Ten Vital Jewish Issues (1964).*

◻

Alan L. Keyes

ENEMY OF RACISM

It's a lie about claims that Jews once dominated the slave trade. It's a lie, and there's a
strange thing about such wickedness. Racism
thrives on darkness and hatefulness. Jews are
people who opposed racial hatred before it
was popular to do so.

*From an address delivered on June 26, 1994
at the twenty-first annual conference of the
American Friends of Hebrew University,
held at the Century Plaza Hotel in Los
Angeles.*

◻

Nikita S. Khrushchev

A DIRE WARNING

If Israel continues her present policy, she
will be destroyed.

*In an October 1957 conversation with
Eleanor Roosevelt, after he admitted that it
is difficult for Jews to immigrate or even visit
Israel.*

◻

Nasser al-Kidiva

JEWS ON THE WEST BANK

I have nothing against [the] religious, as I
have nothing against religious Muslims. The
problem is when they use religion as a political tool to achieve political goals.

*In addressing a group of Zionist leaders in
April 1994, he assured them that he had no
objection to Jews living on the West Bank so
long as they remain peaceful.*

◻

Jane Kinderlehrer

MAMA'S IN THE KITCHEN

Chopped liver with grated black radish,
moistened with rendered chicken fat and a
whisper of chopped onion—pure ecstasy in the
mouth. Fluffy knaidlach swimming in chicken
soup flecked with gold; hot knishes, crisp and
delicious with spicy potato, kasha or cheese
fillings; *hamantaschen* bursting with poppy
seeds or prunes; or honey-soaked *teiglach* or
creamy *kugels*—pure bliss to bite into. Mush-
room and barley soup to warm your bones;
hearty kasha *varnishkas* with hot gravy; strudel
with heavenly fruit and nut fillings. You don't
need a fiddler on the roof to tell you that these

foods spell tradition. Their very names evoke blissful memories of small kibitzers crowding around the big black stove, and a lovely warm feeling that Mama's in the kitchen and all's right with the world.

> *From her* Cooking Kosher: The Natural Way *(1980).*

ADDING NUTRITION TO TRADITION

We can make *kugels* that are kind to the arteries.

We can put a little heart in all our chopped meat dishes.

We can provide delicious nosherai we will be happy to see our families devour because every crumb contributes to health. We can make fabulous creamy, pareve desserts without resorting to that bag of chemicals called "nondairy creamer."

We can avoid dangerous additives—and save money—by making homemade salad dressings, mayonnaise, yogurt, granolas, and convenience mixes.

We can make delicious honey cakes, mandelbrodt, and strudel without sugar and hydrogenated fats.

We can avoid the hormones and antibiotics in beef by occasionally serving delicious high-protein vegetarian meals.

> *Ibid.*

Alan King

MY MOTHER, THE COOK

My mother was the worst cook in the world. Everything had to cook for four days. She never believed the butcher killed it! My mother made chicken soup with fat on the top. It used to congeal and you could skate on it!

> *From one of his comedy routines. Quoted in Darryl Lyman's* Jewish Comedy Catalog *(1989).*

JEWISH SYNDROME

When I was a kid I wanted to be somebody. And then I found that amusing people is a helluva way to make a living. And now you might say it is the syndrome of the Jews: if you don't laugh, you die.

> *Ibid.*

SALAMI AND SEX

Salami and eggs. Now, that's better than sex, but only if the salami is thickly sliced and if you put catsup on the eggs and have a toasted bialy.

> *Ibid.*

"UNZER" FAMILY

It's not that Danny [Kaye] denied being Jewish. It's just that, well, I never considered him what my mother would call *unzer*—ours. Family.

> *Quoted in Martin Gottfried's* Nobody's Fool: The Lives of Danny Kaye *(1994).*

Coretta Scott King

A WIFE REMEMBERS

My husband [Martin Luther King, Jr.] demonstrated a deep sensitivity for Jewish concerns and tradition...and was a sincere friend of the people of Israel.

> *From a January 1995 address in New York before the World Jewish Congress, commemorating what would have been her late husband's sixty-sixth birthday.*

ANTI-SEMITISM AND RACISM

Just as Jewish leaders have condemned racism, like Martin Luther King, Jr., I feel I have a moral obligation to deplore the expressions of anti-Semitism that have polluted our society. Anti-Semitism is as vile and contemptible as racism. Anyone who supports it, including African Americans, does a disservice to his people, his country and his God.

> *Ibid.*

Larry King

ARAFAT'S ISRAELI GUARDS

Charming guy. I told him if my mother were alive to see this, she'd die. He just laughed and laughed. But he's a heavyweight—the terrorist who got reality late in life. His place in history is assured even if he gets knocked off tomorrow. Funny thing. The week I saw him, he was being guarded by two Mossad agents against Israeli terrorists. They later told me they grew quite fond of him.

> *Commenting on his meeting with PLO chief Yasser Arafat. Quoted in* The Jerusalem Report, *March 23, 1995.*

NO GOD EXPERIENCES

I didn't see God when I had my heart attack, no flashes of light, no out-of-the-body experiences. I've interviewed many religious leaders and I liked and respected them. But I don't have faith. I wish I did have faith. I wish I could know I'm going to a better place.

> *Ibid.*

GORBACHEV AND THE KING

Jeez! I can't believe it! I'm going to interview Gorbachev. Me, a Jew from Brooklyn!

King's reaction to the news was reported by CNN senior executive producer Wendy Walker Whitworth.

JUST A CONDUIT

I'm just an interviewer. I'm a conduit. I'm not here to judge people.

Describing his function as host of his popular television show, Larry King Live.

CULTURE AND BEING

Jewish culture was very much a part of my being.

From an interview with Elinor and Robert Slater. Quoted in their Great Jewish Men *(1996).*

GOD DOESN'T ANSWER

Somewhere along the line I stopped liking the God of the Old Testament. I asked great Jewish and other religious leaders why there was a Holocaust or why Hitler lived to sixty-six and a child dies at age eight. I never got good answers.

Ibid.

¤

Martin Luther King, Jr.

OVERCOMING HATRED

It is very unfortunate that you dislike Jews.... Most hate is rooted in fear, suspicion, ignorance and pride. You must be sure that all of these factors are removed from your personality where the Jews are concerned.... You can only remove this by knowing the truth and realizing that no one shortcoming can characterize a whole race. I would suggest that you seek real personal fellowship with Jews and you will discover that some of the finest persons in our nation are members of the Jewish community. Through this type of personal fellowship, you will come to know them and love them and thereby transcend...bigotry.

Advising a fellow black on what to do to overcome his feeling of hate for Jews. From his column "Advice for Living," which King wrote for Ebony *magazine from September 1957 through December 1958.*

ANTI-SEMITISM INJURES NEGROES

The Southern Christian Leadership Conference [SCLC] has expressly, frequently and vigorously denounced anti-Semitism and will continue to do so. It is not only that anti-Semitism is immoral—though that alone is enough. It is used to divide Negro and Jew, who have effectively collaborated in the struggle for justice. It injures Negroes because it upholds the doctrine of racism which they have the greatest stake in destroying.

In a personal letter, dated September 28, 1967, to Ambassador Morris B. Abram, replying to Abrams' objection to anti-Semitic remarks made by some of King's young followers.

NO MONOPOLY ON TRUTH

I strongly disagree with the statement which you quoted from a Southern Baptist Convention pamphlet, to the effect that more than five million five hundred thousand Jews in America are "lost without hope." This type of narrow sectarianism can only lead to an irrational religious bigotry and serve to create a dangerous climate of separation between people of different religious persuasion.

My theological position has always led me to believe that God reveals himself in all of the great religions of the world and no religion has an absolute monopoly on truth. One day, all Christians must come to see that "God has other sheep that are not of this fold"—which, in this context, means the Christian fold.

From a March 1, 1962 response by Dr. King to Dr. Samuel Newman, who sought his reaction to a statement issued by the Home Mission of the Southern Baptist Convention. From an article by Dr. Newman in The Jewish Spectator, *June 1968.*

ETHIC OF JUDAISM

To avoid involvement in behalf of a just cause is to live a sterile life. It is the quality of life that one leads that gives it meaning and value, not length.... I draw [meaning for my life] not from Marxism or any other secular philosophy but from the prophets of Israel; from their passion for justice and cry for righteousness. The ethic of Judaism is integral to my Christian faith. The exhortation of the prophet, "Justice, justice, shalt thou pursue," rings constantly in my ears.

In response to the charge associating Dr. King with Communists and fellow travelers.

PEACE EQUALS SECURITY

Peace for Israel means security, and we must stand with all our might to protect its right to exist, its territorial integrity and the right to use whatever sea lanes it needs. Israel is one of the great outposts of democracy in the world, and a marvelous example of what can be done, how desert land can be transformed into an oasis of brotherhood and democracy. Peace for Israel means security and that security must be a reality.

> *In a speech delivered to rabbis in New York City on March 25, 1968, ten days before he was assassinated.*

ACKNOWLEDGING A DEBT

Many of you have gone down in your pockets and given generous financial contributions to the civil rights organizations.... Some of you have been willing to make a personal witness by actually joining in demonstrations to carry on the struggle. And I can assure you that we will remember this support and these marvelous expressions as long as the cords of memory shall lengthen.

> *From a 1963 address to the Union of American Hebrew Congregations convention.*

AN IMMORAL COURSE

We cannot be victims of the notion that you can substitute one tyranny for another. For the black man to struggle for equality and then turn around and be anti-Semitic is not only an irrational course, but an immoral course.

> *Ibid.*

□

Ben Kingsley

FIRSTHAND ANTI-SEMITISM

We've seen anti-Semitism firsthand and it fills me with despair.

> *During the 1993 filming of Steven Spielberg's* Schindler's List, *in Krakow, Poland, when he witnessed an elderly Polish man insultingly drawing a finger over his throat when he learned that one of the actors was Jewish.*

□

Rudyard Kipling

JEWS CAN AFFORD TO SMILE

The Americans are very sensitive people because they are new, but your people, being so old, can afford to smile.

> *In a comment to Israel Zangwill. Quoted by Zangwill in* The New Jew, *October 24, 1898.*

□

Ephraim Kishon

GOLDMANN'S CONDEMNATION

Dr. Goldmann shouts into the *goyim's* ears—through the biggest loudspeakers and from the pages of the most anti-Israeli publications—everything that we here [in Israel] tell ourselves quietly, in sorrow and in anguish. And he does it *now,* just as the world is standing in a ring around us waiting for this fleeting phenomenon called the State of Israel to fleet already and be done with.

> *Commenting on an article in* Die Welt, *a German left-wing weekly, by the former president of the World Zionist Organization and the World Jewish Congress who at age 85 condemns Israel for its treatment of Arabs and predicts the dissolution of the State. From his article in* The Jerusalem Post, *August 2, 1980.*

□

Henry Kissinger

NO ROOM FOR CRISES

There can't be a crisis next week. My schedule is already full.

> *From* The New York Times Magazine, *June 1, 1969.*

AN AMERICAN FIRST

I was born Jewish, but the truth is that has no significance for me. America has given me everything. A home, a chance to study and achieve a high position. I don't know what other Jews expect of me, but I consider myself an American first.

> *To a Jewish friend in the 1970s. Reported in Walter Isaacson's biography entitled* Kissinger.

THE POWER OF POWER

Power is the great aphrodisiac.

> *Quoted in* The New York Times, *January 19, 1971.*

MEETING FAISAL

His Majesty and I sat side by side for a few minutes overlooking the splendid assemblage while I reflected in some wonder what strange twists of fate had caused a refugee from Nazi persecution to wind up in Arabia as the representative of American democracy.

> *Describing his first visit with King Faisal of Saudi Arabia in 1973. From his* Years of Upheaval *(1982).*

HUGS AND HISSES

When I reach Cairo, Sadat hugs and kisses me, but when I come here [to Israel] everyone attacks me.

A complaint made to Golda Meir during the January 1974 negotiations between Israel and Egypt. Golda responded: "If I were an Egyptian, I would kiss you also."

THE ENTEBBE RESCUE

I expected that Israel would act.... All day Saturday we were getting bits and pieces of information at the State Department. But when I was consulted, I told my people to brush them aside.

When advised by Israeli Ambassador to Washington Simcha Dinitz that a commando team had landed secretly at Entebbe Airport, Uganda, to rescue the planeload of hostages taken by Arab terrorists in July 1976.

EMOTIONAL DR. K

This morning I looked through my hotel window at the Old City [of Jerusalem] and thought how my father would have been happy.

Upon meeting with Golda Meir at the prime minister's office late one evening after returning from a visit to Syria.

ISRAEL'S SECURITY

The security of Israel is a moral imperative for all free peoples.

From a November 13, 1977 speech at the presentation of the Stephen S. Wise Award to Golda Meir.

COMPLEX MRS. MEIR

I loved Golda Meir because of her strength, her warmth, her humanity, her sense of humor.... She was sort of the earth-mother of elemental strength, wariness and profundity.

An evaluation of the prime minister spoken on the day she died, December 8, 1978.

SARCASTIC BUT COMPASSIONATE

Her [Golda Meir's] craggy face bore witness to the destiny of a people who had come to know too well the potentialities of man's inhumanity. Her occasionally sarcastic exterior never obscured a compassion that felt the death of every Israeli soldier as the loss of a member of her family.

From his White House Years *(1979).*

FRUSTRATION WITH EUROPE

In periods of tension the Europeans advocated detente, and in periods of relaxed ten-

sion they feared to cooperate. In crisis, they turned to us to maintain the balance outside Europe, and under the umbrella of risks which we undertook they did not hesitate to seek special advantages for themselves.

Ibid.

FIRST-CLASS MIND

He [Hafez al-Assad] had a first-class mind allied to a wicked sense of humor.

Ibid.

SUPERMODESTY

I am being frank about myself in the book. I tell of my first mistake on page 850.

Referring to the second volume of his memoirs, Years of Upheaval. *Quoted in the* London Observer, *January 2, 1983.*

SADAT'S UNFULFILLED DREAM

In my last conversation with Sadat a few weeks before his assassination, he spoke of his dream of building a mosque, a church, and a synagogue on top of Mount Sinai to symbolize the hope for peace and reconciliation. Would it now be Arafat who at last fulfills that vision?

Reflecting on the Israeli–PLO peace accord signed on September 13, 1993. From an article in Newsweek *magazine, September 27, 1993.*

THE SPIRIT OF AN AGREEMENT

A formidable agenda thus lies ahead. Like all diplomatic documents, the agreement signed in Washington represents a compromise which must be compared not with what each side would consider ideal, but with what would exist in the absence of the agreement. All the parties must now learn to live with what they have built, which is quite different from what is familiar to them. The spirit of the emotional signing should be a huge help in getting the parties to their destination.

Ibid.

WHEN PRESSURE BACKFIRES

After the signing ceremony [of the Israeli–Palestinian peace accord on September 13, 1993], one of the PLO negotiators said to me that the PLO had learned that American pressure on Israel for specific concessions usually backfired and that a settlement could be sold best to the Palestinians if it was freely negotiated.

Noting that the negotiations succeeded because the United States had remained on the sidelines and was uninformed about the deliberations.

HISTORY'S JOURNEY

History knows no resting places and no plateaus.

Ibid.

BALANCE OF POWER

The management of a balance of power is a permanent undertaking, not an exertion that has a foreseeable end.

Ibid.

CURIOSITIES OF BRITISH POLITICS

One of the curiosities of British politics is that the party of the insiders—the Tories — should have produced two great Prime Ministers from among rank outsiders: Benjamin Disraeli, of Jewish origin; and Margaret Thatcher, a grocer's daughter. Both proved extremely controversial. Both helped to define a new role for Britain's Conservatives. Disraeli showed the Conservatives that they need not fear mass democracy; Mrs. Thatcher set out to demonstrate that the Conservatives could prosper while dismantling the role of the state and stressing individual responsibility.

From a review of Margaret Thatcher's Down-ing Street Years (1993) in The New York Times Book Review, November 14, 1993.

INTELLIGENCE AND POWER

Intelligence is not that important as the exercise of power, and is often, in point of fact, useless.

From an interview with Oriana Fallaci in Esquire magazine, June 1975.

INDOMITABLE MR. NIXON

He stood on pinnacles that dissolved in the precipice. He achieved greatly and he suffered deeply. But he never gave up. In his solitude he envisaged a new international order that would reduce lingering enmities, strengthen historic friendships and give new hope to mankind. A visionary dream and possibilities conjoined.

From his eulogy of Richard Nixon, thirty-seventh president of the United States, deliv-ered in Yorba Linda, California, April 27, 1994.

DOING THINGS PROPERLY

He [Nixon] drew strength from the conviction he often expressed to me: the price for doing things halfway is no less than for doing it completely, so we might as well do them properly. That's Richard Nixon's greatest accomplishment. It was as much moral as it was political.

Ibid.

PALESTINIAN STATEHOOD

Paradoxically, the Begin government, against its preferences and ideology, was really proposing what all other nations were certain to treat as an embryo state and to compound the irony, within the 1967 borders since none other was under discussion.

Once there was an elected self-governing authority on the West Bank, an irreversible political fact would be created on the territory over which its authority was supposed to run. However limited this authority, it would soon turn into the nucleus of something like a Palestinian state, probably under PLO control. It would be so treated by almost all the countries of the world except Israel.

It was clearly the main objective of the Israeli (Begin) government to avoid it; its proposal was incompatible with its strategy.

From his Observations (1982). Quoted by Abba Eban in a June 17, 1994 article in Heritage Southwest Jewish Press, in which he states that Palestinian statehood became virtually inevitable the moment Begin agreed to the Camp David test.

IT'S ALL HEARSAY

It's always a privilege to introduce someone who also speaks with an accent.

Introducing President Bill Clinton in February 1995. Quoted in Newsweek magazine, March 13, 1995.

HUMBLE HENRY

I'm a very humble person. Why don't you call me simply Your Excellency.

Recalled by Shimon Peres at a 1995 dinner for the University of Haifa held at the Wal-dorf Astoria in New York. The Israelis weren't sure how to address Kissinger: Mr. Kissinger, Dr. Kissinger, or Mr. Secretary.

¤

Rudolph Kittel

JOYOUS JEWISH FAMILY

Anyone who has had the opportunity of knowing the inner life of present-day Jewish families that observe the Law of the fathers with sincere piety and in all strictness will have been astonished at the wealth of joyfulness, gratitude and sunshine, undreamt of by the outsider, which the Law animates in the Jewish home.

From his Religion of the People of Israel (1925).

Francine Klagsbrun

FROM GENERATION TO GENERATION

There is a collective Jewish consciousness that informs Jewish life—attitudes and values that are passed on from one generation to the next, no matter what the degree of religious observance of any one individual. Those attitudes and ideals play an especially important role in marriage and family life, shaping and influencing the ways partners relate to one another and to their children even when they are not aware of the influences.

> *From her essay entitled "Marriages That Last," which appears in* The Hadassah Magazine Jewish Parenting Book *(1989), edited by Roselyn Bell.*

GENERATION OF CHOICES

We are a generation of choices. But sometimes the choices are not entirely in our hands, and sometimes we must choose from among narrowing options.... There is room within the Jewish community for many kinds of choices and decisions.

> *Ibid. From her essay entitled "Deciding to Have Children."*

Joseph Klausner

NATION AND RELIGION

Judaism is a nation and a religion at one and the same time.

> *From his* From Jesus to Paul *(1944).*

SCHOPENHAUER'S HATE

All of Schopenhauer's hate for Judaism and the Jews...arose largely from the fact that he could not forgive Judaism for its affirmation of life.

> *Ibid.*

ETHICS OF JESUS

Jesus is, for the Jewish nation, a great teacher of morality and an artist in parable.... If ever the day should come and his ethical code be stripped of its wrappings of miracles and mysticism, the Book of the Ethics of Jesus will be one of the choicest treasures in the literature of Israel for all time.

> *From his* Jesus of Nazareth *(1926).*

GLISTENING JEWEL

The Messianic idea is the most glistening jewel in the glorious crown of Judaism!

> *From his* Messianic Idea in Israel *(1955).*

Noah Kleger

PRECIOUS WORDS

I came back because I've got this fantastic feeling that I can say to my driver, "Wait for me at the gate. I will be back in three hours and we'll return to Warsaw."

> *Explaining why he came to the fiftieth anniversary ceremony marking the liberation of Auschwitz on January 27, 1995.*

Morton Klein

ARAB TERRORISM

As long as Arabs are filling Jewish coffins, the United States should not be filling the PLO's coffers with $500 million in aid.

> *In protest to Israel's soft-pedaling terrorist acts by Arabs while discussing a peace accord with the PLO in 1995.*

Robert Klein

HAVING A GOOD TIME

I'm not a teacher, preacher, or prophet.... When I'm on [stage], the audiences have a wonderful time, and it looks like I'm having a wonderful time, too. And sometimes I am. But I'm working. I'm an illusionist, and my illusion is to make everything seem like one big good time.

> *Commenting on his brand of comedy. Quoted in Darryl Lyman's* Jewish Comedy Catalog *(1989).*

Philip M. Klutznick

SPEAKING FRANKLY TO THE ARABS

Should not we Jews have the courage to say to the Arabs, including those who are called Palestinians, that we wish only to protect the independence of Israel, not to deprive you of yours...only to speak with your leaders ready to coexist with and understand us; that we seek not to oppress and dominate, but rather to advance the cause of Israel and her neighbors sharing and living together in brotherhood and peace.

Expressed in October 1981 at the meeting of the Seven Springs Mission to the Middle East, where he was the only Jewish participant. He was criticized for joining in the final report, which was characterized by Moshe Decter, editor of Near East Report, *an Israeli-supported newsletter published in Washington, DC, as "a sinister canard whose unequivocal intent is to vilify Israel by equating the fate of Palestinian Arabs with that of the Jews at the hands of the Nazis."*

GRASPING FOR PEACE

We dare not wait longer to resolve the basic conflict which has separated Arabs and Jews for most of this century—a conflict which continues to play havoc with our best interests and world peace. It has gone on too long, it has cost us all too much, and the dangers of failing to grasp this moment in time to bring it to an end are far too great.

From an address delivered at a March 23, 1984 meeting of the American-Arab Affairs Council.

YEARNING TO BE FREE

If we are to be brutally honest with ourselves, there is in this Palestinian movement for a national homeland something of ourselves, something of our own yearnings to be free from domination by others, to be responsible for ourselves, to be accepted by others as equals, to be proud and strong and independent.

There has been considerable movement in Palestinian intellectual circles. We Jews have all too often chosen only to stress the most negative of Palestinian thinking. And yet all of us know that the Palestinian community has within it brave and dedicated leaders, some of whom have been looking for a path toward coexistence and away from confrontation.

From an address to the Plenary Assembly of the World Jewish Congress in Jerusalem, after he had completed his term as president of the organization.

¤

Alfred A. Knopf

BORN AT THE RIGHT TIME

I was born at the right time. The kind of publishing we did, where a young man with a little capital could start his own company, won't be around again.

A comment to the Academy of Arts and Letters after receiving from them, in 1982 (at age 90), the Award for Distinguished Service to the Arts.

¤

Edward I. Koch

CARTER'S SENSITIVITY TO ISRAEL

Mr. President, you have to understand that the Jews for two thousand years have had people sell them out. There isn't a country on the world's face today except for the United States that hasn't at one point cast its Jews out.... In the past we vetoed resolutions that were one-sided against Israel and that questioned Israeli sovereignty over Jerusalem. Then we got to the point where we simply abstained; and now we are supporting resolutions that have sanctions in them and are denunciatory.

Explaining to President Jimmy Carter, prior to the 1980 election, why Jews were so incensed that his administration did not vote against the UN resolution denouncing Israel, but merely abstained. From his Mayor! (1984).

JEWS AND THE BLACK COMMUNITY

I find the black community very anti-Semitic. I don't care what the American Jewish Congress or the B'nai B'rith will issue by way of polls showing that the black community is not. I think that's pure bull....

Ibid. From his oral memoirs of 1975 and 1976. Koch later amended his comment to say: "A substantial number of blacks are anti-Semitic and substantial numbers of whites are anti-black."

PROUD OF BEING JEWISH

I was always proud of being Jewish, but I had never been a Jewish activist. In my [congressional] district a lot of people did not know I was Jewish.... I had been an activist, to be sure, and in Congress I was soon involved in every civil rights issue for the blacks and Hispanics and women, and worked for every oppressed group in the country—except the Jews. Well, I changed that, and made the Jews one of my priorities.

Ibid.

TRUTH IS TRUTH

The truth is the truth and there is no such thing as a higher truth. That's a falsehood.

Attacking Jewish leaders who wanted to cover up the historically inaccurate 1993 Public Broadcasting System portrayal of a documentary entitled "The Liberators," which attributed the liberation of several Nazi concentration camps to a unit of black American soldiers. The Jewish leaders refrained from commenting in the name of "a higher truth."

◻

Arthur Koestler

ZIONIST GOAL

This is what our philosophy and propaganda aims at. To return to the Land, and within the Land to the soil; to cure that nervous overstrungness of exile and dispersion; to liquidate the racial inferiority complex and breed a healthy, normal earth-bound race of peasants.

From his Thieves in the Night *(1946).*

BREAKING OUT OF HOMELESSNESS

Made homeless in space, they had to expand into new dimensions.... It made them cunning and grew them claws to cling on with as they were swept by the wind...reduced to drift-sand, they had to glitter if they wanted to avoid being trodden on.

Ibid.

MEANING OF ZIONISM

Zionism means one man persuading another man to give money to a third man to go to Palestine.

From his Arrow in the Blue *(1952).*

LOVE AND HATE OF SELF

He who does not love himself, does not love well; and he who does not hate himself, does not hate well.

Ibid.

JEWS ARE LIKE OTHER PEOPLE

The Jews are like other people, only more so.

A popular proverb quoted in his Promise and Fulfillment: Palestine, 1917–1949 *(1949).*

COMMUNICATION FAILURE

God seems to have left the receiver off the hook, and time is running out.

From his Ghost in the Machine *(1967).*

LANGUAGE AND ITS PROBLEMS

Language promotes communication and understanding within the group, but it also accentuates the differences in traditions and beliefs between groups; it erects barriers between tribes, nations, regions, social classes. The Tower of Babel is an archetypal symbol of the process which turns the blessing into a curse and prevents man from reaching into heaven. According to Margaret Mead, among the two million aborigines in New Guinea, 750 different languages are spoken in 750 villages which are at permanent war with one another.

Upon receipt of the Sonning Prize at the University of Copenhagen. Quoted in the Toronto Globe and Mail, *May 6, 1968.*

REACHING FOR THE STARS

Prometheus is reaching out for the stars with an empty grin on his face.

After the first moonlanding. Quoted in The New York Times, *July 21, 1969.*

◻

Helmut Kohl

ON AUSCHWITZ

The warnings emanating from this place must never be forgotten. Unspeakable hurt was inflicted on various peoples here, but above all on European Jews, in the name of Germany.

On a visit to Poland's Auschwitz concentration camp in November 1989.

SINCERE REGRET

I can only be full of shame about what has been done in the name of Germany.

After touring the Yad Va-Shem Holocaust Memorial in June 1995, during his second visit to Israel.

◻

Kaufmann Kohler

STOREHOUSE OF DIVINE TRUTH

Israel could dispense with its State and its Temple, but not with its storehouse of divine truth, from which it constantly derives new life and new youth.

From his Jewish Theology *(1918).*

EMBRACING HUMANITY

As the idea of a common humanity forms its beginning, so Judaism will attain its final goal only in a divine covenant comprising all humanity.

Ibid.

PARADISE AND HELL

When the rabbis speak of paradise and hell...these are only metaphors for the agony of sin and the happiness of virtue.

Ibid.

FEAST OF REDEMPTION

As the springtide of nature fills each creature with joy and hope, so Israel's feast of redemption promises the great day of liberty to those who still chafe under the yoke of oppression.

Ibid.

STRIVING FOR ETERNAL TRUTHS

It is birth, not confession, that imposes on the Jew the obligation to work and strive for the eternal verities of Israel.

Ibid.

THE MAINTENANCE OF NATURE

The maintenance of the entire household of nature is one continuous act of God which can neither be interrupted nor limited in time. God in His infinite wisdom works forever through the same laws which were in force in the beginning and which shall continue through all the realms of time and space.

Ibid.

PHARISAISM AND JUDAISM

Pharisaism shaped the character of Judaism and the life and thought of the Jew for all the future.

From his article "Pharisees" in The Jewish Encyclopedia *(1905).*

¤

Moshe Kohn

NEW NAME FOR KRISTALLNACHT

I again urge Jewish organizations and calendar-makers to adopt the designation "The Night of the Burned Synagogues."

Arguing that the name Kristallnacht *does not convey the tragedy in which 1,300 synagogues throughout Nazi-dominated Europe were vandalized and 270 completely demolished. From an article in* The Jerusalem Post, *November 27, 1993.*

¤

Yitzchak Kolitz

OPPOSITION TO DIALOGUE

The whole concept of interdenominational dialogue is foreign to Judaism. We have the Torah. We don't have to explain anything; we are not interested in converting anybody.

Opposing a planned February 1, 1994 conference that would bring Jewish and Christian leaders together in Jerusalem.

¤

Zvi Kolitz

I DIE A BELIEVER

And these are my last words to You, my wrathful God: nothing will avail You in the least. You have done everything to make me renounce You, to make me lose my faith in You, but I die exactly as I lived, a *believer....*

Hear, O Israel, the Lord is our God, the Lord is One.

Into your hands, O Lord, I consign my soul.

From his "Yossel Rakover's Appeal to God." Quoted in Albert Friedlander's Out of the Whirlwind *(1968).*

¤

Teddy Kollek

REQUISITIONING VS. EXPROPRIATING

Somebody asked me...about the difference between requisitioning and expropriating Jewish property and Arab property. So I said, "The difference is very simple: the Jews call me a bastard, but the Arabs call me a Zionist bastard." I don't think there's anything morally wrong with expropriation. It is happening every day everywhere in the world. It is done much more leniently here than anywhere else, with much higher compensation here than anywhere else.

From a Spring 1977 interview. Reported in Frank Epp's Israelis: Portrait of a People in Conflict *(1980).*

TOLERANT ISRAELIS

When Arabs come back here [after the 1967 War], they are astonished to see that we have Arab street signs...in Jerusalem. We are not a particularly tolerant people, but we are a lot more tolerant than anybody else.

Ibid.

THE UNDIVIDED CITY

With the exception of the years 1948–1967, Jerusalem has always been one undivided city. The Arabs never made it their capital, even though they could have. Instead, they neglected Jerusalem badly. When we entered East Jerusalem in 1967, we found that only 10 percent of the homes had running water.

Why? Because all the money went to building a capital in Amman. Now they want to make Jerusalem their capital because they see that we have it. When they could readily have declared it as their capital, they didn't.

From an October 1993 interview in The Jewish Week.

I Hope I Am Wrong

Jerusalem is now going in a bad direction. I am very sorry about this and can only hope that I am mistaken.

After serving as mayor of Jerusalem for twenty-eight years and then losing to Ehud Olmert in the November 1993 mayoralty contest.

The Cigar-smoking Octogenarian

For the first time in my life [at age 87], I feel truly terrorized not by Arabs nor by Orthodox Jews, but by the anti-smoking lobby.

From a 1995 interview with Jerusalem news correspondent Meir Ronen.

◻

Milton R. Konvitz

Jewish Assertiveness

It is not necessary for the Jew to drift with the mainstream in the world of opportunism, and to become rootless, trivial and alienated;...it is still possible for the Jew to assert himself in his Jewishness through an autonomous decision and a free act.

From a 1964 speech at Harvard University.

Seeding Jewish Education

The organized American Jewish community must act as a Johnny Appleseed, and go up and down the land to plant the seed of Jewish learning.

Urging increased support for the work of the Hillel Foundation.

◻

Abraham Isaac Kook

Not to Be Taken Literally

The idea that there is an evolutionary path upwards provides the world with a basis for optimism.... It is easy enough to see how the two [the Theory of Evolution and the Bible] can be reconciled. Everyone knows that these topics, which belong to life's mystery, are always dominated by metaphor, riddle, and hint.

From his Orot Ha-kodesh *(1938). Quoted in Louis Jacobs'* Jewish Ethics, Philosophy, and Mysticism *(1971), where Jacobs points out that Rabbi Kook indicated that the narrative account in the Book of Genesis belongs to "the secrets of the Torah."*

Garments of the Soul

The soul sings all the time; joy and sweet-

ness are her garments; highminded tenderness envelops her.

Ibid. Quoted in Jacob B. Agus's Banner of Jerusalem *(1946).*

The Reward of Rebuilding

Those who rebuild the land are as favored in the sight of God as the ritually observant.

Stating an unorthodox view.

Where Fear Leads

When man begins to fear to think, he becomes immersed in ignorance, which removes the light of his soul, causes his power to fail, and dims his spirit.

By attribution.

Soul of a People

Erets Yisrael is not something apart from the soul of the Jewish people; it is no mere national possession, serving as a means of unifying our people and buttressing its material, or even its spiritual, survival. *Erets Yisrael* is part of the very essence of our nationhood; it is bound organically to its very time and inner being. Human reason, even at its most sublime, cannot begin to understand the unique holiness of *Erets Yisrael*.

Quoted in Lewis Glinert's Joys of Hebrew *(1992).*

On Becoming Great Jews

I still hope the day will come when the Jews who are great will become great Jews.

One of his last expressed hopes, made prior to his death in 1935. Quoted in Jacob Agus's High Priest of Rebirth *(1970).*

Rabbi with a Big Heart

Our generation is a wonderful generation.... In all of Jewish history it is difficult to find its equal.... It comprises so many opposites. On one hand, mischievous and wild, and on the other hand, exalted and refined; on the one hand, arrogant and shameless and, on the other hand, overwhelmed with a passion for justice and mercy. Its preoccupation with both facts and ideals bursts forth and ascends to Heaven.

Quoted in an article by Emanuel Rackman in The Jewish Week, *May 4, 1984.*

◻

Hillel Kook

Country and Nation

I hope that American Jews will come to recognize that while Israeli and American Jews may share a common history, culture and religion, we have different nationalities. What America is for them, Israel is for me—my country and my nation.

> *Quoted by Louis Rapoport in an article in* Present Tense *magazine.*

SETTLING WITH THE PALESTINIANS

This is the perfect time for a settlement with the Palestinians, and not the PLO. The war [in Lebanon] shattered the equation of the PLO with the Palestinians.... But I'm afraid that Israel as it is presently constituted is incapable of breaking through to make the necessary initiative.

> *Ibid.*

WHO IS AN ISRAELI?

It's absurd to have a Knesset [Parliament] consisting of Jews and non-Jews legislating a religious definition as to who is a Jew. In practice, mixed Jewish and non-Jewish families are admitted into Israel under the Law of Return. The question therefore is not who is a Jew—which is a question for individuals or for rabbis—but who and what is an Israeli nation.

> *Ibid.*

◻

Zevi Judah Kook

FORBIDDEN RETURN

There is not the slightest possibility of permitting that which the Torah forbade absolutely again and again. It is forbidden to turn over any part of our land to non-Jews, and it is most certainly against the Torah to allow them permanent possession. Therefore all Jews, and especially the spiritual authorities, the Cabinet Ministers and the men of the army, are commanded to prevent such action.

> *From a 1978 statement forbidding the return of any land to the Arabs.*

NEEDED MORE LOVE

Sometimes I think that what we need in Israel is more belief for the "believers" and more freedom for the "freethinkers," and above all, love, a bit more love.

> *Quoted in* Commentary *magazine, 1954.*

◻

Ted Koppel

NEVER AGAIN, NEVER

This place and what we commemorate here today demands that we pledge never to close our hearts to the oppressed. Never again. Never.

> *From his remarks as master of ceremonies at the dedication of the United States Holocaust Memorial Museum, in Washington, DC, April 1993.*

◻

Lawrence J. Korb

VISCERAL HATE

I do know that [Secretary of Defense Caspar] Weinberger had almost a visceral dislike of Israel.

> *Commenting on the severe punishment meted out, at Weinberger's insistence, to Jonathan Pollard, who was convicted of spying for Israel.*

◻

Richard Korn

NO NEED FOR A JEWISH HOMELAND

We are not in existence to divide Judaism. On the contrary, we want Jews to come ever closer in their religion. At the same time, we feel that American Jews are welcome in America, that they have no need to feel they are a separatist "Jewish people" who must one day go to a so-called "Jewish homeland."

> *Reported in* The New York Times, *July 16, 1967.*

◻

Jerzy Kosinski

THE SURVIVAL OF SELFHOOD

While at one end of my fiction stands the simple and innocent Chauncy Gardiner of *Being There,* at the other stands Fabian, the morally complex and sexually obsessed hero of *Passion Play*...its essence is the development and survival of one's self-hood.

> *From his* Painted Bird *(1965), a novel about a young Jewish Polish boy wandering in Nazi-occupied Poland.*

THE HOLOCAUST IN PERSPECTIVE

In North America, attempts to erect dignified, soul-stirring and unforgettable monuments to the memory of the Holocaust have regrettably evolved into what can only be termed a second Holocaust: a well-meaning, though often inadvertently Jew-demeaning activity, leading to the most aggravated persecution complex in recent Jewish history....

Remembering the Holocaust and financing

Holocaust-related projects that help to make certain that—never again!—could such an atrocity be repeated is clearly one of our most challenging obligations. But that task must not be carried out at the cost of failing to remember—and to make others know—what preceded the Holocaust and what has come after.

From his Passing By: Selected Essays 1960–1991.

○

Sanford (Sandy) Koufax

Pride of the Pitcher

Pitching is an art in the sense that the driving force is the pride you have in yourself.

From his autobiography, Koufax *(1966).*

Asking for Trouble

It made me ill.... It makes me wonder whether trying to be nice to people is the same thing as asking for trouble.

After discovering that yarmulkes *he had autographed, believing they were to be used as awards to Hebrew school students, were being sold for $75.00 each. Quoted in the* New York Post, *May 12, 1995.*

○

Alex Kozinsky

The Supreme Supreme Court

As it is reviewed and analyzed, the Israeli Supreme Court's decision in the Demjanjuk case will surely become a model of judicial craftsmanship, a luminous example of how a court confronting a difficult and painful subject ought to comport itself. Jews can take pride that Judaism's age-old commitment to the rule of law did not waver.

From an article in The New Republic, *September 13, 1993.*

○

David Kraemer

Life After Death

I think it would be fair to say that the insistence on future resurrection represents a response to the grave injustices and the bitter realities of Jewish history. These authors [of the apocryphal writings such as the Book of Baruch] believed in a just and caring God, but when they looked at the world around them—

at the sufferings of Jews at the hands of people far less righteous than they—they could not understand how their God could permit such horrors. They then concluded that what lay before them was an incomplete picture and that perfect justice would be realized only in a future world.

From an essay in Masoret *magazine, Fall 1993.*

○

Irving Kristol

From Trotskyite to Neoconservative

If America is going to become more Christian, Jews will have to adapt.... Prudence can be relearned.

Expressing warm feelings toward the Christian right, which advises Jews to welcome America as a Christian nation. From a 1991 essay, "The Future of American Jury," included in his Neoconservatism: The Autobiography of an Idea *(1995).*

○

Nachman Krochmal

The Spirit of Religion

When a man is on a low cultural level, he can satisfy his spiritual needs with outward religious observances; but as he becomes more highly developed, he wants to grasp the spirit of religion.

From his Moray Nevuchay Ha-Zeman *(1851).*

Yearning to Know

In our very being there is rooted a mighty desire to know ourselves and our Creator, to understand the primary basis of all real beings.

Ibid.

○

Arthur Krock

Speaking of LBJ

The most political animal to occupy the White House since Andrew Jackson, if not since the creation of the Federal Government, has just completed the first six months of his Presidency.

From his column in The New York Times, *May 24, 1964.*

¤

Dave Kufeld

Mickey Mandel

He overcame adversity, like the Jewish people. I even know some people growing up who tried to make us believe he was Jewish, calling him Mickey Mandel.

Upon the death of the great Yankee baseball player Mickey Mantle in August 1995.

¤

Maxine Kumin

Looking for Matzoh in Kentucky

Can it be
I am the only Jew residing in
Danville, Kentucky,
Looking for *Matzoh* in the Safeway
and the A&P?

From her Living Alone with Jesus *(1972).*

¤

Stanley Kunitz

Universal Attribute

Essentially what I am trying to do is help each person rediscover the poet within himself. I say "rediscover" because I am convinced that it is a universal human attribute to want to play with words, to beat out rhythms, to fashion images, to tell a story, to construct forms.

Describing his teaching goal.

¤

William Kunstler

Defender of Anti-Zionists

[The judge] is a Zionist and therefore has no mercy. He is a Jewish judge who was confronted by a suspected terrorist, and he acted emotionally and against the background of the bombing of the Twin Towers [in New York City].

Statement made in April 1993 after his client, an Arab terrorist, was sentenced in New York to a thirty-year prison term.

Never a Schlemiel

I've been called many things in my almost half-century of lawyering, but never a *schlemiel.*

Taking issue with The New York Times' *Andrea Higbie, who on June 2 called him the "Schlemiel Extraordinaire Lawyer." From his June 7, 1995 letter-to-the-editor of* The Times.

¤

Zvi Kurzweil

Fundamentalist Judaism

I do not believe that Neo-Orthodoxy or, for that matter, even the old-type Orthodoxy, may be aptly characterized as fundamentalist. The concepts of fundamentalism were better relegated to the Christian context from which it has sprung.... The only sect in Judaism that may rightly be termed fundamentalist is that of the Karaites, and it is no mere accident that this religious sect did not survive in any significant manner.

From his Modern Impulse of Traditional Judaism *(1985).*

¤

Harold Kushner

Speech Control

Only God can give us credit for the angry words we did not speak.

From his When All You've Ever Wanted Isn't Enough *(1986).*

Making Our Lives Matter

People are not afraid of dying; they are afraid of not having lived. We can handle mortality. What we cannot accept is anonymity, insignificance. If people would realize that Judaism is not a matter of obeying or pleasing God, it is a matter of changing the world by investing ordinary moments with holiness and making our lives matter in the process, then living Jewishly would no longer be an obligation. It would be an irresistible answer to one of life's most pressing questions.

Quoted in Hadassah Magazine, *June–July 1993.*

Judaism: Means to an End

Judaism, done right, has the power to save your life from being spent entirely on the trivial.... But it can do more than that. Its goal is not just to make your life more satisfying. Its goal is not the survival of the Jewish people. That is a means to an end, not an end in itself. The ultimate goal is to transform the world into the kind of world God had in mind when He created it.

From his To Life! *(1993).*

On the Rejection of Jesus

I was once asked at a public lecture: "Doesn't the history of the Jews' wandering and low status prove that they are being cursed for rejecting Jesus?"

I answered, "No, not at all, because the people who predicted that the Jews would suffer are the same people who persecuted them. It would be as if I predicted that that window would break, and then threw a rock through it. That would say more about my propensity for violence than it would about my gift of prophecy."

Ibid.

□

Abraham Kuyper

CITY OF CITIES

Rome in all its glory cannot compare to the world-historical significance of Jerusalem. Babylon may have searched the heavens, Athens given man his highest literary and aesthetic values—Jerusalem was and remains the city of cities, the Holy City, the heart and soul of humanity. Deeper than any other motif, that of religion has been woven into the texture of mankind's evolution.

Quoted in Pierre van Paasen's Days of Our Years *(1939).*

Fiorello LaGuardia

NOMINATION OF THE "LITTLE FLOWER"

Thanks for the Republican nomination. I am a Republican, but I stand for the Republicanism of Abraham Lincoln; and let me tell you fellows something—some of you Republican leaders east of the Mississippi know as much about Abraham Lincoln as Henry Ford knows about the Talmud.

From a speech made by Congressman La-Guardia when the Republican Party of New York brought him the news that he had been nominated to be their candidate for Mayor of New York City.

□

Bert Lahr

WHAT COMES NATURALLY

Everybody says I've got wonderful timing. Young actors have actually stood in the wings with a stopwatch, charting when a certain laugh would come. But you wanna know something? I don't know what the hell they're talking about.

Quoted in Darryl Lyman's Jewish Comedy Catalog *(1989).*

□

Maurice Lamm

WHEN A NON-JEW CONVERTS

When a non-Jew converts to Judaism, he or she does not convert to the Jewish "faith" but rather accedes to the Jewish covenant—the convert "enters into the covenant of Abraham our Father."

From his Becoming a Jew *(1991).*

JEWISH CONTRIBUTION TO CIVILIZATION

The Jewish religion is not simply a calling; conversion is not simply a profession of faith. It is a network of profound ideas and rich insights, which during its long history has generated the fundamental beliefs of all Western religion. It has contributed to the civilized world its crowning ideals and its most glorious convictions—among them the idea of one God, a system of jurisprudence, a structure of ethics and morals...and numerous ideas, ideals, and institutions.

Ibid. From the Preface.

SEX AND MARRIAGE

For Judaism, the value in human sexuality comes only when the relationship involves two people who have committed themselves to one another and have made that commitment in a binding covenant recognized by God and society. The act of sexual union, the deepest personal statement that any human being can make, must be reserved for the moment of total oneness.

From his Jewish Way in Love and Marriage *(1980).*

THE USES OF HOPE

Religious leaders have consistently used hope to buoy the spirits of their flock. But demagogues have used it for their own nefarious purposes; quacks have bottled counterfeit hope for a quick sale; and politicians have used it to cover up their mistakes.

From his Power of Hope *(1995).*

□

Norman Lamm

LIMITS OF GAY ACCEPTANCE

Regular congregations and other Jewish groups should not hesitate to accord hospitality and membership on an individual basis, to those "visible" homosexuals who qualify for the category of the ill.... But to assent to the organization of separate "gay" groups under Jewish auspices makes no more sense, Jewishly, than to suffer the formation of synagogues that cater exclusively to idol worshippers, adulterers, gossipers, tax evaders, or Sabbath violators.

In his article entitled "Judaism and the Modern Attitude to Homosexuality," included in the Encyclopedia Judaica Yearbook *(1974).*

UNITY OF ALL KNOWLEDGE

The words of the Rav [Soloveitchik], one of the spiritual and intellectual giants of Yeshiva University, and indeed of our generation, voice a principled ideal for the unity of all human knowledge. There is sacred learning and there is learning which is sacred, and at Yeshiva University, while we recognize the distinction between the two, we also affirm their affinities, and mutual enrichment.

The University commits itself to the principle that every advance of knowledge is an advance for humanity and service to life. We have the conviction, as the Rav said, that every enterprise of true learning has its part in religious experience and deserves honor and respect.

In eulogizing Dr. Joseph B. Soloveitchik, who taught at Yeshiva University for fifty years.

THE DIVINE TORAH

The Torah is divine revelation in two ways: It is God-given and it is godly. By "God-given," I mean that He willed that man abide by His commandments and that will was communicated in discreet words and letters.... Hence, I accept unapologetically the idea of the verbal revelation of the Torah.... *How* God spoke is a mystery; how *Moses* received this message is an irrelevancy. *That* God spoke is of the utmost significance.

Explaining the Orthodox position in an essay included in The Condition of Jewish Belief *(1966), compiled by the editors of* Commentary *magazine.*

MIND VS. MACHINE

The real challenge to Jewish belief in our day will come, I believe, from the cyberneticians who have been developing a metaphysics of cybernetics in which they attempt to use theories of communication and control to establish criteria for a materialistic conception of meaning and purpose. If the source of human purpose is in the neuronic feedback circuits of our nervous system, then we have snuffed our freedom and established a new and imposing materialism.

But challenging though it may well be, I do not fear it. The computer is an extension of the human brain even as the scissors is an extension of the hand and the automobile of the foot.

Ibid.

RELYING ON GOD

It's too late to lie, and it may be painful for our fellow Jews to hear. But Federations will not save us and Israel won't save us. We have nothing to rely on but God.

At the inaugural meeting of the North American Orthodox Leadership Conference, November 1993.

THE MARITAL RELATIONSHIP

The Jewish family...the bedrock of the home [was] as solid and reliable as the ancient and sacred traditions from which the character of our people is hewn. Squeamishness never allowed the secular nature of this marital love to be overlooked or minimized; modesty never permitted it to be vulgarized and dishonored.

From his Hedge of Roses *(1966).*

EROSION ON THE PERIPHERIES

While there has been erosion on the peripheries of the Jewish community as a result of intermarriage and assimilation, there has also been an intensification on the part of the committed. This core group will enable us to halt the erosion on the periphery, and can aid in providing the educational resources to make the community aware of the rich intellectual and spiritual resources of our people.

From his inaugural address upon assuming the presidency of Yeshiva University in 1976.

LOOKING AT THE FUTURE

Thirty years ago people said that Judaism had no future in America. Well, today more than one-fourth of all religious school students attend yeshivas. And look at the yarmulke-wearing young men in the streets of New York. We have a future. We will make a future.

Commenting, in the 1990s, on the future of the Jewish community in America.

AN APPEAL FOR OPENMINDEDNESS

I think it's a mistake to base everything upon which rabbis we do or do not recognize, because it then develops into a kind of *ad hominem*...argument. That's divisive and disruptive and not conducive to the communal peace that we desperately need at this critical juncture of history.

Commenting on the advisability of considering conversions valid only if performed by Orthodox rabbis.

CANCER OF EXTREMISM

Extremism is the thin membrane that covers the inner volcano of violence.... Extremism begets fanaticism and fanaticism leads to the worst of evils, bloodshed and the desecration of the Divine Name—the most horrific terms in the lexicon of Judaism—all in the name of high principle and great ideals.

Excerpted from a March 1994 address to newly ordained rabbis of the Rabbi Isaac Elchanan Theological Seminary of Yeshiva University. Delivered two weeks after the February 25th massacre of over forty Moslems in a Hebron mosque in Israel.

Beware of Intolerance

Beware of intolerance, and beware of tolerance for the intolerant. There is a fine line that separates passion from violence and zeal from zealotry.

Beware of the tendency to deny that any other position can have merit, that your concern takes precedence over every other consideration, that the adversary is invariably demonized, that every means is legitimate to achieve your end. Those who passionately take strong positions in Jewish life must know that there are unbalanced people who flock to extremes and who can, with what they consider good intentions, subvert the noblest goals. You who are wise, be careful with your words.

Ibid.

God and Nature

The God of the Bible is beyond, not within, nature: "In the beginning, God created heaven and earth."

From his Faith and Doubt: Studies in Traditional Jewish Thought *(1986).*

Criminal Arrogance

To point an accusing finger at European Jewry...is an unparalleled instance of criminal arrogance and brutal insensitivity. How dare anyone even suggest that any "sin" committed by any significant faction of European Jewry was worthy of all the pain and anguish and death visited upon them by Hitler's sadistic butchers?

From an essay in Theological and Halakhic Reflections on the Holocaust *(1992), edited by Bernard Rosenberg and Fred Heuman.*

¤

Ezekiel Landau

Cruelty in Hunting

How can a Jew kill a living thing without any benefit to anyone, and engage in hunting merely to satisfy the enjoyable use of his time? In the case of one who needs to hunt for a living, we would not say that it is cruel, since we slaughter cattle and birds and fish for the needs of man.... But he who has no need to make a livelihood from it, his hunting is cruelty.

Responding to a question about whether a Jew may hunt with non-Jewish friends, so long as he does not eat the meat of the hunted animal. From his 1776 book of responsa entitled Noda Bi-Yehuda *(on Yoreh Deah 2:10).*

¤

Ann Landers

Constructive Marriage Battles

All married couples should learn the act of battle as they should the art of making love.... Good battle is healthy and constructive, and brings to marriage the principle of equal partnership.

From her Ann Landers Says Truth Is Stranger *(1968).*

American Children

What the vast majority of American children needs is to stop being pampered.

Ibid.

Empathizing with People

You don't have to live through an immense amount of agony and pain in order to relate to people who are suffering.

From a 1989 interview in Time *magazine. Commenting on how she learned to relate to people and advise them in her popular newspaper column.*

How I Grew Up

I really care about what happens to people ...I came from a very solid midwestern Jewish home. You see, I led a very sheltered life. I had never seen a man hit his wife. I had never seen any drunkenness. I had never seen any poverty. I knew these things were happening, but they never happened to me. The mail grew me up in a hurry.

Ibid.

¤

Pearl Lang

The Hidden Voice

"He whom the divine storm of the Spirit inspires not with his instrument of speech alone but with his whole being and life is speaker of the hidden voice."

Quoting Martin Buber, to explain what the dance has meant to her. From Murray Polner's American Jewish Biographies *(1982).*

◻

Ivar Lange

BRAVE DANES

Politics must not be discussed here, because it is punishable. In spite of this, I tell you that I would rather die with the Jews than live with the Nazis.

> *Comment made by the pastor of the Frederiksberg Church after the Danish Lutheran Church condemned the Nazis on October 3, 1943.*

◻

Meyer Lansky

FIGHT BACK

"Jews! Why do you just sit around like stupid sheep and allow them to come and kill you, steal your money, kill your sons and rape your daughters? Aren't you ashamed? You must stand up and fight. You are men like other men. I have been a soldier in the Turkish army. I was taught to fight. A Jew can fight. I will teach you how. We have no arms, but it doesn't matter. Sticks and stones. Even if you're going to die, at least do it with honor. Fight back! Stop being cowards. Stop lying down like stupid sheep. Don't be frightened. Hit them and they'll run. If you are going to die, then die fighting. Protect your beloved ones. Your womenfolk should be able to rely on you."

> *Recalling the words of a young Jewish revolutionary soldier who held a meeting in Meyer's grandfather's house in Grodno, Russian Poland, before Meyer came to America in April 1911 as a ten-year-old boy. Reported in Stephen Birmingham's* The Rest of Us *(1984).*

◻

Tom Lantos

THE PRICE OF SILENCE

The Holocaust did not begin with gas chambers, it began with speech no more repulsive and belligerent than the speech of this man [Muhammad]. One can remain silent—and we have seen in the '30s what silence leads to—or one can stand up and condemn this kind of outrage.

> *In an interview after the March 1994 condemnation by the U.S. House of Representatives (361-34) of the anti-Semitic speech of Nation of Islam official Khalid Abdul Muhammad.*

◻

Claude Lanzmann

ON ACCEPTING LOVE

This is a very strange country. They cannot seem to stand it that somebody loves them. I don't know why.

> *Commenting in 1995 after filming the documentary* Tsahal, *which sings the praises of the Israeli armed forces.*

◻

Dominique LaPierre

O, JERUSALEM!

It was a moment I'll never forget. As the driver approached Jerusalem—it was a Friday—I saw Moslems emerging from the mosque, Jews going to the Western Wall and bells ringing all over Jerusalem. I knew then I was in the city of God.

> *Recalling the reopening of Jerusalem to the Jewish population after the 1948 War of Liberation. In an interview with Lisa Frydman in* The Jerusalem Post, *June 12, 1993.*

◻

Daniel Lapin

THE SCHOOL PRAYER CONTROVERSY

It's not in the interest of the Jewish community to give the impression to millions of observant Christians that Jews—who introduced God to the world—should paradoxically be the ones most vigorous in excavating him from the public square.

> *The head of Toward Tradition, a conservative organization seeking to forge better relations with the religious right, commenting in 1995 on the strong Jewish opposition to a school prayer amendment.*

◻

Walter Laqueur

FINAL SOLUTION

While it is correct that only a handful of Germans knew all about the "Final Solution," very few knew nothing.

> *From his* Terrible Secret *(1982).*

HOLOCAUST DENIERS

The phenomenon of Holocaust denial ought to be studied carefully, but I am not sure there is much point in engaging in academic debates with the perpetrators. Not a single denier of the Holocaust has ever been dissuaded by facts; if one argument is disproved, they think of another. You may as well try to convert a militant anti-Semite by adducing Jewish Nobel Prize winners and violinists.

> *From his review in* The New Republic *of Yisrael Gutman and Michael Berenbaum's* Anatomy of the Auschwitz Death Camp *(1994).*

◘

Harold J. Laski

THE RESTIVE PRIME MINISTER

He will not risk things. He will not see people. He gets restive immediately a hint of criticism appears.... He can't bear a big man near him.

> *Commenting on England's Prime Minister (James) Ramsay MacDonald in a February 1939 letter to Felix Frankfurter.*

POLITICAL SYSTEMS

No political system has the privilege of immortality.

> *From an article in* The New Republic, *May 3, 1939.*

ACHIEVING PEACE

Free enterprise and the market economy mean war; socialism and planned economy mean peace. We must plan our civilization or we must perish.

> *From his* Plan or Perish *(1945).*

◘

Yisrael Meir Lau

THE FIRST SOLUTION

The way in which Aharon Lustiger has chosen to live his life goes hand in hand with the Final Solution.... Here is a man who betrayed his own people at the age of 14, and has no regrets though he has had 55 years to think it over.

> *Objecting to Cardinal Jean-Marie Lustiger, Archbishop of Paris, having been invited to address a conference on "The Silence of God" at Tel Aviv University in April 1995. The Jewish-born Lustiger converted to Christianity at age fourteen.*

◘

Ronald S. Lauder

DENYING HITLER A VICTORY

In 1986 I noticed a gap on Vienna's Tempelgasse amid elegant prewar buildings. I asked passersby what had stood there. No one knew, till one old man answered, "The world's most beautiful synagogue."

"No one else knew?" I asked.

"They knew," he replied, "but they want the world to forget."

...I realized that losing our heritage grants Hitler a victory. Those Jews cherished their Judaism despite determined repression; how could I squander mine? My roots are in Central Europe; my Foundation helps today's Central European Jews reclaim their identity. And this "High Holiday Jew" has become a Jew year 'round.

> *Quoted in* Hadassah Magazine, *March 1994.*

◘

T(homas) E(dward) Lawrence

HOPE FOR ZIONISM

The Jew who leaves the country of his birth or adoption to live in Palestine must for a considerable time remain a stranger in the land of his forefathers. But if Zionism is to have any future, this sacrifice must be faced. The Sultan of Egypt once remarked that a Zionist is a Jew who pays another Jew to live in Palestine. Until this idea can be driven out of the heads of Jew and non-Jew alike, there can be no real hope for Zionism.

> *Reflecting on Chaim Weizmann's call: "Jewish People: Where Are You?" From an interview published in the* Palestine Gazette, *December 26, 1919.*

◘

Bernard Lazare

BECAUSE HE WAS A JEW

Because he was a Jew he was arrested. Because he was a Jew he was convicted. Because he was a Jew the voices of justice and of truth could not be heard in his favor.

> *From a brochure entitled* A Judicial Error: The Truth on the Dreyfus Affair, *published on November 6, 1896.*

PROFOUND EMPATHY

What things of history has the Jew not felt? What has he not experienced? To what shame has he not been subjected? What pain has he not suffered? What triumphs has he not known? What defeats has he not accepted? What resignation has he not shown? What pride has he not displayed? And all that has left profound traces in his soul, just as the flood waters leave their sediments on the valley floor.

> *From the writings of the self-hating French writer who returned to positive Jewish feelings under the influence of Theodor Herzl. Quoted in Raphael Patai's* Jewish Mind *(1977).*

INVENTING THE JEW

If the Jew did not exist as an outlet for the wrath of those who are despoiled,...he would be invented.

> *From his* Nationalism and Jewish Emancipation *(1889).*

□

Morris S. Lazaron

ON NATIONAL RIGHTS

The influence of the immigrant Jew is most definitely in the scale of exclusiveness, clannishness. Such institutions as the Jewish parochial schools, or the tendency to inject into our American political system European conceptions of group rights and minority privileges, must be combated with all our influence and all our power.

> *In a 1920 speech. From the* Central Conference of American Rabbis Yearbook, *Volume XXX.*

UNIVERSAL MESSAGE

In the nationalism of our times, we must cry out the universal message of Israel: Not the blood cult, state cult, hate cult, war cult of nationalism, but one humanity on earth as there is one God in heaven.

> *From his* Common Ground *(1938).*

PRICE OF BEING A JEW

He hath...laughed at my losses, mocked at my gains, scorned my nation, thwarted my bargains, cooled my friends, heated mine enemies; and what's his reason? I am a Jew.

> *Ibid.*

THE JEWISH STATE

If Palestine is to be Jewish it cannot be a State, and if it is to be a State it cannot be Jewish.

> *Ibid.*

JIHAD OF HATE

You cannot conquer the world for the god of love by a jihad of hate.

> *Ibid.*

□

Emma Lazarus

MACCABEAN RAGE

Oh deem not dead that martial fire,
Say not the mystic flame is spent!
With Moses' law and David's lyre,
Your ancient strength remains unbent.
Let but an Ezra rise anew
To lift the Banner of the Jew!

> *From her poem "The Banner of the Jew," included in* Songs of a Semite: The Dance to Death and Other Poems *(1882).*

LIVING SPIRIT

The Spirit is not dead, proclaim the word,
Where lay dead bones, a host of armed
   men stand!
I ope [*sic*] your graves, my people, saith the
   Lord,
And I shall place you living in your land.

> *From her poem "The New Ezekiel," included in her* Songs of a Semite.

YEARNING TO BE FREE

Give me your tired, your poor,
Your huddled masses yearning to breathe
   free,
The wretched refuse of your teeming shore,
Send these, the homeless, tempest-tost
   to me.

> *Inscribed on the pedestal of the Statue of Liberty, which stands in New York's harbor. From her poem "The New Colossus" (1883).*

MOTHER OF EXILES

Here at our sea-washed, sunset
gates shall stand
A mighty woman with a torch
whose flame
Is the imprisoned lightning, and
her name:
Mother of Exiles.

> *Ibid.*

LONG-LIVED PASSION

His cup is gall, his meat is tears,
His passion lasts a thousand years.

> *From her poem "Crowing of the Red Cock" (1881).*

THE NOBLE CONQUERED

If Victory makes the hero, raw Success
The stamp of virtue, unremembered
Be then the desperate strife,
the storm and stress
Of the last Warrior Jew. But if
the man

Who dies for freedom, loving all
things less,...
Nobler the conquered than the
conqueror's end!

From her poem "Bar Kochba" (1888).

NEWPORT SYNAGOGUE

No signs of life are here: the very prayers
Inscribed around are in a language dead;
The light of the "perpetual lamp" is spent
That an undying radiance was to shed....
Nathless, the sacred shrine is holy yet,
With its lone floor where reverent feet once
trod.
Take off your shoes as by the burning bush,
Before the mystery of death and God.

From her second volume of poems, Admetus
and Other Poems *(1871), published when
she was twenty-two and dedicated "To my
friend, Ralph Waldo Emerson," who had
encouraged her to continue writing. Written
in July 1867, the subject of the poem is the
Jewish synagogue of Newport, Rhode
Island.*

THE REAWAKENING

I'm all Israel now! Till this cloud passes I
have no thought, no passion, no desire, save
for my own people.

*After the Russian pogroms of 1881 and
1882, Lazarus became aware of the plight of
her fellow Jews, to which she had paid little
attention theretofore. She is quoted as having once said that she disliked "Jewish
things."*

TO A BETTER LIFE

In two divided streams the exiles part,
One rolling homeward to its ancient source,
One rushing sunward with fresh will, new
heart.
By each the truth is spread, the law un-
furled,
Each separate soul contains the nation's
force,
And both embrace the world.

*A poem for the Jewish New Year 5646
(1882–83), which coincided with the large
migration of Jews from Eastern Europe to
America and Palestine.*

NEWFOUND FAITH

First, in a return to the varied pursuits and
broad system of physical and intellectual education adopted by our ancestors; Second, in a
more fraternal and practical movement towards alleviating the sufferings of oppressed
Jews in countries less favored than our own;
Third, in a closer and wider study of Hebrew
literature and history; and finally in a truer

recognition of the large principles of religion,
liberty, and law upon which Judaism is founded, and which should draw into harmonious
unity Jews of every shade and opinion.

*Expressing the credo of her newfound faith
in a series of articles entitled* An Epistle to
the Hebrews, *which appeared in* American
Hebrew, *November 10, 1882 to February
24, 1883.*

JEWISH VERSATILITY

Jews are the intensive form of any nationality whose language and customs they adopt.

Ibid.

□

Josephine Lazarus

UNGRATEFUL SPECULATION

What Emma Lazarus might have accomplished, had she been spared, it is idle and
even ungrateful to speculate. What she did accomplish has real and peculiar significance. It
is the privilege of a favored few that every fact
and circumstance of their individuality shall
add lustre and value to what they achieve. To
be born a Jewess was a distinction to Emma
Lazarus, and she in turn conferred distinction
upon her race.

*From an evaluation of her sister, who died in
1887 at the age of thirty-nine. Josephine,
older by three years, gathered Emma's
poems, which were published in two vol-
umes in 1888 under the title* The Poems of
Emma Lazarus.

□

Moritz Lazarus

THE UNIVERSAL IDEAL

Israel had to be particularistic in order to
formulate and hold up the universal ideal.

From his Ethics of Judaism *(1901).*

DIVINE MAN

Every house a temple, every heart an altar,
every human being a priest.

Ibid.

□

Norman Lear

IMPECCABLE WORDS

I love being associated with the first amendment. Terrific words. Precise. Impeccable.

*Upon receiving the William O. Douglas
First Amendment Award in 1981 for his
leadership in opposing attempts to censor
television programming.*

Rufus Learsi

AMERICAN AND JEW

So live that when the summons
    comes from men
Or from the Inner Voice you cannot
    still
To say what loyalties command
    your heart.
What proud device your noble
    blazon flaunts,
you will stand forth and hold aloft
    your shield
With words writ large: "American
    and Jew."

From his "Tercentennial Oration," in which he paraphrases the last lines of William Cullen Bryant's poem "Thanatopsis."

Fernande Leboucher

TRUCKS FOR JEWS

In June 1944...the infamous Eichmann suggested to the Allies, through an intermediary, a bizarre exchange: one million Jews, to be "delivered" to North Africa, in return for ten thousand trucks. The reply of Lord Moyne, Deputy Minister of State for North Africa, was: "What could we do with a million Jews? Where would we put them?"

In his Incredible Mission.

Maya Lebovich

THE VIEW FROM ISRAEL

There is an entire generation of young men and women who are ready for a more active part in Jewish life, but they will meet resistance from the older generation.

The father, a neighbor of ours, was rather shocked when he saw me standing on the *bimah* [pulpit] with my son, wearing a *tallit* [prayershawl] and carrying the Torah. He told me he was uncomfortable with it all, but that the food was delicious.

Five minutes later, his 18-year-old daughter came up to me and said: "The best part of the bar mitzvah was when you stood on the *bimah* [pulpit] and held the Torah."

I'd say that describes Israeli society in a nutshell.

Upon her ordination as a Reform rabbi at Hebrew Union College in Jerusalem in 1993.

Fran Lebowitz

GOD'S CHILDREN

All God's children are not beautiful. Most of God's children are, in fact, barely presentable.

From her Metropolitan Life *(1978).*

TIP FOR TEENAGERS

Remember that as a teenager you are at the last stage in your life when you will be happy to hear that the phone is for you.

From her Social Studies *(1981).*

William Lecky

ANTIDOTE TO PERSECUTION

Above all this [medieval persecution] the genius of that wonderful people rose supreme. While those around them were groveling in the darkness of besotted ignorance,...the Jews were still pursuing the path of knowledge, amassing learning, and stimulating progress with the same unflinching constancy that they manifested in their faith.

From his Spirit of Rationalism in Europe *(1868).*

Michele Lee

ANSWER TO ANTI-SEMITISM

The answer to anti-Semitism is education. You have to forgive somebody his poor upbringing. You cannot hold it against him. You can, but at the same time you have to understand.

Quoted in Tim Boxer's Jewish Celebrity Hall of Fame *(1987).*

FEARFUL FANTASIZING

I hate to say this, but as I look around the world I am frightened. I am a Jewish person who has actually had fantasies of, gee, what happens if my plane is hijacked...and I'm Jewish.... I thought of all those things. A lot of Jewish people have thought the same things. I thought of going abroad, going to Paris. Think of the anti-Semitism that has been shown around the world. It's frightening. I don't remember feeling this way when I was younger. It's just getting so strange around the world.

Ibid.

PREJUDICIAL REMARKS

I'm not only concerned about anti-Semitism. Being in California, for some reason people like to make derogatory remarks about Mexicans. I really get infuriated. Everything goes cold in me when anyone says derogatory things about anybody.

Ibid.

◻

Isaac Leeser

JEWISH PHILANTHROPY

To our mind, the whole of the system of distributing charity is defective and wrong in principle. The amount given may suffice to relieve immediate want, but no more. Perhaps under existing circumstances, this is all that can be done; but might not a union of all the charity funds raised in any one city be effected, and they be placed under the control of a central board?

A proposal made in 1849.

CRIME PREVENTION

Society owes something more, much more, than merely providing prisons for delinquents, whilst it does so little, so nothing at all, if we may judge, to prevent crime, and to train those exposed to the danger of contamination in such a manner that they should benefit instead of injuring their fellow mortals.

> *From an 1850 appeal in the pages of* The Occident, *a monthly, for wealthy American Jews to support a foster home.*

THE PLACE OF JEWS

In the synagogue we want Jews; in public matters, only Americans.

Ibid.

◻

Joseph Leftwich

DEFINING A JEW

Reason it away, as we will, define and redefine—something there is which we and the world call a Jew. That is our standard. What the Jew becomes after five generations of intermarriage and assimilation is another matter.

> *From the Foreword to his* Jewish Omnibus *(1933).*

CHARACTERISTICS OF JEWISHNESS

To me the greatest of the constituents [of being Jewish] seems to be living as far as possible as my father lived, according to the traditions of Jewishness and Judaism as they have grown to be today, and for the coming generations as they may evolve.

Ibid.

◻

Herbert H. Lehman

A NATION OF IMMIGRANTS

We are a nation of immigrants. It is immigrants who brought to this land the skills of their hands and brains to make it a beacon of opportunity and of hope for all men.

> *In a July 2, 1947 statement before the House Subcommittee on Immigration and Naturalization.*

GAINING RESPECT

You ask whether I have a comment to make to my fellow Jews who may want some day to become publicly known and feel that Judaism may hold them back because of either discrimination or prejudice. My answer is that I think any man, who is seeking public office and allows his ambition to affect his religious affiliation, is not worthy of the confidence of his fellow citizens. I know of very few instances in which a man was looked down upon because he was a Jew. On the other hand I know of many instances where a man sought to hide his religion [and] lost the respect of his fellow citizens.

> *Responding to a young Jew who asked whether being Jewish affected the senator's career. The letter was read at Lehman's funeral in New York City on December 8, 1963.*

NEVER BE ASHAMED

My advice in a word is: Never be ashamed of being a Jew. Never try to hide it. Never try to compromise with your convictions because they may not agree with those of the group in which you find yourself.

Ibid.

RESPECT ALL RELIGIONS

I believe that all religions play a useful and very necessary part in people's lives, and I respect all religions that teach belief and faith in God.

Ibid.

¤

Nechama Leibowitz

ACCEPTANCE AND REJECTION

One can put a hand into a thornbush without being hurt, but when he tries to pull it out he cannot. So it was with Israel in Egypt; they were welcome at first but afterward could not leave. So it has been with Israel many times in the Diaspora.

From her Studies in the Weekly Sidrah *(1960).*

¤

Yeshayahu Leibowitz

"BEGINNING OF REDEMPTION"

The phenomenon of individuals returning to *halakhic* [legal religious] practice has nothing to do with the "beginning of redemption"; it is, rather, an expression of spiritual struggles that can arise within individuals in any place, at any time, and under any historical circumstances. Israel's return to its God will only come about from an awakening of the Jews themselves, not by virtue of the Israel Defense Force. There is today no sign of this awakening.

From an essay in David Hartman's Conflicting Visions *(1990).*

MEANING OF REVELATION

It is my firm and clearly expressed view that the meaning of Revelation is the *demand* made of man and the *obligation* imposed on him to serve God.

Neither the Sinai Revelation nor the Revelation in the words and deeds of the prophets succeeded in making the demand obeyed and the obligation fulfilled.

From an article in The Jerusalem Post, *November 10, 1984.*

ESSENCE OF DEMOCRACY

One of the best American minds of our time, Justice William Douglas, said that the essence of democracy is the defense of the individual against his *own* government, not against the enemy. He added that the meaning of the American Constitution is to make it harder for the government to do as it pleases with the individual. The more free organizing prevails the weaker the state becomes. The state holds the power of coercion. Therefore, the state is the enemy of the individual. I am not an anarchist and I know that this evil called "state" is a necessity. But its authority should be reduced to the necessary minimum. I know that even this

minimum is still a large threat, and so one should keep it from increasing.

In answer to the question "Do you think policemen should be free to establish their own union?" posed by Israeli journalist Levi Yitzhak Hayerushalmi, a staff member of Maariv. *Reported in* The Jewish Spectator, *Summer 1979.*

NO ACCLAIM FOR THE FIGHTER

Nowhere in Jewish sources is there any of the reverence for the heroism of the fighter that is so prevalent in many non-Jewish cultures, even the most enlightened. Nor on *Chanukah* would we recite the added prayer *Al Ha-nisim* for the Maccabees if they had not fought the Lord's war and saved the holy law. Their heroism in battle is not mentioned at all; it is taken for granted.

Quoted in Contemporary Jewish Religious Thought *(1987), edited by Arthur A. Cohen and Paul Mendes-Flohr.*

MESSIANIC FOOLS

[The Gush Emunim movement was comprised of] messianic fools...who are so presumptuous as to think they know God's will.

From a 1990 interview with journalist Matthew Nesvisky. Reported in The Jewish Week, *September 30–October 6, 1994.*

CREATING JUDEO-NAZIS

Military service in the territories turns our youth into murderers against their will.... I call upon them to refuse to serve there and to refuse to obey the illegal orders of the government.

Ibid. Claiming that to serve on the West Bank and Gaza would transform Jewish youth into "Judeo-Nazis."

¤

Vladimir Ilyich Lenin

HOSTILE MOOD

The idea of a Jewish "nationality" runs counter to the interests of the Jewish proletariat because directly or indirectly it arouses within it a mood hostile to assimilation, a ghetto mood.

Quoted in The Jewish Frontier, *August 1950.*

JEWISH BOURGEOISIE

The Jewish bourgeoisie are our enemies, not as Jews but as bourgeoisie. The Jewish worker is our brother.

From a speech to the Council of People's Commissars, August 9, 1918.

¤

Jack E. Leonard

ON FINDING YOURSELF

Don't worry, Ed, someday you'll find your-self—and you'll be terribly disappointed. There's nothing wrong with you that reincarnation won't cure.

Poking fun at Ed Sullivan during one of his many appearances on The Ed Sullivan Show.

¤

Max Lerner

PRESIDENTIAL STRIDE

A President is best judged by the enemies he makes when he has really hit his stride.

From The New York Star, *January 9, 1949.*

THE HATE LAYER

There is a hate layer of opinion and emotion in America. There will be other Mc-Carthys to come who will be hailed as its heroes.

From his column in the New York Post, *April 5, 1950.*

AGE FIFTY

The real sadness of fifty is not that you change so much but that you change so little.

From his column in the New York Post, *December 18, 1952.*

WORD REJECTION

The crime of book purging is that it involves a rejection of the word.... To reject the word is to reject the human search.

Referring to the McCarthy book burnings. From his column in the New York Post, *June 24, 1953.*

A TOWERING FIGURE

Years from now, when historians can look back and put our time into perspective, they will say that of its towering figures—more truly great than generals and diplomats, business grants and labor grants, bigger than most of our presidents—was a man called Brandeis.

In praise of U.S. jurist Louis D. Brandeis in the early 1970s.

HAVE A GOOD DAY

In any culture the phrases that people use, especially in their impersonal meetings, reveal a good deal. *"Guten Morgen"* used to be the morning greeting phrase in the days of the Weimar Republic. It was replaced by *"Heil Hitler."* A whole society had caved in, been pushed out by another. Happily they are saying *"Guten Morgen"* again in Berlin and Frankfurt.

From his column in the New York Post, *February 20, 1976.*

FROM FREEDOM TO ANARCHY

The concept of freedom had been turned into anarchy, and equality had become a quota system. "The social issues" this [new] class reacted to—affirmative action, pornography, abortion—were not part of the liberal agenda.

A 1981 statement denouncing liberals.

PROTRACTED STRUGGLE

Life is a protracted struggle against the Adversary—who is man himself.

From an article in the Saturday Review, *December 5, 1959.*

YEARNING FOR RECOGNITION

I don't write this in a scolding mood. The other day I was oversharp about the posh people at a nightclub opening who, as the proprietor put it, came "to see and be seen." The fact is that all of us enjoy it, splashing about in whatever our little puddle of a pond may be. Each wants to feel he is in the swim. What we cannot bear is the prospect of being left behind by life.

From a 1966 newspaper column on the nature of human conduct.

SOUR MEMORIES

In a holiday spell like this one I fell with the fallen. In their youth perhaps they rode the wave high, had things going for them, had it made. Now they have only the acrid memory. I am not speaking here only of the many in a big city who live alone, eat and drink alone, sit in movie-houses alone, watch TV alone. I am speaking even more of those—millions of them—who may be sitting among friends and family, at tables heavily loaded with food, amidst talk and laughter and the sound of fun, yet who feel empty—for what they have lost, what perhaps they have never had, for the turnings that went wrong, for the broken life chances, for the promises unkept and the promises unfulfilled.

Ibid.

¤

Michael Lerner

THE JEWISH FUTURE

Many Jews under 50 report they experience the Jewish world as conformist, materialistic, dominated by the wealthy and the fund-rais-ers, undemocratic, sexist, lacking in spirituali-ty and defining everyone who criticizes Israeli policy as "self-hating."...Create an environ-ment in which children growing up in the Jew-ish world see that the people who are respected, really have power and influence, are those with greatest sensitivity, caring for others (including non-Jews), spiritual vitality, Jewish learning, commitment to social change and alive to awe, wonder and radical amaze-ment at God's presence in the world—and you'll guarantee the Jewish future.

From Hadassah Magazine, *June–July 1993.*

TRANSFORMING THE WORLD

The notion that the world could and should be different than it is has deep roots within Ju-daism. But in the late 1980's it is an idea that seems strangely out of fashion—and those who still dare to hope often view themselves as isolated, if not irrelevant. In the context of Western societies, too often intoxicated with their own material and technological suc-cess,...those who talk of fundamental transfor-mation seem to be dreaming.

From Tikkun *magazine's 1986 premier.*

TAKING A COMMITTED STAND

The commitment to change the world, to demand justice and love in a world that has given up on these ideals, is not some pious sentiment clouding one's eyes to a hard-nosed look at reality. On the contrary, the rejection of moral neutrality, the committed stance on be-half of the oppressed, makes possible a deeper understanding of the dynamics of culture and society.

Ibid.

A CONTEXT OF MEANING

Liberals have "framed their intellectual commitments around a belief that the only things that really move people are economic entitlements and political rights"; they miss the fact that "human beings have a deep need to have their lives make sense, to transcend the dynamics of individualism and selfishness that predominate in a competitive market soci-ety and to find a way to place their lives in a context of meaning and purpose."

A concept valued especially by Hillary Clin-ton, wife of U.S. President Bill Clinton. From his article in Tikkun *magazine, July–August 1992.*

A BASIC JEWISH TRADITION

The universalistic dream of a transforma-tion and healing of the world, the belief that peace and justice are not meant for heaven but are this-worldly necessities that must be fought for, is the particularistic cultural and re-ligious tradition of the Jews.

From his essay "To Mend, Repair and Trans-form the World," which appeared in Tikkun *magazine (1986).*

CONCEPTIONS OF GOD

Conceptions of God in Judaism have changed and evolved along with our under-standing of ourselves and our world. The God who takes a stroll in the Garden of Eden (Gen-esis 3:8) made little sense to the rabbis who constructed the Talmud, so they reinterpreted Bible stories in ways that made God into a spiritual entity without a body.

From his Jewish Renewal *(1994).*

LEAP OF FAITH

In the final analysis, then, the assertion about the possibility of overcoming cruelty is not an empirical one but a statement of faith in the God of Israel, just as its denial is a statement of faith in the religion of "cynical re-alism."

Ibid.

MAN'S AFFINITY TO GOD

I believe that God's energy permeates every ounce of Being and every moment of exis-tence, that God is constantly sending us mes-sages and constantly not only making possible our transcendence but demanding and beg-ging us to join with Her/Him in this process.

Ibid.

RELIGION OF PESSIMISM

There are institutions and psychological practices that embody and pass on evil from generation to generation. But there is no Radi-cal Evil working behind these phenomena and making them happen. Our testimony as Jews is to a very different force in the universe.

Ibid.

□

Anatole Leroy-Beaulieu

POETIC FIRE

In the depths of the Ghetto the Jew pre-served his Bible and his Agada, two wells of poetry at which he could ever refresh him-self.... The sons of Jacob had, as it were, a latent, subterranean, poetic fire, ready to burst forth wherever Israel's soul had not become too parched by ritual and form, or too degraded by oppression and dishonoring trades.

From his Israel Among the Nations *(1893).*

ARISTOCRATIC NATION

Viewed as a nation, Israel is the most ancient and perhaps the most gifted of all those which the Germans call *Kultur-Völker.* The breadth and antiquity of her culture have won for her a sort of aristocracy of birth among the nations.

Ibid.

□

Allen Lesser

DEDICATED ZIONIST

She [Emma Lazarus] never attached any great value to poetical fame; a purely literary career seemed to her too unreal, too detached from the world of the living, to offer any genuine reward. But once she enlisted in the army of Jewish nationalism, she lived like a woman possessed, her eyes not upon her own career, but upon the fulfillment of the promise of Israel. It was in that cause that her character had its fullest flowering.

From his Weave a Wreath of Laurel.

□

Gotthold E. Lessing

THE FUTURE TEACHERS

God selected a people for His special education, and precisely the rudest and unruliest, in order to begin with it from the very beginning.... He was bringing up in them the future teachers of the human race.

From his Education of the Human Race *(1778).*

THE EYE OF THE BEHOLDER

That which makes me a Christian in your eyes
Makes you a Jew in mine.

From his Nathan the Wise *(1779). The response of the title character to a monk who praised him for raising an orphaned Christian child.*

NEVER A BETTER CHRISTIAN

Nathan! Nathan! You are a Christian! By

God, you are a Christian! There never was a better Christian!

Ibid.

□

Theodor Lessing

TRUE LOYALTY

I am and shall remain a German; I am and shall remain a Jew; I am and shall remain a Socialist...I am now fighting for justice under my own name, against my own country, which I love.

The closing lines of a letter to the Manchester Guardian *two weeks before Lessing was shot to death by Nazi stormtroopers on August 31, 1933. Lessing's forebears had lived in Hanover for more than three hundred years, and he had taught at the university for twenty-six years before being dismissed without his pension.*

□

Julius Lester

RESPONSE TO RACISM

The most enduring response to racism, and my response to anti-Semitism, is precisely this: To affirm life [and say *Le-chaim!*].

Lester, a black, is a convert to Judaism. From an article in Moment *magazine, April 1980.*

USING SUFFERING

There is only one way to be human and that is found in how we use our suffering. And by suffering I do not mean the sentimentality of those who see themselves as victims, of those who define themselves as oppressed. By suffering I mean the pain which comes when you look at yourself and see yourself as you truly are—a mere mortal, limited, frail, full of pretense, bloated with self-importance, very alone and very afraid. And that is only the beginning.

Ibid.

JEWS ARE HUMAN

Angered and hurt as I was by those Jews who opposed affirmative action, I began to accept that it was wrong, very wrong, to expect Jews to be better than anyone else, to expect Jews to understand more and to be more. Jews were human. That was hard enough, without demanding that they live up to my expectations.

Ibid.

KNOWING WHO YOU ARE

In the winter of 1974, while I was on retreat at the Trappist monastery in Spencer, Massachusetts, one of the monks told me, "When you know the name by which God knows you, you will know who you are."

I searched for that name with the passion of one seeking the Eternal Beloved. I called myself Father, Writer, Teacher, but God did not answer.

Now I know the name by which God calls me. I am Yaakov Daniel ben Avraham v'Sarah.

I have become who I am. I am who I always was. I am no longer deceived by the black face which stares at me from the mirror.

I am a Jew.

From his Lovesong: Becoming a Jew *(1988).*

LESSON OF THE HOLOCAUST

When a non-Jew attacks Israel, I feel threatened. Israel is mine. Don't non-Jews understand that after the Holocaust, Jews feel more alone and isolated in the world than ever? Jews no longer expect non-Jews to approve of them, accept them, and certainly not love them as members of the human family. Jewish survival depends upon the willingness and ability of Jews to act in their own defense. That is the lesson of the Holocaust. That is why Israeli planes are bombing Beirut.

Ibid. In a 1982 statement reversing his earlier attitude, expressed in a 1967 essay, defending the Student Nonviolent Coordinating Committee's condemnation of Israel and Zionism.

TIME FOR TACHLIS

The time has come to stop making apologies for black America, to stop patronizing black America with that paternalistic brand of understanding which excuses and finds reasons for the obscenities of black hatred.... Farrakhan is subtly but surely creating an atmosphere in America where hatreds of all kinds will be easier to express openly, and one day, in some as yet unknown form, these hatreds will ride commuter trains into the suburbs. By then it will be too late for us all.

After Louis Farrakhan had addressed a rally in New York. From an article in The New Republic, *October 1985.*

FORGIVEN BUT NOT FORGOTTEN

Many Jews will, of course, never forgive him [Jesse Jackson] for his anti-Semitic remarks in the 1984 campaign [for President]. But Mr. Jackson has made sincere efforts to educate himself and change his behavior in this regard.

To hold him accountable for what he said eleven years ago is to say a person is incapable of learning and growing and changing.

From an article in the Forward, *October 6, 1995.*

THE MILLION MAN MARCH

Why are we not frightened that the Rev. Farrakhan has a standing and power in black America that Martin Luther King, Jr., never came close to? The attempts to disassociate the Rev. Farrakhan from the marchers is an attempt to evade moral responsibility for making the Rev. Farrakhan the most powerful leader in black American history.

Commenting on the November 1995 Million Man March on Washington orchestrated by Louis Farrakhan, in which an estimated 400,000 to 800,000 blacks participated.

□

Steven Leul

PROMOTING HEALING

The Holocaust must become less of a painful emotional problem for us and remain predominantly in historical, philosophical and intellectual context for our children.... But our obligation, unless we choose to remain wedded to masochism, is to promote healing and foster wellness in our young. We must find a via media between the obligation to remember with its unavoidable sadness, the obligation to lessen the obsessive rumination, the corrosive cynicism regarding human possibilities, the distrust of "the other," all of which point to damaging links to the Holocaust.

From his Psychoanalytic Reflections on the Holocaust *(1985).*

□

Oscar Levant

IMPECCABLE BEHAVIOR

My behavior has been impeccable; I've been unconscious for the past six months.

From his Memoirs of an Amnesiac.

THE UNDERBELLY

Underneath this flabby exterior is an enormous lack of character.

Ibid.

FEELING GOOD

I don't drink. I don't like it. It makes me feel good.

Quoted in Time *magazine, May 5, 1950.*

□

Sam Levenson

THE LIGHTER SIDE OF POVERTY

My mother used to buy one pound of meat and make three pounds of hamburgers. You know how? We had a slogan in our house. It said, "Old rolls never die." Everything went into a hamburger. After a while, my mother learned to make chopped meat completely without meat and I liked it that way.

> *From one of his comedy routines. Quoted in Darryl Lyman's* Jewish Comedy Catalog *(1989).*

FAMILY CAT

In the old days, if you bought an order at the butcher's he threw in the liver for the cat. You remember? I will tell you the truth. We didn't always have a cat but we always had liver—you are looking at the family cat.

> *Ibid.*

BE CONSISTENT

Dear Sir:

It's a free world. You don't have to like Jews but for those of you who don't like Jews, I suggest you boycott certain Jewish products: the Wasserman test for syphilis; Digitalis, discovered by Dr. Nuslin; Insulin, discovered by Dr. Minokofsky; Chlorohydrate for convulsions, discovered by Dr. Casamir Fink; Streptomycin, discovered by Dr. Zalman Waksman; the Polio pill by Dr. Albert Sabin, and the polio vaccine by Dr. Jonas Salk.

> *Responding to an anti-Semite.*

NEVER A MASTER

When I was a boy, I used to do what my father wanted. Now I have to do what my boy wants. My problem is: When am I going to do what I want?

> *From one of his comedy routines.*

□

(Rabbi) Levi

AGENTS OF SIN

The heart and the eye are agents of sin. The eye sees and the heart desires.

> *Quoted in the Jerusalem Talmud Berachot (1:5).*

GIFTS FROM THE POOR

See how the Holy One tried to spare the people expense: if one became liable to sacri-

fice, he was commanded to bring from the herd [Leviticus 1:3]; if he could not afford it, he was told to bring a lamb [4:32]; and if he could not afford that, he could bring a goat [3:12], or a fowl [1:14], or just a measure of fine flour [6:12].

> *Quoted in Midrash Leviticus Rabba (8:4).*

GOD SPEAKS THROUGH OUR BODIES

Six organs serve a person; three are under his control and three are not under his control.

The eye, the ear, and the nose are not under a person's control: he sees what he doesn't want to see, hears what he doesn't want to hear, and smells what he doesn't want to smell.

The mouth, the hand, and the foot are under a person's control. If he wishes, he can use his mouth to study Torah; or if he wishes, he can use it to speak gossip and blasphemy. If he wishes, he can use his hand to distribute charity; or if he wishes, he can use it to steal and kill. If he chooses to, he can use his feet to walk to synagogues or houses of study; or, if he chooses to, he can walk to houses of bawdy entertainment or immorality.

> *Quoted in Midrash Genesis Rabba (67:3).*

THE TASTE OF MATZA

One who eats matza on the eve of Passover [on the day before the first Seder] is like one who has intimate relations with his bride-to-be in his father-in-law's home.

> *Asserting that one deserves flogging if he cannot control himself sufficiently so that the experience of tasting matza will be fresh when the holiday begins. Quoted in the Jerusalem Talmud Pesachim (10:1).*

□

Primo Levi

UNDER THE SKIN

I live in my house as I live inside my skin. I know more beautiful, more ample, more sturdy and more picaresque skins, but it would seem to me unnatural to exchange them for mine.

> *From his* Other People's Trades *(1989).*

□

Levi Yitzchak of Berditchev

LET IVAN BLOW

Let Ivan the Gentile blow the shofar *[Loz*

Ivan der goy blozen dem shoifer]; You have treated him as Your very own.

> *The famous chasidic rebbe refused to blow the* shofar *on Rosh Hashana until God showed the same degree of kindness toward His own people that He showed toward the Gentiles.*

COMPLAINT AGAINST GOD

Good morning to You, Lord of the Universe.
I, Levi Yitzchak, son of Sarah of Berditchev,
Have come with a complaint against You on
behalf of our people Israel.
What do You have against Your people Israel?
Why do You afflict Your people Israel?
And I, Levi Yitzchok, son of Sarah of Berditchev, say:
I shall not stir from here—
From this spot I shall not move!
There must be an end to this!
The exile must come to an end!
Yisgadal V'yiskadash shmay raboh.
Magnified and sanctified be His Name.

> *The famous chant of the outstanding chasidic* rebbe *who dared to chastise and indict God. He was so beloved by his community that a successor was never elected after his death.*

PLEA TO THE ALMIGHTY

Lord of the universe! I saw an ordinary Jew pick up his *tefillin* from the floor, and kiss them; and You have let Your *tefillin*, the Jewish people, lie on the ground for more than two thousand years, trampled by their enemies. Why do You not pick them up? Why do You not act as a plain Jew acts? Why?

> *Quoted in S. L. Hurwitz's* Otzar Ha-Torah.

THERE IS A GOD

I wish to announce that there is a God in the world.

> *By way of reminding his* chassidim *that they were not living a moral and ethical life even though they were observing the rituals. Quoted in William B. Silverman's* Rabbinic Wisdom and Values *(1971).*

THE FOURTH SON

The Haggadah speaks of four sons: One wise, one wicked, one simple, and one who does not know how to ask. Lord of the world, I, Levi Yitzchak, am the one who does not know how to ask. In such a case, does not the Haggadah say that with the child who does

not know how to ask, "You must start with him." The father must take the initiative. Lord of the world, are You not my Father? Am I not Your son? I do not even know what questions to ask. You take the initiative and disclose the answers to me. Show me, in connection with whatever happens to me, what is required of me! What are You asking of me? God, I do not ask You why I suffer. I wish to know only that I suffer for Your sake.

> *Quoted in Martin Buber's* Tales of the Hasidim: The Early Masters *(1947).*

¤

Carl Levin

OIL OR IDEALISM?

Oil and idealism do not mix. If idealism stands between Governor Connally's America [Connally, then a candidate for the 1980 Republican presidential nomination, had delivered a speech condemning the so-called Jewish lobby] and a secure oil supply—then IDEALISM [*sic*] must go. And if Israel—the one democratic state in the Middle East, the one stable, friendly government that exists in the Middle East—if Israel stands between Governor Connally's America and secure oil supply—then Israel must go.

> *The United States senator from Michigan expressing his strong support for Israel in 1979 at the annual dinner of the Jewish Reconstructionist Foundation.*

¤

Louis Levin

THE BEST OF THE PAST

Mr. Zangwill makes a fatal mistake. [The making of a] new type of man does not require that he...throw upon the scrap heap all that he has stood for in the past. On the contrary...maintaining intact [the best of his past is] the real contribution that he can make to the betterment of the New American.

> *From a review of Israel Zangwill's 1908 play* The Melting Pot. *Quoted in J. Vincenza Scarpaci's article "Louis H. Levin of Baltimore: A Pioneer in Cultural Pluralism," which appeared in* Maryland Historical Magazine *77, June 1982.*

¤

Meyer Levin

THE MAGNITUDE OF MAN'S INHUMANITY

I knew already that I would never penetrate

its heart of bile, for the magnitude of this horror seemed beyond human register.

> *Upon entering Buchenwald in 1945 in his capacity as a military reporter. The experience was recalled in his autobiography,* In Search *(1950).*

WHAT AM I DOING IN AMERICA?

I know that Jews everywhere are asking themselves this question. The Jew outside [Israel] must define again not only his own relationship to his people. He must decide how to orient his children, whether to give them more Jewish education or try to relieve them of the burden of Jewishness.

> *Ibid. After dramatizing the* Diary of Anne Frank, *he immigrated to Israel.*

OVERCOMING ANTI-SEMITISM

Anti-Semitism is not to be overcome by getting people to forget us, but to know us.

> *Ibid.*

□

Shemarya(hu) Levin

HEBREW AND YIDDISH

The Jewish people represents the only instance of a people that has created two languages of its own.

> *From his* Arena *(1932).*

SUPREME WONDER

The tree is the supreme wonder...the forest is only a mirage.

> *Ibid.*

A JEWISH LIFE

A Jewish life must have a Jewish land.

> *Ibid.*

THE JEWISH FUTURE

Before 1914, a couple of million Jews went to America, a mighty stream; but each of them thought only about himself or his family. A few thousand went to Palestine, a mere trickle; but every one of them was thinking about the future of our Nation.

> *Quoted in* Furrows, *a monthly of the Habonim Labor Zionist Youth, March 1, 1944.*

LOGICIANS AT WORK

Two Jews were discussing which is more important, the sun or the moon. In the end they decided that the moon was more important: the sun gives light in the daytime when it is light anyhow. The moon gives light at night when it is dark.

> *Quoted in Noah Bee's* Impossible Takes Longer *(1983).*

SPIRITUAL GANGRENE

The man who seeks to wipe out his own past is thrown into a state of constant hatred of himself. Out of this hatred is born in turn a profound sadness. The old spirit cannot be cut out clean. There ensues a sort of spiritual gangrene.

> *From his* Youth in Revolt *(1930).*

UNSUCCESSFUL SINGER

As a singer I was not a success. And if I ever asserted myself during that part of the evening's programme, I was gently requested to listen more attentively.

> *Ibid.*

HAY, STRAW! HAY, STRAW!

People in the Russian army in the 1880s were so ignorant and primitive it took weeks to teach them which was their right and which their left hand. And many could not grasp the abstraction of right and left. We had to put a wisp of straw around their left leg and a wisp of hay around their right leg and call out during the march Hay, Straw! Hay, Straw! instead of left right, left right. And even this was often too complicated for them.

> *Ibid.*

FAILURE STIGMATIZED

Two things it's never too late to do: to die and to become a teacher in a *cheder* [Hebrew school]. Only the Jew who has known the old life can understand the bitterness of that proverb, for to become a teacher in a *cheder* was the last resort of every failure.

> *From his* Childhood in Exile *(1929).*

ON WHIPPING CHILDREN

In every person there is a Good and Evil Spirit. The Good Spirit dwells in the head. The Evil Spirit has his abode in the place where you get your whipping. The Good Spirit always remains at home, whereas the Evil Spirit is forever leaving its house and pushing its way into the head. When both spirits get in the head, it is stuffed and there is no room for new ideas. The thing to be done: Put the boy across the bench and let him have it. The Evil Spirit hears someone knocking at its door, gets frightened and runs back. That leaves the head free again and the boy can learn. "I do you a service when I punish you," explains the teacher. "For my conscience won't allow me to leave you to run about with your heads stuffed up and overcrowded."

Ibid. Explaining why it is proper for teachers to whip children.

KISSES THROUGH A VEIL

Bialik once spoke in New York on the subject of the Bible in translation as compared with the original and he likened the former to a kiss which a son might receive from his mother through the thickness of a veil.

Ibid.

EXILE IN AND OUT

It is easier to take a Jew out of the exile than to take the exile out of the Jew.

Quoted by A. Zeitlin in Hadoar *magazine, June 18, 1954.*

THE MAKING OF EXPERTS

One may eat potatoes for forty years, yet that won't make one a botanist.

Comment made at the 1929 Zionist Congress. Quoted in Hadoar *magazine, June 3, 1955.*

ロ

Gilbert Levine

THE POPE AND THE CONDUCTOR

He was curious to meet this American Jew who had been appointed music director in his home city. He sat me down and said, I read all about you in *Newsweek*, so I know your whole story. He then proceeded to talk to me about Cracow with incredible directness and personal concern....

It is a remarkable gesture that he wants to have that concert. I am deeply moved that he wants to have as one of his legacies better relations between Catholics and Jews.

A comment on the meeting to be held in the fall of 1993 in Colorado between the conductor laureate of the Cracow (Poland) Philharmonic Orchestra and Pope John Paul II. Levine was to conduct the National Repertory Orchestra, the Colorado Symphony Chorus, and the Colorado Children's Chorale at a vigil that was to be part of the Pope's visit for World Youth Day. From a report in The New York Times, *August 7, 1993.*

ロ

Naomi Levine

TEXTURES OF JEWISH LIFE

Unfortunately, many of us, including myself, have substituted Jewish politics for Jewish

culture and literacy. We have made fighting anti-Semitism our religion. And if by chance anti-Semitism were no more, and the Russian Jews were finally free to emigrate, and peace finally came to the Middle East—how in the world would we identify as Jews?

Speaking at a 1981 Federation of Jewish Philanthropies Sunday seminar.

WOMEN'S LIB

Women's liberation will not go away. More and more, your daughters will have careers. Federation should support institutions which help a woman to have a career, and, at the same time, a family life if that is her wish. More attention must be given, too, to the single parent.

Ibid.

ロ

Levitas of Yavneh

BE HUMBLE

Be very, very humble, for the end of man's hope is the worm.

From the talmudic tractate Ethics of the Fathers *(4:4).*

ロ

Felix A. Levy

SLAVES TO LITERALISM

The Samaritans are an eloquent illustration of what happens in Israel to any group which surrenders to the letter of the Torah.

From his Crossroads in Judaism *(1954).*

DEBT OWED THE PHARISEES

Too much credit cannot be given to the greatly maligned and misunderstood Pharisees.... The world owes the Bible with its Psalms, the Sabbath, the church, the school, the hospital, and the gospel of love to these modest and self-sacrificing servants of the Lord. They saved the Jew and Judaism from extinction.

Ibid.

ORTHODOX: A MEANINGLESS WORD

Judaism is inherently liberal, and the word "orthodox" has, strictly speaking, no place in it.

Ibid.

◻

Shalom Levy

THE DEATH TOLL

With the death of a husband, you lose your present; with the death of a parent, the past; but with the death of a child you lose your future.

> *From a comment by a member of Kibbutz Hulata who lost his son Daniel in a 1968 commando action. Quoted in* Understanding Bereavement and Grief *(1977), edited by Norman Linzer.*

◻

Uriah P. Levy

COUNTERATTACK

Two things hindered my advancement in the Navy and hastened my retirement. I began my service at sea as a cabin boy. I served as an apprentice to a sailing master. Each of you began as a midshipman. Thus, by the written rules that govern and the whispered rules that have greater power, you are gentlemen. I am not. The men who made the Revolution, Sirs, the men who built this nation out of their bodies and their blood, cared less about such beginnings.

The second hindrance, Gentlemen, is that I am a Jew. I will not insult the Source of the authority of this court and of this nation, nor will I demean my conscience, by defending or explaining my form of worship. The decision as to the faith into which I was born was God's. I believe the same is true of you. I suggest that it is not within the province of the Navy to alter that fact or to place penalties upon His judgment.

> *Addressing the naval court before which he was brought on charges of insubordination because of his relentless campaign against the Navy's practice of flogging sailors as a means of punishment. He refuses to defend his position and instead accuses his superiors of discriminating against him by refusing to give him good assignments worthy of his proven ability.*

FREEDOM OF CONSCIENCE

My parents were Israelites and I was nurtured in the faith of my ancestors. In deciding to adhere to it, I have but exercised a right guaranteed to one by the constitution of my native state, and the United States—a right given to all men by their Maker—a right more precious to each of us than life itself. But,

while claiming and exercising this freedom of conscience I have never failed to acknowledge and respect the like freedom in others.

> *In his* Manual of Rules, *in which was set forth the conduct to be followed by officers on ships under his command. Only absolutely necessary work was to be performed on Sundays.*

TODAY THE JEW, TOMORROW YOU

Are American Christians now to begin the persecution of the Jew?... And think not, if you once enter on this career, that it can be limited to the Jew. What is my case today, if you yield to this injustice, may tomorrow be that of the Roman Catholic or the Unitarian; the Presbyterian or the Methodist; the Episcopalian or the Baptist. There is but one safeguard; that is to be found in an honest, whole-hearted, inflexible support of the wise, the just, the impartial guarantee of the Constitution.

> *In a statement before the Naval Board of Inquiry, convened in 1857 to reconsider Levy's position after he had been dismissed from the Navy in 1855. Levy had protested the naval practice of corporal punishment.*

◻

Kurt Z. Lewin

JEWISH SELF-HATE

There is an almost endless variety of forms which Jewish self-hatred may take.... Most of them, and the most dangerous forms, are a kind of indirect, undercover self-hatred. If I should count the instances where I have encountered open and straightforward contempt among Jews, I could name but a few.... In most cases, expressions of hatred of the Jew against his fellow Jew or against himself as a Jew is [*sic*] more subtle. This hatred is so blended with other motives that [it] is difficult to decide in any one particular case whether or not self-hatred is involved.

> *In a 1941 sociological analysis of the concept of self-hatred.*

◻

Anthony Joseph Lewis

RAISING UP THE POOR

The lawyers who represent the poor in civil matters are doing conservative work in the most fundamental sense. They are building respect for the law among people who tend to be disconnected from society and give them the sense that they have a stake in the system.

> *From a column attacking U.S. President Ronald Reagan for threatening to end a legal aid program for the poor.*

□

Helen Lewis

SAVED BY A DANCE

I took off my wooden shoes, the excellent accordionist played a South American tango, and I danced. Where was the hunger, the fear, the exhaustion? How could I dance with my frostbitten feet? When I finished, they hugged and kissed me, calling me their "star" and lifted me up on their shoulders. Some gave me bread and a bit of margarine and even jam.

> *Describing how she was saved from extermination by entertaining at the concentration camp's Christmas party. From her* A Time to Speak.

□

Jerry Lewis

BEVERLY HILLS CIRCUIT

I don't want the Beverly Hills circuit. I haven't got time for people who ask you how your grandchild is and don't listen to your answer.

> *Quoted in Darryl Lyman's* Jewish Comedy Catalog *(1989).*

□

John L. Lewis

LABOR AND ISRAEL

Labor, like Israel, has many sorrows.

> *From a September 3, 1937 speech in Washington, DC.*

□

Ludwig Lewisohn

BIRDS OF A FEATHER

I regard it as infinitely right and proper that certain groups of my Gentile fellow-citizens desire to remain among themselves. For I have the same feeling about my group. I know certain Gentiles whom I would gladly admit into the closer circle of my friends, and indeed I do so. But if there came into that circle a group of Gentiles whose chief interests, as is natural and proper for them, given their background and their friends, were in competitive sports, or

in hunting, or in war, or in the manufacture of material things as ends and not as means, or else in *their* ancestral memories and their just pride therein of border chieftains or march-raiders or valiant fighters in all the wars of the world—if such came in too great numbers into the group of my friends and fellows, would we not be, while sincerely respecting the otherness of those others, stricken quite dumb and desolate and cramped and ill at ease?

> *Quoted by Maurice Samuel in a 1939 article entitled "Recalling Ludwig Lewisohn."*

SELF-DESTRUCTION

A people cannot be destroyed except from within.

> *From his* Israel *(1925).*

SPAWNED BY SPIRIT

In the first half millennium of the Christian era, amid darkness, confusion, the conflict of creeds and the downfall of classical civilization, the Jews learned the lesson of being a nation by force of the spirit alone.

> *Ibid.*

ARYAN AND JEW

The Aryan gentleman asks concerning an action: Is it honorable according to a code? Is it correct? Is it gentlemanly? Is it "quite cricket?" The Jewish gentleman asks: Is it righteous? What is its relation to an eternal justice, an eternal mercy? It is perfectly true, that according to the standards of chivalric Europe...the Jew is no gentleman.

> *Ibid.*

FRIEND OF MANKIND

To be a Jew is to be a friend of mankind, to be a proclaimer of liberty and peace.

> *Ibid.*

STARTING FROM SCRATCH

The ruin and desolation of the land was and is to us its glory and its opportunity. Here the creative effort of the Jew must build first the very soil he is to dig, bring the very water that is to make it tillable, fight the diseases of man and beast and plant which to the natives had been mere objects of superstitious fear.

> *Ibid.*

LIFE THROUGH DRAMA

In all ages the drama, through its portrayal of the acting and suffering spirit of man, has been more closely allied than any other art to his deeper thoughts concerning his nature and his destiny.

From his Modern Drama *(1923).*

Joseph Lichten

THE HUMANITY OF PIUS XII

What cannot be questioned is the integrity, the charity, and the deep commitment to humanity of Pius XII. It is idle to speculate about what more he could have done, for unlike most of the leaders of his day, he did very much.

From his Pius XII and the Holocaust: A Reader *(1988).*

Henrik Lichtenson

WE WON!

We won. We're here. We had children, and they gave us grandchildren and I stand here and say to myself, it's 1994 and you're here, alive. Who would believe it?

Comment of one of Schindler's Jews at a screening, for fellow survivors, of Steven Spielberg's Academy Award-winning Schindler's List. *Quoted in* The Jerusalem Report, *March 24, 1994.*

David Lieber

UNKNOWN AND UNKNOWABLE

God, the source of all existence, is unknown and forever unknowable. At the same time, He does seem to reveal Himself in human experience in unexpected moments and in a variety of circumstances. In any case, He functions as the symbol of all human aspirations for self-transcendence, as the ideal limit of man's notion of supreme value. He is "the beyond" in our midst, and faith in Him is an awareness of the ideal possibilities of human life, and of man's ability to fashion his life in the light of them.

From an essay in Condition of Jewish Belief *(1966), compiled by the editors of* Commentary *magazine.*

Elias Lieberman

EMBLEM OF THE PROMISED LAND

The flag of stars and stripes is yours:
It is the emblem of the promised land.

From his essay "I Am An American."

Joseph I. Lieberman

A SENATOR'S CREDO

Part of [my involvement in politics] has to do with my Jewish education and the whole tradition in Judaism of an obligation to try to do justice, to try to better the community and to try to make a difference.

By attribution.

Saul Lieberman

NONSENSICAL SCHOLARSHIP

It is forbidden to have a course in nonsense, but studying the history of nonsense, that is scholarship.

Responding to students' requests to introduce a course on kabbalah.

SMART VS. WISE

The difference between a smart man and a wise one is this: A smart man can work his way out of a difficulty that a wise man will not get into in the first place.

A comment to his students.

Isi Liebler

BLACK–JEWISH RELATIONS

It is not for us to question what might be motivating [Jesse] Jackson to mend fences with us. It could quite conceivably be concern about dangerously deteriorating black-Jewish relations. In which case we could be at the start of a promising breakthrough in black-Jewish relations in the United States. On the other hand, it could be something far less noble, the opportunistic move of a politician, in which case we may have been monumentally suckered. Only time will tell. But for the moment, all of us are obliged to give Jesse Jackson the benefit of the doubt and wait to see if his actions back home match up with his impressive rhetoric in Brussels.

From an address delivered at the World Conference on Anti-Semitism and Prejudice in a Changing World, held in Brussels, Belgium, July 1992.

◻

Charles S. Liebman

ADMIRATION FOR ORTHODOXY

There is a recognition and admiration for Orthodoxy as the only group which today [1965] contains within it a strength and will to live that may yet nourish all the Jewish world.

From his article "Orthodoxy in American Jewish Life," which appeared in The American Jewish Yearbook *(1965).*

◻

Joshua Loth Liebman

DEATH AS A FRIEND

I often feel that death is not the enemy of life, but its friend, for it is the knowledge that our years are limited which makes them so precious.

From his Peace of Mind *(1946).*

DEATH: THE GREAT NURSE

For each one of us the moment comes when the great nurse, death, takes man, the child, by the hand and quietly says, "It is time to go home. Night is coming. It is your bedtime, child of earth. Come; you're tired. Lie down at last in the quiet nursery of nature and sleep. Sleep well. The day is gone. Stars shine in the canopy of eternity."

Ibid.

EACH DAY A YEAR

While we live, we should try to make each day a year as far as beauty, nobility, and a warm sense of brotherhood are concerned. In a time when there is so much cruelty abroad, we must generate the oxygen of love to keep the soul of the world still breathing.

Ibid.

INTENSIFYING LIFE

Religion should summon all of us to deepen the quality of life as a compensation for the diminution of its quantity, to treasure each other in the recognition that we do not know how long we shall have each other, to make life strong and brave and beautiful as our an-swer to the forces of death abroad in the world. We must make up for the threatened brevity of life by heightening the intensity of life.

Ibid.

HEALING PRINCIPLES

It is basic to Jewish tradition that God reveals himself anew in every generation, and some of the channels of this revelation in our day are in the healing principles and insights of psychology and psychiatry.

From his Psychiatry and Religion.

◻

Abraham Liesen

COMBINING SOCIALIST PROPAGANDA

When I learned I was a convinced Marxist, I also discovered I was...not just a human being (which is merely an abstraction), but a Jew. Marxism intensified my sense of reality, and the reality surrounding me was Jewish.... At first I tried to fight off these sinful thoughts...just as ten years earlier I had tried to struggle with the religious doubts which tormented me. But I saw that the struggle was lost. I had become a nationalist.

Quoted in Lucy Dawidowicz's Golden Tradition *(1967).*

◻

Robert Jay Lifton

BOUNDLESSNESS OF HUMAN DESTRUCTION

That is why I called my book about Hiroshima *Death in Life*. The death that survivors carried on in their continuing lives was not the ordinary structured death of individuals; it was grotesque, absurd, collective, unacceptable, unabsorbable death. That's what the politicians don't talk about.

From a 1968 study of the psychological effect on the survivors of the atomic bombing of Hiroshima.

CHURCH, STATE, AND THE AJC

The AJC's [American Jewish Committee's] unique role in the courts is going to have a greater emphasis as the American people, particularly the Jewish people, look to stop the thrust of the religious right breaking down the barrier of church and state.

Upon his retirement in 1994.

¤

Max Lilienthal

THREE ESSENTIAL DOCTRINES

Here are the three doctrines which shall be taught here as the essence of Judaism: First, there is a God, one, indivisible, eternal, spiritual, most holy and most perfect. Second, there is an immortal life and man is a son of eternity. Thirdly, love thy fellow men without distinction of creed or race as thyself.

From his Modern Judaism *(1865).*

THE BEST MOTTO

The best religion is humanity, the best divine service, love thy neighbor as thyself. The motto which we inscribe on our banner is the fatherhood of God and the brotherhood of man.

From an 1876 speech.

¤

Nissan Limor

A MAN FOR ALL SEASONS

[Chaim Herzog is] a man for all seasons. He has a keen sense of humor, high standards, and always sets a shining personal example. He is easy to get along with, a good sport in every sense of the word. His memory is phenomenal.

Spoken during the Israeli presidency of Chaim Herzog (1984–1993).

¤

Abraham Lincoln

RABBIS AS CHAPLAINS

I find that there are several particulars in which the present law in regard to Chaplains is supposed to be deficient, all of which I now design presenting to the appropriate Committee of Congress. I shall try to have a new law broad enough to cover what is desired by you in behalf of the Israelites.

In a December 14, 1861 communication to the Reverend Arnold Fischel, the lecturer of Congregation Shearith Israel, in New York. Dr. Fischel led the delegation urging President Lincoln to use his influence to have Congress amend the Chaplaincy Act so that Jewish clergymen, like Christians, might serve as military chaplains.

AN APPEAL TO FATHER ABRAHAM

"And so the Children of Israel were driven from the happy land of Canaan?"

"Yes," replied Kaskel, "and that is why we have come unto Father Abraham's bosom,

asking protection."

"And this protection they shall have at once."

To a delegation of Jews from Paducah, Kentucky, led by respected merchant Cesar Kaskel, who had come on December 29, 1862 to urge the President to rescind Grants Order #11. On January 7, 1863 the revocation order was issued.

FLESH AND BLOOD

I am blood of your blood, flesh of your flesh.

An assurance from the President to Isaac M. Wise, founder of Reform Judaism. Quoted in the Prologue to Howard M. Sachar's History of the Jews in America *(1992).*

¤

Charles A. Lindbergh

LINDBERGH VS. JEWS

I can understand why the Jewish people wish to overthrow the Nazis. The persecution they have suffered in Germany would be sufficient to make bitter enemies of any race. No person with a sense of dignity of mankind condones the persecution of the Jewish race in Germany. Certainly I and my friends do not.

But though I sympathize with the Jews, let me add a word of warning. No person of honesty and vision can look on their prowar policy here today without seeing the dangers involved in such a policy, both for us—and for them.... Their greatest danger to this country lies in their large ownership and influence in our motion pictures, our press, our radio, and our Government.... We cannot blame them for looking out for what they believe to be their own interest, but we also must look out for ours. We cannot allow the natural passions and prejudices of other peoples to lead our country to destruction.

In an address to an American First rally in Des Moines, Iowa, on September 11, 1941. Quoted in Leonard Mosley's Lindberg: A Biography *(1976).*

THE BRITISH, THE JEWS, AND ROOSEVELT

The three most important groups who have been pressing this country towards war are the British, the Jews, and the Roosevelt administration.... Instead of agitating for war, the Jewish groups in this country should be opposing it in every possible way, for they will be among the first to feel its consequences.

Ibid.

◻

Sol Linowitz

IMAGE OF A WINNER

The Israeli victory in the Six-Day War in 1967 was the end of the image of the Jew as a loser.

Expressing pride in Israel's remarkable feat.

◻

Israel Salanter Lipkin

AN EXPENSIVE HOTEL

The world is an expensive hotel; you pay dearly for each pleasure.

Quoted in D. Katz's Tenuat Ha-musar *(1945).*

THE WRITTEN WORD

Writing is one of the easiest things; erasing one of the hardest.

Ibid.

RABBI WITHOUT ENEMIES

A rabbi whom they don't want to drive out of town isn't a rabbi, and a rabbi whom they actually drive out isn't a man.

Ibid.

KNOW THYSELF

Man lives with himself for seventy years, and doesn't know himself.

Ibid.

WORDS AND THOUGHTS

Not all that is thought should be spoken, not all that is spoken deserves to be written, and not all that is written is meant to be printed.

Quoted in F. Kobler's Treasury of Jewish Letters *(1952).*

IMAGINATION AND REASON

Man is free in his imagination, but bound by his reason.

From his Iggeret HaMusar *(1858). Quoted in M.G. Glenn's* Israel Salanter *(1953).*

IMITATION OF GOD

In imitation of God, it is our duty not only to confer an act of kindness upon those who harm us, but to do it at the very moment we are wronged.

Quoted in Louis Ginzberg's Students, Scholars and Saints *(1928).*

◻

Yisrael Lippel

ACCESS TO HOLY PLACES

The holy places are the heart of our attachment to the land.... Wars have been fought over the holy places. If Jews are denied proper access to them, the peace process will explode.

Pointing out that about two dozen holy sites, most of them ancient graves, are scattered across the West Bank. Quoted in The Jerusalem Report, *December 16, 1993.*

◻

Walter Lippmann

AN OBLIGATION TO BE BETTER

While the Jews are not sharper traders than the Greeks or the Scotch, and while there are not among Jews more blatantly vulgar rich than among other stocks, sharp trading and blatant vulgarity are more conspicuous in the Jew because he himself is more conspicuous....

Because the Jew is conspicuous, he is under all the greater obligation not to practice the vices of our civilization.... For that reason the rich and vulgar and pretentious Jews of our big American cities are perhaps the greatest misfortune that has ever befallen the Jewish people. They are the real fountain of anti-Semitism.

Quoted in Ronald Steel's biography Walter Lippmann and the American Century *(1980). This rare reference to Lippmann's Jewishness appeared earlier in the April 14, 1922 edition of* The American Hebrew.

IDENTIFYING WITH THE CALUMNY

Nothing is more disheartening to me than the kind of tribal loyalty which you ask of me.... You need not expect me to subscribe to the myth of the innocent Jewish people unreasonably persecuted the world over.

Responding in 1905 to his classmate Henry Hurwitz, who chided Lippmann for an article he had written for The New Republic *in which he suggested that "the bad economic habits of the Jew, his exploiting of simple people, has caused victims to assert their own identity."*

ON MENCKEN

[H.L. Mencken was] the most powerful personal influence on this whole generation of educated people.

From a 1926 article in which he laments Mencken's anti-Semitic views.

HARVARD'S JEWISH QUOTA

I do not regard the Jews as innocent victims. They hand on unconsciously and uncritically from one generation to another many distressing personal and social habits, which were selected by a bitter history and intensified by a Pharasaical theology.

Speaking out in 1922 in support of Harvard president A. Lawrence Lowell's appeal for a Jewish quota at Harvard.

ON A UNITED NATIONS

The world state is inherent in the United Nations as an oak tree is in an acorn.

From his One World or None *(1946).*

ALLIANCES

An alliance is like a chain. It is not made stronger by adding weak links to it.

From an article in the New York Herald Tribune, *August 5, 1952.*

SEEKING RECONCILIATION

The complexity of modern civilization is a daily lesson in the necessity of not pressing any claim too far, of understanding opposing points of view, of seeking to reconcile them, of conducting matters so that there is some kind of harmony in a plural society.

Quoted in Lionel Blue's Jewish Guide to the Here and Hereafter *(1988).*

ABANDONING TRADITION

The ancient world, we may remind ourselves, was not destroyed because the traditions were false. They were submerged, neglected, lost. For the men adhering to them had become a dwindling minority who were alien to the traditions, having never been initiated and adopted into them. May it not be that while the historical circumstances are obviously so different, something like that is happening again?

From his Public Philosophy *(1955).*

LIBERTY AND DEMOCRACY

My hope is that both liberty and democracy can be preserved before the one destroys the other. Whether this can be done is the question of our time, what with more than half the world denying and despairing of it.

Ibid.

POWERS OF CHURCH AND STATE

The best that is possible in the human condition, and in the world as it is, is that the state and the churches should each be too strong to be conquered, not strong enough to have unlimited dominion.

Ibid.

¤

Louis Lipsky

CONVERSION OF JUDAH MAGNES

I met Judah L. Magnes when he returned from his studies in Germany...in a kosher restaurant on Canal Street. He insisted that it be kosher. He was a tall, spare young man with a light beard, who smiled generously with an easy friendliness and confessed without provocation that in Berlin he had been converted to Orthodoxy, that he had attended a Zionist Congress and knew Theodor Herzl.

In his book Gallery of Zionist Profiles *(1956). Magnes, raised in a Reform San Francisco family, enrolled in Hebrew Union College, a Reform seminary, at age 17.*

HERZL'S WEAPON

Audacity created the Zionist Congress. It was Theodor Herzl's only weapon.... The Zionist Congress enabled us to regain corporate responsibility of our national destiny. It gave a Galuth [Diaspora] people status and an address. It is the forerunner of the Jewish State.

From his Selected Works *(1927).*

REJOICING IN THE LAND

There is singing again on Mount Scopus. And there is rejoicing in the Holy City of Jerusalem.

From remarks at the inauguration of Hebrew University, in Jerusalem, in March 1925.

¤

Deborah E. Lipstadt

JEWISH SENSITIVITY

Given the reality of their historical experience, Jews are extremely sensitive to any attack on them. It is similar to the situation of the woman who has been raped in a parking lot at dusk. She will be forever sensitive about walking through such places at that time of day. She may jump even when there is no danger. And who can blame her? How much stronger would be her reaction if she had been raped not once but many times. So it is with Jews.

In her Jewish Spectator *column, "Tomer Devorah," Winter 1990.*

DANGER OF DENIAL

There is an obvious danger in assuming that because Holocaust denial is so outlandish, it can be ignored. The denier's worldview is no more bizarre than that [of those who believe in the] *Protocols of the Elders of Zion,* a report purporting to be the text of a secret plan to establish Jewish world supremacy.

From her Denying the Holocaust *(1993).*

THE "OTHER SIDE" OF A NONISSUE

I have, since the publication of my book [*Denying the Holocaust*], declined to appear on many American talk shows because it entailed debating a denier [of the Holocaust]. In all these cases, when I rejected the invitation, the idea for the show was abandoned. All the producers wanted was fireworks—not substance. I categorically refuse to fulfill the deniers' aim of becoming the "other side" of an issue that has no other side.

From a letter-to-the-editor in The Jerusalem Report, *December 30, 1993.*

HOLOCAUST DENIERS

That is exactly what the objective of the denier is—to insert himself into Holocaust debate as "the other side." What other side? This is all part of a world view: "If it is your opinion, even if it is ridiculous, what right do I have to say anything?" Because of this climate, revisionists have become worthy of being heard. Producers are looking for ratings. They don't care one whit about ethics.

From an article about Denying the Holocaust *(1993) in* The Report of Women's American ORT, *Spring 1994.*

EVALUATING OPINIONS

What revisionists have to say is utter nonsense. Our fight against them should be that it's totally nonsensical. Opinion has to be rooted in fact. Just because it's your opinion doesn't mean it has the validity of being worthwhile.

Ibid.

HOLOCAUST IGNORANCE

The danger is in the potential of this [denial of the Holocaust] to spread. There is tremendous ignorance in this country about the Holocaust, people who don't know what the Holocaust is. What I'd like to see you do is to fight ignorance. What we can do is to learn, study and remember.

From an address to a Jewish community center audience.

OYS AND JOYS

[The trick is in finding the right balance between transmitting] the oys and joys of Jewish life. I am sometimes afraid that the message [the community] gives to contemporary and future generations is that the oys are the glue that holds us together.

From a December 1994 address to the annual Sanford Solender Lecture, held at the UJA-Federation headquarters in New York City.

UNIQUENESS OF THE HOLOCAUST

The Holocaust remains unique for two primary reasons. It was the only time in recorded history that a state tried to destroy an entire people, regardless of an individual's age, sex, location, profession or belief. And it is the only instance in which the perpetrators conducted this genocide for no ostensible material, territorial or political gain.

From her essay in The New Republic, *March 6, 1995.*

□

Solomon Liptzin

WILL JEWRY EVER MERGE?

As a Jew who is Orthodox, Conservative, and Reform, my answer is no, they will not merge. And I will give you my reasons for it. Insofar as Jewishness is meaningful to us, insofar as it is a living organism, I envisage it as a sort of tree, with Orthodoxy as the strong and gnarled trunk of this tree whose roots are deep in the earth. It may have excrescences, it may have ugliness about it, but it is strong indeed. I envisage Conservatism as the branches that come out of this trunk. And I envisage Reform Judaism as the beautiful leaves, flowers, and fruits at the end of it; all three are necessary for the health of the tree of Judaism.

In a 1960 dialogue with Rabbi William Berkowitz at the Institute of Adult Jewish Studies in New York. Reported in Berkowitz's Ten Vital Jewish Issues *(1964).*

□

Franklin H. Littell

THE BROTHERHOOD OF MAN

We Protestant Americans need our...Jewish neighbors even more than they need us. Above all we need them because living with them can help us to bury forever the temptation to long for the good old days when we thought to have our way by force.

From his Church and the Body Politic *(1969).*

THE TEST OF CHRISTIANITY

The truth about the murder of European Jewry by baptized Christians is this: It raises in a most fundamental way the question of the credibility of Christianity. Was Jesus a false Messiah? No one can be a true Messiah whose followers feel compelled to torture and destroy other human persons who think differently.

From his Crucifixion of the Jews *(1974).*

NEW CODE WORD

The new code word for anti-Semitism is anti-Zionism. No one can be an enemy of Zionism and be a friend of the Jewish people today.

Ibid.

DEATH CAMP DESIGNERS

The death camps were designed by professors and built by Ph.D.s.

From an article in 1971.

THE GREATEST CRIME

It is not the Jews, but the so-called Christians who need absolution. No crime in human history can equal the guilt which lies upon Christendom.

From his article "Politics, Theology, and the Jews" in the Journal of Ecumenical Studies, *Fall 1965.*

◘

David Lloyd George

THE CREDO OF ANTI-SEMITES

Of all the bigotries that savage the human temper there is none so stupid as anti-Semitism. In the sight of these fanatics, Jews can do nothing right. If they are rich, they are birds of prey. If they are poor, they are vermin. If they are in favor of war, that is because they want to exploit the bloody feuds of Gentiles to their own profit. If they are anxious for peace, they are either instinctive cowards or traitors. If they give generously—and there are no more liberal givers than the Jews—they are doing it for some selfish purpose of their own. If they don't give, then what would one expect of a Jew?

From his article "What Has the Jew Done?" Reported in The American Hebrew, *December 23, 1938.*

A TASK FOR JEWS ONLY

If Palestine is to be restored...it must be by settling Jews on its soil. The condition to which the land has been reduced...is such that restoration is only possible by a race that is prepared for sentimental reasons to make and endure sacrifices for that purpose.

From Hearst Newspapers, July 1923.

◘

John Locke

HYGIENE OF THE JEWS

If the rivers of Italy are warmer, those of Germany and Poland are much colder than any in this our country; and yet in these the Jews, both men and women, bathe all over, at all seasons of the year, without any prejudice to their health.

From his Some Thoughts Concerning Education *(1690), urging the benefits of cold water on his fellow countrymen. Quoted in Cecil Roth's* Jewish Contribution to Civilization *(1940).*

TOLERATION FOR ALL

Neither Pagan nor Mahometan nor Jew ought to be excluded from the civil rights of the Commonwealth because of his religion.... If we allow the Jews to have...dwellings amongst us, why should we not allow them to have synagogs [*sic*]?

From his Letter Concerning Toleration *(1689).*

◘

Betty Loeb

"PUSHY" JEWS

When traveling on a train for short distances, never hurry for the exit when it reaches your stop. People will think you are a pushy Jew.

Advice to her children. Quoted in Stephen Birmingham's Our Crowd *(1967).*

◘

Judah Loew

FUNCTION OF THE MESSIAH

The essential function of the Messiah will consist in uniting and perfecting all, so that this will be truly one world.

Quoted in Ben Zion Bokser's From the World of Cabbalah *(1954).*

DIGNITY OF GOD

The dignity of a neighbor, who was created in the divine image, is equivalent to God's dignity.

Ibid.

ISRAEL AND THE JEWS

Exile is a change and departure from the natural order, whereby the Lord situated every nation in the place best suited it.... The place [the Jews] deserved according to the order of existence was to be independent in the Land of Israel.

Quoted in Haim H. Ben-Sasson's History of the Jewish People *(1976).*

□

Herbert M. Loewe

TRUTH IS INDIVISIBLE

What is false in science cannot be true in religion. Truth is one and indivisible. God is bound by His own laws.

From his Rabbinic Anthology *(1938).*

□

Louis Loewe

CENTURY OF SERVICE

The tree under whose shadows thousands of his brethren found shelter.

From an address delivered at the memorial service for Sir Moses Montefiore, who died in 1885 at age 101.

□

Meyer London

LONDON GOES TO WASHINGTON

When I take my seat in Congress I do not expect to accomplish wonders. What I expect to do is take to Washington the message of the people.... I want to show them what the East Side of New York is and what the East Side Jew is.

At a victory rally promising to defend the good name of New York's East Side Jews.

SOCIALIST AGENDA

We shall not rest until every power of capitalism has been destroyed and the workers emancipated from wage slavery.... I hope that my presence will represent an entirely different type of Jew from the kind that Congress is accustomed to see.

From a speech after his election to Congress in 1914. Reported in the New York Call, *November 9, 1914.*

WHAT AMERICA MEANS TO ME

To me Americanism means not only an opportunity to do better...but an imperative duty to be nobler than the rest of the world.

In a speech before the U.S. Congress, January 18, 1916.

□

Henry Wadsworth Longfellow

EXODUS OF DEATH

The long mysterious Exodus of death...
Pride and humiliation hand in hand
Walketh with them through the whole
    world
where'er they went.
Trampled and beaten were they as the
    sand,
And yet unshaken as the continent.

A tribute to the Jews of Newport, Rhode Island. From a poem entitled "Jewish Cemetery at Newport" (1852).

BEING ON THE SAFE SIDE

When the Jews prosper, ye claim
kindred with them;
When the Jews suffer, ye are
Medes and Persians.

From his "Judas Maccabeus" (1872).

PRECIOUS BOOK

That book of gems, that book of gold,
Of wonders many and manifold.

From his "Wayside Inn" (1863).

SARAH'S BEAUTY

When Abraham went with Sarah into
    Egypt,
The land was all illumined with her beauty.

From his Divine Tragedy, *The First Passover, III.*

□

Stephen Longstreet

WRITING TRUTHFULLY

I hate self pity and most Jewish writers roll in it. I dislike black and white in anything and the relationship of Jews and Gentiles is almost always presented in black and white. My Jews are human beings first.

From a letter by the author of The Pedlocks *(1951), a chronicle of Jewish family life in America.*

Joseph Lookstein

A JEW IN LOVE

I love every Jew except a Jew who doesn't love other Jews.

> *Quoted by his son, Haskel, when he was inducted as president of the Synagogue Council of America in September 1993.*

Courtney Love

NO JEW IN HIM

He had a lot of German in him. Some Irish. But no Jew. I think that if he had a little Jew, he would have stuck it out.

> *Speculating on what it would have taken for her late husband, singer Kurt Cobain, to avoid suicide in 1995.*

James Russell Lowell

THE STATUE'S SONNET

I liked your sonnet about the statue [in "The New Colossus"] better than the Statue [of Liberty] itself. But your sonnet gives its subject a *raison d'être* which it needed as much as it needed a pedestal.

> *From a letter to Emma Lazarus in 1883 after reading her famous sonnet.*

EXCLUSION OF JEWS

England, indeed, may be called a monarchy with democratic tendencies, the United States a democracy with conservative instincts.

One of the most curious of these frenzies of exclusion was that against the emancipation of the Jews. All share in the government of the world was denied for centuries to perhaps the ablest, certainly the most tenacious, race that ever lived in it—the race to whom we owed our religion and the purest spiritual stimulus and consolation to be found in all literature.

> *From an address delivered on October 6, 1884 in Birmingham, England.*

Martin Luther

ANTI-SEMITIC VENOM

I do not intend to quarrel with the Jews, or learn from them how to interpret or understand Scripture; I know all of that very well already. Much less do I intend to convert the Jews, for that is impossible....

They are real liars and bloodhounds who have not only continually perverted and falsified all of Scripture with their mendacious glosses.... The sun has never shone on a more bloodthirsty and vengeful people than they are who imagine that they are God's people who have been commissioned and commanded to murder and to slay the Gentiles. In fact, the most important thing that they expect of their Messiah is that he will murder the entire world with their sword.... They would still like to do this if they had the power, and often enough have made the attempt, for which they have got their snouts boxed lustily.

> *From his treatise* On the Jews and Their Lies *(1543), published after all his efforts to convert Jews had failed.*

THE JEWISH PROBLEM

What shall we Christians do with this rejected and condemned people, the Jews?.... I shall give you my sincere advice.

- First, set fire to their synagogues or schools and bury and cover with dirt whatever will not burn, so that no man will ever again see a stone or cinder of them....
- Second, their houses also should be razed and destroyed, for they pursue in them the same aims as in their synagogues....
- Third, all their prayerbooks and talmudic writings...should be taken from them.
- Fourth, their rabbis should be forbidden to teach henceforth on pain of loss of life and limb....
- Fifth, safe-conduct on the highways should be abolished completely for the Jews....

> *Ibid.*

CONVERSION AND THE JEWS

It is as easy to convert Jews as to convert the devil himself.

> *Quoted in* The Jewish Encyclopedia *(1905), edited by I. Singer.*

TURNING THE OTHER CHEEK

If the apostles...had behaved towards us Gentiles as we Gentiles behave towards the Jews, not one Gentile would have become a Christian.

> *From his* Jesus Was Born a Jew *(1523).*

SOURCE OF GLORY

Though we boast of rank, we must admit that we are but of pagan stock while the Jews are the blood of Christ.... The Glory came from them, not from us.

> *Ibid.*

VIEW OF MOSES

Moses with his law is most terrible; there never was any equal to him in perplexing, affrighting, tyrannizing, threatening, preaching, and thundering.

From his Table Talk *(1569).*

SUCCINCTNESS OF HEBREW

The words of the Hebrew tongue have a peculiar energy. It is impossible to convey so much so briefly in any other language.

Ibid.

WHO CRUCIFIED JESUS?

The Jews crucified Christ with words, but the Gentiles have crucified him with works and deeds.

Ibid.

SITTING ON A WHEELBARROW

The Jews are the most miserable people on earth. They are plagued everywhere, and scattered about all countries, having no resting place. They sit as on a wheelbarrow, without a country, people, or government...but they are rightly served, for seeing they refused to have Christ and his gospel, instead of freedom they must have servitude.

Ibid.

LUTHER THE JUDOPHILE

This rage (against the Jews) is still defended by some silly theologians, and advocated by them; they declare insolently that the Jews are the servants of the Christians, and subject to the emperor. I beg you to tell me who will join our religion, be he the most amiable and patient of men, when he sees that they are treated so cruelly and inimically, and not only in an unchristian way, but even brutally. Most of the Passion Preachers (in Holy Week) do nothing but make the sin committed by Jews against Christ heavier and greater, and embitter the hearts of believers against them.

Ibid. In defense of Jews early in his career, when his Reformation concentrated on vilifying the Church.

MY LOT IS WITH THE JEWS

Those fools, the papists, bishops, sophists and monks, have hitherto so dealt with Jews, that every good Christian would rather have been a Jew. And if I had been a Jew, and seen such stupidity and such blockheads reign in the Christian Church, I would rather have been a pig than a Christian. They have treated the Jews as if they were dogs, not men; they have done nothing but revile them... I beg, therefore, my dear papists, if you become tired of abusing me as a heretic, that you begin to revile me as a Jew.

Ibid.

EVIL OF THE JEWS

Besides all this you still have the Jews, who do great evil in the land. If they could kill us all, they would gladly do so, aye, and often do it, especially those who profess to be physicians—they know all that is known about medicine in Germany; they can give poison to a man of which he will die in an hour, or in ten or twenty years; they thoroughly understand this art. I say to you lastly, as a countryman, if the Jews refuse to be converted, we ought not to suffer them or bear with them any longer.

Ibid. After all his efforts to convert the Jews, Luther turned on them. From a sermon preached shortly before his death in 1546.

LUTHER'S PEEVE

I would threaten to cut their tongues out from their throats if they refuse to accept the Christian proof that God is a trinity, not a plain unity.

Quoted in the Hayim Greenberg Anthology *(1968), edited by Marie Syrkin.*

¤

Edward Luttwak

MILITARY PREPAREDNESS

What has been revealed as empty of strategic significance is not the Soviet brigade in Cuba, but rather the obsessive pursuit of the cumbersome legalisms of SALT at a time when our chief adversary is ceaselessly maneuvering to prevail. While our best minds use their energies to explain away all Moscow tries to do, in Moscow a machine of imperial ambition is at work, whose goal is to exploit all our points of weakness around the world.

Sharp criticism directed in 1979 at the administration of U.S. President Jimmy Carter for failing to understand the goals of the Soviet Union.

¤

Moses Hayyim Luzzatto

PATH OF THE UPRIGHT

There is an unmistakable distinction between fraudulent and honest persuasion. It is perfectly proper to point out to the buyer any good quality which the thing for sale really possesses. Fraud consists of hiding the defects in one's wares.

In his Messilat Yesharim *(1740).*

SAINTLINESS

Abstinence is the beginning of saintliness.

Ibid.

MAN'S PURPOSE

Man came into the world only to achieve nearness to God.

Ibid.

MAN'S DUTY

It is fundamentally necessary both for saintliness and for the perfect worship of God to realize clearly what constitutes man's duty in this world, and what goal is worthy of his endeavors throughout all the days of his life. Our Sages have taught that man was created only to find delight in the Lord, and to bask in the radiance of His Presence. But the real place for such happiness is the world to come, which has been created for that very purpose. The present world is only a path to that goal. "This world," say our Sages, "is like a vestibule before the world to come." Therefore, has God, blessed be His name, given us the miswot [sic]. For this world is the only place where the miswot [sic] can be observed. Man is put here in order to earn with the means at his command the place that has been prepared for him in the world to come.

Ibid. Quoted in Mordecai M. Kaplan's Judaism as a Civilization (1934).

¤

Samuel David Luzzatto

OF WHAT AVAIL INVENTIONS?

When were there seen such great inventions as in our generation? And as a result, have there been less war, murder, theft, poverty, disease, envy, hatred and untimely deaths?

From his Yesoday Ha-Torah *(1880).*

TRUSTING IN PROVIDENCE

The cornerstone of the Torah...is to strengthen in the human heart the quality of mercy and love, to remove confidence in our own power and in the might of our hands, and to put our trust in divine Providence which follows not intelligence but justice and lovingkindness and sincerity.

Ibid.

CHILDREN OF ONE FATHER

Judaism looks upon all human beings as children of one Father; thinks of them all as created in the image of God, and insists that a man be judged not by his religion, but his action.

Ibid.

BASIC JEWISH BELIEFS

Judaism has no future without adherence to the commandments and without belief in miracles and prophecy.

From his Igrot Shadal *(1882).*

EFFECTS OF GREEK PHILOSOPHY

Greek philosophy, especially in this generation, not only does not render its students wiser and better, it does not even make them happier. On the contrary, it turns their natural joy into sadness. How many delightful youths were led by these studies to melancholy, misanthropy and self-hatred, and finally to suicide!

From his Peninay Shadal *(1883).*

Thomas B. Macaulay

WHAT THE JEW IS

The Jew is what we made him.

Quoted in Madison Peters's Jew as a Patriot.

JEWS AND POLITICAL POWER

On every principle of moral obligation I hold that the Jew has a right to political power.

From an address before the British House of Commons, April 5, 1830.

A MOST CIVILIZED PEOPLE

In the infancy of civilization, when our island was as savage as New Guinea, when letters and arts were still unknown to Athens, when scarcely a thatched roofed hut stood on what was afterwards the site of Rome, this condemned people had their fenced cities and cedar palaces, their splendid Temple, their fleets of merchant ships, their schools of sacred learning, their great statesmen and soldiers, their natural philosophers, their historians and their poets.

From an address before the British House of Commons, April 17, 1833.

DOING JUSTICE

Let us do justice to them [the Jews].... Let us open to them every career in which ability and energy can be displayed. Till we have done this, let us not presume to say that there is no genius among the countrymen of Isaiah, no heroism among the descendants of the Maccabees.

Ibid.

WHERE JUDAISM AND CHRISTIANITY DIFFER

The points of difference between Christianity and Judaism have very much to do with a man's fitness to be a bishop or a rabbi. But they have no more to do with a man's fitness to be a magistrate or a legislator than with his fitness to be a cobbler.

Quoted in Joseph Leftwich's Caravan: A Jewish Quarterly Omnibus *(1962).*

J. Ramsay MacDonald

PROMISES, PROMISES

We encouraged an Arab revolt against Turkey by promising to create an Arab kingdom including Palestine. At the same time we were encouraging the Jews to help us, by promising them that Palestine could be placed at their disposal for settlement and government; and also, at the same time, we were secretly making with France, the Sykes-Picot Agreement partitioning the territory which we had instructed our governor-general of Egypt to promise to the Arabs. No one who has felt the undercurrents of Eastern movements can console himself with the belief that the Arab has forgotten or forgiven, or that the moral evil we committed will speedily cease to have political influence. Our treatment of the Moslems has been a madness.

In a statement written for a pamphlet published by the Zionist Labor Party after the British Labor Party leader visited Palestine in 1922. Quoted in Zionism Reconsidered, *edited by Michael Selzer (1970).*

LAND AND PEOPLE

Palestine and the Jew can never be separated. No power on earth can take from this land its magic attractions for its people. I have seen the living, the youth, the believers, planting the waste places and adorning the land as a bride is adorned by gifts from the bridegroom. These things are evidence that in the heart of Judaism there is love, and that in the Jew's mind there is a quest which he will pursue in the face of all obstacles and through wearily long generations, until the prophecies of his ancient teachers and of his own heart have been fulfilled.

From a 1924 statement. Quoted in Joseph Baron's Stars and Sand *(1943).*

◻

Ali MacGraw

WHO AM I?

I want to know who I am. I was brought up in New York as an Episcopalian. I believe there was Jewish blood on my mother's side. Grandfather Maurice Klein came from Budapest at age fourteen and worked in a sweatshop here. To me it says, Jewish family.

It's disturbing that here I am, a grownup, and I have no idea who I am. Everybody who can tell me is dead.

Her questioning was prompted by her having appeared in Herman Wouk's Winds of War, *a seven-part television mini-series.*

IT WAS REALLY HAPPENING

We filmed the exodus from Poland. I escaped in a car with Topol at the wheel. When they called a lunch break, I couldn't join the cast to eat and chat. I went off by myself and cried. I couldn't break the mood. For me, it was really happening.

There's an Orthodox wedding scene, very moving. After the ceremony and joyous dancing, the Nazis came and strafed the village. I found it absolutely devastating.

Ibid.

◻

Charles A. Madison

JEWISH PAGAN POET

Simultaneously a pagan poet who sees things through the prism of earthly beauty and a passionate Jew who must cry out when his people are in pain, he again and again submits to his conscience—to the detriment of his sensuous imagination.

From an article "Sholem Asch," which appeared in Poet Lore, *Winter 1940.*

◻

James Madison

ON JEWISH HISTORY

The history of the Jews must forever be interesting. The modern part of it is at the same time so little generally known, that every ray of light on the subject has its value.... Among the features peculiar to the political system of the United States is the perfect equality of rights which it secures to every religious sect.

In a letter to Dr. Jacob de La Motta, a southern Jew who saw service as an army surgeon

in the War of 1812 and was active in Jewish affairs. De La Motta had sent the former president a copy of his Discourse, *an address he gave in 1820 at the consecration of the synagogue in Savannah, Georgia.*

TO MORDECAI M. NOAH

Sir: I have received your letter of the 6th, with the eloquent discourse delivered at the consecration of the Synagogue. Having ever regarded the freedom of religious opinions and worship as equally belonging to every sect, and the secure enjoyment of it as the best human provision for bringing all, either into the same way of thinking, or into that mutual charity which is the only proper substitute, I observe with pleasure the view you give of the spirit in which your sect partake of the common blessings afforded by our Government and laws.

In response to a communication from Mordecai M. Noah that included Noah's address delivered at the consecration of New York's Mill Street Synagogue on May 28, 1818.

◻

Judah Magnes

PLEA FOR HUMANITARIAN AID

With my own eyes, I have seen the misery, the slow starvation of thousands. The Jews of America are sharing in prosperity as never before. Will they do their duty by their fellow Jews? Give, I beg of you, to the old men and women, to the young wives whose husbands are at war in the different armies, to the numberless sick who have been brought down by privation, to the children who at times still play and sing despite the cold and the hunger that menace them. Give so that the Jewish people may live.

From a letter to M. H. Rosenberg dated December 21, 1915, after a visit to wartorn Eastern Europe, demanding that the Joint Distribution Committee (JDC) set as its goal the raising of ten million dollars for relief of the victims of World War I.

RECIPROCAL INFLUENCES

The entire [Jewish] people must be organized in different forms, in different countries. Palestine should be the connecting link, the summit of organized [Jewish] life. The Jews of the world influence Palestine, Palestine influences the Jews of the world.

From a 1914 letter to Chaim Weizmann.

OUR MOST IMPORTANT POSSESSION

The Jewish spirit, the Jewish soul, is the most important thing we have. In some sense it is all we have, all that is worth having and living and struggling for.

From a 1916 statement. Quoted in Norman Bentwich's For Zion's Sake *(1954).*

THE ROOTS OF THINGS

The Jews have a radical quality which goes to the root of things, whether in capitalism or socialism.

Ibid.

JUSTICE FOR ONE AND ALL

The Jews have more than a claim upon the world for justice, but I am not ready to try to achieve justice to the Jew through injustice to the Arab.

From a 1947 statement.

LONGING FOR FREEDOM

A mighty longing for freedom is what characterizes the Jew.

From his Gleanings *(1948).*

DESTINY OF ISRAEL

The destiny of Israel, more than that of any other people, depends on the establishment of universal freedom.

From a 1941 essay.

¤

Lady Katie Magnus

GHETTO GOLD

The alchemy of home life went far to turn the dross of the Ghetto into gold.

From her Jewish Portraits *(1905).*

¤

Norman Mailer

THE GROWING PROCESS

Every moment of one's existence one is growing into more or retreating into less. One is always living a little more or dying a little bit.

From an article in Western Review, *Winter 1959.*

THE DEVIL'S SHARE

The more a man can achieve, the more he may be certain that the devil will inhabit a part of his creation.

From his Presidential Papers *(1963).*

¤

Solomon Maimon

PERPETUAL ARISTOCRACY

The Jewish people is, aside from accidental modifications, a perpetual aristocracy under the appearance of a theocracy.

From his Autobiography *(1793).*

¤

Moses Maimonides

MEANING OF REPENTANCE

Repentance means that the sinner forsake his sins, cast them out of his mind, and resolve in his heart to sin no more.

From his Mishneh Torah, *Hilchot Teshuva (2:2).*

ON FREE WILL

Free will is granted to every man. If he desires to incline towards the good way, and be righteous, he has the power to do so; and if he desires to incline towards the unrighteous way, and be a wicked man, he has also the power to do so.

Ibid (5:1).

THE CHOICE IS OURS

Pay no attention to those fools among the nations of the world and many stupid Jews who say that God pre-ordains, from birth, whether one will be righteous or wicked. This is not so. Every person can be as righteous as Moses or as wicked as Jeroboam....

Ibid (5:2).

WOMEN'S RIGHTS

If a woman says, "My husband is distasteful to me, and I cannot have intercourse with him," he is compelled to grant her a divorce, because she is not to be considered a captive woman who must satisfy her husband.

Ibid. Hilchot Ishut *(14:8).*

BEING KIND TO THE POOR

[On Purim] one need send "portions [gifts]" to only one friend or neighbor, but must give gifts to at least two poor persons.... It is better to lavish gifts on the poor than to feast heavily or to give presents to your friends. For there is no greater joy than bringing gladness to the poor, the orphan, the widow and all those who have no kin.

Ibid. Hilchot Megilla *(2:16–17).*

LEARNING HOW TO GIVE TO CHARITY

There are eight degrees in the giving of charity. They are as follows, from the least to the most desirable:

He who gives reluctantly, or with regret.

He who gives less than he should, but gives graciously.

He who gives what he should, but only after he is asked.

He who gives before he is asked.

He who gives without knowing to whom he gives, although the recipient may know the identity of the donor.

He who gives without making his identity known.

He who gives without knowing to whom he gives, and the recipient not knowing from whom he receives.

He who helps a fellowman to support himself by a gift, or a loan, or by finding employment for him, thus helping him to become self-supporting.

Ibid. Hilchot Matnot Aniyim (10:8–13).

MARK OF RIGHTEOUSNESS

We should observe the laws of charity more carefully even than all the other commandments. Charity *(tzedaka)* is the mark of the righteous ones of the children of Abraham our Father.... One does not become impoverished as a result of practicing charity. No harm or evil can be its outcome. He who has compassion on others is deserving of compassion. As to the merciless one, who knows no pity, his Jewish extraction may be considered doubtful, because cruelty is usually a characteristic of pagans.

Ibid (10:1).

THE FIRST BEING

The foundation of foundations and the pillar of the sciences is to know that there is a First Being and that He caused the existence of all things; and all things that exist from heaven and earth and intervening space only exist from the reality of His existence. If it could be supposed that He is nonexistent, nothing else could possibly exist.... This Being is the God of the world, Lord of the whole earth. He controls the Universe with a power to which there is neither end nor limit, with a power unceasing.

Ibid. Yesoday Ha-Torah (1:1).

UNITY OF GOD

God is one; He is not two, but one. The oneness of any of the single things existent in the Universe is unlike His Unity. He is not one as a species since this includes numerous individuals; nor one as a body since this is divisible into parts and sections, but a Unity which is unique in the world.

Ibid (1:7).

RATIONALE OF TORAH LAWS

The purpose of the laws of the Torah is not to bring hardship upon man but to bring mercy, lovingkindness, and peace to the world.

Ibid. Hilchot Shabbat (2:3).

TREATMENT OF SERVANTS

One should never put a servant to shame by an unkind action or word.... One should not scold him unduly and in anger, but should speak to him quietly and listen to what he has to say.

Ibid. Hilchot Avadim (9:8).

RULES FOR THE WISE

Even as the sage is recognized by his wisdom and by his character, which set him apart from common people, so should he be distinguished by his conduct, by his mode of eating and drinking, his marital life, his manner of talking, walking, dressing, conducting his affairs, and his business.

Ibid. Hilchot De'ot (5:1).

HARM NO HUMAN

As a general rule, one should be among the persecuted and not among the persecutors, among the abused and not among the abusers. Concerning him who conducts himself thus, Scriptures say: "And He said unto me: Thou art My servant, Israel, in whom I will be glorified" (Isaiah 49:3).

Ibid (5:12).

OBLIGATION TO STUDY

Every Jew is duty bound to study the Torah, whether he is poor or wealthy, sick or healthy, young, or old and weak. Even if one is a pauper who is supported by the community and begs from door to door, and even if he is a married man with children—he must set aside a prescribed time for Torah study during the day and at night.

Ibid. Hilchot Talmud Torah (1:8).

FIRST FUNDAMENTAL PRINCIPLE

I believe with complete faith in the existence of the Creator, blessed be He, who is perfect in all aspects of existence; that He is the cause of all things in existence, and nothing can exist without Him.

> *Based upon his commentary to the Mishna Sanhedrin (10), in which he presents Thirteen Principles (Articles) of Faith every Jew must believe in order to be assured a place in the world-to-come. These principles were recast in poetic form by an unknown author; the composition is known as* Ani Maamin *("I Believe"). Maimonides' Thirteen Principles is also the basis of the* Yigdal *hymn, which was composed in the year 1300 by Daniel ben Judah and which is part of the daily morning* (Shacharit) *liturgy.*

SECOND FUNDAMENTAL PRINCIPLE

I believe with complete faith that the Creator, blessed be He, is One and totally unique, unlike any other species or entity. He alone is our God who was, is, and ever will be.

> *Ibid.*

THIRD FUNDAMENTAL PRINCIPLE

I believe with complete faith that the Creator, blessed be He, is not a physical being. Physical attributes such as movement and rest do not apply to Him.

> *Ibid.*

FOURTH FUNDAMENTAL PRINCIPLE

I believe with complete faith that the Creator, blessed be He, is the absolute first, and everything else that exists is not first in relation to Him.

> *Ibid.*

FIFTH FUNDAMENTAL PRINCIPLE

I believe with complete faith that the Creator, blessed be He—and may He be exalted—is the only One worthy of worship, and that his greatness should be made known to all.

> *Ibid.*

SIXTH FUNDAMENTAL PRINCIPLE

I believe with complete faith that within the human race there are prophets, individuals of outstanding merit and great intellect, from whom prophecy emanates.

> *Ibid.*

SEVENTH FUNDAMENTAL PRINCIPLE

I believe with complete faith that the prophecy of Moses our teacher, peace upon him, was true, and that he was the father of all the prophets—both those who preceded him and those who followed him. All are below him in rank, for he was chosen by God.

> *Ibid.*

EIGHTH FUNDAMENTAL PRINCIPLE

I believe with complete faith that the entire Torah which is found in our hands today comes from Heaven and is the same one that was given through Moses.

> *Ibid.*

NINTH FUNDAMENTAL PRINCIPLE

I believe with complete faith that this Torah will not be abrogated and that no other Torah will come from God. One may not add to it or delete any part of it. This applies to the Written Torah and the Oral Torah.

> *Ibid.*

TENTH FUNDAMENTAL PRINCIPLE

I believe with complete faith that the Exhalted One knows the actions of all men and does not neglect [turn his eyes] from them.

> *Ibid.*

ELEVENTH FUNDAMENTAL PRINCIPLE

I believe with complete faith that the Exalted One rewards those who observe the commandments of the Torah and punishes those who transgress them. The greatest reward is entering the world-to-come and the greatest punishment is extinction.

> *Ibid.*

TWELFTH FUNDAMENTAL PRINCIPLE

I believe with complete faith in the coming of the Messiah, and even though he may tarry, nevertheless I do look forward to his coming every day.

> *Ibid.*

THIRTEENTH FUNDAMENTAL PRINCIPLE

I believe with complete faith that there will be a resurrection of the dead.

> *Ibid.*

BY BIRTH AND BY CHOICE

You may recite every prayer in proper order and you need not make any changes. You may pray in the same manner as every Jew by birth.... Moses separated us from the nations and brought us beneath the wings of the Divine presence and gave to all of us one law. Since you have also entered beneath the wings of the Divine presence, there is no difference between us and you.

> *In response to a letter addressed to him by Obadiah the Proselyte, who had been criticized for using the words "our God and God of our fathers" in his prayers. Maimonides comforted Obadiah by declaring that although he was not a Jew by birth, he had a right to say* our God.

MALIGNING A CONVERT

Go tell your teacher that he owes you an apology. And tell him that he should fast and pray and ask God to forgive him for what he said to you. He must have been intoxicated, and he forgot that in thirty-six places the Torah reminds us to *respect* the convert and that in thirty-six places it admonishes us to *love* the convert. A convert is a child of Abraham, and whoever maligns him commits a great sin.

Ibid.

CONVERTS ARE FULL-FLEDGED JEWS

Your prayer and blessing should be the same as that of any other Israelite, regardless of whether you pray in private or conduct the service. The explanation is as follows: Abraham, our father, taught mankind the true belief and the unity of God, repudiating idolatry; through him many of his own household and also others were guided "to keep the way of the Lord, to do righteousness and justice." Thus he who becomes a proselyte and confesses the unity of God, as taught in the Torah, is a disciple of Abraham, our father.

Ibid.

SOURCE OF GOOD AND EVIL

We seek relief from our own faults; we suffer from evils which we inflict on ourselves, and we ascribe them to God who is far from connected with them.

From his Guide of the Perplexed *(1190).*

FINDING PEACE OF MIND

Only if man knows himself, and has no illusion about himself, and understands every existing thing in relation to itself, will he find real peace [of mind].

Ibid.

THE HIGHEST VIRTUE

The highest virtue to which a man can aspire is to become similar to God as far as this is possible: that means that we must imitate His actions, as has been indicated by our Rabbis in their comment on the words "You shall be holy" (Leviticus 19:2): As He is gracious, so shall you be gracious; as He is merciful, so shall you be merciful.

Ibid.

DEFINING GOD

Existence, life, power, wisdom and will, when applied to God, have not the same meaning as when applied to us.... It cannot be said that His [God's] existence is more stable, His

life more permanent, His power greater, His wisdom more perfect, and His will more pervasive, and that the same definition applies to both of us.... There is no comparison between the essence of God and that of other beings.

Ibid.

KNOWING ONE'S PLACE

An ignorant man believes that the whole universe exists only for him.... If, therefore, anything happens to him contrary to his expectations, he at once concludes that the whole universe is evil.

Ibid.

RECOGNIZING OUR LIMITATIONS

It is ignorance or a kind of madness to weary our minds with subjects which are beyond our reach.

Ibid.

TRUE WORSHIP

True worship is possible only when correct notions of God have previously been conceived.

Ibid.

LOVE EQUALS KNOWLEDGE

Man's love of God is identical with his knowledge of Him.

Ibid.

TRANSFERENCE OF SINS

There is no doubt that sins cannot be carried like a burden and taken off the shoulder of one being to be laid on that of another being.

Ibid.

SCHOLARLY INTEGRITY

When I am troubled by a problem and because of its difficulty find it possible to teach the truth in a manner that will be approved by one worthy man and disapproved by ten thousand fools, I am resolved to impart it to the one and not to be sensitive to the disdain of the great multitude. I wish to help the one worthy man out of his perplexity, to show him a way out of his confusion, so that he may attain perfection and peace.

Ibid.

DISCOVERING GOD

We can only obtain a knowledge of God through His works; His works give evidence of His existence.

Ibid.

MAN AND FREE WILL

The theory that man has free will is one of the fundamental principles of the Law of our Teacher Moses, and of those who follow the Law. According to this principle, man does what is in his power to do, by his nature, his choice, and his will. His action is not due to any faculty created for the purpose.

Ibid.

GOD AND GOODNESS

It cannot be said of God that He directly creates evil.... This is impossible. His works are perfectly good. He only produces existence, and all existence is good.

Ibid.

ACCOLADE FOR ABRAHAM IBN EZRA

I exhort you not to pay attention or divert your mind on commentaries, treatises and books other than those of [Abraham] Ibn Ezra, which alone are meaningful and profitable to all those who study them with intelligence, understanding and insight...for he feared no-one, flattered no-one.

From a letter to his son about the greatness of the twelfth-century scholar.

FROM FATHER TO SON

My son, let your pleasant company be only with our brothers the Sephardim who are called Andalusians, because they have brains and understanding and clarity of thought.... And beware of some of the people who dwell in the West in the place called Jerba and in the Barbary States, for they are dull and have a crude nature. And beware most particularly of the people who dwell between Tunis and Alexandria of Egypt. And also of those who dwell in the mountains of Barbary, for they are to me more ignorant than the rest of mankind, although they are very strong in their faith, and God is my witness that I regard them like the Karaites who deny the Oral Law, and they have no clarity of thought at all.

From a letter to his son Abraham. Contained in Letters and Responsa: Kobez Teshuboth ha-Rambam, *edited by A. Lichtenberg (1859).*

ON DESECRATING GOD'S NAME

Avoid lengthy repetitions, and thus prevent the desecration of the Name, for the rumor has spread among Gentiles that Jews spit and cough and chatter during their prayers.

Ibid.

CONSOLATION IN STUDY

If not the study of the Torah, which is my delight, if not the study of the sciences, which helps me overcome my grief, I would be lost.

Ibid.

MUSLIMS AND MONOTHEISM

The Ishmaelites [Mohammedans] are not considered pagans in any sense; no trace of paganism is left in their speech and in their hearts; they confess the Unity of God in its correct and unconditional meaning. People say that their houses of worship are pagan, that they contain pagan symbols which were revered by their ancestors. But this does not matter. Even if they still bow to them, their hearts are directed toward God. They may be deluded and in error in various matters, but concerning monotheism they are not at all mistaken.

From a responsum *in* Teshuboth ha-Rambam *(1934), edited by A. Freimann.*

FERRETING OUT THE TRUTH

Do not take matters as proven because they are stated so in books. Lies are committed with the mouth as well as with the pen. Only fools will consider a matter truly proven if they find it in writing.

From his Iggeret Teman *(1172). The Jews of Yemen were compelled to choose between accepting Islam or suffering persecution and expulsion.*

INHUMAN SCHEDULE

The Sultan [Alafdhal] lives in Cairo, and I in Fostat; the two towns lie at a distance of two Sabbath journeys [about a mile and one-third] from each other. With the Sultan I have a hard time; I must visit him daily in the morning, and when he, or any of his children, or one of the women of his harem is suffering, I may not leave Cairo. Even when nothing particular happens, I cannot come home till after mid-day. When I enter my house, dying of hunger, I find the hall thronged with people—Jews, Mahometans, illustrious and otherwise, friends and foes, a motley crowd—who await my advice as a physician. There scarcely remains time for me to alight from my horse, wash myself, and take some refreshment. Thus it continues till night, and then, worn out with weakness, I must retire to bed. Only on Sabbath have I time to occupy myself with the congregation and with the Law. I am accustomed on this day to dispose of the affairs of the community for the following week, and to hold a discourse. Thus my days glide away.

From an 1199 communication to Samuel ben Judah ibn Tibbon, who had requested to visit with Maimonides in Egypt before beginning the translation of The Guide of the Perplexed *into Hebrew. Maimonides dissuaded him from making the perilous journey from France because he had little time to spare. Quoted in Heinrich Graetz's* History of the Jews *(1894).*

REMEMBERING ADVERSITY

Man ought to remember his difficult days in his days of prosperity. He will thereby be inclined to thank God repeatedly, to lead a modest and humble life. Therefore, on Tabernacles we leave our houses in order to dwell in booths. We shall thereby remember that this has once been our condition.

Commenting on Leviticus 23:42 and the commandment to dwell in sukkot *(huts).*

REASON'S REALM

Never should a man throw his reason behind him, for his eyes are not in the back, but in the front.

From his epistle to the Jews of Marseilles.

◻

Abdel Salam Majali

EVERYTHING IN ITS TIME

In Arabic, we say, "He who hastens things before its time, God will prevent him from having it." Not to try to push things before it is time. When it is time, it is right, it is delicious, it is good. If it is before its time, if you eat the apple before its time, you will get tummy cramps.

When asked how soon peace would come after King Hussein of Jordan announced that he would meet in Washington, on July 25, 1994, with Prime Minister Yitzhak Rabin of Israel.

◻

(Prophet) Malachi

WE ALL HAVE ONE FATHER

Have we not all one Father?
Did not one God create us all?
Why then do we deal unkindly with one another?

From the Book of Malachi (2:10).

◻

Bernard Malamud

SOMEBODY HAS TO CRY

The suffering of the Jews is a distinct thing for me. I for one believe that not enough has been made of the destruction of six million Jews. Somebody has to cry—even if it's a writer, twenty years later.

In his novels, Malamud did not deal directly with the subject of the Holocaust.

LEST YOU FORGET

If you ever forget you're a Jew, a Gentile will remind you.

An epigraph adopted by Joseph Heller, author of Catch-22.

ALL MEN ARE JEWS

I think I said, "All men are Jews except they don't know it." I doubt I expected anyone to take the statement literally. But I think it's an understandable statement and a metaphoric way of indicating how history, sooner or later, treats all men.

From a 1975 interview.

MIDDLE AGE DEFINED

Middle age...is when you pay for what you didn't have or couldn't do when you were young.

Quoted in Lionel Blue's Jewish Guide to the Here and Hereafter *(1988).*

DEFINING BIOGRAPHY

All biography is ultimately fiction.

From his Dubin's Lives *(1979).*

◻

Irving Malin

A WARM TESTAMENT

Despite the outwardly sarcastic, crazy tone of the novel, it is a warm testament...[suggesting] that Jewishness, however differently it is interpreted [or misinterpreted], is heartfelt and golden.

In a critique of Joseph Heller's Good as Gold *(1979).*

◻

Jerome R. Malino

ABIDING FRIENDSHIPS

Perhaps the most rewarding aspect [of being a congregational rabbi] is the opportunity for abiding personal relationships. I am able, without hesitation...to utter the same prayer of gratitude I spoke after twelve years in my pulpit when I said [that] the rabbi "will feel himself a partner with God in creating souls." As he confirms those he knew as infants, marries those he has confirmed, as he sees his handiwork in happier and better integrated lives, as he grows with his labors and earns the love of those he served, he will say, "The reward was worth the effort."

From his 1980 presidential address before the Central Conference of American Rabbis.

¤

Manasseh ben Israel

MEN ARE TAUGHT BY REASON

The Spanish Inquisition, with all its torments and cruelties, could make any Jew become a Christian. For unreasonable beasts are taught by blows, but men are taught by reason.

From his Vindiciac Judaeorum *(1656).*

¤

Charles T. Manatt

JESSE JACKSON—ANTI-SEMITE?

I do not believe Jesse Jackson is anti-Jewish in any way and that the Democratic Party will not disavow the presidential candidate for his allegedly anti-Semitic remarks.

From a June 1984 statement in The Los Angeles Times.

¤

Morris Mandel

MEASURING PERSONAL WEALTH

The true wealth of a person lies in his hidden strength: his desire to help others without recompense. The best exercise for strengthening the heart is to reach down and lift others up.

From his Heaven, Man and a Carrot *(1963).*

PULLING THE TRIGGER

It is not enough to have a good aim in life; you must also pull the trigger.

Ibid.

LIFE'S CEMENT

Nothing in the world is more powerful than faith. It is the cement that holds life together. Faith is belief, plus will, plus trust, plus work.

Ibid.

THE POWER OF FAITH

Faith is the material that will not shrink when washed in the tears of affliction. Living without faith is like driving a car without headlights on a moonless and starless night.

Ibid.

NATURE OF TRUE WISDOM

A man of wisdom looks below the surface of things; he is not content with the superficial. In humility he goes to the writings of our sages, and conscious of his own limitations, bows his head to Infinite Wisdom and prays, "Write me as one who loves his fellow-man."

True wisdom, therefore, has little to do with books; it is, rather, the possession of those who attune their hearts to that inner voice that whispers in each of us.

From the Introduction to his and Leo Gartenberg's Tomorrow Is Today *(1977) .*

BEAUTY IS GOD'S THERAPY

Today is here. Breathe in the fresh cool air, enjoy the patches of sunshine. Mix with sincere friends. Exchange ideas and see the beautiful, not the ugly side of life. Beauty is God's therapy. It is there for all to enjoy—today.

Ibid.

WALKING WITH THE WIND

Great people are *not* affected by every puff of wind that blows ill. We can walk into the wind and fight it, or we can use the wind to propel us in the direction that we wish to move.

Ibid.

WHAT IS FAITH?

Faith is not to be confused with determination, optimism or imagination. Actually, it is simply *believing*. It is knowing there is an ocean, because you have seen a brook; a mountain, because you have seen a hill; God, because you have seen man.

Ibid.

RELIGION VS. SCIENCE

Science adds to our comfort, knowledge and power. It has helped place man in orbit. It has sent man to the moon and landed its instruments on Mars. But what does it all add up to? Only religion, not science, can add dignity to our lives and make us feel like human beings.

Ibid.

◻

Nelson Mandela

A COMMON BOND

There is a good amount of interaction with the Jewish community. There is a general danger that confronts all of us from the right wing.

To a delegation of American Jewish Committee leaders during Mandela's visit to the United States in July 1993, in which he emphasized "common interests of blacks and Jews and their history of cooperation against racism."

ON ISRAEL

There has never been any doubting the existence, *de facto* and *de jure,* of the State of Israel within secure boundaries.

At a meeting with American Jewish leaders in Geneva on June 10, 1990.

CALLING FOR JEWISH SUPPORT

There are many influential Jewish businesspeople who have an important contribution to make in the partnership between the private sector and the government, which we believe is so crucial for the economic well-being of our country.... We believe that the Jewish community, who have suffered so much under racism and who have a proud history of resistance and humanitarianism, will continue to provide their support to a nonracial and democratic dispensation in South Africa.

Speaking in Johannesburg in April 1994, prior to his expected election as the first black president of South Africa and the subsequent swearing-in on May 10, 1994.

◻

Bernard Mandelbaum

I CONDEMN

I condemn the consistently *highest* salaries for fund-raising administrators, many times the salaries of *educational* administrators and teachers.

I condemn the outrageously large pensions given to retired Federation and UJA executives. They exceed the pensions of U.S. Armed Forces officers which are now being investigated.

I condemn the blatant luxury of the lifestyle of the top professionals of the Jewish Agency in Israel.

The time has come for us to see to it that those who are employed by the Jewish community do not squander charitable funds by a lifestyle of luxury, especially at this time when these funds are sorely needed in Israel and in this country.

From The Jewish Spectator, Fall 1985.

SIGNS OF MATURITY

Just as a child expresses himself and expects answers in terms which are concrete, tangible and specific, so, too, the childish, naive mind expects clear, precise, unequivocal evidence and portrayal of truth, goodness, righteousness, God. The mature, realistic person recognizes the realities of life's complexities—its perplexing paradoxes as well as its continuity.

From the Introduction to his Choose Life (1968).

VITALITY OF IDEAS

Ideas, in contrast to things, have an influence that is way out of proportion to their apparent size or power. They can be in many places at the same time. They have a vitality that can increase, rather than weaken, with time. Ideas are active even when men are asleep.

Ibid.

◻

Itzik Manger

ROAD TO DESTRUCTION

I am the road to destruction,
The blonde death in the sun,
The brown strain of the shepherd's pipe,
The tired sunset glow.
My brother, do not follow me,
To pass down my road is to pass away.

Describing how the roads inside the shtetl lead in a circle—to death.

◻

Barry Manilow

BAR MITZVAH GIFT

I got Willie Murphy as a stepfather for my Bar Mitzvah. He tipped me off to serious music, taking me to my first jazz concert: Gerry Mulligan at Town Hall.

In the late 1950s, Manilow's mother remarried. Her new husband, Willie Murphy, was a truck driver and also a jazz aficionado who shared his love for music with his stepson.

Theodore Mann

ON FULL RECOGNITION

I don't want the State of Israel to tell me that we are something less than Jewish because we do not accept the Orthodox point of view.

In a 1984 statement opposing any amendment to the Law of Return that would redefine who is a Jew.

Thomas Mann

A BORN FABULIST

[Jacob] Wassermann is a storyteller. He is this above all else, a born fabulist.... He is the man who today can still write a real novel of the finer sort.

Evaluating the career and talent of German writer Jacob Wassermann.

Anis Mansour

SPREADING HATE

They [the Jews] have what they call the Easter Feast (Passover), the feast of the unleavened bread, which is celebrated by bleeding a non-Jew. Then they take a piece of flesh and mix it with the *matzoh*. The rabbi himself does the butcher's work. This is the nature of our enemy.

From a 1972 article in the Cairo daily Al Akhbar.

AN OBSCENE EVALUATION

The world is now aware of the fact that Hitler was right and that the cremation ovens were an appropriate means of punishing such contempt of human values, principles, religions, and law [as the Jews exhibit].

Quoted from the Cairo daily Al Akhbar by Le Monde, Paris, August 21, 1973.

Moshe Ma'Oz

BE PREPARED TO TALK

Israel should be prepared to talk to the PLO provided the PLO recognizes the *right* of Israel to exist as a sovereign Jewish state, and agrees to the principle that the status of the West Bank and the Gaza Strip should be determined in the last stage of an overall Arab-Israeli settlement.

From a symposium in Moment magazine, March 1976.

ABRAHAM AND GOD

There were no stories about God. That was indeed perhaps the most remarkable thing: the courage with which Abram represented and expressed God's essence from the first, without more ado, simply in that he said "God."

From Joseph and His Brothers.

JOSEPH: THE IDEAL PERSON

Joseph is the ideal manifested, as the union of darkness and light, feeling and mind, the primitive and the civilized, wisdom and the happy heart—in short as the humanized mystery we call man.

From I Believe (1939), edited by Clifton Fadiman.

David (Mickey) Marcus

HAVE YOU BEEN TO DACHAU?

Have you been to Dachau, Major? Have you ever seen or heard a group of Jewish skeletons singing *Hatikva*?

Responding to the request of Major Yitzhak Shamir, who had come to Marcus's law office on December 7, 1947, to enlist his services as an instructor in the newly formed Jewish army. Shamir was surprised at Marcus's instant positive response.

Yoel Marcus

SILENCE OF THE LION

You know what? I'm fed up seeing [Syrian] President Assad's sourpuss face—his and that of his Foreign Minister, Farouk al-Sharaa. They behave, keep silent and speak as if they are doing us a favor by their very existence. They say one word and rest for a month. They rest for a month and say another word, and again rest for a month. In between, Assad experts, both in Israel and Washington, engage in dialectics, discussing what the poet intended.

Commenting on the slow progress in establishing peace with Syria. From his column in the Israeli newspaper Haaretz. Quoted in The New York Times, October 18, 1994.

◻

David Margolick

COUNTLESS SUITS

I bought a large box of 64 Crayolas so I could identify the colors of Johnnie Cochran's suits.

> *At a barbecue given for the media by Larry Schiller, co-author with O. J. Simpson of* I Want to Tell You *(1995). Cochran, lead defense attorney at the O. J. Simpson murder trial, was known for his extensive wardrobe.*

◻

Jacques Maritain

ISRAEL'S GLORY

If the world hates the Jews, it is because it feels that they will always be supernatural foreigners; it is because it dislikes their passion for the absolute, and the unbearable stimulus it inflicts on the world. It is the vocation of Israel which arouses so much hostility. To be hated by the world, that is Israel's glory.

> *From his* Mystery of Israel.

ANTI-SEMITISM AS A DIVERSION

Anti-Semitism diverts men from the real tasks confronting them. It diverts them from the true causes of their woes.

> *From his* A Christian Looks at the Jewish Question *(1939), in which he continues to condemn anti-Semitism as immoral, stupid, and a sin against the Catholic faith.*

YEAST OF THE WORLD

Israel, which is not of the world, is to be found at the very heart of the world's structure, stimulating it, exasperating it, moving it. Like an alien body, like an activating ferment injected into the mass, it gives the world no peace, it bars slumber, it teaches the world to be discontented and restless as long as the world has not God.

> *Ibid.*

◻

Sidney Marks

A FORTUNATE PEOPLE

We are such fortunate people, such very fortunate people. Here we are, American citizens. We share with the rest of our fellow Americans this wonderful civilization. But think of the double flowering that we Jewish people have. Not only do we partake of this American civilization but also of this Jewish civilization of ours.

> *From a 1960 dialogue with Rabbi William Berkowitz at the Institute of Adult Jewish Studies in New York. Reported in Berkowitz's* Ten Vital Jewish Issues *(1964).*

◻

Christopher Marlowe

TO BE HATED

Who hateth me but for my happiness?
Or who is honored now but for his wealth?
Rather had I, a Jew, be hated thus
Than pitied in a Christian poverty.

> *From his play* Jew of Malta, *Act I (1589).*

ACT OF CHARITY

To undo a Jew is charity, not sin....
I count religion but a childish toy,
and hold there is no sin but ignorance.

> *Ibid. Act IV.*

◻

Louis M. Marshall

SERVING TWO MASTERS

I do not feel that I am guilty of any inconsistency by being president of Temple Emanu-El, a Reform congregation, and at the same time the president of the Jewish Theological Seminary of America, an Orthodox institution [today we call it Conservative; in those early years it was still considered Orthodox], so long as both conscientiously carry out their principles, and they both promote and advance the cause of religion, of morality, of good citizenship, and of Judaism.

> *Responding in 1902 to the question of how he could serve two masters at the same time.*

◻

Arthur Marx

MASTER OF INSULTS

On his climb up the ladder he [his father, Groucho] has enjoyed life to the utmost. He has shaken hands with Presidents, danced cheek to cheek with Marlene Dietrich, played baseball with Lou Gehrig, traded backhands with Jack Kramer, strummed guitar duets with the great Segovia, and he's insulted nearly everyone worth insulting.

> *Quoted in his* Life with Groucho.

Groucho Marx

ACCEPT MY RESIGNATION

I sent the [Friar's] club a wire stating, PLEASE ACCEPT MY RESIGNATION. I DON'T WANT TO BELONG TO ANY CLUB THAT WILL ACCEPT ME AS A MEMBER.

From his Groucho and Me *(1959). Reacting to the Friar Club's policy of not accepting all Jews.*

FRIED EGGS AND LITERATURE

I toy with the idea of doing a cookbook.... I think a lot of people who hate literature but love fried eggs would buy it if the price is right.

Ibid.

BIRTH ANNOUNCEMENT

Although it is generally known, I think it's about time to announce that I was born at a very early age.

Ibid.

GETTING OLD

Age is not a particularly interesting subject. Anyone can get old. All you have to do is live long enough.

Ibid.

HALF A LOAF

Since my little son is only half-Jewish, would it be all right if he went into the pool only up to his waist?

Addressed to a country club that would not admit his son.

LIES, LIES, LIES

They say a man is as old as the woman he feels. In that case I'm eighty-five.... I want it known here and now that this is what I want on my tombstone. Here lies Groucho Marx, and Lies and Lies and Lies. P.S. He never kissed an ugly girl.

From his Secret World of Groucho.

Harpo Marx

TRUE LOVE

For one year and one month he declared my house his house. For one year and one month he ate my food, played my piano, ran up my phone bill, burned cigarette holes in my landlady's furniture, monopolized my record player and my coffeepot, gave his guests the run of the joint, insulted my guests, and never stopped complaining. He was an insomniac. He was an egomaniac. He was a leech and a lunatic... But I loved the guy.

His experience with Oscar Levant. Quoted in Harpo Speaks.

ONE-SIDED RELATIONSHIPS

Oscar was utterly unable to enjoy an equal relationship with anybody. It had to be one-sided, on his side, with the single exception of George Gershwin. Once I understood this and accepted it, I found Oscar to be one of the most rewarding men I had ever known. I lost a house, but I gained a friend.

Ibid.

PLAYING IT BY EAR

I was the same kind of father as I was a harpist—I played by ear.

Ibid.

EXPERIENCE GALORE

I've played piano in a whorehouse. I've smuggled secret papers out of Russia. I've spent an evening on the divan with Peggy Hopkins Joyce. I've taught a gangster mob how to play Pinchie Winchie. I've played croquet with Herbert Bayard Swope while he kept Governor Al Smith waiting on the phone. I've gambled with Nick the Greek, sat on the floor with Greta Garbo, sparred with Benny Leonard, horsed around with the Prince of Wales, played ping-pong with George Gershwin.... The truth is, I had no business doing any of these things. I couldn't read a note of music. I never finished the second grade. But I was having too much fun to recognize myself as an ignorant upstart.

Ibid.

Karl Marx

FOR THE LOVE OF MONEY

Money is the jealous God of Israel, besides which no other gods may exist. Money abases all the gods of mankind and changes them into commodities. Money is the self-sufficient value of all things. It has, therefore, deprived the whole world, both the human world and nature, of their own proper value. Money is the alienated essence of man's work and existence: this essence dominates him and he worships it. The god of the Jews has been secularized and has become the god of this world.

From T. B. Bottomore's Karl Marx: Early Writings *(1963).*

Jews and Jesuits

Thus we find every tyrant backed by a Jew, as is every pope by a Jesuit. In truth, the cravings of oppressors would be hopeless and the practicability of war out of the question, if there were not an army of Jesuits to smother thought and a handful of Jews to ransack pockets.

Ibid.

Emancipating Mankind

The emancipation of the Jews in the last significance is the emancipation of mankind from Judaism.

From his On the Jewish Question *(1844), in which he equates Judaism with commercialism.*

Finding Fault with Jews

As soon as society succeeds in abolishing the empirical essence of Judaism, which is the huckster and the conditions that produce him, the Jew will become impossible, because his consciousness will no longer have a corresponding object.

Quoted in Alan Dershowitz's Chutzpah *(1991).*

¤

Thomas Masaryk

Undoing Anti-Semitism

Mother would forbid us to go near the Lechners because, as she said, Jews were using the blood of Christian children. I would therefore make a wide turn to avoid passing their house; and so did all my schoolmates.... The superstition of Christian blood used for Passover cakes had become so much part and parcel of my existence that whenever I chanced to come near a Jew—I wouldn't do it on purpose—I would look at his fingers to see if blood were there. I for a long time I continued this practice [*sic*].... Would that I may unmake all that anti-Semitism caused me to do in my childhood days.

Quoted in Karel Capek's President Masaryk Tells His Story.

¤

Tzevi Hirsch Masliansky

The Good Speaker

No man is a good speaker who can use his collar again.

Quoted in Abram L. Sachar's Sufferance Is the Badge *(1939).*

¤

Will Maslow

Jewish Assets

The assets at the command of the Jewish community are considerable: a network of Jewish organizations, widely dispersed, manned by skilled professionals and dedicated laymen, alert to Jewish concerns and able to count on the ready support of a committed membership educated and affluent, with many political and governmental contacts and an overriding concern for [liberal issues and the] security of Israel.... If these assets are used prudently, American Jewry can continue to exercise an influence disproportionate to its numbers when focused on its limited and meaningful goals.

From a 1975 statement.

¤

Jackie Mason

English Courtesy

If an Englishman gets run down by a truck, he apologizes to the truck.

Quoted in the London Independent, *September 20, 1990.*

Politically Incorrect

I have been associated with the phrase "politically incorrect" for ten years, ever since the expression became popular. Everyone has always thought of me as politically incorrect. My whole attitude was always politically incorrect; it's my expression of independence.

Comment of the comedian when Comedy Central cable television, which was running a weekly series entitled Politically Incorrect, *went to court to bar Mason from calling his new show* Jackie Mason, Politically Incorrect. *Reported in* The New York Times, *November 3, 1993.*

The Race Race

People have become so frightened of being thought of as a racist that they've lost touch with reality. They are only expressing an irrational panic out of a frightened response to the past history of racism that once permeated our society. White people today are desperately pleading to the black population for forgiveness. They are in a race to top each other in anti-racist zealousness. They are in a search-and-destroy mission to locate a victim to label as a racist. It has taken on the fervor of a Salem witch hunt with McCarthyite fanaticism.

In response to criticism of his use of the word shvartze *(Yiddish for black) when referring to Mayor David Dinkins of New York City. From an article in* The Jewish Week, *October 24–November 4, 1993.*

BUILDING BLOCKS OF HUMOR

The Talmud is the study of logic. Every time I see a contradiction or hypocrisy in somebody's behavior, I think of the Talmud and build the joke from there.

Quoted in Darryl Lyman's Jewish Comedy Catalog *(1989).*

NEED FOR ADORATION

A normal person wouldn't become a comedian. The egomania, the neurosis, the need to overcompensate, the feeling that life is meaningless without stardom—it's too much suffering.

Ibid.

BEING TAKEN FOR GRANTED

The Jewish people took me for granted. The young people saw me as an anachronism. Then I went to Broadway, where I *never* thought I'd succeed. For the longest time I'm considered some bum from the mountains by the same people who think I'm an art form now.

Ibid.

PARANOIA

When I went to a football game, every time the players went into a huddle I thought they were talking about me.

From one of Mason's comedy routines.

HOW DO I KNOW ME?

My analyst said, "We have to search for the real you." I said to myself, "If I don't know who I am, how would I know what I look like? And even if I find the real me, how would I know it's me? Besides, what if I find the real me, and I find that he's even worse than I am? I don't make enough for myself—I need a partner?"

Ibid.

MANISCHEWITZ WINE

A *Seder* without sweet Manischewitz would be like horseradish without tears, like a cantor without a voice, like a *shul* without a complaint, like a *yenta* without a big mouth, like Passover without Jews.

Ibid.

¤

Cotton Mather

O, TO BAPTIZE A JEW!

[I pray] for the conversion of the Jewish nation, and for my own having the happiness to baptize a Jew, that my ministry be brought home unto the Lord.

From a July 19, 1696 entry in his diary. Mather believed that the millennium would come only when the Jews had been converted.

HEAVENLY HOPE

I had advice from Heaven—yea, more than that; that I shall shortly see some Harvest of my Prayers and Pains, and the Jewish Nation also.

From a May 21, 1699 entry in his diary.

¤

Mattathias the Priest

WHO IS FOR THE LORD?

Whoever is for the Lord, let him follow me.

His charge to the people of Israel when leading a rebellion against the Syrian-Greeks in the second century B.C.E.

¤

Cornelius Matthews

A PEOPLE APART

The Jews were as thick with their gloomy whiskers, as blackberries; the air smelt of old coats and hats, and the sideways were glutted with dresses and overcoats and little, fat greasy children. There were country men moving up and down the street, horribly harassed and perplexed, and every now and then falling into the hands of one of these fierce-whiskered Jews, carried into a gloomy cavern, and presently sent forth again, in a garment coat or hat or breeches, in which he might dance, and turn his partner to boot.

A description of the Jews' Chatham Street. From his Guidebook to New York City *(1845).*

¤

W. Somerset Maugham

SOME OF MY BEST FRIENDS...

God knows that I have never been that [anti-Semitic]; some of my best friends both in England and America are Jews.

From a May 1946 letter. Quoted in Ted Morgan's Somerset Maugham *(1980).*

❏

Elisabeth (Betty) Maxwell

KILLING A MYTH

That's complete rubbish. It was totally unnecessary for my husband to have been in the Mossad. He knew absolutely everybody in Israel. He didn't need to be in any form of agency to do anything or see anyone. And to put it crudely, I wouldn't have thought that the Israelis kill their friends.

> *Commenting on the allegation in Victor Ostrovsky's* Other Side of Deception *that her husband, Robert, who died at sea on November 5, 1991, was eliminated by the Mossad when he tried to extort funds for his ailing empire.*

GUILT OF A GOY

My first visit to Auschwitz was in the 1960s. That was traumatic, mostly because Bob's grief was so poignant. In those days you could put your hand in the dirt and you had bones in your hands. It was the first time I had a profound sensation of guilt. I suppose that guilt also reverberated from my husband. All of a sudden, I was really the enemy, the *goy*.

> *From her* Mind of My Own: My Life With Robert Maxwell *(1994), in which she describes what led her, born in a staunchly French Protestant home in France, to become a scholar and lecturer on the Holocaust. Her husband had lost most of his relatives in concentration camps.*

❏

Robert Maxwell

MAN WITH A DREAM

As for my thoughts, I am dreaming about the help which I would like to give to the State of Israel to enable it to become one of the world leaders and a paradise on earth. My dreams very often revolve on this one line. This evening they were brought about by the big opening headline in the American journal, reading in red letters ISRAEL DESTINED TO LEAD MIDDLE EAST IN 10 YEARS, followed by a dispatch from the paper on Hearst, who was there on a visit, justifying the headline.

> *From a 1957 letter to his wife, Elisabeth. Quoted in her* Mind of My Own: My Life with Robert Maxwell *(1994).*

IN LOVE WITH JUDAISM

I and my family were observant Jews. I still believe in God, the God of Israel. I do believe in the ethical lessons of Judaism. I love and admire my people's devotion to the study of

Torah. I definitely see myself as a Jew. I was born as a Jew, and I shall die as a Jew, so help me God.

> *Ibid.*

❏

Egon Mayer

WELCOMING INTERMARRIEDS

You can't just ignore the bad news or dismiss these people as bad people. If you want them in your Sukkah, you've got to let them know [that they are welcome], and the encouragement process is lifelong.

> *The sociologist who did the Jewish Outreach Institute survey on intermarriage urges the Jewish community to extend a welcome to intermarried couples. Quoted in* The Jewish Week, *October 8–14, 1993.*

❏

Jonathan Mayhew

CHOOSING A KING

God gave Israel a king (or absolute monarchy) in His anger, because they had not the sense and virtue enough to like a free commonwealth, and to have Himself for their king.

> *From a sermon on the repeal of the Stamp Act, delivered in Boston on May 23, 1766.*

❏

Jacob Mazé

JEWS PAY THE BILLS

The Trotskys make the revolutions and the Bronsteins pay the bills.

> *A 1921 comment of a Moscow rabbi in 1921 about Leon Trotsky, whose birth name was Lev Bronstein.*

❏

James McReynolds

JEWISH AFFLICTION

Do not afflict the court with another Jew.

> *Advising President Herbert Hoover in 1932, when he was considering a replacement for Oliver Wendell Holmes. The two Jewish justices to whom he was referring were Brandeis, who was then serving on the Court, and Cardozo, the potential nominee.*

SUPREME BIGOT

Huh, seems the only way you can get on

the Supreme Court these days is to either be the son of a criminal or a Jew or both.

Commenting after Hoover nominated Benjamin N. Cardozo to take the seat being vacated by Oliver Wendell Holmes.

◻

George Meany

PLAIN TALK

She speaks my language. For Abba Eban I have to take a dictionary.

Referring to Golda Meir and her midwestern American accent.

◻

Anne Meara

SINCERE CONVERSION

I had ceased to be a Catholic.

Explaining why she had converted to Judaism six years after marrying Jerry Stiller, insisting that it was purely voluntary. Quoted in an interview with Robin Cembalest in the Forward, *August 18, 1995.*

◻

Vladka Meed

MARKING MILA 18

Fifty years have passed. Mila 18, the house which served as the headquarters of the Warsaw ghetto fighters, is no more. A small patch of grass, a few flowers during the summertime, and a big, lonely rock mark the place.

A courier for the Jewish Fighting Organization during the Warsaw Ghetto uprising in April-May 1943 recounted her experiences at the Days of Remembrance ceremony, marking the fiftieth anniversary of the revolt. The ceremony was held in the Capitol Rotunda, Washington, DC, on April 20, 1993.

◻

Aharon Megged

FEELING OF AN OUTSIDER

Although I have had jobs which everyone respected, and did them to the best of my ability, I have always felt myself an outsider, never "one of the crowd." I stood within and observed from without. Perhaps this is a sharpened existential condition of being Jewish for me, rooted in my character. At any rate, this is what has caused all the heroes of my stories and novels to be anti-heroes, characters on

the periphery of society, whose prevailing modes are irony.

From a profile in The Jerusalem Post, *June 4, 1994.*

WRITERS AND REVIEWERS

It is a zoological survey of the relationship between writers and reviewers, like the way someone would study the relationship between cats and dogs. This is the world of a writer. Even someone like Shai Agnon, who received so many positive reviews, would get so angry when someone criticized him.... There are no writers who like bad reviews. Generally, I think about it two or three days, and then move on.

Ibid.

◻

Zubin Mehta

MY ADOPTED COUNTRY

I heard a Tel Aviv flight announcement and suddenly found myself walking toward it. I was adopted by this country and I felt it my duty to be with the Israelis in a time of emergency.

While awaiting a New York-bound plane at the Paris airport, on January 14, 1991, at the height of the Gulf War. Iraq was firing SCUD *missiles at Israel.*

◻

(Rabbi) Meir

CHEWING FOOD

Chew your food well with your teeth and you will feel it in your steps.

Quoted in the talmudic tractate Shabbat (152a).

ENTERING AND LEAVING

A baby enters the world with hands clenched, as if to say, "The world is mine; I shall grab it." A man leaves with hands open, as if to say, "I can take nothing with me."

Quoted in the Midrash Ecclesiastes Rabba (5:14).

ENJOY THE JUICE

When I see a juicy pomegranate, I enjoy its contents and throw away the skin.

Upon being criticized for associating with the excommunicated talmudic scholar Elisha ben Avuya.

MERITING ETERNAL LIFE

Anyone who has settled in the Land of Israel is careful with regard to the consumption of consecrated food [he does not eat sacrificial animals that belong to the *Kohen*], and who speaks in the holy tongue [Hebrew] and recites the Shema mornings and evenings—it is certain that such a person will merit life in the world-to-come.

> *Quoted in the Jerusalem Talmud Shabbat (1:3).*

○

Golda Meir

THE DAY OF ACCOUNTING

Some day my son will ask me by what right I gave up most of the country and I won't know how to answer him.

> *Reacting to the Peel Commission report of 1937, which proposed the partition of Palestine into Jewish and Arab sections.*

ON FORGIVING ARABS

When peace comes, we will perhaps in time be able to forgive the Arabs for killing our sons, but it will be harder for us to forgive them for having forced us to kill their sons.

> *From an interview after the 1967 Six-Day War.*

EICHMANN'S CAPTURE

This is a body that deals with threats to peace. Is this a threat to peace—Eichmann brought to trial by the very people to whose total physical annihilation he dedicated all his energies, even if the manner of his apprehension violated the laws of the Argentine? Or did the threat to peace lie in Eichmann at large, Eichmann unpunished, Eichmann free to spread the poison of his twisted soul to a new generation?

> *From a speech delivered in 1960 before the UN Security Council after Argentina had complained that Israel had breached her sovereignty when it captured Eichmann on Argentinian soil without permission.*

THANK YOU FOR REMAINING JEWS

Thank you for remaining Jews [*A dank eich vos ihr zeit gebliben Yidn*].

> *To the crowds that swarmed around her on Rosh Hashana 1948, when she visited the Moscow synagogue after her appointment as Israeli ambassador to the USSR.*

DELIVERANCE FINALLY

For two thousand years we have waited for our deliverance. Now that it is here it is so great and wonderful that it surpasses words.... *Mazal tov*—congratulations!

> *Spoken in November 1947, before thousands of people gathered at the Jewish Agency in Jerusalem, immediately after the United Nations voted for partition of Palestine and statehood for the Jewish people.*

FREE AT LAST

I want to be able to read a book without feeling guilty or go to a concert when I like.... I do not intend to retire to a political nunnery.

> *Following her retirement from government service.*

SAVIOR ON A WHITE HORSE

Look, Clara, you're an American. You don't like Nixon. I'm an Israeli. I'll never forget that if it hadn't been for Nixon we would have been destroyed.

> *Speaking to her sister during the Watergate scandal. Because of his support of Israel during the Yom Kippur War, to Golda Nixon was a savior on a white horse.*

IN DEFENSE OF KISSINGER

I had bitter arguments with him, very bitter. Israel's statesman will have tough arguments with him more than once and on more than one subject. But to arrive at the conclusion that he is ready to abandon Israel and sell us out to the Arabs—this is groundless and will remain groundless and incorrect.

> *Defending Henry Kissinger against Israelis who argued that he was too pro-Arab.*

LISTEN TO YOUR HEART

I should have listened to the warnings of my heart and ordered a call-up.... I shall live with this terrible knowledge for the rest of my life.

> *From her autobiography,* My Life *(1975), in which she writes about the surprise Arab attack in the Yom Kippur War of 1973.*

A MEANINGLESS WORD

I said to my colleagues, "Surrender? What is this word surrender? It has no meaning in Hebrew!" Then I went to the lavatory to vomit.

> *From an interview towards the end of her life with Alan Hart, reported in his* Arafat: A Political Biography *(1984). Moshe Dayan had suggested at a Kitchen Cabinet meeting that Israel should "surrender" its front-line positions along the Suez Canal to prevent further loss of Israeli life.*

MAINTAINING FORMALITY

When Kissinger was in Israel, my Cabinet

colleagues used to call him Henry and slap him on the back. He responded by slapping them on the back and calling them by their first names. I never allowed that sort of relationship to develop. I always insisted that he call me Mrs. Meir or Madame Prime Minister. And I always called him either Mr. Secretary of State or Dr. Kissinger. I always told my colleagues that it was a mistake to be on first-name terms with such a man.

> *Ibid.*

DESERVING OF AN OSCAR

I don't know about the Nobel Prize, but they certainly deserve an Oscar.

> *When asked her reaction to the suggestion that Anwar Sadat and Menachem Begin be nominated for the next Nobel Peace Prize.*

THE CARPENTER'S DAUGHTER

What's going on here? Me, the daughter of Moshe Mabovitch the carpenter, going to meet the Pope of the Catholics? To which one of her aides quickly replied, "Just a minute, Golda, carpentry is a very respected profession around here."

> *Addressing her aides Lou Kaddar and Simcha Dinitz as she was about to enter the quarters for an audience with Pope Paul VI on January 15, 1973.*

MYERSON MEETS MYERSON

So you're the famous Myerson girl I've been hearing so much about.

> *To Bess Myerson, Miss America of 1945, upon meeting her after Golda had become Prime Minister of Israel in 1969. Golda's married surname was Myerson.*

SERVANT OF PEACE

We share the grief of humanity at the passing away of his Holiness Pope Pius XII. In a generation afflicted by wars and discords, he upheld the highest ideals of peace and compassion. When fearful martyrdom came to our people in the decade of Nazi terror, the voice of the Pope was raised for the victims. The life of our times was enriched by a voice speaking out on the great moral truths above the tumult of daily conflict. We mourn a great servant of peace.

> *Quoted in Pinchas Lapide's* Last Three Popes and the Jews *(1967).*

CONFRONTING THE POPE

Your Holiness, do you know what my own very earliest memory is? It is waiting for a pogrom in Kiev. Let me assure you that my people know all about real harshness, and also that we learned all about real mercy when we were being led to the gas chambers of the Nazis.

> *In response to Pope Paul VI's comment, at their January 15, 1973 meeting, that he found it hard to fathom how the Jewish people, "which should be so merciful," behaves so harshly in its own country.*

WHO ARE THE PALESTINIANS?

There was no such thing as Palestinians. When was there an independent Palestinian people with a Palestinian state? It was either southern Syria before the first World War, and then it was a Palestine including Jordan. It was not as though there was a Palestinian people and we came and threw them out and took their country away from them. They did not exist.

> *In an interview with the* Sunday Times *of* London, *on June 15, 1969. She later tried to retract this position.*

I AM A PALESTINIAN

I am a Palestinian. From 1921 to 1948 I held a Palestinian passport. And I was aware that there were Arabs and Jews in Palestine and that all were Palestinians.

> *From a statement in which she tried to temper her June 15, 1969 statement in which she said, "There was no such thing as Palestinians." See above.*

MASTERS OF OUR OWN FATE

We only want that which is given naturally to all peoples of the world, to be masters of our own fate, only of our fate, not of others, and in cooperation and friendship with others.

> *From an address to the Anglo-American Committee of Inquiry, March 25, 1946.*

APPRECIATING NIXON

Your decision will have a great and beneficial influence on our fighting capability. I knew that in this hour of dire need for Israel, I could turn to you and count on your deep sympathy and understanding. We are fighting against heavy odds, but we are fully confident that we shall come out victorious. When we do, we will have you in mind.

> *In a communication to President Richard Nixon after she learned that he had overridden the view of Secretary of State Henry Kissinger and had ordered that the Department of Defense send Israel a large amount of arms and supplies, which turned the tide in the 1973 Yom Kippur War.*

THE FLIGHT OF OLD AGE

Old age is like a plane flying through a storm. Once you're aboard there's nothing you can do.

> *Quoted in a 1973 article by Oriana Fallaci in* L'Europeo.

LEARNING TO WEEP

Those who do not know how to weep with their heart don't know how to laugh either.

> *Ibid.*

ENOUGH

I have had enough.

> *Upon resigning as prime minister of Israel in 1974.*

PESSIMISM

Pessimism is a luxury that a Jew can never allow himself.

> *From a 1973 interview in the* London Observer.

MOSES' MISADVENTURE

Let me tell you something we have against Moses. He took us forty years through the desert in order to bring us to the one spot in the Middle East that has no oil.

> *Quoted in* The New York Times, *1973.*

NO COMPROMISING

To be or not to be is not a question of compromise. Either you be or you don't be.

> *Quoted in* The New York Times, *December 12, 1974.*

THE "OLD LADY"

Let us at least conclude one thing, the beginning that you have made, with such courage and with such hope for peace—let us decide one thing—it must go on, face-to-face between us and between you so that even an old lady like I am will live to see the day.... You always called me an old lady...will live to see the day, whoever signs on the part of Israel, I want to see that day of peace between you and us, of peace between all our neighbors and us.

> *At a meeting between Sadat and political leaders of Israel on the day after the Egyptian's memorable speech to the Knesset on November 20, 1977. Golda died less than four months before the signing of the Israel–Egypt peace treaty in March 1979.*

PALESTINE: A ROMAN NAME

There is no such thing as a Palestinian Arab nation!... Palestine is a name the Romans gave to Eretz Yisrael with the express purpose of infuriating the Jews. They knew it would burn Jewish souls if they named the land for the Philistines—Israel's arch enemy.

Why should we use the spiteful name meant to humiliate us? Do we call Jerusalem Aelia Capitolina because the Romans wanted to obliterate all memory of Judea?

> *Quoted by journalist Sarah Honig in* The Jerusalem Post International Edition, *December 4, 1993, from news stories she wrote in the 1970s.*

MORE THAN NABLUS AND GAZA

They [the Palestinians] don't just want Nablus and Gaza. They want Tel Aviv and Afula. They want everything. Was there peace here before the Six Day War? Why didn't they make peace before we were occupiers? Why didn't they establish a Palestinian State when they had all the territories?

> *Ibid.*

CRUSHED BUT NOT DEFEATED

We Jews just refuse to disappear. No matter how strong, brutal, and ruthless the forces against us may be—here we are. Millions of bodies broken, buried alive, burned to death, but never has anyone been able to succeed in breaking the spirit of the Jewish people.

> *From a February 19, 1976 speech delivered at the Brussels II conference on the Plight of Soviet Jewry.*

WHAT'S THE CHOICE?

If we have to have a choice between being dead and pitied, and being alive with a bad image, we'd rather be alive and have a bad image.

> *Quoted in Elinor and Robert Slater's* Great Jewish Women *(1994).*

□

Meir of Rothenburg

UNAFFECTED BY TORTURE

After a man has determined to surrender his life in martyrdom, he is absolutely insensible to torture.

> *From his* Responsa *(1891).*

NO FAIR GAME

Who hunts game with dogs will not partake of Leviathan.

> *Ibid.*

DEMEANING ISRAEL

Sinning in Eretz Israel is worse than else-where.... It is like rebellion right within the king's own palace.

> *Ibid.*

ANTI-DEMON DEVICE

I am convinced that no demon can harm a house properly provided with a mezuza.

> *Exhorting Jews to fasten a mezuza to their doorposts. Quoted in Irving Agus's* Rabbi Meir of Rothenburg *(1970).*

✡

Yitzchak Meir

NO USE TO BROOD

He who reflects on the evil he has done is thinking evil, and what one thinks, therein is one caught. Stir filth however you will, it is still filth. In the time that I am brooding, I could be stringing pearls for the sake of Heaven.

> *Commenting on the verse "Depart from evil, and do good" (Psalms 34:15). Quoted in William B. Silverman's* Rabbinic Wisdom and Jewish Values *(1971).*

✡

Albert Memmi

VIVE LA DIFFÉRENCE

Difference is...the condition requisite to all dignity and to all liberation. To be aware of oneself is to be aware of oneself as different. To be is to be different.

> *From his* Portrait of a Jew *(1962).*

✡

Menachem Mendel of Kotzk

MORE THAN JUST A THREAT

Lord of the universe,...send us our Messiah, for we have no more strength to suffer. Show me a sign, O God. Give me the force to rend the chains of exile. Otherwise,...otherwise...I rebel against Thee. If Thou dost not keep thy covenant,...then neither will I keep that agree-ment, and it is all over, we are through being Thy chosen people, Thy peculiar treasure!

> *From "Der Rebbe Fun Kotzk."*

MAN'S PURPOSE

Man was created so that he might lift up the heavens.

> *Quoted in Martin Buber's* Tales of the Hasidim *(1947).*

GOD'S ADDRESS

God dwells wherever man lets Him in.

> *Ibid.*

TO MAKE A CHASID

Ah, but does he know how to make a *chasid* [pious man]?

> *When told that a miracle-worker knew how to make a golem (robot).*

THE SOULS IN KOTZK

In Kotzk we have a soul, not a clock.

> *Explaining why a chasid will often disregard the strict statutory times when one must pray.*

ME AND YOU

If I am I because I am I, then I am I and you are you. But if I am I because you are you, and you are you because I am I, then I am not I and you are not you.

> *Arguing that one must always be true to oneself.*

BELIEVERS AND UNBELIEVERS

For the believer there are no questions and for the unbeliever there are no answers.

> *Quoted in Harold M. Schulweis's* For Those Who Can't Believe *(1994).*

A WHOLE HEART

The only whole heart is a broken one.

> *By attribution.*

OPENING THE DOOR TO GOD

Where is God's dwelling? God dwells wher-ever man lets Him in.

> *By attribution.*

MITZVA'S REAL MEANING

The prohibition against idolatry includes the prohibition against making idols out of the mitzvot [commandments]. We should never imagine that the chief purpose of a mitzva is its outer form; rather it is the inward meaning.

> *Quoted in Louis Newman's* Hasidic Anthology *(1963).*

GIVING AND RECEIVING

The giving [of the Torah] was on Shavuot; the receiving must take place every day.

> *His response to the question, "Why is the holiday of Shavuot called the time of giving the Torah, and not the time of receiving the Torah?"*

◻

Henry L. Mencken

Rich Jewish Heritage

These same Jews, from time immemorial, have been the chief dreamers of the human race, and beyond all comparison its greatest poets. It was Jews who wrote the magnificent poems called the Psalms, the Song of Solomon, and the books of Job and Ruth.... No heritage of modern man is richer and none has made a more brilliant mark upon human thought.

From his Treatise on the Gods *(1930).*

Epitome of Putdowns

The Jews could be put down very plausibly as the most unpleasant race ever heard of. As commonly encountered, they lack many of the qualities that mark the civilized man: courage, dignity, incorruptibility, ease, confidence. They have vanity without pride, voluptuousness without taste, and learning without wisdom. Their fortitude, such as it is, is wasted upon puerile objects, and their charity is mainly a form of display.

Ibid.

America's Humanity

Either we are willing to give refuge to the German Jews, or we are not willing. If the former, then there is one vote for bringing them in by the first available ships, and staking them sufficiently to set them on their feet. That is the only way we can really help them, and that is the only way we can avoid going down into history as hypocrites almost as grotesque as the English.

The initiative should be taken by the so-called Christians who are now so free with weasel words of comfort and flattery, and so curiously stingy with practical aid. In particular, it should be taken by the political mountebanks who fill the air with hollow denunciations of Hitler, and yet never lift a hand to help an actual Jew.

From Mencken's final column in the Baltimore Sun, *January 1, 1939, displaying a compassionate side of his character.*

Short of Libel

The three of us are all in the same business—libel—but Winchell seems to know where to stop.

Addressed to George Jean Nathan. Quoted in Bob Thomas's Winchell.

◻

Mendele Mocher Seforim

A Bundle of Contradictions

A Jew is a great paradox, a living bundle of contrasts: wise and foolish, calculating like a merchant and fanciful like a child, burning like fire and freezing like ice, believer and heretic, scholar and ignoramus, meek and conceited, bashful and arrogant, mighty and innocent, disobedient and prompt performer, soft and hard, brave like a lion and craven like a hare, kind and cruel, spendthrift and miser, dandy and beggar.

From his In a Sturm Tzeit *(1913).*

Birthdays and Yahrzeits

Among Jews, a birthday is no holiday; but the anniversary of a death [*yahrzeit*], that a Jew remembers.

From his Dos Kleine Menshele *(1864).*

◻

Moses Mendelssohn

Dual Loyalty

The House of Jacob can receive no better advice than precisely this: adapt yourselves to the customs and the constitution of the land in which you live; yet, at the same time, adhere firmly to the religion of your ancestors. Carry both burdens as well as you can.

In a call for religious pluralism issued when German Jews had not as yet attained citizenship.

On Making Converts

Your question, why I do not try to make converts, has, I must say, somewhat surprised me. The duty to proselytize springs clearly from the idea that outside a certain belief there is no salvation. I, as a Jew, am not bound to accept that dogma, because, according to the teachings of the Rabbis, the righteous of all nations shall have a part in the rewards of the future world. Your motive, therefore, is foreign to me. As a Jew, I am not allowed publicly to attack any religion which is sound in its moral teachings.

From a letter to a non-Jewish correspondent.

The Sacred Language

God will raise up the tabernacle of David from the dust.... Then He will also send His spirit into our sacred language, to revive it, to put it back upon the pedestal on which it once stood.

Quoted in S. Halkin's Modern Hebrew Literature *(1950).*

THE IMPERISHABLE SOUL

If our souls were mortal, reason would be a dream.... We would be like animals destined only to seek food and perish.

From his essay "Phaedon" (1767).

CHURCH AND STATE TENSION

When church and state are in the field against each other, mankind is the victim of their discord; and when they agree, the brightest jewel of human happiness is gone, for they seldom agree but for the purpose of banishing from their realms a third moral entity, liberty of conscience.

From his Jerusalem *(1783).*

PREPARATION FOR THE FUTURE

It is essential that man should be constantly reminded that with death there is not a complete end of him; on the contrary, an interminable future awaits him, to which his earthly life is only a preparation; the same as all through Nature every present is a preparation for the future.

Ibid.

MIRACLES AND MORAL CERTAINTY

According to my religious teaching, miracles are not the distinguishing marks of Truth and do not provide moral certainty about the divine mission of the prophet. For seducers and false prophets too can perform signs, whether through magic, secret arts, or perhaps a misuse of a gift given to them for a good purpose.

In response to Swiss clergyman John Casper Lavater's challenge, in 1769, that Mendelssohn defend his contention that Judaism is superior to Christianity.

IMPERFECT RELIGIOUS TRADITIONS

I do not deny that I see certain human excesses...that tarnish the beauty of my religion. But is there any friend of truth who can claim that his religion is completely free of man-made accretions?

From his Jerusalem and Other Writings *(1969), in which he discusses religion with a Christian.*

ADEQUATE COMPENSATION

I dote on him [Maimonides] for if he was unwittingly the cause of my physical deformity, has he not compensated my soul with sublime knowledge?

Referring to his hunchback, which he attributes to the long hours he spent bent over studying Maimonides' Guide of the Perplexed *(1190). Quoted in Jacob S. Minkin's essay on Maimonides in* Great Jewish Books.

□

Henry Pereira Mendes

PROTEST AGAINST REFORM JUDAISM

The Union of Orthodox Jewish Congregations of America was formed two and a half years ago to protest against declarations of Reform rabbis not in accord with the teachings of our Torah, Nebiim, and the accepted rulings of recognized sages of Israel. It stands for loyalty to Jewish law and custom. It stands for the establishment of a synod of certified rabbis, elders in official position—men of wisdom and understanding and known able men, God-fearing men—men of truth, hating all self-advantage.

Advocating the establishment of a higher religious authority. From an article in American Hebrew *magazine, January 4, 1901.*

ZIONISM'S SPIRITUAL SIDE

I consider that the spiritual side of Zionism doesn't mean only the possession of a legalized home in the land of our Fathers. It means that, and much more. Our possession is already legalized by Him who gave it to us forever and who gives all lands to whom He pleases.

Ibid. A strong advocate of Torah-centered Zionism carries on his crusade for Palestine as a spiritual home for Jews.

□

Carlos Sául Menem

VICTIM OF GRIEF

In [my] grief, I am also a victim.

Expressing solidarity with the Jews of Argentina after the bombing on July 18, 1994 of a seven-story building in Buenos Aires, Argentina, that housed 130 of the country's Jewish organizations. About 100 people were killed and more than 200 were injured.

□

George Meredith

MAJESTY OF THE JEW

There is not in the sublimest of Gentiles a majesty comparable to that of the Jew elect. He may well think his race is favored of heaven, though heaven chastise them still. The noble Jew is grave in age, but in his youth he is the arrow to the bow of his fiery eastern blood.

From his Tragic Comedians *(1892).*

◘

Yehuda Meshi-Zahav

NO RED CARPET

We'll have everything but a red carpet. A red carpet is a *goyish* idea.

> *Responding to whether those planning the June 1994 visit to Israel of Moshe Teitelbaum, the Satmar Rebbe, would include rolling out of a red carpet. Reported in* The Jerusalem Post, *June 11, 1994.*

THE OFF-LIMITS WALL

Satmar Chasidim don't go to the [Western] Wall because it was conquered by Zionists.

> *Ibid. When asked whether the Satmar Rebbe would visit the Wailing (Western) Wall during his visit to Israel.*

◘

Marshall Meyer

COMMITTED TO HARDSHIP

Someone would call and say, "We know when your son gets out of school. He won't make it home." I lived with that reality for years. A person is known by his enemies as well as his friends. I could not live with myself if I did not denounce the Nazi fascist dictatorship in Argentina. When things got really bad, we contemplated leaving, but didn't. I felt I had a commitment to the thousands of people who depended on me as a voice.

> *Recalling the hardships he endured because of his stance against the cruel dictatorship in Argentina in the 1970s. Quoted in the Epilogue to Eva Fogelman's* Of Conscience & Courage *(1994).*

◘

Harvey M. Meyerhoff

LEARNING TO LEARN

This is an American museum for the American people. It may prove to be more, but it must never be anything less.

This building tells the story of events that human eyes should never have seen once, but having been seen, must never be forgotten. Through this Museum our eyes will always see; our hearts will always feel. It is not sufficient to remember the past. We must learn from it.

> *From remarks delivered at the April 1993 dedication of the United States Holocaust Memorial Museum, in Washington, DC.*

◘

(Prophet) Micah

JUSTICE, MERCY, HUMILITY

It hath been told thee, O man, what is
    good,
And what the Lord doth require of thee:
Only to do justly, and to love mercy,
And to walk humbly with thy God.

> *From the Book of Micah (6:8).*

◘

Leonard Michaels

FEAR OF BEING A COPYCAT

It's so contagious, you don't even know it's happening sometimes. You pick up the peculiar rhythm of another writer, or you find yourself playing with attitudes you discover in some other novelist that are not yours at all. I don't want to be subjected to that kind of temptation when I write.

> *Admitting that he admires writers such as Isaac Babel and Franz Kafka, and he avoids reading their works for fear of copying their style.*

BATTLING WOMEN

I thought again about the women. Anger, identity, politics, rights, wrongs. I envied them. It seemed attractive to be deprived in our society. Deprivation gives you something to fight for, it makes you morally superior, it makes you serious. What was left for men these days? They already had everything. Did they need clubs? The mere sight of two men together suggests a club. Consider Damon and Pythias, Huck and Jim, Hamlet and Horatio. The list is familiar. Even the Lone Ranger wasn't lonely. He had Tonto.

> *From his novel* The Men's Club *(1981), originally a short story that appeared in* Esquire *magazine in 1978.*

◘

Jules Michelet

VICES AND VIRTUES

The Jews' vices are those which we have produced in them; their virtues are their own.

> *From his* Bible of Humanity *(1864).*

◘

Bette Midler

AGING BODY

After thirty, a body has a mind of its own.

> *Quoted in the* Reader's Digest *(1982).*

TOO MUCH ROSH HASHANA

Too much Rosh Hashana. I ate a brisket the size of a Checker cab. And that kugel. Just wait till Arafat tries *kugel.*

After performing an exhausting song-and-dance number to a sell-out crowd at Radio City Music Hall during the 1993 High Holiday season.

OLD-FASHIONED VALUES

In your young life, you rebel against values you think are square. After a while, you realize they are good values and there's a reason they've been around for thousands of years.

After marrying at age thirty-nine and settling down like "old-fashioned" people. Quoted in Darryl Lyman's Jewish Comedy Catalog *(1989).*

◻

Abner Mikva

THE ESSENCE OF JUDAISM

Yiddishkeit for me is the tradition of social justice.

At a May 1995 dinner honoring the judge, sponsored by The Washington Institute for Jewish Leadership and Values.

◻

Sylvia Miles

THE FOUNTAIN OF MY HERITAGE

I felt very strongly that I was privileged to be a Jew because it was part of the hidden source of my desire to better myself and to aspire as an artist. I always felt fed by the fountain of my heritage.

Commenting on her being raised by a Jewish father and Catholic stepmother.

ISRAEL: A COUNTRY SO BEAUTIFUL

I found Jerusalem beautiful, but I found Tel Aviv very exciting because it has the beauty of a resort and the hubbub of a big city. People were very friendly. It was very cosmopolitan. In the afternoon people sat at the cafes. I loved how the old people were treated, with reverence. It was very safe there, and very positive.

Commenting on her first visit to Israel.

◻

Arthur Miller

AVOIDING JEWISH THEMES

I think I gave up the Jews as literary material because I was afraid that even an innocent literary allusion to the individual wrongdoing of an individual Jew would be inflamed by the atmosphere, ignited by the hatred I suddenly was aware of, and my love would be twisted into a weapon of persecution against Jews. No good writer can approach material in that atmosphere. I cannot censor myself without thwarting my passion for writing itself. I turned away from the Jews as material for my work.

From a 1947 speech. Quoted in Harold U. Ribalow's article entitled "American Jewish Writers and Their Judaism."

BUT HE'S HUMAN!

I don't say he's a great man. Willy Loman never made a lot of money. His name was never in the paper. He's not the finest character that ever lived. But he's a human being, and a terrible thing is happening to him. So attention must be paid. He's not to be allowed to fall into his grave like an old dog. Attention, attention must be finally paid to such a person.

From his play Death of a Salesman *(1949).*

WHEN THEY DON'T SMILE BACK

Willy was a salesman. And for a salesman, there is no rock bottom to the life. He don't put a bolt to a nut, he don't tell you the law or give you medicine. He's a man way out there in the blue, riding on a smile and a shoeshine. And when they start not smiling back—that's an earthquake. And then you get yourself a couple of spots on your hat, and your [sic] finished. Nobody dast blame this man. A salesman is got to dream, boy. It comes with the territory.

Ibid.

THE POWER OF PERSONALITY

It's not what you say, it's how you say it—because personality always wins the day.

Ibid.

SENSE OF SELF

I will protect my sense of self. I could not use the name of another person and bring trouble on him.

A statement made in 1953 before the House Committee on Un-American Activities, when he refused to identify some writers who had been accused of being Communist. He was convicted of contempt of Congress.

STRUCTURE OF A PLAY

I used...to keep a book in which I would talk to myself. One of the aphorisms I wrote was, "The structure of a play is always the story of how the birds came home to roost."

From an article in Harper's *magazine, August 1958.*

WALLOWING IN TRAGEDY

There is tragedy in the world, but the world must continue. The Jews can't afford to revel too much in the tragic because it might overwhelm them. I have, so to speak, a psychic investment in the continuity of life.

From a 1966 interview in the Paris Review.

ORGANIZED ABANDONMENT

The concentration camp is the final expression of human separateness and its ultimate consequence. It is organized abandonment.

Ibid.

ART BEFORE POLITICS

Turning her down because of her ideas was unacceptable to me; after all, I suffered the blacklist myself.

Protesting the attempt to deny Vanessa Redgrave, an outspoken supporter of the Palestine Liberation Organization, the role of Fania Fenelon, a "half-Jewish" musician, in his 1980 drama, Playing for Time.

WHEN ART DIES

When the guns boom, the arts die and this law is far stronger than any law man may devise.

From a September 25, 1965 telegram to the White House in which, as a protest against the Vietnam War, he refused to witness the signing of the Arts and Humanities Act.

THEATER DEMANDS RELEVANCE

More than any other art, Theater asks for relevance. A play that convinces us that this is the way it is now can be excused many shortcomings. At any one moment there is a particular quality of feeling which dominates in human intercourse, a tonality which marks the present from the past, and when this tone is struck on the stage, the theater seems necessary again, like self-knowledge.

From an article in The New York Times, *August 15, 1965.*

SHOW BIZ AND THEATER

I believe there is a confusion in many minds between Show Business and the Theater. I belong to the Theatre, which happens at the moment to be in a bad way, but since this word, when capitalized, usually implies something uplifting and boring, I must add that the rarely seen but very real Theater is the most engrossing theater of all; and when it isn't it is nothing.

From an article in Holiday *magazine, January 1955.*

FEARING FAILURE

To Paul Muni, acting was not just a career, but an obsession. Despite enormous success on Broadway and in Hollywood, he threw himself into each role with a sense of dedication that can only be explained one way; he was pursued by a fear of failure.

Quoted in Jerome Lawrence's Actor.

THE THEATER'S DEMISE

I'm the end of the line; absurd and appalling as it may seem, serious New York theater has died in my lifetime.

Quoted in the London Times, *January 11, 1989.*

¤

Henry Miller

CONFUSION

Confusion is a word we have invented for an order which is not understood.

From his Tropic of Capricorn *(1938).*

THE AIM OF LIFE

The aim of life is to live, and to live means to be aware, joyously, drunkenly, serenely, divinely aware.

From his Wisdom of the Heart *(1947).*

ON HEROES

The ordinary man is involved in action, the hero acts. An immense difference.

From his Books in My Life *(1951).*

JEW HATE

Who hates the Jews more than the Jew?

From his Tropic of Cancer *(1979).*

¤

Jonathan Miller

JUST JEW-ISH

In fact, I'm not really a *Jew*. Just Jew-*ish*. Not the whole hog, you know.

From Complete Beyond the Fringe *(1987), by Alan Bennett et al.*

¤

Judith Miller

THE HOLOCAUST IN PERSPECTIVE

We must remind ourselves that the Holocaust was six million. It was one, plus one, plus one.

From her One by One by One *(1990).*

William E. Miller

ONE DEFINITION OF A BIGOT

Barry's a Protestant and a Jew, and I'm [the vice-presidential candidate] a Catholic. Anybody who's against that ticket is a damn bigot.

Comment on his own religion and that of Republican presidential candidate Barry Goldwater during the 1964 campaign for the U.S. Presidency.

Jacob Minkin

LOVE OF NATURE

It came to him [the Baal Shem Tov] simply and naturally from his profound love and knowledge of nature. God did not create the world and then withdraw from it; creation is continuous, progressive, unending.

Claiming the Baal Shem Tov to be a Spinozan pantheist without knowing it. From his Romance of Hassidism *(1955).*

SOUL OF MAIMONIDES

Great books, like human beings, have souls, and long after they have seemingly passed out of existence, they continue to live.

Commenting specifically on Maimonides' Guide of the Perplexed (1190). From his essay in Great Jewish Books.

Jerome R. Mintz

STORYTELLING AND HASIDIM

Storytelling won an established place in the life of the earliest *hasidim* and it became part of the Shabbes ritual. On the Shabbes, the men met three times to pray and share communal meals.... The *hasidim* added a fourth communal meal, the *melaveh malkeh*, at which time it became customary to gather at the Rebbe's table to hear stories of hasidic saints and sages.

In the Introduction to his Legends of the Hasidim *(1974).*

Ruth Finer Mintz

REBEKAH

I knew my sons
Like my own hands.
The younger was a balm,
A cruse of oil.

The older one, a knife.
Cain and Abel were reborn
Out of my wound.
I brought them both to life.

So I made the youngest son a thief,
The older one, a brigand
For a birthright he was glad to sell.
All this I did, for kindness sake,
As I drew water for the stranger
At the well.

From her Darkening Green *(1965).*

(Count) Honoré Mirabeau

VIRTUES OF JEWS EXTOLLED

If you wish the Jews to become better men and useful citizens, then banish every humiliating distinction, open to them every avenue of gaining a livelihood; instead of forbidding them agriculture, handicrafts, and the mechanical arts, encourage them to devote themselves to these occupations.

One of many statements by the eighteenth-century French revolutionist who defended Jews against attack by anti-Semites. Quoted in Heinrich Graetz's History of the Jews *(1894).*

ENCOURAGING JEWISH NEIGHBORS

There is only one thing to be lamented, that so highly gifted a nation should so long have been kept in a state wherein it was impossible for its powers to develop, and every far-sighted man must rejoice in the acquisition of useful fellow-citizens from among the Jews.

Ibid.

Mohammed

CHOOSING ALLIES

O ye believers, choose not Jews and Christians as allies.... He who befriends them is one of them.

From the Koran.

Penina Moise

WELCOME TO THE IMMIGRANTS

If thou art one of the oppressed race,
Whose pilgrimage from Palestine we trace,
Brave the Atlantic—Hope's broad anchor weigh
A Western Sun will gild your future days.

From her Fancy's Sketch Book *(1833).*

¤

Ivy Molotov

DO YOU SPEAK YIDDISH?

I don't speak Hebrew, of course, but I speak Yiddish. Do you speak Yiddish?

Addressing Golda Meir at a reception in her home on November 7, 1948, the anniversary of the Bolshevik Revolution.

DAUGHTER OF ISRAEL

Why, I'm a daughter of Israel.

Mrs. Molotov's response to Golda Meir, who asked: "How do you know how to speak Yiddish?"

¤

Theodore Mommsen

REASONING IS USELESS

You are mistaken if you believe that anything at all can be achieved by reason. In years past I thought so myself and kept protesting against the monstrous infamy that is anti-Semitism. But it is useless, completely useless.

Quoted in Deborah Lipstadt's Denying the Holocaust *(1993).*

¤

Walter Mondale

ADVOCATE FOR ALL TIMES

I've been in Washington a long, long time. I've seen them all; and there is no one, representing any group or any organization, in any aspect of American life, who does it with more brilliance and more decency, and who deserves our respect more than that remarkable human being, Hyman Bookbinder.

A May 1978 statement in praise of Bookbinder, who had, in 1977, been honored by the National Conference of Christians and Jews "for depth of understanding of the meaning of justice and equality."

¤

James Monroe

REJECTION OF NOAH

At the time of your appointment as Consul at Tunis, it was not known that the religion which you profess would form any obstacle to the exercise of your Consular functions. Recent information, however... proves that it would produce a very unfavourable effect. In consequence of which,

the President has deemed it expedient to revoke your commission.

> I am, very respectfully, Sir,
>
> Your obedient servant,
>
> [Signed] James Monroe.

Notification served upon Mordecai Manuel Noah. Monroe, at the time (1824), served as secretary of state under President James Madison. Noah was being recalled as U.S. consul to the kingdom of Tunis, an appointment he held since 1813.

¤

Lily H. Montague

DISCOVERING GOD

Whatever the creed of his father,...a religious man must seek and discover God for himself.

From an article in the Jewish Quarterly Review, *Old Series.*

MY PERSONAL FAITH

I believe in God as the God of truth.... It matters infinitely what we think and believe, for thought and belief do affect conduct. We know that some of the best Jews the world has produced have been unlearned and that learning and the love of truth are not necessarily the same thing.

From her Faith of a Jewish Woman.

KINSHIP WITH GOD

Kinship with God is derived from the actual experience of prayer and from the effort after righteousness. We have no power to explain God. If we could, we should be God ourselves.

Quoted in Elinor and Robert Slater's Great Jewish Women *(1994).*

¤

Claude G. Montefiore

A SECULAR ISRAEL

Israel is a religious people.... A secular, nonreligious Israel is a monstrosity.

From his Rabbinic Anthology *(1938).*

JUDAISM AS A DISCIPLINE

Though liberal Judaism has ceased to be a strictly legal religion, it does not abandon the great Jewish conception that religion is a discipline as well as a faith.

From his Liberal Judaism *(1903).*

A GODLESS WORLD

Hard as it is for the world to explain *with* God, it is harder yet without Him.

Ibid.

GOD IS SO NEAR

When we are told that the Jewish God is distant, we smile with astonishment at the strange accusation. So near is He, that He needs no Son to bring Him nearer to us, no intercessor to reconcile Him with us or us with Him.

Ibid.

RESPONSIBILITY OF BEING A JEW

It is a grave responsibility this—to be a Jew; and you cannot escape from it, even if you choose to ignore it. Ethically or religiously, we Jews can be and do nothing lightheartedly. Ten bad Jews may help to damn us; ten good Jews may help to save us. Which *minyan* [religious quorum] will you join?

From a 1900 address at Cambridge, England.

DAY OF REST

To dedicate one day a week to rest and to God—this is the prerogative and the privilege of man alone.

Quoted in J. H. Hertz's Pentateuch and Haftorahs *(1961).*

THE QUALITY OF RACHMANUS

There is no ethical quality more characteristic of Rabbinic Judaism than *Rachmanus*—pity. The beggar whose point of view is that you are to thank him for allowing him to give you the opportunity for showing *Rachmanus* is a characteristically Jewish figure.

Ibid.

EXODUS FROM EGYPT

The Exodus from Egypt is not only one of the great events and epochs in the history of the Jews, but one of the greatest epochs in history of the world.

Ibid.

◻

Moses Montefiore

PALESTINE AND THE JEWS

Palestine must belong to the Jews, and Jerusalem is destined to become the seat of a Jewish Commonwealth.

Quoted in Nahum Sokolow's History of Zionism *(1919).*

◻

Dwight L. Moody

A UNIQUE PEOPLE

When I meet a Jew, I can't help having a profound respect for them [*sic*], for they are God's people.

From a sermon he preached in 1877. Quoted in Egal Feldman's Dual Destinies: The Jewish Encounter with Protestant America *(1990).*

◻

Ron Moody

THE REAL FAGIN

I found [Alec Guinness's interpretation] to be so anti-Semitic as to be unbearable. But Bart is as Jewish as I am, and we both felt an obligation to get Fagin away from a viciously racial stereotype and instead make him what he really is—a crazy old Father Christmas gone wrong.

Explaining why he finally accepted the role of Fagin in Lionel Bart's stage musical Oliver, *an adaptation of the Charles Dickens novel* Oliver Twist. *Quoted in Darryl Lyman's* Jewish Comedy Catalog *(1989).*

◻

George F. Moore

A UNIVERSAL RELIGION

The Jews were the only people in their world who conceived the idea of a universal religion, and labored to realize it by a propaganda often more zealous than discreet.

From his Judaism *(1927).*

INSTITUTIONS OF JUDAISM

Judaism gave to the world not only the fundamental ideas of the great monotheistic religions but the institutional forms in which they have perpetuated and propagated themselves.

Ibid.

MONUMENT OF THE PHARISEES

Judaism is the monument of the Pharisees.

Ibid.

JUDGING A TREE

Jews have small reason to admire Christian ethics in application, whether ecclesiastical, political, social, or individual. Judging the tree by the fruit it has borne in eighteen centuries of persecution, they not unnaturally [*sic*] resent Christian assertions of its preeminence.

Quoted in Samuel Sandmel's We Jews and Jesus *(1965).*

Thomas Moore

JEHOVAH HAS TRIUMPHED

Sound the loud timbrel o'er Egypt's dark sea! Jehovah has triumphe'd. His people are free.

From Sound the Loud Timbrel.

Julian Morgenstern

ESAU AND EDOM

In rabbinical tradition Esau and Edom came to symbolize Rome, the colossal, temporal, material power, which sought to crush nations, which overran the earth with warfare and bloodshed, and found its highest pleasure in murderous gladiatorial combats. And Jacob continued to represent Israel, the spiritual people, the servant of the Lord, whose mission was to bind up the bleeding wounds of cruelty and oppression and to bring law and order, peace and brotherhood, and the knowledge of God unto all mankind.

From his Book of Genesis.

Saul Levi Morteira

THE EXCOMMUNICATION OF SPINOZA

The chiefs of the council make known to you that, having long known of evil opinions and acts of Baruch de Spinoza, they have endeavoured by various means and promises to turn him from evil ways. Not being able to find any remedy, but on the contrary receiving every day more information about the abominable heresies practised and taught by him and about the monstrous acts committed by him, having this from many trustworthy witnesses who have deposed and borne witness on all this in the presence of the said Spinoza, who has been convicted; all this having been examined in the presence of the rabbis, the council decided, with the advice of the rabbis, that the said Spinoza should be excommunicated and cut off from the Nation of Israel.

The rabbinical court in Amsterdam excommunicated twenty-four-year-old Spinoza on July 27, 1656. The rabbinical pronouncement bore the signatures of other rabbis as well.

Leah Morton

WOMAN AND JEW

We Jews are alike. We have the same intensities, the sensitiveness, poetry, bitterness, sorrow, the same humor, the same memories. The memories are not those we can bring forth from our minds: they are centuries old and are written in our features, in the cells of our brains.

From her I Am a Woman—and a Jew *(1926).*

Moses

MISREPRESENTATION

When a pig lies down, it extends its hooves as if to say: "Look, I am clean!"

By attribution. Quoted in Midrash Genesis Rabba (65:1). The cloven hoof that the swine exposes does not make it kosher; an animal must also chew its cud to be counted as kosher.

CHOOSING THE RIGHT SIDE

Whoever is on the Lord's side, let him come to me.

After seeing the Israelites dancing around the Golden Calf. From the Book of Exodus (32:26).

ONE CALAMITY AT A TIME

It is sufficient to talk about one calamity at a time [*Da'ya le-tzara be-shata*].

Responding to God's command to say to the Children of Israel, "I was with you in this servitude [in Egypt] and I will be with you in the servitude of other kingdoms." Quoted in the talmudic tractate Berachot (9b).

Moses Ben Jacob of Coucy

HONEST MERCHANTS

Point out to your customer, regardless of his creed, the defects in your merchandise.

From his Semag *(1250).*

CLAIMING TO BE A JEW

If people come and claim to be Jews, we do not investigate their story. We drink their wine with them and eat the meat from their slaughtering.

Ibid. Quoted in Solomon B. Freehof's Current Reform Responsa *(1969).*

JEWS HAVE NO LAW

Those who lie to, or steal from, non-Jews are also blasphemous, for it is due to them that some say: "Jews have no law."

Ibid.

THE JEWISH MODEL

We have already explained concerning the remnants of Israel that they are not to deceive anyone whether Christian or Muslim. God has scattered Israel among the nations so that proselytes shall be gathered unto them; so long as they behave deceitfully toward them [non-Jews], who will cleave to them? Jews should not lie either to a Jew or Gentile, nor mislead them in any matter.

Urging his fellow Jews to live exemplary lives despite the atmosphere of hate for Jews that was prevalent in thirteenth-century Spain and France.

¤

Raphael Jacob Moses

CALL ME A JEW

Would you honor me? Call me a Jew. Would you place in unenviable prominence your unchristian prejudices and narrow bigotry? Call me a Jew!

I am not angered, but while I thank you for the opportunity which you have given me to rebuke a prejudice confined to a limited number distinguished for their bigotry and sectarian feelings, of which you are a fit exemplar, I pity you for having been cast in a mold impervious to the many and liberal sentiments which distinguish the nineteenth century.

When Moses, a sixty-four-year-old one-time Confederate soldier, ran for Congress, his anti-Semitic opponent, W.O. Toggle, attacked him viciously. Moses responded with a letter to the Columbus Daily Times, *quoted here in part.*

¤

Moshe Lieb of Sassov

LOVE THY NEIGHBOR

I learned how we must truly love our neighbor from the conversation between two villagers which I overheard. The first said: "Tell me, friend Ivan, do you love me?" The second: "I love you deeply." The first: "Do you know, my friend, what gives me pain?" The second: "How can I, pray, know what gives you pain?" The first: "If you do not know what gives me pain, how can you say that you truly love me?" Understand then, my sons, to love—truly to love—means to know what brings pain to your fellow human beings.

Sharing a newly discovered insight with his followers. Quoted in William B. Silverman's Rabbinic Wisdom and Jewish Values *(1971).*

FROM ATHEISM TO GODLINESS

Even atheism can be uplifted through charity. If someone seeks your aid, act as if there were no God, as if you alone can help.

Quoted in Martin Buber's Tales of the Hasidim *(1947).*

TRUE LOVE

To know the needs of men and to bear the burden of their sorrow—that is the true love of men.

Quoted in Martin Buber's Tales of Hasidim: The Later Masters *(1975).*

¤

Leonard Mosley

PREJUDICES OF LINDBERGH AND FORD

Charles Lindbergh and Henry Ford had known each other since 1927.

...They quickly discovered in subsequent meetings that they had characteristics (and prejudices) in common: Both were lifelong teetotalers and nonsmokers, both believed in God and the puritan ethic, both admired the discipline and efficiency of the totalitarian regimes in Europe, both hated Roosevelt and his Administration for having got them into the wrong war on the wrong side, and both believed that sinister influences were at work in the nation to destroy the moral fiber of the people. Henry Ford came out loud with it and flatly blamed the Jews.

From his Lindbergh: A Biography *(1976).*

¤

Zero Mostel

TRUE ARTISTRY

Painting is a much more creative field than acting. You take up an empty canvas; you fill it. In acting, you've got something to start with.

Quoted in Darryl Lyman's Jewish Comedy Catalog *(1989).*

MEANING OF COMEDY

Comedy is rebellion against falsehood,... against all evil masquerading as true and good and worthy of respect.

Ibid. From his 1962 lecture to Harvard University students.

○

Daniel P. Moynihan

HEADING?

The choice between support for biased United Nations resolutions and support for the peace process is a false choice. Any peace process is only as good as the principles upon which it is built. United States support for prejudicial language on Jerusalem directly undermines the principle of direct negotiations established in Madrid and the Declaration of Principles agreed to in Washington.

> *From comments made on the Senate floor on March 17, 1994, the day before the United Nations Security Council passed a resolution which condemned the massacre by a Jewish extremist of Arabs in a Hebron mosque and which referred to Jerusalem as "occupied" territory. Eighty-one senators urged the U.S. to veto the resolution.*

NO ROOM FOR DOUBT

Simply put, there must be no uncertainty about U.S. conduct toward Jerusalem. It is not helpful to the peace process for there to be any legitimate question about whether our officials might take steps which create damaging precedents or lend any weight to Palestinian claims to Jerusalem. This amendment is intended to end that uncertainty.

> *From a statement explaining the importance of legislation introduced jointly with Senator Jesse Helms. The legislation which protects the status of Jerusalem was adopted by the Senate in July 1994.*

○

Khallid Abdul Muhammad

JOHNNY-COME-LATELY JEWS

Brothers and sisters—the so-called Jew, and I must say so-called Jew, because you're not the true Jew. You are Johnny-come-lately Jew, who just crawled out of the caves and hills of Europe just a little over 4,000 years ago. You're not from the original people. You are a European strain of people who crawled around on all fours in the caves and hills of Europe, eatin' Juniper roots and eatin' each other.

> *From remarks made at Kean College, New Jersey, on November 11, 1993.*

GOD WILL KILL MY ENEMY

I will never apologize to this bastard—never. I want to see my enemy on his back, whining, crying, on his back begging for mercy. No mercy here. If you give the cracker mercy and you turn your back, he will take you out. Don't give the cracker no mercy.

Never will I say I am not an anti-Semite. Whatever he is, God damn it, I'm against him. I pray for my enemy all the time—I pray that God will kill my enemy and take him off the face of the planet earth.

> *Asserting, in Baltimore, Maryland, that he would not apologize for his November 29, 1993 Kean College remarks.*

WICKEDLY GREAT JEWS

You see everybody always talk about Hitler exterminating six million Jews. That's right. But don't nobody ever ask what did they do to Hitler? What did they do to them folks? They went in there, in Germany, the way they do everywhere they go, and they supplanted, they usurped, they turned around and a German, in his own country, would almost have to go to a Jew to get money. They had undermined the very fabric of the society. Now he was an arrogant no-good devil bastard, Hitler, no question about it. He was wickedly great. Yes, he was. He used his greatness for evil and wickedness. But they are wickedly great too, brother. Everywhere they go, and they always do it and hide their head.

> *Ibid.*

NATION OF ISLAM'S PARANOIA

Many of our politicians are in the palm of the white man's hand, but in particular, in the palm of the Jewish white man's hand.... The Jews have told us, the so-called Jews have told us, ve [*sic*], ve, ve suffer like you. Ve, ve, ve, ve marched with Dr. Martin Luther King, Jr. Ve, ve, ve, were in Selma, Alabama. Ve, ve were on the front line of the civil rights marches. Ve have always supported you. But let's take a look at it. The Jews, the so-called Jews, what they have actually done, brothers and sisters, is used us as cannon fodder.

> *Ibid.*

FRAUD PERPETRATORS

It's that old no-good Jew, that old imposter Jew, that old hooknose, bagel-eating, lox-eating Johnny-come-lately perpetrating a fraud, just crawled out of the caves and hills of Europe, so-called damned Jew.

> *Ibid.*

BLACK MAN JESUS

It was the white so-called Jews that set up a kangaroo court to charge Jesus with heresy, and accepted a thief and a robber named Barabbas over the good black man Jesus, and under a system of capital punishment ordered the death penalty for Jesus, the black revolutionary Messiah.

> *Ibid.*

COMPARING HOLOCAUSTS

Our holocaust is a hundred times worse than the so-called Jewish Holocaust. They claim they lost six million. But when you go to the death camps and talk to the scholars, talk to the scientists, talk to the tour guides, there, they say it wasn't six million. They say it wasn't even two million. I didn't say it. They say it's a lie.

> *Remarks made on March 26, 1994, the first night of Passover, at the Camp Curtain YMCA in Harrisburg, PA.*

¤

Herbert J. Muller

CHOSEN PEOPLE

Altogether, both the glory and tragedy of Israel may be traced to the singular idea cherished by its people—the exalted, conceited, preposterous idea that they alone were God's chosen people.

> *From his* Freedom in the Ancient World *(1961).*

¤

Stanislaw Musial

DIALOGUE WITH A GHOST

It is paradoxical that when the Jewish community in Poland constituted ten percent of the population of three and a half million people before the Second World War, the Catholic Church in Poland did not feel right that there should be a commission to set up a dialogue with Jews and Judaism. We lived side by side, but we did not know one another. It was a total indifference if not hostility, especially on the part of the Catholics towards the Jews.... It is only in the 80s that a commission for dialogue with Judaism was created in the Catholic Church. Is it hypocritical in such circumstances to create a commission when there are no longer Jews in Poland? A commission of dialogue? I don't believe so.

> *From an address to the World Conference on Anti-Semitism and Prejudice in a Changing World, held in Brussels, Belgium, July 1992.*

¤

Bess Myerson

LOUIS AND BELLA'S DAUGHTER

They did not use me at all the first year after I won.... The sponsors did not want me. And they asked me to change my name to Bess Merrick. I explained that I live in the Sholem Aleichem Apartment Houses with 250 Jewish families, and no one would know who Bess Merrick is. We were like one family. When someone was evicted, you took in a child, a mother, a bureau. So I should change my name? I am Louis and Bella Myerson's daughter.

> *Commenting in 1996, the seventy-fifth anniversary of the Miss America Pageant, on the endemic anti-Semitism of the period when she won the Miss America title (1945).*

HANDICAPPED JEW

They considered me more severely handicapped [than Heather Whitestone, the 1995 deaf Miss America winner] because I was Jewish.

> *Ibid.*

N

(Rabbi) Nachman

UNFLATTERING NAMES

Haughtiness in women is unbecoming. There were two haughty women [in the Bible] and their names were detestable, one being called hornet [or bee] and the other weasel.

Referring to Deborah (bee) and Hulda (weasel). Quoted in the talmudic tractate Megilla (14b).

¤

Nachman's Mother

COVERED HEADS

Cover your head so that the fear of Heaven may be upon you, and pray [for mercy].

To her son, after being told by astrologers that her son would be a thief. Quoted in the talmudic tractate Shabbat (156b).

¤

Nachman ben Simcha of Bratzlav

UNION WITH GOD

Solitude is the highest stage. Only in solitude can man attain union with the eternal God. Therefore a man must seek to be alone, at least for an hour each day, especially at night, when everyone is asleep and all things are quiet. Solitude in the open air, in the forest or in the desert, is of the utmost importance.

Quoted in S. A. Horodetzky's Leaders of Hasidim *(1928).*

HIDING A MOUNTAIN

A small coin before the eye will hide the biggest mountain.

From Likutay Moharan *(1806), a book of his teachings published by his disciple Nathan.*

MONEY-LUST

Abolish the lust for money, and Messiah will come.

Ibid.

LEAP TO FREEDOM

When you leave Egypt, any Egypt, do not stop to think: "But how will I earn a living out there?" One who stops to make provisions for the way will never get out of Egypt.

Ibid.

POWER OF A SMILE

There are men who suffer terrible distress and are unable to tell what they feel in their hearts, and they go their way and suffer and suffer. But if they meet one with a laughing face, he can revive them with his joy. And to revive a man is no slight thing.

Quoted in Nahum Glatzer's In Time and Eternity *(1946).*

TOPSY-TURVY WORLD

The world is a spinning top. Everything turns and changes: man is turned to an angel, and an angel to man; and the head to the foot, and the foot to the head. Thus all things turn and spin and change, this into that, and that into this, the topmost to the undermost, and the undermost to the topmost.

Ibid.

HOLY LAND OF ISRAEL

All the holiness of Israel clings to Eretz Israel, and every time a man cleanses and purifies his soul, he conquers and liberates a portion of the land.

Ibid.

THE ZADDIK AS TEACHER

If the *Zaddik* [hasidic leader] serves God, but does not take the trouble to teach the multitude, he will descend from his rung.

From Martin Buber's Tales of the Hasidim *(1948).*

DISCIPLES AND TEACHER

The teacher helps his disciples find themselves, and in hours of desolation the disciples help their teacher find himself again.

Ibid.

DOCTORS AND DEATH

It's difficult for the Angel of Death to do all the killing himself, so God provided doctors to help him.

By attribution.

FEARLESS LIVING

The world is a narrow bridge. The key to the crossing is to not be afraid.

Words still sung by devotees of the charismatic chasidic rebbe who died in 1810 at age 38 and was never replaced by a successor.

I WILL NOT FORSAKE YOU

My flame will burn until the end of time. Don't cry, I will not forsake you.

A promise made to all who will spend Rosh Hashana at his burial site in Uman, Ukraine.

▯

Moses Nachmanides

SPEAK SOFTLY

Accustom yourself to speak calmly to all men, at all times, and you will save yourself from anger, which is an ill thing that brings man into sin.

From a letter to his son (c. 1268). Quoted in Nahum Glatzer's In Time and Eternity (1946).

HOW TO AVOID SIN

Humility is the first virtue, for if you are aware of God's greatness and man's lowliness, you will fear God and avoid sin.

Ibid.

▯

Nachman of Kosov

TO THINK OF GOD

Some people think of business when they are at the synagogue. Is it too much to ask them to think of God when they are at business?

From his writings.

▯

(Rabbi) Nachum

LEARNING FROM CHECKERS

Do you know the rules of the game of checkers?.... I shall tell you the rules of the game of checkers [called "draughts" in Great Britain]. The first is that one must not make two moves at once. The second is that one may only move forward and not backward. And the third is that when one has reached the last row, one may move to where he likes.

A lesson to his students who were playing the game of draughts on one of the days of Chanuka. Quoted in Martin Buber's Tales of the Hasidim (1947).

▯

Nachum of Gamzu

ACCENTUATING THE POSITIVE

This, too, is for the best [*Gam zu le-tova*].

The favorite expression of the second-century scholar who would repeat these words no matter what kind of tragedy befell him. Quoted in the talmudic tractate Taanit (21a).

▯

Naftali of Ropshitz

WASTING TIME

"When I [Napoleon] sleep I am no longer king, and what a great loss to sleep away such a fabulous kingdom." Sabbath is our kingdom and we are the monarchs and princes. How dare we waste such a precious kingdom in sleep!

Commenting on the quotation attributed to Napoleon. From Menashe Unger's Chasiduth Un Leben (1946).

▯

Lewis Namier

TRAGIC HISTORY

There is no modern Jewish history, only a Jewish martyrology.

Quoted in Avishai Margalit's essay about Isaiah Berlin in The New Republic, February 20, 1995.

▯

Ora Namir

FOR A NEW IMMIGRATION POLICY

I'm not at all happy with the immigrants from the CIS [Confederation of Independent States] in the last year and a half. A third are elderly, a third are seriously handicapped, and nearly a third are single mothers. [Children were] sending their old parents here so that Israel can spend its resources on them.

Issuing a call for limiting immigration to Israel. In a fall 1994 interview with the liberal daily Ha-aretz.

¤

Napoleon (Bonaparte)

ON ANTI-SEMITISM

Who could believe it that in the year of grace 1812, anyone would still harbor an antipathy to the Jews!

From an 1812 letter to Kubloscher of Danzig.

JEWISH EMANCIPATOR

To the Jews as French, everything; to the Jews as Jews, nothing.

Encouraging the Jews of France to abandon ghetto life and become assimilated in the political life of the country. Quoted in Max Dimont's Jews in America *(1978).*

NAPOLEON'S PROPOSAL

If I would rule a nation of Jews, I would rebuild the Temple.

When asked why he had signed a concordat with the Vatican.

HOPE FOR RECONSTRUCTION

A people that mourns such an ancient national destruction is entitled to have hope for a national reconstruction.

Upon passing a synagogue on Tisha B'Av and noting the people chanting and wailing over the destruction of the Temple.

¤

Pierre Vidal Naquet

DEBATING THE HOLOCAUST

One can and should enter into a discourse concerning the "revisionists"; one can analyze their texts as one might the anatomy of a lie; one can and should analyze their specific place in the configuration of ideologies, raise the question of why and in what manner they surfaced. But one should not enter into debate *with* the "revisionists." It is of no concern to me whether the "revisionists" are neo-Nazi or extreme left wing in their politics: whether they are characterized psychologically as perfidious, perverse, paranoid or quite simply idiotic. I have nothing to reply to them and will not do so. Such is the price to be paid for intellectual coherence.

From his Assassins of Memory *(1993).*

¤

Gamal Abdel Nasser

PALESTINE SOLUTION

The only solution to Palestine is that mat-
ters should return to the condition prevailing before the error was committed—i.e., the annulment of Israel's existence.

In a September 1960 speech before the United Nations General Assembly.

DISMAL PLEDGE

We shall not enter Palestine with its soil covered in sand. We shall enter it with its soil saturated in blood.

In a March 1965 statement, two years before the Egyptians were devastated in the Six-Day War.

READY FOR WAR

The Jews threaten war. We tell them: welcome, we are ready for war.

In a May 22, 1967 speech at an air base in the Sinai Desert in which he announced the closing of the Straits of Tiran to all Israeli ships.

ON THE WARPATH

The problem presently before the Arab countries is not whether the port of Eilat should be blockaded or how to blockade it—but how to totally exterminate the State of Israel for all time.

In a May 25, 1967 address before the Egyptian National Assembly discussing Israel's right of passage through the Straits of Tiran.

¤

Nathan ben Naphtali Herz

REJOICING BEFORE GOD

The whole world is nothing more than a song and a dance before the Holy One, blessed be He. Every Jew is a singer before Him, and every letter in the Torah is a musical note.

Quoted in Maurice Samuel's Prince of the Ghetto *(1948).*

¤

Yitzhak Navon

PAID NOT TO THINK

It's not that I don't have opinions; rather that I'm paid not to think aloud.

Commenting on the nonpolitical office of President of Israel. Quoted in the London Observer, *January 16, 1983.*

◻

Yuval Ne'Eman

THE MASADA SYNDROME

It is my firm belief that if the West Bank and Gaza can ever be used as staging areas by modern Arab forces, Israel would be undefendable. If forewarned, we might manage a Masada.

Jerusalem would be on the border, Tel Aviv's center at ten miles distance from it. An armored penetration such as those achieved by the Syrians on the Golan in 1973 would reach Dizengoff Circle! All our airfields would come under artillery fire in a war. Arab antiaircraft missiles could shoot down any plane over the whole of central Israel.

From a symposium in Moment *magazine, March 1976.*

◻

Ernst Neizvestny

BIG BIBLE MENTALITY

Of course, I'm proud that I have in my blood the blood of big Bible prophet. I like big Jewish Bible mentality, but I'm not so much interested in story of small Jewish town.

From an interview with the highly successful Russian sculptor who arrived in the United States in 1976. Quoted in The Jewish Week, *February 17, 1995.*

BREAD AND FREEDOM

I don't want to say I'm happy. If somebody says they're very, very happy, they're from California. I'm not from California. I'm from Russia.... I don't want to say I'm happy. But I love America. America my home. I think America is the best experience in human history because we have freedom and we have bread.

Ibid.

BROAD OUTLOOK

He [Isaac Bashevis Singer] always told me, "I'm not specifically a Jewish writer. No, what I say about the Jewish people is a universal human view. Universal mystery." I agree. I don't want to be a guy who thinks about Jewish people from small Jewish village. No, for me this is cosmology and the human story.

Ibid.

◻

Howard Nemerov

VIEWING THE WORLD

The end of the war. I took it quietly
Enough. I tried to wash the dirt out of
My hair and from under my fingernails,
I dressed in clean white clothes and went to
    bed.
I heard the dust falling between the walls.

From "Redeployment," a poem from his collection entitled The Salt Garden *(1955).*

◻

Leon Nemoy

WHO IS AN ARAB?

Who is an Arab? The question is almost as difficult to answer as the question: "Who is a Jew?" The definition that seems to be most acceptable to Arab writers is that an Arab is a person whose mother-tongue is Arabic and who considers himself an Arab. Religion is a secondary consideration, for although the overwhelming majority of Arabs are Muslims, a minority is, and was, Christian, and that minority is no less conscious of its Arab identity.

From an article in The Jewish Spectator, *October 1973.*

◻

Mordechai Nessyahu

MEASURE FOR MEASURE

The name of the game regarding the fate of the Palestinians in the territories is independence.... The principle that should guide Israel in talking with the Palestinians has to be the measure of Palestinian independence to the measure of Israeli security.

A statement advising Israeli Prime Minister Yitzhak Rabin on options relating to the future of the territories. Reported in The Jerusalem Post, *January 8, 1994.*

◻

Benjamin Netanyahu

MARCHING TO DESTRUCTION

Israel has suffered a national humiliation.... We are marching toward a PLO state and the destruction of Israel.

Reacting to the proposed peace accord between Israel and the Palestine Liberation Organization, just before it was signed at the White House on September 13, 1993.

ON UPROOTING JEWS

No one disputes that orders must be obeyed, but there are certain orders that must not be given, and uprooting Jews from the Land of Israel is one of them.

From an April 1994 television interview. Commenting on the question of whether soldiers should follow orders requiring the removal of settlers from the West Bank.

IS ANTI-ZIONISM ANTI-SEMITISM?

The libel of "Zionism equals racism" is the...contemporary equivalent of "Christ-killer," "traitor," "usurer," "international conspirator." All this has stolen into vogue under the sham disclaimer of "I'm not anti-Semitic, I'm just anti-Zionist"—the equivalent of "I'm not anti-American, I just think the United States shouldn't exist."

From his Place Among the Nations: Israel and the World *(1993).*

PEACE IN THE GOLAN

What has kept the peace in the Golan during the last 20 years is the fact that we kept the army tanks that stand at a spitting distance from Damascus.

Reiterating the Likud Party's skepticism on reaching a peace agreement with Syria. Quoted in The New York Times, *September 9, 1994.*

THE NOBEL PEACE FARCE

The fact that the prize is given to the person who invented international terrorism, the archmurderer who says he decided to stop killing for a while and whose men killed seven Israelis this year, this fact turns the prize into a farce.

When learning that Yasser Arafat was to receive the Nobel Peace Prize in 1994.

◻

Yonatan Netanyahu

THE LINK THAT BROKE

By "the past" I mean not only my personal past but the pattern of which I see myself as an inseparable part, as a link in the chain of our existence and the independence of Israel.

Yonatan led the daring raid on Entebbe in Uganda on July 4, 1976 that freed the hostages being held at the airport. He lost his life in the engagement.

◻

Abraham A. Neuman

QUINTESSENCE OF JUDAISM

Torah is the quintessence of Judaism. There can be no Judaism worthy of the name without Torah. A Torah-less Judaism would be pulseless, nerveless; a corpse, without life or potency.

From his Landmarks and Goals *(1948).*

ISRAEL'S DIVINE ROLE

Israel has a divine and prophetic role to play in the concert of nations and in the progress of united humanity toward an era of universal justice and peace. The millennial vision abides eternally in the Torah and illumines the hope of all its children.

Ibid.

◻

Jacob Neusner

RELIGION'S POWER

The power of religion is to teach us to look for God's image and likeness in the face of others, but the pathos is that beyond "the others" whom we know and differentiate lies the outsider, "the other," who is left without distinctive traits. The power of religion is to define worthy goals for the social order, setting forth components of public policy that accord with our vision of humanity "in our image, after our likeness." The pathos of religion is that, whether now or a thousand years ago, religion has proved unable to cope with difference and change.

From an article in The Jewish Spectator, *Winter 1990, based on his remark of September 27, 1990 to the Fourth International Meeting for Peace, in Bari, Italy.*

COMMUNITY RESPONSIBILITY

I believe that all schools have a right to community support, and that all Jewish educational ventures and youth programs have a right to turn to the community for assistance.... We should help whoever comes to us to ask our help to study the Torah, whether he be Orthodox, or Reform, or Conservative, or Reconstructionist, or secularist, or Zionist, or Yiddishist, or what have you.

From an article entitled "Jewish Education and Culture and the Jewish Welfare Fund," which appeared in The Synagogue School, *Winter 1967.*

ZIONISM IS NOT ENOUGH

Zionism provides much of the vigor and excitement of contemporary Jewish affairs, but insofar as Jews live and suffer, are born and die, reflect and doubt, raise children and worry over them, live and work—insofar as Jews are human, they require Judaism.

Neusner sees the vitality of the Diaspora as complementary to religious and cultural life in Israel.

HOLY SOCIETY

Jerusalem's *Chevra Kadisha* is deserving of its name, "the holy society." Those beautiful Jews showed me more of what it means to be a Jew, of what Torah stands for, than all the books I ever read. They tended the corpse gently and reverently, yet did not pretend it was other than a corpse.

Quoted in Jewish Reflections on Death *(1974), edited by Jack Riemer.*

ISRAEL AND THE MORMONS

Nothing they do is selfless. Everything they do has the single goal of converting everyone they can. Pure and simple. The proposed BYU [Brigham Young University] Center will provide access, not only to Israeli Jewry, but also (and especially) to large numbers of foreign, including American, Jewish youth who study in Jerusalem....

Commenting on the proposed campus to be established in Jerusalem. Quoted in Egal Feldman's Dual Destinies: The Jewish Encounter with Protestant America *(1990).*

○

Jack Newfield

INVESTIGATIVE REPORTING

When I wanted to understand the nursing-home rackets, I talked to the nurses' aides who bandaged the infected bedsores of [Rabbi Bernard] Bergman's patients. When I wanted to identify the bigoted, malingering and unfit judges, I went to cops and Legal Aid attorneys. When I wanted to understand how they [politicians] rigged the bus-shelter bid, I talked to a civil service auditor. And when I wanted to understand the plague of lead poisoning, I went to the South Bronx and interviewed a woman whose 22-month-old daughter had just died of lead poisoning because of the landlord's callous neglect.

From a 1981 speech when he was being honored as the "conscience of New York" in his role as senior editor of The Village Voice.

○

Al Newman

HELL FACTORY

The hell factory worked by the living dead.

After witnessing the liberation of the Nordhausen concentration camp in April 1945.

○

Arnold Newman

RABIN'S SMILE

It takes a sledgehammer to get [Yitzhak] Rabin to smile.

Commenting on the difficulty he faced when trying to capture the Israeli leader on film. Quoted in The Jerusalem Report, *February 24, 1994, in a profile of one of the twentieth century's great photographers.*

○

Mike Nichols

CENTRAL PARADOX

Life is hopeless—but it isn't; love is fleeting—but eternal; our personal lives are everything—but we are unimportant.

From a conversation with Barbara Gelb in The New York Times Magazine, *May 27, 1984.*

LIVING ON BORROWED TIME

The Holocaust was the central fact of my life, and I have always had a sense of living on borrowed time. It's something you never think about, but it's always there. It's the plight of the alien who's learned perfectly how to imitate the natives. I think the sense of being from somewhere else, of being a Jew in another culture, is the main thing about my work.

From an interview with Sheli Teitelbaum in The Jerusalem Report, *December 16, 1993.*

○

Jack Nicholson

NO COMPETITION

You could make a case that the world has already ended. Certainly that art is dead, that the death of the six million Jews marked the end of art. That no metaphor, nothing of the imagination could ever compete with that.

Spoken in his role as a genteel New York book editor in Mike Nichols' 1994 film, Wolf.

¤

Martin Niemöller

HEARTFELT EMPATHY

No power on earth can force me not to see in the Jew my fellow man.... I have seen with my own eyes and heard with my own ears how Jews have been maltreated. I had a chance to "study" this prison, which is built underground like a cave. When they whipped the Jews and I heard these poor creatures cry out like wounded animals, I knelt down and prayed to God. I never prayed so fervently before in all my life. I almost collapsed.

> *From a conversation in 1937 with fellow concentration camp inmate Leo Stein. Reported in B'nai Brith's* National Jewish Monthly, *May 1941.*

TOO LATE

In Germany, the Nazis first came for the Communists, and I didn't speak up because I was not a Communist. Then they came for the Jews, and I did not speak up because I was not a Jew. Then they came for the Trade Unionists, and I didn't speak up because I wasn't a Trade Unionist.

Then they came for me...by that time there was no one to speak up for anyone.

> *From a statement made during his 1946 visit to the United States.*

¤

Friedrich Nietzsche

BOOK OF RIGHTEOUSNESS

In the Old Testament of the Jews, the Book of Divine Righteousness, there are men, events, and words so great that there is nothing in Greek or Indian literature to compare with it.

> *From his* Beyond Good and Evil *(1885).*

THE PUREST RACE

The Jews are beyond all doubt the strongest, toughest, and purest race at present living in Europe.

> *Ibid.*

CONTEMPT FOR JEWS

People wanted to make them contemptible by treating them scornfully for twenty centuries...and by pushing them all the deeper down into the mean trades—and, indeed, they have not become cleaner under this process. But contemptible? They have never ceased be-

lieving themselves qualified for the highest functions; neither have the virtues of all suffering people ever failed to adorn them.

> *From his* Dawn of Day *(1886).*

FACING PROBLEMS

In time of distress, Jews least of all...try to escape by recourse to drink or suicide.

> *Ibid.*

TO MEET A JEW

To meet a Jew is a blessing, especially if one lives among Germans.

> *Quoted in H. Valentin's* Anti-Semitism *(1936).*

HOW GREEKS BECAME JEWS

When Socrates and Plato began to speak of truth and justice, they were no longer Greeks, but Jews.

> *Quoted by Leo Baeck in his* Judaism and Ethics.

ENVIED AND HATED

The whole problem of the Jews exists only in nation states, for here their energy and higher intelligence, their accumulated capital of spirit and will, gathered from generation to generation through a long schooling in suffering, must become so preponderant as to arouse mass envy and hatred.

> *From his* Human, All-too-Human *(1878).*

BEING OR NOT BEING

The Jews are the most remarkable nation of world history because, faced with the question of being or not being, they preferred, with a perfectly uncanny conviction, being at any price; the price they had to pay was the radical falsification of all nature, all naturalness, all reality, the entire inner world as well as the outer.

> *From his* Anti-Christ *(1888).*

¤

Samuel Niger

A GOOD LIBRARY

Books lead us into the society of those great men with whom we could not otherwise come into personal contact. They bring us near to the geniuses of the remotest lands and times. A good library is a place, a palace, where the lofty spirits of all nations and generations meet.

> *From his* Gathered Works *(1928).*

David Niles

ROOSEVELT AND THE JEWS

There are serious doubts in my mind that Israel would have come into being if Roosevelt had lived.

> *Quoted in Howard Sachar's* History of Israel *(1976).*

Nittai the Arbelite

RETRIBUTION ASSURED

Do not delude yourself into thinking that [divine] punishment will not come.

> *From the talmudic tractate Ethics of the Fathers (1:6).*

Richard M. Nixon

ISRAEL AND THE U.S.

The preservation of the State of Israel is what I regard as one of the essential goals of United States foreign policy.

> *An August 1960 statement, when he was running as the Republican candidate for U.S. President.*

DEGREES OF EVIL

I have great respect for Rabin, but I didn't want to go to the dog and pony show on the White House lawn. I told him later that it takes a strong man to make peace; he's able to do what he's doing because Arafat is weak, and far worse than Arafat is waiting in the wings. Paul Johnson had a line that statesmen must differentiate between different degrees of evil.

> *Commenting on why he did not attend the peace accord ceremony between Israel and the PLO. Quoted in William Safire's column in* The New York Times, *April 28, 1994.*

Mordecai Manuel Noah

THE JEWISH STATE OF ARARAT

I, Mordecai Manuel Noah, Citizen of the United States of America, late Consul of the said States for the City and Kingdom of Tunis, High Sheriff of New York, Counsellor at Law, and by the grace of God Governor and Judge of Israel, do hereby proclaim the establishment of the Jewish State of Ararat.

> *A proclamation delivered by him on September 15, 1825 on Grand Island, a 2,444-acre tract in the Niagara River, near the Canadian border, which he purchased from the New York legislature for $17,000 dollars to serve as a "colony" for the Jews of the world.*

GREAT EXPECTATIONS

Fine Christian that had to be hanged!

> *Responding to an opponent while running for Sheriff of New York County early in the nineteenth century. The opponent had declared: "It would be a pity to have a Jew hang a Christian."*

BRINGING BACK THE FAITH

We will return to Zion as we went forth, bringing back the faith we carried away with us.

> *Quoted in J. H. Hertz's* Book of Jewish Thoughts *(1917).*

DREAMING OF A JEWISH COLONY

I have long been persuaded that this is the only country where the Jews can be completely regenerated, where in the enjoyment of perfect civil and religious liberty...under the protection of the laws, their faculties could be developed, their talents and enterprise encouraged; their persons and property protected and themselves respected and esteemed, as their conduct and deportment shall merit.

> *From a July 24, 1820 letter to Secretary of State John Quincy Adams.*

Benjamin Nones

I AM A JEW

I am a Jew. I glory in belonging to that persuasion, which even its opponents, whether Christian or Mohammedan, allow to be of divine origin—of that persuasion on which Christianity itself was originally founded and ultimately rests—which has preserved its faith secure and undefiled, for near three thousand years, whose votaries have never murdered each other in religious wars, or cherished the theological hatred so general, so inextinguishable among those who revile them.

> *The response of the brave French-born soldier, who served the revolutionary cause in General Casimir Pulaski's Legion, after being accused of "being a Jew, a Republican, and of being poor." The full reply was featured in the Republican newspaper* Aurora, *August 13, 1800. Quoted in Morris V. Schappes'* Documentary History of the Jews in the United States *(1950).*

(Queen) Noor of Jordan

UNTIL WE MEET AGAIN

I hope the day will not be far off when we can meet again in Amman or in Jerusalem.

Expressed to Knesset member Naomi Chazan at a conference of women from the Middle East held at Columbia University after the peace accord between Israel and the Palestinians was signed in September 1993.

Max Nordau

THE JEWISH/ZIONIST CONNECTION

Judaism will be Zionist, or Judaism will not be.

From an April 1899 address delivered in Amsterdam, Holland.

INBRED DETESTATION

"If you have to drown a dog," says the proverb, "you must first declare him to be mad." All kinds of vices are falsely attributed to the Jews, because people want to prove to themselves that they have a right to detest them. But the primary sentiment is the detestation of the Jews.

From an August 1897 speech delivered at the First Zionist Congress.

SYNONYMS

Judaism is Zionism, and Zionism is Judaism.

From an August 1898 address delivered at the Second Zionist Congress.

HERZL AND THE JEWISH PEOPLE

Our people had a Herzl, but Herzl never had a people.

From a July 1905 speech delivered at the Seventh Zionist Congress.

LIFE WITHOUT AN IDEAL

A great people cannot live without an ideal.

From a 1915 address delivered in Madrid, Spain.

HOW TO BE MODERN

We are never more modern, never more progressive, than when we are ourselves.

From a 1907 address.

REINVENTION OF ZIONISM

A day will come when Zionism will be needed by you, proud Germans, as much as by those wretched Ostjuden [East European Jews].... A day will come when you will beg for asylum in the land you now scorn.

From a January 23, 1899 speech delivered in Berlin, Germany.

THE NATURE OF ANTI-SEMITISM

I am sorry for the blindness of Jews who comfort themselves in the evils that face them now, saying that anti-Semitism is ephemeral and will pass away. Abandon that hope!

Ibid.

JEWISH HATRED

The Jews are not hated because they have evil qualities; evil qualities are sought for them because they are hated.

Quoted in Leo Rosten's Treasury of Jewish Quotations *(1972).*

David Novak

REJECTION OF JESUS

The messianic claims made by Jesus's followers in his name are rejected [by Jews] because Jesus did not fulfill two essential messianic criteria: (1) he did not restore the national sovereignty of the Jewish people in the land of Israel and gather in all the exiles; and (2) he did not bring about God's universal kingdom of justice and peace on earth.

Quoted in Moment *magazine, August 1994.*

Ida Nudel

FREEDOM FOR A REFUSENIK

It is the moment of my life. I am home at the soul of my Jewish people. I am a free person among my own people.

Upon arriving in Israel on October 15, 1987 after ten years of imprisonment and exile in Russia. Jane Fonda and Yitzhak Shamir greeted her at the airport.

MY DESTINY IS TO HELP

Every person is born with a destiny. Mine is to help people. To be in some way an essence of national self-preservation. Maybe it is a blessing, maybe a curse, I don't know.

From an interview with Yossi Klein Halevi in The Jerusalem Report, *December 30, 1993.*

MY BEST YEARS

Those were my best years. I saved many people. I watched the prisoners, helped them in their special circumstances. The KGB won against me physically—they kept me there. But I won spiritually.

Ibid. Referring to the fifteen years in the Soviet Union (1972–1987) when she led the struggle to allow Jews to leave the country.

NURSED ILLUSIONS

We nursed many illusions about the Jewish state, but most of them turned out to be fairy tales. We thought it was a cultured society. We came from the same civilization as America and Europe, and found that Israel is not Europe. It's half Europe, half Middle East. It did not match what we thought a Jewish state should be.

From an interview in The Jerusalem Post International Edition, *August 27, 1994.*

ACCEPTING COMPROMISE

The immigrants are doing fine. There are professors cleaning streets, and engineers doing manual labor, but we are not committing suicide, and most do not go back to Russia. We are hardworking people and accept compromises....

Ibid.

LIKUD'S FAILURE

The Likud didn't lift a finger during all the years of *aliya*. And when they finally began to build, where did they build? In places that will go to the Arabs. They knew.

I spoke with Shamir and his advisors. They could have built factories and industry to attract people, but did nothing. They began to build only after the train had left the station.

Ibid.

LIFE IS WAR

Life is not a bed of roses. Life is war. The stronger side will win.

Ibid.

IN DEFENSE OF KAHANISTS

I have a very small head, big enough only for the Jewish people. I can't save the whole world. The Palestinians have Hanan Ashrawi. She is 100 times more clever than I. She speaks for her own, so I will too.... I was de-

tained in Russia to stop me from speaking. Same with these [Kahanists in Israel]. They pushed them in a prison just to silence them. Here I found it was a democratic society but people were facing the same thing.

From an interview, reported in The Jewish Week, *November 11–17, 1994.*

□

Hazem Nusseibeh

A JEWISH CABAL

A Jewish cabal controls, manipulates, and exploits the rest of humanity by controlling the wealth of the world.

From a December 8, 1980 speech to the United Nations General Assembly.

□

Sari Nusseibeh

A FRAGILE AGREEMENT

One wants to keep one's emotions in check. We hope this is a turning point. It opens up a lot of potential for this area and for the two people. But it is a very fragile agreement, fraught with explosives, and one has to nurture it very tenderly to make sure that it grows—on both sides.

On the Palestine side, we have to act very seriously to make sure that no acts are committed that do not bring the peace effort forward and that might actually undermine progress toward a state.

Reacting to the peace accord signed by Israel and the PLO on September 13, 1993, in Washington, DC.

□

Gerald R. Nye

BLAMING THE VICTIM

If anti-Semitism exists in America, the Jews have themselves to blame.

In an August 1941 address. The senator from North Dakota charged Hollywood with making films designed to involve America in a European war.

(Prophet) Obadiah

RECIPROCITY

As you have done, so shall be done to you.

From the Book of Obadiah (1:15).

¤

Howard Vincent O'Brien

PITY THE GERMAN!

Pity the poor German!

If he has heart disease he can't use digitalis, because it was discovered by a Jew, Ludwig Traube.

If his tooth aches, he cannot have the comfort of cocaine; for that would be utilizing the work of a Jew, Solomon Stricker.

If he has syphilis, he cannot allow himself to be cured by salvarsan, because that was discovered by the Jew, Ehrlich.

He may like music, but he can't listen to Toscanini because Toscanini's daughter is married to a Jew, Horowitz.

Selections from his article in The Chicago Daily News, *June 27, 1938.*

¤

Adolph S. Ochs

JEWISH OPPOSITION TO BRANDEIS

To place on the Supreme Bench judges who hold a different view of the function of the Court, to supplant conservatism by radicalism, would...strip the Constitution of its defenses.

From a January 1916 editorial in The New York Times *opposing the selection of Louis Brandeis, who was nominated by President Woodrow Wilson to serve on the U.S. Supreme Court.*

¤

Vanessa L. Ochs

MASTER TEACHER

To have studied with Nehama [Leibowitz] is to have been in analysis with Freud, to have

been educated in a nursery school by Maria Montessori, is to have been inoculated against polio by Dr. Salk.

Expressing admiration for the famous Israeli Bible teacher. From her Words on Fire *(1990).*

¤

Daniel O'Connell

DISRAELI THE MISCREANT

Disraeli's name shows he is by descent a Jew. His father became a convert. He is the better for that in this world, and I hope he will be the better for it in the next. I have the happiness of being acquainted with some Jewish families in London, and among them more accomplished ladies, or more humane, cordial, high-minded, or better-educated gentlemen I have never met. It will not be supposed, therefore, that when I speak of Disraeli as the descendant of a Jew, that I mean to tarnish him on that account. They were once the chosen people of God.

There were miscreants among them, however, also, and it must certainly have been from one of these that Disraeli descended. He possesses just the qualities of the impenitent thief who died upon the cross, whose name, I verily believe, must have been Disraeli.

From a speech at a trades union meeting in Dublin in 1835.

¤

John (Cardinal) O'Connor

SHOCK AT YAD VASHEM

Anything I would say here is banal. This experience is totally indescribable, I can't talk about it. It is a mystery to me.

After a visit to Jerusalem's Yad Vashem Holocaust memorial.

Levi Olan

BETWEEN A PEOPLE AND GOD

Celebrations of historic occasions are incumbent upon us because they represent, preserve, and keep alive chunks of Jewish history. Passover and freedom are obligatory upon a Jew. If all Jews were to cease celebrating Passover, a [vital portion] of Jewish experience would be lost. No Jew has a right to do that!...To be a Jew is to act to preserve the historic experience of the people with God.

From a letter to Rabbi Henry Cohen, author of Why Judaism? *(1973).*

Lionel H. Olmer

ISRAEL'S SECRET ECONOMIC ASSET

There must be a higher concentration of intellectual resources among the four million people in Israel than anywhere in the world. Israelis possess not merely the capacity for academic study, but the power to create, innovate and adapt. Israel is seizing its comparative advantage in the technology era the world has entered and is offering its services to those wise enough to recognize its value.

From a 1984 address to the World Jewish Congress.

Ehud Olmert

THE JEWISH SOUL

I will do all I can to make sure it is united, undivided, and the capital of Israel.... We have not been in Jerusalem since 1948 or 1967. The real date is 3,000 years. That fact must be projected to every person in the world and every policymaker in the U.S. We are not fighting here for territory or a piece of land. We are fighting for the soul of the Jewish people.... While there can be flexibility about some issues, Jerusalem is beyond and above any compromise and is the essence of Jewish existence and the State of Israel.

From a December 1993 address to the Conference of Presidents of Major Jewish Organizations, following his election as Mayor of Jerusalem.

TAKING HIS OWN MEASURE

I checked the size of my feet when I took office [as Mayor of Jerusalem] and found they weren't so small.... I don't have an inferiority complex. I believe I came into this job with no less experience, knowhow, executive skills and international connections than Teddy [Kollek] brought when he was first elected. Maybe more.

From a profile by Barbara Sofer in Hadassah Magazine, *January 1994.*

A PHILOSOPHY OF NEIGHBORHOODS

I'd like a new philosophy of neighborhoods to come out of Jerusalem, one in which a citizen will ask not what one can do to improve his own status, but how one can tolerate the differences of neighbors...a symphony of different voices somehow synchronized into a great melody.

Ibid.

THE INVITED AND UNINVITED

Arafat does not invite and he is not invited. Arafat, who calls for the division of Jerusalem, has no right to invite anyone to visit there, and is certainly not invited himself.

Responding to Yasser Arafat's claim at a July 1994 news conference that he has sole authority to invite people to Jerusalem, and that King Hussein can come only when he (Arafat) invites him.

Eugene O'Neill, Jr.

LITTLE-KNOWN PRIMARY TEXT

The Talmud is undoubtedly one of the world's most important religious writings...also one of the least known of the important religious writings, except, of course, to persons of Jewish faith.

From a comment made in April 1945 when he chaired Invitation to Learning, *a CBS radio program.*

Joseph Opatoshu

DIGGING IN TO FLY HIGH

Have you ever watched children swinging? In order to lift themselves higher they have to dig their toes into the earth.

From his In Polish Woods *(1921).*

DIVINITY EVERYWHERE

In every evil thought there is a spark of divinity, which has sunk to a very low degree, and begs to be elevated.

Ibid.

SOURCE OF STRENGTH

Our strength is rooted not in our being a world power, but in our being the people of the Lord.

From his Last Revolt *(1952).*

◻

Joseph (Süss) Oppenheimer

FATE OF A COURT JEW

I am a Jew and will remain a Jew. I would not become a Christian even if I could become an emperor. Changing one's religion is a matter for consideration by a free man; it is an evil thing for a prisoner.

A statement made to Pastor Rieger, who suggested that he be baptized to save his life. Oppenheimer, appointed in 1732 as finance minister of Württemberg, was accused of embezzling state funds and having sexual relations with Christian women. The novel Jew Süss, *by Lion Feuchtwanger, is based on Oppenheimer's life.*

◻

J. Robert Oppenheimer

FROM SECRECY TO CORRUPTION

We know that the wages of secrecy are corruption. We know that in secrecy, error undetected will flourish and subvert.

From a February 1950 statement.

WHAT A MAN!

A man whose errors take ten years to correct is quite a man.

Commenting on errors in the early scientific work of Albert Einstein. Remarks made at a symposium on Einstein held in Paris, France, December 13, 1965.

BETWEEN GOD AND THE JEWS

Were it not for the Land that God promised on oath to Abraham and to Isaac and to Jacob and to their heirs forever, there would be no covenant. For be it noted that everything in the contract, all the blessings—economic, territorial, political, increase in population, and the like—all these would be forthcoming from God to Israel not in Abraham's native land in Mesopotamia...nor in Egypt, but in the Promised Land.

From his essay "The Biblical Concept of the Land of Israel," which is included in Lawrence A. Hoffman's Land of Israel: Jewish Perspectives *(1986).*

◻

Yair Oron

HOLOCAUST SENSITIVITY

If I demand that the world know the Holocaust, I have to also demand that my own people address the genocide of the Armenians and Gypsies.

Defending his 1994 proposal that students be taught sensitivity to the suffering of other minorities, such as Armenians and Gypsies, at the hands of the Nazis.

UNIQUENESS OF THE HOLOCAUST

I agree that the Holocaust was unique. I think it was an extreme example of genocide, and different from other ones.... [But] how can we know why and how the Holocaust was unique if we don't know what happened to other people?

Ibid.

◻

Amos Oz

NO ALTERNATIVE

Mr. Prime Minister, there can either be a compromise, albeit a painful one, between the two peoples in this land, or else perpetual war. There is no third alternative.

From an open letter to Prime Minister Menachem Begin at the outset of the Lebanese War. Printed in Yediot Aharonot, *June 21, 1982.*

ISRAEL SCAPEGOAT

It is crystal clear to me that if Arabs put down a draft resolution blaming Israel for the recent earthquake in Iran, it would probably have a majority. The U.S. would veto it and Britain and France would abstain.

Quoted in the London Times, *October 24, 1990.*

ENDING YEARS OF SOLITUDE

From a Zionist perspective, people may look back on 1993 as the end of our one hundred years of solitude in the Land of Israel. Now it may be time...to consolidate Israel as a safe, stable, legitimate home for the Jewish people and its Arab citizens.

His immediate reaction to the signing of the peace accord between Israel and the Palestinian Liberation Organization on September 13, 1993.

A BABY IN COMMON

Israel and the PLO have a baby in common

now. They may not love the baby, but both depend on its welfare.

Ibid.

AN ISRAELI-PALESTINIAN DIVORCE

In some circles I am thought to be a raving radical, but I have never been a radical. I have been an evolutionist all my life. I believe in painful compromise vis-à-vis the Palestinians, vis-à-vis the Orthodox, vis-à-vis other segments of Israel.

From an interview in Tikkun *magazine, Vol. 1, No. 2 (1986).*

WHISPERS IN PRIVATE

Conversations I've had with Palestinians have been quite pleasant as long as they were conducted in private and in English over a cozy cup of coffee. Unfortunately, most of my Palestinian partners in those conversations, when addressing their own constituencies in Arabic, have repeated the most savage PLO lines about the need to exterminate Israel altogether, sometimes just days after they talk to me. Over the years I've learned that what those people say in Arabic to their own constituencies weighs a million times more than what they might have whispered in private into my peace-loving ear.

Ibid.

JUDAISM AS A CIVILIZATION

Israeli society is by definition a Jewish society, because I regard Judaism as a civilization, not just a religion. Israeli society operates within the domain of a Jewish language, Hebrew, and also within the domain of a rich sense of Jewish sensibilities, memories and, indeed, lunacies.

Ibid.

WRITER'S EARS

I need to have everything in my ears, like music. Only after that do I put it on paper.

Quoted in Elinor and Robert Slater's Great Jewish Men *(1996).*

◻

Cynthia Ozick

NOTHING IS DEAD

The molecules dance inside all forms, and within the molecules dance the atoms, and within the atoms dance still profounder sources of divine vitality. There is nothing that is Dead. There is no non-life. Holy life subsists even in the stone, even in the bones of dead dogs and dead men.

From her Pagan Rabbi *(1976).*

THE INCOMPARABLE JERUSALEM

They tell us that Boston is our Jerusalem...but Boston has no tragic tradition. Boston has never wept. No Bostonian has ever sung, mourning for his city, "If I do not remember thee, let my tongue cleave to the roof of my mouth"—for, to manage his accent, the Bostonian's tongue is already in that position...Boston has a history of neighborhoods. Jerusalem has a history of histories.

Ibid. From the short story "The Butterfly and the Traffic Light."

JEWISH HALF-GENIUS

Until Jewish women are in the same relation to history and Torah as Jewish men are, and have been, we should not allow ourselves ever again to indulge in the phrase "the Jewish genius." There is no collective Jewish genius.... What we have had is Jewish half-genius. That is not enough for the people who choose to hear the Voice of the Lord of History.

Quoted in The Jerusalem Post, *July 1978.*

TERM OF ENDEARMENT

Gotenyu, a way of addressing God when in despair, is a derivative of familial endearment, of rebuke as well as despair.

From her "Legacies," an essay which first appeared in the London Times Literary Supplement, *May 3, 1983.*

THE FACE TELLS ALL

After a certain number of years, our faces become our biographies. We get to be responsible for our faces.

From an interview in Writers at Work *(1988), edited by George Plimpton.*

CONSCIENCE AND CROCODILE TEARS

A statement of conscience that fails to come on time is worth little or nothing. Nations that were perpetrators, or collaborators, or merely indifferent during the hell of the Holocaust, and which today openly sympathize with the victims of 50 years go, are crying weightless, cost-free crocodile tears. Remorse, whether in nations or writers, is sympathy too long delayed to matter.

From a statement in The Jerusalem Post, *July 10, 1993.*

SECOND-CLASS JEWS

In the world at large, I call myself and am called a Jew. But when, on the Shabbat, I sit among women in my traditional shul and the rabbi speaks the word "Jew," I can be sure that he is not referring to me. For him, "Jew" means "male Jew."

Quoted in the "Hers" column in The New York Times, *August 25, 1983.*

MAKING A WEEK

Among ancient peoples, all the days of the week were alike, and that, of course, was natural; to the trees and the fish and the molecules of air, all the days are alike; nothing makes a week.... Sinai made the Sabbath. The Sabbath is a made, invented, created, given thing; it is not a natural thing.

Quoted in Nahum N. Glatzer's Modern Jewish Thought *(1976).*

TO BE A WRITER

I wanted to use what I was, to be what I was born to be—not to have a "career," but to be that straightforward obvious unmistakable animal, a writer.

From her Metaphor and Memory *(1989).*

EMBLEM OF COMMON SENSE

Just as "Dr. Spock" long ago became a synonym for popular common sense in baby health, so will "Letty Pogrebin" enter the language as an emblem of common sense in prizing children and other human beings.

On the woman (Letty Cottin Pogrebin) who helped found the National Women's Political Caucus in 1971.

MURDER IS MURDER

Yet what is to be gained by setting the two Hebron massacres side by side—and who promotes this ugly twinning? Chronology apart, neither atrocity avenges the other. Murder is murder, and every murder stands alone, an abomination in itself. Nothing can justify murder—no cause, no ideology, no credo, no zealotry, no moral grievance, no principled motive of any kind. In the face of deliberate and unprovoked bloodshed, motives are inadmissible.

Deploring the tendency to compare the 1929 Arab massacre of seventy innocent Jews in Hebron with the 1994 massacre by Jewish extremist Baruch Goldstein of twenty-nine Arabs in a Hebron mosque. From her Op-Ed article in The New York Times, *March 2, 1994.*

TO HELL WITH THE SS MAN

Murder is irrevocable. Murder is irreversible.... Forgiveness is pitiless. It forgets the victim.... Let the SS man die unshriven. Let him go to hell.

Quoted in Simon Wiesenthal's Sunflower *(1976).*

HOLOCAUST DENIAL

This business of Holocaust denial is something new under the sun. What's new is that we think artists always use imagination for make believe—to say that something that isn't there is there. These deniers are saying something that's never been said before—that something that is there, isn't there! They are using imagination to annihilate instead of to create. That is something new in terms of how human beings use imagination.

Commenting on the theme of her first play, Blue Light *(1994), in which she crafted a dramatic condemnation of those who would deny that the Holocaust took place. Quoted in* The Jewish Week, *August 12–18, 1994.*

NOVELIST TURNS PLAYWRIGHT

I've always wanted to write a play for lots of reasons. One reason is I believe in writing and think that a writer should write in all genres. I feel quite passionate about it. One should write short stories, novels, plays, op-ed pieces. I wanted to write a Neil Simon comedy. I also think that as far as a comic play is concerned that *The Importance of Being Earnest* is a masterpiece, and that's what I wanted to write.

Ibid. After writing her Blue Light *under the guidance of director Sidney Lumet. The play is loosely based on her 1989 novella* The Shawl, *portraying the lives of two women who survived the death camps of the Holocaust.*

Tom Paine

THE BIBLE AS FABLE

It is not the antiquity of a tale that is any evidence of its truth; on the contrary, it is a symptom of its being fabulous; for the more ancient any history pretends to be the more it has the resemblance of a fable. The origin of every nation is buried in fabulous tradition; and that of the Jews is as much to be suspected as any other.

From his Age of Reason, *Part II, in which he denies that the Bible is the word of God or was inspired by God.*

TO HELP A JEW

An unbelieving Jew one day
Was skating o'er the icy way,
Which, being brittle, let him in
Just deep enough to catch his chin,
And in that woeful plight he hung,
With only power to move his tongue.
A brother skater near at hand,
A Papist born in foreign land,
With hasty steps directly flew
To save poor Mordecai the Jew;
"But first," quoth he, "I must enjoin
That you renounce your faith for mine,
There's no entreaties else will do,
This heresy to help a Jew."

The first two stanzas of a satirical poem entitled "A Bigot's Immersion," printed in 1775 in the Pennsylvania Magazine *of* Philadelphia.

□

Paul Painlevé

FATE OF THE JEWS

The fate of the Jewish people is the scandal of history. Like Hellenism, Judaism is one of the deep sources of our occidental civilizations: It gave them its Bible, its God, its unquenchable thirst for justice, the majestic poetry of its old prophets hurled like an outcry to the Deity. That such a people could, for

eighteen centuries, be massacred, quartered, dispersed like a vile band over the face of the earth...condemned to endless exile and blamed for this very exile in order to justify new persecutions against them, is an iniquity which has disgusted all generous hearts for many years.

Quoted in Joseph L. Baron's Stars and Sand *(1943).*

□

Grace Paley

WHAT JUDAISM IS ALL ABOUT

I was raised by secular Jews who had a strong Jewish identification, though they weren't religious. My parents believed in an ethical, idealistic way of life. I always assumed that that's what Jews were all about. That and storytelling—we have a tradition of great Jewish storytellers. Look at the Bible!

Recalling her roots.

□

Aimé Pallière

IN LOVE WITH HEBREW

Through the Hebrew syllables with their sonorous cadence, something of the soul of Israel reached me.... When I opened the psalter the words had...an emotional and religious value that I could never again find in French or Latin.

From his Unknown Sanctuary *(1928).*

□

(Lord) Henry Palmerston

EARLY ADVOCATE OF ZIONISM

There exists at the present time, among the Jews dispersed over Europe, a strong notion that the time is approaching when their nation is to return to Palestine.... It would be of manifest importance to the Sultan to encourage the Jews to return and to settle in Palestine.

From an August 11, 1840 letter instructing his ambassador to Constantinople to intercede with the Ottoman rulers on behalf of a Jewish national home. Quoted in Barbara Tuchman's Bible and Sword: England and Palestine from the Bronze Age to Balfour *(1956).*

¤

Murray Pantirer

Three Hours of Pain

When [the President] left, his eyes were wet, and Mrs. Clinton was crying like a baby. That touched me. I'm very grateful the President and Mrs. Clinton went through three hours of pain.

After Bill and Hillary Clinton saw a preview of Steven Spielberg's Schindler's List *on November 30, 1993. The movie depicts the life of Oskar Schindler, who saved 1,100 Jews from the Nazi death camps. Pantirer was one of those saved.*

¤

(Rabbi) Papa

Courtesy to a Wife

If your wife is short, bend down and whisper to her.

A comment made to Abaye. Quoted in the talmudic tractate Bava Metzia (59a).

¤

Joseph Papp

Afraid to Go

I was always afraid to go. I felt I couldn't take it emotionally.

In an interview with Jane Perlez of The New York Times *after his first visit to Israel in 1981.*

¤

James W. Parkes

Origin of Jewish Antipathy

The Jew as devil, the Jew whose badge was a scorpion, the symbol of falsity, owes his origin to religion, not to economics.

From his Judaism and Christianity *(1948).*

God Still Needs the Jews

There must be no surrender whatever by either Jew or Christian of the fullness of his inheritance. God still needs the Jews as Jews.

From his Jews, Christians and God *(1942).*

Need for Scapegoats

So long as the world is a place in which life to the ordinary man means insecurity, frustration and unemployment, so long will he need some scapegoat for his feelings; and the position of the Jews, and their powerlessness, make them the perfect scapegoat.

From his An Enemy of the People: Antisemitism *(1946).*

Short of Full Equality

Even where Jews enjoy complete equality with the rest of the population, they do so by the good will of that population. And that is not complete equality.

Ibid.

The Church and Anti-Semitism

Antisemitism is a unique expression of group prejudice, and arises out of a unique cause. That which changed the normal pattern of Jewish-Gentile relations was the action of the Christian Church. The statement is tragic but the evidence is inescapable.

Ibid.

¤

Talcott Parsons

Hosts and Guests

[The major cause of anti-Semitism was the] arrogance of the claim that a group who are in a sense "guests" in a [Christian] country claim a higher status than the "host" people.

A 1940s comment. Quoted in Jews in a Gentile World *(1942), edited by Isacque Graeber and Steuart Henderson.*

¤

Dolly Parton

Omnipresent Myth

I had this idea to do a series called *High and Mighty* about a country singer that has a near-death experience, then becomes like a gospel singer. But everybody's afraid to touch anything that's religious because most of the people out here [in Hollywood] are Jewish, and it's a frightening thing for them to promote Christianity.

Quoted in Vogue *magazine, January 1994.*

Blaise Pascal

PLACE OF THE JEWS

The carnal Jews hold a middle place between the Christians and the pagans. The pagans do not know God and love only the earth. The Christians know the true God and do not love the earth.

From his Pensées *(1670).*

Abdul Rahman Azzam Pasha

WAR OF EXTERMINATION

This war will be a war of extermination and a momentous massacre which will be spoken of like the Mongol Massacre and the Crusades.

Comment of the Secretary General of the Arab League after Israel declared itself an independent state in May 1948.

Boris L. Pasternak

GIVE UP YOUR IDENTITY

In whose interests is this voluntary martyrdom? Who stands to gain by keeping it going? So that all these innocent old men and women and children, all these clever, kind, humane people should go on being mocked and beaten up throughout the centuries?...Why don't the intellectual leaders of the Jewish people say to them: "That's enough, stop now. Don't hold on to your identity, don't all get together in a crowd. Disperse. Be with all the rest."

Expressing his inner feelings about Jews and Judaism through one of the title character's friends, Misha Gordon, a Jew. From his Doctor Zhivago *(1958).*

Raphael Patai

WHO IS A JEW?

A Jew is a person who considers himself a Jew and is so considered by others.

From his Jewish Mind *(1977).*

Mandy Patinkin

A JEW IN LOVE

My Jewishness informs my entire life. I do the rituals and the holidays, and I love my Jewishness. I love the tradition...belonging to a history of people are what I like most—the comfort that I feel through the ancestral links of centuries.

From his Introduction to Dorothy and Thomas Hoobler's Jewish American Family Album *(1995).*

David Patterson

A PROSELYTE'S MOTIVATION

I declare myself to be a Jew, not to join the victims, but to divorce myself from the executioners and to undo the indifferent ones, to rid myself of the indifference within myself.

From his Pilgrimage of a Proselyte: From Auschwitz to Jerusalem *(1993).*

TRAUMA AT YAD VASHEM

I am dizzy, exhausted, drained, scattered. How much more of this can I stand? I want to leave it all, but it won't leave me. Choosing has nothing to do with it. I am chosen before I choose, summoned before I decide. Six million names cover my name like a shroud, and forever I must identify myself by the name of the other, by my capacity to answer to and for these names. I am terrified....

Ibid. Upon visiting Yad Vashem after his conversion to Judaism.

LIGHT BATTLING DARKNESS

Casting its light over these names, the flame on the floor is itself bathed in the light that comes through the opening in the roof, and from beyond that opening. Yet this large room is dim, dim despite the light, as dim as memory. Here light does battle with darkness, as it reaches for light, touches light, cuts into the eyes, bores into the soul. The struggle between light and darkness is unfair, says Wiesel. Light always wins. But the darkness is not defeated. It goes into hiding. Where does it hide? Inside the light.

Ibid.

A PROCESS OF BECOMING

To be a Jew is to be engaged in the process of becoming more Jewish, of eternally becoming more—more responsible, more thankful, more generous, more loving.

Ibid.

¤

George Patton

A Visit to a Displaced Persons' Camp

[The Jews] were collected in a large wooden building which they called a synagogue. We [he and General Dwight D. Eisenhower] entered the synagogue, which was packed with the greatest stinking bunch of humanity I have ever seen. When we got about half way up, the head rabbi, who was dressed in a fur hat similar to that worn by Henry VIII of England and in a surplice heavily embroidered and very filthy, came down to meet the General [Eisenhower]. Also a copy of the Talmud, I think it is called, written on a sheet and rolled around a stick, was carried by one of the attending physicians.

A notation is his diary after visiting a DP camp near Munich, Germany, on Yom Kippur in September 1945, with General Eisenhower. Patton was commander of the U.S. Third Army, in whose zone of occupation most of the Jewish DPs were congregated.

¤

(Pope) Paul IV

Inequality of the Jews

It is absurd that the Jews, who through their own fault have been condemned by God to everlasting slavery, should claim to be the Christians' equal.

After ordering, in 1555, that the Jews of Rome be confined to a ghetto. Quoted in Sam Waagenaar's Pope's Jews *(1974).*

¤

Robert Peel

Reparations Due the Jew

If there be a class of our fellow-beings to whom reparation is due from every Christian State in Europe...the Jews are that class. I defy you to read the early history of this country narrated, not by indignant Jews, but by the popular historians of your own faith, without shuddering at the atrocities committed by Christian sovereigns and a Christian people.

From a speech to the House of Commons, February 11, 1848.

¤

Pinchas Peli

Blessings

Blessings were instituted by the Rabbis as a means for directing man into the presence of God at all times, thus providing for the continuous preservation of contact with the Creator.

From his essay "Blessings—The Gateway to Prayer," which appeared in Tradition, *Fall 1937.*

To Believe Is Not Enough

To believe is necessary, but it is not enough; one must also feel and sense the existence of God. The presence of the Almighty must be a personal, intimate experience. And if this experience is not common, and if it proves impossible to achieve that devekut [clinging] in Him, blessed be He, and if one feels not the touch of His hand, one cannot be a complete Jew.

From an article in Tradition: A Journal of Orthodox Thought, *Summer 1980.*

Vegetarianism Preferred

The laws of kashrut come to teach us that a Jew's first preference should be a vegetarian meal. If, however, one cannot control a craving for meat, it should be kosher meat, which would serve as a reminder that the animal being eaten is a creature of God, that the death of such a creature cannot be taken lightly, that hunting for sport is forbidden.

From his Torah Today *(1987).*

¤

Noa Ben-Artzi Pelossof

My Grandfather

Please excuse me for not wanting to talk about the peace. I want to talk about my grandfather.... Others greater than I have already eulogized you, but none of them ever had the pleasure that I had to feel the caress of your warm, soft hands, to merit your warm embrace that was reserved only for us, to see your half-smile that always told me so much.

Eulogizing her grandfather, Yitzhak Rabin, on November 6, 1995.

¤

Murray Perahia

Happy Tears

Rather than it being the happiest moment

of my life, it was one of the saddest. It was kind of crazy. All I could do was cry, and I did. It meant life was ahead of me, and I didn't know if I was ready for it.

> *In 1972, after winning first prize in the triennial Leeds (England) International Pianoforte Competition. Andrew Porter of* The New Yorker *wrote, "...judges have awarded first prize not to a hard-hitter or to a conventionally big pianist, but to a poet."*

▱

Shimon Peres

ON KISSINGER

...the most devious man I ever met.

> *Quoted in Walter Isaacson's biography entitled* Kissinger *(1993).*

GREATEST JEW OF OUR GENERATION

With David Ben-Gurion I worked for seventeen years without a pause, sometimes days and nights without a break. I knew him well, and I am bound to say that not only did I see him as the greatest Jew of our generation, but my admiration for him continued to grow throughout the years of our acquaintance. I did not hesitate to admit this in his lifetime, and today, in retrospect, I am proud that I recognized his greatness and called it by its name.

> *From his* From These Men: Seven Founders of the State of Israel *(1979).*

MAN AT HIS BEST

I am not unaware of the theory which claims that the heart of man is essentially evil. But I am convinced that Israel is the story of man at his best. This belief is the torch that guides our footsteps and illuminates our paths, we who walk like men and with men.

> *Ibid.*

PRACTICAL POLITICIAN'S FORESIGHT

Although he saw the desert as the most beautiful of landscapes, he believed that it was possible to change the climate by means of afforestation and he was prepared to cover the entire land surface with poplar trees. He was convinced that sea water could provide the necessary irrigation for a flourishing agricultural economy.

He believed that China would become a world power. He foresaw a united Europe. He believed that in the place of nation-states, communities of nations would arise.

> *Ibid. An evaluation of David Ben-Gurion.*

TERRITORIAL DILEMMA

I see some rabbis, and rabbis are very powerful, opposing most of what we do.... We need to have a real discussion with the religious people [but] they don't have the permission from the Lord to give preference to territory over [Israel's moral] spirit.

> *From an address to the Conference of Presidents of Major American Jewish Organizations, which stirred up a hornet's nest among many of the Orthodox present.*

CLOSING THE CIRCLE OF LIFE

Bob was a man who looked life in the eye and extracted the utmost from it. His spiritual strength was that of the Jewish people. He was a tireless defender of freedom of expression. He was different from other people and yet allowed others to be different from him. He is buried today as a Jew, on the Mount of Olives in Jerusalem. He is closing the circle of life that knew want and plenty, danger and grandeur but never surrender and despair.

> *From his eulogy in 1991 at the Jerusalem funeral of Robert Maxwell. Quoted in Elisabeth Maxwell's* Mind of My Own: My Life with Robert Maxwell *(1994).*

SIZE OF A MAN'S LIFE

He lost his breath in the vast sea but not his soul. It will float above the waves as a marker to anyone believing that a man's life can be bigger than the cards he is dealt.

> *Ibid.*

LAND WITH A MESSAGE

Never was Israel just a country. It was a message as well. Now that we have a country, we haven't forgotten the message. Never in our history did we want to occupy, dominate, or discriminate against another people....

When some people say "Gaza is ours," what do they mean? What is ours? Their poverty, their refugee camps, their lack of future and dignity? Can we, the Jewish people, afford it? Whoever says so is not Jewish!

> *From an address delivered at the Park East Synagogue, in New York City, after the signing of the September 13, 1993 peace accord between Israel and the PLO.*

FROM BULLETS TO BALLOTS

We live in an ancient land and as our land is small, so must our reconciliation be great. As our wars have been long, so must our healing be swift. Deep gaps call for lofty breezes. I want to tell the Palestinian delegation that we are sincere, that we mean business. We do not seek to shape your lives or determine your destiny. Let all of us turn from bullets to ballots, from guns to shovels. We shall pray with you. We shall offer you our help in making Gaza prosper and Jericho blossom again.

> *From an address delivered at the White House on September 13, 1993, before the signing of the peace accord between Israel and the PLO.*

PLO AS A NEGOTIATING PARTNER

Supported by hard evidence we believe the PLO is engaged in terrorist activities and is therefore no partner for any negotiations or dialogue.

> *From a May 3, 1993 letter to the American Zionist Organization.*

ENOUGH VILIFICATIONS!

There is no one in this country who has been as vilified and had so many lies told about him.... My life will not be long enough for me to undo all the lies, beginning with who my mother was and ending with how many factories I own.

I will not take it lying down, and you have no moral right to behave as you are behaving. Enough of your stories, enough of your vilifications; you've hurt me enough and invented enough stories about me.

> *During a speech to the Knesset when it was debating the Israeli–PLO declaration of principles signed in Washington, DC, on September 13, 1993.*

EIGHT WASTED YEARS

What are you shouting about? You wasted our lives for eight years. Eight years of a sit-and-do-nothing prime minister. You did nothing. You did not bring peace.

> *Ibid. Addressing Yitzhak Shamir during the September 1993 Knesset debate.*

IMPEDIMENTS TO THE PEACE PROCESS

We view peace as a process of give and take. Israel has given. It decided to stop settlements. The Arabs said they would put an end to the boycott in return. Israel lived up to its commitment; the Arabs did not.... Peace is a matter of both mutuality and public conduct. It is impossible for one party to take its positions publicly with the other party applauding it in private. If this continues to be the case, Israel will view the Arab side as responsible for slowing and even endangering the peace process.

> *From an interview with William Safire in* The New York Times, *October 4, 1993.*

REDEFINING WHO IS A JEW

In the future, the argument will not be about whether a Jew is one who has a Jewish mother or a Jewish father. A Jew will be one who has Jewish children.

> *Speaking to Jewish community leaders in London in 1992.*

PALESTINIANS' RIGHT

Just as we Jewish people did not ask the Palestinians for permission to become a state, neither do they need our permission to become a people.

> *From his* New Middle East *(1993).*

ISRAEL IS HERE TO STAY

We will not move from the only place on earth where we can renew our independence, achieve security and live with self-respect and honor—our honor, and our neighbors'.

> *Ibid.*

FUTILITY OF WAR

First and foremost, we must all acknowledge the futility of war. The Arabs cannot defeat Israel on the battlefield; Israel cannot dictate the conditions for peace to the Arabs.

> *Ibid.*

RABIN'S DOUBTS

He was skeptical of the Oslo talks; sometimes he wholly disbelieved in them.

> *Describing Yitzhak Rabin's attitude towards the secret 1993 negotiations that led to the Israel–PLO accord. Quoted in his memoirs,* Battling for Peace *(1994).*

A MAP AND A DREAM

We had a dream before we had a map. Now we have a map and a dream together.

> *From his address at the signing of the Israeli-PLO peace accord in Cairo, Egypt, on May 4, 1994.*

A PROMISE

No more terrorism, no more bloodshed, no more violence, [and] no finger will press a trigger anymore.

> *Ibid.*

JUDGING THE PEACE PROCESS

I don't think we should judge the [peace] process by the performance of Yasser Arafat. We're not negotiating with Yasser Arafat. We're negotiating with ourselves—about what sort of people we want to become. I do believe that while the dangers are great, the opportunities are greater.

> *From a May 1994 address to American Jewish leaders after Yasser Arafat had called for "a jihad to liberate Jerusalem" in a speech in Johannesburg earlier in the month.*

IN BUSINESS FOR ONESELF

It breaks up the idea of a united Jewish appeal. They are doing their own thing for political purposes.... Everyone is making *Shabbos* for himself.

> *Referring to the Jewish Federation in Greater Middlesex County, New Jersey, which in 1994 allocated some of its funds to support the 140,000 Jews living in the West Bank and Golan Heights.*

TERRITORIAL COMPROMISE

Without a territorial compromise [with Syria], there can be no chance for peace.

> *From a speech in December 1994 before an assembly of 2,000 people at Sinai Temple in Los Angeles, California.*

HOPE-RAISING MISSION

I am here for hope-raising and not fundraising. There is a new political agenda awaiting us. Indeed, I am not used to seeing Judaism in such good shape. We have five million Hebrew-speaking people in Israel [including one million Arabs who speak Hebrew]. That's more than the total of the Danish-speaking people in Denmark.

> *Ibid.*

ISRAEL AND FUNDAMENTALISM

Fundamentalism in the Moslem world is a greater danger than Syria. Fundamentalists can acquire nuclear bombs. For them we need a new strategy.

> *Ibid.*

MILK, HONEY, AND ELECTRONICS

Israel has become a land of milk and honey—and electronic engineers.

> *Ibid.*

THE SABBATH

Our Sabbath saved us.

> *Ibid. Repeating his answer to U.S. President Bill Clinton and Vice President Al Gore, each of whom wanted to know how it was that Jews were able to survive over the last 2,000 years.*

CASTIGATING KING DAVID

I'm trying to tell the Torah sage, Mr. Gut-

man, that not everything that King David did, on the ground, on the roofs [a reference to the story of his love affair with Bathsheba], is acceptable to a Jew or is something I like.

> *A remark made in December 1994 to Knesset member Shaul Gutman during a verbal duel about the awarding of the Nobel Peace Prize to Peres, Rabin, and Arafat. Peres had said: "Mine is a Jewish truth.... We did not rule over another people, and we shall not."*

I APOLOGIZE

In the name of Bathsheba. I apologize to King David.

> *Ibid. After Knesset member Yosef Ba-Gad shouted at Peres: "It is a shame for you to say that [about King David]. You should be ashamed of yourself."*

MISTAKE OF A FRIEND

When a friend makes a mistake, the friend remains a friend, and the mistake remains a mistake.

> *Commenting on U.S. President Ronald Reagan's May 1985 visit to the military cemetery in Bitburg, Germany, where Nazi officers were buried.*

WE ARE LEADERS

Most of you think we politicians are part of a television show—we handshake to the point we don't represent the people. I believe we lead a people and pave the way even if we are in the minority and act against opposing winds.

> *Commenting in 1995 on the peace process.*

BASEBALL STRIKE PROGNOSTICATION

We will get an interim agreement. It will be a handshake.

> *When a reporter mistaking him for one of the principals in the baseball negotiations being held at the Mayflower Hotel, Washington, DC (where he was staying in February 1995), was asked how he foresaw the strike ending. Peres was referring to the famous September 1993 handshake between Rabin and Arafat.*

TWISTING A POLICY

It never happened before, to the best of my recollection, that Jewish organized life in the United States went to the Capitol to act against the government of Israel. Everyone in America can express their views; I don't suggest that people should keep quiet.

But to go in an organized manner to intervene in the diplomacy of Israel, to try to twist a policy of an elected government of a country is not done, is unheard of, is unprecedented.

The only thing you can do is condemn it, and we shall condemn it.

Condemning American Jews who have been lobbying Congress to place stringent conditions on the PLO in return for continued U.S. aid. At a press conference in New York on October 1, 1995.

DEFINING LEADERSHIP

Leadership has to lead, not only to represent. It's not a beauty contest. And people usually are very conservative.

Ibid.

EGGS FROM OMELETTES

Like trying to make eggs out of an omelette.

Concerning the 1995 deliberations with the PLO on finding a solution to the security of Jewish settlers in Hebron.

DREAMS AND REALITY

Mr. Arafat has the right to have his own dreams, but we told Arafat that the difference between a dream and an agreement is that for a dream it is enough to have one person; for an agreement you have to have two parties.

After Arafat declared at the World Economic Forum, held in Davos, Switzerland, in 1996, that the Palestinians have an "unalienable right" to make East Jerusalem their capital. Peres responded: "Jerusalem is not for division or for sale."

❑

I. L. Peretz

SATAN ON A FISHING EXPEDITION

We are like fish
In this vast sea
And Satan fishes
For you and me.

Quoted in Joseph Leftwich's Golden Peacock *(1939).*

ALIKE BUT DIFFERENT

By nature we are like all human beings, yet our people is unlike others, because our life is different, our history is different, our teacher is the Exile.

From his Idishe Bibliotek *(1890).*

FROM YOUTH TO OLD AGE

Youth is fair, a graceful stag,
Leaping, playing in a park.
Age is gray, a toothless hag,
Stumbling in the dark.

From his play Sewing the Wedding Gown *(1906).*

HEARTS LIKE A SPONGE

Sheer egotism compels us to the purest love of mankind as a whole.... Our hearts are like a sponge, receptive to all the newest humanitarian ideas; and our sympathy goes out to all the unfortunate, all the oppressed.

Quoted in Jewish Affairs, *June 1952.*

DUTY OF JEWISH INTELLECTUALS

Don't assume, Jewish intellectuals, that you are doing your duty by working for so-called Humanity.... You are lighting a fire beneath the open sky, while your own family in your own house is freezing.

From his Bildung *(1890).*

BINDING POWER OF HEBREW

The Hebrew language is the only glue which holds together our scattered bones. It also holds together the rings in the chain of time. It binds us to those who built pyramids, to those who shed their blood on the ramparts of Jerusalem, and to those who, at the burning stakes, cried *Shema Yisrael!*

Ibid.

TASK OF THE JEWISH ARTIST

To find the essence of Judaism in all places, at all times, in all parts of a people scattered throughout the world and to see it illuminated by the prophetic dream of man's future—that is the task of every Jewish artist.

Quoted in Otto F. Best's Yiddish: One Language and Its Literature *(1988).*

A PEOPLE THAT WILL NOT PERISH

Is there any people that changes its languages, a nomad people with no guaranteed frontiers, without its own economic structure, yet this people lives, suffers, does not perish? It is weak and is warred against by the strongest, the most powerful peoples, but it does not capitulate. Such a people must see differently, feel differently, have a different outlook on the world, a different picture of the future of the world, of existence and of man.

From his essay "Roads That Lead Away from Jewishness." Reprinted in Joseph Leftwich's The Way We Think *(1969).*

LOOKING FOR GOD

Zeitlin once wrote: "Peretz has a heaven, but no God in heaven!" The first half of the phrase is a compliment, and I acknowledge it gratefully. And I confirm that the second half is true, too. I don't even know where to look for His dear Name! Before the world—He is its Creator? After the world—He slips out of it?

Ibid.

LIVING WITH IMAGINATION

Life means: having divine imagination and in a certain measure divine will to carry what is imagined into effect, to change the environment to accord with the imagination, creating new forms—a partner in the work of Creation!

I live—therefore I have a divine spark in me; all who live have it—and I feel that all lives!

He who denies God also has the divine spark. So has the blasphemer.

Ibid.

□

Martin Peretz

STRUGGLE FOR MULTICULTURALISM

Let me say that the struggle for multiculturalism is not about culture; it is really a raw struggle for political power.... I do not believe that Jews should do anything else in American society than defend their own interests, because at this moment in history, the interest of the Jews is the interest of an incandescent vision of society under siege. It is the vision of a democratic politics and a democratic culture which judges men and women on their own.

From an address delivered at the World Conference on Anti-Semitism and Prejudice in a Changing World, held in Brussels, Belgium, July 1992.

DISMISSAL OF A SHIBBOLETH

The friendship of the Clinton administration for Israel is not in doubt. It seems even to extend to [Secretary of State Warren] Christopher, who has refused to repeat the mantra, so long reassuring to the Arabs, that the entire West Bank and East Jerusalem are "occupied territories." This vernacular, he says rightly, is "almost theological." If everywhere is occupied territory, then everywhere has to be given up, and that is not at all what the United States intends.

From an article entitled "From Sarajevo to Jerusalem," which appeared in The New Republic, *September 6, 1993.*

POLITICS OF THE 1990S

This flow [of capital and immigrants] actually emboldens Israel, and it should give pause to its neighbors. New capital assures that Israel will remain a cutting-edge scientific society in a region that is still in its first confounding encounters with modernity. The new immigrants have already devastated the Palestinian hope that they will eventually overwhelm the Jews demographically.

Ibid.

THE MIDEAST PEACE TALKS

To the Arabs, the Jews will always be usurpers and interlopers. Xenophobia in our time is not the disposition of the Arabs alone. But in an age when the state conflates politics with identity, Arab Islam, suffering from feelings of inferiority about Israel and the West, is especially xenophobic, thinking of the Middle East as its world and its world alone. However forthcoming the Israelis will be in a settlement, they will still have to live inconclusively, and dangerously.

Ibid.

FACING BETRAYAL

I feel, if not exactly gaiety, some exhilarated sense of the possibilities of the moment. But I also know that Jews have often been betrayed both by their own hopes and by their well-wishers. This is the Middle East, you have to remember, and pessimists have been right here more often than they were wrong. Ben-Gurion's anxiety still shakes my bones.

His reaction to the Israeli-Palestinian peace accord signed in Washington, DC, on September 13, 1993. From a column in The New Republic, *October 4, 1993.*

HISTORIC PRECEDENT

There is not another case in modern history—and perhaps not in all of history—in which a nation so strategically well-positioned as Israel entered a negotiation fated to end in its forfeiting territory to its nemesis. How common is it that a country which wins several wars of self-defense is prepared to hand over (and has already handed over) a goodly portion of its conquests to people who are and always have been at best...well, hostile? Say what the anchorman will about "the lost soul of Israel," the body-politic of Israel is rare in the annals. The Israelis, as Fouad Ajami put it, are "conquerors with scruples...occupiers with a bad conscience." These scruples and this bad conscience are part of the glory of Zionism, or at least of one strain of Zionism, and this is the strain from which Yitzhak Rabin and Shimon Peres come. Peres with unrelenting passion.

Ibid.

THE SECURITY OF ISRAEL

The security of Israel is for me as much a moral issue as Indochina was a decade ago. The Palestinians have a right to decide their own life, but not Israel's life.

From a comment to a New York Times *reporter.*

FREEDOM AND POWER

People whose view of the world has not been affected by the coalition between the oil powers and the communist bloc, in reference to the State of Israel, are the ones who have not seen the important changes in the world. If you ask whether my new appreciation of the role of American power has anything to do with the precariousness of Israel's situation... the answer is yes. It made me think about the predicament of where freedom would be in the world without American power.

From a 1982 statement to the Jewish Student Press Service.

DISTORTED ZIONISM

The new Israeli West Bank settlement Elon Moreh is a nationalist extravaganza which Israel can ill afford. I think Zionism is an ally of democratic values, however that Zionism may be distorted, perverted and tainted by the incumbent (Begin) government in Israel.

From a 1979 letter to The New York Times.

PORTABLE JUDAISM

We do not believe we live in exile. Judaism is portable.

Comment made at the June 1994 conference convened by Israeli President Ezer Weizman to discuss Israel-Diaspora relations.

¤

Richard Perle

THE JACKSON-VANIK AMENDMENT

I, too, plan to offer a tribute to "Scoop" [Senator Henry Jackson], who hired me as his legislative aide while I was still in graduate school, became my spiritual and professional mentor, and who was like a father to me. Indeed, one of the high points of my career remains that day, more than 22 years ago, when I and other Senate aides met in the basement of the Old Senate Office building—now the Russell Building—to forge what came to be known as the Jackson-Vanik Amendment.

Commenting on the amendment that tied trade benefits for the Soviet Union to the granting of exit visas. Senator Jackson's accomplishment was commemorated in Jerusalem in January 1995. Quoted in the Forward, *January 6, 1995.*

¤

Itzhak Perlman

PICK OF THE LOT

Israel's grand tradition of violinists is in safe hands.

After giving a class to some of Israel's brightest young violinists. Quoted in The Jerusalem Report, *April 21, 1994.*

¤

Nathan Perlmutter

PLAIN TALK ABOUT JESSE JACKSON

Let us say it plainly. We are dealing with a person whose recorded expressions are those of an anti-Semite.

How else view a man who, when annoyed by the press, attributes it to "Jewish" domination of the press? And when critical of labor, blames it on "Jewish" control of labor unions?

When displeased by a boxing match between a white South African and a black American, condemns "Jewish" promoters?

In his annual report to the National Commission of the Anti-Defamation League.

¤

Roberta Peters

THE BEAUTY IN BEING JEWISH

I am Jewish down to my toes, my soul. I have always felt that having a Jewish soul has colored my life in the very best sense. I sing better. I have an aliveness. There is a certain beauty in being Jewish that sustains me.

Quoted in Self-Chosen.

¤

Leonid Petlakh

TO BE JEWISH

Being Jewish means much to me: it means advancing the good of my people by sharing the beauty and depth of Judaism; it is to be involved in *tikkun olam,* the healing of the world for the betterment of all people; and it is to be a *rodef shalom,* a pursuer of peace, in a troubled and often violent world.

From his winning essay for undergraduates on the meaning of being Jewish, in a competition sponsored by the American Jewish Committee. Reported in The New York Times, *May 4, 1994.*

THE GIFT OF FREEDOM

I am grateful for the precious gift of freedom. As a Jew, I believe that freedom includes the responsibility to preserve my precious heritage and to transmit it—something my parents and grandparents were not allowed to do. My greatest wish is that I may some day teach my own children the fulfillment of being a Jew.

A member of the Hunter College Class of 1995, he arrived in the U.S. from Russia in 1989 and tasted freedom for the first time.

ⵟ

Jakob Petuchowski

A RETURN TO OBSERVANCE

Not every "ritual" necessarily has to teach an "ethical" lesson...to be a valuable component of religion. A *ritual* serving as an expression of the Jew's love for God...is as much entitled to our consideration as are the more pronounced *ethical* commandments.

Advocating a return to the observance of traditional rituals.

SPEAKING TO GOD

We Jews are so much better at speaking *to* God than we are speaking *of* God. We speak *to* God all the time and not just in moments of formal prayer during worship services. We are asked how our children are, and we answer: "Thank God, they are very well."

"Thank God!" "God Forbid!" "Good God!" "Please God!"—those and similar expressions are constantly on our lips.

From an essay in The Jewish Spectator, *Winter 1984.*

GOD IS CAPABLE OF SAYING "NO"

God cannot be manipulated by man. He can only be *addressed*. He may, or may not grant a specific request. But there is no mechanism of man's devising which would compel Him to do so. In addressing God, man knows that a "No" can be as much of an "answer" as a "Yes."

Ibid.

ⵟ

Leo Pfeffer

STATUS OF AMERICAN JUDAISM

[Judaism] has adjusted itself most completely and most happily to the values of secular humanism. When one compares the Judaism of mid-twentieth-century America with the Judaism of mid-nineteenth-century Eastern Europe, one can see the radical changes effected by the alliance.

From his Creeds in Competition *(1978).*

ⵟ

David Philipson

JERUSALEM: USA

The United States is our Palestine and Washington our Jerusalem.

An 1895 statement by the staunchly anti-Zionist rabbi.

TRADITION DEFINED

Reform Judaism differentiates between *tradition* and *the traditions;* it considers itself, too, a link in the chain of Jewish tradition, the product of this age as Talmudism was of its age.

From his Reform Movement in Judaism *(1907).*

PURPOSE OF THE REFORM MOVEMENT

The all-important truth that Judaism spells development and not stagnation ...is the intent and content of the Reform movement.

Ibid.

ⵟ

Wendell Phillips

IRONY OF IRONIES

A Russian to hate a Jew! Out of the wall of his vast cathedrals he carves the figures of his twelve holy apostles—and every one a Jew. He enters and prostrates himself before the picture of a Hebrew child in the arms of a Hebrew mother. He mutters a creed that declares a Jew to be the Son of God, the Savior of the world—then he goes out and kills the first Jew he meets because he is a Jew. It is irony to move the laughter of devils and the tears of the just.

From a January 21, 1906 speech.

ⵟ

Philo

FATHERLAND VS. MOTHERLAND

Greece is my Fatherland and Palestine my Motherland.

By attribution.

GOD AND PARENTS

What God is to the world, parents are to their children.

From his Honor Due Parents.

ENJOYING THE SEARCH

Nothing is better than to search for the true God, even if the discovery of Him eludes human capacity, since the very wish to learn, if earnestly entertained, produces untold joys and pleasures.

From his Special Laws.

EARLIEST SEDER CELEBRATIONS

The whole nation performs the sacred rites and acts as priests with pure hands and complete immunity.... Every home is invested with the outward semblance and dignity of a temple.

Writing about the ambiance of the Passover Seder in its formative years, during the last century of Second Temple times.

SYMBOL OF OPPRESSION

The burning bush was a symbol of the oppressed people, and the burning fire was a symbol of the oppressors; and the circumstance of the burning bush not being consumed was an emblem of the fact that the people thus oppressed would not be destroyed by those who were attacking them.

From his On the Life of Moses.

UNAPPRECIATED LAWGIVER

I have conceived the idea of writing the life of Moses, who, according to the account of some persons, was the lawgiver of the Jews, but according to others only an interpreter of the sacred laws, the greatest and most perfect man that ever lived, having a desire to make his character fully known to those who ought not to remain in ignorance respecting him, for the glory of the laws which he left behind him has reached over the whole world, and has penetrated to the very furthest limits of the universe...though the historians who have flourished among the Greeks have not chosen to think him worthy of mention.

Ibid.

ATTEMPTS TO BRIBE GOD

If a man practices ablutions and purifications, but defiles his mind while he cleanses his body; or if, through his wealth, he founds a temple at a large outlay and expense; or if he offers hecatombs and sacrifices oxen without number, or adorns the shrine with rich ornaments, or gives endless timber and cunningly wrought work, more precious than silver or gold—let him none the more be called religious. For he has wandered far from the path of religion, mistaking ritual for holiness, and attempting to bribe the Incorruptible, and to flatter Him whom none can flatter. God wel-comes genuine service, and that is the service of a soul that offers the bare and simple sacrifice of truth, but from false service, the mere display of material wealth, He turns away.

Quoted in David Winston's Philo-Judæus of Alexandria *(1981).*

□

Molly Picon

SATISFYING TIMES

We met people who hadn't laughed in seven years and who laughed for the first time. It gave them a sense of normalcy again, to come together and see who was still alive. That was six months of great nights.

Describing her travels throughout Europe after World War II, bringing gifts and entertainment to the people they met in displaced persons' camps. Quoted in Elinor and Robert Slater's Great Jewish Women *(1994).*

YIDDISH POOL

At three feet the poolside sign said, a *mecha'yeh*, at five, *oy vay,* and at ten feet, *gevalt.*

Ibid. Priding herself on having the only Yiddish swimming pool in the world.

A COMEDIENNE'S HOPE

How can I tell you how much your love for me has gladdened my heart through a wonderful life? All I hope is that I have gladdened your hearts too, and brightened your lives as you have mine.

From the closing lines of her autobiography. Quoted in Darryl Lyman's Jewish Comedy Catalog *(1989).*

□

Pinchas of Koretz

KNOWING GOD FULLY

How is it possible to know God in *all* ways? It is, because when God gave the Torah, the whole world was filled with the Torah. Thus there is nothing which did not contain Torah.... Since the beginnings of Hasidism this doctrine has always been regarded as one of its basic principles.

Quoted in Gershom Scholem's Major Trends in Jewish Mysticism *(1933).*

GOOD IS BEST

I am afraid to be more clever than devout. I should rather be devout than clever. But rather than both devout and clever, I should like to be good.

□

Leo Pinsker

ELEMENTS OF JEWISH SURVIVAL

We do not count ourselves as a nation among the nations and we have no voice in the council of peoples even in affairs that concern ourselves. Our Fatherland is an alien country; our unity, dispersion; our solidarity, the general hostility to us; our weapon, humility; our defense, flight; our originality, adaptability; our future, tomorrow. What a contemptible role for a people that once had its Maccabees!

From an 1882 essay.

AN INCURABLE PSYCHOSIS

Judeophobia is a psychosis. As a psychosis it is hereditary and...incurable.

From his Auto-Emancipation *(1882).*

NO ROAD TOO LONG

To the millennial wanderer, no road, however far, need be too long.

Ibid.

CHOSEN TO BE HATED

The Jews are the chosen people of the world's hatred.

Ibid.

CALL FOR A CONGRESS

The national rebirth of the Jews must be launched through a congress of prominent Jews.

Ibid.

NEED FOR A JEWISH STATE

In order that we may not be compelled to wander from one exile to another, we must have a place of refuge, a rallying point, of our own.

Ibid.

GUESTS EVERYWHERE

The Jews have no fatherland of their own, though they have many motherlands.... They are everywhere guests, nowhere at home.

Ibid.

□

Robert Pinsky

INFLUENCE OF A JEWISH UPBRINGING

I'm not fluent in Italian, but I love lan-guages. This [translating Dante's *Inferno*] was like being a child with a new toy.... It's the only writing I have ever done where it's like reading yourself to sleep each night. We have pillowcases stained with ink where my wife took the pen out of my hand at night—you know, one more tercet, one more tercet.

On another level, I grew up with a kind of nominal Orthodox Jewish upbringing, and for such a person, with really quite secularized parents, the imagery and language and usage of the majority culture are going to be very powerful. In some very complicated way that I don't pretend to understand, this is an expression of that complex relationship of interest and desire and longing to appropriate these feelings toward that culture.

From a telephone interview with Lynn Karpen after the publication of Pinsky's Inferno of Dante: A New Verse Translation. *Reported in* The New York Times Book Review, *January 1, 1995.*

□

Otto Piper

UNBRIDGEABLE THEOLOGICAL GAP

If Jews were to recognize Jesus as their Messiah and Savior, they would no longer be Jews.

Explaining why Jews cannot accept Christianity. From his God in History *(1939), which explores the theological gap between the two religions.*

□

(Pope) Pius IV

BANISHMENT OF THE JEWS

We order that each and every Jew of both sexes in our temporal domain, and in all the cities, lands, places and baronies subject to them, shall depart completely out of the confines thereof within with the space of three months and after these letters have been made public.

A decree issued posthumously in 1565.

□

(Pope) Pius X

THE POPE TO HERZL

We cannot encourage this movement. We cannot prevent the Jews from going to Jerusalem, but we can never encourage them.... The Jews have not recognized our

Lord; therefore we cannot recognize the Jewish people.

At a 1904 meeting in which Herzl sought the pontiff's support of Zionism. Quoted in Herzl's Diaries.

STAY OUT OF PALESTINE

If you come to Palestine and settle your people there, we shall have churches and priests ready to baptize all of you.

Ibid.

□

(Pope) Pius XI

ANTI-SEMITISM IS NOT ADMISSIBLE

Christians cannot possibly have a hand in anti-Semitism. Anti-Semitism is not admissible. Spiritually, we are Semites.

After the 1929 agreement in which the king of Italy, represented by Mussolini, buried their differences, and Jews were assured that synagogues would not be shut down, as was feared. Quoted in Sam Waggenaar's Pope's Jews *(1974).*

ANTI-SEMITISM AND CHRISTIANITY

Through Christ and in Christ we are the spiritual descendants of Abraham. No, it is not possible for Christians to participate in anti-Semitism.

In a September 1938 address to Belgian pilgrims. Quoted in Time *magazine, November 14, 1938.*

□

Belva Plain

LIFE'S PATTERN

We can't always see the pattern [of life] when we are part of it.

From her Crescent City *(1984).*

□

W. Gunther Plaut

CANADIAN JEWRY AND ALIYAH

Except for the 20,000 to 30,000 North African Jews who cling to French as their mother tongue, Jews are part of the English cultural ambience.

They are deeply attached to Israel, to a degree that makes them fairly hawkish on questions of Israel policy. Yet this love of Israel has not produced a phenomenal outbreak of *aliyah* [immigration to Israel] fever. Canadian

Jews probably visit Israel in somewhat larger numbers (proportionally speaking) than American Jews, but they too don't stay to settle.

Rabbi Emeritus at Holy Blossom Temple in Toronto and past president of the Canadian Jewish Congress. In a December 1980 article on Canadian Jewry.

HOLOCAUST SURVIVORS AND CANADA

In many ways, the most distinctive feature of Canadian Jewry, one that dramatically distinguishes it from the American community, is the role here of Holocaust survivors. Canada was wide open after the end of the last war. While the United States still operated on an immigration law that dated from the 1920s, Canada welcomed tens of thousands of DPs into its land.

Ibid.

TEACHERS AND PARENTS

The classroom is the laboratory of the living room and the teacher the surrogate of the parents. When these roles are reversed, obscured or neglected, when the child becomes the authority and his pleasure the educational yardstick, the learning process is at best minimized, at the worst, thwarted.

From Jewish Information *magazine, Vol. 6, No. 1 (1966).*

FINDING ONE'S ROOTS

A Jew, by the very condition of his Jewishness, pays the continuing price of Sinai. If Jewishness remains his fate, Judaism remains the framework of his native spiritual existence and God his partner. And therefore, as long as the people as a continuing organism in history keep alive the consciousness of Sinai, each Jew can find his roots.

From his Torah: A Modern Commentary *(1981).*

ALONENESS: BURDEN OF THE JEW

The Jew will be what he was. For his anchorpoint is the awesome, hidden Other One who Himself dwells alone. Aloneness is the existential burden of the Jew. He is, as tradition and meaning convey, *kadosh*, holy and separate at once.

Ibid.

REAPPEARANCE OF AMALEK

The ancient Amalek has appeared and reappeared in Jewish history in many forms and guises: he wore the signet ring of the king as Haman; the royal crown as Antiochus; the general's uniform as Titus; the emperor's toga as Hadrian; the priestly robe as Torquemada; the cossack's boots as Chmielnitzki; or the brown shirt as Hitler. All of them had in common their hatred of Jews and Judaism, and they all failed in their objective to crush the faith and the people of God.

Ibid.

¤

Norman Podhoretz

BASEBALL AND POLITICS

Morally, baseball is what we all would love politics to be—a beautiful abstraction whose clarity is unspoiled by the contradictions that bog us down in life.

From his essay "Achilles in Left Field," a review of Bernard Malamud's The Natural, *which appeared in* Commentary *magazine, March 1953.*

THE GREATNESS OF JUDAISM

I tried to recommend Judaism for its special qualities, and my most powerful weapons were two major attitudes which I ascribed to it. The first was that Judaism entertained no dualism of body and soul—an effective argument, because for us dualism was the ubiquitous villain of Western civilization—and the second was that Judaism remained the only culture beside the Greek which believed in learning for its own sake and which honored the sage more than it did the plutocrat.

From his essay "Jewish Culture and the Intellectuals," which appeared in Commentary *magazine, May 1955.*

WEEPING WITH WOUK

If the Jewish personality can indeed only flourish by rooting itself in a parochial, insulated way of life, and if the suburbs of New York are to become another kind of ghetto to protect the Jew from the assaults of Greenwich Village, then Wouk has a right to his sadness—and then, too, the rest of us can begin weeping along with him.

From his review of Herman Wouk's Marjorie Morningstar, *which appeared in* Commentary *magazine, February 1956.*

A REALLY BIG IDEA

After four thousand years of existence, the Jews are indeed a very big idea in the history of the world, and no person born into this idea can dismiss it or refuse to acknowledge the

loyalties and responsibilities it imposes on him, without doing himself some violence.

From an essay in Commentary *magazine, April 1961.*

EICHMANN AND ARENDT

This habit of judging the Jews by one standard and everyone else by another is a habit Miss Arendt shares with many of her fellow-Jews, emphatically including those who think that the main defect of her version of the story is her failure to dwell on all the heroism and all the virtue that the six million displayed among them. But the truth is—must be—that the Jews under Hitler acted as men will act when they are set upon by murderers, no better and no worse.

Commenting on Arendt's five-part series Eichmann in Jerusalem, *which first appeared in* The New Yorker *(1962–63).*

PRICE OF SURVIVAL

In thinking about the Jews I have often wondered whether their survival as a distinct group was worth one single hair on the head of a single infant. Did the Jews have to survive so that six million innocent people should one day be burned in the ovens of Auschwitz?

From an essay in Commentary *magazine, February 1963.*

VIEW OF JEWISH LIFE

Looking back on the 1950s and the early 1960s we can now see that being absolved of the need to worry about and press for the Jewish interest—the need to face the world with the humiliating question, *Is it good for the Jews?* perpetually on one's nagging lips—was itself one of the more luxurious perquisites of what may some day come to be considered the Golden Age of Jewish security in America.

From a 1982 article in Commentary *magazine.*

REAGAN AT BITBURG

By proposing to lay a wreath at a military cemetery in which Nazi stormtroopers lie buried, Mr. Reagan is for all practical purposes treating Nazi Germany as though it had indeed been just one ordinary nation at war with other ordinary nations.

From one of his syndicated newspaper columns in which he maintained that Reagan's appearance at the military cemetery in Bitburg, Germany, undermined the very foundation on which Mr. Reagan's foreign policy stood and that this was "no casual or minor error on the President's part."

APPREHENSIONS ABOUT PEACE PROSPECTS

In Jeremiah's day the word of these prophets of peace, consoling and popular though it was, never did come to pass. Instead, just as he had foreseen, the kingdom of Judah was destroyed, the Temple sacked, and the people driven into exile. I will conclude this little jeremiad of my own by praying with all my heart and all my soul and all my might that my apprehensions about the negotiations now going on are ill founded, and that those who tell us that peace between Israel and its enemies is only a few territorial concessions away will turn out to be the true prophets and I the false.

Commenting on the Israel–PLO peace process. From an essay in Commentary *magazine, April 1993.*

ULTIMATE ARAB STRATEGY

Now they [the Syrians] are negotiating rather than threatening. I see this as only contributing to the ultimate strategy.

Assad realized that he could simultaneously get the Golan back and please the Americans by negotiating. Well, why shouldn't he negotiate? What does he have to lose? And the Palestinians finally got smart and realized that autonomy is not just the right to collect your own garbage, which they had been saying derisively, but was the first step on the road to statehood.

From an interview with Elli Wohlgelernter in The Jerusalem Post, *July 17, 1993.*

ISRAEL MUST HOLD TIGHT

My view is that Israel has to hold tight as Israel has been doing, and needs to summon the resources necessary.

Ibid.

PEACE MAY TRIGGER WAR

This is the first step toward the establishment of a Palestinian state, which I think will happen sooner rather than later. And far from being a cause of peace and stability, I think it will be the cause of another war.

Reacting to the proposed agreement between Israel and the Palestinians in September 1993. As reported in The New York Times, *September 3, 1993.*

❑

Letty Cottin Pogrebin

FROM GENERATION TO GENERATION

Lifestyles and sex roles are passed from parent to children as inexorably as blue eyes or small feet.

From an article in The First Ms. Reader *(1972), edited by Francine Klagsbrun.*

TWO BIG BATTLES

Jewish women have two battles to fight: against sexism and against anti-Jewish beliefs. Must we identify as Jews within feminism with as much discomfort as we identify as feminists within Judaism?

From an article entitled "Anti-Semitism in the Women's Movement," which appeared in Ms. *magazine, June 1982.*

BATTLE FOR WOMEN'S RIGHTS

Nearly 30 years ago the men in my congregation rejected me when a *minyan* (the quorum of 10 worshipers) was needed for services after my mother's death. I had been schooled at a yeshiva, made Bat Mitzvah and attended Sabbath services every week of my life. Nevertheless, strange men were called to make a *minyan*. A daughter's *kaddish* (prayer for the dead), a woman's *kaddish*, was as inconsequential as a cry in the wind.

From her article in the "Hers" column in The New York Times, *August 25, 1983.*

SUFFERING HOLOCAUST NIGHTMARES

Dreams are a real issue for me. Once or twice a year, every year, I have a Holocaust nightmare. I am neither a survivor nor the child of survivors; I have the pogroms to thank for driving my grandparents to these shores in time to avoid the Nazi scourge. Nevertheless, like others of my generation who were children during the Second World War, I am old enough to remember that I was young enough, lucky enough and American enough to escape. Maybe survivor guilt explains why I carry around memories of things that never happened to me and why they keep intruding in my life.

After viewing a screening of Steven Spielberg's film Schindler's List *in December 1993.*

ON RELIGIOUS HYPOCRISY

Most of us do not expect Jews to be holier than other peoples, but we do expect Jews who proclaim themselves holier than other Jews to fulfill that role and behave themselves.

From Moment *magazine, June 1993.*

I CHEATED MY CHILDREN

My children *felt* Jewish, but had little sense of being part of a historical constituency.... Like many of my anti-religion decisions, I have come to view this as a grievous error of judgment. Because I had a feminist axe to grind, I cheated my children out of a Jewish education and allowed them to reject a rite of tribal inclusion whose significance they were not equipped to evaluate.

From her Deborah, Golda, and Me *(1991).*

◘

Jonathan Pollard
THE ISRAELI HANDLER
I know I can help you.... You have no idea how much vital information the United States is denying Israel.

At his initial meeting with his first Israeli contact, Colonel Aviem Sella. On November 21, 1985, Pollard was arrested by the U.S. government and charged with conspiracy to commit espionage. He was sentenced to life imprisonment on March 4, 1987.

I'M YOUR SPY!
This is all a terrible mistake.... You can't betray an Israeli spy like this!

Screaming upon being ejected from Israel's embassy compound in Washington, DC, on November 21, 1985.

RATIONALIZATION
I watched the threats to Israel's existence grow and gradually came to the conclusion that I had to do something.... I never thought for a second that Israel's gain would necessarily result in America's loss.... How could it?

Explaining his motivation for spying.

GOD'S WILL
God put me in prison for a reason, and when the time is right I'll be released. It is a great *hesed* [act of God's mercy] to be in prison because I still have some cleansing to do. If people really want to help me, they should say Psalms for me.

Reported in 1993 by Rabbi Ezriel Tauber after visiting Pollard in prison.

THE FRUITS OF SPYING
The only thing I pray for is that the pronounced military advantage which Israel will now enjoy over her Arab and Soviet enemies lasts long beyond the point in time when my name is but a distant memory.

From a letter written to a supporter from jail. Quoted in Wolf Blitzer's Territory of Lies *(1995).*

◘

Molly Pollard
YOUNG POLLARD
Right before the Six-Day War...Jay was crying. He said, "They're going to kill Israel. I'll never get to see Israel...." The next day I told him that the Israel Air Force had knocked out the Arabs and the whole war was over. I can't tell you his reaction of unbelievable joy.

Remembering her son, Jonathan, at age twelve.

◘

Murray Polner
WE AREN'T ONE; WE ARE MANY AND DIVERSE
Sadly, most Establishment groups are exhausted and bereft of ideas, a coterie of paper organizations, with little or no rationale anymore....

We aren't "One" as that hackneyed slogan once went. We are instead many and diverse. Most of us are unaffiliated, secular and very much confidently acculturated Americans, thank you. To them—and me—the organizations have nothing to say; they missed the boat.

From an article in The Jewish Week, *October 8–14, 1993.*

A GOOD OLD TRADITION
The third and fourth generations of American Jews tend to associate their interpretation of Judaism with ethical and moral behavior arising from some sense of the prophetic tradition, of doing for others as well as themselves. That's an old Jewish tradition. And it's still a very good one.

From an article in The Jewish Week, *April 25–May 5, 1994.*

◘

David de Sola Pool
RENEWAL IN ZION
The harsh and cramping regulations imposed on Jews immured in medieval ghettos never succeeded in imprisoning the Jewish spirit. Remoteness in time from the Jewish commonwealth of old and distance from the Land of Israel did not blur the vision of the new Jerusalem and Zion rebuilt.

From his Why I Am a Jew *(1957).*

○

Alexander Pope

SHAKESPEARE'S JEW

This is the Jew
That Shakespeare drew.

By attribution. After witnessing a performance of Shylock *by Charles Macklin, February 14, 1741.*

○

Ruth W. Popkin

FOREST AS MEMORIAL

Why a forest? Because trees symbolize life and renewal. They beautify Israel. They create "blankets of green" on desert land. They anchor shifting sands, prevent erosion, allow for irrigation and, thus, enable the building of life in previously desolate wilderness.

In a 1993 joint statement with Leon Ilutovich, chairman of the Polish Jewry Memorial Forest.

○

Menachem Porush

THIS LAND, MY PEOPLE

God promised this land to the Jewish people. That is why, nine generations back, my family came here to Israel: because this land had been promised in the Bible to the Jewish people. Although there had been no Jewish people in Israel for about 2,000 years, we had been expecting all the time to come back to Israel.

From an interview in the spring of 1977. Quoted in Frank Epp's Israelis: Portrait of a People in Conflict *(1980).*

○

Chaim Potok

THE NEVER-ENDING NEED TO DREAM

Yes, most of the gentle Jews are gone.

Yes, the Jew is now solidly inside the affairs of the world.

Yes, we are aware of the resonance of hate that lingers like a stench upon Western civilization.

Yes, we will continue to be the other, to hold to our own view of things.

Yes, we are a single people, capable of loving our separate lands as well as Israel—as one is able to love a mother and a father.

Yes, there will be peace one day.

Yes, we will renew our people.

Yes, we touch millennia of precious history when we walk the streets of Jerusalem, and climb the hills, and journey through the sand wastes of the land.

Yes, there are flowers to plant, seedlings to nurture, young trees to tend, old earth to nourish, and new earth to put in—a garden of new dreams to bring forth, to add to old covenants and messianic hopes, and to offer to ourselves and to our broken and beloved world.

Yes.

From the conclusion of his Wanderings: History of the Jews *(1978).*

THE CHARISMATIC REBBE

He had a way of gesturing minimally that was electrifying. The slightest lift of a finger, the vaguest wave of the wrist. His was the mysterious ability to fill a room simply by being there.

Characterizing Menachem Mendel Schneerson, the charismatic Lubavitcher rebbe.

○

Henry Codman Potter

MAKE AMERICA YOUR ZION

I feel it will grieve you very much if I say that I am not a Zionist. If I understand the term, it means one who would go away and live alone with his own nation. We don't want you to do that. You are a very valuable part of our nation. Make America your Zion.

Expressing how welcome Jews are in America. Spoken in 1901 at a mass meeting of American Jews organized in behalf of the needs of Jews abroad.

○

Ezra Pound

RECOMMENDED READING

For God's sake, read the Protocols.

A supporter of Mussolini, he went to the U.S. in 1939 trying to persuade the administration not to go to war against the axis by blaming the Jews, as purported in the Protocols of Zion.

MY WORST MISTAKE

The worst mistake I made was that stupid, suburban prejudice of anti-Semitism.

In a conversation with Allen Ginsberg in June 1968. Quoted in Humphrey Carpenter's A Serious Character *(1988).*

Colin Powell

SHABBES GOY

On Friday nights I earned a quarter by turning the lights on and off at the Orthodox synagogue, so that the worshippers would observe the Sabbath ban on activity.

> *In describing his youthful years growing up in the Hunts Point section of the South Bronx, New York City. From his autobiography,* My American Journey *(1995).*

NEVER AGAIN

I understood the intensity of Barak's feelings. His nation had survived for the past forty years by taking no guff from its enemies. You could hear the echoes of "Never again" in everything Israeli leaders said.

> *Ibid. Recalling a "soldier to soldier" meeting during the 1991 Gulf War with the then-deputy chief of staff of the Israel Defense Force, Ehud Barak.*

SWAMP OF HATRED

African Americans have come too far and we have too far yet to go to take a detour into the swamp of hatred.

> *From his 1995 commencement address at Howard University, where speakers from the Nation of Islam had denounced Jews.*

TOO GOOD TO DENY

Word got out that I even conducted a private meeting with Prime Minister Yitzhak Shamir in Yiddish; not true, but too good to deny.

> *Writing about a 1990 trip to Israel at which he surprised Lieutenant General Dan Shomron and guests at a party with some Yiddish words.*

MAYBE A BISL

I really do not speak Yiddish. Ah—maybe a *bisl*.

> *From a 1991 speech to AIPAC, the pro-Israel lobby.*

Ferdinand Praeger

WAGNER AND THE JEWS

It [the article] opened with an assertion that one has an involuntary and inexplicable revulsion of feeling towards the Jews; that, as a people, there is something objectionable in them, their person repellent, and manner obnoxious. Now, when it is remembered that Wagner's daily visitor during his first sojourn in Paris was Dessauer, a Jew, and that the man who brought about his own death for love of Wagner was a Jew, and that the music-publisher Schlesinger, his friend, was also a Jew, it will be confessed that this was a startling charge to come from him.

> *Recalling a notorious article, "Judaism in Music," written by Richard Wagner in 1852 in* Die Neue Zeitschrift, *wherein the German composer reveals his antipathy toward Jews by expressing intense dislike of them while accepting favors and friendship from them. From Praeger's* Wagner as I Knew Him.

Dennis Prager

THE JEW AND THE CANARY

The Jews are the world's miners' canary. Canaries are taken down to mines because they quickly die upon exposure to noxious fumes. When the miner sees the canary dead, he knows there are noxious fumes to be fought. So it is with the Jews. Noxious moral forces often focus first on the Jews. But their ultimate targets are the moral values that the Jews represent.

> *From an article entitled "What Bitburg Revealed About the Jews," which appeared in* Ultimate Issues, *Summer 1995.*

THREAT TO ALL MEN OF VALUES

Most Americans, Jews included, regard Jesse Jackson's hostility to the Jews as an unfortunate problem—for Jews. This perception is very wrong. Jesse Jackson is a threat to far more than Jews because to the anti-Semite, the Jews are the embodiment of fundamental moral values of the Western world. It is those values, and ultimately all those who hold those values, that anti-Semites seek to destroy. The Jews are only their first target.

> *Ibid., Winter 1985.*

IS THIS LIFE ALL THERE IS?

If there is nothing after this life, then the Nazis and the Jewish children they threw alive into Auschwitz furnaces have identical fates. If I believed such a thing, I would either become an atheist or hate a God who had created such a cruelly absurd universe.

> *Ibid., Spring 1987.*

SEX IN MARRIAGE ONLY

When Judaism demanded that all sexual activity be channeled into marriage, it changed the world.

> *Ibid., April–June 1990.*

DEFINING AN ISRAEL-HATER

When a person begins talking about the unfairness of Israel's creation, know that you are listening to an Israel-hater. Almost every country on earth was born in bloodshed, yet this person challenges only one's legitimacy—that of the one Jewish state.

Ibid., October–December 1990.

WANTING TO SURVIVE

Because there are a billion Christians in the world and because America is largely Christian, Christians do not perceive intermarriage as a threat to the survival of their faith. For Jews outside of Israel, however, intermarriage is usually a death knell. The children of these marriages are overwhelmingly likely not to identify as Jews. Jews want Judaism to survive.

Answering an accusation that Judaism encourages racism. From Moment *magazine, June 1993.*

MORAL VALUES VS. ECONOMICS

Moral values, not economics, determine people's moral behavior. So long as Jews hold the Left view of evil—that it is caused by the absence of enough money—and deny the Jewish view—that evil is caused by the absence of good values—their religion will remain liberalism, not Judaism.

From an article in Moment *magazine, February 1994.*

JEWS AND LIBERALISM

Given Judaism's instrumental role in Jewish survival, why do so few American Jews take Judaism seriously? The major reason is because they already have a deep and passionate commitment to another religion—liberalism.

Ibid.

DIVINE MISSION

The primary reason I am a committed Jew is that I believe Jews have a divine mission to the rest of humanity. It is nothing less than a tragedy that few Jews feel Judaism has anything to say to the world. It is terrible for the world and for the Jews.

Ibid., June 1994.

JEWISH SPOKESPEOPLE

The Jews who speak to the world are the least committed to Judaism, and the Jews who are most committed to Judaism speak the least to the world.

Ibid.

ETHICAL MONOTHEISM

Judaism's greatest and most revolutionary teaching is that because there is one God for humanity, there is one moral law. We and the stranger are accountable to the same God and to the same morality. We do not need to share one culture or even one religion, just one moral standard.

Ibid.

PREPARING FOR A FULL LIFE

In order for a caterpillar to become a beautiful butterfly taking its beauty out into the world, it must first spend time in a cocoon. In order for a Jew to become a beautiful Jew taking his or her beauty into the world, he or she too must first spend time in a cocoon. Unfortunately, most non-Orthodox Jews don't believe in the cocoon, and most Orthodox Jews don't believe in flying into the world.

Quoted in Joseph Telushkin's Jewish Wisdom *(1994).*

ON ETHICAL MONOTHEISM

If Jews do not teach the world ethical monotheism, they will be victims of a world they didn't influence.

Ibid.

CONFRONTING CHANGE

I believe deeply in *zachor* [remembering], but not if it paralyzes me from acknowledging present reality.... [Just as] most blacks are not willing to confront the fact that most whites have changed, most Jews are not willing to accept that most Christians have changed. They are still voting against the right, associating resurgent Christianity with pogroms, crusades and inquisitions.

Quoted in The Jewish Week, *November 25–December 1, 1994.*

RELIGIOSITY OF JEWS

Jews are the least religious people in United States by every poll that's been taken. They have a religion—it's called liberalism. I place the blame for that 50 percent on religious Jews and 50 percent on others. Jews have made Judaism unappealing to too many Jews.

Ibid.

JEWISH AUTHENTICITY

There is no authentic [Jewish] denomination; there are only authentic Jews.

By attribution.

Gabriel Preil

DECLINE OF HEBREW WRITERS

There is very little secular Hebrew education provided here [in the United States].... The Hebrew education that does exist involves Bible and prayer but hardly any modern literature. It's not a question of blame, though, but simply a recognition of the realities of the situation. The dominant culture is very strong in the United States, in contrast to Lithuania, for instance, so that it is difficult for a small culture to survive.

From a 1982 interview.

William H. Prescott

ACT OF SELF-DEVOTION

There were found but very few, when the day of departure [from Spain] arrived, who were not prepared to abandon their country rather than their religion. This extraordinary act of self-devotion by a whole people for conscience' sake may be thought, in the nineteenth century, to merit other epithets than those of "perfidy, incredulity, and stiff-necked obstinacy," with which the worthy Curate of Los Palacios, in the charitable feeling of that day, has seen fit to stigmatize it.

From his Ferdinand and Isabella *(1837).*

Sally Priesand

FIRST FEMALE AMERICAN RABBI

For thousands of years women in Judaism had been second-class citizens. They were not permitted to own property. They could not serve as witnesses. They did not have the right to initiate divorce proceedings. They were not counted in the *minyan*. Even in Reform Judaism, they were not permitted to participate fully in the life of the synagogue. With my ordination all that was going to change; one more barrier was about to be broken.... I decided to do this so that I would be the first woman rabbi to carry a torch for the feminist movement.

Statement made after her ordination as a rabbi on June 3, 1972.

EVOLVING CONCEPT OF GOD

In rabbinical school I always believed in an all-powerful God, but when you start dealing with real people who suffer, that's not the kind of God you can believe in. I've started to believe in a God who is not all-powerful but loving, who is with us, helping us to cope, somethimes disappointed in us, not able to prevent tragedies from happening to us—a God who weeps with us.

From an interview with Judy Petsonik in Hadassah Magazine, *June–July 1993.*

ON ENGAGING A WOMAN RABBI

We tread on dangerous ground when we separate the contributions that women can make from those that men can make.... When congregations hire women rabbis, they ought to be asking, "What does she as an individual have to offer?" rather than, "What does she, as a woman, have to offer?"

From her Judaism and the New Woman *(1975).*

Joseph Priestly

FEW NOMINAL JEWS

Nominal Christians are numerous, but merely nominal Jews, though there are some, are comparatively very few.

From his Discourse on the Evidence of Revealed Religion *(1794).*

PAST AND FUTURE

Who would not be proud of so illustrious a descent and so glorious a destination as they [the Jews] alone can boast of?

Ibid.

Joachim Prinz

RELIGIOUS INTOLERANCE IN ISRAEL

When I converted David Ben Gurion's daughter-in-law to Judaism in the City of London in 1946, the conversion was not recognized by the Chief Rabbis of Israel, and she had to be reconverted. Yet I am a fully ordained "rabbi in Israel." When my granddaughter, who lives in a kibbutz in Israel, was to be married in that kibbutz, I was not permitted to perform the ceremony. The treatment of non-Orthodox Judaism in Israel is an issue which should, properly, be the subject of world-wide Jewish dissent.

From an article in Moment *magazine, December 1976.*

WAR WON'T SOLVE PROBLEMS

Some time ago, in a letter to *The New York Times,* I expressed the view that war can never solve the problems of the Middle East. And I added that while it would be a catastrophe for Israel were it to lose a war, it would be even more tragic an aggravation were it to win, for that would render a solution to the Arab-Israel dispute impossible. Needless to say, my statement was resented both by Israel and by Israel's friends.

Ibid.

JEWS ON A MISSION

Jews have no right to be normal. We live under laws and tenets which emphasize our chosenness as a people of particularly stringent adherence to Jewish ethics. This refers, among other things, to human attitudes towards neighbors and fellow citizens regardless of creed, color and national origin. Israel does not always adhere to these Jewish restrictions. She claims that political considerations supersede Jewish convictions. If that be so, our interest in the Jewish State of Israel must be redefined and even reconsidered.

Ibid.

¤

Nicholas J. Pritzker

THE WAY TO WEALTH

Never sell your land—lease it.

Advice to his sons by the founding father of the richest Jewish family in America. Pritzker came to Chicago from Kiev in 1880.

¤

Joseph Pulitzer

COURAGE TO FACE INJUSTICE

Always fight for progress and reform, never tolerate injustice or corruption, always fight demagogues of all parties, never belong to any party, always oppose privileged classes and public plunderers, never lack sympathy with the poor, always remain devoted to the public welfare.

Upon his retirement as editor of the St. Louis Post-Dispatch, October 16, 1890.

UNDERSTATED REPORTS

I came here in a suspicious frame of mind, feeling that I would find that many of the terrible reports were exaggerations and propaganda. They have been understatements.

Commented in May 1945 after touring concentration camps together with other journalists.

William Quandt

BRIDGING THE GAP

The only way to bridge the gap between the Israeli and Palestinian positions will be with creative political ideas for which no clear precedents exist....Ideas of shared authority, overlapping sovereignty, and mixed regimes will be needed.

In a study of how the Camp David "territories for peace" stipulation can be fulfilled.

Rabba bar bar Chana

MARRIAGE BROKERING

To effect a union between man and woman is as difficult a task as parting the Red Sea.

Quoting Rabbi Yochanan. From the talmudic tractate Sanhedrin (22a).

¤

Rabba ben Avuha

HUMANE EXECUTIONS

Choose an easy death for him who must be executed.

From the talmudic tractate Sanhedrin (52a).

¤

Rabba ben Chinena

ON SHOWING REMORSE

If one commits a sin and is ashamed of it, all his sins are forgiven.

Indicating that being conscience-stricken is the beginning of rehabilitation. Quoted in the talmudic tractate Berachot (12b).

¤

Rabba ben Joseph

THANKING THE WRONG PARTY

Though the wine belongs to the owner, the thanks are given to the butler.

A popular saying quoted by him in the talmudic tractate Bava Kamma (92b).

THINKING OF OTHERS

Into the well from which you drank water do not throw clods.

Ibid.

MARCH OF TIME

When we were young, we were treated as men [and told not to act like children]; now that we have grown old we are looked upon as babies [unable to take care of ourselves without help].

Ibid.

HOW TO BE ENRICHED

Honor your wives that you may be enriched.

Quoted in the talmudic tractate Bava Metzia (59a).

NO NEED FOR RETRIBUTION

This one [the defendant] derived a benefit, but this one [the plaintiff] suffered no loss.

Quoted in the talmudic tractate Bava Kamma (20b).

PRAYER FOR MODESTY

Three requests have I made from Heaven. Two were fulfilled and the third evaded me. I prayed for [Rabbi] Huna's learning and [Rabbi] Chisda's wealth, and I was granted both. But Rabba bar Huna's modest disposition was not granted me.

Quoted in the talmudic tractate Moed Katan (28a).

DESTINY RULES LIFE

Length of life, children, and sustenance depend not on merit but rather on *mazal* [luck].

Ibid.

ON TAKING THE FIFTH

Every man is considered a relative to himself, and no one can incriminate himself.

A talmudic version of the constitutional right against forcing a person to testify against himself. Quoted in the talmudic tractate Sanhedrin (9b).

EDGE OF RESPONSIBILITY

A man is not held responsible for what he says when he is under duress.

From the talmudic tractate Bava Batra (16b).

A DUTY TO GET DRUNK

On Purim it is man's duty to inebriate himself to the point that he is unable to distinguish between the phrases "cursed be Haman" and "blessed be Mordecai."

Quoted in the talmudic tractate Megilla (7b).

◻

Isidor Isaac Rabi

TESTING THE BOMB

The atomic age came at about five-thirty in the morning of July 16, 1945. It was a sight which I have attempted from time to time to describe. I never felt successful in doing it. One has to go back to the Bible, to witnesses of the ancient miracles, to get some impression of the tremendous emotional experience it produced.

> *A statement made after the first atomic bomb was dropped in the New Mexico desert.*

STUDYING MANKIND

The proper study of mankind is science, which also means that the proper study of mankind is man.

> *From an interview with Jeremy Bernstein in* The New Yorker, *October 20, 1975.*

THE SCIENCE GAME

Science is a great game. It is inspiring and refreshing. The playing field is the universe itself.

> *From a* New York Times *profile, October 28, 1965.*

JEWISH AND AMERICAN

I turned away from the old world. I realized I had to be an American, not a Jewish American.

> *Reflecting upon his school years among a predominately non-Jewish student body. Quoted in Elinor and Robert Slater's* Great Jewish Men *(1996).*

◻

Leah Rabin

THE SILENCE IS BROKEN

The silent majority will be silent no more.

> *Wife of Prime Minister Yitzak Rabin before more than a quarter of a million Israelis gathered to memorialize the slain leader one week after his murder on November 4, 1995.*

BITTER LAMENT

I would prefer my children be Arabs rather than Orthodox Jews.

> *Following the assassination of her husband by an Orthodox student. Quoted in the Hebrew-language publication* Panim Chadashot, *November 10, 1995.*

◻

Yitzhak Rabin

THE BASIS OF REAL PEACE

The very same developments which led up to the Six-Day War can repeat themselves at any time, at any moment, as long as the policy of the Arab States remains belligerency, and as long as they remain unreconciled to the fact of Israel's existence, as long as their declared aim will be the destruction of Israel.

Any real and sincere effort to prevent war in the Middle East must first of all address itself to this problem. Israel seeks peace, with all her heart, but the basic condition for a real peace is mutual recognition and a common understanding. These are the guiding lines of Israel's actions and policy.

> *From his address at the Ninth Annual Policy Conference of the American Israel Public Affairs Committee on March 11, 1968.*

THE CALCULATED RISK

Once the Jewish people decided that here in the Land of Israel we have to establish a Jewish state, we decided also who will be our neighbors—the Arab countries, the Muslim world, hundreds of millions.

And there are two ways to deal with this reality: a prolonged war of violence and terror, or to live in peace. There is no third choice. In wars we took the risks. I believe that for peace, we should take calculated risks.

> *From a statement made in Jerusalem on September 11, 1993 before leaving for the United States to attend the September 13th signing of the peace accord with the Palestine Liberation Organization.*

NO MORE PRETENSES

The Palestinian delegation to the Middle East peace talks had proved ineffectual, and since it took direction from the leadership in Tunis, why not drop the pretense and deal with the puppeteer? You make peace with enemies, not friends.

> *Ibid.*

GIVING PEACE A CHANCE

I'm an old guy. I served 27 years in the military. My son served. Now my grandson serves. Let's give a hope that at least my grandson will not need to fight. If there will be a need, I'm sure that a fourth generation also will do it. But I feel a responsibility to give a chance that it will not happen.

> *Ibid.*

HOPE MIXED WITH APPREHENSION

This signing of the Israeli-Palestinian declaration of principle here today—it's not so easy—neither for myself as a soldier in Israel's wars nor for the people of Israel, nor to the Jewish people in the diaspora, who are watching us now with great hope mixed with apprehension. It is certainly not easy for the families of the victims of the war's violence, terror, whose pain will never heal.... For them this ceremony has come too late.

From a speech delivered on the South Lawn of the White House on Monday, September 13, 1993, just before the peace accord between Israel and the Palestine Liberation Organization was signed.

OPENING A NEW CHAPTER

We wish to open a new chapter in the sad book of our lives together—a chapter of mutual recognition, of good neighborliness, of mutual respect, of understanding.

Ibid.

ENOUGH OF BLOOD AND TEARS

Let me say to you, the Palestinians, we are destined to live together on the same soil in the same land. We, the soldiers who have returned from battles stained with blood; we who have seen our relatives and friends killed before our eyes; we who have attended their funerals and cannot look in the eyes of their parents; we who have come from a land where parents bury their children; we who have fought against you, the Palestinians—we say to you today, in a loud and a clear voice: enough of blood and tears. Enough.

We have no desire for revenge. We harbor no hatred towards you. We, like you, are people—people who want to build a home. To plant a tree. To love. To live side by side with you. In dignity. In empathy. As human beings. As free men. We are today giving peace a chance.

Ibid.

WOUNDED VICTORS

We did not rejoice in battle. We wanted nothing to do with war. It was forced upon us by countries and by organizations that wanted—and some of which still want—to destroy us. We ended every war as victors. We came out of every war wounded. The scars of wars stay with us.

From a November 18, 1993 speech delivered in Montreal, Canada, before the Council of Jewish Federations.

UNANSWERED INVITATION

Syria refuses to hold any kind of secret negotiations. I invited him [Assad] a few times to come to Jerusalem, but he refuses to come and refuses to have me there.

In an interview with the Spanish newspaper El Pais, *November 1993.*

ON KISSINGER

I distinguish between the way that [Henry] Kissinger thinks and operates on the basic issues—which I appreciated, even though I didn't agree all the time—and his personal behaviour, sensitivity, reactions, and gossip, which I believe have harmed his dealings. Thus, Kissinger the thinker, the operator, the statesman, the diplomat, the strategist, I appreciate very much. I'm sorry that Kissinger's personal attitudes and behaviour have not matched his professional qualities.

A comment made in an interview with Robert Slater on November 18, 1976. Quoted in Slater's Rabin of Israel.

ISLAMIC FUNDAMENTALISM

We are not sure that President-elect [Bill] Clinton and his team fully comprehend the danger from Islamic fundamentalism and the critical role of Israel in fighting it. The Arab world, and the world in general, will pay if the cancer of radical-fundamentalist Iran is not halted.

At a fall 1992 meeting with leading American Jews.

FATE OF THE JEWS

It is the fate of the Jews to be slaughtered by our hands.... Torture is the fate of the Jews.... No Jew is innocent; all Jews must be killed; Israel will exist until it is destroyed by Islam.

Statement from the "Covenant" of the Islamic Resistance Movement, compiled by Rabin in 1992.

TERRITORY FOR PEACE

If and when negotiations with Syria reach the point where we can weigh the price to pay for peace against the nature of that peace, we shall have to make a decision. But we shall not divest ourselves of everything and leave ourselves naked. We shall not conclude a peace at any price and on any conditions.

Speaking in June 1993 on the status of the Golan Heights in the framework of establishing peace with Syria.

AN EMBARRASSMENT TO JUDAISM

I am shamed over the disgrace imposed upon us by a degenerate murderer. You are not part of the community of Israel. You are not part of the national democratic camp which we all belong to in this house, and many of the people despise you. You are not partners in the Zionist enterprise. You are a foreign implant. You are an errant weed. Sensible Judaism spits you out. You placed yourself outside the wall of Jewish law.

You are a shame on Zionism and an embarrassment to Judaism.

Addressing the most militant settlers on the West Bank following the slaughter of at least forty Arabs while engaged in prayer at a mosque in Hebron on Friday, February 25, 1994. The perpetrator was an American medical doctor, Baruch Goldstein, who had settled in a West Bank community.

TIP OF THE ICEBERG

We witnessed, you witnessed, the world witnessed the tip of the iceberg of problems that we shall have to overcome in the implementation of even the first phase of the Declaration of Principles, to overcome 100 years of animosity, suspicion, bloodshed. It is not so simple.... We are heading down the new road with great hope. It's a daring road. We have hope, but we have much trepidation, that the two peoples could live on the same tiny patch of land, each under their own fig tree, as the prophets said.

An excerpt from a speech delivered in Cairo on May 4, 1994, at the signing of an accord between Israel and the Palestine Liberation Organization, giving the latter self-rule in the Gaza Strip and Jericho.

LET US BURY THE PAST

I turn to the people, the Palestinian people, our neighbors. A hundred years of animosity has created hatred between us. We have killed you, and you have killed us. Thousands of our graves, thousands of your graves are the painful signposts in your history and in our history. Today, you and we stretch out our hands to each other. We begin a new count. The people of Israel hope that you will not disappoint us.

Ibid.

GREAT FRIEND OF ISRAEL

Israel has lost one of its greatest friends. From our point of view, his supreme test came at a time of tribulation, and he proved himself with honor. During the Yom Kippur War in 1973, Richard Nixon was the driving force in mobilizing the airlift to assist us with weaponry at the most difficult of moments. His contribution to reinforcing the security of the State of Israel merits the highest appreciation.

Upon learning of the death of Richard Nixon on April 22, 1994.

SEEING THE LIGHT

It is dusk at our homes in the Middle East. Soon darkness will prevail. But the citizens of Israel and Jordan will see a great light.

A statement of the Israeli prime minister on July 25, 1994, just before he and King Hussein of Jordan picked up their pens to sign a declaration ending the state of war that existed between Israel and Jordan for 46 years.

AND NOW...THE BATTLE FOR PEACE

If my people did not desire peace so strongly, I would not be standing here today.... I, who sent regiments into the fire and soldiers to their deaths, I say to you, Your Majesty, the King of Jordan, and I say to you, American friends, today we are embarking on a battle which has no blood and no anguish. This is the only battle which is a pleasure to wage: the battle for peace.

From an address on July 26, 1994 before a joint session of Congress which honored the prime minister of Israel and King Hussein of Jordan for concluding an agreement to end the state of war between the two nations.

WE CANNOT WAIT

Friends say to us, "The pace of events is too fast, we cannot keep up. Wait a minute."

Your Royal Highness, our friends in the Hashemite Kingdom of Jordan, we have waited 46 years. We have gone through war, pain and suffering. To prevent further loss and so on, we cannot wait even one more day.

Remarks made on August 9, 1994, when the Israeli leader visited the King of Jordan at his seaside summer palace in Akaba and opened a border crossing between Jordan and Israel.

ALL WINNERS

No one lost, no one won, we all won.

To Jordan's King Hussein on October 17, 1994, after initialing an agreement to sign a peace treaty between Israel and Jordan.

THERE COMES A TIME

There comes a time when there is a need to be strong and to make courageous decisions to overcome the minefields, the drought, the barrenness between our two peoples. We have known many days of sorrow. You [King Hussein] have known many days of grief. But bereavement unites us, as does bravery. And we honor those who sacrificed their lives. We both must draw on the springs of our great spiritual resources to forgive the anguish we caused to each other, to clear the minefields that divided us for so many years and to supplant it with fields of plenty.

An excerpt from remarks made on October 26, 1994, at the signing of the Israel-Jordan peace accord at the Arava Crossing, Israel.

FROM HEART TO HEART

For nearly two generations, desolation pervaded the heart of our two peoples. The time has now come not merely to dream of a better future, but to realize it.... I don't believe that we would have reached this great moment without the desire for peace in the hearts of both peoples, in the hearts of the soldiers and the intellectuals, in the hearts of the farmers and of the lorry drivers who drive to the Arabat highways in Jordan and Israel, in the hearts of teachers and of the little children. Both nations were determined that the great revolution in the Middle East would take place in their generation.

Ibid.

UNITING FOR PEACE

I want to say to you, Chairman Arafat, the leader of the Palestinians, together we should not let the land that flows with milk and honey become a land flowing with blood and tears. Don't let it happen. If all the partners to the peacemaking do not unite against the evil angels of death by terrorism, all that will remain of this ceremony are color snapshots, empty mementos.

At the signing of the peace accord between Israel and the PLO on Thursday, September 28, 1995, at the White House.

RIGHTS FOR ALL

For me what is most important is to have a Jewish state in which at least 80% of its population is Jewish. [But] the non-Jewish citizens—the Palestinians, Muslims, Christians—should entertain all a person's civilian political rights, because I believe that racism and Judaism by essence are in contradiction. The Palestinians in their schools, government-paid schools, are entitled—be they Muslims or Christians—to have their religion, to have their culture, their language, their heritage. I

believe that they can be loyal Israeli citizens while maintaining their special identity.

While visiting New York City in 1995 to celebrate the fiftieth anniversary of the United Nations. From an interview with the editors of Time *magazine.*

HOPING FOR RECONCILIATION

We all love the same children, weep the same tears, hate the same enmity, and pray for reconciliation. Peace has no borders.

Ibid.

DOOMSDAY

This is the greatest day of my life.

Complimenting the former mayor of Tel Aviv for organizing a successful peace rally. Spoken while leaving the stage, moments before being hit by an assassin's bullet on November 4, 1995.

IT HURTS

It hurts, but it's not so bad.

Spoken while being driven by his chauffeur to the hospital where he died. Among his last words.

¤

Louis Rabinowitz

THE BETTER MAN

I always knew the better man would lose.

From a message of congratulations to Rabbi Immanuel Jakobovits after Rabinowitz was defeated by Jakobovits on September 11, 1965 as Chief Rabbi of Britain.

¤

Stanley Rabinowitz

THE STUMBLING-BLOCK PRINCIPLE

Caveat emptor...let the buyer beware...has never been a tenet of Judaism; Judaism operates on the principle: Let the seller beware. The seller must protect the innocent buyer who may be blinded by the stumbling block of ignorance and need.

From his sermon in Best Jewish Sermons of 5727 (1968), *edited by Saul I. Teplitz.*

AROUSING FALSE HOPES

We are mindful that our country is the only great power that can speak to both sides of the [Palestinian-Israeli] dispute, and we are therefore heartened by the broad definition you have given to the concept of peace, but we are somewhat bewildered about the meaning of what was called "The Palestine Question." In your address at Clinton, Massachusetts, you used the phrase "Palestine Homeland" while Vice President Mondale referred to a "Palestinian entity." If these phrases imply the possibility of a Palestine state, then our country may be arousing Arab hopes beyond our capacity to deliver. As far as we are concerned, a Palestinian state already exists in Jordan, where more than half of the people are Palestinians. Do you not fear lest a separate Palestine state introduce a radical and extremist component into the area which will surely abort the peace which you seek?

Addressed to U.S. President Jimmy Carter on July 6, 1977 at a White House meeting of Jewish religious leaders and high governmental officials.

□

Emanuel Rackman

THE HIGH ROAD

Nothing gives my life character, my thought significance, and my activity zest as much as my Jewish loyalty. As one great thinker put it: "I love being Jewish because it is the least difficult way I know of being human."

From his sermon in Best Jewish Sermons of 5713 (1953), *edited by Saul I. Teplitz.*

ON ISRAEL'S CONTINUED EXISTENCE

There is a dimension in Jewish history which even Abba Eban—a secularist—describes as mystical. The laws of universal history simply do not apply to the Jews. And for that reason the optimists can reassure us. Israel exists not because humanity ever wanted her—rather despite the express wishes of the major world powers.

From his column in The Jewish Week, *October 19, 1980.*

FREUD AND HIS JEWISHNESS

The great Sigmund Freud broke with his faith and, for a while, with his people. He wrote books not only denigrating the religious life but books that made Jews lose their pride in their Jewishness, their pride in Moses, their pride in the Jewish contribution to civilization. Freud so broke with his tradition that he insisted his sweetheart—a pious, devout, observant Jew—should prove her love of him by writing him a letter on the Sabbath day.

From his column in The Jewish Week, *November 8–14, 1991.*

MAKING HEROES OF THE MISGUIDED

That President De Klerk of South Africa will receive the [Nobel] prize makes me very happy—he truly deserves it. That his adversary Nelson Mandela will get it sickens me just as I would be sick if Arafat got it. Imagine, Elie Wiesel, Mandela and Arafat laureates of the same award!

From his column in The Jewish Week, *December 3–9, 1993.*

THE PEACE PROCESS MIRAGE

I believe that I speak for many in Israel and abroad that the haste in which everything was done may make a mirage of the entire peace process. There ought be a slowdown as soon as possible. Sure, that slowdown may give the opposition a chance to derail the whole. But the speed with which all is being done may not only derail but also create irreversible tragic conditions approaching anarchy and virtual lawlessness.

Commenting on the Israel–PLO peace accord signed in Washington, DC, on September 13, 1993. From his column in The Jewish Week, *December 3–9, 1993.*

REACHING OUT

Undoubtedly many authorities discouraged the study of anything but Torah. Others were permissive, especially if the purpose was to engage in dialogue with a heretic. Today we do not deem the non-Orthodox and the secularists as heretics. Even the Orthodox must love them as Jews who share the same fate, if not the same faith. To help them back one must understand them.

In an April 1988 article in L'eylah *magazine.*

RIGHT TO OPPOSE AN IMMORAL ORDER

It is the position of our legal system—and this position has support in our Halachic tradition—that one must not obey the orders of a superior when one deems that order immoral. On that theory we prosecuted war criminals. On that theory Israel executed Eichmann. On that theory we expressed our indignation about several massacres in Vietnam....

Does this then mean that any citizen can deny obedience to laws approved by a majority or to officials who are empowered by a majority to give orders? Yes, but not without punishment.

From his column in The Jewish Week– American Examiner, *February 27, 1977.*

TRUTH IS GOD'S NAME

Truth for me is God's name. His total being. It must address itself to my total being. Much I may never be able to explain, but the explanation exists. It exists in God. And to His will I deliver myself—or at least aspire to deliver myself.

From an essay in Condition of Jewish Belief *(1966), compiled by the editors of* Commentary *magazine.*

CERTAINTY AND FANATICISM

Judaism encourages doubt even as it enjoins faith and commitment. A Jew dare not live with absolute certainty, because certainty is the hallmark of the fanatic and Judaism abhors fanaticism, [and] because doubt is good for the human soul.... One apparent reason [why God denies us certainty] is that man's certainty with regard to anything is poison to his soul. Who knows this better than moderns who have had to cope with dogmatic Fascists, Communists, and even scientists?

Ibid.

PLEASE SLOW IT DOWN

In my career I was known as one who made decisions—often hasty ones. But never when life and death hung in the balance. I beg of Prime Minister Rabin: Please, slow it down!

Commenting on the peace process between Israel and the Palestine Liberation Organization started on September 13, 1993. From his column in The Jewish Week, *February 18–24, 1994.*

ACCEPTING "FAST BLEACH" JEWS

When Marilyn Monroe embraced the Jewish faith some years ago in order to marry the famous playwright Arthur Miller, a number of Jewish and Protestant clergy were meeting in Switzerland to discuss interreligious amity and understanding. The conversion was accomplished within a day and the marriage took place.

The reaction of one Protestant theologian was memorable. He said very thoughtfully, "We Protestants will not mourn the loss of one of us—if she had, in fact, been a Christian. But what we cannot understand is how Jews can be so accepting of a *Schnellbleich* [a fast bleach]." I use the German phrase he used because it is so appropriate. Overnight Marilyn was made a Jew! Like the "bleaching" of laundry in a washing machine.

From his article in The Jewish Week, *December 31, 1993–January 6, 1994.*

LETTER TO A SON

The sum-total of all that I have written is that I want you to perform the *mitzvah* [commandment] of *kiddush ha-Shem*—sanctifying God's name in everything that you do. The essence of that *mitzvah* is not martyrdom, although it sometimes calls for that. However, our sages define it differently. "So act," they enjoin us, "that all who behold you will say: 'Blessed is that man's God.'"

It is thus that I pray you will act. And you and we shall rejoice.

From a letter to his son upon his leaving for college. Quoted in This I Believe: Documents of American Jewish Life *(1990), edited by Jacob R. Marcus.*

TRUE LIBERALS

...true liberals should seek to protect the rights of majorities as well as minorities when freedom of expression is involved.

Quoted in his Foreword to Merrill Simon's Jerry Falwell and the Jews *(1984).*

□

Asad Abdel Rahman

NEW ORDER OF MIDDLE EAST ECONOMICS

Even if we would like to, we cannot separate anymore the economies of the area. Whether I love or hate the concept of a [new] Middle Eastern order, we are going to have it that way.

Commenting on the impact of the signing of the peace accord between Israel and the Palestinians on September 13, 1993.

□

Abraham Raisen

A JEWISH HEARTH EVERYWHERE

We have sat by every river,
Not only of Babylon,...
So that now we love
Every inch of earth.
In each far-flung region
There is a Jewish hearth.

From his poem "The Jewish Song." Quoted in Joseph Leftwich's Golden Peacock *(1939).*

□

Yossel Rakover

GOD, I WILL ALWAYS LOVE YOU

My rabbi would frequently tell the story of a Jew who fled from the Spanish Inquisition with his wife and child, striking out in a small boat over the stormy sea until he reached a rocky island. A flash of lightning killed his wife; a storm rose and hurled his son into the sea; then, as lonely as a stone, naked, barefoot, lashed by the storm, terrified by the thunder and lightning, hands turned up to God, the Jew, again setting out on his journey through the wastes of the rocky island, turned to God with the following words: "God of Israel, I have fled to this place in order to worship You without molestation, to obey Your commandments, and to sanctify Your name. You, however, have done everything to make me stop believing in You. Now, lest it seem to You that You will succeed by these tribulations in driving me from the right path, I notify You, my God and the God of my fathers, that it will not avail You in the least. You may insult me, You may castigate me, You may take from me all that I cherish and hold dear in the world, You may torture me to death; but I will always love You, and these are my last words to You, my wrathful God: Nothing will avail You in the least."

Discovered in a small bottle after World War II in the rubble of the Warsaw Ghetto ruins, this is a portion of a testament written on April 28, 1943, hours before the ghetto was finally taken by the Nazis. The story is recorded in Zvi Kolitz's Tiger Beneath the Skin.

◻

Charles Rangel

CHASIDIM IN CITY POLITICS

If the chasidim [*sic*] community is constantly reacting in a way that can cause people to believe that they were screaming too loudly [against Dinkins], that they were making a Jewish thing, it could be personalized and politicized and it could have a backlash.

From a statement by the congressman from New York during the 1994 mayoralty campaign in which the chasidim were critical of the incumbent, Mayor David Dinkins.

◻

Chaim Raphael

MAGICAL BOOK

On the surface, the Passover Haggadah is merely the libretto for the Seder, but it is in fact a book compounded of magic.

From his Feast of History *(1972).*

ASSOCIATIONS OF THE SEDER

Artists and writers have reached out be-yond the words to try and capture the mysterious associations of the Seder—the dangers, joys, fears, and hopes—that have reverberated throughout Jewish history. In every century the Haggadah has been presented afresh with endless commentary and with illustrations ranging from the primitive to the most lavish and beautiful.

Ibid.

◻

Morris J. Raphall

THE BIBLE AND SLAVERY

When you remember that Abraham, Isaac, Jacob and Job—the men with whom the Almighty conversed...were slaveholders, does it not strike you that you are guilty of something very little short of blasphemy?

In an 1861 sermon entitled "The Bible View of Slavery," making the case that the Bible does not prohibit slavery. His statement was a denouncement of abolitionists, particularly Henry Ward Beecher, who preached that "slaveholding is a sin."

GENTLEMAN FROM BROOKLYN

The reverend gentleman from Brooklyn.

Ibid. Referring to Henry Ward Beecher.

◻

Nessa Rapoport

DEFINING A JEW

To be a devoted Jew means to dwell perpetually in the radiance and eclipse of an infinite Being, engaged with us in a mysterious partnership that has been tragic, sustaining, sublime.

From her article "Still Here," in Hadassah Magazine, *March 1994.*

◻

Rashi

ROLE MODEL

If a great man from whom people learn is not careful in his actions, lesser people will denigrate the Torah because of his behavior. They will say: "This one understands that there is nothing worthwhile in the Torah and its commandments." In this manner the name of God is profaned.

From a comment regarding the concept of chilul ha-shem (desecration of God's name) in the talmudic tractate Shabbat (33a).

HISTORY'S WHIPPING BOYS

All manner of outrages come upon the world. Israel must concern itself and say: "This omen came more for us than for all the other nations because Israel is more accustomed to being stricken than all the others."

From his commentary on Sukka 29a *concerning a statement that a solar eclipse is an evil omen for those who hate Jews, having the viciousness of the Crusaders in mind.*

PRESENT GENTILES

Gentiles of the present age are not heathens.

Quoted in Leo Jung's Judaism in a Changing World *(1939).*

◻

P. M. Raskin

GOD'S GREATEST RIDDLE

Israel, my people,
God's greatest riddle,
Will thy solution
Ever be told?

By attribution.

◻

Walter Rathenau

SECOND-CLASS CITIZENS

In the early days of every German Jew there comes a painful moment, which he remembers for the rest of his life, when he first becomes fully aware of the fact that he came into the world as a second-class citizen, and that no proficiency and no merit can release him from that status.

From his Staat und Judentum *(1911).*

◻

Jonathan Rauch

FREEDOM OF SPEECH

Where there is genuine freedom of expression, there will be racist expression. As long as they remain bigoted, bigots will simply find other words. If they can't call you a kike then they will say Jewboy, Judas, or Hebe, and when all those are banned they will press words like "oven" and "lampshade" into their service. The vocabulary of hate is potentially as rich as your dictionary, and all you do by banning language used by cretins is to let them decide what the rest of us may say.

Arguing for the protection of incendiary speech. From Harper's *magazine, May 1995.*

◻

Rav

EDUCATING THE YOUNG

Do not accept pupils who are less than six years old, but from that age on you can accept them and stuff them with learning the way you would stuff an ox.

Advising Samuel ben Shilat. Quoted in the talmudic tractate Bava Batra (21a).

ON DISCIPLINING STUDENTS

When you wish to punish a pupil, hit him with nothing harder than a shoelace.

Ibid.

MADE TO ENJOY LIFE

Man will be called to account in the hereafter for each pleasure he denied himself without sufficient cause.

Quoted in the Jerusalem Talmud, Kiddushin (4:12).

EFFECT OF A SIGH

A sigh [of distress] breaks down half the human body [constitution].

Quoted in the talmudic tractate Ketubot (62a).

CROWNING OF THE RIGHTEOUS

The future world is not like this world. In the world-to-come there will be no eating or drinking, no propagating or business activity, no envy or hatred or contention. The righteous will be sitting on thrones with crowns on their heads, enjoying the brilliance of God's splendor [the *Shechina*].

Quoted in the talmudic tractate Berachot (17a).

DISPASSIONATE HUMANS

Whoever can pray for his fellow man and does not do so must be called a sinner.

Ibid (12b).

EVERYTHING IS FOR THE BEST

A man must always accustom himself to think that whatever the Almighty does is for the best.

Ibid (60b).

TREATMENT OF ANIMALS

One must not eat before feeding his animals.

Ibid (40a).

LIMITED CLASS SIZE

The number of pupils that should be assigned to each teacher is twenty-five.... If there are forty, appoint an assistant.

> *Ibid.*

BASIC FOOD

A meal without salt is no meal.

> *Ibid (44a).*

ON TORAH STUDY

The study of Torah is more important than the rebuilding of the [Jerusalem] Temple.

> *Quoted in the talmudic tractate Megilla (16b).*

WICKED RULERS

If all the seas were ink and all the reeds in the swamps were pens, they would not suffice to describe all the evil torments a ruler can invent for his subjects.

> *Quoted in the talmudic tractate Shabbat (11a).*

PURPOSE OF THE COMMANDMENTS

The Almighty gave us the commandments in order to refine the Jews, just as the goldsmith places gold in his crucible and removes the dross.

> *Quoted in Midrash Samuel (4).*

□

Ronald Reagan

WEST BANK SETTLEMENTS

I disagreed when the previous administration referred to them as illegal; they're not illegal.

> *A February 1981 response to a question about the status of the Israeli settlements on the West Bank. In August 1984 he referred to the settlements as "an obstacle to peace."*

NEGOTIATING JERUSALEM

Jerusalem has to be part of the negotiation if we're going to have peace talks.

> *In May 1984, after Senator Patrick Moynihan of New York proposed moving the U.S. embassy in Israel from Tel Aviv to Jerusalem.*

VOTING ON THE TEN COMMANDMENTS

I have wondered at times what the Ten Commandments would have looked like if Moses had run it through a state legislature.

> *Commenting on his difficulties as governor with the California legislature. Quoted in Morris Mandel's* Affronts, Insults, and Indignities *(1975).*

ON VOLUNTARY PRAYER

I have never known a child who was hurt by exposure to a voluntary prayer.

> *Statement made in the White House Rose Garden in 1983.*

□

(Matriarch) Rebecca

DRINK, MY LORD

Drink, my lord...I will also draw [water] for your camels until they finish drinking.

> *Speaking to Abraham's servant, who was in search of a wife for Isaac.*

□

Walter Reich

DEMISE OF ISRAEL

With their votes, the Israeli Arabs could revoke that Law [of Return], revise the Declaration of Independence, which identifies Israel as a Jewish state, and even change the name of the country to Palestine. In this process, carried out solely through democratic means, Israel would cease to exist, the Jews would no longer have a national home, and Jews being persecuted in other countries would once again have nowhere to flee.

> *Predicting what will happen if Arab Israelis become the majority. From an interview with Rabbi Meir Kahane in* Moment *magazine, January–February 1985.*

DENIERS OF THE HOLOCAUST

The primary motivation for most deniers is anti-Semitism, and for them the Holocaust is an infuriatingly inconvenient fact of history.... What better way to rehabilitate anti-Semitism, make anti-Semitic arguments seem once again respectable in civilized discourse and even make it acceptable for governments to pursue anti-Semitic policies than by convincing the world that the great crime for which anti-Semitism was blamed simply never happened—indeed, that it was nothing more than a frame-up through their control of the media?

> *From his review of Deborah E. Lipstadt's* Denying the Holocaust *(1993) and Pierre Vidal-Naquet's* Assassins of Memory *(1993) in* The New York Times Book Review, *July 11, 1993.*

◻

Theodor Reik

POWER OF THE KOL NIDRE

I remembered the mysterious trembling that possessed the congregation when the cantor began the *Kol Nidre*. I remembered the visible signs of deep contrition exhibited by all these serious men and their emotional participation in the text, and, how I, child as I was, had been carried away by that irresistible wave of feeling.... I sobbed convulsively while hot tears poured from my eyes. Then I ran out into the night; my spirit torn and purified. I believe that in that never-to-be-forgotten hour no single stain remained upon my soul.

From his Psychological Problems of Religion–Ritual, Psycho-analytic Studies *(1931).*

◻

(Joseph) Ernest Renan

THE RELIGION OF ISAIAH

The pure religion which we dream of as the bond that shall in days to come hold together the whole of mankind in one communion will be the realization of the religion of Isaiah, the ideal Jewish religion, freed from all admixture of impurity.

Quoted in G. Karpeles's Jews and Judaism in the Nineteenth Century *(1905).*

LIVING PROTEST AGAINST IDOLATRY

The Jews were a living protest against superstition and religious materialism.

From his Life of Jesus *(1836).*

ISRAEL'S STRENGTH

Even now in our own day synagogues are the strength of Judaism—a strength that others envy, the ground of many a jealous calumny, to which there is but one answer to be made: Go, and do thou likewise.

Ibid.

LEGACY OF THE JEWS

Besides the immense service which the Jews rendered to the world in the matter of religion, by converting it to the belief in one God, we cannot deny that they have also been of the greatest service to us in the matter of science. But for the Jews, the Hebrew Bible, one of the most important monuments of history and philology, would have ceased to exist. It is certain that had Christianity completely absorbed Judaism in the first centuries of our era, the Hebrew text of the Bible would have been lost. Early Christians seem to have very seldom taken the trouble to consult it.

From his Studies in Religious History, *first published as an article entitled "The Translations of the Bible" (1858).*

THE JEW AS LEAVEN

The Jew was designed to serve as leaven in the progress of every country, rather than to form a separate nation on the globe.

From his History of Israel *(1895).*

A STRANGE PEOPLE!

What a strange people, verily—made to set before us every contrast! It gave God to the world, and barely believes in Him.

Ibid.

ORIGINAL CREATION

The synagogue has been the most original and fruitful creation of the Jewish people.

Ibid.

THE JEWISH GENIUS

The Song of Songs and Koheleth [Ecclesiastes] seem like a love-song and a pamphlet of Voltaire found astray among the folios of a theological library. This is what gives them their value.

Ibid.

JEWISH CONTRIBUTION TO GERMANY

Germany, after devoting herself entirely to military life, would have had no talent left if it were not for the Jews, to whom she has been so ungrateful.

From his Recollections of Infancy and Youth *(1883).*

THE JEWISH ENEMY

The enemies of Jewry are for the most part the enemies of the modern spirit.

Quoted in Joseph L. Baron's Stars and Sand *(1943).*

◻

Resh Lakish

DEFINING ADULTERY

You must not assume that only he who has committed the crime with his body is called an adulterer. If he commits adultery with his eyes he is also called an adulterer.

Quoted in the Midrash Leviticus Rabba *(23:12).*

THREATENING A NEIGHBOR

He who raises his hand against his neighbor, even though he does not strike him, is called a wicked man.

Quoted in the talmudic tractate Sanhedrin (58b).

GOD FAVORS PROSELYTES

In the eyes of God a proselyte is preferred to a Jew, even to those Jews who stood at the foot of Mount Sinai [in the days of Moses] and of whom God is so proud. Why? Because were it not for the lightning and thunder and the blowing of the heavenly *shofar* at the time of the giving of the Torah, the Jews would not have accepted it. But a proselyte, who has not seen or heard all this, embraces the Torah of his own free will.

Quoted in the Midrash Tanchuma on Lech Lecha (6).

MAN'S MATE

Every man gets the wife he deserves.

From the talmudic tractate Sota (2a).

BETTER TO MARRY

Rather than remain widowed, 'tis better to marry again.

From the talmudic tractate Ketubot (75a).

BORN AGAIN

A proselyte is like a newborn child.

From the talmudic tractate Yevamot (62a).

REWARDS OF REPENTANCE

Great is repentance: it turns sins into incentives for right conduct.

Quoted in the talmudic tractate Yoma (86b).

¤

Charles Reznikoff

MOTHER'S CALLOUSED HAND

In her last sickness, my mother took my hand in hers
tightly: for the first time I knew
how calloused a hand it was, and how soft was mine.

From his Poems 1937–1975 *(1977).*

¤

Joachim von Ribbentrop

ITALIANS LACK UNDERSTANDING

Italian military circles...lack a proper understanding of the Jewish question.

Complaining to Benito Mussolini in February 1943.

¤

Abraham Ribicoff

PRESIDENTIAL REPRIMAND

What do you do when the President gets you on the phone and eats your consummate ass out? He told me what a low-life bastard I was, and how I'd better get right with God.

Referring to U.S. President Lyndon Baines Johnson.

THE AMERICAN DREAM

Any boy regardless of race, creed or color, has the right to aspire to public office. Abe Ribicoff is not here to repudiate the American dream. Abe Ribicoff believes in that American dream, and I know that the American dream can come true.

Answering those who objected to him during his successful 1954 campaign for governor of Connecticut on the Democratic ticket.

FACING LIBERALS

I don't think you [Senator Jacob Javits] have the guts to face your liberal constituents who have moved to the suburbs to avoid sending their children to school with blacks.

In an attack upon the only other Jewish U.S. senator during a 1971 debate on school desegregation. Ribicoff charged the Republican Javits with "hypocrisy."

THE CONTENTIOUS CONVENTION

With George McGovern as president of the United States we wouldn't need police using Gestapo tactics in the streets of Chicago. With George McGovern, we wouldn't need the National Guard.

During a speech at the 1968 Democratic convention in Chicago when he nominated George McGovern for the presidency. Ribicoff peered directly at Chicago Mayor Richard Daley as he spoke these words because Daley's police had attacked antiwar protesters.

¤

Frank Rich

THE FARRAKHAN PHENOMENON

At a time when white Americans can't agree among ourselves on anything, here at last is one opinion that unites us all, liberal and conservative, Democrat and Republican, rich and poor: Louis Farrakhan is a hate-filled demagogue with a divisive, separatist ideology and an appalling record of racism, sexism, anti-Semitism and homophobia.

From his op-ed piece in The New York Times, *October 18, 1995, two days after the Million Man March of black men on Washington, DC.*

¤

Bernard G. Richards

NAILED TO HISTORY

Whatever one may think of Dr. Magnes' record in Palestine, it was part of the notable career of a striking personality, full of contrasts and contradictions, at once storm petrel and dove of peace; but imbued also with intense human qualities of zeal, ardor, enthusiasm, and in the last analysis, deepest devotion to the people of Israel in a manner and form of belief that was bound up with his complex personality. Thus ended a career that was colorful as it was contradictory, as daring as it was paradoxical, as quixotic and impetuous as it was destined to be beset by disillusionment—yet an arresting figure who nailed his name to history.

From Congress Weekly, *written shortly after the death of Judah L. Magnes in 1948.*

¤

Don Rickles

THE REAL DON RICKLES

I'm still very pious, very conscious of being Jewish. I'm a serious man, serious about my work, my family.

Quoted in Darryl Lyman's Jewish Comedy Catalog *(1989).*

¤

Gerhart M. Riegner

JEWISH RENAISSANCE MAN

He [Nahum Goldmann] was a renaissance man in the sense that his personality transcended any attempt of definition in terms of conventional human categories. He was a man with a global vision, never losing touch with reality, a man with a sense of bigness, with an insatiable thirst for life and beauty, whose interests embraced the totality of human endeavor. They stretched from his own early exercise in poetry, mysticism, astronomy, to philosophy, history, politics, literature, art, music, etc.

But I use the term also in the other meaning of the word: a *Jewish* renaissance man, a man of the Jewish renaissance who at the time of the greatest catastrophe never gave up hope, never despaired and who with his all-embracing global Jewish view and his deep concern for the Jewish people in all its parts, tried to give the best of himself to rebuild Jewish life by creating the conditions for a happier future in the new independent state and in the Diaspora.

From remarks introducing the 1983 Nahum Goldmann Memorial Lecture at the Museum of the Diaspora in Israel.

¤

Jack Riemer

MESSAGE TO TV PRODUCERS

The television screen reaches a lot more Jews in a week than the synagogue and the school do in a decade. How then do we continue to put up with the maligning of Judaism that takes place in the sitcoms and the dramas? How can we tolerate the fact that *Brooklyn Bridge* sends the message that intermarriage is the "American way" and only old fuddy duddies object? That *Cheers* and *L.A. Law* sends the message that Jewish men are wimps. And that the sitcoms send the message that Jewish women are JAPs? No one wants censorship, God forbid, but can't we send back the word that anti-Semitism is unacceptable, whether it comes from non-Jews or from Jews.

From an article in Manhattan Jewish Sentinel, *July 14–20, 1993.*

¤

David Riesman

THE NEED TO BE LIKED

While all people want and need to be liked by some of the people some of the time, it is only the modern other-directed types who make this their chief source of direction and chief area of sensitivity.

From his Lonely Crowd *(1950).*

ARE ALL MEN CREATED EQUAL?

The idea that men are created free and equal is both true and misleading: men are created different; they lose their social freedom and their individual autonomy in seeking to become like each other.

Ibid.

ON BEING ONESELF

The "nerve of failure" is the courage to face aloneness and the possibility of defeat in one's personal life or one's work without being morally destroyed. It is, in a larger sense, simply the nerve to be oneself when that self is not approved of by the dominant ethic of a society.

From his Individualism Reconsidered *(1954).*

¤

Gabriel Riesser

RELIGION OF OUR FATHERS

We have no reason to repudiate the religion of our fathers; we have every reason to love it. We can see in it...the highest ideals which humanity in our days can comprehend.

Quoted in Liberal Judaism, *April 1945.*

¤

Emanuel Ringelblum

VENGEANCE IS THE LORD'S

Spent the two Passover nights at Schachna's. There was an interesting discussion about vengeance. Mr. Isaac, who had been interned in a prison camp in Pomerania, demonstrated that vengeance would never solve anything. The vanquished would in turn plan their own vengeance, and so it would go on forever. There was talk that raising the moral level of humanity was the only solution.

From an entry in his diary, April 13, 1943.

POLAND'S INNATE ANTI-SEMITISM

The blind folly of Poland's anti-Semites has been responsible for the deaths of hundreds of thousands of Jews who could have been saved despite the Germans.

From the history of Jewish–Polish relations about which he was writing while in hiding from the Nazis, before he was discovered in March 1944.

¤

William Z. Ripley

JEWS ARE ONLY A PEOPLE

The Jews are not a race but only a people, after all.

From his Races of Europe *(1899).*

¤

Shlomo Riskin

THE ROAD TO VEGETARIANISM

The dietary laws are intended to teach us

compassion and to lead us gently to vegetarianism.

From his column in The Jewish Week, *August 14, 1987.*

RUTH THE PROTOTYPE

Who says that mixed marriage will lead to more Jews opting out? Perhaps it will enable more gentiles to count themselves in. Was not Ruth the prototypical convert, a Moabite woman who married a Jew and became grandmother to King David and eventually the ancestor of the Messiah?...

Ibid., May 21–27, 1993.

TWO TYPES OF JEWS

There are two types of Jews: the religious and the not-yet-religious.

From a 1980 interview.

INVERTED MARRANOS

America has spawned inverted Marranos: Jews who act out the rituals but have the inner responses of the secularists.

Ibid.

OUR ETHICAL IMPERATIVE

I was always thought of as a liberal. I marched with Martin Luther King and feel very strongly about equal rights.... But we're not fighting an enemy who plays by the rules. The mukhtar of Beit Fajr, who was co-chairperson with me on a committee for the establishment of a hospital in the area was hacked to death by the PLO. His genitals were removed.... One dare not be naive. Given the cruelty and barbarism of the Arabs to their own people, our ethical imperative is not to commit suicide.

Quoted in The Jerusalem Post, *February 12, 1994.*

¤

Ellis Rivkin

SOURCES OF ANTI-SEMITISM

Any serious student of anti-Semitism in its historical manifestations knows that the false, stupid, and shopworn character of the propaganda is no protection against its effectiveness when a society is undergoing major stresses and strains. Anti-Semitism waxes and wanes in direct relationship to economic and social stability.

From Madison C. Peters' Jew as a Patriot *(1902).*

◘

Leonard Roan

A BIGOTED JURY

If Christ and his angels came down here and showed this jury that [Leo] Frank was innocent, it would bring him in guilty.

Comment made to a friend by the presiding judge at the April 1913 Leo Frank murder trial, held in Atlanta, Georgia. Quoted in Elmer R. Murphy's article entitled "A Visit with Leo M. Frank in the Death Cell at Atlanta," which appeared in Rhodes' Colossus, *March 1915.*

◘

Pat Robertson

RELIGIOUS RIGHT PROTESTS

Just like what Nazi Germany did to Jews, so liberal America is now doing to the evangelical Christians.

From a 1994 monograph prepared by the Anti-Defamation League. Quoted in The New Republic, *August, 1, 1994.*

PRAYING FOR ABE

It is painfully obvious that you are a deeply troubled individual who has somewhere along the way lost your Judaic roots, only to seek in radical secularism what only God can give you.

Please know, Abe, that I will pray earnestly that you may indeed meet personally the God of Abraham, Isaac and Jacob, and that his blessing be upon you.

From a 1994 letter to Abraham H. Foxman, executive director of the Anti-Defamation League, critical of the stance of the "Religious Right" on the separation of Church and State. Reported in Heritage Southwest Jewish Press, *July 29, 1994.*

◘

Theodore H. Robinson

SACRED POETS

They are the songs of the human soul, timeless and universal; it is the sacred poets of Israel who, more than any others, have well and truly interpreted the spirit of man.

From his History of Israel *(1932).*

◘

Artur Rodzinski

APPEALING ON HIGH

I finally asked God whom I should take and God said, "Take Bernstein."

When in need of an assistant at the New York Philharmonic in 1943. Quoted in Elinor and Robert Slater's Great Jewish Men *(1996).*

◘

Anne Roiphe

DREAMERS AGAIN

We must once again be dreamers of a better world, binding our children to us with the intensity of our moral worth, the beauty of our historical and ethical vision. Our children will join us if they see us engaged in the heroic and moral journey of Jewish destiny; at least they should.

Quoted in Hadassah Magazine, *June–July 1993.*

FAMILY LIFE IN AMERICA

I know family life in America is a minefield, an economic trap for women, a study in disappointment for both sexes.

From her Lovingkindness *(1987).*

THE NEED TO BUILD HOPE

We can express open anger at the anti-Semitic acts of terrorists or members of a country club. We can mourn the dead of the Hitler era. We can tell our children what we genuinely feel, but we must be sure to tell them about the goodness of people, to express again and again our conviction that the world will get better and that our individual acts of kindness make a difference.

From her essay entitled "Talking to Kids About Anti-Semitism," which appears in The Hadassah Magazine Jewish Parenting Book *(1989), edited by Roselyn Bell.*

COMBUSTIBLE TOPICS

The Jewish family and Jews and money are highly combustible topics, and when you're candid you run the risk of appearing to be anti-Semitic.

Commenting on the risk she took in writing Pursuit of Happiness, *a richly atmospheric novel about the Jewish immigrant experience.*

THE MAKING OF A SAINT

The recognition of Edith Stein, now on the second rung of the ladder to sainthood, serves also to blur the singularity of the Jewish tragedy. If Edith Stein [a Jewish philosopher who converted to Catholicism and joined a Carmelite order] is a saint, then the Holocaust becomes a general disaster belonging to Catholics as well as Jews. The Nazis never intended to rid the world of every last Catholic. They did not believe that Catholic women and children were a cancer in the public body. The Catholic Church in whose sanctuary Nazi war criminals slept should not yet make a Catholic saint out of a Jewish intellectual whatever her religious convictions.

> *From her* Season for Healing *(1988). Edith Stein died as a Jew at the hands of the Nazis.*

CREATING A NORMAL STATE

Israel and Israelis are, as Herzl envisioned, a normal state made up of normal human beings and as such they are tempted, as are all peoples, to abuse power, to hate the stranger, to allow violence and cruelty to replace law. If the Jews can find a way toward peace, even with the difficulties of Arab hostility, then perhaps they will have become the people chosen to show the way toward a benign nationalism.

> *Ibid.*

INTERMARRIAGE QUANDARY

If one of my children married out, I would be sad, I would be grieved, but I would accept it as a consequence of living in the United States.

> *Expressing her deep concern over the explosive problem of intermarriage. Quoted in* The Jerusalem Report, *December 2, 1993.*

THIS MATTER OF JEWISHNESS

Years ago when I was beginning to think about this matter of Jewishness, we were invited to a Seder at the home of our pediatrician.... The Hebrew words went on and on, the guests argued endlessly about the right tune. I felt left out, unknowing, but like a child with my face pressed to the window of a house inside of which a wondrous thing was happening.... I heard the sound of my people. I heard history moving and standing still. I saw generations lifting up cups, washing their hands, saying the same words. I was a guest and not a guest, I belonged: past, present and future.

> *Quoted in* Hadassah Magazine, *March 1994.*

Yisrael Dov Rokeah

CALLING FOR ALIYA

I want to ask the Jews abroad what they are doing here?...Your place is in Eretz Yisrael. Why are you building palaces abroad? What about the *mitzva* to settle Eretz Yisrael?

True, there are countries like Belgium who host guests and treat the Jews nicely. But this is only while the Jews feel and act like guests. Once they think that they are equal citizens, the Gentiles will, heaven forbid, remember that they are guests and foreigners.

> *Speaking at a ground-breaking ceremony for a new educational complex in Antwerp, Belgium, in June 1994. Reported in* The Jerusalem Post, *July 2, 1994.*

Ole Edvart Rolvaag

HOW TO CONTRIBUTE MOST

If they, as individuals or as a group, owe any debt to America, the payment can only be made by their remaining Jews, and the same holds true for all nationalities that have come here.

> *From his* Their Fathers' Gods *(1931).*

Eleanor Roosevelt

VERY JEWISH

An interesting little man but very Jewish.

> *After her first meeting with Felix Frankfurter and before she had overcome the anti-Semitism of her early upbringing. Quoted in Joseph P. Lash's* Eleanor and Franklin *(1971).*

NOT AFRAID OF THE TRUTH

Written by a young girl—and the young are not afraid of telling the truth—it is one of the wisest and most moving commentaries on war and its impact on human beings that I have ever read.

> *From her introduction to* Anne Frank: The Diary of Young Girl *(1967).*

Franklin Delano Roosevelt

ISAIAH REVIVED

Old Isaiah.

> *The name by which he would sometimes call Louis D. Brandeis, appointed to the Supreme Court in 1916.*

DAY OF RECKONING

Citizens, regardless of religious allegiance, will share in the sorrow of our Jewish fellow-citizens over the savagery of the Nazis against their helpless victims. The Nazis will not succeed in exterminating their victims any more than they will succeed in enslaving mankind. The American people not only sympathize with all victims of Nazi crimes but will hold the perpetrators of these crimes to strict accountability in a day of reckoning which will surely come.

> *From a July 17, 1942 letter to Dr. Stephen S. Wise, which was read at a public meeting in New York City on July 21, 1942.*

ON PALESTINE

Palestine should be for the Jews and no Arabs should be in it.... It should be exclusive Jewish territory.

> *Noted in the diary of U.S. Secretary of State Edward R. Stettinius, Jr., November 1944.*

STAYING ABOVE THE FRACAS

The German authorities are treating the Jews shamefully, and the Jews in this country are greatly excited. But this is also not a government affair. We can do nothing except for American citizens who happen to be victims. We must protect them, and whatever we can do to moderate the general persecution by unofficial and personal influence ought to be done.

> *From William E. Dodd's diary entry of June 16, 1933, after consulting with FDR, prior to assuming his duties as U.S. ambassador to Germany in July.*

¤

Theodore Roosevelt

PROVIDING FOR JEWISH SERVICEMEN

...commanding officers [are to] be authorized to permit Jewish soldiers to be absent for attendance at services on the Jewish holy days.

> *Instructions issued to the War Department on September 8, 1904, after Rabbi Henry Pereira Mendes of New York City petitioned the president to provide for the religious needs of Jewish servicemen.*

PRESIDENTIAL REBUKE

Three circumcised Jews and three anemic Christians.

> *A characterization of six editors of* The New Republic, *of which Walter Lipmann was a senior editor. Roosevelt had once called the twenty-five-year-old Lipmann "the most brilliant young man of his age in the United States." The editors were critical of Roosevelt's belligerency toward Mexico.*

A MESSAGE TO THE RUSSIANS

I don't know whether you know it or not, but I want you to become a member of my Cabinet. I have a very high estimate of your character, your judgment and your ability, and I want you for personal reasons. There is still a further reason: I want to show Russia and some other countries what we think of Jews in this country.

> *Statement made to Oscar Straus one day in 1906 after a luncheon at the White House. Straus became Secretary of the Department of Commerce and Labor in the Roosevelt Cabinet.*

IN APPRECIATION OF A STORY WRITER

Mrs. Roosevelt and I and most of the children know your very amusing and very pathetic accounts of East Side school children almost by heart, and I...thank you for them. While I was Police Commissioner I quite often went to the Houston Street public school and was immensely...impressed by what I saw there. I thought there were a good many Miss Bailies [the schoolteacher heroine of Miss Kelly's stories] there, and the work they were doing among their scholars (who were so largely of Russian–Jewish parentage, like the children you write of) was very much like what your Miss Bailey has done.

> *Expressing his appreciation to author Myra Kelly for her stories about Jewish children on New York's Lower East Side. Her touching stories, such as "A Passport to Paradise," which appeared in* McClure's, *November 1904, were favorites of the Roosevelt family.*

PRAISE FROM THE PRESIDENT

My Dear Sir: I am forced to make a rule not to write letters on the occasion of any celebration.... I make an exception in this case because [of] the lamentable and terrible suffering to which so many of the Jewish people in other lands have been subjected.... The Jews of the United States...have become indissolubly incorporated in the great army of American citizenship.... They are honorably distinguished by their industry, their obedience to law, and their devotion to the national welfare.

> *From a letter to Jacob H. Schiff on the occasion of Jewry's celebration in New York's Carnegie Hall, on Thanksgiving Day 1905, of the 250th anniversary of the settlement of Jews in the U.S.*

A Great Play

That's a great play, Mr. Zangwill, a great play!

> *Congratulating the author after the first showing of his play* The Melting Pot *at Columbia Theater, Washington, DC, on October 5, 1908.*

◻

Daniel Rose

Jews and the Civil Rights Movement

I was with Bayard Rustin and Martin Luther King when Dr. King stated that 90 percent of gifts to the movement of over a thousand dollars came from Jews. It is also generally accepted that 40 percent of freedom riders were Jewish and this from a people that constitutes only 2 percent of the American public.

> *Rejecting the assertion of many black leaders that Jewish participation in the civil rights struggle has been exaggerated. From a statement made at a May 1994 conference on the Jewish reaction to black anti-Semitism.*

◻

Moses Rosen

Our Sack of Sorrows

I recall those dreadful days I felt like a man climbing a mountain with a sack full of Jewish sorrows on my back.

But my dream was to reach the top of that mountain, and to throw off that sack laden with the suffering and sorrows of my people.

> *From a 1992 speech, on his eightieth birthday, when he was honored by Israeli leaders. Quoted in the* WJC *[World Jewish Congress] Report, July–August 1994.*

◻

Norman Rosenbaum

Black and White

When the police beat Rodney King, there were calls for justice when the jury acquitted [the police]. When Reginald Denny was pulled from his truck and beaten senseless, we're told

we have to build bridges and heal.... The only difference in the two cases is that Rodney King is black and Reginald Denny is white.

> *Commenting on the murder of his brother, Yankel, after a pogrom in Crown Heights (Brooklyn) in August 1991. Despite the evidence, Lemrick Nelson, a black man, was acquitted in a state court trial on October 29, 1992.*

Jewish Blood

Jewish blood is not cheap!

> *Protesting the verdict exonerating Lemrick Nelson for the August 1991 murder of Norman's brother, Yankel.*

◻

Jay Rosenberg

I Choose the Jewish Cause

From this point on I shall join no movement that does not accept and support my people's struggle. If I must choose between the Jewish cause and a "progressive'" anti-Israel SDS [Students for a Democratic Society], I shall choose the Jewish cause. If barricades are erected, I will fight as a Jew.

> *Redefining his position after Israel's victory in the 1967 Six-Day War. From an article in* The Village Voice, *February 1969.*

◻

Gary Rosenblatt

Discuss and Disagree

All branches of Judaism, despite their serious differences on approaching the issue of intermarriage, should be able to agree on several basic messages: that we recognize the reality of intermarriage, that we want to increase and foster Jewish family life, and that we want Jewish partners to remain Jewish.

After that, let the rabbis discuss, and disagree, about how best to proceed. But the issue is too important to keep decrying without confronting.

> *From his column in* The Jewish Week, *October 8–14, 1993.*

Reviving Hillel on Campus

I have the solution to the problem of heightening Jewish identity on college campuses. But no one takes me seriously. All you have to do is have the Hillel foundation hire Minister Louis Farrakhan, Rev. Al Sharpton and David Duke to address students at college campuses around the country. I guarantee you they will attract more Jewish students, stir them in their *kishkes* and make them feel more Jewish than virtually any speakers we have within the Jewish community.

> *From his column in* The Jewish Week, *December 31, 1993–January 6, 1994.*

¤

Penina Rosenblum

WASTED ENERGY

People are always asking me how I could accept him [her father] after all those years and what he did to us. One thing I've learned in life is not to waste energy on revenge.

> *As a successful adult and CEO of a prosperous cosmetics company in Tel Aviv, she decided to search out her father in Germany, even though he had deserted them when she was a young child.*

¤

Morris Rosenfeld

SONG OF EXILE

With a wanderer's staff in hand,
Without a home, without a land,
No friend, no helper on the way,
No tomorrow and no today.

> *From his "Exile Song." Quoted in J. Leftwich's* Golden Peacock *(1939).*

¤

Samuel I. Rosenman

PRESIDENTIAL STYLE

I do not believe that Franklin Roosevelt, in considering a man's suitability for appointment to office, cared any more about his religion than he did about the color of his hair. Of course, he did follow the usual political style of not appointing too many men of one religion or ethnic group to a court or agency, only because such appointment might give rise to the suspicion that he was prejudiced against other religions and groups. This was not only fair but good politics.

> *From* Presidential Style *(c. 1950), written by his wife, Dorothy.*

¤

Menachem Z. Rosensaft

IT'S A GREAT DAY

From the cradle in Bergen-Belsen to the lawn of the White House with the Israeli Prime Minister and Foreign Minister, Arafat and Bill Clinton. That is somewhat of a momentous journey. It's a great day.

> *Commenting on the Israeli–PLO peace accord, which he saw enacted on the White House lawn on September 13, 1993. An official at Chase Manhattan Bank, the son of Holocaust survivors, Rosensaft himself was born in Bergen-Belsen concentration camp.*

POSITIVE JEWISH THINKING

Commemoration of the Holocaust must be one of the priorities in terms of historic memories and consciousness. [But it] can't be allowed to become an ersatz or alternate religion, and remembering it can't be the principal element and Jewish priority. We must not teach our children that the annihilation of six million Jews is a reason to be Jewish. Anti-Semitism is not a positive force of any kind.

> *Reported in* Hadassah Magazine, *April 1994.*

WE MUST BECOME EDUCATED

In order to understand the Holocaust we must be educated Jews. [It is the] obligation of the Jewish community to make sure what they see in Washington is supplemented to provide a comprehensive awareness of context. If we tell our kids that the [only] reason to be Jewish is that Hitler killed six million Jews, the response is "why be Jewish?"

> *Ibid.*

NO OTHER CEMETERY?

For heaven's sake, let him find another cemetery. There must be at least one in all of Germany which does not contain SS men.

> *Commenting on President Ronald Reagan's planned visit to Bitburg in April 1986 to commemorate the fortieth anniversary of Germany's defeat, and to lay a wreath at the military cemetery where some Nazi officers were also buried.*

¤

A. M. Rosenthal

DANCING WITH WOLVES

If I were an Israeli, and I felt I had to dance with wolves, I would certainly keep counting my toes.

> *Noting how many broken promises Israel has had to contend with in negotiating peace with the Arabs. From his column in* The New York Times, *September 9, 1994.*

THE POWER OF HOPE

Geography has not changed for Israel. Mr.

Rabin, like his predecessors, once believed that the West Bank was essential to give Israel the needed mobilization hours if war came. Now he believes security lies more in peace arrangements than in time and space. Many Israelis and foreign friends of Israel, including me, are nervous about that.

> *From his column in* The New York Times, *September 14, 1993, the day after Yitzhak Rabin and Yasser Arafat shook hands on the White House lawn prior to the signing of the peace accord between Israel and the Palestine Liberation Organization.*

THE HOLOCAUST WAS UNIQUE

The Holocaust was not a civil, ethnic or religious conflict but a methodical effort to annihilate every Jew in every land. Peace was never possible because there were no sides. There were just the gas chambers and those put to suffocation.... The Holocaust was not a war of any kind. It was a Holocaust, you see.

> *Pointing out the inequity in comparing the Bosnian massacre by the Serbs to the Holocaust. From his column in* The New York Times, *April 26, 1994.*

◻

Julius Rosenwald

RICH DOES NOT MEAN SMART

Do not be fooled into believing that because a man is rich he is necessarily smart. There is ample proof to the contrary.

> *By attribution.*

◻

Franz Rosenzweig

YOM KIPPUR JUDAISM

He who knows...what potentialities lie dormant even...in a mere Yom Kippur Judaism... will guard against speaking disdainfully of the synagogue.

> *From his* Bildung und Kein Ende *(1920). Quoted in M. M. Glatzer's* Franz Rosenzweig *(1953).*

THE CAPACITY TO WONDER

Where common sense proceeds in reckless haste, philosophy pauses and wonders. And were it merely a question of this gift, alone, this capacity to wonder, philosophy's rightful claim to superiority could not be disputed. For common sense, as it is said, is not addicted to the ways of wonder.

> *From* Understanding the Sick and the Healthy.

BOOKS AND PEOPLE

Books are not now the prime need of the day. What we need more than ever are human beings—Jewish human beings.

> *By attribution.*

ON THE MAKING OF MAN

As long as God is still creating, he does not in fact say "I." He says "We," an absolute, all-inclusive term which does not refer to an I outside the self but is the plural of all- encompassing majesty. It is an impersonal I, an I that does not face another Thou, that does not reveal anything but lives, like the metaphysical God of pre-creation, only in itself.

> *Commenting on "Let us make man. . ." in Genesis 1:26. From his* Star of Redemption *(1970).*

DREAM OF PERFECTION

The Sabbath is the dream of perfection, but it is only a dream. Only in its being both does it become the cornerstone of life, only as the festival of perfection does it become the constant renewal of creation.

> *Ibid.*

IN LOVE WITH GERMAN

Even if the German Reich ceased to exist, my German identity would remain exactly what it is. Language is, after all, more than blood.

> *By attribution.*

RAPTUROUS ENTHUSIASM

On Saturday I happened into a Hasidic *shtiebel* [small European synagogue].... The songs were the main attraction. I have never heard anything like it. They do not need an organ—such rapturous enthusiasm, young and old all together.

> *From his* Letters and Diaries *(1978), edited by Rachel Rosenzweig and Edith Rosenzweig-Scheinmann.*

NOT YET

Not yet [*a'da'yin lo*].

> *When asked if he practices his religion.*

◻

Barney Ross

MOTHER'S CHOLENT

Ma would peel six pounds of potatoes, then leave them in cold water overnight to prepare it for the *cholent*, a Sabbath delicacy that by tradition among the Jews of Eastern Europe descent is served to the menfolk when they come home from synagogue.... Ma and the other women on our block would blend and season their *cholent* Friday then take it to the bakery...and let it cook all night on a low fire in the baker's stove.

> *Quoted in his autobiography,* No Man Stands Alone *(1957).*

BLASPHEMY OF BOXING

If Pa had lived, I think he would have killed me before he ever would have permitted me to put on a pair of gloves and climb into a ring.

> *Ibid. To the mind of Barney's father, Isidore, "anybody who [even] got into a fistfight on the street was a bum."*

Isidore Ross

BOXING IS ANATHEMA

What shame this [Benny] Leonard has brought to his mother and father.

> *A statement by Barney Ross's father when he was told about the great boxing champion Benny Leonard. Quoted in Barney Ross's* No Man Stands Alone *(1957).*

Leo Rosten

DOUGHNUTS WITH A DEGREE

Bagels are doughnuts with a college education—and the college is probably Yeshiva [University].

> *From his* Joys of Yiddish *(1968).*

Yaacov Rotblitt

THE EXTINGUISHED LIGHT

Let the sun rise, the morning shine,
The most righteous prayer will not bring us back.
Who is the one whose light has been extinguished,
And buried in the earth?
Bitter tears will not wake him, will not bring him back.
No song of praise or victory will avail us.
Therefore, sing only a song of peace.
Don't whisper a prayer—
sing aloud a song of peace.

> *The song sung by Yitzhak Rabin at the November 4, 1995 peace rally in Tel Aviv, a short while before he was assassinated. The lyrics refer to the 1967 Six-Day War.*

Benjamin Roth

AN ETHICAL WILL

Never leave the religion that is yours by birth, the faith of your parents and ancestors. Neither wealth, nor friendship, nor the possibility of a brilliant career in life, nor seduction, nor even the love of a girl should move you or have the power to make you change your religion....

Have no relations with a prostitute. Her breath is poison, her word the bite of a snake; and they are all alike. However, let me add here, in praise of Jewish womanhood, that with a few exceptions they have preserved much purer morals than the girls of other races; and they have contained themselves from selling their charms for money.

> *From a letter to his son Solomon, written in Hechingen, Wuerttemberg, Germany, in 1854. Translated from the German by Albert H. Friedlander. Quoted in* Critical Studies in American Jewish History *(1971).*

FATHERLY ADVICE

Never have any contact with missionaries. You do not have enough knowledge of the Holy Scriptures. That way, you cannot engage in disputations with them; for they could easily lead you astray. Consider them therefore only as self-seeking cheats, or as ranting visionaries, as I have come to know them. And, indeed, in my conversations with them I frequently exhibited them as such in the presence of company, something I could do since I have studied Scripture from my childhood days. And yet, even then it was a difficult task.

> *Ibid.*

Cecil Roth

THE COLORING OF CONVERSATION

Few people can realize today to what an extent their ordinary conversation is colored by the Hebrew Scriptures. When a man escapes by the skin of his teeth, when he goes down to the sea in ships, when he inquires whether a leopard can change its spots, when he threatens to make his enemy lick the dust, he is using biblical phrases which have become an inseparable part of his language.

> *From his* Jewish Contribution to Civilization *(1938).*

THE JEWISH PEPYS

It is no exaggeration to call Glückel [of Hameln] a German–Jewish Pepys. She has all of Pepys's garrulity, frankness, unbound zest in life, and genius for portraiture. Only their spheres were different. He was interested in amours, politics, and courts; she in match-making.

> From his collected essays, Personalities and Events in Jewish History (1953).

SYNONYMOUS WITH OPTIMISM

Judaism teaches that to despair of the future is one of the gravest of all sins, because the perfect age for which every man must work still lies before us.

> Quoted in Great Ages and Ideas of the Jewish People (1956), edited by Leo W. Schwartz.

OUR UNIQUE VOCABULARY

Every age has its own vocabulary, and the vocabulary of our thinking must be our own.... Maimonides' words are not ours nor is his science the science of our generation. The Scriptures still "talk the language of men" but the language of men has changed.

> Quoted in Jacob S. Minkin's essay on Maimonides in Great Jewish Books.

❑

Henry Roth

WHAT IF...

Had I stayed there on the Lower East Side I'm sure I would have been a lot happier and I...might have been a rabbi—who knows? Or a good zoologist, had a happy Jewish family.... The point was I'd have rather been happy, no matter what, instead of this tormented life that I lived.

> In 1993, at age 87, looking back at his early years and speculating on what his life would have been like had his family not moved from the Lower East Side to the more affluent Harlem when he was eight years old. From his autobiographical novel, Mercy of a Rude Stream (1993).

❑

Joel Roth

CONSERVATIVE JUDAISM ON HOMOSEXUALITY

Persons who live openly homosexual lifestyles could not reasonably be accepted as rabbis or cantors precisely because their lifestyle suggests that homosexuality is halachically [according to Jewish law] acceptable.

> Expressing the reason for the 1992 ruling rejecting openly gay and lesbian candidates as students in the rabbinical and cantorial schools of the Jewish Theological Seminary of America.

TRADITION AND CHANGE

The Conservative movement stands firmly committed to the binding authority of Jewish law. For us as a Movement, halakhah is much more than simply "tradition" or "custom." It is law which we are obligated to obey.

> From The United Synagogue Review, Spring 1990.

THE RIGHT TO MODIFY

We affirm that the sages of our day have all of the same power and authority that the sages of antiquity possessed. The authority includes the right to modify, or even to abrogate, precedented norms.

> Ibid.

INTERMARRIAGES UNACCEPTABLE

Intermarriages are legally forbidden in the Conservative movement. They are not recognized as either legally valid or communally acceptable.

> Ibid.

❑

Joseph Roth

CONNECTING WITH OUR FORBEARS

I am an Eastern Jew, and we are at home wherever our dead are buried.... My son will be a complete American, for that is where I will be buried.

> From his Letters 1911–1939 (1970), edited by Hermann Kesten.

❑

Leon Roth

MAN AND GOD

Monotheism means not only the positive search for unity but also, negatively, the refusal to set man in the throne of God.

> From his Jewish Thought (1927).

DIALOGUING ABOUT GOD

It has become fashionable to talk of the relationship between God and man as that of a dialogue. That is as may be; but it should at least be noted that the dialogue involved is not a tea-table conversation. It is rather a call, even a calling to account; and it is curious to observe from the record how some of those called upon found in it terror and suffering and how some, for varying reasons, tried to evade it.

From his God and Man in the Old Testament *(1955).*

¤

Philip Roth

THE JEWISH WRITER

That is why at this point in human history, when power seems the ultimate end of government, and "success" the goal of individual lives; when the value of humility is in doubt, and the nerve to fail hardly to be seen at all; when a willful blindness of man's condition can only precipitate further anguishes and miseries—at this point, with the murder of six million people fixed forever in our imaginations, I cannot help but believe that there is a higher moral purpose for the Jewish writer, and the Jewish people, than the improvement of public relations.

From an article in American Judaism *(1961), in which he is critical of writers such as Leon Uris and Harry Golden, who are admired for having written books that have brought honor and respect to the Jewish people.*

GROWING UP

A Jewish man with parents alive is a fifteen-year-old boy, and will remain a fifteen-year-old boy until they die!

From his Portnoy's Complaint *(1967).*

THE AIM OF WORDS

Words aren't only bombs and bullets—no, they're little gifts, containing meanings.

Ibid.

PUTTING THE "ID" BACK IN "YID"

Doctor, my doctor, what do you say,
LET'S PUT THE ID BACK IN YID!

Ibid.

A KHRUSHCHEV ASSESSMENT

However much it pleases me to accept this award, I must remind you that not only have you repudiated the longstanding judgment of many wise men and women, but what is even more disturbing, you have confirmed the exasperated assessment of the Jews made by none

other than the late Nikita Khrushchev. "They are all individualists," complained Khrushchev, "and are all intellectuals. They want to talk about everything, they want to discuss everything, they want to debate everything—and they come to totally different conclusions!"

From his speech when accepting the 1979 Present Tense Literary Award for his novel The Ghost Writer *(1979).*

TIME OF DEATH

Just like those who are incurably ill, the aged know everything about their dying except exactly when.

From his The Facts *(1988).*

FACT OR FICTION

I write fiction and I'm told it's autobiography, I write autobiography and I'm told it's fiction, so since I'm so dim and they're so smart, let them decide what it is or it isn't.

From his Deception *(1990).*

A TRADITIONAL BURIAL

A suit! He's not going to the office! No! No suit! It's senseless!

In his Patrimony *(1990), when a mortician asks Roth to pick out a suit in which to bury his father instead of the traditional shrouds.*

INSENSITIVE YEAR

They call it image making: whatever works, whatever suits the need of the client, whatever serves the propaganda machine. Marlboro has the Marlboro Man, Israel has the Holocaust Man...FOR THE SMOKESCREEN THAT HIDES EVERYTHING, SMOKE HOLOCAUST.

From his novel Operation Shylock *(1993).*

WHAT TO EXPECT OF A JEW

The fellows who say to you, "I expect more of the Jews," don't believe them. *They expect less.* What they are really saying is "Okay, we know you're a bunch of ravenous bastards, and given half the chance you'd eat up half the world...."

From his Counterlife *(1986).*

¤

Edmond de Rothschild

A "RICH MAN"

A rich man lives on the income of his income. If I agree to give you a large amount of money, I shall no longer be a rich man.

In response to Chaim Weizmann who, in 1931 in Paris, asked the wealthy baron if he would help Jews in Palestine.

Miriam Rothschild

LUCKY AND PROUD

My father really believed that assimilation was a better solution. [However,] I was terribly conscious of anti-Semitism. I lost my husband's whole family and my mother's whole family in the Holocaust. Some people find it difficult to be Jewish. I was one of the lucky people. I was always glad to be Jewish. I always liked being Jewish. I was proud to be Jewish.

Quoted in Elinor and Robert Slater's Great Jewish Women *(1994).*

W. Rottenheim

AMERICA: GREAT COUNTRY

Far, far from where the sun sets
A glorious blessed land
Across the trackless ocean
Extends a brother's hand.
There, there shall be our haven,
To which our course we'll bend
There will the dire oppression
At last forever end.

Encouraging fellow German Jews to emigrate to America as he did. Quoted in the German language weekly Die Deborah, *August 24, 1855.*

Jean Jacques Rosseau

SPEAKING FREELY

I shall never believe that I have seriously heard the arguments of the Jews until they have a free state, schools, universities, where they can speak and dispute without risk. Only then will we be able to know what they have to say.

From his Émile, ou de l'Éducation *(1762).*

TIMID PEOPLE

These unhappy people feel that they are in our power; the tyranny they have suffered makes them timid.

Ibid.

Aryeh Rubenstein

THE RABBINIC TRADITION

Judaism comprises an astonishingly wide array of beliefs and views.... Certain authorities favored asceticism while others deprecated it;

there are rabbis who stressed the cultic and ritual aspects of Judaism, and there are others for whom the social teachings of Judaism seem to be of paramount importance. All these views are within the rabbinic tradition and, as long as their advocates did not negate any of the few basic teachings and remained within the relatively wide framework of *halakhah* [Jewish law], are perfectly legitimate.

From the Introduction to his Hasidism *(1975).*

MIRACLE OF 1948

There can be no doubt whatsoever that the re-establishment of the State of Israel in 1948 is one of the most important events in Jewish history. That a nation cut off—in the main—from its land for nearly two thousand years should regain its sovereignty is amazing enough. That it should do so immediately after suffering the worst disaster any people in recorded history has ever suffered and, from a military point of view, against overwhelming odds, compounds the astonishment and, indeed, awe that any spectator must feel. With good reason, many people, both Jews and gentiles, saw the hand of God in the miracle of 1948.

Ibid.

Richard Rubenstein

A DISTINCTIVE CONTRIBUTION

I believe that Judaism continues to make a unique contribution to the world, more in terms of the quality of its men and women than in terms of any special insight absent from other religions. Judaism will continue to make a distinctive contribution so long as it develops men and women who function as an element of creative discontent before the regnant idolatries of any given time or community.

From an essay in Condition of Jewish Belief *(1966), compiled by the editors of* Commentary *magazine.*

SHARING MORAL FAILURE

I would caution against the tendency in contemporary Judaism to overstress the moral and the ethical. Admittedly, Judaism seeks to inculcate high ethical standards, but one of the most important functions of a religious community is the *sharing of failure*, especially moral failure. We turn to the sanctuary less to be admonished to pursue virtue than out of the need to express and share our inevitable shortcomings in that pursuit.

Ibid.

THE GREAT CHALLENGE

I believe the greatest single challenge to modern Judaism arises out of the question of God and the death camps.... How can Jews believe in an omnipotent, beneficent God after Auschwitz? Traditional Jewish theology maintains that God is the ultimate, omnipotent actor in the historical drama. It has interpreted every major catastrophe in Jewish history as God's punishment of a sinful Israel. I fail to see how this position can be maintained without regarding Hitler and the SS as instruments of God's will.... The idea is simply too obscene for me to accept.

Ibid.

ABANDONING MYTHS

[The greatest obstacle to Jewish–Christian understanding] is that the true dialogue, the genuine meeting of persons, is impossible so long as Jew and Christian are committed to the religion-historic myths of their respective communities. [The Jew must release his hold on the] doctrine of the election of Israel and the Torah as the sole content of God's revelation to mankind [while the Christian, in turn, must de-emphasize] the decisive character of the Christ event in human history [a myth] that must be at best an error and at worst blasphemy.

From his After Auschwitz: Radical Theology and Contemporary Judaism *(1966).*

ALL ALONE

We learned in the crisis that we were totally and nakedly alone, that we could expect neither support nor succor from God nor from our fellow creatures. Therefore, the world will forever remain a place of pain, suffering, alienation and ultimate defeat.

Ibid.

CONFRONTATION WITH GOD

No Jewish theology will possess even a remote degree of relevance to contemporary Jewish life if it ignores the question of God and the death camps.

Ibid.

JEWISH UNITY AND DESTINY

Whatever most diaspora Jews believe, they consider themselves primarily a distinctive religion-ethnic group rather than a community with a common creed. Far more Jews today accept the unity of Jewish destiny than the unity of Jewish belief.

From his essay entitled "Homeland and Holocaust." Quoted in Nathan Glazer's American Judaism *(1957).*

□

Amnon Rubinstein
HUMANISTIC AND GENERAL JUDAIC VALUES

Judaism is too important to be left only in the hands of the Orthodox. It belongs to the entire nation. We must stress excellence in humanistic fields in general, and Jewish studies in particular, alongside excellence in science and technology.

Endorsing a three-year study on the need to expand Jewish studies in Israel's state schools.

THE INFLAMMATORY MR. ARAFAT

If Arafat wants to make do with being head man of the village of Jericho, he should continue with acts like this. But if he wants to reach an historic peace between Palestinians and the State of Israel he must get off his mistaken, stupid path and begin talking like a human being.

After the PLO leader had made a speech in a mosque in South Africa, where he had come to attend Nelson Mandela's inauguration on May 10, 1994. Mandela had said: "You have to come to fight a jihad to liberate Jerusalem, your precious shrine."

□

Anton Rubinstein
NEITHER FISH NOR MEAT

For the Jews I am a Christian, for the Christians a Jew, for the Russians a German, for the Germans a Russian, for the classicists a futurist, for the futurists a retrograde. From this I conclude that I am neither fish nor meat—a sorrowful individual indeed.

Expressing disappointment at his lack of recognition in Russia as a pianist and composer. Quoted in Morris Mandel's Affronts, Insults and Indignities *(1975).*

□

Artur Rubinstein
SPEAKING OF CRITICS

When they praise me, it bores me; when they pan me, it annoys me.

From an article in The New York Times Magazine, *January 26, 1964.*

Helena Rubinstein

A WOMAN'S PREROGATIVE

I have always felt a woman has the right to treat the subject of her age with ambiguity until, perhaps, she passes into the realm of over ninety. Then it is better she be candid with herself and the world.

From her My Life for Beauty *(1966).*

Muriel Rukeyser

THE GIFT OF BEING A JEW

To be a Jew in the twentieth century
Is to be offered a gift. If you refuse,
Wishing to be invisible, you choose
Death of the spirit, the stone insanity.
Accepting, take full life, full agonies...
Daring to live for the impossible.

From her poem "To Be a Jew," included in Breaking Open: New Poems by Muriel Rukeyser *(1973).*

Robert Runcie

CHRISTIAN ANTI-SEMITISM

Without centuries of Christian anti-Semitism, Hitler's passionate hatred would never have been so fervently echoed.

From an article in London's Daily Telegraph, *November 10, 1988.*

Dagobert D. Runes

WHY MAN?

If God could make angels, why did he bother with men?

From his Treasury of World Literature *(1966).*

LIVING FOR GOD

Millions have died for Him, but only a few lived for Him.

Ibid.

ON MORALITY

Morality is the observance of the rights of others.

Ibid.

Damon Runyon

FIGHTING JEW

From that great Valhalla where the souls of all gallant men abide, Sam [Drebin] must be watching with pride the exploits in this war of the Americans of his religious faith that the 5th column propagandists said would not fight....

The Hitlerites were trying to spread the impression that the Jews were somehow different from other Americans—that they would not take up arms in defense of the flag with the same patriotic fervor—an insult to the memory of Drebin and thousands of his faith who fought in our other wars, but nonetheless eagerly whispered about by the totalitarian stooges.

From his column entitled "Brighter Side," in the Milwaukee Sentinel, *May 11, 1942, in which he calls Sam Drebin "my favorite soldier."*

IDEAL COMPANIONS

Walter and I made the ideal companions. He loved to talk, and I couldn't do anything but listen.

Quoted in Bob Thomas's Winchell.

Arthur Ruppin

ANSWER TO ANNIHILATION

Zionism is not a mere national or chauvinistic caprice, but the last desperate stand of the Jews against annihilation.

From his Jews of Today *(1904).*

John Ruskin

INFLUENCED BY THE JEWISH FAITH

In religion, which with me pervaded all the hours of life, I had been moved by the Jewish ideal, and as the perfect color and sound gradually asserted their power on me, they seemed finally to agree in the old article of Jewish faith that things done delightfully and rightfully were always done by the help and spirit of God.

Quoted in Nahum Sokolow's History of Zionism *(1919).*

THE WORD OF THE LORD

Of course you can't imagine such a thing as that the word of God should ever come to you? Is that because you are worse, or better, than Abraham?—because you are a more, or less, civilized person than he? I leave you to answer that question for yourself;—only as I have told you often before, but cannot repeat too often, find out first what the word is.

Commenting on the verse in Genesis 15:1. Quoted in Solomon Goldman's In the Beginning *(1949).*

◻

Bertrand Russell
NAZISM AND CHRISTIANITY

The rejection of humility, of love of one's neighbor and of the rights of the meek, is contrary to Gospel teaching; and anti-Semitism, when it is theoretical as well as practical, is not easily reconciled with a religion of Jewish origin. For these reasons, Nazidom and Christianity have difficulty in making friends, and it is not impossible that their antagonism may bring about the downfall of the Nazis.

From his In Praise of Idleness and Other Essays *(1935).*

◻

Ruth
UNDYING LOYALTY

Entreat me not to leave thee, and to return from following after thee; for whither thou goest, I will go; and where thou lodgest, I will lodge; thy people shall be my people, and thy God, my God; where thou diest, will I die, and there will I be buried; the Lord do so to me, and more also, if aught but death part thee and me.

Imploring her mother-in-law, Naomi, to take her along to Bethlehem. From the Book of Ruth *(1:16).*

◻

Alexandr Rutskoi
RACIAL INTOLERANCE

In many countries, citizens increasingly encounter examples of racism and national xenophobia. Covering themselves with pseudo-patriotic slogans, exploiting economic difficulties, the forces of racial intolerance organize outrageous demonstrations and defile cultural monuments and graves. I am convinced those forces do not have any future in any country, including Russia.

From a speech at a 1992 conference on anti-Semitism held in Paris, sponsored by the United Nations Educational, Scientific, and Cultural Organization and the Simon Wiesenthal Center. Ruskoi's mother was Jewish.

Saadya Gaon

JEWISH RAISON D'ÊTRE

Our nation is a nation only by virtue of its Torah.

> *From his* Emunot Ve-deot *(933).*

WHY SIN IS SINFUL

Sin is not sinful because God forbade it, but God forbade it because it is sinful.

> *Ibid.*

TRADITION AND REASON

The Bible is not the sole basis of our religion, for in addition to it we have two other bases. One is anterior to it, namely, the fountain of reason. The second is posterior to it, namely, the source of tradition.

> *Ibid.*

FORGIVABLE SINS

All sins are atoned for by repentance, except such as entail irretrievable harm—for example, corrupting, misleading and misinforming a multitude; ruining the reputation of an innocent person; and keeping misappropriated articles.

> *Ibid.*

REACHING THE NEXT WORLD

The righteous servant of God loves the life of this world merely because it serves as a step-ladder to the next world.

> *Ibid.*

◻

Muhammad al-Sabah

OUTDOING JEWS

If two Kuwaitis get together, they will come up with four opinions instead of three. Kuwaitis outdo Jews in that regard.

> *During an address to a group of Jewish visitors at the Kuwaiti Embassy in Washington, DC. Quoted in* The Jerusalem Report, *April 21, 1994.*

◻

Abram Leon Sachar

THE LIVING BIBLE

The early Hebrews had created the Bible out of their lives; their descendants created their lives out of the Bible.

> *From his* History of the Jews *(1930).*

HERZL'S GREATNESS

Herzl's redeeming greatness was [that he]...removed the Jewish problem from the waiting rooms of philanthropy and introduced it into the chancelleries of European diplomacy.

> *From his* History of Israel *(1976).*

◻

Andrew M. Sachs

CONSERVATIVE JUDAISM IN ISRAEL

I am a Conservative rabbi living in Israel. Many of our rabbis perform weddings, despite the fact that officiating at a wedding of two Jews, permitted the world over, is forbidden to us under Israeli law. We cannot be registered with the Rabbinate; nonetheless, couples turn to us as an alternative. The officiating rabbi runs the risk of imprisonment, yet we proceed.

> *Discussing the Conservative and Reform struggle for status in Israel. From* Moment *magazine, June 1993.*

◻

Nelly Sachs

LEARNING FROM DEATH

I could not have written, I could not have survived. Death was my teacher.

> *In reflecting on the horror of the Holocaust in which most of her family perished, she made constant use of the German word* Tod, *meaning "death." Quoted in Elinor and Robert Slater's* Great Jewish Women *(1994).*

REPRESENTING TRAGEDY

Agnon represents the State of Israel. I represent the tragedy of the Jewish people.

After receiving the 1966 Nobel Prize in Literature jointly with S. Y. Agnon.

HOLY DARKNESS

I have constantly striven to raise the unutterable to a transcendental level, in order to make it tolerable, and in this night of nights, to give some idea of the holy darkness in which the quiver and the arrow are hidden.

Ibid.

BUILD WHILE THERE IS TIME

Build, when the hourglass trickles,
But do not weep away the minutes
Together with the dust
That obscures the light.

From her poem "To You That Build the New House."

¤

John Sack

WRATH OF THE JEWS

Through the wrath of Jews...the Germans lost more civilians than at Dresden, more than, or just as many as, the Japanese at Hiroshima, the Americans at Pearl Harbor, the British in the Battle of Britain, or the Jews themselves in all of Poland's pogroms.

Arguing that in 1945 Jews behaved like Nazis. From his An Eye for an Eye: The Untold Story of Jewish Revenge Against the Germans in 1945 *(1993).*

SURVIVORS LIKE NAZIS

The worst thing that happened to some Holocaust survivors was that they became like Nazis.

Ibid. From the flap copy.

¤

Jonathan Sacks

MANDATORY JEWISH EDUCATION

The growth in modern times of universal compulsory education has tended to make us forget that such an institution existed in Jewish life almost two thousand years earlier. Already in the late Second Temple period, according to the Talmud (Baba Batra 21a), Joshua ben Gamla had ordained that teachers be appointed to each district and town and that children should enter school at the age of six or seven.

From an article in L'eylah *magazine, April 1988.*

THE GREAT QUESTION

The great question that Jews in the diaspora must ask themselves today is will we have Jewish grandchildren. And only Orthodox Jews can answer in the affirmative with any degree of certainty.

From a message to the inaugural meeting of the North American Orthodox Leadership Conference, November 1993.

NURTURE VERSUS NATURE

There is no other way. The survival of a minority is a matter of nurture, not nature. It is sustained through education, nothing else. So long as Jews learned, they lived. Once they stopped learning, Jewish identity started dying.

From his Will We Have Jewish Grandchildren? Jewish Continuity and How to Achieve It *(1994).*

CHAIN OF CONTINUITY

Not only is intermarriage rising, resistance to it has almost disappeared.... The astonishing chain of Jewish continuity is breaking. American Jewry is assimilating with the speed of the Ten Lost Tribes.

Ibid.

NATIONAL MORTALITY

The Assyrians and Babylonians, Medes and Persians, the Greek and Roman empires, the Third Reich and the Soviet Union rose and fell. The people of Israel lived. Individually, Jews suffered. But collectively, they defied the laws of national mortality.

Ibid.

FATE VS. PRIVILEGE

Jewish continuity will be achieved once education and outreach become our top Diaspora priorities, receiving the best of our leadership and funding. And that will happen when, putting the ghosts of the past behind us, we relearn what our ancestors knew: that being Jewish is not a fate but a privilege.

Ibid.

TURNING POINT

The Six-Day War showed me that Judaism wasn't just a matter of *Shabbos* and *kashrus*, but that it meant being part of an overwhelming Jewish history.

Quoted in The Jerusalem Report, *March 10, 1994.*

□

Anwar al-Sadat

OUT OF THE DEPTHS

We believe as commanded by Allah, that we are a nation elected above all nations.... Jerusalem is not anyone's ownership, it is the property of us all, the property of the Moslem nation....

Nobody can ever decide the fate of Jerusalem. We shall retake it with the help of God out of the hands of those of whom the Koran said: "It was written of them that they shall be demeaned and made wretched."

From a 1972 speech on the occasion of the prophet Mohammed's birthday.

DECEITFUL JEWS

They [the Jews] were the neighbors of the Prophet in Medina...and...they proved that they were men of deceit and treachery, since they allied themselves with his enemies to strike at him in Medina and attack him from within. The most splendid thing that the Prophet Mohammed did was to drive them out of the whole of the Arabian peninsula.... We know our history and their history with the Prophet in the past. They are a nation of liars and traitors, contrivers of plots, a people born for deeds of treachery.

Ibid.

TO HITLER WITH LOVE

I congratulate you from the bottom of my heart. Even if you appear to have been defeated, in reality you are the victor.... You may be proud of having become the immortal leader of Germany or if a new Hitler rises up in your wake.

From an open letter to Hitler published on September 18, 1953 in the Cairo weekly Al Mussawar, *on the occasion of a report that circulated at the time that Hitler was still alive.*

ONE-MILLION-DOLLAR WOMAN

And how do you like a one-million-dollar job? Do you know that the salary for my job is only twelve-thousand dollars a year—and I work day and night?

To Barbara Walters after an interview, when her one-million-dollar contract with ABC in 1976 had become public knowledge.

BRAVE OFFER

I am ready to go to the ends of the earth if this will prevent a soldier or an officer or my sons from being wounded—not being killed, but wounded. Israel will be astonished when it hears me saying now, before you, that I am ready to go to their house, to the Knesset itself to talk to them.

In a speech delivered to the People's Assembly in Cairo, Egypt, on November 9, 1977.

LIVING IN PEACE

Today I tell you, and I declare to the whole world, that we accept living with you in permanent peace based on justice.

In an address delivered to the Israeli Knesset on November 20, 1977.

PRAISE FOR AN OLD FOE

I must record for history that she had been a noble foe during the phase of confrontation between us, which we all hope has ended forever. While we are working to achieve a total and a permanent peace for the people of the area, I must mention that she had an undeniable role in starting this peace process when she signed with us the first disengagement agreement.

She has always proved that she was a political leader of the first category, worthy of occupying her place in your history and worthy of the place she occupied in your leadership. I repeat my condolences to you.

From a personal letter addressed to Golda's children after her death on December 8, 1978.

DAZZLED BY HITLER

I was never sorry for anything that I did. If I were to go back, *I would do the same again....* I had my hair cut in the style of the Prussian generals.... I asked the optician to make me a monocle.... I was dazzled by the German men of war.... I was dazzled by Hitler and became fond of Rommel.

From a series of interviews published in the Cairo magazine after his peace initiative in Jerusalem in November 1977 and after his visit to Yad Vashem, the shrine of the Jewish victims to the Holocaust. Reported in The American Zionist, *June–July 1979.*

NO MORE WAR

Let there be no more war or bloodshed between Arabs and Israelis. Let there be no more suffering or denial of rights. Let there be no more despair or loss of faith.

On the signing of the Egyptian–Israeli peace treaty in Washington, DC, March 26, 1979.

❏

Camelia Sadat

A FATHER'S LEGACY

When I arrived [at Ben-Gurion Airport] and got off the plane and saw the sign "Welcome to Israel," I started crying. I just remembered how...my father [slain Egyptian president Anwar Sadat] came to this place with an initiative and began a process, and now...I was coming to the same place and playing a part in that process. It shook me that this could be happening.

Commenting on how she felt when visiting Israel in November 1994 to study and promote the need for peace education.

FAMILY OF WARRIORS

Peace was very important to me. My ex-husband was in the army. My sisters were married to army officers, my uncles were in the army, my cousins were in the army, and my father, of course, was in the army before he entered politics. That made us like any family here in Israel.

Ibid.

WHEN THE WALL CAME DOWN

When my father went to Israel in 1977, a wall came down for me. A wall that had prevented me from seeing a lot of things, from seeing Jews and Israelis as anything but the enemy. When it went down, I started seeing reality, and I started having great admiration for what the Jewish people have accomplished.

Ibid.

MY FATHER IS ALIVE

My father, and what he believed in, is still alive today. He did a great thing that outlasted his life. Every time anybody talks about peace anywhere in the world, or makes peace anywhere in the world, particularly in the Middle East, we celebrate his life over and over again. He is here.

Ibid.

❏

Jehan Sadat

SONS LIKE BROTHERS

You have treated our sons as if they were your brothers.

Commenting on the humane treatment shown by the Israelis to Egyptian soldiers wounded in combat during the 1973 Yom Kippur War.

❏

William Safire

"HAWK" SPEAKS

I think of Israel as a strategic asset and I'm for treating it as such. Middle East policy really isn't a Democrat-Republican or liberal-conservative issue. It's a hard-line, soft-line. I'm a hardliner. I was a hawk on Vietnam. I think abandoning Taiwan is an indication of a willingness to abandon Israel.

In support of Menachem Begin's government. Quoted in Esquire *magazine, January 1982.*

GENDER EQUALITY

I don't get worked up over Mother Earth and don't expect women to get worked up over Father Time.

Dismissing the overemphasis on delineating gender. From his New York Times *column, "On Language" (1985).*

JUDEO-CHRISTIAN VALUES

We could tell that the Republican candidate Pat Buchanan was reaching out to Jewish voters when he amended Christian values to Judeo-Christian values.

From his New York Times *column, May 7, 1995.*

DECLINING DEMOGRAPHICS

The answer [to the decline of the Jewish population in America from 4% to 2.3%] is not in editors making those who intermarry feel like outcasts or in rabbis setting unenforceable conditions about children's upbringing before performing weddings. That negative strategy just does not work.

Disagreeing with the action of the publisher of the Hartford, Connecticut-based Jewish Ledger, *which refused to publish announcements of intermarriages. From a column in* The New York Times, *July 17, 1995.*

THE JEWISH FAMILY

Judaism is transmitted not by the nation or the tribe or the congregation but by the family.

Jewishness ain't chicken soup or Israeli politics or affection for guilt. Jewish identity is rooted in a distinctive old religion that builds individual character and group loyalty through close family life. That is how the Jewish people have survived through five millennia and is the light the Jews—whatever the number—must continue to offer the world.

Ibid.

PAYBACK TIME

That is what puzzles many whites, in the post-aftermath, about the jubilation that greeted the verdict in so much of the black community. Just as fury rose within Israelis at pictures of Palestinians cheering from the rooftops at incoming Iraqi SCUD missiles, resentment surged among white Americans at the celebration of what so many saw as a wife-beater getting away with murder.

> *Blaming O. J. Simpson for urging his attorney Johnnie Cochran to remind the predominantly black jury in summation of his trial for the murder of Nicole Brown Simpson and Ronald Goldman that this is an opportunity to get even for society's past injustices against blacks. From his essay in* The New York Times, *October 12, 1995.*

WHAT A LANDSLIDE!

"What a landslide!" was President Clinton's telephoned greeting to Benjamin Netanyahu, the Israeli candidate he worked so hard to defeat.

Though the "landslide" joshing was intended as ironic, in one sense it was true: Among Jewish Israelis, Bibi (the short nickname, like Ike, will stick because the headline writers need it) scored a decisive 55 percent victory.

> *From his essay in* The New York Times, *June 3, 1996.*

EITSES-GIVERS

The newly elected leader [of Israel, Benjamin Netanyahu] is surounded by what he calls *eitses*-givers, a combination of Yiddish and English meaning "offerers of advice." The *eitses* to Bibi from this corner: Accept unpopularity in your first year. By keeping your campaign promises, you'll get bad press but make good history.

> *Ibid.*

ROUND ONE TO YELTSIN

Boris Yeltsin brought off a *shturmoushchina.* That's the Russian word for a horse far off the pace who suddenly storms toward the finish line. It also describes a drunken, drugged, stumbling politician who shakes off his lethargy and overwhelms criticism of his sorry record by zestfully demonizing his most dangerous opponent.

> *Commenting on Boris Yeltsin's narrow victory over his communist challenger, Gennadi Zyuganov, in the nonconclusive Russian election of June 16, 1996. From his essay in* The New York Times, *June 17, 1996.*

¤

Mort Sahl

CALL FOR RECIPROCATION

It is said the President is willing to laugh at himself. That is fine. But when is he going to extend that privilege to us?

> *Quoted in Victor Lasky's* J.F.K.: The Man and the Myth *(1966).*

¤

Rachel Salamander

THE LIVING PAST

The past lives only in us. It is our memory that gives it historical reality, making images and words from the past into an aspect of present-day consciousness.

> *From the Foreword to her* Jewish World of Yesterday *(1990).*

¤

Jerome D. Salinger

A BIT OF HUMOR

What I like best is a book that's at least funny once in a while.

> *Words spoken by Holden Caulfield, a character in his* Catcher in the Rye *(1951).*

THE RYE

I keep picturing all these little kids playing some game in this big field of rye.... If they're running and they don't look where they're going I have to come out from somewhere and catch them. That's all I'd do all day. I'd just be the catcher in the rye and all. I know it's crazy.

> *Ibid.*

KNOWLEDGE AND WISDOM

I got the idea in my head—and I couldn't get it out—that college was just one more dopey, inane place.... Sometimes I think that knowledge, when it's knowledge for knowledge's sake, is the worst of all.... I don't think it would have all got me down if just once in a while—just once in a while—there was at least some polite, little, perfunctory implication that knowledge should lead to wisdom.

> *From his* Franny and Zooey *(1961).*

WHO IS THAT FAT LADY?

There isn't anyone anywhere that isn't Seymour's Fat Lady. Don't you know that? Don't you know that goddam secret yet? And don't you know—listen to me, now—don't you know who that Fat Lady really is?.... Ah, buddy. Ah buddy. It's Christ Himself. Christ Himself, buddy.

Ibid.

◘

Jonas Salk

POLIO CONQUERED

The vaccine works!

Announcement made on April 12, 1955 by the young upstart researcher whose experiments to find a cure for the polio epidemic was funded by the National Foundation for Infantile Paralysis.

◘

Jessie Sampter

WRESTLING WITH AN ANGEL

Each one of us alone with God:
Behind the mask of face and deed
Each wrestles with an angel.

From his Brand Plucked from the Fire *(1937).*

◘

Samson

SECRET OF HIS STRENGTH

If I be shaven, then my strength will go from me and I shall become weak and be like any other man.

In revealing to Delilah the source of his strength. Quoted from the Book of Judges (16:17).

◘

(Rabbi) Samuel

DECEPTION DEPLORED

We must not deceive a fellow human whether he be Jew or Gentile.

Insisting that one may not sell nonkosher meat even to a gentile without proper notification. Quoted in the talmudic tractate Chulin (94a).

TALMUDIC ASTRONOMER

I am as familiar with the paths of heaven as with the streets of Nehardea [in Babylonia].

Quoted in the talmudic tractate Berachot (58b).

THE WEDDING FEAST

Hurry and eat, hurry and drink, for the world is like a wedding feast from which we must depart.

Quoted in the talmudic tractate Eruvin (54a).

GOD ARRANGES MARRIAGES

Forty days before an embryo is formed, a heavenly voice proclaims: the daughter of so-and-so will be the wife of so-and-so.

Quoted in the talmudic tractate Moed Katan (18b).

THE CURSE OF POVERTY

This world differs from the Messianic era only in respect to servitude of the exiled [by a foreign power], for it is said, "The poor shall never cease from the land" [Deuteronomy 15:11].

Implying that poverty will be prevalent even in the Messianic Age.

◘

Samuel ben Nachman

IRREPLACEABLE TREASURE

Everything can be replaced, except the wife of one's youth.

Quoted in the talmudic tractate Sanhedrin (22a).

GATES OF PENITENCE

The gates of penitence are always open.

From Midrash Lamentations Rabba (3:44).

◘

Herbert Samuel

BALFOUR DECLARATION

[The Balfour Declaration] means that the Jews, a people who are scattered throughout the world, but whose hearts are always turned to Palestine, should be enabled to find their home, and that some among them, within the limits that are fixed by the numbers and interests of the present population, should come to Palestine in order to help by their resources and efforts to develop the country to the advantage of all its inhabitants. If any measures are needed to convince the Moslem and Christian population...that their rights are really safe, such measures will be taken. For the British Government, the trustee under the Mandate for the happiness of the people of

Palestine, would never impose upon them a policy which that people had reason to think was contrary to their religious, their political, and their economic interests.

From a June 3, 1921 statement.

□

Maurice Samuel

YIDDISH CHARACTER

Classic Yiddish writing derives its stylistic strength and charm from the deliberate emphasis on Hebrew phraseology. Yiddish had a policy which gave it its folk-character—and that was to keep Hebrew alive.

From his Prince of the Ghetto *(1948).*

STRANGE PHENOMENON

The self-critical spirit of the Jews is one of the strangest phenomena in history.... We cannot find an instance of another people which, having been driven from its soil by peoples at least as bad as (actually much more than) itself, should wander about the world saying: "It served us right. We lost our homeland because of our sins."

Ibid.

SCHLEMIEL FULLY DEFINED

To say that a *schlemiel* is a luckless person...is to touch only the negative side. It is the *schlemiel*'s avocation and profession to miss out on things, to muff opportunities, to be persistently, organically, preposterously, and ingeniously out of place. A hungry *schlemiel* dreams of a plate of hot soup, and hasn't a spoon.

From his World of Sholom Aleichem *(1944).*

JEWS AND SEX

Jews were too busy having children to bother with sex.

Ibid.

JEWISH ASSOCIATIONS

If somewhere in China today an individual were to work out for himself all the ethical and theological principles of Judaism, and live up to them, would that make him a Jew? My answer is no. He would be as good a person as any Jew, and better than most Jews; but he would not be a Jew until he had associated himself with the fellowship, and had accepted the responsibilities and instruments of that fellowship.

From his Professor and the Fossil *(1956).*

SACRED DUTY

For others a knowledge of the history of their people is a civic duty, while for the Jews it is a sacred duty.

Ibid.

JOSEPH AND DISRAELI

He [the biblical character Joseph] has been called the Disraeli of the ancient world. The comparison goes much further than is usually perceived, and if it has not yet been done someone should write two Plutarchian parallel lives of Victoria's prime minister and Pharaoh's vizier. There are many differences between the two men, but the similarities are astonishing. Both were brilliant, and brilliant alike in their ability to irritate and to charm. Both were "foreigners," though Disraeli was second-generation English-born. Both were democratic conservatives, concerned with the welfare of the masses as much as with the retention of the traditional authority.

From his Certain People of the Book *(1955).*

EVALUATING ESAU

Esau was huntsman, nothing but huntsman, delivered up, heart and soul, body and spirit, to the ferocious pursuit of food when that stage of human subjection to nature had been left behind. He was a throwback, a case of arrested development. He despised his birthright as a civilized man, and how much more his birthright as the son of Isaac and the grandson of Abraham!

Ibid.

SIGNIFICANCE OF REVELATION

Just as Genesis is an explosive denial of the randomness of the physical universe, so the revelation at Sinai is a repudiation of the meaninglessness of history.

From his Foreword to Solomon Goldman's Ten Commandments *(1956).*

THE POWER OF PHILANTHROPY

Between 1914 and 1929 there was a great revival in American Jewish life. The money spent on social service, schools, hospitals, asylums, and temples doubled and trebled. A building fever set in, for stone is by far the most durable memorial, as well as the most striking evidence, of public generosity.... Charity, too long a disproportionate force in Jewish life, will become the sole force, and Jews will aspire to enter the history of the future on a passport of philanthropy whose visas consist of canceled checks.

From his Jews on Approval *(1932).*

JEWS ON APPROVAL

The Jews are probably the only people in the world to whom it has been promised that their historic destiny is—to be nice.... If the Jews would only temper their voices, their table manners and their ties, if they would be discreet and tidy in their enthusiasms, unobtrusive in their comings and goings, and above all reticent about their Jewishness, they would get along very well.

Ibid.

HALLUCINATING ABOUT JEWS

To say that a man has hallucinations when he is hungry makes sense. To say that a man has hallucinations only about Jews when he is hungry does not.

From his Great Hatred *(1941).*

◻

Rebecca Samuel

LIFE IN AMERICA

One can make a good living here, and all live in peace. Anyone can do what he wants. There is no rabbi in all America to excommunicate anyone. This is a blessing here: Jew and Gentile are one. There is no *galut* [separation] here.

In a 1791 letter to her family in Hamburg, Germany, after she migrated to America and settled in Richmond, Virginia. Quoted in Max Dimont's Jews in America *(1978).*

◻

Howard Samuels

A DEATH CAMP THIRTY YEARS LATER

Exactly 30 years ago, Buchenwald was captured from the Germans. I was there.

I had seen death in battle. I had seen people wounded. I had seen suffering. But I was totally unprepared for Buchenwald.

I had read about the Holocaust. But to tell the truth, for a 24-year-old American G.I., reading that a million children were gassed, six million people tortured, starved, and exterminated simply because they were of a different religion, was unreal and totally unbelievable.

I was there before medical help arrived— the emaciated bodies still on the ground; the flatbed truck with hundreds of dead piled on each other like bales of hay, unburned because the camp had run out of coal; the hanging hooks on the wall near the ovens, which

were served by a little rail truck to efficiently pick up the dead and deliver them into the ovens.

I was so stunned by what I saw, that my mind locked it in. And for almost 20 years, I could never speak about it. It took the sight of the swastikas in an American Nazi Party demonstration in 1966 to loosen my tongue as those memories came flooding back.

From an article in The Jewish Week/American Examiner, *May 10, 1975.*

◻

Carl Sandburg

BEING INVOLVED IN MANKIND

He [Harry Golden] is a fascinating entertainer, telling a good story for the story's sake. Then he shifts to be a reporter or current historian of man's inhumanity to man and telling the world what to do about it. Golden says with John Donne, "I am involved in mankind."

From the Foreword to Harry Golden's For 2¢ Plain *(1959).*

I DON'T UNDERSTAND ANTI-SEMITISM

I don't understand anti-Semitism. I found it among poets and among hoboes. I heard it among Socialists and radicals, and I heard it in the fancy homes of the rich.

From a comment to Harry Golden. Quoted in Golden's autobiography, The Right Time *(1969).*

THE FISH CRIER

I knew a Jew fish crier down on Maxwell Street with a voice like a north wind blowing over corn stubble in January.... His face is that of a man terribly glad to be selling fish.

From his Fish Crier.

◻

Samuel Sandmel

THE SUFFERING OF JESUS

So many Jews became martyrs at the hands of later Christians that his martyrdom seems to us perhaps too unexceptionable for special notice. We Jews have so suffered, because Christians in ages past made us suffer, that it is difficult for us to acknowledge that Jesus suffered unusually.

From his We Jews and Jesus *(1965).*

No Faith Is Superior

I have no disposition to set the one [religion] against the other, and to make meaningless comparisons. Judaism is mine, and I consider it good and I am at home in it, and I love it, and I want it. That is how I want the Christians to feel about their Christianity.

Ibid.

Peter Saniford

The Self-hating Jew

Christians feel nothing but contempt for the Jew ashamed of his faith.

Quoted in J. L. Baron's Stars and Sand *(1943).*

Aaron L. Sapiro

"Protocols" Libel Refuted

Ford maintained that there was a committee of Jews, headed by me, for the purpose of organizing and controlling the primary agricultural products of the world, so that the Jewish bankers could squeeze the nations of the earth of their primary foods. In this connection he named Bernard Baruch, Paul Warburg, Otto Kahn, Albert Lasker, Julius Rosenwald and Eugene Meyer.

I spoke to each one to find out whether they would be available for attendance in Detroit at the trial. Otto Kahn refused, saying, "I am not a Jew anymore." Eugene Meyer refused, saying, "My wife, who is not Jewish, does not want me to be concerned with a Jewish case." Albert Lasker refused, saying, "You can be a damn fool and fight a billion dollars, but don't ask me to do it." Julius Rosenwald declined, saying, "I am too old to go through cross examination these days." Bernard Baruch said that he "would attend from wherever he might be, from anywhere in the world." Paul Warburg said he "would do anything" I wanted.

Commenting on the out-of-court settlement of a damage suit he brought against Henry Ford and on the 1921 attacks on him by the Dearborn Independent, *Ford's newspaper. Quoted in* Western States Jewish Historical Quarterly, *October 1982.*

Yossi Sarid

Assigning Blame

There was one murderer but many sent him.

Muttering bitterly after learning that Israeli Prime Minister Yitzhak Rabin had died after being shot by Yigal Amir, a lone gunman, on November 4, 1995.

Jonathan Sarna

Heaven and Hell

[If America] has not been utter heaven for Jews, it has been as far from hell as Jews in the Diaspora have ever known.

From his article entitled "Anti-Semitism in American History," which appeared in Commentary *magazine, March 1981.*

David Sarnoff

Jewish Responsibility

The essential Jewish identity is worth preserving because it is an influence that conditions the formation of a better type of human being. Jewish ethics, morality, and wisdom are constructive influences. Every individual Jew must therefore assume responsibility for the honor of the entire Jewish people, and realize clearly that improper conduct on his part may be damaging to all Jews by encouraging anti-Semitism.

From an interview with the Jewish Journal, *March 24, 1960. Quoted in Elinor and Robert Slater's* Great Jewish Men *(1996).*

Tomorrow's World

In addition to engineers, the world of tomorrow will also need men and women with deep roots in our moral and spiritual heritage. "It is not brains that matter most," Dostoevski once wrote, "but that which guides them—the character, the heart, the generous qualities."

Surely, it was never the Creator's design that humanity be subordinated to the machine. We cannot program a machine to know good or evil, or to be responsible for the social implications of its performance.

From a 1965 address entitled "Education and the Challenge of the Future," delivered at Hendrix College.

LOOKING BACKWARD

Edmund Burke, one of England's greatest statesmen, spoke with prophetic wisdom when he said: "The public interest requires doing today the things that men of intelligence and good will would wish, five or ten years hence, had been done."

Ibid.

DIVINE UNITY

The microscope, no less than the telescope, has revealed unknown galaxies moving in tune to the same music of the spheres—a clue to the most awesome mystery of all, which is the Divine unity in nature.

From his essay "Youth in a Changing World," June 12, 1954.

VIRTUE AND NOBILITY

The thesis that there is an inherent conflict between science and our immortal souls is simply untrue.... Virtue does not of necessity go hand in hand with primitive plumbing, and nobility can be found in a skyscraper no less than a log cabin.

Ibid.

□

Jean-Paul Sartre

BEAUTIFUL JEWESS

There is in the words "beautiful Jewess" a very special sexual signification, one quite different from that contained in the words "beautiful Rumanian," "beautiful Greek," or "beautiful American," for example. The "beautiful Jewess" is she whom the Cossacks under the czars dragged by her hair through the streets of her burning village.

From his Anti-Semite and Jew (1948).

JEW AS PRETEXT

The Jew only serves [the anti-Semite] as a pretext; elsewhere his counterpart will make use of the Negro or the man of yellow skin.

Ibid.

THE MAKING OF A JEW

The Jew is one whom other men consider a Jew. It is the anti-Semite who makes the Jew.... The sole tie that binds them is the hostility and disdain of the societies which surround them.

Ibid.

INFERIORITY COMPLEX

There is no example of an anti-Semite claiming individual superiority over Jews.

Ibid.

DEFINING "ANTI-SEMITE"

Anti-Semitism, in a word, is fear of man's fate. The anti-Semite is the man who wants to be a pitiless stone, a furious torrent, devastating lightning: in short, anything but a man.

Ibid.

ELITE OF THE MEDIOCRE

The mediocre have their own passionate price, and anti-Semitism is an attempt to give value to mediocrity for its own sake, to create an elite of the mediocre.

Ibid.

□

(King) Saud of Saudi Arabia

CANCEROUS ISRAEL

Israel to the Arab world is like a cancer to the human body, and the only way of remedy is to uproot it just like a cancer.... We Arabs total about fifty million. Why don't we sacrifice ten million of our number and live in pride and self-respect?

From a press release dated January 9, 1954.

□

Uri Savir

MUTUAL AMBIGUITIES

Making peace [with Arab nations] will take a lot of patience. One finds ambiguous feelings among Israelis. On the one hand, there is extreme distrust—and there are historical reasons for that—and on the other hand, a strong desire for reconciliation. I think the same kind of ambiguities exist on the Arab side.

Commenting on the September 13, 1993 Israeli-Palestinian peace accord.

□

Dick Schaap

IRRITATING PRODUCER

To hear his detractors, Merrick combines the delicacy of the Marquis de Sade, the humanity of Attila the Hun, the generosity of Ebenezer Scrooge, and the sophisticated taste of Yogi Berra.

In an article about theatrical producer David Merrick, Schaap voices the criticism of those who accused Merrick of tampering with casting and frequently feuding with persons involved in the production.

◻

Zalman Schachter-Shalomi

KEEPING KOSHER

When someone who eats in a nonkosher restaurant orders beefsteaks instead of pork-chops because he keeps kosher, I can no longer laugh at him. His choice was occasioned by a sort of low-level, yet very genuine, concern not to eat [nonkosher] beasts.... When he refuses butter on it and milk with his coffee because of "seethe not the kid in its mother's milk," I respect him still further. And if he orders a scalebearing fish instead of meat, I see him struggling honestly to do God's will.

From his essay in Condition of Jewish Belief *(1966), compiled by the editors of* Commentary *magazine.*

INTERACTING PEACEABLY

Peace! Here is a noun that functions against its own purpose. As long as we think of "having peace," we treat peace as a product, a commodity and not as an incremental and mutual process. We have such sophistication in destroying lives and we have so little in interpeacing. Here, more than anywhere else, we need an interactive verb and an empirical laboratory to show us how to move from adversary manipulation to interacting peaceably.

In Tikkun *magazine's premier issue (1986).*

PURPOSEFUL LIVING OR DEATH

We must be aware that unless we articulate a clear, ringing, vital message for today's world, then fewer and fewer Jews will be interested in remaining Jews. Either we have something of ultimate value to transmit to the world or we are nothing but Professor Toynbee's fossil, a curio of atavistic religious behaviorism which merits antiquarian interest.

Ibid.

SEARCHING FOR RELEVANCY

We must rediscover the relevant messages of our historical sources. Not everything in the past history of Judaism is either relevant or holy. Judaism was never a monolithic faith.

Ibid.

A CALL FOR REBBE-NESS

We need rebbes, women and men rebbes coming from our own ranks. Don't think that you can do without rebbes and survive as a regenerative religious force. Those of us who still have some of the knowledge of the past and sensitivity for the future need to transmit rebbe-craft to the right candidates for rebbe-ness.

From a November 1994 speech to 850 participants at a Jewish Renewal conference in New York City, at which time he announced his retirement.

◻

William Donald Schaefer

JEWS OF THE CITIES

I've always worried about what would happen if the Jewish community deserted the city and moved out into the country. Without the Jewish community in Baltimore, there'd be no cultural life here—no Baltimore Symphony, no Baltimore Museum of Art, no Walters Art Gallery—no nothing!

Comment to a Jewish visitor to Baltimore, Maryland's City Hall.

◻

Walter Schaffer

THE PROBLEM WITH FUNDAMENTALISM

It is impossible for many educated people today to have a fundamentalist attitude to the Torah—unless they suffer from schizophrenia and are able to believe one thing on Monday and its opposite on Saturday. But the Bible must remain the basis of our teaching because it is the trunk of the tree of our tradition. We have to treat it with reverence, though we cannot treat it as a book of magic of which each verse and each chance group of words has the force of a sacred imperative.

It must be the foundation on which we build, not a prison for our thoughts. If we insist on taking every single verse as equally sacred with the great moral principles which the Bible teaches, we merely make the whole Scripture incredible and unacceptable to people living in the world of today.

From an address delivered at the University of Capetown. Reprinted in Jewish Affairs, *August 1965.*

◻

Dore Schary

MAMMENYU, TOTTENYU, GOTTENYU

In the Jewish life I knew there was a trinity to whom we appealed or expressed our fears. A small accident would evoke *"Mammenyu"* (beloved Mother), a larger mishap would bring forth *"Tottenyu"* (beloved Father), and a shock would provoke *"Gottenyu"* (beloved God). A disaster could evoke an appeal to all three.

Mother, Father and God represented the core of Jewish family life. Every home depended on the warmth and care given by Mother, the strength and security given by Father, and the omnipresence and omnipotence of God. Mother was there when you were ailing or hungry or cold, Father was always handy to protect you, and God was available for everything.

From his For Special Occasions *(1961).*

◻

Mathilde Schechter

THE WOMEN'S LEAGUE GOAL

To serve the cause of Judaism by strengthening the bonds of unity among Jewish women, by learning to appreciate everything fine in Jewish life and literature, to instill the beauty of our ancient observances in the hearts of the children, to cherish the ceremonies of *Shabbat* and holidays and to teach their significance intelligently.

Expressing the goal of the Women's League for Conservative Judaism, founded in 1918 and associated with the United Synagogue of America and the Jewish Theological Seminary of America.

◻

Solomon Schechter

PRAYER AND SYNAGOGUE

Prayer is, of course, not the invention of the synagogue. It is, to use the words of an old mystic, as natural an expression of the intimate relations between heaven and earth as courtship between the sexes. Inarticulate whisperings, however, and rapturous effusions at far intervals are sometimes apt to degenerate into mere passing flirtations. The synagogue, by creating something like a liturgy, appointing times for prayer, and erecting places of worship, gave steadiness and duration to these fitful and uncontrolled emotions, and raised them to the dignity of a proper institution.

From his Studies in Judaism *(1896).*

THE RIGHTS OF OTHERS

When man quits the world, he is asked, according to an ancient Midrash, "Hast thou been busy in the study of the Torah and in works of lovingkindness? Hast thou declared thy Maker as King morning and evening? Hast

thou acknowledged thy fellow-man as king over thee in meekness of spirit?" Man should accordingly perceive in his fellowman not only an equal whose rights he is bound to respect, but a superior whom he is obliged to revere and love. In every person, it is pointed out by these saints, precious and noble elements are latent, not to be found with anybody else.

Ibid.

CONTINUING CREATIVITY

The belief in a single creation after which the Master withdrew from his completed work, is erroneous and heretical. The vivifying power is never withdrawn from the world which it animates. Creation is continuous; an unending manifestation of the goodness of God. All things are an affluence from the two divine attributes of Power and Love, which express themselves in various images and reflections.

Ibid.

A PROTESTING RELIGION

Judaism was always a protesting religion.

Ibid.

INDEPENDENT THINKING

It is not by a personal Amen to every utterance of a great authority that truth or literature gains anything.

Ibid.

INCONSISTENT THEOLOGY

It was said by a great writer that the best theology is that which is not consistent, and this advantage the theology of the synagogue possesses to its utmost extent.

Ibid.

TALMUDIC SEA

The "sea of the Talmud" has also its gulf stream of mysticism.

Ibid.

SALVATION THROUGH LOVE

Indeed we should love all including those who have gone astray. This being the only means of bringing them back into the fold. When a certain pious man came to the saint asking his advice as to what he should do with his son who had left the faith of his ancestors the answer was "love him." The influence of the love will be his salvation.

Ibid.

HEBREW BOOKS

It is indeed a rather unusual coincidence

for the title of a Hebrew book to have any connection with its subject matter.

Ibid.

HAVING SOMETHING TO REGRET

The remarkable thing about these saints is that many among them warned their disciples against asceticism. Of the Gaon of Vilna, the story is that when he remonstrated with his disciple Rabbi Zalman against wasting himself by frequent fasts and vigils through the night, he answered: "But I understand the master himself lived such an ascetic life in his younger days." "Yes," answered the rabbi. "I did, but I regret it deeply now." The rejoinder of Rabbi Zalman was: "I also wish to have something to regret."

Ibid.

BE IN FOCUS

You cannot be everything if you want to be anything.

Ibid.

RELIGION AND NATIONALISM

You can never sever Jewish nationalism from Jewish reform.

> *After attending the 1913 Zionist Congress in Vienna.*

GRATEFUL TO GOD

A certain Jewish saint who had the misfortune to survive the death of his greatest disciple is recorded to have exclaimed: "Oh Lord, Thou shouldst be grateful to me that I have trained for Thee so noble a soul." This is somewhat too bold, but we may be grateful to God for having given us such a great soul as Lincoln, who, under God, gave this nation a new birth of freedom, and to our dear country, which by its institutions and its people rendered possible the greatness for which Abraham Lincoln shall stand forever.

> *From his* Seminary Addresses and Other Papers *(1915).*

LANGUAGES TO LIVE BY

There is no future in this country for a Judaism that resists either the English or the Hebrew languages.

> *Ibid. From an August 28, 1904 address.*

ISRAEL AND JUDAISM

The rebirth of Israel's national consciousness and the revival of Judaism are inseparable. When Israel found itself, it found God.

When Israel lost itself, or began to work at its self-effacement, it was sure to deny its God.

Ibid.

GIFT TO THE WORLD

We did not invent the art of printing; we did not discover America ... we did not inaugurate the French Revolution...we were not the first to utilize the power of steam or electricity.... Our great claim to the gratitude of mankind is that we gave to the world the word of God, the Bible. We stormed heaven to snatch down this heavenly gift, as the Puritanic expression is; we threw ourselves into the breach and covered it with our bodies against every attack; we allowed ourselves to be slain by hundreds and thousands rather than become unfaithful to it; and bore witness to its truth and watched over its purity in the face of a hostile world.

Ibid.

ZIONISM'S ACCOMPLISHMENT

[The Zionist movement] must not be judged by what it has accomplished in Zion and Jerusalem but *for* Zion and Jerusalem, by awakening the national Jewish consciousness. Our American synagogues and homes show plainly the effect.

> *Ibid. Viewing Zionism as "the great bulwark against assimilation."*

THE HEBREW LANGUAGE

If history has anything to say in the matter, the lesson it affords us is that the disappearance of the Hebrew language was always followed by assimilation with their surroundings and the disappearance of Judaism. The Hebrew language is not a mere idiom, it is itself a religious symbol of history, a promise and a hope.

> *Quoted in Norman Bentwich's* Solomon Schechter *(1938).*

ARENA FOR SCHOLARSHIP

What is your college doing? America must be a place of Torah, because the future of Judaism is across the seas. You must make something great out of your institution if the Torah and wisdom are to remain among us. Everything is at a standstill in Germany; England has too few Jews to exercise any real influence. What will happen to Jewish learning if America remains indifferent?

> *Ibid. From a November 1893 letter to Rabbi Alexander Kohut, professor of Talmud at the Jewish Theological Seminary of America.*

HEBREW GRAMMAR

You Christians know Hebrew grammar. We know Hebrew.

In a comment to Robertson Smith, the great authority on Semitics.

THE AIR IS CLEARED

I am a Jew, and you will understand that I hate Jesuits. Now let us be friends.

To Father Nolan, member of the Society of Jesus, who had come to call upon Schechter.

LIBERAL JUDAISM

A Judaism which disowns the Bible, which abolishes our ancient calendar, which is constantly playing with Christian doctrines and puts up Jesus as one of its greatest heroes is to my mind an impossibility,....I scarcely need to tell you that such movements in Jewish history have always resulted in spiritual disaster.

Statement made after coming to America from England in 1901. Expressing alarm at the radical tendencies of Reform Judaism.

RABBIS AND BASEBALL

Unless you can play baseball, you'll never get to be a rabbi in America.

A playful comment to Louis Finkelstein, who later also served as Chancellor of the Jewish Theological Seminary. Quoted in Time *magazine, October 15, 1957.*

CENTRALITY OF THE SYNAGOGUE

It is one of the most interesting of religious phenomena to observe the essential unity that the synagogue maintained.... Dispersed among the nations, without a national center, without a synod to formulate its principles, or any secular power to enforce its decrees, the synagogue found its home and harmony in the heart of a loyal and consecrated Israel.

From his Some Aspects of Rabbinic Theology *(1910).*

SOUL OF ISRAEL

The rebirth of Israel's national consciousness and the revival of Judaism are inseparable. When Israel found itself, it found its God. When Israel lost itself, or began to work at its self-effacement, it was sure to deny its God.

From a 1906 statement. Quoted in J. H. Hertz's Book of Jewish Thoughts *(1917).*

RIGHTS OF THE POOR

According to Israel's law no man has a right to more than bread, water and food, as long as the poor are not provided with the necessaries of life.

From an article in American Hebrew *magazine, January 1916.*

MODERNITY AND ETERNITY

There is something higher than modernity, and that is eternity.

Quoted in Menorah Journal *(1924).*

NEO-PAGANISM

Judaism's mission is just as much to teach the world that there *are* false gods and false ideals, as it is to bring it nearer to the true one. Abraham, the friend of God, began his career, according to the legend, with breaking idols; and it is his particular glory to have been in opposition to the whole world.

Quoted in J. H. Hertz's Pentateuch and Haftorahs *(1961).*

□

Barry Scheck

INVOKING THE HOLOCAUST

I don't think [Johnnie Cochran's remark about Hitler] was outlandish. It's not an exaggeration to say that [Mark Fuhrman's] are fascistic or Nazi views [but] I thought it was a fair comment on the evidence.

Following O. J. Simpson's acquittal, on October 3, 1995, of murdering Nicole Brown Simpson and Ronald Goldman. In his summation, defense attorney Cochran had drawn an analogy between Hitler and Detective Fuhrman that many felt was improper. During an interview on the Charlie Rose television show.

□

Harry Scherman

DISHONESTY'S DANGER

To say "it pays to be honest" is the wrong emphasis. The clearer view is that it is highly dangerous, economically, to be dishonest.

From his Promises Men Live By *(1938).*

ⵀ

Jacob Schiff

THREE INDIVISIBLE PARTS

I am divided into three parts: I am an American, I am a German, and I am a Jew.

From a speech in response to which Shmaryahu Levin, a Zionist, rose and asked Schiff if he divided himself horizontally or vertically and, if horizontally, which part he left for the Jewish people. Quoted in Chaim Weizmann's Trial and Error *(1949).*

FORCES IN CONFLICT

It is quite evident that there is a serious break coming between those who wish to force the formation of a distinct Hebraic element in the United States, as distinct from those of us who desire to be American in attachment, thought and action.

From a statement to The New York Times *(1906) in which he regards Palestine as a spiritual home for Judaism rather than a Jewish state. Quoted in Cyrus Adler's* Jacob H. Schiff: His Life and Letters *(1929).*

AMERICANISM AND ZIONISM

Speaking as an American, I cannot for a moment concede that one can be at the same time a true American and an honest adherent of the Zionist movement.

Ibid. In a communication to Solomon Schechter.

TAKING ON THE RUSSIANS

I pride myself that all the efforts, which at various times during the past four or five years have been made by Russia to gain the favor of the American market for its loans, I have been able to bring to naught.

Boasting to Lord Rothschild in 1904 how he used his financial power to thwart the czar at every turn. Quoted in Ron Chernow's Warburgs *(1993).*

ⵀ

Alexander Schindler

ON THE RIGHT TO CRITICIZE ISRAEL

Yes, it is fair to say that we [American Jews] have been treated with contempt [by Israel]— and we've gone along willingly. But we've crossed a watershed now, and our open criticism will continue and increase.

Following an investigative visit to Israel in the wake of the 1982 Christian militia massacre of Palestinian civilians in the Sabra and Shatila refugee camps in Lebanon. From an interview in New York *magazine.*

DEFINING A CHILD AS JEWISH

I want the genealogical factors to be paternal as well as maternal. Surely the father counts for something when we affix his child's religious identity.

In a 1979 statement proposing that Judaism's Reform movement consider the father's faith as well as the mother's.

ⵀ

Solomon Schindler

FAILURE OF SUNDAY SERVICES

Sunday services are not a failure because they are held on Sunday, but because people do not care for *any* services, and as it is here, it is, I suppose, in other cities.... On Saturday, they say they should not be expected to attend—their business prevents them; and so it is, indeed.... On Friday evening, they say, they are not in fit condition to listen to an earnest discourse because they are tired.... Sunday is entirely out of question.

An 1890 comment explaining to a newspaper editor why his attempt at introducing Sunday morning services was a failure.

ⵀ

Ignacy Schipper

ON PROVING THE HOLOCAUST

Nobody will want to believe us, because our disaster is the disaster of the entire civilized world.... We will have the thankless job of proving to a reluctant world that we are Abel, the murdered brother.

Words spoken by a Holocaust victim who perished in the Maidanek concentration camp.

ⵀ

Arthur M. Schlesinger, Jr.

IF HITLER HAD DIED IN 1916

Suppose...that Lenin had died of typhus in Siberia in 1895 and Hitler had been killed on the western front in 1916. What would the twentieth century have looked like now?

From his Cycles of American History *(1986).*

ANTI-SEMITISM OF THE BUSINESSMAN

Anti-intellectualism has long been the anti-Semitism of the businessman.

From an article in Partisan Review, *March 4, 1953.*

SAVIORS OF THE WORLD

Those who are convinced they have a monopoly on The Truth always feel that they are only saving the world when they slaughter the heretics.

From an address to the Indian Council of World Affairs in 1962.

BASIC QUESTION

I am always amazed that the people who attack me never ask the first question that a historian would ask: Is it true?

Commenting on the criticism of his book A Thousand Days *(1965), about John F. Kennedy.*

BERLIN AND BACALL

The two [Lauren Bacall and Isaiah Berlin] did indeed meet at a dinner in Paris, and, since each supposed the other to be French, they began their conversation in French. When Sir Isaiah said (in French) that he lived in Oxford, Lauren Bacall, remembering the man whom she had been enchanted by some twenty years before in my house in Cambridge, Massachusetts, asked, *"Connaissez-vous mon ami Isaiah Berlin?"* Sir Isaiah replied, *"Cest moi"*—and they both happily continued the conversation in English.

Commenting on a February 20, 1995 essay about Isaiah Berlin. From a letter to the editor of The New Republic.

¤

Helmut Schmidt

COLLECTIVE GERMAN GUILT

The crimes of Nazi fascism, the guilt of the German Reich under Hitler's leadership, lie at the bottom of our responsibility. We Germans of today are not guilty as individuals, but we must take upon us the political heritage of the ones who were guilty. In this lies our responsibility.

Commented when visiting Auschwitz in November 1977.

¤

Menachem Mendel Schneerson

I BELONG HERE

My place is [in the Diaspora] where my words are likely to be obeyed. Here I am listened to, but in the Land of Israel I won't be heard. There, our youth will follow only somebody who has sprung up from its own ranks and speaks its own language. The Messiah will be a man of flesh and blood, visible and tangible, a man whom others will follow. And he will come.

In response to a question posed to him by right-wing politician and journalist Geula Cohen in the pages of the Israeli newspaper Maariv: *"Why don't you come [and order your followers to emigrate to Israel]?"*

ATTENTION TO CHILDREN

Just as it is a *mitzva* to put on *tefillin* every day, it is a *mitzva* for the father to be involved with the children every day.

From a popular calendar issued by the Lubavitcher sect.

ALL ON ONE SIDE

It's not two sides, it's one side, because we are one people in the City of New York, under one administration protected by one God, and may God protect the police and all the residents of the city.

After Mayor David Dinkins visited him, on the Sunday following the Crown Heights riots of 1991, and expressed the hope that he could bring peace to both sides.

CONTEMPORARY MALAISE

We each need to make a new commitment to kindness...we stand poised at leaving the age of materialism and entering the age of knowledge; knowledge that unites rather than materialism that divides us. And with today's technology we can reach and unite with people everywhere.

From his Toward a Meaningful Life: The Wisdom of the Rebbe, Menachem Mendel Schneerson *(1995), adapted by Simon Jacobson.*

THE SOUL'S JOURNEY

In a sense, we have all wandered away from our true selves. Birth is the beginning of our soul's journey, sent off from its divine source to live in an unnatural state, a land of materialism. Throughout our lives, therefore, we crave to be reunited with our real selves. We search for our soul, for the G-dly [sic] spark within ourselves. We long to reconnect with our source.

Ibid.

FEMININE ENERGY

After so many years of male dominance, we are standing at the threshold of a truly feminine era. We are witnessing a return to higher values...we have seen a resurrection of feminine energy, of the power of the serene.

Ibid.

¤

Shalom Dov Baer Schneerson

ZIONISM VS. TRUE JUDAISM

That the Zionists glory in the name of Israel applies purely to the name of the people of Israel which to them constitutes Judaism; but from true Judaism which is the fulfillment of the Torah and the commandments and faith in the Lord and in His holy servants they are completely distant through the Zionist ideal.

From a 1903 statement. Quoted in Zionism Reconsidered *(1970), edited by Michael Selzer.*

CHABAD ON ZIONISM

As for the question you ask about Zionism...we are not permitted to press for redemption, certainly not through physical endeavors and enterprises. It is not permitted for us to leave the Exile through force or might; not in this will be our redemption and salvation.

Views expressed during World War I and appearing in the New York press in 1917. Quoted in Abraham Karp's From Haven to Home *(1985).*

¤

Arthur Schneier

JUST SAY DAYENU

It's a wonderful expression for you to use when you skirmish with the press or City Council. Just say *dayenu* ["enough"].

To New York's Mayor Rudy Giuliani, who was attending Rabbi Schneier's 1995 seder at the Park East Synagogue.

¤

Susan Schnur

CASTING OFF THE SHAYTL

For our immigrant foremothers, the equivalent of losing one's American virginity was throwing the *shaytl* [wig] off the ship's prow in view of the Statue of Liberty.

Examining Jewish identity through the subject of hair. From Lilith *magazine, Spring 1995.*

¤

Arnold Schoenberg

FINALLY GETTING IT

I have now finally grasped what I have been forced to learn during the past year and will never forget it again. Namely that I am not

a German, not a European, perhaps hardly even a human being (at least, the Europeans prefer the worst of their race to me), but that I am a Jew.

From his Selected Letters *(1965), edited by Erwin Stein.*

¤

Gershom Scholem

TOO SOON

It is too soon—too soon after the Holocaust.

Responding to the offer of an academic honor in West Germany.

SOURCE OF RELIGIOUS TRUTH

With no thought of denying Revelation as a fact of history, the mystic still conceives the source of religious knowledge and experience which bursts forth from his own heart as being of equal importance for the conception of religious truth.

From his Major Trends in Jewish Mysticism *(1941).*

HASIDISM AND THE UNLETTERED

The Kabbalists never excluded the possibility that a simple and unlettered man could reach the highest spiritual perfection, nor did Hasidism declare such a "simple man" its highest ideal.

Ibid.

STREAM OF MYSTICISM

The story [of Jewish mysticism] is not ended, it has not yet become history, and the secret life it holds can break out tomorrow in you or in me.

Ibid. From the final paragraph.

ON GOD'S "FEMININITY"

In all the numerous references to the *Shekhinah* in the Talmud and the Midrashim... there is no hint that it represents a feminine element in God.

Ibid.

MITSVAH AS COSMIC EVENT

Every *mitsvah* became [for the Kabbalists] an event of cosmic importance, an act which had a bearing upon the dynamics of the universe.

Ibid.

JEWISH BELIEF AND LOGIC

The more genuinely and characteristically

Jewish an idea or doctrine is, the more deliberately unsystematic is it. Its principle of construction is not that of a logical system.

Ibid.

HASIDISM AND MYSTICISM

Hasidism is practical mysticism at its highest. Almost all the kabbalistic ideas are now placed in relation to values peculiar to the individual life, and those which are not remain empty and ineffective. Particular emphasis is laid on ideas and concepts concerning the relation of the individual to God.

Ibid. Pointing out the new emphasis of Chabad—on psychology over theosophy.

ALLEN GINSBERG SPEAKS

The poet Allen Ginsberg once visited me. A likable fellow. Genuine. Strange, mad, but genuine. I took a strong liking to him. My wife and I had a very interesting conversation with him, and in her inimitable way she asked him, "Why don't you come to live here?"...He looked at us and replied, "Me? Your great ideal is to build a new Bronx here. All my life I've been running away from the Bronx, and here I come to the Jewish State and find that the whole big ideal of the Zionists is to build a giant Bronx here. If I have to go back to the Bronx, I may as well stay in the original one."

From his book of essays entitled On Jews & Judaism in Crisis *(1976).*

ON SETTLING IN ISRAEL

People know whether and when it is time for them to come: that's basic. If people want to come, then it is possible to talk to them about it. But I don't have it in me to tell anyone that he must come to Eretz Yisrael. But my wife is different.

Ibid. Scholem's reaction to his wife's asking Allen Ginsberg why he does not settle in Israel.

EFFECT OF ASSIMILATION

The Jews struggled for emancipation—and this is the tragedy that moves us so much today—not for the sake of their rights as a people, but for the sake of assimilating themselves to the peoples among whom they lived. By their readiness to give up their peoplehood, by their act of disavowal, they did not put an end to their misery; they merely opened up a new source of agony. Assimilation did not, as its advocates had hoped, dispose of the Jewish question in Germany; rather it shifted the locus of the question and rendered it all the more acute.

Ibid.

COMMUNICATING WITH KAFKA

It was almost impossible to talk to Kafka about abstractions. He thought in images and spoke in images. He tried to express what he felt simply and in the most direct manner possible, but nevertheless the result was usually very complicated and led to endless speculation without any real decision.

Ibid. From an essay in which Scholem mentions one of the many characteristic traits that Kafka and Agnon have in common.

THE EICHMANN TRIAL

There can be no possible proportion between this crime [of Adolf Eichmann] and its punishment. Neither could his execution serve to teach a lesson to other murderers of our people. The application of the death penalty for the murder of millions is not a "deterrent" and will not deter any potential murderer likely to arise against us in the days to come. It is not the deterrent power of the hanging of one inhuman wretch that will prevent catastrophes of this kind in the future. A different education of men and nations, a new human awareness—these will prevent it. To achieve such a human awareness was the purpose of the Eichmann trial.

From an article in Ammot *magazine, August-September 1962.*

GRAETZ ON KABBALISTS

I liked [Heinrich] Graetz very much as a historian, but I was extremely critical of his attitude to the *Kabbalah*. It was clear to me that the kabbalists could not possibly have been the kind of scoundrels, swindlers, or idiots he described.

From an interview with Muki Tsur, managing editor of Shdemot *magazine, originally published in Spring 1975.*

CRITIQUE OF FRANZ ROSENZWEIG

What impressed me [about Franz Rosenzweig] was the force of his thinking. But two aspects of his thinking got me angry. One was the ecclesiastical aspect he gave Judaism in his book; the way he saw Judaism as a kind of pietistic Protestant church. The second was the Jewish-German synthesis he wanted to create. I have never been able to tolerate that. The German-Jew that Rosenzweig set up as an ideal was intolerable to me.

Ibid.

DISAPPOINTMENT WITH BUBER

My rebellion against Buber's way of looking at things developed because I was convinced that a person who writes as bellicosely as he was writing could not be a true teacher. Buber was a tremendous force in Germany then; he had a profound influence on the youth. But after the war he was also a disappointment—not only to me, but also the romantic youth, who at a certain point were prepared to swallow whatever he felt like feeding them. Buber said very big things, things that looked very extreme, very radical, but it seemed to me that he drew no conclusions from them.

Expressing disappointment over Martin Buber's pro-German stand during World War I and over the fact that he did not settle in Eretz Yisrael (Palestine) after the war.

ALONE WITH GOD

He who has attained the highest degree of spiritual solitude, who is capable of being alone with God, is the true center of the community, because he has reached the stage at which true communion becomes possible.

Quoted in Polish-Jewish History *(1988), edited by Ulf Diederichs.*

○

Arthur Schopenhauer

POWER BASE OF CHRISTIANITY

The power by virtue of which Christianity was able to overcome first Judaism, and then the heathenism of Greece and Rome, lies solely in its pessimism, in the confession that our state is both wretched and sinful, while Judaism and heathenism were optimistic.

From the Supplement to his World as Will and Idea *(1819), edited by Richard Taylor.*

MOTHER OF MONOTHEISM

Judaism cannot be denied the glory of being the only genuinely monotheistic religion on earth.

Admission of a vocal critic of Judaism. Quoted in Alfred J. Kolatch's Second Jewish Book of Why *(1985).*

○

Ismar Schorsch

THE HOLOCAUST IN PERSPECTIVE

By transforming the Holocaust into a surrogate Judaism, we lend unwitting confirmation to the crucial view that attributes Jewish survival to anti-Semitism. To be sure, hostility can temporarily function as a cohesive force. But not over the millennia. Jews persevered because Judaism was able to satisfy their deepest existential needs. By saturating our young and old with the nightmare of the Holocaust, we will...only generate an ephemeral, secular *Trotzjudentum* [Judaism of defiance], without substance.

Expressing grave reservations at the escalating martyrology. From a 1981 article in Midstream *magazine.*

KEY TO JEWISH SURVIVAL

The key to Jewish survival has always been Jewish education; therefore, it, too, has been pushed to the top of that agenda. That puts the [Jewish Theological] Seminary squarely in the forefront of the battle for Jewish continuity in North America—which is precisely where the Seminary wants to be. The study of Torah has been our link to the past, our gateway to the present and our bridge to eternity.

From Masoret *magazine, Spring 1993.*

JEWISH LITERACY

Jewish literacy remains the best defense against assimilation in America.

Ibid.

RETREAT INTO SILENCE

Shabbat imbues us with a sense of proportion. In the silence of the garden, we hear again God's voice. It comes through in the music of our prayers, the chant of the Torah reading, a walk in the park, and our immersion in the study of sacred texts. We withdraw from conquering the world to conquer ourselves.

From an article in Masoret *magazine, Fall 1995.*

INDIVIDUAL AND COMMUNITY

Shabbat restores a modicum of balance for us between the value of the individual and the value of community. This-worldly salvation, which is what Judaism seeks above all else, can only be found in bonding with each other to repair collectively what we have damaged or destroyed individually.

Ibid.

JEWISH HARVARD

We are the Harvard of Jewish studies. The University of Judaism, in terms of rabbinic education, is a community college.

In a dispute with the University of Judaism of Los Angeles, a Conservative institution, which in 1995 announced that it was establishing a rabbinical seminary.

◻

Olive Schreiner

QUALITIES OF ETHICAL LEADERS

The quality most distinguishing them [the Jews] has been a large idealism; the power of grasping great impersonal conceptions, of tenaciously clinging to them, and living for their practical realization. It is these qualities which have made the Jews in all ages the ethical leaders of the race, and which today find their expression in the fields of social and political reform.

From her "Letter on the Jew," July 1, 1906.

◻

Harold Schulweiss

SHARING PERSONAL STRUGGLES

I feel most fulfilled in and through my relationship to the community. The rabbinate is really far from an occupation or profession in the sense that medicine or law is a profession. Every talk I give is autobiographical. My struggles are expressed in lectures, sermons, comments. I have never withheld from the congregation my wrestlings with the nature of God, prayer, the chosen people. They are quite aware that these are things I have difficulty with.

From a 1982 Present Tense *magazine article in which the popular California rabbi reveals his inner conflicts and aspirations.*

BELIEVERS AND UNBELIEVERS

An old adage says: "For the believer there are no questions and for the unbeliever there are no answers." I have come to know many unbelievers with deep yearnings for serious questions.

From the Preface to his For Those Who Can't Believe *(1994).*

NEITHER/NOR ATTITUDES

In matters of religion, most people do not ask questions or seek answers. They assume a neither/nor neutrality: neither apostate nor believer; neither denier nor affirmer of their faith.

Ibid. From the Introduction.

PSYCHOLOGICAL JEWS

The psychological Jew is *sui generis.* He is radically different from the other familiar types. He is on principle a privatist. For this post-ideological Jew, all community is suspect.... In our times, the danger to ourselves comes from the suffocating demands of community. And while community in part is use-ful, it must be kept at a safe distance lest it drain our energies and dessicate our joys.

From an article entitled "Restructuring the Synagogue," which appeared in Conservative Judaism *magazine, Summer 1973.*

COMMUNICATING WITH GOD

The idea of a progressive and growing revelation is not merely compatible with faith in its divine origin, but is the only view that reckons with the nature of the human participant in the process.

Ibid.

SYNAGOGUE *HAVURAH*

For the individual Jew caught in the interstices of the under-institutionalized home and the over-institutionalized synagogue, a halfway house must be built. The individual needs mediating structures.

The synagogue *havurah* is the liveliest illustration of such a mediating institution. It provides the individual with an association small enough to see and hear him, large enough to move him beyond privatism.

Ibid.

JUDAISM AND THE INDIVIDUAL

Jewish men and women are bleeding. Ways must be found to pay attention to the individual in pain, to prescribe medicine according to the particular ailments. If Judaism is a way of life, not simply a catalogue of rites, the practice and teleology of *halachah* must be greatly enlarged.

From an address delivered in October 1983 at a conference on the Future of the American Synagogue, held at the Jewish Theological Seminary of America.

JUDAISM'S BIFURCATION

If Orthodoxy alone is synonymous with authentic Judaism, then we must choose either Orthodoxy or heresy.... But that bifurcation denies the depth of spirituality in the secular Jew, his yearning for a religious metaphysics freed of Orthodox dogma, for a ritual and liturgy responsive to the cadence of his soul, for a body of norms and guides reflective of his moral sensibilities. The superimposed either/or choice has led the secularist to a vacuum which human nature abhors—and which will predictably be taken up by materialism, hedonism or conversion to traditions inimical to Jewish survival, including Scientology, Hare Krishna and the Rev. Sung Myung Moon.

From a paper delivered at the 1980 American Jewish Congress's American-Israel Dialogue in Jerusalem.

SOPHISTICATED SELFISHNESS

A dangerous form of "selfishness" thrives in Jews who identify politically as neoconservatives.... Neoconservatives such as Norman Podhoretz and Irving Kristol are loathe to talk about what I believe is a special gift from God—the Jewish Conscience—because, for example, they are not in favor of the government helping out the poor, so they ignore the issue. This is a kind of sophisticated selfishness.

From a 1993 Yom Kippur sermon.

JEWISH CONSCIENCE

Many people are reluctant to talk about their Jewish Conscience because it unsettles them. I contend that conscience is a very profound spiritual energy that is getting neglected in Jewish popular thought.

Ibid.

SUPPRESSION OF CONSCIENCE

Silence is something that Jewish people have suffered from throughout history. We are the people who are most aware of what can happen when conscience is suppressed, and therefore we should be first to speak out when we see something that is wrong.

Ibid.

READING GOD'S MIND

Whether you call it [the 1994 Los Angeles earthquake] an act of God depends on your understanding of God....

Most assuredly, profoundly and emphatically, this was not punishment from God. I can think of a lot of other areas that are more deserving, like the heart of Las Vegas. Or the headquarters of the Skinheads....

Theology gets into a lot of trouble trying to read God's mind. If the earthquake is to be seen as punishment, then any catastrophe can be seen as punishment, and I just can't accept that.

From an interview with Ari L. Noonan in Heritage Southwest Jewish Press, *January 21, 1994.*

L. A. DYBBUK

A *dybbuk* full of sound and fury.

Characterization of the devastating earthquake that hit Los Angeles in 1994.

MEANING OF PRAYER

We don't pray that God will stop a catastrophe. For example, with the Holocaust, we can't say that because of our sins, one million Jewish children were killed. The logic is bad. The theology is worse. I don't believe a post-

Holocaust world can think that way.... It turns God into what atheists make of Him—a cruel, wrathful deity. Prayer, instead, is meant to move the God within us.

Ibid.

□

Howard Eilberg Schwartz

IMAGES OF GOD

A father God who has no body, or one who turns his back so that we cannot see his face, is not a father with whom some of us find it possible to be intimate.... I imagine a liturgy in which both male and female images are evoked, in which each of us can see God as nurturing and powerful.

From his God's Phallus: And Other Problems for Men and Monotheism *(1994).*

□

(Sir) Walter Scott

GUIDED BY GOD

When Israel, of the Lord belov'd,
Out of the land of bondage came,
Her father's God before her mov'd
an awful guile in smoke and flame.
When Israel, of the Lord belov'd,
Out of the land of bondage came,
Her father's God before her mov'd
an awful guide in smoke and flame.

From his Ivanhoe *(1819).*

□

Sylvia Seaman

SIZING UP THE NOSE

Any nose, as long as it's not like that man's, Cyrano's, is all right on a Gentile, or even on an Arab, those other Semites. But on a Jewish girl, a nose has to be short, straight, and turned up a little. In America, that is.

From her How to Be a Jewish Grandmother *(1979).*

□

Seer of Lublin

PEACE IS BETTER

Better a false peace than a true *machloket* ["disagreement"].

By attribution.

Erich Segal

TRUE LOVE

Love means not ever having to say you're sorry.

From his Love Story *(1970).*

Jerry Seinfeld

SHARING GIFT

My father taught me a gift is to be given, and just as he gave it to me I hope I am able to give it to you.

In his SeinLanguage *(1993).*

WHINING CELEBRITIES

I love everything about being famous. You hear so many celebrities talk about the price of fame. As I see it, there is no price. It's all free. You can talk to people if you want, and if you don't want to you don't have to. Why are celebrities always whining? What's the problem?

From his article in GQ *magazine, November 1991.*

IT IS TO LAUGH

The greatest Jewish tradition is to laugh. The cornerstone of Jewish survival has always been to find humor in life and in ourselves.

After being criticized severely, in September 1995, for airing an episode of his television show Seinfeld *in which the characterization of a rabbi was deemed offensive.*

Moses Seixas

JEWS OF NEWPORT TO WASHINGTON

Sir:—Permit the children of the stock of Abraham to approach you with the most cordial affection and esteem for your person and merit, and to join with our fellow-citizens in welcoming you to Newport.

With pleasure we reflect on those days of difficulty and danger when the God of Israel, who delivered David from the peril of the sword, shielded your head in the day of battle; and we rejoice to think that the same spirit which rested in the bosom of the greatly beloved Daniel, enabling him to preside over the provinces of the Babylonian Empire, rests and ever will rest upon you, enabling you to discharge the arduous duties of the Chief Magistrate of these States.

Upon the visit of President George Washington on August 17, 1790.

TO BIGOTRY NO SANCTION

Deprived as we hitherto have been of the invaluable rights of free citizens, we now—with a deep sense of gratitude to the Almighty Disposer of all events—behold a government erected by the majesty of the people—a government which to bigotry gives no sanction, to persecution no assistance, but generously affording to all liberty of conscience and immunities of citizenship, deeming every one of whatever nation, tongue or language, equal parts of the great governmental machine.

Ibid.

A BLESSING FOR WASHINGTON

For all the blessings of civil and religious liberty which we enjoy under an equal and benign administration, we desire to send up our thanks to the Ancient of Days, the great Preserver of men, beseeching Him that the angels who conducted our forefathers through the wilderness into the promised land may graciously conduct you through all the difficulties and dangers of this mortal life; and when, like Joshua, full of days and full of honors, you are gathered to your fathers, may you be admitted into the heavenly paradise to partake of the water of life and the tree of immortality.

Ibid.

William Selbie

JOY OF THE COMMANDMENT

To the Jews the Sabbath is a day of happiness. The synagogue liturgy of the Sabbath is full of the joyous note. It is marked by gay dress, sumptuous meals, and a general sense of exhilaration. The Puritans knew nothing of synagogue worship or of Jewish homes. They had no experience of "the joy of the commandment"—a phrase often on Jewish lips and in Jewish hearts.

From his Influence of the Old Testament on Puritanism *(1927).*

John Selden

WHY JEWS THRIVE

Talk what you will of the Jews,—that they are cursed: they thrive wherever they come; they are able to oblige the prince of their country by lending him money; none of them beg; they keep together; and as for their being hated, why Christians hate one another as much.

From his Table-Talk *(1689).*

◻

Hannah Semer

MADE FOR THE JOB

About a year before the Six Day War [in 1967], I attended a "Teddy for Mayor" rally. Golda Meir was very annoyed with me. Teddy Kollek was on the Rafi ticket, running against Mapai's incumbent mayor, but I believed that this special city, Israel's capital, with all its complex problems, needed Teddy Kollek. I still do—perhaps even to a greater extent.... Teddy was practically made for the job.

From a column in The Jerusalem Post, *June 26, 1993.*

◻

Anna Sequoia

ETHNIC HUMOR

I think that the Anti-Defamation League needs a laughectomy.... Jews and blacks are the only people in America who think that if outsiders hear the kinds of jokes we make among ourselves, we'll get whomped.... The truth is that Whoopi is funny. She knows how to use hyperbole to get a laugh—and that's what she's done.

Protesting the criticism of Whoopi Goldberg by Abraham Foxman, of the Anti-Defamation League, for her "Jewish American Fried Chicken Recipe." Sequoia's 1982 "Official JAP Handbook" also came under ADL fire.

◻

Winthrop Sergeant

SILLS IS TOPS

If I were recommending the wonders of New York to a tourist, I would place Beverly Sills at the top of the list—way ahead of such things as the Statue of Liberty and the Empire State Building.

From an article in The New York Times, *March 1, 1969.*

◻

Obadiah Sforno

THE TOWER'S LESSON

The real crime of the builders was that they tried to impose one religion on mankind. God prevented this and, by dispersing the people, kept alive a variety of idolatries. But He knew that out of this diversity would eventually come a recognition of the Supreme Ruler.

From his sixteenth-century commentary on the story of the Tower of Babel.

◻

Nabil Sha'ath

OCCUPATION AND RESISTANCE

If occupation [really ends] at least there will no [longer] be the daily sight of Israelis carrying guns, pointing them at people in the streets. There would be no incitement for the kind of violence that was brought about by the natural urge to resist an occupation.

The essence was, if you want to end the violence of resistance you have to end the violence of occupation. And this agreement will end that confrontation by withdrawing Israeli soldiers from [wherever] they will be in direct confrontation with Palestinians.

The senior political advisor to Yasser Arafat reacting to the proposed peace accord between Israel and the PLO. From an interview with David Makosky in Washington, DC. Reported in The Jerusalem Post, *September 11, 1993.*

A FAST TRACK

We achieved within hours what wasn't achieved [at peace talks] in Washington in two years.

Commenting on the negotiations for implementation of the peace accord signed on September 13, 1993. Quoted in Newsweek *magazine, October 25, 1993.*

ARAFAT'S ENGLISH

[Arafat] really recognizes he is not a very good public speaker, particularly in English. He isn't shying away from doing these appearances, [but] I think he recognizes his forte in many other endeavors. Therefore, he has really been prevailing upon me and others who have more ability to do that explanation, to represent him. But I know in his heart and mind, he is absolutely set in this direction [of opposing terrorism].

Explaining in a satellite appearance before the annual gathering of the National Jewish Community Relations Advisory Council why Arafat hasn't denounced terrorist attacks. Quoted in The Jewish Week, *February 17, 1995.*

LAND GIVEBACK

In the West Bank, every settler and every settlement has to go.... If you return 100,000 Palestinians to Galilee, that's only 10% of the Palestinians in Israel already. Will the Israelis have to go along with that? I think they will have to.

From a 1995 interview in the London daily Independent.

◻

Moshe Shahal

CASINOS IN ISRAEL

My Zionist dream did not include a casino.

In voting in 1995 against a decision to set up a ministerial committee to "favorably review" the establishment of a casino in Eilat.

◻

Ben Shahn

TWENTIETH-CENTURY CRUCIFIXION

Ever since I could remember I'd wished I'd been lucky enough to be alive at that great time—when something big was going on, like the Crucifixion. And suddenly I realized I was. Here I was living through another crucifixion. Here was something to paint!

Referring to his painting in 1932 of a gouache of Sacco and Vanzetti, who had been charged with murder and a payroll theft in 1920. Their conviction and execution aroused international protest.

BASIS OF ART

All art is based on nonconformity.

From an article in Atlantic *magazine, September 1957.*

TOLERATING NON-CONFORMITY

The degree of non-conformity present—and tolerated—in a society might be looked upon as a symptom of its state of health.

From his Shape of Content *(1957).*

TEST OF FAITH

In Russia I went to a Jewish school, of course, where we *really read* the Old Testament. That story was about the ark being brought into the temple, hauled by six white oxen, and balanced on a single pole. The Lord knew that the people would worry about the ark's falling off the pole, so to test their faith He gave orders that no one was to touch it, no matter what happened. One man saw it beginning to totter, and he rushed up to help. He was struck dead. I refused to go to school for a week after we read that story. It seemed so damn unfair. And it still does.

Referring to the story told in the Second Book of Samuel (6). Quoted in James Thrall Soby's Ben Shahn: His Graphic Art *(1957).*

◻

William Shakespeare

HATH NOT A JEW?

I am a Jew: Hath not a Jew eyes? Hath not a Jew hands, organs, dimensions, senses, affections, passions? fed with the same food, hurt with the same weapons, subject to the same diseases, healed by the same means, warmed and cooled by the same winter and summer, as a Christian is? If you prick us, do we not bleed? If you tickle us, do we not laugh? If you poison us, do we not die? and if you wrong us, shall we not revenge?

From his Merchant of Venice *(1597). Shylock speaking to Antonio.*

GOING ONE BETTER

If a Jew wrong a Christian, what is his humility? Revenge. If a Christian wrong a Jew, what should his sufferance be by Christian example? Why revenge! The villainy you teach me, I will execute, and it shall go hard, but I will better the instruction.

Ibid.

PRICE OF PORK

Nay, you need not fear us Lorenzo, Launcelot and I are out,—he tells me flatly there's no mercy for me in heaven, because I am a Jew's daughter: and he says you are no good member of the commonwealth, for in converting Jews to Christians, you raise the price of pork.

Ibid. Jessica speaking to Lorenzo, who is in love with her.

SUFFERANCE IS THE BADGE

Signior Antonio, many a time and oft
In the Rialto you have rated me
About my moneys and my usances:
Still have I borne it with a patient shrug,
(For suff'rance is the badge of all our tribe)
You call me misbeliever, cut-throat dog,
And spet upon my Jewish gaberdine,
And all for use of that which is mine own.

Ibid. Shylock speaking to Antonio and requesting a loan of 3,000 ducats.

FOR THE LOVE OF MONEY

Well then, it now appears you need my help:
Go to then, you come to me, and you say,
"Shylock, we would have moneys," you say so:
You that did void your rheum upon my beard,
And foot me as you spurn a stranger cur

Over your threshold, moneys is your suit.
What should I say to you? Should I not say
"Hath a dog money? is it possible
A cur can lend three thousand ducats?" or
Shall I bend low, and in a bondman's key
With bated breath, and whisp'ring humbleness
Say this:
"Fair sir, you spet on me on Wednesday last,
You spurn'd me such a day, another time
You call'd me dog: and for these courtesies
I'll lend you thus much moneys?"

Ibid.

TEARDROPS

Adieu! tears exhibit my tongue, most beautiful pagan, most sweet Jew!—if a Christian do not play the knave and get thee, I am much deceived; but adieu! these foolish drops do something drown my manly spirit: adieu!

Ibid. Launcelot Gobbo, a clown, Shylock's servant, addressing Jessica.

DAUGHTER IN BLOOD

Farewell good Launcelot.
Alack, what heinous sin is it in me
To be ashamed to be my father's child!
But though I am a daughter to his blood
I am not to his manners: O Lorenzo
If thou keep promise I shall end this strife,
Become a Christian and thy loving wife!

Ibid. Jessica responding to Launcelot.

JEPHTHAH'S TREASURE

O Jephthah, judge of Israel, what a treasure hadst thou!

From his Hamlet *(1600).*

TO MEET AGAIN IN JERUSALEM

So part we sadly in this
troublous world
To meet with joy in sweet
Jerusalem.

From his King Henry VI.

□

Khaled el-Shami

REAL PEACE

A peace treaty is formality. Real peace involves developing relationships between people. My being here [in Israel] is just one small step in this direction.

Commenting on the close associations he formed while doing research at the Weizmann Institute.

□

Yair Shamir

NOT LIKE FATHER

My father thought I was giving up on my ideals, giving up a career officer for money.

Comment of Yitzhak Shamir's son after he became, in 1988, executive vice-president of Scitex, one of Israel's most famous high-tech firms, and abandoned his career as a military officer. From a profile in The Jerusalem Report, *January 27, 1994.*

I'M JUST MYSELF

I was always proud of what my father did, and if there was any flak over it, I bore it with love.... The only burden is when people expect me to be his spokesman. I'm not. I'm just myself.

By attribution.

□

Yitzhak Shamir

BLOODIED HANDS

The hands that vote at the UN encourage and strengthen the hands that murder.

In a statement to the Knesset after the July 20, 1980 PLO terrorist attack on a bus full of Jewish teenagers in Antwerp, Belgium, resulting in the death of one fifteen-year-old boy.

FROM DAVID TO GOLIATH

Our image has undergone change from David fighting Goliath to being Goliath.

Quoted in London's Daily Telegraph, *January 25, 1989.*

MEMORABLE DECISION

Israel's purpose—deferring Iraq's capability to bombard this country with nuclear weapons—had been attained. And during the Gulf War a few years later, when the scuds fell, many people recalled the 1981 bombing of the reactor and asked themselves what would have happened had Saddam possessed nuclear weapons.

They certainly realized that the reason he didn't have them was the decision by Israel's government to destroy his reactor. That decision will go down in history.

In a June 1991 address at Tel Aviv University.

HOW TO LOSE A WAR

It was very rare in the history of nations that in such a short time a government can make so many mistakes.... There was no reason or justification for Israel, which was in an excellent position, to act so forcefully against itself. This chapter of Israel's history will go down as a perfect example of how one can lose the war after winning so many battles.

> *Castigating the Labor Party for making a peace accord with the PLO in Washington, DC, on September 13, 1993.*

FATEFUL DECISION

The man simply lost his mind. I knew I had to make a fateful decision and I never avoided it.

> *Confessing that as head of the Lehi (Stern Gang) pre-State underground he ordered the execution of Lehi member Eliyahu Giladi. Quoted in* The Jerusalem Report, *February 10, 1994.*

KISSINGER'S INCONSISTENCIES

I find it impossible to understand former Secretary of State Henry Kissinger's remarks in an interview with Yediot Achronot's Moshe Vardi recently. In that interview, Kissinger states that Israel will not be able to evade the establishment of a Palestinian state. Such a state will have to return the Golan Heights. But at the same time, he stresses that Israel dare not return to the borders of the pre-1967 war. How is this possible?!

How can you establish a Palestinian state in Judea and Samaria, relinquish the Golan Heights and at the same time not return to the pre-1967 borders?! For Israel to do as Kissinger suggests, we would need a country the size of the United States.

> *From an article in* The Jewish Press, *July 19, 1994.*

SUMMING UP

If history remembers me at all, in any way, I hope it will be as a man who loved the Land of Israel and watched over it in every way he could, all his life.

> *Upon the publication of his autobiography,* Summing Up *(1994).*

CAUSE FOR ALARM

[James] Baker is against us; a new hangman for the Jewish people has arisen...a threat to the Jewish people's very existence.

> *Expressing alarm to Moshe Arens about the attitude of the U.S. Secretary of State towards Israel in the 1980s. Quoted in Moshe Arens's* Broken Covenant *(1995).*

◻

Shammai

WELCOME TO ALL

Receive all people with a pleasant countenance.

> *Quoted in the talmudic tractate Ethics of the Fathers (1:15).*

◻

Harold Shanks

HOMOSEXUALS AND FREEDOM OF CHOICE

Is homosexuality a morally neutral choice for people free to choose?

The Jewish answer would surely be no. My gut tells me that the answer is no. But it is not so easy to explain why that is so for committed homosexual partners leading constructive lives and even engaged in rich Jewish observance....

For reasons not so easy to articulate, apart from religious law, I believe that it is wrong for people who are capable of choice to choose a homosexual lifestyle rather than a heterosexual lifestyle.

> *From* Moment *magazine, June 1993.*

INSUFFERABLE POSTURING

There is a messianic arrogance to Lerner and his self-appointed quest. A relic of the '60s, he bursts out of the blue, flags waving, shotgun blasting, peppering the smug and victorious gatekeepers with a steady stream of buckshot.

> *Criticizing Michael Lerner, editor of* Tikkun *magazine. From an article entitled "Michael: His Magazine and His Movement," which appeared in* Moment *magazine, June 1990.*

◻

Constantine Shapiro

ISRAEL: GOLDEN HARP

A golden harp is Israel,
Its strings
Are heaven's own rays,
That trembling, pour a melody
that sings
Of holiness when poet plays.
Alas, the melody is sad and low,
For God has tuned the harp
strings so.

> *From her Collected Poems. Quoted in Meyer Waxman's History of Jewish Literature (1941).*

Karl J. Shapiro

REAL LOVES

The good poet sticks to his real loves, those within the realm of possibility. He never tries to hold hands with God or the human race.

From an article in The New York Times Magazine, *October 15, 1961.*

ARTISTS AND RELIGION

The artist's contribution to religion must, in the nature of things, be heretical.

From an article in Saturday Review, *April 13, 1963.*

Robert Shapiro

THE RACE CARD

Not only did we play the race card, but we dealt it from the bottom of the deck.

Expressing his own misgivings at the way the O. J. Simpson defense team handled the issue of race in the notorious murder trial. From an interview with Barbara Walters following the trial's conclusion on October 3, 1995.

NO COMPARISON

To me, the Holocaust stands alone as the most horrible human event in modern civilization. And with the Holocaust came Adolf Hitler. And to compare this in any way to a rogue cop, in my opinion, was wrong.

Ibid. After stating that he was "deeply offended" by co-counsel Johnnie Cochran's comparison, in summation, of racist Detective Mark Fuhrman to Adolf Hitler.

Natan Sharansky

I LIVED HONESTLY

Five years ago, I submitted my application for exit to Israel. Now I'm further than ever from my dream. It would seem to be cause for regret. But it is absolutely otherwise. I am happy. I am happy that I lived honestly, in peace with my conscience. I never compromised my soul, even under the threat of death.

Statement to a Moscow court before being sentenced on July 14, 1978.

NEXT YEAR IN JERUSALEM

For more than 2,000 years the Jewish people, my people, have been dispersed. But wherever they are, wherever Jews are found,

every year they have repeated, "Next year in Jerusalem." Now, when I am further than ever from my people, from [my wife] Avital, facing many arduous years of imprisonment, I say, turning to my people, my Avital: Next year in Jerusalem.

Ibid.

CHANUKA IN PRISON

Arkady was the only Jew I ever shared a cell with in the *gulag*. We celebrated Hanukkah together in Chistopol prison in 1980, lighting pieces of wax paper we had stashed away for months and hoping they would last long enough for us to say the prayers over them.

Recalled in an article in The Jerusalem Report, *December 30, 1993.*

PALESTINIAN DEMOCRACY

There are very few people who do not see new opportunities and even fewer who do not see new dangers. Look, on the one hand, we can't wait forever to give autonomy to one and a half million people. But then it's so complicated because there is no tradition of democracy in the Palestinian society. The important thing is how quickly they build democratic institutions within the autonomy—not their relations with us, but relations among themselves. The moment there is a human rights catastrophe, it will have great consequences for them and for Israelis.

Reacting to the signing of the peace accord between Israel and the PLO on September 13, 1993.

PACK YOUR BAGS

My advice to the West is to link support, both economic and political, to the processes it wishes to advance, not to a particular person, no matter how good he looks. For the Jews in Russia, my advice remains the same as always: Pack your bags. But when have Jews been able to take this kind of advice?

After Vladimir Zhirinovsky's surprising showing in the December 1993 Russian elections in which his Liberal Democratic party took 23.2 percent of the vote. From his column in The Jerusalem Report, *January 13, 1994.*

CONNECTING WITH THE PAST

The survival of the Jews as a people depends on our ability to give our children the feeling that there is a special meaning to Jewish existence, that we do have a special role among the nations, and through it an opportunity to contribute to them—a sense that must exist in addition to our desires to be a part of liberal society and/or to be a "normal" country.

Without a mystical connection to a history thousands of years old, Jews lose out both as members of a great, liberal diaspora and as founders of a country that, after all, has been in existence for only 45 years.

From his column in The Jerusalem Report, *February 10, 1994.*

A NEW POLITICAL PARTY

Unfortunately, the policy of Israeli governments in recent years has proven that, in spite of this unique moment, integration of new immigrants is a very low priority. This, coupled with the maturing sentiment of Zionism amongst the *aliya*, makes it more justifiable to contemplate the establishment of an Israeli party for whom the goal of bringing another one million Jews to Israel before the year 2000 will be its *raison d'être*. Any questions regarding the potential of such a party's success, or my involvement in such a party, are certainly premature at this stage.

In response to a question put to him in December 1994 by The Jerusalem Post *as to whether he felt this was the right time to establish an independent Russian party and whether he would head such a list. In June 1995 he decided that the time was ripe.*

TURNING ISRAEL AROUND

The establishment of appropriate absorption conditions for the half-million recent olim [immigrants to Israel] and active assistance in their integration into Israeli society is what can turn Israel into a country which attracts Jews instead of a country which accepts them as refugees.

Ibid.

NO COMPROMISE WITH SELFHOOD

Jewish faith came to mean more to me than simply a part of my cultural background in the days after I was sentenced. It was at that time that I made my decision not to compromise. It wasn't a decision that I reached in any rational way. Rationalization wasn't enough, it was based on an irrational—even mystical—feeling of myself as a Jew created in the image of God. And as that was the case, then there could be no possibility of compromise.

Quoted in Hadassah Magazine, *March 1994.*

PRISONERS OF CONSCIENCE MEET

I don't condemn him as enemy of Israel.

After a meeting with Nelson Mandela in Los Angeles, California, on July 6, 1990. Notwithstanding the fact that they had disagreed over the future of Israeli-occupied territories.

WORKERS FOR HUMAN RIGHTS

Only he who understands his own identity and has already become a free person can work effectively for the human rights of others.

From his Fear No Evil *(1988).*

PRIDE IN SELF

Nothing they can do can humiliate me. I alone can humiliate myself.

Ibid. The principle he followed during his years of incarceration in Soviet prisons.

SUSTAINING PRAYER

Baruch atah Adonai, Eloheinu melech ha'olam, ten li mazal lagur im ishti, ahuvati, Avital Sharon, b'Eretz Yisrael. Ten l'horim sheli, ten l'ishti, ten l'kol mishpachti, ko'ach lisbol kol k'shaim ad p'gishteinu. Ten li ko'ach, g'vurah, sechel, mazal v'savlanut latzeit mi'keleh hazeh, l'hagiah l'Eretz Yisrael b'derech yashar v'ra'ui.

Blessed are You, *Adonai*, King of the Universe. Grant me the good fortune to live with my wife, my beloved Avital Sharon, in the Land of Israel. Grant my parents, my wife, and my whole family the strength to endure all hardships until we meet. Grant me the strength, the power, the intelligence, the good fortune, and the patience to leave this jail and to reach the land of Israel in an honest and worthy way.

The short prayer he composed in Hebrew while languishing in the Soviet gulag. He repeated it daily for nine years, especially when he was led to an interrogation. Quoted in his biography, Fear No Evil *(1988).*

FAMILY VALUES

In the daily bustle of life, we don't always realize that the values we hold dear are actually a vessel, filled by our parents and our ancestors. In my case, that vessel was filled not by empty words but by our family's view of the world, with its good-natured optimism and humor, its curiosity about people and events, and its constant readiness to face life's more difficult moments.

From a letter to his mother in 1978, after he learned that his father had died.

RIDING A TIGER

When you're riding on a tiger, the most dangerous thing to do is to stop.

> *Ibid. Quoting an Indian proverb that helped him deal with the constant interrogations he endured while imprisoned.*

REMEMBERING SCOOP

There are three landmarks in my life before leaving the Soviet Union: the Yom Kippur War, the Entebbe operation, and my arrest. But throughout, there was the Jackson Amendment.

> *Commenting on the 1975 Congressional bill sponsored by Senator Henry "Scoop" Jackson from the State of Washington that denied favored-nation status to any country that did not allow free emigration. This was a boon to Soviet refuseniks and other dissidents. Reported in* The Jerusalem Post, *January 14, 1995.*

UNFORGOTTEN HERO

[History] is made by God through those who are ready to fight. Jackson was a man of noble principles who believed that principles do not contradict practicalities.... Jackson lived at a time when there were clear-cut choices between good and evil. In today's confused world, it's good to look back at those romantic times and to return to the realities of today equipped with the truths and legacies of heroes like Senator Jackson.

> *Ibid.*

AN EXTRA DAY FOR REST

The only bad part of Judaism is that we don't have two *Shabbatot* [Sabbaths].

> *From a 1995 interview with Elinor and Robert Slater. Quoted in their* Great Jewish Men *(1996).*

¤

Moshe Sharett

A PERES DISCLAIMER

I have stated that I totally and utterly reject Peres and consider his rise to prominence a malignant, immoral disgrace. I will rend my clothes in mourning for the State if I see him become a Minister in the Israeli government.

> *From his* Personal Diary *(1957).*

¤

Ariel Sharon

THE SOURCE OF VICTORY

We were fewer in number than the enemy, that is certain. The enemy had the most modern equipment, the most modern tanks and artillery. On the other side were our soldiers. I must admit, they looked like a mob. They are excellent soldiers and have excellent commanders, but they were not dressed properly. And they used all kinds of civilian vehicles, milk trucks, and so forth...but these soldiers had magnificent spirit. The officers...running in front of their men are actually the principle reason why we won—not the tanks and artillery, as good as they are.... The same men who in civilian life are shopkeepers or teachers may the next day be attacking the enemy like demons. I don't know how to explain it, but there's something in this people's spirit which makes it possible.

> *Sharon's evaluation of the men in his division after completing their mission in the Six-Day War.*

I DON'T HATE ARABS

I have many contacts with Palestinians. I don't have any hatred whatsoever. On the contrary, if I have anything against the Arabs it's only their lack of quality. I don't like the way they kill. They are cruel. They are terrible. I have a lot of sympathy towards the Palestinians. When I was still in the army and the advisor to the prime minister for a year, I advocated talking to the Palestinians. Even now I advocate talking to the Palestinians. The problem is whether it will be possible to live and exist here with them. I can tell it will be impossible.

> *From a spring 1977 interview. Reported in Frank Epp's* Israelis: Portrait of a People in Conflict *(1980).*

THIS COUNTRY SPEAKS HEBREW

To us [the Israeli's] this is our homeland. This country speaks Hebrew. The place names are Hebrew. They are all biblical names. This is the Jewish homeland. Even though most of the Jews lived in the diaspora and went into exile, there has been a nonstop Jewish existence here for 4,000 years. Jews have been living here all the time.

> *Ibid.*

NO ROOM FOR RECONCILIATION

The Arabs have reacted to last week's diplomatic developments with quiet restraint, keeping their self-respect and national honor. But among us, hearts pound from hyped-up media reports of "a historic reconciliation." It's like Jewish slaves dancing and singing before their new master, Yasser Arafat, defender of Zion.

By recognizing this murderer's organization, the government has committed an act of madness. By reviewing Israel's greatest enemy on the eve of its disintegration and turning it into Israel's "shield" against Hamas, the government has added crime to folly....

There can be no reconciliation, historic or otherwise, with the man who ordered the murders of schoolchildren in Avivim, Ma'alot and Antwerp; of 11 Jewish athletes in Munich, synagogue worshipers in Istanbul, a child and his pregnant mother in Alfeh Menashe, and a mother and her children on a bus in Jericho.

Commenting in anticipation of the signing of the peace accord between Israel and the PLO at the White House on September 13, 1993.

DISGRACEFUL PERFORMANCE

In a shameful event on the White House lawn, an Israeli prime minister [Yitzhak Rabin] revived the PLO, an organization on the brink of collapse. He shook the hand of a man who murdered women and children, transforming a creature despised by heads of state into a popular figure shuttling ceaselessly from kings' palaces to presidents' residences.

Referring to the signing of the peace accord between Israel and the PLO in September 1993. From his column in The Jerusalem Post, *December 18, 1993.*

A DOUBLE-ENTENDRE ATTACK

Some people come up against difficulties and then try to solve problems by placing the blame on others. Some people are caught with their pants down, in both senses of the term.

In a January 1994 attack upon Likud Party chairman Benjamin "Bibi" Netanyahu, after the Labor government had hit a snag in its talks with the Palestine Liberation Organization. Alluding to Netanyahu's alleged amorous exploits.

WAKE-UP CALL

I call upon our leaders to wake up, lower the PLO flag and hoist the flag of immigration, the true flag of Israel.

Urging Israel to stop catering to the Palestinians and to concentrate on bringing 1.5 million Jews to Israel from Russia. From his column in The Jerusalem Post, *January 1, 1994.*

JERUSALEM'S STATUS

Only one people—the Jewish people—exercises sovereignty of Jerusalem in all its parts—especially our holy sites, and primarily the Temple Mount. We cannot accept any foreign sovereignty over Jerusalem. Full rights of religious worship, yes; sovereign status—never.

From his column in The Jerusalem Post, *August 20, 1994.*

◻

Al Sharpton
D'VAR TORAH

If you go to the synagogue, know that the Torah teaches [that] Moses married Tziporah, an African queen. So don't sit up with the Torah talking about *shvartzes* and niggers when we are the basis of your religion.

A message sent to American Jews at a December 17, 1994 rally at Harlem's Public School 175.

◻

George Bernard Shaw
PAYING FOR VALUE

The Jews generally give value. They make you pay, but they deliver the goods. In my experience, the men who want something for nothing are invariably Christians.

From his play Saint Joan *(1923).*

HITLER AND EINSTEIN

Hitler hasn't solved the Jewish problem. He's created it. It has damaged his intellectual credit to an extraordinary extent. Europe could hardly be more disagreeably surprised if he had revived witch burning.

The exiling of Einstein and the confiscation of his property was Hitler's stupidest single act. Einstein may yet be the winner.

From an interview in the London Daily Express, *March 26, 1938.*

SHAW'S ADVICE

Stop being Jews and start being human beings.

Quoted in Alan Dershowitz's Chutzpah *(1991).*

◻

Irwin Shaw
EARTHLY RELIGION

I got a religion that wants to take heaven out of the clouds and plant it right here on the earth where most of us can get a slice of it.

From his antiwar play Bury the Dead *(1936).*

LOOKING BACK

There are too many books I haven't read, too many places I haven't seen, too many memories I haven't kept long enough.

Ibid.

◘

Jonathan Sheffer

WISDOM WITH AGE

As you get older, you realize that you can't be everything, so you should be *more* of something. Returning to Judaism has made me more of what I am.

After becoming a Bar Mitzvah in 1952, one week before his fortieth birthday.

◘

Levi Sheftal

BLESSING THE PRESIDENT

Sir:—We have long been anxious of congratulating you on your appointment, by unanimous approbation, to the presidential dignity of this country, and of testifying our unbounded confidence in your integrity and unblemished virtue. Yet however exalted the station you now fill, it is still not equal to the merit of your heroic services through an arduous and dangerous conflict, which has embosomed you in the hearts of her citizens....

May the Great Author of the world grant you all happiness—an uninterrupted series of health—addition of years to the number of your days, and a continuance of guardianship to that freedom which under auspices of heaven your magnanimity and wisdom have given these States.

From a letter sent to George Washington in 1790 in behalf of the Hebrew congregations of the City of Savannah, Georgia, upon the president's election.

◘

Yoram Sheftel

TRIAL OF DEMJANJUK

I have a natural desire to disturb, disrupt, spoil and to explode into fragments all provocations by the establishment—and the [John] Demjanjuk case was a provocation from the beginning.... After my first meeting with Demjanjuk I had a very strong feeling he was not "Ivan the Terrible." This, combined with evidence that had no legal value, persuaded me to represent him...

A statement made in August 1993 by Demjanjuk's Israeli attorney after the Israeli Supreme Court ruled that Demjanjuk was not guilty as charged, of being Ivan the Terrible, and thus not responsible for some of the 850,000 murders of the Jews at the Treblinka death camp.

◘

Percy Bysshe Shelly

OUTLIVING THE WORLD'S DECAY

The Jew of whom I spake is old,
    so old
He seems to have outlived a
    world's decay;
The hoary mountains and the
    wrinkled ocean
Seem younger still than he; his
    hair and beard
Are whiter than the tempest-
    sifted snow....
...but from his eye looks forth
A life of unconsumèd thought
    which pierces
The present, and the past, and the
    to-come.

From his "Hellas" (1821).

◘

Abraham Shemtov

FAITH UNDER ATTACK

Everyone who places his faith in God finds that faith tested. You assume that if you pray God will answer you. And suppose the answer is not an evident one? How do you explain it to the nonbeliever, and how do you explain it to that part of yourself which is not a believer? Belief is constantly under attack by logic.

Commenting on the belief by some that the deceased Lubavitcher rebbe, Menachem Schneersohn, was the Messiah. Quoted in New York magazine, February 14, 1994.

◘

Neal Sher

EVERY IVAN WAS TERRIBLE

Let's be clear on this. He [John Demjanjuk] was acquitted on the grounds of not being Ivan the Terrible. As to the other count, his being at the Sobibor extermination camp and Trawniki training camp, the Israeli court did not in the end address it. To have served at

Sobibor is no less horrible than to have served at Treblinka. Every Ivan at those camps was Ivan the Terrible.

> *When the Israeli Supreme Court, on July 29, 1993, overturned the conviction of John Demjanjuk, charged with being Ivan the Terrible.*

¤

Mimi Sheraton

OF MOM AND FOOD

By the time she served herself, those who had been fed earliest were ready for seconds. My vision of my mother eating at those happy, noisy, groaning boards is of a woman jumping up and sitting down, cutting off bites that she chewed on the run to the kitchen to get more for the rest of us, a woman whose plate always seemed to contain what looked like trimmings and odd pieces and quarter portions, who finished what others left.

> *From her* My Mother's Kitchen *(1979)*

¤

Moshe Sherer

NO ROOM FOR THE NON-ORTHODOX

They have sanctioned the outright violation of the Torah laws of the Sabbath, of kashrut, of *Taharas HaMishpacha* [family purity]—and now, with their acceptance of gay rabbis, even of basic moral decency.... [They have] stabbed the Jewish people in its very heart with their version of religion.

> *In criticizing the 1993 recommendations of the committee headed by former Minister of Justice Chaim Zadok that non-Orthodox movements in Israel be afforded government funding equal with that of the Orthodox.*

REFORM JUDAISM REPROVED

We lay the fault of the tremendous amount of assimilation in this country at the doorstep of the Reform movement. It created a brand of Judaism which we feel has enabled the masses to believe in a faith that has no basis in our religion. The same plague should not be imported to Israel.

> *Reported in the* Forward, *November 10, 1995.*

¤

Esra Shereshevsky

RASHI'S MEMORIAL

No monument has ever been erected in Rashi's memory. There was no need for it. He attained immortality by virtue of his life work. He created an indispensable tool for the study of Bible and Talmud, an indestructible key to the great treasury of Jewish law, learning and wisdom.

> *From his* Rashi: The Man and His World *(1982).*

¤

Sherira Gaon

JEWS WHO DO WRONG

If you know that a Jew robbed a Gentile, it is your duty to testify to it in court.

> *Quoted in* The Jewish Encyclopedia *(1905).*

¤

Dan Shevitz

NO JUSTIFICATION FOR MURDER

We must refuse to let it make sense—here, or anywhere else. We must steel ourselves against rationalizations and learned political analysis. We must hang on, as long as possible, to our sense of astonishment.

Be astonished that ideology can make murder understandable. Be astonished that hatred can go unchecked until bodies burn. Let us not be misled by labels, as if calling someone a terrorist gives sense to madness.

> *From a sermon delivered by the conservative rabbi of Emanuel Synagogue in Oklahoma City on the final day of Passover, three days after the bombing of the Alfred Murrah Federal Building on Wednesday, April 19, 1995.*

¤

(Rabbi) Shila

BANNING CAPITAL PUNISHMENT

Since we have been exiled from our land, we have no authority to execute people.

> *Explaining why a person found guilty of adultery was not executed as prescribed in the Bible (Leviticus 20:10). Quoted in the talmudic tractate Berachot (58a).*

¤

Dov Shilansky

RETURN OF A PEOPLE

I speak as a Jew, as a remnant snatched from the great conflagration in which Lithuanian Jewry was consumed.... Why did this happen to us? Why? Why? I know the answer. We were born Jews. We were a people without a homeland...dependent on the good graces of strangers.

When you return to your own country, tell your people that with your own eyes you witnessed the rebirth of the Jewish people.

Responding to president of Lithuania Algirdas Brazauskas's speech to the Knesset in March 1995.

○

Shimon ben Menasya

SIN OF ADULTERY

All the transgressions recorded in the Torah can, if committed, be put right. If a man steals, it is possible for him to restore the theft and make amends.... However, one who cohabits with a married woman and causes her to be forbidden to her husband, is driven from the world and goes his way, for he is unable to put things right in such a way that the wife might be permitted to him [her husband] as before.

Quoted in the Midrash Numbers Rabba (9:6).

○

Joseph Shneersohn

EVIL ZIONISTS

It is far worse and more difficult to be in exile among those evil [Zionists] than it is to be among the evil gentiles, because the *goy* only keeps the Jewish body in captivity [while the Zionists] seek to contaminate not only Jewish souls but also to defile the Holy Land itself. Those of us who are here should be thankful that we are not over there in the Diaspora of the Land of Israel.

From a newspaper account, during the Passover of 1943, when the Warsaw Ghetto was burning.

○

Shneur Zalman of Lyadi

SONG OF THE FROGS

Do you know why our master went to the pond every day at dawn and stayed there for a little while before coming home again? He was learning the song with which the frogs praise God. It takes a very long time to learn that song.

In discussing with colleagues the character and greatness of their master, the chasidic rebbe Dov Ber of Mezritch.

TORAH SPICE

Salt adds flavor to food, though it is not itself a food. The same is true of the Kabbalah. In itself it is hardly comprehensible, and it is tasteless, but it adds flavor to the Torah.

From his Tanya (1796).

STUDY PRECEDES PRAYER

You must not interrupt your study of *halacha* [law] for prayer.

Ibid.

FERVENT WISH

I do not want Your paradise. I do not want Your world-to-come. I want You, O God, and You only.

Exclaimed in a moment of ecstasy while reciting his prayers.

CONCENTRATION IN PRAYER

Prayer must spin out like a thread. The slightest interruption and the thread snaps.

By attribution.

○

Sholom Aleichem

CHANUKAH PANCAKES

Can you guess, children, which is the best of all holidays? Chanukah, of course.... Mother is in the kitchen rendering goose fat and frying pancakes.... You eat pancakes every day.

From his Chanukah Gelt.

RICHER THAN ROTHSCHILD

If I were Rothschild, I'd be richer than Rothschild. First of all, I'd have all of Rothschild's money, and then I'd make a little bit on the side as a tailor.

By attribution.

EPITAPH

*Daw ligt a Yid, a poshuter
Geshribn Yiddish-Deitsch far vaiber.
Un far'n prosten folk hawt er
Geven a humorist, a shreiber.*

From his autobiography, Fun'm Yarid. This poem was later inscribed in his tombstone in 1916, the year of his death. In translation it reads: "Here lies a simple Jew who wrote in Jewish-German for women. For plain folks he was a humorist and writer."

BURY ME AMONG THE POOR

Bury me among the poor, that my grave may shine on theirs and their graves on mine.

From his Last Will and Testament *(1916). Quoted in Irving Howe and Eliezer Greenberg's* Treasury of Yiddish Stories *(1954).*

NO MOTHER-IN-LAW

Adam—the luckiest man! He had no mother-in-law.

From I. D. Berkowitz's Sholom Aleichem Buch *(1926).*

BARKING DOGS

Barking dogs don't bite, but they themselves don't know it.

Ibid. A reference to anti-Semites.

LAWYERS AND PHYSICIANS

Lawyers are just like physicians: what one says, the other contradicts.

From his Finf un Zibetsig Toyzend *(1902).*

GOD AND THE POOR

God must hate a poor man, else why did He make him poor?

Spoken by the title character in his Tevye the Dairyman.

BETTER THAN WORSE

It could have been worse, and there are no limits to how much better.

Ibid.

OF HORSES AND MEN

If a horse with four legs can sometimes stumble, how much more a man with only one tongue.

Quoted in Maurice Samuel's World of Sholem Aleichem *(1943).*

THE HEART IS A FIDDLE

The heart, especially the Jewish heart, is a fiddle: you pull the strings and out come songs, mostly plaintive.

By attribution.

REFERRED PAIN

When it rains in Odessa, they open umbrellas in Kasrilevke.

By attribution.

CONCERN FOR FELLOW JEWS

I doubt if Dreyfus's relatives in Paris awaited his return from the island as anxiously as the Jews of Kasrilevke.... They raced to the post office, read the news, digested it, dis-

cussed, shouted.... More than once the postmaster had to let them know that the post office was not their shul; they heard him the way Haman hears the grogger on Purim.

From a piece written during the anxious days of the Dreyfus trial.

SUFFER THE WOMEN

Women! You suffer before you get them, while you have them, and after you lose them.

Quoted in Morris Mandel's Affronts, Insults and Indignities *(1975).*

ONLY TO LAUGH

I tell you, it is an ugly and mean world and only to spite it one must not weep.... Only to laugh out of spite, only to laugh.

From a 1911 comment about the injection of humor into his own writings. Quoted in Elinor and Robert Slater's Great Jewish Men *(1996).*

ロ

Ahmed Shukeiry

A PLO PROGNOSTICATION

Those [Israelis] who survive will remain in Palestine. I estimate that none of them will survive.

In a comment before the June 1967 Six-Day War, before Yasser Arafat took control of the PLO.

ロ

George P. Shultz

INFALLIBLE ISRAEL

Margaret Thatcher [former British leader], who was no big admirer of Yitzhak Shamir, told me something while I was passing through London. She said, "Yitzhak Shamir said something that stuck with me. He said, 'The United States can make a mistake and it's not fatal. Britain can make a mistake, and it is not fatal. But Israel can only make one mistake. If Israel makes one really big mistake, it could be fatal. So you have to be careful.'" I think that is true. I would not want to push Israel into something that could be a big mistake. I think you have to persuade people, but in the end they have to be the judges.

In his book of memoirs, Turmoil and Triumph *(1993).*

ON THE CONCEPT OF TERRITORY

I think some sort of mixed sovereignty is the way that these sort of issues have to be approached. It's not an idea unique to this region.

In Europe, they are struggling with the Maastricht treaty. What is taking place is a massive rearrangement of the meaning of sovereignty, what an individual country can do and what is done in a broader setting.

I think just as peace is an ambiguous concept, so too territory is an ambiguous concept.

I think that we have to think about these subjects in a more operational way, not in some black-and-white sense.

> *In response to questioning by* Jerusalem Post *reporters on June 18, 1993, during a visit to Israel as the guest of the Israel Democracy Institute.*

Who Speaks for a Nation's Security

[Some people wonder] if I had been nastier to Israel and willing to say to them: if you don't do what I think you should do for your security, I am going to work to have US support for your arms withdrawn or something like that. I think you could make an argument like that.

It never appealed to me. I think when it comes to the security of a country, that is something that an outsider should be very very careful about. I think the key judgments of what kind of risk you want to take with your security must be taken by the political leaders of that country. It's a presumption to put yourself in their place, to take that risk for them.

> *Ibid.*

◻

Seymour Siegel

Women as Rabbis

There are those who say that the *Halachah* [religious law] does not permit women rabbis because rabbis are judges, and women cannot be judges since women cannot be witnesses. But what about Deborah? If a woman can serve as a judge then, she can serve as a rabbi now.

> *From a 1980 address supporting the ordination of women as Conservative rabbis.*

What Binds Jews

[Jews] are *not* a people like all other people, nor a religious society promoting certain metaphysical principles and ideas, but a group joined together in relation to God.

> *Explaining the common bond that unites Jews.*

Halacha and Menschlichkeit

When Jewish law makes us insensitive, less

human and more prone to withhold human rights from our fellow man, then it has lost its primacy in Jewish life. *Halacha* is a means, not an end in itself. The means should be judged by the ends.... For it is clear...that if strict *halachic* conformance frustrates our highest and human instinct, then the *halachic* considerations should be secondary and yield to ethics and *menshlichkeit.*

> *Commenting on the attitude of leading talmudists who, in 1983, were opposed to the proposal that the Jewish Theological Seminary of America (Conservative) ordain women. On October 24, 1983, by a vote of 34 to 8, the faculty voted in favor of ordination.*

◻

Henry Siegman

Holocaust in Bosnia

To compare Bosnia and the Holocaust is to invite angry disagreement from some Jewish critics who correctly see the Holocaust as a unique evil, an unprecedented descent into hell. But the uniqueness of the Holocaust does not diminish the force of powerful parallels that do exist between these two tragedies, and no one should understand these commonalities better than the Jews.

> *From his essay in* The Jewish Week, *July 16–22, 1993.*

Free to Speak Out

Some of our people, for reasons I fully understand, may yearn for a period of respite from the wars we have waged. The thought of acting more "normally" and joining the larger Jewish consensus is surely an inviting prospect. My message for you is: Do not yield to that temptation. If the American Jewish Congress is true to its principles...it must always be wary of too intimate an association with power.

> *From his April 1994 farewell speech as executive director of the American Jewish Congress.*

◻

Moshe Silberg

Severing the Umbilical Cord

Whatever the theological outlook of a Jew in Israel may be—whether he be religious, irreligious, or antireligious—he is inextricably bound by an umbilical cord to historical Jewry from which he draws his language and his festivals and whose spiritual and religious martyrs have nourished his national pride. An apostate cannot possibly identify himself completely with a people which has suffered so much from religious persecution, and his sincere affection for Israel and its people cannot possibly take the place of such identification.

> *By a vote of three to one the Israeli Supreme Court upheld the decision to not consider Father Daniel a Jew although he had been born Oswald Rufeisen of Jewish parents in Poland and had converted only later in life. He had attempted, in 1952, to settle in Israel under the Law of Return.*

LAND OF ISRAEL

This heritage [the Land of Israel] to which virtually all of us to a greater or lesser extent are bound is one of the foundation stones of our right to possess and settle the Land. We were exiled from the Land 1,900 years ago, but were not absent from it for a single day. We thought of it unceasingly, whether awake or dreaming.

> *From a ruling in the 1970 Schalit v. Minister of the Interior case before the Israeli Supreme Court.*

□

Charles E. Silberman

BLACKS, JEWS, AND ANTI-SEMITISM

Black anti-Semitism is not just a mirror image of Jewish racism. There is a lack of symmetry in the relationship between blacks and Jews that gives black anti-Semitism a distinctive and troublesome cast. Whereas Jewish leaders are considerably less racist (and considerably more sympathetic to black aspirations) than the rank and file, the opposite, as we have seen, is true of the black community.

> *From his* A Certain People *(1986).*

□

Marvin Silbermuntz

FOUR *SHEMAS*

Exactly four *Shema Yisraels*.

> *Jay Leno's personal gag writer, who lives in Northridge, California, the epicenter of the 1993 earthquake, responding to his father's question: "How long did the earthquake last?"*

□

Beverly Sills

A MAN I COULD MARRY

My brothers used to fix me up with college friends of theirs, both Jewish and non-Jewish; some of them were even *doctors!* I was the kind of girl that men seemed to get serious about quickly, but until Peter [Greenough] came along I never got really serious about any of them.

There's a small problem, though, Mama. He's still married; he has three children; he's thirteen years older than I, and he's not Jewish.

Mama burst into tears: "Why does everything have to happen to my baby?"

> *In her* Bubbles: A Self Portrait *(1976).*

FREE CONCERTS

I had never considered myself anything but an American Jew, but, like most Jews, I had considerable curiosity about Israel. When I was invited to sing there in 1970 for the first time, with the Israeli Philharmonic Orchestra, my mother said, "Fine, but do the concerts for free. No nice Jewish girl takes any money out of Israel."

> *Ibid.*

AN EMOTIONAL TIE

I still consider myself an American Jew but now I feel a strong emotional tie with the Israelis. They are an incredibly brave people living in a wonderful country.... I made up my mind then that I would do everything I could to help Israel survive. And I told Peter—teasingly—that if he should ever convert to Judaism, it will have to be before the highest *menorah* in history.

> *Ibid. After her first visit to Israel in 1970.*

APPEARANCE WITH ZUBIN MEHTA

You ain't never sung with an exciting conductor unless you've sung with Zubin Mehta. That man can whip an orchestra—and singer—into an unbelievable frenzy and he almost knocked me off the stage. We had the time of our lives, that moment when two artists meld into one.

> *Ibid. Describing her experience during the November 1971 Celebrity Pops Concert in Los Angeles.*

VERY HIGH NOTES

Man plans, God laughs. I have always been a kind of fatalist. I firmly believe that what's going to happen to any of us is already written down in a great big book. Someone up there looked down one day, pointed a long finger at me, and said: That one is going to be a singer with very high notes. I like that notion.

> *Ibid.*

◻

Abba Hillel Silver

CURE FOR HOMELESSNESS

From the infested, typhus-ridden ghetto of Warsaw, from the death-block of Nazi-occupied lands, where myriads of our people are awaiting execution by the slow or the quick method, from a hundred concentration camps which befoul the map of Europe, from the pitiful ranks of our wandering hosts over the entire face of the earth, comes the cry: Enough! There must be a final end to all this, a sure and certain end!...There is only one solution for national homelessness. That is a national home.

In an impassioned address to the delegates at the American Jewish Conference assembled in New York, August 29, 1943.

BUILDING A GOOD SOCIETY

The Land of Israel will be small...but the people of Israel will make it great.... Not in opulence but in eminence will their destiny be fulfilled, and the elixir of their pride will be distilled not out of dominion or far-flung borders, but out of the faithful and skillful building of the good society.

From his Vision and Victory *(1949).*

FINDING COMMON GROUND

For an unbelieving Jew and an unbelieving non-Jew to be tolerant of each other's nonbelief is no achievement. It is when a believing Jew, who is profoundly moved by his faith, and a believing Christian, who is profoundly moved by his, discover a common basis for good will, that a significant event is consummated.

From his Religion in a Changing World *(1931).*

BLEAK PROGNOSIS

Without a vital religion and a replenishing Jewish education and scholarship, the American Jewish community will linger on as a waning and decaying residuum of the past in a twilight zone of drift until some unforeseen storm breaks over it, attacks its weakened frame, and shatters it beyond repair.

From an address delivered in 1950 before the Central Conference of American Rabbis.

A PASSIONATE VOICE

Zionism is not refugeeism.... Philanthropy alone is not the answer.

From one of his sermons. Quoted in Max Dimont's Jews in America *(1978).*

OPPONENTS OF ZIONISM

A messianic hope not bound up with the restoration of Israel in Palestine is simply not found in Jewish religious literature anywhere from the time of the Second Isaiah to our own time, except of course in the writings of these Reformers.

Ibid. In condemnation of the Pittsburgh Platform of Reform Judaism (1885), which opposed Zionism.

CONGREGATIONAL LEADERS

There are neither good nor poor congregations. Jews are the same everywhere. There are only good or poor leaders.

Expressed to Rabbi Leon J. Ferrer, who had been advised by friends that the Collingwood Avenue Temple in Toledo, Ohio, which had offered him the position as rabbi, had a rather poor reputation. Quoted in Critical Studies in American Jewish History *(1971).*

THE REVOLUTIONARY MOSES

How Moses came to entertain his revolutionary ideas is no greater mystery than the revolutionary insights that come to all men of genius.... To be sure, he does not operate in a vacuum, but whatever truth he reveals wells up in his own soul with the force of an immediate and overpowering apprehension. Whatever he conceives of intellectually or experiences spiritually is a new act of creation and is his very own. It is not the product of evolution nor is it derived from his cultural environment, and it possesses timeless relevance.

From his Moses and the Original Torah *(1961).*

JEWS AMONG NATIONS

The Jewish people belongs in this society of nations. Surely the Jewish people is no less deserving than other peoples whose national freedom and independence have been established and whose representatives are now seated here. The Jewish people were your Allies in the war and joined their sacrifices to yours to achieve a common victory.... The representatives of the Jewish people of Palestine should sit in your midst.

From an eloquent appeal, on May 15, 1947, to the General Assembly of the United Nations. From Abba Eban's essay "Tragedy and Triumph," printed in Chaim Weizmann: A Biography by Several Hands (1963).

Daniel Jeremy Silver

THE HOLOCAUST IN PERSPECTIVE

[The Holocaust] *cannot and does not provide the kind of vitalizing and informing myth around which American Jews could marshal their energies and construct a vital culture. Martyrs command respect, but a community's sense of sacred purpose must be woven of something more substantial than tears* [italics in original].

From his essay "Choose Life," which appeared in Judaism *magazine, Fall 1986.*

(Sheikh) Fathallah Silwadi

CLAIMING JERUSALEM

All the Muslims, not only Palestinians, are responsible for Jerusalem and Al-Aqsa. And not only these two places are holy, but the entire land of Palestine. Preserving the holy land can be achieved only through *jihad* [holy war].

From an address to a crowd at Jerusalem's Al-Aqsa Mosque on Friday, January 6, 1995.

PALESTINIANS AND THE SETTLEMENTS

How can people talk about peace and work for it while the Israeli authorities escalate their settlement campaign and confiscate ever more Palestinian land, especially in Jerusalem?

Ibid.

Simeon ben Chalafta

RAVAGES OF AGING

The rocks have grown tall, the near have become distant, two have turned into three, and the peacemaker of the home has ceased.

In response to Judah the Prince, who asked Rabbi Simeon why he no longer comes to visit on the festivals. He replies that he has grown old, that his two legs need the aid of a cane and can no longer function as in the past. Quoted in the talmudic tractate Shabbat (152a).

Simeon ben Eleazar

ON BEING FLEXIBLE

A person should always be as flexible as a reed; never as rigid as a cedar. A reed bends with the wind and resumes its upright position when the wind has spent itself. The cedar can be bent by the wind; it can be broken and up-rooted. The healthy reed ends up as a pen that writes a Torah scroll.

Quoted in the talmudic tractate Taanit (20b).

ON COMFORTING MOURNERS

Do not try to comfort your friend while his deceased relative is not yet buried.

From the talmudic tractate Ethics of the Fathers (4:18).

DOING GOD'S WILL

When Jews do the will of God, the Name is glorified; when they do not, the Name is desecrated.

From the Midrash Mechilta on Exodus (15:2).

Simeon ben Gamaliel

CAPITAL PUNISHMENT

They would multiply murders in Israel!

Commenting on views, expressed in the Talmud, opposing capital punishment. The Rabbis in general held that a Sanhedrin that effects one execution in seven years is branded a murderous court. Eleazar ben Azariah said: "One in seventy years." Tarfon and Akiba were of the view: "Were we members of a Sanhedrin, no one would ever be put to death." See the talmudic tractate Makkot (Mishna 1:10).

THREE PILLARS

The world rests on three things: justice, truth, and peace.

Quoted in the talmudic tractate Ethics of the Fathers (1:18).

ULTIMATE JOY

Israel had no greater days of joy than the fifteenth of Av and the Day of Atonement, when Jerusalem's maidens danced in the vineyards, in borrowed white dresses, so as not to embarrass those who had none of their own.

Quoted in the talmudic tractate Taanit (30b).

ERECTING TOMBSTONES

Tombstones need not be erected on the graves of the righteous. Their teachings are their monuments.

Quoted in the Jerusalem Talmud, Shekalim (2:5).

PARENTAL OVERSIGHT

He who wishes to give a [strange] child a piece of bread must first notify his mother.

Quoted in the talmudic tractate Betza (16a).

SCHOLARS AND THE COMMON MAN

[The people] Israel is like a vine: its branches are aristocracy, its clusters scholars, its leaves common people, its twigs the unlearned people. This is what was meant when word was sent from there [Palestine to Babylonia]: "Let the clusters pay for the leaves, for were it not for the leaves, the clusters would not exist."

Quoted in the talmudic tractate Chulin (92a).

THEORY VS. PRACTICE

What is more essential than study is action.

Quoted in the talmudic tractate Ethics of the Fathers (1:17).

A LOOSE TONGUE

I spent all my life among scholars and found no virtue better for a person than silence. He who talks too much brings on sin.

Ibid.

□

Simeon ben Yehotzadak

PRIDE OF AUTHORSHIP

Every word which is quoted in the name of a scholar causes the lips of its author to move in the grave.

Quoted in the talmudic tractates Yevamot (97a) and Sanhedrin (90a).

□

Simeon ben Yochai

HONORING PARENTS

To honor parents is more important even than to honor God.

Quoted in the Jerusalem Talmud, Mishna Peah (1:1).

SHAMING A NEIGHBOR

Throw yourself into a blazing furnace rather than shame a neighbor in public.

From the talmudic tractate Berachot (43b).

REACHING FOR EXCELLENCE

I have noted that there are few men of character and excellence in this world [who will see the presence of God]. However, if there be only 1,000 such men in the whole world, I and my son want to be among them. And if there should be only 100 such people in the world, I and my son want to be among the

100. But, if by chance, there should be only two such people of merit in the whole wide world, I want that my son and I should be those two.

Quoted in the talmudic tractate Sukkah (45b).

SPEAKING KINDLY

It is better for a man to be cast into a fiery furnace than to bring his fellowman to shame.

Quoted in the talmudic tractates Ketubot (67b) and Bava Metzia (59a).

ACKOWLEDGING FAULTS

A man should recount his virtues in a whisper and his faults in a loud voice.

Quoted in the talmudic tractate Sota (32b).

□

Simlai bar Abba

THE TORAH COMMANDMENTS

The 613 commandments [in the Torah] consist of 365 negative ones, equal to the number of days in the year, and 248 positive commandments, equal to the number of limbs in the human body.

Quoted in the talmudic tractate Makkot (23b).

□

Akiba Ernst Simon

LEPROSY OF FLUENCY

Even a deeply pious Jew will rarely be able to say all prayers at all times with real *kavanah* [total concentration]. All of us, and the most pious persons perhaps even more than others, occasionally succumb to the danger of praying by rote. Martin Buber, in criticizing the way in which the Torah is frequently read in some synagogues, once spoke of "leprosy of fluency." This leprosy of fluency threatens organized prayer, too. Prayer must be alive, not the mechanical mumbling of words. Routine destroys kavanah and transforms prayer from a dialogue with God into the mechanical fulfillment of a routine assignment.

From A Prelude to Prayer.

□

Neil Simon

CULTURAL JEWS

I'm Jewish more culturally than in a religious way. I was brought up in a semireligious way at home. We only followed the holidays. Other than that, my father didn't attend synagogue on weekends and things like that.

After my Bar Mitzvah at thirteen I really didn't keep up the religion. You keep up being a Jew, and your culture is always there and your sense of identity is there, but I didn't follow what I call the dogma; it's very hard for me to believe in it.

When asked why in interviews he rarely mentions his Jewish background and its influence on his writing.

Germans and Jews

I found out then [during his adolescence in Washington Heights, on the Upper West Side of New York City where there was an enclave of Jewish refugees from Germany] the difference between German Jews and Jews from other parts of the world. They had a certain dogmatic, Teutonic attitude. This thing that you've got to be like steel is more German than Jewish.

During an interview before the 1993 opening of the movie version of his play Lost in Yonkers, *for which he won a Pulitzer Prize. Simon was explaining the attitude of the leading character, Grandma Kurnitz, who is a German Jew.*

¤

Frank Sinatra

Expanded Frontiers

I'm going to Israel to see the pyramids.

At a Friar's Club banquet after the 1967 Six-Day War, during which Egypt was swiftly defeated.

¤

Aaron Singer

Just Another Israeli

Now you are really one of us. You get treated like dirt like everyone else.

Dean of the Overseas School explaining to Emil Fackenheim, the esteemed philosopher, why he was being vigorously criticized for his views, now (in 1981) that he decided to settle in Israel and become a citizen.

¤

Howard Singer

Giving Children a Vision

Only Jewish organizations will support an effort to give Jewish children some vision of who they are and why they must remain Jews. And if the children do not absorb that vision who is going to support Jewish philanthropies in another twenty years? It goes even deeper. If Jews are going to support hospitals, fine and dandy. But let Jewish hospitals be as Jewish as Catholic hospitals are Catholic. Every room in a Catholic hospital has a crucifix on the wall.

From his Bring Forth the Mighty Men: On Violence & the Jewish Character *(1968).*

¤

Isaac Bashevis Singer

Belief in God

The belief in God is as necessary as sex.

Quoted in The New York Times, *October 23, 1968.*

God's Vocabulary

Although I came to doubt all revelation, I can never accept the idea that the universe is a physical or chemical accident, a result of blind evolution. Even though I learned to recognize the lies, the clichés, and the idolatries of the human mind, I still cling to some truths which I think all of us might accept someday. There must be a way for man to attain all possible pleasures, all the powers and knowledge that nature can grant him, and still serve God—a God who speaks in deeds, not in words, and whose vocabulary is the universe.

From his lecture upon receiving the Nobel Prize for Literature, delivered before the assembled guests at the Nobel Prize banquet in the city of Stockholm, Sweden, on December 10, 1978.

The Storyteller

I never forget that I am only a storyteller.

Ibid.

Literature's Power

I am not ashamed to admit that I belong to those who fantasize that literature is capable of bringing new horizons and new perspectives—philosophical, religious, esthetical and even social. In the history of old Jewish literature there was never any basic difference between the poet and the prophet. Our ancient poetry often became law and a way of life.

Ibid.

Love and Religion

Religion is not a simple thing and neither is love. You can love a woman and still betray her. In my belief in God there's only one thing which is steady: I never say that the universe was an accident. The word "accident" should be erased from the dictionary. It has some meaning in everyday life but no meaning in philosophy.

> *From Richard Burgin's* Conversations with Isaac Bashevis Singer *(1978).*

ASSIMILATED JEWS

In one sense he [the assimilated Jew] is the salt of humanity with his tremendous energy and ambition. But being salt, he gives humanity high blood pressure. He's neither a real Jew nor a real Gentile. He has no roots in any group. He digs all the time in other people's soil, but he never reaches any roots.... The worst thing about the assimilationist is that he has no pride. He always wants to be where he is not wanted.

> *Ibid.*

IDEAS ABOUT GOD

Everything man says about God is pure guesswork. But since I believe in God's existence and since God created man and formed his brain, I believe also that there must be something of the divine in men's ideas about Him—even if they are far from being adequate.

> *Ibid.*

REDISCOVERING RELIGION

This is how I began to work my own way back to religion. I investigated what religion is all about, and I came to the conclusion that the essence of religion is this: you must not build your own fortune on another person's misfortune.

> *From an interview with Nili Wachtel which appeared in* The Jewish Spectator, *Spring 1975.*

WHO IS CREATIVE?

I believe that we are all creative. I don't think that only a person who writes stories or plays or music is creative. Creativity is in all of us. We all get up in the morning with the desire to do something. Whether you plan a party for your friends, or build a house, or work in a factory—whatever you do, you create. The fact that artists have taken to themselves this privilege of calling themselves creative while all others are noncreative is sheer nonsense. Either we are all creative, or nobody is.

> *Ibid.*

BEGINNING OF A GOD-BELIEF

To me, nature is not a blind thing, as the modern scientists claim. That the sun and the moon and the galaxies operate with no knowl-edge, and that the only ones who have knowledge are a few professors in a few universities—is not what I believe. I said some time ago that if you would come to an island, and you would find there a wrist-watch, and someone would tell you that this wrist-watch made itself—there was a little metal, and a little glass, and in the course of a billion years they come together and became a wrist-watch—you would say: not even in twenty billion years. And I say: is the universe less complicated than a wrist-watch? So, you must recognize that there is some higher power, some idea, some plan. Once you recognize this, you begin to believe in the existence of God.

> *Ibid.*

DESIRE TO LEARN

I was exalted; everything seemed good. There was no difference between heaven and earth, the most distant star, and my red hair. My tangled thoughts were divine.... The laws of nature were divine; the true sciences of God were mathematics, physics, and chemistry. My desire to learn intensified.

> *The conclusion of* In My Father's House *(1966), a memoir of his childhood in Warsaw, where his father served as a rabbi.*

CHILDHOOD FANTASIES

I suffered deep crises, was subject to hallucinations. My dreams were filled with demons, ghosts, devils, corpses. Sometimes before falling asleep I saw shapes. They danced around my bed, hovered in the air.

> *Ibid. Childhood dreams reflected in his memoirs.*

PRAYING A LOT

Whenever I am in trouble, I pray. And since I'm always in trouble, I pray a lot.

> *Ibid.*

SORRY LOT OF ANIMALS

For animals every day is Treblinka. One day [in 1962] I decided: no meat, no fish. I just think it's the wrong thing to kill animals.

> *An allusion to the suffering in concentration camps. From his* Enemies *(1972).*

YIDDISH IS FOR ME

If Yiddish was good enough for the Baal Shem Tov, for the Gaon of Vilna, for Rabbi Nachman of Bratslav, for millions of Jews who perished by the hands of the Nazis, then it is good enough for me.

> *Explaining why he doesn't write in Hebrew. From his* Meshugah *(1994).*

HEIGHT OF UGLINESS

[A wealthy widow] with a nose like a *shofar* and the teeth of a goat.

Ibid.

DOCTORS AND PATIENTS

There are more doctors in Tel Aviv than patients.

Ibid.

ROBOTS AND GOLEMS

I am not exaggerating when I say that the Golem story appears less obsolete today than it seemed 100 years ago. What are the computers and robots of our time if not Golems?

Reflecting on the old legend of the Golem, a robot made of clay to save the Jews of Prague.

MANY FACES OF A JEW

I met a Jew who had grown up in a yeshiva and knew large sections of the Talmud by heart. I met a Jew who was an atheist. I met a Jew who owned a large clothing store with hundreds of employees, and I met a Jew who was an ardent communist.... It was all the same man.

A favorite yarn.

SHADOWS OF THE PAST

Heaven and earth conspire that everything which has been, be rooted and reduced to dust. Only the dreamers, who dream while awake, call back the shadows of the past and braid nets from unspun threads.

From his Spinoza of Market Street *(1961).*

PERMANENT CRISIS

Things may look bad [for Israel], but in our history things look bad all the time, and we have outlived scores of nations. We Jews have been living in an eternal, permanent crisis.

Quoted in Elinor and Robert Slater's Great Jewish Men *(1996).*

◻

Israel Singer

REWRITING HISTORY

What is taking place here is a sham, a fraud, not a commemoration but a lie. This is an unpleasant attempt at rewriting history. It is Holocaust revisionism. Hungary was a fas-

cist participant, with great pleasure and aggressiveness, in Nazi crimes.

From a 1984 speech in Budapest, Hungary, at the fortieth anniversary commemoration of the deportation of 700,000 Jews to death camps. Previous speakers were praising Hungary as a place where Jews were protected from the Nazi onslaught.

◻

(Sir) John Skelton

THE DISTINCTIVE MR. DISRAELI

The potent wizard himself, with his olive complexion and coal black eyes, and the mighty dome of his forehead (no Christian temple, be sure), is unlike any living creature one has met.... The face is more like a mask than ever and the division between him and mere mortals more marked. I would as soon have thought of sitting down at a table with Hamlet, or Lear, or the Wandering Jew.... England is the Israel of his imagination, and he will be the Imperial Minister before he dies—if he gets the chance.

Describing Benjamin Disraeli. From his Table Talk of Shirley.

◻

Marshall Sklare

LOST GENERATION

Only if the child has formed a particularly strong identification with the parent who is Jewish will he be motivated to integrate into the minority community. The majority of the children of intermarried Jews, then, will be Gentiles.

From his American Jews *(1971).*

◻

John M. Slaton

COURAGEOUS GOVERNOR

Two thousand years ago another Governor [Pontius Pilate] washed his hands of a case and turned over a Jew [Jesus] to a mob. For two thousand years that Governor's name has been accursed. If today another Jew were lying in his grave because I had failed to do my duty, I would all through life find his blood on my hands and would consider myself an assassin through cowardice.

Upon commuting the death sentence of Leo M. Frank, a Jew who was falsely accused of murder, one day before the hanging was to take place. Reported in the Atlanta Constitution, *June 10, 1915.*

Curtis Sliwa

A CONTEMPORARY PHILO-SEMITE

[I feel compelled to keep it up to] make up for the sins of my father's and grandfather's generation. I think all non-Jews have to do that or the anti-Semitism we see rearing up is going to haunt a new generation of Jews. It's better to hear it from me—the gentile—than from a Jew who people think is always exaggerating and making the Jews the only victims.

Urging Jews not to run away from their Jewishness but instead to battle anti-Semitism "one on one." From an article in The Jewish Week, *December 16–22, 1994.*

Henry Slonimsky

FANNING THE SPARK

We can't all pray from our own creative resources because we are not all of us religious geniuses, and prayer and religion are as truly a form of genius, a gift from God, as poetry or music or any high endowment. We can't all write Shakespeare's poetry or Bach's music but we can still make it our own: we can open our hearts to it, and enrich and expand ourselves by sharing and appropriating it. And so in prayer we must turn to the great religious geniuses, the Isaiahs and Jeremiahs and Psalmists, and make our own the visions they have seen, the communion they have established, the messages they have brought back.

From his Essays *(1967).*

MAN'S FREEDOM OF WILL

Man has freedom, he can choose God or reject God, he can lead the world to perdition and to redemption. The creation of this being Man with such power of freedom means that God has made room for a co-determining power alongside of Himself. Man is the crossroad of the world.

Ibid.

Nahum Slouschz

AN UNSHAKABLE FAITH

Deep down in the sorely tried soul of the Jewish masses, there reposes a fund of idealism, an ardent faith in a better future unshaken by time or disappointments. Defraud them of

the millennial ideal which sustains their courage,...and you push them into the arms of a demoralization that lies in wait.

From his Renascence of Hebrew Literature *(1909).*

Joe Slovo

MANDELA'S RIGHT-HAND MAN

I'm not defensive at all about being a Jew. I'm quite proud of it. And I regard anti-Semitism and anti-Jewish cultural activities on the same basis as racism in this country.

The lifelong Communist stood at the side of Nelson Mandela in his fight for full racial equality. From a 1994 interview in the South African cultural journal Jewish Affairs. *Quoted in the* Forward, *January 13, 1995.*

Yakov Smirnoff

IN LOVE WITH AMERICA

It's hard to see bad stuff when you're in love, and I'm still in love with this country.

Responding to those who say life in America is not very good. Quoted in Darryl Lyman's Jewish Comedy Catalog *(1989).*

WHAT A COUNTRY!

What a country! In America, you can always find a party. In Russia, party always finds you.

Ibid. From a Miller Lite beer commercial.

Bailey Smith

JEWISH PRAYERS

It is interesting, at great political rallies, how you have a Protestant to pray, a Catholic to pray, and then you have a Jew to pray. With all due respect to those dear people, God Almighty does not hear the prayer of a Jew, or how in the world can God hear the prayer of a man who says that Jesus Christ is not the true Messiah? That is blasphemy.

Comment made in 1980 when he was president of the Southern Baptist Convention.

SPECIAL, BUT...

No prayer gets through that is not prayed through Jesus Christ.... I am pro-Jesus. I believe they are God's special people [but] without Jesus Christ they are lost.

Ibid. Expanding upon his earlier statement after being mystified over the storm of criticism that ensued.

□

Gerald K. Smith

EXPONENT OF ANTI-SEMITISM

When I am cursed by a Jew, when I am hated by a Jew, when a Jew seeks to kill me, or smear me, or brand me as an evil force, then I have fellowship with Jesus Christ.

One of his many anti-Semitic diatribes expressed in the 1940s and 1950s.

□

Samuel G. Smith

LEADERS OF THE HUMAN RACE

If the Hebrew people had left us nothing but the memory of their struggle, they would have left us rich. The knowledge that once in human history the whole genius of a people was spent in search after God is enough to prove that mankind is not wholly base. If they had not given their conceptions glorious form and expression; if their poets and prophets had not hymned the sweetest music, yet the conception of what life is and what it really means, the system of values which they have bequeathed to us, would still leave them the leaders of the race.

From his Religion in the Making *(1910).*

□

Peretz Smolenskin

HOLY TONGUE

We who have no national monuments, no solid ground, and no outer authority, have one treasure, salvaged from the ruins of our sanctuary, and that is our holy tongue.... Who rejects this tongue rejects the entire people.

Quoted in F. Kobler's Jüdische Geschichte in Briefen *(1938).*

□

J. C. Smuts

ISAIAH AND THE LEAGUE

I do not know whether you are aware that the League of Nations was first of all the vision

of a great Jew almost 3,000 years ago—the prophet Isaiah.

Commenting on the statements of Isaiah (2:1-4).

□

(Viscountess) Snowden

JEWISH CHARACTERISTICS

The fundamental facts of the controversy about the Jew are at least two: Firstly, the success of the Jew is due to good habits and an inherited gift of intellect. Secondly, the objectionable characteristics of the Jew are the direct consequence of persecution.

From her Political Pilgrim in Europe *(1922).*

□

Abraham Samuel Sofer

PURPOSE OF FASTING

The Sages say that he who "sits and fasts"—that is, one who fasts longer than the law requires—is a sinner. Also, if he fasts and makes no spiritual progress, or if the fast has no deeper effect on him, then he has afflicted himself without purpose and therefore is considered a sinner. The same is true for other forms of abstinence.

From his Ketav Sofer *(1873). Quoted in Alexander Z. Friedman's* Wellsprings of the Torah II *(1969).*

□

Rena Sofer

SHARED QUALITIES

The family is there. The guilt is there. The only difference is one believes in Jesus and one doesn't.

After winning an Emmy Award in 1995 for her role as Lois Cerullo on television's "General Hospital," in which she plays a tough-talking Catholic girl. Rena is the daughter of an Orthodox rabbi.

□

(King) Solomon

LEARN FROM THE ANT

Lazy one! Look to the ant, study its ways and grow wise.... It lays up its stores in the summer, gathers in its food at the harvest....

From the Book of Proverbs *(6:6–8).*

SEEDS OF HAPPINESS

Cast your bread upon the waters; for after many days you will find it.

Ibid (11:1).

A WORD IN SEASON

A word in due season, how good it is!

Ibid (15:23).

SPEAK GENTLY

A soft answer turneth away wrath: but harsh words stir up anger.

Ibid (15:1).

SERVING UP LOVE

Better a dinner of herbs served with love, than a fattened ox served with hatred.

Ibid (15:17).

THE PRICE OF PRIDE

Pride goes before destruction and a haughty spirit before a fall.

Ibid (16:18).

CHILD DISCIPLINE

He who spares the rod hates his son, but he who loves him is diligent to discipline him.

Ibid (23:13).

A WOMAN OF VALOR

A woman of valor who can find? Her price is far above rubies.

Ibid.

TO EVERYTHING A SEASON

To everything there is a season, and a time to every purpose under the heaven.

From the Book of Ecclesiastes (3:1).

LIFE IS PRECIOUS

A living dog is better than a dead lion.

Ibid.

THE SEA IS NEVER FULL

All rivers run into the sea, yet the sea is not full.

Ibid.

VANITY OF VANITIES

Vanity of vanities, all is vanity.

Ibid (1:2).

THE TASTE OF LOVE

Your love is better than wine.

From the Song of Songs (1:2).

JOY IN THE AIR

The flowers appear on earth, the time of singing has come.

Ibid (2:12).

NATURE ALIVE

The voice of the turtle is heard in the land.

Ibid.

□

Solomon ben Yerucham

ENEMY OF PHILOSOPHICAL REASON

Woe to him who leaves the Book of God and seeks others! Woe to him who passes his time with strange sciences, and who turns his back upon the pure truth of God! The wisdom of philosophy is vain and worthless, for we do not find two who agree upon a single point. They propound doctrines which directly contradict the Law. Amongst them there are some who study Arabic literature instead of always having the word of God in their mouths.

Attacking scholars, such as Saadya Gaon, who studied philosophy and used it in the service of Judaism. Quoted in Heinrich Heine's History of the Jews (1894).

□

Adolphus S. Solomons

TO KNOW LINCOLN

To me, whose good fortune it was to know Mr. Lincoln when he first came to Washington, and to know him was to love him; it would come with natural impulse to glow over the makeup of his remarkable career. All of his inclinations were on the sunny side of life and the beauty spots seen through his hopeful eyes covered many freckles upon his human face divine and made him think well of all his fellow men.

Solomons was active in the inauguration ceremonies of every U.S. President from Abraham Lincoln to Theodore Roosevelt. These comments were made in 1903 at the Lincoln birthday celebration given under the auspices of the Hebrew Educational Society of Brooklyn, New York.

DO YOUR OWN PRAYING

The day that Lincoln issued one of his early war proclamations I chanced to be at the White House with a distinguished New York Rabbi, Dr. Morris J. Raphall, who came to Washington to ask for the promotion of his son, Alfred, from a second to a first lieutenancy in the army. The White House was closed for the day when we got there, but upon sending up my card we gained admittance, and after Lincoln had heard the Rabbi's request he blurted out, "As God's minister is it not your first duty to be at home today to pray with your people for the success of our arms as being done in every loyal church throughout the North, East and West?"

The Rabbi, evidently ashamed at his faux pas, blushing made answer: "My assistant is doing that duty."

"Ah," said Lincoln, "that is different."

The President then drew forth a small card and wrote the following upon it: The Secretary of war will promote Second Lieutenant Raphall to a First Lieutenancy.

Handing the card to the Rabbi he said with a smile all his own: "Now, doctor, you can go home and do your own praying."

Aaron Soloveichik

A BLOODY COURT

The Jewish view on the death penalty is that it should exist but should never be used. How do you explain this apparent variance? You must return to the sources. The Torah provides the death penalty for no fewer than 36 sins. Yet the Talmud, the Oral Law, says that any Sanhedrin [Jewish high court] that enacts the death penalty once in seven years is a bloody Sanhedrin. So you have the Written Law mandating the death penalty and the Oral Law saying, in effect, that you can never apply it.... [It] should be there for use in extraordinary situations, in extraordinary threats to the public order.

Advice given in 1994 to New York's newly elected governor, George Pataki. Quoted in New York magazine, January 30, 1995.

WRACKED WITH SELF-RECRIMINATION

We cannot say that our hands did not shed the blood. We are all responsible. [While] it is primarily the fault of the murderer, the Mishna says it is also the fault of the Jews, of the parents, of the teachers, of the *rosh yeshivas* [heads of yeshivas], who did not try to hammer into the minds of the students and children the terrible abomination of bloodshed.

Accusing himself for failing to speak out strongly against his Orthodox colleagues, whose inflammatory rhetoric encouraged the assassination of Prime Minister Yitzhak Rabin on November 4, 1995.

Joseph B. Soloveitchik

TOWARDS RELIGIOUS AWARENESS

Inconsistency enriches existence, contradiction renews creation, negation builds worlds, and denial deepens and expands consciousness.

From his Halakhic Man (1984), where he asserts tremendous creative power is vested in the antithesis.

HUMBLE MAN

I have many pupils and many disciples, but I never impose my views on anyone.

By attribution.

GOD AS CREATOR

[The religious mind] views God from the aspect of His creation; and the first response to such an idea is a purified desire to penetrate the mystery of phenomenal reality. The cognition of this world is of the innermost essence of the religious experience.

From his Lonely Man of Faith (1965), which explores the dual nature of religious man.

PARTAKING OF THE HUMAN ENDEAVOR

We are committed to God and to observing His laws, but God also wills us to be committed to mankind in general and to the society in whose midst we live in particular. To find fulfillment, one must partake of the human endeavor.

An often expressed view that Orthodoxy can thrive in a constantly changing society.

RELIGION AND POLITICS

I was afraid to be an officer of the state. A rabbinate linked up with the state cannot be completely free.

Commenting on why he turned down an offer to become the chief Ashkenazic rabbi of Israel.

COUNTERTREND TO ASSIMILATION

When I came here in the 1930s [to the United States from Germany], there was a certain naîveté, a great pride, a confidence in the American way of life. I'm not sure what the American way of life was, but everyone—including a great many Jews—thought it was best. Jews wanted to disappear.

Quoted in Abraham Karp's Haven and Home (1985).

THE REAL WORLD IS HERE

The *halacha* [Jewish law] is not at all concerned with a transcendent world. The world-to-come is a tranquil, quiet world that is wholly good, wholly everlasting, and wholly eternal, wherein a man will receive the reward for the commandments which he performed in this world. However, the receiving of a reward is not a religious act; therefore, halachic man prefers the real world to a transcendent existence because here, in this world, a man is given the opportunity to create, act, accomplish.

> *Quoted in* Jewish Reflections on Death *(1974), edited by Jack Riemer.*

WEIGHTY PERSON

In Hebrew, the noun *kavod*, "dignity," and the noun *koved*, "weight, gravitas," stem from the same root. The man of dignity is a weighty person.

> *Ibid.*

WEEPING AND GRIEVING

Halacha [Jewish law] did not like to see the dead interred in silent indifference. It wanted to hear the shriek of despair and to see the hot tear washing away human cruelty and toughness.

> *From a eulogy for the Talne* rebbetzin *Rebecca Twersky, January 30, 1977.*

THE NATURE OF GOD

Who is He who trails me steadily, uninvited and unwanted, like an everlasting shadow, and vanishes into the recesses of transcendence the very instant I turn around to confront this numinous, awesome, and mysterious "He"?

> *From his* Lonely Man of Faith *(1992).*

SEARCHING FOR GOD

[The genuinely inquiring mind] looks for the image of God not in mathematical formula or the natural law but in every beam of light, in every bud and blossom, in the morning breeze and the stillness of a starlit evening.

> *Ibid.*

INTERFAITH DIALOGUES

The great encounter between God and man is a wholly personal private affair incomprehensible to the outsider.... We certainly have not been authorized by our history, sanctified by the martyrdom of millions, to even hint to another faith community that we are mentally ready to revise historical attitudes, to trade favors pertaining to fundamental matters of faith.

> *From an article in* Tradition: A Journal of Orthodox Jewish Thought, *Summer 1964.*

Vladimir Soloviev

A QUESTION OF RIGHTEOUSNESS

The Jewish question is essentially a question of righteousness and justice. Justice is trampled under foot in the person of the Jew, for the persecution to which he is subjected is without the slightest justification. The charges leveled against him by the anti-Semites cannot stand the most indulgent criticism. They are nothing but vicious lies.

> *Quoted in Joseph Baron's* Stars and Sand *(1943).*

Werner Sombart

THE RARE JEW

Rare are seven things:
A nun who never sings,
A maid without a lover,
A fair without a robber,
A goat of beard bereft,
A Jew that knows no thrift,
A granary without mice,
And a Cossack without lice.

> *A German ditty quoted in his* Jews and Modern Capitalism *(1913).*

Stephen Sondheim

MARITAL BLISS

The concerts you enjoy together
Neighbors you annoy together
Children you destroy together
That make marriage a joy.

> *Lyrics to the song "It's the Little Things You Do Together," from the George Furth and Stephen Sondheim musical* Company *(1970).*

Susan Sontag

SHARING MEMORIES

It's a pleasure to share one's memories. Everything remembered is dear, endearing, touching, precious.

> *From an essay in* American Review, *September 1973.*

THE PRIVILEGE OF GIVING

I didn't want to be a tourist here. I want to give something, to contribute.

Commenting on her 1993 visit to the ruined city of Sarajevo, where she directed a production of Samuel Beckett's Waiting for Godot.

A SECULAR JEW

I identify as a Jew but I'm not religous at all. I come from an assimilated family that's been here [in the United States] for several generations. My identification is within the concept of secular America.

Quoted in Elinor and Robert Slater's Great Jewish Women *(1994).*

◻

George Soros

A JEW WITHOUT ROOTS

As I looked around me for a worthy cause, I ran into difficulties. I did not belong to any community. As a Hungarian Jew, I had never quite become an American. I had left Hungary behind and my Jewishness did not express itself in a sense of tribal loyalty that would have led me to support Israel. On the contrary, I took pride in being in the minority, an outsider who was capable of seeing the other point of view.

Quoted in an article in The New Republic, *January 10–17, 1992, in which Michael Lewis analyzes the life of the billionaire.*

ROUNDUP OF HUNGARIAN JEWS

The Jewish Council [in Hungary] asked the little kids to hand out the deportation notices. I was told to go to the Jewish Council. And there I was given these small slips of paper. It was three or four lines.... This was a list of Hungarian Jewish lawyers. He said, "You deliver the slips of paper and tell the people that if they report they will be deported." I'm not sure to what extent he knew they were going to be gassed.

Ibid.

◻

Michael I. Sovern

A BIAS-FREE LIFE

I think I've been terribly lucky to be just young enough to have missed the barriers. Though I was the first Jewish dean of Columbia I was not the first Jewish dean of a major law school by a long shot. And I'm not the first

Jewish president of an Ivy League university. The idea that I've had to overcome something extra to get here is an attractive one; I think it's probably not true.

After being appointed president of Columbia University in 1980, he noted that being Jewish never posed a problem in his life.

◻

Henry D. Spalding

I LIKE IKE

I like Ike.

Appeared on Eisenhower campaign buttons in 1947 when General Eisenhower was being promoted as a presidential candidate. Noted in The New Republic, *October 27, 1947.*

◻

Louis Spanier

MONEY AND THE LAW

I do not fear the law. I have a hundred thousand dollars more than you. I will ruin you.

Responding to Rabbi Isaac M. Wise, who threatened to sue Spanier, president of the congregation, for punching him in the nose in front of the congregation on Rosh Hashana 1850. Quoted in Max Dimont's Jews in America *(1978).*

◻

Arlen Specter

ARAFAT AND TERRORISM

Any comments [by Arafat] renouncing terrorism are tactical only.

From a 1990 statement.

READY FOR A JEWISH PRESIDENT?

I believe America is ready for a Jewish president. And if the answer to that question is no, then I believe America should be ready for a Jewish president. And if the answers to those two questions are no, damn the torpedoes, full speed ahead! I'm running! I think that it's time we put religion aside like it was put aside for Catholics when John Kennedy was elected in 1960.

Comment of the U.S. senator from Pennsylvania after he declared himself a Republican candidate for the presidency on March 30, 1995.

TAKING AIM AT THE RELIGIOUS RIGHT

When Pat Robertson says there is no constitutional doctrine of separation of church and state, I say he is wrong. The First Amendment, Freedom of Religion, is as important today as when the Bill of Rights was first written.

And when Pat Buchanan calls for a "holy war" in our society, I say he is categorically wrong. We do not need holy wars; what we need is tolerance and brotherhood and simple humanity.

> *Ibid. Separating himself from the ultra-right Republicans.*

LISTENING TO MOTHER

And as much as I learned from my father, I learned about compassion and family values from my mother, Lillie Specter. It was my mother who would tell me that in America I could be anything I wanted to be—even president. And I listened to her, and I am still listening to her.

> *Ibid.*

□

Aaron Spelling

MY FATHER, THE TAILOR

My father, *alav ha-shalom* [may he rest in peace], was a tailor and never made more than $45 a week in his life.

> *Probably the richest television producer of all times, whose achievement of 2,800 hours of TV programming is noted in* The Guiness Book of World Records. *From a Tom Tugend column in* Heritage Southwest Jewish Press *supplement, July 1993.*

A *SHVARTZE* TAILOR

My father, *alav ha-shalom* [may he rest in peace], was totally colorblind. He always brought a *shvartze* [black] tailor home for the Seder.

> *Ibid. Who equates his father's Jewishness with a hatred of bigotry.*

MENORAH AND BUSH

We have one room at home, where we light the [Chanuka] menorah. In another room, we have a "Chanukah bush" and invite friends and people who work for us, who have no other place to go.

> *From a 1993 interview during a visit to Israel.*

WE LIKE BEING JEWISH

There are some Jews in this town [Hollywood] and nobody knows about it. But we really like being Jewish.... You don't have to see a bullfrog to hear him croak.

> *Ibid.*

THE OLD JEWISH PUSHKE

My mom was someone who taught me a lot about Israel. She had a little blue-and-white tin can with a slit on top, which she called her *pushke*. Every night, when my dad went to sleep, she would go through his trousers and gather up the change and put it in the *pushke*. And when I got paid for my paper route on Thursday afternoon, I would have to put a dime in the *pushke*.

> *From a speech at a 1993 dinner of the American Friends of the Hebrew University, when he announced the establishment of his family's Foundation for the Performing Arts on the Jerusalem campus.*

□

Oswald Spengler

THE TWAIN SHALL NEVER MEET

The Jew could not comprehend the Gothic inwardness, the castle, the Cathedral; nor the Christian the Jew's superior, almost cynical, intelligence and his finished expertness in moneymaking.

> *From his* Decline of the West *(1928).*

□

Shalom Spiegel

SOCIAL VIRTUE

Justice is the soil in which all the other virtues can prosper. It is the precondition of all social virtue, indeed of all community life.

> *From his essay "Amos vs. Amaziah," which was originally delivered as an address on September 13, 1957 at the Jewish Theological Seminary of America before a distinguished audience including former President Harry S Truman and U.S. Supreme Court Chief Justice Earl Warren.*

THE PURPOSE OF RITUAL

Where ritual becomes estranged from its aim and is pursued for its own sake, instead of facilitating an approach, it may clog and clutter it with impediments and importunities of its own; it may even make the very encounter, if possible, impossible. As an end in itself, ritual may become a stumbling block in religion.

> *Ibid.*

ENCOUNTER WITH GOD

Ritual, like precedent, is a footprint left by the encounter of just and holy men with God who is holiness and justice. Footprints like these deserve to be followed, as they may lead again to the source of holiness and justice.

Ibid.

ALL CHILDREN OF GOD

All these people [Arameans, Philistines, Ethiopians] and races had a variety of observances and practices which differed with the landscape. But all these peoples and races also were held by the biblical faith to be the children of one God, the father of all men. It would seem inconceivable, if underneath their variety a trace or token of their common origin did not remain. Whatever their differences, the fingerprint of the Creator should be discernible in all his creatures, stamping all as fellow-bearers of the divine image.

Ibid.

THE DEVIL SHOULD LEARN TALMUD

The devil, according to Shakespeare, quotes Scripture. But if he is really as clever as he is reputed to be, he ought to quote the Talmud, as there is hardly any view of life for and against which one could not quote the Talmud.

From the second Zunz Lecture of the Menorah Society, delivered at the University of Chicago, December 29, 1920.

□

Steven Spielberg

BEYOND IMAGINATION

I have a pretty good imagination. I've made a fortune off my imagination. My imagination is dwarfed by the events of 1940 to 1945. Just dwarfed. And so I couldn't imagine the Holocaust until I went to Cracow, and to Auschwitz-Birkenau for the first time. And I didn't want a style that was similar to anything I had done before. First of all, I threw half my toolbox away. I canceled the crane. I tore out the dolly track. I didn't really plan a style. I didn't say I'm going to use a lot of handheld cameras. I simply tried to pull the events closer to the audience by reducing the artifice.

Speaking about his award-winning movie Schindler's List. *In an interview with Cathleen McGuigan of* Newsweek *magazine, December 20, 1993.*

LOOKING FOR A JEW

I couldn't find any Jews in Poland to be the Jews in the movie because Hitler had murdered them all.

Explaining why he had to import so many actors from outside Poland to appear in Schindler's List.

PITCHING PENNIES AT THE JEW

When we moved to Phoenix, I was one of only five Jewish kids in elementary and high school. There was a lot of anti-Semitism against me and my sisters. In study hall kids used to pitch pennies at me, which would hit my desk and make a large clatter. It was called "pitching pennies at the Jew," and it was very hurtful.

Quoted in an article by Phyllis Ellen Funke in Hadassah Magazine, *December 1993.*

THE BIRTH OF A SON

I made a very strong choice to raise him Jewish with my first wife, Amy Irving, who was half-Jewish.

When I began to read books to him, I had to make a choice. Do I read books about Santa Claus or do I read books about Moses and Abraham and Isaac?

In 1985, after the birth of his son, he was led to re-examine his connection with Judaism. From an interview with Tom Tugend in The Jewish Week, *December 10–16, 1993.*

A BORN-AGAIN JEW

Her [Kate Capshaw's] conversion was a beautiful experience for all of us because I studied along with her. She studied and I was the beneficiary of everything that she was learning that I had forgotten.

I re-emerged [to Judaism], I would say, through the birth of my children and through a decision I had to make about how I was going to raise them.

I think that's what led me, that and events around the world, very naturally and I think in a very smooth way, to the decision to make *Schindler's List.*

Ibid.

WHY DID SCHINDLER SAVE JEWS?

I was always trying to discover through the survivors who knew him, who saw him, who were saved by him, why he did this. And most of the survivors said, "We don't know why he did this. We only know that he did."

Ibid.

DUTY OF EVERY PARENT

I feel that every parent, every Jewish parent, has a responsibility, as my parents felt they had, to inform their kids, in the very early years, about what happened.

We're running out of witnesses, and everything about the Shoah is going to be second-hand information. This is the time for the oldest survivors to address the youngest children, to let them know what happened. So that the next generation will be vigilant about never letting a thing like this happen again.

From an interview with Tom Tugend in The Jerusalem Post, *December 25, 1993.*

▢

Baruch Benedict Spinoza

THE NATURE OF NATURE
Nature abhors a vacuum.

From his Ethics *(1677).*

SOCIABLE MAN
Man is a social animal.

Ibid.

ETERNAL GOD
God and all the attributes of God are eternal.

Ibid.

TRUE AND FALSE
He who would distinguish the true from the false must have an adequate idea of what is true and false.

Ibid.

FEAR AND HOPE
Fear cannot be without hope nor hope without fear.

Ibid.

GOOD, BAD, AND INDIFFERENT
One and the same thing can at the same time be good, bad, and indifferent—for example, music is good to the melancholy, bad to those who mourn, and neither good nor bad to the deaf.

Ibid.

UNDERSTANDING GOD
The more we understand individual things, the more we understand God.

Ibid.

GOALS OF THE MIND
The mind's highest good is the knowledge of God, and the mind's highest virtue is to know God.

Ibid.

SILENCE IS GOLDEN
Surely, human affairs would be far happier if the power in men to be silent were the same as that to speak. But experience more than sufficiently teaches that men govern nothing with more difficulty than their tongues.

Ibid.

UPSETTING ESTABLISHED RELIGION
I do not know how to teach philosophy without becoming a disturber of established religion.

When offered a chair at Heidelberg University in 1670.

CHARACTERIZING PEACE
Peace is not an absence of war, it is a virtue, a state of mind, a disposition for benevolence, confidence, justice.

From his Theological-Political Treatise *(1670).*

CAUSE AND EFFECT
Nothing exists from whose nature some effect does not follow.

Ibid.

BEYOND COMPREHENSION
These doctrines which certain churches put forward concerning Christ, I neither affirm nor deny, for I freely confess that I do not understand them.

Ibid.

NATURE AND GOD
The power of nature is the power of God.

Ibid.

THE RIGHT WORDS
Nothing can be said so rightly that it cannot be twisted into wrong.

Ibid.

GOD IS ONE
He is One. Nobody will dispute that this doctrine is absolutely necessary for complete devotion, admiration, and love toward God. For devotion, admiration, and love spring from the superiority of one over all else.

Ibid.

THE GREATER REVELATION
What Paul says about Peter tells us more about Paul than about Peter.

Quoted in Erich Fromm's Psychoanalysis and Religion *(1950).*

MEMORY RETENTION

The more intelligible a thing is, the more readily it is retained in the memory, and contrariwise, the less intelligible it is, the more easily we forget it.

From his Tractatus de Intellectus Emendatione *(1677).*

¤

Edith Spitzer

WHEN SUFFERING HEALS

Suffering of itself does not heal. Only suffering that has a meaning, and is accepted willingly, has the power to heal, to transform an individual into a whole person; that is, someone who is undivided, who can come to terms with himself, and even with his enemies, as Jacob did with Esau and Laban.

Jung named this process of growth from one stage of awareness to another, *individuation.*

From her article entitled "A Jungian Midrash on Jacob's Dream," which appeared in The Reconstructionist, *October 1976.*

¤

Howard Squadron

VANESSA REDGRAVE: PLO CHAMPION

Perhaps she will begin to understand that if there had been an Israel during the Nazi era, there would have been no Auschwitz. And perhaps she will recognize at last that the Jewish people have a right to a state of their own, a state on soil that is sacred to them, a state that seeks only to live in peace with its Arab neighbors.

An August 1979 declaration, when pro-Arab Vanessa Redgrave was selected to play the part of a Jewish Auschwitz inmate in the film Playing for Time, *written for television by Arthur Miller.*

¤

Joseph Stalin

A "PAPER" NATION

What sort of nation...is a Jewish nation that consists of Georgian, Daghestanian, Russian, American and other Jews, the members of which do not understand each other,...will never see each other, will never act together, whether in time of peace or war?... No, it is not for such paper "nations" that the Social Democratic Party draws up its national program.

From his Marxism and the National Question *(1913).*

COMMUNISM AND ANTI-SEMITISM

Anti-Semitism, as an extreme form of race chauvinism, is the most dangerous survival of cannibalism. Anti-Semitism benefits the exploiters, for it serves as a lightning conductor to divert from capitalism the blows of the toilers. Anti-Semitism is dangerous for the toilers, for it is a false track which diverts them from the proper road and leads them into the jungle. Hence Communists, as consistent internationalists, cannot but be irreconcilable and bitter enemies of anti-Semitism.

From a reply given on January 12, 1931 to an inquiry made by the Jewish Telegraphic Agency of America.

¤

Judah Stampfer

THE POISON WITHIN

The simple cunning of the wasp,
   the bee,
Is how to sting, and sting, and
   still be free.
The poisons human beings generate
Fix them forever to the things
   they hate.

From his "Jerusalem Has Many Faces" (1950).

¤

Arthur Stanley

REVERSE OF AN ABSTRACTION

The idea of God in the Jewish Church, which can be traced to nothing short of Mount Sinai, was the very reverse of a negation or an abstraction. It was the absorbing thought of the national mind. It was not merely the Lord of the Universe, but "the Lord who had brought thee out of the land of Egypt, out of the house of bondage."

From his History of the Jewish Church *(1862).*

¤

Elizabeth Cady Stanton

DEGRADATION OF WOMEN

We found nothing grand in the history of the Jews nor in the morals inculcated in the Pentateuch.... I know of no other books that so fully teach the subjection and degradation of woman.

From her Eight Years and More *(1898).*

¤

Lincoln Steffens

YOM KIPPUR PERFIDY

Outside the synagogues, the young men stood, laughing, telling jokes while in the synagogue the old men sat, gnashing their teeth, reading their prayers, weeping bitter tears, knowing that two, three thousand years of loyalty, dedication and sacrifice for a principle was being lost in a single generation.

Describing the condition of American Jewry at the beginning of the twentieth century. From his Autobiography of Lincoln Steffens.

¤

Cyril Stein

LORD RABBI

If you want to be a bishop, you should join the Church of England.

In a letter to Immanuel Jakobovits, Chief Rabbi of the United Kingdom, urging him not to accept his appointment to the House of Lords.

¤

Ernst Stein

LIFE IN A CEMETERY

It's not particularly conducive to normal life to live in a cemetery.... People don't change overnight. Do you really think the German people changed between 1933 and 1945? Look at the eastern side. In East Germany they were not allowed to celebrate Hitler's birthday in the Alexanderplatz. Now they are...and they do it.

Following the fall of the Berlin wall in 1989. Rabbi Stein held little hope for the Germans' changing character.

GERMANS SAVING JEWS

The average German will tell you his family saved three Jews. I say I believe them, but I really want to know this: exactly where are these millions of Jews who were supposedly saved?

Ibid.

¤

Gertrude Stein

DEFINING A ROSE

Rose is a rose is a rose is a rose.

From her Geography and Plays: Sacred Emily *(1922).*

CREATIVE MIND

I have been the creative literary mind of the century.

Quoted in John Malcolm Brinnin's Third Rose.

ON AGING

One does not get better but different and older, and that is always a pleasure.

From a letter to F. Scott Fitzgerald, May 22, 1925.

LOST GENERATION

You are all a lost generation.

Quoted in Ernest Hemingway's The Sun Also Rises *(1926).*

FANTASY ROSE

Think of the Bible and Homer, think of Shakespeare and think of me.

Quoted in B. L. Reid's Art by Subtraction: A Dissenting Opinion of Gertrude Stein *(1958).*

WIDE OPEN SPACES

In the United States there is more space where nobody is than where anybody is. That is what makes America what it is.

From her Geographical History of America *(1936).*

THE PRICE OF GETTING RICH

I do want to get rich, but I never want to do what there is to do to get rich.

From her Everybody's Autobiography *(1937).*

EVERYBODY IS

In America everybody is, but some are more than others.

Ibid.

SPEAKING OF ROSES

Speaking of the device of rose is a rose is a rose, it was I who found it in one of Gertrude Stein's manuscripts and insisted upon putting it as a device on the letter paper, on the table linen and anywhere that she would permit that I would put it.

From her Autobiography of Alice B. Toklas *(1955).*

THE MODEST ONE

The Jews have produced only three originative geniuses: Christ, Spinoza, and myself.

Quoted in James R. Mellow's Charmed Circle *(1974).*

Joseph Stein

KEEPING OUR BALANCE

And how do we keep our balance? That I can tell you in a word—tradition!

From his libretto for the musical play Fiddler on the Roof *(1964).*

□

Etan Steinberg

NAZI-HUNTER VS. NAZI-CATCHER

I don't suggest that Wiesenthal wasn't looking for Eichmann. Many people were looking for Eichmann. Simon Wiesenthal may be a Nazi-hunter, but he sure is not a Nazi-catcher.

Claiming that Wiesenthal owes the Jewish people an apology for taking credit for what others have given their lives to accomplish. From a profile in The Jerusalem Post, *February 5, 1994.*

□

Joshua Steinberg

STRIKING A BALANCE

Woe to the man who is hated by all, and woe to the man who is popular with all.

From his Mishlay Yehoshua *(1885).*

□

Milton Steinberg

WORSHIPFUL TEMPER

A musician must practice by pre-arranged schedule, regardless of his inclination at the moment. So with the devout soul. It may not rely on caprice or put its hope in chance. It must work. The man on the other hand who folds his hands, waiting for the spirit to move him to think of God—who postpones worship for the right mood and the perfect setting, a forest or mountain peak, for example—will do little of meditating or praying.

From his Basic Judaism *(1955).*

NATURE'S EVOLUTION

Given the One God concept, the whole universe bursts into lucidity. The rationality of nature, the emergence of life, the phenomena of conscience and consciousness become intelligible. Deny it and the who becomes inexplicable.

From his A Believing Jew *(1951).*

KEEPING MAN HUMAN

...by positing God it [Judaism] inhibits man from laying claim to being God. It prevents his becoming less than man through the arrogance of claiming to be more. In brief, it helps to keep man human.

Ibid.

A JEWISH ZERO

The Jew who knows Judaism has his head and heart too full of positive healthful values ever to be invaded by self-contempt. But the Jew who is a hollow shell, a Jewish zero, a Hebraic cipher, a vacuum, is flooded inevitably with hostile notions about Jews. The anti-Semite convinces him. He comes to doubt his work and to despise Judaism, Jews, and even himself.

Ibid.

CHILDREN OF THE MODERN WORLD

We are the children of the modern world, free to believe or disbelieve, to accept or reject as our reason determines—a glorious freedom.

Ibid.

GOAL OF JUDAISM

A respect for life, a sense of the rights of others, an ideal of family purity, high standards of decency and honor, a strong sympathy for the exploited and persecuted—all these were explicit in the book and implicit in law and custom. When the Jew compared his morality with that of the world, he felt that the contrast favored him immensely.

From his Making of the Modern Jew *(1933).*

DEFINING CONSERVATIVE JUDAISM

Conservative Judaism...consists largely in attempting to strike a "happy medium" between the two extremes, in the effort to hold on to as much of the tradition as is tenable and to make such adjustments in Jewish life and thought as circumstances forcibly compel.

Ibid.

THE BEST MERCHANDISE

Out of rigid necessity the Jew concerned himself with study and instruction. In no other society was education taken so seriously as in the ghetto. Mothers in their lullabies assured their infants that Torah was the best of all wares.

Ibid.

VICARIOUS SALVATION

Judaism...has no doctrine of vicarious salvation.

From a 1947 article in The Reconstructionist.

VOICE OF SINAI

The voice that sounded at Sinai was never silenced.

From his Partisan Guide *(1945).*

THE PROBLEM WITH ATHEISM

If the believer has his troubles with evil, the atheist has more and graver difficulties to contend with. Reality stumps him altogether, leaving him baffled not by one consideration but by many, from the existence of natural law through the instinctual cunning of the insect to the brain of the genius and the heart of the prophet. This, then, is the intellectual reason for believing in God: that, though this belief is not free from difficulties, it stands out, head to shoulders, as the best answer to the riddle of the universe.

From his Anatomy of Faith *(1960).*

MAKING SENSE OUT OF LIFE

To believe in God maturely...is to believe that reality did not just happen, that it is no accident, no pointless interplay of matter and energy. It is to insist rather that things, including man's life, make sense, that they add up to something. It is to hold that the universe, physical and moral, is a cosmos, not an anarchy.

Ibid.

UNITY OF THE WORLD

The universe is one, an organic unity, subject everywhere to the same law, knitted together with interdependence.

Ibid.

□

George Steiner

TRAINING FOR SURVIVAL

When I listen to my children breathing in the stillness of my house I grow afraid. I am utterly trying to teach my children the sense of vulnerability and keep them in training for survival.

Quoted in Anne Roiphe's Season for Healing *(1988).*

□

Adin Steinsaltz

FAMILY OF JEWS

Tolstoi once said that there is no such thing as a Jewish nonbeliever. To a large degree, I agree with him. Sometimes among Jews there is a family quarrel, but it doesn't destroy the family or my connection with the family. You see, many of those who are secularists by their own definition are fighting with the ideas of the Jewish faith, but within the family framework. They fight basic ideas of right and wrong; it's not a loving connection, but it's a positive one in that it exists.

From an article by Lesley Hazelton in Moment *magazine, July–August 1980.*

BETWEEN TWO WORLDS

In many ways, I am an amphibian, living in two worlds: the world of the religious in the most traditional or strict orthodox sense, and the modern secular world. It's certainly not a restful position to be in, but it does mean that I am one of the few who can create a gateway between these two worlds.

Ibid.

SELF-INFLICTED HOLOCAUST

Recently published statistics highlighting the high rate of intermarriage in Jewish communities of the Western world created a shock which was unjustified; the writing had been on the wall for a while. What is happening in the Western world may be termed a "self-inflicted holocaust."

In ancient Rome a person would get into a warm bath and cut his own veins; then he would sit and bleed peacefully to death. This is what is happening to the Jewish people: there is a constant bleeding; not dramatic, but unceasing.

From an article in The Jerusalem Post International Edition, *November 6, 1993, previously delivered at a dinner in his honor at the Jerusalem Great Synagogue.*

PLATONIC LOVE

Personally, I don't believe in platonic love. Well, if the woman is 85 and ugly, and the man is about 90 and impotent, then there is a possibility of platonic love.

From a comment on March 28, 1995, during "Shteig '95," a teaching event via satellite to college students interested in studying Talmud.

ACHIEVING SELF-CONTROL

Self-control is easier to preach than do. It's

something that's far more effective when you tell others to do it.

Ibid.

LOOKING FOR A BIBLE?

I recommend one book.... You don't have to go to hotels to find it.

Ibid.

◻

Krister Stendahl

WE ARE ALL MINORITIES

Judaism has always been a light unto the nations. In God's eyes we are all minorities. We will from time to time have converts, one from the other, but let this be by our example as livers of our respective faiths.

From an address delivered at the conference of the Center for Christian–Jewish Understanding. Quoted in its Summer 1994 newsletter.

◻

Casey Stengel

KID KOUFAX

The Jewish kid is probably the best of them.

In answer to the question, "Who was the finest pitcher in baseball history?" Quoted in Geoffrey C. Ward's Baseball: An Illustrated History *(1994).*

◻

George Stephanopoulos

ON ISRAEL

I think I'm pro-Israel. I believe it has to exist. Israel is our best ally [in the Middle East] and the only democracy.... But unless they address the problem of the Palestinians and the problem in their own country, they'll be overtaken by demographics, if nothing else.

From a statement made in 1986 after a trip to Israel with his boss, Democratic Representative Edward Feighan of Ohio.

◻

Avraham "Yair" Stern

ONLY DEATH FREES ONE

Here we are, without uniforms
We've all been drafted for the rest of our lives

Only death frees us from the ranks.

From a piece entitled "Anonymous Soldiers." The founder of the underground Freedom Fighters of Israel (the Stern Gang), known by its Hebrew acronym Lechi, died on the 25th of Shevat 1942. Stern's essay is read at his grave each year on his Yahrzeit.

◻

Isaac Stern

A MAESTRO'S SUCCESS

Would you give twelve hours a day?

In response to an admirer who, after Stern's concert, exclaimed: "O, Mr. Stern, I would give anything to be able to play the violin as magnificently as you do."

BARELY LITERATE

[Sol] Hurok knows six languages—and all of them are Yiddish.

Emphasizing the fact that the famous impresario was barely literate, even in his native Russian.

◻

Susan Stern

LION OF JUDAH EUPHORIA

He gave greetings and talked of peace, and the place went wild. It was like being in a movie, watching the crown prince of Jordan sitting under the UJA sign that read "We are One." To me it was like an out-of-body experience. It was very exciting. History was being made and we were a part of it.

Commenting on the appearance of Crown Prince Hassan of Jordan, King Hussein's brother, before the Lion of Judah Conference, sponsored by the United Jewish Appeal's women's division. The meeting, held in Washington, DC, during the first week of October 1993, was attended by 1,100 women from forty-two states.

◻

Edward Stettinius

PATRONIZING SECRETARY

It is very likely that efforts will be made by some of the Zionist leaders to obtain from you at an early date some commitments in favor of the Zionist program.... The question of Palestine is...a highly complex one and involves questions which go far beyond the plight of the Jews in Europe.... As we have interests in that area which are vital to the United States, we feel that this whole subject is one that should be handled with the greatest care and with a view to the long-range interests of this country.

> *From a memorandum sent to President Harry Truman in April 1945, five days after Franklin Delano Roosevelt's death. Truman was irritated by Stettinius's patronizing tone.*

□

Adlai Stevenson

THE STORY OF HARRY GOLDEN

The story of Harry Golden reminds me of the story of O. Henry, who spent three years in prison. I suspect that this experience deepened Harry Golden's understanding, lengthened his vision, and enlarged his heart.

> *On Golden's years of prison confinement. From Harry Golden's autobiography,* The Right Time *(1969).*

□

Robert Louis Stevenson

WERE I OF JEWISH BLOOD

Were I of Jewish blood, I do not think I could ever forgive the Christians; the ghettos would get in my nostrils like mustard or lit gunpowder.

> *Quoted in J. L. Baron's* Stars and Sand *(1943).*

THOSE WHO REMEMBER

What a strange idea, to think me a Jew-hater! Isaiah and David and Heine are good enough for me; and I leave more unsaid. Were I of Jew blood, I do not think I could ever forgive the Christians; the ghettos would get in my nostrils like mustard or lit gunpowder.

> *From a letter written in 1891. Quoted in* The Letters of Robert Louis Stevenson *(1899), edited by Sidney Colvin.*

□

Walter Stewart

THE AMAZING REICHMANN FAMILY

If you could live in it, work in it, eat it or drink it, chances were, not long ago O&Y [Olympia & York] had a piece of it.

> *Describing the vast business enterprises operated by the Reichmann brothers of Toronto, Canada. From his* Too Big to Fail *(1993).*

□

Ezra Stiles

A GOOD HONEST CITIZEN

His knowledge in commerce was unbounded and his integrity irreproachable.

> *The inscription he prepared for the tombstone of his friend Aaron Lopez, who died in 1782. Quoted in Eli Faber's* Time for Planting *(1992).*

FAILED CONVERSION

He [Aaron Lopez] was my intimate friend and acquaintance! Oh! how often have I wished that sincere, pious, candid mind could have perceived the evidences of Christianity, perceived the truth as it is in Jesus Christ, known that Jesus was the Messiah predicted by Moses and the prophets.

> *Ibid. From Stiles' diary, written after the death of Lopez.*

MISSIONARY ACTIVITY

Providence seems to make every thing to work for mortification to the Jews, and to prevent their incorporating into any nation; that thus they may continue a distinct people.... The opposition it has met with in Rhode Island forebodes that the Jews will never become incorporated with the people of America any more than in Europe, Asia, and Africa.

> *From Stanley F. Chyet's* Lopez of Newport: Colonial American Merchant Prince *(1970).*

□

Harlan F. Stone

RARE TRIBUTE

Learned in the law, with wide experience in the practice of his profession, he brought to the service of the Court and of his country rare sagacity and wisdom, prophetic vision and an influence which derived power from the integrity of his character and his ardent attachment to the highest interests of the court as the implement of government under a written constitution.

> *From the Chief Justice's formal statement announcing the death of Justice Louis D. Brandeis on October 5, 1941.*

□

Isidor Feinstien (I. F.) Stone

UP THE LADDER OF SAINTHOOD

He [Martin Luther King, Jr.] stood in that

line of saints which goes back from Gandhi to Jesus; his violent end, like theirs, reflects the hostility of mankind to those who annoy it by trying hard to pull it one more painful step farther up the ladder from ape to angel.

> *Quoted in* The Best of I. F. Stone *(1973), edited by Neil Middleton.*

IN TIME TO BE REMEMBERED

Perhaps the truth is that in some ways John Fitzgerald Kennedy died just in time. He died in time to be remembered as he would like to be remembered, as ever-young, still victorious, struck down undefeated, with almost all the potentates and rulers of mankind, friend and foe, come to mourn at his bier.

> *Ibid.*

EMERGING FROM HELL

I had the privilege of seeing my people in some of the greatest moments of their long history—as they emerged from the hells of Auschwitz and Buchenwald—packed into the old freighters which served as the *Mayflowers* on the Mediterranean, fighting against odds which seemed overwhelming to establish a Jewish nation.... The Jews had no recourse [in 1948] but to fight for their lives, and the war was stopped only when the [British] Foreign Office and the State Department suddenly realized that the Arabs were losing.

> *From his newsletter of February 6, 1956, in which the journalist recalled the Passover Seder he had attended on Cyprus in 1948 with homeless Jewish survivors of the Holocaust.*

AGE AND AGING

When you are younger you get blamed for crimes you never committed, and when you're older you begin to get credit for virtues you never possessed. It evens itself out.

> *From the* International Herald Tribune, *March 16, 1988.*

□

Dennis Stoutenberg

JESUS RECONSIDERED

Jesus never attended church one day in his life. He was raised under the Judaic code of his own day, attended synagogue and made festival pilgrimages to the Temple. He never established a new religion.

> *After being reawakened to his Jewish roots. Stoutenberg was raised as an agnostic. Quoted in* The Jerusalem Report, *February 23, 1995.*

□

Harriet Beecher Stowe

COMPASSIONATE LAWS OF MOSES

The laws of Moses, if carefully examined, are a perfect phenomenon; an exception to the laws of either ancient or modern nations in the care they exercised over women, widows, orphans, paupers, foreigners, servants, and dumb animals. No so-called Christian nation but could advantageously take a lesson in legislation from the laws of Moses.... Not the gentlest words of Jesus are more compassionate in their spirit than many of these laws of Moses.

> *From her* Moses and His Laws. *Quoted in Simon Wolf's* American Jew as Patriot, Soldier, and Citizen *(1895).*

□

Lee Strasberg

THE HEART OF "THEATER"

We want to create a "theater," not build one. Formal externals are not important. It is the activity within that counts.

> *In a* New York Times *interview with Paul Gardner, May 5, 1964.*

□

Michael Strassfeld

THE PROCESS CALLED INTERPRETATION

The important texts in Jewish tradition, such as the Bible and the Talmud, are kept alive by being endlessly studied and interpreted rather than by being slavishly followed. It is this commitment, if not commandment, to interpret that makes the one Torah given to all Jews at Sinai a personal Torah for each and everyone.

> *From the Introduction to his* Jewish Holidays *(1985).*

SIGNIFICANCE OF THE HOLOCAUST

The implications of the belief that the significance of the Holocaust is that it helped bring about the State of Israel are no less disturbing. It is blasphemous to suggest that six million died so that the State could be created.

> *Ibid.*

□

Oscar Solomon Straus

ADMIRATION FOR ZIONISTS

You know that I am not Zionist, but that does not prevent me from appreciating the noble idealism of those associated with this movement—an idealism which is very near akin...to the spirit that actuated the founders of our republic, who drew their inspiration from the prophets of Israel and the Hebrew commonwealth.

> *Straus was the first Jew to serve in an American Cabinet, acting as secretary.*

NEW WEST AND OLD EAST

Hebraic mortar cemented the foundations of our American democracy, and through the windows of the Puritan churches, the New West looked back to the Old East.

> *From a November 29, 1905 address.*

BENEFITS OF IMMIGRATION

An unprejudiced study of immigration justifies me in saying that the evils are temporary and local, while the benefits are permanent and national.

> *From a May 22, 1907 address.*

AMERICAN JEWS

The Jew is neither a new comer nor an alien in this country or on this continent; his Americanism is as original and ancient as that of any race or people with the exception of the American Indian and other aborigines. He came in the caravels of Columbus, and he knocked at the gates of New Amsterdam only thirty-five years after the Pilgrim Fathers stepped ashore on Plymouth Rock.

> *From a speech delivered in New York City on January 18, 1911.*

□

Julius Streicher

A VITRIOLIC TONGUE

Your proper gathering place is this mountain, where two thousand years ago, your forefathers gathered before the country had been infected by a race which at that time executed the greatest anti-Semite of all time, Jesus Christ, for high treason. Now this race is an enemy to all peoples and threatens the life of the German people. In front of this blazing fire, dedicate yourself to hatred of a people who goad nations into war to profit by it, to hatred of those who dishonor our women, to hatred of those who torture animals to death.

> *From a June 23, 1935 speech on Hesenburg Mountain. Streicher, the Nazi leader of Franconia and founder of* Der Stürme, *took advantage of the occasion to exhort the boys and girls of the Hitler Youth.*

□

Barbra Streisand

My grandmother couldn't handle me. She called me a *farbrent* ["on fire" in Yiddish]. If I was sick with the chicken pox and I wanted to go out and play, I put on my clothes, climbed out the window, and went out to play.

> *Recalling, in 1983, her childhood years. Quoted in Allison J. Walman's* Barbra Streisand Scrapbook *(1995).*

THE AIDS VIRUS

The moral immune system of this country has been weakened and attacked, and the AIDS virus is the perfect metaphor for it.

> *Quoted in the* London Guardian, *November 26, 1992.*

A CASE OF STAGEFRIGHT

I forgot the words in front of 125,000 people, and I wasn't cute about it or anything. I was shocked; I was terrified. It prevented me from performing all these years.

> *Referring to her 1967 performance in New York City's Central Park and her absence from the stage until her reappearance in Las Vegas on New Year's Eve 1994. From an interview in* Newsweek *magazine, May 23, 1994.*

ON OVERCOMING STAGEFRIGHT

I did it, I did it, I did it!

> *Following her 1994 New Year's weekend concerts.*

SUCCESS

Success to me is having ten honeydew melons and eating only the top half of each one.

> *Quote in* Life *magazine, September 20, 1963.*

FORBIDDEN KISS

You think Cairo is upset? You should have seen the letter I got from my Aunt Rose.

> *Upon hearing that Arab censors were upset that Egyptian movie star Omar Sharif kissed her in* Funny Girl, *which resulted in their banning of the film in 1968. Quoted in* Entertainment Weekly, *April 15, 1994.*

HAD I BEEN NICER

If I had been nicer to him, I could have been the first real Jewish princess—Princess Babs.

> *Joking to the London audience during her second sold-out concert at Wembley Arena, on April 25, 1994. She had met Prince Charles in 1972, but had treated him brusquely due to work pressure. Quoted in* The Jewish Week, *April 29–May 5, 1994.*

GOD'S POSITION

Is God really against gun control and food stamps for poor children?

From her January 1995 speech at Harvard's Kennedy School in which she drew a distinction between those who are "humanist" and "compassionate" and those who follow an "evil" course.

WIDENING FREEDOM

[The debate between left and right is simply] a conflict between those who would widen freedom and those who would narrow it; between those who defend tolerance and those who view it as a threat.

Ibid.

AMERICAN DEMOCRACY

To deny artists, or any of us, for that matter, free expression and free thought—or worse, to force us to conform to some rigid notion of "mainstream American values"—is to weaken the very foundation of democracy.

Ibid.

¤

Juergen Stroops

WARSAW'S JEWS

There is no more Jewish Quarter in Warsaw.

His announcement in May 1943 after the Great Warsaw Synagogue on Tlomackie Street was blown up.

¤

Elazar Sturm

PEACE TALK AS THERAPY

I believe that there is a massive fear of what peace could bring. Right now, the average Israeli is experiencing something bizarre: a trauma that is taking place before the traumatic event has even occurred. Normally, traumas take place after an event. And logically, there shouldn't be a trauma because the peace with Egypt works. Despite the fact that it is a limited peace, it works. When I sat with the producers of the show [his weekly Israeli television show], we said to ourselves, how can we cope with this fear, this trauma, which is so prevalent in Israeli society?

Talking about it is somewhat therapeutic, I believe, and the show, aside from just giving information, is like therapy for Israeli society. I really think that the more we talk about peace

and about the problems we will face when and if it happens, the better off we will be.

From an interview with Allison Kaplan Sommer in The Jerusalem Post, *June 19, 1993.*

TWO TYPES OF JEWS

The *haredi* [ultra-Orthodox] world always yells, "We are Judaism. The authentic one, the real one, the only one that exists." The secular Israeli for years has gotten the message that Judaism equals the *haredi* world. He takes with him the guilt feeling that he is not a real Jew. On his ID card it says his nationality is Jewish. But then he says to himself, "Wait a minute. Being Jewish is religion, not nationality. Being Jewish means keeping *mitzvot* [religious commandments]. I don't keep mitzvot, so why am I a Jew?" There is a national problem with identity here, because if you don't observe *mitzvot*, you keep asking yourself consciously or subconsciously, how am I a Jew?

Ibid.

¤

Peter Stuyvesant

FIRST JEWISH SETTLERS IN AMERICA

The Jews who have arrived would nearly all like to remain here, but learning that they (with their customary usury and deceitful trading with the Christians) were very repugnant to the inferior magistrates, as also to the people...we have, for the benefit of this weak and newly developing place and the land in general, deemed it useful to require them in a friendly way to depart: praying also most seriously in this connection, for ourselves as also for the general community of your worships, that the deceitful race—such hateful enemies and blasphemers of the name of Christ—be not allowed further to infect and trouble this new colony.

Asking permission of the West India Company to expel the thirty-three Jews who had arrived in New Amsterdam on the Hudson River [New York] from Recife, Brazil, in September 1654. His request was denied.

¤

Abdel Rahim Sukar

MANIACAL MARTYR

I cried a little at first, but later I stopped. When I saw the flesh and blood of the Jews, I was happy. It was the best martyrdom possible.... This made us walk tall.

> *Comment by the brother of suicide bomber Anwar Sukar, who in January 1995 killed twenty-one Israeli soldiers at a bus stop near Netanya, north of Tel Aviv. Reported in* The New York Times, *January 25, 1995.*

Leslie Susser

POPE AND PRESIDENT

Pope Paul VI's 1964 visit to the Holy Land was insulting to Israel, as the pontiff, unwilling to recognize any vestige of Israeli statehood, agreed only to travel from Jordan to Megiddo and back along a specially prepared road, and addressed a thank-you note to "Mr." Zalman Shazar in Tel Aviv, although Shazar's official title was "president" and his residence (and office) was in Jerusalem.

> *From an article in* The Jerusalem Report, *April 21, 1994.*

Alexander Süsskind (ben Moses)

FACE DEATH JOYFULLY

My dear children, if ye be called upon to suffer martyrdom, go to your death with whole-hearted joy!

> *From his* Tzavaah (1794). *Quoted in Israel Abrahams'* Hebrew Ethical Wills (1926).

Bertha von Suttner

FIRST OF ALL A FATHERLAND

To be a Zionist, said Bourgeois, means to resist anti-Semitism. Hatred of the Jews is injurious to the rest of the community perhaps even more than to the Jews. It breeds coarseness, it inhibits refinement, and it interferes seriously with the realization of the very ideals in the name of which we are assembled here at the Hague.... One must first of all have a fatherland.

> *From her account of a conversation in 1900 at the Hague Peace Conference, with Léon Bourgeois, chairman of the Arbitration Commission.*

Helen Suzman

I KNOW MANDELA

I know Nelson Mandela well and I have never seen a hint of anti-Semitism in him or other leaders.... Being friendly with Palestinian leaders or the ANC (African National Congress) does not make him or the ANC an enemy of Israel.

> *Assessing Mandela after he sought to mend fences with the Jewish community. From an August 1993 speech to the conference of the Jewish Board of Deputies of South Africa.*

EPITOME OF DISDAIN

Like you? I can't stand you!

> *Interrupting a speech by P. W. Botha, South African president, who commented that Suzman did not like him.*

TIME TO LEAVE

I always believed that it was a good idea to leave while people still thought I ought to stay, rather than waiting until they wondered how to get rid of me.

> *Ibid. After deciding at age 72 not to run once again for a seat in the South African Parliament.*

BATTLER FOR JUSTICE

I never forgot I was Jewish, [but] it wasn't being Jewish that drove me into a liberal philosophy. Rabbis have tried to say to me, "It was the Jewish ethos that made you what you were." They make it more complicated than it was. It was simply a natural revulsion against injustice.

> *Contending that her anti-apartheid stance was not influenced by her Jewish heritage.*

INCENTIVE TO BECOME INVOLVED

I was so appalled by what I had learned—the handicaps on mobility, the restrictions on the right to live with one's family, all the aspects that affected the right of Africans to enter the modern industrial economy and I thought to myself that I must get into politics and do something about this.

> *After spending six months studying the laws applying to urban South Africans. Quoted in Elinor and Robert Slater's* Great Jewish Women *(1994).*

OBVIOUS INJUSTICES

Let me assure you that I have no sentimentality about blacks. I'm not a bleeding heart Liberal who goes around moaning about the noble savage and all that rubbish.... But the injustices are so patently obvious to anybody who has the eyes to see, and it has always worried me.

Ibid. From a 1977 statement.

◻

Jimmy Swaggart

MIDDLE EAST UNREST

The reason there has been so little peace in the Mideast is because Israel as a people turned its back on the God of Abraham, Isaac, and Jacob and embraced pagan idols [and] have yielded too often to philosophies that have been harmful to mankind; such as Marx, Freud, Trotsky and Dewey.

Quoted in Anne Roiphe's Season for Healing *(1988).*

◻

John Franklin Swift

PALESTINE IN DECLINE

When a Jew is good for nothing else, he is good to send to Jerusalem.

Penned in 1868 by a Californian reflecting on the decline of the Holy Land, in fulfillment of the Christian belief that God is punishing the errant Jews.

◻

Daniel B. Syme

WHAT GOD IS OR ISN'T

I deeply respect any Jew who has a firmly rooted Jewish theology, who embraces a particular notion of God and speaks of it proudly and assertively. But I am not prepared to dismiss other Jews whose theology may not be biblical or rabbinic but is deeply held conviction....

The fact is that no one knows what God is or isn't. There is no one authoritative, universally accepted Jewish concept of God.

From his essay entitled "Talking to Kids About God," which appears in The Hadassah Magazine Jewish Parenting Book *(1989), edited by Roselyn Bell.*

◻

Marie Syrkin

THE ARAB PRESENCE

As a Zionist, despite the stormy history of Israel, I am still convinced that the establishment of the Jewish state in a "small notch"—to use Lord Balfour's phrase—of the vast territo-

ries liberated from the Ottoman Empire was an act of absolute, not relative, historic justice. I regret that the tiny area was further truncated by successive partitions and reduced to its present dimensions by painful compromises. Nevertheless, I appreciate the intensity of Arab hostility, however ill-motivated it may appear to me, and the reality of the Arab presence on the West Bank and in Gaza. For moral and demographic reasons the position of Israel as occupier is untenable; withdrawal to recognized borders in a context of peace, as offered by the Labor party, is a possible solution.

From a 1986 essay in Tikkun *magazine. Vol. 1, No. 1.*

FAILURE OF LEADERSHIP

Today, when genocide, gas-chamber, and mass-extermination are the small coin of language, it is hard to reconstruct the more innocent state of mind when American Jews, like the Jews in Europe's ghettos, could not immediately grasp that the ascending series of Nazi persecutions had reached this apex...No one can seriously suggest that an American Jewish population...should have challenged the government in the middle of a popular war on whose outcome hung the fate of the free world, that they should have sabotaged troop trains, or tried to force refugee ships past the Statue of Liberty. Sadly, I still believe that even if we had been psychologically ready for such acts, the only practical effect would have been to infuriate the hostile majority.

Responding to the charge that Zionists and Jewish leaders did not cry out sufficiently about the fate of European Jews during World War II.

THE PURE IN HEART RECOGNIZED

As I think of Ben's [Professor Ben Halpern's] career, I find pleasure in the reflection that not only the noisy are heard, that true achievement finds recognition in the academic and literary marketplace, and that the pure in heart, in addition to more ethereal rewards, also get Guggenheims and even Festschriften.

From Essays in Modern History *(1982).*

◻

Hannah Szenes

BECOMING A ZIONIST

I've become a Zionist. This word stands for a tremendous number of things. To me it means, in short, that I now consciously and strongly feel I am a Jew, and am proud of it.

My primary aim is to go to Palestine, to work for it.

A 1938 entry in her diary, which she kept at age seventeen and was published in Hebrew in 1945.

THE STRUGGLE TO BE A JEW

You have to be someone exceptional to fight anti-Semitism.... Only now am I beginning to see what it really means to be a Jew in a Christian society. But I don't mind at all. It is because we have to struggle, because it is more difficult for us to reach our goal, that we develop outstanding qualities. Had I been born a Christian, every profession would be open to me.

Ibid.

HOME AT LAST

I am home.... This is where my life's ambition—I might even say my vocation—binds me because I would lie to feel that by being here I am fulfilling a mission, not just vegetating. Here almost every life is the fulfillment of a mission.

From a letter written to her mother in September 1939, after she settled down in Palestine at the Girls' Agricultural School in Nahalal.

TO DIE YOUNG

To die, to die in youth,
No, no, I did not want it;
I loved the warmth of sun, the lovely light.
I loved song, shining eyes, and not destruction.
I did not want the dark of war, the night.
No, no, I did not want it.

An entry in her diary, when it was clear that the Nazis would soon reach her in Budapest, in 1944.

THE DIE IS CAST

One-two-three...eight feet long,
Two strides across, the rest is dark...
Life hangs over me like a question mark.
One—two—three...maybe another week,
Or next month may still find me here,
But death, I feel, is very near.

From her last poem, written in prison in Budapest.

BLESSED IS THE MATCH

Blessed is the match that is consumed in kindling the flame.
Blessed is the flame that burns in the secret fastness of the heart.
Blessed is the heart with strength to stop its beating for honor's sake.

Blessed is the match that is consumed in kindling the flame.

From her poem "Blessed Is the Match" (1944).

CONTINUE THE STRUGGLE

Continue on the way, don't be deterred. Continue the struggle til the end, until the day of liberty comes, the day of victory for our people.

The final words to her comrades before she was executed by firing squad in November 1944.

IMMORTALITY

There are stars whose radiance is visible on earth though they have long been extinct. There are people whose brilliance continues to light the world though they are no longer among the living. These lights are particularly bright when the night is dark.

Ibid.

ACCORDING TO PLAN

In my life's chain of events nothing was accidental. Everything happened according to an inner need.

Ibid.

I ASK FOR NO MERCY

I ask for no mercy from hangmen.

Response to her executioners, who asked if she wanted to plead for mercy.

¤

Benjamin Szold

FATHERLAND AND FREEDOM

In the household of our nation there cannot be a reign of two mothers, next to freedom there cannot be slavery, next to a Union there cannot be a Confederation....

To us Jews Lincoln has a special meaning. In the course of history we found many fatherlands. We never knew freedom. It was here in the United States that we found freedom. It was Lincoln, who was so devoted to freedom, that we may, indeed, consider him a son of Israel.... Because of his love for freedom, we Jews must honor his memory.

From his 1865 eulogy for U.S. President Abraham Lincoln, which appeared in his Vaterland und Freiheit.

¤

Henrietta Szold

ZIONISM OR EXTINCTION

If I were ten years younger, I would feel

that my field is here [in Palestine]. I think Zionism a more difficult aim to realize than I ever did before...[but] if not Zionism, then nothing...then extinction for the Jews.

After visiting Palestine for the first time in July 1909 and wrestling with the thought of settling there. She stayed for only one year before returning to America.

TIME FOR ACTION

If we are Zionists, as we say we are, what is the good of meeting and talking and drinking tea? Let us do something real and practical— let us organize the Jewish women of America and send nurses and doctors to Palestine.

From an address to a women's Jewish study group meeting at Temple Emanu-El in New York on Purim, February 24, 1912.

ON THE OFFENSE

They ridicule me on account of my sex, proof positive of the narrow-mindedness of which their thoughtless reform of Judaism is a part.... Is telling me that I am a woman refutation of my charges?

Her response in the American Israelite *to charges of Reform leader Rabbi Isaac Mayer Wise that she, as a woman, had no right to comment on the views of Jewish leaders who were materialistic assimilationists.*

WOMEN AND KADDISH

I believe that the elimination of women from such duties [such as saying Kaddish] was never intended by our law and custom. Women were freed from positive duties when they could not perform them, but not when they could. It was never intended that, if they could perform them, their performance of them should not be considered as valuable and valid as when one of the male sex performed them. And of the Kaddish I feel sure this is particularly true.

In a September 16, 1916 communication addressed to Hayim Peretz, a close family friend who had offered to say Kaddish to honor her mother who had just died.

REJECTING THE KADDISH OFFER

My mother had eight daughters and no son; and yet never did I hear a word of regret pass the lips of either my mother or my father that one of us was not a son. When my father died, my mother would not permit others to take her daughters' place in saying the Kad-

dish, and so I am sure I am acting in her spirit when I am moved to decline your offer. But beautiful your offer remains nevertheless.

Ibid.

ON WOMEN'S ORGANIZATIONS

I further believe that, religion being sexless, no necessity exists for Jewish women's organizations.

In a questionnaire she answered about twenty years before founding Hadassah.

SEARCH FOR A SOLUTION

I believe there is a solution [to the Arab-Israeli conflict], and if we cannot find it, then I consider Zionism has failed utterly.

Commenting on the political situation in Palestine during the Arab riots of the late 1930s.

NOT A GHETTO, BUT A GRAVE

There is a vast storehouse filled with treasures. The key, the Hebrew language, is in our guardianship. Have we a right to throw the key into the ocean of oblivion?.... I fear that, in the case of such dereliction of duty, the twentieth century will have in store for us, not a ghetto, but a grave.

From an article written in 1896.

A JEW OF MANY FACETS

Some men reproach me with being a Jew, others forgive me for it, others again even class it among my merits; but all remember it.

Quoted in Marvin Lowenthal's Henrietta Szold: Life and Letters *(1942).*

◻

Mayyas Szuros

FACING THE PAST

The past must be admitted; there can be no absolution! The soul of a whole nation must not be burned by the glowing embers of silence about such harrowing events and uncleared questions. An unrevealed past breeds prejudice. The only way for a nation to be tolerant of otherness is to be free, independent and clear-eyed about itself.

Pleading for honesty about the Holocaust in a 1989 speech to the Hungarian parliament. Quoted in Randolph Braham's Politics of Genocide *(1993).*

William Howard Taft

NOXIOUS WEED

There is not the slightest ground for anti-Semitism among us. It is a vicious plant. It is a noxious weed that should be cut out. It has no place in free America, and the men who seek to introduce it should be condemned by public opinion.

Responding to Henry Ford's circulation of the forged Protocols of the Elders of Zion. *From a 1920 address.*

□

Hassan Tahbub

NO PRAYING PLEASE

Jews can visit them, but they will not be allowed to pray there.

Announcing in 1995 his intention to bar Jews from praying at the Cave of Machpelah in Hebron, Rachel's Tomb in Bethlehem, and Joseph's Tomb in Nablus if these sites come under Palestinian control.

□

Jacob Tam

WIFE-BEATING UNTHINKABLE

Wife-beating is a thing not done in Israel.

Quoted in Israel Abrahams' Jewish Life in the Middle Ages *(1958).*

□

(Rabbi) Tanchum

ADVANTAGES OF MARRIAGE

When a man is without a wife, he lives without joy, without blessing, and without good.

To which Rabbi Ulla added: "Also without peace." Quoted in the talmudic tractate Yevamot *(62b).*

□

(The) Tanzer Rebbe

PREPARING TO PRAY

I pray that I may be able to pray.

In reply to a disciple who asked: "What does the Rebbe do before praying?" Quoted in Louis I. Newman's Hasidic Anthology *(1987).*

□

(Rabbi) Tarfon

NO TIME TO WASTE

The day is short, the task is great, and the workmen are lazy. But the wages are high and the Master of the house is pressing [for results].

Quoted in the talmudic tractate Ethics of the Fathers *(2:20).*

□

Yosef Tekoa

YISHUV VS. U.N.

I deny that the State of Israel was created by the United Nations. It was created by the will of the *yishuv* [Jewish settlers in Palestine]—in spite of the U.N.

From an interview with David Landau in The Jerusalem Post Magazine, *December 27, 1974.*

□

Edward Teller

ISRAEL AND DEVELOPING TECHNOLOGIES

Israel has made a practice of transforming scientific discoveries into usable reality. I believe that defense, nuclear energy and genetic engineering will be three great revolutions of the twenty-first century.

If Israel can develop a defense against ballistic missiles, the next war in the Middle East may be averted.... I recommend that Israel become involved in the design and manufacture of ultrasafe nuclear reactors.... Research on the new possibilities of genetic engineering is second only to military safety in importance to Israel.

From an essay in Moment *magazine, March 1989.*

BELATED BAR MITZVAH

I'm very sorry [that I never had a Bar Mitzvah]. I hope to make up for it no later than my one hundredth birthday.

Ibid.

HEISENBERG'S DECEPTION

Heisenberg's theory that certain is only uncertain means that because the past is rewritten every Sunday evening, the past becomes imagination.

Heisenberg was a brilliant mathematical physicist. He never made a mistake, never, except later when he worked on the atom bomb for the Nazis. I believe he did it deliberately— he misguided the Nazis on purpose.

Ibid.

REASON ENOUGH

I had a very dear friend, and the older brother of my wife, who were killed by the Nazis. I am Jewish, Hungarian and a scientist. All this acted on me in my work. Nobody needed to tell me that we should hurry to make the bomb.

Justifying his advocating the use of the atomic bomb on Hiroshima in 1945.

◻

Moshe D. Tendler

ONLY ONE TRUE RELIGION

Judaism is a world religion. It is not a compilation of local tribal customs. It speaks to Jew and non-Jew. It is a Torah—a code of conduct for all humanity. It is the only "true" religion.

God promulgated different obligatory behavior for Jew and non-Jew.... The seven Noahide laws are binding on all humanity. They have served as the basis for all civilized codes of conduct. They are the Torah of the non-Jew. In this sense there is but one true religion. There is one true record of the responsibilities demanded by God of man created in His image.

From an essay in Condition of Jewish Belief *(1966), compiled by the editors of* Commentary *magazine.*

◻

Saul I. Teplitz

NEIGHBORS VS. BROTHERS

We live in a world that has become a neighborhood, instead of a brotherhood.

From a sermon in Best Jewish Sermons of 5713 *(1953), for which he served as editor.*

SERMONS AND PREACHERS

The goal of an effective sermon should be to change the person in the pew. Otherwise, it should be changed by the preacher in the pulpit.

From his Introduction to Best Jewish Sermons of 5731–5732 *(1972).*

LEARNING TO SHARE

It is a law of life: You have what you use and what you keep you lose.

Ibid.

◻

William M. Thackeray

CONSECRATED JEWISH MOTHER

I saw a Jewish lady only yesterday with a child at her knee, and from whose face towards the child there shone a sweetness so angelical that it seemed to form a sort of glory round both. I protest I could have knelt before her, too, and adored in her the divine beneficence in endowing us with the maternal storge [*sic*] which began with our race and sanctifies the history of mankind.

From his Pendennis *(1849).*

◻

Bob Thomas

MOVIE MOGUL

A Bavarian Jew of immense cunning.

Characterizing motion picture producer Carl Laemmle. From his Selznick.

◻

M. Carey Thomas

COMMON TRAIT

Jews: Reason for dislike. Like Quakers they stick together.

From a footnote to the appendix of a volume of her early journals and letters entitled The Making of a Feminist *(1979).*

TERRIBLE PEOPLE

The Jews are the same now and were the same then, a most terrible set of people.

From a letter to her mother in 1882.

LOVING RELATIVE

He is Jewish to a degree and as ugly as sin. To think I shall have such a brother-in-law and lots of little Jew nephews and nieces.

From a private letter to her friend Mary Garret when, in 1903, she wrote that her own sister married Simon Flexner, the noted pathologist and later director of the Rockefeller Institute for Medical Research. Quoted in Helen Lefkowitz Horowitz's Power and Passion of M. Carey Thomas *(1994).*

□

Dorothy Thompson

FAILED HUSH-HUSH DIPLOMACY

The American Jewish Committee tried to soft-peddle things. It advised watchful waiting. It refused to participate in parades, demonstrations, protest meetings. It tried to get the government to do something, but very, very quietly. Hush-hush was the word. In short, while the stress of the situation demanded leadership, the American Jewish Committee offered restraint. It did nothing, most diplomatically.

Describing the timidity of American Jewry's foremost organization in the 1930s. Dr. Cyrus Adler was president of the American Jewish Committee in 1933 and was in communication with Secretary of State Cordell Hull, urging him to file a formal protest with the German authorities.

APPEAL TO CONSCIENCE

It is a fantastic commentary on the inhumanity of our time that for thousands and thousands of people a piece of paper with a stamp on it is the difference between life and death.

From a February 1939 appeal to Congress to pass the Wagner–Rogers bill, which would allow 20,000 German-Jewish children under the age of fourteen to enter the U.S.

□

Ahmed Tibi

DUAL LOYALTY

Yasser Arafat is the president of my people. Ezer Weizman is the president of my state. I don't see this as a problem.

From a profile of Arafat's special advisor on the peace process, which appeared in The Jerusalem Post, *January 15, 1994.*

□

Alan Tigay

PROOF OF SURVIVABILITY

Asking whether we will survive as a people is as much a part of Jewish tradition as the rituals of the synagogue. We may never find an answer, but if a century from now we are still asking the same question, that may be good enough.

From Hadassah Magazine, June–July 1993.

KEY TO THE VAULT

In my first week in Kyoto [Japan], I met a Japanese Christian minister, a Swiss Catholic student and an American flower child, all of whom could speak Hebrew. I kept trying my five-years-of-pre-Bar-Mitzva Hebrew and kept getting humiliated. Three Hebrew-speaking gentiles in a week. People speaking to me in my own voice and I couldn't respond. Was God telling me I had struck out? My journey ended a year later not in Europe but in an *ulpan* in Jerusalem. The language pushed aside while I was learning everyone else's turned out to be the key to a vault of Jewish riches.

Ibid. March 1994.

□

Paul Tillich

GERMAN CRUELTY

No nation has contributed more to the cruelty of the Jewish fate in our time, and, nevertheless, no nation shows more similarities in character and destiny with Judaism than the Germans.

From an address by the Protestant theologian on February 16, 1942. Quoted in Congress Weekly, February 27, 1942.

□

Ernst Toller

PARADISE ON EARTH

The *summum bonum*, "Paradise on Earth," will not be created by any social system; the only point is to fight for the comparative best that mankind can find and implement.

Quoted in his Collected Works *(1978), edited by John M. Spalek and Wolfgang Frühwald.*

WHERE I BELONG

Shall I capitulate to the insanity of the persecutors and replace my German airs with Jewish ones?.... If someone asked me where I belonged, I would answer: a Jewish mother bore me, Germany nourished me, Europe educated me, my home is the earth, the world my fatherland.

From his I Was a German Jew *(1934).*

☐

Leo Tolstoy

EMBLEM OF ETERNITY

The Jew is the emblem of eternity. He whom neither slaughter nor torture of thousands of years could destroy,...he who was the first to produce the oracle of God, he who has been for so long the guardian of prophecy, and who transmitted it to the rest of the world—such a nation cannot be destroyed. The Jew is everlasting as is eternity itself.

Quoted in Joseph L. Baron's Stars and Sand *(1943).*

JEWISH NONBELIEVERS

There is no such thing as a Jewish nonbeliever.

By attribution.

THE PATHOLOGY OF ANTI-SEMITISM

Anti-Semitism is...a pathological condition, a peculiar form of sexual perversion.... Among all disgraceful phenomena, it is the most disgusting and abominable.

From an 1880 letter to I. Tenoromo.

TURNING THE OTHER CHEEK

Not long ago, I was reading the Sermon on the Mount with a rabbi. At nearly every verse he showed me very similar passages in the Hebrew Bible and Talmud. When we reached the words "Turn the other cheek," he did not say that this, too, is in the Talmud, but asked with a smile, "Do the Christians obey this command?" I had nothing to say in reply, especially as at that particular time, Christians, far from turning the other cheek, were smiting the Jews on both cheeks.

From his My Religion *(1884).*

☐

Arnold Toynbee

ULTIMATE ZIONIST AIM

The ultimate aim of the Zionists is to liberate the Jewish people from the peculiar psychological complex induced by the penalization to which they have been subject for centuries in the Gentile world.

From his Study of History *(1934).*

GOD'S CHOSEN PEOPLE

The most notorious historical example of the idolization of an ephemeral self is the error of the Jews.... They persuaded themselves that Israel's discovery of the One True God had revealed Israel itself to be God's Chosen People.

Ibid.

☐

Joshua Trachtenberg

RELIGION FOR THE LIVING

For all our wide acquaintance with the teachings of prophets, rabbis, and philosophers, it must be said that we really know little about the Jewish religion—that is, the religion...surely needed as a source for strength in the everyday task of combating a perennially hostile world.

From an article entitled "The Folk Element in Judaism," which appeared in The Journal of Religion, *Vol. 22 (1942).*

☐

Isaac Trainin

VISITING THE SICK

Bikur cholim [visiting the sick] is one of what I call the forgotten *mitzvot* [commandments].

By attribution.

☐

Heinrich von Treitschke

MISFORTUNE

The Jews are our misfortune.

Justifying German anti-Semitism based on the fact that Jews refuse to assimilate. He accused Heinrich Graetz of being anti-Christian.

☐

Leo Trepp

HOMOSEXUALITY AND JEWISH LAW

Homosexuality...cannot be regarded as a willful act of religious disobedience. Judaism as such cannot offer formal recognition to the bond that links homosexual persons, nor allow them any special privileges, but it also cannot deny them their Jewishness and the rights and privileges attached to it.

From his Complete Book of Jewish Observance *(1980).*

Diana Trilling

A SENSE OF BEING JEWISH

Lionel was Bar Mitzvahed. Lionel and I were perfectly in agreement that Jim [their son, who became an art historian] should not be. We weren't in that sense practicing, observant. That doesn't mean we didn't have a sense of ourselves as Jews. I've never been without that sense. This is very important. It's not a negligible fact in my life: ... We were going to go [to Israel] when Lionel died. I haven't traveled since Lionel's death [in 1975].

From an interview with Joseph A. Cincotti in The Jerusalem Report, *December 30, 1993, upon the publication of her new book about her marriage at age 88.*

LIKE WALKING IN THE WIND

He didn't come to terms with his Jewishness, he didn't know how to feel about it. He felt something very strong. Indeed, in a 1928 journal entry, he wrote that "being a Jew is like walking in the wind or swimming; you are touched at all points and conscious everywhere."

Ibid. Commenting on her late husband Lionel's feelings toward Judaism.

Lionel Trilling

PENETRATING BABEL

He was a man to whom the perception of the world...came late and had to be apprehended, but strength and speed, against the parental or cultural interdiction, the Jewish interdiction; it was as if every beautiful violent phrase that was to spring upon reality was a protest against his childhood.

Evaluating Isaac Babel.

WALKING IN THE WIND

Being a Jew is like walking in the wind or swimming: you are touched at all points and conscious everywhere.

From an article in the Partisan Review *50th Anniversary Edition (1985).*

Leon Trotsky

EPITOME OF SELF-HATE

Go home to your Jews and tell them that I am not a Jew, and I care nothing for Jews and their fate.

From remarks to a Jewish delegation in 1921. Quoted in H. Valentin's Anti-Semitism *(1936).*

SUDDENLY OLD AGE

Old age is the most unexpected of all things that happen to a man.

By attribution.

Harry S Truman

AMERICAN VIEW OF PALESTINE

The American view of Palestine is that we want to let as many of the Jews into Palestine as it is possible into that country. Then the matter will have to be worked out diplomatically with the British and the Arabs, so that if a state can be set up there, they may be able to set it up on a peaceful basis.

In an announcement made at a press conference on August 10, 1945 endorsing the proposal that 10,000 refugees be admitted into Palestine by the British. Prime Minister Clement Atlee was incensed, asserting: "No major change in Palestine [would be made] against their will."

DIRECTIVE TO GENERAL EISENHOWER

I know you will agree with me that we have a particular responsibility toward those victims of persecution and tyranny who are in our zone. We must make clear to the German people that we thoroughly abhor the Nazi policies of hatred and persecution. We have no better opportunity to demonstrate this than by the manner in which we ourselves actually treat the survivors remaining in Germany.

In a directive sent to General Dwight D. Eisenhower on August 31, 1945 after receiving a report that Jewish DPs were being treated virtually as war prisoners. He insisted that Jews be removed from DP camps and be given decent housing.

A PROUD MOMENT

One of the proudest days of my life occurred at 6:12 p.m. on Friday May 14 [1948] when I was able to announce recognition of the new State of Israel by the government of the United States. In view of the long friendship of the American people for the Zionist ideal it was particularly appropriate that our government should be the first to recognize the new State.

Ibid.

DISPLACED PERSONS' TRAGEDY

I sincerely wish that every member of Congress could visit the displaced persons' camp in Germany and Austria and see just what is happening to 500,000 human beings through no fault of their own.

In an October 1946 letter to Walter George, chairman of the Senate Finance Committee.

ON ISRAEL

Jesus Christ couldn't please them when he was here on earth, so how could anyone expect that I would have any luck.

Fuming at the intense pressure placed upon him in 1948 by Jewish lobbyists to recognize the State of Israel. Quoted in Alonzo L. Hamby's biography, Man of the People: A Life of Harry S Truman *(1995).*

I AM CYRUS

What do you mean "helped create"? I am Cyrus, I am Cyrus.

Responding to Eddie Jacobson's remark in November 1953 that Truman was the man who helped create the State of Israel. Quoted in an essay by Moshe Davis in With Eyes Toward Zion *(1977).*

¤

Barbara Tuchman

HOW, NOT WHY

I belong to the "How" school rather than the "Why." I am a seeker of the small facts, not the big explanations; a narrator, not a philosopher.

Explaining what kind of historian she is. Quoted in Elinor and Robert Slater's Great Jewish Women *(1994).*

GOOD WRITING

It is this quality of being in love with your subject that is indispensable for writing good history—or good anything for that matter.

Ibid.

¤

Kurt Tucholsky

RESIGNING FROM JUDAISM

I "resigned from Judaism" in the year 1911, and I know that cannot be done.

Quoted in Richard von Soldenhoff's Kurt Tucholsky 1890–1935 *(1985).*

UNAFFECTED BY ANTI-SEMITISM

I remain particularly silent during anti-Semitic attacks—and there is a particular reason

for that. The question of Judaism has never affected me much. You can see from my writings that I rarely even touch upon the whole complex; my knowledge in the field is not very extensive, I do not know if the Zionists are right or wrong, and so I remain silent. The people who want to hit the Jew in me shoot wide of the mark. My heartbeat does not accelerate when someone shouts "dirty Jew" after me; it is as alien to me as if he said "You weed whose name starts with a T—what possible good can there be in you?" I do not say that I am right; I am simply stating my feelings, and not even publicly. The question does not affect me.

Ibid.

¤

Cynthia Tucker

EXPOSING SMUT

The act of publicizing something that is vile and offensive and bigoted is, in fact, an old and respected civil rights tactic.... [T]he significant point here is that Khalid Muhammad up until today was a leading figure in the Nation of Islam. And the Congressional Black Caucus was making an effort to have an alliance with the Nation of Islam. We need to know what their major figures are thinking and saying.

Taking New York Congressman Charles B. Rangel to task on the February 3, 1994 broadcast of the MacNeil/Lehrer News Hour *for criticizing the Anti-Defamation League for publicizing the anti-Semitic speech of Louis Farrakhan's aide, Khalid Abdul Muhammad.*

¤

Gordon Tucker

HOMOSEXUAL RIGHTS

The matter of "civil rights and civil duties" within the Jewish community would appear *halachically* [according to Jewish law] simple: gay and lesbian Jews are Jews, eligible for honors and organizational roles, no matter what one may conclude about the permissibility of their sexual lives.... [It is a] longstanding practice in virtually all Jewish communities to accord membership rights and *bimah* [pulpit] honors to known violators of many commandments, such as Shabbat and *kashrut* observance.

From a symposium on "Homosexuality and Halachik Judaism," which appeared in Moment *magazine, June 1993.*

◻

Sophie Tucker

AGES OF WOMAN

From birth to age eighteen, a girl needs good parents. From eighteen to thirty-five, she needs good looks. From thirty-five to fifty-five, she needs a good personality. From fifty-five on, she needs good cash. I'm saving my money.

> *A comment made at age sixty-nine, in 1958. Quoted by actress Tovah Feldshuh at a Myrtle Wreath Award ceremony of the Nassau (NY) region of Hadassah in November 1994.*

PATH OF VIRTUE

The happiest thing of all is that in becoming a success I hurt nobody. Some people get ruthless. Some hurt others, but I did it the hardest way, and the longest way, too.

> *Quoted in Elinor and Robert Slater's* Great Jewish Women *(1994).*

DOING YOUR BEST

Knowing, as you stretch your tired body out between the sheets with a sigh of relief, that you've done a good job, and the members of your own profession think you have, and say, "Oh, Sophie's a good *schnuck*," goes a hell of a long way.

> *Contemplating her work. From her* Some of These Days *(1945).*

RICH IS BETTER

I have been poor and I have been rich. Believe me, honey, rich is better.

> *Ibid.*

HOW TO LIVE LONG

Keep breathing.

> *When asked on her eightieth birthday, January 13, 1964, the secret of longevity.*

◻

Samuel Turk

KEEPING WOMEN IN THEIR PLACE

The thrust of Jewish tradition is not to make women too conspicuous in the public domain. Their talents and forte are in the domestic sphere. Were Jews to ape the present feminist trends of the secular world, the entire fabric of Judaism would have to be revamped. Let us not follow like blind sheep the pagan trends of the non-Jewish world. That world is not doing all that well.

> *Commenting on the proposal to ordain Jewish women as Orthodox rabbis. From an article in* The Jewish Press, *December 3, 1993.*

◻

Mark Twain

PALESTINE THE DREAMLAND

Palestine is no more of this workaday world. It is sacred poetry and tradition—it is dreamland.

> *From his* Innocents Abroad *(1869), in which he accounts for his visit to the Holy Land in 1867.*

UNITED IN HATE

All classes of people were unanimous only on one thing: being against Jews.

> *Ibid. An observation after a visit to Austria in 1898.*

PUFF OF STARDUST

If the statistics are right, the Jews constitute but one quarter of one percent of the human race. It suggests a nebulous dim puff of stardust lost in the blaze of the Milky Way. Properly, the Jew ought hardly to be heard of; but he is heard of, has always been heard of....

The Egyptians, the Babylonians and the Persians rose, filled the planet with sound and splendor, then faded to dream-stuff and passed away; the Greeks and the Romans followed and made a vast noise, and they are gone; other peoples have sprung up and held their torch high for a time but it burned out, and they sit in twilight now, or have vanished.

The Jew saw them all, survived them all, and is now what he always was, exhibiting no decadence, no infirmities of age, no weakening of his parts, no slowing of his energies, no dulling of his alert and aggressive mind.

> *From his essay entitled "Concerning the Jews," which appeared in* Harper's *magazine, September 1899.*

IMMORTAL JEW

He [the Jew] is as prominent on the planet as any other people.... His contributions to the world's list of great names in literature, science, art, music, finance, medicine, and abstruse learning are also way out of proportion to the weakness of his numbers. He has made a marvelous fight in this world, in all the ages; and has done it with his hands tied behind him. All things are mortal but the Jew; all other forces pass, but he remains. What is the secret of his immortality?

> *Ibid.*

TALENT AND BRAINS

Envy of Jewish talents and brains has moved the Gentiles to behave like wild beasts toward a people in some respects their superior. England has been fair to the Jew and America also, generally speaking, but we cannot boast of being above race prejudice while we retain any sense of superiority to another race.

> *From a comment made in 1901 reported by Clara Clemens in* My Husband Gabrilowitsch *(1938).*

PIGMY MINDS

Even if the Jews have not all been geniuses, their general average of intelligence and intellectuality is far above our general average— and that is one of our reasons for wishing to drive them out of the higher forms of business and the professions. It is the swollen envy of pigmy minds—meanness, *injustice.*

> *Ibid.*

□

Adam Tzerniakow

BEYOND HUMAN ENDURANCE

I am powerless, my heart trembles in sorrow and compassion. I can no longer bear all this.

> *The last entry in his diary before he committed suicide in July 1942 when he was ordered to sign children's deportation orders.*

□

(The) Tzupenester Rebbe

A CHASIDIC REBBE ADVISES

You may learn much wisdom from the rules of this game [of checkers]. You surrender one in order to capture two. You may not make two moves at one time. You must move up and not down. When you reach the top, you may move as you like.

> *Teaching a lesson to his disciples who were playing checkers.*

André Ungar

SERMON AS OPPORTUNITY

With all its shortcomings, the sermon offers the preacher an opportunity to teach, to inspire, to arouse, to comfort, to challenge—and to express and fulfill himself. In how many occupations does a person have the utter freedom, the individual attention, the sense of sacred authority a rabbi enjoys?

From an article in The Jewish Spectator, *Fall 1988.*

٥

Samuel Untermeyer

A MEANS OF SURVIVAL

They say we Jews are clannish. It is true, and I hope it will remain true until conditions change. We are not clannish from choice. We are not willing to be received on sufferance or with reservations. Until the time comes when social barriers are so completely destroyed that we mingle among men and women of all creeds and races without thought of distinction we must needs remain clannish and cling to our own if we would preserve our self-respect.

From an April 27, 1923 speech.

٥

Leon Uris

PROFESSIONAL APOLOGISTS

There is a whole school of Jewish American writers who spend their time damning their fathers, hating their mothers, wringing their hands, and wondering why they were born. This isn't art or literature. It's psychiatry. These writers are professional apologists. Every year you find one of their (sic!) works on the best seller lists.... Their work is obnoxious and makes me sick to my stomach.

In an interview with Joseph Wershba, published in the New York Post. *Quoted in* American Judaism *magazine (1961).*

COMING HOME

At dawn of the second day everyone sighted land at once.

"Palestine!"

"Eretz Ysrael!"

A hysteria of laughing and crying and singing and joy burst from the children.

The little salvage tug came within sight of land and the electrifying news spread through the Yishuv. The children who had brought the mighty British Empire to its knees were arriving!...

Twenty-five thousand Jews poured into the Haifa dock to cheer the creaky little boat. The Palestine Philharmonic Orchestra played the Jewish anthem—*Hatikvah,* "The Hope."

The *Exodus* had come home.

From his Exodus *(1958).*

DEFINITELY PRO-JEWISH

I wrote *Exodus* because I was just sick of apologizing—or feeling that it was necessary to apologize. The Jewish community of this country has contributed far more greatly than its numbers—in art, medicine, and especially literature.

I set out to tell a story of Israel. I am definitely biased. I am definitely pro-Jewish.

Ibid.

THE WRITER'S PLACE

To me a writer is one of the most important soldiers in the fight for the survival of the human race. He must stay at his post in the thick of fire to serve the cause of mankind.

From an article in the New York Herald Tribune, *August 16, 1959.*

RABIN EPITAPH

I think [Yitzhak] Rabin takes his place alongside Ben-Gurion as one of the two great Jews of this century. He soared. I think it was almost biblical, how the team—he as a warrior and Shimon Peres as a poet—the two of them together made peace.

Reflecting on the assassination of Israeli Prime Minister Yitzhak Rabin on November 4, 1995.

◘

Melvin F. Urofsky

THE CURSE OF BIG GOVERNMENT

[Louis D.] Brandeis was a liberal by affirmation and championed his causes not out of disinterest, but out of strong beliefs. A Jeffersonian democrat who passionately feared the "curse of bigness," he fought for the rights of states to use their police powers effectively and experimentally in order to preserve a federal system he considered essential for a democratic society.

From his Mind of One Piece: Brandeis and American Reform.

◘

Menachem Ussishkin

PEOPLE AND LAND

When the Jewish people will have redeemed the Land of Israel, the Land of Israel will redeem the Jewish people.

From his Eretz Israel *(1932).*

HERZL'S LEGACY

Those who came before him carried the ideal [of Palestine] in their hearts but only whispered about it in the synagogue.... Herzl brought us courage and taught us to place our demands before the whole non-Jewish world.

Evaluating Herzl's greatness after his death in 1904 at the age of forty-four.

Abigail Van Buren

OLD AGE

Wisdom doesn't automatically come with old age. Nothing does—except wrinkles. It is true some wines improve with age. But only if the grapes were good in the first place.

From one of her 1978 "Dear Abby" columns.

□

Paul M. Van Buren

GOD OF JEWS AND GENTILES

We are Gentiles, preponderantly, who worship the God of Israel. It is one thing for the Jews to call upon God as Father and to know him immediately and always as their God. That is their right and their duty because of their election.... For Gentiles to call upon this God is another thing.

From his Discerning the Way: A Theology of the Jewish Christian Reality *(1980).*

□

Dmitri Vasilev

THE REAL ZHIRINOVSKY

Vladimir Wolfovich [Zhirinovsky] likes to call himself a Russian, but he is not, if we speak openly. He should be honest and not conceal his nationality.

Accusing ultranationalist Vladimir Zhirinovsky of masquerading as a "true Russian" by concealing his Jewish roots. Quoted in The Jerusalem Report, *February 24, 1994.*

□

Simone Veil

REMEMBERING HUMILIATION

As a Jew, as a concentration camp survivor, as a woman, you feel very much that you belong to a minority that has been bullied for a long time. As for the deportation, what re-

mains with you most is the memory of humiliation, and that's a feeling many women have, too, of trampled dignity.... If this Parliament has a Jew, a woman, for its president, it means everyone has the same rights.

Noting the irony of a Holocaust survivor presiding over the European Parliament. From an October 1979 statement to the Associated Press.

□

Eleutherios Venizelos

JEWS OF GREECE

I profess in general a profound esteem and great veneration for the Jewish people, which has always and everywhere been an element of progress and prosperity. My Government and I regard Greek Jewry as a precious factor toward the economic promotion of our country which is essentially tolerant and where one is not asked whether one is a Jew or a Greek.

From an August 27, 1931 interview which appeared in Istanbul in the Ladino journal La Boz de Oriente, *September 17, 1931.*

□

(Queen) Victoria

NEITHER JEW NOR CHRISTIAN

I don't understand you, Mr. Disraeli. You're not a Jew because you were baptized. You're not really a full Christian either. What are you?

To which Benjamin Disraeli, her prime minister, replied: "I am the blank page between the Old Testament and New Testament."

PECULIAR BUT LOYAL

The present man will do well, and will be particularly loyal and anxious to please me in every way. He is very peculiar, but very clever and sensible and very conciliatory.

From a letter to the Crown Princess of Prussia, February 29, 1868, describing Benjamin Disraeli.

Abe Vigoda

MAN FOR ALL CAUSES

I involve myself in different charities. I give of myself whether it's for Jew, Catholic, Protestant or black children, as well as such causes as Israel Bonds. Whatever charity I help out, I never forget that deep inside me stirs my Orthodox upbringing.

From Tim Boxer's Jewish Celebrity Hall of Fame *(1987).*

Oswald Garrison Villard

AMERICA'S DEBT TO ITS IMMIGRANTS

My pen may have some skill, but I could not begin to measure the debt that this country owes to its Jews and to millions of its foreign-born citizens, first for a jealous guarding of American rights and liberties to which the native-born have too often been indifferent; second, for preserving at all times a great reservoir of idealism and liberalism; and thirdly, for keeping alive a passionate desire for knowledge in every field, which has steadily quickened American life and notably its colleges.

From his Fighting Years: Memoirs of a Liberal Editor.

Bert Voeten

THE TRAIN

There runs through my head a train
full of Jews. I shunt the past
on a siding, and count
the cattle cars with the bolts:
fifty trucks, and in ev'ry one of them fifty
   people. One lies
pinched in between members,
one is carrier or is carried,
prisoners of each other
in the darkness of the train-car
in the darkness without water,
without air,
without hope.

A poem written by the non-Jewish Dutch poet to keep alive the memory of the death transports. From the South African Jewish Affairs *magazine, December 1967.*

François Voltaire

A RATIONAL CONCLUSION

If it were permitted to reason consistently in religious matters, it is clear that we all ought to become Jews, because Jesus was born a Jew, lived a Jew, died a Jew, and he said expressly that he was fulfilling the Jewish religion.

From his Philosophical Dictionary v. Toleration *(1746).*

SINFUL JEWS

You [Jews] have surpassed all nations in impertinent fables, in bad conduct, and in barbarism. You deserve to be punished, for this is your destiny.... Nevertheless, they should not be burned at the stake.

Ibid.

ONCE LOVED BY GOD

Jews: a nation full of amenity and composed of lepers, misers, usurers, and scurvy rogues whom the God of the universe, delighted with their shining qualities, in former days fell in love with.

Ibid.

FANATICAL JEWS

They [the Jews] are, all of them, born with raging fanaticism in their hearts, just as the Bretons and the Germans are born with blond hair. I would not be in the least bit surprised if these people would not some day become deadly to the human race.

Quoted in Chaim Potok's Wanderings *(1978).*

BEWARE OF JEWS

[Jews are] an ignorant and barbarous people [who might someday] become deadly to the human race.

Quoted in Alan Dershowitz's Chutzpah *(1991).*

Kurt Vonnegut, Jr.

RIGHT VS. WRONG

I offer my opinion that Eichmann cannot distinguish between right and wrong—that not only right and wrong, but truth and falsehood, hope and despair, beauty and ugliness, kindness and cruelty, comedy and tragedy, are all processed by Eichmann's mind indiscriminately, like birdshot through a bugle.

From his Mother Night *(1961), a fictional memoir of an American-born writer awaiting trial in an Israeli prison for broadcasting Nazi propaganda during World War II.*

ם

Albert Vorspan

JUDAISM'S ETHICAL VALUES

I believe that the ethical values of Judaism, as they were tested and refined through Jewish history, have something sharp and important to say about these problems and to the real world in our time.

From the Preface to his Jewish Values and Social Crisis: A Casebook for Social Action *(1973).*

THE JEWISH BURDEN

[Jews carry the burden] to face this world and its pain head on; to engage in endless study and moral debate; to cherish human life and to pursue justice; to enhance the life of the mind and to struggle, despite all complexity and despair, to be God's co-partners in repairing His broken and incomplete world.

From his Great Jewish Debates and Dilemmas: Jewish Perspective on Moral Issues in the Eighties *(1980).*

ם

Franz Vranitzky

AUSTRIA'S MORAL RESPONSIBILITY

We have felt and still feel that the connotation of collective guilt does not apply to Austria, but we do acknowledge collective responsibility.

We share a moral responsibility because many Austrians welcomed the *Anschluss* supported by the Nazi regime and helped it to function. We have to live up to this side of our history.

In an address on June 16, 1993 at the Hebrew University on Mount Scopus. Vranitzky was the first Austrian head of state to visit Israel.

PRESERVING HISTORICAL FACTS

...[there are some] who wish to deny what has happened, that all the documentation, films, books, pictures and other means of documentation are a fake, and who say that Auschwitz never existed. Therefore it is extremely important, especially [preserving] Birkenau, which serves as evidence for the future.

In an April 1994 address on the importance of preserving the concentration camps at Auschwitz-Birkenau.

W

Richard Wagner

THE JEWISH "PROBLEM"

Only one thing can redeem you from the burden of your curse—annihilation.

By attribution.

¤

Lech Wałesa

ANTI-SEMITISM RENEWED

Though this is just a marginal part of life, I am ashamed of it. As long as I have anything to say in Poland, I will oppose anti-Semitism.

In a March 1991 meeting with Jewish leaders in New York, after acknowledging the revival of anti-Semitism in Poland.

BELATED APOLOGY

Here in Israel, the land of your culture and revival, I ask for your forgiveness.

In a May 1991 address to Israel's Knesset.

¤

James Walker

MARRED RELIGION

And what shall I say of Judaism? Every thoughtful reader must be struck with the lofty tone of monotheistic morality pervading the Old Testament; but it was never understood to come up with the Christian standard.... Judaism is marred throughout—sometimes in principle, and still oftener in spirit—by the narrowness and arrogance of a people educated in the belief that God was *their* God...not the God of all mankind.

Quoted in Egal Feldman's Dual Destinies: The Jewish Encounter with Protestant America *(1990).*

¤

Barbara Walters

ENCHANTING CHILDREN

Parents of young children should realize that few people, and maybe no one, will find their children as enchanting as they do.

From her How to Talk with Practically Anybody About Practically Anything *(1970).*

THE REWARDS OF SUCCESS

Success can make you go one of two ways. It can make you a prima donna, or it can smooth the edges, take away the insecurities, let the nice things come out.

Quoted in Newsweek *magazine, May 6, 1974.*

¤

Siegmund Warburg

BARBED WIRE SAFETY

Safety in this world can never be guaranteed by more barbed wire. Many Jews inside as well as outside Israel who share the views put forward in this letter are reluctant to speak out publicly because they are afraid that this might be interpreted as lack of loyalty to the cause of Israel. However, loyalty to sound principles and moral precepts must override any other loyalties.

Displaying his displeasure with Menachem Begin and his intransigence toward the Arabs. From an article in The Times *of London, February 18, 1978.*

ANTIPATHY TO CHAUVINISM

I don't believe in German chauvinism, never did. I don't believe in British chauvinism, I don't believe in American chauvinism and I don't believe in Israeli chauvinism.

From an article in the Institutional Investor, *March 1980.*

¤

George Washington

SEPARATING CHURCH FROM STATE

Although no man's sentiments are more opposed to *any kind* of restraint upon religious principles than mine are, yet I must confess, that I am not amongst the number of those who are so much alarmed at the thought of making people pay towards the support of that which they profess, if of the denomination of Christians or declare themselves Jews, Mahometans or otherwise, and thereby obtain proper relief.

In an October 3, 1785 letter to George Mason strongly opposing government support for Christian churches long considered part of the "establishment."

A Blessing on Jews

Gentlemen: I thank you with great sincerity for your congratulations on my appointment to the office which I have the honor to hold by the unanimous choice of my fellow-citizens, and especially the expressions you are pleased to use in testifying the confidence that is reposed in me by your congregations....

May the same wonder-working Deity, who long since delivered the Hebrews from their Egyptian oppressors, planted them in a promised land, whose providential agency has lately been conspicuous in establishing these United States as an independent nation, still continue to water them with the dews of heaven and make the inhabitants of every denomination participate in the temporal and spiritual blessings of that people whose God is Jehovah.

From a May 1790 response to a letter of May 6th addressed to him by Levi Sheftal of the Hebrew Congregation of Savannah, Georgia, in which the president was congratulated upon his election.

A Blessing Acknowledged

The affectionate expressions of your address again excite my gratitude and receive my warmest acknowledgment.

The power and goodness of the Almighty, so strongly manifested in the events of our late glorious revolution, and His kind interposition in our behalf, have been no less visible in the establishment of our present equal government. In war he directed the sword, and in peace He has ruled in our councils. My agency in both has been guided by the best intentions and a sense of duty I owe to my country.

And as my exertions have hitherto been amply rewarded by the approbation of my fellow-citizens, I shall endeavor to deserve a continuance of it by my future conduct.

May the same temporal and eternal bless-

ings which you implore for me, rest upon your congregations.

His response to a congratulatory letter written to him by Manuel Josephson, on December 13, 1790, in behalf of the Hebrew Congregations of Philadelphia, New York, Charleston, and Richmond.

Equality, Not Toleration

It is now no more that toleration is spoken of as if it were the indulgence of one class of people that another enjoyed the exercise of their inherent natural rights, for, happily, the government of the United States, which gives to bigotry no sanction, to persecution no assistance, requires only that they who live under its protection should demean themselves as good citizens in giving it on all occasions their effectual support.

It would be inconsistent with the frankness of my character not to avow that I am pleased with your favorable opinion of my administration and fervent wishes for my felicity.

May the children of the stock of Abraham who dwell in this land continue to merit and enjoy the good will of the other inhabitants; while everyone shall sit in safety under his own vine and fig tree and there shall be none to make him afraid.

Responding to a letter received from Moses Seixas of the Hebrew Congregation of Newport, Rhode Island, after Washington's visit to Newport in August 1790.

◻

Arthur Waskow

Limiting Power

One of the deepest teachings of spiritual traditions is the importance of putting limits to one's own power. It is perhaps one of the most important distinctions between most "spiritual" and most "secular" paths. Distorted, the teaching can lead to self-flagellation among individuals and self-victimization among communities and peoples. Heard in all its richness, it offers solidity, the space and time for developing a path of self-determination for every culture, every nation, every community, every person.

From an article in The Jewish Spectator, *Winter 1980.*

Voice of a Dove

Holding the West Bank/Gaza and insisting that no Palestinian state can emerge there is the one policy that means permanent war; permanent and deepening demoralization of Israel as expressed already in the emigration figures; permanent distortion of the Israeli economy and deepening depression/inflation; permanent dependence on the money and the whims of the U.S. government; deepening isolation from all other political forces in the world, and, already peeping over the horizon, isolation even from increasing parts of U.S. public opinion.

From a symposium in Moment *magazine, March 1976.*

¤

Jakob Wasserman

DUAL LOYALTY

I am a German and a Jew, one as much, as completely as the other. Neither is to be separated from the other.

In his autobiography, My Life as German and Jew *(1933).*

GERMAN JEW

A non-German cannot possibly imagine the heartbreaking position of the German Jew. German Jew—you must place full emphasis on both words. You must understand them as the final product of a lengthy evolutionary process. His twofold love and his struggle on two fronts drive him close to the brink of despair.

Ibid.

POPULIST ACCUSATIONS

The unfortunate fact is that one cannot dispute the truth that the persecutors, promoted agents and volunteers alike, had something to go on. Every iconoclastic incident, every convulsion, every social challenge has seen, and still sees, Jews in the front line. Wherever a peremptory demand for a clean sweep is made, wherever the idea of governmental metamorphosis is to be translated into action with frenzied zeal, Jews have been and still are the leaders.

Ibid.

¤

Wendy Wasserstein

ON NAME CHANGING

If I were 20 years older my name probably wouldn't be Wendy Wasserstein, because of those Jewish movie moguls in Hollywood who made people change their names. I'd probably be Wendy Waters because that's what it would have taken to get it done.

In an interview that appeared in Haddassah Magazine, *May 1993.*

JEWISH INFLUENCES

Jewish writers inspired me, particularly of musical comedy.... Passover is the most meaningful holiday to me, and I spend it with my family.... There is a Jewish tradition of show business which has influenced my career. My Jewishness has made my outlook on life more ironic and earnest.

Commenting on her Jewish background. Quoted in Elinor and Robert Slater's Great Jewish Women *(1994).*

ISN'T EVERYONE JEWISH?

As far as I could make out, everyone around me was Jewish when I was a child. I didn't know anybody who was Protestant except on television.

Ibid.

NUREMBERG LESSON

If you're the daughter of immigrants and you go to Nuremberg and that doesn't resonate in you...

After winning a trip to Europe in 1961 from the Herald Tribune's World Youth Forum *and visiting Nuremberg.*

¤

Tom Watson

ANTI-SEMITISM HURTS

I see acts of anti-Semitism on the rise around in the world.... It hurts. It's a family matter and it's something I cannot accept.

A November 1990 statement issued as he resigned from the Kansas City Country Club when it refused the membership application of a Jew. Watson's wife and children are Jewish.

¤

F. W. Watts

GREAT PAINTERS

My intention has not been so much to paint pictures that will charm the eye as to suggest great thoughts that will appeal to the imagination and the heart, and kindle all that is best and noblest in humanity. I even think that, in the future, art may yet speak, as great poetry itself, with the solemn and majestic ring in which the Hebrew prophets spoke to the Jews of old, demanding noble aspirations, condemning in the most trenchant manner private vices, and warning us in deep tones against lapses from morals and duties.

Quoted in J. H. Hertz's Pentateuch and Haftorahs *(1961).*

Henry Waxman

LIBERAL CHAMPION

God never meant liberals to be stupid.

> *Quoted in* Current Biography Yearbook *(1992).*

Simone Weil

THE IMPOSSIBLE

It is only the impossible that is possible for God.

> *Quoted in* Selected Essays *(1943), edited by Richard Rees.*

POWER OF THE WORD

There is something else which has the power to awaken us to the truth. It is the works of writers of genius.

> *From her essay "Morality and Literature" (1944).*

GOD'S VEIL

Necessity is God's veil.

> *From her* Gravity and Grace *(1947).*

WORTHLESS SCIENCE

A science that doesn't bring us nearer to God is worthless.

> *Ibid.*

GOD IN FACT

We must love all facts, not for their consequences, but because in each fact God is there present.

> *From her* Notebooks of Simone Weil *(1951).*

THE SOUL'S NEED

To be rooted is perhaps the most important and least recognized need of the human soul.

> *From her* Need for Roots *(1952).*

KNOWING SELF

I can, therefore I am.

> *Quoted in Simone Pétrement's* Simone Weil: A Life *(1977).*

Moses Cyrus Weiler

TO ISRAEL WITH LOVE

Before our *aliyah* to Israel from South Africa in 1958, I dedicated my children to the defense of Israel. All my five sons and only daughter received military education because I felt the defense of Israel to be supreme, and that each and every one of our children had to be part of it.

I still abide by my faith in Jewish universalism. My Judaism still follows the teachings of the Prophets and Sages of Israel. I still believe in justice and righteousness as the great ideals of the Jewish people. Every Jew must love God, the Jewish people and every human being, regardless of race, color or creed.

> *Weiler, formerly of the Reform Congregation in Johannesburg and later of Jerusalem, lost one son in the War of Attrition and a second son in the Yom Kippur War. When the remains of his younger son were transferred from a temporary grave in the Jerusalem Military Cemetery, Rabbi Weiler spoke these words first published in the November 8, 1974 issue of* Congress Bi-Weekly.

Steven Weinberg

FATE OF THE UNIVERSE

It is very hard to realize that this present universe has evolved from an unspeakably unfamiliar early condition, and faces a future extinction of endless cold or intolerable heat. The more the universe seems comprehensible, the more it also seems pointless.

> *From his* First Three Minutes *(1977).*

Caspar Weinberger

ON POLLARD'S SENTENCE

It is difficult for me...to conceive of a greater harm to national security than that caused by the defendant.... Pollard should have been shot.

> *After the sentencing of Jonathan Pollard on March 4, 1987 for spying for Israel. The comment was reportedly made by the U. S. Secretary of Defense in a conversation with Meir Rosenne, Israel's ambassador to the United States.*

Harry Weinberger

THE GREATEST RIGHT

The greatest right in the world is the right to be wrong.

> *In* The New York Evening Post, *April 10, 1917.*

Herbert Weiner

ON SEEING GOD

The full nature of the revelation at Sinai is relegated by Judaism to that category of "hidden things which are reserved to God." It is the "revealed matters that are given to man," and by "revealed" Judaism refers mainly to the *mitzvot*—the commandments. Deeply Jewish is the startling invitation which the Talmud attributes to God. "Abandon Me, if you will, but keep My commandments." The implication later suggested is that the keeping of the commandments will in its turn "sensitize" the eyes so that they will be better able to "see" God.

> *From an essay in* Condition of Jewish Belief *(1966), compiled by the editors of* Commentary *magazine.*

Marc Weiner

PURPOSE IN LIFE

If you're young and single, the road is a party and, when you don't have any morality, it's a lot of fun. But for me life was very empty.... Being a comedian is totally consuming: you never know when you're going to think of a joke, so you're always working. I thought there had to be more of a purpose than that. I felt the only reason I was living was to perpetuate my puppets; it was really sick.

> *Quoted in Darryl Lyman's* Jewish Comedy Catalog *(1989).*

Jacob J. Weinstein

MEASURE OF MAN

You can't tell the size of an evergreen until it is cut down.

> *Upon the death of Hayim Greenberg, philosopher and Zionist activist.*

Lotus Weinstock

ONSTAGE HONESTY

Lenny [Bruce] was the turning point of my life. Never again would I play beneath my in-telligence or be anything less than honest onstage.

> *After the death of her mentor and fiancé in 1966.*

BRUCE THE PROPHET

He [Lenny Bruce] was like a prophet.... He knew comedy had to have substance.

> *Ibid. Explaining why in her comedy routines she dropped all "little phony tricks."*

SPLIT PERSONALITY

Lotus is here, but Weinstock is out pursuing her earthly goals. Please leave your number, and we'll call back when we are at one.

> *Ibid. Message on her answering machine.*

Jacob Weisberg

FOND OF FOLKLORE

Does anybody really believe, for instance, that Shali [General Shalikashvili] learned English by watching John Wayne movies in Peoria? The fable radiates idealization; it's half Abe Lincoln, half Horatio Alger. Politicians are always fond of lore that demonstrates character at an early age, which is why we heard about the pre-adolescent Ross Perot breaking wild horses and about Bill Clinton facing down his drunken stepfather.

> *From his "Washington Diarist" column in* The New Republic, *October 11, 1993.*

THE REAL FARRAKHAN

It's not just Jews who believe that it was anti-Semitic for Farrakhan to say, "Jews know their wickedness, not just Zionism, which is an outgrowth of Jewish transgression," or to call Judaism a "dirty religion," or to say he was happy to be compared to Hitler because "Hitler was a very great man." Many non-Jewish whites, and yes, many blacks, take a dim view of these statements, too. Many whites, blacks and Jews object to Farrakhan because he is a demagogue who preaches racial hatred and violence. Many blacks do not admire him because they regard him as the leader of a totalitarian cult, which produces brainwashed, bow-tied zombies.

> *Ibid. In response to Lynn Duke's article in* The Washington Post *in which Louis Farrakhan, leader of the Nation of Islam was mildly characterized as "often controversial."*

✿

Meyer W. Weisgal

LOVE CONQUERS ALL

The Bastille has fallen.

The total content of a telegram received by Maurice Samuel in 1921 on the day Shirley Hershfeld, secretary of the Zionist Organization of America, agreed to marry him after a two-year pursuit. Quoted in The Odyssey of an Optimist: Meyer W. Weisgal *(1967).*

WEIZMANN'S GIFT

Without question, the life of modern Israel is the real expression of Dr. Weizmann's astonishing gift for creation. Perhaps more than any other statesman of our time, he succeeded in effecting an organic fusion between the abstractions of the mind and the practical activities demanded by man's physical existence. This fusion is reflected in the very core of life in Israel today.

From an essay evaluating the life and career of Chaim Weizmann. Quoted in Chaim Weizmann: A Biography by Several Hands *(1963), edited by Weisgal and Joel Carmichael.*

WORLD JEWRY

Now it occurs to me that he [Chaim Weizmann] never said *Israel* or the *Israelis,* that he spoke only of the Jewish people. This, too, was characteristic of his philosophy. To him, World Jewry and the Jewish State were an integral entity. The Jewish people, and not Israel's citizens alone, constituted the generating power that would make his vision a reality.

Ibid.

✿

Hugo Weisgall

THE PARTS AND THE WHOLE

Writing the opera forced me to reinvent and rethink my own mythology.... I am Jewish. So what? I am also American. I am also living in the twentieth century. You cannot separate any of these elements and say it characterizes my music.

From the program notes to his opera Esther, *which was performed as part of the New York City Opera's World Premiere Festival in October 1993.*

✿

Avi Weiss

PEACEFUL DRUMMERS

We view the Jewish community as a symphony orchestra in which there are drummers, flutists, violinists, and so on. We are drummers, peaceful drummers; our goal is not to drown out the flutists and violinists, but to beat steadily, relentlessly, never stopping, and, yes, sometimes sounding the alarm loud and clear. When any one of the instruments is missing, there is no symphony. Each one has an important place in the orchestra. Natan Sharansky, just a few days after arriving on his first U.S. visit, said it best: "Quiet diplomacy can help only if it is supported by strong public pressure."

Explaining the importance of activism. From an article in The Jewish Week, *July 1–7, 1994.*

MAKING AMERICA LAST

When Pat Buchanan was running for president, a number of rabbis—Orthodox, Conservative and Reform—joined in raising a voice against his anti-Semitic and racist statements. At his final "America First" rally on the eve of the Georgia primary [in 1992] I called out, "Your racism and anti-Semitism make America *last.*" He looked down at us and replied, "This is a rally of Americans, for Americans and for the good old USA, my friends." Translation: Jews, if you don't like it, get out of here.

Ibid.

VOTING OUT OF FEAR

Jews are well aware that this [New York City] mayoral election will turn on the Jewish vote. There may be a few in our community who are thinking of voting for the mayor [Dinkins] precisely because they are frightened of being blamed for causing his defeat. It is the beginning of the end of the once-proud Jewish community of New York if fear plays any role in its choice of mayor. The honor and self-pride of the Jewish community of New York are on the line in this election.

Discussing the New York City election and contest in which a black mayor was the incumbent. From an article in Manhattan Jewish Sentinel, *October 27, 1993.*

WAS JUSTICE DONE?

Jonathan Pollard committed a crime as an American, but was sentenced as a Jew.

On the sentencing of Pollard, convicted of spying for Israel.

THE SPIRIT LIVES

They've not seen the last of me.

After suffering a heart attack, the second in nine years, in Jerusalem on August 23, 1995.

◻

Victor F. Weisskopf

HUMAN CARING

The rescue of the Danish Jews deserves a special place in the annals of humanitarian deeds. It was a shining example of an action for freedom and human rights, done at a time when human rights were trampled on at so many places on earth.

From a speech delivered at the fiftieth anniversary commemoration of the rescue of the Jews of Denmark by a collective effort of the Danish people beginning on October 1, 1943.

THE WORST OF TIMES

[It was] a collaboration of decent human beings beyond national borders, dedicated to fight together against murderous persecution and destruction.... We have good reasons to celebrate this testimony that decency existed within the human community even during the worst of times.

Ibid.

◻

Michael Dov Weissmandel

SUFFERING INSENSITIVITY

We cannot understand how you can eat and drink, how you can rest in your beds, how you can stroll the streets. I am sure you are doing all those things.... We have been crying out for months and you have done nothing.

From a December 1942 appeal to world Jewry.

◻

Trude Weiss-Rosmarin

HOME AS SANCTUARY

The home has always been the sanctuary where the Jew found rest and succor from the harshness of a hostile world. Despised and shunted about in the street, his human dignity was restored to him when he crossed the threshold of his home.

From her Jewish Survival *(1949).*

MAN'S VALUE

Man as such is the highest value of Judaism. The degradation of any man to the level of "an animated machine" is unthinkable in the Jewish setting.

Ibid.

BASIC JUDAISM

Not beauty but goodness is the central problem and theme of Judaism.

Ibid.

DEMAND FOR EQUAL RIGHTS

[Women] resent the legal inferiority and disabilities to which Jewish law subjects them. They want legal equality, especially with respect to the laws of marriage and divorce.

From an article in The Jewish Spectator, *1971.*

NO VICTORY PARADES

An even greater victory than the military triumph was won by Israel on the morrow of the Six-Day War of June 1967 when the Israel Defense Forces did *not* stage a victory parade. Victory never misled the Israelis to glorify military strength.

Ibid.

THE RISK OF WITHDRAWAL

Now, when Arafat and the PLO have come around to recognize Israel's existence as of right, Israel must respond and take the risk (the risk is minimal) of withdrawing from the occupied territories so as to enable a Palestinian State to come into being.

Ibid., Fall 1988.

ISRAEL'S "PUSHKA" IMAGE

I am gratified that my diagnosis of the cause of Israel's economic woes has been substantiated by several hundred prominent industrialists, businessmen and economic analysts. The diagnosis is that "the *pushka* image" of Israel projected by the Israel fundraising organizations, notably UJA [United Jewish Appeal], is why investors and businessmen have made few commitments in Israel and why aliya from this and other Western countries can not be set into motion.

Ibid. May 1968. She notes that the April 1968 Economic Conference in Jerusalem agreed with the position she advocated as far back as November 1963.

JEWISH–CHRISTIAN DIALOGUE

I am not afraid of Jewish–Christian dialogues! I am not afraid because Jewish belief need not dread the confrontation with Christian belief on any grounds—biblical, historical, theological and philosophical. I do not belong with those of little faith in the strength of Judaism who tremble lest inter-religious dialogues may sway Jews to convert to Christianity.

Ibid., May 1967.

ACTIVE HEROISM

Graetz was only partially right when he characterized Jewish history as *Leidens und Gelehrtengeschichte* (Martyrology and the History of Scholarship). Jewish history is equally the record of active *heroism!*

Ibid., November 1967. She contends that Josephus fabricated the story of the suicide of the last defenders of Masada.

JUDAISM'S UNIQUENESS

You ask what is "so special about Jewishness?" I shall quote Archibald MacLeish who wrote that to avoid the nuclear destruction of our planet, mankind must recognize that "the dignity of man" must be given first place in our scale of values. He stated:

If man can be taught to believe in the worth of man, in the dignity of man, in the "characteristic perfection" of man, he can be taught not only to survive but to live. If the world can be governed in belief in the worth of man,...it can be governed in peace.

One reason why "only the Jews retained their identity" is that in the ancient world only the Jews believed in the worth and dignity of man.

Ibid., Spring 1984.

REAGAN AND BITBURG

President Reagan's visit to the Bitburg Cemetery was proof, if proof was needed, that Lord Chesterfield was never more right than when he wrote, in 1748, "Politicians neither love nor hate. Interest, not sentiments, directs them."

Ibid., Summer 1985.

EGALITARIAN JUDAISM

I am opposed to women's prayer groups and women's *minyanim* because I am against segregation.... I am delighted that egalitarian *minyanim* of women and men are increasing in numbers *and* that their attendance is growing.

Ibid.

GOD'S GENDER

I am not "turned off" by the *linguistic* gender of God because—the *Torah* is feminine in Hebrew *linguistic* gender and in Jewish life. The Torah is "the bride" of Israel, whom we honor and adorn with silver and velvet and silk, whom we tenderly enfold in our arms, and of whom God, according to a profound symbolism said: "Would that they [Israel] had forsaken Me and clung to the Torah."

Ibid.

ON GAY PRIDE

At the risk of shocking the modern people out there, I hold that Gay–Lesbian synagogues are a travesty and a mockery of the basic Jewish conviction that homosexuality (Jewish law has nothing to say on Lesbianism) is *to'eivah*, that is, a "disgrace." I know that those who judged this sickness so harshly were not schooled in psychiatry and psychology. Neither am I....

I leave it to those who are qualified to decide whether the gay and lesbian inclinations can be redirected into heterosexuality. But I do know that the rhetoric of "Gay Pride" and "Lesbian Pride" and "Gay Parades" are in bad taste. I don't see why there is "pride" in being gay or lesbian. If those who look for love to members of their own sex consider it normal and right, why make so much fuss about it?

Ibid., Fall 1985.

NO ROOM FOR ZIONIST ORGANIZATIONS

I am no longer a member of a Zionist organization; I dropped my membership in consonance with my conviction that today there is no longer any room for Zionist organizations.

In a 1960 dialogue with Rabbi William Berkowitz at the Institute of Adult Jewish Studies in New York City. Reported in Berkowitz's Ten Vital Jewish Issues *(1964).*

THE BOOK OF LIFE

The Bible has nurtured Christianity and Islam, Judaism's two daughter religions. Its word pictures have provided the soil and the seeds for the style and styling of all European languages....

It is sad that many Jews do not know their Book, a book not of preachments, as many people wrongly think, but of sublime literature and superior perfection of the style of word pictures. It is a book which celebrates life, but also knows that life is not a rose garden. It is a book which knows the fierceness of passion and the ash of its consuming fire. It knows the limitless love of parents for their children and the children's insensitivity to this love. It knows the despair of "vanity, all is vanity" and the consolation of "God is my shepherd." It rails with Job, the sufferer, against the misfortunes that happen to good and innocent people, and it takes God to task for what we today call "the existential tragedies of life."

From an essay in The Jewish Week, *August 17, 1984.*

MASTER DOUBLESPEAKER

An all-time master of the game of politics was Franklin D. Roosevelt. Of all American presidents, he was most beloved, and not merely respected, by American Jews as "the great friend" of the Jewish people and of Zionism. It was only when the history of the dark years, *While Six Million Died* was researched, that this great friend of the Jewish Homeland and of Zionism was discovered to be anything but a friend.

From The Jewish Week and American Examiner, *October 1972.*

✡

Ezer Weizman

WOMEN AND PILOTS

The best men go to be pilots, and the best women go to the pilots.

A familiar slogan of the former Israeli Air Force chief.

ELTON IN ISRAEL

Let him go wherever he wants. Who needs Elton John? We have many good groups here in Upper Galilee [where he was visiting]. They at least sing real popular music, not nonsense.

Commenting on Elton John's abrupt cancellation of a scheduled concert in Tel Aviv on June 15, 1993, claiming mistreatment by fans and press photographers. John left for England but returned two days later and performed before 30,000 fans.

REDUCE THE RHETORIC

I appeal to everyone to tone down the public debate...and not to say that following one course of action will lead to a holocaust, while following another will not. We must find a joint approach to such a crucial matter.

We are approaching fateful decisions. Life will be different in the Middle East. I am prepared to say, especially to those my age who remember how it used to be, that we have achieved more than we expected.

Trying to calm the populace prior to the signing of the peace accord between Israel and the PLO on the White House South Lawn on September 13, 1993.

COME HOME

The future of Jews is in Israel. We know what mixed marriages can bring. From a demographic point of view, Israel is the only place. I urge you to make Israel your home.

From a May 1993 Jerusalem Day address to leaders from Diaspora communities around the world.

TOO MANY PRESIDENTS

My uncle Chaim, the first president, used to complain that he presided over a nation of two million presidents.... Don't try and be a president.

Castigating a young Israeli who was trying to make a political statement. Quoted in The Jerusalem Report, *January 27, 1994.*

ZION'S BLACK PAGE

This massacre [at Hebron] is the worst thing that has happened to us in the history of Zionism. Since 1948, 18,000 Israelis have fallen. War is ugly and inhuman but we have tried always to maintain our humanity and have never reacted as one man did, on Ramadan, in a mosque, on a Friday. It is despicable to shoot people in the back when they are bending down to pray to the God shared by the three monotheistic faiths.

From a statement to reporters on Saturday night, March 26, 1994, the day after the murder of approximately forty Moslems, by Jewish extremist Baruch Goldstein as they prayed at a mosque in Hebron.

CALL FOR ALIYAH

Why is there no *aliyah* now like the first and second *aliyah*? Why is Israel not as attractive as it should be to world Jewry? We have 4.3 million Jews here. We are the second largest Jewish community. I hope in four years when we celebrate our fiftieth independence day, we'll be the first largest. That is up to you.

From an address in June 1994 to 240 invited guests to discuss Israel–Diaspora relations.

MAIDELE, STAY HOME!

Maidele [young girl] have you ever seen a man knitting? Have you ever met a woman surgeon? Stay home and forget it.

When Alice Miller, who had been rejected for pilot training in the Israeli Air Force in 1995 on the basis of being a woman, appealed to the president of Israel for support.

A STATE TO BE PROUD OF

I wish Israelis would realize what standing the State of Israel has in the world, how we are respected as people who have achieved what they want, who have science and music and knowledge and the ability to solve certain things. We are in a very, very good position in the world.

> *After returning to Israel in May 1995 from a five-day tour of Europe representing Israel in VE Day celebrations.*

COWARDS

Cowards! Join the army.

> *In ultra-Orthodox Bnei Brak, after he was verbally attacked by yeshiva students in 1995.*

JUMPING THE GUN

Israel is getting rid of the territories too early. When it gets to the stage of discussions on a permanent agreement, it won't have any bargaining chips left.

> *To a group of U.S. rabbis visiting Israel in 1995.*

□

Chaim Weizmann

JEWISH IDENTITY CRISIS

The very crux of the Jewish tragedy is that those Jews who are giving their energies and brains to the Germans are doing it in their capacities as Germans and are enriching Germany and not Jewry, which they are abandoning.... They must hide their Judaism...to be allowed to place their brains and abilities at the disposal of the Germans. They are to no little extent responsible for German greatness. The tragedy of it all is that whereas we do not recognize them as Jews, Madame [Cosima] Wagner does not recognize them as Germans, and so we stand there as the most exploited and misunderstood of people.

> *From a 1914 letter to Lord Arthur Balfour about the Jewish identity crisis.*

A JEWISH PALESTINE

Palestine should be as distinctly Jewish as England is English.

> *A comment made in 1919.*

HOW TO BUILD A STATE

A state cannot be created by decree, but by the forces of a people, and in the course of generations. Even if all the governments of the world gave us a country, it would be only a gift of words. But if the Jewish people go and build Palestine, the State of Israel will become a reality.

> *One of Weizmann's first statements, issued in Jerusalem in January 1921, after he had been elected president of the World Zionist Organization.*

TREATED AS A GUEST

You will always be treated as a guest if you, too, can play the host. The only man who is invited to dinner is the man who can have dinner at home if he likes.

> *From his autobiography,* Trial and Error *(1949).*

CHASING A MIRAGE

Conversations and negotiations with Arabs are not unlike chasing a mirage in the desert: full of promise and good to look at, but likely to lead you to death by thirst.

> *Ibid.*

SMALL COUNTRIES

God has always chosen small countries through which to convey his messages.

> *Ibid.*

ON BALFOUR

He [Balfour] told me he had once had a long talk with Cosima Wagner [Richard Wagner's wife], and that he shared many of her [anti-Semitic] prejudices.

> *Ibid.*

COMPELLING FORCE OF LAW

A law is something which must have a moral basis, so that there is an inner compelling force for every citizen to obey.

> *Ibid.*

DOUBLE EXPOSURE

Our great men were always a product of symbiosis between the ancient, Talmudic learning in which our ancestors were steeped in the Polish or Galician ghettos, or even in Spain, and the modern Western universities with which their children came in contact. There is as often as not a long list of Talmudic scholars and Rabbis in the pedigrees of our modern scientists. In many cases they themselves have come from Talmudic schools, breaking away in their twenties and struggling through to Paris or Zurich or Princeton. It is this extraordinary phenomenon—a great tradition of learning fructified by modern methods—which has given us both first-class scientists and competent men in every branch of academic activity, out of all relation to our numbers.

> *Ibid.*

SALT OF THE EARTH

I do not consider it a compliment to be called "the salt of the earth." Salt is used for someone else's food. It dissolves in that food. And salt is good only in small quantities.

Ibid.

AWAITING JUDGMENT

I am certain that the world will judge the Jewish state by what it will do with the Arabs, just as the Jewish people at large will be judged by what we do or fail to do in this state.

Ibid.

FROM RAGS TO RICHES

We are perhaps the sons of dealers in old clothes, but we are the grandsons of prophets.

From a 1923 address.

RIGHTS OF ARABS

[The transformation of Palestine into a Jewish state was impossible] because we could not and would not expel the Arabs.... Moreover, the Arabs were as good Zionists as we are; they also loved their country and they could not be persuaded to hand it over to someone else. Their national awakening had made considerable progress. These were facts which Zionism couldn't afford to ignore.

From a statement at a meeting of the Zionist General Council in Berlin, August 1930.

GROSS MISCALCULATION

If before I die there are half a million Jews in Palestine, I shall be content because I shall know that this "saving remnant" will survive. They, not the millions in the Diaspora, are what really matter.

From a 1933 communication to Prime Minister James McDonald.

THE MESSIANIC HOPE

I make a sharp distinction between the present realities and the Messianic hope... a hope which the nation cannot forget without ceasing to be a nation. A time will come when there shall be neither enemies nor frontiers, when war shall be no more, and men will be secure in the dignity of man.

From a 1939 speech at the Zionist Congress.

A PAINFUL PARTING

It is with a heavy heart that I take my leave.... If, as I hope, we are spared in life and our work continues, who knows—perhaps a new light will shine upon us from the thick black gloom.... We shall meet again. We shall meet again in common labor for our land and people. Our people is deathless, our land eternal.

Ibid. From his farewell speech to the delegates at the Twenty-first Zionist Congress, held in Geneva, Switzerland, on August 24, 1939.

DARKNESS EVERYWHERE

There is darkness all around us and we cannot see through the clouds.

Ibid.

DEFINING MAN

What a man *is* means more in the long run than what he *does*. The same is true of Nations.

Ibid.

JABOTINSKY'S PROGRAM

Here and there a relaxation of the old traditional Zionist puritan ethics, a touch of militarization, and a weakness for its trappings; here and there something worse—the tragic, futile, un-Jewish resort to terrorism...and worst of all, in certain circles, a readiness to compound with the evil, to play politics with it, to condemn and not to condemn it, to treat it not as the thing it was, namely an unmitigated curse to the National Home, but as a phenomenon which might have its advantages.

Describing the militaristic attitude in 1944 Palestine, whose population was being swayed by Jabotinsky's activism.

THE FIRST SHOT

When I am asked these days to use my "restraining influence," my mind goes back some forty years or more to the day when a poor Jewish tailor shot the Governor-General at Vilna. We were called by Plehwe and commanded to "restrain" our young men, lest worse things befall us. And we told Plehwe that, much as we deplored such acts of violence, they were the inevitable result of the impossible conditions which Russia had herself created for her Jewish population and which deprived the leaders of the community of any influence they might otherwise have possessed. Looking back now, I see that the single shot fired by a little Jewish tailor was the first shot of the "Great Revolution."

From an address on July 9, 1946 before the British Actions Committee and its High Commissioner for Palestine, Sir Alan Cunningham.

NEVER AGAIN

I do not know how many Einsteins, how many Freuds, have been destroyed in the furnaces of Auschwitz and Maidanek. But there is one thing I know: if we can prevent it, it will never happen again.

From a statement before the 1946 Anglo-American Commission of Inquiry investigating the predicament of Holocaust survivors.

A PILOT PLANT

Despite some of the things that have been said in this debate, I retain my belief in the prospect of Arab-Jewish cooperation once a solution based on finality and equality has received the sanction of international consent. The Jewish State in Palestine may become a pilot plant for processes and examples which may have a constructive message for its neighbors as well.

From an address before the United Nations Ad Hoc Committee on the Palestine Question, October 18, 1947.

AS TO THE PRESIDENCY...

With regard to the Presidency, I am in full agreement with you, that the American model would not suit our conditions, but I do not think that the French model is more desirable. I think that the middle course approximates to the Czech model. I am not thinking of it because I may have to serve as President, but more as a general proposition, in the interest of the State. There must be some institution not torn by party strife.

From a June 26, 1948 letter to Moshe Sharett, foreign minister of Israel's provisional government.

THANK YOU, MISTER PRESIDENT

You will never know what this means to my people. We have waited and dreamed and worked for this moment for two thousand years.

After securing, in 1948, President Harry S Truman's support for the establishment of the State of Israel.

THE EGYPTIAN ARMY

The trouble with the Egyptian army is that their officers are too fat and their soldiers too thin.

Displaying confidence in 1948 that Israel could withstand the attack of Arab armies. Quoted in Abba Eban's autobiography, Personal Witness: Israel Through My Eyes *(1992).*

HOPE AND CHEER

In this hour a message of hope and good cheer issues from this place, from this sacred city, to all oppressed people and to all who are struggling for freedom and equality.

From his opening speech to the Knesset, February 14, 1949.

SECOND FIFTY YEARS

To bring water to the thirsty earth, shade to the sun-parched sands, the laughter of children to a countryside where only jackals howl; to unearth the good soil under the rocks, to push back the desert, and remove the last swamps—these are among the tasks of the Jewish National Fund in its second fifty years.

From a statement in The New York Times, *January 19, 1951.*

WHERE THE JEWS LIVE

The world [for the Jew] is divided into places where they cannot live and places where they cannot enter.

Quoted in Joseph Telushkin's Jewish Wisdom *(1994).*

IRONY TO THE END

But there's no one to spit at.

Reported by Isaiah Berlin as having been said by his good friend Weizmann when the latter was on his deathbed, coughing badly, and the doctor told him to spit. Quoted in The New Republic, *February 20, 1995.*

A HOPE THAT WOULD NOT DIE

We were strangers to their [the non-Jewish villagers'] ways of thought, to each other's dreams, religions, festivals, even languages. There were times when the non-Jewish world was practically excluded from our consciousness, as on the Sabbath and, still more, on the spring and autumn festivals.... We were separated from the peasants by a whole inner world of memories and experiences.... My father was not yet a Zionist, but the house was steeped in rich Jewish tradition, and Palestine was at the centre of the ritual.... The Return was in the air, a vague, deep-rooted Messianism, a hope which would not die.

Writing about his village, Motol, located near Pinsk, where he lived until age eleven.

HERZL: A DARING LEADER

The effect produced by [Theodor Herzl's] *The Jewish State* was profound. [Yet] not the ideas, but the personality which stood behind them appealed to us. Here was daring, clarity and energy.... If Herzl had contented himself with the mere publication of the booklet...his name would be remembered today as one of the oddities of Jewish history. What has given greatness to his name is Herzl's role as a man of action, as the founder of the Zionist Congress, and as an example of daring and devotion.

Writing about Herzl after the publication of his famous book.

NOTHING IS IMPOSSIBLE

Difficulties take a long time to solve. The impossible always takes a little longer.

An aphorism he was fond of repeating.

JEWISH MUFTI

The Mufti from Cleveland.

Characterizing Abba Hillel Silver, a leading architect of Zionist policy after World War II, who was rabbi of The Temple, in Cleveland, Ohio.

ROYAL TRIBUTE

He was, I might say, what Gandhi has been to many Indians, what Mazzini was to young Italy a century ago.

His tribute to Ahad Ha-am.

◻

Vera Weizmann

BRAINS AND BEAUTY

My husband liked beautiful women, but they had to have brains as well.

From her Impossible Takes Longer *(1967).*

◻

Richard von Weizsacher

REDEMPTION AND REMEMBRANCE

There can be no reconciliation without remembrance. The experience of millionfold death is part of the very being of every Jew in the world. Seeking to forget makes exile all the longer. The secret of redemption lies in remembrance.

From a speech to the West German Parliament on May 8, 1985.

◻

Julius Wellhausen

JESUS THE JEW

Jesus was not a Christian, he was a Jew. He did not proclaim a new faith, but taught men to do the will of God. According to Jesus, as to the Jews generally, this will of God is to be found in the Law and the other canonical Scriptures.

Quoted in J. Klausner's Jesus of Nazareth *(1926).*

◻

H. G. Wells

NO GREATER EVIL

I am convinced myself that there is no more evil thing in this present world than race prejudice, none at all. I write deliberately—it is the worst single thing in life now. It justifies and holds together more baseness, cruelty and abomination than any other sort of error in the world.

Quoted in Harry Emerson Fosdick's Foreword to Cecil Roth's Jewish Contribution to Civilization *(1940).*

◻

Franz Werfel

UNENDING DIALOGUE

Religion is the everlasting dialogue between humanity and God. Art is its soliloquy.

From his Between Heaven and Earth *(1944).*

THE COMING GRACE

Believe not thy foes when they say thou art forsaken like a useless slave, an old outworn servant who is summarily driven out of the house. Do not believe it, Israel! Between thy God and thee there is an unsettled reckoning that will one day be settled in thy favor, when grace will have struck the balance.

Ibid.

BATTLE OF IDEALS

False ideals cannot be shattered by criticism. Right ideals must take up the battle against them.

Ibid.

MYSTERY OF THE TRINITY

In the mystery of the Trinity...lies the chief infraction against the faith of Israel, which rests on the certainty of a free and direct communion between Creator and Creation.

Ibid.

ORGANIZED HAPPINESS

Just as bad music is nothing else than organized emptiness of time, so materialistic thinking is nothing else than organized emptiness of the spirit.

Ibid.

FRUSTRATED LOVE

The basic formula of all sin is: frustrated or neglected love.

Ibid.

ALIEN, ALIEN, ALIEN

So I was a Jew! I was different! I was not a human being like all the rest!...Alien here and alien there! Alien beyond all imagination! Alienation, the arch-feeling of my life.

From his Collected Works: Tales from Two Worlds (1952–53), *edited by Adolf Klarmann.*

¤

Jack Wertheimer

LEARNING FROM HISTORY

The focus is on the destruction of Jews. There is a lot more American Jewry can learn from European Jewry prior to the Holocaust than [from] the destruction of Jews. I don't know what of a positive nature can be [learned] from that.

Commenting after a visit to the United States Holocaust Memorial Museum in Washington, DC. Reported in Hadassah Magazine, *April 1994.*

¤

Arnold Wesker

I FEEL A JEW

I feel a Jew, I am a Jew—there is no logic to it. Yet my roots though vague are real. And because I am a Jew I feel and write in a particular way.... I feel a Jew because of the way my family spoke, because of the rhythms and patterns of their living [even because of] the rituals I knew of, though I did not perform.

Quoted in Joseph Leftwich's Jewish Caravan *(1962).*

¤

John Wesley

EXPLAINING JEWISH SUFFERING

Outcasts from thee, and scattered wide
Blaspheming whom they crucified,
Unsaved, unpitied, unforgiven,
Branded like Cain, they bear their load,
Abhorred of men, and cursed of God.

From the chapter "For the Jews" in The Works of John Wesley *(1983), edited by Hildebrandt and Beckerlegge.*

DISDAIN OF JUDAISM

I do not wonder that so many Jews (especially those who have any reflection) utterly abjure all religion. My spirit was moved within me, at that horrid, senseless pageantry, that mockery of God, which they called public worship.

Ibid. After attending a synagogue service in the fall of 1738.

¤

Ruth Westheimer

SEXUALITY AND JUDAISM

Part of my being able to talk about issues of sexuality has to do with my being so Jewish. Because for us Jews there's never been a question of sex being a sin, but of sex being a *mitzvah* and an obligation.

Quoted in Elinor and Robert Slater's Great Jewish Women *(1994).*

¤

Burton K. Wheeler

AMERICAN FIRSTER

Gifted in the arts of corruption and bribery, [the movie moguls have] debauched legislatures; they have elected and controlled governors. The tentacles of this octopus reach not only into the state legislatures but at times into the Congress of the United States.

Cautioning native Americans in 1941 about the pro-war propaganda of Jewish "Hollywood Hitlers."

¤

(Lord) Alfred North Whitehead

TRAGIC HISTORY

Jewish history, beyond all histories, is composed of tragedies.

From an article in Atlantic Monthly, *March 1939.*

PALESTINE'S SPARKLE

It was the Jewish genius that bestowed its radiance upon Palestine.

Ibid.

¤

John Greenleaf Whittier

BRAVE SONGSTRESS

Since Miriam sang of deliverance and triumph by the Red Sea, the Semitic race has had no braver singer.

> *Quoted in H.E. Jacob's* World of Emma Lazarus.

◌

Max Wiener

GOD AND MAN MEET

Religion and morality, the way to God and the way to man, coincide.

> *Quoted in S. Bernfeld's* Foundations of Jewish Ethics *(1929).*

◌

Elie Wiesel

ALONE IN THE WORLD

Once, New Year's Day had dominated my life. I knew that my sins grieved the Eternal; I implored His forgiveness.... This day I had ceased to plead. I was no longer capable of lamentation. On the contrary, I felt very strong. I was the accuser, God the accused.

> *In his* Night *(1958).*

KADDISH FOR ONESELF

Auschwitz, 1944...Around us, everyone was weeping. Someone began to recite the kaddish. I do not know if it has ever happened before, in the history of the Jews, that people have ever recited the prayer for the dead for themselves.

> *Ibid.*

ALL ALONE

I was the accuser, God the accused. My eyes were open and I was alone—terribly alone in a world without God and without man.

> *Ibid.*

CONSCIENCE OF THE WORLD

I wanted to show the end, the finality of the event. Everything came to an end—history, literature, religion, God. There was nothing left. And yet we begin again with Night. Only where do we go from there? Since then, I have explored all kinds of options. To tell you that I have now found a religion, that I believe—no. I am still searching. I am still exploring. I am still protesting.

> *Commenting on the publication of his first book,* Night *(1960), originally issued in French as* La Nuit *(1958), which opened up a general discussion about the Holocaust for the first time.*

DISLOYAL JEW

The Jew who repudiates himself, claiming to do so for the sake of humanity, will inevitably repudiate humanity in the end. A Jew fulfills his role as a man only from inside his Jewishness. Only by accepting his Jewishness can he attain universality.

> *From his* One Generation After *(1965).*

TO THE CREDIT OF RABBIS

[In the concentration camps there were *Kapos*] of German, Hungarian, Czech, Slovakian, Georgian, Ukrainian, French, and Lithuanian extraction. They were Christians, Jews, and atheists. Former professors, industrialists, artists, merchants, workers, militants from the right and left, philosophers and explorers of the soul, Marxists and staunch humanists. And, of course, a few common criminals. But not one *Kapo* had been a rabbi.

> *Ibid. Describing the types of individuals who agreed to be Kapos, that is, inmates who were appointed to supervise other inmates.*

SURVIVING TO TESTIFY

Rejected by mankind, the condemned do not go so far as to reject it in turn. Their faith in history remains unshaken, and one may well wonder why. They do not despair. The proof: they persist in surviving not only to survive, but to testify.

The victims elect to become witnesses.

> *From his* One Generation After *(1970).*

TRUTH OF A MADMAN

You'll try to reveal what should remain hidden, you'll try to incite people to learn from the past and rebel, but they will refuse to believe you. They will not listen to you.... You'll possess the truth, you already do; but it's the truth of a madman.

> *From his* Beggar in Jerusalem *(1970).*

LET US FIGHT NO MORE

One more war. The last. They always say that. Let us fight so as to fight no more. Let us kill so as to conquer death. Who knows, perhaps Cain himself aspired to be not just the first murderer in history but the last as well.

> *Ibid.*

WHAT IT MEANS TO BE JEWISH

I know what one must do to be Jewish. He must assume his Jewishness. He must assume his collective conscience. He must assume his past with its sorrows and its joys.

> *From the* Time *magazine cover story of April 10, 1972, on the subject "What It Means to Be Jewish."*

BE MAD, RABBI

One has to be mad today to believe in God and in man—one has to be mad to believe. One has to be mad to want to remain human. Be mad, Rabbi, be mad!

> *From his play* Zalmen, Or the Madness of God *(1974).*

ROOTING OUT FEAR

Tear fear out by the root! Let it not become your night and your universe, your silence and your lie—or, what is worse, your truth, your God.

> *Ibid.*

AFTER MOSES

Moses is the most solitary and most powerful hero in biblical history.... After him nothing else was the same again.

> *From his* Messengers of God *(1975).*

LIVING IN FEAR

...Twice a year, at Easter and Christmas, Jewish schoolchildren would be beaten up by their Christian neighbors. Yes, as a child I lived in fear. A symbol of compassion and love to Christians, the cross has become an instrument of torment and terror to be used against Jews. I say this with neither hate nor anger. I say this because it is true. Born in suffering, Christianity became a source and pretext of suffering to others.

> *Quoted in Eva Fleischner's* Auschwitz: Beginning of a New Era? *(1977), in which he describes life in his hometown of Sighet, then part of Hungary.*

THE RIGHT TO REMEMBER

One Jew was put to death in Jerusalem two thousand years ago and the non-Jewish world has not ceased to speak of his death. Do we [Jews] not have the right, the duty, to keep alive the memory of the six million dead?

> *Ibid.*

MODERN MYSTIC

To be a Jew is to have all the reasons in the world not to have faith...but to go on telling the tale, to go on carrying on the dialogue, and to have my own silent prayers and quarrels with God.

> *A 1979 comment.*

SABBATH SERENITY

I shall never forget Shabbat in my town. When I shall have forgotten everything else, my memory will still retain the atmosphere of holiday, of serenity pervading even the poorest houses; the white tablecloth, the candles, the meticulously combed little girls, the men on their way to the synagogue.

> *In his* A Jew Today *(1979).*

THE GATES OF THE PAST

You open the gates of the past and your words bring back the memories of Jews I have known, somewhere, sometime, in other lands. This is so because you, as the man and poet you are, cannot but seek your brethren among both the dead and the living.

Of course, some people may ask you: and what about the others? The Jews were not the only ones to suffer and perish? After all, there were eleven million who suffered death at the hands of the Nazi killers....

Don't listen to them, keep on not listening to them.

Go your way. Remind yourself that when a Jewish poet sings about Jewish trials and sorrows to the agonies of his own brethren, he includes with them all those others that have met a like fate, although for other causes.

Let's state it precisely: If we Jews commemorate our Six Million victims, the world will remember the others too. If we allow ours to be just a part of an anonymous multitude, all will be forgotten.

> *From the Preface to Herb Brin's* Ich Bin ein Jude *(1982), in which the author traces the steps of the Six Million who were led to Hitler's slaughterhouses.*

STRIKING A FALSE NOTE

The Jew who might feel compelled to renounce his Judaism or to water it down in order to be able to speak better about universal problems would strike a wrong note; his voice would have a false ring.

> *Ibid.*

THANKS FOR A FRIEND

What is a friend? Someone who for the first time makes you aware of your loneliness and his, and helps you to escape so you in turn can help him. Thanks to him you can hold your tongue without shame and talk freely without risk. That's it.

> *Quoted in his* Gates of the Forest *(1982).*

REASON GROPES LIKE A BLIND MAN

On your way through life you'll meet men

who cling to reason, but reason gropes like a blind man with a white cane, stumbling over every pebble, and when it comes up against a wall it stops short and tries to tear it down brick by brick, quite ineffectually, because an invisible hand builds it up again, higher and thicker than ever. We, on the other hand, believe in the power of faith and ecstasy, and no wall can stand against us.

Ibid.

LOVE IS A VICTORY

If you see love as a compromise, a defeat, you're mistaken. It's a victory. Above all in time of war, when men are filled with death, this is the time to love. This is the time to choose. An act of love may tip the balance.

Ibid.

THE TRAGEDY OF THE IMPOSSIBLE

We thought the tragedy was that the possible was impossible. The impossible is possible. That's the tragedy.

Ibid.

HEALING SCARS

Every death leaves a scar, and every time a child laughs it starts healing.

Ibid.

JEWS AND GOD

The Jew may love God, or he may fight God, but he may not ignore God.

Ibid.

INDIFFERENCE

The opposite of love is not hate, it's indifference.

Quoted in U.S. News and World Report, *October 27, 1986.*

JEWS FOR JESUS

I feel less revulsion for Christian missionaries than for their Jewish accomplices. The missionaries are at least honest. They proclaim openly that their aim is to absorb as many Jews as possible into their church. They aim to kill their victim's Jewishness by assimilating it. They give each individual Jew the choice between Judaism and Christianity—always doing their best to influence that choice.

Their Jewish colleagues, however, the "Jews for Jesus," for example, are dishonest. They are hypocrites. They do not even have the courage to declare frankly that they have decided to repudiate their people and its memories.

From his essay "The Missionary Menace," in Smashing the Idols *(1988), edited by Gary D. Eisenberg.*

JEWISH RESILIENCE

I marvel at the resilience of the Jewish people. Their best characteristic is their desire to remember. No other people has such an obsession with memory.

Quoted in London's Daily Mail, *July 15, 1988.*

OBLIGATION TO REMEMBER

As a good Jew, I believe in the obligation to remember. We remember the good and the bad, the friends and the foes. We remember that during the darkest era of our recent history, Spain gave shelter to countless Jews who illegally entered its territory. And I remember that five hundred years ago, clinging to their faith, Jews were forced by your ancestors to leave Spain. Could they have imagined that their descendants would meet five centuries later in an atmosphere of tolerance, understanding, and friendship?

From an address delivered on October 7, 1991 before King Juan Carlos of Spain, when he was awarded the Elie Wiesel Foundation Humanitarian Award.

HATE PRODUCES HATE

All racism is always rooted in ugliness, just as anti-Semitism is irrational, vulgar and stupid. Anti-Semites hate us because we are rich, or poor; believers, or non-believers; fervent nationalists or cosmopolitans; communists or capitalists—Jews, they shout, have too much power. They forget that not all Jews have power, and not all who have power are Jewish. So that hatred is stupid and irrationally logical. They hate us not for what we do, or say, or possess, but for what we are. They hate us because they need to hate somebody—anybody! It is their hate that keeps them alive. Not for long though. Hate produces nothing, but more hate.

From an address delivered at the World Conference on Anti-Semitism and Prejudice in a Changing World, held in Brussels, Belgium, July 1992.

MAKING THE WRONG CHOICE

Granted, in this troubled society not everyone is our brother—far from it. There are those who hate us, those who wish to oppress us, and even eliminate us from history. For we shall never forget that one and a half million Jewish children were wiped out by the enemy. But we have learned one more lesson from Cain's and Abel's tale of fear and trembling. They do represent the two poles of human condition. One is either Cain or Abel, one is either killer or victim. Albert Camus was right:

not to choose is also a choice. And if one chooses neutrality, it is the wrong choice.

> *Ibid.*

NO ACCIDENTS

I don't believe in accidents. There are only encounters in history. There are no accidents.

> Quoted in the International Herald Tribune, *September 15, 1992.*

HOLOCAUST NIGHTMARE

I have an occasional nightmare. I wake up shivering, thinking that when we die, no one will be able to persuade people the Holocaust occurred.

> *Quoted in Edward S. Shapiro's* Time for Healing: American Jewry Since World War II *(1992).*

GENERATION IN FLUX

More than any other generation before, my contemporaries have known not only the paroxysm of evil, but also the realization of a promise; not only the Kingdom of Night, but also the rebirth of a dream; not only the horror of Naziism, but also the end of the nightmare; not only the deaths of Babi-Yar, but also the defiance of young Russian Jews, the first to challenge the Kremlin's police state.

> *In the Introduction to his* Passover Haggadah *(1993).*

A SECOND KILLING

To forget would mean to kill victims a second time. We could not prevent their first death; we must not allow them to be killed again.

> *From a speech delivered on April 22, 1993 at the dedication of the United States Holocaust Memorial Museum, in Washington, DC.*

WHY NO PUBLIC OUTCRY?

This museum is not an answer. It is a question mark. How could murderers do what they did and go on living? Why was there no public outcry, indignation, and outrage?

> *Ibid.*

BASEBALL HERO

I didn't even know what it meant. I had a feeling he was talking mysticism to me.... I was trembling all the time because I wouldn't know what to do. So I prayed and my prayers

were heard and apparently I did the right thing.

> *Reflecting upon his having been invited to Shea Stadium by the baseball commissioner to throw out the first ball at the second 1986 World Series game between the New York Mets and Boston Red Sox. Quoted in a profile by Yosef I. Abramowitz that appeared in* Moment *magazine, February 1994.*

SPEAKING OF HAPPINESS

We don't speak about happiness in our faith, we speak about *simcha ve-sasson* (joy and gladness). What do we ask for? *Shalom,* yes. We mainly ask for *yirat shama'yim* (fear of heaven), for study, for *chayim shel Torah* (life of Torah). What is Torah? Meaning. My life has been the pursuit of meaning, not joy.

> *Ibid. In response to the question, "Is Wiesel happy?"*

RATHER AND MOSES

When Dan Rather speaks, more people listen to him than when Moses spoke.

> *Ibid.*

TO GORBACHEV: "AS A JEW I OWE YOU"

When Gorbachev saw me, he was moved. I asked myself, why was he so moved, with tears in his eyes? Because he had just realized that his friends were not his friends. Every single one had betrayed him. Those whom he had elevated, abandoned him. I have rarely seen a man as lonely as he was. And here comes a young Jew, and says I'm here to help you, to give you support. I was thinking: I'm a *yeshivah bucher* from Sighet [Hungary], and all of a sudden I'm involved with presidents, bring personal messages, and traveling in government planes. I was surprised.

> *Ibid. In 1991, following the unsuccessful coup attempt against Soviet Leader Mikhail Gorbachev, Weisel was sent to Moscow by President François Mitterand aboard a French government plane.*

BIRTH OF A SON

Another kind of joy, even deeper than that [of rejoicing in holidays], and more personal, was the birth of my son...even more, the *brit* [circumcision] of my son. To me in my life, it has the importance of the birth of Israel, the reunification of Jerusalem. I felt it in my body, in *every cell* of my body.

> *Ibid.*

FROM DARKNESS TO LIGHT

What is it about Yad Vashem that moves every visitor who comes from New York or Paris, or Holland or Japan? It is when you leave the museum you see Jerusalem. And somehow it creates a certain balance. You are not staying in Yad Vashem. You are not staring in the place that symbolizes the darkness of humanity. But you see Jerusalem, and you plead. And somehow you say, "Thank God. Thank God that from one place you can move to another."

From a speech at the tenth Annual Dinner of the American and International Societies for Yad Vashem, October 30, 1994.

CHASTISING A PRESIDENT

That place, Mr. President, is not your place, your place is with the victims of the S.S.

At a White House ceremony where he was awarded the Congressional Gold Medal of Achievement. Addressed to President Ronald Reagan, who planned to visit the Bitburg (Germany) Cemetery where members of the Nazi SS are buried.

REACHING FOR GOD

If I want to come closer to God...it is only by coming closer to my fellow human being.... If I am your friend, I am God's friend. If not, I am the enemy of both God and his creatures.

In an April 1994 address at Queens College, New York, urging the rejection of fanaticism and the embracing of tolerance and love.

THE FANATIC AND TRUTH

[Fanaticism is the conviction that] only the fanatic has access to truth, only the fanatic knows what is right and has all the answers.... I believe in questions. To me a human being is a question mark, an opening to adventure.

Ibid.

LEARN TO BE SILENT

The Talmud teaches man never to judge his friend until he has been in his place. But, for the world, the Jews are not friends. They have never been. Because they had no friends they are dead. So learn to be silent.

From his "Plea for the Dead," in which he criticizes the critics of Jews in the Warsaw Ghetto who "failed to resist."

THE VICTIMS

It is true that not all victims were Jews, but all Jews were victims.

At the fiftieth anniversary ceremony of the liberation of Auschwitz on January 27, 1995.

SORTING OUT THE TRUTH

If I told you that I believe in God, I would be lying. If I told you that I did not believe in God, I would be lying. If I told you that I believed in man, I would be lying. If I told you I did not believe in man, I would be lying. But one thing I do know: the Messiah has not come yet.

From his Shadows of Auschwitz.

THE PARADOX OF LIFE

The sun is rising? And yet it will set. A night of anguish? And yet it too will pass.

From his memoirs, entitled All Rivers Run to the Sea *(1995).*

RABIN BASHING

I am behind the peace process, but what worries me is the fanaticism which the peace process engenders. The hatred that exists between opposing the positions is frightening.... The way that they call Rabin "Pétain".... This is indecent, it's obscene, it's horrible.

From an interview with Jonathan Mahler less than twenty-four hours before Yitzhak Rabin was assassinated on November 4, 1995. Henri Phillippe Pétain, premier of the French government at Vichy, was convicted of treason in 1945. Quoted in the Foreward, *November 10, 1995.*

UNDERSTANDING GOD

I am not at peace. I never said I lost my faith in God. I was angry. I still don't understand God's ways. If He was going to explain the Holocaust, I would say no, I want the wound to remain open. And it is.

Commenting in 1995 on his ongoing personal struggle with making sense out of the Holocaust.

THE MOST SACRED WORD

The Holocaust should not be used either for politics or [even] for artistic endeavors. It should be there as a dark presence. We should be filled with fear and trembling before we even mention the word.

Ibid.

TOUCHED BY GREATNESS

When I would see the Rebbe, he touched the depth in me, and that was true of everyone who came to see him. Somehow, when people left, they felt that they lived deeper and higher, on a higher level and with a deeper sense of life, of quest for life and meaning.

Describing the effect on him of the Lubavitcher Rebbe, Menachem Schneerson. Quoted in Moment *magazine, October 1995.*

□

Leon Wieseltier

NEWS AND KNOWLEDGE

The difference between news and knowledge is a little like the difference between breathlessness and breath long held. The one excites you and then leaves you defenseless before the caprices of circumstance, the other arms you against disappointment and then abandons you to a world without release.

> *Reacting to the September 13, 1993 peace accord between Israel and the PLO, and the fact that he was not a fool to have believed this might happen one day. From an article in* The New Republic, *October 4, 1993.*

THE GRUDGING HANDSHAKE

The particulars of the deal between the Israelis and the Palestinians are still in the hands of the negotiators. But the image of that swift, febrile, grudging handshake on the White House lawn will live forever in the hearts of all who saw it.

> *Ibid.*

THE RAPE OF BOSNIA

Of course, there is a difference between the European excruciations of the 1990s and the European excruciations of the 1940s, but the difference is primarily quantitative. It is important to remember, therefore, that genocide is not quantitatively defined. Before millions of Jews, Gypsies, homosexuals and dissenters were killed in Europe, thousands of them were killed; and before thousands of them were killed, hundreds of them were killed; and before hundreds of them were killed, tens of them were killed; and it was, the whole time, with every bullet fired and every switch thrown, genocide.

> *A call for arming the Bosnians. From a December 1993 speech at an event sponsored by PEN, the international writers association. Quoted in* The Jewish Week, *December 10–16, 1993.*

□

Simon Wiesenthal

SEARCHING AND HUNTING

The search for Eichmann was not a "hunt," as it has been called, but a long frustrating game of patience, a gigantic jigsaw puzzle. His capture was achieved through the cooperation of many people, most of whom didn't know each other, in several countries. Each added a few pieces of the puzzle; I was able to contribute some significant pieces.

> *In response to those who claim that he had nothing to do with the capture of Adolf Eichmann. From his* Murderers Among Us *(1967).*

THE WORLD'S PIPIK

We are making a huge mistake looking at everything from the Jewish point of view. We are not the *pipik* [bellybutton] of the world. You know what is *pipik?* That is the mistake that all the other nations made.

> *From an interview with Herb Brin. Quoted in Brin's* Ich Bin Ein Jude *(1982).*

KISSINGER'S TIME

There will come a time when the Jews will say, ah, the time of Henry Kissinger was a very good time.

> *Ibid.*

MIGRATION AND SURVIVAL

We survived because the history of man is the history of migration. For thousands of years people have come to one place from another. Jews are the exception because we don't mix. And this is one of the reasons for anti-Semitism.

> *Ibid.*

PRIDE IN THE SUPREME COURT

At the moment when the judges doubted whether [John] Demjanjuk was really identical with Ivan the Terrible they had no other option but to set him free. As a Jew, I am proud of the way the [Israeli] Supreme Court handled the case.

> *Upon learning, on July 29, 1993, that the court overturned the conviction of John Demjanjuk because the charge that he was Ivan the Terrible had not been proven beyond a reasonable doubt.*

EVERY JEW A SURVIVOR

I've met American Jews who say, "I'm not a survivor, but I'll support you." I answer: "You are a survivor. Hitler's program was to kill all the Jews. If he had won the war, it would have been the same in America as in Europe." Hitler said, "First, give me the Jews," and in every country there were people who gave him these Jews. The French police, the Croatian police, the Slovaks, and so on. And in your country such people would be found too. Because Hitler lost the war, you are a survivor.... Even those born after the war are survivors.

> *Quoted by journalist Tad Szulc in a profile that appeared in a 1977 issue of* New York *magazine.*

THE MEMORY OF THE DEAD

They mean everything to me, but they are of no interest to the general public. Of interest alone is my life in relation to Nazism: I have survived the Holocaust and I have tried to preserve the memory of the dead.

> *From a profile in* The Jerusalem Post, *February 5, 1994, in which he states that he is not interested in talking about his grandchildren or his personal life.*

A LINGERING MEMORY

Since my liberation, there is not one day that I have forgotten that I am a survivor.

> *When asked how he would like to be remembered.*

NAZI RIGHTS

I have been told you are a Jewish lawyer; I don't know whether you are young or old but I can tell you one thing, and you can write it down and hang it up over your bed: "A Jew may be stupid, but it's not obligatory."

> *From a phone conversation quoted in his* Justice Not Vengeance *(1989). He was responding to the argument of an ACLU lawyer that the Nazis have a right to march in Skokie, Illinois, because "the First Amendment permits it." In 1978 the U.S. Supreme Court agreed with the lawyer's position.*

¤

Roger Williams

WALL OF SEPARATION

I humbly conceive it to be the duty of the civil magistrate to break down that superstitious wall of separation (as to civil things) between us Gentiles and the Jews, and freely (without their asking) to make way for their free and peaceable habitation amongst us.

> *From his* Fourth Paper Presented by Major Butler, *edited and published in London (1652).*

¤

Wendell Willkie

PERSECUTION OF GERMAN JEWRY

I have more reason than most of you to feel strongly about this [nomination], because the United States gave to my family their first chance for a free life....

My grandparents lived in Germany. They were supporters of the democratic revolutions in that country, and when the revolutions

failed they fled to the United States. How familiar that sounds! Today, also, people are being oppressed in Europe. The story of the barbarous and worse than medieval persecution of the Jews—a race that has done so much to improve the culture of these countries and our own—is the most tragic in human history.

> *From his August 17, 1940 address, when he accepted the nomination of the Republican Party for the presidency of the United States.*

ZIONIST ADVOCATE

The continued barbaric program of extermination being carried out by Hitler against the Jewish people makes the work being done [by Zionists] in Palestine today even more important.... Homeless Jews who survive the war [must be able] to look forward to a homeland of their own in which they can find peace, security and happiness for themselves and for their children.

> *From an April 1943 speech, during the Warsaw Ghetto Uprising.*

¤

Edmund Wilson

MAKING IT

It purported to be a success story.... It told how Norman had now no accent, had been accepted, entertained, toasted and feted by all the Élite of New York—who were Lillian [Hellman], ourselves, Jackie Kennedy and everybody that everybody saw without anybody else's regarding it as a sign of having made it.

> *In his book* The Sixties: The Last Journal, 1960–1972 *(1993), expressing his contempt for Norman Podhoretz's memoir* Making It.

TIMELESS MYTHS

Most Jews have a dimension of eternity.... Our myths are the temporal myths of Caesar and Pericles, of Charlemagne, Washington, Hitler, but the myths of the Jews are timeless—the patriarchs and prophets who never die, the Messiah who never comes.

> *From an article in* The New Yorker, May 15, 1954.

¤

Woodrow Wilson

DON'T WORRY, DR. WISE

Don't worry, Dr. Wise, Palestine is yours.

> *After a meeting of the 1919 Paris Peace Conference.*

ON PALESTINE

I am persuaded that the Allied nations with the fullest concurrence of our own government and people are agreed that in Palestine there shall be laid the foundation of a Jewish commonwealth.

Addressing the American Jewish Congress delegation to the 1919 Paris Peace Conference.

LEAVEN OF JUDAIC THOUGHT

The laws of Moses as well as the laws of Rome contributed suggestions and impulse to the men and institutions which were to prepare the modern world; and if we could but have the eyes to see the subtle elements of thought which constitute the gross substance of our present habit, both as regards the sphere of private life and as regards the action of the State, we should easily discover how very much besides religion we owe to the Jew.

From his The State *(1890).*

THE FACTS MAN

Dr. Facts.

His sobriquet for the financier Bernard M. Baruch.

THE PEOPLE'S ATTORNEY

He is a friend of all just men and a lover of the right; and he knows more than how to talk about the right—he knows how to set it forward in the face of its enemies.

Replying to those in the U.S. Senate who in 1916 opposed the confirmation of Louis D. Brandeis as a Supreme Court justice.

BRANDEIS THE JEW

But he would not be Mr. Brandeis if he were not a Jew.

Response to a friend who said to the president, shortly after he appointed Louis Brandeis to the Supreme Court in 1916, "Isn't it a pity, Mr. President, that a man as great as Mr. Justice Brandeis should be a Jew?"

BECOMING AN AMERICAN

America does not consist of groups. A man who thinks of himself as belonging to a particular national group has not yet become an American.

From his President Wilson's Addressess *(1918).*

❑

Walter Winchell

A NASSER GUY

It couldn't happen to a Nasser guy. He's just an Arrable rouser.

Expressing elation over the defeat of the Egyptian army of Gamal Abdul Nasser, dubbed Public Enemy #1. Quoted in Henry D. Spalding's Encyclopedia of Jewish Humor *(1969).*

❑

Orde Charles Wingate

UNLIKE OTHER NATIONS

Are you prepared to give up your mission so easily? Did your people suffer in exile for 2,000 years just to become like any other nation?

Admonishing the head of the Egyptian Zionist Organization in Cairo in 1941, after he had said to General Wingate, the Bible-toting Scotch-English soldier friend of Israel (who was assigned the task of liberating Ethiopia from Italian occupation): "I am prepared to give up all this idea of a mission in the world; let us just become a free nation in our own country, just like any other nation." Quoted in Moshe Kohn's column in The Jerusalem Post, *March 26, 1994.*

❑

Shelley Winters

THE VOICE OF SILENCE

Every now and then, when you're on stage, you hear the best sound a player can hear. It's a sound you can't get in movies or in television. It is the sound of a wonderful, deep silence that means you've hit them where they live.

Quoted in Theatre Arts *magazine, June 1956.*

SO COLD

I was so cold I almost got married.

Quoted in The New York Times, *1956.*

HOPE OF THE FUTURE

Because I'm a Jew, of course, but more than that, because I'm a human being, and I care about what goes on in the world. I think the whole world must be concerned with Israel—this country is the hope of the future. It combines the wisdom of the old and the energy of the young. If Israel goes, the whole free world goes.

When asked why she devoted so much effort raising funds for Israel. Quoted in Elinor and Robert Slater's Great Jewish Women *(1994).*

A PROUD JEWISH WOMAN

Producers feel being a Jewish woman is a *yenta.* I have to stop this image.

Ibid.

LOOKING FOR A MAN

I'm only sorry that I didn't marry a nice Jewish man and have lots of children. I guess when you come down to it, I'm basically a woman looking for a man.

Ibid.

□

Louis Wirth

THE MAKING OF A JEW

The Jews are what their history has made them.

From his Ghetto *(1928).*

□

Isaac Mayer Wise

THE AMERICANIZING OF A RABBI

The great Sanhedrin [the U.S. Senate] made a deep impression on me.... I was the first visitor to come and the last to leave, and listened with undivided attention to the greatest speeches of the greatest statesmen of that time...I lived a new life, or, rather, I dreamed a new dream, and my imagination soared to other heights, and disported itself in new fields. My sojourn in Washington had an Americanizing influence on me.

> *After a visit to Washington, DC, in the 1850s. Wise considered it his duty as a Reform rabbi to Americanize himself and the Jews he led.*

OPPOSITION TO POLITICAL ZIONISM

Talmud Torah is the curriculum of this college. We want teachers of Judaism. Judaism, we say, and not nationalism, Judaism and not Zionism, Judaism and not Messianism of any kind; that eternal Judaism which is not tied down to a certain piece of land here or there, or to a certain form of government and peculiar laws and institutions.

> *In a September 1897 address at the opening of the academic year of Hebrew Union College. Kaufmann Kohler, who succeeded Rabbi Wise in 1903 as president of the Reform Seminary, also opposed political Zionism.*

ON WRITING BOOKS

It is much easier to write a long book than a short one.

> *From an article in* Deborah *magazine, January 7, 1897.*

COURT JESTERS

We restless idealists are none other than the court jesters of Providence, who even pay for their own fools' caps.

Ibid.

BOOKS AND SHOES

Bulky books and tight shoes have always been most uncomfortable for me.

Ibid.

THE CHOICE OF GOD

Moses was the greatest of all artists...and he left to posterity that imperishable statue of truth...its pedestal is the earth, its head reaches heaven's dome; the name of that inimitable colossus is Israel, the immortal, a nation graced by the choice of God.

> *From his essay "Moses" in* Selected Writings *(1889).*

REASON TO REJOICE

God gives us a thousand joys for each affliction, a thousand smiles for each tear.

> *From an article in* The American Israelite, *August 31, 1866.*

MARSHALING PUBLIC OPINION

We ought to bear in mind that the Jews of Russia and Prussia are insulted and maltreated simply because they are Jews; hence every Jew in the world is insulted and outraged with them.... Tens of thousands of non-Israelites here, in England, France, in fact in all constitutional countries, will be ready if we move to condemn loudly and publicly the proceedings in Russia and Prussia against Jews. *We propose to marshal the most terrible army,* the public opinion of the most civilized nations.

> *Ibid., August 5, 1881.*

LINCOLN'S GENEALOGY

The lamented Abraham Lincoln believed himself to be bone from our bone and flesh from our flesh. He supposed himself to be a descendant of Hebrew parentage. He said so in my presence.

> *From a eulogy delivered after the assassination of President Abraham Lincoln. Scholars dispute the accuracy of the statement.*

THE ALBANY ROSH HASHANA FRACAS

The people acted like furies. The Poles and Hungarians struck out like wild men. The young people jumped down from the choir galleries to protect me. Within two minutes the whole assembly was a fighting mass. The sheriff and posse who were summoned were belabored and forced out.... Louis Spainier: There is a law to which I can appeal.

Describing what happened at the beginning of the Rosh Hashana service at his Congregation Beth El, in Albany, New York, in 1850. Synagogue president Spanier's hatred for the rabbi and his liberal views could no longer be contained and he punched the rabbi in the nose before the open ark. Quoted in Max Dimont's Jews in America (1978).

□

James Waterman Wise

MAN'S INNER BEING

...the essential quality of the man, that which makes him a significant and luminous figure, is not to be found...in his writings or philosophy, not in the movement he has founded, nor in the words he speaks, but in the man himself, in his *being* the secret must be sought. Some men are not equal to their achievements. Adler's achievements are unequal to himself.

In praise of Felix Adler, founder of the Society for Ethical Culture in 1876.

□

Stephen S. Wise

DEMOCRATIZING THE COMMUNITY

A people is not worthy of respect which does not insist upon the right to be heard touching its own affairs, but surrenders the right of judgment and decision to a company of men, however wise and benevolent, who substitute their own opinions and wishes for the convictions and determinations of the whole people.

At a conference in Philadelphia on March 27–28, 1916, Rabbi Wise laments the fact that the American Jewish Committee will not agree to the formation of an American Jewish Congress.

GOD IS A MYSTERY

But the truth is that we do not know the truth. Dogmatic humanists are much too sure that God is not something-or-other. We on the traditionalist side are much too ready to commit the Master of the universe in writing to one or another of our own pet projects. God is, whatever else, a Mystery, and Judaism must be, whatever else it may be, humble before Him who spoke and theology came to be.

From his On God and Theology.

VISION'S MANY FACES

Vision looks inward and becomes duty. Vision looks outward and becomes aspiration. Vision looks upward and becomes faith.

From his Sermons and Addresses (1905).

UNFULFILLED MISSION

Israel has a mission still: Truth-seeking in the world of thought, and right-doing in the world of action!

Ibid.

MUTUAL RESPONSIBILITY

Wherever a Jew lives, Judaism is on trial.... Every Jew, Atlas-like, bears upon his shoulders the burden of the whole world's Jewry.

Ibid.

NOBLE NATION

Ours is a nation too great to offend the least, too mighty to be unjust to the weakest, too lofty and noble to be ungenerous to the poorest and lowliest.

From a July 4, 1905 address.

SPREADING THE AMERICAN SPIRIT

I am an American. Because I am an American, I am free. Because I am an American, I shall live and labor to the end that all men be set free and that the spirit of American freedom rule over all the sons and daughters of men.

From his As I See It (1944).

BEARERS OF A PRICELESS GIFT

The business of Israel is not to vaunt itself as the historical possessor of a priceless heritage but to live and serve and teach in the sight of all the world as becomes the bearers of a great name and of a glorious tradition....

Whether the heritage is to be carried on depends upon the life of the Jew today, here and everywhere; upon the capacity of the individual Jew to give himself to those noble and consecrated ends of life which were the goal and the guerdon of the bequeathing Jew.

Ibid.

LIVING DIVINELY

Jesus was not a being come down from heaven, but one who attained to heavenly heights. He was not a God who walked on earth like a man but a man who walked with God on earth. He was not a God who lived humanly, but a man who lived divinely.... To us he belongs—not his Church, but he—the man, the Jew, the prophet.

Quoted in I. Landman's Christian and Jew (1929).

WHEN JUSTICE IS MUTE

It is occasion for real regret to me that it is necessary for a Jew to speak touching the case of Leo Frank. It would have been infinitely better if non-Jews had arisen throughout the land, as they ought to have done, to plead on behalf of this man. True, there have been those non-Jews within and without this city [New York] who have lifted their voices on behalf of justice for Frank. But the burden of seeking justice has fallen upon the fellow-Jews of Frank....

Commenting on the unjust sentence imposed upon Leo Frank, falsely accused and convicted for a crime he did not commit. From an article in the Free Synagogue Pulpit, *May 1915.*

PERFECT CONCORD

My Jewishness strengthens my Americanism; my Americanism deepens my Jewishness.

From his article "I Am an American" in Opinion *magazine, July 1942.*

MATERIALISTIC STANDARDS

There is this acquisitive passion—the dominance of things and things and things. Children are given thrills instead of responsibilities. There is too much education and too much psychology, fostering the idea that life is self-expression, self-fulfillment and self-realization until it reaches the newest most tragical and final manifestation—the extinction of life itself.

From a speech before the United Parents Association. Quoted in American Hebrew *magazine, April 1, 1927.*

A JEWISH AMERICAN

I am a Jew who is an American. I was a Jew before I was an American. I have been an American all my life, 64 years, but I've been a Jew for 4,000 years.

Commenting on himself in Time *magazine, June 20, 1938.*

PROUD AMERICAN JEW

I could not speak of myself as an American who is a Jew. I am an American Jew... I am of the American nation, and an American citizen; and there is no conflict between my Jewish race and faith and my American citizenship, of which I am most proud.

From a January 19, 1939 communication to A. B. Horwitz.

DISAPPOINTED MIDDLEMAN

I don't know whether I am getting to be a *Hofjude* [Court Jew], but I find that a good part of my work is to explain to my fellow Jews why our government cannot do all the things asked or expected of it.

Expressing to Felix Frankfurter his exasperation over having failed to have Franklin D. Roosevelt take action, even after the President was surely aware (by September 1942) of Hitler's plan to exterminate the Jews.

THE WISE–WARBURG FEUD

When I saw Brandeis, he told me that the President [Roosevelt] would have acted in March 1933 [to the impending threat of Nazism] if it had not been for the Warburg family. You see, Professor Einstein, how these great philanthropists are our deadliest enemies and a fatal curse to the security and honor of the Jewish people.

From a 1936 letter to Albert Einstein. Quoted in Carl Hermann Voss's Stephen S. Wise: Servant of the People *(1969).*

□

Ruth Wisse

JEWISH MUSEUMS

If there were to be museums for Jewish civilization, I would have no problem. But to have the major Jewish museums consecrated to the destruction of Jewry seems to me exceedingly perverse. What does it communicate to American Jews? What person of dignity, what person of noble Jewish spirit, what person who wants to believe in the eternity of Israel, wants to be presented to his fellow Americans primarily, if not exclusively, through the prism of the destruction of a third of his people?

Commented following the opening of the Simon Wiesenthal Center's Beit HaShoah Museum of Tolerance, in Los Angeles, California. Reported in Hadassah Magazine, *April 1994.*

RABIN'S FUNERAL

They [the Arab leaders] would not have come if he had been killed by an Arab, and accordingly, their presence cannot be taken at face value.

Commenting on the presence of Jordan's King Hussein, Egypt's President Mubarak, and other Arab leaders at the Jerusalem funeral of assassinated Israeli Prime Minister Yitzhak Rabin, on Monday, November 6, 1995.

◻

Simon Wolf

CALL FOR FAIR PLAY

Ignorance is said to be the foundation of prejudice and intolerance. I know not how true this axiom may have been in the remote past; it certainly is not true in the present, for the higher you ascend in the scale of intellect and officers of the public service, the more bigotry and prejudice do you find. My heart is sick, my brain weary, my hopes dampened by these manifestations, not alone in the social, but radiating from the highest official circles....

We have been branded and outraged for four long years, until discretion has ceased to be a virtue, and it is incumbent upon you, the father of the American press, to give us a hearing through the columns of your valuable journal.

Why, when the authorities arrest a criminal, telegraph immediately throughout the Union that a Jew, or another Jew blockader has been caught? Do they, when they catch a James Maloney, say a Methodist or Presbyterian has been caught? Is it, then, a crime to be born a Jew, which has to be expiated upon the altar of public opinion by a life of suffering and abuse?

> *A confidant of U.S. presidents from Buchanan to Wilson, in an 1864 letter to William Cullen Bryant, editor of the* New York Evening Post, *pleading for fair play in reporting about his coreligionists.*

◻

David Wolffsohn

PRAYERSHAWL AS SYMBOL

We have a flag, and it is blue and white: the talith [*sic*] with which we wrap ourselves when we pray—that is our symbol.

> *In suggesting a flag for the Zionist movement.*

◻

Harry A. Wolfson

JUDAISM OF THE FUTURE

Liberal Judaism is the Judaism of the future; it is the only type of Judaism that is valiantly grappling with the intellectual religious problem; it is the most active, the most energetic spiritual force in Judaism today.

> *From an essay in* Menorah Journal *(1921).*

TO BE WHAT WE ARE

To continue to be whatever we happen to

be makes in the long run for the greatest human happiness.

> *Ibid.*

SUBMITTING TO ONE'S FATE

There are certain problems of life for which no solution is possible. Because of our Judaism we must be prepared to give up some of the world's goods even as we must be prepared to make sacrifices because of other disadvantages with which we may happen to be born. All men are not born equal. Some are born blind, some deaf, some lame, and some are born Jews.

> *From his pamphlet entitled* Escaping Judaism *(1922).*

◻

David J. Wolpe

DEEP BELIEVER

A deep believer is that rare person who has worked hard to accomplish a conviction. A deep believer is someone who mines the heart of each question, journeying through all the possible positions before landing on any opinion. A deep believer remains open to other possibilities while retaining the robust certainty of one who is deeply convinced of his position.... Such a believer is rare in any denomination.

> *In a review of Rabbi Harold Schulweis's book* In God's Mirror *(1990).*

HEROES AND ICONS

Our admiration has been so often betrayed that we are skeptical of heroes and wary of icons. The pious are instantly suspect; rulers have been democratized out of divinity; and even the wielders of modern magic, scientists, have fallen from public favor. What remains to us are the scholars.

There is a mystique surrounding scholarship which alone seems to promise salvation.... The scholar has studied. The scholar knows.

> *Discussing the scholarship of Gershom Scholem. From an article in* The Jewish Spectator, *Fall 1988.*

TETHERED JEWS

Judaism without God was unthinkable to an earlier age. Through all the meetings and estrangements of history, in every medium the Jew understood—text, life, and land—God was assigned a role. In joy He was praised; in agony, blamed or supplicated.

> *From his* Healer of Shattered Hearts *(1990).*

GOD AND THE HUMAN QUEST

The human quest, wherever and however defined in Jewish thought, is a joint quest, with humanity and God participating together.... God must be prodded by the prayers of human beings to effect His own salvation! If God cannot seek salvation alone, surely human beings cannot.

Ibid.

FEAR AND FAITH

Faith is grasped first by tones and mood. Before approaching the Jewish conception of God, we must step back to feel the world in which belief is born and nurtured....

We are best touched at night. The day seems harsh and real and rational, but night—even with electric lamps and neon splitting the dark—casts a sensitizing shade over us. There are night thoughts and night imaginings. There are certainties of the night that can be shaken by nothing except the coming of the dawn. Fear is a night child. So is faith.

Ibid.

EVENTUAL REDEMPTION

This world is not an illusion; it is a task. History is not an aimless chronicle of misadventures and brief brightnesses but a disorderly, effortful, and often pitiful march to something better.

From his Why Be Jewish? *(1995).*

SHARING THE WORLD-TO-COME

The corridors of eternity, however they wind, are open to all who live in a way that honors the spark of God inside them.

Ibid.

WHY BE JEWISH?

One reason to be Jewish is that Judaism gives us the inspiration, energy, and will to ensure that even from the midst of the valley of Hinnom a promise of Eden survives.

Ibid.

¤

H. A. Woodruff

FAMILY TIES

One very strong element in Jewish culture which differentiates it from modern Christian culture is the cohesiveness of the Hebrew family. To the Jewish child the fifth commandment, the "first one with a promise," is very real.... From what I have observed, the family ties in a Jewish home are much stronger than in a Christian home. This may prove to be the greatest contribution of the Jew to modern life.

Quoted in Leo Jung's Judaism in a Changing World *(1971).*

¤

Alexander Woollcott

MIRACLE NEEDED

There is absolutely nothing wrong with Oscar Levant that a miracle cannot fix.

Quoted in Margaret Case Harriman's Vicious Circle.

WINCHELL'S ZEST

I suppose it would be easy to assemble evidence in support of the contention that Winchell is lacking in taste. He has a more valuable asset. For want of a better term, let us call it zest.

Quoted in Bob Thomas's Winchell.

¤

William Wordsworth

SOUL-SUBDUING LOOKS

Two lovely sisters still and
    sweet
As flowers, stand side by
    side:
Their soul-subduing looks
    might cheat
The Christian of his pride

From his "Jewish Family" (1828).

¤

Herman Wouk

ALIENATED COMEDIANS

I've never had much of a hang-up about being Jewish, never felt the "alienation" which has been getting such a ride in the books and magazines nowadays.

In his novel Inside, Outside *(1985), self-deprecating Jewish comedians are condemned.*

THE DAY THE GAON WEPT

You have reached high holiness. How have you achieved it? Go down in the market place, Gaon, with the rest of the Jews. Endure their work, their strains, their distractions. Mingle in the world, hear the skepticism and irreligion they hear, take the blows they take. Submit to the ordinary trials of the ordinary Jew. Let us see then if you will remain the Vilna Gaon!

A critic points out how much more difficult it is to be a saint in the real world. From his This Is My God *(1949).*

JEWISH LOSSES

[Jews who assimilate] are lost from Judaism, that is all; lost down a road which has swallowed many more Jews than the Hitler terror ever did.

Ibid.

FAITH IN JUDAISM

Judaism is part of my life and of my family's life.... I believe it is our lot to live and serve in our old identity, until the promised day when the Lord will be one and his name one in all the earth.

Ibid.

GOD AS A CRUTCH

Religious people tend to encounter...a cemented certainty that belief in God is a crutch for the weak and the fearful. It would be just as silly to assert that disbelief in God is a crutch for the immoral and the ill-read.

Ibid.

ロ

Richard Wright

INSIDE THE BLACK WORLD

I had never seen a Jew before and the proprietor of the corner grocery was a strange thing in my life. Until that time I had never heard a foreign language spoken and I used to linger at the door of the corner grocery to hear the odd sounds that Jews made when they talked. All of us black people who lived in the neighborhood hated Jews, not because they exploited us, but because we had been taught at home and in Sunday school that Jews were "Christ killers." With the Jews thus singled out for us; we made them fair game for ridicule.

We black children—seven, eight, and nine years of age—used to run to the Jew's store and shout:

Jew, Jew, Jew
    What do you chew?

Or we would form a long line and weave back and forth in front of the door, singing:

Jew, Jew
    Two for five
That's what keeps

Jew alive.
Or we would chant:
Bloody Christ killers
    Never trust a Jew
Bloody Christ killers
    What won't a Jew do?

There were many more folk ditties, some mean, others filthy, all of them cruel. No one ever thought of questioning our right to do this; our mothers and parents generally approved, either actively or passively. To hold an attitude of antagonism or distrust toward Jews was bred in us from childhood; it was not merely racial prejudice, it was a part of our cultural heritage.

From his Black Boy *(1945).*

ロ

Walter S. Wurzberger

ISRAEL AND DIASPORA JEWS

Free speech is a value, even if it is not absolute, and to ban criticism of Israel's policies categorically is enormously hazardous... American Jews have every right to discuss Israel's policies, even though there is always the possibility that some of the discussion may leak to the public media....

But as long as Jews in the Diaspora fail to exercise this option [of settling in Israel under the Law of Return], they have no political association whatsoever with the State. Hence they can have no claim to any role in Israel's decision-making progress which, after all, is the exclusive prerogative of a sovereign state. Jews in the Diaspora therefore must refrain from any form of criticism which goes beyond the furnishing of opinions and information designed to enable Israelites to arrive at more informed decisions.

From an article in Moment *magazine, December 1976.*

UNIVERSAL VALUES

As a rabbi and a Jew it is my task to teach and preach so that I enable my people to understand and maintain their Judaism and to be loyal. Yet Judaism has universal values that I would like to share with others. This must be accomplished without seeking converts—a practice Judaism, for the most part, has never followed.

From an address at the conference for the Center of Christian–Jewish Understanding. Quoted in its Summer 1994 Newsletter.

⬡
Ed Wynn

EARLY RETIREMENT

This business of involuntary retirement is a crusade with me. What this generation is doing to people my age is a crime against humanity, and sooner or later society will pay for it.

Protesting the call for his retirement in 1959 at age 73. Quoted in Darryl Lyman's Jewish Comedy Catalog *(1989).*

NERVE REMOVED

A husband is what is left of a sweetheart after the nerve has been taken out.

Ibid.

DEFINING A BACHELOR

A bachelor is a man who never made the same mistake once.

Ibid.

⬡
Michael Wyschogrod

FAITH AND THE HOLOCAUST

I cannot see why, if I am a secular, non-believing Jew, it is incumbent upon me to preserve Judaism because Hitler wished to destroy it. What was incumbent upon me was to destroy Hitler, but once this is accomplished, the free choice of every individual is restored and no further Hitler-derived burdens rest on the non-believing Jew.

From a review of Emil Fackenheim's God's Presence in History *in* Judaism *magazine, Summer 1971.*

KISSINGER'S IDENTITY

There have been other American Jews who have risen to high positions in this country, such as Benjamin Cardozo, Felix Frankfurter and Louis Brandeis. All of them were proud, identifying Jews and outstanding Americans who did not find it necessary to downplay their Jewishness [as did Kissinger]. And this was before the Holocaust. None of them lost 13 relatives to Nazi anti-Semitism.

Analyzing Henry Kissinger's discomfort with his Jewish identity. From Moment *magazine, April 1993.*

Yakir

SETTLING IN ERETZ YISRAEL

The truth is that living in Eretz Yisrael is very good for the elderly but not for the young....When you reach seventy and have enough money then you may joyously come here.

A communication from the nephew of the Baal Shem Tov who visited Jerusalem in 1760. Quoted in Lester I. Vogel's To See a Promised Land *(1993).*

◻

Rosalyn Yalow

FOCUS OF FEMINISM

If we [women] were ever to move upwards, we must demonstrate competence, courage, and determination to succeed and must be prepared to challenge and take our place in the Establishment.

Quoted in Elinor and Robert Slater's Great Jewish Women *(1994).*

◻

Zev Yaroslavsky

SELF-RELIANCE

We must live Jewishly. Instead of relying only on the synagogue to educate our children and turn them into Jews, we must teach them ourselves through our own dedication to study, prayer and the welfare of Jews everywhere. Instead of relying on rabbis to inculcate Jewish ethical principles in our young, we should demonstrate those principles in our everyday personal and business dealings. Instead of relying only on summer camp to instill the meaning and spirit of Shabbat we must give our children the experience of *Shabbat shalom* in our homes.

Quoted in Hadassah Magazine, *June–July 1993.*

◻

Peter Yarrow

WHY I WRITE SONGS

I believe that as a Jew and a human being I have an ethical imperative to look at any circumstance that deprives people of their liberty. That's what fuels me. That's why I write the songs, why I sing the songs.

From a portrait of the singer in Hadassah Magazine, *November 1994.*

FROM SADNESS TO CARING

They say the tree of loving grows on the banks of the river of suffering.

From his 1970 song "Weave Me the Sunshine."

LIGHT THE CANDLE

Light one candle for the Maccabee children
With thanks that their light didn't die....
Light one candle for all we believe in
That anger won't tear us apart.
And light one candle to bring us together
With peace as the song in our heart.

Ibid.

◻

A. B. Yehoshua

WRITER'S BLOCK

I couldn't write one sentence. Nothing was going on, and I felt as if I was losing all capacity to write.

Recalling how he felt in the 1970s after receiving a large grant from the Prime Minister's Office that was designed to allow writers to concentrate on their work for a year.

FAMILY FIRST

Family comes before everything. If my son comes home from the army, he is my first priority. All the other engagements of the family come before writing.

From an interview in 1995, after winning the Israel Prize for Literature.

FAVORITE CLASSIC WRITER

I think teaching Agnon is always a pleasure, an unbelievable pleasure, because the work is full of humor. Immediately students are laughing at the stories and the class is alive.

Referring to the writers he favors featuring when teaching this class in literature at Haifa University.

ADVICE TO WRITERS

You have to adapt yourself to work. You have to be there. It's like opening a store. When a person opens his store in the morning and not one client comes in, he is still working. So you have to know that when you are in front of your desk and you are not writing anything, still you have done your work. You have achieved something.

Describing how a writer has to discipline himself. From an interview in The Jerusalem Post, *May 6, 1995.*

□

Yehuda ben Simon

ADAM'S LOST OPPORTUNITY

God almost decided to give the Torah through Adam, and He thought: This man whom I created and who is not of woman born, should I not give the Torah through him? But he immediately decided otherwise and said: I gave one commandment to this man that he should not eat of the fruit of the Tree of Knowledge and he failed to obey Me. How, then, can I give him the Torah with its 613 commandments?

Quoted in the Midrash Genesis Rabba (24:5) and Kohelet Rabba (3:14).

□

Jack Yellen

"MY YIDDISHE MOMMA"

I long to hold her hands once more
As in days gone by
And ask her to forgive me for
Things I did that made her cry.
How few were her pleasures
She never cared for fashion styles.
Her jewels and treasures
She found them in her baby's smiles.
Oh I know that I owe what I am today
To that dear little lady so old and grey,
To that wonderful Yiddishe momma,
Momma mine.

A song popularized by Sophie Tucker.

□

Yevgeny Yevtushenko

SIMPLY A JEW

A mediocre anti-Semitic Russian poet once said to the usually jovial Jewish poet Michael Svitlov: "Why do you look so unhappy today, my dear Michael?"

"I am not unhappy," replied Svitlov. "I am simply a Jew."

In a 1992 Brussels speech recalling the effect of the 1952 Doctor's Plot, which accused Jews of being subversive.

TWENTIETH-CENTURY FLIGHT

The twentieth century is not departing, but trying to flee like a criminal from the punishment it deserves. What verdict would I pass on the twentieth century? Life imprisonment in our memory....

The twentieth century is the killer of many great ideals. A tiny great bullet in the beginning of the century that killed the Archduke Ferdinand in Sarajevo—it was the embryo of the atomic bomb.

In an address delivered at the World Conference on Anti-Semitism and Prejudice in a Changing World, held in Brussels, Belgium, July 1992.

ANTI-SEMITISM'S ADDRESS

But amidst all the readdressed addresses of xenophobia, the address of anti-Semitism remains the same. The Jews. It's almost unthinkable to imagine that in a country that lost some 30 million people in the war with fascism, there could be young people who wear medallions with portraits of Hitler and celebrate his birthday. But unfortunately it's true.

In Moscow there are more than 30 newspapers and magazines of fascist and anti-Semitic persuasion with a combined circulation of more than one million.

Ibid.

FEELING PAIN

Our mother earth is a land of our common pain. We children of the same divided family, we are bad Americans if we don't feel the pain of Russians. We are bad Russians if we don't feel the pain of Jews. We are bad Jews if we don't feel the pain of Palestinians, and we are bad Palestinians if we don't recognize the human right of Jews for peaceful and happy coexistence.

Ibid.

A SIGN OF CULTURE

Man's culture, the degree of being civilized,

is defined by the sense he has for the pain of others.

Ibid.

I AM A TRUE RUSSIAN
There is no Jewish blood in my veins,
But I am hated with a scabby hatred
By all the anti-Semites,
like a Jew.
And therefore
I am a true Russian.

From his Babi Yar *(1961).*

ロ

Anzia Yezierska

POVERTY
Poverty becomes a Jew like a red ribbon on a white horse.

From her Red Ribbon on a White Horse *(1950).*

ロ

Yigal

THE RIGHT MAN
This man is the man [*Ha-ish hu ha-ish*].

A cryptic message sent to Israel by one of the three Israeli secret agents in Argentina who stalked Adolf Eichmann for several months and were able to identify him definitively because of a bouquet of flowers he bought for his wife on their twenty-fifth anniversary of marriage, March 21, 1960. Reported in Moshe Pearlman's Capture of Adolf Eichmann *(1963) .*

ロ

Yochanan ben Nappacha

VALUE OF A SMILE
To smile at your neighbor is more important than to treat him to a drink.

Quoted in the talmudic tractate Ketubot (111b).

THE FAMILY TABLE
When the Temple was in existence, its altar atoned for Jews. Now a man's table is his altar.

From the talmudic tractate Berachot (55a).

A FIRST WIFE
Losing one's first wife is like witnessing the destruction of the Temple.

Quoted in the talmudic tractate Sanhedrin (22a).

DOWNFALL OF THE WICKED
[When the Egyptians were drowning] the ministering angels wanted to chant their hymns, but the Holy One, blessed be He, exclaimed: "The works of my hands are drowning and you want to rejoice!"

Quoted in the talmudic tractate Megilla (10b).

THE LANGUAGE OF ANGELS
Who prays in Aramaic will receive no aid from the angels, for they do not understand Aramaic.

Quoted in the talmudic tractate Shabbat (12b).

SINAI'S VOICES
Each word uttered by God [on Mount Sinai] split itself into the seventy languages of the world.

Quoted in the talmudic tractate Shabbat (88b).

IDOLATRY
Anyone who repudiates idolatry is a Jew.

Quoted in the talmudic tractate Megilla (13a).

ロ

Yochanan ben Zakkai

FORGIVEN IDOLATERS
Anyone who observes the Sabbath properly, even if he be an idolater, is forgiven his sins [against God].

Quoted in the talmudic tractate Shabbat (118b).

LEARNING FROM ANIMALS
Had the Torah not been given to Israel, we might have learned modesty from the cat, respect for the property of others from the ant, chastity from the dove, and proper courtship from the rooster who first coaxes and then mates.

From the talmudic tractate Eruvin (100b).

COMING OF THE MESSIAH
The [Messiah] son of David will come only in a generation that is wholly righteous or wholly wicked.

Quoted in the talmudic tractate Sanhedrin (98a).

THE PROPHETIC TRADITION
Ever since the Temple was destroyed, prophecy was taken from the prophets and given to fools and children.

Quoted in the talmudic tractate Bava Batra (12a–b).

THE OLIVE TREE

Why is Israel compared to an olive tree? Because just as an olive yields its oil only when pounded, so Israel is at its best under oppression.

Quoted in the talmudic tractate Menachot (53b).

A GOOD NAME

Happy is he who grew up with a good name, and departed this world with a good name.

Quoted in the talmudic tractate Berachot (17a).

PLACATING ANGER

We must not try to pacify a person in the heat of his anger.

Quoting Rabbi Jose in the talmudic tractates Berachot (7a) and Avot (4:18), where it is quoted in the name of Simeon ben Eleazar.

UNIVERSAL REVELATION

God's voice, as it was uttered [at Sinai], exploded into seventy languages so that all nations could understand Him.

Quoted in Midrash Exodus Rabba (5:9).

THE MEANS TEST

A person should be taxed according to his means.

Quoted in the talmudic tractate Bava Batra (7b).

REPUDIATING IDOLATRY

Whoever repudiates idolatry is called a Jew.

Quoted in the talmudic tractate Megilla (13a).

PITY THE THIEF

The Holy One, blessed be He, is concerned with the dignity of human beings. For a stolen ox who can walk by himself, the thief must pay a five-fold penalty [for the theft], but for a sheep, which the thief must carry off on his shoulders, he pays only a four-fold penalty [to compensate for the trouble to which he is put].

Quoted in the Tosefta, Bava Kamma (7:10), commenting on Exodus (21:37).

SECRET WEAPON

When Jews do God's will, no nation has power over them. When they do not, He delivers them to the beasts among the low.

Quoted in the talmudic tractate Berachot (66b).

LAST REQUEST

Give me Jabneh [Jamnia] and its sages!

From the talmudic tractate Gittin (56b).

FLEETING EXISTENCE

Here today, and tomorrow in the grave.

Quoted in the talmudic tractate Berachot (28b).

FEAR OF GOD

May your fear of God be as strong as your fear of men.

Advice to his son. Quoted in the talmudic tractate Berachot (28b).

◘

Ovadya Yosef

TO SAVE A LIFE

According to the Palestinian Talmud (Yoma 8:5), if one goes to a rabbi to ask whether he may desecrate the Sabbath or Yom Kippur in order save the life of a person in imminent danger, such a delay [in action] may become a form of murder. While one is busy asking the question, the patient may die. When a life is at stake, one must act [decisively and] quickly.

The former Sephardic Chief Rabbi of Israel arguing in 1994 that one must return land to Arabs for the sake of peace, thereby saving lives.

◘

Yosi ben Chalafta

WIFE IS HOME

I have never called my wife "wife" but "home."

From the talmudic tractate Shabbat (118b).

◘

Yosi ben Chamina

HUMAN DIGNITY

He who endeavors to gain honor at the price of having his fellow man being degraded has no portion in the world-to-come.

Ibid.

◘

Yosi ben Yehuda

SABBATH ANGEL

On Sabbath eve, a good angel and an evil angel accompany a man from the synagogue to his home. If the man finds the candles lit, the table set, and the bed made, the good angel says, "May next Sabbath be like this!" And the evil angel answers perforce, "Amen." Otherwise, the evil angel says, "May next Sabbath be like this!" and the good angel is compelled to respond, "Amen."

Quoted in the talmudic tractate Shabbat (119b).

□

Yosi ben Zimra

ATTRACTING PROSELYTES

He who attracts a gentile to God is as though he created him.

Quoted in the Midrash Genesis Rabba (39:14).

□

Henny Youngman

GREATEST INVENTION

The greatest invention in the world was videotape. It made it possible for me to go home and watch myself and see what I did wrong. I get pretty sick of that! But I'll never stop watching. It's so much fun to see when I do something right.

Quoted in Darryl Lyman's Jewish Comedy Catalog (1989).

Israel Zangwill

THE JEWISH CONTRIBUTION

The literature of Israel in its widest sense comprises the contribution made by Jews to the thesaurus of the world. All alphabets and all vocabularies are drawn into its service.

Quoted in the Foreword to Joseph Leftwich's Caravan: A Jewish Quarterly Omnibus *(1962).*

SCRATCH A CHRISTIAN

Scratch the Christian and you find the pagan—spoiled.

From his Children of the Ghetto *(1892).*

ALL-EMBRACING JEW

I figure the Jew as the eldest born of Time, touching the Creation and reaching forward into the future, the true *blasé* of the Universe; the Wandering Jew who has been everywhere, seen everything, done everything, led everything, thought everything, and suffered everything.

Ibid.

THE JEWISH REPRESENTATIVE

The sons of the Law, inhabitants of the Idea.

From the Preface to the American edition of his Dreamers of the Ghetto *(1898).*

GOD'S PROPHET

There is no God but God, and Israel is His prophet; not Moses, not Christ, not Mohammed, but Israel, the race in whom God was revealed.

From an article in the North American Review, *April 1895.*

HOW TO HONOR LENIN

All Jews should set up a statue to Lenin for not being a Jew.

From his Voice of Jerusalem *(1921).*

LEGAL FICTIONS

There is even something to be said for the "legal fictions" which, corrosive of conscience as they were, were probably meant to show that the unavoidable breach of law in a difficult world did not mean repudiation of the Law.

Ibid.

THE LIVING JEWISH TONGUE

Yiddish far more than Hebrew or neo-Hebrew was the living Jewish tongue. It was the language of the Jewish masses; it vibrates with their history, follows the mold of their life and thought, and colors itself with their moods. It is to Yiddish that we must look for the truest repository of specifically Jewish sociology. From Yiddish we can build up a picture of the life of the Judengasse.

Quoted by Joseph Leftwich in The Jewish Spectator, *May 1952.*

UNACCOMPLISHED MISSION

We are proud and happy in that the dread Unknown God of the infinite universe has chosen our race as the medium by which to reveal His will to the world.... Our miraculous survival through the cataclysms of ancient and modern dynasties is a proof that our mission is not yet over.

Ibid.

THE JEWISH TRINITY

Power, Love, Wisdom—there you have a real trinity which makes up the Jewish God.

Ibid.

THE "WHO IS A JEW" TEST

Since neither birth nor marriage now definitely determines who is a Jew and who not, the chronicler of Judaism is reduced to the test of whether a man is buried with the Jews. We take our census in our cemeteries. But the test of Judaism must be not death but life: how a man lives, not how he is buried.

From his Speeches, Articles and Letters *(1937).*

HOLY LAND REGENERATION

Palestine needs a people; Israel needs a country. If, in regenerating the Holy Land, Israel could regenerate itself, how should the world be other than the gainer?

From his Zion, Whence Cometh My Help.

JEW AS SCAPEGOAT

Nothing gratifies the mob more than to get a simple name to account for a complex phenomenon, and the word "Jew" is always at hand to explain the never-absent maladies of the body politic.

From his Voice of Jerusalem *(1921).*

AN EVER-FORGIVING PEOPLE

If ever there was a race which was forgiving to the point of flabbiness, it is the race which styles itself "the merciful, sons of the merciful," and of which I have written..."[The Jews are] the only Christians in Europe, turning the other cheek."

Ibid.

BARUCH BECOMES BENEDICT

I see how much Benedict owes to Baruch.

From his Dreamers of the Ghetto *(1898).*

UNCONQUERABLE PEOPLE

A people that has learned to live without a country is unconquerable.

From the Future of the Jewish People *(1903).*

VICES AND VIRTUES

Israel's vices are on the surface, his virtues lie deep.

From the North American Review, *April 1895.*

SABBATH PEACE

The Ghetto welcomed the Sabbath Bride with proud song and humble feast, and sped her parting with optimistic symbolisms of fire and wine, of spice and light and shadow. All around, their neighbors sought distraction in the blazing public-houses, and their tipsy bellowings resounded through the streets and mingled with the Hebrew hymns. Here and there the voice of a beaten woman rose on the air. But no Son of the Covenant was among the revellers or the wife-beaters; the Jews remained a chosen race, a peculiar people, faulty enough, but redeemed at least from the grosser vices—a little human islet won from the waters of animalism by the genius of ancient engineers.

Quoted in J.H. Hertz's Pentateuch and Haftorahs *(1961).*

GOD'S MELTING POT

America is God's crucible, the Great Melting Pot, where all races of Europe are melting and reforming...Celt and Latin, Slav and Teuton, Greek and Syrian, black and yellow, Jew and Gentile... How the great Alchemist melts and fuses them with his purging flame!.... Here shall they all unite to build the Republic of Man and the Kingdom of God. Peace, peace unto ye unborn millions fated to fill this giant continent—the God of our children give you peace.

From his play The Melting Pot *(1909), in which he describes how a new nation is being forged.*

GLORY OF AMERICA

What is the glory of Rome and Jerusalem, where all nations come to worship and look back, compared with the glory of America, where all races and nations come to labor and look forward?

Ibid.

□

Eli Zborowski

AN OBLIGATION TO REMEMBER

How could we forget that even as the end of history's most terrible war drew near, the greater part of the Hungarian Jewish community [of 600,000] went to its death? How could we forget that even as the Allied forces liberated France and moved ahead on all fronts against Nazi Germany, that behind the lines the dark forces of terror continued their relentless massacre of innocents? How could we forget that even as happy cheers greeted the liberators, the agonized cries of the tortured and condemned went unheard?...

That is why we are here tonight. That is why we are obligated to remember. That is why we have a duty to forewarn the world that such atrocities must never take place again. That is why we must tell the story of the 600,000 over and over again, so that the martyrs and heroes of the tragic period may live on in our memories.

From a speech on October 30, 1994, at a dinner in New York City commemorating the fiftieth anniversary of the deportation and destruction of Hungarian Jews.

WIESEL'S CONTRIBUTION

Elie Wiesel honors us and the sacred cause of remembrance. It is inconceivable to think of remembrance without Elie Wiesel. He has elevated and articulated remembrance as no one else could. Beyond that, whatever he has achieved personally across the globe has enhanced the status and dignity of all survivors.

Ibid.

❑

Mark Zborowski and Elizabeth Herzog

CENTRALITY OF FAMILY

"My shtetl" is the people who live in it, not the place or the buildings or the street. "My home" is the family and the family activities, not the walls or the yard or the broken-down fence.

From their Life Is with People *(1962).*

❑

(Prophet) Zechariah

PLUCKED BRAND

This is a brand plucked out of the fire.

From the Book of Zechariah (3:2).

❑

Hillel Zeitlin

TREE ON A HILL

On the hill stands a tree,
It stands bending sidewise.
A Jew is going to Palestine,
And tears are in his eyes.

I know that hill, I know the tree, and there was a time when I knew that Jew. I knew the Jew with tears in his eyes. I don't know him now. I can't see him now. Where is he?

From an essay by a writer who represented chasidic thought in modern Yiddish literature.

❑

Solomon Zeitlin

WHO CRUCIFIED JESUS?

The Synoptic Gospels and the founders of Christianity and the creators of the Church never accused the Jewish *people* [as a people] of the death of Jesus. This was a charge conceived in a later period and was introduced in the record of the past.

From his Who Crucified Jesus? *(1964).*

❑

(Rabbi) Zera

BEING A ROLE MODEL

A man should not say to a child, "I will give you something," and then fail to give it to him, because this will teach the child to lie.

From the talmudic tractate Sukkah (46b).

❑

Vladimir Zhirinovsky

I RESPECT JEWS

I respect Jews. I respect Israel. You have a great nation. It's the richest—you live better than anyone in the world. I envy you.

At a December 14, 1993 Moscow press conference.

THE RUSSIAN ORGASM

Today is the beginning of orgasm. The whole [Russian] nation, I promise you, will experience orgasm next year.

As he cast his ballot in the Russian elections on December 12, 1993 when his Liberal Democratic party won more than 23 percent in a parliamentary vote. At his victory celebration, he punched a guest who suggested that he, Zhirinovsky, was a Jew. Many people believe that his father, who died when he was a year old, was Jewish. Reported in Newsweek *magazine, December 27, 1993.*

DUAL CITIZENSHIP SCARE

Dual citizenship permits dual morality. Chazanov can use that dual citizenship on the orders of spy services, and get double pay.

Calling for the arrest of Gennady Chazanov, one of Russia's most popular comedians, for holding dual Israeli and Russian citizenship. Quoted in The Jerusalem Report, *January 13, 1994.*

ULTRA-NATIONALIST COMPLAINT

Why did you compensate the Jews after World War II? Who captured Berlin, the Jews or the Russian soldiers? You should have paid the reparations to us.

From a statement to German cable television station RTL. Quoted in The Jerusalem Post, *January 27, 1994.*

❑

Chaim Zhitlowsky

JEWISH YOUTH IN AMERICA

They have absorbed a certain national pride, not a Jewish nationalism, however, but an American.... They were proud of the fact that they are children of the American people, of its language and of its culture. English is their national language; the English culture their national culture.

Characterizing the second generation of Jews before the Yiddish Culture Society.

□

George Ziad

PHILIP ROTH'S PALESTINIAN FRIEND

The people are coarse and noisy and push you in the street. I've lived in Chicago, in New York, in Boston, I've lived in Paris, in London, and nowhere have I seen such people in the street. The *arrogance!* What have they created like you Jews out in the world? Absolutely nothing. Nothing but a state founded on force and the will to dominate. If you want to talk about culture, there is absolutely no comparison. Dismal painting and sculpture, no musical composition, and a very minor literature—that is what all their arrogance has produced.

Compare this to American Jewish culture and it is pitiable, it is laughable. And yet they are not only arrogant about the Arab and *his* mentality, they are arrogant about you and your mentality. These provincial nobodies look down on *you.* Can you imagine it? There is more Jewish spirit and Jewish laughter and Jewish intelligence on the Upper West Side of Manhattan than in this entire country—and as for Jewish *conscience,* as for a Jewish sense of *justice,* as for Jewish *heart*...there's more Jewish heart in the knish counter at Zabar's than in the whole of the Knesset!

A comment by Roth's one-time fellow-student. Quoted in a review of Roth's Operation Shylock *(1993).*

□

Hans Zinsser

BLAMING THE VICTIM

My father once told me that in the 1840s, in a village along the Rhine, a boy had thrown a stone at a Jew. The missile did not hit the Jew but it broke a windowpane; and the Jew was made to pay for the damage, because, if he hadn't dodged, the pane would not have been broken.

From his As I Remember Him, the Biography of R.S. *(1940).*

□

Nathan Ziprin

BURGEONING HASSIDISM

What was the force behind the unique burgeoning of this mystic movement? By placing exultation above learning, it laid the foundation for democracy in Jewish life. By making prayer a matter of the heart rather than conformity with a set standard, it attracted the untutored, the unlearned, and the infirm. By bringing gaiety and song into worship, it brought uplifting of spirit and soul.... Catastrophe has decimated the area of Europe where Hassidism thrived. Hitler slew Hassidim and *mithnageddim* alike. But a living movement, like a root, knows no obstacles. The root has now spread to Israel and America with deep promise in both lands.

From an article in The Jewish Floridian, *July 5, 1963.*

□

Émile Zola

I ACCUSE

Truth is on the march and nothing can stop it.

Defending the falsely charged French army officer Alfred Dreyfus. From his "J'Accuse" (1898), which appeared in the newspaper L'Aurore.

DREYFUS IS INNOCENT

May all my words perish if Dreyfus is not innocent.... I did not want my country to remain in lies and injustice. One day, France will thank me for having helped to save its honor.

Ibid.

IDIOTIC PERSECUTION

The Jews, such as they are today, are our work, the work of our eighteen hundred years of idiotic persecution.

From his Nouvelle Campagne *(1896).*

□

Elyakum Zunser

GOLDEN OPPORTUNITIES

I came to the land, saw it and lo!
Tears and suffering and tales of woe...
Poverty, misery, darkness, cold—
Everywhere in this "Land of Gold!"

After emigrating from Russia to America, the land he admired from afar. From his "For Whom Is the Gold Country?" (1894).

CALLING FOR SELF-RELIANCE

We dare not rely too much on others
Two thousand years of experience instruct
us in this.
Be patriots—be Americans...
Become citizens—organize!...
Use your vote—vote your interest!
The Jew will no longer be attacked
He will be protected in court
He will not need to complain
The judge will listen to his words...
Only then will you be able to say:
"This land is for the Jew, a secure, serene
place."

From his Twenty Popular Songs, *emphasizing the need for American Jews to establish Jewish political clubs, as did the Germans and Irish who came to America.*

◻

Leopold Zunz

LOFTY SPIRIT

Every lofty spirit is bound to a physical body.

In the Preface to his Journal for the Science of Judaism *(1823).*

ON REFORM JUDAISM

I despise a rabbinical hierarchy, but I also have a contempt for a Reform movement that produces namby-pamby programs.... We must reform ourselves, not our religion.

Quoted in W. Gunther Plaut's Rise of Reform Judaism *(1963).*

NATIONAL TRAGEDY

If there are ranks in suffering, Israel takes precedence of all nations; if the duration of sorrows and the patience with which they are borne ennoble, the Jews can challenge the aristocracy of every land; if a literature is called rich in the possession of a few classic tragedies—what shall we say to a national tragedy lasting for fifteen hundred years, in which the poets and the actors were also the heroes?

From his Synagogale Poesie *(1855). Quoted by George Eliot in* Daniel Deronda *(1876).*

ON REFORMING OURSELVES

We must reform ourselves and not our religion. We should attack only evil practices that crept in our religious life whether from within or from without, but not the holy heritage.

From a letter to Abraham Geiger, May 4, 1845. Quoted in Meyer Waxman's History of Jewish Literature *(1930–1941).*

◻

Arnold Zweig

TRADITIONAL VALUES

Striving for knowledge for its own sake, love of justice bordering on fanaticism, and striving for personal autonomy—these are the traditional themes of the Jewish people that allow me to experience my kinship with them as destiny's gift.

Quoted in Arnold Zweig 1887–1968 (1978), edited by George Wenzel.

JOYFUL JEW

You know how passionately, indeed how joyfully I am a Jew.

Ibid.

◻

Stefan Zweig

ON HERZL

When I wrote my first short story at age nineteen, it never occurred to me to submit it to anyone but him [Theodor Herzl], the beloved author whose word was final. Herzl accepted the story and...published it.... [He] was the first to have confidence in me.

Zweig admired Herzl who, aside from his devotion to the Zionist cause, devoted himself primarily to journalism and literature. Towards the end of his life Herzl was literary editor of the Neue Freie Presse.

MAN OF LETTERS

His [Herzl's] readers were fascinated by his essays, now faintly tinged with melancholy, now brilliantly sparkling, full of profound pathos and yet as lucid as crystal.

Writing about the man of letters he most admired.

AUTHORITY AND LIBERTY

Every nation, every epoch, every thoughtful human being, has again and again to establish the landmarks between freedom and authority: for in the absence of authority liberty degenerates into license, and chaos ensues; and authority becomes tyranny unless it is tempered by freedom.

From his Right to Heresy *(1936).*

THE MESSIANISM STRING

Whenever anyone—prophet or deceiver—throughout the two thousand years of exile plucked this [messianism] string the entire soul of the people was brought into vibration.

> *From his* World of Yesterday *(1943), written one year prior to his death in Rio de Janeiro in a suicide pact with his wife.*

TRAITOR TO HUMANITY

Beneath the yoke of barbarism one must not keep silence; one must fight. Whoever is silent at such a time is a traitor to humanity.

> *Ibid. On the day the Nazis burned his books.*

HOME AS ANCHOR

One has to have an anchorage from which one can set out and to which one can always return.

> *Ibid.*

INCOMPREHENSIBLE FATE

What was most tragic in this Jewish tragedy of the twentieth century was that those who suffered it knew that it was pointless and that they were guiltless. Their forefathers and ancestors of medieval times had at least known what they suffered for; for their belief, for their law. They had still possessed a talisman of the soul which today's generation had long since lost, the inviolable faith in their God....

Only now, since they were swept up like dirt in the streets and heaped together, the bankers from their Berlin palaces and sextons from the synagogues of orthodox congregations, the philosophy professors from Paris and Rumanian cabbies, the undertaker's helpers and Nobel prize winners.... What was the reason, the sense, the aim of this senseless persecution?

> *Ibid.*

MENTAL HEALTH

Health alone does not suffice. To be happy, to become creative, man must always be strengthened by faith in the meaning of his own existence.

> *From his* Mental Healers *(1932).*

□

Ulrich Zwingli

HOLY TONGUE

I found the Holy Tongue beyond all belief cultivated, graceful, and dignified.... No other language expresses so much with so few words and such powerful phrases; no language is so rich in many-sided and meaningful forms of expression and modes of imagery. No language so delights and quickens the human heart.

> *Quoted in Abraham Raisen's* Gentile Reactions to Jewish Ideals.

□

Shmuel Zygielbojm

DESPERATE TO BREAK DOWN INDIFFERENCE

I cannot be silent. I cannot live while the remnants of the Jewish population of Poland, of whom I am a representative, are perishing. My friends in the Warsaw Ghetto died with weapons in their hands in the last heroic battle. It was not my destiny to die together with them but I belong to them and in their mass graves.

> *A farewell note addressed to the president and prime minister of the Polish government-in-exile. As a member of the Polish National Council in London, he had pleaded with the Allied governments to rescue the Jews in the Warsaw Ghetto. On May 12, 1943, at age forty-eight, he committed suicide in London after his wife and child had been killed by the Nazis in Poland.*

CRY OF PROTEST

Let my death be an energetic cry of protest against the indifference of the world which witnesses the extermination of the Jewish people without taking any steps to prevent it. In our day and age, human life is of little value; having failed to achieve success in my life, I hope that my death may jolt the indifference of those who, perhaps even in this extreme moment, could save the Jews who are still alive in Poland.

> *Ibid.*

BIOGRAPHICAL NOTATIONS

Biographical Notations

Abba Aricha
See Rav.

Abba ben Acha
Third-century talmudic scholar.

Abba ben Chanina
Third-century talmudic scholar.

Abba ben Zavda
Third-century talmudic scholar.

Abba ben Zevina
Fourth-century talmudic scholar.

Abbahu
Also known as Avahu.
Third-century talmudic scholar.

Abbas, Mahmoud
Also known as Abu Mazen.
Palestine Liberation Organization
representative at Israeli-PLO peace talks,
Oslo, Norway (1993).

Abbaye (Abaye) [c. 280–339]
Talmudic scholar.

Abbott, Lyman [1835–1922]
U.S. clergyman, editor.

Abdel-Latif
Contemporary of Moses Maimonides
(twelfth century).

Abdo, Rajai
Owner of Hisham Palace Hotel in
Jericho; former Imam in Greenville, South
Carolina.

Abdullah [1882–1951]
King of Transjordan after 1946.

Abella, Irving
Contemporary historian, author.

Abraham (Patriarch) [c. 2000 B.C.E.]
Father of the Jewish people.

Abrahams, Israel [1858–1925]
Anglo-Jewish writer, scholar.

Abram, Morris Berthold [1918–]
U.S. attorney, community leader.

Abramov, S. Z. [1908–]
Member of the Knesset (1970s).

Abrams, Robert [1938–]
New York State attorney general (1980s).

Abu Mazen
See Abbas, Mahmoud.

Abuhayy, Ismail Ibrahim
Gaza Strip resident (1994).

Abzug, Bella [1920–]
U.S. congresswoman from New York
(1970s), attorney.

Acheson, Dean [1893–1971]
U.S. undersecretary of state (1949–1953).

Aciman, André
Contemporary author, educator.

Ackerman, Gary [1942–]
U.S. congressman from New York (1990s).

Acton (Lord)
Contemporary of Benjamin Disraeli
(1804–1881).

Adams, Herbert Baxter [1850–1901]
U.S. historian.

Adams, Joey [1911–]
U.S. comedian, author.

Adams, John [1735–1825]
Second U.S. president (1797–1801).

Adda ben Ahaba
Third/fourth-century talmudic scholar.

Addison, Joseph [1672–1719]
British essayist.

Adler, Alfred [1870–1937]
Austrian psychologist.

Adler, Cyrus [1863–1940]
Third president of the Jewish Theological
Seminary of America.

Adler, Felix [1851–1933]
Leader of the Ethical Culture Society.

Adler, Morris [1906–1996]
U.S. rabbi, author.

Adler, Rachel
Contemporary author, feminist leader
(1970s).

Adler, Samuel [1809–1891]
German-American rabbi.

Agnon, S.Y. (Samuel Yosef) [1888–1970]
Hebrew novelist, Nobel Prize winner.

Agus, Jacob B. [1911–1986]
U.S. rabbi, author, scholar.

Ahad Ha-am [1856–1927]
Né Asher Ginsberg.
Ukrainian-born essayist, philosopher.

Ahikar
Hero mentioned in the apocryphal Book of Tobit.

Akavya ben Mehalalel
First-century talmudic scholar.

Akiba (Akiva) ben Joseph [c. 50–135]
Leading talmudic scholar, activist.

Alaa, Abu
Senior negotiator for the Palestine Liberation Organization (1990s).

Albo, Joseph
Fifteenth-century Spanish rabbi, theologian.

Albright, William Foxwell [1891–1971]
Archaeologist.

Alexandri (Rabbi)
Third-century talmudic scholar.

Ali, Muhammed [1942–]
Né Cassius Clay.
Three-time world heavyweight boxing champion (1964–1967).

Allen, Fred [1894–1956]
Contemporary U.S. humorist.

Allen, George E.
British author.

Allen, Steve [1921–]
U.S. comedian, author.

Allen, Woody [1935–]
U.S actor, writer, film director.

Allon, Yigal [1918–1980]
Israeli soldier, politician.

Almansur, Abu-Yussuff
Thirteenth-century Muslim leader.

Alon, Menachem
Contemporary Israeli jurist.

Aloni, Shulamit [1929–]
Israeli communications minister (1994).

Alroy, Gil Carl
College instructor (1970s), U.S. State Department employee.

Alter, Robert B. [1935–]
Hebrew scholar, literary critic.

Alterman, Nathan (Natan) [1916–1970]
U.S. poet, translator.

Altman, Murray
Contemporary writer.

Amery, Jean
Auschwitz survivor.

Amichai, Yehuda [1924–]
Israeli poet.

Amital, Yehuda
Co-dean of the Har-Etzion Yeshiva on the West Bank (1990s).

Amir, Yigal [1970–]
Law student, assassin of Yitzhak Rabin.

Amos
Eighth-century B.C.E. prophet of Israel.

Amsterdam, Morey [1914–]
U.S. comedian.

al-Anani, Jawad
Contemporary Jordanian official.

Angel, Marc D. [1945–]
U.S. rabbi, author.

Angoff, Charles [1902–]
U.S. novelist.

Anielewicz, Mordecai [1919–1943]
Warsaw Ghetto leader.

Anski, Solomon (Rappoport) [1863–1920]
Yiddish publicist, folklorist.

Antin, Mary [1881–1949]
Russian-born U.S. author.

App, Austin J.
Contemporary author, denier of Holocaust.

Appelfeld, Aharon [1932–]
Israeli author.

Arad, Miriam
Contemporary Israeli author.

Arad, Yitzak
Contemporary Israeli official.

Arafat, Suha Tawil [1963–]
Yasser Arafat's Jerusalem-born wife.

Arafat, Yasser (Yasir) [1929–]
Egyptian-born chairman of the Palestine Liberation Organization.

Arama, Isaac [1420–1494]
Spanish rabbi, talmudist, philosopher.

Aref, Abdel Rahmen
President of Iraq in 1967.

Arendt, Hannah [1906–1975]
German-born sociologist, author.

Arens, Moshe [1925–]
Israeli politician, author.

Arieh, Judah
Contemporary Israeli author.

Arlosoroff, Chaim Victor [1899–1933]
Zionist labor leader.

Armey, Richard K. [1940–]
U.S. congressman from Texas (1990s).

Arnold, Matthew [1822–1888]
English poet, critic.

Arnold, Reuben
Attorney of Leo Frank in 1913.

Arnold, Roseanne
See Barr, Roseanne.

Arthur, Beatrice (Bea) [1926–]
U.S. actress, comedienne.

Artzi-Pelossof, Noa Ben
See Pelossof, Noa Ben Artzi-.

Arzt, Max [1897–1975]
U.S. rabbi, author.

Asch, Sholom (Sholem) [1880–1957]
Polish-born Yiddish novelist, playwright.

Asimov, Isaac [1920–1992]
U.S. writer, scientist.

Asner, Edward [1929–]
U.S. actor, political activist.

al-Assad, Hafez [1930–]
President of Syria (1971–).

Auden, W. H. [1907–1973]
English-born U.S. poet.

Auerbach, Ephraim [1892–]
Yiddish writer.

Avineri, Shlomo
Israeli educator, director general of Israel's
foreign ministry (1970s).

Avira (Rabbi)
Talmudic scholar.

Avishai, Bernard I.
Contemporary writer.

Avital, Colette
Israeli consul general in New York (1990s).

Baal Shem Tov, Israel [c.1700–1760]
Founder of chasidism.

Babel, Isaac [1894–1941]
Russian author.

Bacall, Lauren [1924–]
U.S. actress, author.

Bachya (Bahya) ibn Pakuda
See Ibn Pakuda, Bachya.

Bacon, Roger [1214–1294]
British philosopher.

Baeck, Leo [1873–1956]
German rabbi, theologian.

Bailey, Gamaliel
Nineteenth-century antislavery advocate.

Baker, James A. [1930–]
U.S. politician.

Bakshi-Doron, Eliyahu
Sephardic Chief Rabbi of Israel (1990s).

Baldwin, James [1924–]
U.S. novelist, essayist, playwright.

Balfour, Arthur James [1848–1930]
British statesman, philosopher.

Ball, Lucille [1911–1989]
U.S. actress, comedienne.

Bamberger, Bernard J. [1904–]
U.S. rabbi, Bible scholar.

Bankhead, William [1874–1940]
U.S. congressman.

Barak, Ehud [1942–]
Israeli general, politician.

Bar Bar Chana
See Rabba bar bar Chana.

Bar-David, Molly Lyons
Contemporary writer.

Bar-Ilan, David
Executive editor of *The Jerusalem Post*.

Bar Kappara
Third-century talmudic scholar.

Baron, Salo W. [1895–1989]
U.S. professor, author.

Barr, Rosanne [1953–]
U.S. comedienne, actress.

Barth, Karl [1886–1968]
Swiss theologian, author.

Baruch, Bernard M. [1870–1965]
U.S. financier, public official.

Baruch, Simon
Father of Bernard M. Baruch.

Baruch of Medzebozh [c. 1756–1810]
Chasidic rabbi.

Bass, Lia
First Brazilian woman to be ordained
as a rabbi (1994).

Bauer, Yehuda
Contemporary Israeli historian, author.

Baum, Philip [1925–]
Assistant executive director of the American
Jewish Congress (1990s).

Baum, Vicki [1888–1960]
Austrian-born U.S. novelist.

Bautista, Jose [1964–]
Major League pitcher.

Bea, Augustin Cardinal
President of the Secretariat for Promoting
Christian Unity (1963), who quashed the
charge of deicide against the Jews.

Beaulieu, Anatole Leroy
Late nineteenth-century author.

Bedersi, Jedaiah ben Abraham
[c.1270–c.1340]
French Hebrew poet, physician.

Beerbohm, Max [1872–1956]
British satirist, critic.

Beer-Hofmann, Richard [1866–1945]
Austrian poet, playwright, novelist.

Begin, Menachem [1913–1992]
Israeli prime minister (1977–1983).

Begun, Yosef
Russian refusenik released from Christopol
Prison in 1987.

Behrman, Samuel Nathan (S.N.)
[1893–1973]
U.S. dramatist.

Beilin, Yossi
Israeli deputy foreign minister
(1980s–1990s).

Bejski, Moshe
Israeli Supreme Court justice, saved by
Oskar Schindler.

Belafonte, Harry [1927–]
U.S. actor, singer.

Belkin, Samuel [1911–1976]
U.S. rabbi, scholar, educator.

Bell, August
Nineteenth-century author.

Belloc, Hilaire [1870–1953]
British writer, poet, Roman Catholic
apologist.

Bellow, Saul [1915–]
U.S. novelist.

Belzer, Richard [1944–]
U.S. comedian.

Ben-Aharon, Yossi
Aide to Israeli prime minister Yitzhak
Shamir (1980s).

Benamozegh, Elijah ben Abraham
[1822–1900]
Italian rabbi, philosopher.

Ben Artzi-Pelossof, Noa
See Pelossof, Noa Ben Artzi-.

Ben Azzai (Simeon ben Azzai)
Second-century talmudic scholar.

Ben Bag Bag
First-century talmudic scholar.

Ben-Chorin, Michael
Opponent of the 1993 Israel–Palestine
Liberation Organization peace accords.

Bénet, Stephen Vincent [1898–1943]
U.S. poet, novelist.

Benevisti, Meron
Deputy mayor of Jerusalem (early 1980s).

Ben-Gal, Ely
Museum of the Diaspora historian (1990).

Ben-Gurion, David [1886–1973]
First Israeli prime minister (1948–1953;
1955–1963).

Ben Hey-Hey
First-century B.C.E. talmudic scholar.

Ben-Itto, Hadassa
Israeli jurist (1980s), linguist.

Benjacob, Isaac [1801–1863]
Author, bibliographer.

Benjamin, Judah Philip [1811–1884]
U.S. senator from Louisiana.

Ben-Moshe, Yosef
Contemporary Orthodox Israeli.

Benny, Jack [1894–1975]
U.S. comedian, actor.

Ben-Porat, Miriam
Israeli state comptroller (1994).

Ben Sira
Second-century B.C.E. sage, author.

Bentwich, Norman [1883–1971]
Zionist, professor.

Ben-Ze'ev, Yoram
Deputy director of the Israeli president's
residence (1984–1993).

Berdyayev, Nicholai Aleksandrovich
[1874–1948]
Russian existentialist, author.

Berg, Gertrude [1899–1966]
U.S. actress, comedienne.

Berger, Elmer
Founder of the anti-Zionist American
Council for Judaism (1943).

Bergman, Samuel (Shmuel) Hugo
[1883–1975]
Zionist, philosopher.

Bergmann, Martin
Contemporary author, historian.

Bergson, Henri [1859–1941]
French philosopher, author.

Bergson, Peter
See Kook, Hillel.

Berkovits, Eliezer [1908–1992]
U.S. rabbi, scholar, author.

Berkowitz, William [1924–]
U.S. rabbi, author.

Berle, Adolf
Contemporary U.S. author.

Berle, Milton [1908–]
U.S. comedian, actor.

Berlin, Irving [1888–1989]
Russian-born U.S. composer.

Berlin, Isaiah [1909–]
British political scientist, author.

Berman, Saul
Contemporary U.S. rabbi, scholar,
educator.

Bermant, Chaim [1923–]
British author, columnist.

Bernhardt, Sarah [1844–1923]
French actress.

Bernheim, Isaac W. [1848–1945]
Industrialist, philanthropist.

Bernstein, David S.
Founder and editor of *Diversity*.

Bernstein, Leonard [1918–1990]
U.S. composer, conductor.

Bernstein, Louis, J. [?–1995]
U.S. theologian.

Berri, Claude
Contemporary French film director.

Besser, James D.
Washington correspondent of New York's
Jewish Week (1994).

Best, Karl
German SS leader during World War II.

Bettelheim, Bruno [1903–1990]
Austrian-born psychologist, professor,
educator.

Biale, David
Director of the Center for Jewish Studies at
the Graduate Theological Union, Berkeley,
California (1980s).

Bialik, Chaim Nachman [1873–1934]
Hebrew poet.

Binstock, Louis
Contemporary U.S. rabbi.

Birger, Trudi
Holocaust survivor, Israeli social worker.

Birmingham, Stephen [1931–]
U.S. writer.

Birnbaum, Milton
Contemporary Jew.

Birnbaum, Nathan [1864–1937]
U.S. journalist, political philosopher.

Bishop, Joey [1918–]
U.S. comedian.

Bismarck, Otto von [1815–1898]
Unifier of the German Empire (1871–1890).

Bisna (Rabbi)
Talmudic scholar.

Blackmun, Harry A. [1908–]
Retired (1994) U.S. Supreme Court justice.

Blaine, James G. [1830–1893]
U.S. statesman.

Blake, William [1757–1827]
British poet.

Blankfort, Michael [1907–]
U.S. author, playwright.

Blaustein, Jacob [1892–1970]
U.S. industrialist, community leader.

Bleich, J. David [1936–]
U.S. rabbi, attorney, author.

Blitzer, Wolf
Senior CNN White House correspondent
(1990s).

Bloch, Ernst [1880–1959]
Swiss-American composer.

Bloom, Harold [1930–]
Humanities professor, author.

Bloomberg, Michael
Contemporary Jew.

Blum, Léon [1872–1949]
French socialist, statesman.

Bohn, William E.
Former editor of *The New Leader*.

Bokser, Ben Zion [1907–1983]
U.S. rabbi, scholar, author.

Bonaparte, Napoleon
See Napoléon Bonaparte.

Bono, Sonny [1935–]
Former entertainer, U.S. congressman from
California.

Bookbinder, Hyman (Harry) [1916–]
U.S. community leader.

Boorstin, Daniel J. [1914–]
U.S. librarian, historian, author.

Borge, Victor [1909–]
Danish-born entertainer, comedian, pianist.

Börne, Ludwig [1786–1837]
German journalist, essayist.

Borochov, Ber
  Twentieth-century writer.

Borowitz, Eugene [1924–]
  U.S. rabbi, theologian.

Botstein, Leon
  President of Bard College (1990s),
  musician.

Bottome, Phyllis [1884–]
  British novelist.

Boxer, Barbara [1940–]
  U.S. senator from California (1990s).

Bracker, Milton
  Contemporary journalist.

Brandeis, Louis D. [1856–1941]
  U.S. Supreme Court justice (1916–1939).

Brando, Marlon [1924–]
  U.S. actor.

Brazauskas, Algirdas
  President of Lithuania (1990s).

Breindel, Eric [1955–]
  U.S. editor, columnist, educator.

Brenner, David [1945–]
  U.S. comedian, author, television producer.

Breslin, Jimmy [1930–]
  U.S. newspaper columnist, author.

Breuer, Issac [1883–1946]
  German rabbi.

Breyer, Stephen G. [1938–]
  U.S. Supreme Court justice.

Brice, Fanny [1891–1951]
  U.S. comedienne, singer.

Brickner, Balfour [1926–]
  U.S. rabbi, social activist.

Bright, John [1811–1889]
  British statesman, economist.

Brin, Herb
  Contemporary U.S. Jewish newspaper
  publisher, writer.

Brin, Ruth F.
  Contemporary U.S. poet.

Brisbane, Arthur
  Contemporary U.S. journalist.

Brod, Max [1884–1968]
  Czech-born author, composer.

Brodsky, Joseph A. [1940–1996]
  Poet, Nobel Prize winner for literature
  (1987).

Broder, David [1929–]
  Journalist, political commentator.

Bronfman, Edgar B. [1929–]
  President of World Jewish Congress,
  industrialist.

Bronowski, Jacob [1908–]
  British mathematician, philosopher, writer.

Brooks, Mel [1926–]
  U.S. motion picture producer, director,
  writer, actor.

Brovender, Chaim
  Contemporary Israeli educator.

Brown, Cecil
  Contemporary U.S. writer.

Brown, Robert McAfee
  Contemporary Protestant clergyman,
  professor.

Browning, Robert [1812–1889]
  British poet.

Bruce, Lenny [1925–1966]
  U.S. comedian, satirist.

Buber, Martin [1878–1965]
  German theologian, author.

Buchanan, Patrick Joseph [1938–]
  U.S. journalist, political commentator,
  politician.

Buchwald, Art [1925–]
  U.S. humorist, columnist.

Buck, Pearl [1892–1973]
  U.S. novelist.

Bullock, Roy
  Jewish activist (1990s).

Bunam, Simcha (of Przysucha)
  Chasidic rabbi.

Burg, Avraham
  Head of the Jewish Agency (1995).

Burg, Joseph [1909–]
  Israeli political leader.

Burkhardt, Walter
  Contemporary writer.

Burns, George [1896–1996]
  U.S. comedian, actor, author.

Bush, George [1924–]
  Forty-first U.S. president (1989–1993).

Butcher, Samuel Henry [1850–1910]
  British author.

Buttons, Red [1919–]
  U.S. comedian, actor.

Byron, George Noel Gordon (Lord)
  [1788–1824]
  British poet.

Cadman, S. Parkes [1864–1936]
Founder of the National Conference of
Christians and Jews.

Caesar, Julius [c.100–44 B.C.E.]
Roman general, statesman.

Caesar, Sid [1922–]
U.S. comedian.

Cahan, Abraham [1860–1951]
American Yiddish journalist.

Cahn, Sammy [1913–1993]
U.S. songwriter.

Cain
Eldest son of Adam and Eve.

Calisch, Edward N.
Contemporary British writer.

Cantoni, Raphael
Contemporary writer.

Cantor, Eddie [1892–1964]
U.S. comedian, actor.

Cardin, Nina Beth
Contemporary U.S. rabbi.

Cardozo, Benjamin Nathan [1870–1938]
U.S. Supreme Court justice (1932–1938).

Carlebach, Shlomo [1926–1994]
U.S. rabbi, folksinger.

Carlos, Juan
King of Spain (1975–)

Carmel, Abraham Isaac
Contemporary clergyman.

Caro, Joseph [1488–1575]
Codifer of Jewish law.

Carter, Jimmy [1924–]
Thirty-ninth U.S. president (1977–1981).

Carter, Stephen L.
Contemporary author.

Caspi, Joseph ibn
See Ibn Caspi, Joseph.

Cassuto, David
Architect, urban planner, Jerusalem city
councilman (1990s).

Cassuto, Umberto [1883–1951]
Italian Bible scholar.

Celler, Emanuel [1888–1981]
U.S. congressman from New York
(1923–1972).

Chafetz Chaim
See Kagan, Israel Meir.

Chafetz, Ze'ev
U.S.-born Israeli columnist, director of the
Government Press Office under Menachem
Begin.

Chagall, Marc [1887–1985]
Russian-born artist.

Chama ben Chanina
Third-century talmudic scholar.

Chandler, Walter M.
Early twentieth-century writer.

Chanina
First-century deputy High Priest, scholar.

Chanina ben Dosa
First-century talmudic scholar.

Chanina ben Papa
Third-century talmudic scholar.

Chaplin, Charles (Charlie) [1889–1980]
Motion picture actor, director.

Chavoor, Sherm
Mark Spitz's swimming coach.

Chayim of Zans
Chasidic rabbi.

Chazanov, Gennady
Contemporary rabbi, author.

Chelbo
Fourth-century talmudic scholar.

Cherikover, Eliyohu
Contemporary political writer.

Chernoff, Maxine
Contemporary writer, critic.

Chill, Abraham
Contemporary U.S. rabbi, author.

Chirac, Jacques
President of France (1995–).

Chisda (Hisda)
Third-century talmudic scholar.

Chiya (Hiyya) bar Abba
Third-century talmudic scholar.

Chomsky, Noam [1928–]
U.S. linguist, professor.

Christian X [1870–1947]
King of Denmark (1912–1947).

Christopher, Warren [1925–]
U.S. secretary of state (1992–).

Churba, Joseph
Contemporary political analyst.

Churchill, Winston [1874–1964]
British statesman, author.

Çiller, Tanzu
Prime minister of Turkey (1990s).

Claes, Willy
Belgian minister of foreign affairs (1990s).

Clay, Cassius
See Ali, Muhammed.

Cleveland, Grover [1837–1908]
Twenty-second and twenty-fourth U.S. president.

Clinton, Bill [1946–]
Forty-second U.S. president (1993–).

Clinton, Hillary Rodham [1947–]
U.S. First Lady (1993–).

Cohen, Arthur A. [1928–1986]
U.S. writer, theologian.

Cohen, Eliot A.
Contemporary U.S. editor, author.

Cohen, Gerson D. [1924–1991]
U.S. historian, chancellor of the Jewish Theological Seminary of America (1972–1986).

Cohen, Haim [1911–]
Israeli jurist.

Cohen, Henry [1863–1952]
U.S. rabbi, civic leader.

Cohen, Hermann [1842–1918]
German philosopher.

Cohen, Jack J.
Contemporary Reconstructionist rabbi, author.

Cohen, Jonathan, of Lunel
Thirteenth-century French scholar.

Cohen, Morris Raphael [1880–1947]
U.S. philosopher, professor.

Cohen, Pamela
Contemporary Russian scholar.

Cohen, Rina A.
Member of the Zionist Forum (1994), an advocacy group for Russian immigrants.

Cohen, Seymour
Contemporary U.S. rabbi, author.

Cohen, Steven M.
Sociologist, Hebrew University professor.

Cohn-Sherbak, Dan
Contemporary British scholar.

Cokely, Steve
Aide to Chicago mayor Eugene Sawyer (1988).

Coleridge, Samuel Taylor [1772–1834]
British poet.

Columbus, Christopher [1451?–1506]
Italian explorer.

Conrad, Eric
Contemporary British author.

Coolidge, Calvin [1872–1933]
Thirtieth U.S. president (1923–1929).

Copland, Aaron [1900–1990]
U.S. composer.

Cornill, Carl Heinrich [1854–1920]
German Protestant theologian.

Cosell, Howard (1918–1995)
U.S. sportscaster.

Cotler, Irwin
Contemporary Canadian lawyer, professor.

Cousins, Norman [1912–1990]
U.S. journalist, author.

Cowan, Rachel
Contemporary U.S. Reform rabbi.

Cox, Samuel Sullivan
U.S. congressman (1880s), editor, author.

Craig, Gordon A.
Contemporary writer.

Cronbach, Abraham
Contemporary U.S. rabbi.

Cronkite, Walter [1916–]
U.S. newscaster.

Crossman, Richard [1907–]
British journalist.

Crystal, Billy [1948–]
U.S. comedian, actor.

Csernoch, John Cardinal [1852–1927]
Primate of Hungary.

Curley, Michael J. [1879–]
Archbishop of Baltimore.

Czerniakow, Adam [?–1942]
Warsaw Jewry diarist.

Dalai Lama [1935–]
Traditional High Priest of Lamaism.

Daly, Thomas
Bishop of the Diocese of Brooklyn, New York (1994).

D'Amato, Alfonse [1937–]
U.S. senator from New York (1980s–1990s).

Dan, Uri
Military correspondent for *Maariv* (1970s).

Danforth, John
U.S. senator from Missouri (1980s–1990s).

D'Annunzio, Gabriele [1863–1938]
Italian poet, novelist, dramatist.

Dante [1265–1321]
   Né Durante Alghieri.
   Italian poet.

Danzig, Abraham [1748–1820]
   Rabbinic scholar.

Darwish, Mahmoud
   Poet laureate of the Palestine Liberation
   Organization.

David
   King of Israel, ruled c. 1000–960 B.C.E.

Davidson, Israel [1870–1939]
   U.S. poet, scholar, author.

Davidson, Jo [1883–1952]
   U.S. sculptor.

Davis, Sammy, Jr. [1925–1990]
   U.S. entertainer, author.

Dawidowicz, Lucy [1915–]
   U.S. historian, author.

Day, Clarence [1874–1935]
   U.S. author.

Dayan, Moshe [1915–1981]
   Israeli politician, military leader.

Dayan, Yael [1939–]
   Israeli author, political activist, member
   of Knesset.

D'Azeglio, Massimo [1798–1866]
   Italian statesman.

Dechter, Moshe
   Contemporary U.S. journalist.

De Gaulle, Charles [1890–1970]
   President of France (1959–1969).

De Haas, Jacob [1872–1937]
   U.S. journalist.

De Hirsch, Maurice
   Nineteenth-century writer.

De Jong, Louis
   Contemporary Dutch historian, Holocaust survivor.

Della Femina, Jerry
   New York City restaurateur (1990s).

Del Medigo, Joseph [1591–1655]
   Rabbi, philosopher, author.

DeMille, Cecil B. [1881–1959]
   U.S. motion picture director, producer.

Dershowitz, Alan M. [1938–]
   U.S. professor, attorney.

D'Estaing, Giscard [1926–]
   President of France (1980s–1990s).

Deutsch, Gotthard [1859–1921]
   U.S. historian.

Deutsch, Israel

Early nineteenth-century German rabbi.

Deutscher, Isaac [1907–1967]
   Marxist historian, political scientist.

Diamond, Eliezer
   Contemporary U.S. professor of rabbinics.

Dickens, Charles [1812–1870]
   British novelist.

Dickstein, Morris
   Contemporary U.S. scholar, educator.

Dimi
   Fourth-century talmudic scholar.

Dimont, Max
   Contemporary U.S. author, historian.

Dine, Thomas
   Fundraiser, former executive director of the
   American–Israel Public Affairs Committee
   (AIPAC).

Dinitz, Simcha [1928–]
   Israeli politician, former head of the Jewish
   Agency.

Disraeli, Benjamin [1804–1881]
   British prime minister, novelist.

Dixon, Roland B. [1875–1934]
   U.S. anthropologist.

Dole, Robert (Bob) [1923–]
   U.S. senator from Kansas (1969–1996).

Doubleday, Nelson
   Co-owner of the New York Mets baseball
   team.

Douglas, Kirk [1916–]
   U.S. actor.

Dov Ber of Mezeritch [c. 1710–1772]
   Chasidic leader.

Dow, Lorenzo
   Nineteenth-century author.

Downes, Olin
   Twentieth-century U.S. musicologist.

Drescher, Fran [1958–]
   U.S. actress, comedienne.

Driver, Samuel R. [1846–1914]
   Bible scholar, Hebraist.

Drysdale, Don [1936–]
   U.S. baseball player.

Dubnow, Simon M. [1860–1941]
   Russian historian.

Dubois, Marcel
   Contemporary Dominican monk, professor.

Duker, Abraham G. [1907–1987]
   U.S. educator, historian.

Dulles, John Foster [1888–1959]
   U.S. secretary of state under President
   Dwight D. Eisenhower.

Duran, Profiat [?–1414]
Also known as Efod.
Spanish grammarian, philosopher.

Dworkin, Andrea [1946–]
U.S. feminist critic.

Dylan, Bob [1941–]
Né Robert Zimmerman.
U.S. musician, composer, entertainer.

Eban, Abba (Aubrey) [1915–]
Israeli diplomat, author.

Eckardt, A. Roy
Contemporary Protestant theologian,
author.

Eden, Anthony [1897–1977]
British political leader.

Edmonds, Henry Morris [1878–]
Protestant clergyman.

Edwards, Jonathan [1703–1758]
U.S. theologian.

Eichhorn, D. Max [1906–1987]
U.S. rabbi, author.

Eichmann, Adolf (Adolph) [1906–1962]
Nazi officer executed in Israel.

Eichmann, Ricardo
Professor of archaeology; son of Adolf.

Einhorn, David [1809–1879]
German-born U.S. rabbi.

Einstein, Albert [1879–1955]
German-born U.S. scientist.

Einstein, Judah David [1854–1956]
U.S. encyclopedist, anthologist, author.

Eisendrath, Maurice N. [1902–1973]
U.S. Reform rabbi.

Eisenhower, Dwight David [1890–1969]
Thirty-fourth U.S. president.

Eisenstein, Ira [1906–]
U.S. rabbi, author, educator, lecturer.

Eitan, Rafael
Israeli army general (1980s).

Eiver, William Norman
Contemporary author.

Eizenstat, Stuart E. [1943–]
Attorney, U.S. presidential advisor.

Elazar, Daniel J. [1934–]
U.S. political science professor.

Eldar, Akiva
Contemporary writer.

Eleazar
Second-century talmudic scholar.

Eleazar (Elazar) ben Arach
First-century talmudic scholar; pupil of
Yochanan ben Zakkai.

Eleazar ben Azariah [70–135]
President of the Sanhedrin after Gamaliel II
was deposed.

Eleazar ben Pedat
Third-century talmudic scholar.

Eleazar ben Shammua
Second-century talmudic scholar.

Eleazar ben Yair
Zealot leader at Masada (73 C.E.).

Eleazar Ha-kappar
Third-century talmudic scholar.

Eleazar of Modin (Modi'in)
First/second-century talmudic scholar.

Eliach, Yaffa
Contemporary U.S. professor, author.

Eliahu, Mordechai
Contemporary Orthodox rabbi.

Eliav, Arie Lova
Contemporary author.

Eliezer
Fifth-century talmudic scholar.

Eliezer ben Yaakov
First-century talmudic scholar; pupil of
Rabbi Akiba.

Elijah
Ninth-century B.C.E. prophet of Israel.

Elijah ben Solomon (Zalman) [1720–1797]
Also known as The Vilna Gaon.
Lithuanian-born spiritual leader, talmudist.

Eliot, Charles William [1834–1924]
U.S. chemist, educator.

Eliot, George (Marian Evans Cross)
[1819–1880]
British novelist, poet.

Elisha ben Avuya (Abuya)
Second-century talmudic scholar.

Ellis, Havelock [1859–1939]
British novelist, social reformer.

Ellis, Marc
Contemporary scholar at the Center for the
Study of World Religions, Harvard
University.

Elon, Amos
Contemporary Israeli writer, activist.

Elon, Menachem
Chief Justice of the Israeli Supreme Court
(1987).

Elon, Motti
Rabbi, educator; son of Menachem Elon.

Emden, Jacob [1697–1776]
German talmudist.

Emerson, Ralph Waldo [1803–1882]
U.S. poet.

Engel, Eliot
U.S. congressman from New York (1993).

Engels, Friedrich [1820–1895]
German socialist.

Ephraim, Moshe Chaim [c. 1737–c. 1800]
Also known as Moses of Sadilkov.
Chasidic leader.

Ephron the Hittite
Contemporary of the patriarch Abraham.

Epstein, Benjamin
Contemporary U.S. author.

Epstein, Yechiel Michal
Seventeenth-century scholar.

Erasmus, Desiderius [1465–1536]
Dutch philosopher, humanist.

Erskine, John [1879–1951]
U.S. educator, author.

Esau
Elder twin-brother of Jacob; son of Isaac
and Rebecca.

Eshkol, Levi [1895–1969]
Third Israeli prime minister (1963–1969).

Étienne, Rabaud Saint
Eighteenth-century French statesman.

Eugenius IV [1383–1447]
Pope.

Evans, Eli N.
Contemporary U.S. historian, author.

Eve
Biblical character; wife of Adam.

Evers-Williams, Myrlie
Widow of Medgar Evers; head of NAACP
(1995–).

Evron, Yair
Contemporary Israeli scholar, author.

Eybeshitz (Eybeschuetz), Jonathan
[1690–1764]
German rabbi, scholar.

Eytan, Walter [1910–]
Israeli diplomat.

Eytinge, Rose
Nineteenth-century actress, author.

Ezekiel
Sixth-century B.C.E. prophet of Israel.

Fackenheim, Emil L. [1916–]
Contemporary U.S. rabbi, theologian.

Fadiman, Clifton [1904–]
U.S. literary critic.

Fagen, Lewis
One of the Jews saved by Oskar Schindler.

Falwell, Jerry [1933–]
U.S. clergyman, founder of the Moral
Majority.

Farjoun, Moishe
Contemporary Israeli tourist guide.

Farrakhan, Louis [1933–]
Leader of the Nation of Islam.

Faud (King) [1922–]
Monarch of Saudi Arabia (1980s–1990s).

Feierberg, Mordecai Ze'ev [1874–1899]
Hebrew novelist.

Feiffer, Jules [1929–]
U.S. cartoonist.

Fein, Leonard [1934–]
U.S. writer, editor, educator.

Feingold, Henry L. [1931–]
U.S. historian, author.

Feinstein, Dianne [1933–]
U.S. senator from California (1990s).

Feinstein, Moshe (Moses) [1895–1986]
U.S. rabbi, educator, author.

Feisal (Emir) [1885–1933]
King of Iraq.

Feld, Avraham
Director of Mossad Maccabee in Jerusalem
(1990s).

Feld, Edward
Rabbi of the Society for the Advancement
of Judaism (1990s).

Feldman, David
Contemporary U.S. rabbi, author.

Feldshuh, Tovah [1952–]
U.S. actress.

Ferber, Edna [1887–1968]
U.S. novelist.

Ferdinand and Isabella
Fifteenth-century Spanish rulers.

Ferguson, Max
Contemporary U.S. artist.

Feuchtwanger, Lion [1884–1958]
German novelist, theater critic.

Fichte, Johann [1762–1814]
German philosopher.

Field, Ben
Twentieth-century Anglo-Jewish writer.

Fields, Totie [1931–1978]
U.S. comedienne.

Fineman, Irving
Contemporary U.S novelist.

Finkel, Fyvush
Contemporary U.S. actor.

Finkelman, Louis
Hillel director at Wayne State University.

Finkelstein, Louis [1895–1991]
U.S. rabbi, scholar, author, educator.

Fisher, David "Dudu"
Contemporary Israeli singer, actor.

Fisher, Eddie [1928–]
U.S. singer, actor.

Fisher, Eugene
Director of Catholic–Jewish relations for
the National Council of Catholic Bishops
(1990s).

Fisher, Max M. [1908–]
U.S. industrialist, Republican party
fundraiser.

Flannery, Edward H.
Head of the National Conference of
Catholic Bishops.

Fleg, Edmond [1874–1963]
French poet, playwright.

Flexner, Abraham [1866–1959]
U.S. writer, educator.

Flusser, David [1917–]
Professor at Hebrew University, scholar in
comparative religion.

Foch, Ferdinand [1851–1929]
French World War I general.

Folkman, Jerome D.
Contemporary U.S. Reform rabbi,
psychologist.

Ford, Gerald R. [1913–]
Thirty-eighth U.S. president.

Ford, Henry [1863–1947]
U.S. automobile manufacturer.

Ford, Henry II [1917–]
U.S. automobile manufacturer; son of
Henry Ford.

Fosdick, Harry Emerson [1878–]
Protestant clergyman, author.

Fox, Marvin
Contemporary U.S. rabbi, scholar.

Foxman, Abraham H.
Executive director of the Anti-Defamation
League of Bnai Brith (1990s).

France, Anatole [1884–1924]
French novelist.

Frank, Anne [1929–1945]
Holocaust victim, diarist.

Frank, Barney [1940–]
U.S. congressman from Massachusetts
(1990s).

Frank, Hans
Nazi commander in Posen (Poznan) in
1943.

Frankel, Ellen [1938–]
U.S. magazine editor.

Frankel, Zechariah [1801–1875]
German theologian, rabbi.

Frankfurter, Felix [1882–1965]
U.S. Supreme Court justice (1939–1962).

Frankl, Victor E. [1905–]
Austrian psychiatrist, author.

Franklin, Benjamin [1706–1790]
U.S. scientist, inventor, writer.

Franzos, Karl Emil [1848–1904]
Austrian novelist.

Frederick of Baden [1826–1907]
German statesman.

Fredrickson, George M. [1934–]
U.S. historian, editor.

Freedman, Max
Contemporary U.S. editor.

Freehof, Solomon B. [1892–1990]
U.S. rabbi, scholar, author.

Frej, Eliyah
Contemporary Israeli Arab.

Frémont, Abbé [1852–1912]
French cleric.

Freud, Sigmund [1856–1939]
Austrian-born originator of psychoanalysis.

Friedan, Betty Naomi [1921–]
U.S. feminist leader, author.

Friedberg, Maurice [1929–]
U.S. professor, historian.

Friedenwald, Harry [1864–1950]
U.S. ophthamologist.

Friedlaender, Israel [1877–1922]
U.S. Orientalist.

Friedlander, Michael [1833–1910]
British scholar.

Friedman, Lee M. [1871–1957]
U.S. attorney, historian.

Friedman, Milton [1912–]
U.S. economist.

Friedman, Pauline
See Van Buren, Abigail.

Friedman, Thomas L.
Contemporary U.S. journalist.

Friedmann, Pavel
Czech poet.

Frishman, David [1865–1922]
Hebrew author.

Fromm, Erich [1900–1980]
U.S. psychologist, author.

Gatni, Moshe
United Torah Judaism Knesset member
(1990s).

Galiber, Joseph
New York State senator (1994).

Gallico, Paul [1897–]
U.S. journalist, author.

Galsworthy, John [1867–1933]
British author.

Gandhi, Mohandas K. [1869–1948]
Hindu nationalist leader.

Gardner, Hy [1904–]
U.S. journalist.

Gaster, Moses G. [1856–1939]
U.S. rabbi, scholar.

Gaster, Theodor H. [1906–1922]
U.S. folklorist.

Gay, Peter
Contemporary U.S. author, historian.

Geiger, Abraham [1810–1874]
German rabbi, scholar, religious reformer.

Gellman, Marc
Contemporary U.S. writer.

Genovese, Eugene [1930–]
U.S. historian.

George, Henry [1839–1897]
U.S. political economist.

Gephardt, Richard [1941–]
U.S. congressman from Missouri (1990s).

Gerer Rebbe
Polish chasidic leader, author.

Gersonides [1288–1344]
Also known as Levi ben Gershom.
French-born philosopher, Bible scholar.

Gertel, Elliot
Contemporary U.S. rabbi, writer.

Gerville, Bon Claude [1752–1796]
French statesman.

Getty, Estelle [1924–]
U.S. actress.

Gide, André [1869–1951]
French writer, critic.

Gies, Miep
Contemporary author.

Gilman, Neil
Contemporary U.S. rabbi, theologian.

Gingrich, Newt [1943–]
Speaker of the U.S. House of
Representatives (1990s).

Ginsberg, Allen [1926–]
U.S. poet, activist.

Ginsberg, Asher Hirsch
See Ahad Ha-am.

Ginsburg, Martin D.
Husband of Ruth Bader Ginsburg.

Ginsburg, Ruth Bader [1933–]
U.S. Supreme Court justice (1990s).

Ginzberg, Louis [1873–1953]
U.S. talmudic scholar, professor.

Ginzburg, Natalia Levi [1916–1991]
Italian novelist, playwright.

Giuliani, Rudolph [1944–]
Mayor of New York City (1994–).

Gladden, Washington [1836–1918]
U.S. Congregationalist clergyman, author.

Glaser, Joseph B. [1925–1994]
Contemporary U.S. rabbi.

Glatstein, Jacob [1896–1971]
Yiddish author, critic.

Glückel of Hameln [1645–1724]
Yiddish author.

Goebbels, Paul Joseph [1897–1945]
Nazi minister of propaganda.

Goering, Hermann (Wilhelm) [1893–1946]
Nazi field marshal.

Goethe, Johann Wolfgang von [1749–1832]
German poet, dramatist.

Goffin, Sherwood
Contemporary U.S. lyricist.

Gold, Herbert [1924–]
U.S. novelist.

Gold, Michael [1893–1967]
U.S. journalist, author.

Goldberg, Arthur J. [1908–1990]
U.S. Supreme Court justice (1962–1965).

Goldberg, Hank
Prosecuting attorney in the 1995 O. J. Simpson murder trial.

Goldberg, J. J.
New York correspondent of *The Jerusalem Report* (1993).

Goldberg, Michael
Contemporary U.S. author, rabbi.

Goldberg, Reuben (Rube) [1883–1970]
U.S. cartoonist.

Goldberg, Whoopi [1955–]
Née Caryn Johnson. U.S. actress, comedienne.

Golden, Harry [1902–1981]
U.S. newspaper publisher, author.

Goldhirsch (Goldhurst) Lieb (1860–1942)
U.S. journalist, Hebrew teacher.

Golding, Louis [1895–1958]
British novelist.

Golding, William [1911–1993]
British author.

Goldman, Abraham
Father of Emma Goldman.

Goldman, Ari
Contemporary U.S. journalist, Columbia University professor (1994).

Goldman, Emma [1869–1940]
Lithuanian-born anarchist, author.

Goldman, Fred
Father of 1994 Los Angeles murder victim Ronald Goldman.

Goldman, Solomon [1893–1953]
U.S. rabbi, scholar, author.

Goldmann, Nahum [1894–1982]
Zionist leader.

Goldstein, Herbert
Contemporary U.S. rabbi.

Goldstein, Israel [1896–1986]
U.S. rabbi, Zionist leader, author.

Goldstein, Jonah J.
New York City Republican judge during World War II.

Goldwater, Barry [1909–]
U.S. senator, Republican presidential candidate (1964).

Goldwyn, Samuel [1882–1974]
U.S. film producer.

Goliath
Biblical character betrayed by Delilah.

Golomb, Abraham [1888–1982]
Yiddish writer.

Golovensky, David
Contemporary U.S. rabbi.

Goodman, Ellen Holtz [1941–]
U.S. syndicated columnist.

Goodman, Hirsh [1935–]
Israeli journalist, editor of *The Jerusalem Report*.

Goodman, Paul [1875–1949]
British communal worker.

Gorbachev, Mikhail [1931–]
Russian politician.

Gordimer, Nadine [1923–]
South African writer.

Gordin, Jacob [1853–1909]
Ukrainian-born playwright, journalist.

Gordis, Robert [1908–1992]
U.S. rabbi, professor, author.

Gordon, Aaron David [1856–1992]
Zionist philosopher.

Gordon, Judah Leib (Löb) [1830–1892]
Hebrew poet.

Gore, Albert, Jr. [1948–]
U.S. vice president (1992–).

Goren, Shlomo [1917–1994]
Chief Rabbi of Israel (1972–1983).

Gorki, Maxim [1868–1936]
Russian novelist, playwright.

Grade, Chaim [1910–1982]
Lithuanian-born Yiddish poet, novelist.

Graetz, Heinrich [1817–1891]
German historian, Bible scholar.

Graham, Billy [1918–]
U.S. evangelical Christian minister.

Granach, Alexander [1890–1945]
German Yiddish actor, novelist.

Grant, Ulysses S. [1822–1885]
Eighteenth U.S. president (1869–1877).

Gratz, Rebecca [1781–1869]
U.S. social welfare activist.

Grayzel, Solomon [1896–1980]
U.S. rabbi, historian.

Greeley, Andrew M.
Director of the Center for the Study of American Pluralism (1970s).

Green, Arthur
Contemporary U.S. rabbi, professor of philosopy.

Green, Hannah [1932–]
Née JoAnne Greenberg. U.S. author, psychologist.

Green, Mrs. J. R.
British writer.

Greenberg, Blu
Contemporary U.S. writer.

Greenberg, Hayim (Chaim) [1889–1953]
Russian-born journalist, Zionist leader.

Greenberg, Henry ("Hank") [1911–1986]
U.S. baseball player.

Greenberg, Irving [1933–]
U.S. rabbi, author, educator.

Greenberg, JoAnne
See Green, Hannah.

Greenberg, Sidney [1917–]
Contemporary U.S. rabbi, author.

Greenberg, Uri Zevi [1894–1981]
Israeli poet, Zionist leader.

Greenebaum, Gary
Contemporary U.S. rabbi.

Gregory VII [c. 1020–1085]
Pope (1073–1085).

Gresham, William Lindsay
Contemporary U.S. author.

Grey, Joel [1932–]
U.S. actor.

Grobman, Alex
Director of the Martyrs' Memorial and
Museum of the Holocaust, Los Angeles.

Grollman, Earl A.
Contemporary U.S. rabbi, author.

Gromyko, Andrei [1909–]
Soviet diplomat.

Grose, Peter
Contemporary U.S. author.

Grossman, David [1954–]
Israeli writer.

Grossman, Richard
Contemporary U.S. author.

Guedalla, Phillip [1889–1944]
British essayist.

Guest, Edgar A. [1881–1959]
U.S. poet.

Gur, Bettya
Contemporary Israeli mystery writer.

Guthman, Sidney
Contemporary U.S. rabbi.

Guttmann, Jakob (Jacob) [1845–1919]
German historian, philosopher.

Habakkuk
Eighth-century B.C.E. minor prophet.

Habibi, Emile
Contemporary Israeli-Arab author.

Hacohen, Gershon
Contemporary Israeli colonel, brigade
commander.

Ha-Cohen, Solomon (Shalom) [1772–1845]
Hebrew poet.

Hai Gaon [939–1038]
Last head of the academy in Pumbedita,
Babylonia.

Halberstam, David [1934–]
Journalist, author.

Halberstam, Devorah [1956–]
Mother of slain yeshiva student.

Halbertal, Moshe
Contemporary U.S. author.

Haldeman, H. R. [1926–1993]
U.S. president Richard Nixon's chief
of staff (1969–1973).

Halevi, Eliezer
Fourteenth-century scholar.

Halevi, Yehuda [1075–1141]
Poet, philosopher.

Halivni, David Weiss
Contemporary U.S. rabbi, professor of
Talmud.

Halkin, Hillel [1939–]
Israeli author, translator.

Hall, Granville Stanley
Nineteenth/twentieth-century writer.

Hall, Monty [1925–]
U.S. television personality.

Halpern, Ben [1912–1990]
U.S. scholar, Zionist leader.

Hameed, Shaul
Contemporary Arab scholar.

Hamizrachi, Yoram
Contemporary Israeli writer, activist.

Hammerslough, Julius
Friend of president and Mrs. Abraham
Lincoln.

Hamnuna
Third-century talmudic scholar.

Hand, Learned [1872–1961]
U.S. jurist.

Hanina
See Chanina.

Hannah
Biblical character, mother of the prophet
Samuel.

Harby, Isaac H. [1788–1828]
U.S. editor, author, playwright.

Harding, Warren Gamaliel [1865–1923]
Twenty-ninth U.S. president (1921–1923).

Harkabi, Yehoshafat
Contemporary Hebrew University
professor.

Harris, Cyril
Contemporary Chief Rabbi of South Africa.

Harris, Maria [1932–]
U.S. author, educator.

Harrison, Leon [1866–1928]
U.S. rabbi.

Hart, Alan
Contemporary U.S. author.

Hart, Jeffrey
Contemporary U.S. author, professor.

Harte, Bret [1836–1902]
U.S. poet, short-story writer.

Hartman, David
Canadian-born contemporary Israeli
author, rabbi.

Hassan, Khalad
Roving ambassador of the Palestine
Liberation Organization (1990s).

Hassan
Crown Prince of Jordan; brother of King
Hussein.

Hauptman, Judith
Contemporary U.S. educator.

Hauser, Rita E. [1934–]
U.S. attorney, feminist leader.

Hausner, Gideon [1915–1990]
Israeli lawyer, prosecutor of Adolf
Eichmann (1961).

Hawn, Goldie [1945–]
U.S. actress.

Hay, John (Milton) [1838–1905]
U.S. statesman.

Hay, Malcolm
Contemporary U.S. author.

Hearst, William Randolph, Jr. [1863–1951]
U.S. publisher.

Hecht, Abraham
Contemporary U.S. Orthodox rabbi.

Hecht, Ben [1894–1964]
U.S. author, playwright, screenwriter.

Hecht, Eli
Contemporary U.S. rabbi.

Heifetz, Jascha [1901–1987]
Lithuanian-born violinist.

Heilman, Samuel
Contemporary U.S. writer.

Heimler, Eugene
Contemporary U.S. author.

Heine, Heinrich [1797–1856]
German poet.

Heller, Joseph [1923–]
U.S. novelist, playwright.

Hellman, Lillian Florence [1906–1984]
U.S. playwright, author.

Hemingway, Ernest [1899–1961]
U.S. novelist.

Henderson, Brian
Contemporary Canadian news
commentator.

Hendricks, Burton
Contemporary author.

Henkin, Louis [1917–]
U.S. attorney, law professor.

Henry, Michael [?–1874]
British writer.

Hentoff, Nat (Nathan Irving) [1925–]
U.S. journalist.

Herberg, Will [1901–1977]
U.S. theologian, social critic.

Herder, Johann Gottfried [1744–1803]
German author.

Herford, Robert Travers [1860–1950]
Scholar, author.

Herman, Agnes G.
Contemporary U.S. writer.

Herman, Jerry [1932–]
U.S. musical theater composer, lyricist.

Hermon, Ruhama
Contemporary member of Israel's Labor
Party, soldier.

Hersey, John [1914–]
U.S. author.

Hersh, Seymour [1937–]
U.S. journalist.

Hershfield, Harry [1885–1974]
U.S. journalist, cartoonist.

Hertz, Joseph H. [1872–1946]
Chief Rabbi of England, scholar, author.

Hertzberg, Arthur [1921–]
U.S. rabbi, scholar, author.

Hertzler, J. O.
Contemporary U.S. sociologist, educator.

Herzl, Theodor [1860–1904]
Viennese journalist, father of political
Zionism.

Herzog, Aura
Wife of Chaim Herzog.

Herzog, Chaim H. [1918–]
Israel's sixth president.

Herzog, Isaac Halevi [1888–1959]
Ashkenazic Chief Rabbi of Israel
(1936–1959).

Heschel, Abraham Joshua [1907–1972]
U.S. rabbi, theologian, author, activist.

Hess, Moses [1812–1875]
German social philosopher, Zionist.

Hevesi, Alan
Comptroller of the City of New York,
elected in 1992.

Hevesi, Ferenc
Nineteenth-century Hungarian professor.

Heydrich, Reinhard [1904–1942]
Nazi leader.

Hezekiah (Rabbi)
Third-century talmudic scholar.

Hier, Marvin
Director of the Simon Wiesenthal Center
(1990s).

Hikind, Dov
New York City councilman (1990s).

Hilberg, Raoul
Contemporary U.S. author.

Hill, Ben
Contemporary radio talk-show host.

Hillel (the Elder)
First-century scholar, founder of an
academy of learning.

Hillel's Disciples
See Hillel (the Elder).

Hillquit, Morris
New York socialist candidate for U.S.
Congress (1908).

Himmelfarb, Gertrude [1922–]
U.S. author.

Himmelfarb, Milton [1918–]
U.S. writer, researcher.

Himmler, Heinrich [1900–1945]
Nazi leader.

Hindenburg, Paul von [1847–1934]
Second president of the Weimar Republic.

Hirsch, Emil G. [1852–1923]
U.S. Reform rabbi.

Hirsch, Richard G.
Contemporary U.S. Reform rabbi.

Hirsch, Samson Raphael [1808–1888]
German rabbi, scholar, author.

Hirsch, Samuel [1815–1889]
German rabbi.

Hisda
See Chisda.

Hitler, Adolf [1889–1945]
Nazi dictator of Germany (1933–1945).

Hiyya
See Chiya.

Hoeckman, Remi
Secretary to the Holy See's Commission for
Religious Relations with Jews (1994).

Hoenlein, Malcolm
Executive director of the Conference of
Major American Jewish Organizations
(1990s).

Hoffer, Eric
Contemporary U.S. longshoreman,
philosopher.

Hoffman, Abbie
Contemporary U.S. political activist.

Hokuzan, Atago
Contemporary Japanese writer.

Holdheim, Samuel [1806–1860]
German rabbi.

Hollings, Ernest F. [1922–]
U.S. senator from South Carolina (1990s).

Holmes, Abiel
Contemporary U.S. author, son-in-law of
Ezra Stiles.

Holmes, John Haynes [1879–1964]
U.S. Protestant theologian, preacher.

Holmes, Oliver Wendell [1809–1894]
U.S. poet, physician.

Holtz, Barry
Contemporary U.S. author.

Hooks, Benjamin [1925–]
Executive director of NAACP (1977–1995).

Hooton, Earnest A. [1887–]
U.S. anthropologist.

Hoover, Herbert [1874–1964]
Thirty-first U.S. president (1929–1933).

Horowitz, Levi Isaac
Also known as the Boston Rebbe.
Contemporary U.S. rabbi.

Hosea
Eighth-century B.C.E. minor prophet.

House, Edward M. [1858–1938]
U.S. diplomat, advisor to President
Woodrow Wilson.

Howard, Oliver Otis [1830–1909]
U.S. Civil War general.

Howe, Irving [1920–1993]
U.S. novelist, educator, editor.

Hughes, Langston [1902–1967]
U.S. poet, writer.

Hull, Cordell [1871–1955]
U.S. statesman, jurist.

Humphrey, Hubert H. [1911–1978]
U.S. senator from Minnesota.

Huna
Third-century talmudic scholar.

Huna ben Yehoshua
Fourth/fifth-century talmudic scholar.

Hurok, Sol [1890–1974]
Music impresario.

Hurst, Fanny [1889–1968]
U.S. novelist, playwright.

Hussein [1935–]
King of Jordan since 1952.

al-Husseini, Faisal
West Bank senior political leader (1990s).

Huxley, Thomas H. [1825–1895]
British poet, writer, biologist.

Hyacinthe, Père [1827–1912]
Founder of the Catholic Church of
Switzerland.

Hyman, Paula
Contemporary U.S. educator, historian.

Ibn Caspi, Joseph (c. 1280–c. 1340)
Philosopher, grammarian.

Ibn Chasdai, Abraham
Thirteenth-century Spanish scholar, author.

Ibn Ezra, Abraham [1089–1164]
Spanish scholar, poet.

Ibn Ezra, Moses [c. 1055–1135]
Spanish Hebrew poet.

Ibn Gabirol, Solomon [c. 1021–c. 1056]
Spanish poet, philosopher.

Ibn Pakuda, Bachya (Bahya) [c. 1050–1120]
Spanish philosopher, author.

Ibn Sina, Alsaid [980–1037]
Also known as Avicenna.
Arab philosopher.

Ibn Tibbon, Judah [c. 1120–c. 1190]
Spanish translator, physician.

Ibn Verga, Solomon
Fifteenth/sixteenth-century Spanish
historiographer.

Ibsen, Henrik [1828–1906]
Norwegian playwright, poet.

Iddi
Third-century talmudic scholar.

Ila'i
Second-century talmudic scholar.

Ilutovich, Leon
Chairman (1993) of the Polish Jewry
Memorial Forest.

Imber, Naftali Herz [1856–1909]
Hebrew poet.

Imber, Samuel Jacob [1889–1942]
Galician-born Yiddish poet.

Inge, William Ralph [1860–1954]
British theologian.

Innocent III [c. 1161–1216]
Pope (1198–1216).

Innocent IV [?–1254]
Pope (1243–1254).

Ionesco, Eugene [1912–]
Rumanian-born French playwright.

Isaac
Biblical patriarch. Son of Abraham and
Sarah; father of Jacob and Esau.

Isaac
Third-century talmudic scholar.

Isaac, Moses
Medieval scholar.

Isaac ben Nappacha
Third-century talmudic scholar.

Isaac Benjacob [1801–1863]
Hebrew author, bibliographer.

Isaacson, Walter
Contemporary U.S. biographer.

Isabella
See Ferdinand and Isabella.

Isaiah
Eighth-century B.C.E. prophet of Israel.

Ishmael ben Elisha
First/second-century talmudic scholar.

Israel, Edward L.
Contemporary U.S. rabbi.

Israel, Richard J.
Contemporary U.S. rabbi.

Israeli, Isaac [c. 855–c. 955]
Egyptian physician, philosopher.

Isserles, Moses [1525–1572]
Polish rabbi, talmudist, philosopher.

Jabotinsky, Vladimir [1880–1940]
Russian novelist, Zionist leader.

Jackson, Henry "Scoop" [1912–1983]
U.S. senator from Washington State; author of the Jackson–Vanik amendment.

Jackson, Jesse [1941–]
U.S. black leader, politician.

Jackson, Michael [1958–]
Contemporary U.S. singer.

Jacob
Biblical patriarch. Son of Isaac and Rebecca; brother of Esau.

Jacob, Benno [1862–1945]
German Bible exegete.

Jacobs, Joe [1896–1940]
U.S. boxing manager.

Jacobs, Joseph [1854–1916]
Australian-born historian, folklorist.

Jacobs, Louis [1920–]
British rabbi, scholar, author.

Jacobson, Edward (Eddie)
U.S. president Harry Truman's business partner.

Jakobovits, Immanuel (Lord) [1921–]
Former Chief Rabbi of the British Commonwealth.

Javits, Jacob K. [1904–1986]
U.S. senator from New York.

Jefferson, Thomas [1743–1826]
Third U.S. president (1801–1809).

Jellinek, Adolph [c. 1821–1893]
German rabbi, scholar.

Jeremiah
Sixth-century B.C.E. prophet of Israel.

Jessel, George A. [1898–1981]
U.S. entertainer, toastmaster, author.

Jesselson, Erica
Wife of U.S. philanthropist Ludwig Jesselson.

Jibril, Ahmed
Leader of the Popular Front for the Liberation of Palestine (1993).

Jiddah, Ali
Palestinian journalist and political activist (1980s–1990s).

Job
Biblical character.

Joel, Richard M.
International director of B'nai B'rith Hillel Foundation (1990s).

Johanan
See Yochanan.

John I of Castille
Fifteenth-century Spanish ruler.

John XXIII [1881–1963]
Pope (1958–1963). Force behind Vatican II.

John Paul II [1920–]
Pope, consecrated in 1978.

Johnson, Lyndon B. [1908–1973]
Thirty-sixth U.S. president (1963–1969).

Johnson, Paul
Contemporary U.S. historian, author.

Johnson, Richard Mentor [1781–1850]
Ninth U.S. vice-president.

Jolson, Al [1886–1950]
U.S. entertainer, actor.

Jonathan ben Joseph (Jose)
Second-century talmudic scholar.

Jones, Leroi [1934–]
Also known as Imamu Amiri Baraka. U.S. poet, playwright.

Jong, Erica [1942–]
U.S. author.

Jose (Rabbi) [471–520]
Talmudic scholar.

Josef, Czarny
Witness at the Jerusalem trial of John Demjanjuk (1990s).

Joseph (Rabbi)
Third/fourth-century talmudic scholar.

Joseph, Jacob
Chief Rabbi of New York City (1880s).

Joseph, Morris [1848–1930]
British Reform rabbi, theologian.

Josephus, Flavius [c. 37–c. 95 C.E.]
Historian.

Joshua
Successor to the biblical Moses.

Joshua ben Chananya [c. 50–130]
Talmudic scholar.

Joshua ben Karcha (Korcha)
Second-century talmudic scholar.

Joshua ben Levi
Third-century talmudic scholar.

Josiah
Second-century talmudic scholar.

Jossy (Dr.)
Contemporary Israeli medical doctor.

Joyce, James [1892–1941]
Irish novelist.

Judah
Biblical character; fourth son of Jacob and Leah.

Judah bar Ila'i
Second-century talmudic scholar.

Judah ben Tema
Third-century talmudic scholar.

Judah Loew of Prague
See Loew, Judah.

Judah the Prince [c. 135–c. 219]
Also known as Yehuda Ha-nasi.
Palestinian patriarch, talmudic scholar.

Jung, Leo [1876–1949]
U.S. rabbi, author.

Kaddoumi, Farouk
Yasser Arafat's "foreign minister" (1994).

Kael, Pauline [1919–]
U.S. writer, critic.

Kafka, Franz [1883–1924]
Czech author.

Kagan, Israel Meir [1835–1933]
Also known as the Chafetz Chaim.
Polish rabbi, scholar.

Kahane, Meir [1932–1991]
U.S.-born rabbi, political activist.

Kahn, Madeline [1942–]
U.S. actress, comedienne.

Kalb, Bernard [1922–]
Contemporary U.S. journalist, professor.

Kalmanson, Carmela Efros
Hadassah president (early 1990s).

Kalonymos ben (bar) Kalonymos
[1286–1328]
French philosopher, author, translator.

Kalonymos ben Yehuda
Nephew of the Baal Shem Tov.

Kant, Immanuel [1724–1804]
German philosopher.

Kaplan, Aryeh
Contemporary U.S. rabbi, author.

Kaplan, Chaim
Warsaw Ghetto uprising victim, diarist.

Kaplan, Deborah B.
Hadassah president (early 1990s).

Kaplan, Louis [1905–]
U.S. educator.

Kaplan, Mordecai M. [1881–1983]
U.S. rabbi, Reconstructionist movement founder.

Karas, Attar Abu
Leader of the Fatah's Intifada Committee in Gaza (1990s).

Kasher, Menachem M. [1895–1983]
Polish-born Israeli author, scholar.

Katsch, Abraham Isaac [1908–]
U.S. educator, author.

Katz, Shmuel
Contemporary political commentator, historian.

Katznelson, Berl [1887–1944]
Zionist labor leader.

Kaufmann, David [1852–1899]
Austrian scholar.

Kaufmann, Walter [1921–]
U.S. humanistic philosopher.

Kaufmann, Yehezkel [1889–1963]
Ukrainian-born Israeli Bible scholar, philosopher.

Kazin, Alfred [1915–]
U.S. author, book reviewer, editor.

Kelman, Wolfe [1923–1990]
Contemporary U.S. rabbi, Rabbinical Assembly vice-president.

Kemal, Attaturk [1881–1938]
Also known as Mustofa Kemal.
First president of Turkey.

Kemp, Jack [1935–]
U.S. athlete, politician.

Keneally, Thomas
Contemporary U.S. writer.

Kennedy, John F. [1917–1963]
Thirty-fifth U.S. president (1961–1963).

Kennedy, Robert F. [1925–1968]
U.S. senator from New York; brother of John F. Kennedy.

Kerler, Joseph
Contemporary Soviet poet.

Kern, Jerome [1885–1945]
U.S. musician, composer.

Kertzer, Morris N.
Contemporary U.S. rabbi, author.

Keyes, Alan L. [1950–]
Contemporary black diplomat, politician.

Khrushchev, Nikita S. [1895–1971]
Premier of the Soviet Union (1958–1964).

al-Kidiva, Nasser
Palestine Liberation Organization representative to the United Nations (1994).

Kinderlehrer, Jane
Contemporary U.S. cookbook author, nutritionist.

King, Alan [1924–]
U.S. comedian, actor.

King, Coretta Scott [1927–]
Wife of Martin Luther King, Jr.

King, Larry [1933–]
Talk-show host, columnist.

King, Martin Luther, Jr. [1929–1968]
Clergyman, black civil rights leader.

Kingsley, Ben [1943–]
British actor.

Kipling, Rudyard [1865–1936]
British writer.

Kishon, Ephraim [1924–]
Hungarian-born Israeli satirist.

Kissinger, Henry [1923–]
German-born professor, author, U.S. secretary of state.

Kittel, Rudolph [1853–1929]
German Protestant theologian, Bible scholar.

Klagsbrun, Francine
Contemporary U.S. author, social activist.

Klausner, Joseph [1874–1958]
Lithuanian-born critic, historian.

Kleger, Noah [1928–]
Auschwitz survivor living in France.

Klein, Morton
President of the Zionist Organization of America (1995).

Klein, Robert [1942–]
U.S comedian, actor.

Klutznick, Philip M. [1907–]
U.S. government official.

Knopf, Alfred A. [1892–1984]
U.S. book publisher.

Koch, Edward I. [1924–]
U.S. politician, radio talk-show host, author.

Koestler, Arthur [1905–1983]
British author.

Kohl, Helmut [1930–]
West German chancellor (1980s).

Kohler, Kaufmann [1843–1926]
Bavarian-born U.S. rabbi, leader of Reform Judaism.

Kohn, Moshe
Contemporary Israeli writer.

Kolitz, Yitzchak
Contemporary Chief Rabbi of Jerusalem.

Kolitz, Zvi
Contemporary U.S. writer.

Kollek, Teddy (Theodor) [1911–]
Mayor of Jerusalem (1965–1993).

Konvitz, Milton R. [1908–]
Israeli-born U.S. legal scholar, professor.

Kook, Abraham Isaac [1865–1935]
Ashkenazic Chief Rabbi of Palestine after 1919; founder of Yeshiva Mercaz Ha-rav.

Kook, Hillel
Also known as Peter Bergson. Contemporary Israeli writer, Irgun leader (late 1940s).

Kook, Zvi Judah [1891–1982]
Yeshiva head; successor to his father, Abraham Isaac Kook.

Koppel, Ted [1940–]
U.S. broadcast journalist.

Korb, Lawrence J.
U.S. Department of Defense official (1980s).

Korn, Richard
President of the American Council for Judaism (1960s).

Kosinski, Jerzy (Nikodem) [1933–1991]
Polish-born author.

Kotzker Rebbe
See Menachem Mendel of Kotzk.

Koufax, Sanford (Sandy) [1935–]
U.S. baseball pitcher.

Kozinsky, Alex
Contemporary U.S. writer.

Kraemer, David
Contemporary U.S. writer.

Kristol, Irving [1920–]
U.S. writer, editor.

Krochmal, Nachman [1785–1840]
Galician philosopher, historian.

Krock, Arthur [1886–1974]
U.S. editor, political commentator.

Kumin, Maxine [1925–]
U.S. poet, author.

Kunitz, Stanley [1905–]
U.S. poet, educator.

Kunstler, William [1919–1995]
U.S. attorney.

Kurzweil, Zvi
Contemporary author, editor.

Kushner, Harold [1935–]
U.S. rabbi, author.

Kuyper, Abraham [1837–1920]
Dutch statesman, Calvinist theologian.

LaGuardia, Fiorello H. [1882–1947]
Mayor of New York City (1934–1945).

Lahr, Bert [1895–1967]
U.S. comedian.

Lamm, Maurice
Contemporary U.S. rabbi, author.

Lamm, Norman [1927–]
U.S. rabbi; president of Yeshiva University
since 1976.

Landau, Ezekiel [1713–1793]
Rabbi of Prague, scholar, author.

Landers, Ann [1918–]
U.S. newspaper columnist.

Lang, Pearl [1922–]
U.S. dancer, choreographer.

Lange, Ivar
Contemporary Protestant clergyman.

Lansky, Meyer [1902–1983]
U.S. underworld figure.

Lantos, Tom (Thomas Peter) [1928–]
U.S. congressman from California (1990s).

Lanzmann, Claude [1925–]
Director of the documentary film *Shoah*.

Lapierre, Dominique
Contemporary French author.

Lapino, Daniel
Contemporary U.S. political activist, rabbi.

Laqueur, Walter [1921–]
German-born U.S. historian.

Laski, Harold J. [1893–1950]
British Fabian socialist, professor.

Lau, Yisrael Meir
Ashkenazic Chief Rabbi of Israel (1990s).

Lauder, Ronald S.
Contemporary U.S. businessman,
community leader.

Lawrence, Thomas Edward [1888–1935]
Also known as Lawrence of Arabia.
British adventurer, writer.

Lazare, Bernard [1865–1903]
French author.

Lazaron, Morris S. [1888–]
U.S. Reform rabbi.

Lazarus, Emma [1849–1887]
U.S. poet.

Lazarus, Josephine [1846– ?]
Sister of Emma Lazarus.

Lazarus, Moritz [1824–1903]
German philosopher, psychologist.

Lear, Norman [1922–]
U.S. television producer.

Learsi, Rufus (Israel Goldberg) [1887– ?]
"Learsi" is Israel spelled backward.
U.S. author.

Leboucher, Fernande
Contemporary French author.

Lebovich, Maya [1947–]
Israeli-born Reform rabbi, ordained in 1993.

Lebowitz, Fran [1951–]
U.S. author.

Lecky, William [1838–1903]
Irish historian.

Lee, Michelle [1942–]
U.S. actress.

Leeser, Isaac [1806–1868]
U.S. rabbi.

Leftwich, Joseph [1892–1983]
British author.

Lehman, Herbert H. [1878–1963]
U.S. senator from New York (1949–1957).

Leibowitz, Nechama [1905–]
Israeli Bible scholar, author.

Leibowitz, Yeshayahu [1903–1994]
Israeli professor, biochemist.

Lenin, Vladimir Ilyich [1870–1924]
Russian leader of the 1917 Communist
revolution; Soviet premier (1917–1924).

Leonard, Jack E. [1911–1973]
U.S. comedian.

Lerner, Max [1902–1992]
U.S. journalist, author, political scientist.

Lerner, Michael [1943–]
Environmental educator, author.

Leroy-Beaulieu, Anatole [1842–1912]
French publicist.

Lesser, Allen
Nineteenth-century author.

Lessing, Gotthold E. [1729–1781]
German poet, critic.

Lessing, Theodor [1872–1933]
German philosopher.

Lester, Julius [1939–]
U.S. professor, author.

Leul, Steven
Contemporary psychologist, author.

Levant, Oscar [1906–1972]
U.S. author, actor, musician.

Levenson, Sam [1914–1980]
U.S. comedian.

Levi (Rabbi)
Third-century talmudic scholar.

Levi ben Gershom
See Gersonides.

Levi Yitzchak (Isaac) of Berditchev
[1740–1809]
Chasidic rabbi.

Levin, Carl [1934–]
U.S. senator from Michigan, elected in 1978.

Levin, Louis
Early nineteenth-century Baltimore
journalist, educator.

Levin, Meyer [1905–1981]
U.S. novelist, Zionist, journalist.

Levin, Shemarya(hu) [1867–1935]
Russian-born Zionist leader, preacher,
Hebrew and Yiddish author.

Levine, Gilbert
Conductor of Poland's Cracow
Philharmonic Orchestra.

Levine, Naomi
Executive Director of the American Jewish
Congress (1980s).

Levitas of Yavneh
Second-century talmudic scholar.

Levy, Felix A. [1884–1963]
U.S. rabbi.

Levy, Shalom
Israeli kibbutznik.

Levy, Uriah P. [1792–1862]
U.S. Navy commander.

Lewin, Kurt Z. [1890–1947]
German psychologist.

Lewis, Anthony Joseph [1927–]
U.S. newspaper columnist.

Lewis, Helen
Contemporary choreographer, dancer,
author.

Lewis, Jerry [1926–]
U.S. comedian, actor.

Lewis, John L. [1880–1969]
U.S. labor leader.

Lewisohn, Ludwig [1882–1955]
U.S. novelist, editor.

Lichten, Joseph
Contemporary executive of the Anti-
Defamation League of B'nai B'rith.

Lichtenson, Henrik
One of those saved by Oskar Schindler.

Lieber, David [1925–]
U.S. rabbi, scholar, educator.

Lieberman, Elias
Contemporary U.S. educator, author.

Lieberman, Joseph I. [1942–]
U.S. senator from Connecticut (1990s).

Lieberman, Saul [1898–1983]
Byelorussian-born U.S. rabbi, talmudic
authority, educator.

Liebler, Isi
Contemporary Israeli leader.

Liebman, Charles S.
Contemporary sociologist, author.

Liebman, Joshua Loth [1907–1948]
U.S. rabbi, author.

Liesen, Abraham [1872–1938]
Yiddish poet.

Lifton, Robert Jay [1926–]
President of American Jewish Congress
(1988–1994).

Lilienthal, Max [1815–1882]
German-born Reform rabbi, educator.

Limor, Nissan
Director general of the Israeli president's
residence (1984–1993).

Lincoln, Abraham [1809–1865]
Sixteenth U.S. president (1861–1865).

Lindbergh, Charles A. [1902–1974]
U.S. aviator.

Linowitz, Sol [1913–]
U.S. attorney, diplomat, corporate
executive.

Lipkin, Israel Salanter [1810–1883]
Lithuanian rabbi, moralist.

Lippel, Yisrael
Contemporary Israeli political activist.

Lippmann, Walter [1889–1975]
U.S. journalist, columnist.

Lipsky, Louis [1876–1963]
U.S. journalist, Zionist.

Lipstadt, Deborah E.
Contemporary U.S. historian, author.

Liptzin, Solomon [1901–1995]
U.S.-born professor, Yiddishist, author.

Littell, Franklin Hamlin [1917–]
Methodist theologian.

Lloyd George, David [1863–1945]
British prime minister (1916–1923).

Locke, John [1731–1804]
British philosopher.

Loeb, Betty
Contemporary Jew.

Loew, Judah [c. 1525–1609]
Rabbi of Prague, kabbalist.

Loewe, Herbert M. [1882–1940]
British scholar.

Loewe, Louis [1809–1888]
British Orientalist, author, educator.

London, Meyer [1871–1926]
Russian-born New York socialist leader
(early 1900s).

Longfellow, Henry Wadsworth [1807–1882]
U.S. poet.

Longstreet, Stephen [1907–]
Contemporary chronicler of Jewish life.

Lookstein, Joseph H. [1902–1979]
U.S. rabbi, professor.

Love, Courtney
Contemporary U.S. singer.

Lowell, James Russell [1819–1891]
U.S. poet, essayist.

Luther, Martin [1483–1546]
German theologian, leader of Protestant
Reformation.

Luttwak, Edward [1942–]
U.S. military strategist, author.

Luzzatto, Moses Hayyim [1707–1746]
Italian kabbalist, Hebrew poet, author.

Luzzatto, Samuel David [1800–1865]
Italian scholar, philosopher.

Lyons, Molly Bar-David
Contemporary author.

Macaulay, Thomas B. [1800–1859]
British historian, essayist, statesman.

MacDonald, J. Ramsay [1866–1937]
British prime minister (1924; 1929–1935).

MacGraw, Ali [1938–]
U.S. actress.

Madison, Charles A.
Contemporary U.S. author.

Madison, James [1751–1836]
Fourth U.S. president (1809–1817).

Magnes, Judah [1877–1948]
U.S.-born rabbi, educator, communal
leader.

Magnes, Lady Katie [1844–1924]
British author.

Mailer, Norman [1923–]
U.S. novelist, politician.

Maimon, Solomon [1754–1800]
Lithuanian philosopher.

Maimonides, Moses [1135–1204]
Spanish rabbi, physician, scholar,
philosopher, author.

Majali, Abdel Salam
Prime minister of Jordan (1994).

Malachi
Fifth-century B.C.E. prophet of Israel.

Malamud, Bernard [1914–1986]
U.S. novelist.

Malin, Irving [1934–]
U.S. essayist, critic.

Malino, Jerome R. [1911–]
U.S. rabbi.

Manasseh ben Israel [1604–1657]
Dutch rabbi.

Manatt, Charles T.
Democratic Party national chairman
(1980s).

Mandel, Morris [1911–]
U.S.-born psychologist, author, educator.

Mandela, Nelson [1918–]
First black president of South Africa,
elected in 1994.

Mandelbaum, Bernard [1922–]
U.S. rabbi, educator, author.

Manger, Itzik [1901–1969]
Yiddish poet.

Manilow, Barry [1946–]
U.S. pop singer.

Mann, Theodore [1928–]
U.S. lawyer, president of the American
Jewish Congress (1984).

Mann, Thomas [1875–1955]
German novelist.

Mansour, Anis
Contemporary Egyptian intellectual,
journalist.

Ma'oz, Moshe
Contemporary writer.

Marcus, David (Mickey) [1902–1948]
U.S. soldier, military advisor to the
Haganah (1948).

Marcus, Yoel
 Contemporary Israeli newspaper columnist.

Margolick, David
 Contemporary *New York Times* reporter.

Maritain, Jacques [1882–1973]
 French Catholic philosopher.

Marks, Sidney
 Contemporary U.S. Zionist leader.

Marlowe, Christopher [1564–1593]
 British dramatist, poet.

Marshall, Louis M. [1856–1929]
 U.S. attorney, jurist, communal leader.

Marx, Arthur [1921–]
 Son of Groucho Marx, author.

Marx, Groucho [1895–1977]
 Né Julius Marx.
 U.S. comedian, actor, author.

Marx, Harpo [1893–1964]
 Né Adolph Marx.
 U.S. comedian, actor, musician.

Marx, Karl [1818–1883]
 German revolutionary leader, founder of
 modern socialism.

Masaryk, Thomas [1850–1937]
 First president of Czechoslovakia
 (1918–1935).

Masliansky, Tzevi Hirsch [1856–1943]
 Russian-born Zionist leader, preacher.

Maslow, Will [1907–]
 Executive vice-president of the American
 Jewish Congress.

Mason, Jackie [1931–]
 U.S. comedian, actor, author.

Mather, Cotton [1663–1728]
 U.S. clergyman, writer.

Mattathias the Priest [?–167 B.C.E.]
 First leader of the Hasmonean uprising.

Matthews, Cornelius
 Nineteenth-century guidebook author.

Maugham, W. Somerset [1874–1965]
 British novelist, playwright.

Maxwell, Elisabeth (Betty) [1921–]
 Author; wife of Robert Maxwell.

Maxwell, Robert [?–1991]
 British communications entrepreneur.

Mayer, Egon [1944–]
 U.S. sociologist, professor.

Mayhew, Jonathan
 Eighteenth-century U.S. clergyman.

Mazé, Jacob [1860–1925]
 Russian rabbi.

McReynolds, James [c. 1862– ?]
 U.S. Supreme Court justice (1930s).

Meany, George [1894–1980]
 U.S. labor leader.

Meara, Anne [1929–]
 U.S. actress, comedienne.

Meed, Vladka
 Participant in the Warsaw Ghetto uprising
 (1943).

Megged, Aharon [1920–]
 Israeli novelist.

Mehta, Zubin [1936–]
 Indian-born musical conductor.

Meir (Rabbi)
 Second-century talmudic scholar.

Meir, Golda [1898–1978]
 Née Golda Myerson.
 Israeli prime minister (1969–1974).

Meir (ben Baruch) of Rothenburg
 [1215–1293]
 Talmudic scholar, poet.

Meir, Yitzchak
 Nineteenth-century chasidic rabbi.

Memmi, Albert [1920–]
 Tunisian-born French author.

Menachem Mendel of Kotzk [1787–1859]
 Also known as the Kotzker Rebbe.
 Polish-born chasidic leader.

Menachem Mendel of Vitebsk [1730–1788]
 Chasidic rabbi.

Mencken, Henry L. [1880–1956]
 U.S. writer, editor.

Mendele Mocher Seforim [1835–1917]
 Né Shalom Jacob Abramowitsch.
 Byelorussian-born Hebrew-Yiddish author.

Mendelssohn, Moses [1729–1786]
 German philosopher, Bible scholar.

Mendes, Henry Pereira [1852–1937]
 U.S. rabbi.

Menen, Carlos Sául
 President of Argentina (1994).

Meredith, George [1828–1909]
 British novelist.

Meshi-Zahav, Yehuda
 Organizer of the Satmar rebbe's 1994
 visit to Israel.

Meyer, Marshall [1930–1993]
 U.S. rabbi, educator.

Meyerhoff, Harvey M.
 Chairman of the U.S. Holocaust Memorial
 Museum (1987–1993).

Micah
Eighth-century B.C.E. prophet of Israel.

Michaels, Leonard [1933–]
U.S. professor of English.

Michelet, Jules [1798–1874]
French historian.

Midler, Bette [1945–]
U.S. comedienne, actress, singer.

Mikva, Abner [1926–]
U.S. Federal judge.

Miles, Sylvia [1932–]
U.S. actress.

Miller, Arthur [1915–]
U.S. playwright, novelist.

Miller, Henry [1891–1980]
U.S. author.

Miller, Jonathan [1934–]
U.S. actor, author, television director.

Miller, Judith
Contemporary U.S. author.

Miller, William E.
U.S. Republican vice-presidential
candidate (1964).

Minkin, Jacob
Contemporary U.S. rabbi, author.

Mintz, Jerome R.
Contemporary U.S. professor, author.

Mintz, Ruth Finer [1919–]
U.S. poet.

**Mirabeau, Honoré Gabriel Riqueti di
[1749–1791]**
French count, statesman, orator,
revolutionist.

Mohammed [570?–632]
Arabian prophet, founder of Islam.

Moise, Penina [1797–1880]
U.S. poet, teacher.

Molotov, Ivy
Wife of the Soviet foreign minister (1948).

Mommsen, Theodore
Nineteenth-century German historian.

Mondale, Walter [1928–]
U.S. politician, ambassador.

Monroe, James [1758–1831]
Fifth U.S. president (1817–1825).

Montague, Lily (Lilian) H. [1873–1963]
British social worker, liberal religious
leader.

Montefiore, Claude G. [1858–1938]
British scholar.

Montefiore, Moses [1784–1885]
British philanthropist.

Moody, Dwight L. [1837–1899]
U.S. evangelist.

Moody, Ron [1924–]
British comic actor.

Moore, George F. [1851–1931]
U.S. Orientalist, theologian, Bible scholar.

Moore, Thomas [1779–1852]
Irish poet.

Morgenstern, Julian [1881–1977]
U.S. rabbi, Bible scholar, educator.

Morterira, Saul Levi [1596–1661]
Italian rabbi, scholar.

Morton, Leah [1890–1954]
Polish-born U.S. writer.

Moses
Bible hero; leader of the Children of Israel.

Moses ben Jacob of Coucy
Thirteenth-century French scholar, codifier.

Moses, Raphael Jacob [1812–1893]
U.S. lawyer, state legislator.

Moshe Leib of Sassov [1744–1807]
Chasidic rabbi.

Mosley, Leonard
Contemporary U.S. author.

Mostel, Zero [1915–1977]
U.S. actor.

Moynihan, Daniel [1927–]
U.S. senator from New York (1990s).

Muhammad, Khallid Abdul
Aide to Louis Farrakhan (1990s).

Muller, Herbert J.
Contemporary author.

Musial, Stanislaw W.
Contemporary Polish Church leader.

Myerson, Bess [1924–]
U.S. consumer advocate, public speaker.

Nachman (Rabbi)
Fourth-century talmudic scholar.

**Nachman ben Simcha of Bratzlav
[1772–1810]**
Chasidic rabbi.

**Nachmanides (Moses ben Nachman)
[1194–1270]**
Spanish talmudist, physician.

Nachman of Kosov
Eighteenth-century Galician rabbi.

Nachum (Rabbi)
Twentieth-century rabbi of Rizhyn.

Nachum of Gamzu (Gimzo)
Second-century talmudic scholar.

Naftali of Ropshitz [1760–1827]
Founder of a chasidic dynasty in Galicia.

Namier, Lewis [1888–1960]
Galician-born British historian, Zionist.

Namir, Ora [1930–]
Israeli minister of welfare (1990s).

Napoléon Bonaparte [1769–1821]
Emperor of France (1804–1815).

Naquet, Pierre Vidal
Contemporary author.

Nasser, Gamal Abdel [1918–1970]
Egyptian leader.

Navon, Yitzhak [1921–]
Israeli president (1980s).

Ne'eman, Yuval [1925–]
Israeli physicist.

Neizvestny, Ernst [1926–]
Russian sculptor.

Nemerov, Howard [1920–1991]
Poet, critic.

Nemoy, Leon [1901–]
U.S. scholar, librarian.

Nessyahu, Mordechai
Advisor to Israeili prime minister Yitzhak
Rabin (1994).

Netanyahu, Benjamin "Bibi" [1949–]
Israeli political leader, prime minister
(1996–).

Netanyahu, Yonatan [1963–1976]
Israeli soldier.

Neuman, Abraham A. [1890–1970]
U.S. rabbi, educator.

Neusner, Jacob [1932–]
U.S. rabbi, scholar, author.

Newfield, Jack [1939–]
U.S. author, editor.

Newman, Al
Contemporary journalist.

Newman, Arnold [1919–]
U.S. portrait photographer.

Nichols, Mike [1931–]
U.S. film and stage director.

Nicholson, Jack [1937–]
U.S. actor.

Niemöller, Martin [1892–]
German Protestant leader.

Nietzsche, Friedrich W. [1844–1900]
German philosopher.

Niger, Samuel [1883–1956]
Yiddish critic.

Niles, David
Assistant to U.S. president Franklin D.
Roosevelt.

Nitai the Arbelite
Second-century B.C.E. scholar.

Nixon, Richard M. [1913–1994]
Thirty-seventh U.S. president (1969–1974).

Noah, Mordecai Manuel [1785–1851]
U.S. playwright, statesman.

Nones, Benjamin N. [1757–1826]
Major in the American Revolution, political
activist.

Noor, Queen of Jordan
U.S.-born wife of King Hussein.

Nordau, Max [1849–1923]
Hungarian-born physician, Zionist leader.

Novak, David
Contemporary U.S. professor of Judaic
studies, author.

Nudel, Ida [1931–]
Russian-born Jewish activist.

Nusseibeh, Hazem
Palestinian political leader (1980s).

Nusseibeh, Sari
Contemporary Palestinian writer.

Nye, Gerald R.
U.S. senator from North Dakota (1941).

Obadiah
Fourth of the twelve minor prophets.

O'Brien, Howard Vincent [1888–]
U.S. journalist.

Ochs, Adolph S. [1858–1935]
U.S. publisher.

Ochs, Vanessa L.
Contemporary U.S. author.

O'Connell, Daniel
Nineteenth-century adversary of
Benjamin Disraeli.

O'Connor, John (Cardinal) [1920–]
Archbishop of New York (1985–).

Olan, Levi [?–1984]
U.S. rabbi, author.

Olmer, Lionel H.
U.S. undersecretary of commerce (1984).

Olmert, Ehud
Mayor of Jerusalem, elected in 1993.

O'Neill, Eugene, Jr.
Contemporary professor of Greek at Yale
University.

Opatoshu, Joseph [1887–1954]
Polish-born Yiddish writer.

Oppenheimer, Joseph (Süss) [1698–1738]
German financier.

Oppenheimer, J. Robert [1904–1967]
U.S. nuclear physicist.

Oron, Yair
Contemporary Israeli educator.

Oz, Amos [1939–]
Israeli writer, activist, novelist.

Ozick, Cynthia [1928–]
U.S. author, playwright.

Paine, Thomas [1737–1809]
American revolutionary, patriot, writer.

Painlevé, Paul [1863–1933]
French statesman.

Paley, Grace [1922–]
U.S. author.

Pallière, Aimé [1875–]
French advocate of Judaism.

Palmerston, Henry John Temple (Lord)
[1784–1865]
British statesman.

Pantirer, Murray
Holocaust survivor.

Papa (Rabbi)
Also known as Rav Papa.
Fourth-century talmudic scholar.

Papp, Joseph [1921–1991]
U.S. theater producer.

Parkes, James W. [1896–1981]
British clergyman, historian.

Parson, Talcott
Contemporary U.S. sociologist, educator.

Parton, Dolly [1946–]
U.S. country singer, entertainer.

Pascal, Blaise [1623–1662]
French physicist, mathematician,
philosopher.

Pasha, Abdul Rahman Azzam
Secretary general of the Arab League (1948).

Pasternak, Boris L. [1890–1960]
Russian novelist.

Patai, Raphael [1910–1996]
Hungarian-born anthropologist, editor,
educator.

Patinkin, Mandy [1952–]
U.S. actor, singer.

Patterson, David [1948–]
U.S. author, professor.

Patton, George [1885–1945]
U.S. Army general.

Paul IV
Pope, consecrated in 1555.

Peel, Robert [1788–1850]
British prime minister (1834–1835;
1841–1846).

Peli, Pinchas
Contemporary Israeli scholar, author.

Pelossof, Noa Ben Artzi- [1978–]
Yitzhak Rabin's granddaughter.

Perahia, Murray [1947–]
U.S. poet, pianist.

Peres, Shimon [1923–]
Israeli political leader, prime minister
(1984–1986; 1996).

Peretz, Isaac Leibush [1852–1915]
Polish-born Yiddish novelist, poet, critic.

Peretz, Martin [1939–]
U.S. editor, magazine publisher.

Perle, Richard
U.S. assistant secretary of defense (1980s).

Perlman, Itzhak [1929–]
Israeli-born U.S. violinist.

Perlmutter, Nathan
Director of the Anti-Defamation League
(1980s).

Peters, Roberta [1930–]
U.S. opera singer.

Petlakh, Leonid
Contemporary Jewish esssayist.

Petuchowski, Jakob [1925–1991]
U.S. professor, theologian.

Pfeffer Leo [1910–1993]
U.S. attorney, writer.

Philipson, David [1862– 1949]
U.S. Reform rabbi.

Phillips, Wendell [1811–1884]
U.S. abolitionist, reformer, orator.

Philo [c. 20 B.C.E.–40 C.E.]
Alexandrian philosopher, Bible scholar,
author.

Picon, Molly [1898–1992]
U.S. actress, comedienne.

Pinchas of Koretz [1726–1791]
Also known as Pinchas ben Abraham Abba
Shapiro.
Ukrainian chasidic rabbi.

Pinsker, Leo [1821–1891]
Polish-born physician, Zionist leader,
writer.

Pinsky, Robert [1940–]
U.S. writer.

Piper, Otto
U.S. Protestant theologian.

Pius IV
Pope, consecrated in 1559.

Pius X [1835–1914]
Pope, consecrated in 1903.

Piux XI [1857–1939]
Pope, consecrated in 1922.

Plain, Belva [1919–]
U.S. novelist.

Plaut, Gunther W. [1912–]
German-born rabbi, author, Bible scholar.

Podhoretz, Norman [1930–]
U.S. editor, author.

Pogrebin, Letty Cottin [1939–]
U.S. author, editor, feminist leader.

Pollard, Jonathan [1954–]
U.S. government employee.

Pollard, Molly
Mother of Jonathan Pollard.

Polner, Murray
Contemporary U.S. writer, editor.

Pool, David de Sola [1885–1970]
U.S. rabbi, author.

Pope, Alexander [1688–1744]
British poet.

Popkin, Ruth W.
President of the Jewish National Fund
(1993).

Porush, Menachem
Contemporary Israeli political leader.

Potok, Chaim [1929–]
U.S. rabbi, historian, novelist.

Potter, Henry Codman
Episcopal bishop of New York (early
1900s).

Pound, Ezra [1885–1972]
U.S. poet, critic.

Powell, Colin
Chairman of U.S. Joint Chiefs of Staff
(1989–1993).

Praeger, Ferdinand
German biographer.

Prager, Dennis
Contemporary U.S. editor, author, radio
talk-show host.

Preil, Gabriel Joshua [1911–]
U.S. Hebrew poet.

Prescott, William H. [1796–1859]
U.S. historian.

Priesand, Sally [1946–]
First U.S. female rabbi.

Priestly, Joseph [1733–1804]
Founder of Unitarianism in the U.S.

Prinz, Joachim [1902–1988]
German-born U.S. rabbi, community
leader.

Pritzker, Nicholas J.
Nineteenth-century Kiev-born U.S.
financier.

Pulitzer, Joseph [1847–1911]
Hungarian-born U.S. newspaper publisher.

Quandt, William
Middle East expert; advisor to U.S.
president Jimmy Carter.

Rabba bar bar Chana
Third/fourth-century talmudic scholar.

Rabba ben Avuha
Third/fourth-century talmudic scholar.

Rabba ben Chinena
Third-century talmudic scholar.

Rabba ben Joseph [c. 280–352]
Often referred to simply as Rabba.
Talmudic scholar.

Rabbenu Tam
See Tam, Jacob.

Rabi, Isidor Isaac [1898–1988]
Austro-Hungarian-born U.S. physicist,
Nobel Prize winner (1944).

Rabin, Leah
 Wife of Israeli prime minister Yitzhak
 Rabin.

Rabin, Yitzhak [1922–1995]
 Israeli prime minister (1992–1995).

Rabinowitz, Louis [1906–1984]
 Deputy editor-in-chief of *Encyclopedia
 Judaica*.

Rabinowitz, Stanley [1917–]
 Contemporary U.S. rabbi.

Rackman, Emanuel [1910–]
 U.S.-born Orthodox rabbi, scholar,
 educator.

Rahman, Asad Abdel
 Member of the Palestine National Council
 of the PLO (1993).

Raisen, Abraham
 Contemporary U.S. poet.

Rakover, Yossel
 Victim of the Warsaw Ghetto uprising.

Rangel, Charles [1930–]
 U.S. congressman from New York City
 (1990s).

Raphael, Chaim [1908–]
 British author, scholar.

Raphall, Morris [1798–1868]
 Swedish rabbi of New York City's
 Congregation B'nai Jeshurun.

Rapoport, Nessa
 Contemporary U.S. author, editor.

Rashi [1040–1105]
 French Bible and Talmud commentator.

Raskin, P. M.
 Contemporary U.S. poet.

Rathenau, Walter [1867–1922]
 German industrialist, statesman, author.

Rauch, Jonathan
 Contemporary U.S. writer.

Rav
 Also known as Abba Aricha.
 Third-century Babylonian scholar.

Reagan, Ronald [1911–]
 Fortieth U.S. president (1981–1989).

Rebecca
 Wife of the biblical patriarch Issac.

Reich, Walter
 Contemporary U.S. journalist, author.

Reik, Theodor [1888–1970]
 Viennese psychologist.

Renan, Joseph Ernest [1823–1892]
 French historian, essayist, theologian.

Resh Lakish
 Also known as Rabbi Shimon (Simeon).
 Second/third-century talmudic scholar.

Rezinkoff, Charles [1894–1976]
 U.S. poet.

Ribbentrop, Joachim von [1893–1946]
 German Nazi foreign minister (1938–1945).

Ribicoff, Abraham [1910–]
 U.S. senator from Connecticut
 (1963–1981).

Rich, Frank [1949–]
 U.S. journalist.

Richards, Bernard G.
 Contemporary U.S. writer.

Rickles, Don [1926–]
 U.S. comedian.

Riegner, Gerhart M.
 Co-chairman of the World Jewish Congress
 (1980s).

Riemer, Jack
 Contemporary U.S. rabbi, author.

Riesman, David [1909–]
 U.S. sociologist, author.

Riesser, Gabriel [1806–1863]
 German publicist, jurist.

Ringelbaum, Emanuel [?–1944]
 Warsaw Ghetto diarist.

Ripley, William Z. [1867–1941]
 U.S. economist, anthropologist.

Riskin, Shlomo [1940–]
 U.S.-born Israeli rabbi, columnist.

Rivkin, Ellis [1918–]
 U.S. historian, professor.

Roan, Leonard
 U.S. judge.

Robertson, Pat
 Contemporary evangelical Christian leader.

Robinson, Theodore H. [1881–]
 British historian, Orientalist.

Rodzinski, Artur [1892–1958]
 Dalmatian-born musical conductor.

Roiphe, Anne Richardson [1935–]
 Contemporary U.S. writer.

Rokeah, Yisrael Dov
 Contemporary leader of the Belzer chasidic
 sect.

Rolvaag, Ole Edvart [1876–1931]
 Norwegian-born U.S. novelist.

Roosevelt, Eleanor [1884–1962]
 Wife of U.S. president Franklin D.
 Roosevelt, writer, delegate to the United
 Nations.

Roosevelt, Franklin Delano [1882–1945]
Thirty-second U.S. president (1933–1945).

Roosevelt, Theodore [1858–1919]
Twenty-sixth U.S. president (1901–1909).

Rose, Daniel
Contemporary U.S. businessman, civil
rights advocate.

Rosen, Moses [1912–1994]
Chief Rabbi of Romania (1948–1994).

Rosenbaum, Norman
Australian brother of 1991 murder victim
Yankel Rosenbaum.

Rosenberg, Jay
Contemporary U.S. journalist.

Rosenblatt, Gary
Contemporary U.S. journalist, newspaper
publisher.

Rosenblum, Penina
Contemporary Israeli entrepreneur.

Rosenfeld, Morris [1862–1923]
Yiddish poet.

Rosenman, Samuel I. [1896–1973]
U.S. president Franklin D. Roosevelt's
advisor and speechwriter.

Rosensaft, Menachem Z.
Founding chairman of the International
Network of Children of Jewish Holocaust
Survivors.

Rosenthal, A. M. [1922–]
U.S. journalist.

Rosenwald, Julius [1862–1932]
U.S. business leader, philanthropist.

Rosenzweig, Franz [1886–1929]
German philosopher, theologian.

Rosmarin, Trude Weiss
See Weiss-Rosmarin, Trude.

Ross, Barney [1909–1967]
U.S. boxing champion.

Ross, Isidore
Father of Barney Ross.

Rosten, Leo [1907–]
U.S. author, humorist.

Roth, Benjamin
Nineteenth-century German writer.

Roth, Cecil [1899–1970]
British historian, author.

Roth, Henry [1907–]
U.S. novelist.

Roth, Joel
Contemporary U.S. rabbi, legal scholar.

Roth, Joseph [1894–1939]
Austrian novelist, journalist.

Roth, Leon [1896–1963]
English-born philosopher, scholar, Hebrew
University professor.

Roth, Philip [1933–]
U.S. novelist.

Rothschild, Edmond de [1845–1934]
French financier, philanthropist.

Rothschild, Miriam [1908–]
British naturalist, author.

Rottenheim, W.
Nineteenth-century German émigré to
the U.S.

Rousseau, Jean Jacques [1712–1778]
French political philosopher, author.

Rubenstein, Aryeh
Contemporary historian, author.

Rubenstein, Richard [1924–]
U.S. rabbi, author, professor.

Rubinstein, Amnon
Israeli minister of education (1994).

Rubinstein, Anton [1829–1894]
Russian pianist, composer.

Rubinstein, Artur [1886–1982]
Polish-born pianist.

Rubinstein, Helena [1870–1965]
Polish-born cosmetician.

Rukeyser, Muriel [1913–]
U.S. poet, author.

Runcie, Robert [1921–]
Archbishop of Canterbury.

Runes, Dagobert D.
Contemporary U.S. philosopher, author,
publisher.

Runyon, Damon [1884–]
U.S. journalist, short-story writer.

Ruppin, Arthur [1876–1943]
German sociologist.

Ruskin, John [1819–1900]
British writer, art critic, social reformer.

Russell, Bertrand [1872–1970]
British philosopher.

Ruth
Moabite ancestor of King David; daughter-
in-law of Naomi.

Rutskoi, Alexandr
Contemporary Russian historian,
sociologist.

Saadya (ben Joseph) Gaon [882–942]
Babylonian scholar, liturgist.

al-Sabah, Muhammad
Kuwaiti ambassador to the U.S. (1990s).

Sachar, Abram Leon [1899–1993]
U.S. rabbi, historian.

Sachs, Andrew M.
Contemporary U.S. Conservative rabbi.

Sachs, Nelly [1891–1970]
German-born poet.

Sack, John
Contemporary U.S. author.

Sacks, Jonathan [1948–]
Chief Rabbi of Great Britian (1991–).

al-Sadat, Anwar [1918–1981]
President of Egypt (1970–1981).

Sadat, Camelia [1947–]
Anwar Sadat's daughter from his first
marriage to Ekbal Madi.

Sadat, Jehan
Wife of Anwar Sadat.

Safire, William [1929–]
U.S. columnist, linguist, author.

Sahl, Mort [1927–]
U.S. humorist.

Salamander, Rachel
Contemporary U.S. historian, author.

Salanter, Israel
See Lipkin, Israel Salanter.

Salinger, Jerome D. [1919–]
U.S. author.

Salk, Jonas [1914–1995]
U.S. scientist.

Sampter, Jessie Ethel [1883–1938]
U.S.-born author, poet, Zionist.

Samson
Biblical character who battled the
Philistines.

Samuel [165–257]
Also known as Samuel bar Abba.
Talmudic scholar.

Samuel ben Nachman
Third-century talmudic scholar.

Samuel, Herbert [1870–1963]
British statesman.

Samuel, Maurice [1895–1972]
Rumanian-born essayist, novelist.

Samuel, Rebecca
Late eighteenth-century American immigrant.

Samuels, Howard
Contemporary New York politician.

Sandburg, Carl [1878–1967]
U.S. poet, writer.

Sandmel, Samuel
Contemporary U.S. theologian, educator.

Saniford, Peter [1882–]
Canadian educator.

Sapiro, Aaron L.
Contemporary of Henry Ford.

Sarid, Yossi
Contemporary Israeli politician.

Sarna, Jonathan
Contemporary U.S. historian, author.

Sarnoff, David [1891–1971]
U.S. industrialist.

Sarte, Jean-Paul [1905–1980]
French philosopher, playwright, novelist.

Saud, King
Saudi Arabian monarch (1990s).

Savir, Uri
Israel's chief negotiator with the Palestine
Liberation Organization (1993).

Schaap, Richard J. (Dick) [1934–]
U.S. sports broadcast journalist.

Schachter-Shalomi, Zalman [1924–]
U.S. rabbi, mystic, educator.

Schaefer, William Donald
Mayor of Baltimore, Maryland (1990s).

Schaffer, Walter
South African physics professor (1960s).

Schary, Dore [1905–1980]
U.S. playwright, film and theater producer.

Schechter, Mathilde
Wife of Solomon Schechter.

Schechter, Solomon [1847–1915]
Rumanian-born scholar, author, educator.

Scheck, Barry
Contemporary U.S. attorney.

Scherman, Harry [1887–1969]
U.S. publisher; Book-of-the-Month Club
president.

Schiff, Jacob H. [1847–1920]
German-born U.S. financier, philanthropist.

Schindler, Alexander [1925–]
U.S. rabbi, Reform leader.

Schindler, Solomon [1842–1915]
German-born U.S. Reform rabbi.

Schipper, Ignacy (Yitzhak) [1884–1943]
Polish historian.

Schlesinger, Arthur, Jr. [1917–]
U.S. historian, author.

Schmidt, Helmut [1918–]
German political leader.

Schneerson, Menachem Mendel
[1902–1994]
Spiritual leader of the Chabad (Lubavitcher)
chasidic sect.

Schneerson, Shalom Dov Baer [1866–1920]
Lubavitcher rabbi.

Schneier, Arthur
Contemporary U.S. rabbi.

Schnur, Susan
Contemporary U.S. rabbi.

Schoenberg, Arnold [1874–1951]
Austrian-born music composer.

Scholem, Gershom [1897–1982]
German-born historian, authority on
mysticism.

Schopenhauer, Arthur [1788–1860]
German philosopher.

Schorsch, Ismar [1925–]
U.S. rabbi, historian, Jewish Theological
Seminary of America chancellor.

Schreiner, Olive
Nineteenth/twentieth-century writer.

Schulweiss, Harold [1925–]
U.S. rabbi, author.

Schwartz, Howard Eilberg
Contemporary U.S. author.

Scott, Sir Walter [1771–1832]
Scottish poet, novelist.

Seaman, Sylvia
Contemporary U.S. author.

Seer of Lublin [1745–1815]
Also known as Jacob Isaac Ha-chozeh
Mi-Lublin.
Founder of the chasidic movement in
Poland.

Segal, Erich [1937–]
U.S. novelist.

Seinfeld, Jerry [1954–]
U.S. comedian, actor.

Seixas, Moses
Warden of the Hebrew congregation of
Newport, Rhode Island (1790).

Selbie, William B. [1862–1944]
British theologian.

Selden, John [1584–1654]
British jurist, Orientalist.

Semer, Hannah
Contemporary Israeli journalist.

Senesh (Szenes) Hannah
See Szenes, Hannah.

Sequoia, Anna
Contemporary U.S. essayist.

Sergeant, Winthrop
Contemporary U.S. writer.

Sforno, Obadiah (ben Jacob) [c. 1475–1550]
Italian physician, Bible commentator.

Sha'ath, Nabil
Senior political advisor to Yasser Arafat
(1990s).

Shahal, Moshe
Israeli police minister (1990s).

Shahn, Ben [1898–1969]
Lithuanian-born artist, author.

Shakespeare, William [1564–1616]
British playwright, poet.

el-Shami, Khaled
Contemporary Egyptian scientist.

Shamir, Yair
Business executive; son of Yitzhak Shamir.

Shamir, Yitzhak [1915–]
Israeli prime minister (1983–1984;
1986–1992).

Shammai
First-century B.C.E. talmudic scholar,
founder of an academy of learning.

Shanks, Harold
Contemporary U.S. publisher of *Moment*
magazine.

Shapiro, Constantine [1841–1900]
Russian-born Hebrew poet.

Shapiro, Karl J. [1913–]
U.S. poet.

Shapiro, Robert
Contemporary U.S. attorney.

Sharansky, Natan (Anatol) [1948–]
Russian refusenik, author, Israeli political
leader.

Sharett, Moshe [1894–1965]
Israeli prime minister (1963–1973).

Sharon, Ariel [1928–]
Israeli general, author, political leader.

Sharpton, Al
Contemporary black leader, clergyman.

Shaw, George Bernard [1856–1950]
Irish playwright, scholar.

Shaw, Irwin [1913–1984]
U.S. novelist.

Sheffer, Jonathan [1952–]
Hollywood composer.

Sheftal, Levi
Eighteenth-century spiritual leader.

Sheftel, Yoram
Contemporary Israeli attorney.

Shelly, Percy Bysshe [1792–1822]
British poet.

Shemtov, Abraham
Washington, DC emissary of the Chabad
movement (1990s).

Sher, Neal
U.S. Department of Justice official, Nazi
hunter (1990s).

Sheraton, Mimi
Contemporary cookbook author, restaurant
critic.

Sherer, Moshe
Contemporary U.S. Orthodox religious
leader.

Shereshevsky, Esra
Contemporary U.S. scholar, author.

Sherira, Gaon [906–1006]
Leading Babylonian scholar.

Shevitz, Dan
Contemporary U.S. Conservative rabbi.

Shila (Rabbi)
Second/third-century talmudic scholar.

Shilansky, Dov
Holocaust survivor, member of Israeli
Knesset (1990s).

Shimon ben Menasya
Second/third-century talmudic scholar.

Shneersohn, Joseph
Warsaw Ghetto victim (1943).

**Shneur Zalman ben Baruch of Lyady
[1747–1813]**
Founder of the Chabad Movement.

**Sholom (Shalom, Sholem) Aleichem
[1859–1916]**
Ukrainian-born author, Yiddish humorist.

Shukeiry, Ahmed
Founder of the Palestine Liberation
Organization (1960s).

Shultz, George P. [1920–]
U.S. secretary of state (1982–1988).

Siegel, Seymour [1927–1988]
U.S. rabbi, author, professor.

Siegman, Henry
Executive director of the American Jewish
Congress (1990s).

Silberg, Moshe (1900–)
Lithuanian-born Israeli jurist.

Silberman, Charles Eliot [1925–]
U.S. journalist, author.

Silbermuntz, Marvin
Contemporary U.S. comedy writer.

Sills, Beverly [1929–]
U.S. opera singer.

Silver, Abba Hillel [1893–1963]
U.S. rabbi, Zionist leader.

Silver, Daniel Jeremy
Contemporary U.S. rabbi, historian.

Silwadi, Fathallah
Senior member of the Palestine Liberation
Organization's ministry of religion (1990s).

Simeon (Simon) ben Chalafta
Second-century talmudic scholar.

Simeon (Simon) ben Eleazar (Elazar)
Second-century talmudic scholar.

Simeon ben Gamaliel
First-century talmudic scholar.

Simeon ben Lakish
See Resh Lakish.

Simeon ben Yehotzadak
Third-century talmudic scholar.

Simeon (Shimon) ben Yochai
Second-century talmudic scholar.

Simlai bar Abba
Third-century talmudic scholar.

Simon, Akiba Ernst [1899–1988]
Israeli educator.

Simon, Neil [1927–]
U.S. playwright.

Sinatra, Frank [1915–]
U.S. singer.

Singer, Aaron
Contemporary U.S. educator.

Singer, Howard [1922–]
U.S. rabbi, author.

Singer, Isaac Bashevis [1904–1991]
Polish-born novelist, Nobel Prize winner.

Singer, Israel
Secretary general of the World Jewish
Congress (1990s).

Skelton, (Sir) John
Nineteenth-century British author.

Sklare, Marshall [1921–1992]
U.S. sociologist.

Slaton, John
Governor of Georgia (1915).

Sliwa, Curtis [1954–]
U.S. radio talk-show host; organizer of the
Guardian Angels.

Slonimsky, Henry [1884–1970]
U.S. philosopher, professor.

Slouschz, Nahum [1871–1966]
Russian-born historian, archaeologist,
traveler.

Slovo, Joe [1927–1995]
Member of the South African Cabinet.

Smirnoff, Yakov [1951–]
Ukrainian-born U.S. comedian.

Smith, Bailey
President of the Southern Baptist
Convention (1980s).

Smith, Gerald L. K.
Founder of the Christian Nationalist Party
(1948).

Smith, Samuel G. [1852–1915]
U.S. educator, sociologist.

Smolenskin, Peretz [1842–1885]
Austrian-born Hebrew novelist, editor.

Smuts, Jan Christian (J. C.) [1870–1950]
South African prime minister (1919–1924;
1939–1948).

Snowden, Viscountess [1881–]
British author; wife of Philip Snowden.

Sofer, Abraham Samuel [1815–1871]
Rabbi in Pressburg, Slovakia.

Sofer, Rena
Contemporary U.S. actress.

Solomon
Third king of Israel; son of David.

Solomon ben Yerucham
Tenth-century scholar.

Solomons, Adolphus S. [1826–1910]
U.S. social welfare pioneer.

Soloveitchik, Aaron [1918–]
U.S. rabbi, Chicago-based educator.

Soloveitchik, Joseph B. [1903–1993]
U.S. rabbi, scholar, professor.

Soloviev, Vladimir [1853–1900]
Russian philosopher, poet.

Sombart, Werner [1863–1941]
German economist.

Sondheim, Stephen [1930–]
U.S. composer, lyricist.

Sontag, Susan [1933–]
U.S. writer.

Soros, George
Hungarian-born industrialist.

Sovern, Michael I. [1931–]
U.S. legal scholar.

Spalding, Henry D. [1915–]
U.S. author, editor, humorist.

Spainier, Louis
Nineteenth-century congregational
president.

Specter, Arlen
U.S. senator from Pennsylvania (1990s).

Spelling, Aaron [1925–]
U.S. television producer.

Spengler, Oswald [1880–1936]
German author.

Spiegel, Shalom [1889–1984]
U.S. author, educator.

Spielberg, Steven [1947–]
U.S. movie director, producer.

Spinoza, Baruch (Benedict) [1632–1677]
Dutch philosopher, author.

Spitzer, Edith
Contemporary U.S. scholar, author.

Squadron, Howard
Attorney, president of the American Jewish
Congress (1970s).

Stalin, Joseph [1879–1953]
Soviet premier (1941–1953).

Stampfer, Judah [1923–]
U.S. rabbi, poet.

Stanley, Arthur [1815–1881]
British church historian.

Stanton, Elizabeth Cady [1815–1902]
U.S. women's rights activist.

Steffens, Lincoln [1866–1936]
U.S. poet.

Stein, Cyril
Twentieth-century leader of English Jewry.

Stein, Ernst
Contemporary German-born Reform rabbi.

Stein, Gertrude [1874–1946]
U.S.-born writer.

Stein, Joseph [1912–]
U.S. contemporary playwright.

Steinberg, Etan
Executive director of the World Jewish
Congress (1990s).

Steinberg, Joshua [1825–1908]
Russian linguist, rabbi, author.

Steinberg, Milton [1903–1950]
U.S. rabbi, author, scholar.

Steiner, George [1929–]
Author, literary critic, teacher in the U.S.
and England.

Steinsaltz, Adin [1937–]
Israeli rabbi, talmudic scholar, author.

Stendahl, Krister
U.S. bishop, Christian-Jewish scholar (1994).

Stengel, Casey [1890–1975]
U.S. baseball manager.

Stephanopoulos, George
Advisor to U.S. president Bill Clinton
(1990s).

Stern, Avraham ("Yair") [1907–1942]
Israeli underground leader.

Stern, Issac [1920–]
U.S. violinist.

Stern, Susan
Leader of the United Jewish Appeal's
Women's Division (1990s).

Stettinius, Edward R. [1900–1949]
U.S. secretary of state (1940s).

Stevenson, Adlai [1900–1965]
U.S. political leader.

Stevenson, Robert Louis [1850–1894]
Scottish novelist.

Stewart, Walter
Contemporary author.

Stiles, Ezra [1729–1795]
U.S. university president, church minister.

Stone, Harlan F. [1872–1946]
Chief Justice of the U.S. Supreme Court
(1941–1946).

Stone, I. F. (Isidor Feinstein) [1907–1989]
U.S. journalist.

Stone, Irving [1903–1984]
U.S. novelist.

Stoutenberg, Dennis [1951–]
Bible scholar, theologian.

Stowe, Harriet Beecher [1811–1896]
U.S. author.

Strasberg, Lee [1901–1982]
U.S. theater director, teacher.

Strassfeld, Michael
Contemporary U.S. rabbi, author.

Straus, Oscar Solomon [1850–1926]
U.S. statesman.

Streicher, Julius [1885–1946]
German Nazi leader.

Streisand, Barbra [1942–]
U.S. singer, actress, movie producer.

Stroops, Juergen
Polish citizen (1940s).

Sturm, Elazar
Contemporary Israeli television host.

Stuyvesant, Peter [1592–1672]
Last Dutch governor of New Netherland.

Sukar, Abdel Rahim
Contemporary Palestinian.

Susser, Leslie
Contemporary writer.

Süsskind, Alexander ben Moses
Eighteenth-century scholar.

Suttner, Bertha von [1843–1914]
Austrian novelist, baroness, 1905 Nobel
Peace Prize winner.

Suzman, Helen [1917–]
South African politician, member of
Parliament (1961–1974).

Swaggart, Jimmy
Contemporary U.S. evangelist.

Swift, John Franklin
Nineteenth-century U.S. Christian.

Syme, Daniel B.
Contemporary U.S. rabbi.

Syrkin, Marie [1900–1989]
U.S. writer, teacher, Zionist.

Szenes, Hannah [1921–1944]
Hungarian-born poet, heroine.

Szold, Benjamin [1829–1902]
Hungarian-born U.S. rabbi, Bible scholar.

Szold, Henrietta [1860–1945]
U.S. writer, founder of Hadassah.

Szuros, Mayyas
Contemporary Hungarian politician.

Taft, William Howard [1857–1930]
Twenty-seventh U.S. president
(1909–1913).

Tahbub, Hassan
Palestinian minister of religious affairs
(1995).

Tam, Jacob (Rabbenu) [1100–1171]
French talmudist, grandson of Rashi.

Tanchum
Third-century talmudic scholar.

Tanzer Rebbe
Nineteenth-century chasidic rabbi.

Tarfon [c. 70–132]
Talmudic scholar.

Tawil, Suha
See Arafat, Suha Tawil.

Tekoa, Yosef
Contemporary Israeli political leader.

Teller, Edward [1908–]
Hungarian-born U.S. physicist, nuclear
scientist.

Tendler, Moshe D.
Contemporary U.S. scholar.

Teplitz, Saul I. [1921–]
U.S. rabbi, author.

Thackeray, William M. [1811–1863]
British novelist.

Thomas, Bob
Contemporary U.S. author.

Thomas, M. Carey [1857–1935]
U.S. feminist, Bryn Mawr College president.

Thompson, Dorothy
Contemporary U.S. columnist.

Tibi, Ahmed
Special advisor to Yasser Arafat (1990s).

Tigay, Alan
Hadassah Magazine editor (1990s).

Tillich, Paul Johannes [1886–1965]
German-born U.S. theologian.

Toller, Ernst [1893–1939]
German dramatist.

Tolstoy, Leo [1828–1910]
Russian novelist, social reformer.

Toynbee, Arnold J. [1889–1975]
British historian.

Trachtenberg, Joshua
Contemporary U.S. rabbi, author.

Trainin, Isaac
Religious affairs director of UJA–Federation (1980s).

Treitschke, Heinrich von [1834–1896]
German historian.

Trepp, Leo
Contemporary U.S. rabbi, author.

Trilling, Diana [1905–]
U.S. literary critic.

Trilling, Lionel [1905–1975]
U.S. author, professor.

Trotsky, Leon [1879–1940]
Russian revolutionist.

Truman, Harry S [1884–1972]
Thirty-third U.S. president (1945–1953).

Tuchman, Barbara W. [1912–]
U.S. journalist, author.

Tucholsky, Kurt [1890–1935]
German journalist, political analyst, satirist.

Tucker, Cynthia
Contemporary U.S. journalist.

Tucker, Gordon
Contemporary U.S. rabbi.

Tucker, Sophie [1884–1966]
U.S. entertainer.

Turk, Samuel
Contemporary U.S. writer.

Twain, Mark [1834–1910]
U.S. writer, humorist.

Tzerniakow, Adam [?–1942]
Head of the Warsaw Jewish Council.

Tzupensester Rebbe
Contemporary chasidic leader.

Ungar, André
Contemporary U.S. rabbi, author.

Untermeyer, Samuel [1858–1940]
U.S. attorney.

Uris, Leon [1924–]
U.S. novelist, screenwriter.

Urofsky, Melvin F. [1939–]
Contemporary U.S. historian, professor.

Ussishkin, Menachem [1863–1943]
Russian-born Zionist leader, writer.

Van Buren, Abigail [1918–]
Née Pauline Friedman.
U.S. newspaper columnist.

Van Buren, Paul M.
Contemporary Protestant theologian.

Vasilev, Dmitri
Leader of Russia's anti-Semitic Pamyat organization (1990s).

Veil, Simone [1927–]
French politician, president of European Parliament (1979–1982).

Venizelos, Eleutherios [1864–1936]
Greek prime minister (1930s).

Victoria [1819–1901]
Queen of Great Britain and Ireland (1837–1901).

Vigoda, Abe [1922–]
U.S. actor.

Villard, Oswald Garrison [1872–1942]
Journalist, editor.

Vilna Gaon
See Elijah ben Solomon (Zalman).

Voeten, Bert
Contemporary Dutch poet.

Voltaire, François [1694–1778]
  French author.

Vonnegut, Kurt, Jr. [1922–]
  U.S. novelist, playwright.

Von Hindenburg, Paul
  See Hindenburg, Paul von.

Von Suttner, Bertha
  See Suttner, Bertha von.

Von Treitschke, Heinrich
  See Treitschke, Heinrich von.

Von Weizsacher, Richard
  See Weizsacher, Richard von.

Vorspan, Albert [1924–]
  Leader in U.S. Reform movement, author.

Vranitzky, Franz [1937–]
  Chancellor of Austria (1980s).

Wagner, Richard [1813–1883]
  German composer.

Wałesa, Lech
  Polish politician (1990s).

Walker, James
  Nineteenth-century Protestant preacher,
  scholar.

Walters, Barbara [1931–]
  U.S. broadcast journalist.

Warburg, Siegmund
  Contemporary British writer.

Washington, George [1732–1799]
  First U.S. president (1789–1797).

Waskow, Arthur [1933–]
  U.S. writer, theologian.

Wasserman, Jakob [1873–1934]
  German novelist.

Wasserstein, Wendy [1950–]
  U.S. playwright.

Watson, Tom
  Contemporary U.S. professional golfer.

Watts, F. W.
  Contemporary British artist.

Waxman, Henry A. [1939–]
  U.S. congressman from California (1990s).

Weil, Simone [1909–1943]
  French philosopher, author.

Weiler, Moses Cyrus
  Contemporary South African Reform rabbi.

Weinberg, Steven
  Contemporary U.S. author.

Weinberger, Caspar
  U.S. secretary of defense (1980s).

Weinberger, Harry [1885–]
  U.S. attorney.

Weiner, Herbert
  Contemporary U.S. author.

Weiner, Marc [1952–]
  U.S. comedian.

Weinstein, Jacob J.
  Contemporary U.S. rabbi.

Weinstock, Lotus [1943–]
  U.S. comedienne

Weisberg, Jacob
  Contemporary U.S. columnist.

Weisgal, Meyer W. [1894–1977]
  Polish-born educator, Zionist.

Weisgall, Hugo [1912–]
  Moravian-born U.S. composer, conductor.

Weiss, Avi
  Contemporary U.S. rabbi, social activist.

Weisskopf, Victor F. [1908–]
  Austrian-born U.S. physicist.

Weissmandel, Michael Dov [?–1957]
  Slovakian rabbi; World War II resistance
  leader.

Weiss-Rosmarin, Trude [1908–1989]
  German-born U.S. magazine publisher,
  author, lecturer.

Weizman, Ezer [1924–]
  Israeli president, elected in 1993.

Weizmann, Chaim [1874–1952]
  Russian-born chemist, Zionist leader, first
  president of Israel (1948–1952).

Weizmann, Vera [1882–1966]
  Russian-born wife of Chaim Weizmann.

Weizsacher, Richard von
  West German president (1980s).

Wellhausen, Julius [1844–1918]
  German theologian, Bible critic.

Wells, H. G. (Herbert George) [1866–1946]
  British novelist.

Werfel, Franz [1890–1945]
  Czech-born poet, playwright, novelist.

Wertheimer, Jack
  Contemporary U.S. rabbi, historian.

Wesker, Arnold [1932–]
  British playwright.

Wesley, John [1703–1791]
  British clergyman, evangelist.

Westheimer, Ruth [1928–]
German-born U.S. sex therapist, author.

Wheeler, Burton K. [1882–]
U.S. senator from Montana (1940s).

Whitehead, (Lord) Alfred North
[1861–1947]
British mathmetician, philosopher.

Whittier, John Greenleaf [1807–1892]
U.S. poet, author.

Wiener, Max [1882–1950]
German-born Reform rabbi.

Wiesel, Elie [1928–]
Rumanian-born author, professor.

Wieseltier, Leon
Contemporary U.S. writer.

Wiesenthal, Simon [1908–]
Nazi hunter, author.

Wilkie, Wendell [1892–1944]
U.S. politician, industrialist.

Williams, Roger [1599–1683]
British clergyman, founder of Rhode Island.

Wilson, Edmund [1895–]
U.S. writer.

Wilson, Woodrow [1856–1924]
Twenty-eighth U.S. president (1913–1921).

Winchell, Walter [1897–1972]
U.S. radio commentator, journalist.

Wingate, Orde Charles [1903–1944]
British soldier, Christian Zionist.

Winters, Shelley [1923–]
U.S. actress.

Wirth, Louis [1897–1952]
German-born sociologist.

Wise, Isaac Mayer [1819–1900]
German-born U.S. Reform rabbi, educator.

Wise, James Waterman [1901–]
U.S. editor, author.

Wise, Stephen S. [1874–1949]
U.S. rabbi, Zionist leader, educator.

Wisse, Ruth
Contemporary Canadian author, scholar.

Wolf, Simon [1836–1923]
U.S. lawyer, communal leader.

Wolffsohn, David [1856–1914]
Lithuanian-born Zionist leader.

Wolfson, Harry A. [1887–1974]
Byelorussian-born philosopher, historian.

Wolpe, David J.
Contemporary U.S. rabbi, author, educator.

Woodruff, H. A.
Contemporary Christian author.

Woollcott, Alexander [1887–1943]
U.S. writer, critic.

Wordsworth, William [1770–1850]
British poet.

Wouk, Herman [1915–]
U.S. author.

Wright, Richard [1908–1960]
U.S. novelist.

Wurzburger, Walter S. [1920–]
U.S. rabbi, professor, philosopher.

Wynn, Ed [1886–1966]
U.S. actor.

Wyschogrod, Michael
Contemporary U.S. author.

Yakir
Eighteenth-century chasid.

Yalow, Rosalyn [1921–]
U.S. medical physicist.

Yaroslavsky, Zev [1948–]
U.S. politician, Los Angeles city
councilman (1990s).

Yarrow, Peter
Contemporary U.S. entertainer; member of
the Peter, Paul, and Mary trio.

Yehoshua, A. B. [1936–]
Israeli novelist.

Yehuda ben (bar) Simon
Also known as Yehuda ben Pazzi.
Fourth-century talmudic scholar.

Yehuda Ha-nasi
See Judah the Prince.

Yellen, Jack [1892–1991]
U.S. lyricist.

Yevtushenko, Yevgeny Alexandrovich
[1933–]
Russian poet.

Yezierska, Anzia [1885–1970]
Russian-born U.S. novelist.

Yigal
Israeli secret agent who stalked Adolf
Eichmann in Argentina (1960).

Yochanan ben (bar) Napacha [190–279]
Talmudic scholar.

Yochanan ben Zakkai
First-century talmudic scholar.

Yosef, Ovadya [1920–]
Baghdad-born Sephardic Chief Rabbi of

Israel (1970s).

Yosi (Jose) ben Chalafta
Second-century talmudic scholar.

Yosi (Jose) ben Chanina.
Third/fourth-century talmudic scholar.

Yosi ben Yehuda (Judah)
Second-century talmudic scholar.

Yosi ben Zimra
Second-century talmudic scholar.

Youngman, Henny [1906–]
U.S. comedian.

Zangwill, Israel [1864–1926]
British author.

Zborowski, Eli
Contemporary author, editor, chairman of
Societies for Yad Vashem.

Zborowski, Mark
Contemporary U.S. author.

Zechariah
Sixth century B.C.E. prophet of Israel.

Zeitlin, Hillel [1871–1942]
Russian-born Hebrew and Yiddish scholar,
journalist.

Zeitlin, Solomon [1892–1976]
Russian-born scholar, historian.

Zera (Rabbi)
Second-century talmudic scholar.

Zhirinovsky, Vladimir
Contemporary Russian politician.

Zhitlowsky, Chaim [1865–1943]
Russian-born Yiddish philosopher, essayist.

Ziad, George
Contemporary Palestinian.

Zinsser, Hans [1878–1940]
U.S. bacteriologist, author.

Ziprin, Nathan
Contemporary U.S. writer.

Zola, Émile [1840–1902]
French novelist.

Zunser, Elyakum [1836–1913]
Lithuanian-born Yiddish poet, songwriter.

Zunz, Leopold [1794–1886]
German scholar.

Zweig, Arnold [1887–1968]
German author.

Zweig, Stefan [1881–1942]
Austrian biographer, playwright, essayist.

Zwingli, Ulrich [1484–1531]
Swiss Protestant Reformer.

Zygielbojm, Shmuel (Samuel) [1895–1943]
Warsaw Ghetto leader.

INDEX

Index

The names of the individuals quoted in this volume are not necessarily included in the index. They appear in alphabetical order in the body of the text.

O